Waitrose
GOOD FOOD
GUIDE
2015

Distributed by Littlehampton Book Services Ltd
Faraday Close, Durrington, Worthing, West Sussex, BN13 3RB

Copyright © Waitrose Ltd, 2014

Base mapping by Cosmographics Ltd
Data management and export by AMA DataSet Ltd, Preston
Printed and bound by Charterhouse, Hatfield

A catalogue record for this book is available from the British Library

ISBN: 978 0 95379 832 2

Maps designed and produced by Cosmographics Ltd, www.cosmographics.co.uk
Mapping contains Ordnance Survey data © Crown copyright and database right 2014
UK digital database © Cosmographics Ltd, 2014
Greater London map and North and South London maps © Cosmographics Ltd, 2014
West, Central and East London map data © Cosmographics Ltd, 2014 used with kind
permission of VisitBritain
Illustrations for features courtesy of Shutterstock

Consultant Editor: Elizabeth Carter
Editor: Rochelle Venables
Editorial Assistant: Ria Martin

The *Waitrose Good Food Guide* makes every effort to be as accurate and up to date as possible. All inspections are anonymous, but Main Entries have been contacted separately for details. As we are an annual Guide, we have strict guidelines for fact-checking information ahead
of going to press, so some restaurants were dropped if they failed to provide the information
we required. The editors' decision on inclusion and scores in the *Good Food Guide* is final,
and we will not enter into any discussion with individual restaurants.

The publisher cannot be held responsible for any errors or omissions, or for changes in the
details given in this Guide. Restaurants may close or change chefs during the Guide's lifetime,
and readers should always check with the restaurant at the time of booking.

We would like to extend special thanks to the following people: Iain Barker, Francesca Bon-
naud, Ruth Coombs, Tom Fahey, Alan Grimwade, Phil Harriss, Oliver Moyce, Joanne Murray,
Emma Sturgess, Mark Taylor, Andrew Turvil, Steve Trayler, Stuart Walton, Jenny White,
Lisa Whitehouse and Gavin Yam. And a special thanks to all of our hard-working inspectors.

www.thegoodfoodguide.co.uk

"You can corrupt one man. You can't bribe an army."

Raymond Postgate
founder of The Good Food Guide, 1951

Contents

Introduction

Elizabeth Carter
Consultant Editor

Welcome to the 2015 edition of the *Good Food Guide*, the UK's most trusted, best-loved and bestselling restaurant bible. In these pages we aim to present to you the very best of what UK restaurants have to offer.

It's a complicated business, eating. A meal outside of the home is more than just a plate of food; whatever the quality, it is a social event. Meals can be memorable for the occasion, the conversation, the hospitality of the staff or the atmosphere in the restaurant itself. Indeed, the cooking may be some way down the list of why the meal was enjoyed so much. As the British dining scene has grown in confidence, so too

has the total restaurant experience grown dynamically in importance. Dining out is about so much more than the food.

Moreover, fine dining has become democratised. 'Ordinary' people are now saving up to visit high-end restaurants a few times a year, as if they were cultural experiences on a par with seeing a West End show or a major sporting event. It's worth noting that a three-course meal (without drinks) in a restaurant scoring 8 or 9 in this Guide would cost approximately £85 per head, yet premium tickets for *The Book of Mormon* on a Saturday night are more than £100 a person; best seats at Robbie Williams' 2014 O2 appearance £108; and Centre Court tickets for the men's final

> *"As the British dining scene has grown in confidence, so too has the total restaurant experience grown dynamically in importance"*

at Wimbledon would have set you back £148 this year – if you were lucky enough to bag one in the ballot.

Top restaurants in Britain today differ dramatically from their time-honoured image of stiff and formal service, rich and exotic cuisine and a generally 'posh' atmosphere. In fact, the very best (and not just the top-scoring) restaurants have excellent but informal service, a relaxed dress code and offer creative, memorable, satisfying food based on quality seasonal produce; butter and cream, the traditional ingredients of fine dining, are no longer the mainstays of top-flight cooking. In short, these restaurants are there for enjoyment. The *Good Food Guide*, now in its 64th year, celebrates that.

A high-wire act

From among that highly individual group of chefs who currently dominate the UK's dining scene, Clare Smyth of Restaurant Gordon Ramsay has emerged as one of our top chefs. After a break of a decade, Ramsay's Chelsea flagship has once again been awarded a perfect 10. Now the domain of Smyth, with support from what is, without doubt, one of the best front-of-house teams in the UK, this most impressive of London's premier restaurants is back in that elite club. It's a delight to see Smyth's brilliantly artistic, elegant, modern French cooking perfectly complementing the witty, cerebral Fat Duck and the sensual farm-to-table delights of L'Enclume at the pinnacle of our Top 50 list.

2014 was a great year for debuts

Some of the best new restaurants reviewed for this edition of the Guide came from chefs or owners who are relatively unknown. We were greatly impressed by Gareth Ward, who has found a stage at Ynyshir Hall for his remarkably nuanced, unforgettable creations. And by Jordan Annabi, now heading the brigade at Airds Hotel in Port Appin; a smart, accomplished chef whose cooking is noted for vibrant seasoning and ultra-fresh ingredients. And when Tyron Ellul emerged from the kitchen of Glenapp Castle displaying an impressive set of skills and a sure sense of what's delicious, there was no doubt in our minds – these are definitely young chefs to watch.

And there are some terrifically enjoyable new restaurants from seasoned veterans like André Garrett at Cliveden, James Sommerin at Restaurant James Sommerin, Nuno Mendes at the Chiltern Firehouse and Simon Rogan at Fera. Each has achieved the kind of excellence you both feel in the dining room and taste in the food; an excellence born of experience and skill. While the bottom line is always about exploring quality produce through classical skills and modern methods, it is the vividness of the imagination displayed by each chef, and their brilliance in execution, that is so exciting.

> ## "Across the years you, the Guide's readers, have helped us document the resurgence of pride in British cooking"

But that's not the full story. Mid-market venues are also thriving, as canny restaurateurs exploit the public's demand for eating well without spending a fortune. Notable examples are the Ox in Bristol, Timberyard in Edinburgh, Coast (with former La Bécasse chef Will Holland) in Wales, and Angela Hartnett's affordable, casual Café Murano in Mayfair.

We've cast a critical eye over budget eating, too. We felt 'Also Recommended' was no longer a fitting description for our neighbourhood restaurants. Instead, with the emphasis on more value-for-money choice, you will find 'Local Gems'. As a collection they are an odd bag – cafés, bistros, seafood shacks, pubs and more – but they are linked by a single theme: they all serve good food at affordable prices. There are a few eccentrics – the Upton Fish Shop in Lincolnshire, the only fish and chip shop with a coal-fired range in the country; the basic Beachhouse café on the South Milton Sands in Devon – but on the whole our Local Gems are all about everyday eating at everyday prices.

Over to you

Across the years you, the Guide's readers, have helped us document the resurgence of pride in British cooking. Each year may bring new ideas, fresh thinking and some great food, but to discover it all we still need pointing in the right direction.

Some guidebooks have a small, dedicated band of paid inspectors who do the groundwork and deliver assessments. Many rely on support from within the industry they are assessing, take advertisements, or charge for entries in the publication itself. That's not us; the *Good Food Guide* has never worked that way. There are no advertisements, no free meals, no paid-for entries. Its reporters are no small band but the whole army of its readers who fill the office inbox daily with comments.

The Guide's essence lies in these reports, backed up by anonymous inspections by our experts. It is the *Good Food Guide* team's function to report the conclusions in each year's edition. Of course we make checks, make some judgement on the prejudices and enthusiasms of the reporter. But each entry must draw a clear recommendation in favour from readers and inspectors. Where there is doubt, the restaurant is left out. It has been thus for 64 years – you really couldn't ask for a more straightforward formula for success.

And whether you agree or disagree with what you find in the following pages, your voice can be heard. All you have to do is log on to thegoodfoodguide.co.uk. Every scrap of information is useful, so even if you don't have the time to go into great detail, a short paragraph telling us about the food you ate, the feel of the place and the quality of the service will be hugely important for the next edition. Be a part of history, a part of the *Good Food Guide*. There's no one else like us.

Top 50 Restaurants

1. L'Enclume, Cumbria (10)
2. The Fat Duck, Berkshire (10)
3. Restaurant Gordon Ramsay, London (10)
4. Restaurant Nathan Outlaw, Cornwall (9)
5. Hibiscus, London (9)
6. Pollen Street Social, London (9)
7. Restaurant Sat Bains, Nottinghamshire (9)
8. The Square, London (8)
9. Le Champignon Sauvage, Gloucestershire (8)
10. The Ledbury, London (8)
11. Andrew Fairlie at Gleneagles, Tayside (8)
12. Midsummer House, Cambridgeshire (8)
13. Le Manoir aux Quat'Saisons, Oxfordshire (8)
14. The French, Manchester (8)
15. Le Gavroche, London (8)
16. Whatley Manor, The Dining Room, Wiltshire (8)
17. Fraiche, Merseyside (8)
18. André Garrett at Cliveden, Berkshire (7)
19. Fera at Claridges, London (7)
20. Marcus, London (7)
21. Dinner by Heston Blumenthal, London (7)
22. The Kitchin, Edinburgh (7)
23. The Waterside Inn, Berkshire (7)
24. Pied-à-Terre, London (7)
25. Alain Ducasse at the Dorchester, London (7)
26. Michael Wignall at the Latymer, Surrey (7)
27. Restaurant Martin Wishart, Edinburgh (7)
28. Artichoke, Buckinghamshire (7)
29. Fischer's Baslow Hall, Derbyshire (7)
30. Restaurant James Sommerin, Glamorgan (7)
31. The Peat Inn, Fife (7)
32. Murano, London (7)
33. Paul Ainsworth at No. 6, Cornwall (7)
34. Gidleigh Park, Devon (7)
35. Hedone, London (7)
36. Hambleton Hall, Rutland (7)
37. Restaurant Story, London (7)
38. The Pass, West Sussex (7)
39. Casamia, Bristol (7)
40. Ynyshir Hall, Powys (7)
41. Freemasons at Wiswell, Lancashire (7)
42. Hélène Darroze at the Connaught, London (6)
43. The Hand & Flowers, Buckinghamshire (6)
44. Yorke Arms, Ramsgill, Yorkshire (6)
45. Paris House, Bedfordshire (6)
46. Simon Radley at the Chester Grosvenor, Cheshire (6)
47. The Raby Hunt, Durham (6)
48. Chiltern Firehouse, London (6)
49. Northcote, Lancashire (6)
50. The Clove Club, London (6)

Top 50 Pubs

At the request of our readers, and following the success of our Top 50 Restaurants, we are delighted to list our Top 50 Pubs for the first time. Ranging from rustic locals to stylish inns, the list has been compiled from the pub's score in the *Good Food Guide*, inspection reports and our readers' feedback.

1. Freemasons at Wiswell, Lancashire
2. The Hand & Flowers, Buckinghamshire
3. The Red Lion, East Chisenbury, Wiltshire
4. The Royal Oak, Paley Street, Berkshire
5. The Sportsman, Kent
6. The Pipe and Glass Inn, Yorkshire
7. The Gunton Arms, Norfolk
8. The White Oak, Cookham, Berkshire
9. The Butchers Arms, Eldersfield, Gloucestershire
10. The Treby Arms, Devon
11. The Hardwick, Abergavenny
12. The Nut Tree Inn, Oxfordshire
13. The Stagg Inn, Titley, Herefordshire
14. The Star Inn, Harome, Yorkshire
15. The Harwood Arms, Fulham, London
16. The Plough, Bolnhurst, Bedfordshire
17. The Plough Inn, Longparish, Hampshire
18. The Hinds Head, Berkshire
19. The Masons Arms, Knowstone, Devon
20. The Broad Chare, Tyne & Wear
21. The Springer Spaniel, Cornwall
22. The Wellington Arms, Baughurst, Hampshire
23. The British Larder, Suffolk
24. The Sir Charles Napier, Oxfordshire
25. The Pony & Trap, Chew Magna, Somerset
26. The Star Inn, Sparsholt, Oxfordshire
27. The Felin Fach Griffin, Powys
28. The Duke of Cumberland Arms, West Sussex
29. The Richmond Arms, West Ashling, West Sussex
30. The Foxhunter, Gwent
31. The White Hart, Lydgate, Greater Manchester
32. The General Tarleton, Yorkshire
33. The Kinmel Arms, Conway
34. The Wheatsheaf, Combe Hay, Somerset
35. The Five Alls, Oxfordshire
36. The Bay Horse, Hurworth-on-Tees, Durham
37. The Bildeston Crown, Suffolk
38. The Malt House, Fulham, London
39. The Earl of March, West Sussex
40. The Kingham Plough, Oxfordshire
41. The Star @ Sancton, Yorkshire
42. The Black Swan, Oldstead, Yorkshire.
43. Beckford Arms, Wiltshire
44. The Wheatsheaf Inn, Northleach, Gloucestershire
45. The Duke of York Inn, Grindleton, Lancashire
46. The Rummer, Bristol
47. Camberwell Arms, Camberwell, London
48. The Crown, Old Basing, Hampshire
49. Smokehouse, Islington, London
50. The White Horse, Brancaster Staithe, Norfolk

Longest Serving

The *Good Food Guide* was founded in 1951.
The following restaurants have appeared consistently since their
first entry into the Guide.

The Connaught, London, *62 years*
Gravetye Manor, West Sussex, *58 years*
Porth Tocyn Hotel, Gwynedd, *58 years*
Le Gavroche, London, *45 years*
Ubiquitous Chip, Glasgow, *43 years*
Plumber Manor, Dorset, *42 years*
The Druidstone, Pembrokeshire, *42 years*
The Waterside Inn, Berkshire, *42 years*
Airds Hotel, Argyll & Bute, *39 years*
Farlam Hall, Cumbria, *38 years*
Corse Lawn House Hotel,
    Gloucestershire, *36 years*
Hambleton Hall, Rutland, *36 years*
The Pier at Harwich, Essex, *36 years*
Magpie Café, Whitby,
    North Yorkshire, *35 years*
RSJ, London, *34 years*
The Seafood Restaurant, Padstow,
    Cornwall, *34 years*
The Sir Charles Napier, Oxfordshire,
    34 years
Le Caprice, London, *33 years*
Little Barwick House, Somerset, *33 years*
Inverlochy Castle, Fort William, *32 years*
Ostlers Close, Fife, *32 years*
The Angel Inn, Hetton, *31 years*
Brilliant, London, *30 years*
Clarke's, London, *30 years*

Le Manoir aux Quat'Saisons,
    Oxfordshire, *30 years*
Roade House, Northamptonshire,
    30 years
Blostin's, Somerset, *29 years*
Read's, Kent, *29 years*
The Castle at Taunton, Somerset,
    29 years
The Three Chimneys, Isle of Skye,
    29 years
Northcote, Lancashire, *28 years*
The Old Vicarage, Ridgeway, *27 years*
Cnapan, Pembrokeshire, *27 years*
Kensington Place, London, *26 years*
Le Champignon Sauvage,
    Gloucestershire, *26 years*
Quince & Medlar, Cumbria, *26 years*
Silver Darling, Aberdeen, *26 years*
Plas Bodegroes, Gwynedd, *25 years*
Bibendum, London, *25 years*
The Great House, Suffolk, *25 years*
Ynyshir Hall, Powys, *25 years*
The Creel, Orkney, *25 years*
Dylanwad Da, Gwynedd, *25 years*
Crannog, Fort William, *25 years*
Eslington Villa, Tyne & Wear, *24 years*
Castle Cottage, Harlech, *23 years*

Readers' Awards

The Readers' Restaurant of the Year Awards celebrate local restaurants, pubs and cafés, as nominated by members of the public. The winner of the overall award is picked by the editors of the *Good Food Guide* and announced in September 2014.

The regional winners are as follows:

East England
The Ingham Swan
Ingham, Norfolk

Northern Ireland
James Street South
Belfast

London
Charlotte's Bistro
Chiswick

Scotland
The Birch Tree
Delny

Midlands
Carters of Moseley
Birmingham

South East
Stovell's
Chobham, Surrey

North East
The Spiced Pear
Holmfirth, Yorkshire

South West
Menu Gordon Jones
Bath

North West
Lunya
Liverpool

Wales
Bar 44
Cowbridge, Glamorgan

Editors' Awards

The editors of the *Good Food Guide* are delighted to confer the following awards on the following restaurants and chefs who have shown excellence in their field.

— ♦ —

Chef(s) of the Year
Jonray and Peter Sanchez-Iglesias
Casamia, Bristol

— ♦ —

Chef to Watch
Gareth Ward
Ynyshir Hall, Powys

— ♦ —

Best New Entry: Restaurant
André Garrett at Cliveden, *Berkshire*

— ♦ —

Best New Entry: Pub
The Broad Chare, *Newcastle*

— ♦ —

Wine List of the Year
The Sun Inn
Dedham, Essex

— ♦ —

Pub of the Year
Freemasons at Wiswell, *Lancashire*

— ♦ —

Local Gem of the Year
Delilah
Nottingham

— ♦ —

Best Set Lunch
Tuddenham Mill, *Suffolk*

How to use the Good Food Guide

In our opinion, the restaurants included in the *Good Food Guide* are the very best in the UK; this means that simply getting an entry is an accomplishment to be proud of, and a Score 1 or above is a significant achievement.

The *Good Food Guide* is completely rewritten every year and compiled from scratch. Our research list is based on the huge volume of feedback we receive from readers, which, together with anonymous inspections by our experts, ensures that every entry is assessed afresh. Please keep the reports coming in! Visit thegoodfoodguide.co.uk for details.

Symbols

We contact restaurants that we're considering for inclusion ahead of publication to check key information about opening times and facilities. They are also invited to participate in the £5 voucher scheme. The symbols against each entry are intended for at-a-glance identification and are based on the information given to us by each restaurant.

Accommodation is available

£30 It is possible to have three courses, excluding wine, at the restaurant for less than £30.

V The restaurant has a separate vegetarian menu.

£XX The average price of a three-course dinner, excluding wine.

£5 OFF The restaurant is participating in our £5 voucher scheme. See vouchers for terms and conditions.

The restaurant has a wine list that our experts have considered to be outstanding, either for strong by-the-glass options, an in-depth focus on a particular region, or attractive margins on fine wines.

Scoring

We add and reject many restaurants when we compile each guide. There are always subjective aspects to rating systems, but our inspectors are equipped with extensive scoring guidelines to ensure that restaurant bench-marking around the UK is accurate. As we take into account reader feedback on each restaurant, any given review is based on several meals.

'New chef' in place of a score indicates that the restaurant has had a recent change of chef and we have been unable to score it reliably; we particularly welcome reports on these restaurants.

Readers Recommend

These are direct quotes from our reader feedback and highlight places that have caught the attention of our loyal followers. Reports are particularly welcome on these entries also.

Local Gem

This year Local Gems replace our Also Recommended entries, bringing you more choice of venue at better value for money. Simple cafés, bistros and pubs, these are the places that sit happily on your doorstep, delivering good, freshly cooked food; the perfect neighbourhood venue.

Score 1 Capable cooking with simple food combinations and clear flavours, but some inconsistencies.

---------------- ◆ ----------------

Score 2 Decent cooking, displaying good technical skills and interesting combinations and flavours. Occasional inconsistencies.

---------------- ◆ ----------------

Score 3 Good cooking, showing sound technical skills and using quality ingredients.

---------------- ◆ ----------------

Score 4 Dedicated, focused approach to cooking; good classical skills and high-quality ingredients.

---------------- ◆ ----------------

Score 5 Exact cooking techniques and a degree of ambition; showing balance and depth of flavour in dishes.

---------------- ◆ ----------------

Score 6 Exemplary cooking skills, innovative ideas, impeccable ingredients and an element of excitement.

---------------- ◆ ----------------

Score 7 High level of ambition and individuality, attention to the smallest detail, accurate and vibrant dishes.

---------------- ◆ ----------------

Score 8 A kitchen cooking close to or at the top of its game. Highly individual with impressive artistry. There is little room for disappointment here.

---------------- ◆ ----------------

Score 9 Cooking that has reached a pinnacle of achievement, making it a hugely memorable experience for the diner.

---------------- ◆ ----------------

Score 10 Just perfect dishes, showing faultless technique at every service; extremely rare, and the highest accolade the Guide can give.

London Explained

London is split into six regions: Central, North, East, South, West and Greater. Restaurants within each region are listed alphabetically. Each main entry and Local Gem entry has a map reference.

The lists below are a guide to the areas covered in each region.

London — Central
Belgravia, Bloomsbury, Covent Garden, Fitzrovia, Green Park, Holborn, Hyde Park, Lancaster Gate, Leicester Square, Marble Arch, Marylebone, Mayfair, Oxford Circus, Piccadilly, Pimlico, Soho, Westminster

London — North
Archway, Camden, Finsbury Park, Golders Green, Hampstead, Islington, Kensal Green, Kentish Town, King's Cross, Maida Vale, Muswell Hill, Neasden, Primrose Hill, Stoke Newington, Swiss Cottage, Willesden

London — East
Barbican, Bethnal Green, Canary Wharf, City, Clerkenwell, Dalston, Farringdon, Hackney, Hoxton, St Paul's, Shoreditch, Spitalfields, Tower Hill, Whitechapel

London — South
Balham, Battersea, Bermondsey, Blackheath, Borough, Brixton, Camberwell, Clapham, East Dulwich, Elephant & Castle, Forest Hill, Greenwich, Herne Hill, Peckham, Putney, South Bank, Southwark, Stockwell, Tooting, Victoria, Wandsworth, Wimbledon

London — West
Belgravia, Chelsea, Chiswick, Ealing, Earl's Court, Fulham, Gloucester Road, Hammersmith, Kensington, Knightsbridge, Ladbroke Grove, Notting Hill, Olympia, Parsons Green, Shepherd's Bush, South Kensington

London — Greater
Barnes, Croydon, Crystal Palace, East Sheen, Harrow-on-the-Hill, Kew, Richmond, Southall, Surbiton, Teddington, Twickenham, Walthamstow, Wood Green

LONDON

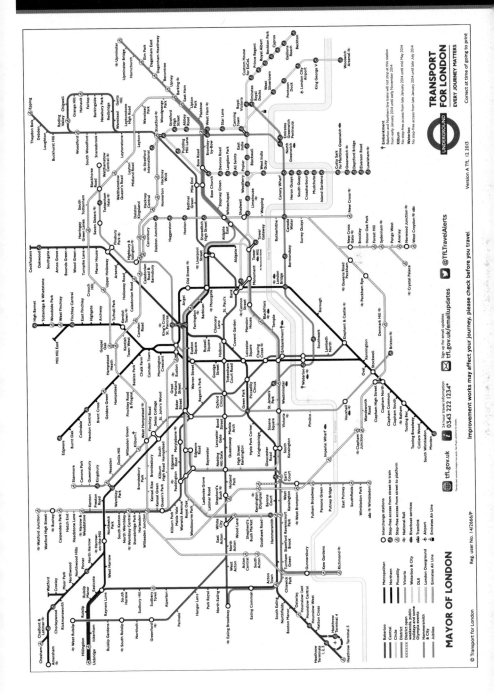

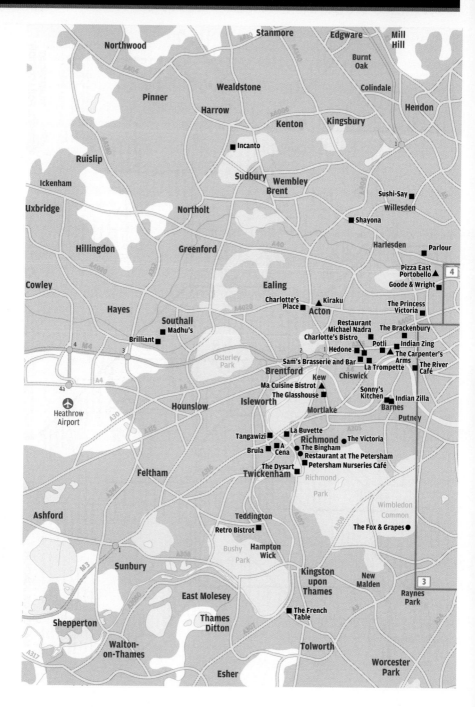

Stanmore
Edgware
Mill Hill
Northwood
Burnt Oak
Wealdstone
Colindale
Pinner
Harrow
Hendon
Kenton
Kingsbury
Ruislip
Incanto
Ickenham
Sudbury
Wembley
Brent
Uxbridge
Northolt
Sushi-Say
Willesden
Shayona
Hillingdon
Greenford
Harlesden
Parlour
Pizza East Portobello ▲
Goode & Wright
4
Cowley
Ealing
Charlotte's Place
Kiraku
The Princess Victoria
Hayes
Southall
Acton
Madhu's
Restaurant Michael Nadra
The Brackenbury
Brilliant
Charlotte's Bistro
Potli
Indian Zing
Hedone
The Carpenter's Arms
Osterley Park
Sam's Brasserie and Bar
La Trompette
The River Café
Brentford
Chiswick
Heathrow Airport
Kew
Sonny's Kitchen
Ma Cuisine Bistrot ▲
The Glasshouse
Indian Zilla
Hounslow
Isleworth
Mortlake
Barnes
Putney
La Buvette
Tangawizi
Richmond
The Victoria
Brula
A Cena
The Bingham
Restaurant at The Petersham
Petersham Nurseries Café
The Dysart
Feltham
Twickenham
Richmond Park
Wimbledon Common
Ashford
Teddington
Retro Bistrot
The Fox & Grapes
Bushy Park
Hampton Wick
Kingston upon Thames
New Malden
Raynes Park
3
Sunbury
East Molesey
The French Table
Shepperton
Thames Ditton
Tolworth
Walton-on-Thames
Worcester Park
Esher

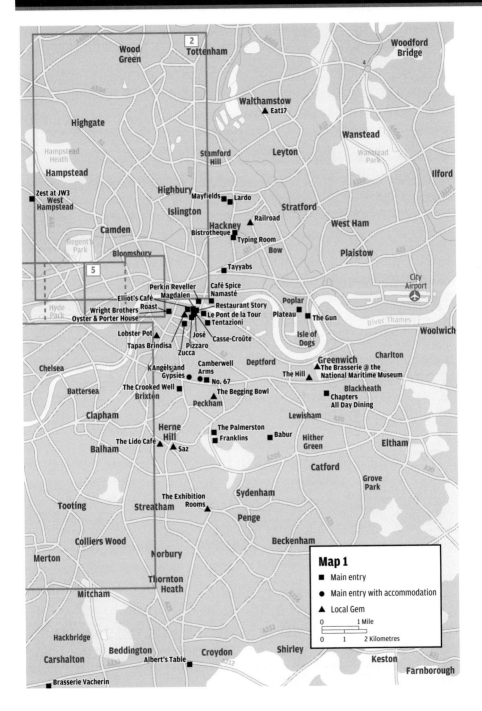

Wood Green
Tottenham
Woodford Bridge

Highgate

Hampstead Heath

Hampstead

Walthamstow
▲ Eat17

Wanstead

Wanstead Park

Ilford

Stamford Hill

Leyton

Zest at JW3
West Hampstead

Highbury
Mayfields ■ Lardo ■

Islington

Stratford

Camden

Hackney
Bistrotheque ■
Typing Room ■

Railroad ▲

West Ham

Plaistow

Bow

Regent's Park

Bloomsbury

Tayyabs ■

City Airport

Hyde Park

Perkin Reveller ■ Café Spice Namasté
Elliot's Café Magdalen
Roast ■
Wright Brothers
Oyster & Porter House

Restaurant Story
Le Pont de la Tour
Tentazioni

Poplar

Plateau ● ■ The Gun

River Thames

Woolwich

Lobster Pot ▲
Tapas Brindisa
José
Pizzaro
Zucca
Casse-Croûte

Isle of Dogs

Charlton

Chelsea

K Angèls and Gypsies
The Crooked Well ■
Brixton

Camberwell Arms
■ ■ No. 67

Deptford

The Hill ●

Greenwich
▲ The Brasserie @ the National Maritime Museum

Battersea

The Begging Bowl

Peckham

Blackheath
Chapters
All Day Dining ■

Clapham

Lewisham

Herne Hill
The Lido Café ▲
▲ Saz

The Palmerston
■ Franklins ■ Babur

Hither Green

Eltham

Balham

Catford

The Exhibition Rooms ▲

Sydenham

Grove Park

Tooting

Streatham

Penge

Beckenham

Colliers Wood

Norbury

Merton

Thornton Heath

Mitcham

Map 1

■ Main entry
● Main entry with accommodation
▲ Local Gem

0   1 Mile
0   1   2 Kilometres

Hackbridge

Beddington
Albert's Table ■

Croydon

Shirley

Keston

Carshalton

Farnborough

Brasserie Vacherin ■

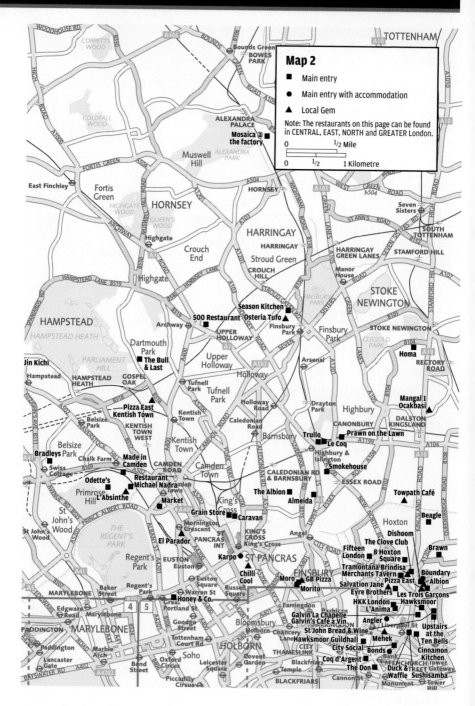

Map 2

- ■ Main entry
- ● Main entry with accommodation
- ▲ Local Gem

Note: The restaurants on this page can be found in CENTRAL, EAST, NORTH and GREATER London.

0 ———— 1/2 Mile
0 ———— 1/2 ———— 1 Kilometre

TOTTENHAM

WOODHOUSE RD
CORPETTS WOOD
BOUNDS GREEN
Bounds Green
BOWES PARK
COLDFALL WOOD
ALEXANDRA PALACE
Mosaica @ the factory
Muswell Hill
ALEXANDRA PARK
East Finchley
Fortis Green
FORTIS GREEN
HORNSEY
HIGHGATE WOOD
QUEEN'S WOOD
HARRINGAY
HARRINGAY
Stroud Green
CROUCH HILL
Seven Sisters
SOUTH TOTTENHAM
HARRINGAY GREEN LANES
STAMFORD HILL
Highgate
Crouch End
Manor House
STOKE NEWINGTON
STOKE NEWINGTON
HAMPSTEAD LANE B519
Highgate
HAMPSTEAD
HAMPSTEAD HEATH
Season Kitchen
500 Restaurant
Osteria Tufo
FINSBURY PARK
Finsbury Park
Finsbury Park
CLISSOLD PARK
Homa
RECTORY ROAD
Jin Kichi
Dartmouth Park
PARLIAMENT HILL
UPPER HOLLOWAY
Upper Holloway
Hampstead
HAMPSTEAD HEATH
GOSPEL OAK
The Bull & Last
Holloway
Arsenal
Pizza East Kentish Town
Tufnell Park
Tufnell Park
Holloway Road
Drayton Park
Highbury
Mangal 1 Ocakbasi
DALSTON KINGSLAND
Belsize Park
KENTISH TOWN WEST
Kentish Town
Caledonian Road
CANONBURY
Belsize Park
KENTISH TOWN
Kentish Town
Barnsbury
Trullo
Prawn on the Lawn
Bradleys
Chalk Farm
Made in Camden
CAMDEN ROAD
Camden Town
Le Coq
Highbury & Islington
Swiss Cottage
Odette's
Restaurant Michael Nadra
CALEDONIAN RD & BARNSBURY
Smokehouse
ESSEX ROAD
Primrose Hill
L'Absinthe
Camden Town
The Albion
Almeida
Towpath Café
St John's Wood
Market
King's Cross
Beagle
THE REGENT'S PARK
Grain Store
Caravan
Hoxton
St John's Wood
El Parador
Mornington Crescent
PANCRAS INT
KING'S CROSS
Angel
Dishoom
The Clove Club
Brawn
Regent's Park
EUSTON
Euston
Karpo
ST PANCRAS
King's Cross
FINSBURY
Fifteen London
8 Hoxton Square
Baker Street
Regent's Park
Chilli Cool
Moro
GB Pizza
Tramontana Brindisa
Merchants Tavern
Pizza East
Boundary
MARYLEBONE
Euston Square
Warren St
Russell Square
Morito
Salvation Jane
Eyre Brothers
Les Trois Garçons
Albion
Hawksmoor
Honey & Co.
Great Portland St
Farringdon
HKK London
L'Anima
Edgware Road
Marylebone
Goodge Street
Bloomsbury
Barbican
Galvin La Chapelle
Galvin's Café a Vin
Angler
Upstairs at the Ten Bells
PADDINGTON
MARYLEBONE
Tottenham Court Rd
Holborn
Chancery Lane
St John Bread & Wine
Hawksmoor Guildhall
Mehek
Cinnamon Kitchen
Paddington
Marble Arch
Soho
Oxford Circus
Leicester Square
Covent Garden
HOLBORN
CITY
THAMESLINK
City Social
Bonds
Coq d'Argent
Bank
Duck & Waffle
Sushisamba
Lancaster Gate
Bond Street
Blackfriars
Temple
Coq d'Argent
The Don
FENCHURCH STREET GATEWAY
BAYSWATER RD
Piccadilly Circus
BLACKFRIARS
Cannon St
Monument
Tower Hill

4 5

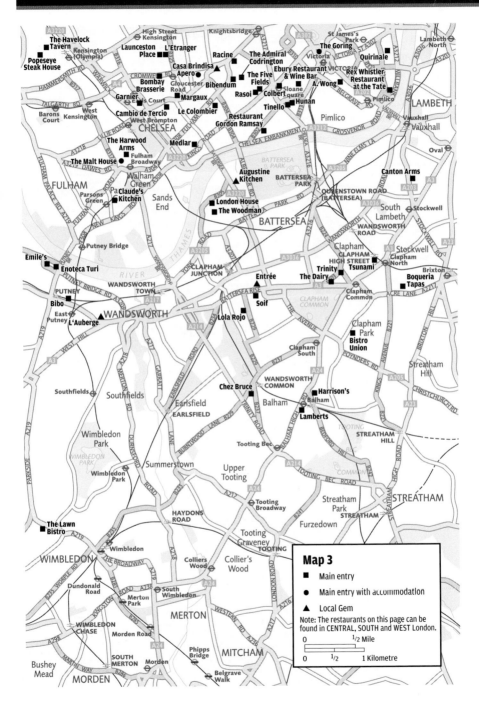

Map 3

■ Main entry

● Main entry with accommodation

▲ Local Gem

Note: The restaurants on this page can be found in CENTRAL, SOUTH and WEST London.

0 .... 1/2 Mile

0 .... 1/2 .... 1 Kilometre

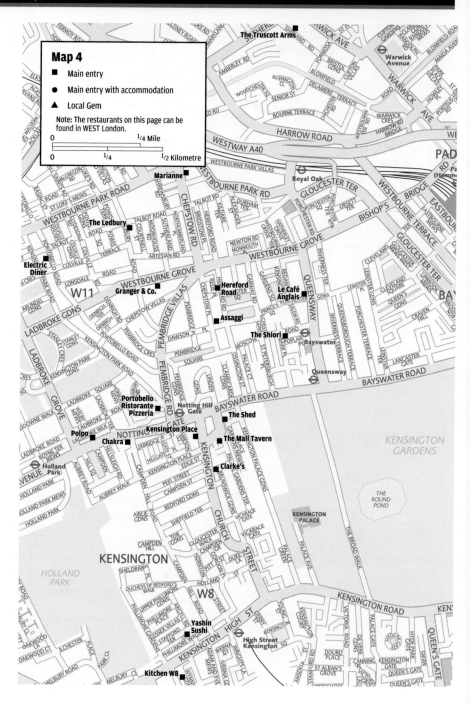

Map 4

- ■ Main entry
- ● Main entry with accommodation
- ▲ Local Gem

Note: The restaurants on this page can be found in WEST London.

0 — ¼ Mile

0 — ¼ — ½ Kilometre

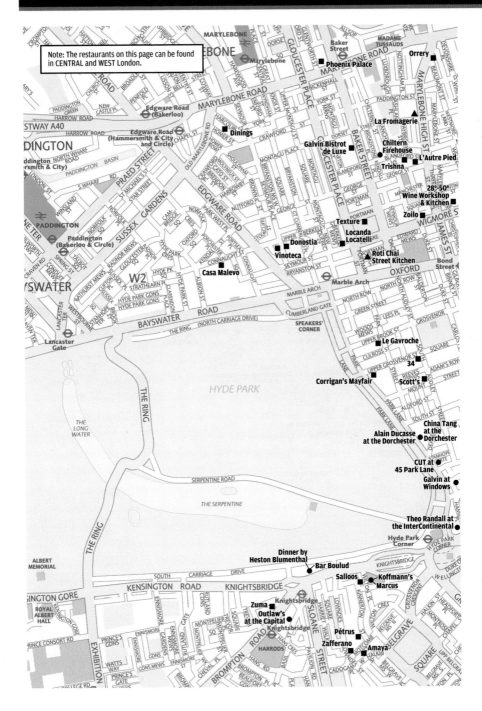

Note: The restaurants on this page can be found in CENTRAL and WEST LONDON.

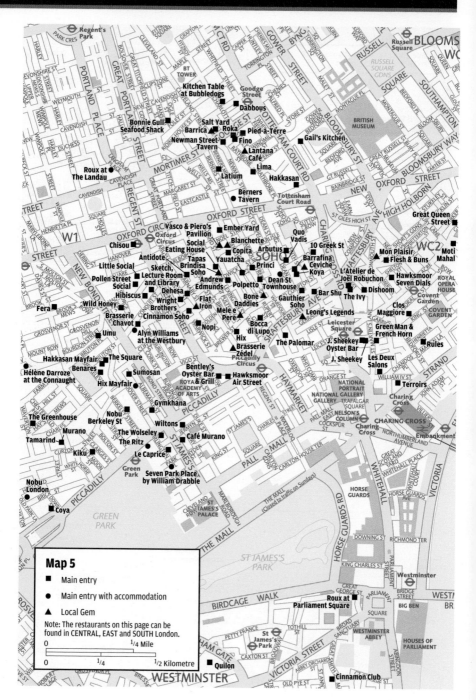

Map 5

- ■ Main entry
- ● Main entry with accommodation
- ▲ Local Gem

Note: The restaurants on this page can be found in CENTRAL, EAST and SOUTH London.

0   1/4 Mile

0   1/4   1/2 Kilometre

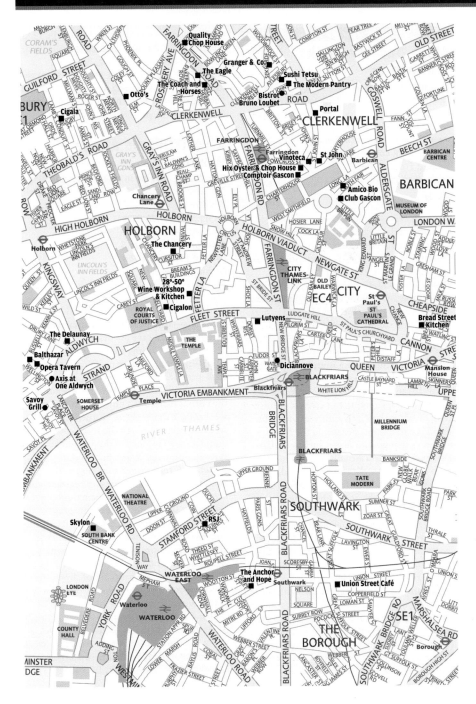

★ TOP 50 ★
Alain Ducasse at the Dorchester
A corner of France on Park Lane
The Dorchester Hotel, 53 Park Lane, Hyde Park, W1K 1QA
Tel no: (020) 7629 8866
www.alainducasse-dorchester.com
⊖ Hyde Park Corner, map 4
Modern French | £90
Cooking score: 7

🍴 V

Alain Ducasse's name continues to be the icing on an ornately decorated cake. Among the old London grandees, the Dorchester is more plentifully equipped with good eating than any other hotel. Here, in an almost provocatively understated room, with white seating and amorphous white screens dividing a blond wood space, Jocelyn Herland brings panache and sophistication to the interpretation of Ducasse's philosophy. Menus evolve slowly, yet retain a seasonal note, with many preparations being founded on the methodology and compositional genius of classic haute cuisine. From the arrival of the amuse (perhaps a mousse of celeriac garnished with diced apple) it's clear that attention to detail is paramount, sustaining the fine materials that go into dishes such as caviared Dorset crab in delicate jelly, sautéed lobster with chicken quenelles and pasta, and the grandiose seared duck foie gras with citrused white asparagus. Meats might come with top French pedigree (Anjou pigeon, milk-fed Roquefortin lamb), while other ingredients hail from closer to home, such as Hereford snails, or Scottish salmon (served with spring vegetables). True depth of impact, if not necessarily complexity, characterises most dishes, through to strawberry tart with clotted cream, or baba laced with whichever rum you fancy. The wine list is a Francophile's fantasy. Start at £30 for bottles, £9 for small glasses. (This establishment is part of the Sultan of Brunei's Dorchester Collection: see entries for CUT at 45 Park Lane and China Tang.)

Chef/s: Jocelyn Herland. **Open:** Tue to Fri L 12 to 1.30, Tue to Sat D 6.30 to 9.30. **Closed:** Sun, Mon, 2 weeks Christmas, 2 weeks Aug, bank hols. **Meals:** Set L £65 (2 courses). Set D £90 (3 courses) to £105 (4 courses). Tasting menu £125 (7 courses). **Details:** 82 seats. Wheelchair access. Car parking. Children over 10 yrs only.

Alyn Williams at the Westbury
Painstaking cooking in preened surroundings
The Westbury Hotel, 37 Conduit Street, Mayfair, W1S 2YF
Tel no: (020) 7078 9579
www.alynwilliams.co.uk
⊖ Oxford Circus, map 5
Modern European | £58
Cooking score: 6

🍴 V

With its recessed entrance off Bond Street, where top-hatted commissionaires await, the Westbury could give the nearby Ritz a run for its money. The dining room consecrated to Alyn Williams is a more prosaically modern, dark-panelled place patrolled by keen international staff. Central to the operation are the tasting menus, the only choice at weekends, a shorter carte also available in the week. Progress through the seven courses is an undulating affair, the dazzling eminences thrown into relief by less breathtaking stretches. A reimagined tom yum with langoustines and lemongrass in coconut-chilli broth makes an exuberant opener, subsequent highlights including sticks of foie gras semifreddo with prunes, celeriac and bacon on espresso syrup, a serving of Ibérico pork in tarragon emulsion, and duck breast with artichoke barigoule and wild garlic. At the end comes the booming bass note of chocolate marquise and melilot (sweet clover), lightly salted. Wines from a glitzy list start at £24. **Chef/s:** Alyn Williams. **Open:** Tue to Sat L 12 to 2.30, D 6 to 10.30. **Closed:** Sun, Mon, 26 to 28 Dec, 2 weeks Jan, 2 weeks Aug. **Meals:** Set L £28. Set D £58. Tasting menu £65. **Details:** 50 seats. Separate bar. Wheelchair access. Music. Car parking.

Andrew Edmunds
Wine-loving Soho stalwart
46 Lexington Street, Soho, W1F 0LW
Tel no: (020) 7437 5708
www.andrewedmunds.com
⊖ Oxford Circus, Piccadilly Circus, map 5
Modern European | £30
Cooking score: 2

The nature of this Soho favourite presents a dilemma. At both street level and in the basement, the 'cramped' but charming 18th-century town house would be more comfortable if it were near-deserted. But it's the squash and squeeze of relaxed close-quarters dining – alongside low light, friendly quickfire service and plenty of interesting wine – that generates the atmosphere. Cooking is plain, seasonal and muscular, with straightforward plates such as dressed crab with mayonnaise or a salad of mozzarella, roast red onion and Jerusalem artichoke, to start. Comfort is favoured over balance and finesse; it's not unheard of for four out of five main courses to feature potatoes, perhaps with crisped-up confit duck leg or a chunky cod fillet with clams and salsa verde. All this ballast (sticky toffee pudding is the pick of the puds) goes well with an exceedingly good-value wine list, starting at £18.50.
Chef/s: Bob Cairns. **Open:** all week L 12 to 3.30 (12.30 Sat, 1 to 4 Sun), D 5.30 to 10.45 (6 to 10.30 Sun). **Closed:** 24 Dec to 2 Jan. **Meals:** alc (main courses £13 to £23). **Details:** 58 seats.

NEW ENTRY
Antidote
Dynamic plates of modern food
12A Newburgh Street, Soho, W1F 7RR
Tel no: (020) 7287 8488
www.antidotewinebar.com
⊖ Oxford Circus, map 5
Modern European | £34
Cooking score: 5

Whatever Antidote purports to be the antidote to, it's clear that it is the cure and not the poison. With the involvement of Mikael Jonsson of Hedone fame (see entry) and with Chris Johns at the stove, this kitchen is turning out dynamic plates of contemporary food that deliver exciting flavours. The décor is bare-bones minimalist in a fashionable Scandi way. The ground-floor wine bar – 'no poorer cousin' – offers fab charcuterie, small plates and daytime tartines. Alternatively, head upstairs for a bit more space and the full-throttle menu. Sourdough bread is 'the best'. A first-course chicken salad comes glammed up with crispy shards of skin and a garden's worth of herbs, then main-course pollack arrives in the heady company of a courgette-fest and crispy deep-fried mussels. Salt marsh lamb is a 'simply stunning main', followed by a dessert of chocolate and cherries that displays stellar technique. Drink organic and biodynamic wines from £20.
Chef/s: Chris Johns. **Open:** Mon to Sat 11 to 11 (10am Sat). **Closed:** Sun. **Meals:** alc (main courses £20 to £22). Set L £19 (2 courses) to £27 (4 courses). Tasting menu £40. **Details:** 45 seats.

Arbutus
Groundbreaking Soho eatery
63-64 Frith Street, Soho, W1D 3JW
Tel no: (020) 7734 4545
www.arbutusrestaurant.co.uk
⊖ Tottenham Court Road, map 5
Modern European | £35
Cooking score: 5

It helped kick-start a little revolution back in the noughties with its enlightened attitude to butch ingredients and humble cuts, resolutely pegged-back prices and virtuoso displays of seasonal gastronomy – and Arbutus still has the power to thrill. Closely packed beech-wood tables and striking contemporary artwork add extra vitality to the jam-packed dining room, while the kitchen continues to nail it with comforting but refined nourishment: ravioli of veal and goats' curd 'explodes with mint, parsley and Moroccan lemon'; roast cod holds its own alongside caramelised endive, curly kale, sea purslane and blood-orange; ox cheek keeps earthy company with smoked polenta and punchy bourguignon sauce. For afters, it's worth the wait for a 'flavour-packed' raspberry clafoutis with vanilla ice cream. Invitingly priced 'working lunches' and pre-theatre deals are tailored for a speedy turnaround, and the trailblazing global wine list displays its credentials with everything available by the glass or 250ml carafe; bottles from £19.50. **Open:** all week L 12 to 2.30 (3 Sun), D 5 to 11 (6 to 9.30 Sun). **Closed:** 25 and 26 Dec, 1 Jan. **Meals:** alc (main courses £16 to £21). Set L £18 (2 courses) to £20. **Details:** 72 seats.

L'Atelier de Joël Robuchon
An indulgent line-up
13-15 West Street, Covent Garden, WC2H 9NE
Tel no: (020) 7010 8600
www.joelrobuchon.co.uk
⊖ Leicester Square, map 5
Modern French | £85
Cooking score: 6

V

Concept dining at its swishest is the Robuchon way. The ground-floor Atelier is a hermetically encased environment of gleaming rosewood table and counter surfaces, offset with the deep-red tones of Japanese lacquerwork and walls of trailing foliage. Xavier Boyer now heads the open-to-view kitchen, and knows the style well, having worked within the international Robuchon stable for a dozen years. Full-sized and tapas servings of contemporary French food are the drill, and once you start exploring the menu, the revelations come thick and fast. Lobster and cauliflower salad arrives with a delicately tempura-battered courgette flower and pesto, spaghetti and chanterelles with a soft-boiled egg in parsley emulsion. A diner subjected to uncoordinated service had any doubts stilled by slow-roast lamb curry with fondant carrots and cumin foam ('absolutely stunning'). Desserts go all classical, with rum baba, or Guanaja chocolate soufflé and pistachio ice cream. Thoroughbred wines start at £8 a 150ml glass, £38 a bottle.

Chef/s: Xavier Boyer. **Open:** all week L 12 to 3, D 5.30 to 11 (10.30 Sun). **Closed:** 25 Dec, 1 Jan, Aug bank hol. **Meals:** alc (main courses £24 to £48). Set L and early D £31 (2 courses) to £41. Tasting menu £95 (5 courses) to £129. **Details:** 43 seats. Separate bar. Wheelchair access.

L'Autre Pied
Classy little metropolitan eatery
5-7 Blandford Street, Marylebone, W1U 3DB
Tel no: (020) 7486 9696
www.lautrepied.co.uk
⊖ Bond Street, map 4
Modern European | £50
Cooking score: 6

£5 OFF **V**

It may lack the poise of its elder sibling Pied-à-Terre (see entry), but classy little L'Autre Pied is no slouch. Tables are perhaps too close for comfort, yet the dining room is convivial with its raspberry-hued banquettes, utilitarian chairs and attentive service. The kitchen deals in bold contemporary food, displaying intelligent ideas, seasonal resonance and sympathetic flavours: from baked Crapaudine beetroot with smoked eel, crème fraîche, radishes and dried olives to roe deer cooked in cocoa and juniper with Hispi cabbage cannelloni, carrot and kohlrabi. Turbot might receive exotic treatment with celeriac, fennel, black quinoa, ras-el-hanout and soya beans, while desserts proffer unashamed indulgence: witness Valrhona Caramelia chocolate crémeux with honeycomb, pistachio and tonka bean ice cream. All the details are in place and superb breads help to mop up the sauces – 'is that a "no-no" these days?', enquired one reader who got stuck in. Exemplary wines from trustworthy sources start at £27.

Chef/s: Andrew McFadden. **Open:** all week L 12 to 2.30 (3.30 Sun), Mon to Sat D 6 to 10.30. **Closed:** 23 to 28 Dec. **Meals:** alc (main courses £28 to £30). Set L and pre-theatre D £23 (2 courses) to £28. Sun L £35. Tasting menu £70 (8 courses). **Details:** 50 seats. 12 seats outside. Music.

Axis at One Aldwych
Cosmopolitan interior and satisfying food
1 Aldwych, Covent Garden, WC2B 4BZ
Tel no: (020) 7300 0300
www.onealdwych.com
⊖ Covent Garden, map 5
Modern British | £37
Cooking score: 2

£5 OFF 🛏

Located in the basement of the One Aldwych Hotel, Axis has its own entrance at street level, with stairs leading down to a large, high-ceilinged dining room done out with comfort in mind – think well-padded leather chairs and well-spaced tables. The menu is an appealing modern British repertoire where the range might extend from tartare of salt marsh lamb dressed with roasted shallots, capers, black olives, charcoal oil and Berkswell cheese, to roasted brill teamed with roasted garlic, salsify, braised kale and maple syrup shallots, finishing with chocolate and caramel tart with buttermilk ice cream. The deal for early dinner (from 5.30 to 6.30pm) is particularly good: consider smoked trout rillettes, then line-caught Brixham plaice or roasted loin of Suffolk pork with pulled pork, pumpkin and sage gremolata. The global wine list opens at £29.
Chef/s: Dominic Teague. **Open:** Tue to Sat D only 5.30 to 10. **Closed:** Sun, Mon, 21 Dec to 13 Jan, Apr 17 to 22, 11 Aug to 2 Sep. **Meals:** alc (main courses £16 to £24). Early D £20 (2 courses) to £24. Tasting menu £45. **Details:** 120 seats. Separate bar. Wheelchair access. Music. Car parking.

Balthazar
Star-spangled brasserie
4-6 Russell Street, Covent Garden, WC2E 7BN
Tel no: (020) 3301 1155
www.balthazarlondon.com
⊖ Covent Garden, map 5
Modern European | £45
Cooking score: 2

Balthazar is a true urban eatery, like the all-day French brasseries to which it pays homage. Open all week in Covent Garden and New York, from breakfasts and brunches to after-dinner brandies, it's filled with an infectious air of motoric efficiency. Shelves crammed with bottles, counter seating and a seafood bar contribute to the impression of all bases being covered, as does the classically constructed menu, which can be as French as garlic-buttered escargots or gratinated onion soup, or as *autre terre* as whopping cheeseburgers and fries with Heinz ketchup. The seafood platters are crammed with goodies, and there's oscietra caviar for the minted. Mains bring earthy comfort food: spatchcocked chicken basquaise, duck confit with roasties, sea bass in a paper envelope with mussels, fennel and Jerusalem artichokes. Finish with lemon tart and raspberries, or berry pavlova. The French wines soar from vins de pays to grands crus, starting at £19 (£5 a glass).
Chef/s: Robert Reid. **Open:** Mon to Fri L 12 to 3.30, all week D 5.30 to 10 (11 Sun). **Meals:** alc (main courses £13 to £36). **Details:** 150 seats. Separate bar. Wheelchair access. Music.

Bar Shu
Red-hot Szechuan lip-tingler
28 Frith Street, Soho, W1D 5LF
Tel no: (020) 7287 8822
www.barshurestaurant.co.uk
⊖ Leicester Square, map 5
Chinese | £45
Cooking score: 4

It may be just a short walk from Soho's Chinatown, but the red-hot Szechuan food served in this two-floored eatery is far from the Cantonese norm. The atmosphere is typical of the area's Chinese restaurants, however, 'a bit rushed, bright lighting and thin on ambience'. Staff also like to pack diners in upstairs leaving the ground floor free for walk-ins. But you're here to experience the fiery temperament of traditional Szechuan cuisine, and you should brace yourself for the sensory overload 'with enough spicy flavour per dish to power an entire restaurant'. Daring diners might try ducks' tongues and pig's trotters, in a sea of wok-fried red chillies, depicted on the menu above ominous words such as 'lip–tingly' and 'numbing'. Gentler alternatives include sticky tender ribs and biltong-like dried beef; deep, warming meat hotpots; gong-bao chicken or prawn, fried with vegetables and honeyed peanuts; and braised beef. Wine costs from £23 a bottle. **Chef/s:** Xiao Zhong Zhang. **Open:** all week 12 to 11 (11.30pm Fri and Sat). **Closed:** 24 and 25 Dec. **Meals:** alc (main courses £10 to £29). **Details:** 100 seats. Wheelchair access. Music.

Barrafina
Crammed with good things
54 Frith Street, Soho, W1D 4SL
Tel no: (020) 7813 8016
www.barrafina.co.uk
⊖ **Tottenham Court Road, map 5**
Spanish | £30
Cooking score: 5

'Had a wonderful light lunch here, everything so fresh and perfectly cooked, from a fabulous dish of cavolo nero (who would have thought?) to a perfect tortilla.' So runs one glowing report, perfectly catching the tone of Sam and Eddie Hart's tapas bar, considered one of London's most consistent addresses for Spanish food. Authentically reservation free, it's first come, first served at the long counter, but many are happy to queue for assured cooking that's driven by well-sourced produce and intelligent simplicity – especially given the good-natured staff. The repertoire is modern yet rooted in tradition: hand-carved jamón Señorio de Montanera, ham croquetas, grilled quail with allioli, chipirones (baby squid) and sardines a la plancha. Or look to the daily specials for fantastic prawns, razor clams, red king crab, even lobster. Come dessert, it's hard not to resist the hugely popular crema catalana. Cracking sherries and Spanish regional wines provide the accompaniment (from £19). A new Covent Garden branch is to be found at 10 Adelaide Street, WC2N 4HZ. **Chef/s:** Nieves Barragán Mohacho. **Open:** all week L 12 to 3 (1 to 3.30 Sun), D 5 to 11 (5.30 to 10 Sun). **Closed:** 24 and 26 Dec, bank hols. **Meals:** alc (main courses £7 to £16). **Details:** 23 seats. 8 seats outside.

LOCAL GEM
▲ Barrica
62 Goodge Street, Fitzrovia, W1T 4NE
Tel no: (020) 7436 9448
www.barrica.co.uk
⊖ **Goodge Street, map 5**
Spanish | £20

With its chequerboard floor and sunny hues, Barrica makes a good stab at recreating an *auténtico* Spanish tapas bar on Goodge Street. A bar counter replete with hanging jamón adds to the vibe, and there are some excellent snifters to be had from sherries, regional wines and pacharán (a sloe-flavoured liqueur). Rabbit comes with Jerusalem artichokes in a stew rich with oloroso; bacalao is served with assorted beetroots; and mussels make their way into croquetas. Wines start at £25. Open Mon to Sat.

Benares
Supercharged Indian high-roller
12a Berkeley Square, Mayfair, W1J 6BS
Tel no: (020) 7629 8886
www.benaresrestaurant.com
⊖ **Green Park, map 5**
Indian | £60
Cooking score: 4
V

Atul Kochhar's stylish Mayfair haven of pan-Indian elegance is a first-floor room decorated in sober dark-brown tones. For those with an eye to the action, there's a chef's table where the kitchen is on wide-angle view through glass panels. Among all the Asian cuisines in London, Indian food has reached out the most venturesomely – not just for technical polish, but for innovation too. Start here with crispy soft-shell crab and chilli squid salad with passion-fruit salsa, or smoky tandoor-roasted scallops and cauliflower textures, before explosively seasoned main courses such as roasted lamb rump with a samosa, Kolkata chickpeas and pickled baby artichoke, or a witty take on fish and chips, with John Dory in Cobra beer batter, cumined mushy peas and smoked tomato chutney. The unmissable

finisher is raspberry and rose bhapa doi (cooked yoghurt) with a pistachio barfi sweetmeat. Intelligently chosen, Mayfair-priced wines start at £29, or £6.50 a small glass.
Chef/s: Atul Kochhar. **Open:** Mon to Sat L 12 to 2.30, D 5.30 to 11. **Closed:** Sun, 24 to 26 Dec, 1 Jan. **Meals:** alc (main courses £24 to £36). Set L and D £29 (2 courses) to £35. Tasting menu £82 (6 courses). **Details:** 150 seats. Separate bar. Wheelchair access. Music. No children after 7.30.

Bentley's Oyster Bar & Grill
Venerable West End institution
11-15 Swallow Street, Piccadilly, W1B 4DG
Tel no: (020) 7734 4756
www.bentleys.org
⊖ Piccadilly Circus, map 5
Seafood | £40
Cooking score: 5
🍷

In 2015 Richard Corrigan will clock up ten years as owner of this venerable West End institution. On the ground floor is the compact oyster bar, the beating heart of the operation – pure English, the fittings glowing – where those in the know prefer to be. The heated terrace outside seats 35, but this doesn't reduce the crush within; the more sedate dining room upstairs tends to be favoured by tourists. Corrigan is crazy about the raw materials – the oysters are wonderful, the fish spanking fresh – and unapologetic about the prices. The old guard is cajoled by dressed crab, fish pie and fish and chips, but the kitchen also has plenty of contemporary aces up its sleeve: grilled octopus and artichoke, say, or Dover sole with sea kale and citrus. Seafood may be the predominant theme, but the grill supplies excellent meat dishes, bread-and-butter pudding is a must, and the strong wine list delivers fish-friendly whites, a good slate of sherries and excellent choice by the glass; bottles from £27.
Chef/s: Richard Corrigan. **Open:** all week L 12 to 6, D 6 to 12. **Closed:** 25 Dec, 1 Jan. **Meals:** alc (main courses £8 to £85). **Details:** 100 seats. 35 seats outside. Separate bar. Music.

Berners Tavern
The West End's most seductive tavern
10 Berners Street, Fitzrovia, W1T 3NP
Tel no: (020) 7908 7979
www.edition-hotels.marriott.com
⊖ Tottenham Court Road, Oxford Circus, map 5
Modern British | £42
Cooking score: 5
🛏

With more stardust than sawdust, Jason Atherton's 'tavern' at the smartest Marriott hotel in town offers grown-up glamour all day. The vast, high-ceilinged room – filled with framed art, elaborate cornicing, flickering candles and purposeful staff – is grand but seductive. Atherton's precise, sometimes playful dishes, overseen from the semi-open kitchen by chef-lieutenant Phil Carmichael, have equal appeal. Notes on provenance don't stop with roast Romney Marsh lamb shoulder or Lake District steak (this is a hotel, after all). Vivid wild garlic soup, poured over snails, tiny Jersey Royals and soft morels, comes with a foie gras toastie fresh from the Breville. Mains played with a straight bat include roast sea bass with brown shrimps, spinach and the breezy acidity of a grain-mustard velouté, while a cinnamon doughnut with almond sorbet oozes fun as well as silky chocolate sauce. Wine, chosen and sold by an attentive team, is from £21 (£7 a glass of Muscadet).
Chef/s: Jason Atherton and Phil Carmichael. **Open:** all week L 12 to 2.30, D 6 to 10.30. **Meals:** alc (main courses £19 to £28). **Details:** 163 seats. Separate bar. Wheelchair access.

Symbols
🛏 Accommodation is available
💷30 Three courses for less than £30
V Separate vegetarian menu
£5 OFF £5-off voucher scheme
🍷 Notable wine list

LOCAL GEM
▲ Blanchette
9 D'Arblay Street, Soho, W1F 8DR
Tel no: (020) 7439 8100
www.blanchettesoho.co.uk
⊖ Tottenham Court Road, Oxford Circus, map 5
French | £27

This lively eatery, patriotically French right down to its wine list (from £18.50), is worth knowing about. Owned by three brothers, it's a rough-hewn one-off, a pretty tiled front bar with counter seating giving way to exposed brick, rickety furniture and candles. The display of charcuterie and cheeses tempts, and there's a line-up of kindly priced small sharing plates: simple things like chunky terrine; crispy frogs' legs with bois boudran sauce; braised lamb shoulder with anchovy, rosemary and soubise; good leeks vinaigrette; frites with a rich béarnaise. Closed D Sun.

Bocca di Lupo
Dishes bursting with Italian flavours
12 Archer Street, Piccadilly, W1D 7BB
Tel no: (020) 7734 2223
www.boccadilupo.com
⊖ Piccadilly Circus, map 5
Italian | £30
Cooking score: 2

Bocca di Lupo's casual concept suits the way people want to eat and drink these days, but regulars advise grabbing a seat at the bar rather than enduring the cramped tables in the back dining room. Jacob Kenedy makes every effort to bring the essence of modern Italian cooking to this corner of Piccadilly via a menu that turns its back on conventional courses, offering instead a choice of large and small plates. Inspiration comes from all over: Puglia may supply burrata with aubergines, tomato, chilli and mint; Trentino the venison tartare with Parmesan and capers; and from the Veneto could come sea bream carpaccio with orange and rosemary. Alternatively, there is grilled wild boar sausage and roast red onions or spaghettini with half a lobster, mussels and ginger, and you could finish with chocolate-covered almond and orange cake. The wine list is an Italian regional blockbuster; bottles start at £21.75 but rise steeply.
Chef/s: Jacob Kenedy. **Open:** all week L 12.15 to 3 (12.30 to 3.30 Sun), D 5.15 to 11 (9.30 Sun). **Meals:** alc (main courses £10 to £27). **Details:** 70 seats. Wheelchair access. Music.

LOCAL GEM
▲ Bone Daddies
31 Peter Street, Soho, W1F 0AR
Tel no: (020) 7287 8581
www.bonedaddiesramen.com
⊖ Leicester Square, Piccadilly Circus, map 5
Japanese | £24

Headed by Ross Shonhan (ex-Zuma and Nobu), Bone Daddies is one of several no-frills ramen noodle bars to hit London recently. It delivers ramen 'so deep in flavour and seriously unctuous' you must be 'prepared to queue, sit next to strangers in a cramped room and shout above the pumping music'. Regulars order tonkatsu ramen, which comes in a cloudy, richly flavoured 20-hour pork bone broth with a perfectly cooked marinated soft-boiled egg and tender chashu pork belly. Wine from £16; otherwise, explore the cocktails, shochu or beer. Open all week.

Bonnie Gull Seafood Shack
A handy local asset
21A Foley Street, Fitzrovia, W1W 6DS
Tel no: (020) 7436 0921
www.bonniegull.com
⊖ Oxford Circus, Goodge Street, map 5
Seafood | £35
Cooking score: 2
£5
OFF

It looks every inch the seafood restaurant, from its blue-and-white striped awning outside to the cramped, nautically themed room with clattery floorboards and closely packed tables. Big windows on two sides keep it light and bright and everyone finds the service cheerful. What's offered is a short, daily changing menu built around the freshest seafood, fashionable pairings and reasonable

prices. The kitchen likes to keep things simple – and seasonal. Cumin-cayenne spiced sprats with aïoli; mussels with bacon, cider and crème fraîche; Cornish mackerel with mesclun salad and lemon; and a very fresh tranche of brill meunière with Poularde clams and samphire are typical of the style. These might be backed up by sides of chunky beef-dripping chips or a seasonal green. Desserts, such as a superb chocolate brownie with salted-caramel ice cream and candied hazelnuts, close proceedings. Fish-friendly wines from £18. Note: a second Bonnie Gull has opened at 55-57 Exmouth Market, EC1R 4QL; tel: (020) 3122 0047.
Chef/s: Luke Robinson and Gavin Gordon. **Open:** all week L 12 to 3 (4 Sat and Sun), D 6 to 10. **Meals:** alc (main courses £15 to £35). **Details:** 32 seats. 12 seats outside. Separate bar. Music.

Brasserie Chavot
Classical themes for belt-loosening gluttony
41 Conduit Street, Mayfair, W1S 2YF
Tel no: (020) 7078 9577
www.brasseriechavot.com
⊖ Oxford Circus, map 5
French | £40
Cooking score: 5

Oh, the glamour – the beautiful mosaic floors, the voluptuous chandeliers, the mirrored walls, the red-leather booths – this is a Parisian dream and the food fits it like a kid glove. Eric Chavot may have shifted down a gear since his days at the Capital, but that's no bad thing, because here he's free to promote relaxation, nostalgia and shameless, belt-loosening gluttony. Flavour rules supreme in an 'utterly wonderful' starter of grilled asparagus with Parmesan foam and melting slivers of Parmesan, while a main course of 'accurately cooked', pearly sea bass ('a perfect piece of fish') with caramelised ratatouille niçoise showcases top ingredients. A side order of pommes frites certainly won't disappoint, nor will a dish of intense smoky chickpeas and chorizo. For dessert, look to classics such as

rum baba or îles flottantes. The wine list covers France well, and offers a decent choice from the rest of the world, starting at £22.
Chef/s: Eric Chavot. **Open:** Mon to Sat L 12 to 2.30, D 6 to 10.30. Sun 12.30 to 9 Sun. **Meals:** alc (main courses £18 to £26). **Details:** 72 seats. Separate bar. Wheelchair access. Music.

LOCAL GEM
▲ Brasserie Zédel
20 Sherwood Street, Soho, W1F 7ED
Tel no: (020) 7734 4888
www.brasseriezedel.com
⊖ Piccadilly Circus, map 5
French | £23

The London equivalent of Paris' legendary Chartier, Brasserie Zédel doesn't yet boast a century of history but it's off to a good start. Run by the smooth operators behind the Wolseley (see entry), Zédel is 'far from haute cuisine' but its charm lies instead in the nostalgic pleasures of its old-fashioned brasserie menu and 'expansive', glamorous dining room. Egg mayonnaise, escargots, oysters, gateau 'Opéra', choucroute and confit de canard keep the capital's impecunious Francophiles well fed and happy. House wine, £17.75. Open all week.

NEW ENTRY
Café Murano
Smart-casual Mayfair hangout
33 St James's Street, Green Park, SW1A 1HD
Tel no: (020) 3371 5559
www.cafemurano.co.uk
⊖ Green Park, map 5
Italian | £33
Cooking score: 4

Offering a simple approach to north Italian cooking, this casual offshoot of Murano (see entry) is hard to trump, perfectly pitched in both pricing and atmosphere. The long, narrow room is done out in fashionable neutral shades with plenty of polished wood and gentle lighting. Whether you are perched on stools at the bar or ensconced at a small table, the place runs like a well-oiled machine

thanks to excellent staff. Angela Hartnett is giving people what they like to eat: cicchetti to nibble with drinks (do try the fabulous truffle arancini), antipasti of comforting ribollita, primi of gloriously buttery gnocchi of pumpkin and chestnut with a hint of sage. Secondi could bring a great dish of tender ox cheek with wet polenta and chestnuts, but there is really no obligation to have multi courses. Add the good-value set lunch and this is just what the area wants. Wines from £19.50.
Chef/s: Samantha Williams. **Open:** Mon to Sun L 12 to 3 (11.30 to 4 Sun), Mon to Sat D 5.30 to 11. **Closed:** 25 and 26 Dec. **Meals:** alc (main courses £15 to £22). Set L and D £18 (2 courses) to £22. Sun L £45. **Details:** 85 seats.

Le Caprice

Famous Mayfair brasserie with loyal fans
Arlington House, Arlington Street, Mayfair, SW1A 1RJ
Tel no: (020) 7629 2239
www.le-caprice.co.uk
⊖ Green Park, map 5
Modern British | £45
Cooking score: 4

V

When it comes to giving the people what they want, the folks at Caprice Holdings know a thing or two. The place isn't even that audaciously expensive for this part of town, although readers are still bemused by the need for a four quid cover charge. It's a swanky brasserie with David Bailey's photos on the walls and a faint expectation that Princess Di might walk in at any moment. The menu, however, has shifted with the sands of time, so the likes of slow-roasted Blythburgh pork belly with wild garlic mash or fillet of cod with crab and sea vegetable risotto have a contemporary ring, while grilled calf's liver with crispy pancetta is a long-time classic that isn't going anywhere. There are also Med flavours aplenty, a few Asian interlopers and a good showing of British ingredients. Finish with a cherry cola sundae and expect occasional jazzy interludes. Wines from £23.50.

Chef/s: Andrew McLay. **Open:** all week 12 to 12 (11.30am Sat, 11 to 11 Sun). **Closed:** 25 and 26 Dec. **Meals:** alc (main courses £17 to £35). Set D £20 (2 courses) to £25. **Details:** 74 seats. 16 seats outside. Separate bar. Wheelchair access. Music.

Casa Malevo

Warm-hearted Argentinian dining
23 Connaught Street, Marylebone, W2 2AY
Tel no: (020) 7402 1988
www.casamalevo.com
⊖ Marble Arch, map 4
Argentinian | £38
Cooking score: 2

In the four years it has been open in 'Connaught Village', this unassuming Argentinian wine bar has gathered something of a following. It's all rollickingly informal – exposed brick, wooden floors and closely packed small tables see to that – and the emphasis is firmly on Argentinian food and drink. Ingredients are impeccable (beef is imported from Argentina), so settle down with a patriotic carafe from the all-Argentinian wine list and order some empanadas or grilled chorizo on toast served with onions and braised ox cheeks. Steaks may be the star of the show, but the grill can also deliver rump of lamb with red quinoa, broccoli and 'anchovies' salsa verde, or half a free-range chicken with rosemary and lemon. Typical of the style, too, is the chimichurri beef burger, but do save room for the famed dulce de leche crème brûlée with banana split ice cream. Carafes from £11.95, bottles from £19.95.
Chef/s: Diego Jacquet. **Open:** all week L 12 to 2.30 (3.30 Sat and Sun), D 6 to 10.30 (10 Sun). **Closed:** 25 and 26 Dec. **Meals:** alc (main courses £14 to £28). **Details:** 37 seats. 6 seats outside. Music.

╽╽• Visit us Online

To find out more about *The Good Food Guide*, please visit www.thegoodfoodguide.co.uk

LOCAL GEM
▲ Ceviche
17 Frith Street, Soho, W1D 4RG
Tel no: (020) 7292 2040
www.cevicheuk.com
⊖ Tottenham Court Road, map 5
Peruvian | £30

Mixing a mean pisco sour, Ceviche is all about the flavours of Peru, from that oh-so trendy cocktail to little plates of marinated seafood with a South American sparkle. The ceviche bar steals the show with its output of drunk scallops with pisco, pomegranate and the kick of chilli and lime, or sea bass in amarillo chilli tiger's milk (the lime-based marinade that's the bedrock of ceviche). There's cooked stuff, too, but it doesn't reach the same heights. Wines from £17.50. Open all week.

The Chancery
Fine-tuned cooking in lawyerland
9 Cursitor Street, Holborn, EC4A 1LL
Tel no: (020) 7831 4000
www.thechancery.co.uk
⊖ Chancery Lane, map 5
Modern European | £35
Cooking score: 4

The intimately proportioned Chancery, a suite of little rooms over two floors on a Holborn corner, is popular with legal eagles. It buzzes with custom at lunchtimes particularly. Hung with contemporary British artworks and space-expanding mirrors, this is an unmistakably 21st-century eating space, and the menu reflects that with modern European dishes built from strong seasonal, often unexpected, flavours. If you've tumbled in on a winter's day in search of a bowl of something hot, helianthus artichoke velouté should do the trick. Alternatively, start with scared scallops, caviar and crème fraîche (and no cauliflower purée!). Pork main courses never lack for takers, especially when composed of smoked Ibérico, BBQ rib and crackling, with creamed Savoy and pickled pear, while fish could be roast halibut with blood orange, pine nuts and monk's beard. Finish with that latter-day classic, Brillat-Savarin cheesecake with rhubarb. A compact choice of wines opens with house French at £17.50.
Chef/s: Graham Long. Open: Mon to Fri L 12 to 2.30, Mon to Sat D 6 to 10.30. Closed: Sun, 23 Dec to 4 Jan, bank hols. Meals: alc (main courses £12 to £22). Tasting menu £48.50 (6 courses) to £70. Details: 108 seats. 14 seats outside. Separate bar.

★ TOP 50 ★

NEW ENTRY
Chiltern Firehouse
Just simple, delicious food
1 Chiltern Street, Marylebone, W1U 7PA
Tel no: (020) 7073 7676
www.chilternfirehouse.com
⊖ Baker Street, Bond Street, map 4
Modern American | £60
Cooking score: 6

🛏

The attempt to turn this former fire station into a landmark of the London dining scene has been a disarming success. The listed Victorian red-brick building (also a hotel, owned by André Balazs of LA's Chateau Marmont and New York's The Mercer), is decorated in casual, modernistic style creating a large, vibrant, tightly packed room. The result is atmospheric or a crush, depending on your perspective, but everyone is courteously accommodated by a smart, knowledgeable crew. Prized tables are banquettes, though some feel the counter seating overlooking the action-packed open kitchen is where to be. Behind it all is Nuno Mendes, who made a strong impression at Viajante with his hard-to-classify molecular cooking, but has now embraced a more orthodox style, cooking with astonishing vigour, authority and a master's touch. This is delicious food in all its seasonal glory. Unabashed simplicity is the key to a staggeringly fine plate involving char-grilled Ibérico pork, sweet-roasted garlic purée and collard greens. And there's brilliance in the fish department, too: from a starter of grilled octopus with aubergine, daikon and mushrooms to a tender monkfish cooked over pine, scattered with crisp, puffed

barley and needing nothing more than fennel (whole and puréed). The kitchen can also deliver light-as-air crab doughnuts to nibble, and bring things to a conclusion with an extraordinary and very modern frozen apple pannacotta with herb granita and dried meringue. The wine list opens at £19.
Chef/s: Nuno Mendes and Dale Osborne. **Open:** all week L 12 to 2 (11 to 3 Sat and Sun), D 5 to 10.30 (6 Sat and Sun). **Meals:** alc (main courses £18 to £30). **Details:** 200 seats. Separate bar. Wheelchair access. Music.

China Tang at the Dorchester
Scintillating Shanghai glitz
The Dorchester Hotel, 53 Park Lane, Hyde Park, W1K 1QA
Tel no: (020) 7629 9988
www.chinatanglondon.co.uk
⊖ Hyde Park Corner, map 4
Chinese | £50
Cooking score: 4

Anyone weaned on plates of roast duck on rice in Soho's Chinatown is in for a shock at this glamorous subterranean dining room in the bowels of the Dorchester hotel. Invoking the sultry excesses of 1930s Shanghai, China Tang resembles a set from a decadent movie with its sumptuous chinoiserie, Art Deco artefacts, silken swathes, carved woodwork and calligraphy. While the menu contains much for the five-star-luxury hotel set (with three-figure price tags), it also has very correct Chinese food cooked to a standard that you'll rarely find in London. The Peking duck, for instance, is the proper three-course meal (including duck soup and the crispy skin), roast pigeon is a classic Cantonese dish, as is steamed pork patty with salted fish. Set menus and lunchtime dim sum are kinder on the wallet, but the wine list jets skywards from £27. The restaurant is part of the Sultan of Brunei's Dorchester Collection (see entries for Alain Ducasse and CUT at 45 Park Lane).

Chef/s: Chong Choi Fong. **Open:** all week 12 to 11.45 (11.30 Sun). **Closed:** 24 and 25 Dec. **Meals:** alc (main courses £10 to £42). Set L £27.50. **Details:** 120 seats. Separate bar. Wheelchair access. Music.

Chisou
Authentic, unobtrusive Japanese favourite
4 Princes Street, Mayfair, W1B 2LE
Tel no: (020) 7629 3931
www.chisourestaurant.com
⊖ Oxford Circus, map 5
Japanese | £40
Cooking score: 4
£5 OFF **V**

The elbow-to-elbow craziness of Oxford Street is just a short walk away, making Chisou a great escape from all the chain offerings churning out noodles by the truck load. The harmonious neutrality of blond wood provides the décor, and there are tables at the counter for a bit of sushi action (plus a couple of private dining rooms in the basement). The izakaya style of sharing is the way to go, with a choice of little plates: from sushi of braised eel and razor clam, to yellowtail sashimi and squid tempura. The fish and shellfish are top-notch, fresh as can be and prepared with skill. Beef teriyaki, grilled sea bass, black cod marinated in white miso paste – bring them on, until body or wallet reaches maximum capacity. There are noodles, too, such as tanuki udon, and the saké list is helpfully informative. Wines from £19. Branches in Knightsbridge and Chiswick.
Chef/s: Dham Kodi. **Open:** Mon to Sat L 12 to 2.30 (12.30 to 3 Sat), D 6 to 10.30. Sun 1 to 9. **Closed:** 25 and 26 Dec, bank hols. **Meals:** alc (main courses £9 to £27). Set L £15. **Details:** 75 seats. Music.

Cigala

Friendly neighbourhood tapas
54 Lamb's Conduit Street, Bloomsbury, WC1N 3LW
Tel no: (020) 7405 1717
www.cigala.co.uk
⊖ Holborn, Russell Square, map 5
Spanish | £27
Cooking score: 1

£30

White walls, birch pews and globe lights lend a Scandinavian modernity to this convivial tapas restaurant. Although there's a handful of mains, most diners stick to the tapas menu, which, although bewilderingly long, combines the classics (jamón Ibérico, croquetas, tortilla) with more unusual Basque tongue-twisters like txangurro (baked crab). Some dishes arrive with almost alarming speed, though their quality is seemingly undiminished. A plate of organic scrambled eggs with chorizo ticks the comfort-food box as do the croquetas, their insides pleasingly gooey – and don't miss the walnut tart. The all-Spanish wine list is informative on regions and grape varieties. House wine £15 per 500ml carafe.
Chef/s: Clayton Felizari. **Open:** all week 12 to 10.45 (12.30 Sat, 9.45 Sun). **Closed:** 25 and 26 Dec, Easter. **Meals:** alc (main courses £14 to £20). Set L £18 (2 courses) to £20. Sun L £16. **Details:** 64 seats. 30 seats outside. Separate bar.

Cigalon

Provence on a plate
115 Chancery Lane, Holborn, WC2A 1PP
Tel no: (020) 7242 8373
www.cigalon.co.uk
⊖ Chancery Lane, map 5
French | £30
Cooking score: 3

£5 OFF

You don't need to jump on a plane in search of the sunny Riviera. Taking its name from an obscure 1930s French movie about restaurant rivalry, Cigalon conjures up just the right vibe with olive trees outside, ivy-clad trellises, pastel-striped canvas seats and a soundtrack of chirping cicadas in the glass-ceilinged dining room. The menu also fuels fantasies by offering nostalgia-inducing plates of salade niçoise, pissaladière, fennel and mussel soup laced with pastis, or red mullet carpaccio with limoncello dressing – as well as provençale and Corsican charcuterie, assorted pastas (smoked aubergine and ricotta ravioli, for example) and more robust seasonal ideas including grilled haunch of venison with pumpkin and trompette mushrooms. Finish in style with ewes' cheese and fig pickle, candied chestnut parfait or a chocolate bar with Tropézienne cream. The regionally biased drinks list features pungent native aperitifs such as thyme-based farigoule and peachy Rinquinquin, plus a compendium of French wines from £19.50.
Chef/s: Julien Carlon. **Open:** Mon to Fri L 12 to 2.15, D 5.45 to 10. **Closed:** Sat, Sun, 2 weeks Christmas and New Year. **Meals:** alc (main courses £9 to £20). Set L and D £20 (2 courses) to £25. **Details:** 68 seats. Music.

Cinnamon Club

Exhilarating new-wave Indian cuisine
30-32 Great Smith Street, Westminster, SW1P 3BU
Tel no: (020) 7222 2555
www.cinnamonclub.com
⊖ Westminster, map 5
Indian | £60
Cooking score: 4

£5 OFF

Ensconced rather grandly in premises that once housed the Westminster Library, the Cinnamon Club has been part of the transformation of Indian food in the capital since 2001. The august Victorian surroundings somehow suit Vivek Singh's vision perfectly, although the dining room itself is light and airy, with white walls and smartly laid tables. The cooking is distinctly in the modern idiom, with plenty to enthral. A char-grilled breast of Anjou squab and pigeon tikki come with chilli-walnut salad to start, while grilled king crab is boosted with garlic and pepper, and accompanied by smoked crab purée. Seafood is always interesting, as in mains of

tandoori king prawns with malai curry sauce and dried shrimp rice, and vegetarian dishes are inspired. Try braised snake gourd filled with spiced paneer, served with yellow lentils and rice. Finish with milk chocolate and pecan pudding, bitter chocolate mousse and thandai (spiced almond) ice cream. Wines start at £27.
Chef/s: Vivek Singh. **Open:** Mon to Sat L 12 to 2.45, D 6 to 10.45. **Closed:** Sun, 26 Dec, 1 Jan, bank hols.
Meals: alc (main courses £16 to £35). Set L £22 (2 courses) to £24. Set D £26 (2 courses) to £30.
Details: 210 seats. Separate bar. Wheelchair access.

Cinnamon Soho
Vivid Indian flavours for Soho hipsters
5 Kingly Street, Soho, W1B 5PF
Tel no: (020) 7437 1664
www.cinnamonsoho.com
⊖ Oxford Circus, map 5
Indian | £20
Cooking score: 3

£5 £30
OFF

The third of Vivek Singh's group of dynamic Cinnamon-branded gaffs (see entries for Club and Kitchen), this one is aimed at the Soho crowd for an express lunch or a full-on feast whenever the mood strikes. It all takes place in a slick space rich with dark wood, leather banquettes and modern art: like a contemporary canteen for the media classes, with a menu that deals in classy modern stuff presented with pizazz. Start with slow-braised pork belly with honey and chilli glaze, or share something from the 'Balls!' section – Bangla Scotch eggs, maybe, or vegetable shikampur. Spicing is spot-on throughout. Lucknow-style chicken biryani is made with a free-range bird, rump of Kentish lamb comes with Rajasthani corn sauce, and black lentils simmer for 24 hours. There's afternoon tea, too (high chai), and desserts include the likes of black carrot cake with stem ginger ice cream. Wines from £18.
Chef/s: Vivek Singh and Ramachandran Raju. **Open:** Mon to Sat 11 to 11. Sun L 12 to 4. **Closed:** 1 Jan.
Meals: alc (main courses £11 to £17). Set L and D

£15 (2 courses) to £18. Sun L £24. Tasting menu £35.
Details: 70 seats. 24 seats outside. Wheelchair access. Music.

Clos Maggiore
A seductive French experience
33 King Street, Covent Garden, WC2E 8JD
Tel no: (020) 7379 9696
www.closmaggiore.com
⊖ Covent Garden, map 5
French | £38
Cooking score: 2

⬧ V

Tables are mainly for two at Clos Maggiore, one of Covent Garden's most romantic spots. In summer, the conservatory roof comes back to allow for starlit dinners, while candlelight and flickering fires create the mood in the other dining spaces. From France via the rest of the Med, the food is a good match for the old-school, 'on-the-ball' hospitality, and vegetarians aren't forgotten among all the Limousin veal and Ibérico pork. To start, braised shoulder of Loire rabbit comes with sweet and sour black radish, while rack of Welsh lamb has less modish accompaniments involving black olive and goats' cheese. Paris-Brest, vanilla pain perdu and a Valrhona mille-feuille are among the very Frenchest of desserts. Given the location, the pre-theatre menu is especially handy, though being waylaid by the vast wine list is always a possibility. Big on France, with a selection listed by grape variety, it starts at £18.50.
Chef/s: Marcellin Marc. **Open:** all week L 12 to 2.30, D 5 to 11 (10 Sun). **Closed:** 24 and 25 Dec. **Meals:** alc (main courses £18 to £33). Set L and D £18 (2 courses) to £22. Sun L £25. **Details:** 67 seats. Music. Children at L only.

⫴⬥ Average Price
The average price listed in main-entry reviews denotes the price of a three-course meal, without wine.

Copita

Big flavours in small packages
27 d'Arblay Street, Soho, W1F 8EP
Tel no: (020) 7287 7797
www.copita.co.uk
⊖ Oxford Circus, Tottenham Court Road, map 5
Spanish | £18
Cooking score: 3

🍶 £30

Owned by the people behind Barrica (see entry), this Soho hangout is small, fun and noisy – certainly not the place for an intimate tête-à-tête, but everyone has a good time. If you can squeeze in at one of the perilously high stools, you're in for a treat: this is not your average tapas. Unorthodox is the word for a choice that runs from Jerusalem artichoke with peanut aïoli to salted ox tongue with sweet chilli and mustard, via smoked eel with pork crackling, and pheasant with butter-bean stew and sage. Elsewhere, you can graze on hand-carved jamón Ibérico de Bellota and nibble on mushroom croquetas or truffled goats' cheese with almond and honey. Service is perfectly timed. If you've got a sweet tooth, round things off with churros and chocolate. Wash it all down with delectable sherries and Spanish regional wines by the glass or carafe. Bottles from £20.
Chef/s: Nacho Pinilla. **Open:** Mon to Sat L 12 to 4 (1 Sat), D 5.30 to 10.30. **Closed:** Sun, 24 to 26 Dec, 1 Jan, bank hols. **Meals:** alc (tapas £3 to £8). **Details:** 36 seats. 8 seats outside. Music.

Corrigan's Mayfair

Gilded Mayfair flagship
28 Upper Grosvenor Street, Mayfair, W1K 7EH
Tel no: (020) 7499 9943
www.corrigansmayfair.com
⊖ Marble Arch, map 4
Modern British | £60
Cooking score: 4

V

Deep in gilt-edged Mayfair, Corrigan's has many of the trappings expected of restaurants in this area: a dimly lit, clubby sheen, polished service and plenty of custom from hedge-fund managers who are unlikely to flinch at the prices. Diners come, though, for the no-nonsense cooking rich with classic combinations and packing a culinary punch. Richard Corrigan's food is rooted in regional provenance, mainly first-class British and Irish produce. When it comes to game – say roast mallard with chestnuts and sprouts, game pie or a very good version of venison shepherd's pie – he's the business. There's praise, too, for the likes of crab and chilli linguine, whole Dover sole meunière and for the Sunday roast beef carved at the table. And dessert? By all accounts the rhubarb crumble soufflé is hard to skip. The excellent-value set lunch offers some financial relief, but not so the extensive wine list, where prices zoom skywards from £29.
Chef/s: Richard Corrigan and Chris McGowan. **Open:** Sun to Fri L 12 to 3 (4 Sun), all week D 6 to 10.30 (9.30 Sun). **Closed:** 24 to 30 Dec, 1 Jan. **Meals:** alc (main courses £24 to £40). Set L £25 (2 courses) to £29. Sunday L £27. Tasting menu £75. **Details:** 84 seats. Separate bar. Wheelchair access. Music.

Coya

Slick, modern Peruvian cooking
118 Piccadilly, Mayfair, W1J 7NW
Tel no: (020) 7042 7118
www.coyarestaurant.com
⊖ Hyde Park Corner, Green Park, map 5
Peruvian | £50
Cooking score: 4

Arjun Waney of Roka and Zuma fame has delivered another rip-roaring destination: slick, funky and polished. The colourful, moodily lit lower-ground floor incorporates on-view chefs and a lively bar. It's a place that happily accommodates all comers, from big-occasion bashes to cool, romantic assignations. Small plates are the mainstay of a menu that deals in highly assured, evolved Peruvian cooking – exhibiting a touch of worldly sophistication in yellowfin tuna ceviche (with soy, sesame seeds and shrimp cracker) or sashimi-style tiraditos of cobia fish (served with dashi, truffle oil and chives). Large plates

are big on flavour, perhaps lamb chops with crushed aubergines or beef ribs with black Cusqueña (Peruvian beer) and aji limo. Corn sundae, with sweetcorn ice cream and popcorn, makes a brilliant finale. The sheer expense of it all can grate (especially when table turning is ruthlessly enforced), and the modern wine list (from £28) takes no prisoners.
Chef/s: Gareth Rhodes. **Open:** Mon to Sat L 12 to 3, all week D 6 to 10.30 (11 Thur to Sat). **Closed:** 25 to 27 Dec, 1 Jan. **Meals:** alc (main courses £15 to £72). Set L £20 (2 courses) to £27. **Details:** 140 seats. Separate bar. Wheelchair access. Music.

CUT at 45 Park Lane
Glitzy all-American steakhouse
45 Park Lane, Mayfair, W1K 1PN
Tel no: (020) 7493 4545
www.45parklane.com
⊖ Hyde Park Corner, map 4
North American | £80
Cooking score: 4

Some hotel dining rooms pretend they're a stand-alone restaurant, others have hotel-lobby entrances that are so concealed you need to be directed. Not so CUT, the London offshoot of Wolfgang Puck's high-gloss modern American steakhouse chain. Glide past the foyer of the opulent 45 Park Lane (part of the Sultan of Brunei's Dorchester Collection) and you're there: a lush, mirrored brown-gold room with soaring double-height door frames giving focus, full-drop windows letting in natural light. Reporters usually skip starters, partly due to the Mayfair prices, but as one explained 'when I'm having a good steak I go straight to the main event'. And good they are, with cuts ranging from south Devon Angus filet mignon to an Australian Wagyu, served with an extensive choice of sauces such as tempura onion rings or French fries. Bread is excellent, brûléed banana cream pie remains the star dessert. The US-favouring wine list starts high at £35.

Chef/s: David McIntyre. **Open:** all week L 12 to 3, D 6 to 11 (10.30 Sun). **Meals:** alc (main courses £21 to £92). Set L £34 (2 courses). **Details:** 70 seats. Separate bar. Wheelchair access. Music.

Dabbous
Ferociously seasonal food
39 Whitfield Street, Fitzrovia, W1T 2SF
Tel no: (020) 7323 1544
www.dabbous.co.uk
⊖ Goodge Street, map 5
Modern European | £48
Cooking score: 6

It may be easier to get a table nowadays, but Ollie Dabbous helped define a genre when he landed on this grungy street corner in 2012 with his deceptively simple, ferociously seasonal food that (with hay, pebbles and wild flowers) might have just blown in from the wild. Outward simplicity with underlying sophistication defines the cooking, seen in English asparagus teamed with virgin rapeseed oil mayonnaise, meadowsweet and chopped, toasted hazelnuts; a 'quite astonishingly gorgeous' coddled egg with smoked butter and flecks of mushroom; and buttery-rich, crisp-skinned chicken matched with generously dressed lettuce cut through with fenugreek and rounded off with a creamy, silken, egg-based sauce. And where else would you get a coconut filled with ethereal foam, glacial sorbet and a layer of sweet baked coconut that steams like an Icelandic geyser when you dig into it? The European-weighted wine list offers plenty by the glass or carafe, with bottles starting at £25.
Chef/s: Ollie Dabbous. **Open:** Tue to Sat L 12 to 3, D 5.30 to 11.30 (6.30 Sat). **Closed:** Sun, Mon, 2 weeks Christmas, 2 weeks Aug. **Meals:** Set L £28 (4 courses). Set D £48 (4 courses). Tasting menu £59 (7 courses). **Details:** 40 seats. Separate bar.

Dean Street Townhouse

Glamorous Soho rendezvous
69-71 Dean Street, Soho, W1D 3SE
Tel no: (020) 7434 1775
www.deanstreettownhouse.com
⊖ Tottenham Court Road, map 5
Modern British | £50
Cooking score: 3

Soho House founder Nick Jones certainly nailed all-day dining in Soho when he opened this British brasserie in an oh-so-cool Georgian town house some five years ago. It has played to a packed house ever since. The dining room is all dark wood and red leather clubby masculinity, its long, stool-lined bar and noisy *Mad Men* vibes creating a thunderous babble. The menu looks back with affection, sourcing the UK's best seasonal foodstuffs and presenting them simply. How about a plate of mince and potatoes, a Suffolk pork T bone with apple and crackling or even good old fish and chips? The dishes come thick and fast, from Dorset crab soup to treacle tart and clotted cream via ribeye steak with fat chips and béarnaise, Sunday roasts, savouries such as Welsh rarebit, and well-reported breakfasts and afternoon teas. The wine list provides a snappy global tour, with prices from £22.
Chef/s: Harvey Ayliff. **Open:** all week 7am to midnight (8am Sat, 8am to 11pm Sun). **Meals:** alc (main courses £14 to £60). Sun L £24 to £28.
Details: 120 seats. Separate bar. Music.

Dehesa

Gregarious tapas pit-stop
25 Ganton Street, Oxford Circus, W1F 9BP
Tel no: (020) 7494 4170
www.dehesa.co.uk
⊖ Oxford Circus, map 5
Tapas | £35
Cooking score: 2

Whole legs of jamón hanging in the window are a reminder that Dehesa is named after the woodland region of Spain where the tastiest acorn-munching porkers roam.

Unsurprisingly, top-drawer Ibérico charcuterie is a must-have at this enthusiastically run, jazzy sibling of Salt Yard (see entry). The menu also promises myriad Iberian and Italian tapas treats at very gentle prices. Aside from breads, artisan cheeses and cured meats, look for spot-on plates of confit octopus with pink fir potatoes and sautéed sprouting broccoli, braised wild boar with grilled polenta, or 'nduja and green olive croquetas with guindilla chilli-spiked aïoli. Nibbles of Padrón peppers, boquerones or pork rillons go down well with a glass of Palo Cortado at the bar. Otherwise, delve into the fascinating list of Italian and Spanish regional wines (from £19). Tables are tightly packed in the gregarious room, and there are discreet window booths for those who pitch up early.
Chef/s: Gianni Vatteroni. **Open:** Mon to Fri L 12 to 3, D 5 to 11. Sat and Sun 12 to 11 (10 Sun). **Closed:** 25 and 26 Dec, 1 Jan. **Meals:** alc (tapas £5 to £11).
Details: 46 seats. 60 seats outside. Separate bar. Music.

The Delaunay

Strikingly handsome high-roller
55 Aldwych, Covent Garden, WC2B 4BB
Tel no: (020) 7499 8558
www.thedelaunay.com
⊖ Temple, map 5
Modern European | £35
Cooking score: 3
V

'I loved the old-fashioned atmosphere and that rather continental feel of the place. Quite expensive, but worth it for the occasion.' Chris Corbin and Jeremy King (of Wolseley fame, see entry) spared no effort in their reincarnation of a Central European grand café. Three years down the line, the kitchen continues to do a remarkable job reworking classic principles and maintaining a grandeur in the cuisine to match the room's panelled splendour. Hungarian goulash is served alongside choucroute à l'alsacienne, and you can also expect excellent schnitzel Cordon Bleu ('so long since I have seen this on a menu') or a simple fillet of sea trout served on finely

sliced braised leeks and greens with a tangy lemon sauce. Desserts took one reader back to the Viennese and Hungarian restaurants of the old-school: ice cream coups 'just as they should be', Sachertorte and passion fruit gugelhupf. Wines from £19.
Chef/s: Malachi O'Gallagher. **Open:** all week 11.30am to midnight (11pm Sun). **Closed:** 25 Dec. **Meals:** alc (main courses £12 to £28). **Details:** 160 seats. Wheelchair access.

Les Deux Salons

Barnstorming French brasserie
40-42 William IV Street, Covent Garden, WC2N 4DD
Tel no: (020) 7420 2050
www.lesdeuxsalons.co.uk
⊖ Charing Cross, map 5
French | £30
Cooking score: 4
£5 OFF

From the same stable as Arbutus and Wild Honey (see entries), this barnstorming brasserie delivers its founders' distinctive take on French-accented food in high-gloss surrounds. Deliberately tarnished mirrors, mosaic tiled floors and brass fittings conjure up shades of fin de siècle Paris. Eat in the boisterous ground-floor space, or the more intimate tier upstairs, from a menu that bristles with cheap cuts and chart-topping ideas: fish soup, salade niçoise and confit duck with butter beans appear right on cue; snail and bacon pie has become a Covent Garden classic; and the Josper grill turns out hefty slabs of calf's liver, massive veal chops and steak-frites – as well as andouillettes with mustard sauce for the purists. To follow, gâteau Opéra or île flottante also whistle 'La Marseillaise'. The pre-theatre deal is popular, and everything on the brief, well-chosen wine list is offered by the glass or carafe; bottles from £16.50.
Chef/s: Barry Tonks. **Open:** all week 12 to 11 (12 to 6 Sun). **Closed:** 25 Dec, 1 Jan. **Meals:** alc (main courses £15 to £29). Set L and pre-theatre D £13 (2 courses) to £23. **Details:** 170 seats. Separate bar. Wheelchair access.

Dinings

Teeny-weeny Japanese thriller
22 Harcourt Street, Marylebone, W1H 4HH
Tel no: (020) 7723 0666
www.dinings.co.uk
⊖ Marylebone, map 4
Japanese | £85
Cooking score: 3

This pocket-sized sushi space in Marylebone is small in stature, big in reputation. The 'concrete-floored basement', 'tight, winding staircase' and rock-hard chairs are the very definition of cool minimalism – and not terribly comfortable. But all that's forgotten once the first 'small plate' arrives. Here, these are called 'Japanese tapas': a gimmicky-sounding concept yet one that makes perfect sense in the form of chef Masaki Sugisaki's lobster with miso américaine, smoked wild venison tataki and sweet mustard miso, and Iberian pork shabu-shabu with chojang sauce. The ex-Nobu chef is on better than nodding terms with luxury, so don't scrimp. Try the 'melt in the mouth' Wagyu sushi with ponzu jelly and truffle salsa, or scallop sushi with foie gras mousse. Desserts such as wasanbon (Japanese sugar) crème brûlée are similarly creative. Wines start high (£33); the quirkily annotated saké list is a better bet.
Chef/s: Masaki Sugisaki. **Open:** Mon to Sat L 12 to 2.30 (3 Sat), D 6 to 10.30. **Closed:** Sun, 23 Dec to 4 Jan. **Meals:** alc (main courses £11 to £49). **Details:** 28 seats. Music.

Dishoom

Funky all-day Indian café
12 Upper St Martin's Lane, Covent Garden, WC2H 9FB
Tel no: (020) 7420 9320
www.dishoom.com
⊖ Leicester Square, Covent Garden, map 5
Indian | £20
Cooking score: 2
£30

Dishoom takes its style cue from the Iranian-run all-day cafés of old Mumbai, bringing a shot of Subcontinental convivium to Covent

Garden and Shoreditch (see entry, east London). Opening early enough to provide breakfast bites that will bring the blood-sugar levels back up (bacon naan roll, or a bowl of fortifying porridge), the kitchen motors industriously through the day, offering frankies (open-ended naan parcels filled with red beans in minty chutney, or minced lamb and peas) and salad plates to the lunchers. The main menus are full of pop and crackle, from warmly spiced vegetable samosas to principals such as charred masala prawns, lamb chops in lime juice and jaggery, paneer tikka with red and green peppers, and slow-cooked biryanis. Otherwise, have a Bombay chip butty, sprinkled with hillbilly ghati masala. Finish luxuriously with salted chocolate-chilli mousse garnished with shrikhand yoghurt and blackberries. Drinks include an IPA beer brewed in Hackney, and wines from £18.90.
Chef/s: Naved Nasir and Arun Kumar. **Open:** all week 8am to 11pm (midnight Thur and Fri, 9am to midnight Sat, 9am to 10pm Sun). **Closed:** 25 Dec, 1 Jan. **Meals:** alc (main courses £6 to £22). Set L and D £20 (2 courses) to £35. **Details:** 140 seats. 20 seats outside. Separate bar. Wheelchair access.

Donostia
Where to snack like the Basques
10 Seymour Place, Marylebone, W1H 7ND
Tel no: (020) 3620 1845
www.donostia.co.uk
⊖ **Marble Arch, map 4**
Spanish | £30
Cooking score: 3

Tiny, a little off the beaten track and decidedly 'more modern and formal than the normally rustic pintxo bars in the Basque region', Donostia is a boon for anyone in the Oxford Street area, thanks to engaging service and some skilfully made dishes. You can chat to the chefs at the marble counter or eat on shiny white table tops, and staff are more than happy to talk through the menu. Freshness and care distinguish the cooking, with a nice balance between simple and more labour-intensive food. Arriving in random order, dishes range from the familiar ham croquetas, hand-carved

jamón Ibérico and pimientos de Padrón to the more unusual octopus in a Basque marinade, cod cheeks with squid-ink aïoli, and pigeon breast with chestnut purée. Finish with torrija with fresh mint ice cream. Drinks also champion the Basque cause (try Txakoli), otherwise the all-Spanish list starts at £18.
Chef/s: Damian Surowiec. **Open:** Tue to Sun L 12 to 3.30 (1 to 4 Sun), all week D 6 to 11 (10 Sun). **Closed:** 25 and 26 Dec, 1 Jan. **Meals:** alc (tapas £9 to £20). **Details:** 40 seats. 10 seats outside. Music.

NEW ENTRY
Ember Yard
Small plates, big flavours in Soho
60 Berwick Street, Soho, W1F 8SU
Tel no: (020) 7439 8057
www.emberyard.co.uk
⊖ **Tottenham Court Road, Oxford Circus, map 5**
Modern European | £28
Cooking score: 4
🍷 £30

'The trick here is to be selfish and not share', confessed a visitor to this latest Spanish-Italian tapas bar from Simon Mullins and Ben Tish (see entries for Dehesa, Opera Tavern, Salt Yard). The small plates provoke a dilemma: who's getting the last bite? That question came up with the wonderful oak-smoked Basque beef burger with Idiazabal cheese and chorizo ketchup. And we could imagine arguing over the tender, full-flavoured char-grilled salt marsh lamb (served atop roasted aubergine and salsa verde) and the char-grilled squid with pancetta, peas and chilli. That said, there's also charcuterie and cheeses and larger plates of Old Spot pork belly and beef skirt steak. Anchor yourself in the basement at counter seating looking over the kitchen or perch at a ground-floor high table – it's great fun, especially with the switched-on service and an Italian-Spanish wine list (from £25) that's in danger of hogging the limelight.
Chef/s: Ben Tish and Jacques Fourie. **Open:** all week 12 to 12 (10.30pm Sun). **Closed:** 25 and 26 Dec, 1 and 2 Jan. **Meals:** alc (main courses £8 to £12). **Details:** 100 seats. Separate bar. Music.

★ TOP 50 ★

NEW ENTRY

Fera at Claridges

Phenomenally dynamic food
49 Brook Street, Mayfair, W1K 4HR
Tel no: (020) 7107 8888
www.claridges.co.uk
⊖ Bond Street, map 5
Modern British | £85
Cooking score: 7

🍷 🍴

What we want from luxury restaurants is changing, along with our notions of luxury, and Simon Rogan nails the new mood perfectly. His latest London opening in the more exclusive of the capital's grand hotels is cool, relaxed and unstuffy. There's a classy subtlety to the grand room decorated in soft greens, creams and gold, with Art Deco touches and mirrored, silvered pillars – and while there's no doubt that Fera delivers a special-occasion feeling, it is free of any ostentation. The staff are very friendly, with a breadth of knowledge that makes it a pleasure to speak with them about food. Dan Cox heads the kitchen and the sheer breadth of his cooking can be gauged immediately from the terrific opening salvo that takes in a tiny crisp of puffed barley topped with smoked eel and ox-eye daisy, and a bowl of exquisite potato and Winslade cheese purée tempered by a few pieces of tender duck heart. Standards are maintained throughout: salad grilled over embers is a masterclass in how to do charred vegetables; sea bass, cooked with faultless timing, shares its chunky plate with razor clams, baby turnips, broad beans, some new-season girolles and anise hyssop; and raw veal teamed with oysters, smoked cauliflower, gooseberry and sweet cicely is a brilliant updating of steak tartare. For dessert, the kitchen is judicious with sugar and quite comfortable with vegetables, coaxing astonishing flavour and textural contrasts from a confection of pineapple weed, butterscotch and celery (diced and syrup) and camomile snow. A sommelier is on hand to present the fine wines, and the glass selections with the tasting menu often spark engaged debate. Glasses start at £8.
Chef/s: Simon Rogan and Dan Cox. **Open:** all week L 12 to 2.30, D 6.30 to 10. **Meals:** alc (3 courses £85). Set L (Mon to Fri) £45. Tasting menu £105. **Details:** 90 seats. Separate bar. Wheelchair access.

Fino

Big-hitting tapas restaurant
33 Charlotte Street (entrance in Rathbone Street), Fitzrovia, W1T 1RR
Tel no: (020) 7813 8010
www.finorestaurant.com
⊖ Goodge Street, map 5
Spanish | £45
Cooking score: 3

Nigh-on a dozen years since opening, Fino is wearing well. The appeal, in a nutshell, is contemporary and traditional Spanish tapas served in a tastefully modern basement dining room. With its low-key décor, dark leather and soft lighting, this original of Sam and Eddie Hart's trio (see entries for Barrafina and Quo Vadis) presents a cool, mature setting. Whether you perch at the bar or occupy a closely set table (this is no place for a quiet head-to-head), you can look forward to hand-carved jamón de Bellota Señorio or a plate of pimientos de Padrón before going on to chickpeas with spinach and smoked pancetta, crab croquetas, some acorn-fed duck with celeriac purée and Marsala, and a rather good whole sea bream from the plancha. Menus are adjusted to reflect native seasonal produce and fine Spanish imports – wonderful ingredients, simply cooked with precision. The all-Spanish wine list opens at £19.
Chef/s: Nieves Barragán Mohacho. **Open:** Mon to Fri L 12 to 2.30, Mon to Sat D 6 to 10.30. **Closed:** Sun, bank hols. **Meals:** alc (tapas £9 to £23). Set tapas L £18 (5 courses) to £20 (6 courses). **Details:** 85 seats. Separate bar. Wheelchair access.

LOCAL GEM
▲ Flat Iron
17 Beak Street, Soho, W1F 9RW
www.flatironsteak.co.uk
⊖ Leicester Square, map 5
Steaks | £20

What started life as a pop-up has become part of the Soho scene, with punters happy to queue at this steak-only, no-bookings venue. Dark and buzzy, with a basement cocktail bar and cramped communal tables, it's ideal for a good-value feed with friends. The carefully sourced steaks cost a tenner, then you pay for extras such as 'crisp and perfectly portioned' chips and 'moreish' roast aubergine, tomato, basil and Parmesan. Pass on the one dessert. Wines from £16. Open all week. A new branch is at 9 Denmark Street, WC2H 8LS.

NEW ENTRY
Flesh & Buns
Fast-food izakaya that's bang on target
41 Earlham Street, Covent Garden, WC2H 9LX
Tel no: (020) 7632 9500
www.fleshandbuns.com
⊖ Covent Garden, map 5
Japanese | £30
Cooking score: 1

Last year Ross Shonhan brought us Bone Daddies (see entry); this is his Japanese fast-food izakaya: bang on target with its pleasing informality, switched on service, and low-lit industrial vibes (think concrete floor, bare wood tables, iron pillars, white painted brick and a not too obtrusive soundtrack). Grab a seat at the central communal table or a side booth, and expect sparky ideas from the very busy open kitchen. 'Buns' are New York chef David Chang's oft-copied steam buns, 'flesh' the steaks, lamb chops, crispy duck leg, chicken, salmon and sea bass – with various Japanese-style accompaniments – that make the DIY filling. There's a variety of sashimi, chicken yakitori or prawn tempura to start; finish with kinako doughnuts filled with black sugar custard. Wines from £17.20.

Chef/s: Joe McCafferty. Open: all week L 12 to 3 (4.30 Sat and Sun), D 5 to 10.30 (11.30 Wed to Sat, 9 Sun). Closed: 24 and 25 Dec, 1 Jan. Meals: alc (main courses £13 to £20). Set L £20. Set D £23. Details: 145 seats. Separate bar. Wheelchair access.

LOCAL GEM
▲ La Fromagerie
2-6 Moxon Street, Marylebone, W1U 4EW
Tel no: (020) 7935 0341
www.lafromagerie.co.uk
⊖ Baker Street, Bond Street, map 4
Modern European | £20

Large windows offer glimpses from the street of a fabulous array of cheeses, but venture in to bag a table and you'll find yourself surrounded by a veritable emporium of good things. Over the years legions of regulars have grown used to having the luxury of Patricia Michelson's cheese shop/deli/café at hand, and they pile in for lunches or early suppers of soup, cheese or charcuterie plates, terrines or a chorizo and cannellini bean stew, and excellent cakes. Wines by the glass from £4.20. Open all week.

Gail's Kitchen
A successful step from bakery to kitchen
11-13 Bayley Street, Bloomsbury, WC1B 3HD
Tel no: (020) 7323 9694
www.gailskitchen.co.uk
⊖ Tottenham Court Road, map 5
Modern British | £29
Cooking score: 2
£30

A dining offshoot of the bakery chain, Gail's Kitchen aims to extend the nationally popular pastime of baking to an informal restaurant ethos. Since last year, Jonathan Levy has stepped up to oversee operations out the back, and the successful drill remains the same. Choose from a wide range of small plates and get stuck into each other's selections in a happily mixing-and-matching approach, beginning with nibbles of polenta chips and olives. Grilled mackerel with al dente vegetables; sticky chicken with roast garlic, carrots and almonds; and butternut and mascarpone ravioli, dressed in lemon, sage and Parmesan – all are mentioned in dispatches, and the coffee is good and strong. The relentless upselling (often a modus operandi in small-plate dining) can be tiresome, but not so chocolate and marmalade tart, or buttermilk pannacotta with spiced poached quince and a gingersnap. A tiny slate of wines starts from £19, or £5 a glass.

Chef/s: Jonathan Levy. **Open:** all week L 12 to 3 (4 Sun), Mon to Sat D 5.30 to 10.30 (11 Fri and Sat). **Closed:** 25 Dec. **Meals:** alc (small plates £7 to £9). **Details:** 54 seats.

Galvin at Windows

Precision-tuned food with a view
Hilton Hotel, 22 Park Lane, Mayfair, W1K 1BE
Tel no: (020) 7208 4021
www.galvinatwindows.com
⊖ Hyde Park Corner, Green Park, map 4
French | £68
Cooking score: 6

Perched atop the Park Lane Hilton with London unfurled below, how could you not fall in love with this place? There's an Art Deco flavour to the fittings, and a friendly, smart efficiency to the service. Most importantly, Joo Won's cooking rises to the occasion with heart-stopping brilliance. Take a velvety, verdant pea velouté for instance, shifted up a gear with a crunch of Bayonne ham, then made delightful with melting Sainte-Maure cheese; or fillet of potato-crusted wild sea bass that falls into fleshy flakes under the fork, served on shellfish and gnocchi and sharpened with parsley and citrus. The peripheries are perfect too: warm, crunchy French bread, firm slices of wholemeal, a fresh amuse of tart apple jelly with earthy parsnip purée and coconut foam. The classic European bent extends to a dessert of mini tarte Tatin – a whole caramelised apple in crisp pastry – served with the richest vanilla ice cream. The ample wine list (from £20) includes sections for English and 'natural' (organic, biodynamic) wines.

Chef/s: Joo Won. **Open:** Sun to Fri L 12 to 2.30 (11.45 to 3.30 Sun), Mon to Sat D 6 to 10 (10.30 Thur to Sat). **Closed:** bank hols. **Meals:** Set L £25 (2 courses) to £29. Set D £68. **Details:** 109 seats. Separate bar. Wheelchair access. Music. Car parking.

Galvin Bistrot de Luxe

Big flavours and persuasive Gallic charm
66 Baker Street, Marylebone, W1U 7DJ
Tel no: (020) 7935 4007
www.galvinrestaurants.com
⊖ Baker Street, map 4
French | £37
Cooking score: 4

The Galvin brothers' empire runs from London to Edinburgh, well, London *and* Edinburgh, and it all began here some nine years ago. The pair are adept at creating authentic-feeling venues that somehow combine old-world propriety with contemporary swagger. Bistrot de Luxe gives a fine impression of an upmarket Parisian gaff, complete with leather banquettes and lots of dark wood. The spruce service team can occasionally buckle under the strain, but are generally 'charming' nonetheless. The menu sticks to the programme, with a rendition of classy bistro classics. Escargots à la bourguignonne sets the pace, lasagne of Dorset crab is a fixture, while main-course warm Roscoff onion tart with caramelised walnuts and Roquefort shows that even vegetarians get a look in. Magret of duck with morteau sausage and lentils was the highlight for one reader, and, among desserts, tarte Tatin is hard to skip. The mostly Gallic wines start at £21.

Chef/s: Kevin Tew. **Open:** all week L 12 to 2.30 (3 Sun), D 6 to 10.30 (11 Thur to Sat, 9.30 Sun). **Closed:** 25 and 26 Dec, 1 Jan. **Meals:** alc (main courses £17 to £30). Set L £20. Set D £22. **Details:** 128 seats. 26 seats outside. Separate bar.

Gauthier Soho

Cosseting vibes and virtuoso food
21 Romilly Street, Soho, W1D 5AF
Tel no: (020) 7494 3111
www.gauthiersoho.co.uk
⊖ Leicester Square, map 5
Modern French | £40
Cooking score: 6

£5 OFF ♦ V

'We have just been to heaven . . . again!'
enthused a regular who rang the doorbell and
ascended the stairs of this discreet Georgian
town house in search of 'superb lunching,
cosseting vibes and remarkable value'. Serene
Gauthier really is an 'oasis of calm' in raffishly
foodie Soho. Open fireplaces, well-spaced
tables and soothing colours set the mood;
service is low-key professional; and the food is
a triumph of virtuosity, intricate detailing and
delicacy. Menus are built around a procession
of bijou, pretty 'plats', all worthily calorie-
counted: seared scallops with leeks, celery,
nuts and sultanas; 'divinely rich' chervil pasta
with foie gras and truffle oil; halibut with
purple artichokes, fondant fennel and confit
tomatoes . . . the list goes on. To finish,
everyone drools over the astonishing Louis
XV: dark chocolate mousse and praline topped
with gold leaf and ganache 'so shiny you can
practically see your face in it'. Gauthier's
sommelier is also on top form, advising on
suitable wine matches from the patrician list.
Prices from £25.
Chef/s: Alexis Gauthier and Gerard Virolle. **Open:**
Tue to Sat L 12 to 2.30, Mon to Sat D 6.30 to 10.30.
Closed: Sun, 25 and 26 Dec, Aug bank hol.
Meals: Set L £18 (2 courses) to £25. Set D £40 to
£60 (5 courses). Tasting menu £70 (8 courses).
Details: 45 seats. Children over 6 yrs only.

❚❘ Visit us Online

To find out more about
The Good Food Guide, please visit
www.thegoodfoodguide.co.uk

★ TOP 50 ★

Le Gavroche

Supreme gastronomic artistry
43 Upper Brook Street, Mayfair, W1K 7QR
Tel no: (020) 7408 0881
www.le-gavroche.com
⊖ Marble Arch, map 4
French | £120
Cooking score: 8

It is worth remembering that Le Gavroche,
which opened in 1967, introduced top-class
gastronomy to the UK and as a restaurant is
considered an institution. As the grown-up
alternative (with full dress code) to the hip
new restaurants with Glastonbury noise levels,
backless benches and no-booking policies, it is
genteel, sedate even. The opulent, sepulchrally
lit basement dining room induces a feeling of
wellbeing – there are comfortable chairs,
plenty of fine linen and lots of elbow room.
Some things never change on the menu, from
the soufflé suissesse to the omelette
Rothschild, but Michel Roux Jnr's cooking
moves with the times, whether dealing with a
mesmerising stone bass with 'its magnificent
Arabian spices' and red Camargue rice, or a
clever combination of boudin noir, crumbed
egg, asparagus salad, spiced tomato chutney
and 'a touch of perfect crackling'. Attention to
detail is paramount, sustaining the fine
materials that go into dishes such as grilled
fillet of Scottish beef with wild mushrooms
and red wine shallot sauce, and even the
handsome cheeseboard, which is served with
knowledge and generosity. Given the frankly
astronomical à la carte prices, one way of
ensuring customer loyalty is through the
gentler-on-the-pocket set lunch – which
continues to impress readers. Le Gavroche is
not in the habit of sending us a wine list, but
reports tell of a magisterial list of pedigree
stars at prices that take no prisoners; bottles
start at £32.
Chef/s: Rachel Humphrey. **Open:** Mon to Fri L 12 to
2, Mon to Sat D 6 to 10. **Closed:** Sun, 2 weeks
Christmas to New Year, bank hols. **Meals:** alc (main
courses £27 to £61). Set L £55. **Details:** 100 seats.
Separate bar.

A PRIZE MEAL AT LE GAVROCHE

Monisha Khandker, winner of the Waitrose Good Food Guide Restaurant Critic competition, with an excerpt from her review of Le Gavroche. Read the full review at thegoodfoodguide.co.uk

From the cloud of soufflé Suissesse that melts in your mouth at the beginning, to the impish little nougat squares peeking out of their enamelled box at the end, each dish on the Menu Exceptionnel delights like the surprise discovery of hidden treasure.

We began our journey with crunchy, warm mushroom toast, spice-crusted foie gras and cubes of Madeira jelly, before leaving shore for sea with seared langoustines, peas and Bayonne ham, the soft pink flesh surrounded by tides of velvety green pea foam.

Stone bass with rich, succulent, chewy red rice and pastilla scented with Arabian spices took us to *One Thousand and One Nights* against the soft hum of the ras-el-hanout and sweet fennel, while collapsingly tender smoked-pork cheek and crispy golden belly ravioli with pungent red cabbage appeared like a celebration of autumnal colour, a thin crisp of pork crackling adorning the plate like a wisp of smoke. Squab pigeon, sweet and fatty with a sharp jolt of blackcurrant continued the magical forest theme.

Finally, a bitter chocolate truffle with cherries steeped in eau de vie; a decadent yet enlivening dessert before the petits fours grand finale – a myriad of miniatures: chocolate ganache pastries, toffee-appled kumquats, macaroons and the enchanted little nougat squares. The magic had finally come to an end, but I remained spellbound.

Great Queen Street
Humming, no-frills eatery
32 Great Queen Street, Covent Garden, WC2B 5AA
Tel no: (020) 7242 0622
⊖ Covent Garden, map 5
Modern British | £26
Cooking score: 3
£30

Happy vibes, brisk service, keen prices and a twice-daily menu of unreformed Brit-accented grub keep customers satisfied in this humming eatery. It's all about the seasons as the kitchen moves from wintry plates of pig and game rillettes, quick-cured pollack with fennel and clementine salad or roast partridge with bread sauce, to summertime hits such as whole crab with rouille or gnocchi with asparagus, peas and girolles. Like its sibling the Anchor & Hope in Waterloo (see entry), this place makes a feature of trencherman sharing dishes such as rabbit pie or 'very slowly roasted' suckling pig. Communal, family-style feasting menus are ideal for Covent Garden's fun-loving throngs – particularly with chocolate fritters or steamed lemon and buttermilk pudding to close. Zesty cocktails, craft beers and guest ales compete with tumblers of quaffable wine on the enterprising drinks list. Vins de pays cost £16 a bottle. **Chef/s:** Tom Norrington-Davies and Sam Hutchins. **Open:** all week L 12 to 2.30 (1 to 4 Sun), Mon to Sat D 6 to 10.30. **Meals:** alc (main courses £12 to £18). Set L £15 (2 courses) to £18. **Details:** 60 seats. 12 seats outside. Separate bar.

Green Man & French Horn
The Loire Valley explored in food and wine
54 St Martin's Lane, Covent Garden, WC2N 4EA
Tel no: (020) 7836 2645
www.greenmanfrenchhorn.co
⊖ Leicester Square, map 5
Modern French | £26
Cooking score: 2
£30

Amid the bustle of activity on St Martin's Lane, it would be easy to miss a venue whose compound name makes up in length what the place itself lacks in outward dimensions. Inside, the old pub has been transformed into a brisk London bistro, dedicated to the demotic food and heavenly wines of the Loire Valley. The journey from the river's source in central France to the port of St-Nazaire is traced here in an itinerary that leads from pea soup with Vendée ham and mint, to turbot with crispy artichoke, capers and oregano, or spring lamb in soubise with anchovies and chard. Big, pungent flavours are in evidence, so loins should be girded for oxtail with turnips, grelot onions and horseradish. Tarte vigneronne (apple tart glazed in red wine jelly) is the obvious way to finish. The wine list breast-strokes its way along the Loire's course: Sancerres and Pouillys, sharp Chenin and earthy Cabernet Franc, traditional-method fizz, stickies and Muscadet that tastes of something. Prices open at £18.75.

Chef/s: Ed Wilson. **Open:** Mon to Sat L 12 to 3, D 5.30 to 11. **Closed:** Sun, 23 Dec to 2 Jan, bank hols. **Meals:** alc (main courses £11 to £20). **Details:** 48 seats. Separate bar. Wheelchair access. Music.

The Greenhouse
Rarefied Mayfair oasis
27a Hay's Mews, Green Park, W1J 5NX
Tel no: (020) 7499 3331
www.greenhouserestaurant.co.uk
⊖ Green Park, map 5
Modern European | £75
Cooking score: 4

Fronted by a leafy garden, this rarefied oasis in a residential corner of Mayfair has a formal air and very smart staff. The interior – glass panels with ivy pattern, classic table settings and shades of coffee, cream and green – offers simple sophistication and really dim lighting: 'you'll wish you'd brought a torch'. Arnaud Bignon achieves a distinct blend of creativity and fashion in his modern menus. Top-notch ingredients are the building blocks, from 'huge, oversized' green asparagus wrapped in barely there slivers of lardo di colonnata and served with big, salty morels, liquorice and rocket coulis (the highlight of a test meal), to John Dory with tandoori spices, celeriac and

crab sauce. To finish, a pre-dessert of fresh pineapple basil sorbet could be followed by a sugary silver sphere filled with apple, caramel sauce and ice cream: a marvel to behold. The weighty wine list (from £28) is for other people, note the 'under £100' section.

Chef/s: Arnaud Bignon. **Open:** Mon to Fri L 12 to 2.30, Mon to Sat D 6.30 to 10.30. **Closed:** Sun, 25 Dec, 1 Jan, bank hols. **Meals:** alc (main courses £45). Set L £30 (2 courses) to £35. Set D £85. Tasting menu £98. **Details:** 60 seats.

NEW ENTRY

Gymkhana
Top-notch Indian food
42 Albermarle Street, Mayfair, W1S 4JH
Tel no: (020) 3011 5900
www.gymkhanalondon.com
⊖ Piccadilly Circus, Green Park, map 5
Modern Indian | £60
Cooking score: 5

V

Gymkhana's somewhat clichéd Raj-inspired interior may not win design/décor awards, but – proving you shouldn't judge a restaurant by its designer – it serves top-notch Indian cuisine. This being modern India, there are three kinds of poppadoms, tasting menus and a real sense of excitement about the food, for the kitchen offers an update on traditional ideas: 'brilliant' wild muntjac biryani, for example, served with pomegranate and mint raita. Dishes impressing reporters include a potato chaat with chickpeas, tamarind and sev (a crisp vermicelli); spicy Chettinad duck with coconut chutney and papery dosa; and, from the tandoor, a superb head of broccoli with green chilli raita, and oh-so-tender guinea fowl breast, which arrives with its slow-cooked leg, green mango chaat and a mint-coriander chutney. Portions are generous, and prices, particularly at lunch, are fair for Mayfair. The sommelier makes a reasonable stab at recommending wines to drink with various dishes; bottles from £25.

Chef/s: Karam Sethi. **Open:** Mon to Sat L 12 to 2.30, D 5.30 to 10.30. **Closed:** Sun, 23 to 28 Dec, 1 to 4 Jan. **Meals:** alc (main courses £8 to £40). Set L £20

(2 courses) to £25. Set D £25. Game menu £65 (5 courses). **Details:** 90 seats. Separate bar. Wheelchair access. Music. No children after 7.30.

Hakkasan

Thrillingly seductive new-Cantonese food
8 Hanway Place, Fitzrovia, W1T 1HD
Tel no: (020) 7927 7000
www.hakkasan.com
⊖ **Tottenham Court Road, map 5**
Chinese | £65
Cooking score: 5

V

When this original (and some say best) Hakkasan opened in 2001, it set a radical new tone for Eastern dining in London. Still a surreal place – a subterranean world of moodily lit rooms divided by dark-wood fretwork screens – it no longer rocks to a fashionable crowd, but the highly glamorised, nominally Cantonese cooking remains 'staggeringly expensive'. So it's worth concentrating on 'Dim Sum Sunday' lunch, costing about £58 a head (including drinks): best value of the various fixed-price options. There were no dud notes among the procession of beautifully crafted dishes tried at inspection, including crispy duck salad with lovely sweet and sour notes from pomelo, pine nut and shallot; XO scallop dumpling with Thai asparagus and lingzhi mushrooms; the fabulous baked venison puff; the famed Chilean sea bass with Chinese honey, pak choi and sticky rice in a lotus leaf for main course; and a cross-cultural hazelnut and chocolate dessert. Wines from £29.
Chef/s: Tong Chee Hwee. **Open:** all week L 12 to 3 (4 Sat and Sun), D 6 to 11 (11.30 Thur to Sat). **Closed:** 25 Dec. **Meals:** alc (main courses £9 to £61). Set L and early D £35 (3 courses). Sun L £48 (6 courses) to £58. **Details:** 210 seats. Separate bar. Wheelchair access. Music.

Hakkasan Mayfair

Slinky Chinese opulence
17 Bruton Street, Mayfair, W1J 6QB
Tel no: (020) 7907 1888
www.hakkasan.com
⊖ **Green Park, Bond Street, map 5**
Chinese | £65
Cooking score: 4

V

Not quite as sleek as the original Hakkasan (see entry), this Mayfair-chic sibling is still an oh-so-cool hideaway for big-spending fans of top-end Chinese cuisine. The scent of jasmine mingles with the smell of new money, a booming soundtrack energises the cocktail bar, and the cacophonous din continues in the icy-blue dining room. That said, it's not all bluster – particularly as regards food. Hakkasan is famed for dim sum, and the list of revelatory morsels doesn't disappoint: from baked venison puffs to jasmine tea-smoked organic pork ribs. Otherwise it's all virtuosity, invention and extravagance as the kitchen sends out plates of Peking duck with Qiandao caviar, stir-fried Australian lobster with lily bulbs, and the now-legendary roast silver cod in Champagne and Chinese honey. Desserts go west for the likes of pistachio and orange roulade. The wine list (from £28) invites exploration with its cute categories ('terroir intense', etc) and selections by the glass.
Chef/s: Tong Chee Hwee. **Open:** all week L 12 to 3.15 (4.15 Sat and Sun), D 6 to 11.15 (12.15 Thur to Sat). **Closed:** 24 and 25 Dec. **Meals:** alc (main courses £16 to £61). Set L £40. Set D £65 to £130 (10 courses). **Details:** 212 seats. Separate bar.

¶|◐ Average Price

The average price listed in main-entry reviews denotes the price of a three-course meal, without wine.

Hawksmoor Air Street
A temple to seafood and steak
5a Air Street, Soho, W1J 0AD
Tel no: (020) 7406 3980
www.thehawksmoor.com
⊖ Piccadilly Circus, map 5
British | £45
Cooking score: 3

Will Beckett and Huw Gott do seem to have that magic touch. This Piccadilly branch of their big-statement Hawksmoor group makes a confident first-floor destination (not always easy to pull off), with a lively bar out front and a massive wood, leather and stained-glass dining room beyond. While it may seem 'bizarre to see people who run steak restaurants do such an accomplished seafood restaurant', there's no need for die-hard fans to panic. There's still satisfaction to be had from the likes of expertly aged porterhouse, bone-in prime rib and fillet with all the trademark sauces and sides (macaroni cheese, triple-cooked chips, buttered greens, for instance). But plump for roast shoulder of turbot with béarnaise sauce or char-grilled Dover sole – fresh, simple and perfectly timed – and you certainly won't feel you're getting the second-best item on the menu. Service is alert as well as friendly, and wines start at £21.
Chef/s: Richard Turner and Liam Kirwin. **Open:** Mon to Fri L 12 to 3, D 5 to 10.30 (11 Fri). Sat and Sun 12 to 11. **Closed:** 24 to 27 Dec, 1 Jan. **Meals:** alc (main courses £20 to £48). Set L and D £23 (2 courses) to £26. Sun L £20. **Details:** 235 seats. Separate bar. Wheelchair access. Music.

Hawksmoor Seven Dials
British beef at its best
11 Langley Street, Covent Garden, WC2H 9JG
Tel no: (020) 7420 9390
www.thehawksmoor.com
⊖ Covent Garden, map 5
British | £45
Cooking score: 4

With four branches (and more promised), Hawksmoor's waggon train trundles through the capital, winning hearts and palates. The Seven Dials branch of this revivalist steakhouse is manna for *Mad Men* execs, tourists and lovers of tub-thumping, red-blooded grub, who head to the barrel-vaulted basement for some of London's best British beef. It's noisy, dark and heavily dosed with testosterone, but great fun – whether you're knocking back brilliant cocktails at the bar or sitting in a leather chair amid the steel girders, industrial piping and gentlemanly trappings of the clubby dining room. 'Big chunks of cooked cow' are advertised on blackboards and described by persuasive servers. So, gorge on a 'bloody lovely' 55-day aged D-rump, ribeye steak or thickly carved bone-in rib, with beef-dripping fries and terrific sauces. Not into steak? How about 'suitably unctuous' bone marrow and onions followed by grilled lobster, with salted-caramel Rolos to finish. Admirable wines from £21.
Chef/s: Richard Turner and Miroslaw Dawid. **Open:** Mon to Sat L 12 to 3, D 5 to 10.30 (11 Fri and Sat). Sun 12 to 9.30. **Closed:** 24 to 27 Dec. **Meals:** alc (main courses £13 to £50). Set L and D £23 (2 courses) to £26. Sun L £20. **Details:** 140 seats. Separate bar. Wheelchair access. Music.

★ TOP 50 ★

Hélène Darroze at the Connaught
Complex avant-garde thrills
16 Carlos Place, Mayfair, W1K 2AL
Tel no: (020) 3147 7200
www.the-connaught.co.uk
⊖ Bond Street, Green Park, map 5
Modern French | £92
Cooking score: 6

🛏 V

There's a certain dialectical tension nowadays in the old Connaught dining room: its august oak-panelled shell having been invaded by boldly patterned fabrics in violet and lime; the room now displaying food stylisations under glass cloches (rhubarb, lemons, a golden bull). It all chimes with Hélène Darroze's expansively resourceful menus, which carefully pick and exuberantly mix prime materials from across France with seafood from Northern Ireland and culinary influences from east Asia. The many surprising treasures include foie gras offset with cacao, pear, ginger and sorrel, while Ulster lobster comes in ozone-fresh array with bottarga, seaweed and white asparagus. Basque lamb, tender as can be, appears in a cosmopolitan hubbub of tandoori spices, mint and Greek yoghurt, while veal sweetbreads are gently spiced with vadouvan and sweetened with Muscat grapes. Purists, note: your baba will be doused in Armagnac, served with rhubarb and scented with galangal. A wine list to suit a grand hotel, in mark-ups and majesty, starts at £39.

Chef/s: Hélène Darroze. **Open:** Tue to Sat L 12 to 2.30 (brunch 11 to 2.30 Sat), D 6.30 to 10.45. **Closed:** Sun, Mon, 2 weeks Aug. **Meals:** Set L £30 (2 courses) to £45. Set D £52 (3 courses) to £125. Tasting menu £92 (6 courses) to £155 (9 courses). **Details:** 62 seats. Separate bar. Wheelchair access.

★ TOP 10 ★

Hibiscus
Wildly creative, knockout dishes from a master
29 Maddox Street, Mayfair, W1S 2PA
Tel no: (020) 7629 2999
www.hibiscusrestaurant.co.uk
⊖ Oxford Circus, map 5
Modern French | £88
Cooking score: 9

🍷 V

It is 15 years since Hibiscus first opened in Ludlow, and almost eight since Claude Bosi made the decision to up sticks and move the restaurant to London. Initially, the choice of showcasing Bosi's inimitable talent in the capital appeared a strange one: a crowded Mayfair street, a small ground-floor dining room that lacked soul. But all this has changed. Last year's complete overhaul and this year's buy out of backers, leaving Bosi as sole owner, reaffirms the chef's own value and stance. The whole effort seems to have fused the rest of the operation. There's now an unfussy mood in the dining room, and the cooking – always intuitive, always with

plenty of provocative combinations – has taken a deep breath and forged ahead. One minute Bosi will do the unadorned, non-interventionist thing more typical of a Japanese chef: sweet scallops, shown heat for just seconds, given a mere hint of acidity by a slick of strawberry sauce vierge. The next he will blindside you. Native lobster, enlivened by spring onion and black pepper sauce, sweet-and-sour pickled cucumber, and on the side, a quasi-oriental version of that French Riviera speciality barbajuan (mini-stuffed pastries), is totally irresistible. And then there are the little flavour bombs. The rich, fleeting, teasing contrasts in a foie gras cone, the umami hit of a gougère filled with liquid cheese, the pure lusciousness of 'en cocotte' pea mousse with coconut and curry. Equally notable is John Dory with a Lancashire mead sauce, the sweetness cut by a blob of onion and lime purée; and tender, slow-cooked kid, served with razor clams, samphire and sea beet sauce. Burrata, pulled into focus by a sweet/acidic apple-sorrel sauce and frozen raspberries, is the perfect curtain-raiser for fresh strawberry salad layered with celeriac jelly and Szechuan pepper ice cream, while olive oil parfait with kaffir lime, white chocolate and mango carpaccio is the final trump card. Controlling front-of-house is Laurent Gilis, who chats amiably, dismantles the formalities and sets people at ease while staying vigilant. And wine? It's a fascinating list with many desirable bottles and small, interesting producers galore (from £28), so it's worth thinking about a matching flight or giving sommelier Bastien Ferreri a budget to get the best out of it.

Chef/s: Claude Bosi. **Open:** Tue to Sat L 12 to 2.30, D 6 to 10. **Closed:** Sun, Mon, 24 to 26 Dec, one week Aug, bank hols. **Meals:** Set L £29.50 (2 courses) to £35. Set D £65 (2 courses) to £88. Tasting menu £100 (6 courses), £120 (8 courses). **Details:** 48 seats.

Hix

über-cool Brit brasserie
66-70 Brewer Street, Soho, W1F 9UP
Tel no: (020) 7292 3518
www.hixsoho.co.uk
⊖ Piccadilly Circus, map 5
British | £60
Cooking score: 3

V

Mark Hix is synonymous with new-Brit foodie patriotism, and while his all-day Soho flagship may come with high decibels and equally lofty prices, there's no disputing the valiant intent behind it. The kitchen plucks the best from artisan producers across the land and the straightforward menu has plenty to please. There has been praise for Hix's signature dish of 'heaven and earth', an 'absolutely delicious', big-on-flavour ball of wild boar black pudding, mashed potato and apple, and a mustard and gravy sauce. Plaudits, too, for Webster's fish fingers and chips, a perennial favourite that comes with good mushy minted peas; a Herdwick mutton shank curry; and steamed blood-orange marmalade pudding. The kitchen's output, and hence reports, are mixed, yet it's worth remembering the good-value set-price menus. Most reporters praise staff who have 'got the right mix of being knowledgeable without being stuck up'. Drinks also champion the British cause, with wines from £22.
Chef/s: Damian Clisby. **Open:** all week 12 to 11.30 (10.30 Sun). **Closed:** 24 to 26 Dec. **Meals:** alc (main courses £17 to £37). Set L and D £20 (2 courses) to £25. Sun L £24. **Details:** 85 seats. Separate bar. Music.

Hix Mayfair

Old-school charm and regional goodies
Brown's Hotel, 30 Albemarle Street, Mayfair, W1S 4BP
Tel no: (020) 7518 4004
www.roccofortehotels.com
⊖ Green Park, map 5
British | £46
Cooking score: 4

🛏 **V**

Located within Brown's Hotel – a bastion of old-school civility if ever there was one – Mark Hix's restaurant celebrates great British ingredients and great British artworks side by side. The fact that it's Tracey Emin and Bridget Riley as opposed to John Constable and Edwin Landseer on the walls shows how the place has moved with the times: and that goes for the updated British classics on the menu, too. It's possible to keep things simple with steamed Wye Valley asparagus and hollandaise followed by Aberdeenshire fillet steak cooked on the bone. But an alternative route would be pan-fried Launceston lamb's sweetbreads with Peter Hannan's guanciale (a cured pork cheek) and ramsons, then pan-fried Beesands scallops with inked spelt and sea sandwort. Finish with a modern take on Bramley apple pie or New Forest trifle. A lunchtime trolley delivers a roast of the day. Service remains 'attentive and available', but house wine is a whopping £35.
Chef/s: Lee Streeton. **Open:** all week L 12 to 3 (4 Sun), D 5.30 to 11 (7 to 10.30 Sun). **Meals:** alc (main courses £20 to £43). Set L and D £27.50 (2 courses) to £32.50. Sun L £36.50. **Details:** 70 seats. Separate bar. Wheelchair access.

Honey & Co

Unique, freethinking cooking
25a Warren Street, Fitzrovia, W1T 5LZ
Tel no: (020) 7388 6175
www.honeyandco.co.uk
⊖ Warren Street, map 2
Middle Eastern | £27
Cooking score: 2

£30

'How can anyone fail to love Honey & Co?' asked one reporter of this tiny, cramped venue which opened to a burst of enthusiasm in 2012. It's one of those special places that radiate warmth, with a ramshackle charm and a genuine love of feeding customers. Everything 'appears thrown together in the most accidentally perfect way'. The concise menu delivers some unique, freethinking Middle Eastern cooking – and it's 'fabulous' food. The kitchen rarely falters with the likes of Yemeni-style falafel or grilled octopus with spiced lentils and roasted peppers, while mains bring Tunisian meatballs, prawn and fennel tagine, and rabbit braised in red wine with tomatoes and mountain herbs. The baking is good, too: whether soft, pillowy flatbread or rich, luscious cakes such as 'melt-in-the-mouth' chestnut and whiskey cake with salt caramel sauce, or a warm marzipan cake with roasted rhubarb. A list of ten or so European wines starts at £20.
Chef/s: Sarit Packer and Itamar Srulovich. **Open:** Mon to Sat 8am to 10pm (9.30am Sat). **Closed:** Sun. **Meals:** alc (main courses £11 to £15). Set D £27 (2 courses) to £30. **Details:** 26 seats. 6 seats outside.

The Ivy

A timeless classic
1-5 West Street, Covent Garden, WC2H 9NQ
Tel no: (020) 7836 4751
www.the-ivy.co.uk
⊖ Leicester Square, map 5
Modern European | £39
Cooking score: 1

Stained glass, wood panelling, leather banquettes, crisp napery, smooth, efficient service – there's something timeless about The Ivy. Early-evening tables chase the opening times of surrounding theatres, and the food satisfies without ever reaching for the stars. A simple dressed Dorset crab with celeriac rémoulade has plenty of flavour; spiced-roasted duck breast (which arrives with charred greens, crispy duck roll and orange and soy) is rich and savoury; and late spring brings asparagus treated to nothing other than hollandaise. Raspberry and elderflower trifle makes a splendid finish, if Welsh rarebit doesn't take your fancy. Wines start at £24.
Chef/s: Gary Lee. **Open:** all week 12 to 11.30 (10.30 Sun). **Closed:** 25 Dec. **Meals:** alc (main courses £10 to £39). Set L and pre/post-theatre D £22 (2 courses) to £27. **Details:** 105 seats. Separate bar. Wheelchair access.

J. Sheekey

Theatreland's seafood star
28-32 St Martin's Court, Covent Garden, WC2N 4AL
Tel no: (020) 7240 2565
www.j-sheekey.co.uk
⊖ Leicester Square, map 5
Seafood | £37
Cooking score: 4

V

The plum location amid the theatres and bookshops of the West End is not the smallest asset that the Sheekey operation has going for it. In the relative seclusion of St Martin's Court, the original restaurant and its more recent outgrowth, the Oyster Bar (see entry below), are consecrated to the delivery of respectfully treated seafood, via cookbook and restaurant kitchen. Variously sourced oysters (Gillardeau, Jersey, Lindisfarne) extend through the long season, alongside the likes of de-shelled dressed crab, lobster mayo on the half-shell, and more distant hints of the ocean wave in grilled asparagus with a gull's egg and shaved bottarga. There are fish-based stews, roasts and grills at main course, as well as the house fish pie, and specials such as monkfish with smoked aubergine and cuttlefish in harissa. Finish with plum tart and amaretti ice cream. Vegetarians are looked after, too, and there are appealing fish-friendly wines from £21.

Chef/s: James Cornwall. **Open:** all week L 12 to 3 (3.30 Sat and Sun), D 5 to 12 (5.30 Sat, 5.30 to 11 Sun). **Closed:** 25 and 26 Dec. **Meals:** alc (main courses £16 to £42). Weekend Set L £26.50 (3 courses). **Details:** 93 seats. 26 seats outside. Separate bar. Wheelchair access.

J. Sheekey Oyster Bar

Sheekey offspring with speciality seafood
33-34 St Martin's Court, Covent Garden, WC2N 4AL
Tel no: (020) 7240 2565
www.jsheekeyoysterbar.co.uk
⊖ Leicester Square, map 5
Seafood | £26
Cooking score: 4
£30

A reader who feared the ambience of an Oyster Bar might be fearfully stuffy and clubby found the scales falling from his eyes as he set about a hefty prawn, crab and avocado cocktail. Diners around him were being efficiently processed, so they could get to the opera on time. It's a measure of the professionalism with which this and the original Sheekey's next door are run that everything happens with lightning efficiency. Which is not to say you can't tarry, over scallops in their shells with garlic and chilli, tandoori prawns and raita, or the oysters themselves – perhaps crisped in tempura and wasabied up, or garnished with spicy boar sausage. Then move on to a shrimp and scallop burger, sea bass ceviche with plantain crisps, or the signature fish pie. Brownie, tiffin and Eccles could be a firm of Dickensian solicitors, or just a collection of sweet treats. Wines from £21.

Chef/s: James Cornwall. **Open:** all week L 12 to 3 (3.30 Sat and Sun), D 5 to 12 (5.30 Sat, 5.30 to 11 Sun). **Closed:** 25 and 26 Dec. **Meals:** alc (main courses £9 to £21). **Details:** 51 seats. Wheelchair access.

Kiku

Stalwart of classical Japanese cooking
17 Half Moon Street, Mayfair, W1J 7BE
Tel no: (020) 7499 4208
www.kikurestaurant.co.uk
⊖ Green Park, map 5
Japanese | £40
Cooking score: 3

Kiku has been serving classical Japanese cuisine since 1978 and remains popular with Japanese families and business folk. There's a sense of calm when stepping into the dining room, decked out with stone floors and swathes of pale wood. On the upper level, the sushi counter is a popular spot to perch. Grilled mackerel with boiled rice from the set-lunch menu – arriving perfectly cooked with crispy skin – has been praised, as has the miso soup. Sushi (razor clam, scad and handroll of white crabmeat) 'will not disappoint'; and grilled aubergine topped with bonito flakes in a light soy sauce is stirred into life by the gentle heat of ginger. Kiku does Japanese comfort food well: agedashi tofu is well made, for instance, and delicious crisp-fried chicken is nicely paired with a dollop of English mustard. Black sesame ice cream makes a pleasant finish. The wine list (from £16.50) is brief and gently priced.

Chef/s: H Shiraishi, Y Hattori and M Anayama. **Open:** Mon to Sat L 12 to 2.30, all week D 6 to 10.15 (5.30 to 9.45 Sun). **Closed:** 25 to 27 Dec, 1 Jan. **Meals:** alc (main courses £15 to £40). Set L £22. Set D £55. **Details:** 98 seats. Wheelchair access.

Kitchen Table at Bubbledogs

The ultimate chef's table
70 Charlotte Street, Fitzrovia, W1T 4QG
Tel no: (020) 7637 7770
www.kitchentablelondon.co.uk
⊖ Goodge Street, map 5
Modern British | £78
Cooking score: 5

Nineteen counter-side seats encircling the most open of kitchens, 12 or more courses assembled right before diners, 'up close and personal' service from hosts passionate about what they do – Kitchen Table offers a unique experience. Dishes are kept small and simple: necessary as the menu changes daily, depending on the market. Opening salvos could be a 'lovely' nugget of oyster with apple pieces, shiso granite and apple vinegar; a crisp, crumbly choux bun stuffed with luscious, pungent cod's roe mousse; and the famous crisp of chicken skin bearing rosemary-laced mascarpone and a dollop of sugary-salty bacon jam. There's innovative cooking and there's straightforward: perfectly roasted lamb rump with glossy sauce, Jersey Royals, garlic leaves and salted wild garlic buds, for example. But the meal can drag, with so many 'frustratingly small' tasters, consistency not always achieved – due to the restrictions imposed by this format. Could James Knappett reach far greater heights were he cooking in a traditional kitchen? Wines from £35.

Chef/s: James Knappett. **Open:** Tue to Sat D only 6 to 10. **Closed:** Sun, Mon, 24 to 27 Dec, first 2 weeks Jan, 1 week Apr. **Meals:** Tasting menu £78 (12+ courses). **Details:** 19 seats. Music.

Koya
Noodles with oodles of love and care
49 Frith Street, Soho, W1D 4SG
Tel no: (020) 7434 4463
www.koya.co.uk
⊖ Tottenham Court Road, map 5
Japanese | £19
Cooking score: 3
£30

'There were people waiting all the time we were there' is testament to the popularity of this Japanese eatery. The advice, from those in the know, is to choose from the blackboard menu, which is 'really something . . . some really, really good ingredients being used'. Perch at the chef's counter 'pretty much in the kitchen' to get the full experience. Since the tiny Koya Bar opened next door, the focus is also on non-noodle dishes: pickled ox tongue, pickled beetroot and horseradish, say, or sea bass, beautifully steamed and treated very simply with a dressing of steamed julienne of

ginger and a light soy sauce. But if you are here for noodles, then consider ten hiya atsu (cold noodle with hot broth) with 'perfect' prawn and vegetable tempura, and hiyashi udon (cold udon and cold sauce) with smoked mackerel and green leaves. To drink, saké, shochu or beer may be preferable to wine (from £20).
Chef/s: Junya Yamasaki. **Open:** all week L 12 to 3, D 5.30 to 10.30 (10 Sun). **Closed:** 24 Dec to 2 Jan. **Meals:** alc (main courses £7 to £15). **Details:** 46 seats.

LOCAL GEM
▲ Lantana Café
13 Charlotte Place, Fitzrovia, W1T 1SN
Tel no: (020) 7637 3347
www.lantanacafe.co.uk
⊖ Goodge Street, Tottenham Court Road, map 5
Australian | £20

The sunny global flavours that the Aussies do so well are everywhere in this no-frills all-day café off Goodge Street. Corn fritters star at breakfast, and the daily repertoire takes in Asian shredded pork salad with fennel, bean shoots, coriander, mint and crispy noodles, or crispy chicken and bacon burger with coriander aïoli and winter slaw. With no bookings taken you should expect to queue at popular times. Fortunately, staff are good-natured. Wines from £18. Open all week, closed evenings.

Latium
Old-school Italian with winning ways
21 Berners Street, Fitzrovia, W1T 3LP
Tel no: (020) 7323 9123
www.latiumrestaurant.com
⊖ Goodge Street, Oxford Circus, map 5
Italian | £36
Cooking score: 3

Unashamedly old-school, but with a winning streak nonetheless, Latium continues to please its regulars with a blend of cosseting service, elegant surroundings and food with a heartfelt personal touch. Leather chairs and abstract artworks brighten up the rather sedate dining room, while the cooking spotlights chef/

patron Maurizio Morelli's passion for pasta – there's even a separate menu devoted to his beloved ravioli. These little parcels are stuffed with all manner of ingenious fillings, from an oxtail version with celery sauce to a fish selection dressed with sea bass bottarga (cured roe). The carte features distinct regional accents and clever combos such as stewed baby octopus with chickpea sauce and oregano; or roast lamb with broad beans, roasted new potatoes and oven-dried tomatoes. Sweet ravioli also appear among the desserts, or you could try dark chocolate and almond tart. The wine list (from £16) is a tempting oenophiles' tour of Italy.

Chef/s: Maurizio Morelli. **Open:** Mon to Fri L 12 to 3, all week D 5.30 to 10.30 (11 Sat). **Closed:** 25 and 26 Dec, 31 Dec to 2 Jan, bank hols. **Meals:** alc (main courses £10 to £21). Set L £17 (2 courses) to £23. Set D £30 (2 courses) to £36. **Details:** 56 seats. Wheelchair access.

LOCAL GEM
▲ Leong's Legends

4 Macclesfield Street, Soho, W1D 6AX
Tel no: (020) 7287 0288
www.leongslegends.co.uk
⊖ Leicester Square, map 5
Taiwanese | £21

Known for its curious door policy – which requires a hard knock to gain admittance – Leong's Legends offers relaxed, even sleepy service, dim lighting and a muted atmosphere. It's a welcome change to Gerrard Street's brisk one-in-one-out affairs. Classic dim sum for lunch is exceptional, as are homemade Taiwanese snacks such as siu long bao (pork and prawn soup dumplings): so good they're served all day. Dinner is less reliable. Wine (from £17) is available, but dim sum is best enjoyed with beer. Open all week.

Lima

Contemporary Peruvian cooking
31 Rathbone Place, Fitzrovia, W1T 1JH
Tel no: (020) 3002 2640
www.limalondon.com
⊖ Tottenham Court Road, map 5
Peruvian | £55
Cooking score: 2

£5
OFF

If you hanker after a bit of trendy South American action, note that Fitzrovia's Lima is the domain of a chap who is positively white-hot in Peru, Virgilio Martinez. His restaurant, Central (in Lima), gets global attention. In London, where he's executive chef, the deal is to take British and South American ingredients and deliver modern little plates packed with Latin style. It's contemporary stuff, served in pretty patterns on the plate, and everything takes place in a spruce room with banquette seating and jazzy artworks. There's nothing overly radical in the output, despite appearances, with ceviche such as a vibrant plate of sea bream and traditional potato-based causa among the starters (an organic salmon version, maybe). Follow on with suckling pig with giant corn and red and green peppers, or duck escabèche, and finish with a dessert made from top-quality cacao Porcelana. House Spanish is £19.

Chef/s: Virgilio Martinez and Robert Ortiz. **Open:** Mon to Sat L 12 to 2.30, D 5.30 to 10.30. **Closed:** Sun, 23 to 27 Dec. **Meals:** alc (main courses £9 to £29). Set L and D £20 (2 courses) to £23. **Details:** 70 seats. 8 seats outside. Music.

Little Social

Gregarious little blockbuster
5 Pollen Street, Mayfair, W1S 1NE
Tel no: (020) 7870 3730
www.littlesocial.co.uk
⊖ Oxford Circus, map 5
Modern European | £35
Cooking score: 6

♦ V

Jason Atherton's imperious Pollen Street Social may be 'the special one', but this 'stonking' sibling across the road has a kind of magic too. Fun-loving Little Social rocks to an ebullient tune, enveloping everyone with its seductive London-meets-Paris vibe and 'blinding' Anglo-European food. Consider a tapas dream plate involving milky burrata, lightly pickled quince and pear, truffled honey and pickled walnut, or a delicately detailed combo of raw hand-dived scallop accented with Japanese notes – dashi jelly, apple, shiso and pungent wasabi. Big flavours also hit the bull's-eye: juicy pork chops with artichoke purée; melting lamb shank with soft, pulpy polenta; magnificent braised ox cheek on horseradish mash with sourdough crumb and roast marrow bone – all enriched with lip-sticking juices. After that, wickedly tempting maple-glazed cinnamon doughnuts will keep you rooted to your red banquette a while longer. Aproned staff charm the place with bubbly enthusiasm, while the savvy, offbeat wine list packs a real punch, with Gallic glugs aplenty by the glass; bottles from £26.
Chef/s: Cary Docherty. **Open:** Mon to Sat L 12 to 2.30, D 6 to 10.30. **Closed:** Sun, 25 and 26 Dec, 1 and 2 Jan, bank hols. **Meals:** alc (main courses £15 to £26). Set L £21 (2 courses) to £25. **Details:** 55 seats. Wheelchair access. Music.

Locanda Locatelli

Silky-smooth Italian flagship
8 Seymour Street, Marble Arch, W1H 7JZ
Tel no: (020) 7935 9088
www.locandalocatelli.com
⊖ Marble Arch, map 4
Italian | £60
Cooking score: 4

♦

Giorgio Locatelli's name is synonymous with smart Italian cooking in London's swisher neighbourhoods, and the dashing celeb chef knows exactly how to win over his worldly clientele. Located within the Hyatt Regency Churchill Hotel, this flagship dining room sets the silky-smooth tone with its cosseting surrounds, tasteful drapes, fish-eye mirrors and retro fittings. It's an oh-so-chic backdrop for cooking that relies on top ingredients, thoughtful sourcing and meticulous craftsmanship. Perfect pastas prove the point (think oxtail ravioli or tubular 'mezze maniche' with red gurnard, black olives and tapenade), while antipasti are all about daisy-fresh seasonal assemblages – as in Jerusalem artichoke salad with pea shoots and heritage carrot. Locatelli's mastery also shows through in high-end 'secondi' such as char-grilled spring lamb with morels, pea and mint purée or roast monkfish with samphire, accompanied by walnut and caper sauce. To finish, don't miss the daring Gorgonzola pannacotta with chocolate crumble. The deeply patriotic, patrician wine list tours the byways of Italian regional winemaking, with revelatory results; prices from £17 (£5 a glass).
Chef/s: Giorgio Locatelli. **Open:** all week L 12 to 3 (3.30 Sat and Sun), D 6.45 to 11 (11.30 Fri and Sat, 10.15 Sun). **Closed:** 25 to 27 Dec, Aug bank hol. **Meals:** alc (main courses £19 to £33). **Details:** 75 seats. Wheelchair access.

LOCAL GEM
▲ Mele e Pere
46 Brewer Street, Soho, W1F 9TF
Tel no: (020) 7096 2096
www.meleepere.co.uk
⊖ Piccadilly Circus, map 5
Italian | £28 £5 OFF

A classic Soho venue with a few tables on the ground floor, but more in the basement, 'Apples and Pears' specialises in simple yet dynamically seasoned Italian food of considerable charm. Small sharing plates for starters include deep-fried squid with smoked aïoli, followed by pastas such as tagliatelle with beef ragù, and mains like veal chop with Borettane onions in balsamic. The star dessert is lemon custard with lychee ice cream and marshmallow. Cocktails and digestifs supplement the short Italian wine list (from £18). Open all week.

▲ Mon Plaisir
21 Monmouth Street, Covent Garden, WC2H 9DD
Tel no: (020) 7836 7243
www.monplaisir.co.uk
⊖ Covent Garden, map 5
French | £35

A Covent Garden fixture for more than 40 years, Alan Lhermitte's bistro remains undilutedly Gallic. The Tricolore flies outside and posters cover every inch of wall space. The menu is a familiar run through country pork and chicken liver terrine, coq au vin, navarin d'agneau and ribeye steak with béarnaise. However, salmon marinated in coconut, lime, tomato and chives, and wild boar casserole with fresh tagliatelle give a more contemporary feel. Finish with chocolate mousse or crème brûlée. Patriotic wines from £19. Closed Sun.

Moti Mahal
Indian regional cook's tour
45 Great Queen Street, Covent Garden, WC2B 5AA
Tel no: (020) 7240 9329
www.motimahal-uk.com
⊖ Covent Garden, map 5
Indian | £35
Cooking score: 3
£5 OFF

The Grand Trunk Road might not have the same historical resonance as the Silk Route or the Khyber Pass, say, but here in Covent Garden the thoroughfare gets the appreciation it deserves – well, the culinary traditions of those that live along it are celebrated. Anirudh Arora's classy modern Indian restaurant takes its inspiration from the 2,500km highway that runs from Kolkata to Peshawar. Hand-picked crab comes Malabar-style with chickpeas and curry leaves, and Keralan flavours enrich a red mullet parcel (hold on, where's the map?). The tandoor and thatee grill add authenticity to lamb chops flavoured with caraway seeds and Kashmiri chillies, and there's braised rabbit with cumin from Jaipur. A contemporary sheen to the presentation confirms the new-wave credentials of the place, as do glam cocktails and the open-to-view kitchen. The wine list offers some advice as to what goes with what, prices starting at a steep £28.
Chef/s: Anirudh Arora. **Open:** Mon to Fri L 12 to 3, Mon to Sat D 5.30 to 11. **Closed:** Sun, 24 to 28 Dec. **Meals:** alc (main courses £12 to £24). Set L £16. Set D £21 (2 courses) to £35. **Details:** 85 seats. Music.

★ TOP 50 ★

Murano

Flawless, fine-tuned cooking
20 Queen Street, Mayfair, W1J 5PP
Tel no: (020) 7495 1127
www.muranolondon.com
⊖ Green Park, map 5
Italian | £65
Cooking score: 7
🍷

Angela Hartnett's flagship is part of a growing family that now includes a 'little sister', Café Murano in St James (see entry). One side effect of this might be to make Murano, with its neat frontage and tastefully pale interior, seem stiff or dull by comparison. Yes, the airy plushness of the dining room is tailor-made for Mayfair, but readers report that the atmosphere is relaxed and friendly – even a little excitable. Hartnett's reputation for flawless, fine-tuned cooking will do that to a room, or perhaps it's the thrill of having carte blanche to choose anything between two and five courses from a 'flexible' menu that's strongly but not slavishly Italian. Delicate ingredients like sweetbreads, served with apple and walnuts, or turbot paired with purple sprouting and almond purée do especially well here. There's a hint of woodsy comfort in baked potato gnocchi with fontina, wild mushrooms and speck, while venison loin with a matching shepherd's pie is 'the star of a very impressive show'. Desserts embrace the classic: try Amalfi lemon tart or pear and chocolate mousse with hazelnut praline and pear sorbet. The three-course lunch at £30 is a good entry point. Marc-Andréa Lévy's wine list makes for good reading on Italy and the French regions. It starts at an accessible £20, or £4.50 by the glass – but it goes up.
Chef/s: Angela Hartnett and Philippa Lacey. **Open:** Mon to Sat L 12 to 3, D 6.30 to 11. **Closed:** Sun, 23 to 26 Dec. **Meals:** alc (main courses £15 to £35). Set L £25 (2 courses) to £30. Set D £50 (2 courses) to £65. **Details:** 55 seats. Wheelchair access.

Newman Street Tavern

Seasonal bounty from the regional larder
48 Newman Street, Fitzrovia, W1T 1QQ
Tel no: (020) 3667 1445
www.newmanstreettavern.co.uk
⊖ Goodge Street, map 5
British | £30
Cooking score: 2
🍷

What was a sparsely populated Fitzrovia drinking den has been spruced up and re-branded as a modern-day 'tavern': a hostelry devoted to seasonal bounty from new Albion's regional larder. Stake your claim in the lively 'raw bar' or head upstairs (past the jumbled prints of fish, flesh and fowl) to the quieter, more discreet dining room. Either way, feast from a menu that stands or falls by the quality of its ingredients. Smoked herring roes on toast, wild brown trout with fennel and cucumber, Blackface lamb with roasted beetroot, and Cobb chicken with bread sauce are typical calls from the plain-speaking line-up. Neal's Yard Dairy cheeses maintain the patriotic theme, as do desserts such as lemon cheesecake with blackthorn (sloe) jelly. Lamentably slow service is a regular gripe, but there's no arguing with a wine list that punches well above its weight for quality and value. Offbeat themed categories such as 'thirst' or 'skin and clay' conceal charms and surprises at every turn; prices from £18.50 (£3.60 a glass).
Chef/s: Peter Weeden. **Open:** all week L 12 to 3 (4.30 Sun), Mon to Sat D 5.30 to 10.30. **Closed:** 25 and 26 Dec, bank hols. **Meals:** alc (main courses £13 to £20). Set L and D £17 (2 courses) to £20. **Details:** 90 seats. 12 seats outside. Separate bar. Wheelchair access. Music.

Nobu Berkeley St
High-gloss celebrity hangout
15 Berkeley Street, Mayfair, W1J 8DY
Tel no: (020) 7290 9222
www.noburestaurants.com
⊖ **Green Park, map 5**
Japanese | £80
Cooking score: 4

Two floors of thrilling glitz, the Mayfair branch of Nobu is a diamond-bright celebrity hangout. Tree silhouettes and foliate design constitute an ironic nod to the natural world amid the brushed-steel sheen of the interior. The group menu, under the aegis of executive chef Mark Edwards, continues to deliver the goods for precisely seasoned, exquisitely presented mouthfuls of umami, chilli-heat and acid edge. Osusume (recommended) dishes served from 6pm may begin an evening with lemon and garlic lobster, or an anticucho ribeye skewer, but the main business is in Japanese classics like tempura veg, maki rolls, sashimi and melt-in-the-mouth Wagyu beef cuts such as truffled rump. Nor do lunch-counter bento-boxers need to miss out on these treasures. Creative desserts play their part too: contemplate an array of white chocolate mousse, pistachio sponge, mango cream and kalamansi sorbet. Drinking will send the bill heavenwards, bottles of wine starting at £37.
Chef/s: Mark Edwards. **Open:** Mon to Sat L 12 to 2.30 (3 Sat), all week D 6 to 11 (12 Thur, Fri and Sat, 9.45 Sun). **Closed:** 25 Dec. **Meals:** alc (main courses £7 to £34). Tasting menu £70. **Details:** 180 seats. Separate bar. Wheelchair access. Music.

Nobu London
Japanese fusion pioneer
Metropolitan Hotel, 19 Old Park Lane, Mayfair, W1K 1LB
Tel no: (020) 7447 4747
www.noburestaurants.com
⊖ **Hyde Park Corner, map 5**
Japanese | £75
Cooking score: 4
£5 OFF 🛏

The glamour, the gossip and the paparazzi have moved on, leaving Nobu's original London establishment to don a more civilised pose. It may feel slightly tame these days, but at least the kitchen still knows how to excite, even if many of its emblematic dishes have been replicated across the land: think black cod in miso, creamy shrimp tempura or yellowtail sashimi with jalapeño dressing. Nobu made its name by bringing Latin influences to the Japanese table in the form of boat-shaped tacos, ceviches and chilli-spiked anticuchos skewers, but it can also deliver delicate artistry. Classic sushi such as sparkling nigiri and handrolls sit happily alongside 'new style' sashimi dressed with dry miso, clean-flavoured salads and specials such as soft-shell crab kara-age with ponzu or grilled poussin with truffle teriyaki. Intimidating prices and strictly enforced table-turning are perennial bugbears, while the high-rolling, plutocratic wine list (from £30) inflicts financial pain, yet also potable pleasure.
Chef/s: Mark Edwards and Hideki Maede. **Open:** all week L 12 to 2.15 (12.30 to 2.30 Sat and Sun), D 6 to 10.15 (11 Fri and Sat, 10 Sun). **Closed:** 25 Dec, 1 Jan. **Meals:** alc (main courses £10 to £42). Set L £24 (2 courses) to £30. Set D £35 (2 courses) to £75. **Details:** 150 seats. Separate bar. Wheelchair access. Music.

Nopi

Sunny ingredients and striking flavours
21-22 Warwick Street, Soho, W1B 5NE
Tel no: (020) 7494 9584
www.nopi-restaurant.com
⊖ Piccadilly Circus, map 5
Middle Eastern/Mediterranean | £40
Cooking score: 3

TV chef, *Guardian* columnist and deli king Yotam Ottolenghi went deliberately upmarket when he opened Nopi – although this stylish venue still trumpets the Med-influenced fusion food that put him on London's gastronomic map. Soho trendies and Yotam disciples feel right at home amid the polished marble floors, shiny white-tiled walls and clean-lined contemporary furnishings, while the kitchen conjures up vibrancy, colour and striking flavours from myriad sunny ingredients. The menu leavens its now-familiar veggie offering with a contingent of meat and fish surprises: perhaps lamb's sweetbreads with wasabi peas and miso glaze, or octopus with red quinoa and Botija olive purée. Otherwise, seek out the pleasures of Persian 'love rice' wrapped in vine leaves with pickled kohlrabi, burnt butter and courgette tzatziki, before sweetening the deal with some coffee and pecan financiers. Creative cocktails add extra pep to the zesty global wine list; bottles from £24.
Chef/s: Yotam Ottolenghi. **Open:** Mon to Fri and Sun 8am to 3 (10 to 4 Sun), Mon to Fri D 5.30 to 10.30. Sat 10am to 10.30pm. **Closed:** 25 and 26 Dec, 1 Jan. **Meals:** alc (main courses £17 to £30). **Details:** 102 seats. Separate bar. Music.

Opera Tavern

Vibrant theatreland venue with lively tapas
23 Catherine Street, Covent Garden, WC2B 5JS
Tel no: (020) 7836 3680
www.operatavern.co.uk
⊖ Covent Garden, map 5
Tapas | £40
Cooking score: 4

Competition is fierce in the bustling streets of Covent Garden, but this classy former pub more than holds its own. The combination of convivial ground-floor bar and sedate restaurant upstairs (where tables are bookable) is immediately appealing, while Spanish and Italian culinary influences jostle on a menu that's geared for casual satisfaction. Like its chart-topping siblings Salt Yard, Dehesa and Ember Yard (see entries), Opera Tavern deals in modern tapas – trademarks include excellent charcuterie and cheeses, a superb mini Ibérico pork and foie gras burger, and the never-off-the-menu goats' cheese-stuffed courgette flower with honey. Alternatively, there's braised pig's cheek with celeriac mash and crispy kale, or char-grilled octopus with chickpea fritter, red pepper and mojo verde. A glass of something from the fine selection of sherries makes an apt accompaniment, or explore the enticing Italian-Spanish treasures on a well-annotated wine list packed with good bottles. Prices from £19.
Chef/s: James Thickett. **Open:** all week L 12 to 3 (5 Sat and Sun), Mon to Sat D 5 to 11.30. **Closed:** 25 and 26 Dec, bank hols. **Meals:** alc (main courses £6 to £10). **Details:** 76 seats. 6 seats outside. Separate bar. Music.

NEW ENTRY
Orrery

Slick professionalism at Marylebone grandee
55 Marylebone High Street, Marylebone, W1U 5RB
Tel no: (020) 7616 8000
www.orrery-restaurant.co.uk
⊖ Baker Street, Regent's Park, map 4
French | £30
Cooking score: 4

🍷 V

Hidden above the Conran Store, Orrery makes a virtue of discretion, going about its business with cool aplomb. The long, narrow dining room with arched windows looking over a churchyard may look less cutting edge than in its Chris Galvin heyday, but the clean lines, pastel shades and blond wood still have currency. Likewise, the modern French cooking shows 'top skill' as chef Igor Tymchyshyn (here since 2008) has brought stability to the kitchen. His confident, refined dishes are as light and smart as the surroundings, built around top-notch ingredients with balance and depth of flavour a given. At a test meal, a beguiling opener of succulent roasted quail (breasts and legs) came with standout fig compote, crispy pancetta and stellar Madeira jus, while mains of steamed Dorset sea bass fillet was 'teamed with the balanced citrus of agrumes and a coriander jus to counter the bitter note of endive'. Professional service and a cracking wine list (from £25) add allure.
Chef/s: Igor Tymchyshyn. **Open:** all week L 12 to 2.30 (3 Sun), D 6.30 to 10 (10.30 Fri). **Meals:** Set L £25 (2 courses) to £40. Set D £30 (2 courses) to £50. Sun L £30. **Details:** 80 seats. 20 seats outside. Separate bar. Wheelchair access.

NEW ENTRY
Otto's

Gallic food with a theatrical bent
182 Gray's Inn Road, Bloomsbury, WC1X 8EW
Tel no: (020) 7713 0107
www.ottos-restaurant.com
⊖ Chancery Lane, map 5
French | £45
Cooking score: 2

A historical curiosity that's relatively newly minted, Otto's celebrates the culinary theatre of another place and time. In a narrow, characterful room crammed with kitsch and serious silverware, old-school French dishes are served with a flourish. The house special, which must be pre-ordered, is duck squeezed in a Christofle press, but there are also lesser-spotted rarities including creamy calf's brain (with capers, parsley and fatty pan juices) and smoked salmon carved and garnished at the table. With performance often taking precedence over consistency, it pays to cleave to more traditional dishes – tournedos Rossini, with a rewardingly generous lump of seared foie gras, instead of characterless sole with garlic tortellini, for example. Puddings are hit and miss, but if your eyebrows are feeling chilly then Grand Marnier soufflé, flamed at the table, makes for a powerfully boozy remedy. Wine is mainly French, with a fixed mark-up, from £19.50.
Chef/s: Matt Burns. **Open:** Mon to Fri L 12 to 1.45, Mon to Sat D 6 to 9.45. **Closed:** Sun, 25 Dec to 5 Jan. **Meals:** alc (main courses £18 to £30). Set L £24 (2 courses) to £28. **Details:** 40 seats. Children over 10 yrs only.

NEW ENTRY
The Palomar

Hot ticket cooking from Jerusalem
34 Rupert Street, Soho, W1D 6DN
Tel no: (020) 7439 8777
www.thepalomar.co.uk
⊖ Piccadilly Circus, map 5
Middle Eastern | £30
Cooking score: 4

With its 16 first-come, first-served kitchen counter seats, bookable backroom tables and warmly welcoming attitude, this tiny, relaxed Israeli eatery is just right for its location at the Chinatown end of Rupert Street. And what a hot ticket it's turned out to be, with queues right from the get go for the vibrantly flavoured Sephardic dishes – a blend of Middle Eastern and Mediterranean styles – that chefs from Jerusalem's famed Machneyuda restaurant belt out with gusto. This is non-kosher Israeli cooking – note mussels, corn-fed chicken cooked in buttermilk and pork belly tagine – that packs a major punch. Assorted mezze includes several ways with aubergine and delicious homemade labneh, the umami hit of the 'Jerusalem style' polenta is worth the queue, shakshukit is a deconstructed kebab of minced meat, yoghurt and tahini, and there's a delicate, rose-scented milk pudding with raspberry coulis to finish. Wines from £20.50.
Chef/s: Tomer Amedi. **Open:** Mon to Sat L 12 to 2.30, D 5.30 to 12.30. **Closed:** Sun. **Meals:** alc (main courses £9 to £15). **Details:** 56 seats. Music.

Phoenix Palace

Hong Kong opulence and superior dim sum
3-5 Glentworth Street, Marylebone, NW1 5PG
Tel no: (020) 7486 3515
www.phoenixpalace.co.uk
⊖ Baker Street, map 4
Chinese | £35
Cooking score: 2

The interior designers did not stint when decking out Phoenix Palace – there are enough oriental bits and bobs to fill a couple of dozen market stalls. The opulent space of red and gold is regularly packed (and the venue seats 250 people), with happy punters seated at circular tables to enable sharing. Quite a buzz is generated. Dim sum (last orders 4.45pm) is the real deal, with ducks' tongues in a sesame dressing alongside more familiar food such as pork and prawn dumplings. The main menu has plenty of old favourites (kung po chicken, say), but lots more besides – abalone with sea cucumber, venison with lemongrass, and a casserole of braised beef brisket and lettuce. Start with a mixed platter or focus on breaded scallop with mango sauce, and finish with cold sago cream with yam. There are set and party menus galore, and wines from £19.
Chef/s: Zhan Hong Yu. **Open:** all week 12 to 11.30 (11 to 10.30 Sun). **Closed:** 25 Dec. **Meals:** alc (main courses £10 to £54). Set D £33. **Details:** 250 seats. Separate bar. Wheelchair access. Music.

★ TOP 50 ★

Pied-à-Terre

Bijou Fitzrovia aristocrat
34 Charlotte Street, Fitzrovia, W1T 2NH
Tel no: (020) 7636 1178
www.pied-a-terre.co.uk
⊖ Goodge Street, map 5
Modern French | £80
Cooking score: 7

🍸 V

Among the long-established destination dining rooms of London, Pied-à-Terre has always been one of the least ostentatious. To this day, the modestly proportioned premises feel intimate in the best way: quietly civilised and relaxing, even if determinedly monochrome, the sombre-panelled walls offset by a skylight. David Moore has kept a reassuring hand on the tiller here since the early 1990s, and in concert with present chef Marcus Eaves continues to keep the place in the first division. The cooking is a little more obviously French in its modernism than British, with a greater willingness to aim for complexity in dishes paying off handsomely. The quail starter that sees the two breast cuts, a crispy leg and a dear little Kiev accompanied by a purée of Douglas fir and hazelnut vinaigrette is something of a signature now, or there may be Chinese-inspired langoustine and prawn dumplings with steamed choi sum in shellfish consommé. Roasted monkfish blackened with spice gains from its supporting cast of mussels, butternut, Amalfi lemon, coriander and mint, while guinea-fowl appears more conventionally with morels and braised leek in rosemary jus, its sweet shallot purée spiked with liquorice. Chocos will find it hard to resist Valrhona crème with caramel sauce, peanut ice cream and chocolate jelly, but there's also cardamom-scented rhubarb mille-feuille served with matching sorbet. Any weightier and the wine list would have to arrive by forklift truck. It's a massive, but deeply engaging tome, full of unimpeachable class and idiosyncrasy, from Japanese Koshu to Uruguay Viognier, starting at £28.

Chef/s: Marcus Eaves. **Open:** Mon to Fri L 12.15 to 2.30, Mon to Sat D 6 to 11. **Closed:** Sun, 1 week Dec, 1 week Jan. **Meals:** Set L £28 (2 courses) to £34. Set D £65 (2 courses) to £80. Tasting menu £105. **Details:** 44 seats. Separate bar. Music.

★ TOP 10 ★

Pollen Street Social

Utterly brilliant uptown eatery
8-13 Pollen Street, Mayfair, W1S 1NQ
Tel no: (020) 7290 7600
www.pollenstreetsocial.com
⊖ Oxford Circus, map 5
Modern British | £55
Cooking score: 9

♦ V

Man of the moment Jason Atherton seems to be everywhere these days, generously spreading his wares across the capital like whipped goats' curd on sourdough – although Pollen Street Social remains his special project. Hidden on a Mayfair alleyway just wide enough to accommodate a black cab, this utterly brilliant eatery is as electrifying and as classy as they come. The suave dining room has seen some cosmetic improvements of late – new artwork and furniture, a few tweaks to the layout – and a seemingly endless supply of rabbits pulled from the hat. Note the galaxy of appetisers brought to the table on a wooden 'cake stand' and the trolley loaded with potted fresh herbs for those requiring tea. Atherton has the knack of picking the right man for the job when it comes to head chef. The current incumbent is on blistering form, and the cooking has acquired new levels of finesse and refinement – witness a sublimely simple dish of John Dory with oh-so-sweet crayfish and four riffs on garlic, all dressed with a shellfish broth of near-unbelievable depth and intensity. A chart of food miles on the menu is a reminder that seasonal British produce underpins just about everything here, and it is used to startling effect: 'mind-blowing' mushroom tea poured into a demi-tasse of Parmesan foam; Orkney scallop carpaccio, kohlrabi and lemon skin purée sprinkled with frozen pink grapefruit; roast squab pigeon and offal with honey-spiced beetroots, pickled pear, date and black tea purée. And then there are the high-wire thrills of the dessert bar – nitro-blasted wizardry, billowing smoke, velvety ice creams coddled in dry ice, cocktail glasses filled with caramel popcorn and the sheer, nerve-tingling complexity of, say, bergamot and verbena sorbet with frozen citrus and bergamot jam. Astonishing-value set lunches (deliberately pegged below £30) remain the best deal in Mayfair, while hugely confident staff leaven their full-dress professionalism with spirited good humour. The scintillating global wine list is bigger and better than ever, with imperious French vintages alongside astonishing artisan obscurities and terroir-led discoveries; also note the top-end Coravin selections by the glass. Bottles from £23.

Chef/s: Jason Atherton and Ross Bryans. **Open:** Mon to Sat L 12 to 2.30, D 6 to 10.30. **Closed:** Sun, bank hols. **Meals:** alc (main courses £30 to £39). Set L £26 (2 courses) to £30. Tasting menu £85 (7 courses). **Details:** 65 seats. Separate bar. Wheelchair access. Music. No children after 8.

NEW ENTRY
Polpetto
Fashionable food in a cosy trattoria
11 Berwick Street, Soho, W1F OPL
Tel no: (020) 7439 8627
www.polpo.co.uk
⊖ Oxford Circus, Piccadilly Circus, map 5
Italian | £25
Cooking score: 3
£30

This year, Polpetto made the move from poky room above the French House pub to chic stand-alone trattoria, while its chef Florence Knight went from supporting player in Russell Norman's Polpo Group to a leading star. A summer inspection of the cosy little candlelit restaurant left us with some reservations but in no doubt we were in the presence of a fine cook. From the short seasonal sharing menu, grey mullet under a near-transparent sheet of lardo was perfectly seasoned, perfectly cooked. Its raw sea vegetable garnish, however, was – alas – like chewing the cud. Soft braised rabbit to follow in its pool of clear, golden broth was similarly unenhanced by aggressive Douglas fir. Knight signatures of burrata with monk's beard and her excellent pasta (beef shin strozzapreti, for instance) are safer bets, and dessert (a wobbly maple tart with impeccable pastry) was faultless. The Italian wines (from £18), cocktails and bitters are a classy, enjoyable selection. For more casual eating of a similar ilk, try the original Polpo nearby (41 Beak Street), the other West End branch (6 Maiden Lane in Covent Garden) or head west to Notting Hill Gate.
Chef/s: Florence Knight. **Open:** all week 12 to 11 (12 to 4 Sun). **Meals:** alc (tapas £4 to £12). **Details:** 70 seats. Separate bar.

¦¦¦• Visit us
¦¦¦ Online
To find out more about
The Good Food Guide, please visit
www.thegoodfoodguide.co.uk

Princi
Good ingredients, good value, good buzz
135 Wardour Street, Soho, W1F OUT
Tel no: (020) 7478 8888
www.princi.com
⊖ Tottenham Court Road, Piccadilly Circus, map 5
Italian | £20
Cooking score: 2
£30

'Spirito di Milano', they say, for Princi has its roots in the great city in Lombardy, where the owners have a gaggle of bakeries. The Wardour Street outpost has a self-service café attracting punters for pastries, sandwiches, stews and the like, but it's the pizzeria that fires up the Soho crowd. A staple of Naples, maybe, but these Milanese have brought in a wood-fired oven and can knock-up a bang-on version. The kitchen can also produce simple starters such as a salad with baccalà (salt cod), chicory and taggiasche olives, and a main-course char-grilled squid with chickpeas and chilli, but, really, folk come for the pizza. And, boy, do they come! Seated at simple wooden tables, served by an *autentico* service team, the crowds might tuck into 'Diavola' with Ventricina salami and chilli, or perhaps a veggie version with courgettes and peppers. The wine list (from £19) sticks to the Italian homeland.
Chef/s: Matteo Cocchetti. **Open:** all week 8am to 11.30pm (8.30am to 10pm Sun). **Meals:** alc (main courses £8 to £12). **Details:** 46 seats. Separate bar. Wheelchair access. Music.

Quilon
Spot-on south Indian flavours
41 Buckingham Gate, Westminster, SW1E 6AF
Tel no: (020) 7821 1899
www.quilon.co.uk
⊖ St James's Park, Victoria, map 5
Indian | £45
Cooking score: 4
£5 OFF

With its own separate entrance on Buckingham Place Road, Quilon just manages to avoid the straitjacket of a big-hotel

dining format. The décor is elegant, with well-spaced, white-clothed tables, and the kitchen offers a good, gentle introduction to a fascinating palette of mainly Goan and Keralan influences and flavours. The focus is on seafood and vegetarian food (though several meat dishes are offered) and Sriram Aylur's cooking shows flashes of innovation. Very gentle spicing can be seen in delicate crab cakes; in cauliflower florets tossed in yoghurt, green chilli and curry leaves; and in seafood moilee (halibut, prawns and potato in a coconut, ginger and chilli sauce). Malabar lamb biryani and an east-meets-west dessert of white chocolate mousse in a chocolate cup with cassata ice cream show creativity. Effort has been put into finding wines (from £25) that go with spicy food, and there are also fascinating globally sourced beers.
Chef/s: Sriram Aylur. **Open:** all week L 12 to 2.30 (12.30 to 3 Sat and Sun), D 6 to 10.30 (10 Sun). **Closed:** 25 Dec. **Meals:** alc (main courses £15 to £31). Set L £24. Set D £48. Sun L £24. **Details:** 82 seats. Separate bar. Music.

Quirinale

Intimate Westminster Italian
1 Great Peter Street, Westminster, SW1P 3LL
Tel no: (020) 7222 7080
www.quirinale.co.uk
⊖ Westminster, map 3
Italian | £35
Cooking score: 3
£5 OFF

A light-filled basement a short trot along the embankment from the Palace of Westminster, Quirinale does old and new Italian things in considerable style. It's possible to feast on carpaccio with rocket and Parmesan, whole grilled sea bass, and tiramisu while you try not to look as though you're earwigging on what MPs are saying to journalists all around you, but there's a more innovative vein, too. That latter tendency might bring on shallot-crusted turbot fillet with pumpkin and liquorice, but it's the tried-and-true route that probably results in the deepest satisfaction, as in fortifying main dishes of roast venison with

soft polenta and wild mushrooms. The Italian cheeses are excellent, if you can tear yourself away from the prospect of hot chocolate pudding with vanilla ice cream. The wine list (from £21) explores the Italian regions, with Alto Adige Gewürztraminer and Sardinian Carignano leading you off the beaten track.
Chef/s: Stefano Savio. **Open:** Mon to Fri L 12 to 2.30, D 6 to 10.30. **Closed:** Sat, Sun, 1 Aug to 1 Sept, 24 Dec to 5 Jan. **Meals:** alc (main courses £19 to £29). Set L and D £19 (2 courses) to £23. **Details:** 50 seats. Music.

Quo Vadis

Simply a Soho legend
26-29 Dean Street, Soho, W1D 3LL
Tel no: (020) 7437 9585
www.quovadissoho.co.uk
⊖ Tottenham Court Road, map 5
Modern British | £45
Cooking score: 4

'I remember coming here years ago when it was all dark gloom and Italian grovelling,' an old hand reminds us, adding 'now the dining room looks bright as a pin, with antique mirrors, glass panels, lots of white and some neat Art Deco touches'. It's seven years since Sam and Eddie Hart revived this old theatreland address, while the more recent arrival of frontman Jeremy Lee has refocused the kitchen admirably. Lee's style revolves around unusual combinations of fresh seasonal ingredients put together with flare: a kind of rekindled British cooking if you like, delivered via a short, regularly changing menu. Smoked trout with sea kale and butter sauce, mains of pork belly with pickled fennel and plums, or mutton shoulder with chickpeas and kale, may seem uncomplicated, but it's the impeccable sourcing that gives them a lift. Among desserts, rum baba with raspberries has shone. The modern, wide-ranging wine list opens at £21.
Chef/s: Jeremy Lee. **Open:** Mon to Sat L 12 to 2.30, D 5.30 to 10.45. **Closed:** Sun, bank hols. **Meals:** alc (main courses £12 to £21). Set L and D £17.50 (2 courses) to £20. **Details:** 70 seats. 15 seats outside. Separate bar.

NEW ENTRY
Rex Whistler at the Tate
Seasonal promise at a rejuvenated gallery
Millbank, Pimlico, SW1P 4RG
Tel no: (020) 7887 8825
www.tate.org.uk
⊖ Pimlico, map 3
British | £29
Cooking score: 2
£30

The Rex Whistler Restaurant at Tate Britain
has reopened following a two-year closure
during the gallery's refurbishment. The Deco-
style dining room (open lunch and afternoon
tea only) has never looked better: the Rex
Whistler mural that wraps around the room
has been restored to glory, and the gleaming
columns and pristine napery look
wonderfully grand. On a springtime visit, the
menu sang with seasonal promise. To start,
devilled lamb's kidneys were impeccable, and
smoked eel and mackerel with golden
beetroot jelly delivered clean, clear flavours.
Mains took in black bream teamed with sea
purslane, samphire and saffron liquor, and a
wild garlic and goats' cheese soufflé (which
sadly came collapsed in a heap), while brûléed
custard tart made a safe if not outstanding
finish. Surprisingly, service lacked the
commanding presence that would do the
room and famous wine list justice.
Nevertheless, the half-bottles, rare finds and
keen prices (from £21) remain impressive.
Chef/s: Nathan Brewster. **Open:** all week L only 12
to 3. **Closed:** 23 to 25 Dec. **Meals:** alc (main courses
£17). Set L £24 (2 courses) to £29. Sun L £17.
Details: 90 seats. 20 seats outside. Wheelchair
access.

NEW ENTRY
The Ritz
One of the capital's great old dining rooms
150 Piccadilly, Mayfair, W1J 9BR
Tel no: (020) 7300 2370
www.theritzlondon.com
⊖ Green Park, map 5
French | £75
Cooking score: 6
🍽 V

This is one of the capital's great dining rooms,
lavish and enchanting in an elegant Louis XVI
style: all gilt and pastel, marbled and
chandeliered. It's definitely the place for an
old-fashioned special occasion in beautiful
surroundings. John Williams has done a
remarkable job reworking classic principles
and maintaining a grandeur in the cuisine to
match the hotel's Edwardian splendour. Here
you can taste cooking in the grand tradition –
Bresse chicken demi-deuil en vessie and sea
bass en croûte with sauce Mireille – at a
punishing price. The smart move is to go at
lunchtime and eat from the set menu, which
mixes classic and modern French ideas and
doesn't stint on luxury ingredients (or 'the
lovely fresh, carefully and prettily prepared'
amuse-bouches and petits fours). One such
meal got off to a fine start with good, baked-
on-the-premises bread and a faultless pea soup
teamed with mushroom, Parmesan and
truffle, went on to navarin of lamb and
finished with the lightest of chocolate soufflés
and, with attentive service, 'we were not
treated as poor cousins'. Expect, too, a good-
looking cheese trolley, and a wine list that
heads skywards from £48, with glasses
from £17.
Chef/s: John Williams MBE. **Open:** all week L 12.30
to 2, D 5.30 to 10. **Meals:** alc (main courses £37 to
£40). Set L £49. Menu Surprise £95. Sun L £59.
Details: 110 seats. 27 seats outside. Separate bar.
Wheelchair access. Car parking.

Roka

Stylish urban Japanese eating
37 Charlotte Street, Fitzrovia, W1T 1RR
Tel no: (020) 7580 6464
www.rokarestaurant.com
⊖ Goodge Street, map 5
Japanese | £50
Cooking score: 4

The original London branch of Roka (there's another at Canary Wharf) made a super-cool Japanese-style splash when it landed here a decade ago. Full-drop windows let in the bristling Medialand daylight, and although there's a subterranean bar (the Shochu Lounge), the main action takes place around a wood-built robata counter with chefs a-broil right before your eyes. The buzz of the place makes an enlivening change from the Zen tranquillity of other Japanese eateries, and the repertoire, while familiar, remains as sharp and fresh as if the whole cuisine were newly minted. Sea bass sashimi in white miso, Wagyu beef with Wafu tomatoes in teriyaki, maki rolls stuffed with soft-shell crab and kim-chee, glazed back ribs with sansho and cashews: everything is tippling over with sour, salt and umami intensity. Nor are the sweet elements devoid of interest; try raspberry shochu trifle with black sesame ice cream. Saké starts at £8 a small cup.
Chef/s: Damon Griffin. **Open:** all week L 12 to 3.30 (12.30 to 4 Sat and Sun), D 5.30 to 11.30 (10.30 Sun). **Closed:** 25 Dec. **Meals:** alc (dishes from £5 to £15). **Details:** 88 seats. 24 seats outside.

LOCAL GEM

▲ Roti Chai Street Kitchen

3 Portman Mews South, Marylebone, W1H 6HS
Tel no: (020) 7408 0101
www.rotichai.com
⊖ Marble Arch, Bond Street, map 4
Indian | £18

With its canteen vibe and Indian street food menu, Roti Chai is a handy pit-stop just off Oxford Street (behind Marble Arch M&S). The ground floor is the place to go for plates of idli sambar (rice cakes in a lentil and vegetable stew) or railway lamb curry, plus classic bhel puris and Keralan spiced chicken wings (or chicken lollipops as they call them). There's an evening dining room in the basement serving the likes of Chettinad chicken and desserts such as 'delicious' pistachio kulfi. Open all week.

Roux at Parliament Square

Luxe Anglo-French dining
11 Great George Street, Parliament Square, Westminster, SW1P 3AD
Tel no: (020) 7334 3737
www.rouxatparliamentsquare.co.uk
⊖ Westminster, St James's Park, map 5
Anglo-French | £55
Cooking score: 4
£5 OFF

The arrival of *MasterChef: The Professionals* winner Steve Groves has given this hushed dining room within the Royal Institution of Chartered Surveyors quite a fillip. Top-drawer British ingredients get the fine French treatment – Michel Roux Jnr is a consultant – on a 'limited' but elegant and quietly innovative menu. Venison tartare with sloe gin, Douglas fir and walnuts to start is 'small, but so tasty', while a Herdwick hogget 'tasting' with Jerusalem and violet artichokes and crosnes puts the spotlight on oft-overlooked ingredients. 'Everything was of the highest quality' sighs one reader, singling out the excellent cheeseboard (up against stiff competition from desserts such as banana soufflé, Valrhona chocolate and peanut-butter ice cream). This is a serious Westminster restaurant designed for fine dining and fine conversation; tables are well spaced and the thick carpets muffle political gossip. A predominantly French wine list (from £24) boasts 'acceptable prices – for London'.
Chef/s: Steve Groves. **Open:** Mon to Fri L 12 to 2, D 6.30 to 10. **Closed:** Sat, Sun, 24 Dec to 2 Jan, bank hols. **Meals:** alc (main courses £18 to £29). Set L £35 (3 courses). **Details:** 55 seats. Separate bar. Wheelchair access.

Roux at the Landau

A paean to sumptuous luxury
The Langham, 1c Portland Place, Oxford Circus,
W1B 1JA
Tel no: (020) 7965 0165
www.rouxatthelandau.com
⊖ Oxford Circus, map 5
Modern European | £63
Cooking score: 3
🛏

The Landau has its own access to one side of
the Langham Hotel. Inside is all high-toned
elegance: a panelled oval space with a broad
window vista and spiky modernist light
fittings. Behind it is the formidable pairing of
Albert and Michel Roux Junior, working via
Chris King to bring a gentle style of modern
French cooking to the West End's northern
fringe. Menus embrace the fanciful (seared
scallops with Jerusalem artichokes, pickled
kumquats and long pepper) and the familiar
(dry-aged beef sirloin with garlic potatoes in
sauce albuféra) to equally positive effect. A
summer reporter enjoyed smoked chicken and
Serrano ham ballotine with violet artichoke
salad, then crisped sea bream with yellow-
bean purée in tomato butter, finishing with
coconut and lime mousse with white
chocolate and rum ice cream, and a superlative
plate-load from the cheese trolley. A classically
based wine list finds quality outside the old
heartlands, with prices from £30.
Chef/s: Chris King. **Open:** Mon to Fri L 12.30 to 2.30,
Mon to Sat D 5.30 to 10.30. **Closed:** Sun. **Meals:** alc
(main courses £22 to £56). Set L and early D £35 (3
courses) to £47. **Details:** 82 seats. Separate bar.
Wheelchair access.

Symbols

🛏 Accommodation is available

£30 Three courses for less than £30

V Separate vegetarian menu

£5 OFF £5-off voucher scheme

🍷 Notable wine list

Rules

Britannia rules in Covent Garden
35 Maiden Lane, Covent Garden, WC2E 7LB
Tel no: (020) 7836 5314
www.rules.co.uk
⊖ Covent Garden, Leicester Square, map 5
British | £55
Cooking score: 3

Well into its third century of feeding central
London's hordes, Rules defiantly celebrates
British tradition. The place seems never less
than packed to the gills, and the clubbable
ambience provided by theatrical portraits and
red plush banquettes is augmented by a nerve-
twanging mural of the late Baroness Thatcher
as Britannia, her hair lacquered into a gigantic
battle-helmet. Amid all that, a menu of
smoked salmon, steak and chips, and lemon
meringue pie may come as clunking bathos,
but the lure has always been fabulous seasonal
game, now from the owner's Lartington Estate
in Teesdale. Don't miss whole roast birds such
as grouse or red-leg partridge, or take a spin on
pheasant curry. If lemon meringue isn't your
bag, try the new-fangled chocolate and
espresso tart. New World interlopers pop up
among the French classic wines that suit the
food best, with prices from £24.50, or £7 a
glass.
Chef/s: David Stafford. **Open:** all week 12 to 11.45
(10.45 Sun). **Closed:** 25 and 26 Dec. **Meals:** alc
(main courses £18 to £36). **Details:** 95 seats.
Separate bar.

Salt Yard

Versatile tapas hot spot
54 Goodge Street, Fitzrovia, W1T 4NA
Tel no: (020) 7637 0657
www.saltyard.co.uk
⊖ Goodge Street, map 5
Tapas | £28
Cooking score: 2
£30

It's ten years since this new-wave tapas bar
opened amid a parade of Goodge Street shops,
and it has gathered quite a following – as well
as three siblings (see entries, Ember Yard,

Dehesa, Opera Tavern). Salt Yard is tightly packed and rollickingly informal, whether you sit in the ground-floor bar or basement dining room. Italy and Spain provide the inspiration for sharing plates and the tipples to go with them. There are crowd-pleasers aplenty, perhaps 18-month cured Serrano ham, a classic tortilla or crisp baby squid with a gentle saffron aïoli. But look for creative spins on classics, too, for instance char-grilled chorizo with broad bean dressing and piquillo purée or smoked eel croquetas with horseradish and beetroot purée. Everyone loves the courgette flowers with goats' cheese and honey, but give the almond, polenta and citrus cake a try. Sherries by the glass open a snappy wine list, with bottles from £19.
Chef/s: Dan Sherlock. **Open:** Mon to Fri L 12 to 3, D 5.30 to 11. Sat 12 to 11. **Closed:** Sun, 25 and 26 Dec, 31 Dec, 1 Jan. **Meals:** alc (tapas £4 to £10). **Details:** 70 seats. 8 seats outside. Separate bar. Music.

Savoy Grill
An evocation of flavours past
The Savoy, Strand, Covent Garden, WC2R 0EU
Tel no: (020) 7592 1600
www.gordonramsay.com
⊖ Charing Cross, map 5
Anglo-French | £45
Cooking score: 2

To call the Savoy Grill 'clubby' may be to under-egg the pudding; on one midweek evening in early summer the clientele was predominantly groups of men 'tucking into T-bones'. But the place does have a sense of occasion – 'glorious', thought one (female) visitor – and along with gleaming wood panelling, noise-absorbing carpet and trundling trolleys, this cosseting Art Deco dining room is confirmed as one of London's more traditional eating spaces with food to match. Familiar strains resound in omelette Arnold Bennett, lobster thermidor, Dover sole meunière, beef Wellington or the various grills. There's little more to it than that, apart from the popular lunch-only roast trolley, its

cargo changing daily (on Mondays expect salt-baked leg of lamb with mint sauce), and desserts of chocolate marquise with dark chocolate ganache and peppermint ice cream or lemon sorbet with pineapple. The wine list has a strong base in France, with bottles from £25.
Chef/s: Andy Cook. **Open:** all week L 12 to 3 (4 Sun), D 5.30 to 11 (6 to 10.30 Sun). **Meals:** alc (main courses £19 to £38). Set L £30. Pre-theatre weekday D £24 (2 courses) to £28. Sun L £38. **Details:** 95 seats. Wheelchair access. Music.

Scott's
It's about luxury, comfort and indulgence
20 Mount Street, Mayfair, W1K 2HE
Tel no: (020) 7495 7309
www.scotts-restaurant.com
⊖ Green Park, map 4
Seafood | £45
Cooking score: 4

V

It may be party central for paparazzi staking out the pavement terrace, but on the whole Scott's caters for a well-heeled rather than hip crowd. As such the décor is stylish, the service attentive and the cooking confident, though not attention-grabbing. Some regulars prefer to perch at the seafood bar, others would rather bag the green leather banquettes edging the oak-panelled dining room. But all are here for the broad, predominantly seafood menu where British classics are mixed with a splash of Mediterranean colour: from octopus carpaccio with chilli, spring onion and coriander, to slip soles with seaweed butter and cockles. You'll also find comfort food (deep-fried haddock with mushy peas, lobster thermidor), a few meat dishes (say chicken, bacon and quail's egg pie or char-grilled veal rib steak with salsa verde) and a decent vegetarian menu. Given the Mayfair setting, there should be no surprise that the wine list moves swiftly past £30.
Chef/s: David McCarthy. **Open:** all week 12 to 10.30 (10 Sun). **Closed:** 25 and 26 Dec. **Meals:** alc (main courses £19 to £30). **Details:** 120 seats. 28 seats outside. Separate bar. Wheelchair access.

Seven Park Place by William Drabble

Fastidiously detailed French food
St James's Hotel and Club, 7-8 Park Place,
Mayfair, SW1A 1LS
Tel no: (020) 7316 1600
www.stjameshotelandclub.com
⊖ Green Park, map 5
Modern French | £62
Cooking score: 6

There's plenty of distraction at this bijou, standalone restaurant within the floridly designed St James's Hotel & Club – a riotous clash of extravagantly patterned wallpaper, patterned carpets and outré portraits. Ironically, fastidious detailing is a hallmark of William Drabble's finely honed contemporary French cuisine, evidenced by a regularly praised assiette of pork with a rectangle of black pudding, caramelised apple purée, Madeira jus and crispy onion 'crackling'. The food isn't intended to startle, but it's meticulous and classically moulded: from pot-roast quail with crispy sweetbreads, foie gras, 'marmalade' orange and hazelnut dressing, to poached native lobster tail with cauliflower and lobster butter sauce (a satisfying blend of delicacy and richness). However, Drabble's dexterity really shines with desserts, judging by his potently flavoured chocolate mousse cake with fresh raspberries or 'exceptional' vanilla-roast pineapple with coconut sorbet and coconut crème. Assured service never misses a trick, while the premier-league global wine list screams quality, with top producers, desirable varietals, peerless vintages and prices from £29 (£7 a glass).
Chef/s: William Drabble. **Open:** Tue to Sat L 12 to 2, D 6.30 to 10. **Closed:** Sun, Mon. **Meals:** Set L £26 (2 courses) to £30. Set D £55 (2 courses) to £61. Tasting menu £72 (6 courses). **Details:** 26 seats. Separate bar. Wheelchair access.

Sketch, Lecture Room & Library

An extravagant pleasure palace
9 Conduit Street, Mayfair, W1S 2XG
Tel no: (020) 7659 4500
www.sketch.uk.com
⊖ Oxford Circus, map 5
Modern European | £95
Cooking score: 6
V

Some feel that the design conceptualism of Sketch is a triumph of form over function, as did a reader who emerged from the tenebrous murk of the bathroom ('Comb your hair? Forget it!') a little tousled, but with dignity intact. Pierre Gagnaire's cooking must similarly take its chances in a dining room of hot lemon, where multiple mirrored panels reflect the elongated Chinese lanterns. Dishes appear to have been subjected to a quasi-bureaucratic classification. The various components are assigned to a multitude of little plates within each course, as the menu ushers you from shellfish and foie gras (duck jelly, razor clams, artichoke, foie gras, tapioca, cockles, winkles, almonds, port and blackcurrant syrup) through almost every possible cut of lamb with aubergine, Roquefort and tamarind, to chocolate from multifarious origins in numerous guises, with Muscat jelly and saffroned apricots. A compendious list of glorious wines starts at £25, and soon takes leave of its senses.
Chef/s: Pierre Gagnaire. **Open:** Tue to Fri L 12 to 2.15, Tue to Sat D 7 to 11. **Closed:** Sun, Mon, last 2 weeks Aug. **Meals:** alc (main courses £46 to £55). Set L £35 (2 courses) to £40. **Details:** 50 seats. Music.

Social Eating House

Smart-casual Soho hangout
58 Poland Street, Soho, W1F 7NR
Tel no: (020) 7993 3251
socialeatinghouse.com
⊖ Oxford Circus, map 5
Modern British | £45
Cooking score: 6
🍷 V

Poland Street is such a mishmash of signs and shopfronts that it's easy to miss this comparatively discreet restaurant. Considered the most casual of Jason Atherton's expanding group of 'Social' restaurants, the Eating House has functional furnishings, artfully distressed walls and a low, mirrored ceiling – which fit the Soho location to a T. Paul Hood heads the kitchen, a talented chef with a cool, mature approach and an intelligent streak of novelty, seen in a well-wrought starter of smoked Shetland salmon with miso crème fraîche, barbecue cucumber and spring truffle, and in roast turbot with sweet millet, yellow carrot and sour cream flavoured with black curry – star turns at a meal where delivery was uniformly impressive. The cooking also has a sense of seasonality, expressed in Norfolk lamb (rump, confit neck, kidney) with peas and mint, asparagus and girolles. The 70% chocolate nemesis with Vin Santo, mascarpone and espresso essence has been praised, bread is another hit, and the wine list works its magic at all levels, offering plenty by the glass and bottles from £17.
Chef/s: Paul Hood. **Open:** Mon to Sat L 12 to 2.30, D 6 to 10.30. **Closed:** Sun, 25 and 26 Dec, 1 and 2 Jan, bank hols. **Meals:** alc (main courses) £16 to £29. Set L £19 (2 courses) to £23. **Details:** 75 seats. Separate bar. Music.

🍴 Average Price

The average price listed in main-entry reviews denotes the price of a three-course meal, without wine.

★ TOP 10 ★

The Square

World-class gastronomy
6-10 Bruton Street, Mayfair, W1J 6PU
Tel no: (020) 7495 7100
www.squarerestaurant.com
⊖ Green Park, map 5
Modern French | £90
Cooking score: 8
🍷 V

Can it really be 23 years since Philip Howard moved here, swapping St James's Square for Berkeley? If the pace of change in London gastronomy can be a head-spinning blur, this has become a longue durée. And yet the place still looks new-minted, its teasing frosted frontage half-concealing the golden glow within, the red phone-box outside adding to the iconic identity. If the Square looks a little like a luxury liner, it's one that sails in calm seas: the front-of-house run with civility and charm, Gary Foulkes heading the kitchens since 2013. The cooking here was arguably in the modern European mode before others had even considered the genre, and some of the long-standing dishes reflect that: a sauté of langoustines with Parmesan gnocchi in truffled potato emulsion; roast veal sweetbreads with crushed broad beans, almonds and girolles; the famous Brillat-Savarin cheesecake, its lactic density given angles with passion fruit and lime. Dishes are exquisitely sculpted, colourful and seductive in their aromatic allure: witness the roast foie gras with sweet-and-sour plum top layer, garnished with macadamias and plum saké; or the ruby-red aged fillet and short rib of beef with beer-glazed onions, fermented ceps, smoked bone marrow and an epaulette of wilted kale. The chocolate praline pavé with olive oil caviar looks neat and compact enough to pack into a travelling trousse. A list of thoroughbred wines teems with quality – and not all of the forbidding variety. Wines by the glass, from £9 for Grüner Veltliner, are a fabulous bunch. For bottles, you'll need at least £28. Details overleaf.

Chef/s: Philip Howard and Gary Foulkes. **Open:** Mon to Sat L 12 to 2.30, all week D 6.30 to 10 (10.30 Fri and Sat, 9.30 Sun). **Closed:** 24, 26 Dec, bank hols. **Meals:** Set L £35 (2 courses) to £40. Set D £90. Tasting menu £115. **Details:** 70 seats. Wheelchair access.

Sumosan

Glamorous modern Japanese
26b Albemarle Street, Mayfair, W1S 4HY
Tel no: (020) 7495 5999
www.sumosan.com
⊖ Green Park, map 5
Japanese | £50
Cooking score: 4

V

Russian by birth but Japanese by name, this London outpost of a Moscow-based group attracts A-listers and financial hotshots who couldn't care one jot about bonsai portions and punishing, sumo-sized bills. Sumosan is set within an exclusive grey-toned dining room screened from the outside world by full-length blinds. Its pulse rate quickens and the din increases as the night progresses and appetites graduate from sushi and slabs of Wagyu beef to cocktails, saké flights and bottles of Cristal. Given its parentage and target audience, the food unsurprisingly has international inflections and ample luxury ingredients. Goose liver and Peking duck appear alongside sea urchins and top-grade tuna on the sushi list, there are tiraditos among the tartares, and the line-up also runs to swanky salads, lobster teppanyaki and duck breast with buckwheat risotto. By comparison, lunch is low-key, where customers are encouraged to create relatively affordable bento boxes from a list of different components. Wines from £33.
Chef/s: Bubker Belkhit. **Open:** Mon to Fri L 12 to 2.45, all week D 6 to 11.30 (10.30 Sun). **Closed:** 25 and 26 Dec, 31 Dec. **Meals:** alc (main courses £8 to £65). Set L £25. Set D £65. **Details:** 100 seats. Separate bar. Wheelchair access. Music.

Tamarind

A masterclass in Moghul cuisine
20 Queen Street, Mayfair, W1J 5PR
Tel no: (020) 7629 3561
www.tamarindrestaurant.com
⊖ Green Park, map 5
Indian | £60
Cooking score: 5

£5 OFF **V**

Tamarind was not just one of the first Indian restaurants in London, but one of the first in the world to be elevated into the international firmament. Its basement dining room, all gold and silver sheen, features sturdy pillars, an ostentatious floral display and smartly attired tables. Peter Joseph is comfortable with the multi-faceted and dynamic foodways of the Subcontinent, and there's a profound understanding at work of the resonances that marinating and long simmering produce. The fixed-price menus offer a heady tour through the likes of kingfish in turmeric, ginger, chillies and yoghurt; tilapia and mint chutney gram-batter rolls; and mains such as lamb masala with peppers – and even chicken tikka as you've never tasted it before. Nor does the aromatic shimmer fade at dessert stage, when basmati in clove milk or mango and basil sorbet are to hand. Wines from £28 are fine, but will amplify the bill.
Chef/s: Alfred Prasad and Peter Joseph. **Open:** Sun to Fri L 12 to 2.45, all week D 5.30 to 11 (6 to 10.30 Sun). **Closed:** 25 and 26 Dec, 1 Jan. **Meals:** alc (main courses £20 to £40). Set L £21 (2 courses) to £24. Set D £33. Sun L £32. Tasting menu £56. **Details:** 80 seats. Music. No children under 5 yrs after 7.

LOCAL GEM

▲ Tapas Brindisa Soho

46 Broadwick Street, Soho, W1F 7AF
Tel no: (020) 7534 1690
www.brindisa.com
⊖ Oxford Circus, map 5
Spanish | £20

People-watching and plate-picking are two of the joys of Brindisa's Soho drop-in. A flexible (though ambitiously priced) menu of small and larger dishes – cod buñuelos, ox cheeks with dried fruit and red wine sauce, jamón and cheese – makes it all very easy. London's Spanish food scene has grown and changed around Brindisa and there's more refinement to be found elsewhere, but this is still a good (and popular) venue for the tapas equivalent of a fry-up, mopped up with pan de pincel. House wine is £21.95. Open all week.

10 Greek Street

Nice vibes, sharp cooking, no reservations
10 Greek Street, Soho, W1D 4DH
Tel no: (020) 7734 4677
www.10greekstreet.com
⊖ Tottenham Court Road, map 5
Modern European | £30
Cooking score: 4

'Love, love, love this place,' declares a supporter of this oh-so-casual Soho eatery. Basic décor reflects an aim to provide great food and drink without breaking the bank, and judging by the friendly buzz of contentment radiating from the cramped space, there's no doubt the kitchen knows how to deliver satisfaction. Cameron Emirali's cooking is a tribute to great British produce and plays off the seasons with mainly Eurozone-influenced dishes: say duck confit with crumbled egg, green beans and mustard or octopus served with n'duja, baby spinach and peperonata. Dishes show minimum posturing but are always comforting and big-flavoured, whether a main course of Gloucester Old Spot pork teamed with spring onion mash, kale and apple chutney, or a well-made custard tart for dessert. The reasonable prices extend to the stash of modern wines, most of them available by the glass. Bottles from £16. Note, no reservations at dinner.
Chef/s: Cameron Emirali. **Open:** Mon to Sat L 12 to 2.30, D 5.30 to 10.45. **Closed:** Sun, Christmas, bank hols. **Meals:** alc (main courses £12 to £21). **Details:** 30 seats. 2 seats outside. Separate bar. Music.

Terroirs

Crowd-pulling bistro with great wines
5 William IV Street, Covent Garden, WC2N 4DW
Tel no: (020) 7036 0660
www.terroirswinebar.com
⊖ Charing Cross, map 5
French | £32
Cooking score: 3
🍷

Six years after opening, Terroirs has lost none of its X-factor. In the ground-floor wine bar you can enjoy small plates and *plats du jour* while seated at close-packed tables or perched at the long zinc-topped bar watching the chefs at work. Down in the cellar it feels like a secret restaurant – a hugely atmospheric one with bare brick, burgundy colours and gentle lighting. Wherever you eat, the mood is casual, the décor functional, prices refreshing and the menu adds Mediterranean vibrancy to the core French repertoire. Downstairs, bouillabaisse with rouille, Gruyère and croûtons represents the old guard, while Welsh lamb chops with merguez, couscous and harissa aïoli strikes a contemporary note. The wine bar brings excellent duck rillettes, or snails with garlic, parsley and bacon. All-day nibbles of charcuterie and cheese are also available, along with many wines by the glass or 500ml pot. The full wine list is a fascinating France-led triumph, an insightful selection of organic and biodynamic wines – noted for diversity, style and quality. Prices start at £17.25.
Chef/s: Ed Wilson. **Open:** Mon to Sat L 12 to 3, D 5.30 to 11. **Closed:** Sun, 24 Dec to 1 Jan, bank hols. **Meals:** alc (main courses £12 to £22). **Details:** 110 seats. 6 seats outside. Separate bar. Music.

Texture

High calibre Nordic-inspired cuisine
34 Portman Street, Marble Arch, W1H 7BY
Tel no: (020) 7224 0028
www.texture-restaurant.co.uk
⊖ **Marble Arch, map 4**
Modern French/Nordic | £62
Cooking score: 4

🍷 V

Behind the Georgian façade of 'hidden gem' Texture lies a 'cool, calm oasis of soft lighting and Scandinavian design'. Agnar Sverrisson's tautly executed Nordic-influenced modern European cooking suits the linen-free tables and understated flowers, and the contrasting grandeur of this high-ceilinged converted bank. Sverrisson is famous for his 'light touch' and eschewal of butter and cream: a stance not to the detriment of 'incredible tastes and, of course, textures'. Readers praise the 'sensational' tasting menus where key Texture dishes of 'superb' salted Icelandic cod, Anjou pigeon with sweetcorn, bacon popcorn and red wine essence, and Icelandic skyr with gariguette strawberries often appear. Scottish halibut in a 'stunning bonito broth with little jewels of quinoa', and beef rib, ox cheek and horseradish also make their mark. Set lunch is easier on the wallet. The dazzling wine list (from £38) is upfront about its obsessions, with Rieslings, Champagnes and Burgundies stealing the show.
Chef/s: Agnar Sverrisson. **Open:** Tue to Sat L 12 to 2.30, D 6.30 to 10.30. **Closed:** Sun, Mon, 23 Dec to 9 Jan, 1 week Easter, 2 weeks Aug. **Meals:** alc (main courses £28 to £38). Set L £22 (2 courses) to £25. Tasting menu £79 (7 courses). **Details:** 50 seats. Separate bar. Wheelchair access. Music.

Theo Randall at the InterContinental

Spirited regional Italian cooking
InterContinental London Hotel, 1 Hamilton Place, Mayfair, W1J 7QY
Tel no: (020) 7318 8747
www.theorandall.com
⊖ **Hyde Park Corner, map 4**
Italian | £60
Cooking score: 6

£5 OFF 🍽 V

Once the unsung hero of Hammersmith's River Café (see entry), Theo Randall has spent the past eight years carving out a niche in the rather unlikely corporate surroundings of the InterContinental Hotel. He has brushed up his Italian, made trips in search of ingredients and slowly refined his brand of spirited regional cooking. The result is heroically unadorned food that resonates with rusticity: although prices are more Mayfair than Montepulciano. Given Randall's CV, it's no surprise he understands seasonality and the mysteries of the wood-fired oven: a device used to triumphant effect in dishes such as turbot with Roseval potatoes, Soave Classico and violet artichokes. Daisy-fresh flavours and rich, intense undercurrents are everywhere: from smoked eel with red and golden beetroot, Italian leaves and horseradish, or linguine with Dorset blue lobster and San Marzano tomatoes, to ricotta cheesecake with Marsala-marinated pears. The wallet-denting wine list (from £34) is a veritable gazetteer of Italian viticulture.
Chef/s: Theo Randall. **Open:** Mon to Fri L 12 to 3, Mon to Sat D 5.45 to 11. **Closed:** Sun, bank hols. **Meals:** alc (main courses £27 to £38). Set L and D £27 (2 courses) to £33. **Details:** 200 seats. Separate bar. Wheelchair access. Music. Car parking.

34

Mayfair opulence and thrilling grilling
34 Grosvenor Square (entrance on South Audley
Street), Mayfair, W1K 2HD
Tel no: (020) 3350 3434
www.34-restaurant.co.uk
⊖ Bond Street, Green Park, map 4
Modern British | £45
Cooking score: 2

V

Within a handsome Mayfair block (entered
via South Audley Street), 34 has many of the
trappings expected in this postcode: a
moneyed, clubby sheen and a rather snazzy
modern art collection. But the star of the show
is the parilla grill, imported from Argentina.
It's just the business when it comes to cooking
prime protein. Beef is brought down from
Scotland (from Black Angus, Charolais and
Hereford herds among others), or further
afield if it's Wagyu or USDA Prime. The steaks
– ribeye, bavette, T-bone, New York Strip –
are cooked bang-on. The rest of the menu is
worth exploring too, with cured meats, a
bonanza of asparagus dishes in season (with
truffled hollandaise maybe), and fish such as
fillet of John Dory with mousserons and
cauliflower purée. There's a vegetarian menu,
too. Champagne pannacotta seems like a good
way to go out. Wines start at £24.
Chef/s: Harvey Ayliffe. **Open:** all week 12 to 10.30
(11.30am Sat and Sun). **Closed:** 25 and 26 Dec.
Meals: alc (main courses £18 to £32). Set L £23 (2
courses) to £28. **Details:** 90 seats. Separate bar.

Trishna

Indian seafood star
15-17 Blandford Street, Marylebone, W1U 3DG
Tel no: (020) 7935 5624
www.trishnalondon.com
⊖ Marylebone, Bond Street, map 4
Indian/Seafood | £40
Cooking score: 4

🍶 V

Some things have changed at Karam Sethi's
seafood-focused Marylebone star, with a
thorough refurbishment rendering the

previously hardline interior almost as warm
and soft as the tandoor-cooked breads. The
new look provides a more comfortable,
nostalgia-rich backdrop for a menu that's still
full of greatest hits: haldi chipirones in a crisp
turmeric and fennel coating, quail pepper-fry
big on black pepper, ethereal biriyanis (it's not
just sister restaurant Gymkhana – see entry –
that can do them right) and succulent herb-
and chilli-coated hariyali bream. All the bits
and pieces – salads, raitas, pickles and
chutneys – are classy, and though the lunch
deal is a no-brainer for shoppers and business
people, there are tasting menus to show off
every aspect of the kitchen's skill. Occasional
upselling can mar the experience somewhat,
but sommelier Sunaina Sethi's considered
wine list is flexible and full of discoveries, with
real choice by the glass or carafe and bottles
from £23.
Chef/s: Karam Sethi. **Open:** all week L 12 to 2.45
(3.15 Sun), D 6 to 10.45 (9.45 Sun). **Closed:** 23 to 26
Dec, 1 Jan. **Meals:** alc (main courses £12 to £25). Set
L £19 (2 courses) to £24. Early D £28. Tasting menu
£70. **Details:** 80 seats. 6 seats outside. Music.

28°-50°

Wine-centric bistro
15-17 Marylebone Lane, Marylebone, W1U 2NE
Tel no: (020) 7486 7922
www.2850.co.uk
⊖ Bond Street, map 4
French | £30
Cooking score: 3

🍶

Xavier Rousset and Agnar Sverrisson, who
operate on a higher plane at Texture (see
entry), also excel at easy, good-quality bistros
via their small group of 'wine workshops'.
Pitch-perfect service and simple good
cooking make this Marylebone branch (split
between ground level and a smaller basement)
handy to know about. A plate of charcuterie,
grilled spatchcock chicken with béarnaise
sauce and vanilla cheesecake with raspberry
sorbet are the simpler options, though more
involved dishes include scallops with
cauliflower and brioche purée, coco beans,

chorizo and fennel. But it's not just about the food. The main room is a comfortable, buzzy triangular space dominated by a zinc-topped bar, reflecting the importance and versatility of a 30-bin wine list available in various quantities: from 75ml pours (from £2.40) to bottles from £21. A programme of wine events adds extra interest, and a 'collectors list' harbours the fine and rare. Head to the Mayfair branch for the group's first Champagne bar: 17-19 Maddox Street, W1S 2QH; tel: (020) 7495 1505.
Open: Mon to Sat L 12 to 2.30, D 6 to 10 (10.30 Thur to Sat). **Closed:** Sun, 25 and 26 Dec, 31 Dec, 1 Jan. **Meals:** alc (main courses £13 to £22). Set L £16 (2 courses) to £19. **Details:** 60 seats. Music.

Umu
Ravishing Japanese virtuosity
14-16 Bruton Place, Mayfair, W1J 6LX
Tel no: (020) 7499 8881
www.umurestaurant.com
⊖ **Green Park, Bond Street, map 5**
Japanese | £90
Cooking score: 5

Ultra-discreet and anonymous, with access via a security touchpad, Umu reveals all once you've whooshed through the curtain and entered its muted dining room: a softly lit space with high-spec furnishings, Murano glassware and vintage pottery. Such trappings ain't cheap, and Umu's gilt-edged Kyoto cuisine is brutally expensive, rising to the imperial majesty of a multi-course kaiseki menu – although the pay-off is a procession of ravishing, exquisitely fashioned dishes. Sushi and sashimi here are among London's best: from traditional nigiri to 'new-style' renditions such as lobster with pesto and plum. The kitchen's virtuosity also shows in plates of saké-cured langoustine with tomato jelly; a 'kaminabe' hotpot of Ibérico pork shoulder, Chinese cabbage and yuzu; and in grilled Welsh eel kabayaki with hot egg yolk and Périgord truffles – prime ingredients at their peak. Lunchtime bento boxes are

relatively affordable (provided you resist the euphoria-inducing saké list). Showy wines start at £30.
Chef/s: Yoshinori Ishii. **Open:** Mon to Fri L 12 to 2.30, Mon to Sat D 6 to 11. **Closed:** Sun, 24 Dec to 3 Jan, bank hols. **Meals:** alc (main courses £21 to £65). Set L £25 to £38. Kaiseki menu £115 (8 courses). **Details:** 60 seats. Wheelchair access. Music.

LOCAL GEM
▲ Vasco & Piero's Pavilion
15 Poland Street, Soho, W1F 8QE
Tel no: (020) 7437 8774
www.vascosfood.com
⊖ **Oxford Circus, map 5**
Italian | £35 £5 OFF

Vasco Matteucci and family have been serving no-frills Umbrian food to Soho's media and film movers-and-shakers for decades. Vasco is still on hand to ensure that quality ingredients take centre stage on the handwritten daily menu – whether in the burrata pugliese with vine tomatoes and basil, the homemade pasta accompanying traditional beef ragù, or the roast duck with fennel pollen and borlotti beans. This is a simple set-up with a warm welcome, and it draws a loyal crowd. Wine starts at £19.50. Closed Sat L and Sun D.

Vinoteca
Welcoming, buzzy, bibulous brasserie
15 Seymour Place, Marylebone, W1H 5BD
Tel no: (020) 7724 7288
www.vinoteca.co.uk
⊖ **Marble Arch, map 4**
Modern European | £29
Cooking score: 2
🍾 £30

'It was all terribly informal and European,' pronounced one reporter of this bibulous brasserie, adding 'the food reflected this, with Spanish and Italian influences'. An offspring of Vinoteca in Farringdon (see entry), it's a charming, off-the-main-drag Marylebone bolt-hole, a combination of wine shop, on-view kitchen and laid-back dining room.

Everything on the seasonally aware, daily changing menu arrives in an unfussy style that perfectly matches the simple, rustic surroundings: perhaps lamb sweetbreads with braised peas, bacon and gem lettuce; braised wild rabbit with smoked bacon and new-season garlic; or poached smoked haddock with champ and mustard cream. Drop in, too, for a plate of Spanish-cured meats or a selection of British cheeses from Neal's Yard Dairy. And accompany your repast with a glass of something from the ever-evolving wine list, which is sourced with an eye for little-known gems and quality drinking. Bottles from £15.75. Another branch of Vinoteca is in Soho, at 53-55 Beak Street, W1F 9SH; tel: (020) 3544 7411.
Chef/s: Dan Richards. **Open:** all week L 12 to 3 (4 Sun), Mon to Sat D 6 to 10. **Closed:** bank hols. **Meals:** alc (main courses £10 to £18). **Details:** 55 seats. Music.

Wild Honey
Grown-up food in an upbeat setting
12 St George Street, Mayfair, W1S 2FB
Tel no: (020) 7758 9160
www.wildhoneyrestaurant.co.uk
⊖ Oxford Circus, Bond Street, map 5
Modern European | £45
Cooking score: 5

£5
OFF

The urbane younger sibling of Arbutus (see entry) can sometimes feel like a high-decibel gentlemen's club with its warm oak-panelled walls and quirky artwork. But no one grumbles when the kitchen can deliver intelligent, grown-up food at reasonable prices (at least for Mayfair). It's upbeat yet civilised, with a menu that gives oft-neglected seasonal ingredients the respect they deserve – be it crisp ox tongue with a winter salad and pickled mushrooms, or cod with spiced lentils and onion fritters (both from the admirably titled 'working lunch'). That said, there's nothing humble or penny-pinching about the results, as movers and shakers seal deals over plates of white truffles with fresh macaroni, rosemary and Parmesan, or wild sea bass with braised endive and carrot purée. To finish, it has to be wild honey ice cream (perhaps accompanied by Yorkshire rhubarb). Happily, there's the option of drinking wine by the carafe; alternatively, bottles start at £28.
Chef/s: Anthony Demetre and Patrick Leano. **Open:** Mon to Sat L 12 to 2.30, D 6 to 11. **Closed:** Sun, bank hols. **Meals:** alc (main courses £24 to £36). Set L £29. **Details:** 55 seats. Separate bar.

Wiltons
Upholding the best of British traditions
55 Jermyn Street, Mayfair, SW1Y 6LX
Tel no: (020) 7629 9955
www.wiltons.co.uk
⊖ Green Park, map 5
British | £55
Cooking score: 4

'This was a real treat – so well done, so fabulously old-fashioned and so expensive,' purred one contented reporter, who noted 'a lesser restaurant would have ceded to the pressure of modern fashion long ago'. But Wiltons, with its thick carpet, heavy linen-draped tables and velvet booths, stuffed carp and hunting scenes 'regally continues, and oh, how good it is'. Fish and shellfish have always been a speciality; this is where to try proper lobster thermidor. There's no such thing as a new take on old ideas here, dishes are prepared and served in true old-school manner. Those on a budget should stick to the seasonal set menu, offering, say, classic crab and avocado cocktail, Dover sole with brown shrimp and samphire or a daily choice from the silver carving trolley ('Monday's roast lamb is excellent'), followed by proper puddings and cheese. The fulsome wine list takes no prisoners – wines start at £35.
Chef/s: Daniel Kent. **Open:** Mon to Fri L 12 to 2.30, Mon to Sat D 5.30 to 10.30. **Closed:** Sun, Christmas, 1 Jan, bank hols. **Meals:** alc (main courses £17 to £52). Set L and D £30 (2 courses) to £38. **Details:** 100 seats. Separate bar. Wheelchair access.

The Wolseley

High-impact all-day brasserie
160 Piccadilly, Mayfair, W1J 9EB
Tel no: (020) 7499 6996
www.thewolseley.com
⊖ Green Park, map 5
Modern European | £35
Cooking score: 2

Twelve years on, Messrs Corbin and King's take on continental café culture is still going strong. It's a grand venue: a high-impact building of marble floors, high stone ceiling, arches and tall, black opal-effect columns. There's more than a touch of the big French brasserie about the place and the menu reinforces this impression, even if a Viennese café is frequently mentioned – down to the presence of Weiner schnitzel and Holstein on the menu. From the suits in for breakfast at 7am, via the afternoon tea set, to the post-theatre crowd still teeming in after 11pm, the day is a long one. Invariably packed, undoubtedly high decibel, this is where to come for the sort of dishes you can eat every day – coq au vin (Monday's *plat du jour*) and grilled halibut with béarnaise sauce, right through to omelette Arnold Bennett and Welsh rarebit. The all-European wine list opens at £19.75.
Chef/s: Lawrence Keogh. **Open:** all week 7am to midnight (8am Sat, 11pm Sun). **Meals:** alc (main courses £12 to £35). **Details:** 150 seats. Wheelchair access.

Wright Brothers

Good-value Soho seafood bar and restaurant
13 Kingly Street, Soho, W1B 5PW
Tel no: (020) 7434 3611
www.thewrightbrothers.co.uk
⊖ Oxford Circus, map 5
Seafood | £33
Cooking score: 2

After a refurbishment closure, the original Wright Brothers is back (there's also a branch in Southwark, see entry). The venue extends over three floors just off Regent Street, furnished with blood-red buttoned banquettes behind tiny tables. A cheeringly laid-back ambience permeates the place, helped by candidly friendly service. Fresh shellfish are treated with integrity, with a range of oyster varieties in the right months. Sharp east Asian seasonings enliven many dishes. Soft-shell crab in tempura batter incorporating rings of jalapeño chilli comes with bitingly zesty vinaigrette, while thickly sliced salmon is ceviched in a mixture of citrus and soy, garnished with salmon roe and a little sorbet. Mains feature glorious cod with pancetta, leeks and samphire in smoky cream sauce, and a side of char-grilled peppers dressed with aged sweet balsamic and topped with plump, fresh boquerones. Wines – from £4.90 a glass, £13 a half-litre carafe or £19.50 a bottle – suit the food.
Chef/s: Sasha Ziverts. **Open:** all week L 12 to 3 (3.30 Sat, 6 Sun), Mon to Sat D 5.30 to 10.45. **Closed:** 24 to 28 Dec, 1 and 2 Jan, bank hols. **Meals:** alc (main courses £12 to £18). Set L and D £14.50 (2 courses) to £16.50. Set D £16.50 (2 courses) to £18.50. **Details:** 96 seats. 24 seats outside.

Yauatcha

Chinese foodie delights
15-17 Broadwick Street, Soho, W1F 0DL
Tel no: (020) 7494 8888
www.yauatcha.com
⊖ Tottenham Court Road, map 5
Chinese | £30
Cooking score: 3

V

Sublime dim sum, esoteric teas, famously good cakes and luscious crossover desserts are just some of Yauatcha's delights. The clean-lined, blue-tinted street-level 'café' is the place for dim sum, tea and cakes – if you don't mind the crowds or the frenetic pace. Reward comes in the shape of mustard-greens and edamame dumplings, spinach balls with prawns and cuttlefish, roast duck and pumpkin puffs or starchy helpings of pork and preserved egg congee: blindingly good stuff delivered with pizazz and artistry. Alternatively, head to the moody basement for an extended menu offering anything from braised sea bass with

shiitake mushrooms, bamboo shoots and wolfberries to sweet-and-sour pork. As for those puds and patisserie: how about a grand macaron with Cassis, vanilla and violet or salted caramel with walnut and iced coffee to accompany one of Yauatcha's fabulous selection of teas? Otherwise, drinks run from trendy smoothies, cocktails and saké to appetising global wines (from £26).
Chef/s: Tong Chee Hwee. **Open:** all week 12 to 11.30 (10.30 Sun). **Closed:** 25 and 26 Dec. **Meals:** alc (dishes £5 to £30). **Details:** 191 seats. Separate bar. Wheelchair access.

Zafferano

Top Italian performer
15 Lowndes Street, Belgravia, SW1X 9EY
Tel no: (020) 7235 5800
www.atozrestaurants.com
⊖ Knightsbridge, Hyde Park Corner, map 4
Italian | £50
Cooking score: 5

For ten years now Zafferano has been dishing out classy plates of Italian food to the residents of Knightsbridge and those in the know. It's the sort of gaff that matches this postcode well with its polished service, dignified finish and faint sense of Mediterranean glamour. Diners come, though, for the no-nonsense menu that is rich in classic combinations presented with a bit of panache. Crab salad with lemon and pesto is full of the joys of summer, or go for Culatello di Zibello (a top-notch salume) with pickled mushrooms. Linguine with lobster catches the eye among the ace pasta options, spiked with chilli and fresh tomatoes, while osso buco is packed into ravioli and served with gremolata. Calf's liver with balsamic sauce, char-grilled monkfish with puntarelle, sea bass with fennel and olives . . . winning combinations all. The regional wine list is true to the motherland, with bottles from £28.
Chef/s: Miles Nixon. **Open:** all week L 12 to 3, D 6 to 11.30 (Sun 11). **Meals:** alc (main courses £16 to £33). Set L £21 (2 courses) to £30. **Details:** 140 seats. Separate bar. Wheelchair access.

Zoilo

Drink to an Argentinian crowd-pleaser
9 Duke Street, Marylebone, W1U 3EG
Tel no: (020) 7486 9699
www.zoilo.co.uk
⊖ Bond Street, map 4
Argentinian | £30
Cooking score: 2

This intimate bar-bistro is proving to be a welcoming beacon of hospitality in an area (behind Selfridges) not generally noted for good, reasonably priced restaurants. It's on two levels, including a narrow ground floor with bright-red leather banquettes, six cramped tables, a chequered tiled floor and stool seating along the bar that dominates the room. Downstairs there's an open kitchen with counter seating where you can watch the chefs at work – 'this is where I would head next time'. The cooking is contemporary Argentinian, served tapas-style. An obviously Spanish-influenced menu is divided into empanadas (try the spinach, goats' cheese, raisin and pine nuts), seafood such as scallops with sweet potato, caramelised pork belly and chorizo, and meat (perhaps grilled quail with lentil ragù, cauliflower and sherry sauce). Reporters continue to applaud the neighbourly feel, the good, engaged service and the all-Argentinian wine list, which opens at £21.95.
Chef/s: Diego Jacquet. **Open:** Mon to Sat L 12 to 3, D 5.30 to 10.30. **Closed:** Sun. **Meals:** alc (tapas £4 to £11). Set L £10 (2 courses). **Details:** 48 seats. 4 seats outside. Music.

LOCAL GEM
▲ L'Absinthe

40 Chalcot Road, Primrose Hill, NW1 8LS
Tel no: (020) 7483 4848
www.labsinthe.co.uk
⊖ Chalk Farm, map 2
French | £24

It's a hive of activity here on Chalcot Road. Café-deli, wine shop and restaurant, with pavement tables to enhance the Gallic vibe, L'Absinthe turns out plates of 'keenly priced' French bistro food. Classic onion soup is just that, snails get the garlic butter treatment, followed by confit duck or steak-frites (Aberdeen Angus ribeye no less). It's tarte Tatin or crêpes suzette for dessert. House wine is £16.95, or buy something in the shop and add £10 corkage. Closed Mon.

The Albion

Lively local with no-frills Brit food
10 Thornhill Road, Islington, N1 1HW
Tel no: (020) 7607 7450
www.the-albion.co.uk
⊖ Angel, Highbury & Islington, map 2
British | £30
Cooking score: 2

There's a grand 'rus in urbe' charm to Barnsbury's Albion that evokes those lovely Cotswold villages to which A-listers flee at weekends. Its pristine tongue-and-groove paintwork, vintage furniture and, mostly, its glorious garden would amount to a 'destination' even if the food were poor – which, happily, it isn't. New chef Nathan Andrews has maintained established standards, so if you can get further than the glossy sausage rolls at the bar, you will be in for seasonally adjusted roasts such as pork belly with potato salad or salt marsh lamb with fondant potato and minted lamb jus or, on a lighter tip, sea bass with a 'Caesar-esque' anchovy dressing or dressed crab with radish, fennel and herb salad. For afters, chocolate cake with vanilla ice cream with cherries and

honeycomb shards delivers more than it promises on paper. Trendy cocktails and classic wines (from £16) suit this stylish setting.
Chef/s: Nathan Andrews. **Open:** Mon to Sat L 12 to 3 (4 Sat), D 6 to 10. Sun 12 to 9. **Closed:** 25 Dec, 1 Jan. **Meals:** alc (main courses £13 to £24). **Details:** 101 seats. 128 seats outside. Separate bar. Wheelchair access. Music.

Almeida

An appetising pre-theatre warm-up
30 Almeida Street, Islington, N1 1AD
Tel no: (020) 7354 4777
www.almeida-restaurant.co.uk
⊖ Angel, Highbury & Islington, map 2
French | £34
Cooking score: 2

It's showtime at this Guide veteran come evening, as a pre-theatre crowd arrive for a warm-up act of good-value dining. Almeida might be getting a bit scruffy around the edges (the 1990s décor needs updating), but it's as accommodating as ever, gaining plaudits for its continued efforts to inject some excitement via the kitchen. Chef Tommy Boland (ex-head chef at Tom Aikens) brings his own take on modern British food with a French accent, so diners might encounter wild garlic velouté with onion tarte fine or a colourful salad of grilled mackerel, smoked eel, beetroot and sorrel as starters. Main courses could include flavoursome roasted chicken with super-rich creamed potatoes, or a risotto rated 'excellent' by one Italian visitor. On inspection, a Barkham Blue bavarois with pear and savoury granola was the standout dessert, and equal praise comes for the extensive wine list (from £20), which regulars rate 'a delight'.
Chef/s: Tommy Boland. **Open:** Tue to Sun L 12 to 2.30 (3.30 Sun), Mon to Sat D 5.30 to 10.30. **Closed:** 26 Dec, 1 Jan. **Meals:** alc (main meals £15 to £25). Set L and D £17 (2 courses) to £20. Sun L £20 (2 courses) to £25. **Details:** 120 seats. 10 seats outside. Separate bar. Wheelchair access.

Bradleys

Long-running French favourite
25 Winchester Road, Swiss Cottage, NW3 3NR
Tel no: (020) 7722 3457
www.bradleysnw3.co.uk
⊖ Swiss Cottage, map 2
French | £34
Cooking score: 3

For a restaurant trading for over 20 years, and run by the same hands-on couple for that entire period, Bradleys seems remarkably contemporary. Simon and Jolanta Bradley's place (close to the Hampstead Theatre) has a light-grey finish (inside and out) and an easy charm that keeps the punters coming back. Simon's cooking has its roots in French classicism, but has moved with the times to deliver dishes that, like the venue itself, meet 21st-century expectations. That means lots of excellent British ingredients and combinations that deliver flavour and impact. Smoked haddock stars in a first course with curried leeks and an onion bhajia, for example, while main-course rack and shoulder of West Country lamb comes with a kidney brochette and potato croquette. Finish with pear tarte Tatin with sherry vinegar ice cream, or excellent British/French cheeses. There's also a bargain set (and pre-theatre) menu and a prix fixe option. Wines start at £19.
Chef/s: Simon Bradley. **Open:** all week L 12 to 3, Mon to Sat D 5.30 to 10.30. **Meals:** alc (main courses £17 to £22). Set L £16 (2 courses) to £20. Set D £16 (2 courses) to £20. Sun L £25 (2 courses) to £29. **Details:** 60 seats.

The Bull & Last

Tried-and-true modern Brit dishes
168 Highgate Road, Hampstead, NW5 1QS
Tel no: (020) 7267 3641
www.thebullandlast.co.uk
⊖ Tufnell Park, Kentish Town, map 2
Modern British | £34
Cooking score: 3

Rather like a country pub in the metropolis, the Bull & Last has a rustic finish and even a stuffed animal or two about the place.

Hampstead Heath is just across the way if you're hankering for a bit of green space before or after a visit. The ground-floor bar packs in punters for pints of proper beer and food that is hale and hearty, presented in a rustic, modern manner (maybe on a wooden board). There's a first-floor dining room for a more chilled-out vibe, but that might be being used for a function. Among first courses, beef tartare comes with cornichons and toast, and there are sharing boards of charcuterie or seafood, with main courses running to Gloucester Old Spot chop with smoked eel and turnip tops, or orecchiette pasta with wild mushrooms, treviso and truffle oil. It's baked chocolate mousse for pud. Wines start at £18.
Chef/s: Oliver Pudney. **Open:** all week L 12 to 3 (4 Sat and Sun), D 6.30 to 10 (9 Sun). **Closed:** 24 and 25 Dec. **Meals:** alc (main courses £14 to £24). **Details:** 80 seats. 30 seats outside. Separate bar. Music. Car parking.

Caravan

High-decibel King's Cross bolt-hole
Granary Building, 1 Granary Square, King's Cross, N1C 4AA
Tel no: (020) 7101 7661
www.caravankingscross.co.uk
⊖ King's Cross, map 2
Global | £28
Cooking score: 2
£30

'Food is good, atmosphere always excellent,' just about sums up this high-impact all-day eatery that's handy for King's Cross-St Pancras. The massive, bare-brick space plays to the crowds and no one seems to mind the packed tables and high decibel levels. With a concept of warm informality and menus that allow for nibbling as much as three-coursing, Caravan suits the way London wants to eat these days. Its modestly priced menu of small and large plates delivers a punchy, uncluttered ensemble of flavours. Influences are mainly Mediterranean with some Asian and North African notes. Octopus, chorizo, piquillo and mojo picon; or mackerel with nori purée, daikon rémoulade and sticky soy are typical

choices. Still hungry? Pizzas are popular, there's Wagyu ribeye, and, to round things off, cinnamon doughnuts with pistachio cream and Turkish delight. Breakfast, cakes and good coffee tempt, too. Wines from £17.
Chef/s: Miles Kirby. **Open:** all week 8am to 10.30pm (10am Sat, 10 to 4 Sun). **Closed:** 25, 26 and 31 Dec, 1 Jan. **Meals:** alc (main courses £14 to £22). **Details:** 125 seats. 50 seats outside. Separate bar. Wheelchair access. Music.

LOCAL GEM
▲ Chilli Cool
15 Leigh Street, King's Cross, WC1H 9EW
Tel no: (020) 7383 3135
www.chillicool.com
⊖ Russell Square, King's Cross, map 2
Chinese | £22 £5 OFF

It may sound oxymoronic, but chilli really is cool at this terrific Szechuan canteen on a forgettable side street near King's Cross. Hip foodies mingle with students and commuters while the kitchen lets rip with a barrage of eye-wateringly punchy flavours. Spice and fire meet 'nose to tail' in the shape of ducks' tongues, ox tripe, sliced pig's ears in sesame oil, beef offal and chilli hotpot, or 'dry-stewed' sea bass in soya paste with noodles. Wines from £13.80, although tea and Tiger beer are the coolers of choice. Open all week.

READERS RECOMMEND
Chriskitch
Modern British
7a Tetherdown, Muswell Hill, N10 1ND
Tel no: (020) 8411 0051
www.chriskitch.com
'Tiny café, bit cramped but a great place to hang out. Delicious salads, lovely breads, gorgeous cakes.'

NEW ENTRY
Le Coq
Buzzy neighbourhood rotisserie in Highbury
292-294 St Paul's Road, Islington, N1 2LH
Tel no: (020) 7359 5055
www.le-coq.co.uk
⊖ Highbury & Islington, map 2
Modern European | £22
Cooking score: 2
£30

From the name-board out front to the small flock of chickens rotating over the spit inside, Le Coq is a restaurant particular about poultry. Or, to be precise, organic chickens from Sutton Hoo, Suffolk – roasted until sublimely crispy and served as the only main course on the rather monogamous menu at this Highbury newcomer. It's a simple premise, and likewise the dining space décor doesn't over-complicate: whitewashed walls, tables packed like sardines and big, bright windows facing St Paul's Road. Weekly changing starters are a worthy warm-up; tabbouleh with wondrously gloopy labneh impressed on inspection. That said, rotisserie chicken is the headline act that everyone's here for: generous in flavour and portion-size, served with seasonal accompaniments (piquant salsa verde and braised piattone beans on one visit). Puddings pale somewhat in comparison and service is sometimes skew-whiff: nonetheless, no-one is pecking at the excellent-value prices. House wines from £22.
Chef/s: Benjamin Benton. **Open:** Tue to Sat L 12 to 3, D 5 to 10.30. Sun 2 to 9. **Closed:** Mon, 24 Dec to 3 Jan. **Meals:** Set L and D £17 (2 courses) to £22. **Details:** 45 seats. Music.

500 Restaurant

Genuine neighbourhood Italian
782 Holloway Road, Archway, N19 3JH
Tel no: (020) 7272 3406
www.500restaurant.co.uk
⊖ Archway, map 2
Italian | £30
Cooking score: 2
£5
OFF

Giorgio Pili and Mario Magli's orange-fronted neighbourhood restaurant in Archway – which should properly be pronounced 'Cinquecento' after the Fiat model – is a brightly burning beacon of warm Italian hospitality. Locals continue to throng to the place for characterful, sun-splashed food that draws notably on the traditional foodways of Sardinia. This produces a lasagnette starter composed of layers of carasau crispbread filled with crabmeat in tomato salsa, or Campidano ham with marinated baby onions in balsamic vinegar. Intermediate dishes of gnocchi with salsiccia, or rich risotto with celeriac and blue sheep's cheese, prepare the way for char-grilled lamb cutlets with roasted pumpkin in anchovy and almond dressing, or sea bass with spinach and walnuts. Finish with warm panettone in crema inglese, lightly spiced chocolate mousse or classic cantuccini with vin santo. A very reasonably priced Italian list with useful notes opens with a quartet of house wines (Chardonnay, Grechetto, Shiraz and Cannonau) at £15.50.
Chef/s: Mario Magli. **Open:** Fri to Sun L 12 to 3, all week D 6 to 10.30 (9.30 Sun). **Closed:** 2 weeks Christmas, 2 weeks Aug. **Meals:** alc (main courses £12 to £17). **Details:** 38 seats. Music.

Grain Store

Raising the bar in King's Cross
1-3 Stable Street, King's Cross, N1C 4AB
Tel no: (020) 7324 4466
www.grainstore.com
⊖ King's Cross, map 2
Global | £30
Cooking score: 4
V

Trendy, bohemian and definitely coming up in the world, the King's Cross development is well placed to support a restaurant of serious intent. Bruno Loubet's Grain Store rises effortlessly to the occasion. Housed in an old grain warehouse with high ceilings, rough brick walls, stripped-back ambience and exposed kitchen, it's a versatile space where vegetables are both the medium and the message. The unfussy, purposeful cooking is based on snappy global ideas and deep, precise flavours, seen in dishes such as a Moroccan carrot and orange salad teamed with spiced goats' labneh and flatbread, or wild mushroom croquettes with pine nuts. Meat or fish often play bit parts, as in cabbage pierogi served alongside caramelised onion, grain-mustard crème fraîche and homemade smoked game sausage, or in grilled leeks with apple and pickled walnut salsa and confit pork belly. Sweet things include coconut and kaffir lime tapioca with sweet potato and banana water. Wines from £22.
Chef/s: Bruno Loubet. **Open:** all week L 12 to 2.30 (Sat 11 to 3, Sun 11 to 4), Mon to Sat D 6 to 10.30. **Closed:** 25 and 26 Dec, 1 Jan. **Meals:** alc (main courses £10 to £17). **Details:** 140 seats. 75 seats outside. Separate bar. Wheelchair access. Music.

Homa

Trendy brasserie with sunny food
71-73 Stoke Newington Church Street, Stoke
Newington, N16 0AS
Tel no: (020) 7254 2072
www.homalondon.co.uk
⊖ Arsenal, map 2
Modern European | £35
Cooking score: 3

There's much love for Stokey on show at
Homa, where everything from the furniture
to the coffee is sourced from local suppliers.
The husband-and-wife team behind it hail
from Turkey and Italy respectively, which
explains the Pan-European approach of the
menu and the sunny Mediterranean climes it
evokes. Everything takes place in a hefty
residential property done out with a trendy
designer neutrality that works a treat in this
setting. The kitchen starts up for brunch
(sourdough with borlotti beans, goats' curd
and poached egg) before shifting up a gear for
lunch of slow-cooked pork neck with apple
and Dijon mustard. There are decidedly Italian
leanings throughout, with pasta dishes such as
potato and thyme ravioli in an octopus and
courgette ragù available in two sizes. Braised
ox cheek with truffled potato purée is present,
too, as well as desserts such as amaretti
chocolate and pear cake. Wines, mostly French
and Italian, start at £16.50.
Open: Mon to Sat L 10 to 3 (4 Sat), all week D 6.30
to 10.30. **Closed:** 25 and 26 Dec. **Meals:** alc (main
courses £12 to £21). **Details:** 80 seats. 20 seats
outside. Separate bar. Music.

LOCAL GEM

▲ Jin Kichi

73 Heath Street, Hampstead, NW3 6UG
Tel no: (020) 7794 6158
www.jinkichi.com
⊖ Hampstead, map 2
Japanese | £30

Stepping inside Jin Kichi can feel like you've
been plunged into an izakaya bar on a Tokyo
backstreet. At the heart of the cosy dining
room is a robata grill, which fires out tasty

skewers of chicken (including its gizzards),
pork with shiso leaf or ox tongue. Yakitori
may be the highlight here, but premium tuna
sushi, prawn tempura and sautéed shiitake
mushrooms are worth a punt. Wines (from
£28) are pricey, so opt for the saké or shochu
instead. Closed Mon.

Karpo

A terrific asset in King's Cross
23 Euston Road, King's Cross, NW1 2SD
Tel no: (020) 7843 2221
www.karpo.co.uk
⊖ King's Cross, map 2
Modern European | £28
Cooking score: 1
£5 OFF 🛏 £30

With its bold interior, easy-going service,
gentle pricing and honest intent in the
kitchen, the hugely likeable Karpo is quite a
local asset. The venue is part of the Megaro
Hotel, sited across the road from King's Cross
station, and strikes just the right chord with its
all-day opening, deliberately playing many
roles from coffee shop to full-on restaurant.
The simple Med-influenced lunch and dinner
menus offer the likes of charred Cornish
herrings with sorrel, cucumber and mustard
seeds, followed by haunch of venison with
creamed potato and green peppercorn sauce,
then Vacherin cheesecake with quince and
walnuts. Wines from £20.
Chef/s: Joseph Sharratt. **Open:** all week L 12 to 3.30
(8 to 4 Sat and Sun), D 5.30 to 10.30 (9.30 Sun).
Meals: alc (main courses £15 to £26). Set L £14 (2
courses) to £18. **Details:** 60 seats. Separate bar.
Wheelchair access. Music.

Symbols

🛏 Accommodation is available

£30 Three courses for less than £30

V Separate vegetarian menu

£5 OFF £5-off voucher scheme

🍷 Notable wine list

Made in Camden

A kaleidoscope of captivating sharing plates
Roundhouse, Chalk Farm Road, Camden,
NW1 8EH
Tel no: (020) 7424 8495
www.roundhouse.org.uk
⊖ Chalk Farm, map 2
International | £25
Cooking score: 3

V £30

Made is a cool, curvy and casual joint tacked on to the Roundhouse, offering sharing plates with a Mediterranean aspect. The glassy appendage to the iconic venue has posters covering one wall – a reflection of the artistic outpourings hereabouts – and it functions very nicely as a bar and diner for those heading to a gig. But it's well worth popping in here if you're ticket-less and in the neighbourhood. Drink cocktails, or beer from the Camden Town Brewery, and tuck into calamari with yuzu aïoli and chilli jam, sea bass with tahini cream and yoghurt flatbread, or the MiC lamb burger. There's a global spin to proceedings and a good few North African flavours on show. The place is open for breakfast and brunch, too, and there are inventive sandwiches at lunchtime alongside a bargain set menu. Finish with white chocolate and ginger cheesecake. Wine prices start at £18. **Chef/s:** Jean-Baptiste Barbosa. **Open:** Tue to Sun L 12 to 2.30 (11 to 3 Sat and Sun), D 6 to 10.30. **Closed:** Mon, 25 and 26 Dec. **Meals:** alc (main courses £14 to £15). Set L £7 (1 course) to £12 (3 courses). **Details:** 54 seats. Separate bar.

LOCAL GEM

▲ Mangal 1 Ocakbasi

10 Arcola Street, Stoke Newington, E8 2DJ
Tel no: (020) 7275 8981
www.mangal1.com
⊖ Dalston Kingsland, map 2
Turkish | £18

First firing up the ocak grill in 1990, Mangal 1 has been packing in hungry punters for 25 years and doesn't look like slowing down anytime soon. It's a basic sort of place with a few Turkish rugs on the walls to bring splashes of colour to the interior. Kick off with meze of stuffed vine leaves and lahmacun (a sort of pizza topped with minced lamb) before something from the grill: dinky quails, chicken wings or a classic shish kebab. Open all week.

Market

Trendy eatery with plucky Brit food
43 Parkway, Camden, NW1 7PN
Tel no: (020) 7267 9700
www.marketrestaurant.co.uk
⊖ Camden Town, map 2
Modern British | £29
Cooking score: 2

£30

With its bare-brick walls, plank floor and closely packed tables, humble little Market is one of those down-to-earth restaurants that only make a show of themselves where it matters: on the plate. And seven years on, the venue continues to enjoy faithful support. Big, bold flavours prevail on a menu that emphasises seasonality and lets well-sourced ingredients shine. Brit-accented dishes such as duck egg atop wild mushrooms on toast, and beetroot, pickled walnuts and watercress have been winter first-course hits. Next might come guinea fowl, bacon and leek pie with a side of greens, its earthiness perfectly echoing the surroundings, though alternatives could be Cumbrian lamb saddle with bubble and squeak and carrots, or lemon sole with mussels and samphire. Desserts tempt, especially chocolate mousse with honeycomb and salted caramel ice cream. Modest prices (the set lunch is a bargain) extend to the short modern wine list, which opens at £18.25. **Chef/s:** Richard Teague. **Open:** all week L 12 to 2.30 (11 to 3 Sun), Mon to Sat D 6 to 10.30. **Closed:** 24 Dec to 2 Jan, bank hols. **Meals:** alc (main courses £14 to £18). Set L £10 (2 courses). Set D £18 (2 courses) to £20. **Details:** 38 seats. 4 seats outside. Music.

Odette's

Letting quality ingredients do the talking
130 Regents Park Road, Primrose Hill, NW1 8XL
Tel no: (020) 7586 8569
www.odettesprimrosehill.com
⊖ Chalk Farm, map 2
Modern British | £34
Cooking score: 5
£5 OFF **V**

In the gastronomic enclave of Primrose Hill, Odette's has always been leader of the pack, having plied its trade under various owners since the late 1970s. Bryn Williams has been chef/patron since 2008, and in February 2014 unveiled a brand-new, supremely stylish look in greens and browns. The culinary compass point has gradually shifted from south of the Channel to the contemporary British idiom, and the present repertoire is replete with bright ideas. A glazed pig cheek in apple and lobster bisque is a bravura starter, or there may be delightful Cornish mackerel with rhubarb and hazelnuts. Mains don't overelaborate, but stay within the satisfying bounds of whole lemon sole with salsify, potted shrimps and capers, or roast pheasant stuffed with chestnuts and bacon, accompanied by honeyed parsnips. Finish with a tranche of pistachio cake, served with apple terrine and sorbet. House Spanish is £19.75, or £5.20 a glass.
Chef/s: Bryn Williams and Jamie Randalls. **Open:** Mon to Sat L 12 to 2.30 (3 Sat), D 6 to 10 (10.30 Fri and Sat). Sun 12 to 10. **Closed:** 25 Dec, 1 Jan. **Meals:** alc (main courses £16 to £20). Set L £13 (2 courses) to £15. Set D £17 (2 courses) to £20. Sun L £30. **Details:** 54 seats. 28 seats outside. Music.

LOCAL GEM

▲ Osteria Tufo

67 Fonthill Road, Finsbury Park, N4 3HZ
Tel no: (020) 7272 2911
www.osteriatufo.co.uk
⊖ Finsbury Park, map 2
Italian | £30

'It feels like good, Italian home cooking, imbued with love and care,' thought one visitor to this cherished local eatery. Tables are

'crammed in higgledy-piggledy', you can spill on to a little terrace in warmer weather and the cooking is simplicity itself. Start, say, with char-grilled squid, shredded red cabbage, lemon and olive oil, or hot, crisp potato croquette, smoked mozzarella and 'earthy, savoury and moreish' puréed broccoli and mushroom; then very fresh cod, squid and mussels with garlic, white wine and tomato sauce. Open D Tue to Sun, and Sun L.

▲ El Parador

245 Eversholt Street, Camden, NW1 1BA
Tel no: (020) 7387 2789
www.elparadorlondon.com
⊖ Mornington Crescent, map 2
Spanish | £20 £5 OFF

Tapas are the name of the game at El Parador, which has been offering a little piece of Iberian sunshine since 1988. The colour scheme and basic décor may well recall sunny holidays, while a table in the terrace garden ups the ante. The menu extends beyond old favourites to deliver rolled pork bell braised in cider, and swordfish with a romesco sauce, but there are commendable versions of the classics, too: tortilla, jamón Ibérico and the like. Wines from £15.50. Closed L Sat and Sun.

NEW ENTRY
Parlour

All-day comfort food pit-stop
5 Regent Street, Kensal Green, NW10 5LG
Tel no: (020) 8969 2184
www.parlourkensal.com
⊖ Kensal Green, map 1
British | £30
Cooking score: 2

Stepping boldly into the culinary vacuum of Kensal Green, Parlour styles itself 'an all-day and late-night serving parlour', opening its doors at 8am for breakfasts and closing after craft-beer sessions in the wee hours. Interiors match the multi-purpose motto: a bar area with crisp white tiling and scuffed wooden furniture, a smarter dining room plus a patio for balmy evenings. Cleverly constructed comfort food rules throughout the day. An inspection dinner opened auspiciously with chunky pork pâté matched with piccalilli and sublime beer bread. Mains are fulsomely flavoured too: think cow pie, mackerel burger and (on inspection) a triumphantly gooey, tennis ball-sized chicken Kiev, balanced atop a potato rösti. Crumbles and cheesecakes lead the puds. One grumble is the number of cryptic references on the menu ('back door' smoked salmon?) – though helpful staff can decode. House wines from £17, but the 'beeropedia'and cocktail list are worth a look. **Chef/s:** Jesse Dunford-Wood. **Open:** all week 10am to 11pm. **Closed:** 23 Dec to 1 Jan. **Meals:** alc (main courses £14 to £20). Set L £10 (2 courses) to £13. Set D £20 (2 courses) to £25. Sun L £30. **Details:** 100 seats. 30 seats outside. Separate bar.

LOCAL GEM
▲ Pizza East Kentish Town
79 Highgate Road, Kentish Town, NW5 1TL
Tel no: (020) 3310 2000
www.pizzaeastkentishtown.com
⊖ Kentish Town, map 2
£25

With cured meats hanging above the counter and wood-fired ovens burning away in the open kitchen, it's evident this is a pizza joint with a bit of va-va-voom. Part of a trio of joints (see entries in Portobello and Shoreditch), the Kentish Town operation has an urban industrial finish and offers classy rustic pizzas with toppings such as veal meatballs, prosciutto and cream or speck with asparagus. Salt-baked salmon and lasagne are alternatives.Wines from £19.50. Open all week.

||◦ Average Price
The average price listed in main-entry reviews denotes the price of a three-course meal, without wine.

NEW ENTRY
Prawn on the Lawn
Neighbourhood fishmonger dabbling in dining
220 St Paul's Road, Highbury, N1 2LL
Tel no: (020) 3302 8668
www.prawnonthelawn.com
⊖ Highbury and Islington, map 2
Seafood | £35
Cooking score: 3

In its first year of opening, this fishmonger's (in a former butcher's shop) with a sideline serving simple seafood dishes, earned itself many dining disciples. Building on its success, Prawn on the Lawn continues as a modest operation with diners choosing to eat in the 'absolutely tiny'cellar dining room or to perch atop stools in the modish white-tiled shop, sharing surface space with chefs busy filleting: 'you feel like you're sat in the kitchen'. Very fresh fish and shellfish is delivered from Cornwall to star in tapas-sized dishes (generally served cold). The scrupulously sourced seafood is served plain and simple: oysters, say, or whole Padstow lobster or half a crab with ratatouille and tangy salsa verde (one of the few warm dishes). Clear, precise flavours shine through in the likes of wild sea trout with cool tabbouleh and mint. Desserts are straightforward – lime posset, chocolate ginger crunch – with wines starting at £19.50. **Chef/s:** Rick Toogood. **Open:** Tue to Sat 12 to 11 (12 Thur to Sat). **Closed:** Sun, Mon. **Meals:** alc (main courses £9 to £29). **Details:** 32 seats.

Restaurant Michael Nadra
Lively canal-side cooking
42 Gloucester Avenue, Primrose Hill, NW1 8JD
Tel no: (020) 7722 2800
www.restaurant-michaelnadra.co.uk
⊖ Chalk Farm, map 2
Modern European | £36
Cooking score: 4
£5 OFF

The original Michael Nadra is in Chiswick (see entry, West London), but this branch is easily recognisable as it occupies the only

Grade II-listed horse tunnel on the Regent's Canal. There's a conservatory and Martini bar too, along with a lovely garden and a brick-walled, low-lit dining room with caramel banquettes. The kitchen produces lively, modern European cooking, with pin-sharp seasonings and incisive sauces in multi-layered dishes. Open with soft-shell crab tempura in a dressing of daikon, black sesame, ginger and chilli, and move on to Scotch beef fillet and braised cheeks with wild mushrooms and truffled mash in Madeira jus, or continue the east Asian seafood theme via sea bass with scallop and prawn dumplings, greens, carrot and ginger purée and lemongrass bisque. You'll find plenty of chocolate, caramel and treacle for dessert, and also vanilla rice pudding with rhubarb compote. Wines are classified by grape variety, with bottles of house Languedoc at £18.
Chef/s: Michael Nadra. **Open:** all week L 12 to 2.30 (4 Sat and Sun), D 6 to 10 (10.30 Fri and Sat, 9 Sun). **Closed:** 25 and 26 Dec, 1 Jan. **Meals:** alc (main courses £18 to £25). **Details:** 90 seats. 32 seats outside. Separate bar. Wheelchair access. Music.

Season Kitchen
Down-to-earth neighbourhood restaurant
53 Stroud Green Road, Finsbury Park, N4 3EF
Tel no: (020) 7263 5500
www.seasonkitchen.co.uk
⊖ Finsbury Park, map 2
Modern British | £25
Cooking score: 3
£5 OFF   £30

The inhabitants of Finsbury Park look kindly on Neil Gill's gregarious, good-natured little restaurant and it is easy to see why. Season Kitchen strikes just the right note for a neighbourhood venue, with a concept that suits the way London wants to eat and drink these days: an unfussy atmosphere, dishes that go in for minimum posturing, and a compact wine list blessed with a minimal mark-up policy (from £15.50). No surprise, then, that the place is usually buzzy. It keeps regulars returning with a changing menu that plays off the seasons and straddles the Eurozone and

beyond – perhaps mackerel ceviche with poached rhubarb, crispy skin and horseradish cream or char-grilled broccoli with Ally Pally white (cheese), sorrel and egg. Mains might include comforting, big-flavoured ox cheek daube with parsnip purée or a perfect veal T-bone, while Ben's rhubarb and custard doughnuts are firm favourites.
Chef/s: Ben Wooles. **Open:** Sat and Sun L 12 to 4, Tue to Sun D 5.30 to 10.30. **Closed:** Mon, 25 and 26 Dec, 1 Jan. **Meals:** alc (main courses £13 to £19). Pre-theatre D £10. **Details:** 35 seats. Music.

LOCAL GEM
▲ Shayona
56-62 Meadow Garth, Neasden, NW10 8HD
Tel no: (020) 8965 3365
www.shayonarestaurants.com
⊖ Stonebridge Park, map 1
Indian Vegetarian | £15

Right by the magnificent Swaminarayan Hindu temple that is a Neasden (and national) landmark, Shayona serves sattvic food that is entirely vegetarian and excludes onion and garlic (among other things). It's a quietly modern space with light wood, chrome and curvy high-backed chairs, and flashes of vivid colour from spiritually minded artworks. A Gujarati-style buffet sets the pace midweek lunchtimes, with the main menu offering pan-Indian street food like khasta kachori chaat, sev dahi puri and dosas. Curries run to bhindi masala and dhal makhani, with excellent breads such as aloo paratha to accompany them. No alcohol. Open all week.

¦¦• Please send us your feedback
To register your opinion about any restaurant listed in the Guide, or a new restaurant that you wish to bring to our attention, please visit the web address at the bottom of the page. Your feedback informs the content of the book and will be used to compile next year's reviews.

NEW ENTRY

Smokehouse

Hearty grilled meats in a refined setting
63-69 Canonbury Road, Islington, N1 2DG
Tel no: (020) 7354 1144
www.smokehouseislington.co.uk
⊖ Highbury & Islington, map 2
Modern British | £32
Cooking score: 3

Neil Rankin made his name at barbecue joint Pitt Cue – and proved barbecues aren't just for summer. He's now making his mark behind the grill at this refined pub, working in a semi-open kitchen at one end of a dining room, which in turn flows around a bar featuring no less than 25 beers. It's totally laid-back with a 'stark tastefulness' to the wooden floors, mismatched wood tables and whitewashed walls. The generously portioned food 'packs a serious punch': duck spring rolls are more like wraps in size, bulging with meat; Scotch egg-style brisket roll comes with Korean mustard sauce; bourguignon is long-marinated beef piled on mahogany-coloured, BBQ-sauce glazed ribs; ox cheek is peppered and tender, served with cauliflower cheese; and a hefty Barnsley chop sits 'in a fat puddle of deeply savoury gravy'. If you've room, try sticky toffee apple cobbler or a dense 'Double D' chocolate tart. Wines from £17.95.
Chef/s: Neil Rankin. **Open:** Sat and Sun L 11 to 4, all week D 6 to 10. **Meals:** alc (main courses £13 to £19). **Details:** 60 seats. Separate bar.

Sushi-Say

Japanese delicacies from a sushi master
33b Walm Lane, Willesden, NW2 5SH
Tel no: (020) 8459 7512
⊖ Willesden Green, map 1
Japanese | £29
Cooking score: 3
£30

Honourable, family-run Sushi-Say has been lighting up the backwaters of NW2 since 1995 and remains a go-to for foodie adventurers. 'How delightful to see Europeans enjoying old-fashioned Japanese dishes over saké,' says owner Katsuharu Shimizu. The narrow, contemporary dining room isn't much to look at, but readers reckon the food can compete with the best in town – thanks to a combination of top-notch ingredients and considerable culinary technique. 'Brilliant fish' is the key to faultless nigiri, seaweed rolls and sashimi, but the sushi master also oversees other textbook offerings from the traditional repertoire. Zensai appetisers of jellyfish with vinegar sauce, sliced turbot wing with sticky, fermented soya beans or salmon roe with grated daikon tease the palate, ahead of grilled black cod with salt, king prawn tempura or chicken teriyaki. Saké, shochu and Japanese beer are the drinks of choice; wines from £20.
Chef/s: Katsuharu Shimizu. **Open:** Sat and Sun L 12 to 3, Wed to Sun D 6.30 to 10 (10.30 Sat, 6 to 9.30 Sun). **Closed:** Mon, Tue, 31 Dec to 2 Jan, 2 weeks Sept. **Meals:** alc (main courses £11 to £29). Set L £15 to £23. Set D £29 (6 courses) to £48. **Details:** 41 seats. Wheelchair access.

Trullo

Effortlessly likeable Italian eatery
300-302 St Paul's Road, Islington, N1 2LH
Tel no: (020) 7226 2733
www.trullorestaurant.com
⊖ Highbury and Islington, map 2
Italian | £32
Cooking score: 3

Amid the din and hurly-burly of Highbury Corner, Trullo does well to maintain a sense of calm. The dead-simple dark brown and white décor, with bistro chairs and bare floorboards, makes a neutral ambience for the kind of Italian cooking that impresses London these days – simple, authentic and big on natural flavour. Fish and meats cooked over charcoal, pasta churned out of the hand-turner shortly before service and decent Italian wines are the name of the game. New season's agretti with lamb's tongue in anchovy sauce is a palate-priming opener, and might be followed by a plate of pappardelle in a rich ragù of beef shin. Mains include roast hake with mussels or, from the char-grill, a sizzled chop of Black

Hampshire pork with baked borlotti beans and salsa rossa. Finish with salty caramel ice cream. Wines start at £20, with half-bottle carafes from £11.

Chef/s: Conor Gadd. **Open:** Mon to Sun L 12.30 to 2.45 (3 Sun), D 6 to 10.15. **Closed:** 24 Dec to 4 Jan. **Meals:** alc (main courses £15 to £30). **Details:** 90 seats. Music.

NEW ENTRY

The Truscott Arms

Fine production with some artistic touches
55 Shirland Road, Maida Vale, W9 2JD
Tel no: (020) 7266 9198
www.thetruscottarms.com
⊖ Warwick Avenue, map 4
British | £32
Cooking score: 3

The Fishwicks – an ex-theatre husband and wife duo – deliver an accomplished production with their first pub venture. While hipsters swill pints from London's best craft breweries on the ground floor, the dining room above (evenings only, apart from weekends) delivers some plate-based artistry, with photogenic starters such as razor-thin slivers of red wine-dried Wagyu beef with gazpacho and sour cream ice cream, or scallops with chicken wings, pearl barley and spinach – tasting as good as they look. Main courses are no less impressive, and intricately designed dishes such as suckling pig with Ibérico loin, grapefruit purée and braised chicory; or plaice with lettuce emulsion, smoked mussels, asparagus and beans, see interesting flavours balanced with great skill. The Truscott's neutral-toned décor and contemporary artworks serve as an understated backdrop. Its wine list (from £18) broadens the usual repertoire to include enticing bottles from Croatia, the Lebanon and the USA.

Chef/s: Barry Snook. **Open:** Sat L 12 to 4, Mon to Sat D 6.30 to 10. Sun 12 to 9.30. **Meals:** Set L £18 (Sat only, 2 courses) to £22. Set D £27 (2 courses) to £32. Sun L alc (main courses £12 to £18). **Details:** 60 seats. Separate bar.

NEW ENTRY

Zest at JW3

Boldly flavoured food with a sunny disposition
341-351 Finchley Road, Swiss Cottage, NW3 6ET
Tel no: (020) 7433 8955
www.zestatjw3.co.uk
⊖ Finchley Road, map 1
Jewish | £30
Cooking score: 3

The point about Zest is that it redefines the notion of Jewish food in London. For this is modern kosher Jewish cooking (under the supervision of the Sephardi Kashrut Authority) that takes inspiration from the Middle East, rather than the more familiar Ashkenazi cooking of eastern Europe. On the lower-ground floor of the Jewish Community Centre, the infectiously bustly space (part-café/part-restaurant) offers vibrant minimalism and cheery vibes. It strikes just the right note for boldly flavoured food with a sunny disposition. There's no meat, but fish dishes include an excellent salt-baked salmon salad served on a potato and butternut squash pashtida (an Israeli dish similar to a frittata). Vegetarian dishes are vivid and fresh: perhaps sweet potato gnocchi with burnt aubergine, sage butter, crispy shallots, Greek yoghurt and pomegranate. Bread-and-butter challah with crème anglaise, lemon thyme, pistachio roasted peaches and passion fruit makes a fine finish. Wines from £18.

Chef/s: Eran Tibi. **Open:** Mon to Thur L 12 to 3, D 6 to 10. Sun 10.30 to 3. **Closed:** Fri, Sat. **Meals:** alc (main courses £15 to £22). **Details:** 60 seats. 32 seats outside. Wheelchair access.

EAST A to Z | London

LOCAL GEM
▲ Albion

2-4 Boundary Street, Shoreditch, E2 7DD
Tel no: (020) 7729 1051
www.albioncaff.co.uk
⊖ Shoreditch, Liverpool Street, map 2
British | £25

Forget greasy spoons, Sir Terence Conran's
trendy 'caff' puts on a clean-lined design-
conscious face for hungry Shoreditch locals,
tourists, shoppers and others at his expansive
Boundary hotel/restaurant project. Breakfast,
home-baked cakes and afternoon tea keep
everyone happy, while the all-day menu
heroically invokes 'cool Britannia': new riffs
on patriotic favourites such as Welsh rarebit or
kedgeree, plus baked sea trout with braised
chicory or skirt and chips with marrow bone,
followed by rhubarb crumble or Cambridge
burnt cream. Wines from £18.50. Open all
week. No bookings.

Amico Bio

Green-thinking Italian veggie
44 Cloth Fair, Barbican, EC1A 7JQ
Tel no: (020) 7600 7778
www.amicobio.co.uk
⊖ Barbican, map 5
Vegetarian | £24
Cooking score: 1

V £30

Smithfield meat market may be nearby, but
this handsome Georgian building is a rare
outpost of vegetarianism in the City. Pasquale
Amico's informal, family-friendly Italian
proves that meat-free organic cookery can
appeal to suit-wearers as much as sandal-
wearers. Produce from the family's farm in
Italy ends up in keenly priced dishes of
beetroot, buffalo mozzarella and basil salad, or
pumpkin squash and potato tortino served
with pearl barley and green beans. The organic
wine list starts from £16. There's a branch at 43
New Oxford Street, WC1A 1BH; tel: (020)
7836 7509.

Chef/s: Pasquale Amico. **Open:** Mon to Sat L 12 to 3,
D 5 to 10.30. **Closed:** Sun, 25 and 26 Dec, bank hols.
Meals: alc (main courses £8 to £10). Set L £12. Set D
£18. **Details:** 48 seats. Music.

NEW ENTRY
Angler

Diverting seafood in high-flying City setting
South Place Hotel, 3 South Place, Moorgate,
EC2M 2AF
Tel no: (020) 3215 1260
www.anglerrestaurant.com
⊖ Moorgate, map 2
Seafood | £48
Cooking score: 4

The glass-walled restaurant atop D&D
London's trendy South Place Hotel does away
with the nautical knick-knacks of traditional
seafood specialists in favour of monochrome
stripes, mirrored ceiling, plush carpets and
city views. It all provides a contemporary
context for contemporary cuisine, courtesy of
Tony Fleming whose skilled British seafood
cookery encompasses classics, new creations
and combinations of the two. At inspection,
sautéed langoustines, slow-cooked lamb
breast and asparagus proved a bold 'surf and
turf' pairing, the strong flavours accentuated
by candied lemon and anchovy purée – to
diverting, if not entirely coherent, effect.
Monkfish and lobster pie to follow was rich
and comforting, though too large to maintain
interest. Warm hazelnut cake with salted
caramel and zesty lime sorbet made a brighter
finish. Staff are uniformly effusive, as
delighted to serve the generous set lunch as
they are to explore the classic wine list. Bottles
from £21 and plenty by the glass.
Chef/s: Tony Fleming. **Open:** Mon to Fri L 12 to 2.30,
Mon to Sat D 6 to 10. **Closed:** Sun, 24 to 26 Dec, 1
week Jan. **Meals:** alc (main courses £20 to £36). Set
L and D £28 (2 courses) to £33. **Details:** 80 seats.
40 seats outside. Separate bar. Wheelchair access.
Music.

L'Anima

Gorgeous modern Italian food
1 Snowden Street, City, EC2A 2DQ
Tel no: (020) 7422 7000
www.lanima.co.uk
⊖ Liverpool Street, map 2
Italian | £50
Cooking score: 5

An exquisitely stylish Italian venue in the heart of the City, L'Anima goes for transparency with a glass-fronted look, and a spacious interior with white seating and bar stools. It suits the busy whizzkid as much as those who have time to enrol in Saturday pasta classes. Southern Italy and the islands are where Francesco Mazzei's heart lies, and his food is distinguished by freshness and integrity. Salt cod with olive oil mash, anchovy sauce and black olives is brimming with umami; octopus is grilled on the plancha and served with 'nduja, ricotta and paprika oil; and there's fine fritto misto. For main, rabbit siciliana, or fish stew with Sardinian fregola, offer a taste of island cuisine, while sea bass comes with fashionable monk's beard and red onion purée. Finish with iced chocolate truffle. Italian wines are priced for City slickers, but start at £22 for Greco and Gaglioppo southern varietals.
Chef/s: Francesco Mazzei. **Open:** Mon to Fri L 11.45 to 3, Mon to Sat D 5.30 to 11 (11.30 Sat). **Closed:** Sun. **Meals:** alc (main courses £15 to £36). Set L and D £17 (2 courses) to £19. **Details:** 100 seats. Separate bar. Wheelchair access. Music.

Beagle

Great Brit cooking, seductive Med flavours
397-399 Geffrye Street, Hoxton, E2 8HZ
Tel no: (020) 7613 2967
www.beaglelondon.co.uk
⊖ Hoxton, map 2
British | £30
Cooking score: 3

£5
OFF

If you are a devotee of TV crime dramas, you might think railway arches are only good for hiding stolen goods or dead bodies, but here

by Hoxton station three of them have been turned into a thrilling restaurant, bar and coffee shop. The industrial neutrality remains intact – exposed brick and suchlike – and you'll also find plenty of the hip attitude that is expected in this part of town. The menu has the kind of rustic British/Med combos that make foodies go weak at the knees: grilled cuttlefish with winter tomatoes and fregola, braised English kid with pearl barley and green sauce . . . great stuff. There's a brunch menu and an express deal that's a steal for mid-week lunches and early evenings. Puddings run to steamed treacle sponge or a seductive chocolate and salted-caramel pot. The wine list has a decent range by the glass, with bottles from £19.
Chef/s: James Ferguson. **Open:** Wed to Sun L 12 to 3 (11 Sat, 11 to 5 Sun), Mon to Sat D 6 to 10.30. **Closed:** 25 Dec and 1 Jan. **Meals:** alc (main courses £14 to £21). **Details:** 65 seats. 40 seats outside. Separate bar. Wheelchair access. Music. Car parking.

Bistrot Bruno Loubet

Cutting quite a dash
The Zetter Hotel, 86-88 Clerkenwell Road, Clerkenwell, EC1M 5RJ
Tel no: (020) 7324 4455
www.bistrotbrunoloubet.com
⊖ Farringdon, Barbican, map 5
Modern French | £30
Cooking score: 3

Since returning from his eight-year sojourn down under, Bruno Loubet has made a big impact on London, opening the Grain Store at King's Cross (see entry) and this bistrot on the ground floor of the Zetter Hotel. The venue cuts quite a dash with its white walls, contorted metallic curios, fanciful furniture and floor-to-ceiling windows overlooking St John's Square, and the cooking surpasses the bourguignon bistro norm. Breads arrive in little flowerpots and the menu is a refreshingly eclectic assortment of 'plates' large and small: from niçoise-style octopus terrine or the famed combo of snails and meatballs mauricette, to sautéed veal kidney with pumpkin polenta and devilled sauce, or roast sea bass stuffed with prawn mousse and braised fennel. Salads and steaks revert to type, likewise desserts such as crème brûlée or pear and hazelnut brownie with tonka bean ice cream. Wines (from £19.95) give equal billing to the Old and New Worlds.

Chef/s: Bruno Loubet and Dominique Goltinger. **Open:** all week L 12 to 2.30 (11 to 3 Sat and Sun), D 6 to 10.30 (10 Sun). **Closed:** 24 to 26 Dec. **Meals:** alc (main courses £14 to £25). **Details:** 85 seats. 40 seats outside. Separate bar. Wheelchair access. Music.

Bistrotheque

Achingly cool east London pioneer
23–27 Wadeson Street, Bethnal Green, E2 9DR
Tel no: (020) 8983 7900
www.bistrotheque.com
⊖ Bethnal Green, map 1
French | £35
Cooking score: 2

White-painted minimalism combines with Bethnal Green's industrial heritage to create a little slice of urban cool in a former sweatshop. Colour is provided by the clientele, while the menu aims to satisfy with its take on bistro-style tucker. Brunch is a weekend treat, with a pianist on hand to accompany pancakes with bacon and syrup or salmon and brown crab cake. The evening menu plays to the gallery with cod and chips or cheeseburger with pancetta and caramelised onions, but equally you might kick off with curried mussel soup and follow on with a lamb broth with peas, broad beans and monk's beard. There's a bar where stools at the counter await and even a private dining room. Desserts run to lemon granita and île flottante. The wine list shows allegiance to the European mainland, and beers range from Breton cider to local pale ale. House French is £19.

Chef/s: Christopher Branscombe. **Open:** Sat and Sun L 11 to 4 (5 Sun), all week D 6 to 10.30 (11 Fri and Sat). **Closed:** 24 to 26 Dec. **Meals:** alc (main courses £12 to £32). Set D £18 (3 courses). **Details:** 80 seats. Separate bar.

Bonds

Solid City-pleaser
Threadneedle Hotel, 5 Threadneedle Street, City, EC2R 8AY
Tel no: (020) 7657 8088
www.bonds-restaurant.co.uk
⊖ Bank, map 2
Modern European | £41
Cooking score: 4

Now that nobody is fond of banks any more, there's something even more reassuring about seeing the magnificent old pillared halls of finance being reconstituted as gastronomic palaces. The Bank of England itself may be nearby, but Bonds has made a good job of softening the forbidding grandeur of this space into something more suited to elite hospitality. Stephen Smith furnishes the place in his own way, with modern European dishes that utilise many ingredients that have entered the British mainstream. Start with sustaining winter veg, chorizo and butter-bean stew with a confit duck leg on top, as an opener for sea bass with crab and saffron risotto, truffled wild mushroom tortellini with roasted artichokes and Parmesan, or Cumbrian mountain lamb with celeriac and pancetta, garnished with rosemary and lemon gnocchi. Concluding crowd-pleasers include chocolate tart with orange marmalade jelly. An enterprising wine list with useful notes shows plenty of discernment, with bottles from £22.

Chef/s: Stephen Smith. **Open:** Mon to Fri L 12 to 2.30, D 6 to 11. **Closed:** Sat, Sun, bank hols. **Meals:** alc (main courses £15 to £26). Set L and D £24 (2 courses) to £27. **Details:** 80 seats. Separate bar. Wheelchair access. Music.

Symbols

🛏 Accommodation is available

£30 Three courses for less than £30

V Separate vegetarian menu

£5 OFF £5-off voucher scheme

🍾 Notable wine list

Boundary

Full-dress restaurant with a very posh wine list
2-4 Boundary Street (entrance in Redchurch
Street), Shoreditch, E2 7DD
Tel no: (020) 7729 1051
www.theboundary.co.uk
⊖ Shoreditch, Old Street, map 2
Modern French | £80
Cooking score: 3

🚗

The Conran group's Boundary is a Shoreditch
style-hub, reached down a deliberately faintly
grotty staircase. The intrepid are rewarded
with a formal dining room under a ceiling
painted with zodiacal motifs, and a service
tone that wouldn't disgrace the Hôtel
Splendide. (There's a glassed-in rooftop café
too, if you've a head for heights and a yen to see
east London spread before you.) Frederick
Forster cooks modern French, with rather
more innovative energy than is the Conran
norm: expect panko-crumbed egg with
Bayonne ham and peas, then poached turbot
with dill gnocchi and mussels, or roast pigeon
with provençale veg and puréed celeriac.
Couples can share a whole garlic-buttered
bream or herb-crusted lamb rack. Finish with
tarte Tatin flamed in Calvados, caramelised
banana with chocolate mousse and mango
coulis, or something from the cheese chariot.
Wines are very snooty, though not all French,
with prices from £20.
Chef/s: Frederick Forster. **Open:** Mon to Sat D 6.30
to 10.30, Sun L 12 to 3.30. **Closed:** 25 and 26 Dec, 1
Jan, bank hols. **Meals:** alc (main courses £10 to
£36). Set D £26. Sun L £20. **Details:** 120 seats.
Separate bar. Wheelchair access. Music.

Brawn

Unbuttoned neighbourhood eatery
49 Columbia Road, Shoreditch, E2 7RG
Tel no: (020) 7729 5692
www.brawn.co
⊖ Shoreditch, map 2
French | £28
Cooking score: 4

💷30

'All in all, we ate very well in a convivial and
relaxed atmosphere, and the prices are
reasonable to boot, which in London is never
to be taken for granted,' is how one visitor
described his meal at this neighbourhood
eatery on Columbia Road. Delivering the
same pared-back, functional style as siblings
Terroirs, Soif, Green Man and French Horn
(see entries), Brawn offers an interesting menu
focusing (as the name suggests) on offal and
less popular meat cuts. There are some very
good things to eat. Start, appropriately, with
firm, flavourful brawn (potted pig's head), and
buffalo mozzarella teamed with purple
sprouting broccoli and an anchovy and chilli
dressing, then go on to grilled duck hearts
with parsnip purée and rosemary or hake
grenobloise with mashed potato. Afterwards,
vanilla cheesecake should provide the right
sweet hit. There's a good, modern stash of
(mostly French) wines by the glass or carafe;
bottles from £19.75.
Chef/s: Owen Kenworthy. **Open:** Tue to Sun L 12 to 3
(4 Sun), Mon to Sat D 6 to 10.30 (11 Fri and Sat).
Closed: 24 Dec to 2 Jan, bank hols. **Meals:** alc (main
courses £6 to £16). Sun L £28. **Details:** 70 seats.
Wheelchair access. Music.

Bread Street Kitchen
Ramsay's buzzy all-dayer
One New Change, 10 Bread Street, St Paul's,
EC4M 9AJ
Tel no: (020) 3030 4050
www.gordonramsay.com/breadstreet
⊖ St Paul's, map 5
Modern British | £48
Cooking score: 2

A vast space of industrial scale and design from
the Gordon Ramsay group, Bread Street
Kitchen has a brasserie attitude and an all-day
menu that covers every base from posh burger
to a salad packed with superfoods. Mustard-
coloured banquettes and a chequerboard floor
add to the continental feel, and there are two
bars to pull in the City crowd for cocktails
(with live music on a Sunday, too). Breakfast
deals in everything from eggs Benedict to the
full works and a detox option, while the main
menu aims to satisfy with its broad approach.
The Josper grill works its magic on an English
rose veal chop and Casterbridge ribeye steak,
with hand-cut chips an optional extra. A
starter of tamarind-spiced chicken wings is
contemporary comfort food, followed
perhaps by sea trout with palourde clams and
an aromatic broth. Finish with blood-orange
baked Alaska. The wine list kicks off at £22.
Chef/s: Erion Karaj. **Open:** all week 11 to 11 (11 to 8
Sun). **Closed:** 25 and 26 Dec. **Meals:** alc (main
courses £13 to £35). **Details:** 312 seats. Separate
bar. Wheelchair access. Music.

Café Spice Namasté
High-rolling modern Indian
16 Prescot Street, Tower Hill, E1 8AZ
Tel no: (020) 7488 9242
www.cafespice.co.uk
⊖ Tower Hill, map 1
Indian | £30
Cooking score: 2
£5
OFF

Cyrus Todiwala was born in Mumbai and
moved to London in the early 1990s, just as
Indian food in the UK was moving up a gear
and heading into 'modern' territory. His

experience in the upmarket Taj group stood
him in good stead to make an impact, and in
1995 Café Spice Namasté was opened, a short
distance from the Tower of London. It's still
going strong, featuring colourful décor and a
menu that never fails to excite with its
combinations rooted in Indian traditions and
peppered with high-quality British
ingredients. Venison from Suffolk's Denham
Estate is used in tikka aflatoon, with the
flavours of fennel and star anise deftly
handled, while Goan prawn curry is served
with organic red rice. Todiwala is a Parsee, so
the properly authentic dhansak is an eye-
opener, and everything from the breads to
desserts (like rose kulfi) are a cut above. Wines
start at £23.
Chef/s: Cyrus Todiwala. **Open:** Mon to Fri L 12 to 3,
Mon to Sat D 6.15 to 10.30 (6.30 Sat). **Closed:** Sun,
25 Dec to 1 Jan, bank hols. **Meals:** alc (main courses
£15 to £20). Set L and D £30 (2 courses) to £35.
Tasting menu £75. **Details:** 140 seats. Wheelchair
access. Music.

Cinnamon Kitchen
Sharp-suited City Indian
9 Devonshire Square, City, EC2M 4YL
Tel no: (020) 7626 5000
www.cinnamon-kitchen.com
⊖ Liverpool Street, map 2
Modern Indian | £40
Cooking score: 4
£5
OFF

This offspring of Westminster's Cinnamon
Club (see entry) is an ultra-cool former spice
warehouse with an open-minded, inventive
kitchen, perfect for feeding the City throngs.
It's cool, energetic and full of pulsating action.
The house style of creatively configured
modern Indian food makes lively use of spice,
with well-chosen British ingredients. It works
to great effect in such deceptively simple dishes
as grilled aubergine with sesame, tamarind
and peanut, in smoked saddle of Kentish lamb
with saffron sauce, and in tandoori red deer
with root vegetables and yoghurt sauce.
Tandoori kebabs, rich biryanis and a
traditional Rajasthani curry of wild rabbit and

corn with 'miso' roti are vibrant assemblies, and if an agony of indecision overtakes you, a cleverly compiled tasting menu helps narrow down your selections. Set lunch and dinner are a steal for cooking of this calibre. The wine list (from £19) has a broad span and matches the food's incisive flavours.
Chef/s: Vivek Singh and Abdul Yaseen. **Open:** Mon to Fri L 12 to 3, Mon to Sat D 6 to 11. **Closed:** Sun, bank hols. **Meals:** alc (main courses £13 to £32). Set L and D £15 (2 courses) to £18. Tasting menu £57 (7 courses). **Details:** 130 seats. 50 seats outside. Separate bar. Wheelchair access. Music.

NEW ENTRY

City Social

City humdinger
Tower 42, 25 Old Broad Street, City, EC2N 1HQ
Tel no: (020) 7877 7703
www.citysociallondon.com
⊖ Liverpool Street, map 2
Modern British | £52
Cooking score: 6

🍾

As Rhodes 24 this was one of London's original up-in-the-clouds venues. Now that it's a Jason Atherton restaurant, the airport-style security that bedevilled entry to Tower 42 has been solved – by giving City Social its own entrance. A lift whisks you to the 24th floor, to a classy wood and leather-toned bar and dining room strategically designed to optimise the spectacular view. Here, Paul Walsh hits exactly the right notes: from City crowd-pleasers (grilled Dover sole, lobster, côte de boeuf) via the odd Atherton classic (heritage and heirloom tomato salad, burrata, chilled tomato consommé, frozen basil), to cross-cultural kicks (a super-fresh tuna tataki amalgamated with cucumber, blobs of avocado, a tangle of shaved radish and zingy ponzu dressing). British ingredients loom large in a fabulous dish of rabbit (saddle and sausage), tarragon and hazelnut pesto, asparagus and 'utterly delicious' mini cassoulet. As a finale, there's a 'wicked' strawberry soufflé. Impeccably chosen wines from £24.

Chef/s: Paul Walsh. **Open:** Mon to Sat L 12 to 2.30, D 6 to 10.30. **Closed:** Sun. **Meals:** alc (main courses £18 to £38). **Details:** 90 seats. Separate bar. Music.

★ TOP 50 ★

The Clove Club

Fashion-forward roots
Shoreditch Town Hall, 380 Old Street, Shoreditch, EC1V 9LT
Tel no: (020) 7729 6496
www.thecloveclub.com
⊖ Old Street, Shoreditch High Street, map 2
Modern European | £35
Cooking score: 6

V

The Clove Club's scuffed, back-to-basics ground-floor rooms in Shoreditch's former town hall suit its blend of new-Brit culinary cool. The vibe is youthful and casual – like most (though by no means all) of its customers – with Isaac McHale and brigade on full display in the kitchen-slash-dining room. There's no doubt the place has matured in the past year, morphing successfully from hot ticket into that rare thing for trafficky Old Street: a destination restaurant. There's delight at the accessible, ambitious cooking, at the first-class seasonal ingredients, and in the nugget of buttermilk-fried chicken that's part of the opening salvo (on the eight-course tasting menu). What dazzles, though, is a sweet Scottish langoustine and accompanying mousserons (mushroom) and elderflower purée and oh-so-tender fennel; an unbelievably flavoursome nugget of 30-day dry-aged Challans duck breast; and raspberry cranachan, a superb riff on oats, cream, raspberries and whisky. Details such as fresh baked bread, the extra little treats thrown in and genuinely committed staff are much appreciated, likewise the excellent advice given by the young sommelier on a modern wine list that opens at £20.
Chef/s: Isaac McHale. **Open:** Tue to Sat L 12 to 2.30, Mon to Sat D 6 to 12. **Closed:** Sun, 23 Dec to 4 Jan. **Meals:** alc (main courses £14 to £23). Set L £35. Tasting menu £55 (8 courses) to £95 (14 courses). **Details:** 70 seats. Separate bar. Music.

Club Gascon

A lively sea of surrealist cooking
57 West Smithfield, City, EC1A 9DS
Tel no: (020) 7600 6144
www.clubgascon.com
⊖ Barbican, Farringdon, map 5
Modern French | £60
Cooking score: 6

♦ V

Pascal Aussignac was one of the first chefs to abandon conventional courses and catch the modern mood for eating a multiplicity of small dishes. What he offers is a tasting menu minus the no-choice factor. The initial inspiration is south-west France (from where many high-class ingredients are sourced), but his creations go off on a tangent from there. Aussignac's high-definition collection of little dishes, listed under headings such as 'la route de sel' and 'les paturages', is played out in a softly illuminated, jewel-like room with foie gras at the heart of things – 'superb' duck foie gras 'chocobar' with gingerbread and crazy salt, say. But the kitchen also applies its skills to 'wonderful' sweet-tasting ambre tulip stuffed with a quinoa risotto and served with a smear of truffled pumpkin; and a fine Charolais beef variation (fillet, beef-cheek ravioli, tartare, bone marrow). Wines from the south-western appellations make for fascinating exploration, but the list also reaches out to Provence and Corsica, with big boys from Bordeaux getting in on the act too; bottles from £20.
Chef/s: Pascal Aussignac. **Open:** Mon to Fri L 12 to 2, Mon to Sat D 6.30 to 10 (10.30 Fri and Sat). **Closed:** Sun, 23 Dec to 4 Jan, Easter, bank hols. **Meals:** alc (main courses £10 to £26). Set L and D £25 (2 courses) to £60. 5 courses with wine £90. **Details:** 42 seats. Separate bar. Wheelchair access. Music.

The Coach & Horses

British pub grub with a swagger
26-28 Ray Street, Clerkenwell, EC1R 3DJ
Tel no: (020) 7278 8990
www.thecoachandhorses.com
⊖ Farringdon, map 5
Modern British | £24
Cooking score: 2

£5 OFF £30

A Victorian tavern that has held on to most of its period character, the Coach & Horses remains a 'proper' pub thanks to owner Giles Webster's attention to detail and respect for the past. The River Fleet runs by: underground these days, so dipping toes is off the agenda. Both beer and food are given equal weight. There are bar snacks such as biltong and shepherd's pie croquettes to keep you going; alternatively, head through to the dining area for some classy food that brings both British and European flavours to the table. Salmon is cured in Sipsmith gin in a starter that fits the bill to a T, followed by chicken liver with sage, brown butter and pappardelle, or a nifty fish and chips made with coley and a Portobello Ale batter. Desserts take a similarly Pan-European approach, with good old bread-and-butter pudding made with panettone and Marsala. Wines start at £16.75.
Chef/s: Leigh Norton. **Open:** Mon to Fri L 12 to 3, D 6 to 10. **Closed:** Sat, Sun, 24 Dec to 3 Jan. **Meals:** alc (main courses £10 to £23). Set L £10. **Details:** 72 seats. 50 seats outside. Separate bar. Music.

¶¶♦ Please send us your feedback

To register your opinion about any restaurant listed in the Guide, or a new restaurant that you wish to bring to our attention, please visit the web address at the bottom of the page. Your feedback informs the content of the book and will be used to compile next year's reviews.

Comptoir Gascon
Welcoming bistro-deli, simple Gascon cooking
61-63 Charterhouse Street, Clerkenwell, EC1M 6HJ
Tel no: (020) 7608 0851
www.comptoirgascon.com
⊖ Farringdon, Barbican, map 5
French | £30
Cooking score: 4

'Sometimes there's nothing I want more than a really hearty slap-up meal and a glass or three to boot . . . this is just the place to be when in that mood.' So ran the notes of one seasoned reporter who went on to enjoy a deeply flavoured leek and potato soup and a rich cassoulet toulousain 'packed with sausage, white beans and other meats'. An offshoot of Pascal Aussignac and Vincent Labeyrie's nearby Club Gascon (see entry), this welcoming bistro-deli is a smart-casual place with a short repertoire specialising in the victuals of south-west France. It may do a roaring trade with its duck burger (add foie gras for a luxury take) and double-cooked, duck-fat chips ('an event in themselves'), but grilled squid in rich bisque, and ox cheeks pot-au-feu are worthy alternatives. Apple croustade with Armagnac and cinnamon ice cream makes a good finish. The proudly Gascon wine list starts at £17.
Chef/s: Jeremy Evans. **Open:** Tue to Sat L 12 to 2.30, D 6.30 to 10. **Closed:** Sun, Mon, 29 Dec to 5 Jan, Easter, bank hols. **Meals:** alc (main courses £10 to £15). Set L £15 (2 courses). **Details:** 55 seats. 8 seats outside. Wheelchair access. Music.

Coq d'Argent
City slicker with spectacular views
1 Poultry, City, EC2R 8EJ
Tel no: (020) 7395 5000
www.coqdargent.co.uk
⊖ Bank, map 2
Modern French | £41
Cooking score: 2

V

Nothing screams 'summer in the city' more than Coq d'Argent's seductive garden terrace: a top-of-the-world rallying point for the City's sharp suits in holiday mode. Whether you're admiring the panoramic vistas or sitting pretty in the smart, airy dining room, you can look forward to generous servings of bourgeois Gallic food *comme il faut* – from hand-cut beef tartare and garlicky escargots to thyme-roasted turbot on the bone with lemon butter, or beef fillet with asparagus, salsify, baby onions and watercress aïoli. Oysters, plateaux de fruits de mer, high-protein grills and desserts such as Paris-Brest with praline cream also feature, not forgetting caviar for the City bonuses brigade. If you're not in that league, make a beeline for the more affordable fixed-price menu, and bypass the bottles of Louis Roederer Cristal in favour of something more modest from the gargantuan all-encompassing wine list. Wine from £21.50.
Chef/s: Mickael Weiss. **Open:** Mon to Sun L 11.30 to 3 (12 to 3.45 Sat, 12 Sun), D 5.30 to 10. **Meals:** alc (main courses £25 to £38). Set L £26 (2 courses) to £29. Set D £29. Sun L £26 (2 courses) to £29. **Details:** 150 seats. 200 seats outside. Separate bar. Wheelchair access. Music.

Diciannove
Convivial City Italian
Crowne Plaza Hotel, 19 New Bridge Street, City, EC4V 6DB
Tel no: (020) 7438 8052
www.diciannove19.com
⊖ Blackfriars, map 5
Italian | £35
Cooking score: 2

🛏

The bright-yellow colour scheme brings a shot of Mediterranean sunshine to the concrete canyons of the City, as the Crowne Plaza's Italian eatery piles on the style. You can sit in booths, up at the counter, at dinky tables for two or share one of the big round communal tables – and the experience is uniformly pleasing. A traditionally constructed menu opens with antipasti such as grilled aubergine in tomato, basil and chilli, or pancetta-crumbed scallops with butternut purée, before gliding on through the risottos and pastas (ravioli filled with luganica sausage, scattered with toasted pine nuts and sage, is a hot bet), to the mains. Robust fish dishes (grilled swordfish, monkfish in artichoke, chickpea and tomato stew) alternate with satisfying meats like rolled lamb loin with roasted fennel and zucchini. The signature desserts are amarena cherries served warm with pistachios and ricotta, and dense-textured chocolate mousse. Wines start at £21. **Chef/s:** Alessandro Bay. **Open:** Mon to Fri 12 to 10.30. Sat D only 6 to 10. **Closed:** Sun. **Meals:** alc (main courses £18 to £26). Set D £25 (3 courses) to £65 (6 courses). **Details:** 100 seats. Separate bar. Wheelchair access. Music.

Dishoom

Buzzy all-day Bombay café
7 Boundary Street, Shoreditch, E2 7JE
Tel no: (020) 7420 9324
www.dishoom.com
⊖ Old Street, Liverpool Street, map 2
Indian | £20
Cooking score: 2
£30

The second branch of the 'Bombay café' concept, Shoreditch's Dishoom has proved even more of a hit than the Covent Garden original (see entry). The 'startlingly good value' eatery obviously speaks to the hip young locals. Even those who find the vintage artefacts and industrial chic somewhat laboured concede that the 'lively' cavernous space works. More importantly, so does the food. The all-day menu, in sub-sections such as 'Frankies' (filled naans), 'Ruby Murray' and 'Small Plates', announces dishes both familiar and quirky. Chilli cheese toast, roomali roti bread and 'bhel' (a 'moreish mix' of puffed rice, pomegranate, tomato and tamarind) are Bombay standards and favourites here, too. Crisp Gujarati samosas, chicken tikka and the 'classic warming dish' of Kacchi lamb and rice also get great feedback. Dishes arrive when ready, which, at inspection, meant before the drinks. Sip lassis, coolers or chai for the full experience. Wine from £20.

Chef/s: Naved Nasir. **Open:** all week 8 to 11 (12 Thur to Sat). **Closed:** 25 and 26 Dec, 1 and 2 Jan. **Meals:** alc (main courses £6 to £22). Set L and D £20 (2 courses) to £35. **Details:** 230 seats. 30 seats outside. Separate bar. Wheelchair access. Music.

The Don

Fine wines and enterprising cooking
The Courtyard, 20 St Swithin's Lane, City,
EC4N 8AD
Tel no: (020) 7626 2606
www.thedonrestaurant.co.uk
⊖ Bank, Cannon Street, map 2
Modern European | £37
Cooking score: 2
£5 OFF

A sacred spot for port and sherry buffs, The Don is comfortably established in Sandeman's old offices. There's a cellar bistro and a second restaurant (the Sign of the Don) next door, but the main dining room, splashed with John Hoyland abstracts, has a sense of order that makes for an unflashy City experience. To start, beef consommé, salty and restorative, is poured over shreds of brisket, tiny alphabet pasta and a few perfectly fresh herbs. There's a modish (more modish than the doily under the soup, anyway) wafer of salmon skin in full sail on the subtly smoked mash that comes with butter-soft poached salmon, dollhouse pieces of bacon, kale and snails; it's harmonious without being dull. Desserts are heavily Frenchified, with a flawless passion fruit soufflé inspiring confidence in the rest. As you'd expect, the wine list is full of characterful twists, with port, sherry and larger formats bolstering choice, from £22. **Chef/s:** James Walker. **Open:** Mon to Fri L 12 to 2.30, D 6 to 10.30. **Closed:** Sat, Sun, 23 Dec to 4 Jan, bank hols. **Meals:** alc (main courses £17 to £32). Set D £30. **Details:** 90 seats.

Duck & Waffle
High-flyer with a bird's-eye view of the City
Heron Tower, 40th floor, 110 Bishopsgate, City,
EC2N 4AY
Tel no: (020) 3640 7310
www.duckandwaffle.com
⊖ Liverpool Street, map 2
International | £46
Cooking score: 3

Understandably, the highest restaurant in the UK is 'made by the view', which makes the next-door Gherkin seem cocktail-sized by comparison. But the 'local suits and gastro-tourists' who ascend to the Heron Tower's 40th floor are also drawn by the buzzy atmosphere and 24-hour opening. Taken at 3am with the city spread like a quilt below, a spicy ox cheek doughnut with apricot jam is just the tonic for any jaded Londoner. Juggling small plates and bigger sharing dishes for the table brings indulgence in a variety of forms: foie gras crème brûlée with buttered lobster or smoked chilli pig's cheeks with cheesy polenta and fried pickles, perhaps, followed by the signature waffle topped with duck confit, fried duck egg and mustard maple syrup. Oysters and shellfish from the raw bar are an option for the clean-living, though puddings such as brownie sundae with peanut crunch revert to type. Wine from £29.
Chef/s: Daniel Doherty. **Open:** all week 24-hour opening. **Meals:** alc (small plates £9 to £16, 'for the table' £14 to £36). **Details:** 100 seats. Separate bar. Wheelchair access. Music.

The Eagle
The pub that launched 1,000 imitations
159 Farringdon Road, Clerkenwell, EC1R 3AL
Tel no: (020) 7837 1353
⊖ Farringdon, map 5
Modern European | £16
Cooking score: 2

£30

'One on every street please', was the 1992 Guide's comment on first including this mould-breaking pub, which virtually defined the new 'gastropub' genre when it opened.

Nowadays, proprietor Michael Belben proudly describes the Eagle as 'the pub that launched 1,000 imitations (at least)'. It continues to thrive on that bare-bones look, space is still fought over by drinkers and diners, but the robust British-Mediterranean cooking is interesting and the prices are always fair. The concise list of stand-alone dishes is chalked up over the bar, where you order and pay, and might include smoked haddock and clam chowder; braised whole partridge with borlotti beans, pancetta and sage; or onglet steak (served rare) with roast potato, beetroot, watercress and horseradish. Steak sandwich is never off the menu, nor are pasteis de nata, which along with a cake – say chocolate and walnut – could provide a sweet finish. Wines from £14.70.
Chef/s: Ed Mottershaw. **Open:** all week L 12 to 3 (3.30 Sat, 4 Sun), Mon to Sat D 6.30 to 10.30. **Closed:** 1 week Christmas, bank hols. **Meals:** alc (main meals £6 to £17). **Details:** 65 seats. 24 seats outside. Music.

NEW ENTRY
8 Hoxton Square
Impressive newcomer in hipsterland
8-9 Hoxton Square, Hoxton, N1 6NU
Tel no: (020) 7729 4232
www.8hoxtonsquare.com
⊖ Old Street, map 2
Modern European | £30
Cooking score: 4

With this new venture in the hipster heartland of Hoxton Square, the brains behind 10 Greek Street (see entry) have followed the same imaginative naming tradition. Inside, all is sleek and modish: blackboards mounted on whitewashed walls; beards and tattoos on the staff. Look past the faux-industrial clichés to the kitchen, however, and there's the same studied craft that has earned the Soho sister legions of fans. A starter might be as subtle and satisfying as prawns with chorizo and aïoli, or a cockle-warming nettle, leek and potato soup. Mains are as spirited as they are diverse: taking inspiration from the Veneto in a tender cuttlefish swimming in risotto nero; or from rainy valleys closer to home in the form of Welsh Black beef with duck-fat potatoes, kale and horseradish. Puds are splendidly good fun – pistachio and rice crema catalana begs for a thwack of a spoon. Fairly priced wines start at £15.

Chef/s: Cameron Emirali. **Open:** all week L 12 to 3 (1 Sat, 1 to 4 Sun), Mon to Sat D 6 to 10.30. **Closed:** bank hols. **Meals:** alc (main courses £12 to £19). **Details:** 57 seats. 12 seats outside. Music.

Eyre Brothers

Gutsy Iberian cooking
68-70 Leonard Street, Shoreditch, EC2A 4QX
Tel no: (020) 7613 5346
www.eyrebrothers.co.uk
⊖ **Old Street, map 2**
Spanish-Portuguese | £37
Cooking score: 4

'Whatever you do, have the pork,' advises one reader, a happy beneficiary of Eyre Brothers' way with acorn-fed Ibérico pig. This sleek (one reporter thinks 'slightly dated') Shoreditch restaurant brings together the culinary tics of Spain and Portugal, representing them with humble Portuguese soup, Galician-style octopus and piquillo peppers stuffed with salt cod to start, then a no-messing clam and pork cataplana to share afterwards. That grilled pork, best medium-rare, comes marinated with pimentón, thyme and garlic and served with crisp oven potatoes. Shetland cod gets the Iberian treatment with a tomato, black olive and caper sauce and fried Padrón peppers. It's gutsy stuff, tempered by a calm approach to service and, perhaps, the smooth sweetness of poached quinces or a custard tart or two. Refer to the map in the wine list for a brush-up on Iberian vineyard regions before making your choice, from £19.

Chef/s: David Eyre and João Cleto. **Open:** Mon to Fri L 12 to 2.30, Mon to Sat D 6 to 10.30 (7 Sat). **Closed:** Sun, 25 Dec to 1 Jan, bank hols. **Meals:** alc (main courses £12 to £24). **Details:** 85 seats. Separate bar. Wheelchair access. Music.

Fifteen London

Modern British revamp from brand Jamie
15 Westland Place, Shoreditch, N1 7LP
Tel no: (020) 3375 1515
www.fifteen.net
⊖ **Old Street, map 2**
British | £45
Cooking score: 3
£5 OFF

It doesn't seem 12 years since Jamie Oliver's not-for-profit philanthropic venture opened on this two-storey site in Shoreditch, and yet *tempus fugit*. Over that time, Fifteen has launched the careers of many previously disadvantaged young people, unleashing their creativity in ways that chime harmoniously with the youthful London mood. Generously loaded sharing plates of British modernism pour forth from Jon Rotheram's busy kitchen, into the laid-back basement. The menu changes daily, and may feature braised cuttlefish with sea beets, fennel and saffron aïoli; smoked ricotta pizza with baby chard and black olives; grilled hake with cockles, peas and trendy Tokyo turnips; or pig's cheek with Pentland Dell potatoes, cucumber and sea trout caviar. It's vigorous, brightly seasoned fare, all the way to sides of Jersey Royals with truffled Cheddar, and finishers such as pear and Prosecco jelly with shortbread. The ground-floor bar is a jumping joint, where cocktails, quality beers and wines (from £21) pack them in.

Chef/s: Jon Rotheram. **Open:** all week L 12 to 3, D 6 to 11 (10 Sun). **Closed:** 25 and 26 Dec, 1 Jan. **Meals:** alc (main courses £17 to £32). **Details:** 110 seats. Separate bar. Wheelchair access. Music.

Galvin Café à Vin

Good-value Galvin offshoot
35 Spital Square, Spitalfields, E1 6DY
Tel no: (020) 7299 0404
www.galvinrestaurants.com
⊖ **Liverpool Street, map 2**
French | £30
Cooking score: 3

It may be bijou compared to the stately
grandeur of Galvin La Chapelle next door (see
entry), but this cheery eatery is Gallic to the
core. It's a good-looker, too, with its classic
livery, painted mirrors, parquet floors, smart
wooden furniture and long metal bar running
the length of the room. A pianist plays two
nights a week. The venue's winning charms are
backed by some honest, good-value food
straight from the bistro mould: pear,
Roquefort and endive salad with walnuts;
tarte flambée from the wood-fired oven; roast
rabbit leg with Savoy cabbage and mustard
sauce; Shorthorn bavette with braised beef
hash and red wine jus. Occasionally the
kitchen goes off-piste, serving Saddleback
pork burgers with black pudding and apple
sauce, but it's back to France for tarte Tatin and
rum baba. All-day nibbles go well with a glass
or pichet from the astutely assembled French-
led wine list. Bottles from £18.50.
Chef/s: Jack Boast. **Open:** all week 11.30 to 10.30
(9.30pm Sun). **Closed:** 24 to 26 Dec, 1 Jan.
Meals: alc (main courses £14 to £19). Set L and
early D £20. Sun L £17 (2 courses) to £20.
Details: 65 seats. 80 seats outside. Separate bar.
Wheelchair access. Music.

Galvin La Chapelle

Head-turning French class
35 Spital Square, Spitalfields, E1 6DY
Tel no: (020) 7299 0400
www.galvinrestaurants.com
⊖ **Liverpool Street, map 2**
Modern French | £49
Cooking score: 6
🍾

Standing firm against the muscular warehouse
look that passes for décor in many a
Spitalfields restaurant, this listed Victorian
school hall cuts quite a dash with its high-
vaulted ceiling, dramatic stone arches and
spectacular mezzanine. Regulars love the
conversational mood of the place and the
solicitous staff – although coming here is
mainly about the food (and wine). Jeff Galvin's
pedigree is a given, and he proves his mettle
with subtle invention as well as absolutely
precise technique and timing. A rich and
indulgent lasagne of Dorset crab piles on the
luxury with a beurre nantaise; breast of red-
legged partridge comes with macerated
kumquats, redcurrant salad and truffle
dressing; and fillet of sea bream is assigned
black rice, brown shrimps, parsley and
horseradish. For dessert, few can resist the
classic apple tarte Tatin. The wine list has a
heavy price tag, but is a glittering array,
starting with a prolonged exploration of
France, which naturally includes rarities from
La Chapelle – the jewel of Maison Jaboulet in
the Rhône Valley. House selections start
at £24.50.
Chef/s: Jeff Galvin and Eric Jolibois. **Open:** all week
L 12 to 2.30 (3 Sun), D 6 to 10.30 (9.30 Sun). **Closed:**
25 and 26 Dec, 1 Jan. **Meals:** alc (main courses £23
to £34). Set L and early D £24 (2 courses) to £29.
Sun L £29. Tasting menu £70 (7 courses).
Details: 110 seats. 16 seats outside. Wheelchair
access.

LOCAL GEM
▲ GB Pizza Co
50 Exmouth Market, Farringdon, EC1R 4QE
Tel no: (020) 7278 6252
www.greatbritishpizza.com
⊖ Farringdon, map 5
Italian | £15

Everyone has a good word to say about GB Pizza in Margate (see entry, Kent); indeed, some reckon there's no place like it. Still, it's quite a coup to open a branch in Exmouth Market. This is a smarter version of the older sibling, incorporating a pared-back interior and the same vigorously championed British produce. You can expect the trademark wood-fired, thin-crust pizzas: from 'margate-rita' to specials of beef pepperoni with red onions and mushrooms. Margate's much-loved chocolate brownies and Gelupo ice creams are also here, along with some London-brewed ales, and organic house wine from £13. Open all week.

NEW ENTRY
Granger & Co.
Lovely, zingy cross-cultural cooking
50 Sekforde Street, Clerkenwell, EC1R 0HA
Tel no: (020) 7251 9032
www.grangerandco.com
⊖ Farringdon, map 5
Australian | £30
Cooking score: 2

It's a glossier version of the Westbourne Grove original (see entry), housed more commodiously in a spacious, light-filled upper-ground-floor dining room on the edge of Clerkenwell Green. What is constant, though, is the level of informality and the cross-cultural cooking of Aussie chef Bill Granger. You can't book, and good-value prices draw a lively young crowd – but no queues (yet), perhaps because reporters feel the place is still finding its feet in such sleek surroundings. Nevertheless, the food certainly packs a punch. This is casual all-day dining at its very best: from breakfast bowls of brown rice and sweet miso porridge with dairy-free yoghurt and mango ('ruined me for oatmeal

porridge forever'), and those famous ricotta hot cakes, via pizzas, salads, sandwiches and burgers, to sticky chilli pork belly or the crab, chorizo and house kim-chee fried brown rice that was the undoubted highlight at inspection. Wine from £19.50.
Chef/s: Tom Cajone. **Open:** Mon to Sat 8am to 11pm (9am Sat). Sun 10 to 6. **Meals:** alc (main courses £13 to £23). **Details:** 92 seats.

The Gun
Docklands socialising and robust food
27 Coldharbour, Canary Wharf, E14 9NS
Tel no: (020) 7515 5222
www.thegundocklands.com
⊖ Canary Wharf, map 1
Modern British | £35
Cooking score: 1

Found at the end of a well-heeled residential cul-de-sac, this white-painted early 18th-century hostelry (announced by a pub sign punctured by a big bullet hole) doesn't look large enough to house its warren-like collection of rooms and truly glorious river-facing terrace. But the Gun is a real crowd puller, popular not only for its tried-and-trusted bar food (black pudding Scotch egg, fish finger sandwich, beef-shin burger), but also for the smart restaurant menu that mixes influences in true modern-British style: say smoked trout and mussel rillettes; then herb-crusted cod with peas, broad beans, smoked bacon and pearl onions; with a passion-fruit posset to finish. Wines from £19.
Chef/s: Quinton Bennett. **Open:** all week L 12 to 3 (4 Sat and Sun), D 6 to 10.30 (6.30 to 9.30 Sun). **Closed:** 25 and 26 Dec. **Meals:** alc (main courses £15 to £32). **Details:** 70 seats. 40 seats outside. Separate bar. Wheelchair access. Music. No children in the bar after 8.

🍴 Average Price
The average price listed in main-entry reviews denotes the price of a three-course meal, without wine.

Hawksmoor Guildhall
A sizzling advert for British beef
10-12 Basinghall Street, City, EC2V 5BQ
Tel no: (020) 7397 8120
www.thehawksmoor.com
⊖ Bank, map 2
British | £45
Cooking score: 4

Many list this City offshoot of Will Beckett and Huw Gott's Hawksmoor group as their favourite, citing the rich wood and leather sheen of the low-ceilinged basement dining room, the first-class service and the invariably thunderous babble from satisfied diners. This 'modern-day meat shrine' may deliver starters of smoked salmon, Brixham crab or shrimps on toast, even a main course of char-grilled monkfish (all satisfying) – but really, eat the beef, for that's what it's all about. Whether you're sharing a massive porterhouse or chateaubriand, or going solo and tucking into a fillet, ribeye or sirloin, you'll experience that peerless combination of perfectly charred outside with succulent red inside. Reporters praise the choice of sauces, the creamed spinach (a classic American steakhouse side) and the triple-cooked chips. Finish with pear Bakewell tart, think about returning to try 'divine' weekday breakfasts and brace yourself for the bill – it doesn't come cheap. Wines from £21.
Chef/s: Richard Turner and Richard Sandiford. **Open:** Mon to Fri L 12 to 3, D 5 to 10.30. **Closed:** Sat, Sun, 19 Dec to 2 Jan, bank hols. **Meals:** alc (main courses £13 to £50). Set early D £23 (2 courses) to £26. **Details:** 160 seats. Separate bar. Wheelchair access. Music.

Hawksmoor Spitalfields
Prime British steakhouse
157a Commercial Street, City, E1 6BJ
Tel no: (020) 7247 7392
www.thehawksmoor.co.uk
⊖ Liverpool Street, Aldgate East, map 2
British | £45
Cooking score: 3

When it comes to prime protein, the Hawksmoor group (see entries: four in total) is a prime mover, dealing in quality British beef cooked over charcoal with minimum faffing about. The meat isn't cheap, but it is very good. This Spitalfields original branch set the tone, with acres of dark wood (tables, chairs, floors) giving the impression of a brooding brasserie. So, to the beef. Sourced from British herds like Yorkshire Longhorn, the cuts range from T-bone to fillet, via bone-in prime rib. The flavours speak for themselves. Carbohydrate comes as extras – triple-cooked chips and macaroni cheese – with starters running to Brixham crab on toast and puds to banana and bourbon tart. The express menu (lunch and early evening) is a good bet and the Sunday roast very nearly steals the show. A basement bar serves nifty cocktails. Hawksmoor's wine list (from £19), like its menu, is big on the red stuff.
Chef/s: Richard Turner and Paul O'Dowd. **Open:** all week L 12 to 2.30 (4.30 Sun), Mon to Sat D 5 to 10.30. **Closed:** 24 to 27 Dec, 1 Jan. **Meals:** alc (main courses £13 to £50). Set L and D £23 (2 courses) to £26. Sun L £20. **Details:** 116 seats. Separate bar. Wheelchair access. Music.

Hix Oyster & Chop House
A personal take on British ingredients
35-37 Greenhill Rents, Cowcross Street,
Clerkenwell, EC1M 6BN
Tel no: (020) 7017 1930
www.hixoysterandchophouse.co.uk
⊖ Farringdon, map 5
British | £45
Cooking score: 3

V

This Smithfield operation, the first of Mark
Hix's expanding collection of restaurants,
gives equal billing – as the name suggests – to
steak and oysters. The day's oyster specials
(River Fal natives, Porthilly rocks, etc) and the
presentation of the day's meat cuts are a major
part of the experience. The contemporary art-
hung, white-tiled brasserie wouldn't be what
it is, however, without the creative flair of
Mark Hix, a long-time champion of foraged,
forgotten foods. Alas, at inspection, a dish of
Herefordshire snails with whipped cauliflower
and ramsons that should have been the
standout arrived barely warm. Simpler plates
such as Webster's fish fingers and char-grilled
halibut with rich béarnaise were, by
comparison, stronger. Nutty 'shipwrecked
tart' made a generously boozy finish. Hix
opens through the day and is ideal for long,
late lunches as second (third and fourth)
bottles are ordered from the predominantly
Old World list, which starts at £18.75.
Chef/s: Jamie Guy. **Open:** Mon to Fri and Sun L 12 to
4.30, all week D 5 to 11 (10 Sun). **Closed:** 25 and 26
Dec. **Meals:** alc (main courses £17 to £37). Set L £20
(2 courses) to £25. Sun L £28. **Details:** 65 seats. 6
seats outside. Music.

HKK London
Chinese cooking doesn't get any better
Broadgate West, Worship Street, City, EC2A 2BF
Tel no: (0203) 535 1888
www.hkklondon.com
⊖ Liverpool Street, map 2
Chinese | £45
Cooking score: 6

V

It's an odd place, a ground-floor space in an
anonymous office block not far from
Liverpool Street station with bland décor: so
unlike HKK's opulent Hakkasan cousins (see
entries). The more arresting visual flourishes
are in chef Tong Chee Hwee's dishes – his
cooking revealing London's need for more
establishments that give Chinese food the kind
of treatment that French, Italian, Japanese,
even Indian, routinely receive. For this is
Chinese cooking with a difference, not a twist,
and with a modern, Western perspective.
Some reporters have been confused by 'the
context of eating Cantonese food as if it were
French', but then confess 'the Peking duck was
the best I've ever tasted – otherworldly.' Other
wondrous constructions include the star-of-
the-show dim sum trilogy, exquisite char-
grilled Chilean sea bass, and the jasmine-tea
smoked Wagyu beef. After that, for sheer
occidental indulgence, finish with almond
brûlée tart with wine-poached plum. Prices
are high, but go for lunch and there are set-
price options. Wines start at £29.
Chef/s: Tong Chee Hwee. **Open:** Mon to Sat L 12 to
2.30, D 6 to 9.45. **Closed:** Sun, 25 Dec, bank hols.
Meals: alc (main courses £14 to £38). Set L £28.50
(4 courses), £42 (5 courses) to £48 (8 courses).
Tasting menu £95 (15 courses). **Details:** 72 seats.
Separate bar. Wheelchair access. Music.

Lardo

Hip-yet-homely pizzeria
205 Richmond Road, Hackney, E8 3NJ
Tel no: (020) 8985 2683
www.lardo.co.uk
⊖ **Hackney Central, map 1**
Italian | £30
Cooking score: 2

One of the first on the scene that's now developing around Hackney's London Fields, Lardo is a hip eatery in a converted factory. Its forte is pizza, which is consistently good: both the black anise and pepperoni version, and the egg, spinach and lardo (cured back fat) version really work. The menu also pulls in bright seasonal ideas from across Italy, such as nettle tagliatelle, mushrooms and Taleggio; lamb sweetbreads with parsley and St George's mushrooms; and pistachio cannoli. The restaurant's own artisan charcuterie and a small selection of Italian cheeses open up snacking possibilities well suited to Lardo's all-day opening. Brunch and Sunday roasts are now served at the weekend. Nifty cocktails such as the 'Boozy Chinotto' and 'Amaretto Sour' both feature homemade liquor, and Italophile drinkers get the lion's share of the wine list, too (from £20). It changes completely twice-yearly, favouring northern wines in the winter, southern in the summer.
Chef/s: Damian Currie. **Open:** all week 12 to 11 (10pm Sun). **Closed:** 24 to 26 Dec, 1 Jan. **Meals:** alc (main courses £8 to £16). **Details:** 60 seats. 40 seats outside. Wheelchair access. Music.

Lutyens

Classy, confident Conran classic
85 Fleet Street, City, EC4Y 1AE
Tel no: (020) 7583 8385
www.lutyens-restaurant.com
⊖ **Chancery Lane, St Paul's, Temple, map 5**
Anglo-European | £45
Cooking score: 4

Designed by Sir Edwin Lutyens and once home to the London outpost of Reuters, this City megalith is now part of the Conran empire: a slab of patrician Edwardian grandeur transmuted into a salubrious bar, restaurant and members' club. Inside, the vast all-white space has 'thundering noise-bounce', smartly clothed tables and supremely professional, regimented staff contributing to a classy, confident, worldly-wise set-up. Conran's DNA is everywhere, and the menu is a showcase for first-rate produce – think zingy salmon tartare from the 'raw bar', Lincolnshire smoked eel with celeriac and apple or Cornish lamb with salt-baked beetroot and anchovy. Dover sole tops the popularity stakes, and a plate of 55-day aged Middle White pork with sauerkraut and heritage carrots has yielded some 'mind-blowing' meat, including silky pink loin and a crackled tranche of belly ('pure porcine goo'). French aristocrats dominate the illustrious, high-spend wine list, although entry-level selections (from £26) are German.
Chef/s: Henrik Ritzen. **Open:** Mon to Fri L 12 to 3, D 6 to 10. **Closed:** Sat, Sun, Christmas, New Year, bank hols. **Meals:** alc (main courses £16 to £36). Set L and D £22 (2 courses) to £26. **Details:** 130 seats. Wheelchair access. Music.

NEW ENTRY
Mayfields

Wild ambition in a petite package
52 Wilton Way, Hackney, E8 1BG
Tel no: (020) 7254 8311
www.mayfieldswiltonway.co.uk
⊖ **Hackney Central, map 1**
Modern European | £35
Cooking score: 3
🍾

The spirit of Parisian hipster bistros comes to Hackney in the form of Formica-tabled, timber-walled, very tiny Mayfields. From a sliver of a kitchen, chef Matthew Young (ex Wapping Food) proffers a daily 'small plates' menu that goes in (occasionally wild) jags from Italy to Asia. Dishes vary not only in culinary derivation but also complexity; some are simple assemblies, others are staggeringly 'haute'. How well the sharing plates concept works is debatable, though, as the likes of salt-cod brandade with its tangle of monk's beard on toast; lemon sole, lemon butter, daikon and liquorice; and lamb's leg with green tomato, anchovy and dandelion are dishes for hogging, not splitting. Likewise, dark chocolate mousse served – spoiler alert – warm with kaffir lime ice cream. The taut list of intriguing organic and biodynamic wines is a collaboration with Borough Wines; all come by the glass from £4.25, bottle £22.

Chef/s: Matthew Young. **Open:** Fri and Sat L 12 to 3, Mon to Sat D 6 to 10.30. **Closed:** Sun. **Meals:** alc (main courses £5 to £16). **Details:** 34 seats. 8 seats outside. Wheelchair access.

LOCAL GEM
▲ Mehek
45 London Wall, Moorgate, EC2M 5TE
Tel no: (020) 7588 5043
www.mehek.co.uk
⊖ Moorgate, Liverpool Street, map 2
Indian | £24 £5 off

The name means 'fragrance' and this lavish pan-Indian restaurant on historic London Wall continues to live up to its translation, with aromatic dishes and well-defined spicing. Popular with City suits, the eye-catching Bollywood film set-inspired interior sets the scene for regional specialities including Bay of Bengal king prawns in 'royal' sauce; Goan fish curry; and a piquant Hyderabadi duck marinated in coconut, peanuts, sesame seeds and mustard. Finish with an Indian ice cream. Wines from £18.50. Open Mon to Fri.

NEW ENTRY
Merchants Tavern
A grown-up restaurant of serious intent
36 Charlotte Road, Shoreditch, EC2A 3PG
Tel no: (020) 7060 5335
www.merchantstavern.co.uk
⊖ Old Street, map 2
Modern European | £45
Cooking score: 5

It's a sign of how much Shoreditch has changed that what was Cantaloupe – a mid-90s hot spot – is now a grown-up restaurant of serious intent. This collaboration between

Angela Hartnett and the founders of the Canteen chain fills the cavernous brick space with the sound of an inter-generational crowd having a terrific time. The bar (where you can eat well on charcuterie and snacks) is abuzz, as is the open kitchen where chef Neil Borthwick toils, head down, throughout service. Take a cue from him: ignore the din and focus on the plate. Start, perhaps, with a plump ham raviolo in a puddle of deliciously oily-salty Parmesan and chicken broth, the soft meat contrasting with mustardy greens. Next might be brill with creamy toasted almond milk, broccoli and caper raisin purée: vivid flavours in comfort mode. Overwhelmingly chocolatey Mont Blanc concluded an otherwise successful test meal. European wines from £24.

Chef/s: Neil Borthwick. **Open:** Tue to Sat L 12 to 3, D 6 to 11. Sun 12 to 9. **Closed:** Mon, 25 and 26 Dec. **Meals:** alc (main courses £16 to £25). Set L £18 (2 courses) to £22. **Details:** 65 seats. Separate bar. Wheelchair access. Music.

The Modern Pantry
Flexible fusion in Clerkenwell
47-48 St John's Square, Clerkenwell, EC1V 4JJ
Tel no: (020) 7553 9210
www.themodernpantry.co.uk
⊖ Farringdon, map 5
Fusion | £35
Cooking score: 3
🍷

Take one desirable Georgian town house, divide it up into a cluster of spaces for eating, drinking and socialising, call on the services of fusion queen bee Anna Hansen MBE and, *voilà*, you have the Modern Pantry. The interior is an exercise in restrained minimalism, and the food challenges all those crossover clichés with delicate, surprising and cohesive flavours garnered from the world larder. Mingle with the creatives over breakfast in the cramped street-level café, or take a global trip through the main menu upstairs: from the now-legendary sugar-cured Caledonian prawn omelette with smoked chilli sambal, to pineapple tarte Tatin with

miso and tamarind caramel, turmeric-yoghurt sorbet and pineapple sherbet. Dig deeper into Hansen's box of tricks and you might also find great plates of slow-roast Gloucester Old Spot pork belly with chorizo grits, kale and green pepper relish. Organic tipples (from £20) lead the charge on the joyfully freewheeling, agreeably priced global wine list.
Chef/s: Anna Hansen. **Open:** Mon to Fri 8am to 10.30pm (10pm Mon). Sat 9 to 4, 6 to 10.30. Sun 10 to 4, 6 to 10. **Closed:** 25 and 26 Dec, Aug bank hol. **Meals:** alc (main courses £16 to £22). Set weekday L £22 (2 courses). Sun L £27. **Details:** 100 seats. 36 seats outside. Music.

Morito

Tiptop tapas
32 Exmouth Market, Clerkenwell, EC1R 4QE
Tel no: (020) 7278 7007
www.morito.co.uk
Ө Farringdon, map 2
Tapas | £20
Cooking score: 4
£30

It's plain, bare and cramped. Staff squeeze you in where they can – stools at the bar are popular as you can watch the chefs at work – and they don't take bookings in the evening (you're safe at lunch). Yet young urbanites flood in to Morito to devour its simple, pared-back modern tapas. Seasonal, unfussy offerings lay bare the credentials of big brother Moro (next door, see entry), and everything is suited to shared-plate dining. There's tenderness in spiced lamb with aubergine, yoghurt and pine nuts; freshness in the blood-orange, olive and pistachio salad; and tenderness and freshness in scallops with slow-cooked cauliflower, barberries and saffron. Tapas classics have a place, too – salt cod croquetas, patatas bravas or cocido (chorizo, jamón and chickpea stew) – although tortilla might be given a spring reboot with wild garlic. Finish with crema catalana. The concise, all-Spanish wine list (from £18) includes many sherries.

Chef/s: Samuel and Samantha Clark. **Open:** all week L 12 to 4, Mon to Sat D 5 to 11. **Closed:** 23 Dec to 3 Jan, bank hols. **Meals:** alc (tapas £3 to £9). **Details:** 35 seats. 10 seats outside. Wheelchair access. Music.

Moro

Good-time vibes and earthy Moorish food
34-36 Exmouth Market, Clerkenwell, EC1R 4QE
Tel no: (020) 7833 8336
www.moro.co.uk
Ө Farringdon, map 2
Spanish-North African | £35
Cooking score: 4

Fashions have come and gone since 1997, but Moro's regulars' appetite for the likes of char-grilled lamb with green-tomato bulgur, and yoghurt cake with pistachios and pomegranate, seems undiminished. Sam and Sam Clark's Exmouth Market stalwart has changed little over the years. Join the Sadler's Wells set here after a performance, or pop in for patatas bravas or Syrian lentils at the bar, and you'll discover the dining room (now somewhat weathered, admittedly) as exuberant as ever. Feedback from readers hasn't been uniformly brilliant; heavy-handed seasoning and a poor-quality finish let the side down sometimes, but when on the ball, Moro's powerful Moorish cuisine can floor you. Spiced labneh with tomatoes, broad beans and anchovies, and char-grilled mackerel with chermoula, red peppers and black olive sauce are characteristically punchy. The all-Iberian wine list (from £19) is usefully annotated, making the 'interesting gems' all the more accessible.
Chef/s: Samuel and Samantha Clark. **Open:** all week L 12 to 2.30 (12.30 to 2.45 Sun), Mon to Sat D 6 to 10.30. **Closed:** 23 Dec to 3 Jan, bank hols. **Meals:** alc (main courses £17 to £21). **Details:** 90 seats. Separate bar. Wheelchair access.

Perkin Reveller

Tipples and tuck by the Tower
East Gate, Tower of London, St Katherine's Way,
Tower Hill, EC3N 4AB
Tel no: (020) 3166 6949
www.perkinreveller.co.uk
⊖ Tower Hill, map 1
British | £30
Cooking score: 2

£5
OFF

Perkin the Reveller popped up in the Cook's story of *The Canterbury Tales*: rather apt, given this rollicking restaurant, bar and terrace is pitched close to touristy Tower Wharf (a building project overseen by Chaucer in his role as 'clerk of the king's works'). Banqueting-style tables, earthenware beer jugs and 'ye olde' artefacts set the scene for trencherman British tuck and tipples. Determined gluttons can gorge on well-rendered plates of Trealy Farm cured meats, Cornish fish stew or pork belly with cabbage, bacon, apple and ginger purée – although the kitchen ups the ante by gilding its ham hock and duck terrine with jellied beetroot, and embellishing venison cottage pie with truffled potato foam. To finish, apple crumble and steamed orange sponge joust with the likes of peanut parfait and caramel ice cream. Quaffable booze in the twin bars ranges from gins and punch bowls to vintage cocktails and wines (from £17).
Chef/s: Andrew Donovan. **Open:** all week L 11.30 to 3.30 (5 Sun), Mon to Sat D 5.30 to 10.30. **Closed:** 24 to 26 Dec. **Meals:** alc (main courses £14 to £28). Set L £17 (2 courses) to £20. Set D £30 (2 courses) to £35. Sun L £15. **Details:** 120 seats. 80 seats outside. Separate bar. Wheelchair access. Music.

Symbols

🛏 Accommodation is available

£30 Three courses for less than £30

V Separate vegetarian menu

£5
OFF £5-off voucher scheme

🍾 Notable wine list

LOCAL GEM

▲ Pizza East

56 Shoreditch High Street, Shoreditch, E1 6JJ
Tel no: (020) 3310 2000
www.pizzaeast.com
⊖ Liverpool Street, Old Street, map 2
Italian-American | £25

It's hard to miss the Tea Building, which houses Pizza East on its ground floor (the vast warehouse has the word 'TEA' on the roof in giant letters). The industrial vibe matches the casual mood of other branches (see entries in Portobello and Kentish Town). Pizzas are cooked in a wood-fired oven and topped with the likes of heirloom tomatoes, caprino fresco cheese and wild garlic. Mac 'n' cheese and short rib of beef are offered, too, plus wines from £20. Open all week.

NEW ENTRY

Plateau

Modern dining with high-rise vista
4th Floor, Canada Place, Canary Wharf, E14 5ER
Tel no: (020) 7715 7100
www.plateau-restaurant.co.uk
⊖ Canary Wharf, map 1
Modern European | £38
Cooking score: 4

🍾 V

There's a wow factor in the setting, on the fourth floor of a striking steel and glass building in the heart of Canary Wharf. With its masculine city edge softened by an outdoor terrace, Plateau is a very individual venue. It operates as both a restaurant and a grill (doing mod brasserie-style food), the two areas divided by a semi-open kitchen – and it certainly attracts the local sharp suits (especially at lunch). In the restaurant, Allan Pickett delivers fine-tuned modern cooking underpinned by classical French roots and driven by prime ingredients and seasonality. A test meal opened with Josper-grilled asparagus, neatly teamed with truffled goats' curd, toasted hazelnut and nasturtium leaves. That same light, skilful touch was seen in a main course of fresh halibut accompanied by fashionable kale and lardo, plump cockles, cauliflower, black olives and piquant red pepper, which, like everything else, 'doesn't hold back on flavour'. Wines are a key feature, with superb by-the-glass or bottle choice (from £19.75).

Chef/s: Allan Pickett. **Open:** Mon to Sat L 12 to 3, D 6 to 10.30. **Closed:** Sun, 25 Dec, 1 Jan. **Meals:** alc (main courses £17 to £32). Set L and D £15 (2 courses) to £20. **Details:** 150 seats. 40 seats outside. Separate bar. Wheelchair access. Music. Car parking.

NEW ENTRY
Portal
Architectural gem with sophisticated cooking
88 St John Street, Farringdon, EC1M 4EH
Tel no: (020) 7253 6950
www.portalrestaurant.com
⊖ Farringdon, Barbican, map 5
Portuguese | £35
Cooking score: 2

The green-tiled and black façade of this handsome Portuguese restaurant gives little hint of the architectural gem within. Beyond the stylish bar area, the space widens out to reveal a bare-bricked warehouse conversion, then a breathtaking glass-walled extension, backing on to a compact cobbled courtyard. While the Portuguese influence is evident in a classic fish soup or a main of bacalhau (salt cod), it's more subtle in a starter of plump scallops with a light smattering of farinheira (tangy smoked sausage), or the umami-rich mushroom purée. In keeping with the surroundings, dishes are beautifully presented, ranging from super-minimal – a few gorgeously fatty slices of aged pata negra ham – to full-blown works of art, as with a main of lamb rump, parsnip purée and wild mushrooms. Save room for classic pasteis de nata (custard tarts). The mostly Portuguese wine list (from £22) is a corker and staff are happy to make recommendations.

Chef/s: Vitor Veloso. **Open:** Mon to Fri L 12 to 3, Mon to Sat D 6 to 10.15. **Closed:** Sun. **Meals:** alc (main courses £16 to £25). Set L £23 (2 courses) to £28. **Details:** Separate bar.

Quality Chop House
A Victorian gem reincarnated
94 Farringdon Road, Clerkenwell, EC1R 3EA
Tel no: (020) 7278 1452
www.thequalitychophouse.com
⊖ Farringdon, map 5
British | £35
Cooking score: 3

Opened in 1869 under its present name, around the corner from Exmouth Market, the Chop House is an evocative reminder of Victorian London – only without the street urchins pickpocketing outside. The Grade II-listed dining room is furnished with dark wooden booth seating at tables on wrought-iron legs, with a black-and-white tiled floor. And the cooking comes from heritage Britain too, though with modern presentational standards. A daily changing set-dinner menu opens with an array of bites such as brown crabmeat on toast, pork rillettes with pickles, Galloway beef with onion, and a bowl of peas with lemon and horseradish, before the main spread arrives: perhaps Somerset kid with kale, pink fir potatoes in nettle pesto, and boquerones with courgettes and almonds. Tapas treats head the bar menu, followed by dishes such as monkfish with sea veg, or Middle White pork with mushroom ketchup. Finish with chocolate and raspberry mille-feuille. Wines start at £21.

Chef/s: Shaun Searley. **Open:** all week L 12 to 3 (4 Sun), Mon to Sat D 6 to 10.30. **Meals:** alc (main courses L only £10 to £20). Set D £35. **Details:** 80 seats. 6 seats outside. Separate bar.

LOCAL GEM
▲ Railroad
120-122 Morning Lane, Hackney, E9 6LH
Tel no: (020) 8985 2858
www.railroadhackney.co.uk
⊖ Bethnal Green, map 1
Global | £25

A cramped Hackney café with communal tables and a pocket-sized open kitchen, Railroad is a relaxed daytime hangout serving delicious cakes, good coffee and daily changing light lunches such as aromatic duck with broth, purple sprouting broccoli, walnuts and jasmine rice. From Wednesday to Saturday, it is transformed into an atmospheric dinner venue with bold, international dishes such as lamb kofte, raw beetroot and almond salad; and chicken haleem with naan bread and radish. Wines from £16. Closed Mon and Tue.

St John

Nose-to-tail pioneer
26 St John Street, Clerkenwell, EC1M 4AY
Tel no: (020) 7251 0848
www.stjohngroup.uk.com
⊖ Farringdon, map 5
British | £40
Cooking score: 5

Honesty is the clarion call at St John: a defunct Smithfield smokehouse reinvented as the spiritual home of 'nose-to-tail' eating. The notion of serving reinvented poorhouse victuals, butcher's offcuts and pickings from almost-forgotten regional curiosities was revolutionary in the 1990s. These days it's *de rigueur* for self-respecting chefs to show some familiarity with bone marrow, ducks' hearts and pig's ears – probably with dandelion leaves or alexanders on the side. What sets this place apart from its imitators is an unswerving devotion to provenance, blood-and-guts freshness and flavour; the devil is in the detail (or the uncompromising lack of it). Ignore the rather clinical, pared-backed interiors and get stuck into plates of rabbit offal with green beans and pickled walnut, calf's liver and beetroot, or roast suckling kid with carrots and wild garlic, followed by freshly baked madeleines or Eccles cake with Lancashire cheese. Wines (from £24) look to France for inspiration.
Chef/s: Chris Gillard. **Open:** Sun to Fri L 12 to 3 (1 to 3 Sun), Mon to Sat D 6 to 11. **Closed:** 23 Dec to 2 Jan, bank hols. **Meals:** alc (main courses £14 to £29). **Details:** 110 seats. Separate bar.

St John Bread & Wine

The chilled out younger sibling of St John
94-96 Commercial Street, Spitalfields, E1 6LZ
Tel no: (020) 3301 8069
www.stjohngroup.uk.com
⊖ Liverpool Street, map 2
British | £35
Cooking score: 3

Like its big brother in Clerkenwell (see entry), St John Bread & Wine has a love of nose-to-tail dining and a horror of unnecessary garnishes. This City-fringes venue is a simple, minimalistic affair, the square room featuring whitewashed walls and wooden tables that are quickly filled, producing a buzzy atmosphere. Informative, attentive staff can explain how each robust, plain dish is cooked, and they deliver them without fanfare. Both menu and daily specials are devised for sharing, with many dishes demonstrating Fergus Henderson's love of less popular cuts of meat: kidney or chitterlings, for instance. Small dishes include medium-rare quail, or delectably fatty bone marrow on toast with a tangy parsley salad. Ox tongue with Jersey Royals or pigeon cooked rare might be among the larger plates. Desserts are typically British; the warm ginger loaf with butterscotch sauce proved a hit at inspection. Wine (from £21) consists of a well-considered selection of French favourites.
Chef/s: Tristram Bowden. **Open:** all week 9am to 11pm (9pm Sun). **Closed:** 25 and 26 Dec, 1 Jan. **Meals:** alc (main courses £13 to £25). **Details:** 56 seats.

LOCAL GEM
▲ Salvation Jane

Unit 2, 1 Oliver's Yard, 55 City Road, Shoreditch, EC1Y 1HQ
Tel no: (020) 7253 5273
www.salvationjanecafe.co.uk
⊖ Old Street, map 2
Australian | £20

This Shoreditch offshoot of the popular Lantana Café in Fitzrovia (see entry) delivers the same Aussie-flavoured breakfast/brunch, superb coffee, great service and no-booking policy as its big brother. What sets the place apart is the more spacious feel and the evening opening, when crowds pile in for smoked tomato and roasted red onion risotto or beef brisket open sandwich on caraway rye with pickled slaw and mustard aïoli, and the fabulous double chocolate brownie. Wines from £18. Open all week.

Sushi Tetsu

Supreme Tokyo-style sushi
12 Jerusalem Passage, Clerkenwell, EC1V 4JP
Tel no: (020) 3217 0090
www.sushitetsu.co.uk
⊖ Farringdon, map 5
Japanese | £30
Cooking score: 4

Secreted in a Clerkenwell backwater, Sushi Tetsu consists of just seven seats and a wooden counter that requires the full attention of Kobe-trained master Toru Takahashi. Eating sushi in London doesn't come any more exclusive, and it's arguably the nearest thing to Tokyo legends such as Sukiyabashi Jiro. It pays to pre-order the full omakase experience: a two-hour show that allows Toru to show off his knife skills and talent for hand-moulding clumps of just-warm seasonal rice. Everything hinges on meticulous sourcing, supreme freshness and scalpel-sharp precision, whether the subject is mackerel, turbot, baby shrimp, snow crab or one of many cuts of tuna. And then there are the details: home-pickled ginger, exemplary soy, real Japanese (and English) wasabi grated to order, tiny squares of sweet omelette signalling the final act, and totally beguiling service. Tea, beer and saké are proffered for refreshment. The only downside is snagging a seat: the phones are jammed on the first Monday morning of each month when reservations are released.
Chef/s: Toru Takahashi. **Open:** Tue to Fri L 11.45 to 2 (last sitting 12), Tue to Sat D 5 to 9.30 (last sitting 7.30). **Closed:** Sun, Mon. **Meals:** Sushi from £3.60 (1 piece), sashimi from £9 (3 pieces). Sashimi set £18 to £45. Sushi set £26 to £46. Omakase £60 to £80. **Details:** 7 seats.

Sushisamba

Mixing Japanese and South American cuisines
Heron Tower, 110 Bishopsgate, City, EC2N 4AY
Tel no: (020) 3640 7330
www.sushisamba.com
⊖ Liverpool Street, map 2
Japanese-South American | £75
Cooking score: 1
V

At 38 floors up, everyone loves the view here and the oh-so-cool bar and terrace. But they come, too, for a kitchen that takes South American influences and blends them nicely with more traditional Japanese ideas. Stars of the show are undoubtedly black cod miso, Wagyu gyoza and the tempura prawns, though there's also excellent lemon sole with fennel, celery, Peruvian salad, and orange, chilli and honey-orange ponzu. Come here, too, for nigiri and sashimi, and finish in style with the stunning red chocolate chilli dessert. Creative cocktails and an extensive selection of saké add extra pep to the global wine list. Bottles from £30.
Chef/s: Cláudio Cardoso. **Open:** all week 11.30am to 1am (midnight Sun and Mon). **Meals:** alc (main courses £16 to £49). **Details:** 124 seats. 54 seats outside. Separate bar. Wheelchair access. Music.

Tayyabs

Rollicking Punjabi canteen with wicked spicing
83-89 Fieldgate Street, Whitechapel, E1 1JU
Tel no: (020) 7247 6400/9543
www.tayyabs.co.uk
⊖ Whitechapel, Aldgate East, map 1
Pakistani | £20
Cooking score: 2
V £30

Opened in 1972, Mohamed Tayyab's seminal Whitechapel restaurant remains one of the capital's foremost specialists when it comes to Punjabi and Pakistani-style grilled meat. 'The minted lamb chops are still the best in London' noted one visitor, who also enthused about the 'magnificent' naan breads. Other options include chef's specialities such as the punchy karahi mutton tikka masala or chicken biryani, but there is more to Tayyabs than hunks of grilled meat and poultry. A range of interesting and well-priced vegetarian dishes includes dhal baingun with lentils and baby aubergines; and methi aloo gajar with fenugreek, potato and carrot. Although you can book online now, queuing for food at this canteen-style restaurant is part of the experience, as is the occasionally brusque service and tightly packed tables. It's all balanced by the reasonable prices and the fact you can BYO booze without a corkage fee, which keeps bills low. **Chef/s:** Wasim Tayyab. **Open:** all week 12 to 11.30. **Meals:** alc (main courses £6 to £12). **Details:** 400 seats. Music.

LOCAL GEM
▲ Towpath Café
42 De Beauvoir Crescent, Dalston, N1 5SB
www.towpathcafe.wordpress.com
⊖ Old Street, map 2
Modern European | £20

The setting is as pastoral as a London restaurant can get: right on the Regent's Canal with boats, ducks, cyclists, walkers and dogs passing all day. Lori de Mori and Jason Lowe's all-day café is at its best when the sun shines (little is under cover), but is always good for morning coffee and things on toast. Enticing, seasonally inspired daily lunch specials could bring glorious asparagus with ajo blanco, rump of lamb with white sprouting broccoli and anchovy butter, and wine from £21.50. Open Tue to Sun, Mar to Oct only. Cash only.

▲ Tramontana Brindisa
152 Curtain Road, Shoreditch, EC2A 3AT
Tel no: (020) 7749 9961
www.brindisa.com
⊖ Old Street, map 2
Spanish | £20

There's a strong Spanish atmosphere, all-day opening and an unerring authenticity to the kitchen's tapas output at Brindisa's Shoreditch branch. Flavours ring true thanks to impeccable sourcing from the home country:

Ibérico de Bellota ham, chorizo riojano, single-estate bomba and carnaroli rice, goats' and sheep's milk cheeses – the list goes on. Otherwise there could be pork shoulder loin with flambé orange and raisin, gambas à la plancha, Galician-style octopus and crema catalana. The all-Spanish wine list opens at £18.50. Open all week.

Les Trois Garçons
High camp and vigorous French cooking
1 Club Row, Shoreditch, E1 6JX
Tel no: (020) 7613 1924
www.lestroisgarcons.com
⊖ Liverpool Street, map 2
French | £45
Cooking score: 2

Les Trois Garçons is guaranteed to leave a lasting impression on anyone who ventures across its threshold. A cane-wielding crocodile; Bambi wearing a bejewelled choker; a bulldog with butterfly wings – welcome to a riotous high-camp extravaganza within the audaciously transmogrified shell of a former Shoreditch boozer. It's a hard act to follow, but the kitchen has its moments: witness Szechuan-cured tuna with baby gem, wasabi crisps and a slow-poached egg yolk; or pork belly and fillet with runner beans, amaranth, gluten-free celeriac gnocchi, ginger and honey sauce. The cooking is notionally French, incorporating signature plates of foie gras cured in Sauternes or organic salmon with spinach, salsify and Champagne butter sauce. Desserts fly the tricolour, with quince tarte Tatin and mulled wine sorbet or crème brûlée accompanied by milk jam doughnuts. Fine cheeses from Androuet are a constant temptation, and the wine list flaunts its French credentials, with bottles from £26. **Chef/s:** Michael Chan. **Open:** Wed and Fri L 12 to 2, Mon to Sat D 6 to 9.30 (10.30 Fri and Sat). **Closed:** Sun, 22 Dec to 5 Jan, bank hols. **Meals:** alc (main courses £17 to £33). Set L £18 (2 courses) to £22. Tasting menu £66 (6 courses). **Details:** 65 seats. Music.

28°-50°
Dedicated to the fruit of the vine
140 Fetter Lane, City, EC4A 1BT
Tel no: (020) 7242 8877
www.2850.co.uk
⊖ Chancery Lane, map 5
French | £40
Cooking score: 3
🍾

The original branch of the 28-50 group is a stolid, woody, brick-walled room consecrated to the enjoyment of wine – as studiously or hedonistically as you prefer. There's some food too, mostly French-influenced bistro stuff such as goose and mustard terrine, onglet with béarnaise, steaming main-course bowls of mussels in shallots, fennel, garlic and lemon, and gooseberry crème brûlée. Venturing beyond may take you to the wilder shores of gravadlax, butternut risotto, or perhaps a hefty Cheddar burger. There's also a condensed menu for bar dining, but the focus is on wine. It isn't necessarily the most extensive selection, but there is intelligent choosing written all over it. Lallier's rosé Champagne, Boeckel Pinot Gris from Alsace, Jura Savagnin, Xinomavro from Greece's Naoussa region, von Kesselstatt's Riesling Spätlese are just some of the alternatives to the beaten path, and the digestifs are great, too. Prices open at £21, or £3.90 for the smaller glass.
Chef/s: Imran Rafi. **Open:** Mon to Fri L 12 to 2.30, D 6 to 9.30. **Closed:** Sat, Sun, bank hols. **Meals:** alc (main courses £14 to £19). Set L £16 (2 courses) to £19. **Details:** 60 seats. Separate bar.

NEW ENTRY
Typing Room
A new star in the East
Patriot Square, Town Hall Hotel, Bethnal Green, E2 9NF
Tel no: (020) 7871 0461
www.typingroom.com
⊖ Bethnal Green, map 1
Modern British | £43
Cooking score: 5

Nuno Mendes' departure for Chiltern Firehouse (see entry) left big shoes to fill at Bethnal Green's Town Hall Hotel, but Jason Atherton protégé Lee Westcott is the man to fill them. Westcott's Typing Room took over the Viajante space in May 2014, bringing marble-topped tables, Scandinavian-style chairs and an informal vibe fostered by rock soundtrack, open kitchen and chipper staff. All very hip, but also inclusive, matching Westcott's style. Witness brill with heritage tomato, courgette and squid, or lamb with blackened aubergine emulsion, wild garlic and onions (two early fixtures on both carte and six-course tasting menu): 'safe' pairings, certainly, but executed with visual flair and great technique. The yoghurt accompaniment with suckling pork belly, peach and (underpowered) mustard was a rare example of one too many items on the plate. To finish, an artful array of chocolate, almond and Amaretto textures was delightful. The wine list (from £23) revels in English and biodynamic finds.
Chef/s: Lee Westcott. **Open:** Wed to Sun L 12 to 2.30 (3.30 Sun), Wed to Sat D 6 to 10.30. **Closed:** Mon, Tue. **Meals:** alc (main courses £22 to £26). Tasting menu (6 courses) £55. **Details:** 36 seats. Separate bar. Wheelchair access. Music.

Upstairs at the Ten Bells
Uber-cool Spitalfields hangout
84 Commercial Street, Spitalfields, E1 6LY
Tel no: (07530) 492986
www.tenbells.com
⊖ Liverpool Street, Aldgate East, map 2
Modern British | £32
Cooking score: 4

Timeworn original features rub shoulders with striking modern artworks to generate a perfect storm of shabby-chicery at this joint above a pub that has associations with the Ripper murders – they say Mary Kelly worked the street outside. The easy-going staff keep everything chilled, and the kitchen, headed by Giorgio Ravelli, takes inspiration from some of the culinary world's leading lights (we're talking about Brett Graham and René Redzepi here). Lunch is a shorter express job to suit local workers, with the full-on menu firing up in the evening. Expect bang-on flavours, exciting combinations and first-rate British ingredients. Start with 'snacks' such as buttermilk fried chicken before ravioli rich with fallow deer, plus broad beans and mousserons, and lamb's rolled breast and sweetbreads with 'sandy' carrots. The kitchen's good sense and acute skills continue into a dessert of gloriously caramelised pineapple with goats' milk rice pudding and wicked Madras sorbet. Clever stuff. Wines from £19.
Chef/s: Giorgio Ravelli. **Open:** Tue to Sun L 12 to 2.30 (4 Sun), Tue to Sat D 6 to 10.30. **Closed:** Mon. **Meals:** alc (main courses £16 to £18). Set L £17 (2 courses) to £21. **Details:** 44 seats.

Vinoteca
Mediterranean flavours and interesting tipples
7 St John Street, Farringdon, EC1M 4AA
Tel no: (020) 7253 8786
www.vinoteca.co.uk
⊖ Farringdon, Barbican, map 5
Modern European | £29
Cooking score: 2

🍾 £30

With its good-time mix of buzz, bonhomie and fairly priced food and drink, Vinoteca goes about its business with gusto, proud of its wares. The open-to-view kitchen keeps up, as the close-packed tables are constantly turned. Indeed, there's something reassuring about the simple, well-prepared food with its penchant for strong European flavours and a keen eye for the seasons. And with nothing incidental on the daily changing menu, no after-thoughts, everything is geared towards satisfaction. The plates of Spanish cured meats and the British cheeses from Neal's Yard Dairy have always been popular, but other hits have included game terrine with pickles and wholegrain mustard, grilled poussin with roast sweet potato, coriander and a guindilla chilli sauce, and a straightforward rare bavette steak with porcini butter, chips and horseradish. On the wine front, the owners stay on top of emerging trends and offer exemplary choice by the glass. Bottles from £15.75.
Chef/s: Will Robertson. **Open:** Mon to Sat L 12 to 2.45 (4 Sat), D 5.45 to 10. **Closed:** Sun. **Meals:** alc (main courses £10 to £18). **Details:** 35 seats. Music.

A. Wong

Chinese good fortune in Victoria
70-71 Wilton Road, Victoria, SW1V 1DE
Tel no: (020) 7828 8931
www.awong.co.uk
⊖ Victoria, map 3
Chinese | £35
Cooking score: 4
£5 OFF

'You know when you're looking forward to a restaurant and it's just not as good as you were hoping? Very unusually, this is better.' Like a benevolent fortune cookie deposited in the Victoria hinterlands, A. Wong promises Chinese surprises in a modest package – in this case a minimalist, open-plan dining room with polished floors, gleaming copper lights and a visible kitchen. Andrew Wong has cooking in his blood (the premises were once his parents' restaurant) and aims to please foodies as well as locals with a blend of high-street staples and big-league small plates. There are thrills aplenty on the 10-course tasting menu: delights such as Shanghai steamed dumplings with ginger-infused vinegar, Xinjiang barbecued lamb with cumin, chilli and pomegranate salad or 'white-cut' chicken dressed with peanuts, 'gong bao' sauce and Szechuan aubergine – all artily presented on wood, stone or porcelain platters. The lunchtime dim sum menu is full of sparky new-wave crackers such as quail's egg croquettes, dry-braised tiger prawns or 25-second aerated sponge cake. Wines from £15.
Chef/s: Andrew Wong. **Open:** Tue to Sat L 12 to 2.30, Mon to Sat D 5.30 to 10.30. **Closed:** Sun, 23 Dec to 3 Jan. **Meals:** alc (main courses £8 to £23). Set L and D £13. Tasting menu £45 (10 courses). **Details:** 70 seats. 12 seats outside. Separate bar. Wheelchair access. Music.

The Anchor & Hope

Hearty stuff from a foodie boozer
36 The Cut, South Bank, SE1 8LP
Tel no: (020) 7928 9898
www.anchorandhopepub.co.uk
⊖ Waterloo, Southwark, map 5
British | £27
Cooking score: 3
£30

A firm favourite of Waterloo's theatre-going contingent, the Anchor & Hope is a serious contender fashioned from a workaday pub. The house style is, shall we say, unpolished: a characteristic that defines the haphazard service and bohemian (bordering on basic) interior as well as the cooking. The kitchen takes a 'flavour first' approach, so if the food seems almost defiantly unpretty (Longhorn ragù and gnocchi, we're looking at you), it will still taste terrific. This is 'modern British' of the 'gastropub' old-school, meaning immaculate ingredients, particularly fish and meat – perhaps whole crab with mayonnaise and Middle White porchetta and Jersey Royals – plus a few stray dishes from France and Italy. The menu, changing twice daily, cleverly intuits what you want, be it globe artichoke vinaigrette in early summer or choucroute in winter. European wines from £16, pints of bitter and cocktails at pub prices keep things lively. No reservations.
Chef/s: Jonathan Jones. **Open:** Tue to Sat L 12 to 2.30, Sun L 2 (1 sitting), Mon to Sat D 6 to 10.30. **Closed:** Christmas through New Year, bank hols. **Meals:** alc (main courses £11 to £25). Set L £15 (2 courses) to £17. Sun L £32. **Details:** 40 seats. 30 seats outside. Separate bar. Wheelchair access. Music.

Angels and Gypsies
Take a pew for saintly tapas
33 Camberwell Church Street, Camberwell,
SE5 8TR
Tel no: (020) 7703 5984
www.angelsandgypsies.com
map 1
Spanish | £22
Cooking score: 2
£30

Holy moly! It's tapas with an authentic flavour in a room done out with stained glass depicting – you guessed it – angels and gypsies, plus churchy arches, old chapel chairs and moody lighting. If the place sounds a bit 'theme park', fear not: it has rough urban edges and a cool attitude. The menu matches quality UK produce with some *excelente* Spanish imports such as jamón, lomo and salchichón. Dishes cover all bases from Galicia to the Med. Sourdough bread is made in-house, and there's plenty of old favourites to choose from, but the kitchen also turns out the likes of fennel salad with feta and pomegranate, or Sephardic-style albondigas with apricots and chickpeas. Hand-carved meats are a good bet, though everything else from salt-cod tortilla to slow-cooked ox cheek also hits the spot. Drink manzanilla or splash out on cocktails; house Spanish wine starts at £18. There's breakfast, brunch and lunchtime burritos, too. **Chef/s:** Mel Raido. **Open:** all week L 12 to 3 (3.30 Sat, 4 Sun), D 6 to 10.30 (11 Fri and Sat). **Closed:** 25 to 27 Dec, 1 and 2 Jan. **Meals:** alc (tapas £4 to £13). Set L £12 (2 courses) to £15. Set D £15 (2 courses) to £18. **Details:** 45 seats. Separate bar. Music.

LOCAL GEM
▲ L'Auberge
22 Upper Richmond Road, Putney, SW15 2RX
Tel no: (020) 8874 3593
www.ardillys.com
⊖ East Putney, map 3
French | £30

French-owned and family-run, Pascal Ardilly's small neighbourhood bistro is loved by Putney locals. It reminds regulars and first-time visitors just how satisfying genuine Gallic cooking can be. Nostalgic Francophiles are well served by familiar classics of snails and mushrooms baked in creamy garlic and white wine sauce, or ribeye steak in green peppercorn sauce. Finish with pear poached in red wine and blackcurrants. Midweek fixed-price menus are good value at £18 for three courses. Wines from £15.95. Tue to Sat D only.

▲ Augustine Kitchen
63 Battersea Bridge Road, Battersea, SW11 3AU
Tel no: (020) 7978 7085
www.augustine-kitchen.co.uk
map 3
French | £26 £5 OFF

This relaxed French eatery is ideal for a bit of midweek comfort food and a nice glass of wine. Beyond the slightly Spartan interiors are hospitable staff and a chef who cannot do enough to please his diners. Star dishes include a starter of bone marrow with shallot and anchovy crust, and delicately smoked fera fish with crème fraîche. Hearty mains follow: slow-cooked pork shank, a 28-day entrecôte steak, or rack of lamb with gratin dauphinois to share. Wines from £18. Closed D Sun and all Mon.

Babur
Classy surrounds, creative cooking
119 Brockley Rise, Forest Hill, SE23 1JP
Tel no: (020) 8291 2400
www.babur.info
map 1
Indian | £26
Cooking score: 2
£5 OFF £30

One of south-east London's most enduringly popular restaurants, this 30-year-old veteran is a smart, professionally run outfit. Against a backdrop of exposed brick, stone, glass and wood veneers, customers can sample skilfully rendered modern Subcontinental cooking. The fusion of old and new in some creations has considerable appeal. Scallops aromatised with ginger, garlic and crushed spice butter and teamed with roasted cumin and onion

cauliflower purée and cauliflower popcorn is a different way to start. You could follow on with sea bass with pickled vegetables and moilee sauce, pot-roasted mustard rabbit with garlic roti, or a memorable rendition of spice-crusted lamb shoulder served with beetroot khichadi (a yoghurt-based Keralan-style curry). Finish with spiced apricot and fig crumble served with saffron custard. Sunday lunch is a leisurely family buffet, and wines (from £19.25) are well chosen to accompany the spicy food, with excellent by-the-glass recommendations.
Chef/s: Jiwan Lal. **Open:** all week L 12 to 2.30 (4 Sun), D 6 to 11.30. **Closed:** 25 and 26 Dec. **Meals:** alc (main courses £12 to £17). Sun L £13 (buffet). **Details:** 72 seats. Music.

LOCAL GEM
▲ The Begging Bowl
168 Bellenden Road, Peckham, SE15 4BW
Tel no: (020) 7635 2627
www.thebeggingbowl.co.uk
⊖ Peckham Rye, map 1
Thai | £25

It's no reservations at this cheerful Thai eatery, so expect to queue or to wait at a nearby pub. Small plates of flavour-packed street food arrive in no particular order and diners are encouraged to share, tapas-style. Sticky free-range pork belly is worthy of Bangkok's finest vendors, as is the grilled aubergine salad with crispy prawns. Unlimited rice only costs a quid. The laudable wine list has been chosen with spicy food in mind (from £16.90). Closed Sun D and Mon L.

Symbols
🛏 Accommodation is available

£30 Three courses for less than £30

V Separate vegetarian menu

£5 OFF £5-off voucher scheme

🍷 Notable wine list

NEW ENTRY
Bibo
A refreshingly independent Italian local
146 Upper Richmond Road, Putney, SW15 2SW
Tel no: (020) 8780 0592
www.biborestaurant.com
⊖ East Putney, map 3
Italian | £32
Cooking score: 1

'Nice airy space, service is excellent', noted a visitor to this latest opening from Rebecca Mascarenhas (Sonny's Kitchen, Kitchen W8, see entries). Inside, petrol-blue wood panels complement clean white walls and well-spaced tables. The Italian menu kicks off with tempting antipasti such as salted friggitelli (like Spanish pimientos de Padrón), and moreish 'nduja croquettes. Simple but flavoursome pork tortellini primi with sage butter might follow. Mains have a less obvious Mediterranean identity but the lemon sole was buttery-soft, and the pork belly succulent. Bomboloni make the perfect dessert: warm sugared doughnut balls with ample Amalfi lemon curd. The all-Italian wine list opens at £18.
Chef/s: Chris Beverley. **Open:** all week 12 to 11. **Meals:** alc (main courses £13 to £17). **Details:** 70 seats. Separate bar.

Bistro Union
Straight-talking British bistro
40 Abbeville Road, Clapham, SW4 9NG
Tel no: (020) 7042 6400
www.bistrounion.co.uk
⊖ Clapham South, map 3
British | £35
Cooking score: 2

Adam Byatt's second gaff (see entry, Trinity) has quite a swagger with its big windows giving lots of light and street views. Punters lured in to sit at the bar counter or grab a table for the longer haul don't leave disappointed. The big attraction is good-value menus that aim to please all-comers. Alongside trusty, standard British fare – such as mussels cooked in perry; steak, chips and mushroom ketchup; and roast chicken for two with pigs in blankets and bread sauce – the menu strikes at the heart of the modern foodie. This is a kitchen that can turn out duck breast with pickled beetroot and dandelion, and whole grilled lemon sole with monk's beard, chilli and red onion. To finish, expect ale cake with clotted cream and treacle toffee sauce or custard tart with Agen prunes. Book for Sunday supper and BYO (free corkage); otherwise, wines start at £19. **Chef/s:** Karl Goward. **Open:** all week L 12 to 3 (9.30 to 3 Sat and Sun), D 6 to 10 (8 Sun). **Closed:** 24 to 27 Dec, 1 to 2 Jan. **Meals:** alc (main courses £11 to £24). Sunday supper £26. **Details:** 39 seats. 10 seats outside.

Boqueria Tapas
Sparklingly fresh, authentic tapas
192 Acre Lane, Brixton, SW2 5UL
Tel no: (020) 7733 4408
www.boqueriatapas.com
⊖ Clapham North, Brixton, map 3
Spanish | £22
Cooking score: 3
£30

It may look a little sterile at first, with its rows of desk-like tables and worksheet menus in a clinically white room under skylight windows, but once it's filled with drinkers and nibblers, Boqueria is a riot of conviviality. There's private dining in the basement (even though tapas eating seems to chafe at the very concept), and the place has a solid, enthusiastic fanbase. The little bites include *tradicionales* like squid in lemon mayo, Ibérico croquetas and fresh boquerones in vinegar, but there are more speculative creations too, such as beef tenderloin with foie gras and PX on toast, or suckling pig with parsnip, sweet potato crisps, apple sauce and lemon sorbet. Fried milk cubes dusted with cinnamon, or the irresistible triple chocolate tart, fill any remaining gaps. A short Spanish wine list opens at £16 a bottle (£4.50 a glass). There's another branch at 278 Queenstown Road, Battersea SW8 4LT.

Chef/s: Jose Luis Gil. **Open:** Mon to Fri D 5 to 11.30. Sat L 12.30 to 3.30, D 5.30 to 12. Sun 12.30 to 10.30. **Closed:** 25 and 26 Dec. **Meals:** alc (tapas £4 to £9). **Details:** 75 seats. Separate bar. Wheelchair access. Music.

LOCAL GEM
▲ The Brasserie @ the National Maritime Museum
King William Street, Greenwich, SE10 9NF
Tel no: (020) 8305 0445
www.brasseriegreenwich.co.uk
⊖ Cutty Sark, map 1
Modern British | £30

Roaming mariners and museum-goers are well served by this upmarket modern steel, glass and poured-concrete adjunct at the back of the museum. If slightly functional, it's warmed by friendly service and has great alfresco dining potential for sunnier days. Aside from the occasional hiccup, the solid brasserie menu of smoked chicken salad with roasted butternut squash and feta; confit of duck leg on butter-bean cassoulet; or pan-seared cod loin on roasted anya potatoes, chorizo and sun-dried tomatoes is competently delivered. Wine from £18. Closed D Sun, Mon and Tue.

★ TOP 50 PUB ★
NEW ENTRY
Camberwell Arms
Under-the-radar with great potential
65 Camberwell Church Street, Camberwell, SE5 8TR
Tel no: (020) 7358 4364
www.thecamberwellarms.co.uk
map 1
Modern British | £25
Cooking score: 3
£30

'One to watch' seems to be the word on this latest venture from the team behind the Anchor & Hope and Canton Arms (see entries). There's a real buzz to the intimate,

candlelit pub where tables are shared and stools shoehorned in, ready for the onslaught of hungry throngs. Snack on toast spread with pork fat and hot-and-sweet Scotch bonnet before sampling the casual but considered cooking. Diverse influences mean that dishes might include super-sweet Datterini tomatoes and buffalo mozzarella, rich macaroni and meatballs; sweet soused herring; or asparagus with a salad of salmon ceviche and chopped egg. The addition of monk's beard to brill with rich cream sauce, or homemade (from the rooftop smokehouse) cured pig's cheek in quail with braised peas, smacks of commitment to seasonality and quality. For dinner *à deux*, sharing options might include a whole rabbit or char-grilled double pork chop. Wine from £15.
Chef/s: Mike Davies. **Open:** Tue to Sun L 12 to 2.30 (4 Sun), Mon to Sat D 6 to 10. **Closed:** 25 and 26 Dec. **Meals:** alc (main courses £11 to £17). **Details:** 70 seats. Separate bar. Wheelchair access. Music.

Canton Arms
Revitalised local boozer
177 South Lambeth Road, Stockwell, SW8 1XP
Tel no: (020) 7582 8710
www.cantonarms.com
⊖ Stockwell, map 3
Modern British | £25
Cooking score: 1
£30

Like a right and proper pub, bookings are not taken at the Canton Arms, so rock up and be lucky. A corner boozer that has no truck with contemporary design shenanigans, this place is unreconstructed and all the better for it. Betty Stogs on draught, bottles of Newky Brown and a good few whiskies smooth the way on the bar side, while the eating takes place in the diminutive dining room out back. It's Med-focused stuff, hearty and spirited: grilled sardines with tapenade, chopped goat curry or hake with little white beans and aïoli. Wines start at £15.

Chef/s: Trish Hilferty. **Open:** Tue to Sun L 12 to 2.30 (4 Sun), Mon to Sat D 6 to 10. **Closed:** 24 Dec to 2 Jan. **Meals:** alc (main courses £13 to £16). **Details:** 70 seats. Separate bar. Music.

NEW ENTRY
Casse-Croûte
French from beginning to end
109 Bermondsey Street, Bermondsey, SE1 3XB
Tel no: (020) 7407 2140
www.cassecroute.co.uk
⊖ London Bridge, Borough, map 1
French | £27
Cooking score: 4
£30

Sitting in this tiny corner restaurant at one of the cramped, red-checked tables looking at walls covered in paintings and posters, made a trio of diners feel they had been transported to Paris. A feeling reinforced by the young, hospitable French staff and the scrawled blackboard menu of typical brasserie dishes. Pâté de foie de volaille, rognons de veau à la moutarde, and paleron (beef) à la bourguignonne all make appearances. The daily changing menu consists of just three starters, mains and desserts: all refreshingly moderately priced. There are no pretensions or unnecessary garnishes – flavours are direct and enjoyable, whether a classic bouchée à la reine (sweetbreads and mushrooms in a creamy sauce) served in a puff pastry vol-au-vent, or a slow-cooked ('and tender') civet de chevreuil served atop potato purée and cabbage. Desserts? Think Paris-Brest or tarte Tatin. French to the end, the short wine list opens at £19.
Chef/s: Sylvain Soulard. **Open:** Mon to Sat 12 to 10 (9am Sat). Sun 9 to 4. **Closed:** 24 to 28 Dec. **Meals:** alc (main courses £15 to £19). **Details:** 25 seats. 2 seats outside. Music.

Chapters All Day Dining

User-friendly neighbourhood brasserie
43-45 Montpelier Vale, Blackheath, SE3 0TJ
Tel no: (020) 8333 2666
www.chaptersrestaurants.com
map 1
Modern British | £28
Cooking score: 3
£30

Delivering upbeat, user-friendly food right through the day, Chapters also knows how to put on the style. Art Deco mirrors, clean lines, polished surfaces and exposed brickwork scream contemporary brasserie, while the menu proves its point with big flavours and keen prices. Kick-start your day with kippers or pancakes, drop by for some charcuterie and risotto balls at the bar or take a more leisurely stroll through the main menu while gazing out towards the heath from the floor-to-ceiling windows. The Josper grill works its smoky magic on venison burgers, Barnsley chops, spatchcock chicken and ribeye steaks, but the line-up also promises lively plates of slow-roast pork belly with black pudding mash or Loch Duart salmon with couscous, pak choi and saffron sauce. To start, try a warm salad or some grilled sardines; to finish, consider warm treacle tart with quince compote. Wines from £16 (£11.50 a pichet). **Chef/s:** Alex Tyndall. **Open:** all week L 12 to 3, D 6 to 11 (9 Sun). **Closed:** 2 to 4 Jan. **Meals:** alc (main courses £11 to £25). Set L £13 (2 courses) to £15. Set D £15 (2 courses) to £18. **Details:** 100 seats. 20 seats outside. Separate bar. Wheelchair access. Music.

Chez Bruce

Big-hitting neighbourhood star
2 Bellevue Road, Wandsworth, SW17 7EG
Tel no: (020) 8672 0114
www.chezbruce.co.uk
⊖ Balham, map 3
Modern British | £45
Cooking score: 6

Bruce Poole's residency in one of London's most fondly regarded neighbourhood restaurants is nearing 20 years. Fronting Wandsworth Common, it's a supremely relaxing place, the pristine white walls decorated with bold statement artworks. Time has refined the originally earthy French cuisine into something sleeker and more international in outlook, but Poole still believes in strong, forthright flavour over ethereal delicacy. How else to explain a starter that surrounds mackerel with the various pungencies of smoked eel, pickled rhubarb and horseradish? Mains offer calf's tongue and kidney in peppercorn sauce, among the more obvious prime cuts; otherwise, go Moroccan for lamb tagine and kofta with harissa aubergine and coriander-speckled couscous. Expect a little gilding of the lily for a tiramisu finale, with poached pear, salted caramel and amaretti. A regionally exhaustive list of thoroughbred wines provides informed satisfaction at all levels (though glasses, from £4.50, are in small measures). Bottles from £22. **Chef/s:** Matt Christmas. **Open:** all week L 12 to 2.30 (3 Sat and Sun), D 6.30 to 10 (10.30 Fri and Sat, 9.30 Sun). **Closed:** 24 to 26 Dec, 1 Jan. **Meals:** Set L £24 (2 courses) to £34. Set D £35 (2 courses) to £56. **Details:** 90 seats. Wheelchair access. Children at L only.

The Crooked Well

A hunky-dory home from home
16 Grove Lane, Camberwell, SE5 8SY
Tel no: (020) 7252 7798
www.thecrookedwell.com
map 1
Modern British | £30
Cooking score: 3
£5 OFF

Bring a like-minded friend here and you can tuck into rabbit and bacon pie, or roast lamb with spiced aubergine, for the Crooked Well excels at sharing plates. It's an old boozer done up a treat, with a retro vibe that makes you want to hang around all day. Handily, an all-day menu is provided, plus cocktails, and you're welcome just to pop in for a drink. Dishes arrive looking rustically appealing and full of flavour, indicating a steady hand (or two) in the kitchen. Expect modern British food not restricted by international borders, so Roquefort ravioli comes with pear and sweet chilli salsa, and red mullet escabèche with an olive tapenade. To follow, a main-course crisp pork belly arrives with marjoram polenta and butternut squash purée. Among desserts, the hot chocolate pudding with Chantilly and salted-caramel ice cream requires the involvement of a willing accomplice once again. House Spanish is £15.50.
Chef/s: Matt Green-Armytage. **Open:** Tue to Sun L 12.30 to 3 (4 Sun), all week D 6.30 to 10 (10.30 Fri and Sat, 7 to 9 Sun). **Closed:** 24 to 26 Dec. **Meals:** alc (main courses £13 to £19). Set L £10 (2 courses). **Details:** 56 seats. 40 seats outside. Wheelchair access. Music.

The Dairy

Ingredient-driven foodie hot spot
15 The Pavement, Clapham, SW4 0HY
Tel no: (020) 7622 4165
www.the-dairy.co.uk
⊖ Clapham Common, map 3
Modern British | £30
Cooking score: 5
£5 OFF V

With its wood floor, exposed brick, bare tables and neutral tones, the Dairy achieves a stylish informality. It has also become a foodie hot spot, for there's something about Robin Gill's 'beautiful grown-up food'. His flawlessly executed dishes, characterised by powerful British ingredients and an interest in foraging, deliver the finest materials at their seasonal best. The kitchen rolls out a succession of little dishes: venison Scotch egg with Brussels tops and toasted hazelnuts; charred leeks with three-cornered garlic and egg yolk; Cornish wild sea bass with Swiss chard and bonito butter. Short-rib nuggets with leek ketchup has been described as 'a masterclass in simplicity, flavour and plain old-fashioned deep-fried irresistibility'. Malty bread is moreish, salted caramel with biscuits and malted barley ice cream startlingly good – ditto the old-fashioned tin of delights at the end with hibiscus doughnuts, buttery shortbread and tart apple jellies. Good European wines from £21.50.
Chef/s: Robin Gill. **Open:** Wed to Sun L 12 to 2.45 (4 Sun), Tue to Sat D 6 to 10. **Closed:** Mon. **Meals:** alc (small plates £9 to £10). Set weekday L £25. Tasting menu £40 (7 courses). **Details:** 65 seats. 4 seats outside. Separate bar. Music.

Elliot's Café

On-trend foodie canteen
12 Stoney Street, Borough, SE1 9AD
Tel no: (020) 7403 7436
www.elliotscafe.com
⊖ London Bridge, map 1
Modern European | £30
Cooking score: 3

An easy-going eatery opposite Borough
Market, Elliot's Café has heaps of character.
Brick walls, rustic furniture, cheery staff, even
a wood-burner: all encourage a sense of
bonhomie. This helps, as you'll be squeezed in
– but it's the down-to-earth cooking and
seasonal British produce that have locals and
City types competing for space. Asparagus,
crab, wild brown trout and Jersey Royals all
appear the very day you first crave them, but
the kitchen excels at coaxing flavour out of
cheap, unshowy cuts of meat: grilled chicken
hearts with lardo, for instance, or beef shin
ragù with fazzoletti pasta, and a bollito misto
of ox tongue with cotechino (sausage) and
chicken. The cheeseburger (a must-try), squid
ink risotto, and blue cheese soufflé have all
struck a chord with reporters this year, as have
the reasonable food prices. In contrast, entry to
the excellent organic-biodynamic wine list is
a rather steep £28.
Chef/s: Adam Sellar. **Open:** Mon to Sat L 12 to 3 (4
Sat), D 6 to 10. **Closed:** Sun, 25 and 26 Dec, bank
hols. **Meals:** alc (main courses £14 to £30).
Details: 44 seats. 9 seats outside. Music.

Emile's

Long-serving Putney favourite
96-98 Felsham Road, Putney, SW15 1DQ
Tel no: (020) 8789 3323
www.emilesrestaurant.co.uk
⊖ Putney Bridge, map 3
Anglo-French | £30
Cooking score: 1

£5 OFF

Emile's is a neighbourhood joint in a nice
neighbourhood, with prices set to encourage
regular return. It has been run by Emil Fahmy
and chef Andrew Sherlock since 1990. The

dining rooms – two on the ground floor, the
third a moody basement – are smart and
unassuming, while the French/Med menu has
widespread appeal and some intelligent
combinations. A starter of confit sea bass is a
full-flavoured dish with red pepper and green
olive salad, and main courses run to roasted
guinea fowl breast with black pudding and
leek stuffing and a chorizo cream sauce. Wine
starts at £16.50.
Chef/s: Andrew Sherlock. **Open:** Mon to Sat D only
7.30 to 11. **Closed:** Sun, 24 to 30 Dec, 2 Jan, Easter
Sat, bank hols. **Meals:** Set D £26 (2 courses) to £30.
Details: 90 seats. Music.

Enoteca Turi

Italian oenophile heaven
28 Putney High Street, Putney, SW15 1SQ
Tel no: (020) 8785 4449
www.enotecaturi.com
⊖ Putney Bridge, map 3
Italian | £39
Cooking score: 3

The traditions of forthright regional Italian
cooking are alive and well in Giuseppe and
Pamela Turi's pleasant restaurant not far from
Putney Bridge. The kitchen looks to
Piedmont, Puglia and beyond for ideas and
the menu changes twice every season. The
food is colourful, working a classic vein that
brings on salad of slow-cooked rabbit
marinated in olive oil with sage, garlic,
Controne beans and asparagus chicory (a
bitter leafy green). Pasta dishes are well
rendered – crab with spaghettini, garlic, chilli
and samphire, say – and meat dishes are
cleverly handled, perhaps calf's kidney sautéed
with garlic and parsley, spinach and potato
mash. Prune and almond tart and blood-
orange pannacotta are the kinds of desserts to
expect. Wines are a superb collection from all
corners of Italy: a skilful blend of modern
styles and traditional flavours, all thoughtfully
annotated with fascinating tasting notes and
providing an apt complement to the cuisine.
Prices start at £19.50. Details overleaf.

Chef/s: Baldo Amodio. **Open:** Mon to Sat L 12 to 2.30, D 7 to 10.30 (11 Fri and Sat). **Closed:** Sun, 25 and 26 Dec, 1 Jan. **Meals:** alc (main courses £9 to £26). Set L £19 (2 courses) to £22. Set D £29 (2 courses) to £34. **Details:** 85 seats. Wheelchair access.

LOCAL GEM
▲ Entrée
2 Battersea Rise, Battersea, SW11 1ED
Tel no: (020) 7223 5147
www.entreebattersea.co.uk
⊖ Clapham South, map 3
Modern European | £30

A hit with Clapham locals, Entrée strikes a quietly confident note despite an unpromising location at the top of Battersea Rise. Inside, there's a lively ground-floor piano bar – it's the upstairs brasserie that delivers imaginative, European-influenced food. You could take a well-tried route with pork rillettes followed by steak, chips and béarnaise. Otherwise, head off into the world of seared wood pigeon with wild mushroom and butternut squash, and wild bream with cauliflower, parsley pasta and salsify. Wines from £19. Open Tue to Sat D.

The Fox & Grapes
Fancy food in relaxed surroundings
9 Camp Road, Wimbledon, SW19 4UN
Tel no: (020) 8619 1300
www.foxandgrapeswimbledon.co.uk
⊖ Wimbledon, map 1
British | £35
Cooking score: 3

A stone's throw from Wimbledon Common, this lovely wood-framed pub (sister to Fulham's Malt House, see entry) continues to impress. Exercised dogs laze around the sensitively refurbished interior (light and airy, high ceiling, original lead windows and wood panelling) while their owners refuel on impressively rendered pub classics. These might include Jenga-style burger with English mustard mayo and Ogleshield cheese, or a ploughman's with Godminster Cheddar

and terrine – but the real action is in the seasonal menu. Here, typical choices are slow-poached egg with smoked duck breast and sweet, tangy mushroom ketchup; a verdant wild garlic risotto with chanterelles and pecorino; or casserole of mussels with bacon and dark ale, and triple-cooked chips. Finish with a spot-on chocolate marquise with pistachios and frozen cherry yoghurt. Sunday lunches are a firm favourite, with well-sourced roasts made for sharing. The wine list opens at £19, but the pub is also a good spot for a quiet pint.
Chef/s: Andrew Horton-Jones. **Open:** Mon to Sat L 12 to 3, D 6 to 9.30. Sun 12 to 8.30. **Closed:** 25 Dec. **Meals:** alc (main courses £13 to £25). **Details:** 90 seats. Wheelchair access.

Franklins
Trencherman food with patriotic overtones
157 Lordship Lane, East Dulwich, SE22 8HX
Tel no: (020) 8299 9598
www.franklinsrestaurant.com
map 1
British | £30
Cooking score: 2

With a rumbustious, gilt-topped bar out front, a mellow, bare-bones dining room and a terrific farm shop across the road, long-serving Franklins is a thumpingly good local destination offering patriotic food and drinks without frills or furbelows. The kitchen ticks all the boxes for local, seasonal and organic, although it never rams provenance down people's throats. Instead, the menu keeps it short and tight, proffering the likes of cured pork belly with piccalilli or ox heart with radish, capers and frisée ahead of trencherman plates loaded with anything from rabbit, cider, carrots and turnip to whole plaice with chicory, artichokes and olives. For afters, the ghost of Mrs Beeton looms over gentlemanly savouries (Scotch woodcock, black pudding on toast), as well as folksy desserts such as Yorkshire curd tart or rhubarb fool. Sunday lunch is a hit, cocktails are a top shout for the locals and wines start at £16 (£4 a glass).

Chef/s: Ralf Wittig. **Open:** all week 12 to 12 (10am Sat, 10.30pm Sun). **Closed:** 25 and 26 Dec, 1 and 2 Jan. **Meals:** alc (main courses £14 to £22). Set L £14 (2 courses) to £17. Sun L £15. **Details:** 70 seats. 16 seats outside. Separate bar. Wheelchair access. Music.

Harrison's

Easy neighbourhood option
15-19 Bedford Hill, Balham, SW12 9EX
Tel no: (020) 8675 6900
www.harrisonsbalham.co.uk
⊖ Balham, map 3
Modern British | £29
Cooking score: 1
£30 ▼

Utterly at ease with its neighbourhood go-to status, this venture from namesake Sam (with backing from Rick Stein, among others) has broad appeal. The open kitchen, concrete floors, copper lights and comfy banquettes strike a balance between casual and buttoned-up dining. Young professionals sip cocktails in the bar. An inexpensive brasserie menu, generally capably executed, means yesterday's macaroni might be today's fritters with smoked bacon and mustard mayo; or there could be Nashville hot chicken with celeriac and apple slaw alongside more quotidian burgers and steaks. The focus is squarely on having a good time, which Harrison's delivers well. Wines from £18.50.
Chef/s: Mark Baines. **Open:** all week L 12 to 4, D 6 to 10.30 (10 Sun). **Closed:** 24 to 26 Dec. **Meals:** alc (main courses £12 to £23). Set L and D £14 (2 courses) to £17. Sun L £22. **Details:** 90 seats. 12 seats outside. Separate bar. Wheelchair access. Music.

¶¶• Visit us
||• Online
To find out more about
The Good Food Guide, please visit
www.thegoodfoodguide.co.uk

LOCAL GEM
▲ The Hill
89 Royal Hill, Greenwich, SE10 8SE
Tel no: (020) 8691 3626
www.thehillgreenwich.com
⊖ Greenwich, map 1
Mediterranean | £30

An asset to the Greenwich area, the cooking at this restaurant-cum-bar is spot-on for the local crowd. The Hill is a casually garbed, straight-talking kind of place, with a pleasant courtyard for when the sun shines, and a kitchen that mixes Mediterranean and South American influences. A plate of hand-carved Ibérico ham; Ecuadorian ceviche; fresh egg pasta with wild boar ragù; Argentinean fillet steak with peppercorn sauce; paella valenciana; excellent thin-crust pizzas; tiramisu . . . say no more. Wines from £17.50. Open all week.

José

Custom-built for grazing and sipping
104 Bermondsey Street, Bermondsey, SE1 3UB
Tel no: (020) 7403 4902
www.josepizarro.com
⊖ London Bridge, Borough, map 1
Spanish | £20
Cooking score: 3
£30 ▼

All-conquering José Pizarro's dashing tapas and sherry bar is the no-bookings bebé sibling to his big-name restaurant, Pizarro, further down Bermondsey Street (see entry). In true Spanish fashion, it encourages standing up to eat, especially when the place fills up. Fine-looking legs of carefully sourced jamón Ibérico Manuel Maldonado hang from the low ceilings; patterned tiles brighten up exposed brickwork; and a zinc counter separates punters from the modest kitchen with its sizzling plancha grill – in short, the place is custom-built for grazing. Anchor yourself by a sturdy barrel and work your way through little plates of top-drawer tapas – sea bream with morcilla and peppers; chorizo with lentils; pisto with crispy duck egg;

tomato salad with vermouth vinegar – plus inviting one-offs from the daily specials board. 'Seco' and 'dulce' sherries from peerless producers are the sips of choice, although the short wine list has splendid stuff from £19.50 (£5 a glass).

Chef/s: José Pizarro. **Open:** all week 12 to 10.30 (12 to 5.30 Sun). **Closed:** 24 to 26 Dec, 1 Jan. **Meals:** alc (tapas £3 to £10). **Details:** 20 seats. Wheelchair access. Music.

Lamberts

Good-natured local asset
2 Station Parade, Balham High Road, Balham, SW12 9AZ
Tel no: (020) 8675 2233
www.lambertsrestaurant.com
⊖ Balham, map 3
Modern British | £35
Cooking score: 2
£5
OFF

'Seasonal British food' is the mantra at this neighbourhood joint, where produce is king and efforts are made to source from small-scale producers and seek out organic ingredients. There's a contemporary neutrality to the dining room, along with pictures of foodstuffs, a few pavement tables and doors that open up when the sun shines on Balham. In addition to British fare, the menu shows an appreciation of pan-European culinary techniques. A starter of wild rabbit with truffled herb mayonnaise and spring vegetables is a winning combo, followed by Telmara Farm duck breast with a little hotpot made from the leg meat, or herb-crusted hake with creamed leek and wild mushroom cannelloni. Desserts such as custard tart, Earl Grey and nutmeg ice cream also have plenty of flavour. Set lunch and midweek market menus are worthwhile entry points. The wine list has natural options and a varied choice by the glass or carafe; bottles from £18.

Chef/s: Ryan Lowery. **Open:** Tue to Sun L 12.30 to 2.30 (12 to 5 Sun), Tue to Sat D 6 to 10. **Closed:** Mon, 25 and 26 Dec. **Meals:** alc (main courses £17 to £23). Set mid-week D £17 (2 courses) to £20. Sun L £28. **Details:** 53 seats. 8 seats outside. Music.

The Lawn Bistro

A godsend for Wimbledon Village
67 High Street, Wimbledon Village, Wimbledon, SW19 5EE
Tel no: (020) 8947 8278
www.thelawnbistro.co.uk
⊖ Wimbledon, map 3
Modern French | £35
Cooking score: 3
£5
OFF

When it comes to the bistro moniker, the Lawn is definitely at the posher end of the smart-casual spectrum. That goes for the good-looking food, too, which shows a soupçon of refinement. And then there are the prices, which are clearly set for the postcode. That said, Lawn Bistro is much appreciated in an area not over-endowed with free-spirited places that make high-quality food their top priority. A 'working lunch menu' is a low-level entry point; otherwise it's straight to the carte for French-focused cooking with some contemporary touches. A poached duck egg comes in a clever combo with Jerusalem artichoke and pesto purée and a blackcurrant jus, followed by a whopping côte de boeuf to share, or the somewhat lighter pan-fried bream with Roseval potato salad and pomegranate vinaigrette ('a beautiful summer dish'). Finish with a baked Alaska, which is set alight at the table. Wines from £21.

Chef/s: Neal Cooper. **Open:** Tue to Sun L 12 to 2 (2.30 Sat, 3 Sun), Tue to Sat D 6.30 to 10.30. **Closed:** Mon. **Meals:** alc (main courses £14 to £33). Set L £15 (2 courses) to £19. Set D £24 (2 courses) to £28. Sun L £21. **Details:** 70 seats. Separate bar. Wheelchair access. Music.

¶⦿ Please send us your feedback

To register your opinion about any restaurant listed in the Guide, or a new restaurant that you wish to bring to our attention, please visit the web address at the bottom of the page. Your feedback informs the content of the book and will be used to compile next year's reviews.

LOCAL GEM
▲ The Lido Cafe
Brockwell Park, Dulwich Road, Herne Hill,
SE24 0PA
Tel no: (020) 7737 8183
www.thelidocafe.co.uk
⊖ Brixton, map 1
Modern British | £27

An Art Deco gem, Brockwell Lido was built
in 1937 to satisfy the nation's craving for
exercise. The big change these days is the
spruced up café, where swimmers and locals
congregate from breakfast through to dinner.
The Prosecco breakfast probably isn't wise if
you're taking a dip, but it's a winner just the
same. In the evening the lights are dimmed
and the mood softens for potted mackerel and
guinea fowl braised in red wine. Wines from
£18.50. Closed D Mon, Tue and Sun.

▲ Lobster Pot
3 Kennington Lane, Elephant and Castle, SE11 4RG
Tel no: (020) 7582 5556
www.lobsterpotrestaurant.co.uk
⊖ Kennington, map 1
Seafood | £50

With a wooden ship's cabin evoking the
Brittany seaside, seagull soundtrack,
waitresses dressed like ship's stewards and a
moustachioed chef/patron (Hervé) straight
out of *Asterix*, this local legend has sailed
through 20-odd years in business. It's
tremendous fun to don a bib and crack claws:
whether super-fresh langoustines with
homemade mayo or Scottish lobster. More
innovative dishes include monkfish cheeks in
cider and orange, while seafood platters are
available for a *grande bouffe*. House wine is
£19.50. Closed Sun and Mon. Next door is
sister venue Toulouse Lautrec, a bar/brasserie
with live music.

Lola Rojo
Creative contemporary tapas
78 Northcote Road, Battersea, SW11 6QL
Tel no: (020) 7350 2262
www.lolarojo.net
⊖ Clapham South, map 3
Spanish | £25
Cooking score: 2
£30

Lolo Roja is an exponent of modern tapas and
is furnished with white walls and splashes of
brilliant red from chairs, woodwork and
artworks (that must be Lola looking sultry).
The modernity is revealed in combinations
such as confit of suckling pig with vanilla and
apple purée, or broken duck eggs with confit
potatoes and wild mushrooms, but there are
classic options too. With both restaurant and
deli to supply, the owners source products
from Spain and the authenticity of the output
is palpable. White anchovies come with a
salmorejo dressing (a puréed tomato and bread
number), while cured meats include Iberian
chorizo and jamón from Guijuelo in the
Salamanca region. There's a paella to share
(minimum two people), and, when it comes to
desserts, the creativity continues with an
intriguing combo of bread, chocolate, olive
oil and salt. Drink sherry or regional wines
from £18.
Chef/s: Antonio Belles. Open: Mon to Thur D only 6
to 10.30. Fri to Sun 12 to 10.30. Closed: 25 and 26
Dec. Meals: alc (tapas £6 to £13). Sun L £16.
Details: 50 seats. 17 seats outside.

NEW ENTRY
London House
Glam Ramsay venue
7-9 Battersea Square, Battersea, SW11 3RA
Tel no: (020) 7592 8545
www.gordonramsay.com/londonhouse
⊖ Clapham Junction, map 3
Modern European | £35
Cooking score: 3

The Georgians were rather partial to oysters
and this sizeable chunk of real estate was built
for the consumption of the bivalves (in 1780, it

says on the gable). Mr G Ramsay saw potential in the place and its location and has produced a deliciously glam venue with a swanky cocktail bar (where blue is the colour) and a series of classy dining spaces. Talking of potential, chef Anna Haugh-Kelly is setting about realising hers by turning out some nicely judged plates using fine British ingredients. British veal carpaccio gets a boost from its accompanying courgette and basil purée and green almonds. Next, a superb piece of hake stars in a main course with cauliflower purée and brown shrimps. Not every flavour hits the mark, but this is a welcome addition to the south side of the river. Wines from £22.

Chef/s: Anna Haugh-Kelly. **Open:** Fri to Sun L 12 to 3 (2.30 Fri), Tue to Sun D 6 to 10 (9.30 Sun). **Closed:** Mon. **Meals:** Set L £28. Set D £35. Sun L £28. **Details:** 70 seats. 16 seats outside. Separate bar. Wheelchair access. Music.

Magdalen

Intelligently crafted seasonal food
152 Tooley Street, Southwark, SE1 2TU
Tel no: (020) 7403 1342
www.magdalenrestaurant.co.uk
⊖ London Bridge, map 1
Modern British | £33
Cooking score: 3

Chef/proprietor James Faulks brings warmth and personality to the environs of London Bridge with this handsome, burgundy-hued neighbourhood restaurant. Polished wood floors, mirrors and bentwood chairs keep things appealing but low-key, while the kitchen exhibits intelligence and confident craftsmanship. The results are sometimes robust, sometimes refined, but big, true flavours always shine through – from a well-reported starter of braised cuttlefish with chickpeas and gremolata to an equally laudable dish of baked Somerset kid with lentils, shallots and turnip tops. Otherwise, expect duck ham with trevise, pickled pears and walnuts; bowls of fish stew with aïoli; and notable desserts including 'perfect' apple tart, steamed lemon sponge with custard or French toast with marmalade and vanilla ice cream. In short, 'lovely seasonal food, good service and no pretension'. The admirable assortment of predominantly Old World wines (from £20) includes plenty by the glass or carafe.

Chef/s: James Faulks. **Open:** Mon to Fri L 12 to 2.30, Mon to Sat D 6.30 to 10. **Closed:** Sun, 25 Dec, 1 Jan, 17 to 30 Aug, bank hols. **Meals:** alc (main courses £17 to £21). Set L £16 (2 courses) to £19. **Details:** 90 seats. Wheelchair access.

No. 67

Laid-back gallery restaurant
South London Gallery, 67 Peckham Road,
Peckham, SE5 8UH
Tel no: (020) 7252 7649
www.number67.co.uk
⊖ Peckham Rye, map 1
Modern European | £25
Cooking score: 1
£30

A boon for Peckhamites, this laid-back café seems happy in its own skin. The menu doesn't punch above its weight, nor does the service, which seems 'like being served by your mates'. By day it's just sandwiches, tarts, cakes and a couple of more substantial dishes, with dinner delivering good-looking brasserie food: say, pork and pistachio terrine, then cod fillet with bobby beans and pancetta, with lemon tart to finish. It's all very homely, and there's a sweet courtyard garden. Wines from £17.

Chef/s: Nick Hardman. **Open:** Tue to Sat 8am to 11pm (10am Sat). Sun 10 to 6.30. **Closed:** Mon. **Meals:** alc (main courses £12 to £14). **Details:** 44 seats. 28 seats outside.

Symbols

🛏 Accommodation is available

£30 Three courses for less than £30

V Separate vegetarian menu

£5 £5-off voucher scheme
OFF

🍷 Notable wine list

The Palmerston

A solid dining pub that's on the up
91 Lordship Lane, East Dulwich, SE22 8EP
Tel no: (020) 8693 1629
www.thepalmerston.net
map 1
Modern British | £35
Cooking score: 1
£5
OFF

It has been ten years since Jamie Younger took over this hostelry and turned it into an appealing pub-cum-restaurant – good news for Dulwich. Most come here to eat, drawn by a menu that touts Brit-inspired dishes with a few sunny Mediterranean nuances. Home-made pork pie (with piccalilli) sits alongside scrambled eggs with black winter truffles, and there are generous plates of sea bass with lentils, marinated fennel and salsa verde or roast venison loin and faggot with champ to follow. After that, a made-to-order chocolate and pecan clafoutis should suffice. Reporters continue to be impressed by Ellis Dickerson, who runs front-of-house. Wines from £18.
Chef/s: James Donnelly. **Open:** all week L 12 to 2.30 (3 Sat and Sun), D 7 to 10 (9.30 Sun). **Closed:** 25 and 26 Dec, 1 Jan. **Meals:** alc (main courses £14 to £22). Set L £14 (2 courses) to £17. **Details:** 70 seats. 30 seats outside. Separate bar. Wheelchair access. Music.

Pizarro

Thrilling fare from a Spanish food hero
194 Bermondsey Street, Southwark, SE1 3TQ
Tel no: (020) 7378 9455
www.josepizarro.com
⊖ London Bridge, Borough, map 1
Spanish | £30
Cooking score: 4

José Pizarro is a savvy Spaniard who is fast becoming the go-to guy when it comes to Iberian culinary matters. As seen on TV and in print, Señor Pizarro offers traditional flavours with a bit of contemporary swagger at this restaurant on Bermondsey Street, and at his original gaff a few yards down the road (see entry for José). An unprepossessing block is home to a venue that combines an authentic *cocina* vibe with a touch of current cool. If you're after tapas, head down the road, for here you can expect three courses running from scallops 'Mum's style' to lamb cutlets with apple compote. There's an unerring authenticity to the kitchen's output and flavours ring true with the likes of ribeye steak with Idiazabal cheese sauce and a dessert of the northern speciality leche frita, with avocado and pomegranate. Sherries and cava catch the eye on a wine list that starts at £19.
Chef/s: José Pizarro. **Open:** Mon to Fri L 12 to 3, D 6 to 11. Sat and Sun 12 to 11 (10pm Sun). **Meals:** alc (main courses £12 to £19). **Details:** 80 seats.

Le Pont de la Tour

Old-fashioned French favourite
36d Shad Thames, Bermondsey, SE1 2YE
Tel no: (020) 7403 8403
www.lepontdelatour.com
⊖ Tower Hill, London Bridge, map 1
Modern French | £45
Cooking score: 1

The riverbank location in an old shipping warehouse – with its ringside views of Tower Bridge and, distantly, Canary Wharf – has kept the Pont de la Tour popular for years, as is attested by the crowds that swirl through the bar and grill. In the full-dress dining room, a more elaborate menu comes into play: swordfish ceviche in tomato-lime vinaigrette; guinea fowl breast with braised baby gem and grilled spring onions; Valrhona mousse with salted-caramel ice cream. The slight air of treading water here is at odds with the ambitious pricing, which the wine list augments significantly. A scintillating global spread starts at £19.50.
Chef/s: Tom Cook. **Open:** all week L 12 to 3 (4 Sat and Sun), D 6 to 11 (10 Sun). **Meals:** alc (main courses £15 to £38). Set L and D £15 (2 courses) to £20. Sun L 20 (2 courses) to £25. **Details:** 100 seats. 70 seats outside. Separate bar. Wheelchair access. Music.

★ TOP 50 ★

Restaurant Story

A Story of spirited individuality
201 Tooley Street, Bermondsey, SE1 2UE
Tel no: (020) 7183 2117
www.restaurantstory.co.uk
⊖ London Bridge, map 1
Modern British | £70
Cooking score: 7

🍸 V

The unassuming modern glass-and-wood construction overlooks a tiny triangle of municipal garden, various bus stops and the distant Shard. It seems an unlikely place to find one of the brightest talents to be let loose in a British kitchen. Tom Sellers has picked up on the zeitgeist of seasonal ingredients, small plates and radical ideas, which he presents in a succession of wildly creative dishes. Off-menu canapé-style bites begin the adventure: among them a squid-ink biscuit sandwiching smoked eel mousse; razor clams with toasted barley and Champagne snow; and a rabbit 'sandwich' with tarragon, cream and bergamot. After the overtures, razor-sharp imagination and peerless technique take flight as the kitchen wheels out dish after dish noted for subtle nuances or an inspired finishing touch. Slices of perfect scallop cured in meadowsweet vinegar with cucumber and dill ash, and a dill oil and horseradish milk emulsion; exquisite Jacob's Ladder cooked in a low oven for 48 hours, offset by watercress purée, sloe berry reduction and spelt, barley and wheat grains; and an ethereal foie gras brûlée with pear and sorrel, a hint of vinegar cutting the richness – all are knockout dishes, no question. And that extends to the signature nursery-rhyme beef-dripping candle (which wouldn't look out of place at the Fat Duck), the finely wrought desserts and the Tunnock's dark chocolate teacake served with coffee. Alert service receives glowing praise, as does the French-accented wine list (despite steep mark-ups), bottles from £24.

Chef/s: Tom Sellers. **Open:** Tue to Sat L 12 to 2, D 6.30 to 9.30. **Closed:** Sun, Mon, 21 Dec to 5 Jan, last 2 weeks Aug. **Meals:** Set L £35 (Tue to Thur). Tasting menus £60 (6 courses), £80 (10 courses). **Details:** 40 seats. Separate bar. Wheelchair access.

Roast

Valiant British foodie patriot
Floral Hall, Stoney Street, Southwark, SE1 1TL
Tel no: (0845) 034 7300
www.roast-restaurant.com
⊖ London Bridge, map 1
British | £40
Cooking score: 2

V

Ten years on, Roast continues to enjoy faithful support. Lodged above the crowds thronging Borough Market, the lofty space cuts quite a dash with its vast expanse of glass, chic bar, white-clad tables and market views. The menu resounds with plucky British flavours, whether it's Jersey oysters, Devon crab or Lancashire chicken. Come here if your palate warms to straight-talking British staples of slow-roasted pork belly with mashed potatoes and Bramley apple sauce or char-grilled Barnsley chop with bubble and squeak and minted hollandaise sauce. There's fish, too, perhaps Severn and Wye cold-smoked mackerel and chicory salad, served with a soft-boiled bantam's egg, or a main course of tandoori-spiced fillets of red gurnard and spiced yoghurt. Desserts might usher in sea buckthorn berry posset or chocolate mousse cake with caramelised blood oranges. There's praise, too, for good British cheeses and the excellent business breakfasts. Wines from £22. **Chef/s:** Marcus Verberne. **Open:** Mon to Sat L 12 to 3.45, D 5.30 to 10.45. Sun 11.30 to 6.30. **Closed:** 25 Dec and 26 Dec, 1 Jan. **Meals:** alc (main courses £16 to £35). Set L and D £30. Sun L £35. **Details:** 126 seats. Separate bar. Wheelchair access. Music.

RSJ

Excellent-value food and astonishing wines
33 Coin Street, Southwark, SE1 9NR
Tel no: (020) 7928 4554
www.rsj.uk.com
⊖ Waterloo, Southwark, map 5
Modern European | £30
Cooking score: 3

♨ V

RSJ's charming blend of fine organic Loire wines and modern European cooking has secured its presence in the Guide for 34 years. A favourite with theatre-goers for its snappy service and good-value fixed-price menu, the Waterloo veteran continues to delight year after year. At a test meal 'fresh seasonal dishes on a lovely menu' delivered starters of a particularly vibrant courgette, mint and ricotta roll drizzled with honey and sultanas, and Cornish mackerel fillet with pickled red cabbage. Next came a delicately roasted hake with colourful beetroot, heritage radishes and a wonderfully zingy lemon shallot dressing, followed by an apricot and almond tart with indulgent amaretti ice cream to finish. The real treat though is the wine list, which offers an exploration of the Loire Valley's biodynamic cellars. An extensive by-the-glass and half-bottle selection provides wonderful value and choice, from Sancerre and Vouvray through to Chinon. A bottle of house Sauvignon is £19.50.
Chef/s: Matthew Pepperall. **Open:** Mon to Fri L 12 to 2.30, Mon to Sat D 5.30 to 11. **Closed:** Sun, 24 to 26 Dec, Easter bank hols. **Meals:** alc (main courses £16 to £23). Set L and D £17 (2 courses) to £20. **Details:** 90 seats. 12 seats outside.

¦¦¦ Visit us Online
To find out more about
The Good Food Guide, please visit
www.thegoodfoodguide.co.uk

LOCAL GEM

▲ Saz

23 Norwood Road, Herne Hill, SE24 9AA
Tel no: (020) 8671 3772
www.saz-hernehill.co.uk
map 1
Turkish | £16 £5 OFF

The name references a stringed instrument (or group of stringed instruments) from Turkey, and it is the food of Türkiye that brings the punters to this joint on Norwood Road. The mangal (charcoal grill) is the star of the show, here for all to see in the open kitchen and turning out marinated lamb ribs, chicken wings and patlican kebabi (aubergine and minced lamb skewers). Meze run to traditional cacik, calamari and stuffed vine leaves. Wines from £11.50. Open all week.

Skylon

A riverside stunner in the Royal Festival Hall
Southbank Centre, Belvedere Road, South Bank, SE1 8XX
Tel no: (020) 7654 7800
www.skylon-restaurant.co.uk
⊖ Waterloo, map 5
Modern British | £48
Cooking score: 2

V

'This smart 1950s beauty – rich reds, chocolate browns and amber crystal ware – could grace the set of *Mad Men*,' thought one visitor to the third-floor restaurant at the Royal Festival Hall. The best tables are by the vast windows with views of the Thames, but there's a relaxed feel wherever you sit and service is both accommodating and attentive. Skylon diners know what they are about, and whether it's a pre-performance dine-and-dash or a special celebration, in the hands of chef Adam Gray they are well served. The seasonally changing menu sports a mixed bag of smart metropolitan dishes for big-city palates: crisp Cornish mackerel is served with rhubarb chutney and dandelion-leaf salad, Great Garnetts Farm pork belly is slow-roasted and

arrives with lobster and tarragon risotto, while chestnut cake comes with pumpkin cream and muscovado ice cream. Wines from £23.50.
Chef/s: Adam Gray. **Open:** all week L 12 to 2.30 (4 Sun), Mon to Sat D 5.30 to 10.30. **Closed:** 25 Dec. **Meals:** Set L £25 (2 courses) to £29. Sun L £28 (2 courses) to £32. **Details:** 80 seats. Separate bar. Wheelchair access.

Soif

Friendly neighbourhood hangout with a winning wine list
27 Battersea Rise, Battersea, SW11 1HG
Tel no: (020) 7223 1112
soif.co
⊖ Clapham South, map 3
Modern European | £30
Cooking score: 1

Welcome to Soif where everyone is a friend. That's the vibe projected on any given evening at this Battersea hangout. Regulars and staff know each other by name, which gives license to a vibrant and chatty atmosphere (rather like big brothers Terroirs and Brawn, see entries). The décor is consistently styled too: the split-level space filled with rustic wooden tables on a terracotta tiled floor. The food is French-cum-Italian with a choice of winning sharing snacks such as the moreish duck rillettes, and the peppery sopressa trentina (salami) – you'll need plenty of bread to accompany both. Standout meaty mains include rabbit leg with Alsace bacon, and a juicy steak haché with enough crisp chips to feed two. Dessert can bring a simple chocolate pudding. Allow time to study the huge wine list, which takes in everything from classic Bordeaux to New World varieties from New Zealand and Argentina. Bottle prices start at £19.
Chef/s: Michal Chacinski. **Open:** Tue to Sun L 12 to 3 (4 Sun), Mon to Sat D 6 to 10.30. **Closed:** bank hols. **Meals:** alc (main courses £15 to £17). **Details:** 56 seats. Music.

¶¶ JOHN WILLIAMS
The Ritz

What inspired you to become a chef?
Graham Kerr - the galloping gourmet - travelling around the world's best restaurants and learning the specialities of the chefs who work in them.

What would you be if you weren't a chef?
A vintner - I love the history of wine and what goes into making it.

What food could you not live without?
Vanilla, it's sublime, it is the equivalent of a good stock in the kitchen, it can flavour the base of many dishes.

Are there any ingredients that evoke strong memories for you?
Jersey Royal potatoes as I always helped my mother to scrape them. I adore the flavour, but they must be cooked in their robes, or scraped.

And finally... tell us something about yourself that will surprise your diners.
I am on a diet permanently. I hate butter, olive oil, bread, lobster, caviar, sugar, desserts, vegetables, beef and lamb. I am gluten/dairy free and vegan. I am also a very bad liar!

LOCAL GEM
▲ Tapas Brindisa
18-20 Southwark Street, Southwark, SE1 1TJ
Tel no: (020) 7357 8880
www.tapasbrindisa.com
⊖ London Bridge, map 1
Spanish | £20

'Bursting at the seams on a Friday lunchtime', the original link in this small, well-known tapas chain is a perennially popular spot on the curved outer edge of Borough Market. It feels Spanish, from the cramped, no-frills décor and fast-paced service right down to the menu, which is driven by top-drawer ingredients imported from Spain. Soak up the happy, bustling atmosphere while tucking into grilled smoked chorizo on toast, and cuttlefish, with some good and tangy gremolata-style dressing. The all-Spanish wine list starts at £18.50. Open all week.

Tentazioni
Popular Italian cooking with a Sardinian tang
Lloyds Wharf, 2 Mill Street, Bermondsey, SE1 2BD
Tel no: (020) 7237 1100
www.tentazioni.co.uk
⊖ Bermondsey, London Bridge, map 1
Italian | £38
Cooking score: 3
£5 OFF

Look for the neon sign pointing the way down a little alley off Mill Street. Riccardo Giacomini's Italian outfit is a relatively formal set-up with rich red walls, tables dressed up in linen cloths and large modern canvases on the walls – but the service lightens the tone with a dose of old-school charm. The kitchen turns out some enticing food with Sardinian flavours to the fore. A starter of swordfish and yellowfin carpaccio is simple stuff done well, or go for the creamy comfort of burrata with gratinated asparagus and classic Sardinian bottarga. Pasta is a good bet too, judging by pheasant ravioli with spinach guazzetto. Main courses can be as trad as Dover sole with sautéed potatoes or extravagant as pigeon breast with foie gras mousse and a potato purée

flavoured with truffles. Tiramisu comes in a Martini glass, and the Italian wine list kicks off at £18.
Chef/s: Alessandro Cattani. **Open:** Sun to Fri L 12 to 2.45, all week D 6 to 10.45 (9 Sun). **Closed:** 24 to 26 Dec, bank hols. **Meals:** alc (main courses £7 to £24). Set L £12 (2 courses) to £15. Tasting menu £50 (7 courses). **Details:** 50 seats. Music.

Trinity
Truly wonderful neighbourhood restaurant
4 The Polygon, Clapham, SW4 0JG
Tel no: (020) 7622 1199
www.trinityrestaurant.co.uk
⊖ Clapham Common, map 3
Modern British | £46
Cooking score: 5
V

Adam Byatt's Trinity flies against fashion by staying true to its fine-dining ideals. But beneath the formal trappings – dapper staff, crisply laundered linen, gleaming stemware – beats the heart of a neighbourhood restaurant. It is, enthuses one inspector, an 'off-radar gem' delivering 'great cooking' and 'warm passionate service'. Choose from the set lunch, vegetarian, à la carte and five-course tasting menus, all at 'scrupulously fair' prices. Build on a delicious beginning of homemade bread and homemade butter with a classic Trinity first course of crispy trotters, gribiche, quail's egg and crackling, then roast halibut, caramelised cauliflower, cockles and grapes. For dessert, the meringue sphere with raspberry, crème Chantilly and lychee sorbet is 'a genius take on Eton Mess'. Trinity's 'value-oriented approach' extends to the wine list (from £19) which delves into the world's vinous regions (including New York State and Croatia) while keeping largely within the £20-£50 bracket.
Chef/s: Adam Byatt. **Open:** Tue to Sun L 12.30 to 2.30 (3 Sun), Mon to Sat D 6 to 10. **Closed:** 24 to 26 Dec. **Meals:** alc (main courses £25 to £32). Set L £22 (2 courses) to £27. Sun L £32. Tasting menu £55. **Details:** 61 seats. Wheelchair access.

Tsunami

Sleek Japanese fusion favourite
5-7 Voltaire Road, Clapham, SW4 6DQ
Tel no: (020) 7978 1610
www.tsunamirestaurant.co.uk
⊖ Clapham North, map 3
Japanese | £28
Cooking score: 3
£30

Refashioned in a sultrily lit mix of blacks, greys and sunflower-yellow, Tsunami continues to offer bright, fresh Japanese food to Clapham's smart set (and there's a Charlotte Street branch for West Enders). The menu construction follows traditional lines, but dishes are intended for sharing in the tapas or dim sum fashion. Tofu fried in tempura batter comes in dashi broth and grated daikon, and there are exemplary salmon sashimi and chicken gyozas for the well versed. Less obvious choices are oyster shooters with ponzu, spring onions and quail's egg, roast pork belly with green beans and peri-peri hoisin, and creamed leeks and oyster mushrooms in wasabi. The modern Japanese classic, black cod in sweet miso, has its stalwart champions, too. Meals end with the likes of pineapple carpaccio and coconut and mango ice cream. A late bar licence at weekends makes for extended interfacing with the cocktails, cold and warm sakés, and global wines (from £20).
Chef/s: S W Cheung. **Open:** Sat and Sun L 12.30 to 4, all week D 5.30 to 10.30 (11 Fri and Sat, 10 Sun). **Closed:** 24 to 26 Dec. **Meals:** alc (main courses £8 to £28). Set L £15 (2 courses). Set D £37 to £42. **Details:** 86 seats. 22 seats outside. Separate bar. Wheelchair access.

NEW ENTRY

Union Street Café

Ramsay does neighbourhood Italian
47-51 Great Suffolk Street, Southwark, SE1 0BS
Tel no: (020) 7592 7977
www.gordonramsay.com
⊖ Southwark, map 5
Italian | £40
Cooking score: 3

We're not in Hammersmith, but Gordon Ramsay's Italian 'café' evokes Ruth Rogers' riverside original. Daily menus are in twiddly blue script, seasonal ingredients come from the mammaland and the dishes are 'about simplicity'. The dining room is a big, semi-industrial shell glammed up with polished wood, navy leather and statement art. Aperitivi might be immaculately crisp, tomatoey arancini dusted with dried herb salt, or quality assemblies such as a salad of roast peppers, anchovies and fresh ricotta. A pasta special of tagliolini with crumbled veal sausage and asparagus shavings comes with a robust, salty sauce. Pudding includes silky-sharp Amalfi lemon cream matched with the cool blandness of milk ice cream. Readers note with relief that there's 'no overdoing of the celebrity chef thing: it's just a good neighbourhood restaurant'. Wine from £19.50.
Chef/s: Davide Degiovanni. **Open:** Mon to Sat L 12 to 3 (4 Sat), D 6 to 11 (10.30 Sat). Sun 12 to 8. **Closed:** 25 and 26 Dec, 1 Jan. **Details:** 120 seats. Separate bar. Wheelchair access. Music.

The Woodman

Unpretentious pub with civilised dining room
60 Battersea High Street, Battersea, SW11 3HW
Tel no: (020) 7228 2968
www.woodman-battersea.co.uk
⊖ Clapham Junction, map 3
British | £24
Cooking score: 2
£5 OFF £30

The hugely likeable Woodman is quite a local asset, the rejuvenated pub playing the role of casual drinkers' den and full-on restaurant

with great style. The wood-burning stove, scuffed wooden floors and junk shop furniture chime perfectly with rustic cooking that makes a good fist of celebrating seasonal ingredients. The formula is simple. Menus deal in well-wrought dishes that are fresh and flavourful – an excellent foie gras and chicken liver pâté with red onion and thyme marmalade, perhaps, or garlic and herb wild mushroom risotto, followed by wild rabbit cooked in a rich mustard sauce and served with creamy mash or a plate of cod and chips. Nor is there a word to be said against the wild boar Scotch egg or sticky toffee pudding with vanilla-pod ice cream. The sheltered patio is a secret worth knowing, and prices are deemed 'reasonable', including the wines from £15.
Chef/s: James Rogers. **Open:** all week L 12 to 6, D 6 to 10 (9 Sun). **Meals:** alc (main meals £10 to £18). **Details:** 80 seats. 40 seats outside. Separate bar. Music.

Wright Brothers Oyster & Porter House
Bivalves and 'black stuff'
11 Stoney Street, Southwark, SE1 9AD
Tel no: (020) 7403 9554
www.thewrightbrothers.co.uk
⊖ London Bridge, map 1
Seafood | £40
Cooking score: 2

Celebrating its tenth year in 2015, and still packing a punch in the exciting foodie enclave of Borough Market, the Wright Brothers' original seafood emporium (see Wright Brothers, Soho) is an informal, bustly eatery that uses a daily delivery of fish and shellfish to popular effect. It's a bare-bricks kind of place where you have the choice of perching at the bar or grabbing a space at communal tables – and it's filled with laughter and life. Combinations are straightforward yet attractively varied, from the widely approved seafood platters, fish soup and moules marinière to daily specials of, say, wild black bream with purple sprouting broccoli and beurre blanc or roast pollack with clams and chorizo. There's beef, Guinness and oyster pie

if you're not in the mood for fish, and a rather good crème brûlée if you've room for dessert. Drinks include a good section of porters, ales and stouts, and wines from £20.
Chef/s: Phillip Coulter. **Open:** all week L 12 to 3 (4 Sat and Sun), D 6 to 11 (10 Sun). **Closed:** bank hols. **Meals:** alc (main courses £8 to £19). **Details:** 35 seats. 6 seats outside. Separate bar. Wheelchair access.

Zucca
Get-stuck-in, good-value Italian cooking
184 Bermondsey Street, Bermondsey, SE1 3TQ
Tel no: (020) 7378 6809
www.zuccalondon.com
⊖ London Bridge, Borough, map 1
Italian | £40
Cooking score: 3

The consensus on Sam Harris's super-busy Italian eatery is that 'everything about it is right'. The large, square room is a lesson in simplicity – furnishings are on the plain side (think bare tables and muted walls) – but light pours in through the plate-glass windows, and the open-to-view kitchen produces unpretentious, confidently rendered Italian dishes. The seasonal menu is full of promise with a meal in April, for example, bringing antipasti of burrata teamed with wild garlic, capers and chilli, and grilled purple sprouting broccoli topped with trapanese (tomato and almond pesto). Homemade pasta is excellent, especially an unusual maltagliati with walnuts, ricotta and lentils. Fillets of mackerel could arrive with beetroot, greens and porcini; reporters continue to drool over the never-off-the-menu 'Zucca' fritti (pumpkin in tempura batter); and there's an unusually delicate banana and panettone pudding with caramel ice cream to finish. The all-Italian wine list opens at £28.
Chef/s: Sam Harris. **Open:** Tue to Sun L 12 to 3 (3.30 Sat, 4 Sun), Tue to Sat D 6 to 10. **Closed:** Mon, Christmas, New Year, Easter. **Meals:** alc (main courses £15 to £19). **Details:** 55 seats. Wheelchair access.

The Admiral Codrington
All-purpose Chelsea bolt-hole
17 Mossop Street, Chelsea, SW3 2LY
Tel no: (020) 7581 0005
www.theadmiralcodrington.co.uk
⊖ South Kensington, map 3
Modern British | £32
Cooking score: 2

Once a rampaging boozer with an appetite for excess, the 'Cod' now seems a more genteel kettle of fish: a bar at the front still attracts local suits and Chelsea girls, while others find comfort in the affable L-shaped dining room towards the back. Piscine prints and a ship's wheel ram home the maritime point, and a retractable roof adds some faux alfresco vibes. If seafood is your wish, consider Inverawe sea trout with blinis and crème fraîche, battered haddock and chips or crab linguine with samphire and citrus butter. If red meat is required, try the Admiral's burger, spatchcock chicken or rump of new season's lamb with rosemary and sauce gribiche. Steaks with triple-cooked chips are spot-on, and desserts such as sticky toffee pudding, apple crumble or rhubarb syllabub offer a blast from the past. A few vintage Bordeaux add depth to the modest wine list; bottles from £19.
Chef/s: Orett Hoilett. **Open:** Mon to Sat L 12 to 3 (4 Sat), D 6 to 10 (11 Fri, 7 to 11 Sat). Sun 12 to 9. **Closed:** 24 to 26 Dec. **Meals:** alc (main courses £12 to £28). **Details:** 55 seats. 20 seats outside.

Amaya
Indian grazing food served with style
15 Halkin Arcade, Motcomb Street, Knightsbridge, SW1X 8JT
Tel no: (020) 7823 1166
www.realindianfood.wn
⊖ Knightsbridge, map 4
Indian | £43
Cooking score: 4

'Amaya opened in 2004, and a decade on, it still delivers some of the best Indian food in town,' enthused one reader, who went on to praise the captivating interior (buffed up by rosewood and walnut) and the 'crisp' service.

When it comes to ordering, the grazing menu is the restaurant's calling card. Dishes are like 'tempting little snippets' served directly from the open-plan kitchen: perhaps a delicately spiced blue swimmer crab cake, or succulent char-grilled lamb chops infused with lime and ginger, both highlights of a February test meal. Vegetables are taken seriously here, including 'delightfully cool and piquant' sweet potato with tamarind and yoghurt. Presentation ensures that dishes look the part – note a gratifying dessert of lime tart with limoncello jelly and blueberry compote, which was 'as eye-catching as the interior'. Wines are cannily assembled to match the spicy dishes, but rise quickly from £32 (glasses from £7).
Chef/s: Karunesh Khanna. **Open:** all week L 12.30 to 2.15 (12.45 to 2.45 Sun), D 6.30 to 11.30 (10.30 Sun). **Meals:** alc (main courses £22 to £26). Set L £21 to £33. Sun L £24 to £33. Tasting menu £43 to £110. **Details:** 100 seats. Separate bar. Wheelchair access. Music. Children before 8pm only.

Apero
Stylish Italian all-day dining
The Ampersand Hotel, 2 -10 Harrington Road, South Kensington, SW7 3ER
Tel no: (020) 7591 4410
www.aperorestaurantandbar.com
⊖ South Kensington, map 3
Mediterranean | £30
Cooking score: 3

🛏 V

Down in the vaults beneath the boutique Ampersand Hotel is a little slice of Mediterranean sunshine. Open from breakfast to dinner, Apero really is very bright and breezy for somewhere on the lower-ground level, helped along by whitewashed walls, shiny white tiles and splashes of colour from the stylish leather seats. The main menu takes a sharing approach, with copious plates of Italian-inspired dishes. Braised cuttlefish come with spinach, bottarga and polenta, the trendy 'nduja perks up a tranche of roast hake, and ribeye arrives in the company of golden enoki mushrooms and snails. There's a long

marble bar if you're up for perching on stools
– very comfy, as it happens. The cocktails are
inspired by the Victoria and Albert Museum
down the road (fancy a Wordsworth sour?)
and desserts extend to Sicilian lemon curd
with hazelnut crumble and meringue. Wines
from £19.
Chef/s: Chris Golding. **Open:** all week L 12 to 2.30, D
6 to 10.30. **Meals:** alc (main courses £9 to £18). Set
L £12 (2 courses) to £15. **Details:** 40 seats. Separate
bar. Wheelchair access. Music.

Assaggi

Fine-tuned rustic Italian food
39 Chepstow Place, Notting Hill, W2 4TS
Tel no: (020) 7792 5501
⊖ Notting Hill Gate, map 4
Italian | £40
Cooking score: 4

Nino Sassu's laid-back Italian eaterie occupies
the first floor of a converted pub in the
Bayswater hinterland, accessed via a mews
entrance on Rede Place. A peach and violet
colour scheme and some Rothko-ish abstracts
lend a vigorous air to the bare-floorboarded
space. The untranslated menu shouldn't tax
veteran Italian vacationers too sorely. What
you can expect is generous platters of
succulent antipasti, perhaps San Daniele ham
with pecorino and rocket, or burrata with
grilled aubergine, and then nicely judged
standbys such as halibut with puréed cress and
saffron, meltingly tender calf's liver or fritto
misto. Sides of tomato and basil, or potatoes
with garlic and rosemary, keep things
motoring, and you won't want to miss a
concluding slab of torta al cioccolato. It's all
served forth with bags of cheering
Mediterranean warmth and a list of prudently
chosen, though heftily marked-up, Italian
wines: from £25.95 for the house Sardinian.
Chef/s: Nino Sassu. **Open:** Mon to Sat L 12.30 to
2.30 (1 Sat), D 7.30 to 11. **Closed:** Sun. **Meals:** alc
(main courses £20 to £30). **Details:** 40 seats.

Bar Boulud

Razzle-dazzle brasserie, New York style
Mandarin Oriental Hyde Park, 66 Knightsbridge,
Knightsbridge, SW1X 7LA
Tel no: (020) 7201 3899
www.barboulud.com
⊖ Knightsbridge, map 4
French | £30
Cooking score: 4

New York-based superstar Daniel Boulud may
love the Big Apple, but this razzle-dazzle
Knightsbridge outpost makes much of his
French birthright, as well as knocking out
some stateside riffs. Located in the bowels of
the Mandarin Oriental Hotel, it's a glamorous,
wood-toned joint with a buzzing open
kitchen. France shows its colours with pâté en
croûte, salade frisée lyonnaise and coq au vin,
while the US brings emblematic burgers –
including a 'piggie' version with BBQ pulled
pork, green chilli and red cabbage slaw.
Sausages are present in abundance (try the
cumin-spiced smoked version with lentil
stew), as are extravagant sharing platters piled
with charcuterie and fruits de mer. Desserts
such as Suzette flottante (steamed lemon
meringue with blood-orange and Grand
Marnier anglaise) go straight for the high-
calorie jugular, while the appealing wine list is
dedicated to bottles from Boulud's beloved
Burgundy, Rhône and regions surrounding
his home town of Lyon; prices from £22.50.
Chef/s: Dean Yasharian. **Open:** all week 12 to 11 (10
Sun). **Meals:** alc (main courses £12 to £32). Set L
and pre-theatre D £24. **Details:** 168 seats. Separate
bar. Wheelchair access. Music.

NEW ENTRY
Bar Margaux
Fancy Eurozone dining
152 Old Brompton Road, SW5 0BE
Tel no: (020) 7373 5753
www.barmargaux.co.uk
⊖ Gloucester Road, map 3
Modern European | £35
Cooking score: 1

Down in the 21st arrondissement (aka South Kensington), this exposed brick, copper and brushed-metal wine bar-cum-restaurant sees an international crowd congregate for a glass of wine (good selection) and something to eat from the modern European menu. Wild sea bass ceviche with Amalfi lemon and lime marinade, green apple and celery salad, makes a good start. Then try slow-cooked Ibérico pork with baby fennel and pineapple compote, finishing with dark chocolate dessert in seven 'textures'. Perhaps unsurprisingly for this part of town, good value can feel elusive, especially on the wine list where bottles start at £25 and quickly rise above £30.
Chef/s: Xavier Castella. **Open:** all week L 12 to 3.30 (4 Sat and Sun), D 6 to 10.30 (11 Sat and Sun). **Closed:** 24 to 26 Dec, 1 Jan. **Meals:** alc (main courses £15 to £20). **Details:** 81 seats. Separate bar. Music.

Bibendum
Aristocratic South Ken landmark
Michelin House, 81 Fulham Road, South Kensington, SW3 6RD
Tel no: (020) 7581 5817
www.bibendum.co.uk
⊖ South Kensington, map 3
French | £50
Cooking score: 4

🍷 V

Cosseted away on the first floor of the beautiful Art Deco building that once housed Michelin HQ, Bibendum seems a world away from the commotion of the capital. Inside, it's a commodious cocoon, tailor-made for long lunches amid walnut screens, etched glass and framed caricatures of the bulbous 'tyre man'. Here, well-heeled regulars work their way through a menu of high-pedigree Franco-European classics – from foie gras terrine with Armagnac jelly or truffled wild mushroom pithiviers to gâteau St Honoré. In between, there's plenty of seasonal generosity in the shape of braised ox cheeks with prunes, bacon and chestnuts, the irreplaceable roast chicken with tarragon, or tapenade-crusted halibut with gremolata. Bibendum's illustrious wine list (from £24.50) is a formidable 800-bin treasury with the added advantage of numerous satisfying samplings by the glass or carafe. And there's plenty more deco design to ogle at downstairs in the Oyster Bar.
Chef/s: Matthew Harris. **Open:** all week L 12 to 2.30 (12.30 to 3 Sat and Sun), D 7 to 11 (10.30 Sun). **Closed:** 25 and 26 Dec, 1 Jan. **Meals:** alc (main courses £19 to £30). Set L £28 (2 courses) to £31. Sun L and D £34. **Details:** 90 seats. Separate bar.

Bombay Brasserie
Born-again Indian veteran
Courtfield Road, South Kensington, SW7 4QH
Tel no: (020) 7370 4040
www.bombaybrasserielondon.com
⊖ Gloucester Road, map 3
Indian | £50
Cooking score: 3

Offering Indian fine dining in the capital since 1982, the Bombay Brasserie endured the new-wave openings of the 1990s and beyond to emerge as the granddaddy of upmarket Asian cuisine. The space looks spruce these days, like a high-end gaff of indeterminate denomination, but one glance at the menu and a sense of place is restored: this is Indian regional cooking with a bit of pizazz. The menu contains some familiar names, but presentation is on the arty side and spicing is clear and true. Patrani macchi is a first course of lemon sole steamed in a banana leaf in the company of coriander, chilli and coconut. Main courses such as nihari lamb shank and Goan fish curry (halibut as it happens) also deliver the promised flavours. A goodly choice

of vegetarian dishes adds to the appeal, and there's a tasting menu to confirm the fine-dining intentions. Wines start at £22.
Chef/s: Prahlad Hegde. **Open:** all week L 12 to 3 (3.30 Sat and Sun), D 6 to 11.30 (10.30 Sun). **Closed:** 25 Dec. **Meals:** alc (main courses £15 to £31). Set L £24. Set D £43. Sun L £31. Tasting menu £48. **Details:** 200 seats. Separate bar. Wheelchair access. Music.

NEW ENTRY
The Brackenbury
Pleasant peasant cooking in the suburbs
129-131 Brackenbury Road, Hammersmith, W6 0BQ
Tel no: (020) 8741 4928
www.brackenburyrestaurant.co.uk
⊖ Hammersmith, map 1
Modern British | £32
Cooking score: 2

The little purlieu of west London now known as Brackenbury Village sits in the interstices of Shepherd's Bush and Hammersmith. It's a well-heeled resort of Victorian villas and polite shopping parades such as the one where you'll find this small bistro makeover, retooled in obstinate beige for modernists. Pleasantly peasanty cooking is the focus of Humphrey Fletcher's output here, with French and Italian accents overlaid on humble, earthy ingredients. A heap of deep-fried anchovies with punchy aïoli is blameless in every way, while more dramatic visual impact comes via stripy Chioggia beetroot, blood orange, mint and milk curd. At main, a whole grilled mackerel is a thing of beauty, its charred skin fit to pop with rich juices, done in chilli gremolata with garlic-dressed puntarelle – or there may be confit rabbit leg in spring vegetable broth. Finish if possible with iced Paris-Brest filled with pistachio ice cream, in hot chocolate sauce. Wines from £17.50.
Chef/s: Humphrey Fletcher and Andy Morris. **Open:** Fri to Sun L 12 to 3, Tue to Sat D 7 to 10. **Closed:** Mon. **Meals:** alc (main courses £16 to £19). **Details:** 50 seats. 20 seats outside.

Le Café Anglais
Big-hearted brasserie pleasures
8 Porchester Gardens, Notting Hill, W2 4DB
Tel no: (020) 7221 1415
www.lecafeanglais.co.uk
⊖ Bayswater, map 4
Modern European | £35
Cooking score: 4
£5 OFF

Rowley Leigh's sweeping Art Deco eatery on the second floor of the Whiteleys shopping complex promises sharply crafted brasserie pleasures. Whether you are finger-picking crustacea at the all-day seafood bar or embarking on a full meal in the bright white dining room, the mood is convivial and cosmopolitan. Light streams in through vast windows and cheery staff go about their business, on the floor and in the open-to-view kitchen. Rich, warm Parmesan custard with anchovy toast continues to 'ping with flavour', although the famed hors d'oeuvre selection also spans everything from raw tuna with ginger dressing to rabbit rillettes with pickled endive. After that, fish pie gets good notices, alongside the likes of steamed red mullet with salsa verde, a 'carpet' burger (oyster included) or veal chop with lemon and sage butter. To finish, chocolate fondant brings a 'flattened dome of richness with a crisp sugar-dusted crust'. Classy, Euro-accented wines start at £22.50.
Chef/s: Rowley Leigh. **Open:** all week L 12 to 3.30 (11 to 4 Sat), D 6.30 to 10.30 (11 Fri and Sat, 10 Sun). **Closed:** 24 to 27 Dec, Aug bank hol. **Meals:** alc (main courses £13 to £30). Set L and D £20 (2 courses) to £25. Set D £30 (2 courses) to £35. Sun L £30. **Details:** 120 seats. Separate bar. Wheelchair access. Car parking.

Cambio de Tercio
Dazzling Spanish innovator
163 Old Brompton Road, Earl's Court, SW5 0LJ
Tel no: (020) 7244 8970
www.cambiodetercio.co.uk
⊖ Gloucester Road, map 3
Spanish | £40
Cooking score: 5
♦

Rafael Nadal reputedly drops in during
Wimbledon fortnight – a reminder that
Cambio de Tercio not only has celebrity clout,
but also cuts it in the authenticity stakes. Black
slate floors, Rioja-red ceilings and dazzling
artworks on Seville-orange walls hit you like
an ace from the tennis star's racquet, while the
kitchen deals in bold, innovative flavours far
removed from tapas-joint clichés. Dry-aged
Wagyu beef 'ham' is an alternative to top-
grade jamón, but that's just the beginning:
'new' patatas bravas and Galician octopus with
paprika give way to signature plates of scallop
ceviche with fino sherry, pea shoots and
parsnip salad; duck breast with liquid
sweetcorn ravioli, vanilla oil and foie gras; or
crispy roast suckling pig with grilled lettuce,
pickled kumquat and shallots. Also don't miss
clever desserts such as the crispy Cuban mojito
in a blown caramel ball. The 350-bin, all-
Spanish wine list (from £25.95) revels in the
glories of native grape varieties and fine
vintages from regional vineyards; also note
the astonishing collection of sherries.
Chef/s: Alberto Criado. **Open:** all week L 12 to 2.30
(3 Sat and Sun), D 6.30 to 11.30 (11 Sun). **Closed:** 2
weeks Christmas, 2 weeks Aug. **Meals:** alc (main
courses £20 to £28). Set L £25 (2 courses) to £30.
Set D £35 (2 courses) to £45. Sun L £27. **Details:** 95
seats. 8 seats outside. Separate bar. Music.

LOCAL GEM
▲ The Carpenter's Arms
89-91 Black Lion Lane, Hammersmith, W6 9BG
Tel no: (020) 8741 8386
www.carpentersarmsw6.co.uk
⊖ Stamford Brook, Ravenscourt Park, map 1
Modern European | £25

A corner pub that can generate quite a noise
when firing on all cylinders, the Carpenter's
Arms is a local worth knowing about. There's a
terrific beer garden out back for eating
outdoors (or puffing a ciggy), and rustic
wooden tables inside affording easier access to
the bar. The food is modern bistro stuff, so a
Scotch egg with salad and pickles, coq au vin
and grilled ribeye with chips fit the bill nicely.
Wines start at £17.70. Open all week.

▲ Casa Brindisa
7-9 Exhibition Road, South Kensington, SW7 2HE
Tel no: (020) 7590 0008
www.brindisa.com
⊖ South Kensington, map 3
Spanish | £20

Part of the Brindisa family with tapas outlets
and shops around the capital, the South Ken
outpost is fairly brimful of Spanish goodies:
from charcuteria (salchichón de Vic, Ibérico de
Bellota chorizo) to cheeses (Picos de Europa,
Idiazabal). There's a basement deli and a high-
energy attitude all round. Go for tapas such as
sautéed squid with cauliflower and Jerusalem
artichoke purée or Ibérico pork cheeks cooked
for 18 hours, and drink sherry and Spanish
wine (bottles from £18.50). Open all week.

Chakra
Subcontinental sizzle and Notting Hill opulence
157-159 Notting Hill Gate, Notting Hill, W11 3LF
Tel no: (020) 7229 2115
www.chakralondon.com
⊖ Notting Hill Gate, map 4
Indian | £40
Cooking score: 3

Citing the Vedic scriptures as its source of
inspiration, Chakra plays the spiritual card
from the off, while also seeking exaltation by

association with the culinary traditions of the royal palaces of old. That's a lot to live up to, but luckily the cooking is pretty good and harmony is maintained. The venue is made up of spaces that evoke either a gentlemen's club or a nightclub, the latter in a room with a white leather wall and chandeliers. Modern Indian fine dining is the name of the game, which amounts to some classy plates of food incorporating familiar combinations and a few surprises along the way. From the tandoor comes smoked Gressingham duck with papaya, or Jalandhar chicken in a creamy masala sauce. There are kebabs like venison galouti and excellent veggie choices including Rajasthani-style crispy okra. Cocktails increase the glam stakes even further. Wines start at £23.

Chef/s: Andy Varma. **Open:** all week L 12 to 3, D 6 to 11 (10.30 Sun). **Closed:** 25 and 26 Dec, 1 Jan. **Meals:** alc (main courses £9 to £29). Set L £9 (2 courses) to £13. Set D £15 (2 courses) to £29. Sun L £15. Tasting menu £45 to £60. **Details:** 75 seats. 15 seats outside. Separate bar.

★ READERS' RESTAURANT OF THE YEAR ★
LONDON

Charlotte's Bistro
Slick neighbourhood eatery
6 Turnham Green Terrace, Chiswick, W4 1QP
Tel no: (020) 8742 3590
www.charlottes.co.uk
⊖ Turnham Green, map 1
Modern European | £27
Cooking score: 3
£30

Competition might be fierce in restaurant-heavy W4, but readers 'can't recommend this enough'. The team behind Charlotte's Place, Ealing (see entry), are the talk of Chiswick with their seasonal cocktails and bar snacks out front. On the first floor it's dining as neat as the décor – don't be fooled by the 'bistro' title and lack of white linen. The 'good imaginative cooking' is no less considered than at the Ealing original. Starters might include gin-cured salmon with lemon and pickled cucumber, or Dorset snails with pig's

head croquette, baby gem and peas, while main courses could be slow-roast garlic risotto with cream cheese and chervil. Desserts, such as a Granny Smith doughnut with crunchy salted caramel, are rated absolute 'winners'. The 'genuinely friendly' staff come in for high praise, eager to offer advice on some 'stunning' wines from a mainly European portfolio full of promise, starting at £18 a bottle.
Chef/s: Lee Cadden. **Open:** all week 12 to 10. **Meals:** alc (main courses £14 to £18). Set L £16 (2 courses) to £19. **Details:** 60 seats. Separate bar. Music.

Charlotte's Place
Dependable, pleasing cooking and great value
16 St Matthew's Road, Ealing, W5 3JT
Tel no: (020) 8567 7541
www.charlottes.co.uk
⊖ Ealing Broadway, Ealing Common, map 1
Modern European | £33
Cooking score: 4

Readers rate this idyllic neighbourhood restaurant – now expanded into Chiswick with Charlotte's Bistro (see entry) and with a further venue in the offing – 'a real treat'. Overlooking the common, the light, if rather cosy dining room (there's more seating in the basement) showcases an ostensibly simple menu punctuated by top-notch ingredients: crispy lamb belly rashers were the highlight of a dish of white asparagus, burrata and tomato relish; violet artichoke is teamed with radish, dandelion and barigoule mayonnaise; and braised rabbit in a rich tarragon cream with potato dumplings and broccoli is just 'pure indulgence'. Finish with a fun dessert of homemade raspberry ripple ice cream sandwich with Chambord. Readers love the 'attentive but not intrusive' service, and recommend a relaxed schedule as you simply 'have to have all three courses'. The wine list takes a grand tour through Europe with forays into the New World and starts at £18.
Chef/s: Lubos Vaskanin. **Open:** all week L 12 to 3 , D 6 to 9.30. **Meals:** Set L £18 (2 courses) to £22. Set D £28 (2 courses) to £33. Sun L £25. **Details:** 54 seats. 16 seats outside. Music.

Clarke's

Pioneering Notting Hill favourite
124 Kensington Church Street, Notting Hill,
W8 4BH
Tel no: (020) 7221 9225
www.sallyclarke.com
⊖ Notting Hill Gate, map 4
Modern British | £38
Cooking score: 3

It's hard to believe that Sally Clarke has been holding court on Kensington Church Street for 30 years. Her ground-floor dining room remains a popular destination 'bustling on a Friday night, with a nice chatty vibe'. The 'inviting' menu still has the knack of delivering punchy, forthright flavours with a sunny Mediterranean outlook. A clay oven is put through its paces for glazed squab pigeon breast and Welsh lamb rump with pomegranate, although the renowned char-grill reigns supreme – try the 'butterflied' Cornish monkfish with black olive and celery tapenade, beetroot and baked fennel. Starters could feature gravadlax with marinated beetroot and pea leaves, and a 'delicious' cheese soufflé. Dessert might bring more soufflé (perhaps a 'tasty' chocolate version) or lemon posset with candied lemon peel. Top-notch organic and biodynamic bottles loom large on the pedigree wine list, alongside bottles from Sally's beloved California; prices from £22.
Chef/s: Sally Clarke. **Open:** Mon to Sat L 12.30 to 2 (12 Sat), D 6.30 to 10. **Closed:** Sun, 10 days Christmas and New Year, 10 days Aug. **Meals:** alc (main courses £20 to £28). **Details:** 90 seats. Separate bar. Wheelchair access.

NEW ENTRY
Claude's Kitchen

Neighbourhood restaurant with big ideas
51 Parsons Green Lane, Parsons Green, SW6 4JA
Tel no: (020) 7371 8517
www.amusebouchelondon.com
⊖ Parsons Green, map 3
Modern British | £30
Cooking score: 4
£5 OFF

Upstairs from buzzy Champagne bar, Amuse Bouche, Claude's Kitchen initially looks like a modest operation: a dining room with scuffed wooden surfaces, artfully mismatched furniture and Bob Dylan on the stereo. Yet this humble veneer disguises fine breeding. Claude (Compton) is formerly of culinary aristocrats Club Gascon and Petersham Nurseries (see entries), and brings this lineage to bear in his kitchen. The menu isn't chatty – a starter might read 'raw beef/kohlrabi/beetroot/wild garlic' – but elements are masterfully assembled judging from an inspection opener: cured sardines balanced with dill pesto and horseradish, crisply offset with iced cucumber. Follow with whole Cornish mackerel improbably matched with rosemary yoghurt and spicy strawberries, or a virtuoso main of lamb chump, surrounded by swirls of squid ink and Jerusalem artichokes. Conclude in the same spirit of originality: 70% aerated chocolate with eucalyptus ice and parsnip foam, perhaps. Service is slick, and wallets are treated kindly. Wines from £19.
Chef/s: Claude Compton. **Open:** Sat and Sun L 12 to 3, Tue to Sat D 6 to 10. **Closed:** Mon, 24 to 26 Dec. **Meals:** alc (main courses £15 to £18). **Details:** 44 seats. Separate bar. Music.

Colbert

Feels like a lovely treat
50-52 Sloane Square, Chelsea, SW1W 8AX
Tel no: (020) 7730 2804
www.colbertchelsea.com
⊖ Sloane Square, map 3
French | £33
Cooking score: 2

A hit since the day it opened in October 2011, Colbert has a reputation that has spread far beyond its Chelsea locale – but then it is owned by dream-team restaurateurs Jeremy King and Chris Corbin of Wolseley, Delauney and Brasserie Zédel fame (see entries). There's a real sense of the Parisian brasserie here, from the black-and-white tiled floor and red-leather booths to the 1930s monochrome posters. The place plays to the crowds from its 8am start for breakfast until the doors close at 11pm. In trademark fashion the kitchen makes the most of a tried-and-tested French repertoire that includes tian de crabe, artichaut farci, and salade niçoise, as well as rognons à la moutarde ('lovely to see them on the menu'), magret de canard à l'orange, and chicken paillard. Finish with lemon tart, described by one fan as 'simply perfect'. Service is 'prompt and very pleasant'. The French wine list opens at £19.75.
Chef/s: Christian Turner. **Open:** 8am to 11pm (11.30pm Fri and Sat, 10.30pm Sun). **Closed:** 25 Dec. **Meals:** alc (main courses £7 to £32). **Details:** 118 seats. 22 seats outside. Separate bar. Wheelchair access. Music.

Le Colombier

Pleasing French classics
145 Dovehouse Street, Chelsea, SW3 6LB
Tel no: (020) 7351 1155
www.le-colombier-restaurant.co.uk
⊖ South Kensington, map 3
French | £42
Cooking score: 2

The address is the clue – a *colombier* is a dovecote – as Didier Garnier's *restaurant du quartier* fits snugly into the Chelsea scene, offering an undiluted French-restaurant

experience of yesteryear to patrons who had never tired of it. The look couldn't be more intuitive. A deep blue awning extends over the terrace, while inside bare boards contrast with smartly dressed tables and bistro chairs, with a well-stocked bar at one end. The menu is written in both languages ('Salade de Crabe' is crab salad), and is full of the sustaining, protein-rich, creamy-buttery dishes of old. Start with fresh shellfish 'au naturel', or oeufs en meurette, before turning to grilled sole, veal chop with thyme and garlic confit, or rack of lamb provençale with tomato and courgettes. Rest assured that crêpes will be flamingly suzetted at the end. French wines start at £18.50, and there are legions of half-bottles.
Chef/s: Philippe Tamet. **Open:** all week L 12 to 3 (3.30 Sat and Sun), D 6 to 10.30. **Meals:** alc (main courses £19 to £38). Set L £20. Sun L £24. **Details:** 65 seats. 25 seats outside. Wheelchair access.

★ TOP 50 ★

Dinner by Heston Blumenthal

A taste of history
Mandarin Oriental Hyde Park, 66 Knightsbridge, Knightsbridge, SW1X 7LA
Tel no: (020) 7201 3833
www.dinnerbyheston.com
⊖ Knightsbridge, map 4
British | £65
Cooking score: 7

🛏

Heston Blumenthal's status as one of the most gifted chefs in the land was given a boost when he opened his homage to British culinary history in the Mandarin Oriental Hotel in 2011. The day-to-day running is in the hands of Ashley Palmer-Watts, who dedicated himself to this comfortably laid-out but sedate Knightsbridge hotel dining room from the very beginning. Every ounce of his accumulated skill and devotion to the craft of cooking is channelled into dishes that are immaculately conceived, fastidiously worked through and hugely enjoyable. But what is it about the food that makes it so special? It's not just the meat fruit (the beautifully worked mandarin jelly encasing chicken liver parfait and foie gras), which feels like an old friend, even to first-timers; or the faultless Earl Grey tea-cured salmon served with a zippy lemon salad, gentleman's relish, wood sorrel and smoked roe; or the chicken cooked with lettuces, a brilliant reworking of an old theme, where slicks of grilled onion emulsion and spiced celeriac sauce evoke the flavours of old-fashioned bread sauce, and slivers of fabulously crisp chicken skin almost steal the show. This is nothing less than a reinvention of our culinary heritage, a startling update of six centuries of British food. The left-field approach also enlivens desserts, even updating the ice cream cart, which is rolled to your table on request. Ice cream is made on the spot with lots of liquid nitrogen and your choice of sprinklers with the ensuing small cone. Excellent staff pitch the tone just right, and the wine list is stuffed with pedigree drinking, but comes at unapologetic Knightsbridge prices – from £35.

Chef/s: Ashley Palmer-Watts. **Open:** all week L 12 to 3, D 6.30 to 11. **Meals:** alc (main courses £28 to £42). Set L £38. **Details:** 105 seats. Separate bar. Wheelchair access. Music. Car parking.

Ebury Restaurant & Wine Bar

Steadfast commitment to enjoyment
139 Ebury Street, Belgravia, SW1W 9QU
Tel no: (020) 7730 5447
www.eburyrestaurant.co.uk
⊖ Victoria, map 3
Modern European | £36
Cooking score: 2

£5 OFF

With its trompe l'oeil wall illustrations and colourful floral displays, the Ebury continues to resist the rise of the minimalist contemporary makeover. The reassuring, old-school nature of the restaurant has charmed many generations (it opened in 1959), with the current custodian – Nigel Windridge –

having been involved with the place since 1973. Tables are closely packed, the service team maintain maximum pampering and the kitchen shows its respect to classical traditions without seeming stuck in the past. Warm salad of rabbit confit with a tarragon cream, or seared scallops with aubergine caviar, might start a meal, before braised ox cheek with parsnip purée. There are brunch and bar options (a nifty burger, maybe), plus an entirely gluten-free menu. Desserts run to mango 'cannelloni' with passion fruit mousse and raspberry coulis. The wine list kicks off at £18.50 and has a decent selection by the glass.
Chef/s: Bernard Dumonteil. **Open:** all week L 12 to 3, D 6 to 10.15. **Closed:** 24 Dec to 2 Jan. **Meals:** alc (main courses £15 to £34). Set L and D £21 (2 courses) to £27. **Details:** 70 seats. Separate bar. Music.

Electric Diner

Fast food? You'll be hard-pressed to find better
191 Portobello Road, Notting Hill, W11 2ED
Tel no: (020) 7908 9696
www.electricdiner.com
⊖ Ladbroke Grove, map 4
French-American | £35
Cooking score: 2

Where once a film outing might be provisioned by a quick burger or pizza afterwards, matters are now a sight more appetising. Next door to the Electric House movie palace is its adjunct, the Diner. Here the action goes on all day, from breakfast to past midnight, with bar and booth seating lending the place an air of smallish-town America. The menu casts its net wide for the kinds of food bound to please most of the people all of the time – lobster roll, pork spare ribs, honey-fried chicken. Squid with pickled peppers, steak tartare, or shrimp cocktail set you up for mains such as grilled salmon in sauce vierge, crispy duck leg on lentils, and steak-frites with béarnaise. Finish with apple fritters and honeycomb ice cream. Early-evening diners going to the flicks eat half-price. The short batch of wines starts with house Languedoc in all three colours at £20.

Chef/s: Gilbert Holmes. **Open:** all week 8am to 11pm (midnight Thur to Sat, 10pm Sun). **Closed:** 25 Dec. **Meals:** alc (main courses £9 to £19). **Details:** 75 seats. 6 seats outside.

L'Etranger

Idiosyncratic Franco-Japanese alliance
36 Gloucester Road, South Kensington, SW7 4QT
Tel no: (020) 7584 1118
www.etranger.co.uk
⊖ **Gloucester Road, South Kensington, map 3**
Modern French | £50
Cooking score: 4

🍷

A cool customer in Kensington for many years, idiosyncratic L'Etranger melds edgy 1980s minimalism, mirrors and expanses of leather with black-lacquered tables and neutral wood tones. The food also looks east and west for inspiration, offering a full menu of sushi and sashimi as well as four kinds of caviar and thoroughly modern French creations such as smoked duck cooked two ways with foie gras, beetroot and Cassis. It's not fusion, but a gently convincing alliance of two gastro-cultures who occupy separate rooms but occasionally pop into bed together – witness lamb fillet and sweetbread with miso aubergine and spicy tomato, or veal chop with salsify, celeriac purée and sancho pepper jus. Desserts such as chocolate fondant with green tea ice cream also offer the excuse for a cross-border get-together. L'Etranger's wine list is one of the best in town, a stupendous collection of grande marque Champagne, vintage French grandees and classy New World contenders with prices from £28. Casual spin-off Meursault is in the basement. **Chef/s:** Jérôme Tauvron. **Open:** all week L 12 to 3, D 6 to 11 (11.30 Fri and Sat, 10 Sun). **Meals:** alc (main courses £10 to £70). Set L £18 (2 courses) to £23. Early D Mon to Fri £23 (2 courses) to £26. Tasting menu £95. **Details:** 65 seats. Separate bar.

The Five Fields

Upping the ante in Chelsea
8-9 Blacklands Terrace, Chelsea, SW3 2SP
Tel no: (020) 7838 1082
www.fivefieldsrestaurant.com
⊖ **Sloane Square, map 3**
Modern British | £50
Cooking score: 5

V

Taylor Bonnyman really upped the ante in Chelsea when opening his intimate town-house restaurant near Sloane Square. Within, the elegant, smooth-toned dining room (restrained colours, just-so fittings) creates an air of civilised comfort, an oh-so-chic backdrop for cooking that relies on top ingredients (mainly British), thoughtful sourcing and meticulous craftsmanship. The food is a triumph of delicate, intricate detailing and virtuosity, with menus built around pretty plates (of three or eight courses). Vegetables and unusual herbs share the limelight with meat, fish, even desserts (a pea and mint cassonade with coconut sorbet and chocolate soil has fans aplenty). Otherwise, expect a herb-strewn smoked eel, sea urchin and English caviar; quail teamed with aubergine, artichoke and black garlic; monkfish with caper, romanesco and brown butter; or fallow deer with shiitake, jamón and morels. Recent reports of 'beautifully judged dishes' prove the Five Fields is riding high on confidence. The French-leaning wine list opens at £25. **Chef/s:** Taylor Bonnyman. **Open:** Tue to Sat D only 6 to 10. **Closed:** Sun, Mon, first 2 weeks Jan, first 2 weeks Sept. **Meals:** Set D £38 (2 courses) to £50. Tasting menu £75. **Details:** 40 seats. Separate bar. Wheelchair access. Music. Car parking.

Garnier

As French as they come
314 Earl's Court Road, Earl's Court, SW5 9BQ
Tel no: (020) 7370 4536
www.garnier-restaurant-london.co.uk
⊖ Earl's Court, map 3
French | £38
Cooking score: 2
£5 OFF

Didier and Eric Garnier have clocked up a formidable wealth of service to London gastronomy between them, joining forces in 2012 to open a traditional French venue in Earl's Court. It wears a bright modern look, with cream walls, framed prints and large mirrors, but the cuisine is unabashedly *ancien régime*. Escargot fricassee in parsley velouté with garlic croûtons is a possible opener. Not a snail fan? Smoked eel with a beetroot and horseradish mousse and saffron potatoes might delight, prior to entrées of rabbit leg stuffed with black pudding, beef fillet in béarnaise, or a positively new-fangled tranche of grilled tuna, seasoned with five-spice and accompanied by butternut purée and Jerusalem artichoke. If you haven't room for profiteroles or cheeses, at least allow staff to drench a sorbet in Mandarine Napoléon. An entirely French wine list contains some glittering treasures. Bottles from £18.50.
Chef/s: Daniele Zaffora. **Open:** all week L 12 to 3 (3.30 Sun), D 6 to 11 (10 Sun). **Meals:** alc (main courses £14 to £32). Set L £18 (2 courses). Sun L £21. **Details:** 45 seats. Wheelchair access.

Goode & Wright

Egalitarian bistro with a Notting Hill swagger
271 Portobello Road, Notting Hill, W11 1LR
Tel no: (020) 7727 5552
www.goodeandwright.co.uk
⊖ Ladbroke Grove, map 1
Anglo-French | £29
Cooking score: 3
£30

There's no mistaking the Francophile leanings here: from the chequerboard flooring, via the leather banquettes, to the menu bursting with Parisian bistro-inspired dishes delivered with a bit of Notting Hill swagger. There are pavement tables – for a cheeky Gauloises maybe – and an open kitchen to confirm the place is fully on-trend. An all-day menu delivers bavette steak with a fried egg and the house croque, with the evening output getting going with a salad of salt-baked beetroot with goats' curd and grilled Little Gem, before a main course of braised ox cheek with Jerusalem artichoke purée and tarragon mustard. The presence of a kids' menu shows the egalitarian nature of the place. When it's time for dessert, take a gander at the specials board to check out the éclair of the day (dark chocolate and pistachio if you're lucky). The drinks list includes absinthe cocktails, and wines from £20.
Chef/s: Finlay Logan. **Open:** Tue to Sun L 11 to 5 (10 to 4 Sat and Sun), Tue to Sat D 6 to 10. **Closed:** Mon, 24 to 27 Dec. **Meals:** alc (main courses £13 to £19). **Details:** 42 seats. 4 seats outside. Wheelchair access. Music.

NEW ENTRY

The Goring

A splendid old-stager gets a new lease of life
15 Beeston Place, Belgravia, SW1W 0JW
Tel no: (020) 7396 9000
www.thegoring.com
⊖ Victoria, map 3
Modern British | £55
Cooking score: 4

Fêted as London's oldest privately owned hotel and holder of a Royal Warrant, there is something splendidly solid and traditional about the Goring – a fact underlined by bowler-hatted door staff, a glorious bar and the David Linley-designed dining room. Since Shay Cooper, last seen in the Guide at the Bingham in Richmond (see entry), has taken over as executive chef, the food is vastly improved. Cooper is doing a good job, modernising the menu but respecting tradition. The daily roast trolley and the never-off-the-menu specials such as potted shrimps and Dover sole continue, but now

there are modern British choices such as an excellent artichoke salad with marinated mushrooms, hollandaise and cep vinaigrette, or salt marsh lamb with hotpot potatoes, haggis, pickled red cabbage and mint. A superb all-British cheeseboard increases the appeal, and service is good, too. The wine list puts the emphasis on Bordeaux and Burgundy, opens at £28 and then soars.
Chef/s: Shay Cooper. **Open:** Sun to Fri L 12 to 2.30, all week D 6 to 10. **Meals:** Set L £43. Set D £33 (2 courses) to £53. Sun L £48. **Details:** 70 seats. 35 seats outside. Separate bar. Wheelchair access. Car parking.

Granger & Co.
A ray of sunshine in Notting Hill
175 Westbourne Grove, Notting Hill, W11 2SB
Tel no: (020) 7229 8944
www.grangerandco.com
⊖ Notting Hill Gate, map 4
Australian | £30
Cooking score: 3

Aussie chef and TV star Bill Granger is dubbed 'the egg master of Sydney' down under, and his all-day eatery brings a ray of sunshine to Notting Hill. You can't book and queuing is inevitable, but it's worth waiting for Granger's stunning line up of flavours – think pepped-up pan-Asian and Pacific Rim, augmented by home-grown ideas. Those famous ricotta hot cakes, sweetcorn fritters and (of course) the must-order scrambled eggs open the show, ahead of 'bowls and grains', 'big plates', BBQ specials, burgers, sandwiches and more. Grazers might fancy shaved kohlrabi with taramasalata and ground sesame or fried calamari with green papaya, nuoc cham (fish sauce), herbs and crispy shallots, while those with heartier appetites could fill up on Parmesan-crumbed chicken with creamed corn and fennel slaw or masala bream with cumin-roast tomatoes. Cakes hit the sweet spot, likewise puds such as lemon curd and ginger nut cheesecake. Wines from £19.50.

Chef/s: Mark Welch. **Open:** all week 7am to 10.30pm (8am to 9.30pm Sun). **Closed:** 25 and 26 Dec. **Meals:** alc (main courses £11 to £18). **Details:** 70 seats. 6 seats outside. Wheelchair access. Music.

★ TOP 50 PUB ★

The Harwood Arms
Gastronomic excellence and a fine wine list
Walham Grove, Fulham, SW6 1QP
Tel no: (020) 7386 1847
www.harwoodarms.com
⊖ Fulham Broadway, map 3
British | £40
Cooking score: 5
🍷

This laid-back hostelry on a very residential street behind Fulham Broadway has flourished triumphantly since launching in 2008 and now has a reputation that spreads far beyond its locale. The Harwood Arms remains a pub at heart with a large central bar, real ales and weekly quiz nights, though food is very much top of the agenda. The menu taps into the UK's regional network and there's plenty to applaud; the famed venison Scotch egg and shared rib of beef with excellent Yorkshire pudding remain firm favourites. The kitchen makes the most of top-notch ingredients, and a summer meal delivered crisp pressed shoulder of rabbit with carrots, dandelion and lovage, and perfectly timed roast Cornish cod with Jersey Royals, tenderstem broccoli and laverbread. Buttermilk pudding with English strawberries and toasted almonds made a perfect finish. Keenly competitive prices are a laudable feature of the vibrant, up-to-the-minute wine list, which opens at £16.50.
Chef/s: Alex Harper. **Open:** Tue to Sun L 12 to 3 (4 Sun), all week D 6.30 to 9.30 (7 to 9 Sun). **Closed:** 24 to 28 Dec, 1 Jan. **Meals:** alc (main courses £20 to £25). Set L £20 (2 courses) to £25. **Details:** 50 seats. Separate bar. Music.

The Havelock Tavern
Bona fide local with eclectic food
57 Masbro Road, Shepherd's Bush, W14 0LS
Tel no: (020) 7603 5374
www.havelocktavern.com
⊖ Shepherd's Bush, Olympia, map 3
Modern British | £25
Cooking score: 2
£30

When it comes to the restaurant-pub conundrum, the Havelock Tavern has always seemed more pub than restaurant, and so it continues. The old corner boozer maintains its original streetwise demeanour with chunky wooden tables and floorboards, and a lack of interior artistic embellishment. While the bar serves up a changing array of real ales, the kitchen turns out feel-good flavours like steamed mussels with smoked bacon and cider, or Butcher's Dog sausage with a milk bun and chilli mustard. There's warm leek tart if meat-free is the order of the day, or a full-on meat-fest where fillet of beef comes with triple-cooked chips and béarnaise. Sticky ginger pudding with vanilla ice cream seems like an appropriate way to sign off. Wines from £17.50.
Chef/s: James Howarth. **Open:** all week L 12.30 to 2.30 (3 Sun), D 7 to 10 (9.30 Sun). **Closed:** 25 and 26 Dec. **Meals:** alc (main courses £10 to £25). **Details:** 80 seats. 20 seats outside. Separate bar. Wheelchair access.

★ TOP 50 ★

Hedone
A unique dining experience
301-303 Chiswick High Road, Chiswick, W4 4HH
Tel no: (020) 8747 0377
www.hedonerestaurant.com
⊖ Chiswick Park, map 1
Modern European | £50
Cooking score: 7

Our readers have been in and out of love with Mikael Jonsson's restaurant for the last two years, but the high rating reflects their (and our) current enthusiasm for the phenomenal amount of creative cooking going on here –

even the bread is addictive. Jonsson's style relies unequivocally on the quality of ingredients. In the height of the English asparagus season, he imports asparagus from the Luberon (because the flavour is more intense) and combines it with avocado, pistachio and wild garlic to give a vivid springtime hit of lush greenness. The sweetness of Roscoff onion consommé is offset by the umami hit from a raviolo improbably filled with a warm Parmesan liquid. Beautifully cooked breast and leg of squab pigeon is given edge with endive, sweetness and acidity from beetroot and blackcurrant. Warm chocolate mousse – served over a passion fruit jelly, covered with a 'biscuit' of raspberry powder and topped with vanilla ice cream – takes an age of intricate care to construct and has about one minute of shelf life before starting to disintegrate. The almost unanimous verdict is that for quality of cooking and the kitchen's care and attention to detail, it's hard to beat. Hedone is not without critics, though. There are those who bemoan the passing of a menu with choice; others long for a little more atmosphere and more of the folderol expected of a restaurant at this level – after all, this is a dining experience not to be approached in a hurry. As for wine, by-the-glass pairing complements the food and 'is done very well'.
Chef/s: Mikael Jonsson. **Open:** Thur to Sat L 12 to 2.30, Tue to Sat D 6.30 to 9.30. **Closed:** Sun, Mon. **Meals:** Set L £35. Set D £55 (Tue and Wed only). Tasting menus £75 to £95. **Details:** 40 seats.

Hereford Road
Cherished local with no-nonsense Brit cooking
3 Hereford Road, Notting Hill, W2 4AB
Tel no: (020) 7727 1144
www.herefordroad.org
⊖ Bayswater, map 4
British | £26
Cooking score: 2
£30

Seven years on, Tom Pemberton's converted butcher's shop continues to enjoy faithful support. 'I'd say a pretty-near perfect

neighbourhood restaurant,' confided one reporter, mightily impressed by the modern, relaxed feel to the two-tier dining space and by her Brit-accented, no-nonsense meal. This is food that deserves credit for its lack of ostentation. Scrupulously seasonal, the kitchen moves from winter platefuls of marinated salt pollack served with potato spiked with eye-wateringly pungent horseradish, or red-legged partridge atop lentils, squash and mushrooms, to springtime hits such as potted crab or soft herring roes and black butter, followed by roast lamb rack with purple sprouting broccoli and anchovy. Desserts will tempt, even if you didn't think you needed one. Chocolate terrine and blood orange, and poached pear with meringue, chocolate and hazelnuts are highly recommended. Wines start at £19.50.
Chef/s: Tom Pemberton. **Open:** all week L 12 to 3 (4 Sun), D 6 to 10.30 (10 Sun). **Closed:** 23 Dec to 2 Jan, 30 Aug to 2 Sept. **Meals:** alc (main courses £10 to £16). Set L £13 (2 courses) to £16. **Details:** 66 seats. 8 seats outside. Wheelchair access.

Hunan
Regional Chinese food served with a twist
51 Pimlico Road, Chelsea, SW1W 8NE
Tel no: (020) 7730 5712
www.hunanlondon.com
⊖ Sloane Square, map 3
Chinese | £51
Cooking score: 3

V

'Hunan's approach may be unconventional but it is enjoyable', noted a first-time visitor to this unique, no-menu Chinese restaurant. State what you can't or won't eat, then leave it to chef/proprietor Michael Peng to deliver a succession of tapas-style dishes, mostly influenced by the food of Taiwan. The set-price dinner might bring up to 18 dishes, among them pork, mince and bamboo broth; octopus salad; pork dumplings with pineapple and bitter melon; and cod with a sliver of thousand-year-old egg. Hunan's crowning glory (at additional cost) is 'light, fresh' crab soup with homemade noodles served with huge chunks of unshelled crab: 'expect to get your hands dirty'. The interior is simple, stark even, but tempered by 'attentive and cheerful' service. The chef might come out to check progress, and ask 'you hungry, you want more?' which 'really adds to the enjoyment factor'. Drink wine (from £19) or saké.
Chef/s: Michael Peng. **Open:** Mon to Sat L 12.30 to 2, D 6.30 to 11. **Closed:** Sun, bank hols. **Meals:** Set L and D £33 (2 courses) to £51. Chef's menu £80. **Details:** 48 seats. 4 seats outside.

Indian Zing
Cool vibes, thrilling food
236 King Street, Hammersmith, W6 0RF
Tel no: (020) 8748 5959
www.indianzing.co.uk
⊖ Ravenscourt Park, map 1
Indian | £35
Cooking score: 3

V

Maharashtra-born Manoj Vasaikar has a distinguished CV, having worked for both the Taj and Oberoi groups in India. Ravenscourt Park may seem a less intuitive locale for his eclectic new-wave approach, but the place has become a destination. The white-walled spaces, hung with colourful artworks, have been designed with elemental harmony in mind – as have the menus, which blend old and new styles in elegant synthesis. A starter of bhaji-like vegetable bhanavla is baked and griddled, then dressed in tamarind and herb relish, while jumbo prawn and aubergine kharphatla is finished with caramelised onions and tomato masala. Main-course ingredients are top drawer, as evidenced by the Khyber lamb shank in ginger and poppy seed sauce, karwari fish curry scented with the peppery west-coast spice tirfal, or good old chicken jalfrezi, thick with peppers, chillies and herbs. Finish with tandoori apricot in spiced Cointreau. Wines start at £16.
Chef/s: Manoj Vasaikar. **Open:** all week L 12 to 3 (1 to 4 Sun), D 6 to 11 (10 Sun). **Meals:** alc (main courses £9 to £22). Set L £12 (2 courses) to £15. Sun L £12 (2 courses) to £15. **Details:** 51 seats. 20 seats outside. Wheelchair access. Music.

Kensington Place
Long-running brasserie icon
201-209 Kensington Church Street, Notting Hill, W8 7LX
Tel no: (020) 7727 3184
www.kensingtonplace-restaurant.co.uk
⊖ Notting Hill Gate, map 4
Modern British | £32
Cooking score: 2

Kensington Place virtually defined London's hotshot brasserie scene back in the 1980s: a high-decibel, plate-glass celeb magnet frequented by Princess Di and famed for its freewheeling approach. Following a refit, the venue has regained some of its special charge, even if it isn't quite the iconic eatery of yore. The din and the glass remain, although there's now a trompe l'oeil lily pond, splashes of yellow and some curious bovine prints. The French-inspired bistro menu leans heavily on pickings from the on-site fishmonger, so expect the likes of spiced Devon crab with chapatis, the legendary KP fish pie, or sea bass fillet with cauliflower, 'brown beech' mushrooms and chicken sauce. You can also order your 'market fish' simply grilled or steamed – or head down the carnivorous route with foie gras parfait and port jelly followed by braised suckling pig with pulled pork, celeriac, apples and black garlic. Perky brasserie wines from £22.
Chef/s: Daniel Loftin. **Open:** Tue to Sun L 12 to 3 (3.30 Sun), Mon to Sat D 6.30 to 10 (10.30 Fri and Sat). **Closed:** 24 to 26 Dec, 1 and 2 Jan, bank hols. **Meals:** alc (main courses £13 to £22). Set L and D £25 (2 courses) to £30. **Details:** 110 seats. Wheelchair access. Music.

Symbols
🛏 Accommodation is available
£30 Three courses for less than £30
V Separate vegetarian menu
£5 £5-off voucher scheme
🍷 Notable wine list

LOCAL GEM
▲ Kiraku
8 Station Parade, Uxbridge Road, Ealing, W5 3LD
Tel no: (020) 8992 2848
www.kiraku.co.uk
⊖ Ealing Common, map 1
Japanese | £35 £5

An antidote to the familiar Japanese chains, Kiraku is a family-run joint that offers a few more esoteric options among the old favourites. It won't intimidate a first-timer, though, with its simple, modern décor and easy-going attitude. Sushi and sashimi are a good bet – squid and shiso-leaf roll and hirame (turbot) respectively – while the hot stuff includes grilled salted mackerel and generous bowls of udon noodles. Wines start at £15, though saké is a more enticing option. Closed Mon.

Kitchen W8
Big-city brio and neighbourhood glitz
11-13 Abingdon Road, Kensington, W8 6AH
Tel no: (020) 7937 0120
www.kitchenw8.com
⊖ High Street Kensington, map 4
Modern European | £43
Cooking score: 6

There's a pulled-together, tightly modern look to this place that suits its Kensington location to a T. The cooking is every bit as classy, treating top-drawer ingredients with pinpoint accuracy and a flair for arty, poised presentation. Each dish has numerous elements – witness an opening salad of cauliflower with brown shrimps, young squid, samphire, seaweed and an oyster beignet; or a main course of roast Creedy Carver duck with bulgur wheat, minced livers, chestnuts, turnips and sprouts. Flavours are deftly handled; one reporter was thrilled by a main course in which 'scorched onions combined with venison to produce flavours that lingered like chocolate'. In comparison to the savoury courses, desserts are relatively straightforward: maybe roast comice pear with gingerbread ice cream and spiced wafers or Yorkshire rhubarb and blood-orange mess. The international wine list includes a decent selection by the glass or carafe, and kicks off at £20 a bottle.

Chef/s: Mark Kempson. **Open:** all week L 12 to 2.30 (12.30 to 3 Sun), D 6 to 10.30 (6.30 to 9 Sun). **Closed:** 24 to 26 Dec, bank hols. **Meals:** alc (main courses £20 to £28). Set L £21 (2 courses) to £23. Set D £22 (2 courses) to £25. Sun L £33. **Details:** 75 seats. Wheelchair access.

Koffmann's

The old master rides on
The Berkeley, Wilton Place, Belgravia, SW1X 7RL
Tel no: (020) 7235 1010
www.the-berkeley.co.uk
⊖ Knightsbridge, Hyde Park Corner, map 4
French | £55
Cooking score: 5

🛏

Anyone who remembers the glory days when Pierre Koffmann ruled at La Tante Claire might be surprised by the old master's return to form in an affable dining room full of flowers. Some formality may have gone, but the food is as forthright as ever – well-aged, supremely crafted and packed with potency. Monsieur K's emblematic glazed pig's trotter stuffed with sweetbreads and morels is still wickedly earthy; Dover sole grenobloise shouldn't be overlooked; and roast grouse is 'classic Gascony to a T', presented with girolles, celeriac mousse, game chips, bread sauce and a rich confit spread on fried bread. After that, the equally legendary pistachio soufflé with pistachio ice cream shows matchless technique and perfect timing. Less expensive are the hugely enjoyable 'proper lunches' of, say, Russian salad, halibut with broad beans and pear Bourdaloue with vanilla ice cream. The ample regional wine list lingers long in Koffmann's beloved south-west France. Bottles from £26.

Chef/s: Pierre Koffmann. **Open:** all week L 12 to 2.30 (3 Sat and Sun), D 6 to 10.30. **Meals:** alc (main courses £25 to £34). Set L £22 (2 courses) to £26.

Set D £24 (2 courses) to £28. Sun L £23 (2 courses) to £26. **Details:** 120 seats. Separate bar. Wheelchair access. Music.

Launceston Place

Fashionable food without frivolity
1a Launceston Place, South Kensington, W8 5RL
Tel no: (020) 7937 6912
www.launcestonplace-restaurant.co.uk
⊖ Gloucester Road, map 3
Modern British | £52
Cooking score: 6

Urbane, clubby surrounds create an air of civilised formality at chi-chi Launceston Place – a series of cosy, interconnecting rooms in a quirky Kensington town house, with big windows, restrained colour schemes and elegant, just-so fittings. Appropriately, the kitchen eschews wild frivolity in favour of clear flavours, well-honed technique and intricate detailing. Scallops are regularly mentioned in dispatches – perhaps served with truffle cassonade, confit chicken wing and sorrel, or in a 'perfectly balanced' combo alongside pork belly, apple and celeriac. Readers have raved about 'sublime' Ibérico pork with broad beans, too, but you might also encounter luxurious Wagyu beef rump with stuffed Cévennes onions or a vibrant dish of lemon sole with Padrón pepper and brandade, squid, brown shrimps and fennel. To finish, share a whole roasted pineapple with lime and bourbon cheesecake. Proceedings run at a gentle pace, overseen by a brigade of impeccably trained staff who strike just the right balance between 'chat and service'. The serious-minded wine list offers a classy mix of 'classic' and 'eclectic' bottles from £25.

Chef/s: Tim Allen. **Open:** Wed to Sun L 12 to 2.30, Tue to Sun D 6 to 10 (6.30 to 9.30 Sun). **Closed:** Mon. **Meals:** Set L £30. Set D £52. Sun L £35. Tasting menu £70 (6 courses). **Details:** 50 seats. Separate bar. Wheelchair access. Music.

The Ledbury

Astonishing food from an Aussie star
127 Ledbury Road, Notting Hill, W11 2AQ
Tel no: (020) 7792 9090
www.theledbury.com
⊖ Notting Hill Gate, Westbourne Park, map 4
Modern British | £80
Cooking score: 8

🍸 V

Brett Graham's career has taken him from 15-year-old apprentice in a New South Wales fish restaurant to the creative ferment of Philip Howard's Square (see entry) and, since 2005, his own show here. The Ledbury may look rather sombre outside, but within is a refined scene of gathered drapes, mirrors and diffused light, creating a sense of community that the flawless front-of-house staff do much to augment. Graham has been a pioneer in the development of British modernism, with the kind of cooking that reaches tirelessly for innovation and produces gasps of delight. Clay-baked beetroot with a roll of smoked eel and its mousse is a typically bold opening statement, then surpassed by tender mackerel grilled over naked flame, alongside pickled cucumber, shiso and Celtic mustard. Turbot arrives with what one reader calls a retinue of 'courtiers and foreign ambassadors': bulgur, quinoa, sea kale and crab. Pigeon receives star billing – roast breast and confit leg served with quince and red vegetables – or there may be Belted Galloway fillet with junipered celeriac, bone marrow and garlic flowers. Desserts perform incredible tricks with sweetness, for a brown-sugar tart with Sauternes-poached grapes and ginger ice cream, or pear cooked in brown butter, with walnuts, barley meal and caramelised goats' milk. A ripsnorter of a wine list is only fitting, the glass selection alone furnishing enough choice (from £9) to get you through, but piling on with Alsacians, Spaniards, Australians and more, of unarguable class. Bottles from £25.

Chef/s: Brett Graham. **Open:** Tue to Sun L 12 to 2 (2.30 Sun), all week D 6.30 to 10.15 (7 to 10 Sun). **Closed:** 25 and 26 Dec, Aug bank hol. **Meals:** alc (main courses £30 to £32). Set L £30 (2 courses) to £35. Set D £80. Sun L £50. Tasting menu £105 (10 courses). **Details:** 55 seats.

The Mall Tavern

Comfort food with a dash of good humour
71-73 Palace Gardens Terrace, Notting Hill, W8 4RU
Tel no: (020) 7229 3374
www.themalltavern.com
⊖ Notting Hill Gate, map 4
Modern British | £29
Cooking score: 2

£30

Local spies confirm little has changed at this 'terribly well-heeled Notting Hill pub' despite a change of chef. The Victorian hostelry continues to charm, with its dark-wood and leather interior. The big central bar acts as a divider, creating a sunny street-side bar and a back dining room with closely packed tables. To eat, the trademark mac and cheese, 'PGT' salmon (smoked on the premises and accompanied by own-made soda bread), and 'big beefy pie with a bone-marrow trough' remain on the menu, served in generous portions. A mixed mid-winter salad with 'our ham' and a tangled heap of chicory leaves, caperberries and spicy slaw, topped with a deep-fried egg, gets the thumbs-up this year, with the general consensus being that 'this is cooking from someone who has a genuine love of food, clear flavoured and big of heart'. Too full for dessert? Then order the salted-caramel chocolate Rolos. Wine from £19.50. **Chef/s:** Asher Abramowitz. **Open:** all week 12 to 10. **Meals:** alc (main courses £9 to £18). **Details:** 85 seats. 20 seats outside. Separate bar.

The Malt House
Raising the bar for the Broadway
17 Vanston Place, Fulham, SW6 1AY
Tel no: (020) 7084 6888
www.malthousefulham.co.uk
⊖ Fulham Broadway, map 3
British | £30
Cooking score: 4

Marcus
New look, special-occasion feeling
The Berkeley, Wilton Place, Belgravia, SW1X 7RL
Tel no: (020) 7235 1200
www.marcus-wareing.com
⊖ Hyde Park Corner, Knightsbridge, map 4
Modern British | £85
Cooking score: 7

V

Good eateries are feeling less marooned among the burger shops and kebabery of Fulham Broadway. The Harwood Arms (see entry) is nearby, and fairly new to the party is this younger sibling of Wimbledon's Fox & Grapes (see entry). A sympathetic reboot has brought a cleaner, lighter, fresher feel to the Malt House, with neutral notes and Victorian features. Similarly elevated is the usual round of pub classics: the pie might now be rabbit, smoked sausage and mushroom, for example. Look to the seasonal menu for some delicate, deft cooking: malt-braised pork belly with exemplary Dorset snails, celeriac purée and purple sprouting broccoli, say, or a quadripartite salad of onions (pickled, sweet, roasted, puréed) teamed with potatoes and grated Ardrahan cheese, or a risotto-like creamed Jerusalem artichoke with leek, truffle and pearl barley with ash brittle. The courtyard entices in good weather, and rooms are available. Wine starts at £19.
Chef/s: Philip Harrison. **Open:** Mon to Sat L 12 to 3, D 6 to 10. Sun 12 to 10. **Closed:** 25 Dec. **Meals:** alc (main courses £14 to £21). **Details:** 80 seats. 20 seats outside. Separate bar. Wheelchair access. Music.

Visit us Online
To find out more about *The Good Food Guide*, please visit www.thegoodfoodguide.co.uk

Gone is the claret colour scheme, the lampshades, the petite chandeliers – after an extensive refurb Marcus Wareing at the Berkeley has been replaced by the more informal Marcus, though in the world of five-star luxury hotels this still means white tablecloths and a battalion of formally dressed staff. Nevertheless, the mood is lighter, as is the wood and cream-coloured room, and the aforementioned staff are more relaxed, even chatty. But the new Marcus is not the Marcus Wareing restaurant for which fans of the chef have been hoping. Meals still proceed at a measured pace, napkins folded if you leave the table, there's a lot of crumbing down, but at these prices, well, you expect it. There is no hiding the fact that a meal here is expensive, and while the cooking is elegant, it is not quite on a par with the very best in the city. Yet there are some surprising treasures, for Wareing achieves a rare degree of refinement in what he does: foie gras perfectly matched by the sweetness of mango, given texture by granola; an 'absolutely stunning' salmon and delicate langoustine, the whole infused with just a hint of lime; a seriously fresh piece of turbot in a tangle of Dorset snails, shallot and excellent gnocchi. The fennel and potato bread shines, too; the cheeseboard is superb, as is a beautifully rendered iced vanilla cream topped with gariguette strawberries and flavoured with basil and lime. The sommelier's wise counsel is priceless when it comes to navigating the stupendous wine list, which is high on quality and generously inclusive outside France (its main port of call). Bottles from £35. Details overleaf.

Chef/s: Marcus Wareing and Mark Froydenlund.
Open: Mon to Sat L 12 to 2.30, D 6 to 11. Closed:
Sun, 1 Jan. Meals: Set L £30 (2 courses) to £38. Set
D £60 (2 courses) to £85. Tasting menu £120.
Details: 92 seats. Wheelchair access.

Medlar
Bold flavours and immaculate culinary skill
438 King's Road, Chelsea, SW10 0LJ
Tel no: (020) 7349 1900
www.medlarrestaurant.co.uk
⊖ Sloane Square, Fulham Broadway, map 3
Modern European | £35
Cooking score: 5

Joe Mercer Nairne's 'remarkable' food, French
in character but wider-ranging in influence,
impresses visitors to his World's End
restaurant: 'I get the feeling they know what
they're doing in this kitchen' being a typical
comment. Medlar's long, narrow dining
room, accented with pale green, opens on to
the street in summer. On the menu, seasonal
variation is balanced with popular mainstays –
duck egg tart with red wine sauce, for
instance, and 'under blade' fillet with Café de
Paris snails. Generous platefuls and bold
flavours, combined with immaculate culinary
skill, command the attention: witness the hare
with semolina tagliatelle, chestnuts,
chanterelle, celery and Lincolnshire Poacher,
or 'outstanding' roast grouse. Finish with a
'triumphant' cherry clafoutis, pink grapefruit
and Campari sorbet with pomegranate and
brandy snaps, or the excellent cheeseboard.
The wine list (from £26) contains plenty
from Europe alongside carefully chosen New
World bottles. Everything is available by the
carafe.
Chef/s: Joe Mercer Nairne. Open: all week L 12 to 3,
D 6.30 to 10.30. Closed: 24 to 26 Dec, 1 Jan.
Meals: Set L Mon to Fri £22 (2 courses) to £27. Set L
Sat £30. Set D £38 (2 courses) to £45. Sun L and D
£35. Details: 75 seats. 8 seats outside.

Outlaw's at the Capital
Flat-out excellent seafood
Capital Hotel, 22-24 Basil Street, Knightsbridge,
SW3 1AT
Tel no: (020) 7589 5171
www.capitalhotel.co.uk
⊖ Knightsbridge, map 4
Seafood | £55
Cooking score: 6

🍽 V

Just behind Harrods, amid some of the more
expensive real estate on earth, Outlaw's at the
Capital Hotel offers one of the best-value
lunchtime deals in town. For one reporter –
whose visit to the Nathan Outlaw flagship in
Rock, Cornwall (see entry) made her all-time
top five – lunch here of 'piping hot fishcakes',
silky carrot soup with chunk of tender ham
hock, mackerel cooked 'just right', dark
chocolate mousse on peanut ice cream, treacle
tartlets and rich chocolate truffles more than
lived up to expectations. Peter Biggs heads the
kitchen, perfectly in tune with the timing that
is everything in fish cookery. He delivers not
surprise or innovation, but freshness (fish is
delivered daily from Cornwall) and a feel for
flavour; each dish has a central taste and others
support it. So, from the pricier à la carte, the
flavour of lobster risotto is accentuated by
orange and basil, and red mullet gains depth
from olives, saffron and mussel sauce. The
heavyweight wine list has prices to match
(from £30), but there's a decent selection by
the glass.
Chef/s: Nathan Outlaw and Peter Biggs. Open: Mon
to Sat L 12 to 2, D 6.30 to 10.30. Closed: Sun.
Meals: alc (main courses £26 to £34). Set L £20 (2
courses) to £25. Set D £45 (2 courses) to £54.
Tasting menu £70 (6 courses). Details: 34 seats.
Separate bar. Wheelchair access. Music.

Pétrus
Blue-blooded Ramsay outpost
1 Kinnerton Street, Knightsbridge, SW1X 8EA
Tel no: (020) 7592 1609
www.gordonramsay.com
⊖ Knightsbridge, map 4
Modern French | £65
new chef/no score

V

Gordon Ramsay's rebooted Pétrus is big on low-key comforts, with just enough luxury to soothe the Knightsbridge set and make them feel at home. A glass-fronted wine store holds pride of place in the highly civilised dining room, while deep claret tones emphasise the oenophile theme. As the Guide went to press it was announced that Neil Snowball was taking over from resident chef Sean Burbidge, although few details were available. However, given that Snowball is a Ramsay protégé – and more recently senior development chef at the Fat Duck (see entry) – it's likely the kitchen will continue to deliver fastidious, French-accented food for sophisticated palates. As for the wine list, expect serried ranks of ultra-rare Château Pétrus for those with bulging wallets, plus a treasure trove of slightly less arcane tipples from elsewhere: all lurking within the aforementioned wine store. Prices rarely dip below £40. Reports please.
Chef/s: Neil Snowball. **Open:** Mon to Sat L 12 to 2.30, D 6.30 to 10.30. **Closed:** Sun, 25 and 26 Dec, 1 Jan. **Meals:** Set L £35. Set D £65. **Details:** 54 seats. Separate bar. Wheelchair access. Music.

LOCAL GEM
▲ Pizza East Portobello
310 Portobello Road, Ladbroke Grove, W10 5TA
Tel no: (020) 8969 4500
www.pizzaeastportobello.com
⊖ Ladbroke Grove, map 1
Italian-American | £25

An old corner boozer has been stripped out, pared back and given a dose of urban cool by the folk at Pizza East (see also entries in Kentish Town and Shoreditch). The venue occupies two floors, with an open kitchen at ground level showing off the wood-fired oven. Expect top-drawer pizzas: crispy pork belly, tomato and mushrooms, say, or burrata and black olives. There's roast chicken with aïoli, too, and ace cured meats and cheeses. Wines from £20. Open all week.

NEW ENTRY
Polpo
Upscale of Soho Original
126-128 Notting Hill Gate, Notting Hill, W11 3QG
Tel no: (020) 7229 3283
www.polpo.co.uk
⊖ Notting Hill Gate, map 4
Italian | £25
Cooking score: 2
£30

As the tentacles of Russell Norman's Polpo empire extend beyond its Soho heartland, *The Restaurant Man* has a challenge on his hands to stay true to his vision of the Venetian bàcaro (or casual eatery). This Notting Hill newcomer is the largest so far: a distressed, bare light bulbs, red banquettes and tiled affair. Diners are encouraged to order several small dishes, ranging from cicchetti (small bites) like spicy salami butter and broad bean crostini, via light pizzette (white, flatbread-style pizza, perhaps with cured pork shoulder and pickled pepper), to spicy pork and fennel meatballs or sliced flank steak with rocket and Parmesan. Fish-wise, there's the mascot octopus with potato salad. To conclude, a dessert of affogato al caffè might be all you can manage. Dishes aren't universally successful, but the place scores well for flexibility and value. Wine starts at £18, with an Aperol spritz or a Bellini possible aperitifs. No bookings.
Chef/s: Jason Wass. **Open:** all week 12 to 11 (10.30 Sun). **Meals:** alc (tapas £3 to £14). **Details:** 120 seats. Separate bar.

Popeseye Steak House

A red-blooded steak-fest
108 Blythe Road, Olympia, W14 0HD
Tel no: (020) 7610 4578
www.popeseye.com
⊖ Olympia, map 3
Steaks | £30
Cooking score: 1
£5 OFF

Hitting the 20-year mark in 2015, Ian Hutchinson's steak joint continues to offer red-blooded satisfaction to a local crowd. There's no unnecessary distraction from the business of the consumption of fillet, sirloin and rump (or popeseye in the Scottish vernacular). The steaks come from Aberdeen Angus cattle raised north of the border, 100% grass-fed, the meat hung for 28 days and cooked on an open grill. The big news is there's also T-bone and ribeye on the blackboard these days. Wines from the almost exclusively red list start at £14.50. There's another branch at 277 Upper Richmond Road, Putney; tel: (020) 8788 7733.
Chef/s: Ian Hutchinson. **Open:** Mon to Fri D only 6.45 to 10. **Closed:** Sat, Sun, Christmas, New Year, bank hols. **Meals:** alc (steaks £12 to £66). **Details:** Cash only. 34 seats. Wheelchair access.

Portobello Ristorante Pizzeria

Eat-me pizza and more
7 Ladbroke Road, Notting Hill, W11 3PA
Tel no: (020) 7221 1373
www.portobellolondon.co.uk
⊖ Notting Hill Gate, map 4
Italian | £30
Cooking score: 2

'Pretty, and very Notting Hill,' thought a fan of this old-school pizzeria that's fronted by a large terrace and serves 'the best sort of Italian food: minimal cooking, maximum flavour and freshness'. Inside it's surprisingly modern, all exposed brick and stripped pine, solid tables and proper napery, with views of the open kitchen and wood-fired pizza oven. There's further seating in the basement where the wine cellar is 'a bit of a feature'. Come here for satisfyingly large portions of creamy, silky burrata con melanzane al funghetto, or a 'spot-on' margherita pizza with a super-sweet tomato base and salty, crisp crust (the kitchen will make it traditional-style by the metre for parties of two or more). There's high-quality pasta, too: seafood linguine consisting of mussels, squid and clams in a deep tomato sauce redolent with the flavours of olive oil and seafood. The coffee is good and the wines (from £19) all Italian.
Chef/s: Andrea Ippolito. **Open:** all week 12 to 11. **Closed:** 25 and 26 Dec, 1 Jan, Easter Sun. **Meals:** Set L £15. Party menu £25. **Details:** 60 seats. 30 seats outside. Music.

Potli

Authentic Indian street food
319-321 King Street, Hammersmith, W6 9NH
Tel no: (020) 8741 4328
www.potli.co.uk
⊖ Ravenscourt Park, Stamford Brook, map 1
Indian | £25
Cooking score: 3
£5 OFF £30

The flavours and energy of Indian street bazaars is the inspiration behind Jay Ghosh and Uttam Tripathy's restaurant, and, by all accounts, they've made a jolly good go of it. With its vivid turmeric-coloured frontage and infectiously enthusiastic staff, Potli does indeed offer something a little different. It's a simply stylish space with nifty artefacts and wooden tables, plus a basement where the chefs can be glimpsed working in the semi-open kitchen. This is regional street food inspired by the likes of Chandni Chowk market in Delhi – piayzi (onion bhajia) or the enigmatic 'chicken 65' – and grilled dishes cooked on the tawa such as Patrani prawns or marinated tilapia. Chutneys and all the incidentals are a cut above and there's plenty of choice for non-meat eaters: stir-fried okra, say, or baby aubergines in a sauce flavoured with five-spice. Drink lassi, Indian-inspired cocktails, beer or wine from £18.

Chef/s: Jay Ghosh. **Open:** Mon to Sat L 12 to 2.45, D 6 to 10.30 (11 Fri and Sat), Sun 12 to 10.30. **Meals:** alc (main courses £9 to £12). **Details:** 72 seats. 16 seats outside. Separate bar. Wheelchair access. Music.

The Princess Victoria
Superior pub food and glorious wines
217 Uxbridge Road, Shepherd's Bush, W12 9DH
Tel no: (020) 8749 5886
www.princessvictoria.co.uk
⊖ Shepherd's Bush Market, map 1
British | £30
Cooking score: 2
£5 OFF 🍾

A godsend for Shepherd's Bush, this cavernous, characterful Victorian gin palace combines a comfortable laid-back demeanour with mismatched pubby good looks, cheerful and competent service, and a kitchen noted for producing unfussy, full-flavoured dishes. Witness the unadulterated simplicity of ox kidney and caramelised balsamic onions on dripping toast, or a whopping ribeye steak with outrageously good chips. Representatives of this gutsy style pepper the menu: gnocchi, baby onions and Parmesan sauce; scallops with pancetta and Palourde clam chowder – even bar snacks like Tamworth Scotch egg or the shared charcuterie board. Puds such as dark chocolate and Guinness cake with honeycomb ice cream are top-notch, too. Mind you, the Vic's trump card is ultimately its wine list, containing insightful selections from Europe and the New World: biodynamics, organics and naturals included. There's plenty of choice by the glass or carafe with bottles from £16.90. **Chef/s:** Matt Reuther. **Open:** all week L 12 to 3 (4.30 Sun), D 6 to 10.30 (9.30 Sun). **Closed:** 24 to 28 Dec. **Meals:** alc (main courses £11 to £26). Set L £13 (2 courses) to £15. **Details:** 155 seats. 40 seats outside. Separate bar. Wheelchair access. Music. Car parking.

Racine
Classic and comforting French food
239 Brompton Road, Knightsbridge, SW3 2EP
Tel no: (020) 7584 4477
www.racine-restaurant.com
⊖ Knightsbridge, South Kensington, map 3
French | £35
Cooking score: 3

Henry Harris's well-established eatery is a bourgeois bistro fit for aristocratic Knightsbridge. There's a pleasant hum of activity about the place even at quieter times, when local residents mingle with well-fixed tourists and the pre-theatre crowd (the Royal Albert Hall is five minutes away). Taken side by side, the specials and à la carte demonstrate Harris's appreciation of unreconstructed Gallic cuisine: from the unsophisticated pleasure of raclette comtoise with cornichons to signature tête de veau and seasonal Norfolk asparagus with mousserons and ventrèche. Dishes at inspection included pan-fried skate, wild garlic, cucumber, tarragon and beurre blanc; unfortunately eggy clafoutis aux griottines was a game of 'find the cherry'. Lighting was a concern too; the waiter's face was barely discernible. Wine-wise, classic French bottles start at £23. **Chef/s:** Henry Harris. **Open:** Mon to Fri L 12 to 3, D 6 to 10.30. Sat and Sun 12 to 10.30 (10 Sun). **Closed:** 25 Dec. **Meals:** alc (main courses £17 to £30). Set L and D £18 (2 courses) to £20. Sun L £20 (2 courses) to £22. **Details:** 75 seats.

Rasoi
Luxurious Indian flagship
10 Lincoln Street, Chelsea, SW3 2TS
Tel no: (020) 7225 1881
www.rasoi-uk.com
⊖ Sloane Square, map 3
Indian | £65
Cooking score: 5

The elegant town house off the King's Road is a sultry, inviting homage to modern Subcontinental cooking. Ring the doorbell, then step into an ambience of subdued lighting, rich draperies and Indian artefacts, where Vineet Bhatia has raised his culinary patrimony to a peak of innovative excitement. Nothing is quite what you expect, least of all familiar-sounding items such as lamb rogan josh and chicken tikka. The Menu Prestige offers the scenic route, beginning with a crab lollipop and coconut-lime soup, then mustard-marinated tilapia steamed in a banana leaf, accompanied by giant couscous grains and aubergine. Spice-grilled foie gras with medallions of lemongrass-crusted liver and green apple chutney is a revelation, and then comes the tikka, infused in mango, with coriander-tamarind rice, and a terrific white tomato sauce. Rose-petal sorbet precedes smoked lamb rack with gojis and Stilton tikki, and the conclusion may be pistachio mousse with rosehips, spiced hazelnuts and a chocolate truffle boozed with Chivas Regal. Wines from £35.

Chef/s: Vineet Bhatia. **Open:** Tue to Fri and Sun L 12 to 2.30, Tue to Sun D 6 to 10.30 (10 Sun). **Closed:** Mon, 25 and 26 Dec, 1 and 2 Jan. **Meals:** alc (main courses £32 to £40). Set L £23 (2 courses) to £28. Set D and Sun L £53 (2 courses) to £65. Tasting menu £89 (7 courses). **Details:** 55 seats.

★ TOP 10 ★

Restaurant Gordon Ramsay

A flagship evolves
68-69 Royal Hospital Road, Chelsea, SW3 4HP
Tel no: (020) 7352 4441
www.gordonramsay.com
Sloane Square, map 3
Modern French | £95
Cooking score: 10

Gordon Ramsay may be name-checked at the front door, but inside, Restaurant Gordon Ramsay is now Clare Smyth's realm – with support from what is, without doubt, one of the best front-of-house teams in London. After all these years, this remains the most impressive of London's premier French restaurants, providing the requisite amuse-bouches and petits fours, the epic wine list: all served in a surprisingly small room given airiness by a neutral colour palette. Smyth has stayed true to the Ramsay identity while adapting to changing times. The goal has always been of accessible elegance, of classic French indulgence with a contemporary flair. But now, more than ever, global currents inform and influence what emerges from the kitchen. That's why, among overtures, there could be a delicate dim sum-style steamed bun flavoured with Jerusalem artichoke and topped with a sliver of truffle. That's why Smyth enlivens a fantastic piece of halibut with cauliflower couscous, Atlantic king crab and a ras-el-hanout-flavoured broth – an infusion of herbs and spices, each of which registers a fleeting, teasing impression. And, naturally, she makes modern adjustments to the richness of traditional French cooking. To lend excitement to Bresse pigeon, Smyth serves it with foie gras, smoked ventrèche, grilled polenta, braised shallots and dates, producing an exquisite balance of flavours and textures. Elsewhere, there's brilliant choreography behind a dish of turbot baked on the bone, the lusciousness of the fish brightened by the sweetness of broccoli, fennel and romanesco, which is in turn offset by the saltiness of seaweed and palourde clams. Then a pestle and mortar arrives, straight out of the freezer, containing freeze-dried leaves of mint, borage and verbena. The instruction is to crush, then add the accompanying spoonful of cucumber sorbet. It's the perfect curtain-raiser for a real French classic for dessert (just to show she can do it) of tarte Tatin for two – crisp, sweet, buttery. There's an unfussy mood in the dining room, sustained by genuinely committed and engaging staff, led by Jean-Claude Breton. The prestigious wine list has global breadth and excellence of pedigree. There are mighty offerings from the French classical regions, with dazzling gems from elsewhere and rarities sprinkled throughout. If your budget is tight, the sommelier's advice is exemplary, and there is plenty to enjoy by the 125ml glass, from £6.

Chef/s: Clare Smyth. **Open:** Mon to Fri L 12 to 2.15, D 6.30 to 10.15. **Closed:** Sat, Sun, 1 week Dec. **Meals:** Set L £55 (3 courses) to £95. Set D £95. Tasting menu £135. Inspiration menu £185 (D only). **Details:** 44 seats. Music.

NEW ENTRY
Restaurant Marianne
Elegant space, modern classic cooking
104 Chepstow Road, Notting Hill, W2 5QS
Tel no: (020) 3675 7750
www.marianrestaurant.com
⊖ Royal Oak, map 4
Modern European | £48
Cooking score: 5

It may be tiny but Marianne Lumb's soft-toned, pretty dining room is cocooning, not claustrophobic, akin to 'being in a Laudré box', purred one reporter. Glimpses into the even tinier kitchen are fascinating ('how do they all fit in?'), and with just six white-clad tables the place has never been so busy. Lumb's short, fixed menus are a classic of modern fashion, starring first-class ingredients in delicate constructions that are beautiful to behold. It's delicious food, too, with a little bit of luxury to increase that special-occasion feeling, so expect black summer truffle linguine or pan-fried foie gras with confit baby beetroot, spiced orange compote and fingers of toasted brioche, followed by steamed turbot with Scottish langoustines, white asparagus, Jersey Royals and Champagne sauce. Desserts draw plenty of enthusiasm, especially a featherlight vanilla and wild strawberry soufflé with a scoop of gariguette sorbet. The well-rounded wine list starts at £19.
Chef/s: Marianne Lumb. **Open:** Fri to Sun L 12 to 3, Tue to Sun D 6 to 11. **Closed:** Mon, 22 Dec to 6 Jan, Aug bank hols. **Meals:** Set L £38 to £50 (4 courses). Set D £55 to £65 (4 courses). Tasting menu L £65 (5 courses), D £85 (6 courses). **Details:** 14 seats. Music.

Restaurant Michael Nadra
Tasteful and satisfying Chiswick favourite
6-8 Elliott Road, Chiswick, W4 1PE
Tel no: (020) 8742 0766
www.restaurant-michaelnadra.co.uk
⊖ Turnham Green, map 1
Modern European | £36
Cooking score: 4

Tasteful, stylish, cosmopolitan – this elegant Chiswick favourite has its dimly lit, low-ceilinged dining room furnished in contemporary brasserie style, complete with closely packed tables. Leather banquettes and slate flooring emphasise the penchant for understated urban chic. Chef/patron Michael Nadra's respectful way with seafood is impressive: a delicate starter of soft-shell crab tempura with crunchy daikon and carrot salad 'lets superlative flavours speak for themselves', while herb-crusted hake might be presented on pearl barley and leek risotto with romanesco, cauliflower purée and parsley foam. The kitchen also knows how to extract real potency, richness and oomph from meat and game – as in a satisfying, wholesome plate of roast rump and braised neck of lamb with turnips, new potatoes, spinach and shallots. To finish, indulge in well-wrought classics such as tarte Tatin, chocolate fondant or sticky toffee pudding. The 200-bin wine list, a classy compendium, includes ample house selections from £18.
Chef/s: Michael Nadra. **Open:** all week L 12 to 2.30 (3.30 Sat and Sun), Mon to Sat D 6 to 10 (10.30 Fri and Sat). **Closed:** 25 to 27 Dec, 1 Jan. **Meals:** Set L £20 (2 courses) to £25. Set D £30 (2 courses) to £36. Tasting menu L £44, D £55 (6 courses). **Details:** 50 seats. Wheelchair access. Music.

The River Café
Italian icon by the river
Thames Wharf, Rainville Road, Hammersmith,
W6 9HA
Tel no: (020) 7386 4200
www.rivercafe.co.uk
⊖ Hammersmith, map 1
Italian | £70
Cooking score: 6

Down by the river, though this be
Hammersmith, you could almost forget you
were in London. A happy family atmosphere,
with the sun shining on outdoor tables, makes
a lovely spring or summer scene at the River
Café, and the friendly, efficient attentions of
staff help make the legendary experience
complete. Inside is all under-emphasised
functional form, the back-projection wall-
clock lurking behind a large, log-burning
oven. To an uncomfortable degree,
appreciation of the fresh, simply constructed
Italian dishes depends on comparisons with
their mostly formidable cost. An unfilleted,
but strongly salted, Dover sole at £38 seems
to need more justification, or accompaniment
even, but prime materials are impeccable.
Plates of salumi misti, crab linguine with
fennel, superb Anjou pigeon ('the best I've
eaten') roasted in Chianti – all come up
triumphantly to the high mark, while the
famous chocolate nemesis never shifts from
the menu. Italian wines at sky-high mark-ups
accompany, from £30.
Chef/s: Ruth Rogers. **Open:** all week L 12.30 to 2.15
(2.30 Sat, 12 to 3 Sun), Mon to Sat D 7 to 9 (9.15 Fri
and Sat). **Meals:** alc (main courses £36 to £38).
Details: 120 seats. 100 seats outside. Wheelchair
access. Car parking.

Symbols
🛏 Accommodation is available

£30 Three courses for less than £30

V Separate vegetarian menu

£5 OFF £5-off voucher scheme

🍾 Notable wine list

Salloos
Long-serving Pakistani stronghold
62-64 Kinnerton Street, Knightsbridge, SW1X 8ER
Tel no: (020) 7235 4444
www.salloos.co.uk
⊖ Knightsbridge, map 4
Pakistani | £50
Cooking score: 2

Muhammad Salahuddin ('Salloo' to his
friends) opened this restaurant on the first
floor of a Knightsbridge mews house in 1978,
and it has become a stronghold for affluent
Pakistani cuisine in London. Inlaid silk panels,
crystal chandeliers and white latticework
shades set the scene in the dining room: a
fitting backdrop for food full of piquant
flavours. Chef Abdul Aziz trained with
Salloo's mother and has been at the stoves since
day one, reinterpreting family recipes and
following the old ways to the letter. The menu
hasn't changed in years, and its status is
measured by the output of the charcoal-fired
tandoor. Everyone talks about the 'colour-
free' lamb chops, but also expect tikkas, seekh
kebabs, king prawns and more. Other dishes
will be familiar from curry houses (bhuna
gosht, chicken jalfrezi), but also look for the
cheese-crusted chicken, stir-fried kidneys and
haleem akbari (shredded lamb cooked with
wheatgerm and lentils). House wine is £20.
Chef/s: Abdul Aziz. **Open:** Mon to Sat 12 to 11.
Closed: Sun, 25 and 26 Dec. **Meals:** alc (main
courses £11 to £25). **Details:** 45 seats. Children over
5 yrs only.

Sam's Brasserie & Bar
Busy, buzzy neighbourhood brasserie
11 Barley Mow Passage, Chiswick, W4 4PH
Tel no: (020) 8987 0555
www.samsbrasserie.co.uk
⊖ Chiswick Park, Turnham Green, map 1
Modern European | £30
Cooking score: 2

The generous proportions of a former paper
factory give Sam's a voluminosity that,
combined with the vestiges of its industrial
past, make for a happy marriage between

brasserie and bar. It's the sort of feel-good place where families can break bread or young couples can chillax over the cocktail of the day (Grapefruit Grin, maybe), and the lucky office workers above can pop down for breakfast and dinner (and everything in between). The kitchen deals in hearty stuff like New England clam and slab-bacon chowder, and Nashville hot chicken with coleslaw, or more European-focused plates of venison polpette with Parmesan polenta. There are sharing boards and even a set menu based on recipes suitable for the 5:2 diet (if you don't know, you probably don't want to know). Finish with warm honey tart with a yoghurt sorbet. The wine list has good choice by the glass and carafe, with bottles starting at £17.50.
Chef/s: Mark Baines. **Open:** all week L 12 to 3 (4 Sat and Sun), D 6.30 to 10.30 (9.30 Sun). **Closed:** 24 to 26 Dec. **Meals:** alc (main courses £12 to £24). Set L and D £14 (2 courses) to £17. Sun L £22 (2 courses) to £26. **Details:** 100 seats. Separate bar. Wheelchair access. Music.

The Shed

All about big flavours and good provenance
122 Palace Gardens Terrace, Notting Hill, W8 4RT
Tel no: (020) 7229 4024
www.theshed-restaurant.com
⊖ **Notting Hill Gate, map 4**
Modern British | £35
Cooking score: 2

The brothers Gladwin from West Sussex haven't pulled any punches when it comes to reflecting their farming roots and farm-to-fork ethos in their restaurant – there's a tractor bonnet as a design feature at the bar. It's a family affair, with the youngest bro down on the farm, the middle one at the stoves and big bruv front-of-house. They've nailed the 'shed' vibe to a T, with the 'quirky country aesthetic' running to reclaimed wood, steel drums and a 'relaxed' attitude. Small plates is the deal, with seasonality a given. Everything that isn't home-grown is sourced with earnestness. The menu – split between 'slow' and 'fast' cooking – offers rustic and colourful plates such as a salad of celeriac, pears and lentils, a veal ragù

with pappardelle, and hake with rocket pesto and their own lardo. The brothers make their own wine back in Sussex, too, with house French coming in at £22.
Chef/s: Oliver Gladwin. **Open:** Tue to Sat L 12 to 3 (4 Sat), Mon to Sat D 6 to 11. **Closed:** Sun, 20 Dec to 2 Jan. **Meals:** alc (small plates £7 to £10). Set L £25 (6 courses) to £32. Set D £25 (6 courses) to £37. **Details:** 50 seats. 12 seats outside. Separate bar. Wheelchair access. Music.

The Shiori

Exquisite Kyoto cuisine
45 Moscow Road, Notting Hill, W2 4AH
Tel no: (020) 7221 9790
www.theshiori.com
⊖ **Bayswater, map 4**
Japanese | £70
Cooking score: 3

From drop-in sushi joint to high-art kaiseki ceremonials is quite a jump, but that's what chef Takashi Takagi achieved when moving his base camp from Euston's Drummond Street to Bayswater. Occupying a minimalist dining room with just 16 seats, the Shiori is devoted to exquisite Kyoto cuisine: multi-course banquets showcasing the full range of traditional Japanese cooking styles. Hitomi Takagi is a sweet hostess, whose gentle guidance is much appreciated, while Takashi's food is all about clarity, delicacy and subtly nuanced flavours. An appetiser of octopus with taro potato and azuki might precede a little salad involving junsai (an aquatic vegetable), 'lady fish' consommé, sashimi, tofu and a grilled dish of scallops with mustardy vinegared miso. After that, bamboo shoots with seasoned rice and pickles signals the meal is drawing to its close. All that remains is a modest dessert: perhaps yuzu sorbet. Matcha tea and saké are *de rigueur,* although wines (from £27) are available.
Chef/s: Takashi Takagi. **Open:** Tue to Sat L 12.30 to 3, D 6.30 to 10.30. **Closed:** Sun, Mon, 2 weeks Christmas and New Year, 10 days Aug, bank hols. **Meals:** Set L £50 (6 courses). Set D £70 (8 courses) to £95 (10 courses). **Details:** 16 seats. Wheelchair access. Music.

Tinello

The Italians' Italian
87 Pimlico Road, Chelsea, SW1W 8PH
Tel no: (020) 7730 3663
www.tinello.co.uk
⊖ Sloane Square, map 3
Italian | £40
Cooking score: 4

As Giorgio Locatelli protégés, Federico and Max Sali know the recipe for a quality neighbourhood restaurant. With its bare-brick walls, dangling metal lamps and utilitarian style, Tinello is very low-key, but the food is far from understated. The kitchen is rooted in solid technique, the menu driven by excellent raw ingredients. Fashionable 'small eats' such as 'delicious' baby squid or Tuscan chicken liver crostini and wild chicory and caper salad are perfect for sharing before a 'moreish' secondi of homemade tagliatelle, Parma ham and Parmesan, then a 'juicy and well-flavoured' pork fillet. So good is the food that, for one reporter, uncharacteristic lapses in the normally sharp service couldn't detract from the meal, especially when such a light, flavour-packed tiramisu was finally produced for dessert. The Italian-heavy wine list (from £16.60) ticks all the boxes when it comes to quality and value.
Chef/s: Federico Sali. **Open:** Mon to Sat L 12 to 2.30, D 6.30 to 10.30. **Closed:** Sun, bank hols. **Meals:** alc (main courses £18 to £27). **Details:** 74 seats. 6 seats outside.

¶¶● Please send us your feedback

To register your opinion about any restaurant listed in the Guide, or a new restaurant that you wish to bring to our attention, please visit the web address at the bottom of the page. Your feedback informs the content of the book and will be used to compile next year's reviews.

La Trompette

Cherished Chiswick star
5-7 Devonshire Road, Chiswick, W4 2EU
Tel no: (020) 8747 1836
www.latrompette.co.uk
⊖ Turnham Green, map 1
Modern European | £45
Cooking score: 5
🍾

Chiswick's most cherished restaurant is looking good and feeling great after its lavish 2013 refurb. Smart features such as funky paintings and gold banquettes have added extra gloss to the elegant, ever-crowded dining room – although one local die-hard thought the place had lost some of its 'soul' along the way. Chef Rob Weston's cooking is all about big European flavours and clever ideas, with lots of intricate detailing on the plate. A starter of salt-baked beetroot, smoked eel, horseradish and apple is enhanced with salt-and-pepper sand eels; breast and thigh of guinea fowl might appear with Jerusalem artichokes, salsify, chestnut pesto and trompette mushrooms (naturally). There are also more robust servings of caramelised suckling pig, BBQ shoulder of Welsh lamb and seasonal treats such as Dorset hogget. Desserts show the kitchen's classic side: think warm pear and almond tart, or tiramisu with dulce de leche ice cream. A triumphant, gloriously comprehensive 600-bin wine list has superb pickings galore, with prices from £22.
Chef/s: Rob Weston. **Open:** all week L 12 to 2.30 (12.30 to 3 Sun), D 6.30 to 10.30 (7 to 9.30 Sun). **Closed:** 24 to 26 Dec, 1 Jan. **Meals:** Set L £24 (2 courses) to £28. Set D £40 (2 courses) to £45. Sun L £28 (2 courses) to £33. **Details:** 82 seats. 14 seats outside. Wheelchair access.

Yashin Sushi
Sushi with a daring twist
1a Argyll Road, Kensington, W8 7DB
Tel no: (020) 7938 1536
www.yashinsushi.com
⊖ High Street Kensington, map 4
Japanese | £45
Cooking score: 3

V

Launched by two chefs from Nobu London (see entry), hot-ticket Yashin Sushi has a daring way of doing things. 'Without soy sauce – but if you want to' proclaims a sign, and the menu enters the world of contemporary fusion and crossovers. Although the kitchen team has been properly trained in the art, mystery and founding principles of traditional nigiri, maki rolls and sashimi, the guys are more interested in pushing the envelope. The blowtorch gets much use and there are numerous hot dishes: perhaps layered tofu with sweet wasabi sauce or slow-cooked pork belly with mustard cream. Also, don't miss the selection of creative appetisers such as pickled cherry tomatoes and Bella di Cerignola olives or Maldon oysters with spicy tosazu jelly. Wines start at £22 and there's premium saké for an additional outlay. The chefs also run Yashin Ocean House, a seafood restaurant at 117–119 Old Brompton Road, SW7 3RN.
Chef/s: Yasuhiro Mineno and Shinya Ikeda. **Open:** all week L 12 to 3, D 6 to 11. **Closed:** 24 to 26 Dec, 31 Dec, 1 to 3 Jan. **Meals:** alc (main courses £15 to £60). Set L £20 (2 courses) to £30. Set D £35 (2 courses) to £60. **Details:** 37 seats. Music.

Zuma
Slinky Knightsbridge high-roller
5 Raphael Street, Knightsbridge, SW7 1DL
Tel no: (020) 7584 1010
www.zumarestaurant.com
⊖ Knightsbridge, map 4
Japanese | £75
Cooking score: 5

The Zuma experience extends over three continents, bringing exquisitely stylish Japanese food and design to constituencies from Hong Kong to Miami, via Istanbul and Knightsbridge. Enter a world of discreetly lit stone and marble, calming as a Buddhist temple, but giving way to the hard-edged modernity of perforated bare-wood screens and undressed tables. Counter seating at the robata grill is the spectator-sport option. The food is as impeccably styled as the surroundings: high on umami, searing heat and the marine pungency of fresh seafood. Yellowfin tuna with green-chilli relish, ponzu and pickled garlic; fried langoustines with sour dashi and onions; robata Wagyu with aïoli and daikon – these are morsels to awaken the taste-buds. The precision-cooking of grilled sea bass in ginger and chilli, or spiced lamb chops with miso tofu, is not to be impugned, either. Prices are sky-high, from the tasting menus to the bank-loan drinks list of aged sakés, Champagnes and glittering wines (though the latter start at just £22).
Chef/s: Bjoern Weissgerber. **Open:** all week L 12 to 2.30 (12.30 to 3.30 Sat and Sun), D 6 to 11 (10.30 Sun). **Closed:** 25 Dec. **Meals:** alc (sharing plates £7 to £75). Tasting menu £68 to £118. **Details:** 175 seats. Separate bar. Wheelchair access. Music.

A Cena

Attractive local Italian with reliable food
418 Richmond Road, Twickenham, TW1 2EB
Tel no: (020) 8288 0108
www.acena.co.uk
⊖ Richmond, map 1
Italian | £30
Cooking score: 2

A decade of operations has refined the simple allure of Twickenham's simpatico Italian neighbourhood restaurant. Its unfussy furnishings consist of a dark-wood bar with stools and a row of booth tables extending down a long, white, many-mirrored room. Nicola Parsons keeps things fresh and straightforward, cooking to the traditional Italian menu template of antipasti and primi before mains and desserts. Appetising openers include Sicilian-style fried swordfish with pickled mussels, as well as buffalo mozzarella with lentils, herbed crème fraîche and basil oil. Gratinated ricotta gnocchi with spinach in Gorgonzola cream may be the transition to something like rump of lamb with black olives and Parmesan, or marinated hake with cime di rapa, capers and lemon. To finish, there's a capable take on the River Café's famously fiendish chocolate nemesis, or ciambelle – Florentine doughnuts with raspberry sauce. Wines, entirely Italian apart from Champagne, start at £18.50.
Chef/s: Nicola Parsons. **Open:** Tue to Sun L 12 to 2.30, Mon to Sat D 7 to 10.30. **Meals:** alc (main courses £11 to £24). **Details:** 55 seats.

Albert's Table

Confident and sophisticated local bistro
49b/c Southend, Croydon, CRO 1BF
Tel no: (020) 8680 2010
www.albertstable.co.uk
map 1
Modern British | £35
Cooking score: 3
£5 OFF V

Chef/proprietor Joby Wells earned his stripes in big-hitting London kitchens such as the Square and La Trompette (see entries), but his current mission is to give suburban Croydon some culinary clout. Albert's Table has all the attributes of a confident neighbourhood bistro: keen prices, enterprising food and a proper local vibe without too much affectation. Flavours ring true, sourcing is on the money and the menu is stuffed with dishes that scream 'eat me'. If you fancy a change from the signature shortcrust of Dorset crab, order a salad of roast salsify and baby artichokes with truffle mayonnaise, before sampling a casserole of South Down mutton with yoghurt and caper scones, or lightly curried Cornish monkfish with Kentish leeks and lentil purée. After that, regional cheeses with fig chutney and piccalilli beckon – unless you're tempted by sherry soufflé or egg custard and cranberry tart. Wines also offer great value, with bottles from £18.
Chef/s: Joby Wells. **Open:** Tue to Sun L 12 to 2.30 (3.30 Sun), Tue to Sat D 6.30 to 10.30. **Closed:** Mon. **Meals:** Set L £20 (2 courses) to £23. Set D £28 (2 courses) to £35. Sun L £20. Tasting menu £23. **Details:** 60 seats. Wheelchair access. Music. Car parking.

The Bingham

Accomplished cooking by the Thames
61-63 Petersham Road, Richmond, TW10 6UT
Tel no: (020) 8940 0902
www.thebingham.co.uk
⊖ Richmond, map 1
Modern British | £47
Cooking score: 5
£5 OFF ☕ V

'Discreet, calm and quietly upmarket', this riverside hotel is noted for its romantic dining area softened by twinkling chandeliers, plump leather seating and a particularly inviting Thames view. Following the departure of Shay Cooper (to the Goring, see entry), Mark Jarvis, formerly head chef at the Blueprint Café, has taken over the kitchen. His expertise is in modern British cooking and his menus are fresh, seasonal and inventive – but not far-fetched. Witness a test meal that produced a stylish starter of squid, scallop and cuttlefish on inked quinoa with foamy garlic

dressing, and a creamy bacon risotto with a perfectly poached egg yolk. Mains yielded impressive, tender Telmara Farm duck served atop Hispi cabbage, prunes and kohlrabi, and grass-fed beef teamed with roasted onion, buttermilk and oxtail. A velvety mascarpone mousse infused with lemon thyme made a fitting finale. The global wine list ranges far and wide. Bottle prices start at £13.
Chef/s: Mark Jarvis. **Open:** all week L 12 to 2.30 (4 Sun), Mon to Sat D 6.30 to 10 (10.30 Fri and Sat). **Meals:** alc (main courses £23 to £28). Set L £15. Sun L £38. Tasting menu £65. **Details:** 38 seats. 14 seats outside.

Brilliant
Chart-topping north Indian stalwart
72-76 Western Road, Southall, UB2 5DZ
Tel no: (020) 8574 1928
www.brilliantrestaurant.com
⊖ Hounslow West, map 1
Indian | £23
Cooking score: 3
£5 OFF £30

The Anand family business has been a pillar of the Southall community for 40 years, and its modestly named restaurant has spawned a cookery school, outdoor catering and a banqueting suite – not to mention consistent accolades in the world of restaurant awards and TV. While Indian cooking in central London has taken off into all sorts of unexplored avenues, the focus here has always been on conscientiously rendered Punjabi cooking, in which everything seems familiar apart from the elevated quality. Start with tandoori tilapia, fried prawns in filo or a spiced lamb chop, before plunging into a cornucopia of north Indian classics. Chicken keema, palak lamb, kofta, and king prawn biryani are all present and correct, with healthy eating options flagged up on the menu for weight watchers. Indian breads and traditional sweets add to the full package. A small slate of wines from £11 supplements the lassi and cocktail lists.

Chef/s: Jasvindersit Singh. **Open:** Tue to Fri L 12 to 3, Tue to Sun D 6 to 11.30. **Closed:** Mon, 25 Dec, bank hols. **Meals:** alc (main courses £5 to £14). Set L and D £20. **Details:** 220 seats. Music. Car parking.

Brula
Pretty and hospitable
43 Crown Road, St Margarets, Twickenham, TW1 3EJ
Tel no: (020) 8892 0602
www.brula.co.uk
⊖ Richmond, map 1
French | £35
Cooking score: 3
V

Thanks to its pretty stained-glass exterior, this charming French bolt-hole is unmissable from the street. But intricately crafted windows and bistro décor only go so far. It's the food, as well as the ambience, that readers say 'consistently delivers' at Brula – and the venue has been in operation since the 1990s. Dishes designed to please might include cream of Jerusalem artichoke soup with trompettes de la mort or 'wonderful' scallops with celeriac purée in Calvados broth, followed by sea bass with garlic mash, pine nuts, golden raisins and parsley, or onglet with garlic butter and 'super' chips. Afterwards there's chocolate and Kirsch cherry mousse with honeycomb and cherry sorbet, or an Agen prune clafoutis with hazelnuts and Armagnac ice cream. Notwithstanding the 'little moan' that portions can lack generosity, Brula is 'always a treat'. The same can be said of the neat, slightly offbeat wine list, starting at £19.50.
Chef/s: Jamie Russell. **Open:** all week L 10 to 5, D 5 to 10.30. **Closed:** 26 Dec. **Meals:** alc (main courses £15 to £25). Set L and D £15 (2 courses) to £20. **Details:** 45 seats. 10 seats outside.

La Buvette

Textbook French favourites
6 Church Walk, Richmond, TW9 1SN
Tel no: (020) 8940 6264
www.labuvette.co.uk
⊖ Richmond, map 1
French | £25
Cooking score: 3
£5 OFF £30

The checked tablecloths, blackboard menus and bentwood chairs in the cosy dining room and secluded courtyard at Richmond's Buvette say 'classic French bistro' like nothing else. Chef Buck Carter matches the mise-en-scène with gloriously, unapologetically, Gallic cuisine – garlic butter doused snails, sticky tarte Tatin, fondue, moules and all. The list of old favourites also includes fish soup with rouille, onglet steak and frites, not forgetting crème brûlée. Pot-au-feu with pork shin, cheek and chou farci (stuffed cabbage) comes highly recommended. International influences do sneak on to the plate here and there, with preserved lemon, tomato relish and beetroot garnishing ox tongue, and an 'amazing' waffle with smoked fudge sauce. The wine list is 'interesting and well priced' (from £16.75) with serious producers from France's major regions well represented and new 'wine flights' (£16/three glasses) that prove there's more to French wine than Chablis.
Chef/s: Buck Carter. **Open:** all week L 12 to 3, D 5.45 to 10 (9 Sun). **Closed:** 25 and 26 Dec, Good Fri, Easter Sun. **Meals:** alc (main courses £14 to £19). Set L £17 (2 courses) to £20. Set D and Sun L £19 (2 courses) to £22. Sun L £19 (2 courses) to £22.
Details: 44 seats. 32 seats outside.

NEW ENTRY

The Dysart

Precision and invention in bucolic surrounds
135 Petersham Road, Richmond, TW10 7AA
Tel no: (020) 8940 8005
www.thedysartarms.co.uk
⊖ Richmond, map 1
Modern British | £39
Cooking score: 6
£5 OFF V

There's 'superbly inventive and precise cooking' from Roux Scholar Kenneth Culhane in this former pub, now definitely a restaurant. In pretty grounds facing south over Richmond Park, the Arts and Crafts interior is 'striking yet unfussy', with bountiful greenery. Canapés start at 'stunning', with a soy and mirin-marinated scallop on sushi rice with black truffle mayonnaise. From the à la carte, parsnip soup (a creamy purée topped with light coconut foam and bursts of lime zest) shows Culhane giving traditional dishes an ambitious twist. Veal sweetbreads (tasting menu) are cooked to crisp-then-gooey and served with Cevenne onion and fennel and a verjus-spiked sauce. The theme of 'subdued rusticity' continues into lemon bergamot sorbet and a plank laden with admirable cheeses. If service feels slightly 'unconvincing' in places, it's of minor concern to readers who regard the Dysart as a special destination. From a list with much choice under £50, wine starts at £18.50.
Chef/s: Kenneth Culhane. **Open:** all week L 12 to 3 (3.30 Sat, 4 Sun), Mon to Sat D 6 to 9.30. **Meals:** alc (main courses £16 to £27). Set L and D £19 (2 courses) to £23. Sun L £32. Tasting menu £60.
Details: 50 seats. 40 seats outside. Wheelchair access. Music. Car parking.

LOCAL GEM
▲ Eat17

28-30 Orford Road, Walthamstow, E17 9NJ
Tel no: (020) 8521 5279
www.eat17.co.uk
⊖ Walthamstow Central, map 1
British | £25

Purveyor of bacon jam (a modish and moreish condiment) and a grand Walthamstow postcode pun, Eat17 also includes a food-shop-with-integrity next door. Eating-in combines Brit dishes such as ham hock salad or the rarely seen beef plate pie, with more fashionable favourites including pulled pork with slaw and cornbread or chorizo jam with mascarpone on brioche. The unifying theme is comfort, and it all fits nicely with a pint of Meantime Pale Ale in faux-plush surroundings. Wines start at £16. Closed Sun D. A new branch can be found in Clapton, 64-66 Brooksby's Walk, E9 6DA.

▲ The Exhibition Rooms

69-71 Westow Hill, Crystal Palace, SE19 1TX
Tel no: (020) 8761 1175
www.theexhibitionrooms.com
map 1
Modern British | £26

Taking inspiration from the famous (and former) glass structure that hosted the Great Exhibition in 1851, the Exhibition Rooms is a thriving and buzzy outfit with twin personalities of restaurant and cocktail lounge. Exposed bricks and a mellow vibe set the scene for satisfying mod Brit/brasserie-inspired stuff such as Cornish sardines with beetroot and walnut relish, a nifty burger or a risotto of forest mushrooms. The cool bar has a heated terrace and DJs. Wines from £16.75. Open Fri to Sun L, all week D.

The French Table

Fantastic neighbourhood restaurant
85 Maple Road, Surbiton, KT6 4AW
Tel no: (020) 8399 2365
www.thefrenchtable.co.uk
map 1
French | £40
Cooking score: 4

V

Sarah and Eric Guignard have hit on a winning formula at their combined restaurant and boulangerie. With a sparkling-clean white interior, offset by leaf-green banquettes, its focus is on modern French cuisine drawing on pedigree British ingredients. Pheasant breast makes a tempting opener, served with smoked celeriac cream, sautéed Brussels and apple fondant. This may precede a Bayonne ham package of monkfish with lentils, carrots and a herb froth. A young reporter already versed in contemporary cuisine enjoyed his Piedmont goats' cheese and roast beetroot with cumin-flavoured beetroot hummus, and also relished a main-course sea bream with foaming cauliflower cream, grilled leeks and a crab tortellino. Finish with featherlight lavender crème brûlée, or full-throttle chocolate fondant with griottines and cherry sorbet. Quarterly cheese and wine evenings add to Surbiton's quality of life. Wines are classified by style, opening at £16.95 a bottle, £12.50 a half-litre carafe or £7 a glass.

Chef/s: Eric and Sarah Guignard. **Open:** Tue to Sat L 12 to 2.30, D 7 to 10.30. **Closed:** Sun, Mon, 25 to 27 Dec, 2 weeks Aug. **Meals:** alc (main courses £20 to £29). Set L £19.50 (2 courses) to £23.50. Tasting menu £45 to £75. **Details:** 55 seats. Music.

The Glasshouse
Low-key high-achiever
14 Station Parade, Kew, TW9 3PZ
Tel no: (020) 8940 6777
www.glasshouserestaurant.co.uk
⊖ Kew Gardens, map 1
Modern European | £43
Cooking score: 5

The glasshouses of nearby Kew Gardens may be filled with exotic flora from steamier climes than ours, but the many-windowed namesake restaurant in the parade of shops by the tube station carries on its own traffic with the world beyond our shores. Once securely French in orientation, the cooking has since trained its sights in a broader European arc, a trend maintained under new chef Berwyn Davies. Dishes aim high for complexity, as when a starter serving of Bresse pigeon comes with a spicy pastilla of the leg meat, along with foie gras, king cabbage, hazelnuts and glazed fig. Up next could be cod in garlic velouté with gnocchi, morels and smoked pine nuts. Finish royally with burnt vanilla cream garnished with rhubarb, pistachio biscotti and Champagne foam. Wines are a hearteningly democratic selection in both physical range and pricing, with many at the relatively affordable end. Hungary, Croatia and Japanese Koshu all get a look-in; Italian and regional French selections are excellent. Prices open at £19.
Chef/s: Berwyn Davies. **Open:** all week L 12 to 2.30 (12.30 to 3 Sun), D 6.30 to 10.30 (7 to 10 Sun). **Closed:** 24 to 26 Dec, 1 Jan. **Meals:** alc (main courses £20 to £27). Set L £24 (2 courses) to £28. Set D £38 (2 courses) to £43. Sun L £33. **Details:** 66 seats.

Incanto
Creative Italian food and fascinating wines
41 High Street, Harrow-on-the-Hill, HA1 3HT
Tel no: (020) 8426 6767
www.incanto.co.uk
⊖ Harrow-on-the-Hill, map 1
Italian | £35
Cooking score: 4

£5 OFF V

Occupying a one-time post office within shouting distance of Harrow's blue-blooded public school, Incanto delivers a telling mix of 'exceptional food', knowledgeable service and enticing wines in a light, airy space that encourages lingering. There's a cracking deli attached, helping make this a 'faultless local amenity catering to its community'. Top-drawer seasonal ingredients provide the building blocks for a raft of thrilling dishes cooked with 'real panache, style and insight'. Everyone adores the sensational duck egg ravioli, but glowing recommendations span the entire repertoire – from a lasagnetta of Scottish langoustines with bisque sauce and Prosecco foam or a trio of quail with quince, baby onions, celeriac and apple, to fillet of Scotch beef with guanciale, oxtail, smoked garlic purée and a broad bean croquette. To finish, the chestnut pannacotta with Amarone-poached pear and candied chestnuts is 'just perfect'. Fascinating organic and biodynamic wines get star billing on the enlightened, Italian-led list; bottles from £18.50.
Chef/s: Ciprian Marginean. **Open:** Tue to Sun L 12 to 2.30 (12.30 to 4 Sun), Tue to Sat D 6.30 to 10.30. **Closed:** Mon, 24 to 26 Dec, 1 Jan, bank hols. **Meals:** alc (main courses £15 to £23). Set L £18 (2 courses) to £20. Set D £20 (2 courses) to £24. Tasting menu £55 (7 courses). **Details:** 64 seats. Wheelchair access. Music.

Indian Zilla
Style, creativity and Indian pizazz
2-3 Rocks Lane, Barnes, SW13 0DB
Tel no: (020) 8878 3989
www.indianzilla.co.uk
map 1
Indian | £29
Cooking score: 3
£30

A zilla is an administrative district in India – a neighbourhood, if you will – and Indian Zilla serves Barnes (and the broader SW communities) with some crack regional Indian cuisine. There's a simple and smart modernity to the space, in keeping with the postcode. The menu acknowledges the diversity of the Subcontinent, with inspiration coming from everything from street food to royal banquets. Manoj Vasaikar and his team are skilful when it comes to handling spices, and dishes such as mussel rasam (in a tomato and tamarind broth) and duck Chettinad have spirited flavours. The thalis are a good bet to get a real taste of the place – served in trad metal bowls – while tandoori figs and a masala bread-and-butter pudding are well-crafted Anglo-European desserts. A bargain lunch menu ups the neighbourhood ante, and wines start at £16. **Chef/s:** Manoj Vasaikar. **Open:** Fri to Sun L 12 to 3, all week D 6 to 11. **Closed:** 25 Dec. **Meals:** alc (main courses £9 to £22). Set L £12 (2 courses) to £15. **Details:** 75 seats. 2 seats outside. Separate bar. Wheelchair access. Music.

LOCAL GEM
▲ Ma Cuisine Bistrot
9 Station Approach, Kew, TW9 3QB
Tel no: (020) 8332 1923
www.macuisinebistrot.co.uk
⊖ Kew Gardens, map 1
French | £34 £5 OFF

A stone's throw from Kew Gardens tube station, this former post office is everyone's idea of a cheerful neighbourhood French bistro – right down to the gingham tablecloths, black-and-white chequered floor and Toulouse-Lautrec posters. The greatest-hits menu of carefully prepared brasserie classics includes 'astonishingly good' onion soup, which might precede full-flavoured coq au vin or saddle of venison, Savoy cabbage with lardons, chestnut purée and Armagnac sauce. Leave room for crêpes suzette. House wine is £14.50. Open all week.

Madhu's
High-gloss Punjabi specialist
39 South Road, Southall, UB1 1SW
Tel no: (020) 8574 1897
www.madhus.co.uk
map 1
Indian | £24
Cooking score: 3
£5 OFF V £30

First opening its doors in 1980, Madhu's is a proper brand these days, with outside catering and a glitzy new gaff in the Sheraton Skyline Hotel at Heathrow. It all started in Southall, and the punters they still do come – 'amazing', 'service with a smile', 'best main curry I have ever eaten'. Sanjay Anand's restaurant looks startlingly modern with its shiny surfaces and designer staircase snaking to the upper level. The cooking, though, deals in classic Punjabi flavours and reveals a few influences from the family's time in Kenya. Jeera chicken is cooked on the bone for maximum effect with roasted cumin seeds. Vegetarian dishes are always a good bet, too: the classic aloo papri chaat, say, or aloo raviya (stuffed baby aubergines: a firm favourite). Spicing is clear and true throughout, exemplified in a punch-packing main course of karahi murg, featuring succulent chicken and a spicy sauce. House French is a bargain £11. **Chef/s:** Mr Rakesh Verma. **Open:** Mon and Wed to Fri L 12.30 to 3, Wed to Mon D 6 to 11.30. **Closed:** Tue, 25 Dec. **Meals:** alc (main courses £5 to £12). Set L £17 (2 courses) to £20. Set D £20 (2 courses) to £24. **Details:** 104 seats. Separate bar. Music. Car parking.

Mosaica at the Factory
Funky flavour-fest
Chocolate Factory, 5 Clarendon Road, Wood
Green, N22 6XJ
Tel no: (020) 8889 2400
www.mosaicarestaurant.com
⊖ Wood Green, map 2
Modern European | £30
Cooking score: 3

Not the easiest place to find, Mosaica is located
in what looks like an office block in the heart
of a redeveloped industrial area. But once
you're inside the defunct chocolate factory,
you'll discover a quirky, lively New York-style
loft offering 'loads of space', fairy lights
hanging from the ceiling, art on the walls and
an open kitchen. It's all rollickingly informal.
The kitchen may not have a sense of
adventure, but it sends out confident, well-
priced modern classics: mainly no-frills dishes
such as black tiger prawns with chilli and
garlic; slow-roast belly pork with crisp
crackling, red cabbage and mustard mash; and
'very good' ribeye steak. Sticky toffee pudding
with Nutella ice cream, and warm chocolate
brownie are typical desserts. The package also
runs to a well-reported Sunday lunch. Wines
from £15.
Chef/s: Phil Ducker. **Open:** Mon to Fri and Sun L 12
to 2.30 (1 to 4 Sun), Mon to Sat D 7 to 9.30 (10 Sat).
Meals: alc (main courses £14 to £23). **Details:** 80
seats. 30 seats outside.

Petersham Nurseries Café
**Italian-inspired menus using home-grown
produce**
Church Lane, off Petersham Road, Richmond,
TW10 7AG
Tel no: (020) 8940 5230
www.petershamnurseries.com
⊖ Richmond, map 1
Modern British | £45
Cooking score: 3
£5 OFF

Not so much rustic-chic as gardening-chic,
Petersham Nurseries sits between the park and
the river, with its lunchtime café located in a
greenhouse filled with an abundance of
flowers and trees. Herbs and heritage
vegetables make their way the short distance
from the walled kitchen garden to the kitchen,
then to the table. What isn't gown in situ is
sourced with care from natural and small-scale
producers and growers. This is no veggie
outfit, though, with the Italian-inflected
menus running to coppa di Parma with
greenish camone tomatoes, grumolo rosso and
artichokes hearts, plus some Parmesan
shavings, and wild sea bass with lentils and
cime di rapa. There might be steak, too,
cooked in red wine, and desserts like
pannacotta with blood-orange and ginger
caramel. Service is by a cool-looking bunch in
long aprons, and despite the casual setting,
prices are high. Wines start at £18.
Chef/s: Lucy Boyde. **Open:** Tue to Sun L only 12 to 3.
Closed: Mon, 25 and 26 Dec. **Meals:** alc (main
courses £21 to £30). Set L £23 (2 courses) to £28.
Details: 120 seats. 100 seats outside. Wheelchair
access. Car parking.

Restaurant at The Petersham
River views and stately dining
Nightingale Lane, Richmond, TW10 6UZ
Tel no: (020) 8939 1084
www.petershamhotel.co.uk
⊖ Richmond, map 1
Modern European | £42
Cooking score: 4

🍽 V

A Richmond landmark 'overlooking the
Thames since 1865', the Petersham continues
to make much of those glorious panoramic
vistas stretching across meadows and the river
towards Hampton Court. Guests in the hotel's
determinedly old-fashioned restaurant can
view the sights from a dramatic wall of
windows – a welcome diversion from the
heavy carpeting and hushed tones that are the
norm here. Die-hards still demand smoked
salmon, breaded veal escalope and fillet steak
from dapper, dutiful staff, but the kitchen also
displays its considerable talents with precisely
rendered contemporary ideas: think rabbit

and black pudding on tomato and courgette risotto, or sea bass with honey-roasted pancetta, spiced lentils, courgettes, fennel and lemon soubise. For afters, pavlova and baked apple with cinnamon pastry are fail-safes, although it's worth waiting for a plate of chocolate moelleux with caramelised banana and pistachio ice cream. Unsurprisingly, the wine list (from £22.50) is firmly rooted in the Old World. **Chef/s:** Alex Bentley. **Open:** all week L 12.15 to 2.15 (12.30 to 3.30 Sun), D 7 to 9.45 (9.15 Sun). **Closed:** 25 and 26 Dec, 1 Jan. **Meals:** alc (main courses £17 to £34). Set L and D £23 (2 courses) to £27. Sun L £35. **Details:** 60 seats. Separate bar. Wheelchair access. Car parking.

Retro Bistrot
Warm, buzzy French bistro
114-116 High Street, Teddington, TW11 8JB
Tel no: (020) 8977 2239
www.retrobistrot.co.uk
map 1
French | £35
Cooking score: 3
£5 OFF V

This much-loved high-street eatery, at once flamboyant and cosy, is clearly dear to the foodies of Teddington. It's 'reliable and always delivers' both in terms of food and first-rate service – maître d' Vincent Gerbeau and his well-trained team ensure that diners are well looked after. A clear, compact menu of French brasserie classics is superbly executed, diners raving about starters of 'sublime' endive, Roquefort and walnut salad, and garlic snails. The chateaubriand steak to share gets the thumbs-up from many, too. Try also a pan-fried skate wing with green beans, shallots, almonds and caper beurre noisette, or tender confit pork belly, spiced apple purée and pickled white cabbage. Whatever you choose, don't leave without a taste of the 'terrific' dark chocolate soufflé and double chocolate ice cream. There's confident advice on wines and plenty to drink by the glass and carafe, as well as bottles from £17.50.

Chef/s: Michael Collins. **Open:** all week L 12 to 3.30, Mon to Sat D 6.30 to 11. **Closed:** 25 and 26 Dec. **Meals:** alc (main courses £14 to £28). Set L £13 (2 courses) to £16. Set D £18 (2 courses) to £20. Sun L £13. **Details:** 90 seats. Wheelchair access. Music.

Sonny's Kitchen
Well-rehearsed neighbourhood favourite
94 Church Road, Barnes, SW13 0DQ
Tel no: (020) 8748 0393
www.sonnyskitchen.co.uk
map 1
Modern European | £32
Cooking score: 2
£5 OFF

This long-established Barnes eatery strikes just the right note: warm and convivial, good for everyday dining as well as easy celebrations. Owner Rebecca Mascarenhas, now in collaboration with chef Philip Howard of the Square (see entry), has implemented a menu of well-rehearsed Anglo-European dishes; Mascarenhas knows her customers and doesn't seek to inflict shocks to their systems. Foie gras and chicken liver parfait, langoustines with lemon mayonnaise or pizza margherita indicate the palette of flavours on the daily changing menu, followed, perhaps, by roast cod and chips, calf's liver with creamed potatoes and bacon or roast chicken and mushroom pie. There are no surprises, either, when it comes to desserts. Old faithful puddings take in treacle tart and warm chocolate fondant. Charming, friendly and relaxed service enhances the experience, which is completed by a modern wine list that offers wide choice and kind prices. Bottles from £17.25.

Chef/s: James Holah. **Open:** all week L 12 to 2.30 (3.30 Sat and Sun), D 6.30 to 10 (10.30 Fri and Sat, 9.30 Sun). **Closed:** 25 and 26 Dec, 1 Jan, Aug bank hol. **Meals:** alc (main courses £13 to £20). Set L and early D £17 (2 courses) to £19. Sun L £22 (2 courses) to £25. **Details:** 100 seats. Separate bar. Music.

Tangawizi

Upmarket local Indian
406 Richmond Road, Twickenham, TW1 2EB
Tel no: (020) 8891 3737
www.tangawizi.co.uk
⊖ Richmond, map 1
Indian | £25
Cooking score: 2
£30

Close to 'fortress Twickenham' and not far from Richmond Bridge, this clean-cut, upmarket Indian adds some glitz and gloss to its tandooris and curries in the form of chic purple-toned interiors, sultry lighting and stylish, cosmopolitan vibes. The cooking is a cut above, too, with duck samosas, grilled paneer cheese in mango dressing and daily fish curries spicing up the repertoire. If you want to keep it old school, look to the line-up of enticingly flavoured favourites: keema peas, chicken jalfrezi, lamb chops masala, prawn biryani and suchlike, backed by a big contingent of vegetable sides, rice and breads (try the stuffed onion kulcha). Consistently high standards mean regular full houses, so book ahead at peak times. To drink, there's Cobra beer and a list of exotic cocktails such as Mumbai Bite (gin, orange and pineapple juice with lemonade and grenadine) – plus mango lassi if you're driving. Wines from £18.50.
Chef/s: Surat Singh Rana. **Open:** all week D only 6 to 11 (10.30 Sun). **Closed:** 25 and 26 Dec, 1 Jan. **Meals:** alc (main courses £7 to £15). **Details:** 56 seats. Music.

---

⑪♦ Please send us your feedback

To register your opinion about any restaurant listed in the Guide, or a new restaurant that you wish to bring to our attention, please visit the web address at the bottom of the page. Your feedback informs the content of the book and will be used to compile next year's reviews.

The Victoria

Appealing all-rounder
10 West Temple Sheen, East Sheen, SW14 7RT
Tel no: (020) 8876 4238
www.thevictoria.net
⊖ Richmond, map 1
Modern British | £30
Cooking score: 3
£5 OFF 🍽

Hugely popular among readers for its Richmond Park location, relaxed atmosphere and positive, family-friendly approach, this pub and restaurant-with-rooms is a 'haven of tranquillity'. Chef Paul Merrett, not unknown to TV audiences, has established a reputation for 'honest, interesting and well-sourced food, cooked with heart'. It takes a variety of forms: summer barbecues from the outdoor kitchen, much-loved burgers and baps (including the 'charity burger', with a £2 donation included in the price of a Moroccan spiced patty with tzatziki and tomato jam) from the bar menu, and a more serious, but still reasonably priced, à la carte. From here, warm confit duck salad with black pudding, green beans, celeriac and a duck egg; Serrano ham-wrapped pollack with skordalia potato and monk's beard; and a thyme blossom honey semifreddo – all satisfy both the creative chef and the instinctive eater. Wines from an extensive list start at £17.
Chef/s: Paul Merrett. **Open:** all week L 12 to 2.30 (11 to 4 Sat, 12 to 4 Sun), all week D 6 to 10 (5 to 9 Sun). **Meals:** alc (main courses £14 to £20). Set L and D £15. **Details:** 70 seats. 50 seats outside. Separate bar. Wheelchair access. Music. Car parking.

ENGLAND

Bedfordshire, Berkshire,
Buckinghamshire, Cambridgeshire,
Cheshire, Cornwall, Cumbria, Derbyshire,
Devon, Dorset, Durham, Essex,
Gloucestershire & Bristol,
Greater Manchester,
Hampshire (inc. Isle of Wight),
Herefordshire, Hertfordshire, Kent,
Lancashire, Leicestershire and Rutland,
Lincolnshire, Merseyside, Norfolk,
Northamptonshire, Northumberland,
Nottinghamshire, Oxfordshire, Shropshire,
Somerset, Staffordshire, Suffolk, Surrey,
Sussex – East, Sussex – West,
Tyne & Wear, Warwickshire,
West Midlands, Wiltshire, Worcestershire,
Yorkshire

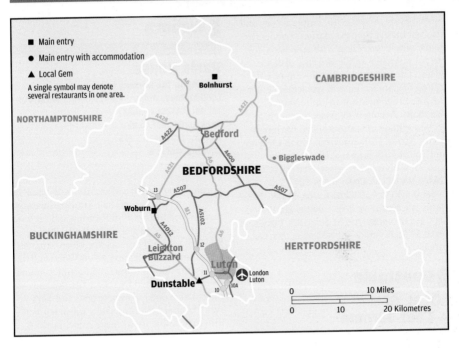

- ■ Main entry
- ● Main entry with accommodation
- ▲ Local Gem

A single symbol may denote several restaurants in one area.

NORTHAMPTONSHIRE

CAMBRIDGESHIRE

■ Bolnhurst

Bedford

BEDFORDSHIRE

● Biggleswade

Woburn

Leighton Buzzard

Luton

London Luton

Dunstable

BUCKINGHAMSHIRE

HERTFORDSHIRE

0   10 Miles

0   10   20 Kilometres

Biggleswade

READERS RECOMMEND

The Croft Kitchen

Modern British
28 Palace Street, Biggleswade, SG18 8DP
Tel no: (01767) 601502
thecroftbiggleswade.com

'Absolutely delicious, relaxed and efficient service, fantastic presentation. Some of the best food we've eaten.'

♨ Please send us your feedback

To register your opinion about any restaurant listed in the Guide, or a new restaurant that you wish to bring to our attention, please visit the web address at the bottom of the page. Your feedback informs the content of the book and will be used to compile next year's reviews.

Bolnhurst

★ TOP 50 PUB ★

The Plough

Big, true flavours and cracking wines
Kimbolton Road, Bolnhurst, MK44 2EX
Tel no: (01234) 376274
www.bolnhurst.com
Modern British | £35
Cooking score: 5

🍷

A whitewashed, 15th-century inn, the Plough has a light, uncluttered look featuring unclothed tables, floral wallpaper and bare-boarded floors – yet this is more than simply a charming country pub. There are thrilling things going on here, including steaks of pedigree Aberdeenshire beef cooked in a Josper charcoal oven. Martin Lee sources wisely from near and far. Grilled cuttlefish with chickpea salad in lime and chilli dressing will make you forget the landlocked location, or you might choose pheasant and slow-cooked blade of beef with white cabbage and 'the best mash I have ever tasted'. For dessert, go the whole sweet hog with rum baba, fig tart, or pistachio soufflé and chocolate ice cream. The wines are sourced from Noel Young of Cambridge, and speak eloquently of the nice judgements of an authoritative merchant. Arranged by style, they include such sought-after names as Glen Carlou in South Africa, Domaine Drouhin in Oregon and Tuscany's Selvapiana. Prices start at £16.95, with standard glasses from £4.75. **Chef/s:** Martin Lee. **Open:** Tue to Sun L 12 to 2, Tue to Sat D 6.30 to 9.30. **Closed:** Mon, 31 Dec, first 2 weeks Jan. **Meals:** alc (main courses £16 to £29). Set L £16 (2 courses) to £20. Sun L £25. **Details:** 90 seats. 30 seats outside. Wheelchair access. Car parking.

■ Dunstable

LOCAL GEM
▲ Chez Jerome

26 Church Street, Dunstable, LU5 4RU
Tel no: (01582) 603310
www.chezjerome.co.uk
French | £30 £5 OFF

Jerome and Lina Dehoux's rustic, beamed restaurant 'never fails to please'. Regulars confirm its status as Dunstable's pick of the crop: a warm-hearted, cosy antidote to the town's soulless junk-food joints. The owners are on first-name terms with most customers, staff are always chirpy and the food scores for value as well as quality. Generous French provincial flavours prevail: from confit foie gras and smoked duck to crêpes suzette, via Bordeaux-laced beef fillet and chicken breast with tarragon sauce. Wines from £14.25. Closed Sun D.

■ Woburn

★ TOP 50 ★

Paris House

Cooking in the present tense
London Road, Woburn Park, Woburn, MK17 9QP
Tel no: (01525) 290692
www.parishouse.co.uk
Modern European | £75
Cooking score: 6
£5 OFF V

Formerly part of Alan Murchison's ill-fated '10 in 8' group, this genteel half-timbered oasis is now owned by chef Phil Fanning and his wife – a move already paying dividends. Paris House is set amid immaculate green expanses, with muntjacs frolicking across Woburn Park. Inside, the dining room's staid country-house conformity is lifted by kooky fittings and male staff dressed in baggy shirts and 'very short' trousers. Fanning's new role has given him the confidence to create some startling, risky culinary feats. His show-stopping, witty spin on gammon and pineapple is a welcome blast from the past, but he can also cook in the present tense: witness hamachi fish matched with assorted seaweeds, strands of daikon, capsules of olive oil and a quenelle of miso sorbet. To finish, there are 'great little puddings' including a complex play on strawberries with dots of lemon curd and popping candy. The substantial, well-balanced wine list starts at £30. **Chef/s:** Phil Fanning. **Open:** Wed to Sun L 12 to 2, Wed to Sat D 7 to 9. **Closed:** Mon, Tue, 24 Dec to 4 Jan. **Meals:** Set L £37 (6 courses). Set D £75 (8 courses) to £98 (10 courses). Sun L £55. **Details:** 25 seats. Separate bar. Music. Car parking.

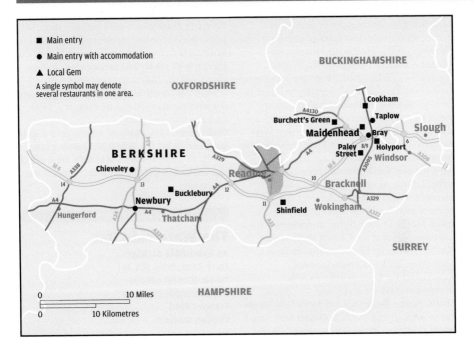

Bray

★ TOP 10 ★

The Fat Duck

The experience of a lifetime
1 High Street, Bray, SL6 2AQ
Tel no: (01628) 580333
www.thefatduck.co.uk
Modern British | £195
Cooking score: 10

V

No grand entrance, no doormen in top hats announce the most famous restaurant in Britain. The venue, a former pub, is surprisingly modest but plays on the high expectations of diners – the tone is that of all truly great eating places, a quiet hum of people enjoying and discovering. There is no question that Heston Blumenthal's food is sensational, the cooking demonstrating a flair that leaves others still bewildered at the starting line. Jonny Lake, Blumenthal's able lieutenant, runs a highly disciplined kitchen where dishes have

been honed and polished to the nth degree, to the point where most can be considered in the 'signature' category. Even readers who have never eaten here may be familiar with some of them: the legendary grassy green and buttery snail porridge; the briny-sweet 'Sounds of the Sea' with accompanying iPod feed of plashing waves and screeching gulls; the Mad Hatter's tea party built around mock turtle soup, a gilded pocket watch and toast sandwiches. For those in a position to try the food, it's the sheer brilliance of the technique that makes all the difference: the gone-in-a-mouthful beetroot and horseradish macaroon palate cleanser; that big-flavoured hit of red cabbage gazpacho with Pommery grain-mustard ice cream; the luxurious indulgence of quail jelly layered with crayfish cream, chicken liver parfait and pea purée, served amid swirls of foaming liquid nitrogen with delicious truffle toast; the sticky richness in a slender finger of British Wagyu beef (with piccalilli components); and then there are those we-want-more whisk(e)y jellies. These are knockout, no question, but outstanding this year was the rich, sensuous

roast foie gras, its consistency that of set cream, served on a thin sliver of kombu (seaweed) and topped with delicate crab biscuit – a umami-sweet riff made more intense by a slick of rhubarb giving a welcome acidic bite. Yet if one dish is going to linger in your thoughts it is Blumenthal's grandest finale to date: botrytis cinerea (noble rot), a dazzling, playful exploration of dessert wine flavours through texture and temperature. The beautifully realised assemblage of grapes (all jelly, mousse, ice, brittle and liquid) proving to be, for one reporter 'the most unusual, memorable and inventive dessert I've ever come across'. And hold it in our memory we must, for the Duck is flying 'down under' for a six-month stint at the Crown Melbourne Resort, Australia. The doors shut in Bray in December 2014 and a reinvigorated, refurbished Fat Duck will be back in September 2015.
Chef/s: Heston Blumenthal and Jonny Lake. **Open:** Tue to Sat L 12 to 2, D 7 to 9. **Closed:** Mon, Sun, 2 weeks Christmas. **Meals:** Tasting menu L and D £195. **Details:** 40 seats.

★ TOP 50 PUB ★

The Hinds Head
The English country pub, Blumenthal-style
High Street, Bray, SL6 2AB
Tel no: (01628) 626151
www.hindsheadbray.com
British | £45
Cooking score: 5

The village pub branch of the Blumenthal operation in Bray is only a stone's throw from the Fat Duck (see entry). Behind the whitewashed frontage is a classic Tudor inn, all dark oak panelling, brick fireplaces and rustic furniture. Extending over two floors, the operation may be less rustic than before, but the guest ales and bar snacks keep things reasonably real. Otherwise, the attraction is Kevin Love's skilful renditions of British dishes such as fortifying pea and ham soup, stickily rich oxtail and kidney pudding, and treacle tart. Newer experiments meet with uproarious approval, as evidenced by the

February diner who found nothing short of perfection in the tea-smoked salmon with brilliant soda bread and sour cream butter, the pigeon with salsify and parsley roots in date sauce, and the chocolate wine slush with millionaire shortbread. An enterprising wine list with plenty by the glass starts at £19.95 (£5.10 a standard glass).
Chef/s: Kevin Love. **Open:** all week L 12 to 2.30 (4 Sun), Mon to Sat D 6.15 to 9.30. **Closed:** 25 Dec. **Meals:** alc (main courses £18 to £32). Set L £18 (2 courses) to £22. **Details:** 135 seats. Separate bar. Car parking.

★ TOP 50 ★

The Waterside Inn
An irresistible package
Ferry Road, Bray, SL6 2AT
Tel no: (01628) 620691
www.waterside-inn.co.uk
French | £140
Cooking score: 7

'It may not be at the cutting edge, compared with its near neighbour, but our meal here demonstrated that it doesn't have to be molecular to be brilliant.' So concludes the report of a mightily satisfied customer of the good old Waterside, which sits as serenely as a swan on the Thames, having once invented Bray as a destination. The picture-book view from the dining room windows soothes the soul, as does the front-of-house performance: 'every single member of staff knew exactly what was expected, and how to interact with customers to make them feel valued'. Perfect punctiliousness extends to the husbandry of a French haute cuisine that the Waterside wears as a badge of honour, marshalled by Michel Roux's son Alain. Lobster is a treat, whether generously loaded into a salad on mixed citrus jelly in raspberry vinaigrette, or in the long-running sauté in white port with gingered vegetable julienne. Main courses arrive like dignitaries on state visits: fillets of rabbit on celeriac fondant with marrons glacés in Armagnac sauce, or the glorious venison Wellington with broccoli in Hermitage and blackcurrant vinegar. Exquisite sugar-work goes into memorable dessert creations like lime-garnished pineapple parfait on pain d'épices sablé, or a perfectly pneumatic mirabelle plum soufflé. An encyclopedic guide to French wines is offered by a list that starts at £29 and disappears into the ether.

Chef/s: Alain Roux. **Open:** Wed to Sun L 12 to 2 (2.30 Sun), D 7 to 10. **Closed:** Mon, Tue, 26 Dec to 28 Jan. **Meals:** alc (main courses £50 to £59). Set L £50 (2 courses) to £62 (weekdays). Sun L £80. Tasting menu £153. **Details:** 70 seats. Separate bar. Car parking. Children over 12 yrs only.

LOCAL GEM
▲ The Crown at Bray
High Street, Bray, SL6 2AH
Tel no: (01628) 621936
www.thecrownatbray.com
British | £30

This centuries-old pub in the village centre is full of promise and possibilities. Heston Blumenthal may be the owner, but his commitment to maintain the Crown as the village pub can be seen in the selection of real ales, in hearty British cooking, and in the reasonable prices. Potted mackerel, char-grilled Irish Black Angus bavette with fries and marrowbone sauce, or roast hake with shrimps, capers, anchovies, cucumber and brown butter are typical choices. Wines from £17.75. Open all week.

■ Bucklebury
The Bladebone Inn
Versatile village inn
Chapel Row, Bucklebury, RG7 6PD
Tel no: (0118) 9712326
www.thebladeboneinn.com
Modern British | £28
Cooking score: 1
£5 OFF £30

Cosy, with a wood-panelled bar, beams and an open fire, this village pub feels English to a T. It's a suitably rustic setting for food that takes account of seasonal supplies and local produce,

and reporters have been delighted with the honest food. Recent favourites have included the truffled ham, egg and chips Scotch egg that has become something of a signature dish, and saffron ravioli with trompette de la mort, egg yolk, truffle and black olive oil, but you might also choose steak, sausages or fish and chips. Finish with hot chocolate fondant with yoghurt sorbet. Wines from £16.

Chef/s: Kiren Puri. **Open:** all week L 12 to 2.30 (4 Sun), Mon to Sat D 6.30 to 9 (9.30 Sat). **Meals:** alc (main courses £12 to £20). Set L £13 (2 courses) to £15. **Details:** 36 seats. 30 seats outside. Separate bar. Music. Car parking.

■ Burchett's Green
NEW ENTRY
The Crown
Big flavours in a diminutive pub
Burchett's Green, SL6 6QZ
Tel no: (01628) 824079
www.thecrownburchettsgreen.com
Modern British | £26
Cooking score: 3
£30

'Simon Bonwick is an economical and creative cook who puts wonderful food on the table for ridiculously fair prices,' noted a reader who remembers the chef's cooking when at the Blackboys Inn in Hurley. Now Bonwick has taken over this 'cute' country pub – just two small rooms decorated 'on the most austere of shoestrings' with jumble-sale oddments and scuffed wooden tables. But the cooking is 'superb', ingredients of a high quality, food 'rarely less than delicious'. A knockout Ardèche pâté with ravigote sauce opened a meal that went on to pheasant crown roasted on the bone, served on mash and covered in a subtle sauce of dates, cashews, mushrooms and chunks of cured wing meat, and finished with a cherry jam-laced frangipane slice topped with poached rhubarb, Seville orange segments and a dollop of vanilla ice cream. Wines from £17.50.

Chef/s: Simon Bonwick. **Open:** Sun L 12 to 3, Mon to Sat D 6 to 9. **Meals:** alc (main courses £12 to £16). **Details:** 28 seats. Separate bar.

Chieveley
The Crab at Chieveley
Fresh seafood for landlubbers
Wantage Road, Chieveley, RG20 8UE
Tel no: (01635) 247550
www.crabatchieveley.com
Seafood | £35
Cooking score: 3

🛏 V

With its thatched roof and views over Berkshire fields it may look like a classic country inn (with fabulous bedrooms), but the interior tells a very different story. Nets, lobster pots and other seafaring curios point up the theme, and there's no mistaking the orientation of the menu, with daily deliveries straight from West Country ports. You'll find whole Salcombe crab, of course – with either thermidor sauce, garlic and lemon butter, or curried coconut, lime and coriander – and platters of fish and shellfish, but the kitchen also turns out a satisfying smoked haddock chowder, and follows up strongly with wild sea bass with Parmesan gnocchi, artichoke cream and mushrooms. Not fanatical about fish? The menu obliges with pigeon breast, raisin purée and deep-fried quail's egg, and Dijon and herb-crusted rack of lamb with baked moussaka. To finish there's strawberry Pavlova. Wines start at £18.50.
Chef/s: David Horridge. **Open:** all week L 12 to 2.30, D 6 to 9.30. **Meals:** alc (main courses £16 to £29). Set L £19 (2 courses) to £23. Sun L £23 (2 courses) to £26. **Details:** 80 seats. Separate bar. Wheelchair access. Music. Car parking.

Symbols
🛏 Accommodation is available

£30 Three courses for less than £30

V Separate vegetarian menu

£5 £5-off voucher scheme
OFF

🍷 Notable wine list

Cookham
Maliks
Bright, lively Home Counties Indian
High Street, Cookham, SL6 9SF
Tel no: (01628) 520085
www.maliks.co.uk
Indian | £30
Cooking score: 1

Malik Ahmed set up his long-running restaurant in a former pub in 1999. His extensive menu goes where most suburban high-street Indian venues love to tread, with the likes of onion bhajia, chicken tikka masala and various tandoori dishes, but these form part of a good range of bright, lively dishes cooked with fresh ingredients. There has been praise for tandoori monkfish cooked in coconut milk, and spiced and skewered duck breast. Nevertheless, while it's clear the cooking is well attuned to local requirements, the restaurant can sometimes lose sight of the finer points in a rush to feed the throngs. House French is £18.
Chef/s: Malik Ahmed. **Open:** all week L 12 to 2.30, D 6 to 11 (10.30 Sun). **Closed:** 25 and 26 Dec. **Meals:** alc (main courses £8 to £16). Set L £12 (2 courses) to £15. Set D £24 (2 courses) to £40. Sun L buffet £12. **Details:** 66 seats. Wheelchair access. Car parking.

★ TOP 10 PUB ★
The White Oak
Village pub that follows the seasons
The Pound, Cookham, SL6 9QE
Tel no: (01628) 523043
www.thewhiteoak.co.uk
Modern European | £33
Cooking score: 5
£5
OFF

The red-brick White Oak is a classy pub in a classy village, with a focus firmly on its culinary output. That said, you'll still find a decent pint of real ale in the bar. The restaurant occupies a smart space with a fashionably neutral colour scheme and an upmarket country finish. Clive Dixon is a produce-led, reactive cook who changes the menu daily and delivers dishes that combine culinary good sense with technical know-how. There's an addictive quality to a luscious crab macaroni starter, and Asian inclinations in a pollack sashimi, but there is a unifying theme: this is stuff you actually want to eat. 'Pristine' hake fillet with wood-roasted peppers and quinoa spiced up with chipotle reflects the overall approach: first-class produce, relatively simple plates, the odd creative flourish. And it's a brave chef who puts on suckling pig for two in a Berkshire dining pub at £55, but the result is superb. To finish, who can resist apple tart 'baked to hit caramel on top, gooey in the middle, crisp on the bottom'? House French is £17.

Chef/s: Clive Dixon. **Open:** all week L 12 to 2.30 (5 Sun), Mon to Sat D 6 to 9.30. **Meals:** alc (main courses £15). Set L £14 (2 courses) to £16. Set D £21. **Details:** 70 seats. 30 seats outside. Separate bar. Wheelchair access. Music. Car parking.

▉ Holyport
The Belgian Arms
Good pub food at exactly the right price
Holyport, SL6 2JR
Tel no: (01628) 634468
www.thebelgianarms.com
British | £25
Cooking score: 3
£5 OFF   £30

'Good friendly service, well-presented food, lovely atmosphere,' enthused one fan of Nick Parkinson's village boozer (he also owns the Royal Oak, Paley Street). 'Just what the area needs,' noted another, drawn by the keenly priced menu. Opened up and modernised it may be, but there's a friendly, unpretentious charm to this white-painted pub that anchors the village green and pond. Locals are clearly delighted to have it on their doorstep. And what's not to like? Brakspear ales mean drinkers are welcome, and the kitchen attempts to please all palates – a policy that seems to work well. Upbeat British classics could include the likes of fried scampi and squid with aïoli, pot-roast chicken or braised

faggots with caramelised onions, as well as confit duck leg with celeriac purée, and spiced lamb burger with cucumber and yoghurt. Praise, too, for sticky toffee pudding with vanilla ice cream. Wines from £15.95.

Chef/s: David Thompson. **Open:** all week L 12 to 2.30 (3.30 Sun), Mon to Sat D 6.30 to 9.30 (10 Fri and Sat). **Meals:** alc (main courses £10 to £15). Set L £10 (2 courses). Sun L £22 (2 courses) to £26. **Details:** 60 seats. 40 seats outside. Separate bar. Music. Car parking.

▉ Maidenhead
Boulters Riverside Brasserie
A river runs past it
Boulters Lock Island, Maidenhead, SL6 8PE
Tel no: (01628) 621291
www.boultersrestaurant.co.uk
Modern British | £35
Cooking score: 2
£5 OFF

You can't fault the characterful location of the Dennis family's modern brasserie, which sits on the edge of a lock island in the Thames, surveying the peaceful view downstream. Perhaps the interior could be accused of a certain chilly minimalism, but the thinking was presumably not to distract from the riparian tranquillity of the surrounds. Daniel Woodhouse's cooking is appealing modern brasserie fare, with a few old faves such as truffled wild mushroom risotto or moules marinière pitched in. Otherwise, good reports are forthcoming about pea pannacotta with Serrano ham and a Parmesan crisp, pavé of hake on pistou risotto, and well-judged steaks of local beef served with triple-cooked chips. Dessert might be delightful mango and passion fruit soufflé, or chocolate-coated blackberry parfait with vanilla ice cream. A serviceable wine list offers a good choice by various sizes of glass, with standards (175ml) starting at £4.40. Bottles from £15.95.

Chef/s: Daniel Woodhouse. **Open:** all week L 12 to 2.45, Tue to Sat D 6.30 to 9.30. **Meals:** alc (main courses £12 to £20). Set L £16 (2 courses) to £20. **Details:** 70 seats. 70 seats outside. Separate bar. Wheelchair access. Music. Car parking.

Newbury

The Vineyard
French cooking and epic wines
Stockcross, Newbury, RG20 8JU
Tel no: (01635) 528770
www.the-vineyard.co.uk
Modern French | £65
Cooking score: 5
£5 OFF 🍷 🍽 V

The Rancho Newburyo architectural style is
rather surprising for first-timers, but the
Vineyard was conceived with unique selling
points all over the show. Not the least of these
is a burning commitment to the best in global
wine – now celebrated with more Dionysian
abandon than ever in the form of a hundred
choices by the glass or carafe. Hoorah! Daniel
Galmiche endeavours to maintain the culinary
excitement to back it all up, and while the
production is uneven, there are good things to
be had. Crisp-skinned guinea-fowl terrine
with orange, almonds and chicory is a fine
opener, and then there's monkfish with fennel
and both shades of asparagus, or corn-fed
duck breast with puréed carrot and mixed rice
pilaf. Chocolate and salty caramel mousse
with fromage blanc ice cream and a gooey
fondant doughnut tries hard to please at
dessert stage. The cooking needs sharper focus,
though, to keep pace with the wine treasures,
which are served forth on little paper mats to
identify them. The opening price is £25.
Chef/s: Daniel Galmiche. **Open:** all week L 12 to 2, D
7 to 9. **Meals:** alc (main courses £22 to £28). Set L
£29 (3 courses). Set D £65 (4 courses) to £75. Sun L
£39. **Details:** 90 seats. 60 seats outside. Separate
bar. Wheelchair access. Music. Car parking.

🍴 **Visit us**
Online
To find out more about
The Good Food Guide, please visit
www.thegoodfoodguide.co.uk

READERS RECOMMEND

Brebis
French
16 Bartholomew Street, Newbury, RG14 5LL
Tel no: (01635) 40527
www.brebis.co.uk
'Delightful surprise to discover this
Francophile gem in downtown Newbury.
Delicious, and good value for this level of food
in Berkshire.'

Paley Street

★ **TOP 10 PUB** ★

The Royal Oak
Turning great ingredients into stunning dishes
Littlefield Green, Paley Street, SL6 3JN
Tel no: (01628) 620541
www.theroyaloakpaleystreet.com
Modern British | £42
Cooking score: 6
🍷

The Royal Oak is a Berkshire institution with
14 years under its belt. It has a formidable local
reputation thanks to Nick Parkinson, who has
imbued the place with an air of civilised
charm. Visitors lap up the atmosphere in its
gentrified rural-chic interior (beams, polished
wood and leather, with contemporary
paintings). Dominic Chapman may have
departed but his replacement (former sous
chef Michael Chapman: no relation) sets a
high standard. He share's his former boss's
ability to turn great ingredients into stunning
flavour-packed dishes, whether it's a simple
Scotch egg or luxuries like foie gras or turbot.
Asparagus served with a pheasant egg and
hollandaise proves the point, as does a haunch
of venison (with creamed spinach and sauce
poivrade). Chocolate fondant with toffee
sauce and coffee ice cream shows standards
don't slip at dessert. A well-chosen page of
wines by the glass, carafe and bottle thriftily
opens a list that offers grandees from the classic
French regions alongside some fine southern-
hemisphere contenders. Prices start at £19.50.

Chef/s: Michael Chapman. **Open:** all week L 12 to 2.30 (3.30 Sun), Mon to Sat D 6.30 to 9.30 (10 Fri and Sat). **Meals:** alc (main courses £16 to £34). Sun L £26. **Details:** 80 seats. Separate bar. Music. Car parking. Children over 3 yrs only.

▌Shinfield

L'Ortolan

Prosperous, cultured Berkshire destination
Church Lane, Shinfield, RG2 9BY
Tel no: (01189) 888500
www.lortolan.com
Modern French | £65
Cooking score: 6

£5 OFF ▌ V

Although chef Alan Murchison's '10 in 8' restaurant group went into liquidation at the end of 2013, the Berkshire flagship is still going strong with Murchison heading the kitchen and continuing to get plaudits from readers. Occupying a former vicarage surrounded by resplendent mature gardens to the south of the M4, L'Ortolan belongs to Berkshire's gastronomic aristocracy. It's a prosperous, elegant and cultured destination with a comfortably appointed bar and dining rooms run by an army of professional staff. Murchison's exquisitely wrought dishes meld the trappings of contemporary French cuisine with overt British detailing and a thoroughly modern sensibility – hence confit salmon with pink grapefruit and fennel salad; ballotine of oxtail with bacon, smoked pomme purée and parsnips; or caramel mousse with honeycomb and aerated chocolate. Service is discreet, advice is delivered with authority and diners 'feel as if they really matter' in this eminently civilised rendezvous. The resourceful, conscientiously assembled wine list also plays its part, mixing vintage class with a penchant for organic and 'natural' viticulture. Prices start at £24.

Chef/s: Alan Murchison. **Open:** Tue to Sat L 12 to 2, D 7 to 9 (9.30 Fri and Sat). **Closed:** Sun, Mon, 24 Dec to 3 Jan. **Meals:** Set L £28 (2 courses) to £32. Set D £58 (2 courses) to £65. Tasting menu £70 (7 courses) to £105. **Details:** 58 seats. Separate bar. Music. Car parking.

▌Taplow

NEW ENTRY

André Garrett at Cliveden

Harmonious balance in a celebrated setting
Cliveden House, Taplow, SL6 0JF
Tel no: (01628) 607100
www.clivedenhouse.co.uk
Modern European | £65
Cooking score: 7

£5 OFF ▌ ➞ V

The celebrated Italianate country seat has been the scene of salacious goings-on for the past century, from the days of the Astor family's social maelstrom to its key role in the Profumo affair, conceived at the very poolside here. Cliveden has seen some highly elevated cooking over the years too, André Garrett's residency currently setting the pace in the ineffably elegant dining room (formerly The Terrace) where ornate chandeliers and framed oil portraits provide the adornments and full-height windows give garden views. Precise, harmonious balance is the hallmark of Garrett's dishes, be they sporting two flavours or ten, as dishes captivate the palate without needing to shock it senseless. A take on sole véronique features a hefty rolled fillet in luscious verjus butter, with pine nuts, semi-dried grapes and fennel. That might be preceded by foie gras ballotine parcelled in Cumbrian ham with salt-baked celeriac, golden raisins and hazelnuts in a sweet-savoury syrup, while dessert could produce a multi-layered pressed Cox's apple construction on a pastry base with walnut ice cream and rosemary caramel. Service is flawless. The wine list – fabulous not just for its expected treasures, but for true catholicity – holds a little relative price relief at the everyday end. Bottles start at £29.

Chef/s: André Garrett. **Open:** all week L 12.15 to 2.30, D 7 to 9.45. **Meals:** alc (main courses £38). Set L £28. Set D £65. Sun L £50. Tasting menu £90. **Details:** 70 seats. Separate bar. Music. Car parking.

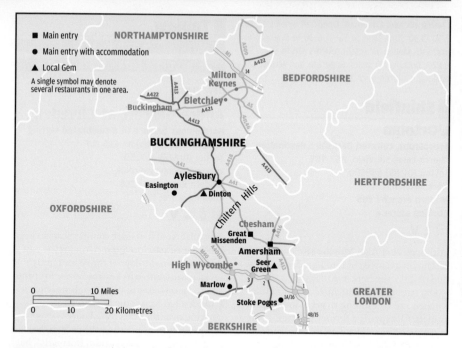

- ■ Main entry
- ● Main entry with accommodation
- ▲ Local Gem

A single symbol may denote several restaurants in one area.

NORTHAMPTONSHIRE

BEDFORDSHIRE

Milton Keynes

Bletchley

Buckingham

BUCKINGHAMSHIRE

Aylesbury

Easington

▲ Dinton

OXFORDSHIRE

Chiltern Hills

HERTFORDSHIRE

Chesham

Great Missenden

Amersham

Seer Green

High Wycombe

Marlow

Stoke Poges

GREATER LONDON

0   10 Miles
0   10   20 Kilometres

BERKSHIRE

■ Amersham

★ TOP 50 ★

Artichoke

Exhilarating seasonal adventures
9 Market Square, Amersham, HP7 ODF
Tel no: (01494) 726611
www.artichokerestaurant.co.uk
Modern British | £48
Cooking score: 7

🍷 V

Laurie and Jacqueline Gear's Artichoke is the kind of restaurant that begs for return visits, a place to cherish. There's something immensely appealing about its honest intent and highly personal style: just look at the muted grey, ivory and amethyst tones, the exquisite cutlery, the detailed fabrics and the willow-resin screens fronting the open kitchen. You can feel the character and confidence as soon as you arrive. Despite long-serving Ludovic Cosson's move to Pollen Street Social (see entry), service remains as keen as mustard and

fully clued-up about the 'stunning' food – so sit back and revel in Laurie's exhilarating seasonal adventures. This is big-city cooking, full of impact, complexity, razor-sharp detailing and clear, clean flavours: from pan-fried scallops with thick slabs of home-cured pork belly, cauliflower and caramel purée to smoked wood-pigeon with pickled artichokes, truffle gel and toasted crumb. Hogget is paired with alliums of every description (including a ribbon of wild garlic), brill gets a sharp wake-up call from young rhubarb, and there's a truly astonishing dish of roasted salsify buried in crispy edible 'soil' with tiny golden enoki mushrooms and a sweep of chervil emulsion: testament to the chef's time with Noma superstar René Redzepi. New desserts are often trailed on the remarkable-value set lunch, perhaps jellied chocolate with passion fruit curd or pear cake with liquorice ice cream. The knowledgeably chosen wine list pulls together fine drinking from reputable names and forward-looking producers worldwide; bottles from £24.

Chef/s: Laurie Gear and Ben Jenkins. **Open:** Tue to Sat L 12 to 3, D 6.30 to 11 (6 Fri and Sat). **Closed:** Sun, Mon, 1 week Christmas, 1 week Easter, 2 weeks Aug. **Meals:** alc (main courses £20 to £24). Set L £22 (2 courses) to £25. Set D £42 (2 courses) to £48. Tasting menu L £35 (5 courses), D £68 (7 courses). **Details:** 48 seats. 2 seats outside. Music.

LOCAL GEM
▲ Gilbey's
1 Market Square, Amersham, HP7 0DF
Tel no: (01494) 727242
www.gilbeygroup.com
Modern British | £34

Staff are 'always on form' at this Amersham stalwart, family-run by people who know wine as well as food. In a 17th-century former grammar school (with courtyard garden), Adam Whitlock produces 'classics with flair', adding interest to pressed confit duck with fig gel and spiced pears, and giving vegetarians comfort by way of a savoury bread-and-butter pudding with Rachel goats' cheese, walnuts and thyme. For a sweet pudding, try pistachio parfait. House wine is £16.25. Open all week.

Aylesbury
Hartwell House
Luxurious dining at a magnificent mansion
Oxford Road, Aylesbury, HP17 8NR
Tel no: (01296) 747444
www.hartwell-house.com
Modern European | £52
Cooking score: 2

£5 OFF 🛏

The French heir-presumptive Louis XVIII roughed it at Hartwell for five years during his exile, which gives you some idea of the grandeur of this Jacobean hall, sitting in 90 acres of parkland in the majestic serenity of the Vale of Aylesbury. There is a sense that the kitchen hasn't quite decided on its point of orientation, but winter diners thoroughly approved a dinner that incorporated monkfish with Bombay potatoes in yuzu sauce, and pork belly with aubergine gnocchi, to start,

and then a winning main course of plaice fillets in fine seafood sauce, accompanied by a crab and potato cake and spinach. Desserts such as dark chocolate macaroons with clementine, orange jelly and white chocolate mousse add allure, and there are pedigree British cheeses with homemade chutney. An exhaustive wine list holds many treasures, with plenty in the £30–40 price range. House Spanish is £28.75.
Chef/s: Daniel Richardson. **Open:** all week L 12.30 to 1.45, D 7.30 to 9.30. **Meals:** alc (main courses £25 to £38). Set L £25 (2 courses) to £32. Set D £25 (2 courses) to £32. Sun L £27 (2 courses) to £35. **Details:** 90 seats. Separate bar. Wheelchair access. Car parking. Children over 4 yrs only.

▌ Buckingham

READERS RECOMMEND
Nelson Street Restaurant
Modern British
53/54 Nelson Street, Buckingham, MK18 1BT
Tel no: (01280) 815556
www.nelsonstreetrestaurant.co.uk
'Just something a bit different and always tastes very fresh. Have been several times for lunch and dinners and was impressed by regular menu changes and new choices each time.'

▌ Dinton
LOCAL GEM
▲ La Chouette
High Street, Dinton, HP17 8UW
Tel no: (01296) 747422
www.lachouette.co.uk
Belgian | £43

'Belgian restaurants are rare in the UK,' writes chef/proprietor Frédéric Desmette, so don't be fooled by this quaint English village inn. The menus rarely venture beyond the canon of classic French and Belgian cooking: grilled scallops with a chicory sauce; rump steak with a green peppercorn sauce, or partridge with cabbage; a chocolate soufflé (for two). Wondrous bread, glorious French wines (from £18.50), Belgian beers and an appealing, time-warp dining room displaying the owner's photographs of *les chouettes* (owls), complete the scene. Closed Sat L and Sun.

Easington

The Mole & Chicken

Sympathetically gentrified pub-with-rooms
Easington Terrace, Easington, HP18 9EY
Tel no: (01844) 208387
www.themoleandchicken.co.uk
Modern British | £30
Cooking score: 1

In summer, alfresco tables on the gorgeous terrace are much in demand at this sympathetically gentrified pub-cum-restaurant overlooking swathes of Buckinghamshire countryside; in winter, log fires and cosy comforts beckon in the warren of little rooms. As for food, recent recommendations suggest the kitchen has a broad remit – from devilled kidneys on toast or Mediterranean-style pot-roast chicken with chive linguine to flaked confit duck salad with Thai herbs or pan-fried cod with pea risotto. There are 28-day-aged steaks, roasts, pub staples and British cheeses, too, plus desserts such as caramelised banana and hazelnut meringue. Wines offer sound drinking from £19.50 (£4.90 a glass).
Chef/s: Steve Bush. **Open:** all week L 12 to 2.30 (3 Sat, 4 Sun), D 6.30 to 9.30 (6 to 9 Sun). **Closed:** 25 Dec. **Meals:** alc (main courses £13 to £26). Set L and D £15 (2 courses) to £20. **Details:** 60 seats. 65 seats outside. Wheelchair access. Music. Car parking.

Great Missenden

La Petite Auberge

Bastion of French virtues
107 High Street, Great Missenden, HP16 0BB
Tel no: (01494) 865370
www.lapetiteauberge.co.uk
French | £35
Cooking score: 2
£5
OFF

An immutable bastion of French culinary virtues and a *chère amie* to the folk of Great Missenden, Hubert and Madame Martel's petite dining room has been accommodating the local crowd for almost a quarter of a century. French is the lingua franca in the kitchen and on the menu – although translations are provided for most items. This is the world of 'foie gras de canard cuit en terrine', 'escargots de bourgogne préparés en surprise' (wait and see!) and 'noisettes de chevreuil poêlées au chou rouge' (medallions of venison with red cabbage, in case you were wondering). Otherwise, pan-fried scallops with julienne of carrot and soy dressing is about as adventurous as it gets. Main courses invariably appear with 'les legumes du marché', while dessert is a roll call of chart-topping evergreens (crème brûlée, nougatine glacée, tarte au citron). Wines (from £19.50) never stray beyond the French borders.
Chef/s: Hubert Martel. **Open:** Mon to Sat D only 7 to 10. **Closed:** Sun (except Mothering Sun L), 2 weeks Christmas, 2 weeks Easter. **Meals:** alc (main courses £18 to £21). **Details:** 28 seats. Wheelchair access.

Marlow

★ TOP 50 / TOP 10 PUB ★

The Hand & Flowers

Big-hearted, resourceful cooking
126 West Street, Marlow, SL7 2BP
Tel no: (01628) 482277
www.thehandandflowers.co.uk
Modern British | £45
Cooking score: 6

Tom Kerridge is the man of the moment, the chef du jour: on the telly, in print, and taking the pub to an exalted level. For one reader, the experience here was more than just nostalgia it was 'truly phenomenal'. The classy pub finish – now enhanced by a totally in-keeping bar extension (a light, comfortable room in pale wood and leather) – is backed by staff who know their onions and a menu that can hit the heights. A glazed omelette rich with smoked haddock and Parmesan has a high comfort factor, while slow-cooked duck breast with duck-fat chips is still thought to be the 'star of the show' for some. Essex lamb 'bun' looks the business and has a superb piece of meat at its heart. Puddings such as pear soufflé with caraway crumble also rise to the occasion. The wine list (from £25) has good options (some organic) by the glass and carafe. Top tip for those who can't get a table or have given up on the booking system: there are four stools in the bar that are available for walk-ins, no booking, full menu . . . take a chance.
Chef/s: Tom Kerridge. **Open:** all week L 12 to 2.45 (3.15 Sun), Mon to Sat D 6.30 to 9.45. **Closed:** 24 to 26 Dec. **Meals:** alc (main courses £24 to £32). Set L Mon to Sat £15 (2 courses) to £19.50. **Details:** 50 seats. 20 seats outside.

Average Price

The average price listed in main-entry reviews denotes the price of a three-course meal, without wine.

The Vanilla Pod

Modern cooking that delivers every time
31 West Street, Marlow, SL7 2LS
Tel no: (01628) 898101
www.thevanillapod.co.uk
Modern European | £45
Cooking score: 5

£5 OFF V

Michael Macdonald's small town house restaurant gives the lie to the notion that there's only one culinary show in Marlow. Readers find a 'very relaxing' atmosphere in the 'cosy, historic' building where TS Eliot once lived, and they value the consistency of the kitchen's focus on flavour, quality and, especially at lunch, value. Plates are prettily worked, but dishes aren't fussy. Start with venison carpaccio or quail with asparagus and Parma ham, followed by one of Macdonald's favourite uses of the eponymous pod: in a well-judged cream sauce with poached sea bass. Loin of venison with potato fondant and turnips in brown butter, or lamb rump with white beans and mustard, show a solid understanding of how to flatter good meat. Pudding might be a beer cake made with local Rebellion ale and served with spiced plum and lemon cheese cream, or a bitter chocolate fondant with caramel. Wine from £19.50.
Chef/s: Michael Macdonald. **Open:** Tue to Sat L 12 to 3, D 7 to 10. **Closed:** Sun, Mon, 23 Dec to 6 Jan, 1 week Jun, 1 week Aug. **Meals:** Set L £15 (2 courses) to £20. Set D £30 (2 courses) to £45. **Details:** 36 seats. 16 seats outside. Separate bar.

Seer Green

LOCAL GEM
▲ The Jolly Cricketers

24 Chalfont Road, Seer Green, HP9 2YG
Tel no: (01494) 676308
www.thejollycricketers.co.uk
Modern British | £28 £5 OFF

Fans of the game can wallow in the cricketing memorabilia and giggle at the jokey references on the menu at this wisteria-clad, 150-year-old Chiltern watering hole. Local ales quench thirsts in the cluttered bar, while ambitious pub grub satisfies hunger pangs in the adjoining 'parlour' – a snug setting for 'openers' and 'main play' dishes ranging from crispy squid with chilli and lemon sauce to braised faggots or pan-fried stone bass with wild mushrooms, braised fennel and potato purée. Wines from £16.50. No food Sun D.

▌Stoke Poges

The Garden Room

Thoroughly modern kind of cooking
Stoke Place, Stoke Green, Stoke Poges, SL2 4HT
Tel no: (01753) 534790
www.stokeplace.co.uk
Modern European | £45
Cooking score: 4

Stoke Place is a modern country house hotel in grounds designed by 'Capability' Brown. It aims to be a hot ticket for corporate events, glam parties and well-to-do weddings, but it's also home to the Garden Room restaurant, which is a very interesting proposition indeed. With its mismatched chairs, linen-free tables and garden theme, the restaurant is in sync with the boutique ambitions of the hotel. Chef Craig van der Meer is a proponent of a thoroughly modern kind of cooking, with each plate looking as pretty as a picture. Smoked eel comes with feather-light Serrano ham croquettes, pickled kohlrabi and passion fruit; cannon of lamb is dressed with a miso froth; and wild sea bass comes with vanilla and corn purée, crayfish and samphire. Desserts are equally complex (but ethereally light): cinnamon doughnut, perhaps, with gingerbread ice cream and poached pear. The excellent wine (and water) list has good tasting notes; bottles from £19.
Chef/s: Craig van der Meer. **Open:** all week L 12 to 2, D 7 to 9.30. **Meals:** Set L £35 (2 courses) to £45. Tasting menu £55. **Details:** 30 seats. 25 seats outside. Separate bar. Wheelchair access. Music. Car parking. Children at L only.

▟▙ CLIVE DIXON
The White Oak, Berkshire

What do you enjoy about being a chef?
The fact I surround myself with quality ingredients and passionate people.

What would you be if you weren't a chef?
I was five years old when I decided to become a chef. I have not for a moment given thought to doing anything else since.

Do you have a favourite new restaurant opening?
The most exciting restaurant opening for a long time has been Brasserie Chavot.

What food could you not live without?
Quality beef! It's so versatile and I love the different flavours and textures you get from different cuts.

Is there a dish that evokes strong memories for you?
My dad's bacon rib and cabbage sandwich, cooked for me on Saturday lunchtimes when I was a young boy.

Do you have a guilty foodie pleasure?
After Eight mints and jelly babies.

Photo: Martin Wilson

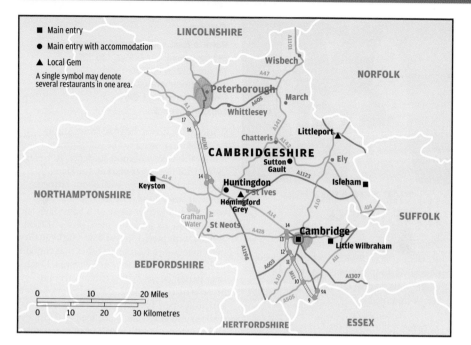

Map legend:
- ■ Main entry
- ● Main entry with accommodation
- ▲ Local Gem

A single symbol may denote several restaurants in one area.

LINCOLNSHIRE

NORFOLK

Wisbech

Peterborough

March

Whittlesey

Chatteris

Littleport

CAMBRIDGESHIRE

Sutton
Gault

Ely

Isleham

Keyston

Huntingdon
St Ives

Hemingford
Grey

Grafham
Water

St Neots

Cambridge

Little Wilbraham

SUFFOLK

NORTHAMPTONSHIRE

BEDFORDSHIRE

HERTFORDSHIRE

ESSEX

0   10   20 Miles
0   10   20   30 Kilometres

■ Cambridge

Alimentum
Hot ticket with high-impact food
152-154 Hills Road, Cambridge, CB2 8PB
Tel no: (01223) 413000
www.restaurantalimentum.co.uk
Modern European | £49
Cooking score: 6

Alimentum's funky minimalism and stark, clubby décor aren't to everyone's taste (think black chairs, black walls and sharp red tones), but they're a precise fit for the dramatic contemporary food offered in this hot-ticket restaurant. 'Painstaking preparation and exquisite presentation' only tell half the story: this is bold, high-impact cooking – although some readers have occasionally found the results a tad 'bland'. Cheddar cheese soup with pickled onion and red grape is a cheeky pub trade-off; breast of grouse with sourdough, elderberry and leek provides a concentrated blast of flavours. The kitchen raises the bar even further with 'sensational' mains such as ozone-fresh stone bass with crab, pistachio and turnip, but it can also do 'earthy', as proved by lamb with haggis bolognese, swede and lettuce. Desserts have included an 'absolutely stunning' chocolate ganache with toffee and rice. Service is faultless, and the grown-up wine list (from £15 a carafe) offers a palate-illuminating tour, particularly through France and Italy.
Chef/s: Mark Poynton. **Open:** all week L 12 to 2, D 6 to 10. **Closed:** 23 to 31 Dec, bank hols. **Meals:** Set L and early D £19 (2 courses) to £25. Set menu £36 (2 courses) to £49. Tasting menu £72. **Details:** 62 seats. Separate bar. Wheelchair access.

Visit us Online
To find out more about *The Good Food Guide*, please visit www.thegoodfoodguide.co.uk

THE THEATRE OF SERVICE

Once in danger of becoming extinct, the art of gueridon service has been revived of late. At our picks, you can see your waiter finish a dish tableside - and it's worth tipping for.

At Otto's, tableside theatre has its ultimate expression in canard á la presse. The juices of a rare roast duck are extracted in a silver duck-press, and used to enrich a red wine sauce served with slices of the duck breast.

At the Galvin brothers' restaurants, at-table flourishes seem perfectly natural. The Pompadour's house special is poulet en vessie. Chicken is cooked in a pig's bladder which is opened at the table, and the contents served with truffle and mushroom sauce.

It may not always say so on the menus, but Heston Blumenthal's restaurants are gueridon hotspots. Look out for the liquid nitrogen ice cream trolley at Dinner.

A soufflé split at the table, to accommodate sauce or ice cream, is a favourite restaurant trick. Try the Don's rhubarb version, perhaps preceded by Dover sole filleted before your very eyes.

Cotto

Hard-to-fault sourcing and flavours
183 East Road, Cambridge, CB1 1BG
Tel no: (01223) 302010
www.cottocambridge.co.uk
Modern European | £55
Cooking score: 3

Cotto is just down the road from Anglia Ruskin University, but the prices probably put it out of the reach of most students. To be fair, they're not the target market, for Hans Schweitzer's restaurant is all about refined, contemporary food. The fixed-price menu costs 55 quid (a fiver more on a Saturday), and for that you get some dynamic plates of food cooked with precision and flair. High-quality ingredients are a feature of dishes that contain well-judged combinations of flavours. Duck liver parfait comes with a truffle jelly and brioche in a starter with classical roots, before a main course of grey mullet with queen scallops and gazpacho, or sautéed veal kidneys and sweetbreads with wholegrain mustard sauce. Everything looks pretty on the plate, not least desserts like the 'chocolate composition' (Hans is a skilled chocolatier) – and the service team are entirely on the ball. Wines from £17.50.
Chef/s: Hans Schweitzer. **Open:** Wed to Sat D only 6.30 to 10 (6 Sat). **Closed:** Sun, Mon, Tue. **Meals:** Set D £55. **Details:** 45 seats. Music. Car parking. Children over 10 yrs only.

Fitzbillies

Vintage Cambridge haunt
51-52 Trumpington Street, Cambridge, CB2 1RG
Tel no: (01223) 352500
www.fitzbillies.com
British | £26
Cooking score: 1
£30

A vintage Cambridge haunt attracting hungry mouths, Fitzbillies is a populist, urban-minded eatery with bags of vigour and a bakery upfront. The utilitarian but convivial set-up has a tub-thumping approach to British classics – so during the day expect hefty sausage rolls, bacon and egg pie, Welsh rarebit and the famous Chelsea buns. Most dishes cost under £10. Thursday to Saturday evenings, however, the kitchen ups its game (and prices) with the likes of scrambled duck egg and black pudding on toast, grilled venison haunch with Burgundy sauce and truffle mash, and Seville orange tart. Wines from £16.

Chef/s: Rosie Sykes. **Open:** all week L 12 to 3, Thur to Sat D 6 to 9.30. **Closed:** No D in Aug. **Meals:** alc (main courses £13 to £17). **Details:** 65 seats.

★ TOP 50 ★

Midsummer House

Cambridge's class act
Midsummer Common, Cambridge, CB4 1HA
Tel no: (01223) 369299
www.midsummerhouse.co.uk
Modern British | £75
Cooking score: 8

V

The Victorian villa on Midsummer Common, beside the tranquil river Cam, has over the past 16 years become one of the nation's outstanding venues. Some places aim to satisfy with a sense of stately perfection; others fire the imagination, prompting excited word of mouth. The unison of reports to the Guide suggests Daniel Clifford has successfully positioned Midsummer in the latter category. Readers are impressed by the whole deal, from sympathetic, relaxing service to the serenity of the setting, and the sensational cooking. Fixed tasters are the format, for five, seven or ten courses as you see fit. With so many dishes in prospect, and many of formidable intricacy, it's all the more remarkable that reporters recall them in such detail. But they do. Highlights for one February diner included precision-timed scallop with apple and truffle, rich duck confit with celeriac baked for 12 hours on open coals, as well as miraculously tender Wagyu beef with braised oxtail and puréed spinach in concentrated cooking juices. Fish dishes rise to the occasion too, as in a duo of turbot and Scottish squat lobster with roasted cauliflower. Desserts to evoke rhapsodies have included Yorkshire rhubarb

with hickory-wood ice cream and sorrel, or poached banana with chocolate crémeux, caramelised brioche and chocolate yoghurt sorbet. Opting for the wine flight is one way to keep a lid on the drinks bill. The quality-laden list is nearly all stiff peaks, starting at £28.

Chef/s: Daniel Clifford. **Open:** Wed to Sat L 12 to 1.30, Tue to Sat D 7 to 9. **Closed:** Sun, Mon, 2 weeks Christmas. **Meals:** Tasting menus £45 (5 courses) to £75 (7 courses) to £95 (10 courses). **Details:** 62 seats. Separate bar.

Hemingford Grey

LOCAL GEM
▲ The Cock

47 High Street, Hemingford Grey, PE28 9BJ
Tel no: (01480) 463609
www.thecockhemingford.co.uk
Modern British | £25

'Another lovely meal at our local favourite,' concluded one couple, admiring this rustic village pub-cum-restaurant. One side houses a proper drinking gaff, the other a casual restaurant with blackboard menus offering ample choice. Fish is a forte (hake with butter-bean, chorizo and tomato stew), but you might also find homemade sausages with a choice of mash and sauce. Tuesday's steak and chop night is recommended for 'cooked to perfection' butler's steak and 'very good' pork T-bone. Wines from £18.50. Open all week.

Huntingdon
The Old Bridge Hotel

Eat, drink and enjoy
1 High Street, Huntingdon, PE29 3TQ
Tel no: (01480) 424300
www.huntsbridge.com
Modern British | £35
Cooking score: 2

'How lovely to sink into the comfort of this delightful hotel restaurant,' enthused one visitor to this 18th-century building overlooking the River Ouse. Well-heeled

locals love it, coming to feast on a menu that bursts with classics – think asparagus with poached egg and hollandaise, lemon sole with parsley butter, crème brûlée with Champagne rhubarb. A starter of Brixham crab cries out for less creaminess and more crabbiness, but a simple pear and Colston Bassett Stilton salad is sublimely crunchy, sweet and salty. Pork belly might have benefited from longer cooking, but bream, perfectly pan-fried and served with a sparky chilli risotto, restores confidence. With an MW in charge here, it's not surprising that wine-lovers linger. A vast list whisks guests on a magic carpet ride to an Aladdin's cave of vinous treasures, all succinctly described, with bottles from just £17.95. Favourites can be bought in the hotel's outstanding wine shop.
Chef/s: Jack Woolner. **Open:** all week L 12 to 2, D 6.30 to 10. **Meals:** alc (main courses £14 to £26). Set L and D £17 (2 courses) to £21. Sun L £30. **Details:** 80 seats. 50 seats outside. Separate bar. Car parking.

▌Isleham

The Merry Monk
Classic flavours in tucked-away village eatery
30 West Street, Isleham, CB7 5SB
Tel no: (01638) 780900
www.merry-monk.co.uk
British | £29
Cooking score: 2
£5 OFF   £30

This village eatery might be deep in the Fens, but it still attracts loyal diners, hungry for chef/patron Adrian Smith's classically inspired cooking. Nibbles ('beware, they are big nibbles!') include crisp, moreish deep-fried duck 'lollipops' with hoisin sauce, while a starter of crumbed boiled egg and brioche 'soldiers' comes with oh-so-sweet pork belly. To pursue the crisp theme, lamb scrumpet (breaded, deep-fried breast of lamb) accompanies slow-cooked leg of spring lamb, with a nod to health in the form of wilted greens. For something lighter, try the cod fillet with brown shrimps, cauliflower purée and curly kale. Or there's the steak menu, with

cuts ranging from a refined fillet to a whopping double-cut rib steak for two, served with a choice of sauce and triple-cooked chips. A lemon curd pudding may have lacked tartness, but a deeply chocolatey brownie with refreshing yoghurt orange sorbet was a hit. Wine from £17.95.
Chef/s: Adrian Smith. **Open:** Wed to Sun L 11.45 to 2, D 6.30 to 9. **Closed:** Mon, Tue, 25 and 26 Dec. **Meals:** alc (main courses £15 to 21). Set D £19. **Details:** 60 seats. 24 seats outside. Separate bar. Music. Car parking.

▌Keyston

The Pheasant
Vigorous metropolitan flavours
Loop Road, Keyston, PE28 0RE
Tel no: (01832) 710241
www.thepheasant-keyston.co.uk
Modern British | £27
Cooking score: 2
£5 OFF   £30

Chef Simon Cadge and his front-of-house partner Gerda Coedijk now have their names above the door of this thatched hostelry deep in the Cambridgeshire countryside – but little else has changed at the well-groomed, affluent Pheasant. Inside, beams and open fires add to the rustic feel, although the food is all about vigorous metropolitan flavours: from pan-fried swordfish with chickpeas, chermoula and purple sprouting broccoli to roast corn-fed chicken with borlotti beans, confit celeriac, cavolo nero and pancetta. There are also plenty of honest-to-goodness Brit classics for those who prefer fishcakes with samphire or homemade black pudding with mash and fried onions. Desserts promise the best of both worlds: pannacotta with rhubarb compote, for instance, or bread-and-butter pudding with custard. Former owner and respected oenophile John Hoskins MW still oversees the brilliant 100-bin wine list, which offers bags of top drinking by the glass, excellent half-bottles and modern thrills on every page. House selections start at £17 (£5 a glass).

Chef/s: Simon Cadge. **Open:** Tue to Sun L 12 to 2 (3.30 Sun), Tue to Sat D 6.30 to 9.30. **Closed:** Mon, 2 to 16 Jan. **Meals:** alc (main courses £10 to £22). Set L £15 (2 courses) to £20. Sun L £25. **Details:** 80 seats. 50 seats outside. Separate bar. Car parking.

Little Wilbraham
The Hole in the Wall
Spirited food and folksy trappings
Primrose Farm Road, Little Wilbraham, CB21 5JY
Tel no: (01223) 812282
www.holeinthewallcambridge.com
Modern British | £30
Cooking score: 1
£5 OFF

MasterChef finalist turned restaurateur Alex Rushmer is making a good fist of things at this 16th-century free house in a pretty Fenland village. Weathered beams, open fires and folksy trappings provide the requisite rusticity, while the kitchen keeps it fresh and modern with spirited dishes such as courgette, asparagus and smoked goats' cheese risotto or beef cheek and shin with roast cauliflower, celeriac and crispy kale. Duck with spiced caramel and pickled cucumber is a 'great new take on sweet-and-sour', and everyone rates the mini doughnuts with warm chocolate dipping sauce. Wines from £18.
Chef/s: Alex Rushmer. **Open:** Wed to Sun L 12 to 3 (4 Sun), Tue to Sat D 6 to 10 (11 Fri and Sat). **Closed:** Mon. **Meals:** alc (main courses £13 to £27). Set L £16 (2 courses) to £18. Tasting menu £45 (8 courses). **Details:** 80 seats. 25 seats outside. Separate bar. Wheelchair access. Music. Car parking.

Littleport

LOCAL GEM
▲ The Fen House
2 Lynn Road, Littleport, CB6 1QG
Tel no: (01353) 860645
Modern British | £40

David Warne has been quietly going about his business since 1987, drawing customers to this exclusive white-fronted Fenland cottage with the promise of dinner two nights a week.

Meals run at a leisurely pace, but there's much to savour on the fixed-price four-course menu (£40 including cheese). A warm salad of slow-cooked pork belly, pear and fennel might precede sea bass in puff pastry with spinach and ginger butter sauce, while desserts could bring white chocolate tart with raspberries. Wines from £16.75. Open Fri and Sat D only.

Sutton Gault
The Anchor Inn
Unshowy country pub on peaceful Fens
Bury Lane, Sutton Gault, CB6 2BD
Tel no: (01353) 778537
www.anchor-inn-restaurant.co.uk
Modern British | £30
Cooking score: 1
£5 OFF 🛏

Super-fresh bread and a jug of chilled water, delivered with a smile and without asking, make a great start to a meal at this unpretentious Fenland pub. Ignore the slightly tired décor and enjoy the food. A beetroot, goats' cheese and candied walnut starter is a wild, slightly over-sweet assembly of everything a chef can do with beetroot. Confit belly of pork with black pudding and Jerusalem artichoke is a more conventional option. Follow with sea bass served with the freshest of samphire, peppery crushed potatoes and vivid broccoli purée. To finish, indulge yourself with a double chocolate and peanut brownie. Wines from £14.30.
Chef/s: Maciej Bilewski. **Open:** all week L 12 to 2 (2.30 Sun), D 7 to 9 (6 Sat, 6.30 Sun). **Meals:** alc (main courses £12 to £23). Set L £14 (2 courses) to £18. Sun L £13. **Details:** 60 seats. 30 seats outside. Wheelchair access. Car parking.

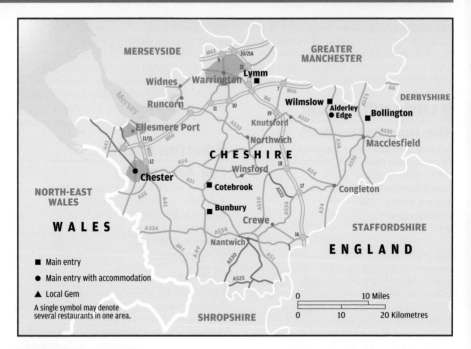

▮ Alderley Edge

Alderley Edge Hotel

Cheshire favourite with serious food
Macclesfield Road, Alderley Edge, SK9 7BJ
Tel no: (01625) 583033
www.alderleyedgehotel.com
Modern British | £48
Cooking score: 3

🍽 V

The wooded slopes of Alderley Edge provide a pleasingly pastoral backdrop to the Victorian Gothic trappings of this locally renowned hotel: a favourite with emigrés from south Manchester and beyond. A major attraction is the ambitious food served in the swish conservatory-style dining room. Here, guests are treated to seriously crafted food with strong regional credentials – as in Reg Johnson's Goosnargh duck three ways with quince, Muscat and pain d'epice, or slow-cooked loin of Cheshire lamb with sun-dried tomato purée, basil jam and a 'hotpot' cake. There are classy fish dishes too (grilled lemon sole with new season's squash, chanterelles and tarragon, say), while desserts might feature hibiscus-poached rhubarb (from the Yorkshire 'triangle') with frozen Cheshire yoghurt and rhubarb soup. The cheese menu is also worth a sniff. Alternatively, seek out the all-day brasserie for open sandwiches and reinvented retro classics such as shepherd's pie with pickled red cabbage. House wines from £21.50.
Chef/s: Chris Holland. **Open:** all week L 12 to 2 (4 Sun), Mon to Sat D 7 to 10. **Closed:** 1 Jan. **Meals:** alc (main courses £24 to £25). Set L £23 (2 courses) to £28. **Details:** 70 seats. Separate bar. Wheelchair access. Music. Car parking.

🍴 Visit us Online

To find out more about
The Good Food Guide, please visit
www.thegoodfoodguide.co.uk

▌Bollington
The Lord Clyde
A country pub pushing the foodie boundaries
36 Clarke Lane, Kerridge, Bollington, SK10 5AH
Tel no: (01625) 562123
www.thelordclyde.co.uk
Modern British | £32
Cooking score: 3
£5
OFF

South African Ernst Van Zyl and his English partner Sarah have big ambitions for this little pub on a quiet country lane just outside Macclesfield. Since opening, their 'next level food' (as one reader put it) has attracted a considerable following. Treats like wafer-thin pork skin with 'little squirts of flavour' and sourdough bread in a hessian sack with smoked butter indicate that 'pub food this ain't'. At a test meal, succulent sous-vide-style quail with sweet (carrot) and bitter (chicory) salad was 'very good indeed', as was a whole salt-baked beetroot that came with homemade cheese, watercress and 'hints of coffee'. Next, 'a really clever' dish of tenderloin of pork was rolled with dried black pudding and teamed with broccoli, grape and buckwheat, and a 'tender with deep flavour' venison arrived with a very rich jus and aubergine, beetroot and spelt. Desserts push the boundaries, too, while the global wine list starts at £15.50. **Chef/s:** Ernst Van Zyl. **Open:** Tue to Sun L 12 to 2.30 (2 Sun), D 6.30 to 9. **Closed:** Mon. **Meals:** alc (main courses £14 to £19). Set L £17 (2 courses) to £19. Sun L £17 (2 courses) to £19. **Details:** 24 seats. 20 seats outside. Music. Car parking.

Symbols
 Accommodation is available
£30 Three courses for less than £30
V Separate vegetarian menu
£5 OFF £5-off voucher scheme
 Notable wine list

▌Bunbury
The Yew Tree Inn
Smart country local
Long Lane, Spurstow, Bunbury, CW6 9RD
Tel no: (01829) 260274
www.theyewtreebunbury.com
Modern British | £25
Cooking score: 2
£5 OFF £30

Built by the Earl of Crewe in the 19th century with a mock-Tudor spin, the Yew Tree's leafy aspect and period charm are part of its appeal. There's a real sense of Englishness and character to the place, with an opened-up contemporary finish and Victorian-style eccentricity. Real ales and craft beers rubber-stamp its pub credentials, while the kitchen shows not a jot of pretension. There are 'pub classics' like homemade pie of the day or beer-battered cod with chips and a choice of peas (mushy or garden, you decide), but the kitchen can also turn its hand to crab and chorizo risotto, or slow-braised shin of beef with boulangère potatoes and bourguignon sauce. Desserts of apple crumble and bread-and-butter pudding come with crème anglaise. Wines start at £14.50. **Chef/s:** Rob McDiarmid. **Open:** Mon to Fri L 12 to 2.30, D 6 to 9.30 (10 Fri). Sat and Sun 12 to 10 (8 Sun). **Closed:** 25 Dec. **Meals:** alc (main courses £10 to £24). Set L and D £13 (2 courses) to £24. **Details:** 65 seats. 70 seats outside. Separate bar. Wheelchair access. Music. Car parking.

▌Chester
Joseph Benjamin
Lively deli/eatery with foodie pleasures
134-140 Northgate Street, Chester, CH1 2HT
Tel no: (01244) 344295
www.josephbenjamin.co.uk
Modern European | £26
Cooking score: 2
 £30

There are two people behind the eponym, brothers Joe and Ben Wright, and their deli-restaurant by Chester's historic city walls draws in custom from 9am breakfasts to the last port and cheese of evening. Straightforward, well-executed brasserie dishes form the backbone of the operation: the likes of duck terrine with rhubarb, antipasti tasting plates, steak burgers on brioche buns, and salmon with niçoise salad. Food is far more attractively presented than the laid-back ambience might lead you to expect, but without veering into primping. Joe is a versatile chef, as much at home producing a vegetable curry of cauliflower, lentils and spinach with coconut rice and an aubergine bhaji, as with roasting guinea fowl breast or braising ox cheek in soy. Finish with affogato, or fruitcake and Stilton. The wine list is a model of thoughtful concision, full of heterogeneous interest from £17.50 up to £50 or thereabouts, inspiring confidence all the way from Castilian Verdejo/Viura to an opulently ripe Bolgheri red.

Chef/s: Joe Wright. **Open:** Tue to Sun L 12 to 3 (4 Sun), Thur to Sat D 6 to 9.30. **Closed:** Mon, 25 Dec to 1 Jan. **Meals:** alc (main courses £11 to £19). Sun L £20 (3 courses). **Details:** 35 seats. 20 seats outside. Separate bar. Wheelchair access. Music.

Michael Caines at ABode Chester

High-level dining in more ways than one
Grosvenor Road, Chester, CH1 2DJ
Tel no: (01244) 347000
www.michaelcaines.com
Modern British | £45
Cooking score: 5
£5 OFF 🛏

The Chester branch of Michael Caines' ABode group occupies a prime position in a predominantly glass building that was once the HQ of Cheshire police force. From the fifth-floor dining room, you have a panoramic view of Chester racecourse (pick your race-day carefully, punters), as well as the city centre and the Welsh hills beyond. You get the full gastronomic package, with early-bird, grazing, tasters and kids' menus supplementing the à la carte. Many of the group's familiar dishes are rendered with

convincing panache, as in slow-cooked salmon with wasabi yoghurt in honey-soy vinaigrette, and mains such as Cumbrian beef strip-loin with watercress purée, smoked butter croquettes and horseradish shallots in red wine, or salt cod with mussels, kohlrabi and cauliflower in Indian-spiced sauce. Finish with mandarin and dark chocolate millefeuille and mandarin sorbet, or classic lemon tart. Wines have been selected with gusto and imagination, with bottles from £19.

Chef/s: Thomas Hine. **Open:** Mon to Sat L 12 to 2.30, D 6 to 10. **Closed:** Sun. **Meals:** alc (main courses £13 to £25). Set L £15 (2 courses) to £20. Set D £17 (2 courses) to £23. **Details:** 76 seats. Separate bar. Wheelchair access. Music.

★ TOP 50 ★

Simon Radley at the Chester Grosvenor

Tradition and innovation meet in Chester
Eastgate, Chester, CH1 1LT
Tel no: (01244) 324024
www.chestergrosvenor.com
Modern European | £69
Cooking score: 6
£5 OFF 🍷 🛏 V

This mighty hotel right in the centre of the city is a Chester landmark. At its heart is Simon Radley's modern temple to fine wines and classy food: a comfortable, classic dining room that, quite effortlessly, exudes both sophistication and old-fashioned charm. Over the years Radley has perfected a highly personal style with an eye for detail and appreciation of quality that is beyond reproach. His cooking pleases, excites and soothes. Highlighted dishes this year range from a sweet pea vichyssoise with duck liver carpaccio and smoked magret ('an utterly divine array of silky textures'), to an 'earthy' whip of new-season Jersey Royals with morels, asparagus, sweetbread and langoustine. Also exceptional was 'a really well-conceived dish' of Edge's rare-breed beef – poached fillet, salt cheeks – teamed with pickle purée and snail pasta. A real strength

here is the selection of breads, all made on the premises and uniformly magnificent. Service is top-notch, too. The wine list (from £22) is exemplary and, refreshingly, offers plenty of interest without breaking the bank.
Chef/s: Simon Radley. **Open:** Tue to Sat D only 6.30 to 9. **Closed:** Sun, Mon, 25 Dec, 1 to 7 Jan. **Meals:** Set D £69. Tasting menu £90 (8 courses). **Details:** 45 seats. Separate bar. Wheelchair access. Car parking. Children over 12 yrs only.

Sticky Walnut
Unstuffy food, sharply executed
11 Charles Street, Chester, CH2 3AZ
Tel no: (01244) 400400
www.stickywalnut.com
Modern European | £25
Cooking score: 4
£30

Deep satisfaction emanates from readers dining at chef/owner Gary Usher's neighbourhood bistro, deceptively close to Chester and the station. Housed over two floors of a converted terrace, informal but nicely pulled together with its recipe books and blackboards, it relies on quality for its appeal. The eponymous nuts, more crunchy than sticky, are used for contrast in a 'simple and straightforward' starter of roasted beetroot, spicy pumpkin seeds and fresh ricotta. There's a strong but not self-flagellating sense of seasonality, and cuts from the less glamorous end of the beast appear with pleasing frequency; rolled and stuffed pork belly with smoky bacon lentils stars melting, tender meat and properly crisped crackling. Like the 'excellent' rosemary and thyme focaccia, the fat truffle and Parmesan chips are an indulgence on the side. Pudding could be dark chocolate and cherry mousse with fresh honeycomb, or Amaretto chocolate truffles with coffee. Wine is from £16.
Chef/s: Gary Usher. **Open:** all week L 12 to 3, Mon to Sat D 6 to 10. **Closed:** 25 to 26 Dec, 1 to 2 Jan. **Meals:** alc (main courses £14 to £30). Sun L £16. **Details:** 50 seats. Music.

Cotebrook
Fox & Barrel
Reinvigorated country boozer
Foxbank, Cotebrook, CW6 9DZ
Tel no: (01829) 760529
www.foxandbarrel.co.uk
Modern British | £25
Cooking score: 1
£5 £30
OFF

The curious and, apparently, unique name refers to an incident where a former landlord of this reinvigorated hostelry played the good Samaritan and allowed a fox on the run to escape via the pub's cellar. These days, drinkers still pile into the quarry-tiled bar, although most attention focuses on the generous food served in the pleasingly appointed dining room. The menu is a mixed bag, offering everything from sandwiches, burgers and honey-glazed gammon to kedgeree, twice-baked Appleby's Cheshire cheese soufflé or pan-fried hake fillet with chorizo, red peppers and basil cream. To finish, try Yorkshire rhubarb pannacotta or Belgian waffles with butterscotch sauce. Wines from £16.45.
Chef/s: Richard Cotterill and Aaron Totty. **Open:** all week 12 to 9.30 (9 Sun). **Closed:** 25 Dec. **Meals:** alc (main courses £10 to £19). **Details:** 100 seats. 110 seats outside. Separate bar. Car parking.

Lymm
The Church Green
British pub food with optional frills
Higher Lane, Lymm, WA13 0AP
Tel no: (01925) 752068
www.aidenbyrne.co.uk
Modern British | £34
Cooking score: 2
V

The arrival of glossy, ambitious Manchester House (see entry) means that this substantial converted pub has been demoted to the status of Aiden Byrne's 'other' restaurant. But on its side the Church Green has longevity, and a menu adapted to suit its customers. Tasting menus are an option: five or eight courses of carefully composed modern European dishes such as ajo blanco with green apple, or lamb with courgette, goats' cheese and pine nuts. Nevertheless, the smart pub setting provides a good argument for sticking with the grill: perhaps burgers with myriad toppings or a sweet-cured pork chop with smoked apple purée and puffy crackling. 'Homely classics' include great pies and an ox cheek hotpot; attention to detail means that chips are fried in beef dripping; and cheffy touches (such as foie gras and a duck egg to top a Cheshire dry-aged steak) keep things interesting. Wine is from £18.

Chef/s: Aiden Byrne. **Open:** all week 12 to 11. **Meals:** alc (main courses £12 to £25). Tasting menu £60. **Details:** 65 seats. Separate bar. Wheelchair access. Music. Car parking.

▌Marton

READERS RECOMMEND
La Popote
French
Manchester Road (A34), Marton, SK11 9HF
Tel no: (01260) 224785
www.la-popote.co.uk
'Brilliant! An intimate, family-run restaurant emphasising classic French cooking without skimping on ingredients.'

▌Wilmslow

NEW ENTRY
Stolen Lamb
Refined Greek cooking
70a Grove Street, Wilmslow, SK9 1DS
Tel no: (01625) 419571
www.stolenlamb.com
Greek | £28
Cooking score: 2
£30

George Yiannis specialises in refined, but not bloodless, Greek cooking at his smartly done-out restaurant overlooking Wilmslow's main shopping street. Clutch the thick rope bannister and follow your nose upstairs, where (pre-ordered) whole roast lambs issue from the wood-fired clay oven and neat takes on Greek classics do the rest. Dinner starts with warm, fragrant olives with good bread, and early highlights are the cool, limpid cucumber gazpacho, which forms part of a take on Greek salad, and chunks of haloumi crusted winningly with sesame seeds and served with sweet onion purée. House kleftiko could, on occasion, be more melting, but the flavour's there and the accompanying dolmades, peas and artichokes are a positive diversion. To finish, try pistachio-rich baklava with a poached pear and honeycomb ice cream. If you want to explore Greek wine, this is the place to do it, with prices from £21 (£16.95 for a French house bottle).

Chef/s: George Yiannis. **Open:** Fri to Sun L 12 to 3 (5 Sun), Tue to Sat D 6 to 11. **Closed:** Mon. **Meals:** alc (main courses £14 to £20). Set L £12. House meze £27 (2 persons min). Tasting menu £42. **Details:** 62 seats.

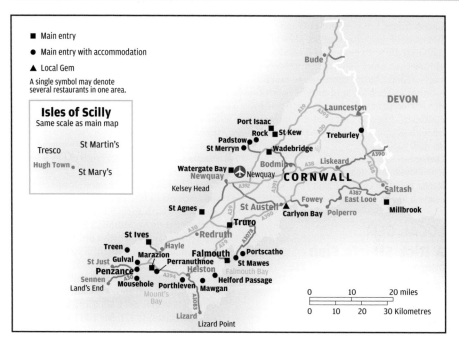

- ■ Main entry
- ● Main entry with accommodation
- ▲ Local Gem

A single symbol may denote
several restaurants in one area.

Isles of Scilly
Same scale as main map

Tresco   St Martin's

Hugh Town   St Mary's

Bude

DEVON

Port Isaac
Rock   St Kew
Padstow   Treburley
St Merryn   Wadebridge
Watergate Bay   Bodmin   Liskeard
Newquay   Newquay   Saltash
Kelsey Head   CORNWALL
St Austell   Fowey   East Looe
St Agnes   Carlyon Bay   Polperro   Millbrook
Truro
St Ives   Redruth
Treen   Hayle
Marazion   Falmouth   Portscatho
St Just   Gulval   Perranuthnoe   St Mawes
Penzance   Helston   Falmouth Bay
Sennen   Helford Passage
Land's End   Mousehole   Porthleven   Mawgan
Mount's Bay
Lizard
Lizard Point

| 0 | 10 | 20 miles |
| 0 | 10 | 20 | 30 Kilometres |

▌Carlyon Bay

LOCAL GEM
▲ Austell's
10 Beach Road, Carlyon Bay, PL25 3PH
Tel no: (01726) 813888
www.austells.co.uk
Modern British | £28

'I wonder if the locals realise what a treasure
they have on their doorstep,' mused one visitor
to this contemporary restaurant pitched on the
road leading to the beach. Brett Camborne-
Paynter, an ambitious chef, lays down an
emphatic marker with the likes of mustard and
potato bread, warm salad of ham hock and
apple with pea mousse. A generous streak runs
through mains such as haddock with pea
purée, mushrooms and leeks in a smoked
salmon sauce, but don't skip dessert: sticky
toffee pudding is 'a blinder'. Wines from
£16.95. Closed Mon and L Tue to Sat.

▌Falmouth

NEW ENTRY
Oliver's
Cute, down-to-earth bistro
33 High Street, Falmouth, TR11 2AD
Tel no: (01326) 218138
www.oliversfalmouth.com
Modern British | £30
Cooking score: 3

V

'A cute little bistro serving mildly ambitious
food at super-fair prices' just about sums up
Ken and Karen Symons' enthusiastically run
bistro wedged in among Falmouth's surfing-
gear outlets. Oliver's all-glass frontage gives
way to a clean-cut, stripped-back room with
polished floors and whitewashed walls, where
chirpy staff hawk the day's menu from table to
table on an orange plastic board. To start,
mackerel fillet on roasted Tregassow asparagus
with citrus dressing chimes with the region.
Mains show a touch more enterprise (and
fiddly work): think venison with coppa,

squash fritter, broad beans, peas and Jägermeister jus; or a complex plate of stuffed rabbit saddle with braised de-boned legs in gloopy cider sauce and herb gnocchi. A strong vegetarian presence reflects the restaurant's location and boho neighbours. Desserts throw in a few surprises: perhaps a rich, decadent combo of chocolate, caramel and malt jazzed up with popping candy. Wines (from £14.50) do their job.

Chef/s: Ken Symons. **Open:** Tue to Sat L 12 to 2, D 7 to 9. **Closed:** Sun, Mon, Nov, 24 Dec to 4 Jan. **Meals:** alc (main courses £13 to £24). Set L £14 (2 courses) to £20. **Details:** 28 seats. Music.

LOCAL GEM

▲ Rick Stein's Fish

Discovery Quay, Falmouth, TR11 3XA
Tel no: (01841) 532700
www.rickstein.com
Seafood | £25

It's another winner from seafood aficionado Rick Stein (see Padstow). This light, clean, modern space has fish and chips at the heart of the menu (there's a popular take-away section, too), though also delivers simple seafood dishes such as moules marinière and grilled hake with spring onion mash. But this wouldn't be a Rick Stein establishment without some well-travelled flavours, so look out for a cod curry from southern India, say, or lemon sole with lemongrass butter. Wines from £19.50. No bookings. Open all week.

▌ Gulval

The Coldstreamer Inn

Village local with fresh flavours
Gulval, TR18 3BB
Tel no: (01736) 362072
www.coldstreamer-penzance.co.uk
Modern British | £25
Cooking score: 2
£5 OFF 🛏 £30

In the centre of a sprawling village that is almost a suburb of Penzance, and across from a 12th-century church, this Victorian pub-

with-rooms has an opened-up contemporary attitude with beams, a real fire and Cornish-brewed ales. Locals may gather for a pint in the bar, but there's good nourishment to be had as the kitchen supports local and regional suppliers and has realistic ambitions, turning out traditional but polished food. There are plenty of takers for comforting pork and green peppercorn terrine or Newlyn crab rarebit, for hake and prawns with crushed new potatoes and broccoli, or lamb chops with celeriac gratin, red cabbage and red wine sauce. The refreshingly honest, low-key approach extends to desserts – say yoghurt pannacotta with apple doughnut and blueberry sorbet – although the south west cheeseboard is also worth a punt. The balance between pub and restaurant is spot-on, too. Wines from £16.

Chef/s: Roger Hoskin. **Open:** all week L 12 to 3, D 6 to 9. **Closed:** 25 and 26 Dec. **Meals:** alc (main courses £11 to £18). Set L £15 (2 courses) to £17. Set D £17 (3 courses) to £21. Sun L £17. **Details:** 55 seats. 12 seats outside. Separate bar. Music.

▌ Helford Passage

Ferryboat Inn

Reinvented riverside hostelry
Helford Passage, TR11 5LB
Tel no: (01326) 250625
www.thewrightbrothers.co.uk
Seafood | £25
Cooking score: 2
🛏 £30

Part of the Wright Brothers group (see entries for a brace of London seafood joints), the Ferryboat Inn takes pride of place on the waterfront by the Helford River – with ready access to the county's stellar ingredients. It's a 'beautiful spot', with a pint of Tribute to be had while watching the bobbing boats. The 300-year-old inn doesn't only offer seafood; meat options run to ox cheeks with pickled red cabbage and boulangère potatoes. Start with white onion and cider soup, though the oysters from the Duchy of Cornwall farm down the river are hard to resist. Battered haddock with mushy peas and chips is a trad way to follow, or go for hake with samphire and one of those oysters duly poached. There are sandwiches at lunchtime (Cornish crab roll with chips), and desserts such as Bramley apple and blackberry crumble served with custard. Wines start at £16.

Chef/s: Robert Bunny. **Open:** all week L 12 to 3, D 6 to 9 (9.30 Fri and Sat). **Meals:** alc (main courses £8 to £12). **Details:** 80 seats. 116 seats outside. Separate bar. Music. Car parking.

▌Marazion
Ben's Cornish Kitchen
Understated bistro making waves in Cornwall
West End, Marazion, TR17 0EL
Tel no: (01736) 719200
www.benscornishkitchen.com
Modern British | £30
Cooking score: 5
£5
OFF

The bistro-style dining room on Marazion's main street is very understated with its polished wooden floor, simple white-painted walls and modest tables and chairs. But factor in Ben Prior's classy contemporary cooking, clear-sighted, harmonious ideas and 'incredible pricing' and it's no wonder fans insist they 'would recommend this place to anyone'. A glance at the menu will tell you the kitchen is dedicated to proper sourcing: home-spice cured Devon trout; home-smoked fish chowder; roast Bodmin venison haunch; shoulder of Trevaskis lamb (with red cabbage, celeriac, port and rosemary gravy). Reporters who have visited in winter tell of the spiced caramel that made scallops and parsnip so memorable, venison ham that was served with roasted beetroot and pickled pear purée, and a simple roast and poached Cornish chicken. For pudding, everyone loves the sweet curry plate (mango curd, spicy rice, coconut purée, spiced caramel, ginger jelly). The cracking wine list starts at £16.

Chef/s: Ben Prior. **Open:** Tue to Sat L 12 to 2, D 6 to 9. **Closed:** Sun, Mon, 25 and 26 Dec, 1 Jan. **Meals:** alc (main courses £12 to £24). Set L £16 (2 courses) to £18. **Details:** 30 seats. Wheelchair access. Music.

▌Mawgan
New Yard Restaurant
A kitchen with its money on local produce
Trelowarren Estate, Mawgan, TR12 6AF
Tel no: (01326) 221595
www.trelowarren.com
Modern British | £30
Cooking score: 3

'There are few better spots in which to sit back and relax', noted one visitor to this rustic, isolated courtyard restaurant on the 1000-year-old Trelowarren Estate. It's a former coach house with floor-to-ceiling arched windows creating an open, airy feel. A hearth burns at one end, while at the other an open kitchen keeps proceedings lively. The cooking is guided by local produce, the menu deliciously straightforward: pigeon terrine with watercress and rhubarb chutney; wild garlic soup; grilled lemon sole with brown shrimps and samphire; and a flat-iron, ribeye and côte de boeuf all cut from cattle reared on Bodmin – fine ingredients, which the kitchen handles simply and well. At a test meal, well-flavoured bouillabaisse came stuffed with just-cooked mussels, hake, sole, monkfish and a few Cornish Earlies, and there was nutmeg and custard tart to finish. Staff showed 'real enthusiasm'. Wine from £15.

Chef/s: Max Wilson. **Open:** all week L 12 to 2.15, D 6.30 to 9. **Closed:** January. **Meals:** alc (main courses £14 to £24). **Details:** Cash only. 70 seats. 30 seats outside. Separate bar. Wheelchair access. Music.

▌Millbrook
The View
Outstanding clifftop package
Treninnow Cliff, Millbrook, PL10 1JY
Tel no: (01752) 822345
www.theview-restaurant.co.uk
Modern British | £35
Cooking score: 2

Matt and Rachel Corner pitched camp on the cliffs overlooking Whitsand Bay in 2004 and have made their modest family eatery a real

destination, especially in summer. The titular views stretch as far as the Lizard Peninsula, with the beams of Eddystone Lighthouse piercing the night sky – although there's more than sightseeing offered here. Matt cooks with the seasons, takes full advantage of fish from local boats and keeps customers interested with a rolling menu of cosmopolitan dishes. Fans of seafood might fancy a bowl of bouillabaisse, grilled monkfish with peppered crevettes and calamari, or roast sea bass with crispy ham, sun-blush tomatoes and basil, while carnivores could go for confit Gressingham duck with creamed leeks and pomegranate reduction. Savoury tarts please vegetarians and there are also tempters for those requiring a sugar fix: think blueberry clafoutis or iced honeycomb parfait. Wines from £16.95. Ring for winter opening hours.
Chef/s: Matt Corner. **Open:** Wed to Sun L 12 to 1.45, D 7 to 8.45. **Closed:** Mon, Tue, Jan. **Meals:** alc (main courses £17 to £21). Set L £14 (2 courses) to £16. **Details:** 48 seats. 32 seats outside. Car parking.

Mousehole
The Old Coastguard
Coastal inn with confident local food
The Parade, Mousehole, TR19 6PR
Tel no: (01736) 731222
www.oldcoastguardhotel.co.uk
Modern British | £25
Cooking score: 3
£5 OFF 🍽 £30

A bright, cheerful dining room with farmhouse tables and a log fire creates the same unfailingly welcoming, informal tone here as at Charles and Edmund Inkin's other ventures (the Gurnard's Head nearby in Treen and Felin Fach Griffin in Mid Wales – see entries). It's not the only selling point: a lush tropical garden with glorious views across Mounts Bay is quite a draw, too. That said, food remains top of the agenda and everything has an instantly recognisable thumbprint. The kitchen goes about its work with flair and dexterity, whether serving smoked cod's roe on toast with a soft-boiled egg or an equally deceptively simple whole plaice with

Jerusalem artichoke and brown shrimp butter. You might also choose venison ragù with tagliatelle or ale-braised ox cheek with onions, turnips and horseradish. Cheeses fly the flag and desserts are familiar creations along the lines of apple and almond tarte fine. Wines from £17.50.
Chef/s: Tom Symons. **Open:** all week L 12.30 to 2.30 (12 Sun), D 6.30 to 9 (9.30 Fri and Sat). **Closed:** 1 week Dec. **Meals:** alc (main courses £13 to £20). Set L £14 (2 courses) to £18. Sun L £14 (1 course) to £24. **Details:** 70 seats. 20 seats outside. Separate bar. Wheelchair access. Music. Car parking.

2 Fore Street
Unpretentious Cornish bistro
2 Fore Street, Mousehole, TR19 6PF
Tel no: (01736) 731164
www.2forestreet.co.uk
Modern British | £27
Cooking score: 3
£30

Joe Wardell's brand of straightforward cooking based on good seasonal produce is proving a winning formula at this light-filled restaurant close to the harbour. It's all very casual: a mix of wood tables, bare boards and washed-out colours. Add to this liberal helpings of genuine bonhomie and the contentment of lunch or dinner, and the result is pure pleasure. Fresh-from-the-boats seafood gets a good airing, perhaps scallops with caramelised cauliflower purée and crispy pancetta, or John Dory fillets with crisp oyster and creamed leeks. Those with other preferences might fancy a twice-baked Bath Blue soufflé with walnut and beetroot or the homespun flavours of slow-roasted, black treacle-glazed pork belly with apple cider sauce. Chocolate délice with white chocolate ice cream and hazelnut crumb stands out among the comfort desserts. There's praise for fine-weather alfresco opportunities, and the well-spread wine list opens at £14.74.
Chef/s: Joe Wardell. **Open:** all week L 12 to 3.30, D 6 to 9.30. **Closed:** Mon (Feb and Nov), 5 Jan to 12 Feb. **Meals:** alc (main courses £15 to £17). **Details:** 36 seats. 24 seats outside. Music.

Padstow

★ TOP 50 ★

Paul Ainsworth at No. 6
Padstow's premier gastronomic address
6 Middle Street, Padstow, PL28 8AP
Tel no: (01841) 532093
www.number6inpadstow.co.uk
Modern British | £48
Cooking score: 7

🍷 V

The Georgian town house is tucked in Padstow's little warren of streets. Inside, the charming small dining rooms on ground and first floors are decorated in distinctly domestic fashion. Yet if it all looks unassuming, think again. Paul Ainsworth is an ambitious, ingenious presence in the kitchen, realising an exciting vision of modish, technically resourceful, regionally based cooking. His menu encompasses interesting variants on tried-and-true dishes: livery parfaits of duck or goose, the former accompanying pickled duck with a toasted clotted cream brioche, the latter appearing with roast red peppers and smoked almonds. Fish is as fresh as you'd expect in a harbour town, in starters such as torched mackerel with celeriac rémoulade, Parma ham and cucumber, and mains like cod with radish yoghurt and curried cauliflower, or monkfish with bone marrow, sour cream and a veal shin salad. Two meat eaters might consider lamb rump roasted on the bone in 'hay and bay', or Hereford short rib with beef tartare, red chicory and horseradish. Memorable finishers could be pistachio 'caramac' and dark chocolate sorbet, or a more detoxy yoghurt with raspberries and hazelnut muesli. Such full-on flavours call for equally forthright wines, and the list is teeming with imaginative choices, from New York State Riesling to Puglian Primitivo and Galician Albariño. Prices open at £29.

Chef/s: Paul Ainsworth. **Open:** Tue to Sat L 12 to 2.30, D 6 to 10. **Closed:** Sun, Mon, 24 to 26 Dec, 13 Jan to 4 Feb. **Meals:** alc (main courses £27 to £35). Set L £19 (2 courses) to £25. **Details:** 45 seats. 6 seats outside. Music. Children over 4 yrs only.

🍴 PAUL AINSWORTH
Paul Ainsworth at No. 6

What do you enjoy about being a chef?
As a chef I love how things evolve, whether it's a dish, a member of the team, the restaurant and also yourself - there's no other industry like it.

What food trends are you spotting at the moment?
Barbecue, smoking, pit cooking and dirty burgers. I think that we're really embracing simple comfort food, but cooked really well.

What food could you not live without?
Probably meat, from a good steak to amazing charcuterie meats and roast chicken. And then there's slow-cooked shoulder of lamb. I could go on...

What would you be if you weren't a chef?
Easy - JCB driver by day, house music DJ by night.

Do you have a guilty food pleasure and if so what is it?
The Colonel's Zinger Tower burger!

Rojano's in the Square

Excellent pizzas pull the crowds
9 Mill Square, Padstow, PL28 8AE
Tel no: (01841) 532796
www.rojanos.co.uk
Italian | £23
Cooking score: 1

£30

Since Paul Ainsworth of nearby No 6 (see entry) acquired the business, this rejuvenated Italian in the heart of Padstow has become a step up from the usual pizza joint. It is flexible, family friendly, and whatever your definition of popular Italian dining – be it Italian charcuterie, fried baby squid, a good selection of pizzas and pasta – the menu is likely to satisfy. Portions are generous, but salads, arancini and great tomato bread plug any gaps. Cornish sea salt and pistachio brownie with cherry compote and pistachio ice cream makes a satisfying finish. Italian wines open at £18.95.
Chef/s: Paul Dodd. **Open:** all week L 12 to 3, D 5 to 10. **Closed:** 24 to 26 Dec, 3 weeks Jan. **Meals:** alc (main courses £8 to £25). **Details:** 70 seats. 24 seats outside. Music.

The Seafood Restaurant

Rick Stein's seafood original
Riverside, Padstow, PL28 8BY
Tel no: (01841) 532700
www.rickstein.com
Seafood | £60
Cooking score: 5

🛏 V

The flagship of Rick Stein's ever-expanding gastronomic flotilla, this hotel/restaurant overlooking Padstow harbour is where it all began back in 1975. Things have changed greatly since those early years: you won't now find Stein himself in the kitchen, and the artily decorated, white-walled dining room has been bolstered by a cut-price seafood bar. Nevertheless, exemplary fresh fish from the local boats still forms the menu's backbone – augmented by specialities such as Carlingford oysters that have much further to travel – and

the repertoire is peppered with eclectic ideas lifted from Stein's TV gastro-travelogues. Cruise your way through deep-fried Amritsari plaice with chaat masala, Indonesian seafood curry or crab with wakame, cucumber and dashi salad: not forgetting lobster thermidor, cod and chips or char-grilled Dover sole with lime. To finish, the lemon tart is simply 'delectable'. Stein's thumbprint is all over the auspicious wine list, which offers bespoke, hand-picked selections from £27.95.
Chef/s: Stephane Delourme. **Open:** all week L 12 to 2, D 6.30 to 10. **Closed:** 25 and 26 Dec. **Meals:** alc (main courses £18 to £51). Set L £30 (winter), £39 (summer). **Details:** 90 seats. Separate bar. Wheelchair access. Children over 3 yrs only.

LOCAL GEM

▲ Rick Stein's Café

10 Middle Street, Padstow, PL28 8AP
Tel no: (01841) 532700
www.rickstein.com
Seafood | £28

There's a New England feel to this likeable and informal café, with its fresh, light, understated look, and modern paintings and posters adorning the walls. It does a roaring trade in pastries and breakfast, then snacky lunches all day long, evident in a cod curry from Pondicherry, and a small mound of 'gougons of fish' with salad and tartare sauce – although you can find ribeye steak on the menu, too. At busy times those in the know join the swifter queue at Stein's Fish and Chips by the harbour. Wines from £19.50. Open all week.

🍴 Please send us your feedback

To register your opinion about any restaurant listed in the Guide, or a new restaurant that you wish to bring to our attention, please visit the web address at the bottom of the page. Your feedback informs the content of the book and will be used to compile next year's reviews.

▌Penzance

The Bakehouse

Funky eatery with good local food
Old Bakehouse Lane, Chapel Street, Penzance,
TR18 4AE
Tel no: (01736) 331331
www.bakehouserestaurant.co.uk
Modern European | £25
Cooking score: 2

£30

Tucked away off Chapel Street in a palm-filled courtyard, Andy and Rachel Carr's funky two-tiered restaurant has been going for more than a decade. Walls covered with exhibits from local artists, and the original bread oven from the building's days as a bakery, add to the quirkiness of this Penzance favourite, which has close links with fishermen from nearby Newlyn. The robust, straightforward Anglo-European dishes look to the coast for much of their inspiration: Helford mussels are served with rosemary, white wine and cream; cod fillet is matched with sweet potato and pistachio and lemon dressing. Cornish Angus beef steaks from the butcher up the road are served with a multiple choice of sauces, rubs and butters. Char-grilled vegetables with roasted beetroot purée and haloumi is one vegetarian alternative. For dessert, try zingy lemon tart with vanilla ice cream or rich chocolate nemesis with clotted cream. Wines from £14.95.
Chef/s: Andy Carr. **Open:** Wed to Sat L 10 to 4, Wed to Sun D 6.15 to 9. **Closed:** Mon, Tue, 24 to 27 Dec, 2 weeks Jan. **Meals:** alc (main courses £9). Early D £13 (2 courses). **Details:** 56 seats. 10 seats outside. Music.

Symbols

🛏 Accommodation is available

£30 Three courses for less than £30

V Separate vegetarian menu

£5 OFF £5-off voucher scheme

🍷 Notable wine list

The Bay

Art, views and Cornish flavours
Hotel Penzance, Britons Hill, Penzance, TR18 3AE
Tel no: (01736) 366890
www.thebaypenzance.co.uk
Modern British | £34
Cooking score: 3

£5 OFF 🛏 V

The setting is fresh and airy – a broad hotel balcony with plenty of outdoor seating and bright bay views, plus a roomy glass-walled interior with bistro-style tables and modern artwork. There's no corner cutting in The Bay's kitchen, where everything from bread to ice cream is made in house and, just as importantly, is very good. Slices of nigella-peppered loaf, for example, are perfect for mopping up the liquor that scents and soaks steamed local mussels. Crab linguine with chilli, shallot and fresh coriander typifies the clear-tasting cooking, while crayfish risotto is beautifully handled: firm, flowing rice, with rounded flavours and faultless seasoning. Pineapple, cherry chocolate and mocha ice cream make a satisfactory lunchtime dessert, but evening options, such as a pressing of apple with cider reduction, cinnamon ice cream and walnut praline, catch the eye. Drinks range from cocktails to international wines (including some Cornish options) starting at £17.50 a bottle.
Chef/s: Bruce Rennie. **Open:** all week L 12 to 2.30, D 5 to 9.30. **Closed:** 1 to 14 Jan. **Meals:** Set L £18. Set D £26 (2 courses) to £34. Sun L £20. **Details:** 60 seats. 9 seats outside. Music. Car parking.

Harris's

Veteran bistro with big Cornish flavours
46 New Street, Penzance, TR18 2LZ
Tel no: (01736) 364408
www.harrissrestaurant.co.uk
Modern European | £35
Cooking score: 2

In a cobbled side street in the heart of Penzance, not far from the Humphry Davy statue, Roger and Anne Harris have run their tiny bistro for more than four decades. They're a hard-working couple who know what their customers want, and Roger's passion for food remains undimmed. You won't find cutting-edge dishes or fancy-pants presentation: rather, sound cooking and solid technique hold sway. Prime Cornish produce (including daily fish and seafood deliveries from nearby Newlyn) and a watchful eye on the seasons steer the menu. A meal could start with a simple but precisely cooked dish of grilled scallops with salad leaves and a punchy herb vinaigrette. John Dory roasted on the bone with a delicate saffron and white wine sauce is one enjoyable main course, followed perhaps by a light, zesty iced lemon soufflé encased in thin, dark chocolate and coupled with fresh raspberry sauce. Wines from £17.50.

Chef/s: Roger Harris. **Open:** Tue to Sat L 12 to 2, Mon to Sat D 6.30 to 9. **Closed:** Sun, Mon (Nov to May), 25 and 26 Dec, 2 weeks Feb, 2 weeks Nov. **Meals:** alc (main courses £13 to £32). **Details:** 39 seats. Music. Children over 5 yrs only.

▌Perranuthnoe

Victoria Inn
Historic inn with appealing cooking
Perranuthnoe, TR20 9NP
Tel no: (01736) 710309
www.victoriainn-penzance.co.uk
Modern British | £28
Cooking score: 2

£5 OFF   £30

Its lovely food may merit a detour, but at first glance the Victoria Inn does a good impression of a regular village pub. The unassuming pink-washed façade hides an interior kitted out in traditional fixtures and fittings – which, naturally, include a wood-burner, bare floorboards and mismatched country pine furniture. Exceptional homemade seeded bread, perhaps served with a superb provençale fish soup and punchy aïoli, is the first sign the kitchen is a cut above. The European theme continues with a pearlescent hunk of roasted cod with creamy champ, greens, chorizo and chickpea stew, but there are also pubby options such as ham, eggs and chips with homemade ketchup, or a big juicy

ribeye steak with chips. Even the simpler-sounding dishes are relatively sophisticated: witness a dessert that marries the nursery comforts of rice pudding with tangy stewed fruit, melting vanilla ice cream and a boozy Pedro Ximénez syrup. International wines start at £15.

Chef/s: Stewart Eddy. **Open:** all week L 12 to 2 (2.30 Sun), D 6.15 to 9. **Closed:** Mon (Oct to Mar), 25, 26 and 31 Dec, 1 week Jan. **Meals:** alc (main courses £11 to £20). **Details:** 60 seats. 20 seats outside. Separate bar. Music. Car parking.

▌Port Isaac

NEW ENTRY
Outlaw's Fish Kitchen
Delightful newbie from Nathan Outlaw
1 Middle Street, Port Isaac, PL29 3RH
Tel no: (01208) 880237
www.outlaws.co.uk
Seafood | £25
Cooking score: 5

£5 OFF   £30

'Honestly, I would travel to Cornwall again just to eat here,' confessed a reporter from Wales, who also enjoyed the cosy intimacy of the whitewashed, 'knobbly beamed hidey-hole' of a dining room, its seaside freshness topped off with harbour views. With Nathan Outlaw's name over the door, 'you have a right to expect good things', and the chef's newest venture scores highly for satisfaction, especially as the relatively small plates are so kindly priced. The delicious smoked haddock Scotch egg is a must, set off by a light curry sauce. Other goodies include meaty cured brill with garden-fresh peas and bright slivers of mint, battered John Dory with a glorious chilli-spiked pickled carrot salad, and terrific queenie scallops in fabulous seaweed butter sauce. To finish, cream-cheese and lime ice cream make perfect partners for grilled pineapple glossed with passion fruit syrup, or there's a brilliant soft brownie with salted-peanut caramel. Wines from £20.

Chef/s: James Lean. **Open:** all week L 12 to 3, D 6 to 9. **Closed:** 5 Jan to 1 Feb. **Meals:** alc (main courses £6 to £15). **Details:** 24 seats. Music.

Fresh from the Sea

Seafood
18 New Road, Port Isaac, PL29 3SB
Tel no: (01208) 880849
www.freshfromthesea.co.uk

'Tiny harbour village café. Very small, simple menu. Enjoyed lobster salad with a glass of crisp white wine, crab salad and smoked salmon sandwich. Everything was an absolute delight.'

█ Porthleven

Kota

All about seasonality, balance and flavours
Harbour Head, Porthleven, TR13 9JA
Tel no: (01326) 562407
www.kotarestaurant.co.uk
Fusion-Modern European | £33
Cooking score: 3

The Kereamas' restaurant-with-rooms is the kind of place that wins you over in an instant. It occupies a converted harbour-head corn mill and weaves its magic with a blend of personable courtesy backed by cooking that knows all about seasonality, balance and flavours that work. Falmouth Bay scallops, for example, come teamed with crisp pork belly, parsnips and an apple-ginger dressing, while a fine main course of local brill takes a more classical approach with its accompaniments of crab raviolo, samphire, spinach, fennel cream and shellfish sauce. Praise, too, for pan-roast sirloin and tempura rib of beef with horseradish mash, baby turnips, wild garlic leaves, oyster mushrooms, white onion purée and port wine jus, described as 'one of the best dishes I have ever eaten'. Thoroughbred West Country cheeses are the alternative to indulgences such as tarte Tatin with Granny Smith apple sorbet. Wines from £15.25.
Chef/s: Jude Kereama. **Open:** Tue to Sat D only 6 to 9. **Closed:** Sun, Mon, Nov to Feb. **Meals:** alc (main courses £12 to £20). Set D £18 (2 courses) to £21. **Details:** 40 seats. Separate bar. Wheelchair access. Music.

█ Portscatho

Driftwood

Elegant clifftop hotel with stylish food
Rosevine, Portscatho, TR2 5EW
Tel no: (01872) 580644
www.driftwoodhotel.co.uk
Modern European | £53
Cooking score: 5

Modern European Driftwood near pretty Portscatho bears comparison with counterparts across the Channel; it is 'if anything, better', reports one frequent diner. Chris Eden is a Cornish chef cooking Cornish produce in a Cornish boutique hotel. His commitment to the local cause is clear in a seasonal, seafood-oriented starter of courgette flower with lobster mousse and bisque ('wonderful') and turbot with tarama, kale crisps and St Austell Bay mussels. The glorious coastal position and the dining room's subtly maritime blue and white interior suggest seafood, though Eden often leans towards richer, earthier flavours – duck boudin, celeriac, pickled plums and port; or venison with beetroot, turnip tops and cocoa being cases in point. Golden raisin and cider soufflé with apple sorbet, English cheeses, and coffee on the deck round things off nicely. Service is 'courteous and friendly'. The wine cellar has some 'very good but modestly priced' bottles (from £19).
Chef/s: Chris Eden. **Open:** all week D only 6.30 to 9.30. **Closed:** early Dec to early Feb. **Meals:** Set D £53 (3 courses). **Details:** 40 seats. Separate bar. Wheelchair access. Music. Car parking.

LOCAL GEM

▲ Rosevine

Rosevine, Portscatho, TR2 5EW
Tel no: (01872) 580206
www.rosevine.co.uk
Modern British | £30 £5 OFF

It's a grand Victorian house in lovely gardens with the beach a stroll away and sea views from the dining room. Visitors return for the setting and for the capable British cooking, which has a strong sense of seasonal cohesion. Duck burger with Sharpham rarebit and homemade ketchup is a deserved favourite, but deft contemporary touches can be seen in starters of pickled mackerel with heritage carrots, rocket and ciabatta, and desserts of Sicilian orange cake with lemon sorbet and honey custard. Wines from £18. Closed Sun D and Mon L in winter.

Rock
Outlaw's
A breath of fresh air
St Enodoc Hotel, Rock Road, Rock, PL27 6LA
Tel no: (01208) 863394
www.nathan-outlaw.com
Seafood | £45
Cooking score: 4

If you only associate Mr Outlaw with things fishy, prepare to be enlightened by a couple of glorious hogget chops covered in a verdant minty sauce. The more casual restaurant in the St Enodoc Hotel (the other is the powerhouse that is Restaurant Nathan Outlaw – see next entry) does have a menu rich with strikingly fresh seafood, but much more besides. There's a terrace overlooking the Camel Estuary and a dining room that hits the casual-chic balance right on the nose. A three-course fixed-price menu is the deal, with regional produce from land and sea dominating. If shore and velvet crab soup doesn't quite pack the desired punch, those chops certainly do, or go for butterflied mackerel with wild garlic dressing. Add desserts such as lemon pavlova with yoghurt sorbet, British cheeses and dynamite sourdough bread, and Outlaw's is 'pretty much perfect'. Wines start at £20.
Chef/s: Tom Brown. **Open:** all week L 12 to 2.30, D 6 to 9.30. **Closed:** 23 Dec to 1 Feb. **Meals:** Set L and D £35 (2 courses) to £45. **Details:** 50 seats. 20 seats outside. Wheelchair access. Music. Car parking. Children over 10 yrs only at D.

★ TOP 10 ★

Restaurant Nathan Outlaw
Impressive seafood from a top talent
St Enodoc Hotel, Rock Road, Rock, PL27 6LA
Tel no: (01208) 862737
www.nathan-outlaw.com
Seafood | £99
Cooking score: 9

Nathan Outlaw's reputation now reaches far beyond Cornwall, and anyone who makes the trip to see what the fuss is about will not be disappointed – 'the total experience is top-class'. Restaurant Nathan Outlaw is part of the smart St Enodoc Hotel and is not to be confused with the less formal offering, Outlaw's, which is under the same roof. It's a comfortable room with cushion-strewn banquettes, bold artwork by Sir Terry Frost and soft modern-retro lighting: the backdrop for a delicately nuanced seafood tasting menu that is like no other. The first two courses are served together: slices of raw scallop in a tangy dressing topped with tiny, punchy pieces of cured herring and sprinkled with crisp powdered bacon; and meaty cured brill peppered with almond pieces, scented with wild garlic and magically lifted by sweet slivers of white grape. Then come sweet Port Isaac crabmeat and a buttery avocado pâté, which are squared with the crunch of raw asparagus and the toasted brioche served on the side; and discs of crisp kohlrabi counter the silky softness of red mullet in a sensuous crab-based Porthilly sauce. Turbot on the bone arrives with perfectly salted potato terrine, tiny pickled mushrooms, a darkly beautiful mushroom purée and an unforgettable sweet-savoury gravy made with roast chicken and a red wine reduction. An unexpectedly rustic pastry case filled with Ragstone goats' cheese sweetened with beetroot jam and candied walnuts formed an effective bridge between the savoury courses and desserts, which, while slightly less thrilling than the main courses, are still note perfect. Juicy blood orange and rhubarb in jelly with frozen yoghurt was a breezy palate-cleanser, while the intense sweetness of a pistachio and banana ice cream sandwich (made with crisp coconut tuiles) was countered with espresso syrup. Professionalism and ease define the service, including the wine advice. There's much to fascinate on a fine list divided by style, which includes a good number of organic and biodynamic wines. If you're on a budget, the impressive £20 house wine, chosen because it sits well with most dishes on the menu, is a good choice.

Chef/s: Nathan Outlaw and Christopher Simpson. **Open:** Tue to Sat D only 6.45 to 9. **Closed:** Sun, Mon, 23 Dec to 1 Feb. **Meals:** Tasting menu £99 (£80 vegetarian). **Details:** 22 seats. Separate bar. Wheelchair access. Music. Car parking. No children.

St Agnes

NEW ENTRY

No.4 Peterville

Friendly, stylish village gem
Peterville Square, St Agnes, TR5 0QU
Tel no: (01872) 554245
www.no4peterville.co.uk
Modern British | £30
Cooking score: 3

Every village should have a restaurant like No. 4. This particular village's charms include picture-book cottages and a pub that's clearly a community hub. No. 4 slots in neatly next door, looking like a cross between an urban hipster joint and something far more rustic, with whitewashed wood panelling, industrial lighting and an abundance of ceramic tiles. Service is leisurely (occasionally too leisurely) and the food is broadly European, but not exclusively so; pan-fried cuttlefish is partnered by merguez sausage, broth and aïoli, for instance. Wild garlic potato dumplings with girolles, purple sprouting broccoli and deep-fried Tunworth cheese is a meat-free charmer; at the other end of the spectrum might be pork ribeye with black pudding, cockles, cider roast carrots and crispy pig's ears. A 'choc ice' of malted semifreddo, topped with salted caramel and peanuts, is an impressive way to end. The modest international wine list kicks off at £15.50.

Chef/s: Adam Vasey. **Open:** Tue to Sat D only 7 to 10.30. **Closed:** Sun, Mon, Tue (winter only), 2 Jan to mid Feb. **Meals:** alc (main courses £14 to £22). Set D £20. **Details:** 30 seats. 6 seats outside. Wheelchair access. Music.

St Ives

Alba

Ex-lifeboat house that lifts the spirits
Old Lifeboat House, Wharf Road, St Ives, TR26 1LF
Tel no: (01736) 797222
www.thealbarestaurant.com
Modern European | £30
Cooking score: 3
£5
OFF

The main attraction of any waterside restaurant is likely to be fish, and on that score Alba, the former lifeboat house on St Ives' harbour front, comes up trumps. Surroundings are smart, modern and spread over two floors. At ground level there's the bustle of an open-to-view kitchen, while upstairs delivers unbeatable panoramic coastal views from its large picture window. An intensely flavoured, 'redolent of the warm south' provençale fish soup, and a delicate fillet of very fresh hake neatly paired with crunchy beans, pleased one autumn visitor, but the bright, user-friendly repertoire also embraces steamed Fowey mussels, Cornish crab linguine, and miso-marinated cod with prawn tempura, vermicelli noodles and cashew nut salad. Meat dishes share equal billing in the evening – say Primrose Herd pork belly or confit five-spiced duck – while kaffir lime crème brûlée with toasted coconut ice cream is a splendid way to finish. Wines from £13.95.

Chef/s: Grant Nethercott. **Open:** all week L 12 to 2, D 5 to 10. **Closed:** Sun and Tue (Nov to Mar), 25 and 26 Dec. **Meals:** alc (main courses £11 to £23). Set L and D £17 (2 courses) to £20. **Details:** 60 seats. Wheelchair access. Music.

Alfresco

Buzzy seafood eatery with harbour views
The Wharf, St Ives, TR26 1LF
Tel no: (01736) 793737
www.alfresco-stives.co.uk
Modern British | £25
Cooking score: 2

£5 OFF £30

Just a few paces across the road to the harbour wall, this open-fronted, no-frills restaurant has a distinctly Mediterranean feel. Fresh Cornish seafood and cracking bay views are the big draw, as are the outdoor seats, but the cheerfulness of the staff and lively atmosphere play their part. Focused, modern dishes allow local flavours to shine, whether the please-all appeal of daytime specials of fish with duck-fat chips or 'luxury' crab sandwiches, or in the evening when a starter of silky asparagus, pea and wild garlic soup might precede wild sea bass with celeriac and apple textures, purple sprouting broccoli, crispy oyster and cider sauce. A cooked-to-order rhubarb tarte Tatin with stem ginger ice cream is a winning combination and worth the wait. For those in search of a bargain, the set-lunch menu doesn't skimp on quality. Wines from £14.95.
Chef/s: Jamie Phillips. **Open:** all week L 12 to 3, D 6 to 10. **Closed:** Jan, 2 weeks Feb. **Meals:** alc (main courses £15 to £21). Set L and D £17. **Details:** 26 seats. 12 seats outside. Wheelchair access. Music.

The Black Rock

Imaginative cooking from friendly local gem
Market Place, St Ives, TR26 1RZ
Tel no: (01736) 791911
www.theblackrockstives.co.uk
Modern British | £26
Cooking score: 2

£5 OFF £30

'This is a great little local,' exclaimed a first-time visitor to David Symons' restaurant (for decades his family's hardware shop). It's a modest place, tucked behind the harbour, close to the Barbara Hepworth museum. Splashes of primary colours lift the monochrome effect of black slate floors and white tables – walls are a mix of teal, sunflower yellow or white. Paintings and ceramics from local artists are displayed. From the partially open kitchen come dishes championing local seafood and meat from nearby farms. The cooking is 'hard to fault', whether a generous portion of St Ives Bay crab claws poached in garlic butter; soy-marinated bavette steak, which arrives with beef-dripping chips and greens; or 'perfectly cooked' lemon sole with lemon and dill butter, purple sprouting broccoli and a separate ramekin of 'moreish' crab risotto. End with hot chocolate doughnuts, toasted almonds and homemade almond ice cream. The inexpensive wine list starts at £14.95.
Chef/s: David Symons. **Open:** Mon to Sat D only 6 to 10.30. **Closed:** Nov to Feb. **Meals:** alc (main courses £12 to £17). Set D £17 (2 courses) to £20. **Details:** 36 seats. Separate bar. Music.

Blas Burgerworks

Feel-good eco-friendly burger bar
The Warren, St Ives, TR26 2EA
Tel no: (01736) 797272
www.blasburgerworks.co.uk
Burgers | £15
Cooking score: 1

V £30

Industrial chic meets surfer cool at Blas, a wee granite property once used for storing fishing nets and now hauling in punters wanting a damn fine burger. A passion for sustainability leads to a proactive, eco-friendly approach (no mere lip service), with the burgers made from 100% Cornish beef. Hunker down at chunky wooden communal tables and tuck into a patty cooked on the char-grill and topped with Old Smokey Cheddar and homemade piccalilli (all burgers come with fries). There are veggie and chicken versions, too, and sustainable fish makes an appearance occasionally. The short wine list starts at £16.
Chef/s: Marie Dixon, Jack Williams. **Open:** all week D only 5.30 to 9.30 and 12 to 10 (school hols). **Closed:** Nov to mid Feb. **Meals:** alc (main courses £10 to £12). **Details:** 30 seats. Music.

Halsetown Inn
Passionate commitment to local sourcing
Halsetown, St Ives, TR26 3NA
Tel no: (01736) 795583
www.halsetowninn.co.uk
Modern British | £25
Cooking score: 2

£30

'Nice pub with plenty of character and the welcome couldn't have been warmer,' commented one reader after visiting this granite-stone hostelry in a village on the outskirts of St Ives. The Halsetown Inn has gained quite a band of followers since opening in May 2012. The owners also run the popular Blas Burgerworks in St Ives (see entry) and reporters have noted a similar level of high-quality service and excellent value. The menu looks mainly to the Mediterranean for inspiration, although tip-top ingredients tend to come from local producers. The cooking can reveal a splendidly rustic, unrefined edge, and reporters have praised courgette and sweetcorn fritters with whipped feta and avocado salsa, rabbit pie with clementine hummus and pickled carrot salad, and the pub's own beef burger. And dessert? Who can resist grilled banana split with honeycomb and salted caramel. Wines from £16.
Chef/s: Angela Baxter. **Open:** all week L 12 to 2 (4 Sun), Mon to Sat D 5.30 to 9. **Closed:** 6 to 19 Jan. **Meals:** alc (main courses £11 to £18). Set L £12 (2 courses) to £15. Sun L £11. **Details:** 60 seats. 20 seats outside. Separate bar. Wheelchair access. Music. Car parking.

Porthgwidden Beach Cafe
An idyllic setting to sample local seafood
Porthgwidden Beach, The Island, St Ives, TR26 1PL
Tel no: (01736) 796791
www.porthgwiddencafe.co.uk
Modern British | £27
Cooking score: 1

£30

Tucked away on an unspoilt, secluded beach overlooking St Ives Bay, and popular with in-the-know locals, this relaxed Aussie-style seaside café is the little sibling of the grander Porthminster Beach Café (see entry). The simple whitewashed room echoes the uncomplicated spirit of the kitchen, which champions locally sourced seafood. A starter of Cornish scallops with white miso dressing and Thai celery might be followed by local crab linguine, mussels, lemon, chilli, garlic and parsley; or pan-fried sea bass, shellfish bouillabaisse, saffron potatoes and rouille. Laid-back breakfasts and simple lunches such as fish and chips are also served. Wines from £14.50.
Chef/s: Robert Michael. **Open:** all week L 12 to 3, D 6 to 9.30 (Apr to Oct). Tue to Sun L 12 to 3 and Thur to Sat D 6 to 9.30 (Nov to Mar). **Closed:** 25 Dec, Mon (winter). **Meals:** alc (main courses £10 to £14). **Details:** 34 seats. 40 seats outside.

Porthmeor Beach Café
Tapas and stunning St Ives sunsets
Porthmeor, St Ives, TR26 1JZ
Tel no: (01736) 793366
www.porthmeor-beach.co.uk
Tapas | £25
Cooking score: 1

V £30

Just below the Tate gallery, this beachside venue is in an unbeatable location, perfect for catching those St Ives sunsets, surfers riding the waves below, and even glimpsing the occasional dolphin. You'll notice a discernible Antipodean feel to the conservatory-style café with its colourful and cheery interior, white tables, lime-green chairs and pink plastic buckets of cutlery. From the open kitchen come robustly flavoured tapas such as good-value monkfish tail with pineapple chilli caramel, and 'suppers' like crispy skinned pork belly with carrot purée and crab coleslaw. Wines from £14.50. Sister beach cafés at nearby Porthminster and Porthgwidden (see entries).
Chef/s: Cam Jennings and Nathan Madden. **Open:** all week B 9 to 11.15, L 12 to 4.30, D 6 to 10. **Meals:** alc (tapas and main courses £4 to £21). **Details:** 30 seats. 70 seats outside. Separate bar. Music.

Porthminster Beach Café

Beach hangout with enticing global dishes
Porthminster Beach, St Ives, TR26 2EB
Tel no: (01736) 795352
www.porthminstercafe.co.uk
Seafood | £48
Cooking score: 3

'I've been eating here once or twice every year for the past decade . . . such is the lure of the place and its stunning location'. The Art Deco café on one of Cornwall's finest beaches is a veteran provider of good things, with breakfast, morning coffee and afternoon tea thrown into the mix. As you'd hope, the local catch appears in dishes such as blow-torched mackerel fillet served with labneh, spicy nuts and lemon, or mild Indonesian monkfish curry – the Middle Eastern/Asian notes courtesy of Aussie chef Michael Smith. But there's meat too, perhaps sticky pork cheeks with tempura prawn, peanuts and wasabi pea purée, and a Cornish beef fillet salad with foraged herbs, rocket, beetroot, horseradish and crème fraîche. Any room? A Pimm's deconstruction consisting of strawberry bavarois, Pimm's lemonade jelly, apple and cucumber sorbet, wild mint ice cream and summer berry sherbet makes the ideal finale. Wines from £15.50.
Chef/s: Michael Smith. **Open:** all week L 12 to 4, D 6 to 10 (D Thur to Sat only in winter). **Closed:** Mon (Nov to Feb). **Meals:** alc (main courses £9 to £22). **Details:** 60 seats. 70 seats outside. Music.

▌St Kew

St Kew Inn

Ancient charm with locally rooted cooking
St Kew, PL30 3HB
Tel no: (01208) 841259
www.stkewinn.co.uk
Modern British | £26
Cooking score: 2
£30

Everybody has a good word to say about the St Kew Inn. With a lovely garden taking in views of the church and river, a full contingent of beams, worn flagstones, scrubbed tables and a roaring fire in the bar, plus bags of atmosphere throughout, this 15th-century hostelry certainly puts on a convincing show. Its unpretentious approach is matched by some appealingly soothing food. The menu offers a familiar run through the modern pub catalogue: farmhouse pâté or salt-and-pepper squid, say, ahead of braised steak and mushroom pie or Ruby Red rump steak with all the trimmings. Generous portions of wild mushroom tortellini with wilted spinach and herb cream, the smoked haddock chowder with bacon and sweetcorn, very good Sunday roasts, and lemon tart with mandarin sorbet have received recent endorsements. Welcoming service is praised too. Drink St Austell Brewery ales or wines from £15.95.
Chef/s: David Trainer and Martin Perkins. **Open:** all week L 12 to 2, D 6 to 9. **Closed:** 25 Dec. **Meals:** alc (main courses £11 to £21). Set L £14 (2 courses) to £17. Set D £16 (2 courses) to £20. Sun L £11. **Details:** 70 seats. 80 seats outside. Separate bar. Car parking.

▌St Mawes

Hotel Tresanton

Stylish seaside bolt-hole
27 Lower Castle Road, St Mawes, TR2 5DR
Tel no: (01326) 270055
www.tresanton.com
Modern European | £40
Cooking score: 3
£5 OFF 🍴

A trailblazer for the newly trendified Cornwall when it opened back in the 1990s, Tresanton is perhaps no longer the *belle de jour* of the south west, but it can still hold its own. The seaside-boutique vibe remains appealing, and the location overlooking the Fal Estuary and St Anthony's lighthouse is a winner all day long. The restaurant maintains the seaside-chic attitude with its neutral, natural tones and windows that open on to the splendid terrace, and the sea view. The menu has modern European leanings, glimpsed through a prism made in Italy. Fish and chips is a regular (with crushed peas and tartare sauce) and seafood gets a good showing all round: wild bass with

Fal prawns, mussels and fregola, for example. A winter starter might combine celeriac soup with Welsh rarebit. For dessert, Tunisian orange cake with yoghurt sorbet hits the spot. Wines start at £20.

Chef/s: Paul Wadham. **Open:** all week L 12.30 to 2.30, D 6.15 to 9.30. **Closed:** 2 weeks Jan. **Meals:** alc (main courses £20 to £26). Set L £22 (2 courses) to £26. **Details:** 60 seats. 60 seats outside. Separate bar. Wheelchair access. Car parking. Children over 6 yrs only at D.

St Merryn

NEW ENTRY
The Cornish Arms
New, relaxed Stein offering
St Merryn, PL28 8ND
Tel no: (01841) 532700
www.rickstein.com
British | £22
Cooking score: 2

This country inn has survived its absorption into the Rick Stein empire with its pubby heart intact. A light touch with the styling has made the most of its natural assets, from beams to raw stonework, while chunky modern furniture makes it clear this is no throwback, despite its traditional looks. Pub classics, from burgers to fish and chips, dominate the menu, but there are also plentiful fresh fish options and some interesting regional curries. Stand-out dishes include pau bhaji – think colourful curried mash, served with a blast of mint chutney – and fat mussels in a buttery liquor with fluffy chips and golden mayonnaise. The big, crumbly burger, its bun sogged by juices, was not a high point, but the treacle pudding was just as it should be. Almost everything on the international wine list is available by the glass or carafe. Bottles start at £15.95.

Chef/s: Alex Clark. **Open:** all week L 12 to 3, D 5.30 to 9. **Meals:** alc (main courses £10 to £17). **Details:** 91 seats. Separate bar. Wheelchair access. Music. Car parking.

Treburley

★ TOP 50 PUB ★

NEW ENTRY
The Springer Spaniel
Smart pub with pitch-perfect food
Treburley, PL15 9NS
Tel no: (01579) 370424
www.thespringerspaniel.org.uk
Modern British | £30
Cooking score: 4

Following on swiftly from the success of chef/patron Anton Piotrowski's Treby Arms in Devon (see entry), the Springer Spaniel treads the same sure-footed path. This smart country pub strikes a well-judged balance between everyday food and fancier fare 'for the interested minority' and also provides good value and 'warm, bend-over-backwards' service. The dining area, classy but not over-dressed, retains a relaxed feel and the kitchen turns out a roster of pitch-perfect dishes: from pub favourites such as steak and Guinness suet pudding with horseradish mash and green beans in Parma ham, or white-wine battered fish and chips, to a more ambitious terrine of rabbit and duck with pickled carrots and dots of red cabbage purée, and 'seafood wreck', a 'superb' plate of various fish – hake, brill, anchovy, shrimps – presented in different ways. To finish, the signature plant-pot 'Treby's gone carrots', is a novel spin on carrot cake. Wines start at £16.50.

Chef/s: Anton Piotrowski. **Open:** Tue to Sun L 12 to 3, D 6 to 9. **Meals:** alc (main courses £13 to £20). **Details:** 68 seats. 20 seats outside. Separate bar. Music. Car parking.

Treen

The Gurnard's Head

Clifftop pub with a local flavour
Treen, TR26 3DE
Tel no: (01736) 796928
www.gurnardshead.co.uk
British | £30
Cooking score: 3
£5 OFF

On the winding road that snakes along the coast from St Just to St Ives, the Gurnard's Head is a stopover to warm the cockles of a traveller's heart. It's a dining pub run by the team behind the Felin Fach Griffin near Brecon and the Old Coastguard down the road in Mousehole (see entries). There's a proper bar with three draught ales on the go, plus colourful spaces where diners choose from a menu that has a regional flavour and no lack of ambition. The kitchen lights up the blow-torch to give mackerel that char-grilled flavour (served with celeriac rémoulade and pickled cucumber), while leek and potato soup is enriched with truffle cream. Main-course braised ox cheek follows (with parsnip purée), and desserts run to apple and almond tart. Wines start at £17.50, with a host available by the carafe.
Chef/s: Bruce Rennie. **Open:** all week L 12.30 to 2.30 (12 Sun), D 6.30 to 9. **Closed:** 5 days Dec. **Meals:** alc (main courses £12 to £18). Set L £16 (2 courses) to £19. **Details:** 73 seats. 40 seats outside. Music. Car parking.

Truro

Tabb's

Gently evolving, sensitive food
85 Kenwyn Street, Truro, TR1 3BZ
Tel no: (01872) 262110
www.tabbs.co.uk
Modern British | £35
Cooking score: 5
£5 OFF

A beguiling Cornish favourite since 2005, Nigel Tabb's intimate little restaurant is impressively furnished in pale lilac hues, slate floors and high-backed leather chairs – although some visitors find the atmosphere somewhat 'bland', with 'no candles or flowers on the tables'. In the end it's all about Nigel's gently evolving, sensitive and increasingly confident food, not forgetting his terrific home-baked breads and the handcrafted chocolates that end every meal. He serves breast of pigeon with a deep-fried egg, homemade pasta and sun-dried tomato dressing; matches grilled hake fillet with provençale leeks and mushrooms, spring onion velouté and basil oil; and finishes off roast breast of duck with a smoked paprika reduction. After that, desserts such as tonka bean pannacotta provide a satisfying conclusion. Global tapas hold sway at lunchtime (three plates for £12) – think tempura courgettes or pork belly with harissa couscous. The wine list has some choice selections from £16.95.
Chef/s: Nigel Tabb. **Open:** Tue to Fri L 12 to 2, Tue to Sat D 5.30 to 9. **Closed:** Sun, Mon. **Meals:** alc (main courses £16 to £21). Set L and D £25. **Details:** 30 seats. Separate bar. Music.

Wadebridge

NEW ENTRY
Little Plates

Stylish sharing plates in a relaxed setting
Polmorla Road, Wadebridge, PL27 7ND
Tel no: (01208) 816377
www.littleplatesbar.co.uk
Mediterranean | £22
Cooking score: 3
£30

The sea may be several miles downriver, but there's more than a hint of surfside café to this laid-back 'bar and eatery' in the heart of Wadebridge. Vintage plates on sea-blue walls, distressed metal chairs and Formica tables – this is lifestyle-magazine Cornwall, but with a Mediterranean twist. Generous portions, big flavours and sprightly ingredients characterise sharing plates such as Spanish meatballs in a muscular tomato and basil sauce; squid brightened by the smart crunch of deep-fried breadcrumbs and almonds; and arancini with melting mozzarella hearts. Don't miss the white gazpacho dip made with sourdough breadcrumbs, sweet grapes and sharp sherry vinegar – it is stunning on its own, but works wonders with arancini or fresh local bread. Buttery-smooth crema catalana is a perfect way to end, maybe with an intense, rounded espresso. Stronger drinks include craft beers and Mediterranean wines, from £16.75. **Chef/s:** Fergus Coyle and Eddie Thomson. **Open:** Mon to Sat L 12 to 2, D 5 to 9. **Closed:** Sun. **Meals:** alc (main courses £8 to £11). **Details:** 44 seats. Music.

Watergate Bay
Fifteen Cornwall
Zealously sourced ingredients with rustic punch
On the beach, Watergate Bay, TR8 4AA
Tel no: (01637) 861000
www.fifteencornwall.co.uk
Italian | £40
Cooking score: 4

Refurbishment in January 2014 resulted in an even brighter, breezier look at the Cornish outpost of Jamie Oliver's Fifteen charitable enterprise, which has lately taken to the high seas aboard a cruise-liner. The big canteen-like space with its office chairs and teardrop light-fittings looks out over the honeyed sands and scintillant waters of the bay, from an elevation of (naturally) 15 feet. Andy Appleton is a capable ambassador for the group's presentation of simple but flavour-laden Italian food, the kind of pukka, lovely-jubbly, gnarly nosh that Oliver has made all his own. Start with a sharply dressed serving of burrata in blood-orange with little leaves and pistachios, skip lightly through gnocchi with Vulscombe goats' cheese, and square up to turbot in clam and mussel brodo, or wood-fired lamb loin in lardo with artichokes, pecorino and mint. Then join the crowds stampeding towards Amadei chocolate torte with espresso ice cream. House Italian is £19.95.

Chef/s: Andy Appleton. **Open:** all week L 12 to 2.30, D 6.15 to 9.15. **Meals:** alc L (main courses £17 to £29). Set L £28. Set D £60 (5 courses) to £80. **Details:** 120 seats. Children over 4 yrs only at D.

LOCAL GEM
▲ The Beach Hut
Watergate Bay Hotel, Watergate Bay, TR8 4AA
Tel no: (01637) 860877
www.watergatebay.co.uk
Modern British | £25

'We have visited Watergate many times and the Beach Hut has never disappointed us – amazing location, great food, friendly welcoming service, and what could be better than staring out over the ocean?' So ran the notes of one reporter, neatly summing up the charms of this beachside hangout. Regulars come for risk-free, uncluttered modern dishes with a local flavour, from Cornish crab cakes and moules marinière, to ribeye steak, pulled pork sandwiches and classic burgers. Vegetarians do well, too. Breakfast is served, as well as tea and cakes, and there's wine from £11. Open all week.

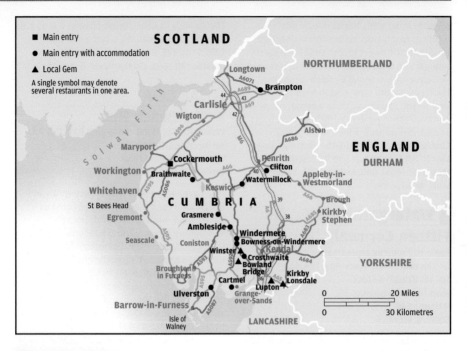

- ■ Main entry
- ● Main entry with accommodation
- ▲ Local Gem

A single symbol may denote several restaurants in one area.

Ambleside

The Drunken Duck Inn

Glorious old inn with modern tucker
Barngates, Ambleside, LA22 ONG
Tel no: (015394) 36347
www.drunkenduckinn.co.uk
Modern British | £35
Cooking score: 2

The Drunken Duck is at a crossroads (not metaphorically, literally) high above Ambleside with views to inspire any budding poets. Its own on-site Barngates Brewery's beer is on hand to provide assistance if further 'inspiration' is required. This classic old pub (a smart one, mind) has log fires in the bar and a restaurant that serves up ethically sourced, local produce in a creative modern British manner. At lunchtime, place your order at the bar and tuck into a ploughman's, a steak and onion sandwich or smoked haddock and Lancashire cheese soufflé. The ante is well and truly upped in the evening with a clever take on the Scotch egg – a kipper version, with brown sauce – followed by venison (loin and ragoût) with Douglas fir and broad beans, and raw apple crumble with smoked maple and wood-sorrel ice cream to finish. Wines start at £24.

Chef/s: Jonny Watson. **Open:** all week L 12 to 4, D 6 to 9. **Meals:** alc (main courses £14 to £24). **Details:** 64 seats. 70 seats outside. Separate bar. Wheelchair access. Car parking.

NEW ENTRY

Old Stamp House

Ambitious food in Ambleside
Church Street, Ambleside, LA22 OBU
Tel no: (015394) 32775
www.oldstamphouse.com
Modern British | £35
Cooking score: 4

V

Since opening in February 2014, the Old Stamp House has won local approval with its innovative menus and genuinely warm welcome. The simple basement restaurant has rough, whitewashed stone walls, plain tables and low carver chairs and is the former workplace of poet William Wordsworth (in his role as Distributor of Stamps). It's the first venture for chef Ryan Blackburn, who arrives from The Cottage in the Wood (see entry), and he continues to use much seasonal and foraged produce. Black pudding bonbon with sweet Cumberland sauce gives notice of big flavours, while goats' curd with beetroot, wild herbs and pickled damson shows off locally sourced credentials perfectly. Among mains, braised cheek of local beef paired with pea risotto proved to be an excellent dish at inspection. Desserts pleased, too, particularly a light dish of strawberries with whipped custard, crumble and sweet cicely. The short wine list opens at £24.

Chef/s: Ryan Blackburn. **Open:** Tue to Sat L 12.30 to 2, D 6 to 9 (9.30 Fri and Sat). **Closed:** Sun, Mon, 25 and 26 Dec, 2 Jan, 1 Feb. **Meals:** alc (main courses £19 to £23). Set L £19 (2 courses) to £23. **Details:** 32 seats. Music.

▌Bowland Bridge

LOCAL GEM
▲ Hare & Hounds
Bowland Bridge, LA11 6NN
Tel no: (015395) 68333
www.hareandhoundsbowlandbridge.co.uk
British | £20

An idyllic prospect, with glorious views across the Winster Valley, this smartly maintained 17th-century coaching inn-with-rooms comes with beams, slate floors and winter fires. It can provide you with a Lancashire cheese and chutney sandwich and a pint of local ale, but primarily it's a dining destination. Chose from a menu with a strong regional flavour and no lack of ambition: perhaps local black pudding and Bishops Blue cheese potato cake with mustard cream sauce, then braised local lamb shank with a redcurrant and mint gravy. Wines from £15.95. Open all week. Accommodation.

▮▮● RYAN BLACKBURN
Old Stamp House

What do you enjoy about being a chef?
The thing I enjoy most about being a chef is the learning. A supplier, a fellow chef or a historian, you can always find something new and interesting to keep you excited about food.

What is your favourite time of year for food?
Spring; wild garlic is the most exciting ingredient to see because it means the worst of winter is over, and it's not long until the rest follows.

What's your newest ingredient discovery?
Iron Age pigs from a farmer in Wasdale, who also supplies our kid goats.

Is there an ingredient that evokes strong memories for you?
Wild salmon; I spent most of my childhood (when I wasn't in a kitchen!) fishing for them with my father and grandfather.

And finally... tell us something about yourself that will surprise your diners.
I was in Coniston Mountain Rescue when I was younger and attended more than 100 call-outs.

Photo: Phil Rigby, Cumbria Life

Bowness-on-Windermere

Linthwaite House

Quality cooking at a delightful hotel
Crook Road, Bowness-on-Windermere, LA23 3JA
Tel no: (015394) 88600
www.linthwaite.com
Modern British | £52
Cooking score: 5
£5 OFF ♦ ⊨ V

Surrounded by 15 acres of enchanting woodland with spectacular views of Lake Windermere, this lovely old house started life as an Edwardian gentleman's residence and still has that personal touch. It's also a highly professional set-up, particularly when it comes to the elegant restaurant with its wall of mirrors, patterned banquettes and rich Regency-style furnishings. The kitchen takes an eclectic view of things, but allows regional ingredients their due in elaborately fashioned dishes such as a witty combo of gin-cured salmon with lemon purée and tonic sorbet, or roast duck breast with confit leg, celeriac and poached plums. Cod is given a spicy Bombay crust; pan-fried stone bass comes with crab and fennel risotto and a puff of Champagne foam; and vegetarians might fancy mascarpone agnolotti with broccoli purée, egg yolk and chicory. Otherwise, Cumbrian lamb is always a good shout, likewise the 'simply wonderful' soufflés that often conclude proceedings. Informative, drinker-friendly notes add clout to the well-spread, authoritative wine list; bottles from £19.50.
Chef/s: Chris O'Callaghan. **Open:** all week L 12 to 2, D 7 to 9. **Meals:** Set L £15 (2 courses) to £20. Set D £52 (4 courses). Sun L £25. **Details:** 64 seats. 30 seats outside. Separate bar. Wheelchair access. Car parking.

Braithwaite

The Cottage in the Wood

Warm hospitality and good food
Whinlatter Forest, Braithwaite, CA12 5TW
Tel no: (01768) 778409
www.thecottageinthewood.co.uk
Modern British | £50
Cooking score: 4
£5 OFF ⊨ V

'A joy from start to finish' was the verdict of one visitor to this 17th-century 'cottage' in the heart of the Whinlatter Forest, taken by the kind hospitality from people 'who you feel really love what they do'. There are breathtaking views over Bassenthwaite Lake and the Skiddaw mountain range from the attractive semi-circular dining room, but it's the cooking that steals the show. Chris Archer's 'innovative' menus celebrate seasonality and draw on as much local produce as he can find – note a 'beautifully presented' dish of Curthwaite goats' curd with Cumbrian ham and white asparagus, artichoke and truffle dressing. Mains follow suit with a 'perfect dish' of Whitehaven turbot teamed with roasted cauliflower, wild asparagus, girolles and plump mussel nage. To finish, there's apricot délice with poached apricot, lemon curd and Earl Grey or mint pannacotta with pink ginger and almond. The wine list (from £19.75) is short and well chosen.
Chef/s: Christopher Archer. **Open:** Wed to Sat L 12.30 to 2, Tue to Sat D 6 to 9. **Closed:** Sun, Mon, Jan. **Meals:** Set L £25 (3 courses). Set D £50 (3 courses). Tasting menu £65. **Details:** 40 seats. 20 seats outside. Wheelchair access. Car parking. Children over 6 yrs only at D.

Brampton

Farlam Hall
Generous hospitality in a Lakeland retreat
Brampton, CA8 2NG
Tel no: (016977) 46234
www.farlamhall.co.uk
Modern British | £47
Cooking score: 3

🛏 V

'A bit of a time warp in some ways, but they really know how to do hospitality here,' noted one visitor to this handsome country house that has been in the Quinion family for over three decades. Dinner is the main event, served in the 'opulent' dining room at tables laid with beautiful silver-plated cutlery and starched clothes. Everybody sits down at 8pm for a short-choice, four-course menu, plus coffee. Barry Quinion cooks in a gentle Anglo-French style: say, confit of Gressingham duck leg with raspberry vinegar and walnut oil dressing; salmon with asparagus, dill and dry sherry cream with marsh samphire; or a simply executed and 'really excellent' local beef fillet with griddled potato and spring onion galette, and peppercorn and brandy sauce. For afters there could be orange and marmalade jelly with Grand Marnier ice cream, or well-kept English cheeses. The short, global wine list opens at £20.75.
Chef/s: Barry Quinion. **Open:** all week D only 7.30 for 8 (1 sitting). **Closed:** 25 to 30 Dec, 5 to 22 Jan. **Meals:** Set D £47.50 (4 courses). **Details:** 40 seats. Music. Car parking. Children over 5 yrs only.

Symbols
🛏 Accommodation is available

💷30 Three courses for less than £30

V Separate vegetarian menu

💷5 OFF £5-off voucher scheme

🍷 Notable wine list

Cartmel

★ TOP 10 ★
L'Enclume
Miracles of nature
Cavendish Street, Cartmel, LA11 6PZ
Tel no: (015395) 36362
www.lenclume.co.uk
Modern British | £120
Cooking score: 10

🍷 🛏 V

Great chefs place excellence of raw materials first in their list of essentials. Simon Rogan's take here is a bit left of centre: while many restaurant kitchens are currently doing the grow-your-own thing, Rogan has his own farm growing fruit, vegetables and herbs to exact specifications; added support from local producers ensures that his cooking is firmly rooted in the surrounding countryside. Serious and fun at the same time, the 21-course, mini-portion extravaganza may well last for four hours, but the opening salvo of compact flavour-bombs draws notice from the start. Consider the famed oyster pebble, an exquisite oxtail dumpling, a nibble of smoked eel, or a very sweet raw scallop minimally but effectively matched by dots of strawberry gel and English caviar. With Rogan having restaurants in Manchester and London to look after (see entries for the French, and Fera at Claridge's), the day-to-day running of L'Enclume's kitchen is in the hands of executive chef Mark Birchall, who hits the high notes as effortlessly as his boss. Indeed, nearly everyone who has eaten here in the past year has reported brilliantly successful meals. It's a busy, highly worked approach with dishes defined by their look-at-me artistry, but every detail makes sense: the sheer satisfaction to be found in creamed celeriac and chicken gizzards in a rich Tunworth cheese sauce; a winning version of wild venison tartare that layers smoky flavour from charcoal oil, sweetness from candied fennel and blistering heat from dots of mustard; the finely tuned control on rustic flavours in Reg's duck and sweetbread with beetroot, leek and elderflower. Other zeniths include an elegant turnip cream containing crunchy baby turnips, a just-set Marans egg yolk and peppery nasturtium leaves, and a spicy, aromatic dish of potatoes in onion ashes with lovage and wood sorrel – indeed, some of the real pleasures here are often to be found among the vegetable dishes. Equally deft are desserts, whether an evocative sweet-and-sour assemblage of gooseberries, sheep's milk and anise hyssop snow; the understated hum of sweetness in a dish of green strawberries, apple marigold custard and beach leaf; or a beautifully realised meadowsweet mousse enlivened with cherries and dots of the most exquisite reduced cider. The deal is sealed by the unfussy mood in the understated dining rooms, by the engaging and genuinely committed staff, and by the masterful wine service which is on hand to guide you through the impressively arranged list (from £30), or to match a series of glasses.

Chef/s: Simon Rogan, Mark Birchall and Tom Barnes. **Open:** Wed to Sun L 12 to 1.30, all week D 6.30 to 9. **Meals:** Set L £45. Set D £120. **Details:** 55 seats. Wheelchair access. No children under 10 yrs at D.

NEW ENTRY
Pig & Whistle
A real village local
Aynesome Road, Cartmel, LA11 6PL
Tel no: (015395) 36482
www.pigandwhistlecartmel.co.uk
British | £28
Cooking score: 2
£30

This basic, edge-of-village boozer remains strongly rooted in the community thanks to owner Simon Rogan's respect for the past. It's run as a 'proper' pub where both beer and food are given equal weight. There are bar snacks such as Scotch egg with spiced brown sauce or XB ale cheese on toast to keep you going; alternatively, head through to the simple dining room for some feel-good food that brings big Brit flavours to the table. 'Utterly delicious' pea and mint soup with cheese

fritters, is one way to start, with a classy burger topped with Blacksticks blue and relishes a trad way to follow; or go for hogget suet pudding, which comes with a potato and vegetable bake and cockles and capers. The pub may seem run down and the mis-matched furniture has definitely seen better days, but it is truly welcoming, staff are attentive and pleasant, and prices reasonable. Wines from £13.

Chef/s: Gareth Webster. **Open:** all week L 12 to 2, D 5 to 8.30. **Closed:** 25 Dec. **Meals:** alc (main courses £13 to £22). **Details:** 28 seats. 40 seats outside. Separate bar.

Rogan & Company
A talented young chef at the helm
The Square, Cartmel, LA11 6QD
Tel no: (015395) 35917
www.roganandcompany.co.uk
Modern British | £40
Cooking score: 5
£5 OFF

'Really enjoyed the whole experience . . . has improved out of all recognition since our last visit.' Reporters have been quick to spot the change of chef at Simon Rogan's other Cumbrian restaurant and to praise the 'fantastic' food and 'knowledge and enthusiasm' of the service. But then Kevin Tickle is no stranger to Rogan's methods, having spent several years at L'Enclume; he now brings his considerable skill to Rogan & Company. Mr Tickle starts with local ingredients and balances their flavours with judgement, thanks in part to some tried-and-tested L'Enclume signature dishes ('an à la carte version of L'Enclume', thought one reader), and his own unique twists. Recent hits have included Marans egg with salt-baked turnip, truffle and toasted seeds, and Langdale mutton with parsnips and kale. Summer flavours shone through in cured rainbow trout with English mace, soured cream, cucumber and bronze fennel, and an impressive, big-on-flavour guinea hen with peas, marjoram, bacon and celeriac. Wines from £22.

Chef/s: Kevin Tickle. Open: Tue to Sat L 12 to 2, Mon to Sat D 6.30 to 9. Closed: Sun. Meals: Set L £29 (four courses). Set D £40. Details: 40 seats. Wheelchair access. Music.

Clifton
George & Dragon
Strong on local produce
Clifton, CA10 2ER
Tel no: (01768) 865381
www.georgeanddragonclifton.co.uk
British | £28
Cooking score: 3

£5 OFF 🍴 £30

Built as a coaching inn in the 18th century, the white-painted George and Dragon is an old village pub that is definitely seeing better days, thanks to the vision and dedication of Charles Lowther. It's a well-bred place of stone and slate, heritage colours and bare tables, and it glows with confidence. Where possible, ingredients are reared or grown on the Lowther Estate, or sourced within 20 miles, and everybody seems to find everything 'seriously good'. The seasonally based cooking delivers all kind of plain-speaking dishes. Homespun pub die-hards (a rather well-made burger) or a crusty roll filled with lambs' kidneys, bacon and mushroom in wholegrain mustard sauce, sit happily beside generous gutsy plates of roast cod with a bouillabaisse-style sauce or herb-crusted lamb shoulder rack with gratin dauphinois. Desserts are in keeping, especially an apple and cinnamon sponge with custard, but there's an intriguing mix of local cheeses, too. Wines start at £16.50.
Chef/s: Ian Jackson. Open: all week L 12 to 2.30, D 6 to 9. Closed: 26 Dec. Meals: alc (main courses £11 to £22). Set L £13 (2 courses) to £17. Details: 110 seats. 60 seats outside. Separate bar. Music. Car parking.

Cockermouth
Quince & Medlar
Long-serving Lakeland veggie
11-13 Castlegate, Cockermouth, CA13 9EU
Tel no: (01900) 823579
www.quinceandmedlar.co.uk
Vegetarian | £27
Cooking score: 2

V £30

Serving vegetarian food in Cockermouth since 1989, Quince & Medlar has a very loyal following that continues to enjoy the comfortable, smart surroundings in this listed Georgian building. A meal here 'feels more like an occasion' than at other veggie haunts. An early summer inspection found attentive service, a full dining room on an early weekday evening and dishes that provided tasty combinations. Generous starters included spiced aubergine sticks with pumpkin seed oil-dressed greens and poppy seed pancakes, and courgette and shallot garam fries with okra and raita. To follow, mushroom suet wrap with balsamic red onion, red rice, toasted walnuts and watercress reduction may have been a 'very brown dish' but was full of flavour. Puddings find favour, especially 'a very rich and silky' dark chocolate pot. Wines from £16.50.
Chef/s: Colin Le Voi. Open: Tue to Sat D only 6.30 to 9.30. Closed: Sun, Mon, 24 to 26 Dec. Meals: alc (main courses £14). Details: 26 seats.

Crosthwaite
The Punch Bowl
Keen prices and cosmopolitan ideas
Lyth Valley, Crosthwaite, LA8 8HR
Tel no: (015395) 68237
www.the-punchbowl.co.uk
Modern British | £32
Cooking score: 3

£5 OFF 🍴

Settled in next to St Mary's church in the Lyth Valley, which should one day have an *appellation contrôlée* for its incomparable damsons, the Punch Bowl is a country inn and

then some. The décor emphasises Lakeland elegance, with quality furniture and table appointments, and framed prints abounding. Outdoor summer tables are a must for the views. Scott Fairweather makes a good fist of providing an extensive menu of modern British creativity. It can get as exotic as seared scallops with truffled white chocolate risotto, followed by monkfish in chorizo and mussel stew, or maple-roasted duck breast with braised red cabbage and dauphinois, dappled with orange and raisins. Then again, a Sunday lunch of roast beef and Yorkshire with deeply flavoured gravy pushes many buttons too. Finish with lemon posset, served with mulled wine jelly and cranberries and a granola flapjack. Wine prices open at £21.95, or £5.25 a standard glass.
Chef/s: Scott Fairweather. **Open:** all week L 12 to 5.30 (4 Sat and Sun), D 5.30 to 9. **Meals:** alc (main courses £11 to £20). Sun L £15. **Details:** 92 seats. 30 seats outside. Wheelchair access. Music.

Culgaith

READERS RECOMMEND
Mrs Miller's
British
Hazel Dene Garden Centre, Culgaith, CA10 1QF
Tel no: (01768) 882520
www.mrsmillersculgaith.co.uk
'During the day, an excellent café; on Friday and Saturday evenings it really shines with imaginative and varied menus.'

Grasmere

The Jumble Room
Global cooking in the heart of Lakeland
Langdale Road, Grasmere, LA22 9SU
Tel no: (015394) 35188
www.thejumbleroom.co.uk
Global | £35
Cooking score: 1
£5
OFF

In a village swamped with cutesy tea rooms, it's refreshing to experience the Jumble Room's exuberant, music-fuelled

atmosphere: not to mention the lively flavours created by its kitchen. Local produce features strongly – Morecambe Bay shrimps, beef from the southern fells, Goosnargh poultry – but the menu also happily visits Thailand for a coconutty choo chee seafood curry, or China for a five-spiced monkfish (seasoned with a restraint that enhances the fish). Starters attract the odd gripe ('doughy' spring onion bhajias), and reports on the tempura batter oscillate from 'soggy, thick' to 'light, crisp', but advocates recommend the 'stunning' gingerbread crumble. Wine from £16.
Chef/s: Simon Boden. **Open:** Wed to Mon D only 5.30 to 9.30. **Closed:** Tue, Mon to Fri (Jan), 14 to 27 Dec. **Meals:** alc (main courses £7 to £26). **Details:** 50 seats. Music.

READERS RECOMMEND
Oak Bank Hotel
Modern British
Broadgate, Grasmere, LA22 9TA
Tel no: (01539) 435217
www.lakedistricthotel.co.uk
'Main course was pork, with four different aspects, each full of flavour, and each different. The small helping of pork black pudding was beautifully light and still tasty other selections, Herdwick lamb and Scottish scallops, were equally appreciated.'

Kirkby Lonsdale

LOCAL GEM
▲ The Sun Inn
6 Market Street, Kirkby Lonsdale, LA6 2AU
Tel no: (015242) 71965
www.sun-inn.info
Modern British | £29

This fine old Cumbrian pub-with-rooms has fetching beams, wood fires and fashionable menus driven by seasonal produce – with pub classics offered during the day. The evening-only three-course set menu does a good line in modern British brasserie dishes, with smoked haddock risotto alongside the likes of slow-braised pork belly with crispy squid, pineapple gel and crushed heritage potatoes, and Yorkshire rhubarb and ginger sponge trifle to finish. Drink local real ales, or wines from £17.50. Closed Mon L. Accommodation.

▌ Lupton

LOCAL GEM
▲ The Plough
Cow Brow, Lupton, LA6 1PJ
Tel no: (015395) 67700
www.theploughatlupton.co.uk
British | £24 £5 OFF

'No one's walking away from the Plough still hungry,' noted a visitor to this engaging roadside pub, a few handy miles from junction 36 of the M6. All-day eating in a relaxed, casual setting is the modus operandi, with ploughman's and fisherman's boards served alongside ham hock terrine, whole baked Camembert and mains such as coq au vin and slow-cooked belly pork. Finish with the likes of hot chocolate fondant with raspberry sorbet or local cheeses. Wines from £17.95. Open all week. Accommodation.

▌ Ulverston

The Bay Horse
Romantic charm and breathtaking views
Canal Foot, Ulverston, LA12 9EL
Tel no: (01229) 583972
www.thebayhorsehotel.co.uk
Modern British | £35
Cooking score: 3

🍽 V

There were once stage-coaches hurtling across the sands at Morecambe Bay, but the only hastening thing you're likely to see now is the tide racing in – and the Bay Horse's dining room provides a ringside seat of this, through conservatory-style windows. It's a restful prospect, with the towering fells of Lakeland as a backdrop. The long comfortable room is furnished in light green tones. It's worth trading up from snacks in the bar (good though the lunchtime sandwiches are) to sit here. A gently modernised version of Anglo-French cuisine is the kitchen's norm, with

some excursions into South African cooking for bobotie (spiced minced lamb and fruit with a quiche-like topping) and malva pudding (the Cape's answer to sticky toffee). For the rest, expect mains such as smoked haddock on mushroom and onion pâté in white wine cream, or lamb shank braised in ginger, orange and red wine. Wines start at £17.50.
Chef/s: Robert Lyons. Open: all week L 12 to 3 (4 Sat and Sun), D 7.30 for 8. Meals: alc (main courses £15 to £27). Details: 50 seats. 16 seats outside. Separate bar. Wheelchair access. Music. Car parking. Children over 9 yrs only at D.

The General Burgoyne
Hospitable Lakes pub
Church Road, Great Urswick, Ulverston, LA12 0SZ
Tel no: (01229) 586394
www.generalburgoyne.com
British | £28
Cooking score: 3
£5 OFF £30 ⬇

Craig and Louise Sherrington stay true to the spirit of Lakeland hospitality at their 17th-century Furness pub, maintaining the charm of fire-warmed snugs alongside the more contemporary Orangery restaurant. All-comers receive a 'pleasant and cheerful welcome' and 'enthusiastic', efficient service. A balance is struck between soups and sandwiches, afternoon tea, pub standards and more creative dishes. Fig tarte Tatin with Manchego or goats' cheese bonbons with home-dried tomatoes pack a punch before a game-bird trio of 'beautifully cooked' pigeon, pheasant and partridge with cavolo nero and thyme and game jus. A map shows where many of the main ingredients come from. Generous portions are especially welcome on Sundays. To finish, the kitchen delights in boozy jellies, as in a dessert of Old Tom chocolate ale with vanilla pannacotta, salted caramel and peanut iced parfait. There's more Robinsons beer on tap, and house wine is £14. Details overleaf.

Chef/s: Craig Sherrington. Open: Wed to Sun L 12 to 2, Tue to Sun D 6 to 9 (8 Sun). Closed: Mon, first week Jan. Meals: alc (main courses £11 to £17). Sun L £18. Tasting menu £45. Details: 33 seats. 12 seats outside. Separate bar. Music. Car parking.

■ Watermillock

Rampsbeck Country House Hotel

Gracious comforts and fine contemporary food
Watermillock, CA11 0LP
Tel no: (017684) 86442
www.rampsbeck.co.uk
Anglo-French | £60
Cooking score: 5

🛏 V

No modern tweaks here: this is a classic country hotel, complete with oil paintings, wood panelling and flock wallpaper. It's a pristine delight – in a Cluedo mansion kind of way – and the grounds, with their views of Ullswater, are immaculate. For all the classicism, the kitchen has a few surprises up its sleeve and cooks local ingredients with plenty of flair and imagination. A salad of roasted and pickled beetroot with goats'cheese cream, candied walnuts, orange and sherry vinegar dressing trumpets freshness and quality, while a superb piece of pan-fried fillet of sea bass with pickled celery, braised lettuce, Morecambe Bay shrimps and chicken juices boasts interesting textures and 'vibrant flavours'. There's intelligence and subtlety at dessert, too, where you might find warm, marzipan-filled cherries teamed with chocolate pudding, almond milk ice cream, cherry sorbet and crunchy chocolate 'soil'. A decent choice of international wines starts at £17.
Chef/s: Ben Wilkinson. Open: all week L 12 to 1.30, D 6.30 to 9. Meals: Set L £32. Set D £60. Sun L £32. Details: 45 seats. 20 seats outside. Separate bar. Wheelchair access. Music. Car parking. Children over 10 yrs only.

■ Windermere

Gilpin Hotel & Lake House

Lakeside elegance and innovative cooking
Crook Road, Windermere, LA23 3NE
Tel no: (015394) 88818
www.thegilpin.co.uk
Modern British | £65
Cooking score: 5

£5 OFF 🍷 🛏 V

A homely country lodge extending through a series of luscious rooms, the Gilpin is nothing if not eclectic. The interior ranges from a metropolitan-style bar to a classic country-house lounge, taking in everything from chinoiserie to venerable oil paintings along the way. Its windows look out on verdant grounds coaxed from the rugged Lakeland landscape. The menu draws much from these surroundings, while taking a broader view in terms of flavours and techniques. The hickory-smoked bone marrow with cep purée and kale crisps is a 'magnificent-looking dish' – a big half-bone filled with the purée and topped with pieces of marrow, some breaded and deep-fried. Grilled hake with tomato, chorizo, broad beans and 'crispy squid' proved big on flavour, though the squid lacked the desired crunch. For dessert, the classic sherry trifle is a 'show stopper'. The extensive but approachable wine list, priced from £24, offers plenty of choice and excellent notes.
Chef/s: Alex O'Kane. Open: all week L 12 to 2, D 6.30 to 9.15. Meals: alc L (main courses £6 to £18). Set D £58 (5 courses). Sun L £35. Details: 65 seats. 30 seats outside. Separate bar. Wheelchair access. Car parking. Children over 7 yrs only.

Holbeck Ghyll

The finer things of life
Holbeck Lane, Windermere, LA23 1LU
Tel no: (015394) 32375
www.holbeckghyll.com
Modern British | £65
Cooking score: 5

£5 OFF 🛏 🍴 V

Holbeck Ghyll's elevated position provides fine views over Lake Windermere and the Langdale fells. 'You move into a different world of tranquillity and comfort,' reckoned one visitor to this well-proportioned former hunting lodge. Though it isn't a place for cutting-edge cuisine, menus are thoughtful and well balanced, relying on classic treatments of scrupulously sourced raw materials for impact. Indeed, chef David McLaughlin takes the sourcing of materials seriously – hand-dived scallops may come from Scotland (perhaps served with smoked bacon and Jerusalem artichoke purée, with sherry vinegar dressing), but the best end of lamb, praised in several reports this year, is Cumbrian, as is roast loin of venison, which may arrive with herb spätzle and squash purée. Meals are unhurried, taking in canapés served in the drawing room, a trundling cheese trolley laden with French and British specimens, and an ever-evolving wine list where the 'personal house selection' (from £31) and 'fantastic finds' are obvious places to start. France makes the biggest splash in the array of intriguing wines (in both colours).
Chef/s: David McLaughlin. **Open:** all week L 12.30 to 2, D 7 to 9.30. **Closed:** first 2 weeks Jan. **Meals:** Set D £65. Gourmet menu £85. **Details:** 40 seats. Separate bar. Wheelchair access. Music. Car parking. Children over 8 yrs only at D.

▌Winster

LOCAL GEM
▲ The Brown Horse Inn
Winster, LA23 3NR
Tel no: (015394) 43443
www.thebrownhorseinn.co.uk
Modern British | £28

There's plenty of old-school character on show at the Brown Horse: a venerable inn with the original features intact. It's a proper pub, even operating a micro-brewery, with old beams, flagged floors, simple bedrooms and a fire or two in winter. The kitchen produces some good stuff that hits the pub brief, but aims higher than the norm: tarte fine with caramelised onion and glazed goats' cheese, for example, followed by sticky roast corn-fed poussin, or homemade pie of the week. Wines from £15.95. Open all week.

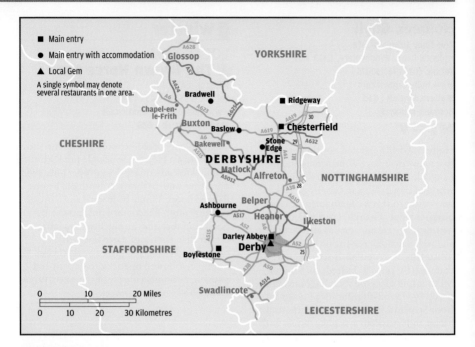

- ■ Main entry
- ● Main entry with accommodation
- ▲ Local Gem

A single symbol may denote
several restaurants in one area.

Ashbourne

The Dining Room
Finely honed tasting plates
33 St John Street, Ashbourne, DE6 1GP
Tel no: (01335) 300666
www.thediningroomashbourne.co.uk
Modern European | £40
Cooking score: 5

🛏 V

'Peter Dale is a craftsman who has spent the last 10 years working alone in the same kitchen, carving out a style that is entirely his own' – so writes an admirer of this highly personal set-up. Occupying an endearingly wonky 17th-century building, the diminutive Dining Room blends ancient beams and timbers with polished light-wood floors and high-back chairs. Dinner consists of finely honed, labour-intensive tasting plates backed by miraculous spelt bread, home-churned cultured butter, clever 'finger food' nibbles, carefully nurtured British cheeses and more. There are no duff ideas here, witness slices of almost-gamey flat-iron steak draped over a nugget of slow-cooked beef cheek embellished with red rice, wild garlic leaves, onion shoots and coriander. Other hits have ranged from a 'cliché-free' scallop dish involving crispy crab balls, slivers of radish, apple and horseradish cream to poppy-seed sponge with grapefruit cream and blood-orange purée. Service has oodles of charm and personality. Wines from £24.

Chef/s: Peter Dale. **Open:** Thur to Sat D only 6 to 10. **Closed:** Sun to Wed, 1 week Sept, 25 Dec to 7 Jan. **Meals:** Set weekday D £40. Sat D £48. **Details:** 18 seats. Music. Children over 12 yrs only.

Symbols
🛏 Accommodation is available

£30 Three courses for less than £30

V Separate vegetarian menu

£5 OFF £5-off voucher scheme

🍶 Notable wine list

Baslow

★ TOP 50 ★

Fischer's Baslow Hall
Blisteringly fine food in a stellar retreat
Calver Road, Baslow, DE45 1RR
Tel no: (01246) 583259
www.fischers-baslowhall.co.uk
Modern European | £72
Cooking score: 7

🍷 ⊨ V

Built in 1907 at the behest of a local family with a penchant for the past, Baslow Hall is nattily attired in full baronial garb, although it never succumbs to lordly posturing on the hospitality front. The kitchen takes its cue from France and the Mediterranean, yet also flies the flag for British ingredients. A seasonal harvest of home-grown herbs and vegetables is supplemented with moorland venison, Derbyshire lamb, Yorkshire rhubarb, Sheffield honey and more besides. There are wallet-friendly deals at lunchtime, but it pays to blow the budget on Rupert Rowley's top-end dinner menu – a parade of fashionable riffs, on-trend techniques and blisteringly fine assemblages that sometimes seem at odds with the sedate, traditional dining room. A Cornish crab 'sandwich' dressed up with fennel, wasabi and crab jelly sets the tone, before the kitchen conjures up plates of richly flavoured oxtail braised in St Petersburg stout (with smoked bone marrow and potato purée as accompaniments) or fragrant miso-glazed turbot with coconut, lime leaf broth and wakame seaweed. To finish, the jokey 'winter tree trunk' with mandarin sorbet and chocolate mousse will get tongues wagging, likewise the spectacular cheese trolley (consult the owners' cheese 'bible' for guidance). Readers confirm that both food and service are 'to the highest standard'. The classy, worldwide wine list doesn't lag behind either, with fastidiously chosen star names for connoisseurs and everyday drinkers alike. Prices start at £22.

Chef/s: Rupert Rowley. **Open:** all week L 12 to 1.30, D 7 to 8.30. **Closed:** 25 and 26 Dec. **Meals:** alc (main courses £25, L only). Set L £21 (2 courses) to £28. Set D £55 (2 courses) to £72. Sun L £32. **Details:** 50 seats. Separate bar. Car parking. Children over 5 yrs at L (exc Sun); over 8 yrs at D.

Rowley's
Stylish all-purpose venue
Church Lane, Baslow, DE45 1RY
Tel no: (01246) 583880
www.rowleysrestaurant.co.uk
Modern British | £32
Cooking score: 1

There's a freewheeling modernity to Rowley's, sibling venue to the fine-dining grandee that is Fischer's Baslow Hall (see entry). The one-time village pub still looks the part from the outside with its reliable stone stolidity, but within it's all shades of purple and lime, and contemporary swagger. Both a restaurant and bar are incorporated, so popping in for a coffee or pint is positively encouraged. The culinary output extends to some bright, British-focused food like pan-fried mackerel with sweet chilli dressing, and slow-braised ox cheek with bone marrow and oxtail dumplings. Wines from £16.95.
Chef/s: Jason Kendra and Max Fischer. **Open:** Tue to Sun L 12 to 2.30 (4 Sun), Tue to Sat D 5.30 to 9 (6 to 9.30 Sun). **Closed:** Mon, 25 Dec. **Meals:** alc (main courses £12 to £21). Set L £16 (2 courses) to £20. Sun L £20 to £24. **Details:** 65 seats. 12 seats outside. Separate bar. Wheelchair access. Music. Car parking.

Boylestone
The Lighthouse Restaurant
A discreet gastronomic beacon
New Road, Boylestone, DE6 5AA
Tel no: (01335) 330658
www.the-lighthouse-restaurant.co.uk
Modern British | £38
Cooking score: 3

A third successful year proves this rural Derbyshire restaurant to be no flash-in-the-pan, despite its incongruous setting behind a scruffy country pub. The modern barn-like dining room with pine-beamed rafters might frustrate with its limited opening times, but the kitchen rewards patience, delivering good produce inventively cooked. Avoiding needless affectations, the nicely paced tasting menu (tried at inspection) delivered a perfectly caramelised scallop atop a luscious saffron risotto laced with a dice of its roe; a 'pleasure to eat' tranche of duck with leg-meat croquette; and an accomplished set lemon custard pre-dessert. The carte offers heartier dishes along the lines of Derbyshire Longhorn fillet steak with triple-cooked chips, and wild Cornish turbot with clams, shellfish beurre blanc and Charlotte potato – enjoyable food cooked without unnecessary flimflam. The friendly front-of-house staff could be better organised, and more attention also needs paying to the 'almost nonexistent' wine list, which starts at £14.95.

Chef/s: Jonathan Hardy. **Open:** Sun L 12 to 4, Wed to Sat D 7 to 12. **Closed:** Mon, Tue, 1 to 14 Jan. **Meals:** alc (main courses £12 to £25). Tasting menu £50. **Details:** 36 seats. Wheelchair access. Music. Car parking.

▌Bradwell

The Samuel Fox Inn
Cut-above country pub
Stretfield Road, Bradwell, S33 9JT
Tel no: (01433) 621562
www.samuelfox.co.uk
British | £31
Cooking score: 3
£5
OFF

A pub for our times, the Samuel Fox Inn (named after the chap who invented the modern umbrella back in 1852) has been spruced up and gently revamped. There's now an opened-up interior where drinkers are welcomed – but food is the prime concern. The chef/proprietor, James Duckett, has worked at some top-end gaffs, and 2014 saw the introduction of a tasting menu to showcase his talents. The main menu reveals a flair for appealing combos such as crumbed cod cheeks with tartare sauce, or game terrine with spicy

carrot pickle. There are daily specials on the blackboard and main courses of local sirloin with chunky chips or pan-fried cod with clam casserole. Lemon and blueberry trifle might round things off. Glorious countryside views are an ever-present distraction, and bedrooms, real ales and roaring fires complete the package. Wines start at £15.50.

Chef/s: James Duckett. **Open:** Wed to Sun L 12 to 2.30 (3.30 Sun), Tue to Sat D 6 to 9. **Closed:** Mon, 5 to 22 Jan. **Meals:** alc (main courses £14 to £22). Set L £19 (2 courses) to £24. Sun L £19 (2 courses) to £24. **Details:** 40 seats. 30 seats outside. Separate bar. Wheelchair access. Music. Car parking.

▌Chesterfield

Non Solo Vino
Trailblazing Italian wine shop-cum-restaurant
417 Chatsworth Road, Brampton, Chesterfield, S40 3AD
Tel no: (01246) 276760
www.nonsolovino.co.uk
Italian | £40
Cooking score: 3
£5
OFF

Not just wine, as the name says, for Non Solo Vino is a little powerhouse of contemporary Italian cooking. The cracking wine shop plays its part, for sure, with its cutting-edge Enomatic machine allowing customers to sample a fab range by the glass, but it's worth sticking around to eat in the contemporary looking restaurant. Staff are happy to serve up three-course convention if necessary, but this place is all about the multi-course experience, centred on a tasting menu full of little plates of dynamic food. How about venison tartare with blackberry gel and gin-and-tonic ice? Modern cooking techniques are used to good effect in dishes like scallops with Jerusalem artichoke purée and candied pancetta, or duck breast with horseradish foam and bitter orange purée. There's an inexpensive 'bocconcini' set lunch too, and a lounge bar on the first floor. The wine list (starting at £20) is loyal to the motherland.

Chef/s: Matt Bennison. **Open:** Tue to Sun L 12 to 3, D 6 to 10. **Closed:** Mon, 25 and 26 Dec, 1 to 7 Jan. **Meals:** Set L £10 (2 courses) to £15. Set D £20 (2 courses) to £30. Tasting menu £40 (6 courses) to £50. **Details:** 40 seats. Separate bar. Music. Car parking.

LOCAL GEM
▲ Calabria
30 Glumangate, Chesterfield, S40 1TX
Tel no: (01246) 559944
www.calabriacucina.co.uk
Italian | £30 £5 OFF

In a world of corporate uniformity and blandness, this eatery on the wonderfully named and cobbled Glumangate positively overflows with attitude and charisma. Family-run with its roots in Calabria (Italy's toe), it is open for breakfast and lunch of hearty platefuls, and then in the evening for perky modern stuff such as swordfish carpaccio with salsa and caper dressing, and Derbyshire lamb shank with fregola and apricots. There's a tasting menu, too, plus regional Italian wines from £16.50. Closed Sun.

Darley Abbey
Darleys
Tourist hot spot with capable food
Darley Abbey Mills, Haslams Lane, Darley Abbey, DE22 1DZ
Tel no: (01332) 364987
www.darleys.com
Modern British | £40
Cooking score: 3

V

The setting in a north-country World Heritage Site could hardly be more appealing. Darley's occupies a converted cotton mill on the edge of a weir on the Derwent, with a riverside terrace under canopies. To be seated there on a summer's day with hardly a ripple to disturb the watery scene is idyllic indeed. The inside room is smart, too, with linen-clad tables, wall lighting and gathered curtains. The kitchen makes an impressive job of turning locally sourced food into contemporary British cuisine. Start with tartare of cured sea trout and Bloody Mary garnish, prior to mains such as rose veal with cauliflower cheese and piccalilli potato, or turbot fillet with roast cucumber, citrus polenta and clams. Desserts feature plenty of fun components like rhubarb ripple milkshake, salted peanut cream, or chocolate crunch, but also the more classical likes of apple and red berry soufflé with green apple sorbet. House Chilean is £17.50.
Chef/s: Jonathan Hobson and Mark Hadfield. **Open:** all week L 12 to 2 (2.30 Sun), Mon to Sat D 7 to 9.30. **Closed:** 25 Dec to 10 Jan, bank hols. **Meals:** alc (main courses £20 to £23). Set L £20 (2 courses) to £23. Sun L £25. **Details:** 60 seats. 10 seats outside. Separate bar. Music. Car parking.

Derby

LOCAL GEM
▲ Masa
The Old Wesleyan Chapel, Brook Street, Derby, DE1 3PF
Tel no: (01332) 203345
www.masarestaurantwinebar.com
Modern European | £30

Housed in a listed Wesleyan chapel just off Derby's inner ring road, Masa is one of the city's more quirky venues. Eat in the atmospheric, tiered gallery restaurant from a concise Euro-accented menu that might run from chicken and black pudding mousse with crumpets and shallot compote via sea bass fillet with cauliflower purée, pak choi and cumin velouté to treacle sponge with crème anglaise. Lighter bistro-style food is served in the ground-floor lounge bar. Global wines from £18. Closed Mon and Tue.

Average Price
The average price listed in main-entry reviews denotes the price of a three-course meal, without wine.

▌Ridgeway
The Old Vicarage
A temple of natural-born cooking
Ridgeway Moor, Ridgeway, S12 3XW
Tel no: (0114) 2475814
www.theoldvicarage.co.uk
Modern British | £75
Cooking score: 6

£5 OFF

Standing amid undulating lawns and shady copses, the stone-built Victorian vicarage opposite the village church is a picture of pastoral contentment – and only ten minutes' drive from Sheffield. Tessa Bramley has run the show since 1987, offering seasonal cooking in a setting from where it's easy to imagine most ingredients hail. Menus take a while to read, descriptions extending for three lines per dish, but what turns up mostly makes triumphant sense. Begin with chicken terrine: breast and leg layered with spring greens and bacon, garnished with tubes of creamy liver parfait and a glazed confit of the wing. Main might be rump, shoulder and sweetbreads of lamb in a glossy reduction with puréed peas and roasted cherry tomatoes, or sevruga-topped cod with mussels and saffron potatoes. Dessert could be something unimaginably complex involving chocolate, or a straightforward Tatin with cinnamon ice cream and butterscotch sauce. The artfully constructed wine list embraces a style range from 'chic rustique' to 'crème de la crème', with abundant quality throughout. Prices from £24.
Chef/s: Tessa Bramley and Nathan Smith. **Open:** Tue to Fri L 12.30 to 2, Tue to Sat D 6 to 9 (9.30 Fri and Sat). **Closed:** Sun, Mon, 26 Dec to 5 Jan, 2 weeks Aug, bank hols. **Meals:** Set L £40 (3 courses). Set D £75 (4 courses) to £85. **Details:** 46 seats. 24 seats outside. Wheelchair access. Car parking. Children over 6 yrs only at D.

▌Stone Edge
Red Lion Pub & Bistro
Seriously scrubbed-up rural package
Peak Edge Hotel, Darley Road, Stone Edge, S45 0LW
Tel no: (01246) 566142
www.peakedgehotel.co.uk
Modern British | £37
Cooking score: 2

With a modern hotel tacked on, this self-styled 'pub and bistro' in the moorland fringes of the Peak District is a surprisingly upbeat package. You'll find strong foodie credentials here and a fondness for self-sufficiency: note the kitchen garden, orchard and free-ranging chickens. Inside, it has been seriously scrubbed-up, with open fires, low lights and leather sofas adding to the smart-casual vibe – plus plenty of cask ales. The kitchen aims high, serving mackerel with red cabbage gazpacho and Pommery mustard pannacotta as a starter, before offering stone bass with confit radishes, pak choi and chicken 'oysters', or poached and roasted rabbit with baby gem, carrot 'variations' and rabbit bolognese. There's plenty of local game in season, while desserts might bring a modish combo of Granny Smith apple semifreddo with cinnamon doughnut, ricotta and malt crumb. Wines from Renishaw Hall vineyard add local colour to the wine list; otherwise, bottles start at £15.95.
Chef/s: Daniel Laycock. **Open:** all week 12 to 9. **Meals:** alc (main courses £11 to £25). Set L £20. Sun L £16. **Details:** 80 seats. 40 seats outside. Separate bar. Wheelchair access. Music. Car parking.

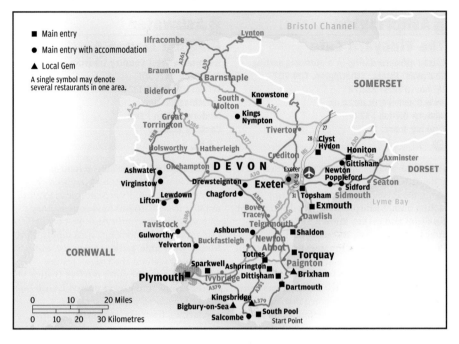

- ■ Main entry
- ● Main entry with accommodation
- ▲ Local Gem

A single symbol may denote several restaurants in one area.

■ Ashburton

Agaric

Heartfelt natural cooking
30 North Street, Ashburton, TQ13 7QD
Tel no: (01364) 654478
www.agaricrestaurant.co.uk
Modern British | £35
Cooking score: 4

£5 OFF

With a cook shop by the restaurant, B&B rooms available in a Georgian town house two doors up and a smallholding where they grow produce for the table, Nick and Sophie Coiley certainly don't let the grass grow under their feet. Loyal support is shown to local organic growers and producers, as just about everything is sourced within 20 miles of Ashburton. The Coileys have even planted olive trees in the hope of producing their own olive oil. These ingredients in fine fettle are cooked with skill and care – flavour not fashion is the driving force. Start with a cheesy twice-baked smoked haddock soufflé or a classic provençal fish soup, with Quickes Cheddar bringing a regional flavour to the trad accompaniments. Main-course turbot has a Euro flavour, too, via grilled fennel and Seville orange hollandaise. For dessert, those oranges might feature again in a soufflé with toast ice cream. Wines start at £19.50.

Chef/s: Nick Coiley. **Open:** Wed to Fri L 12 to 2, Wed to Sat D 7 to 9. **Closed:** Sun, Mon, Tue, 2 weeks Dec, 2 weeks Aug. **Meals:** alc (main courses £16 to £23). Set L £16 (2 courses). **Details:** 28 seats. 14 seats outside. Separate bar. Wheelchair access.

🍴 Please send us your feedback

To register your opinion about any restaurant listed in the Guide, or a new restaurant that you wish to bring to our attention, please visit the web address at the bottom of the page. Your feedback informs the content of the book and will be used to compile next year's reviews.

▌Ashprington
The Vineyard Café

Classy alfresco dining in a stunning setting
Sharpham Estate, Ashprington, TQ9 7UT
Tel no: (01803) 732178
www.thevineyardcafe.co.uk
Modern British | £22
Cooking score: 2
£30

Across the Sharpham Estate you can see
vineyards, find lush, green riverside trails
along the River Dart and visit a 'quaint' shop
selling homemade produce. But the highlight
for locals and in-the-know visitors is this
simple café set on a sun-facing deck – the
beautiful location really comes into its own on
a summer's day. The kitchen deals in good,
generous cooking that's inventive and
seasonal. Fritters made with Sharpham's own
rustic cheese mixed with green pea and mint
and served with chive crème fraîche makes an
excellent starter, as does leek and potato soup
with homemade bread, or pork, pistachio and
prune terrine. A Spanish-style fish stew, rich
in paprika, fennel, peppers and tomato, might
follow, or thick slices of pork belly on braised
lentils. For afters, there could be locally made
ice cream or the splendid Sharpham
cheeseboard. All wines are from the
Sharpham Estate, with bottles from £16.95.
Chef/s: Rosie Weston, Charlie Goddard and Angie
Chappell-Howard. **Open:** Mon to Fri L 12 to 2 (2.30
Sat and Sun). **Closed:** Oct to Apr. **Meals:** alc (main
courses £11 to £15). **Details:** 60 seats outside.
Separate bar. Wheelchair access. Car parking.

▌Ashwater
Blagdon Manor

Hospitable West Country treasure
Ashwater, EX21 5DF
Tel no: (01409) 211224
www.blagdon.com
Modern British | £40
Cooking score: 2
£5 OFF 🚗 V

The Moreys' one-time Devon long-house
dating from the 16th century has been coaxed
very elegantly into its present role as a stylish
restaurant-with-rooms (and conservatory
extension) in the countryside west of
Dartmoor. Neighbouring farms supply Steve
Morey with lamb, pork and poultry, and
south-west seafood and cheeses feature
prominently too. Voguish modern British
flavours come into play in starters such as
smoked mackerel with horseradish
pannacotta, beetroot, yoghurt and orange,
while main courses show off those local
ingredients to their best advantage in rack of
lamb with duck confit ravioli and braised
turnips in port and cinnamon, or brill with
creamed leeks, Indian-spiced cauliflower and
mussels. Labour-intensive desserts might take
in red berry soufflé with blackberry sorbet and
a gingery doughnut, as well as the must-have
chocolate tasting, which includes a ravishing
dollop of chocolate and prune porridge. Wines
start at £17, or £5.25 a glass, for Chilean
Chardonnay.
Chef/s: Steve Morey. **Open:** Thur to Sun L 12 to 1.30,
Wed to Sun D 7 to 9. **Closed:** Mon, Tue, 2 weeks Jan.
Meals: Set L £17 (2 courses) to £20. Set D £35 (2
courses) to £40. **Details:** 26 seats. Separate bar.
Wheelchair access. Car parking. Children over 12 yrs
only.

Bigbury-on-Sea

LOCAL GEM
▲ The Oyster Shack
Milburn Orchard Farm, Stakes Hill, Bigbury-on-Sea, TQ7 4BE
Tel no: (01548) 810876
www.oystershack.co.uk
Seafood | £38 £5 OFF

'Don't come here if you don't like fish,' exclaimed one regular at this quirky, hugely popular seafood restaurant just off the A379. Sit under the giant sail on 'deck' (the covered terrace) and tuck into oysters – 'au naturel' or with a multitude of dressings – Salcombe lobster, crab and Fowey mussels. The kitchen keeps things equally uncomplicated when it comes to ozone-fresh locally landed fish: a whole roasted gilthead bream being simply anointed with garlic butter. House wine £15.75. Open all week.

Brixham

LOCAL GEM
▲ The Brixham Deli
68a Fore Street, Brixham, TQ5 8EF
Tel no: (01803) 859585
www.thebrixhamdeli.co.uk
Modern British | £18

Roy and Gill Hakin are hands-on owners and their deli is a thriving enterprise selling cheese, wine, charcuterie and the like, but you can also stick around and tuck into carefully crafted dishes on the premises. It's open for breakfast with the likes of organic porridge or sausage bap, and then moves on to sandwiches (hand-picked Brixham crab), deli platters and hot stuff like garlicky Exe mussels in cream and wine or a burger topped with smoked bacon. Wine starts at £11. Open daytime all week.

Chagford

★ TOP 50 ★

Gidleigh Park
Seductive Dartmoor setting
Chagford, TQ13 8HH
Tel no: (01647) 432367
www.gidleigh.com
Modern European | £115
Cooking score: 7

🍷 🚗 V

Gidleigh sits on its Dartmoor hillside, almost as aloof from the common thoroughfare as it is from the village of Chagford. A pot-holed road leads to the sublimely remote house. Within you'll find panelled period rooms, the Arts and Crafts mannerisms worked up for an Australian shipping potentate in the 1920s. The dining rooms can take on a little of the ponderous beatitude of the Rare Books Room at the British Library when partially full – so, Michael Caines' cooking comes as a dynamic surprise. There are some unusual combinations, if unusualism is your bag, but nothing to cause the wrong kind of palpitation. A warm pigeon salad with apple and caramelised hazelnuts comes with a lobe of roasted foie gras, as a possible prelude to Cornish sea bass roasted in anise, with lobster tortellini and bouillabaisse sauce, or local venison with a chaperone of braised pork belly, red cabbage and twin purées of figs and chestnuts. Improbable connections can do their bit at dessert, when banana parfait works well with lime and butterscotch, but it's hard to resist the more classical approach – orange and Grand Marnier soufflé with orange sorbet. The august wine list, replete with names to conjure with, from Burgundy's Côte de Nuits to the Judean Hills of Israel, at least has the air of true discernment rather than lazy profiteering, and there are plenty by the glass, from £8 (bottles from £20).
Chef/s: Michael Caines MBE. Open: all week L 12 to 2.30, D 7 to 9.30. Meals: Set L £44 (2 courses) to £57. Set D £115. Details: 50 seats. Separate bar. Wheelchair access. Car parking. Children over 8 yrs only.

▌Clyst Hydon

NEW ENTRY
The Five Bells Inn
Well-executed dishes in a thatched village pub
Main Street, Clyst Hydon, EX15 2NT
Tel no: (01884) 277288
www.fivebells.uk.com
British | £30
Cooking score: 1

Under the same ownership as the Jack in the
Green in Rockbeare, the Five Bells is
considerably harder to find, skulking on a
bend in a hair-raisingly narrow road. It's a
thatched village pub of obvious charm, much
devoted to dining but with a pool room too.
The kitchen turns out well-executed dishes
such as chicken rillettes with leek in sage
dressing, deeply flavoured cauliflower cheese
soup, accurately rendered mushroom risotto
and rump steaks with beef-dripping chips and
peppercorn sauce. Sundays bring traditional
roasts and perhaps a thunderously
cinnamoned apple and rhubarb crumble. A
short card of wines from Christopher Piper
(starting at £13.50) suffices.
Chef/s: Ian Webber. **Open:** Mon to Sat L 12 to 2
(2.30 Sat), D 6 to 9. Sun 12 to 9. **Meals:** alc (main
courses £11 to £18). Mon to Fri Set L £15 (2 courses).
Sun L £19 (2 courses) to £23. **Details:** 70 seats.
Separate bar. Wheelchair access. Music. Car
parking.

▌Dartmouth
Rockfish Seafood and Chips
Proper seaside fish and chips
8 South Embankment, Dartmouth, TQ6 9BH
Tel no: (01803) 832800
www.rockfishdevon.co.uk
Seafood | £25
Cooking score: 1
£30

Mitch Tonks' winning combination of
simplicity and sustainability makes this a
seafood haven. The décor is nautically themed,
there's a 'really lovely atmosphere here, relaxed
and informal yet efficient', and the kitchen
delivers 'some of the best fish and chips I've
had'. But look out, too, for smoked fish
chowder, crisp, fried salt-and-pepper shellfish
platters (soft-shell crab, squid, oysters,
prawns), as well as dressed crab, grilled plaice
and New England garlic shrimp rolls. Sides
include mushy peas, and jalapeño tartare
sauce; desserts take in chocolate brownie and
Knickerbocker glory. Look out for the
restaurant's own rosé cider. Wines
from £16.95.
Chef/s: Kirk Gosden. **Open:** all week 12 to 9.
Meals: alc (main courses £8 to £17). **Details:** 60
seats. Wheelchair access. Music.

The Seahorse
Enlightened seafood eatery
5 South Embankment, Dartmouth, TQ6 9BH
Tel no: (01803) 835147
www.seahorserestaurant.co.uk
Seafood | £40
Cooking score: 5
🍷 V

Pitched centre stage on Dartmouth's riverside
Embankment, this enlightened eatery quickly
wins friends with its daily supplies of ozone-
fresh seafood, zingy cooking and
exceptionally friendly, 'eagle-eyed' staff. The
dining room, kitted out in easy-going style,
features lofty ceilings, banquettes and Art
Deco lamps, but all eyes are on the open
kitchen. This delivers everything from raw sea

bass simply dressed with new season's olive oil and lemon, or fritto misto with 'wonderfully pungent' aïoli, to whole Dover sole or monkfish sizzling from the charcoal oven. The sunny Mediterranean accent is unmistakable, but the kitchen can also rustle up 'stunning' roast beef for Sunday lunch. No wonder chef/proprietor and seafood guru Mitch Tonks is being tipped as the heir apparent to Rick Stein's crown in the West Country. The keenly priced 'locals' menu is a bargain, and it's also worth perusing the day's selection of wines by the glass or carafe. Otherwise, the bullish Old World list bristles with imaginative stuff from artisan producers; bottles from £19.
Chef/s: Mitch Tonks and Mat Prowse. **Open:** Wed to Sun L 12 to 2.30, Tue to Sat D 6 to 9.30. **Closed:** Mon, 1 week Christmas. **Meals:** alc (main courses £18 to £32). Set L and early D £20 (2 courses). **Details:** 40 seats. 4 seats outside.

Dittisham
Anchorstone Café
Seafood lovers' paradise
Manor Street, Dittisham, TQ6 0EX
Tel no: (01803) 722365
www.anchorstonecafe.co.uk
Seafood | £23
Cooking score: 3
£30

Even 'a bag of crisps' would be gastronomic heaven in these environs, coos one visitor to the Anchorstone Café on the banks of the River Dart. Whether you're outside on the terrace or inside the 'basic', 'brightly painted clapperboard café', the setting calls for local seafood 'cooked without fuss'. Clare Harvey provides exactly that, specialising in shellfish and day-boat fish from fishermen with whom she's on first-name terms. Look to the blackboard for the specials: everybody else does. A 'deliciously sweet spider crab big enough to serve a party of four' is hard to beat, but bouillabaisse, char-grilled monkfish with fresh herbs and steamed mussels with fries aren't far behind. Dependable versions of cod and chips, prawn cocktail and ploughman's lunch appear on the regular menu. Though it's

open summertime only, and hard to reach (boat is best), the café's fans promise it's worth the effort. House wine, £16.
Chef/s: Clare Harvey and Jasmine Harvey. **Open:** Wed to Sun 12 to 4. **Closed:** Nov to Mar. **Meals:** alc (main courses £9 to £13). **Details:** 28 seats. 50 seats outside. Wheelchair access.

Drewsteignton
The Old Inn
Exclusive little restaurant-with-rooms
Drewsteignton, EX6 6QR
Tel no: (01647) 281276
www.old-inn.co.uk
Modern European | £46
Cooking score: 3

The whitewashed 17th-century inn is shoehorned in amid the hair-raisingly narrow streets of a pint-sized Dartmoor village: just the sort of location that Devon does best. Two retrievers may lollop over to greet you, and the welcome matches the warmth of the snug sitting room on winter evenings. A pair of small dining rooms provide the setting for the concise well-rounded menus of Duncan Walker. Every dish seems to have earned its place. One couple who have become happy regulars write to applaud starters of duck breast with a croquette, foie gras and pea purée, and saffron-fragrant lobster risotto, while memorable mains have included lamb three ways (including a dinky shepherd's pie and boulangère potatoes), as well as loin and confit leg of rabbit with veal sweetbreads. At the finishing line comes chocolate pithiviers with cherries and crème fraîche ice cream. Wines start at £22, or £6.60 a glass.
Chef/s: Duncan Walker. **Open:** Fri and Sat L 12 to 2, Wed to Sat D 7 to 10. **Closed:** Sun, Mon, Tue. **Meals:** Set L and D £41 (2 courses) to £46. **Details:** 17 seats. Children over 12 yrs only.

▌Exeter

The Magdalen Chapter
Sturdy bourgeois nourishment and cheeky riffs
Magdalen Street, Exeter, EX2 4HY
Tel no: (01392) 281000
www.themagdalenchapter.com
Modern British | £27
Cooking score: 3

£5 OFF 🍴 £30

Exeter's Victorian eye hospital has been lavishly transformed into a snazzy boutique hotel complete with a spa and this eye-catching restaurant. The glass-fronted dining room takes the form of a huge 'marquee' with fanned-out, arched ceiling and a central tent-pole, plus dramatic dangling lights, an open theatre kitchen and French windows leading to a walled garden. TV chef/author Simon Hopkinson acts as culinary consultant, so expect clear flavours, rock-solid technique and sturdy bourgeois nourishment with creative riffs. Meze plates, steaks and roast cod with chips sit alongside rare tuna dressed with orange, chilli and capers or slow-cooked pork belly with leeks, white beans and morcilla. Desserts proffer comfort in the guise of Swedish apple cake or peanut-butter parfait with chocolate mousse and caramel sauce. The wine list, presented on an iPad, holds plenty to enjoy – especially if you fancy drinking by the glass or 500ml pichet. Bottles from £17.50.
Chef/s: Ben Bulger. **Open:** all week L 12 to 2.30 (12.30 to 3 Sun), D 6 to 10 (9.30 Sun). **Meals:** alc (main courses £10 to £26). Set L and D £14 (2 courses) to £17. Sun L £20. **Details:** 75 seats. 30 seats outside. Separate bar. Wheelchair access. Music. Car parking.

Michael Caines at ABode Exeter
A polished set-up
Royal Clarence Hotel, Cathedral Yard, Exeter, EX1 1HD
Tel no: (01392) 223638
www.abodeexeter.co.uk
Modern European | £39
Cooking score: 5

£5 OFF 🍴

Facing the green and the soaring Gothic west façade of the cathedral, the Exeter branch of ABode is housed in the Royal Clarence Hotel. It's a spacious, mirrored room done in cream, grey and natural wood, and run with much-appreciated professional aplomb. There has been frequent change in the kitchens in recent years, but with Nick Topham's arrival comes a sense of stability. Local materials feature prominently, as they always have, with confit cod and Brixham crab taking starring roles in a starter incorporating lemon-dressed chorizo salad. Creedy Carver duck turns up at main in five-spice jus, with braised turnips, cabbage and roast garlic. Skate wing in cumin velouté with romanesco is a fish possibility, while a vegetarian pasta dish like spinach and Parmesan agnolotti with chestnut purée and rosemary cream lacks nothing in savoury richness. Finish with apple tart and cider ice cream. A varietally arranged wine list opens at £22.50.
Chef/s: Nick Topham. **Open:** Mon to Sat L 12 to 2.30, D 6 to 10. **Closed:** Sun. **Meals:** alc (main courses £10 to £27). Set L £15 (2 courses) to £20. Set D £17 (2 courses) to £23. **Details:** 65 seats. Separate bar. Wheelchair access. Music.

▌Exmouth

Les Saveurs at the Seafood Restaurant

A neighbourhood bistro making a splash
9 Tower Street, Exmouth, EX8 1NT
Tel no: (01395) 269459
www.lessaveurs.co.uk
French | £32
Cooking score: 2

The Guyard-Mulkerrins have made quite a splash in Exmouth with their homely neighbourhood restaurant along a little backstreet. The crowds pour in for menus that ingeniously combine classic French seafood cookery with familiar modern British flourishes. There's an agreeable bistro feel to the premises, and a world of satisfaction to be had from well-made classic fish soup with heaps of grated Emmental and spicy rouille, or from local mussels done more or less marinière. Main-course fish is soundly cooked, as in gilthead bream on chive mash with sauce armoricaine, or the heady cosmopolitanism of Bombay potatoes and Egyptian curry that comes with locally landed cod. You'll find plenty of meat dishes, too, such as duck breast or lamb rump, mostly served with dauphinois, and good French bistro finishers like apricot clafoutis with mascarpone, or oeufs à la neige in Baileys. The French wines open with house Ardèche at £18.
Chef/s: Olivier Guyard-Mulkerrin. **Open:** Tue to Sat D only 7 to 10.30 (6.30 Fri and Sat). **Closed:** Sun, Mon, Jan. **Meals:** alc (main courses £17 to £25). **Details:** 54 seats. Separate bar. Music. Children over 10 yrs only.

▌Gittisham

Combe House

Seductive hotel with seriously good dining
Gittisham, EX14 3AD
Tel no: (01404) 540400
www.combehousedevon.com
Modern British | £54
Cooking score: 5

🛏 V

The splendid Elizabethan manor house near Honiton stands in 3,500 panoramic acres of east Devon – a view the dining-room windows don't stint on. Hadleigh Barrett has Combe's own hens' eggs and organic fruit and veg at his disposal, with fish from Lyme Bay and pedigree local meats. But he looks further afield for culinary inspiration, to Morocco for a starter of spiced quail with salted lemon couscous, sweet potato purée and almonds. Brill may be ornately coated in foie gras, alongside roasted artichokes and girolles in Madeira sauce, or there may be roast loin and suet pudding of lamb with crushed roots and Savoy. Form an orderly queue for chocolate and peanut délice with salted caramel and chocolate sorbet, or take a West Country cheese tour. A tiny, painstakingly chosen list of outstanding wines is a model of informative concision that will change seasonally, starting at around £25.
Chef/s: Hadleigh Barrett. **Open:** all week L 12 to 2, D 7 to 9.30. **Closed:** 2 weeks Jan. **Meals:** Set L £29 (2 courses) to £36. Set D £54. Sun L £39. **Details:** 75 seats. Separate bar. Wheelchair access. Music. Car parking.

Gulworthy
The Horn of Plenty
Ravishing views and confident cooking
Gulworthy, PL19 8JD
Tel no: (01822) 832528
www.thehornofplenty.co.uk
Modern British | £50
Cooking score: 4

🛏

A soul-soothing cornucopia for anyone hankering after the earthly delights of civilised country living, this aptly named Devon retreat seems to have everything. It is set in five acres of gardens and orchards, with ravishing views over the Tamar Valley and easy access to Dartmoor. Guests are courted with crackling log fires, plump furnishings, elegant comforts and the promise of confident modern cooking. Ingredients from far and wide come together on a monthly changing menu that might open with a pressing of rabbit, Ibérico ham and white asparagus, or beetroot mousse with goats' cheese and gingerbread. Next could come something more classically inclined: perhaps poached and grilled duck breast matched with chicory and orange, or skate wing in brown butter with caper and raisin purée. To finish, there's an updated version of peach Melba – or you might prefer the pleasures of banana parfait with lime and peanuts. A well-spread wine list starts at £19.50.
Chef/s: Scott Paton. **Open:** all week L 12 to 2, D 7 to 8.45. **Meals:** Set L £20 (2 courses) to £25. Set D £50. Sun L £20 (2 courses) to £25. Tasting menu £65 (7 courses). **Details:** 40 seats. 20 seats outside. Wheelchair access. Music. Car parking.

Symbols

🛏 Accommodation is available

£30 Three courses for less than £30

V Separate vegetarian menu

£5 £5-off voucher scheme
OFF

🍷 Notable wine list

Honiton
The Holt
Honest pub food
178 High Street, Honiton, EX14 1LA
Tel no: (01404) 47707
www.theholt-honiton.com
Modern British | £26
Cooking score: 1

£30

There are Otter ales on draught at the bar of this waterside pub, and maybe even a glimpse of the real thing in the River Gissage if you're (very) lucky. Brothers Joe and Angus McCaig run the place with an industrious enthusiasm, laying on quarterly music events, cookery classes and a menu packed with carefully sourced regional ingredients. Their own smokehouse turns out the chicken served in a pie with mushroom and tarragon, while there's an Asian spin to grilled sea bream with crisp squid and a sauce of soy, ginger and lime. The bar menu includes tapas options. Wines from £16.50.
Chef/s: Angus McCaig. **Open:** Tue to Sat L 12 to 2, D 6.30 to 9 (9.30 Fri and Sat). **Closed:** Sun, Mon, 25 and 26 Dec, 1 Jan. **Meals:** alc (main courses £13 to £17). **Details:** 60 seats. Separate bar. Wheelchair access. Music.

Kings Nympton
The Grove Inn
Proper country inn with local food
Kings Nympton, EX37 9ST
Tel no: (01769) 580406
www.thegroveinn.co.uk
British | £21
Cooking score: 2

£5 🛏 V £30
OFF

A 17th-century thatched inn in a peaceful north Devon village, the Grove has all the requisite trimmings inside. The ceilings are beamed, the walls of roughcast stone. There are two big fireplaces, and a portrait gallery of Devon notables from yesteryear to now. It isn't hard to see why Robert and Deborah Smallbone forsook London in 2003 to open here. 'The Grove is still not haunted,' they confess, rather tempting providence, but it does boast hearty, regionally sourced superior pub food such as cider-braised pig cheeks with broad beans, pollack with mashed potato in herb sauce, beef Wellington and fish pie, together with a list of international specials. Tempting puddings include blood-orange burnt cream, and treacle tart with clotted cream. Sunday lunch is a reliable local draw, bringing the pick of local meats like crackled pork and beef topside. A concise, well-chosen drinks list opens with Portuguese house wines from Esporão at £15.

Chef/s: Deborah and Robert Smallbone. **Open:** Tue to Sun L 12 to 2 (3 Sun), Tue to Sat D 6.45 to 9. **Closed:** Mon. **Meals:** alc (main courses £8 to £18). Sun L £10. **Details:** 28 seats. 12 seats outside. Separate bar. Wheelchair access.

Kingsbridge

LOCAL GEM
▲ Beachhouse

South Milton Sands, Kingsbridge, TQ7 3JY
Tel no: (01548) 561144
www.beachhousedevon.com
Seafood | £35 £5 OFF

'A tiny place with a big reputation,' noted one reporter of this accommodating all-day eatery on South Milton Sands. Beautiful views help, but everyone comes for the food, whether early birds arriving for breakfast, the local lunch brigade or friends looking for supper. The kitchen delivers perfect renditions of mussels with chips, herby crab salad, and crispy squid, but look out, too, for beef burgers, wild mushroom linguine, 'beautiful' chocolate brownies and Salcombe Dairy ice cream. Wines from £16.50. Open all week (check D opening out of school hols).

Knowstone

The Masons Arms

Fine dining in a village pub
Knowstone, EX36 4RY
Tel no: (01398) 341231
www.masonsarmsdevon.co.uk
Modern British | £42
Cooking score: 5

A charming Exmoor village of ancient cottages, Knowstone looks superficially as if the rest of the world has passed it by for at least 200 years. At its heart is this thriving, thatched pub with a cosy bar and separate dining room. In the bar the open fire, simple furniture and local ales keep up traditional appearances; the restaurant, with its 'eccentric pastoral fantasy' ceiling, is more formal. Raw, often local materials, are spot-on and Mark Dodson's concise menus deal with some complex combinations – monkfish wrapped in prosciutto, served with a salmon mousse sausage and a fennel and cider cream sauce, for example – with satisfying results. Seared peppered tuna with oriental salad has made an excellent first course, followed by 'perfectly cooked' brill in a potato crust. Homemade bread and petits fours have delighted, too, but there have been niggles about the 'unschooled' service. Wines from £15.50.

Chef/s: Mark Dodson. **Open:** Tue to Sun L 12 to 2, Tue to Sat D 7 to 9. **Closed:** Mon, first week Jan, Feb half term, last week Aug. **Meals:** alc (main courses £19 to £25). Set L £20 (2 courses) to £25. Sun L £37. **Details:** 32 seats. 16 seats outside. Separate bar. Music. Car parking. Children over 5 yrs only at D.

Lewdown

The Harris Arms

Robust country cooking
Portgate, Lewdown, EX20 4PZ
Tel no: (01566) 783331
www.theharrisarms.co.uk
Modern British | £25
Cooking score: 2
£5 OFF £30

Homely and traditional, the Harris Arms has not forsaken its pub roots – expect log fires in winter and drinks on the decked back terrace on sunny days. Countryside rolls out across the valley, the views from the dining room are stunning (it is all very peaceful) and the emphasis is on good food. The menu takes its cue from local, seasonal ingredients and offers pub classics such as home-cooked ham, egg and chips or local sausages with mash and onion gravy alongside twice-baked goats' cheese soufflé and 24-hour slow-roasted pork with cider sauce, as well as seasonal fish and game listed on the specials board. Wonderful warm treacle sponge pudding with butterscotch sauce and ice cream stands out among straightforward comfort desserts, and there are West Country cheeses, too. Real ales are on draught and a thoroughly accessible wine list opens at £15.
Chef/s: Andy Whiteman. **Open:** Tue to Sun L 12 to 2, Tue to Sat D 6.30 to 9. **Closed:** Mon, 24 to 26 Dec, 1 Jan. **Meals:** alc (main courses £11 to £19). Sun L £16 (2 courses) to £19. **Details:** 60 seats. 30 seats outside. Separate bar. Car parking.

Lewtrenchard Manor

Personable charm and fine seasonal food
Lewdown, EX20 4PN
Tel no: (01566) 783222
www.lewtrenchard.co.uk
Modern British | £50
Cooking score: 5
V

James and Sue Murray owned Lewtrenchard up to 2003, sold it, but missed it achingly enough to buy it back. And long may they

reign. This former Devon long house was reinvented in the Victorian era as a Jacobean manor by the Revd Sabine Baring-Gould, hymnist. Weathered oak panelling decorates the lounge and the mullioned dining room where family portraits in oils stare affably down. Matthew Peryer arrived in 2013 from the Atlantic Hotel, Jersey (see entry), and has committed himself firmly to Devon localism. A first course of citrus-marinated salmon with crabmeat, radish, wasabi mayonnaise and toasted sesame seeds shows a keen understanding of flavour balancing, while mains might bring on rump and sweetbread of lamb with garlicky spinach purée and morels. Desserts could do with more uplift, but mango parfait with coconut sorbet and pineapple satisfies. A leather-bound wine list (from £25) has been chosen with classical quality in mind.
Chef/s: Matthew Peryer. **Open:** all week L 12 to 2, D 7 to 9. **Meals:** Set L £20 (2 courses) to £24. Set D £50. Sun L £25. **Details:** 50 seats. 15 seats outside. Separate bar. Wheelchair access. Car parking. Children over 8 yrs only at D.

Lifton

The Arundell Arms

Civilised sporting retreat
Fore Street, Lifton, PL16 0AA
Tel no: (01566) 784666
www.arundellarms.com
Modern British | £45
Cooking score: 4
£5 OFF V

Master of all it surveys, the Arundell was named in honour of a noted family of Cornish Royalists, and has stood in its present form since not long after the Civil War. A stone-built village inn and more, it's at the heart of the local country sports set, with a plush lounge and bar, and a chandeliered dining room furnished in panels of unassuming taupe. Steven Pidgeon naturally capitalises on the local seasonal game and produce, and cooks a menu that makes wholehearted sense, without falling over itself to be cutting edge. Gently braised, pillowy pig cheeks with

pancetta in forthright cider jus might be followed by a fillet of crisply grilled sea bass, attended by an honour guard of scallops in saffron cream sauce with diced tomato, and then exotically scented rose-water pannacotta with warm confit pineapple and golden syrup ice cream. Wines, mostly from Piper's of Ottery, start at £19.50 (£4.90 a glass).
Chef/s: Steven Pidgeon. **Open:** all week L 12 to 2, D 6 to 10. **Meals:** Set L £20 (2 courses) to £27. Set D £42 (2 courses) to £47. Sun L £23. **Details:** 80 seats. 30 seats outside. Separate bar. Wheelchair access. Music. Car parking.

▌ Newton Poppleford

Moores'
Ticking all the right boxes
6 Greenbank, High Street, Newton Poppleford, EX10 0EB
Tel no: (01395) 568100
www.mooresrestaurant.co.uk
Modern British | £23
Cooking score: 1

£5 OFF 🛏 £30

There's evident passion for the county's produce on the menu at this restaurant-with-rooms run with hands-on dedication by Jonathan and Kate Moore. It's a homely sort of place, devoid of any affectation, where the seasonal menus are the star of the show. Wild boar and Armagnac terrine might precede turbot with sea salt-baked potatoes and River Exe mussels, or a Devonshire fillet steak with root vegetable rösti. Ace West Country cheeses could conclude a meal, or desserts such as ginger, lemon and treacle tart. Outside tables in the garden are a summertime hit. Wines from £13.95.
Chef/s: Jonathan Moore. **Open:** Tue to Sun L 12 to 1.30, Tue to Sat D 7 to 9.30. **Closed:** Mon, first 2 weeks Jan. **Meals:** Set L £17 (2 courses) to £23. Set D £20 (2 courses) to £26. Sun L £17. **Details:** 32 seats. 12 seats outside. Wheelchair access. Music.

▌ Plymouth

Rock Salt
Accommodating all-day eatery
31 Stonehouse Street, Plymouth, PL1 3PE
Tel no: (01752) 225522
www.rocksaltcafe.co.uk
Modern British | £26
Cooking score: 2

£30

David and Steven Jenkins did Plymouth foodies a big favour when they took over the old Mechanics Arms and turned it into Rock Salt. This accommodating all-day eatery serves the needs of early birds, local lunchers, tea fanciers and everyone else looking for 'consistently excellent food and great value' in a rather insalubrious quarter of town. 'Parking is a nightmare', notes one fan, although few care when the kitchen delivers impeccable renditions of Salcombe crab bisque with nutmeg cream, burgers with tomato and chorizo chutney or Brentor venison with slow-braised ox cheek, red-cabbage ketchup and Jerusalem artichokes. David has a penchant for oriental flavours, so don't be surprised to find hand-dived scallops tempura, Creedy Carver duck confit with shrimp noodles and Asian salad, or pandanus pannacotta with mango, passion fruit and honeycomb on the dinner menu. To drink: cold juices, hot chocolate, Thatchers cider, Spanish Mahou beer and wines from £13.95.
Chef/s: David Jenkins. **Open:** all week 10 to 4 (9am Wed to Fri, 8am Sat), D 5 to 10. **Closed:** 24 to 26 Dec, 1 to 8 Jan. **Meals:** alc (main courses £9 to £22). **Details:** 60 seats. Music.

🍴 Average Price
The average price listed in main-entry reviews denotes the price of a three-course meal, without wine.

Tanners

Contemporary cooking in an ancient setting
Prysten House, Finewell Street, Plymouth,
PL1 2AE
Tel no: (01752) 252001
www.tannersrestaurant.co.uk
Modern British | £42
Cooking score: 3

A 'certain atmosphere' pervades Grade I-listed
Prysten House, which dates from 1490 and has
the features, including an imposing courtyard,
to prove it. The place has been 'well adapted for
fine dining' by brothers Chris and James
Tanner. Along with chef Martyn Compton,
they produce outward-looking, 'well-
handled' modern British dishes within
medieval walls. Hand-picked Devon crab
with salsa verde, pickled turnip, rye bread and
caviar combines home and away in pleasing
style, while lemon sole is seared and served
with mussels from the Fowey, fennel pollen
and heritage potatoes – strange to think that
the early residents of Prysten House may have
looked at these askance. Texture-conscious
puddings might be buttermilk pannacotta
with roast pineapple and granola or Valrhona
chocolate pavé with banana ice cream and
salted-peanut and oat crumble. Wine is from
£18.95, with a generous selection (including a
Sharpham white from Totnes) by the glass
from £3.25.
Chef/s: Martyn Compton, Chris and James Tanner.
Open: Tue to Sat L 12 to 2, D 6.45 to 9 (9.30 Fri and
Sat). **Closed:** Sun, Mon, 24 to 31 Dec, first week Jan.
Meals: alc (main courses £19 to £25). Set L £14 (2
courses) to £17. Set D £17 (2 courses) to £20. Tasting
menu £55. **Details:** 60 seats. 50 seats outside.
Wheelchair access. Music.

Symbols

🛏 Accommodation is available

£30 Three courses for less than £30

V Separate vegetarian menu

£5 OFF £5-off voucher scheme

🍾 Notable wine list

▲ Lemon Tree Café & Bistro
2 Haye Road South, Elburton, Plymouth, PL9 8HJ
Tel no: (01752) 481117
www.lemontreecafe.co.uk
Modern European | £25

On Plymouth's outskirts, the Lemon Tree is a
neighbourhood venue popular for its
unhurried ambience and big-flavoured bistro
food. Private parties of ten or more can order
an appetising Spanish/Moroccan meze spread
(£25 a head), but blackboard specials form the
mainstay, such as split-pea soup with spiced
butter; pork with borlotti beans, sweet potato
and crème fraîche with French bread; and rice
pudding with toasted almonds and cranberry
compote. House wines are £13.95. Open Tue
to Sat L, evenings for private parties of 10 or
more.

▌Salcombe
South Sands Beachside Restaurant
Local seafood beside the seaside
Bolt Head, Salcombe, TQ8 8LL
Tel no: (01548) 845900
www.southsands.com
Seafood | £35
Cooking score: 2
🛏

It's a glorious spot when the weather is benign
(let's not talk about the winter of 2013/14),
with the restaurant opening on to a terrace and
shimmering blue waters. This beachside hotel
has boutique credentials, a New England
finish that maximises the 'beside the seaside'
vibe, and a menu that looks to the sea for
inspiration. The kitchen team in the sunny
Beachside Restaurant give local ingredients a
bit of an international spin, so you might kick
off with salt-and-pepper cuttlefish with
saffron aïoli and move on to River Exe mussels
marinière-style. Find a willing accomplice
and Start Bay wild black bream awaits (served
whole with chorizo jam). There's also a meaty
route through the menu with black pudding

Scotch egg followed by ribeye cooked on the bone. The bar has cocktails to go with the sea views and there's a children's menu too. Wines start at £21.

Chef/s: Darren Swales. **Open:** all week L 12 to 2.30 (3 Sat and Sun), D 6.30 to 9 (9.30 Sat). **Meals:** alc (main courses £15 to £48). **Details:** 75 seats. 35 seats outside. Separate bar. Wheelchair access. Music. Car parking.

Shaldon
Ode Dining
Dazzling combinations from an organic champion
21 Fore Street, Shaldon, TQ14 ODE
Tel no: (01626) 873977
www.odetruefood.co.uk
Modern British | £40
Cooking score: 5

A pretty three-storey Georgian town house in a quaint fishing village, Ode makes the most of the wonderful produce available from the nearby coast and countryside. Chef/proprietor Tim Bouget, a longtime advocate of organic, sustainable principles, produces food 'whose excellence is matched by the ethical principles that underlie it'. His eclectic, modern style pulls in influences from places as diverse as Japan, America and Italy. Sugar-cured duck breast with a salad of pickled turnip and poached pear is a good way to start. Next, the decent showing of fish dishes could include seared Brixham haddock with local brown crab, purple sprouting broccoli, crushed potatoes and red pepper chowder. There's plenty of textural contrast here, as in a dessert of organic clementine iced parfait with clove and candied orange-leather and honeycomb. The wine list has an organic and biodynamic focus, and offers plenty for under £30. Bottles start at £18.

Chef/s: Tim Bouget. **Open:** Wed to Sat D only 7 to 9.30. **Closed:** Sun, Mon, Tue, Christmas, 2 weeks Oct. **Meals:** Set D £35 (2 courses) to £40. **Details:** 24 seats. Music. Children over 8 yrs only.

Sidford
The Salty Monk
Industrious cooking and personal hospitality
Church Street, Sidford, EX10 9QP
Tel no: (01395) 513174
www.saltymonk.co.uk
Modern British | £45
Cooking score: 3
£5 OFF 🍽 V

In the 16th century, the premises were a salt-store for Benedictine monks who traded in that precious medieval commodity at Exeter cathedral. A little way up from the east Devon coast, the Salty Monk is the focal point of bustling village life, offering guest rooms and work by local artists – as well as Andy Witheridge's modern English menus. Things are kept simple at lunchtime, but the full-dress dining room plays host in the evenings to the likes of goats' cheese pannacotta in lentil relish, or pheasant tartlet with cranberry coulis, and then griddled sirloin and ravolied shin of local beef on herbed tagliatelle with celeriac purée, or a marine chorus line of salmon, brill and scallops on ink linguine in saffron-scented white wine sauce. Desserts aim to linger in the memory, with chocolate and pecan tart and salty caramel ice cream, or marmalade pudding with warm orange jelly and clotted cream. Wines from around £17.

Chef/s: Andy Witheridge. **Open:** Thur to Sun L 12 to 1.30, all week D 6.30 to 9.30. **Closed:** Jan, 2 weeks Nov. **Meals:** Set L £25 (2 courses) to £30. Set D £40 (2 courses) to £45. Sun L £25. **Details:** 36 seats. 18 seats outside. Separate bar. Wheelchair access. Music. Car parking.

ANTON PIOTROWSKI
The Treby Arms

What do you enjoy about being a chef?
I love using all local/new produce to create my ever-changing menu, from growing my own veg in my allotment to stalking my own venison.

What would you be if you weren't a chef?
A paramedic! Completely different!

What is your favourite time of year for food?
Spring time, a new year has started as soon as I smell wild garlic in the hedgerows, it's an exciting time for chefs.

What's your newest ingredient discovery?
Yoghurt acid – a yoghurt-based powder that brings acidity/balance to a dish.

What food could you not live without?
Salt and pepper. Season, season, season!

What is your signature dish?
Pigeon wellington, cep purée, morels and English asparagus.

Do you have a guilty foodie pleasure?
Chocolate éclairs – I can eat a whole packet by the time I've got home – and custard creams! I've had to cut back slightly after discovering I am diabetic.

South Pool
The Millbrook Inn
French food in a proper village pub
South Pool, TQ7 2RW
Tel no: (01548) 531581
www.millbrookinnsouthpool.co.uk
French | £36
Cooking score: 2
£5 OFF

A ravishing location on the Salcombe estuary is only the half of it. The Millbrook advertises itself as 'reassuringly pubby', alongside images of the owners and chef clutching feathered game and pigs' heads. Real food is in prospect then, and Jean-Philippe Bidart has remodelled the culinary side of the operation after the fashion of a French auberge, with local sourcing to the fore and a shed selling fresh produce. A meal can be as hearteningly simple as crab bisque followed by bouillabaisse, alike garnished with Gruyère croûtons, but there is innovation in evidence too, seen in a main dish of haunch, rump and fillet of roe deer with braised red cabbage, smoked bacon, Reblochon and onion tartiflette, and juniper sauce. Veggies might approve of pearl barley risotto with a poached duck egg, and then there's chocolate bombe, filled with a suitably ballistic mixture of popping candy and cherry ice cream. Wines from £16.95.
Chef/s: Jean-Philippe Bidart. **Open:** all week L 12 to 2 (3 Sun), D 6 to 9. **Meals:** Set L £10 (2 courses) to £12. Sun L £16. **Details:** 40 seats. 40 seats outside. Wheelchair access.

▌Sparkwell

★ TOP 10 PUB ★

The Treby Arms
It doesn't get much better...
Sparkwell, PL7 5DD
Tel no: (01752) 837363
www.thetrebyarms.co.uk
Modern British | £35
Cooking score: 5

The Piotrowskis' unassuming village inn ticks all the right boxes – stone floors, well-worn tables, crackling winter fire – combining the dual roles of local hostelry and upmarket eatery with agility. Anton's food works as an up-to-the-minute showcase for top-notch local and regional produce. His menu strikes many alluring modern British chords, whether it's crackling coated eel, smoked eel mousse blackened with charcoal, olive crumble and radish soaked in gin and tonic ('an absolutely astonishing riot of tastes and textures') or tender scallops beautifully matched with bacon-wrapped loin of hare and complemented by braised lettuce and a parsley root purée. Elsewhere, sirloin of beef appears with haggis bonbons, chestnut mushrooms, kale and pancetta, while recent crowd-pleasing finales have included 'Treby's gone carrots': carrot cake in a small plant pot with a carrot top sticking out, served with orange sorbet. The mainly West Country cheese selection is a boon, too. Wines from £16.50.
Chef/s: Anton Piotrowski. **Open:** Tue to Thur L 12 to 3, D 6 to 11. Fri to Sun 12 to 11 (10.30 Sun). **Closed:** Mon, 25 and 26 Dec, 1 Jan. **Meals:** alc (main courses £14 to £26). Set L £20. Sun L £25. **Details:** 65 seats. 15 seats outside. Separate bar. Wheelchair access. Music. Car parking.

▌Topsham

La Petite Maison
Engaging 'auberge' with assured cooking
35 Fore Street, Topsham, EX3 0HR
Tel no: (01392) 873660
www.lapetitemaison.co.uk
Modern European | £32
Cooking score: 4
£5 OFF

The 'little house' is just that: a pint-sized property in a charming former port town on the Exe estuary, showing its age architecturally with higgledy-piggledy rooms that have been stylishly spruced up in modern monochrome style. It's a warmly hospitable place, thanks to Elizabeth Pestell's capable front-of-house ministrations. Douglas takes care of business out back, transforming pedigree Devon produce into sleekly executed dishes that balance modernity with traditional French and Italian modes. First out of the blocks might be a lasagne of crab and scallops in old-school white wine beurre blanc, followed hard on its heels by roast chump and confit shoulder of lamb with boulangère potatoes, baby carrots and asparagus in rosemary jus, or perhaps fillet of brill with vegetable 'spaghetti' and a potato and spinach cake in a buttery, dill-fragranced sauce. Finish with pear Tatin, served with butterscotch sauce and vanilla ice cream. Wines on a serviceable list are keenly priced from £18.
Chef/s: Douglas Pestell and Sara Bright. **Open:** all week L 12 to 2.30 (12.30 to 3 Sat and Sun), D 6 to 10.30 (6.30 to 9.30 Sun). **Meals:** Set L and D £33 (2 courses) to £39. **Details:** 28 seats.

Torquay

The Elephant

Torquay's classiest destination
3-4 Beacon Terrace, Torquay, TQ1 2BH
Tel no: (01803) 200044
www.elephantrestaurant.co.uk
Modern British | £70
Cooking score: 5

V

Simon Hulstone's harbourside restaurant continues to keep the Torquay eating scene afloat with a relaxed, welcoming ambience in both the all-year ground-floor Brasserie and the summer-season first-floor Room. It's for the Room menu that we award the rating, the apogee being the eight-course taster menu that embraces prime Devon ingredients, from beetroot with Vulscombe goats' cheese in truffled mustard dressing, to plaice with almond purée in squid ink, and guinea fowl with yin-yang beans, to the closing pair of desserts: strawberry and verbena pannacotta, then apple and soy Tatin. However, you'll also find plenty of stimulating, flavour-first, trimly presented food in the Brasserie, where slow-cooked pig's cheeks with crispy squid, salt-baked celeriac and horseradish cream might be the prelude to duck breast with confit leg pastilla and salsify in clove jus. Finish with glazed plum Bakewell and yoghurt sorbet. Wines start at £19.50 (£4.80 a glass).

Chef/s: Simon Hulstone. **Open:** Brasserie: Tue to Sat L 12 to 2, D 6.30 to 9. Restaurant: Tue to Sat D only 6.30 to 8.30. **Closed:** Brasserie: Sun, Mon, 1 to 21 Jan. Restaurant: Sun, Mon, Oct to Mar. **Meals:** alc (main courses £16 to 24). Set L £15 (2 courses) to £17. Tasting menu £70. **Details:** 84 seats. Separate bar. Wheelchair access. Music. Children in Brasserie only.

Visit us Online

To find out more about
The Good Food Guide, please visit
www.thegoodfoodguide.co.uk

LOCAL GEM

▲ The Orange Tree

14-16 Parkhill Road, Torquay, TQ1 2AL
Tel no: (01803) 213936
www.orangetreerestaurant.co.uk
Modern European | £35

The Wolfs' charming, white-fronted backstreet venue is yards from the harbour, and perfectly fits its Local Gem status. Smartly dressed tables and landscape pictures look the part, but the chatty ambience ensures no starchiness. Bernd Wolf cooks modern English dishes such as fennel- and tarragon-scented crab bisque with seared scallops, honeyed duck breast in rhubarb and ginger jus, and dark chocolate mousse with coconut pannacotta and mango sorbet. Villa Wolf varietals from the Pfalz add interest to the house wine selection (from £17). Open Tue to Sat D.

Totnes

NEW ENTRY

Rumour

A lively, welcoming all-day venue
30 High Street, Totnes, TQ9 5RY
Tel no: (01803) 864682
www.rumourtotnes.com
International | £28
Cooking score: 1

£5 OFF £30 ▼

Not quite under the Eastgate bridge on the High Street, this maroon-fronted wine bar-cum-restaurant has been a Totnes fixture for years. It's a cheerful venue with an interior remodelled in reclaimed timber. Choose from the big blackboard menu. Crespelle filled with wild mushrooms and leeks topped with Taleggio and sage might open a meal of carefully considered cooking, with nicely timed cod fillet on green veg, minted potatoes and pesto to follow. Large sharing pizzas with your choice of toppings are abidingly popular, and there are tempting desserts such as apple and prune crumble tart with honey mascarpone. Good-value wines from £13.55.

Chef/s: Lee Hegerty. **Open:** Mon to Sat L 12 to 3, all week D 6 to 10 (9 Sun). **Closed:** 25 and 26 Dec. **Meals:** alc (main courses £13 to £18). **Details:** 70 seats. Wheelchair access. Music.

▌Virginstow

Percy's

Pedigree ingredients in an alluring setting
Coombeshead Estate, Virginstow, EX21 5EA
Tel no: (01409) 211236
www.percys.co.uk
Modern British | £40
Cooking score: 3

£5 OFF ⇆

The Bricknell-Webbs' west Devon farmstead, conjured out of a dilapidated ruin in the 1990s, makes a wonderfully remote bolt-hole. They run it industriously as a working farm, with fresh produce, livestock and egg-laying hens all pitching in, as well as a cookery school and boutique hotel. A modern lounge area leads into a more obviously ancient cottagey dining room: its white walls hung with food-themed prints, a ginger cat peeping in at the window. Tina Bricknell-Webb cooks a fixed dinner menu of four or five courses, depending on whether you've room for cheese, with pedigree raw materials in the starring role. New season's asparagus bathed in scented béarnaise is outstanding, and might be followed by a serving of crab and smoked salmon on luxuriant saladings, and then pink-cooked Barbary duck breast in an orange and thyme glaze. Strawberry shortcake with vanilla ice cream might close the show. The short wine list opens at £20.
Chef/s: Tina Bricknell-Webb. **Open:** all week D only 7 to 8.30. **Meals:** Set D £40. **Details:** 20 seats. Separate bar. Wheelchair access. Music. Car parking. Children over 10 yrs only.

▌Yelverton

Prince Hall Hotel

Eat the view
Yelverton, PL20 6SA
Tel no: (01822) 890403
www.princehall.co.uk
British | £43
Cooking score: 2

£5 OFF ⇆ V

'We stayed for a weekend and were very pleasantly surprised by the quality of the food at what is otherwise a quiet, remote country house hotel,' recalls a visitor to this 18th-century house in the middle of Dartmoor. Reporters appreciate the comfortable surroundings, the stunning views, the care and attention of the staff ('a happy bunch'), and the cooking, which is perfectly pitched, from 'tasty canapés to the chocolates with coffee'. Local sourcing is a strength. Of particular note is 'fabulous' West Country lamb and the West Country cheeseboard. Scallops teamed with pork belly, the richness offset by pickled apple and a shallot and pancetta velouté, could open a meal, then loin of West Country venison, which arrives with fondant potato, red-wine-braised onions, courgette roulade, butternut squash cream and truffle jus. For dessert, try the 'sublime' hot chocolate fondant. Wines from £20.95.
Chef/s: Richard Greenway. **Open:** all week L 12 to 2.30, D 7 to 8.45. **Meals:** Set L £21 (2 courses) to £27. Set D £37 (2 courses) to £43. Sun L £20 (2 courses) to £23. **Details:** 22 seats. 20 seats outside. Separate bar. Wheelchair access. Car parking.

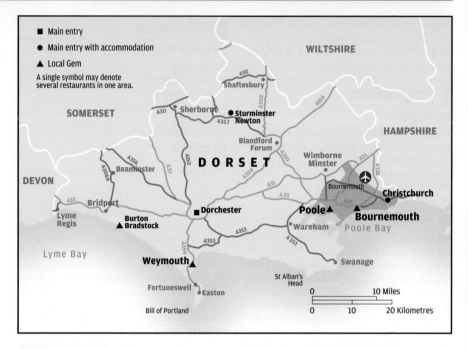

Bournemouth

LOCAL GEM
▲ WestBeach
Pier Approach, Bournemouth, BH2 5AA
Tel no: (01202) 587785
www.west-beach.co.uk
Seafood | £45

When it comes to seaside seafood joints, there aren't many quite as beside the seaside as WestBeach. Right by the sand, a table on the terrace is a thrill on a sunny day, but the place is spruce indoors, too, with a fresh colour scheme of blond wood and brilliant white. The menu isn't entirely of seafood, though salmon ceviche with pickled white radish and soy jelly, and cider-braised plaice, cockles and black trumpet mushrooms are hard to ignore. Wines from £17.50. Open all week.

Burton Bradstock

LOCAL GEM
▲ Hive Beach Café
Beach Road, Burton Bradstock, DT6 4RF
Tel no: (01308) 897070
www.hivebeachcafe.co.uk
Seafood | £15

The Hive Beach Café delivers on the promise of its premise – right by the sea, with views of Lyme Bay and the Jurassic Coast. It's family-friendly (just plain friendly in fact) with a chilled-out vibe and marquee-style awnings to offer some protection if the weather isn't playing ball. Order at the bar and tuck into fresh seafood such as gurnard with roasted scallops and samphire or hot shellfish platter for two. Wines from £15. Open all week for breakfast and L.

▌Christchurch
The Jetty
Slick harbourside restaurant
Christchurch Harbour Hotel & Spa, 95 Mudeford,
Christchurch, BH23 3NT
Tel no: (01202) 400950
www.thejetty.co.uk
Modern British | £35
Cooking score: 4

🛏 V

Alex Aitken's ecologically sound harbourside
venue looks out over the spangling waters
towards Mudeford Quay. It's the sort of place
that's equally magical at sunset as in the glare
of a bright midday. The green philosophy
carries over into the kitchen, where
sustainable fish, foraged items and the produce
of local markets find their way into dishes such
as a ritzy take on macaroni cheese, with lobster
in brandy cream underneath. Sensitively
handled fish and meats follow: turbot is
poached on the bone and attended by prawns,
scallops and herb gnocchi in vermouth sauce;
or there may be three ways with duck (roast
breast, confit leg and 'shepherd's pie') with
greens in port sauce. Or go for both together,
as in veal breast, sweetbreads and prawns, or
hake wrapped in prosciutto. Fig Tatin with
crème fraîche, or chocolate fondant with
banana ice cream, make fitting finales. The
inspiring single-page wine list starts at £17.95.
Chef/s: Alex Aitken. **Open:** Mon to Sat L 12 to 2.30,
D 6 to 10. Sun 12 to 8. **Meals:** alc (main courses £17
to £29). Set L and D £18 (2 courses) to £22. Sun L
£30. **Details:** 80 seats. 40 seats outside. Separate
bar. Wheelchair access. Music. Car parking.

▌Dorchester
Sienna
Tiny restaurant with big ideas
36 High West Street, Dorchester, DT1 1UP
Tel no: (01305) 250022
www.siennarestaurant.co.uk
Modern British | £45
Cooking score: 5
V

The Browns' high-street restaurant is a classic
neighbourhood venue, with nothing showy
or over-elaborate about its pint-sized, red-
banquetted interior. Indeed, the faintly dated
air adds to the charm, especially when Russell
Brown's cooking so obviously punches above
its weight. Elena Brown manages front-of-
house with efficient, friendly aplomb, and it's
clear from the arrival of impressive canapés
that you're in good hands. A fillet of just-
caramelised brill on roasted cauliflower and
spinach with splots of lemon gel is a carefully
considered opener, as is duck liver parfait that
comes with rhubarb both pickled and
marmaladed. At main, there's a world of
straightforward allure in plaice and king
prawns with blanched monk's-beard, crushed
potatoes and tomato salsa, or in roast breast
and confit leg of duck with Puy lentils, roots
and kale. Dessert might be silky chocolate
délice with salted caramel and crème fraîche
ice cream. An appealing list of fairly priced
wines starts at £21.
Chef/s: Russell Brown. **Open:** Wed to Sat L 12.30 to
2, Tue to Sat D 7 to 9. **Closed:** Sun, Mon, 2 weeks
spring, 2 weeks autumn. **Meals:** Set L £26 (2
courses) to £29. Set D £39 (2 courses) to £45.
Tasting menu £65. **Details:** 15 seats. Music. Children
over 12 yrs only.

Poole

LOCAL GEM
▲ Guildhall Tavern
15 Market Street, Poole, BH15 1NB
Tel no: (01202) 671717
www.guildhalltavern.co.uk
French | £35

This staunchly Gallic restaurant continues to pull in locals and visitors to Poole's Old Town after 15 years, such is the draw of chef/owner Frederic Seweryn's traditional French cooking. Booking is advisable for the dining room, where locally caught fish and seafood turn up in tried-and-tested favourites such as scallops in garlic butter followed by pan-fried halibut suprême with Champagne hollandaise. The set-lunch menu is good value at £15 for two courses and £18 for three. Wines from £17.50. Open Tue to Sat.

Sturminster Newton

Plumber Manor
'What eating out in England should be'
Sturminster Newton, DT10 2AF
Tel no: (01258) 472507
www.plumbermanor.com
Anglo-French | £36
Cooking score: 2
£5 OFF

Built by Charles Brune in the 17th century, this fine country manor has remained in the family ever since. It has been a hotel for more than 40 years, thriving as a low-key family affair noted for its comfy, romantic feel, warm heart and good food. With lawns shaded by mature trees, a flagged hallway, a sweeping staircase and walls lined with family portraits, the place exudes a homeliness that is matched by Brian Prideaux-Brune's cooking, which deals in comfort and familiarity. No one is about to rush or get too excited – although the food is immensely pleasurable from start to finish. Come here for crab mousseline in a light curry sauce, pigeon breast on black pudding bubble and squeak or lemon sole with grapes and white wine, and a medley of

puddings: American cheesecake, chocolate torte, lemon meringue roulade and fresh berries. House wines from £17.50.
Chef/s: Brian Prideaux-Brune. Open: Sun L 12 to 2, all week D 7 to 9.30. Closed: Feb. Meals: Set D £29 (2 courses) to £36. Sun L £28. Details: 65 seats. Separate bar. Wheelchair access. Car parking.

Weymouth

LOCAL GEM
▲ Crab House Café
Ferryman's Way, Portland Road, Weymouth, DT4 9YU
Tel no: (01305) 788867
www.crabhousecafe.co.uk
Seafood | £29

It's a simple enough proposition: super-fresh seafood eaten right by the beach in a wooden shack or outside under pink parasols. The Café has its own oyster farm (right out front), so the Portland Royals are must-haves for fans of the bivalves (either natural or with pesto/Parmesan or bacon/cream). Follow on with a whole crab to crack, or baked wing of skate with chorizo, then finish with peanut butter parfait or local cheeses. Wines from £14. Closed Tue and early Dec to early Feb.

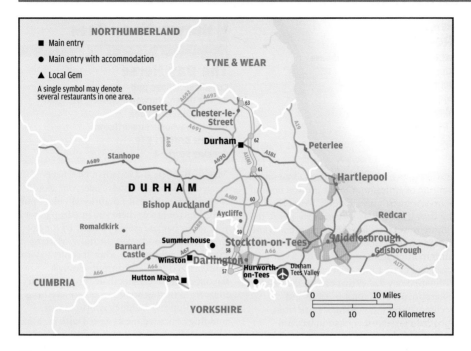

Durham
Bistro 21
Dressed-up comfort food with style
Aykley Heads House, Aykley Heads, Durham,
DH1 5TS
Tel no: (0191) 3844354
www.bistrotwentyone.co.uk
Modern British | £28
Cooking score: 3

V £30

The country cousin of local food hero Terry
Laybourne's Newcastle-based '21' group, this
converted 17th-century farmhouse a few
miles outside Durham is a home from home
for city-based foodies who come for smart,
contemporary cooking at prices that seldom
offend. Bistro 21's pretty courtyard, cellar bar
and upbeat dining room find favour with the
assembled company, while the menu offers a
savvy mash-up of North Country ingredients
and eclectic flavours (plus the odd Asian add-
on): from Gruyère cheese and leek soufflé or a
salad of kippers, pink fir potatoes and soft-
boiled egg to warm chocolate and peanut-
butter pudding or soft coconut meringue
with mango purée and pineapple salsa. In
between, mains such as plaice fillets with
purple sprouting broccoli and caper butter or
slow-cooked pork belly with apple, apple
and black pudding purée deliver dressed-up
comfort food with a touch of style. Around
four dozen wines promise respectable
drinking from £17.50 (£4.70 a glass).
Chef/s: Ruari MacKay. **Open:** all week L 12 to 2
(3.30 Sun), Mon to Sat D 5.30 to 10. **Closed:** 25 Dec,
1 Jan, bank hols. **Meals:** alc (main courses £17 to
£23). Set L and D £16 (2 courses) to £19. Sun L £21.
Details: 90 seats. 24 seats outside. Separate bar.
Wheelchair access. Music. Car parking.

Visit us Online
To find out more about
The Good Food Guide, please visit
www.thegoodfoodguide.co.uk

NEW ENTRY
Restaurant DH1
Whizzy cooking in a guesthouse
The Avenue, Durham, DH1 4DX
Tel no: (0191) 3846655
www.restaurantdh1.co.uk
Modern British | £38
Cooking score: 3

£5 OFF V

Formerly the Gourmet Spot, Restaurant DH1 is still a gourmet spot, or at least a fine-dining venture of ambition. On the ground floor of a four-star guesthouse, Farnley Tower (built in 1870 with a touch of Victorian swagger), the dining room seats just 22 and won't win any design awards. Chef/patron Stephen Hardy aims to impress, though, with his fixed-price carte and tasting menus of creative and contemporary dishes that can hit the heights. There are modern combinations and techniques on show: hanger steak from Neasham Grange is cooked in hay and matched with various preparations of carrot and a Jersey milk curd; pork jowl is slow-cooked and comes in a winning combination with smoked eel and Granny Smith apple. The kitchen hits full throttle when a salted caramel sauce is poured into an aerated chocolate dessert that comes with a scoop of 'fabulous' popcorn ice cream. Wines from £18.50.
Chef/s: Stephen Hardy. **Open:** Tue to Sat D only 6 to 11. **Closed:** Sun, Mon, 25 and 26 Dec, 1 week Jan. **Meals:** Set D £30 (2 courses) to £38. Market menu £18 (2 courses) to £23. Tasting menu £50. **Details:** 22 seats. Separate bar. Wheelchair access. Music. Car parking.

Symbols

🛏 Accommodation is available

£30 Three courses for less than £30

V Separate vegetarian menu

£5 OFF £5-off voucher scheme

🍷 Notable wine list

▋Hurworth-on-Tees

★ TOP 50 PUB ★
The Bay Horse
Cut-above village pub
45 The Green, Hurworth-on-Tees, DL2 2AA
Tel no: (01325) 720663
www.thebayhorsehurworth.com
Modern British | £34
Cooking score: 4

Marcus Bennett and Jonathan Hall have created the kind of hostelry everyone would love as a local. It's still a traditional village pub – the kind of place where you can drop in for a pint in the bar and warm yourself by the open fire – but the food steals the show. Marcus's kitchen is on the money when it comes to local sourcing and fresh, forthright seasonal flavours. British themes share the stage with ideas from further afield, so expect anything from scallop and haddock risotto to suet pudding of braised meats served with herb and garlic crushed potatoes, onions puréed and fricasseed, red wine jus and parsley oil. For dessert, steamed fig roly-poly with apple ice cream and hazelnut custard goes down well. The dinner menu constitutes great value given the quality of the output, while the set lunch is a veritable bargain. Wines from £16.95.
Chef/s: Marcus Bennett. **Open:** all week L 12 to 2.30 (4 Sun), D 6 to 9.30 (8 Sun). **Closed:** 25 and 26 Dec. **Meals:** Set L £14 (2 courses) to £17. Set D £20 (2 courses) to £25. Sun L £20. **Details:** 60 seats. 40 seats outside. Separate bar. Wheelchair access. Music. Car parking.

The Orangery
Classic-meets-modern with panoramic views
Rockliffe Hall, Hurworth-on-Tees, DL2 2DU
Tel no: (01325) 729999
www.rockliffehall.com
Modern British | £60
Cooking score: 4

🛏

Rockliffe Hall has a multitude of red-brick gables, a host of luxurious facilities and, in the shape of the Orangery restaurant, a compelling dining option. It's one of three places to eat in the hotel and the smartest of the bunch, with columns soaring up to the glass roof and a swish finish. There are lovely parkland views. The menu combines classical elements with touches of modernity, and everything arrives looking pretty as a picture. Things can be as traditionally indulgent as oscietra caviar (30 grams for 55 quid) followed by lobster thermidor, but equally you might start with beetroot-cured salmon with Jersey Royals and pickled beets and move on to wood pigeon with wild garlic gnocchi and hazelnut vinaigrette. Rack of lamb is carved at the table and there's a full-dress 'Signature Menu'. Finish with rhubarb and vanilla custard tart. The wine list includes plenty of big guns, with bottle prices starting at £27. **Chef/s:** Paul O'Hara and Paul Bussey. **Open:** all week D only 6.30 to 10. **Meals:** alc (main courses £17 to £30). **Details:** 65 seats. Separate bar. Wheelchair access. Music. Car parking. Children over 12 yrs only at D.

Hutton Magna
The Oak Tree Inn
Village hostelry with high standards
Hutton Magna, DL11 7HH
Tel no: (01833) 627371
www.theoaktreehutton.co.uk
Modern British | £33
Cooking score: 3

'Satisfaction and perfection guaranteed!' exclaimed a fan after visiting the Oak Tree Inn: a spruce village hostelry tucked among the rugged hues of the north Pennines. Alastair and Claire Ross have created an immensely appealing gastronomic oasis behind the pub's rough stone walls – although you must book to sample the dinner menu. Comfy sofas and bottle-green upholstery add sophistication, while the food is defined by precise flavours and picture-pretty presentation. Anything featuring local lamb is a 'must-have', although the menu could run from home-cured salmon with crab jelly, beetroot and cream cheese or John Dory fillet with provençal vegetables, pesto potato,

aubergine and fennel, to seared duck breast with caramelised endive and sweet potato. Desserts such as hot chocolate fondant with chocolate mousse and salted-caramel ice cream also display the kitchen's prowess. Home-baked breads, tasty nibbles, great beer and 'superb staff' are much appreciated, likewise the list of reasonably priced wines from £15.50.
Chef/s: Alastair Ross. **Open:** Tue to Sun D only 6 to 9. **Closed:** Mon, 24 to 27 Dec, 31 Dec to 2 Jan. **Meals:** alc (main courses £20 to £25). **Details:** 20 seats. Separate bar. Car parking.

Summerhouse
★ TOP 50 ★
The Raby Hunt
Remarkable cooking of subtle power
Summerhouse, DL2 3UD
Tel no: (01325) 374237
www.rabyhuntrestaurant.co.uk
Modern British | £58
Cooking score: 6

A mid-Georgian inn on the old drovers' road leading to Northumberland and points north, the Raby Hunt was once a gathering-point for the tally-ho brigade. Its village location suited it perfectly for transformation to an ambitious country restaurant, and the dining room is a nice mix of smart and shoestring elements: whitewashed walls, sanded board floors and floral-patterned chairs. Self-taught James Close has achieved remarkable things here over the past five years, and the successes keep flowing. Multi-course tasters are the foundation, the dishes full of imaginative flair, sound judgement and a light touch. Foie gras parfait wrapped in smoked eel dusted with powdered beetroot is a triumph of subtle power. Fish could be superb roast halibut with nutmegged spinach and dots of fish-roe emulsion, or there might be mesmerising suckling pig loin, belly and shoulder with pickled celeriac, morels, apple, hazelnuts and dandelion leaves. At the end comes salt-baked pineapple with cardamom ice cream, tarragon shoots and toasted coconut. A magisterial list of pedigree wines inspires confidence, with quality and value in impressive balance throughout. Prices open at £22.50, or £15.50 for a half-litre carafe.

Chef/s: James Close. **Open:** Wed to Sat L 12 to 2, D 6 to 9.30. **Closed:** Sun, Mon, Tue, 1 week each season. **Meals:** Set L £29. Set D £58. Tasting menu £80. **Details:** 28 seats. 6 seats outside. Separate bar. Wheelchair access. Car parking.

▌Winston

The Bridgewater Arms
Character, warmth and local ingredients
Winston, DL2 3RN
Tel no: (01325) 730302
www.thebridgewaterarms.com
British | £36
Cooking score: 1

Much to the relief of its many fans, Paul Grundy is back doing sterling service at this welcoming, listed village pub – no longer as landlord, but as chef/proprietor. Once again, the fire roars, drinkers are welcome and a crowd-pleasing menu of straightforward British food is offered. Few seem able to resist the seafood pancake thermidor, but Cheddar and spinach soufflé comes a close second, and there has been praise for fillet of sea bass with scallops, stir-fried greens and sweet chilli sauce, and 'superb' fillet steak with béarnaise sauce. Finish with roast pineapple and lemongrass ice cream. Wines from £15.

Chef/s: Paul Grundy. **Open:** Tue to Sat L 12 to 2, D 6 to 9. **Closed:** Sun, Mon, 24 to 26 Dec. **Meals:** alc (main courses £18 to £30). **Details:** 50 seats. Wheelchair access. Music. Car parking.

▌▌ JAMES CLOSE
Raby Hunt, Durham

What do you enjoy about being a chef?
I enjoy everything about being a chef, it's my passion, it's challenging both mentally and physically but I think that's what I like about it - it's an all-encompassing job. We have a very small team at the Raby Hunt so we do everything together - there are no sections, just solid team work.

What inspired you to become a chef?
I get asked this a lot, especially as I am untrained and had never cooked for paying customers before we opened the Raby Hunt. I have been fortunate enough to travel the world with my parents and have eaten at some of the world's best restaurants. While I was at El Celler de Can Roca I had a steak tartare with mustard ice cream - I was blown away! At that moment I knew I wanted to be a chef.

What is your favourite time of year for food?
Spring - after a hard autumn and winter I love to see all the new fresh English produce coming through the door; it reinvigorates you for fresh and light dishes. Menus change a lot from April into May.

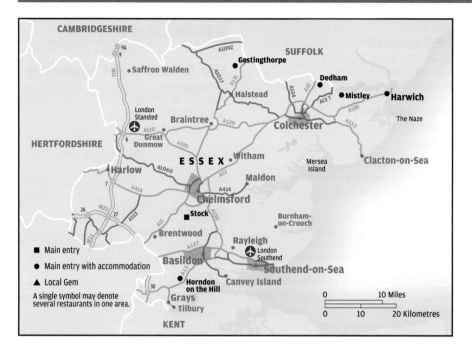

Dedham

★ WINE LIST OF THE YEAR ★

The Sun Inn

Classic inn with an Italian heart
High Street, Dedham, CO7 6DF
Tel no: (01206) 323351
www.thesuninndedham.com
Italian | £27
Cooking score: 3

Piers Baker's Sun Inn is a clever operation designed to appeal to all comers. The transition from ancient village hostelry to a successful food pub, with beams and open fire still intact (and a blackboard bar menu), shows what can be done with a little ingenuity and common sense. Italian is the orientation of the monthly changing menus and there's no shortage of imagination in the kitchen. Pheasant tortellini is teamed with sage butter, balsamic and pomegranate, for example, while grilled leg of salt marsh lamb arrives with a gratin of parsnip, Oxford Blue cheese and kale, and fillet of cod with ricotta and spinach dumplings and tarragon sauce. There's a good-value set deal, own-baked bread, excellent service that is 'quick, organised and friendly', and 'delicious' puddings and ice cream. Winning the Guide's Wine List of the Year Award, the Sun Inn's 'confident, concise, accessible' list offers fantastic value for money. Wines are a blend of Old World and New, well annotated and arranged simply by style: 'Rich & Structured' or 'Succulent & Aromatic', say, with 'Desert Island' wines – sold at a remarkably gentle mark-up – being praised as particularly exciting. There's a lovely by-the-glass list, and bottles start at £15.
Chef/s: Ugo Simonelli. **Open:** all week L 12 to 2.30 (3 Sat and Sun), D 6.30 to 9.30 (10 Fri and Sat). **Closed:** 25 and 26 Dec. **Meals:** alc (main courses £10 to £18). Set L and D £14 (2 courses) to £18. **Details:** 70 seats. 30 seats outside. Music. Car parking.

NEW ENTRY
Le Talbooth
Classy food, classy location
Gun Hill, Dedham, CO7 6HP
Tel no: (01206) 323150
www.milsomhotels.com
Modern British | £48
Cooking score: 4

£5 OFF 🚗

Andrew Hirst is back in his home county, turning out a menu of confidently executed classics at this special riverside restaurant where manicured gardens drift down to the lazy Stour. A starter of local asparagus comes with confit egg yolk in a pool of tangy mustard mayonnaise, crumbs of salty Parma ham scattered over by way of seasoning. Next, seafood foam is perhaps *de trop* on a dish of exquisite red mullet, but herby arancini, delicate leeks and punchy chorizo make this main sing. Pedigree cooking permeates the clear menu: look out for Dover sole, tournedos Rossini and chateaubriand. The remarkable collection of French and English cheeses will satisfy non-pudding lovers, while a nutmeggy egg custard with lively pickled ginger and rhubarb sorbet will tempt the sweet-toothed. The sky's the limit on the carefully annotated wine list (from £19.25), but there's plenty by the glass. Don't expect a cheap night out; relish a memorable one.
Chef/s: Andrew Hirst. **Open:** all week L 12 to 2 (3.30 Sun), Mon to Sat D 6.45 to 9 (9.30 Sat). **Meals:** alc (main courses £20 to £32). Set L £25 (2 courses) to £31. Sun L £35. **Details:** 80 seats. 50 seats outside. Separate bar. Wheelchair access. Music. Car parking.

🍴 Readers Recommend

A 'readers recommend' review is a genuine quote from a report sent in by one of our readers. We intend to follow up these suggestions throughout the year to come.

▌Fuller Street

READERS RECOMMEND
The Square and Compasses
Modern British
Fuller Street, CM3 2BB
Tel no: (01245) 361477
www.thesquareandcompasses.co.uk
'As pub food goes it is exceptional – in the winter, a lot of local game with a very interesting and varied wine list that changes regularly.'

▌Gestingthorpe
The Pheasant
Indulge in some comfort eating
Gestingthorpe, CO9 3AU
Tel no: (01787) 461196
www.thepheasant.net
Modern British | £25
Cooking score: 1

£5 OFF 🚗 £30

Diana and James Donoghue's rural roadside pub has bags of traditional character – the low-beamed series of rooms provide something of a retirement home for lost country furniture. The menu doesn't punch above its weight and stays local (as does the beer), with seasonal produce including estate game (pheasant breast wrapped in bacon and stuffed with pork and leek, perhaps), or a muscular plate of slow-roasted pork belly with caramelised cider gravy. For afters, how about poached pears with warm chocolate and orange sauce? Beehives, chickens, a productive garden and smokehouse complete the picture. Wines from £15.95.
Chef/s: James Donoghue. **Open:** all week L 12 to 2 (2.30 Sat and Sun), D 6.30 to 9. **Closed:** 25 and 26 Dec, 2 weeks Jan. **Meals:** alc (main courses £7 to £19). **Details:** 40 seats. 25 seats outside. Separate bar. Music. Car parking.

Harwich

The Pier at Harwich, Harbourside Restaurant

Fine seafood and estuary views
The Quay, Harwich, CO12 3HH
Tel no: (01255) 241212
www.milsomhotels.com
Seafood | £38
Cooking score: 2
£5 OFF

There are no prizes for guessing the location or the main business at this long-serving hotel dining room overlooking Harwich quay. Nautical vibes and views of the confluent Stour and Orwell estuaries provide an ideal backdrop for some open-minded seafood cookery. Prime piscine pickings arrive fresh at the door each morning, and the kitchen enlivens its classic repertoire with some upbeat modern assemblages. Lobsters are the stars of the show, closely followed by crabs every which way (try the tacos with guacamole and chipotle dressing), but other bright ideas also catch the eye: from pan-fried queenie scallops with broad beans, apple, fennel and oyster leaf, or seared mackerel on Thai papaya salad, to seafood fritura with saffron aïoli. Moules marinière, skate with capers and grilled lemon sole won't rock the boat, and there are options for meat eaters (Dedham Vale steak and kidney pud, for example) and veggies too. Wines from £19.25.
Chef/s: John Goss. **Open:** Wed to Sun L 12 to 2 (3 Sun), D 6 to 9.30 (8.30 Sun). **Closed:** Mon, Tue. **Meals:** alc (main courses £17 to £30). Set L £23 (2 courses) to £26. **Details:** 80 seats. 30 seats outside. Separate bar. Music. Car parking.

Horndon on the Hill

The Bell Inn

Medieval pub with a modern menu
High Road, Horndon on the Hill, SS17 8LD
Tel no: (01375) 642463
www.bell-inn.co.uk
Modern European | £30
Cooking score: 2

It may be a 15th-century coaching inn with many period attributes, but the family who have run the Bell for the past 70 years haven't preserved it in aspic. They provide bedrooms in a Georgian house next door (and upstairs in the pub), and a new decidedly modern dining option in the form of Ostlers grill (open Fri and Sat evenings and Sun lunch), which can turn out a nifty char-grilled ribeye. Otherwise, there are traditional bar areas, confirming this is a proper pub, and the restaurant with its oak beams and panels. The menu is anchored by contemporary constructions such as first-course tea-smoked salmon with wasabi cream cheese, keta and, wait for it . . . Yorkshire pudding. For mains there might be slow-roast shoulder of lamb with devilled kidneys and black pudding mash, while dessert could bring all the comfort of steamed plum pudding. Wines from £14.95, and there are local ales on tap.
Chef/s: Stuart Fay. **Open:** all week L 12 to 1.45 (2.30 Sun), D 6.30 to 9.45 (7 Sun). **Closed:** 25 and 26 Dec. **Meals:** alc (main courses £12 to £25). **Details:** 80 seats. 36 seats outside. Separate bar. Wheelchair access. Car parking.

Mistley

The Mistley Thorn
Upbeat eatery with bright, vibrant food
High Street, Mistley, CO11 1HE
Tel no: (01206) 392821
www.mistleythorn.co.uk
Modern European | £24
Cooking score: 2
🛏 £30

Back in the 17th century, this solid coaching inn had connections with the infamous Witchfinder General, but these days it concentrates on serving good victuals and proper lubrication. American owner Sherri Singleton is 'wonderfully well connected to her restaurant' noted one local resident, referring to her genuine rapport with staff and customers. There are plenty of seaside flavours on the menu, overlaid with bright, sunny influences from the Med and beyond. The oyster bar purveys 'natives' and 'rocks' from the River Deben, seafood platters stand out and the day's fish specials are always worth trying – perhaps grilled mackerel with beetroot, apple and frisée. Other tastes are satisfied by the likes of Suffolk Red Poll burgers, char-grilled leg of Suffolk lamb with Puy lentils, or gnocchi with roasted butternut squash. Dessert might bring mascarpone semifreddo with pistachio praline and poached winter fruits, and breakfast gains plaudits too. Wines from £14.95.
Chef/s: Karl Burnside. **Open:** all week L 12 to 3 (4 Sat, 5 Sun), D 6.30 to 9.30 (6 to 10 Fri and Sat). **Meals:** alc (main courses £11 to £21). Set L and D £13 (2 courses) to £15. Sun L £15 (2 courses) to £18. **Details:** 75 seats. 16 seats outside. Separate bar. Music. Car parking.

Stock

The Oak Room at the Hoop
Enthusiastically run local asset
21 High Street, Stock, CM4 9BD
Tel no: (01277) 841137
www.thehoop.co.uk
Modern British | £30
Cooking score: 1
£5 OFF

Loyal regulars reckon the Hoop is one of the best eating options for miles around. The ground floor is a traditional country pub (with an independent beer festival every summer), while the Oak Room upstairs is given over to very dependable rustic cooking utilising quality ingredients. Expect chickpea fritters with pomegranate and mango yoghurt, or devilled mackerel and beetroot, first up, followed perhaps by seafood linguine in tomato and chilli, or one of the classic roasts on Sunday, served with duck-fat roasties and Yorkshire. Pistachio cake with white chocolate ice cream and candied orange is a tempting finish. Wines start at £14.
Chef/s: Phil Utz. **Open:** Tue to Fri and Sun L 12 to 2.30 (3 Sun), Tue to Sat D 6 to 9 (9.30 Fri and Sat). **Closed:** Mon, 23 to 28 May. **Meals:** alc (main courses £13 to £27). Sun L £25. **Details:** 40 seats. Separate bar. Music.

🍴 **Average Price**
The average price listed in main-entry reviews denotes the price of a three-course meal, without wine.

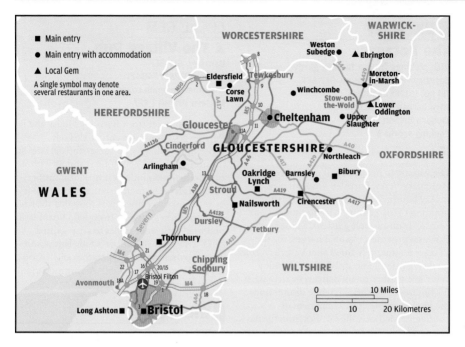

▌Arlingham
The Old Passage

Pin-sharp seafood and fresh flavours
Passage Road, Arlingham, GL2 7JR
Tel no: (01452) 740547
www.theoldpassage.com
Seafood | £40
Cooking score: 3

£5 OFF 🛏

Found on the banks of the River Severn, this secluded former Georgian farmhouse may be tucked away on a road leading to nowhere, but Sally Pearce's welcoming restaurant-with-rooms still draws the crowds. Seafood is the speciality, served in a light-filled dining room with walls lined by the work of local artists. Feast on fruits de mer or the shellfish tasting menu, or go à la carte with seared scallops, crispy pork terrine, apple purée and rum-soaked raisins, followed by roast wild halibut, beer-braised onion purée, salsify, wild mushrooms and mussels. Alternatively, try roast pheasant, game chips, bread sauce, roasted root vegetables and game jus. To finish, maybe crema catalana, port-poached pears and shortbread biscuits. The quality of the food and friendly service are hard to fault, but some reporters have flinched at the prices. White wines start at £19, but reds kick off at a stiffer £25.50.

Chef/s: Mark Redwood. **Open:** Tue to Sun L 12 to 2 (2.30 Sun), Tue to Sat D 7 to 9. **Closed:** Mon, 25 and 26 Dec. **Meals:** alc (main courses £19 to £48). Set L £15 (2 courses) to £20. **Details:** 40 seats. 26 seats outside. Wheelchair access. Music. Car parking. Children at L only.

⫴ **Please send us your feedback**

To register your opinion about any restaurant listed in the Guide, or a new restaurant that you wish to bring to our attention, please visit the web address at the bottom of the page. Your feedback informs the content of the book and will be used to compile next year's reviews.

Barnsley

The Potager
Rich pickings from a famous garden
Barnsley House, Barnsley, GL7 5EE
Tel no: (01285) 740000
www.barnsleyhouse.com
Modern British | £37
Cooking score: 3

🛏

Once home to horticultural queen bee
Rosemary Verey, Barnsley House is now a
snazzy boutique hotel that celebrates the
building's 17th-century heritage and, of
course, its unmissable gardens. Those verdant
expanses provide a seasonal harvest for the
Potager restaurant (named after Verey's famous
kitchen garden). The aptly titled 'Barnsley
vegetable garden' menu delivers exactly what
it promises at lunchtime, while dinner finds
the kitchen creating an assortment of
confident, Med-accented dishes from the day's
rich pickings. Salads, pastas and risottos figure
prominently (try the homemade gnocchi with
purple kale and Berkswell cheese), although
the menu also deals in small plates such as
grilled mackerel with tomato on toast. After
that, go large with a generous serving of stone
bass with parsley mash, clams and anchovy
butter or aged skirt steak with hand-cut chips.
For afters, how about Venetian rice pudding or
almond and prune tart? House wine is £22.
Chef/s: Graham Grafton. **Open:** all week L 12 to 2
(2.30 Sat, 3 Sun), D 7 to 9.30 (10 Fri and Sat).
Meals: alc (main courses £11 to £32). Set L £22 (2
courses) to £26. **Details:** 40 seats. 30 seats outside.
Separate bar. Music. Car parking. No children under
14 yrs at D.

Symbols
🛏 Accommodation is available

💷30 Three courses for less than £30

V Separate vegetarian menu

💷5 £5-off voucher scheme

🍾 Notable wine list

LOCAL GEM

▲ The Village Pub
Barnsley, GL7 5EF
Tel no: (01285) 740421
www.thevillagepub.co.uk
Modern British | £27

A casual spin-off from Barnsley House and its
Potager restaurant (see entry), this self-
proclaimed 'village pub' successfully creates an
illusion of genteel boozy Englishness with its
rustic-chic surrounds, real fires, real timbers
and real ales. The food also ticks the necessary
boxes thanks to a line-up of thoughtful Brit-
accented dishes ranging from wild boar black
pudding with cider apples to char-grilled
calf's liver with champ, or whole lemon sole
with brown butter, new potatoes and seasonal
greens. Wines from £17.50. Accommodation.
Open all week.

Bibury

NEW ENTRY
Origin
Contemporary country-house cooking
Bibury Court Hotel, Bibury, GL7 5NT
Tel no: (01285) 740337
www.biburycourt.com
Modern British | £40
Cooking score: 4

From the outside, this extravagant Jacobean
manor is straight out of a period drama:
mullioned windows, a sweeping drive, views
over lush grassland – it's a vintage delight. The
interior is surprisingly contemporary, the
original features sitting comfortably alongside
pale apple paintwork and stylish lighting. The
restaurant occupies a chunky wooden
conservatory with exquisite garden views: a
perfect setting for James Graham's modern
British food, which is built on the best the
countryside can offer. Wye Valley asparagus
with a Scotch pheasant egg and foraged leaves
typifies the style, while a main of belly and
loin of Tamworth pork with salt-baked
celeriac, braised chard and wonderful brittle,
salty crackling is perfectly executed. The same

could be said of an airy banana soufflé for dessert. Unfortunately, slow service can 'put a dampener on things', so plan to sit back and enjoy something from the wide-ranging wine list where bottles start at £23.

Chef/s: James Graham. **Open:** all week L 12 to 2, D 7 to 9. **Meals:** alc (main courses £16 to £28). Tasting menu £75 (Tue to Sat only). **Details:** 22 seats. Separate bar. Music. Car parking.

█ Bristol

Bell's Diner

Full-frontal eclectic flavours
1-3 York Road, Montpelier, Bristol, BS6 5QB
Tel no: (0117) 9240357
www.bellsdiner.com
Mediterranean | £30
Cooking score: 5

A converted grocer's shop in graffiti-splattered Montpelier/Stokes Croft, this funky veteran comprises three rooms stuffed with cookery books, vintage meat mincers, typewriters and other curios. The owners even provide emergency cigars and roll-ups for customers craving an alfresco puff: very boho Bristol. The food is also spot-on for the neighbourhood, with sharply trimmed prices, full-frontal eclectic flavours and lots of chillies. Nibbles of salt cod fritters with aïoli get the juices flowing, before punters tackle the punchy Med-influenced sharing plates: perhaps 'splodgy, cartoon-style' fried quails' eggs with spiced morcilla and piquillo peppers, or a beautifully light dish of clams and mussels in a sherry-laced broth studded with nuggets of jamón. Char-grilling is a forte – witness juicy onglet with new season's artichokes and pungent salsa verde. To finish, homemade ice creams compete with 'fab' puds such as chocolate nemesis or lemon meringue tart. Beers are from artisan Brits, while wines (from £17.50) favour sunnier climes.

Chef/s: Sam Sohn-Rethel. **Open:** Tue to Sat L 12 to 3, Mon to Sat D 6 to 10. **Closed:** Sun, 25 to 28 Dec. **Meals:** alc (main courses £13 to £24). **Details:** 45 seats. Separate bar. Music.

NEW ENTRY

Birch

Earthy and astute British cooking
47 Raleigh Road, Bristol, BS3 1QS
Tel no: (01179) 028326
www.birchbristol.co
Modern British | £25
Cooking score: 4

£30
▼

Sam Leach and Beccy Massey used to run supper clubs in Bristol, but learnt their trade in notable London establishments – Sam was a pastry chef at St John. When they opened their sleek neighbourhood eatery in May 2014, word of mouth was such that it quickly became one of the city's hottest tickets. With white walls and minimalist design, the dining room is as unbuttoned and unfussy as the food, which veers towards earthy British heritage cooking. There's an unwavering commitment to seasonality, provenance and local produce (including some from the owners' smallholding). Thus a rich, herby slice of brawn with mustard, pickles and excellent sourdough might precede an impressively fresh piece of turbot teamed with spring vegetables and brown crab. For dessert, there's a very good treacle tart with local cream. The interesting wine list kicks off at £19 and rarely looks beyond rising-star producers of France and Italy.

Chef/s: Sam Leach. **Open:** Wed to Sat D only 6 to 10. **Closed:** Sun to Tue. **Meals:** alc (main courses £13 to £16). **Details:** 24 seats. Wheelchair access.

Bravas

Wonderfully atmospheric buzzy tapas bar
7 Cotham Hill, Bristol, BS6 6LD
Tel no: (0117) 3296887
www.bravas.co.uk
Spanish | £15
Cooking score: 2

£30
▼

Kieran and Imogen Waite have recreated their own little corner of Spain in this cramped tapas bar. What began as an underground supper club run from the couple's flat has rapidly become one of Bristol's coolest eateries. Although stools at the elm wood-topped bar cannot be reserved, bookings for the handful of tables at the back are pretty much essential. With its exposed brickwork, copper piping and shelves of Spanish ingredients and cookbooks, the room conjures up the effervescent atmosphere of a Barcelona tapas bar. From a concise daily changing menu comes fried aubergine and molasses, or fried duck's egg with chanterelles and jamón, while from the plancha, there's grilled Ibérico pork or silver mullet. Rice pudding with caramel apple is one reason not to overlook dessert. The vibrant, carefully considered all-Spanish wine list starts at £15.95.

Chef/s: Imogen Waite. **Open:** Tue to Thur D only 5 to 11. Fri and Sat 12 to 11. **Closed:** Sun, Mon, 24 to 26 Dec, 2 to 7 Jan. **Meals:** alc (tapas £3 to £7). **Details:** 46 seats. Separate bar. Music.

★ TOP 50 ★

★ CHEF(S) OF THE YEAR ★

Casamia

Proud, vital and very much worth a visit
38 High Street, Westbury on Trym, Bristol, BS9 3DZ
Tel no: (0117) 9592884
www.casamiarestaurant.co.uk
Modern British | £68
Cooking score: 7

£5 OFF V

As the score shows, Casamia is not an eccentric restaurant run by two charming brothers in an out-of-the-way Bristol suburb, but one of the most enjoyable places to eat in the UK. It's also a serious restaurant, using the finest ingredients in a menu of range and subtlety. There's no doubting that Jonray and Peter Sanchez-Iglesias have grown in stature to rank with the best. Everyone who has eaten here in the last year has reported blisteringly successful meals. A cool, relaxed and unstuffy dining room is run with candid friendliness; this is a place where junior chefs amble out of the open kitchen to explain each dish in the (one per season) ten-course tasting menu. Try

this amalgam from spring: a porcelain 'breakfast egg' topped with a sliver of crisp bacon and filled with delicious egg custard from which you scoop black pudding, mushroom, ketchup, a tiny tomato; a bright, flower-strewn micro salad; lemon sole with a slick of creamy cider sauce, apple jelly contributing acidity, broccoli and deep-fried kale adding crisp texture; lamb, its predictable partner, mint, offered as a restrained purée with a supporting cast of dried-crisp leeks, a single, perfect potato and lick of rich gravy. Among the three desserts, it's the crossover dish that's the triumphant standout – a carrot sponge topped with dried carrot and a thyme-milk and nitrogen-poached ice cream. On the wine front, there's quality drinking all the way from France to the southern hemisphere, with prices from £28.

Chef/s: Jonray and Peter Sanchez-Iglesias. **Open:** Tue to Sat L 12.30 to 1.45, D 7 to 9. **Closed:** Sun, Mon, 21 Dec to 1 Jan. **Meals:** Tasting menu L £38 (5 courses) to £68 (10 courses). Tasting menu D £68 (Tue to Thur) to £88 (Fri and Sat). **Details:** 40 seats. Separate bar. Music.

Flinty Red

Vibrant Med cooking and lively wine list
34 Cotham Hill, Bristol, BS6 6LA
Tel no: (0117) 9238755
www.flintyred.co.uk
Modern European | £30
Cooking score: 4

A diminutive local restaurant just behind Whiteladies Road, Flinty Red has a distinctly Mediterranean feel about it. The operation is run in conjunction with an independent wine shop a few doors away. You can eat at tables or perch at the marble bar where you may find yourself 'striking up a conversation with staff only too happy to share their wine wisdom'. The Italian-leaning menu is driven by imported and local ingredients of faultless provenance and many of the tapas-sized dishes can be doubled up for sharers. Robust, punchy flavour combinations are highlights of starters such as blood-orange, red onion and rhubarb salad with black olive, which might precede a

main course of kid shoulder with lentils, sprouting broccoli and anchovy butter. Doughnuts with whipped yoghurt and maple syrup is one dessert that wins many friends. Wines from £16 (£3 a glass).
Chef/s: Matthew Williamson. **Open:** Tue to Sat L 12 to 3, Mon to Sat D 6.30 to 10. **Closed:** Sun, 24 to 26 Dec, first week Jan. **Meals:** alc (main courses £12 to £16). Set L £10. **Details:** 36 seats. Music.

Greens

Welcoming bistro with wonderful food
25 Zetland Road, Bristol, BS6 7AH
Tel no: (0117) 9246437
www.greensbristol.co.uk
Modern European | £25
Cooking score: 3

V £30

Martin Laurentowicz and Nick Wallace took over this neighbourhood restaurant in 2012 and it remains much loved by locals, who are drawn by the quality of the cooking and the good-value menus. Laurentowicz is a confident chef, noted for straightforward, deceptively simple modern European dishes that pack a real flavour punch. A starter of ham hash cake, poached egg and hollandaise has become something of a signature dish, and it could be followed by precisely cooked spiced roast duck breast with creamed Savoy cabbage, celeriac mash and a rich Madeira sauce. A separate vegetarian menu offering three choices per course might feature udon noodles with tofu, mushroom and pak choi soup and sesame oil. Orange posset with milk crumb and blackberry compote is a good way to finish. The concise, well-designed wine list starts at £15 and offers plenty of good drinking under £20.
Chef/s: Martin Laurentowicz. **Open:** Tue to Sun L 12 to 2.30 (4 Sun), Tue to Sat D 6 to 10. **Closed:** Mon, 25 and 26 Dec. **Meals:** alc (main courses £11 to £20). Set L £10 (2 courses) to £14. Set D £15 (2 courses) to £20. Sun L £15. **Details:** 37 seats. 8 seats outside. Music.

Lido

Aromatic food in awesome surrounds
Oakfield Place, Clifton, Bristol, BS8 2BJ
Tel no: (0117) 9339530
www.lidobristol.com
Mediterranean | £33
Cooking score: 3

'Our favourite place in Bristol, the whole experience is just wonderful,' enthused one regular of this stylish restaurant, which boasts its own open-air swimming pool and spa. Saved from demolition by visionary owner Arne Ringner, the Victorian lido is now a unique urban oasis in the heart of leafy Clifton. Grab a table on the terrace next to the blue-tiled pool, or a window seat overlooking the candy-striped changing cubicles, and enjoy chef Freddy Bird's vigorous cooking. A searing wood-fired oven is the workhorse of the kitchen, the menu inspired by North Africa, the Middle East and the Med. A starter of wood-roast quail, fennel, radish and pomegranate salad might be followed by black rice, cuttlefish, parsley and garlic, while dessert brings the likes of Seville orange curd tart and an enticing list of homemade ices including salted butter caramel. Wine from £17.50.
Chef/s: Freddy Bird. **Open:** all week L 12 to 2.45, Mon to Sat D 6 to 9.45. **Closed:** 25 and 26 Dec. **Meals:** alc (main courses £16 to £19). Set L and D £16 (2 courses) to £20. **Details:** 130 seats. 50 seats outside. Separate bar. Wheelchair access. Music.

Manna

Flavours from around the Med
2B North View, Westbury Park, Bristol, BS6 7QB
Tel no: (0117) 9706276
www.mannabar.co.uk
Mediterranean | £25
Cooking score: 2

£30

Sibling to Prego across the road (see entry), this restaurant/bar is much loved by locals, who are happy to nibble tapas dishes at the window counter or grab a table and dive into the main menu. Spain and Italy are the

kitchen's main influences, though the menu also takes occasional trips to North Africa and the Middle East. Start with crispy pumpkin with ricotta, blossom honey and oregano, or prawn pil pil with Wye Valley asparagus, cumin and chickpeas. Next, move on to roast mutton shoulder with Pardina lentils, salt-baked aubergines and salsa verde, or crispy Old Spot belly, scallop, morcilla and glazed quince. Spiced Persian carrot cake with pistachio, almond and rose-water cream is a typical dessert. The short, punchy wine list kicks off at £14.95 and there's a range of American craft ales and bottled beers from local breweries.
Chef/s: Olly Gallery. **Open:** Mon to Sat D only 5.30 to 10. **Closed:** Sun, 25 to 27 Dec, 30 Dec to 1 Jan. **Meals:** alc (main courses £13 to £15). Set D £25 (3 courses). **Details:** 38 seats. Separate bar. Wheelchair access. Music.

NEW ENTRY
The Ox
Locally sourced steaks and cool cocktails
The Basement, 43 Corn Street, Bristol, BS1 1HT
Tel no: (0117) 9221001
www.theoxbristol.com
British | £30
Cooking score: 3
£5 OFF

In the heart of Bristol's old banking district, this atmospheric subterranean steakhouse occupies the former premises of the Ocean Safe Deposit vaults. The Ox is run by the team behind the nearby Milk Thistle speakeasy bar, and attracts a similarly cool crowd for cocktails in the cosy snug. The dining room is elegant, with Art Deco grape-cluster lamps and vintage mirrors on the distressed panelled walls. It draws comparisons to London's Hawksmoor (see entry), especially as locally sourced steaks cooked over charcoal are the main draw. But don't ignore the rest of the menu. An inspection meal of 'precisely cooked, very fresh' scallops teamed with Puy lentils with a well-balanced apple sauce, followed by a perfectly executed main of duck breast, carrot purée, date sauce and greens,

then a light, seasonal dessert of delicate passion fruit and white chocolate cheesecake with Yorkshire rhubarb and blood orange, was deemed 'pitch perfect'. Wines from £19.
Chef/s: Todd Francis. **Open:** Thur to Fri L 12 to 2.30, Tue to Sat D 5 to 10.30. **Closed:** Sun, Mon. **Meals:** alc (main courses £13 to £30). Set L £13 (2 courses) to £15. **Details:** 80 seats. Separate bar. Music.

Prego
Tiptop local Italian
7 North View, Bristol, BS6 7PT
Tel no: (0117) 9730496
www.pregobar.co.uk
Italian | £28
Cooking score: 3
£30

Now into its fifth year, this neighbourhood bistro continues to pack in the locals as well as drawing customers from far and wide. Chef/proprietors Julian Faiello and Olly Gallery have Italian roots and that country remains the geographical axis, resulting in a style that's regional and rustic. Although they're not afraid to call upon specialist Italian ingredients, much of the produce is seasonal and local to the restaurant: a salad of heirloom tomatoes, perhaps, with black olives and mozzarella, basil and balsamic dressing. Pizzas are a popular option, but the carte and specials board may prove too tempting with typical main courses of cannon of mutton with aubergine and anchovy paste, saffron, courgette, pea and mint risotto, or homemade ricotta ravioli with slow-roasted cherry tomatoes, asparagus and nutty butter. End with vanilla bean pannacotta with rhubarb and blood orange. A lively, all-Italian wine list starts at £15.95.
Chef/s: Olly Gallery. **Open:** Tue to Sat L 12 to 2, all week D 5.30 to 10 (6 Mon). **Closed:** 23 to 26 Dec, 30 Dec to 3 Jan. **Meals:** alc (main courses £13 to £20). Set L £10 (2 courses) to £14. Set D £25. **Details:** 54 seats. 20 seats outside. Wheelchair access. Music.

The Pump House

Waterfront venue with bold seasonal food
Merchants Road, Hotwells, Bristol, BS8 4PZ
Tel no: (0117) 9272229
www.the-pumphouse.com
Modern British | £30
Cooking score: 3
£5 OFF **V**

Positioned on the quayside where Bristol's regenerated docks meet the River Avon, this former Victorian hydraulic pumping station is now a waterside pub with a separate mezzanine restaurant. Chef/proprietor Toby Gritten is a passionate supporter of local produce and also an enthusiastic forager. His frequently changing menus in both bar and dining room mirror this uncompromising allegiance to provenance and seasonality. Grab one of the scrubbed-pine farmhouse tables in the bar and enjoy local onglet with bone marrow, beef-dripping onions and chips. Alternatively, order from the carte, which might kick off with Cotswold Legbar egg, mushroom cream and truffle oil, and then proceed with steamed hake, field mushrooms, cider, thyme cream and leeks. Still hungry? Why not order the cherry and almond trifle with macaroons? A choice of ales from south west breweries in the bar is supplemented by an engaging wine list with bottles from £17.
Chef/s: Toby Gritten. **Open:** all week L 12 to 3, D 7 to 9.30. **Closed:** 25 Dec. **Meals:** alc (main courses £12 to £20). Set L and D £15 (2 courses) to £18. Tasting menu £35 (5 courses) to £50. **Details:** 80 seats. 80 seats outside. Separate bar. Music. Car parking. No children in restaurant.

riverstation

Confident cooking at this waterfront veteran
The Grove, Bristol, BS1 4RB
Tel no: (0117) 9144434
www.riverstation.co.uk
Modern European | £30
Cooking score: 3
£5 OFF

This modernist two-storey former river-police station has been a firm part of Bristol's ever-evolving harbourside restaurant scene for the best part of two decades. Downstairs there's a bustling café/bar with good quayside alfresco potential, while upstairs the light and minimalist restaurant with its partially open kitchen remains one of the city's most consistent performers with a daily changing menu that rarely misses the beat when it comes to seasonality and solid technique. Tiptop ingredients are treated with respect in a broad range of Mediterranean dishes. Start with precisely cooked seared cuttlefish dusted with herb breadcrumbs and served with samphire and tamarillo salsa before moving on to a more Middle Eastern-influenced ras-el-hanout marinated lamb rump with three-seed freekeh, herb salad and labneh. Tonka bean and pistachio frangipane, morello cherries and clotted cream ice cream is one of the well-executed desserts. An intelligently written, interesting wine list starts at £16.50.
Chef/s: Toru Yanada. **Open:** all week L 12 to 2.30 (3 Sun), Mon to Sat D 6 to 10.30 (11 Fri and Sat). **Closed:** 24 to 26 Dec. **Meals:** alc (main courses £16 to £20). Set L £13 (2 courses) to £16. Set D £15 (2 courses) to £19. Sun L £20. **Details:** 120 seats. 22 seats outside. Separate bar.

Rockfish Grill

Quality seafood brasserie
128-130 Whiteladies Road, Bristol, BS8 2RS
Tel no: (0117) 9737384
www.rockfishgrill.co.uk
Seafood | £32
Cooking score: 4

£5 OFF

Sea-green leather banquettes, floaty linen curtains and sandy driftwood floors and tables set the scene at Mitch Tonks' stylish yet informal seafood brasserie, sister restaurant to the Seahorse, Dartmouth (see entry). Walls adorned with photos of Brixham fishermen emphasise the fact that the Devon fish market supplies the daily catch. Locals in the know might pop in for a plate of oysters with a glass of Prosecco, but the menu also delivers an enticing mix of classics such as Dartmouth crab with bread and mayonnaise, or halibut with béarnaise, plus new ideas like cured herring with fennel and blood orange. Hard-to-fault mains range from fresh fillet of char-grilled sea bass teamed with sweet, juicy clams and Sicilian tomatoes, to charcoal-grilled bavette with red wine and rosemary (one of several meat options). Wines are taken seriously, with a daily selection by the glass or carafe; bottles start at £19.
Chef/s: James Davidson. **Open:** Tue to Sat L 12 to 2.30 (3 Sat), D 6 to 10 (10.30 Sat). **Closed:** Sun, Mon, 24 Dec to 4 Jan. **Meals:** alc (main courses £13 to £25). Set L and D £13 (2 courses) to £15. **Details:** 45 seats. Music.

★ TOP 50 PUB ★

NEW ENTRY

The Rummer

Inventive modern cooking in historic hostelry
All Saints Lane, Bristol, BS1 1JH
Tel no: (0117) 9294243
www.therummer.net
British | £31
Cooking score: 3

Set in the heart of the busy St Nicholas Market, with its cornucopia of food stalls, the Rummer is one of Bristol's most notable

buildings, dating in part from the 13th century. It has been a pub since Georgian times and once served as a Berni Inn, but these days the reborn dining room in the medieval cellar (atmospheric, candlelit) provides a lot more than steak and chips. Chef Andrew Clatworthy looks north for inspiration, and his Scandinavian-style, produce-driven cooking comes with a passion for wild and foraged ingredients. The result is unusual dishes with inventive flavour combinations and textures. An early spring meal, for example, started with a warm, mosaic-like terrine of lamb sweetbreads teamed with pea, mint and hyssop, and was followed by braised ox cheek, wild garlic, raw kohlrabi and sweet-roasted onion. Desserts can be more conventional, as in warm chocolate sponge accompanied by whipped coffee cream. House wine from £17.45.
Chef/s: Andrew Clatworthy. **Open:** all week 10 to 5 (11 Sat, 12.30 Sun), Mon to Sat D 6 to 10. **Closed:** 25 and 26 Dec, 1 Jan. **Meals:** alc (main courses £14 to £17). **Details:** 22 seats. Separate bar. Music. Over 18s only.

NEW ENTRY

Wallfish Bistro

Cooking from the heart
112 Princess Victoria Street, Bristol, BS8 4DB
Tel no: (0117) 9735435
www.wallfishbistro.co.uk
British | £30
Cooking score: 4

The blue plaque outside is a permanent reminder that this was the site of Keith Floyd's original restaurant, as are well-thumbed copies of the celebrity chef's books inside. After honing their skills with the likes of Mark Hix and Rowley Leigh, Seldon Curry and Liberty Wenham opened this intimate bistro in the summer of 2013 and it has quickly established itself as a regular haunt for Bristol foodies. With its toffee-coloured leather banquettes, colander lampshades and fish-shaped water jugs (complete with satisfying glug), the Wallfish is a modest, quirky place. Curry cooks from the heart and his menus are uncompromisingly seasonal; an early spring meal kicked off with just-picked Wye Valley asparagus and wild garlic-spiked creamed morels. Fish is a strength, a precisely cooked gilthead sea bream roasted whole with rosemary and charred lemon. Desserts don't hold back – Negroni jelly with blood-orange sorbet packing a serious punch. Wines from £15.

Chef/s: Seldon Curry. **Open:** Wed to Sun L 12 to 3 (10am Sun), D 6 to 10 (9 Sun). **Closed:** Mon, Tue, 24 to 30 Dec, 2 weeks Feb. **Meals:** alc (main courses £10 to 24). **Details:** 40 seats. 4 seats outside. Music.

Wilks

Local favourite with top-class cooking
1-3 Chandos Road, Bristol, BS6 6PG
Tel no: (0117) 9737999
www.wilksrestaurant.co.uk
Modern European | £38
Cooking score: 4

£5
OFF

Since Wilks opened in autumn 2012, James Wilkins and Christine Vayssade have made an indelible mark on the Bristol dining scene. Their stylish neighbourhood restaurant is tucked down a quiet side street in one of the city's leafier suburbs. James previously worked for celebrated French chef Michel Bras and also the Galvin brothers in London. He has that ability to conjure up boldly flavoured inventive dishes from predominately local produce, including some grown exclusively for him at a nearby walled garden. A technically astute poached quail and foie gras ballotine with butternut squash, pickled walnuts and wild leaves might precede a main-course squab pigeon 'royale' complete with a confit leg, violet artichokes, pearl barley and organic beetroots, which displayed extraordinary care and attention to detail. A zesty finale of citrus meringue, lemon curd, mandarin and yuzu sorbet has garnered particular praise. The conscientiously sourced, French-heavy wine list starts at £17.50.

Chef/s: James Wilkins. **Open:** Wed to Sun L 12 to 2 (3 Sun), D 6.30 to 10 (9 Sun). **Closed:** Mon, Tue, 3 weeks Jan, 2 weeks Aug, bank hols. **Meals:** alc

(main courses £16 to £26). Set L £17 (2 courses) to £20. **Details:** 35 seats. 6 seats outside. Wheelchair access. Children over 5 yrs only at D.

Cheltenham

★ TOP 10 ★

Le Champignon Sauvage

A culinary big-hitter
24-26 Suffolk Road, Cheltenham, GL50 2AQ
Tel no: (01242) 573449
www.lechampignonsauvage.co.uk
Modern French | £59
Cooking score: 8

David and Helen Everitt-Matthias are fast approaching their third decade in Cheltenham with their restaurant still as 'brilliant as ever'. Le Champignon Sauvage manages, quite effortlessly, to exude both sophistication and a relaxed, unbuttoned mood for such a culinary big-hitter. David Everitt-Matthias' modern culinary approach comes underpinned by a classical theme, his carefully crafted dishes allowed to evolve rather than chase fashion – after all, this is a chef who was championing seasonal, foraged and locally sourced produce long before it became *de rigueur*. Indeed, much depends on sourcing, and Everitt-Matthias has an enviable, unchallenged reputation for garnering faultless raw materials at their seasonal peak. First courses lay down a marker for what is to follow, perhaps a 'beautifully cooked and beautifully presented' pigeon breast, served the right side of rare, with a pigeon pastilla and teamed with beetroot, pistachios, beetroot and rosehip purée. Centrepiece dishes exhibit upfront flavours and forceful simplicity, witness Cinderford lamb, its accompanying roasted sweetbreads, wilted dandelion and roasted root, orange and goats' curd: exquisite counterpoints of texture and flavour. That this is cooking constructed with real passion can be seen in the likes of frozen bergamot parfait partnered with liquorice cream and an intense orange jelly. Wine is taken seriously, too: reasonable prices (house wines from £20), reliable producers, plenty for the French purists, but with some good southern-hemisphere specialists. **Chef/s:** David Everitt-Matthias. **Open:** Tue to Sat L 12.30 to 1.15, D 7.30 to 8.30. **Closed:** Sun, Mon, 10 days Christmas, 3 weeks Jun. **Meals:** alc (£48 2 courses, £59 3 courses). Set L and Tue to Fri D £26 (2 courses) to £32. **Details:** 38 seats.

The Daffodil
Modern cooking, Art Deco surroundings
18-20 Suffolk Parade, Cheltenham, GL50 2AE
Tel no: (01242) 700055
www.thedaffodil.com
British | £34
Cooking score: 3

Settings don't come more deliciously retro than this former Art Deco cinema, which, despite living through a ragbag of incarnations before becoming a restaurant, has plenty of original features intact. The kitchen sits where the screen once was, and very often there's a live band up there too. Amid the glamour of yesteryear you can expect smart, modern cooking that combines classic European influences and excellent native ingredients – maybe a twice-baked Double Gloucester soufflé with a 'sensational' truffled cheese sauce, and then Cornish cod with Wye Valley asparagus, Jersey Royals and brown shrimp butter. Alternatively, there are steaks from the Josper grill (the buttery, pungent blue cheese sauce is a must). Finish with coconut arancini with rum ice cream and roasted pineapple: 'a fun twist on classic rice pudding'. The international wine list offers plenty of choice by the glass or carafe, with bottles starting at £29.
Chef/s: Tom Rains. **Open:** Mon to Sat L 12 to 2.30, D 6 to 10. **Closed:** Sun. **Meals:** alc (main courses £15 to £25). Set L and early D £14 (2 courses) to £16. **Details:** 80 seats. Separate bar.

Lumière
Complex food in a low-key setting
Clarence Parade, Cheltenham, GL50 3PA
Tel no: (01242) 222200
www.lumiere.cc
Modern British | £55
Cooking score: 5

V

An understated Cheltenham favourite, with enough culinary clout to turn heads and tease palates, Jon and Helen Howe's classy Lumière sits comfortably in a petite Regency house not far from the town centre. Rich purple hues, cream tones, elegant mirrors and comfy banquettes suggest formality, although the mood is never reverential. Against this backdrop, Jon delivers food brimming with on-trend gastronomic complexity, confident gestures and flashes of brilliance: witness smoked sea trout and salmon roe topped with smoked eel wrapped in a sheath of cucumber jelly ('one of the best things we've eaten this year') or a surprising combo of rabbit, white pudding, wheat beer, hedgehog mushrooms and Agen prunes. Palate-cleansers 'extraordinaire' and scintillating desserts also get rave reviews: from Tequila sorbet with salt crisp and milk-shot ball to a 'superb display of tastes, textures and temperatures' involving fresh strawberries, sorbet 'boules' and Aero-style white chocolate. The well-constructed wine list promises serious drinking from £18.
Chef/s: Jon Howe. **Open:** Wed to Sat L 12 to 1.30, Tue to Sat D 7 to 9. **Closed:** Sun, Mon, 2 weeks winter, 2 weeks summer. **Meals:** Set L £28. Set D £55. Tasting menu L £60 (7 courses), D £75 (9 courses). **Details:** 26 seats. Music. Children over 10 yrs only.

NEW ENTRY

No. 131

Cool styling and big-hearted cooking
131 Promenade, Cheltenham, GL50 1NW
Tel no: (01242) 822939
www.no131.com
British | £35
Cooking score: 4

Expect hipster beards aplenty at this stylish town-centre hotel, especially in the basement bar where the cool décor blends beautiful tiled floors and character furniture with offbeat photography and retro industrial lighting. The ground-floor restaurant continues in a similar vein, referencing most decades of the 20th century and coming off feeling like a cross between a gentlemen's club and a 1960s student common room. For all the edgy styling and carefully chosen music, the cooking is big-hearted and unpretentious, from a 'sensational' sizzling crab gratin to a big, pearlescent piece of cod with chickpeas, tender squid and cherry tomatoes. There are manly steaks, too, with luxury extras like foie gras or garlic snails and crisp, rustic duck-fat fries. A hearty pud of treacle tart typifies the comfortable, often nostalgic flavour of the whole operation. Wine-wise, there's a decent international selection, with plenty from France and 19 by the glass. Bottles start at £19.
Chef/s: Antony Ely. **Open:** all week L 12 to 3 (4 Sun), D 6 to 10 (11 Fri and Sat). **Meals:** alc (main courses £12 to £30). **Details:** 46 seats. Separate bar. Music.

Purslane

The perfect neighbourhood restaurant
16 Rodney Road, Cheltenham, GL50 1JJ
Tel no: (01242) 321639
www.purslane-restaurant.co.uk
Seafood | £33
Cooking score: 6

In just a short time Stephanie Ronssin and Gareth Fulford have established Purslane as one of the best restaurants in town. The small dining room, housed in a pale yellow Georgian building in a quiet street off the main shopping drag, 'feels like a neighbourhood restaurant where everyone is very friendly and welcoming'. Gareth Fulford oversees a regularly changing, concertedly seasonal menu that majors in seafood, tries out some artful combinations but doesn't overreach itself in ambition. This was certainly the case with a February meal, which brought veal cheek terrine with Jersey milk curd, romanesco, bone-marrow crumb and pickled mushrooms ahead of black sea bream with monk's beard and mussel stew, salsify, and celery sponges. Or take an April dinner, where a reporter waxed lyrical about cod cheeks with boudin noir, sea bass with Wye Valley asparagus, and rhubarb soufflé made with Evesham rhubarb. Service is 'relaxed and unpretentious'; wines start at £19.
Chef/s: Gareth Fulford. **Open:** Tue to Sat L 12 to 2.30, D 6.30 to 9.30. **Closed:** Sun, Mon, 24 to 31 Dec, 24 Aug to 10 Sept. **Meals:** alc (main courses £16 to £18). **Details:** 34 seats. 4 seats outside. Music. Children at L only.

LOCAL GEM

▲ The Tavern

5 Royal Well Place, Cheltenham, GL50 3DN
Tel no: (01242) 221212
www.thetaverncheltenham.com
Modern British | £28

Flying the flag for the special relationship, the Tavern is a one-time boozer turned Anglo-American joint where chilli dogs can be washed down with pints of British ale. There's an upbeat urban vibe – Soho meets Brooklyn – with bottled beers and cocktails confirming the place's credentials as a drinking den. Food is the mainstay, though, with burgers, sliders and salads (goats' cheese with roast grapes and walnuts), plus British steaks served with French fries. Drink beer or wines from £16. Open all week.

Cirencester

Jesse's Bistro
Folksy bistro with big ideas
The Stableyard, Black Jack Street, Cirencester, GL7 2AA
Tel no: (01285) 641497
www.jessesbistro.co.uk
Modern British | £40
Cooking score: 1

£5 OFF

'The atmosphere is warm, the building is pretty, the location is a gift,' remarked one visitor who enjoyed a real sense of discovery on encountering this pretty bistro in an old brick stable yard. Inside, it's all exposed stone, beams, polished tables and wicker chairs – with plenty to watch in the open kitchen. Reports are mostly positive: twice-baked cheese soufflé, and roast loin and mini shepherd's pie of lamb with Anna potatoes, shallot purée and Savoy cabbage, gaining praise. The set menu is laudable, too, as is the all-British cheeseboard. Desserts such as dark chocolate cheesecake with malted milk ice cream should send you away happy. Wines from £21.50.
Chef/s: David Witnall and Andrew Parffrey. **Open:** Mon to Sat L 12 to 2.30 (3 Sat), Tue to Sat D 7 to 9.30. **Closed:** Sun, 25 to 28 Dec, 1 to 4 Jan. **Meals:** alc (main courses £14 to £30). Set L and D £18 (2 courses) to £26. **Details:** 45 seats. 25 seats outside. Wheelchair access. Music.

Made by Bob
Deli-dining in a Cotswold town
26 Market Place, Cirencester, GL7 2NY
Tel no: (01285) 641818
www.foodmadebybob.com
Modern European | £30
Cooking score: 3

'They don't take bookings and we were advised to arrive early – glad we did,' noted one visitor to this 'deliciously trendy deli' that is 'a worthy diversion even if you don't eat'. Warehouse windows and white-painted walls create a clean, modern look. Beyond a counter piled high with cakes is the open kitchen: a hive of industry, with a stool-lined bar so you can watch the action. The rest is all shiny wooden tables and bustling waiters, who'll bring anything from breakfast onwards through the day. Expect simple brasserie food, perhaps 'perfectly cooked' linguine with charcuterie cream, peas and mint or grilled ribeye with béarnaise and fries. There are no real starters, just lighter options such as fish soup, charcuterie, wild mushroom risotto, salads or sandwiches. A rustic bread-and-butter pudding to finish is 'perfect comfort food'. The keenly priced international wine list starts at £16.
Chef/s: James (Bob) Parkinson. **Open:** Mon to Sat 7.30am to 5.30 (8am Sat). Thur and Fri D 7 to 9. **Closed:** Sun, Jan to Feb for D. **Meals:** alc (main courses £11 to £25). **Details:** 70 seats. Wheelchair access.

Corse Lawn

Corse Lawn House Hotel
Elegance and classic cooking
Corse Lawn, GL19 4LZ
Tel no: (01452) 780771
www.corselawn.com
Anglo-French | £35
Cooking score: 3

£5 OFF 🍽 V

The pond in front of this gracious Queen Anne building was originally a coach wash; nowadays, bobbing ducks are the only things taking a dip. Owned by the Hine family since the 1970s, Corse Lawn House feels family-run, with staff 'a bit stiff but well meaning and very well drilled' and 'good personal touches throughout'. The interior features plenty of period furnishings and 'faded famous prints in frames'. Chef Martin Kinahan is approaching two decades at the stove here. His cooking ranges from the comfortably familiar (as in canapés of smoked salmon on toast or mini pizzas) to harmonious takes on local ingredients, such as Severn and Wye smoked eel with horseradish cream, beetroot and smoked pancetta. Pollack with samphire and saffron sauce is a sure-footed main, while sticky toffee pudding has been described as 'gooey perfection'. The notable wine list (from £20) covers all major French regions and offers decent international coverage.

Chef/s: Martin Kinahan. **Open:** all week L 12 to 2, D 7 to 9.30. **Closed:** 24 to 26 Dec. **Meals:** alc (main courses £15 to £23). Set L £23 (2 courses) to £26. Set D £34. **Details:** 50 seats. 40 seats outside. Separate bar. Wheelchair access. Car parking.

Ebrington

LOCAL GEM
▲ The Ebrington Arms
Ebrington, GL55 6NH
Tel no: (01386) 593223
www.theebringtonarms.co.uk
Modern British | £27

Draught real ales from the owners' Yubberton Brewing Company are the latest crowd-pulling asset at this classy Cotswold pub-with-rooms overlooking Ebrington village green. The food is also a shining star, mixing jazzed-up staples such as fish and chips or venison burgers, with sophisticated ideas ranging from spiced aubergine won tons with red pepper salsa or chilled game Wellington to poached cod with spinach, chorizo and prawn butter. Warm, knowledgeable staff are 'the icing on the cake'. House wine is £18. Open all week. Accom.

Eldersfield

★ TOP 10 PUB ★

The Butchers Arms
Proper pub, confident cooking
Lime Street, Eldersfield, GL19 4NX
Tel no: (01452) 840381
www.thebutchersarms.net
Modern British | £43
Cooking score: 5

James and Elizabeth Winter's 'little gem' is the personification of a small rustic pub: friendly, gratifyingly comfortable, full of warmth (thanks to two wood-burners) and honest intent. According to a pair of regulars 'the entire experience is enormously enjoyable'.

The mood is mellow and James' cooking a beacon of quality defined by clear flavours and pin-sharp accuracy. Among some fortifying cold-weather dishes 'meltingly tender' roast deer loin served with 'strikingly flavoursome' haggis, neeps and tatties has proved a winter hit. Fish is a strength, whether a bowl of Cornish fish soup with smoked haddock, brill and fried brown shrimps or 'beautifully cooked' cod with crab tortellini, pea purée and crab bisque. To conclude, visitors have been impressed by 'perfectly timed' chocolate fondant with vanilla ice cream and honeycomb, and a menu favourite – macarons with pistachio ice cream. Local ales tapped from the cask emphasise pubby credentials. Wines from £23.50.

Chef/s: James Winter. **Open:** Fri to Sun L 12 to 1 (bookings only), Tue to Sat D 7 to 9. **Closed:** Mon, 24 to 27 Dec, 2 weeks Jan, last 2 weeks Aug. **Meals:** alc (main courses £19 to £27). **Details:** 25 seats. Separate bar. Car parking. No children under 10 yrs.

Long Ashton

The Bird in Hand
Handsome village pub on the up
17 Weston Road, Long Ashton, BS41 9LA
Tel no: (01275) 395222
www.bird-in-hand.co.uk
British | £25
Cooking score: 2
£30

With pages from Mrs Beeton cookbooks on the walls and shelves lined with homemade chutneys, the Bird in Hand sets its stall out as an affable village pub that takes food seriously. Locals still huddle around the bar, but in-the-know foodies make a beeline for the teal-coloured dining room, which is adorned with vintage advertising signs and filled with scrubbed wooden tables. Chef Jack Williams has moved across from Toby Gritten and Dan Obern's other pub, the Pump House (see entry). His food is less rustic than his predecessor's, the dishes better presented, although flavours are just as robust and menus strongly seasonal. An early May meal showcased plenty of late-spring produce:

English asparagus with goats' curd and hazelnut vinaigrette; wet garlic-infused barley and greens accompanying rich braised beef tongue and cheek; light and refreshing rhubarb jelly with vanilla custard ice cream. Wines from £17.

Chef/s: Jack Williams. **Open:** all week L 12 to 3 (4 Sun), Mon to Sat D 6 to 9. **Closed:** 25 Dec. **Meals:** alc (main courses £11 to £18). Set L £14 (2 courses) to £16. **Details:** 35 seats. 40 seats outside. Music.

■ Lower Oddington

LOCAL GEM
▲ The Fox Inn
Lower Oddington, GL56 0UR
Tel no: (01451) 870555
www.foxinn.net
British | £27

You'll feel instantly at ease in this Cotswold-stone village inn-with-rooms. With interlinked rooms, rug-strewn stone floors, low-beamed ceilings, open fires, plus a pretty garden, it has the kind of relaxed feel that lifts the spirits. Since taking over in 2013, Peter and Louise Robinson have wisely resisted the urge to change any of it. On the food front, expect a modern British-Mediterranean influenced menu (venison ragù with pappardelle, perhaps) and a handful of pub classics (baked ham, fried eggs and chips). Open all week.

■ Moreton in Marsh

Horse & Groom
Consistently satisfying hilltop inn
Bourton on the Hill, Moreton in Marsh, GL56 9AQ
Tel no: (01386) 700413
www.horseandgroom.info
Modern British | £28
Cooking score: 2
£5 OFF 🛏 £30

Brothers Tom and Will Greenstock restored this honey-coloured Grade II-listed Georgian stone coaching inn-with-rooms ten years ago and it continues to draw locals and Cotswolds visitors. Punters pop in for a quick pint of locally brewed Goff's Jouster, or perhaps tarry longer and order from the menu of no-frills modern British dishes. The kitchen takes local sourcing seriously and the seasonal menus often change during service. Start with home-cured salt beef, roasted beetroot, soft-boiled quails'eggs, gherkin and horseradish cream, then continue with pan-fried fillet of Cornish hake, sautéed leeks and Café de Paris butter, or shin of Dexter beef braised with garlic, ginger and soy, steamed greens and sesame noodles. Banana and hazelnut Eton mess with butterscotch sauce makes a satisfying conclusion. A concise but interesting wine list with plenty of good drinking under £20 starts at £14.75.

Chef/s: Will Greenstock. **Open:** all week L 12 to 2 (2.30 Sun), Mon to Sat D 7 to 9 (9.30 Fri and Sat). **Closed:** 25 Dec, 1 week Jan. **Meals:** alc (main courses £12 to £20). **Details:** 75 seats. 56 seats outside. Separate bar. Car parking.

■ Nailsworth

Mark@street
Doing things properly
Market Street, Nailsworth, GL6 0BX
Tel no: (01453) 839251
www.marketstreetnailsworth.co.uk
Modern British | £32
Cooking score: 2
£5 OFF

Mark Payne brings his experience to bear on the simple food at his solo restaurant, opened after his years in London and the Cotswolds. The venue may be small, and relatively tucked away, but that doesn't prevent the menu having serious appeal and a touch of background flair. Payne does things the proper way, with reports praising the silky-smooth smoked mash served with crisp breast and rare rump of lamb, and the homemade chutneys brought out with parfaits and cheeses. There's a pleasing seasonal (and local) rhythm to a menu featuring wild rabbit and apple rillettes with raisin purée, roe deer with pearl barley and parsley risotto, and glazed rice pudding with port-baked plums and coconut crisps. A blind five-course tasting menu is a popular way to explore further, and the amiable service has the warmth required to get people coming back. Wines are from £16.

Chef/s: Mark Payne. **Open:** Tue to Sun L 12 to 2.30, Tue to Sat D 7 to 9.30. **Closed:** Mon, 26 Dec, 2 weeks Jan, 1 week Sept, bank hols. **Meals:** alc (main courses £16 to £20). Sun L £16 (2 courses) to £20. Tasting menu £40 (5 courses). **Details:** 24 seats. Separate bar. Music. Car parking.

■ Northleach

★ TOP 50 PUB ★

The Wheatsheaf Inn

Captivating Cotswold coaching inn
West End, Northleach, GL54 3EZ
Tel no: (01451) 860244
www.cotswoldswheatsheaf.com
Modern British | £28
Cooking score: 3

A handsome country inn bursting with attributes, the Wheatsheaf brings modern sensibilities to a classic Cotswold village setting. It's a well-bred place that glows with confidence. The interior is kitted out with immense panache while keeping the historic feel of the building. Attention to detail is shown where it matters. Alongside wood fires, real ales on tap and a serious wine list, creature comforts extend to smart accommodation. Such flair also informs the cooking. The kitchen has judged to a nicety what local people want from a country pub. That means devilled kidneys on toast, twice-baked Cheddar soufflé or linguine with crab, chilli, tomato and garlic among starters, and mains of lamb shank with soft polenta, peppered flat-iron steak or haunch of venison with red wine sauce. End proceedings with traditional desserts such as sticky toffee pudding with honey and ginger ice cream. Carefully chosen wines start at £17.

Chef/s: Antony Ely. **Open:** all week L 12 to 3 (4 Sun), D 6 to 9 (10.30 Fri and Sat). **Closed:** 1 day Jan. **Meals:** alc (main courses £10 to £25). Weekday set L

£13 (2 courses) to £15. **Details:** 90 seats. 80 seats outside. Separate bar. Wheelchair access. Music. Car parking.

■ Oakridge Lynch

The Butchers Arms

A tucked-away treat
Oakridge Lynch, GL6 7NZ
Tel no: (01285) 760371
www.butchersarmsoakridge.com
Modern British | £34
Cooking score: 2

With its low-beamed ceiling, exposed stone walls, unclothed tables and beer garden for when the weather turns fine, the unassuming Butchers Arms is exactly what you might expect to find in a genuine village inn. It seems Michael and Sarah Bedford (formerly of the Chef's Table in nearby Tetbury) have worked their magic once again, mixing bags of rustic appeal with local beers – and making food the star of the show. While much is made of local sourcing of ingredients, the short menu mixes French bistro dishes with upbeat British classics, offering a homemade Scotch egg (served with pickled gherkin and celery salt) alongside chicken liver parfait or moules marinière. Equally impressive main courses range from beautifully cooked coq au vin, to rump of beef forestière or a well-made burger served on a homemade sesame roll. There's crème brûlée or sticky toffee pudding to finish. Wines from £17.25.

Chef/s: Michael Bedford. **Open:** Tue to Sun L 12 to 3, Tue to Sat D 7 to 9.30. **Closed:** Mon. **Meals:** alc (main courses £13 to £23). **Details:** 50 seats. 32 seats outside. Separate bar. Wheelchair access. Car parking.

¶¶● Visit us Online

To find out more about *The Good Food Guide*, please visit www.thegoodfoodguide.co.uk

▌Thornbury
Ronnie's of Thornbury
Low-key gem
11 St Mary Street, Thornbury, BS35 2AB
Tel no: (01454) 411137
www.ronnies-restaurant.co.uk
Modern European | £28
Cooking score: 3
£5 OFF £30

'First-class food, service and atmosphere' was the verdict of one visitor to this well-appointed restaurant hidden away in Thornbury's otherwise unremarkable shopping precinct. Despite its quirky location, this 17th-century former schoolhouse continues to attract as many destination diners as it does locals. The bare stone walls, warm lighting and neutral colours make for a relaxed, smart setting for chef/proprietor Ron Faulkner's please-all menus of seasonal, produce-driven modern European food. An early summer meal might begin with cured Brixham mackerel, Jersey Royals, beetroot, yoghurt and horseradish followed, perhaps, by an accurately cooked fillet of wild sea bass, leeks, potato gnocchi and 'well-balanced' mussel and saffron sauce. For dessert, go for the trio of mini brûlées – Madagascan vanilla, latte and orange – or the board of British cheeses. A good-value international wine list starts at £15 but the 'lucky dip' may bag you a wine valued at between £30 and £139.
Chef/s: Ron Faulkner. **Open:** Tue to Sun L 12 to 2.30, Tue to Sat D 6 to 9.30 (10 Sat). **Closed:** Mon, 25 and 26 Dec, 1 to 8 Jan. **Meals:** Set L £20 (2 courses) to £25. Set D £25 (2 courses) to £28. Sun L £18 (2 courses) to £21. **Details:** 52 seats. 18 seats outside. Separate bar. Wheelchair access. Music. Car parking.

▌Upper Slaughter
Lords of the Manor
Cooking with a high degree of technical gloss
Upper Slaughter, GL54 2JD
Tel no: (01451) 820243
www.lordsofthemanor.com
Modern British | £69
Cooking score: 4
£5 OFF ♦ ⊨

The village name belies the fact that it's one of the handful of England's 'thankful' settlements: communities that recorded no losses in either world war. And certainly the serenity pervading the manor house, amid its eight acres of gardens and lake, suggests a place at ease with itself. A dining room in full starched-linen kit makes an elegant setting for Richard Edwards' carefully worked modern British combinations. A serving of Cornish crab, the brown meat in a light potato roll, the white on creamed cucumber and caviar, is all assertiveness rather than ethereal delicacy, while mains such as tender loin and faggot of venison with red cabbage in sloe gin is impeccably timed. Desserts, like an eight-layered mille-feuille of apple and chestnut with clotted cream ice cream, end things on a high. The wine list is a masterpiece that inspires confidence in lesser-known European byways (including England) and the New World, as unerringly as it does in the headline French regions. Bottles from £24.
Chef/s: Richard Edwards. **Open:** Sun L 12.30 to 1.30, all week D 6.45 to 8.45. **Meals:** Set D £69. Sun L £40. **Details:** 50 seats. Car parking. Children over 7 yrs only at D.

■ Weston Subedge
The Seagrave Arms
A pub success story
Friday Street, Weston Subedge, GL55 6QH
Tel no: (01386) 840192
www.seagravearms.co.uk
Modern British | £30
Cooking score: 3

£5 OFF

The listed former Georgian farmhouse built from Cotswold stone makes a heart-warming country inn – big on atmosphere, with crackling fires in winter and a sheltered courtyard for fair-weather alfresco. It's a delightful setting for some distinctly superior cooking. The kitchen knows what is required, and delivers in fine fashion. Basic materials are well sourced (many locally) and well handled, the short-choice menu offering pigeon breast with onion squash and watercress pesto as one way to start. Main dishes run a broadly based course from whole grilled Cornish lemon sole teamed with caper butter sauce and potato gratin, to Madgett's Farm duck confit served atop braised red cabbage and caramelised apples. To finish, the selection of Cotswold cheeses is highly rated or there's lemon curd cheesecake with raspberry coulis. Service is kind and accommodating, and wines from a short list start at £16.95.
Chef/s: Julien Atrous. **Open:** Tue to Sun L 12 to 2.30, Tue to Sat D 6 to 9. **Closed:** Mon, first 2 weeks Jan. **Meals:** alc (main courses £14 to £17). **Details:** 40 seats. 40 seats outside. Separate bar. Wheelchair access. Music. Car parking.

■ Winchcombe
5 North Street
Pint-sized eatery with stellar food
5 North Street, Winchcombe, GL54 5LH
Tel no: (01242) 604566
www.5northstreetrestaurant.co.uk
Modern European | £47
Cooking score: 6

V

Shoehorned into a crooked, half-timbered house on Winchcombe's main drag, Kate and Marcus Ashenford's cosy, pint-sized eatery is a family affair noted for its romantic vibes, warm heart and thoughtful, highly cohesive modern cooking. It's a flexible set-up, with diners offered a choice of three set menus – although mixing and matching is encouraged, with prices adjusted accordingly. After some marvellous home-baked mini loaves and clever canapés, you might be treated to a hand-dived scallop with confit duck, creamed and crispy artichokes, ceps and salsify, followed by seasonal meat or game: perhaps roast Winchcombe partridge with truffle sausage, choucroute, figs and sauce 'aigre doux'. To finish, sticky toffee pudding might appear in unexpected company with Guinness ice cream, pineapple and salted caramel, but don't miss the artisan British cheeses served with a warm onion loaf, oatmeal biscuits, wine jellies and homemade fruit chutney. The well-spread, carefully curated wine list starts at £22.
Chef/s: Marcus Ashenford. **Open:** Wed to Sun L 12.30 to 1.30, Tue to Sat D 7 to 9. **Closed:** Mon, 1 week Jan, 2 weeks Aug. **Meals:** alc (main courses £22 to £24). Set L £24 (2 courses) to £28. Set D £33 (2 courses) to £50. Sun L £33. **Details:** 24 seats. Music.

The Lion Inn
An authentic pub that's a cut above
37 North Street, Winchcombe, GL54 5PS
Tel no: (01242) 603300
www.thelionwinchcombe.co.uk
Modern British | £30
Cooking score: 1

Behind wonky walls of honeyed stone lies a pub with the requisite sleeping dogs, interesting ales and locals propping up the bar. Flagstones and floorboards, rugs and beams, a big toasty fire and fresh paintwork in pale heritage colours add up to a setting that feels venerable but not faded. Rustic leanings colour such offerings as 'country-style soup' or devilled mushrooms on toast – but perfectly roasted salmon with purple potatoes, Jerusalem artichokes, spring greens and hollandaise is not your average pub fare. Finish with zingy homemade lemon tart. Wines start at £18.
Chef/s: Alex Dumitrache. **Open:** all week L 12 to 3, D 6 to 9. **Meals:** alc (main courses £13 to £20). **Details:** 46 seats. 60 seats outside. Separate bar. Music.

Wesley House
Refined home-style dishes
High Street, Winchcombe, GL54 5LJ
Tel no: (01242) 602366
www.wesleyhouse.co.uk
Modern European | £40
Cooking score: 2

What a quirky place Wesley House is, moving from the delightfully archaic (the ramshackle, beamed exterior), to downright old-fashioned (the lobby with its clutter of granny's-front-room furniture). By contrast, the long, thin dining room is cosy and smart, offering white cloths, fresh flowers, candlelight, bare stone and black-on-white beamed walls; it's run with a kind of formal yet friendly efficiency. The kitchen delivers a repertoire of straightforward, enjoyable modern dishes. Recent successes have included smoked haddock soufflé with grilled leek and mustard cream sauce; roast pheasant with celeriac purée, mushroom and game sauce; and lemon sole with cauliflower, truffle, pine nut and fish red wine sauce. For dessert, almond and pistachio cake with brown-bread ice cream has been singled out. The compact wine list offers modest prices and focuses its by-the-glass selection on well-made but reasonably priced grape varieties that diners will recognise. Bottles start from £19.
Chef/s: Cedrik Rullier. **Open:** Tue to Sun L 12 to 2.30, Tue to Sat D 6.30 to 10. **Closed:** Mon, 26 Dec. **Meals:** alc (main courses £15 to £28). Set L £15 (2 courses) to £19. Set D £22 (2 courses) to £28. **Details:** 60 seats. Separate bar.

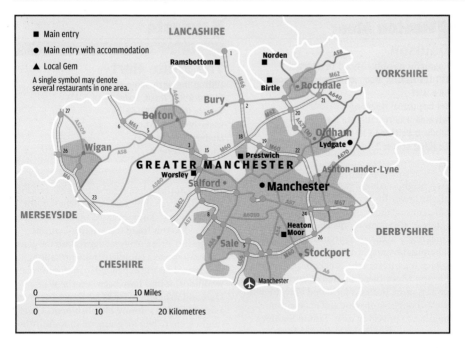

■ Ashton-under-Lyne

READERS RECOMMEND

Lily's Vegetarian Indian Cuisine

75-83 Oldham Road, Ashton-under-Lyne, OL6 7DF
Tel no: (0161) 339 4774
'Bhel puri was as fine an example as you'd want to come across. Masala dosa was a belter.'

■ Birtle

The Waggon at Birtle

Hearty modern British cooking
131 Bury and Rochdale Old Road, Birtle, BL9 6UE
Tel no: (01706) 622955
www.thewaggonatbirtle.co.uk
Modern British | £30
Cooking score: 2

£5
OFF

Affable service and consistent output from the kitchen is what the Waggon is all about. Few traces remain of its former pub identity, except on the outside, for nowadays it's very much a restaurant with polished tables and a warm colour scheme – an oasis in an area with few decent eateries. It's popular, too, so booking is advisable. The kitchen trades in local produce and a modern British outlook, which means a range of influences: from straightforward lunchtime 'light bites' of spicy lamb meatballs with tomato and basil sauce, or battered haddock and chips, to the more complex tempura of Chadwick's Bury black pudding, and roasted 'Johnson and Swarbrick' duck breast with its slow-cooked leg, beetroot fondant and duck and potato croquette in a fig and red wine sauce. There's no stinting on the generosity, especially for dessert when warm mini Eccles cakes arrive with clotted cream and spiced syrup. Wines from £15.95.

Chef/s: David Watson. **Open:** Thur and Fri L 12 to 2, Wed to Sat D 6 to 9 (9.30 Sat). Sun 12.30 to 7. **Closed:** Mon, Tue, 26 to 30 Dec, 1 to 7 Jan, last week Jul, first week Aug. **Meals:** alc (main courses £11 to £23). Set L and D £16 (2 courses) to £18. **Details:** 48 seats. Separate bar. Wheelchair access. Music. Car parking.

Heaton Moor

Damson

Colourful neighbourhood restaurant
113-115 Heaton Moor Road, Heaton Moor,
SK4 4HY
Tel no: (0161) 4324666
www.damsonrestaurant.co.uk
Modern British | £30
Cooking score: 2

£5
OFF

As a neighbourhood restaurant, Damson 'ticks all the boxes' for readers in search of friendly, efficient staff and a menu that holds the interest. What's more, 'the chef can cook better than many in the area', according to reports. The suitably purple dining room is the smartest address in the Stockport suburb of Heaton Moor (head to MediaCity for the newer, more business-oriented branch), with well-thought-out wine and cheese lists helping to provide a treat. Simon Stanley's food – which includes long-standing favourites like the subtly flavoured Whitby crab and parsley risotto with cockles – is rooted in the north. 'Classic modern British' plates like Goosnargh duck with lentils and shredded cabbage tend to be the most successful. Readers note with pleasure that there are 'deals to be had'; dessert from the set lunch might be a none-too-shabby chocolate shortbread with pistachio ice cream. Wine by the bottle from £17.95.
Chef/s: Simon Stanley. Open: Fri L 12 to 2.45, Mon to Sat D 5.30 to 9.30. Sun 12 to 7.30. Meals: alc (main courses £13 to £26). Early D £16 (2 courses) to £19. Sun L £16. Details: 80 seats. 10 seats outside. Wheelchair access. Music.

Lydgate

★ TOP 50 PUB ★

The White Hart

Hilltop inn with some stellar food
51 Stockport Road, Lydgate, OL4 4JJ
Tel no: (01457) 872566
www.thewhitehart.co.uk
Modern British | £31
Cooking score: 4

£5 ⊨ V
OFF

'There's nothing like it for degrees of cooking and price, excluding central Manchester, for miles around.' Thus summed up one who returned to this listed top-of-the-Pennine village inn after a ten-year gap to find the place had undergone a complete transformation. Smartened up and expanded (to accommodate weddings) it may have been, yet the White Hart still manages to strike a balance between a drinking and a dining establishment. There might seem to be a lot going on in some dishes (a tasting menu features), but the food itself, much to its credit, does not appear fussy. Priorities are where they should be: good-value set lunches (Dorset crab salad, roasted-and-poached chicken with BBQ sauce and air-dried skin, passion-fruit soufflé); well-priced brasserie dishes (calf's liver, braised ox cheek); and the posher end of the spectrum represented by slow-roast pork belly with langoustine and shellfish sauce. 'Excellent' service, and wines from £16.50, complete a satisfying package.
Chef/s: Michael Shaw. Open: Mon to Sat L 12 to 2.30, D 6 to 9.30. Sun 12 to 8. Closed: 26 Dec, 1 Jan. Meals: alc (main courses £12 to £21). Set L £14 (2 courses) to £17. Sun L £23. Tasting menu £48 (7 courses). Details: 100 seats. Separate bar. Wheelchair access. Music. Car parking.

Manchester

Albert Square Chop House

Boldly British chophouse
The Memorial Hall, Albert Square, Manchester,
M2 5PF
Tel no: (0161) 8341866
www.albertsquarechophouse.com
British | £29
Cooking score: 2
£5 OFF 🍷 £30

Roger Ward is Manchester's chophouse king, with a mini-chain of boldly British eateries dotted around the city. This Albert Square outlet – housed in Thomas Worthington's iconic Memorial Hall – is reckoned to be the pick of the crop, with its fabulous Victorian Gothic architecture, enlightened seasonal food and top-class wine list. Of course, aged chops and steaks from reputable North Country farms are the headline acts, but the kitchen is also famed for its corned beef hash, steak and kidney pud and cheeky heritage ideas including black pea and celeriac hotpot with pickled red cabbage. Specials such as warm braised ox tongue and cheek with parsley mash are worth considering, while desserts keep it old-fashioned with the likes of ginger parkin or rhubarb trifle. You can drink from the hand-picked wine list in the clubby basement dining room or at the street-level bar: either way, expect quality at realistic prices, with around 30 by the glass and bottles from £16.95.
Chef/s: Paul Faulkner. **Open:** Mon to Fri L 12 to 3, D 5 to 9.45. Sat and Sun 12 to 9.45 (8.30 Sun). **Closed:** 25 Dec. **Meals:** alc (main courses £12 to £29). Set L £14 (2 courses) to £17. **Details:** 25 seats. 74 seats outside. Separate bar. Wheelchair access. Music.

🍴 **Visit us Online**
To find out more about
The Good Food Guide, please visit
www.thegoodfoodguide.co.uk

Australasia

Feel the funk and do it anyway
1 The Avenue, Spinningfields, Manchester, M3 3AP
Tel no: (0161) 8310288
www.australasia.uk.com
Pan-Asian | £30
Cooking score: 2

Cleverly designed and lit to evoke long Antipodean afternoons, this funk-ridden subterranean escape is entered via Manchester's answer to the Louvre pyramid. The similarly glassed-in kitchen sends out pan-Asian small plates (octopus with pickled hijiki and watermelon; chicken, lime and coconut salad), sushi and sashimi (lots of California rolls), and bigger dishes like crispy suckling pork belly with pineapple curry. It's all neat, colourful and fairly safe, but lively enough to provoke conversation with the parade of good-looking, casually dressed staff. Perhaps surprisingly, soufflés (passion fruit with pistachio ice cream and coconut sauce, or chocolate with raspberry sorbet) are a house signature. At the far end, the bar (and 'late lounge') provides a major part of the action, serving cocktails infused with tropical fruits, and wine (from £18). Australasia now also incorporates the adjacent venue, Grand Pacific Australasia, which majors in sushi and small plates.
Chef/s: Dave Spanner. **Open:** all week 12 to 12. **Closed:** 25 and 26 Dec, 1 Jan. **Meals:** alc (main courses £14 to £60). Set L £11 (2 courses) to £15. **Details:** 150 seats. Separate bar. Wheelchair access. Music.

Damson

Fine ingredients and a plum location
MediaCity, Manchester, M50 2HF
Tel no: (0161) 7517020
www.damsonrestaurant.co.uk
Modern British | £30
Cooking score: 2
£5 OFF

Next to the Lowry theatre and with sweeping views of the shiny MediaCityUK complex, Damson is right in the mix when it comes to attracting the workers and visitors of the revitalised Salford Quays. Like its suburban sister (see entry, Heaton Moor), there are plummy colour tones and swirly patterned rugs, but you'll also find a slick, city-smart edge, too, helped by floor-to-ceiling windows and that urban panorama. There's northern soul to the kitchen's output, but this is modern stuff, where grilled scallops come with shiitake mushrooms and soy purée in a starter (plus a prawn won ton and choi sum), and main-course 28-day aged Cheshire beef fillet arrives with its braised shin in hash brown form. A set menu functions as a pre-theatre version in the early evening, and desserts run to the trendy combo of salted caramel tart with confit orange and chocolate sorbet. Wines begin at £17.95.

Chef/s: Simon Stanley. **Open:** all week L 12 to 2.30 (5.30 Sun), Mon to Sat D 5 to 9.30 (9.45 Fri and Sat). **Meals:** alc (mains £14 to £26). Set L and D £17 (2 courses) to £20. Sun L £17. **Details:** 150 seats. 10 seats outside. Separate bar. Wheelchair access. Music. Car parking.

★ TOP 50 ★

The French

Country in the city
16 Peter Street, Manchester, M60 2DS
Tel no: (0161) 2363333
www.the-french.co.uk
Modern British | £59
Cooking score: 8

🍽 V

By bringing the country to the city, Simon Rogan's first grand hotel restaurant (the second, Fera, is at London's Claridges, see entry) 'adds a spark' to Manchester's food scene. The historic dining room's moss-toned 'makeunder' is restrained, but helps draw customers into the earthy rhythms of Rogan's food, overseen to 'impeccable' standards by chef Adam Reid. Tasting menus (6 or 10 courses) are front-loaded with excitement, starting with intense, herb-strewn bites, perhaps with smoked eel and crisped elvers. Vegetables are taken seriously in silky-sweet swede dumplings with crisp, slightly bitter

onions and an eggshell of velvet duck yolk sauce; caramelised cabbage with warm pickled mushrooms, mussels, garlic and shards of chicken skin makes the same point in luxurious fashion. Readers say the French is 'comparable with l'Enclume, but different', and that's evident in the signature ox in coal oil: an arresting play on the venison tartare served at the Cumbrian mothership, bouncing with mini ping-pong balls of kohlrabi and all-enveloping slick of charcoal flavour. Rogan looks upon each ingredient as the source of a new idea, so the seeds strewn over almost-translucent hake provide unusual rattle and crunch, and chamomile scents a puffy 'custard' served with a rhubarb compote. Staff have the 'obvious knowledge' needed to carry it all off, and though the set pairings seem the wisest choice there's no shortage of sommeliers to help with wine, from £22.

Chef/s: Adam Reid and Simon Rogan. **Open:** Wed to Sat L 12 to 2, Tue to Sat D 6.30 to 9. **Closed:** Sun, Mon, 2 weeks Aug, 1 week Dec. **Meals:** Set L and D £59 (6 courses) to £84. **Details:** 58 seats. Separate bar. Wheelchair access. Children over 8 yrs only.

Greens

Well-loved veggie with a thrill-factor
43 Lapwing Lane, West Didsbury, Manchester, M20 2NT
Tel no: (0161) 4344259
www.greensdidsbury.co.uk
Vegetarian | £25
Cooking score: 2

V £30

Back in 1990, Simon Rimmer and a mate somewhat spontaneously decided to open a restaurant with the intention of producing vegetarian food of quality and ambition. You could almost call it visionary. It's still going strong and looking rather dapper these days with its dark-wood finish, olive-green banquettes and posh retro wallpaper. Rimmer is a busy man, with lots of telly work and four cookbooks to his name, but all is well in Lapwing Lane. The menu crosses international borders like a gap year student with a round the world ticket, and flavour is the driving

force. Thai-spiced potato cake with Asian slaw is the kind of punchy, feel-good food to expect, though Europe fights its corner with Roquefort, pecan and tarragon cheesecake. Follow on with Jamaican pepper-pot stew or cauliflower and aubergine rogan josh, and finish with crème brûlée with an orange blossom biscuit. Wines start at £15.50.
Chef/s: Simon Rimmer. **Open:** Tue to Sat L 12 to 2 (2.30 Sat), Mon to Sat D 5.30 to 9.30 (10 Fri and Sat). Sun 12.30 to 9.30. **Closed:** 25 and 26 Dec, 1 Jan. **Meals:** alc (main courses £12 to £14). Set D £15 (2 courses). Sun L £12.95. **Details:** 80 seats. 8 seats outside.

The Lime Tree
Long-serving local trouper
8 Lapwing Lane, West Didsbury, Manchester, M20 2WS
Tel no: (0161) 4451217
www.thelimetree.co.uk
Modern British | £30
Cooking score: 3
♦

With its sunny disposition, abundant greenery, open-minded menus and easy prices, this long-serving trouper continues to play to full houses in trendy Didsbury. The kitchen has a magpie attitude to ingredients, although intricate plates of rare-breed pork and lamb from the owners' farm near Macclesfield add some home-grown clout to proceedings. To start, you might try a bowl of Shetland mussels with cider and bacon, or chicken, leek, shiitake mushroom and Parma ham terrine. Mains could offer anything from calf's liver with celeriac and truffle mash, onion confit and crispy onion rings to seared fillet of sea bass with butternut squash risotto, pine nuts and red pepper compote. Dry-aged Cheshire steaks are always in demand, while desserts head down memory lane for treacle sponge pudding or Eccles cake with a hunk of crumbly Lancashire cheese. The smart, contemporary wine list confidently balances quality and value, with excellent monthly highlights, a decent selection of half-bottles and prices from £16 (£5.50 a glass).

Chef/s: Jason Parker and Gary Hinchcliffe. **Open:** Tue to Fri L 12 to 2.30, Mon to Sat D 5.30 to 10. Sun 12 to 9. **Closed:** 25 and 26 Dec, 1 Jan. **Meals:** alc (main courses £13 to £25). Set L and D £15 (2 courses) to £18. **Details:** 75 seats. 20 seats outside. Music.

NEW ENTRY
Manchester House
Aiden Byrne's biggest stage yet
Tower 12, 18-22 Bridge Street, Manchester, M3 3BZ
Tel no: (0161) 8352557
www.manchesterhouse.uk.com
Modern European | £52
Cooking score: 4
V

In a bobby-dazzler of a room in a Manchester office block, Aiden Byrne finds his biggest stage yet. Customers enter through a substantial open kitchen and are seated among knowing references to the city's past. It's a world apart, where diners are both 'cocooned and challenged' and waiters kneel at the tables as they chat: a matey approach that works only when backed up with the 'excellent knowledge' some readers have observed. Dishes are finely wrought and 'imaginative', if 'not without glitches'. Byrne has pigeon nailed in both à la carte and tasting-menu iterations: the latter a confit with gingerbread and spiced cherry. He also plays cleverly with technique and texture in both foie gras and hazelnut mousse and a modernist sardine rice crisp. At the less delicate end, belted Galloway beef with salsify and potato 'sticks and stones', presented *Flintstones*-style, is a signature. Note: on Saturday nights, it's tasting menu only. Wines from £25.
Chef/s: Aiden Byrne. **Open:** Tue to Sat L 12 to 2.30, D 7 to 9.30 (6 to 10 Fri and Sat). **Closed:** Sun, Mon, last 2 weeks Jun. **Meals:** alc (main courses £24 to £39). Set L £22.50 (2 courses) to £28. Tasting menu £95 (12 courses). **Details:** 62 seats. Separate bar. Wheelchair access. Music.

Michael Caines at ABode Manchester

Classy city-centre dining
107 Piccadilly, Manchester, M1 2DB
Tel no: (0161) 2005678
www.michaelcaines.com
Modern European | £50
Cooking score: 5

🛏 V

With galloping gastronomic advances happening all about it, Michael Caines' diffusion venture has been bumped down the list of Manchester must-tries. Yet chef Robert Cox shows deft skill with top-notch ingredients both in Caines' signature dishes and his own. Plates are almost handsome enough to divert the eye from the now rather dated basement dining room. There's pleasing technique in a truffled potato and egg yolk raviolo with mushroom consommé (the potato moat neatly containing a perfect runny yolk), and also in flavour-forward combinations like a smoked haddock 'salad' with curried mayo, crunchy-crisp onions and apple batons. Wild game is a highlight, but out of season consider roast guinea hen with salt-baked celeriac and a ballotine of the leg. For pudding, soufflés are deservedly popular, and classic matches – as in a silken chocolate mousse with confit orange purée – are well handled. Wine, listed by grape, with lots of bubbles, is from £23.50.
Chef/s: Robert Cox. **Open:** Mon to Sat L 12 to 2.30, D 6 to 10. **Closed:** Sun, 25 Dec to 1 Jan. **Meals:** alc (main courses £17 to £25). Set L £14.50 (2 courses) to £19.50. Set D £16.50 (2 courses) to £22.50. Tasting menu £60. **Details:** 65 seats.

Symbols

🛏 Accommodation is available

£30 Three courses for less than £30

V Separate vegetarian menu

£5 OFF £5-off voucher scheme

🍾 Notable wine list

The Northern Quarter

Well-established Mancunian brasserie
108 High Street, Manchester, M4 1HQ
Tel no: (0161) 8327115
www.tnq.co.uk
Modern British | £29
Cooking score: 2
£5 OFF £30

Ignore the shop frontage, the regimented tables and shabby, utilitarian wood interior, because this evergreen Manchester eatery has a rock-solid reputation for rejigged British dishes that chimes well with readers. The cooking is generally excellent in a homespun way, the kitchen advertising its wares in bald, straight-talking lingo: lamb sweetbreads with peas, broad beans and salsa verde; asparagus, pea and white bean risotto; sea bream with peperonata, chorizo-stuffed squid and lemon and parsley dressing; Barry Pugh's roast suckling pig with onion and sage confit, pancetta potatoes and Bury black pudding jus. Chicken and mushroom pot pie with chips goes down a treat, as does the 10oz flat-iron steak with fat chips and béarnaise – and there might be sticky toffee pudding, chocolate cheesecake or a fine selection of British cheeses to finish. Wines from £18.
Chef/s: Anthony Fielden. **Open:** all week 12 to 10.30 (12 to 7 Sun). **Closed:** 24 to 26 Dec, 1 Jan. **Meals:** alc (main courses £11 to £23). Set L £14 (2 courses) to £17. Sun L £14. **Details:** 60 seats. 64 seats outside. Wheelchair access. Music.

The Rose Garden

Keeping it quirky on Burton Road
218 Burton Road, West Didsbury, Manchester, M20 2LW
Tel no: (0161) 4780747
www.therosegardendidsbury.com
Modern British | £32
Cooking score: 1

Less bucolic than the name might suggest, this pared-back restaurant sits easily on indie-friendly Burton Road. The offer is deliberately quirky, nodding to culinary fashion in dishes like scallops and samphire

with broccoli ketchup and beer-battered coral, or guinea fowl with leg and redcurrant nuggets. Some good cooking lurks beneath a high pun level (the beef dish encourages diners to 'steak your pick' between bavette or fillet marinated in Merlot). It's all delivered by willing staff, including steamed 'choccy, poppy' orange pudding with popping candy ganache. House wine is £16.95.
Chef/s: William Mills. **Open:** Mon to Sat D only 6 to 10.30 (11 Sat). Sun 12.45 to 7.30. **Meals:** alc (main courses £14 to £22). Set D £18 (2 courses) to £20. **Details:** 58 seats. 4 seats outside. Separate bar. Music.

Second Floor

A room with a view
Harvey Nichols, 21 New Cathedral Street, Manchester, M1 1AD
Tel no: (0161) 8288898
www.harveynichols.com
Modern European | £40
Cooking score: 3

V

Score the right table in Harvey Nichols' glass-fronted restaurant and you're master of all you survey: shoppers, Selfridges and heritage rooftops. The cool, spare interior is looking less sharp these days, but there's still a frisson in the glide of the Champagne trolley – and in chef Sam Everett's thoroughly garnished (some might say fiddly) food. Start with Cheshire rabbit, complete with a tiny faggot and earthy watercress pesto, or Loch Duart salmon, gravadlax-style, with an irresistible smoked eel and apple crème fraîche. At inspection, a lemon sole with onion risotto and crab beignets was plagued by acid, undercooked carrots but lifted with a zingy caper dressing; corn-fed Goosnargh chicken, with striking, slippery red wine tapioca and soft confit leg, was much better. Chocolate mousse with hazelnut shortbread shows some fine pastry skills. The wine list is an extension of the fun to be had in Harvey Nicks' wine shop, from £18.50.

Chef/s: Sam Everett. **Open:** Tue to Sun L 12 to 3 (4 Sun), Tue to Sat D 6 to 9.30. **Meals:** Set L and D £32 (2 courses) to £40. Tasting menu £55. **Details:** 90 seats. Separate bar. Wheelchair access. Music.

Solita

Satisfying a primal need
Turner Street, Manchester, M4 1DW
Tel no: (0161) 8392200
www.solita.co.uk
Italian-American | £21
Cooking score: 1
£30

Distinguished by a quick, inventive approach to 'dude' food, Solita is prized for its lively local spirit. Good basics (snappy hot dogs, succulent beef patties) are pimped with outrageous extras: candied bacon, 'Big Manc' sauce and, on a sopping-wet Solita burger, copious amounts of subtly spicy smoked brisket chilli. Add chicken-skin scratchings, melting deep-fried mac 'n' cheese and peanut-butter chocolate fudge brownies and you've several answers to an urgent, primal need. The basement dining room eases the queues, but is soulless compared to the street-level buzz. No bookings taken for small tables. House wine is £14.75, though cocktails or draught beer are preferable.
Chef/s: Martin Trunec. **Open:** all week 12 to 10 (11 Fri and Sat, 9 Sun). **Meals:** alc (main meals £7 to £22). **Details:** 100 seats. Separate bar. Music. Car parking.

Wing's

Cantonese big hitter
Heron House, 1 Lincoln Square, Manchester, M2 5LN
Tel no: (0161) 8349000
www.wingsrestaurant.co.uk
Chinese | £30
Cooking score: 3

V

Fans of Manchester's Chinese scene may remember the original Wing's in Cheadle Hulme, but since moving to the city centre this Cantonese big hitter has gone from

strength to strength. Some reckon the interior resembles an 'Asian airport circa 1995', though its private booths, laminated pine surfaces and celebrity memorabilia are tailor-made for the suited-and-booted business crowd as well as local shoppers. The menu is a 200-dish monster, weaving through appetisers, stir-fries, hotpots, roast meats, noodles, one-plate rice dishes and more. Given the regional bias, it's no surprise that seafood is a strong suit – from steamed king prawns with garlic and soy to a clay pot of monkfish, fried beancurd and vegetables. The kitchen also plunders China's provinces for the likes of Shanghai sliced lamb with chilli, kung-po chicken and Hakka-style belly pork with yams. Dim sum rules at lunchtime: think scallop dumplings with crab roe, crispy duck pancakes, etc. Wines start at £21.50.
Chef/s: Mr Chi Wing Lam. **Open:** all week 12 to 12 (4 to 12 Sat, 1 to 11 Sun). **Meals:** alc (main meals £12 to £55). Set D £45 (4 courses). **Details:** 85 seats. Separate bar. Wheelchair access. Music.

Yuzu

Japanese comfort cooking
39 Faulkner Street, Manchester, M1 4EE
Tel no: (0161) 2364159
www.yuzumanchester.co.uk
Japanese | £20
Cooking score: 3
£30

There's nothing complicated about this proudly independent Japanese joint. What you'll get is good, fresh, flavour-forward comfort cooking with bags of savour – accompanied by pure, sticky white rice as far as the eye can see. Clinging to tradition, Yuzu doesn't try to do sushi without a sushi master in the house, though sashimi comes as a donburi bowl of scallops, tuna, organic salmon and prawns or as a set with rice and miso soup. To start, chicken kara-age hits the spot every time, and the masterful frying continues with vegetable tempura (which pays more than lip service to seasonality) and tonkatsu (which also comes in chicken and salmon variations). Set lunches are popular,

though regulars know not to pull up a seat at one of the wooden tables or counters if in a hurry: service can dawdle alarmingly. There's no pudding and no wine, but saké starts at £28 and beer at £3.
Chef/s: David Leong. **Open:** Tue to Sat L 12 to 2, D 5.30 to 10. **Closed:** Sun, Mon. **Meals:** alc (main courses £8 to £17). Set L £7 to £9. **Details:** 28 seats. Music.

LOCAL GEM

▲ Teacup Kitchen

55 Thomas Street, Manchester, M4 1NA
Tel no: (0161) 8323233
www.teacupandcakes.com
Modern British | £20

Manchester DJ Mr Scruff loves a nice cup of tea and you can't quarrel with the fine loose-leaf selection offered in his freewheeling Northern Quarter café. The menu has expanded over the years, now providing a variety of breakfast eggs (served all-day), lunchtime soups, sandwiches and pies (try the Long Horn beef in puff pastry) alongside the famed three-tiered afternoon tea and wonderful cakes. Queues are possible, but most agree it's worth the wait. Wine from £16.50. Open all week.

▮ Norden
Nutters

Wacky indulgence and serious purpose
Edenfield Road, Norden, OL12 7TT
Tel no: (01706) 650167
www.nuttersrestaurant.co.uk
Modern British | £34
Cooking score: 3
V

Moving beyond any juvenile inferences from the name, the Nutter family business does indeed possess a charmingly English eccentricity. It's run with passion and Northern soul by Rodney, Jean and Andrew, with the latter as chef and some time TV personality. The restaurant occupies a Victorian Gothic manor surrounded by more

than six acres of gardens, yet the bar area is reminiscent to one reader of a 'city-centre hotel' – which only adds to the quirky charm. The food is all about regional produce and full-on flavours. A starter of lentil and spring onion fritters with mango and coriander raita shows the kitchen can borrow from further afield, but mostly this is modern British cooking inlaid with French classical thinking. Caramelised Goosnargh duck breast comes with confit leg, creamy cabbage and port reduction, for example, and bread-and-butter pudding ends proceedings in the comfort zone. Wines kick off at £15.40.
Chef/s: Andrew Nutter. **Open:** Tue to Sun L 12 to 2 (4 Sun), D 6.30 to 9.30 (8 Sun). **Closed:** Mon, 1 or 2 days after Christmas and New Year, bank hols. **Meals:** alc (main courses £18 to £23). Set L £14 (2 courses) to £17. Set D £42 (6 courses). Sun L £24. **Details:** 146 seats. Separate bar. Wheelchair access. Music. Car parking.

Prestwich

Aumbry
Thoughtful revivals and northern flavours
2 Church Lane, Prestwich, M25 1AJ
Tel no: (0161) 7985841
www.aumbryrestaurant.co.uk
British | £40
Cooking score: 6
£5 OFF **V**

If you're at Aumbry, you're in Manchester, and it's the sophisticated bit. That's not true necessarily of the Prestwich location, an easy tram ride from the city, but it is of Mary-Ellen McTague's open-minded, delicately northern food. That spoonable black pea and vinegar canapé is rooted in Lancashire bonfire tradition; the black pudding Scotch egg (now relegated to the lunch menu) is a tribute to Bury; the coffee is roasted in Stockport. Old culinary texts are the other influence on food that just keeps getting better, so tasting menus feature hare loin with turnip, English truffle and barley-grass, slow-cooked kid with sprout tops and roast cauliflower, and ratafia pudding. The revivals are thoughtfully done and 'extremely enjoyable', as is time spent in

the small, pale, calm cottage dining room. Cheeses are from Settle's acclaimed Courtyard Dairy, and tea, coffee, beer and wine are carefully chosen, with the latter from £21.
Chef/s: Mary-Ellen McTague. **Open:** Fri to Sun L 12 to 2, Tue to Sun D 6.30 to 9.30. **Closed:** Mon, 25 and 26 Dec, 1 and 2 Jan. **Meals:** Set L £20 (2 courses) to £25. Tasting menus £55, £70, £90. **Details:** 32 seats. Separate bar. Wheelchair access. Music.

Ramsbottom

Hearth of the Ram
Classy food in relaxed surroundings
13 Peel Brow, Ramsbottom, BL0 0AA
Tel no: (01706) 828681
www.hearthoftheram.com
Modern British | £27
Cooking score: 3
£5 OFF £30

Euan and Dena Watkins, aided by ex-Ramsons chef Abdullah 'Naz' Naseem, have got off to a flying start at their converted Ramsbottom coaching inn, launched in 2012. The pub garden, crackling fires and traditional features contribute to a 'superb atmosphere' and booking is getting close to essential as the fanbase grows. The kitchen takes a twin-pronged approach by day, offering a 'simple' menu leaning towards 'traditional pub nosh' alongside the full, vegetarian-friendly 'modern British' menu you'll find in the evening. From the former, a homemade muffin with ham shank, piccalilli and 'excellent' fat chips and half pints of prawns have been well received; from the latter, there's high praise for 'perfectly pink' partridge breast with a black pudding 'bonbon' and lamb rump with ras-el-hanout, chickpeas and merguez. The 'helpful, friendly' staff know their onions, and can talk you through the cask ales and good by-the-glass wine selection (bottles from £14.50).
Chef/s: Abdullah Naseem. **Open:** all week 12 to 10.30 (11.30 Fri and Sat). **Meals:** alc (main courses £10 to £20). Sun L £21 (2 courses) to £25. **Details:** 90 seats. 50 seats outside. Separate bar. Wheelchair access. Music. Car parking.

Sanmini's

Terrific Indian with pitch-perfect flavours
7 Carrbank Lodge, Ramsbottom Lane,
Ramsbottom, BL0 9DJ
Tel no: (01706) 821831
www.sanminis.com
Indian | £25
Cooking score: 3
£5 OFF **V** £30

The Sankar family's southern Indian-influenced venue in the heart of town is 'quite a change from your average Indian restaurant both in location and food quality'. The kitchen turns out 'fresh and perfectly spiced' dishes influenced by Mini's (part-owner, hence Sanmini) recipes. Try cauliflower florets with sliced okra coriander or beautifully judged paneer (Indian cheese) that really soak up the fragrant spice blend. Other choices include chicken cooked with poppy, fennel and cashew nuts, mutton Madras or 'a dosai to die for' – one reader's description of the light crispy pancake served with green chilli chutney. For a sweet finish sample the badam delight (almonds cooked with milk and saffron) or a traditional Indian pudding of milk, vermicelli and cashew. To drink, quaff local India Pale Ale or rose milk, or choose something from the short wine list that contains interesting Indian offerings. House Australian is £13.95.
Chef/s: Mr Sundaramoorthy and Mr Sathyanand. **Open:** Sat and Sun L 12 to 3, Tue to Sun D 6.30 to 10.30. **Closed:** Mon, 2 weeks Jan. **Meals:** alc (main courses £9 to £16). Sun L £9. **Details:** 40 seats. Separate bar. Wheelchair access. Music.

READERS RECOMMEND

Eagle & Child

3 Whalley Road, Ramsbottom, BL0 0DL
Tel no: (01706) 557181
www.eagle-and-child.com
'Second visit was on a Saturday night, good menu with seasonal specials; so good it convinced us to have our wedding reception there!'

▮ Worsley

Grenache

Intimate neighbourhood bistro
15 Bridgewater Road, Walkden, Worsley, M28 3JE
Tel no: (0161) 7998181
www.grenacherestaurant.co.uk
Modern British | £35
Cooking score: 2
£5 OFF

Locals love this 'jewel of the north west' with its 'superb atmosphere' and 'consistent food'. Indeed, there is a genuinely warm welcome at Hussein Abbas's intimate, laid-back neighbourhood restaurant where generous portions of familiar modern British dishes are served by 'friendly, attentive staff'. There is nothing cutting edge or overcomplicated about the food, but everything is cooked from scratch using high-quality ingredients. Start with pan-fried scallops, Bury black pudding and pea and ham salad or chicken liver parfait with rhubarb and ginger salad, followed by roast rump of lamb with 'hotpot' potatoes, kale, beetroot and roasted garlic oil, or mixed fish bouillabaisse with saffron aïoli. A zesty lemon tart with crème fraîche ice cream and berries is one of the go-to desserts, as is the bread-and-butter pudding with Baileys anglaise. Starting at £14.25, house wines are based on the grape variety that inspired the restaurant's name.
Chef/s: Mike Jennings. **Open:** Sun L 1 to 5, Wed to Sat D 5.30 to 9 (9.30 Fri and Sat). **Closed:** Mon, Tue, first 10 days Jan, 1 week Aug. **Meals:** alc (main courses £12 to £25). Set L and D £18 (2 courses) to £21. Sun L £18 (2 courses) to £21. **Details:** 36 seats. Separate bar. Wheelchair access. Music. No children after 8.30.

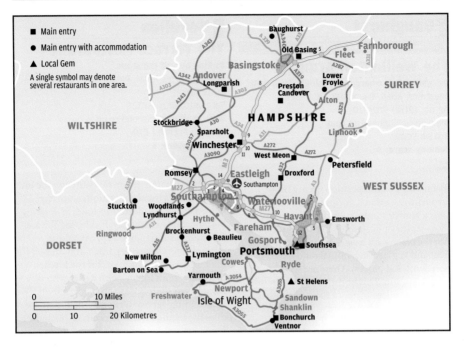

- ■ Main entry
- ● Main entry with accommodation
- ▲ Local Gem

A single symbol may denote several restaurants in one area.

WILTSHIRE
SURREY
HAMPSHIRE
Baughurst
Old Basing 5
Fleet
Farnborough
Basingstoke
Andover
Longparish
Preston Candover
Lower Froyle
Alton
Liphook
Stockbridge
Sparsholt
Winchester
West Meon
Petersfield
Romsey
Eastleigh
Droxford
WEST SUSSEX
Southampton
Stuckton
Woodlands
Lyndhurst
Hythe
Waterlooville
Havant
Emsworth
Ringwood
Brockenhurst
Fareham
Gosport
Southsea
DORSET
Beaulieu
New Milton
Lymington
Portsmouth
Barton on Sea
Cowes
Ryde
Yarmouth
Newport
St Helens
Freshwater
Isle of Wight
Sandown
Shanklin
Bonchurch
Ventnor

0   10 Miles
0   10   20 Kilometres

Barton on Sea
Pebble Beach

Glorious clifftop eatery with sparkling seafood
Marine Drive, Barton on Sea, BH25 7DZ
Tel no: (01425) 627777
www.pebblebeach-uk.com
French | £34
Cooking score: 3

🛏 V

'Loved it. Went Saturday evening, saw the Needles!' gasps a reporter, remarking on the prime geographical feature visible from the sea-facing windows of Mike Caddy's enjoyable clifftop restaurant. Pebble Beach's fresh seafood is equally alluring. Pierre Chevillard knows to let the simplest preparations speak for themselves, so expect plateaux, assiettes and bouillabaisses, alongside dressed Lymington crab, whole lobster thermidor and rock oysters. There are meat dishes, too, for the dissenters, as in slow-cooked wild boar sauced with red wine and juniper, served with truffled mash, or steak and kidney pie made with mushrooms and Guinness. A decent choice of vegetarian mains is a plus, as are puddings such as bread-and-butter made with banana and laced with rum. Appreciable effort has been put into sourcing a broadly based spread of global wines, with house selections from £18.65.
Chef/s: Pierre Chevillard. **Open:** all week L 11 to 2.30 (3 Sat, 12 to 3 Sun), D 6 to 11 (6.30 to 10.30 Sun). **Closed:** 1 Jan. **Meals:** alc (main courses £14 to £26). Sun L £15. **Details:** 90 seats. 36 seats outside. Separate bar. Music. Car parking.

🍴 Please send us your feedback

To register your opinion about any restaurant listed in the Guide, or a new restaurant that you wish to bring to our attention, please visit the web address at the bottom of the page. Your feedback informs the content of the book and will be used to compile next year's reviews.

Baughurst

★ TOP 50 PUB ★

The Wellington Arms
Delightful pub where everything's done well
Baughurst Road, Baughurst, RG26 5LP
Tel no: (0118) 9820110
www.thewellingtonarms.com
British | £30
Cooking score: 4

'Been awarded top position on my list of favourite restaurants,' commented one reader after a bonzer summer lunch at this pretty 18th-century pub. Jason King and Simon Page run the place with hands-on passion, growing fruit and veg, rearing animals and handling bees (with kid gloves). There are stylish bedrooms, too. This holistic approach results in some excellent plates of food, the dishes written up on a blackboard as if to emphasise the daily-changing nature of it all. The cooking allows the carefully gathered, seasonal produce to shine, with robust flavours and just the right amount of refinement. Razor clams are baked with red wine syrup and come with home-cured bacon; whole roasted grouse is stuffed with herbs and arrives in the company of horseradish chips and sticky red cabbage; and, for dessert, steamed vanilla sponge is served with homemade lemon and lime marmalade. Wine starts at £18.
Chef/s: Jason King. **Open:** all week L 12 to 2 (1.30 Sat, 3 Sun), Mon to Sat D 6 to 8.30 (8.45 Fri and Sat). **Meals:** alc (main courses £11 to £21). Set L £16 (2 courses) to £19. **Details:** 40 seats. 20 seats outside. Wheelchair access. Music. Car parking.

Beaulieu

The Terrace Restaurant
Pulling out all the stops
Montagu Arms Hotel, Palace Lane, Beaulieu,
SO42 7ZL
Tel no: (01590) 612324
www.montaguarmshotel.co.uk
Modern French | £70
Cooking score: 5

There has been an inn on this site since the 16th century and several generations since have helped create the gloriously English-looking hostelry that exists today. Inside, the Terrace Restaurant has a timeless appeal, and an outlook over the pretty garden. It is dressed for the business of fine dining, for the kitchen here has serious intent, with a chef who is turning out sharply defined modern food. The 'outstanding' service team play their part, as does the region's splendid produce (including home-grown ingredients). Spiced diver-caught Scottish scallops with cauliflower purée and cumin velouté is a fashionable opener, the flavours finely judged, followed perhaps by a fillet of local Dexter beef with a Jerusalem artichoke gratin. There's a tasting menu and a decent-value set-lunch option, too. Finish with an applefest: pannacotta, sorbet and mini Tatin. The wine list, starting at £25, has a good showing of organic and biodynamic bottles.
Chef/s: Matthew Tomkinson. **Open:** Wed to Sun L 12 to 2, Tue to Sun D 6.30 to 9. **Closed:** Mon. **Meals:** Set L £23 (2 courses) to £28. Set D £70. Sun L £27. **Details:** 70 seats. Separate bar. Wheelchair access. Music. Car parking. Children over 11 yrs only.

Brockenhurst

The Pig
Self-sufficient foodie enterprise
Beaulieu Road, Brockenhurst, SO42 7QL
Tel no: (01590) 622354
www.thepighotel.com
Modern British | £35
Cooking score: 4

🛏 V

Sturdy New Forest oaks provide a pastoral backdrop for the Pig: an ivy-clad Georgian house turned boutique hotel, with a 'greenhouse' dining room full of potting-shed paraphernalia. There are touches of leather-clad, country-squire gentility, but at heart this is a self-sufficient foodie enterprise driven by a green agenda. Produce comes from the walled garden and an experimental polytunnel; poultry and pigs are reared as free-rangers; and a forager scours the countryside for wildings. The result is a bright, sparky '25-mile menu' that sticks to its topographical parameters, from 'piggy bits' to 'fresh this morning' salads. Tachbury Farm black pudding comes with a duck egg, nasturtiums and mustard dressing; line-caught Lymington mackerel appears with garden beets and chilli sauce; New Forest wood pigeon is matched with pickled quails' eggs and spiced sloe sauce. There are pies and steaks too, plus blueberry and lemon trifle for afters. Organic tipples and 'varietal classics' (from £16.50) figure prominently on the wine list.
Chef/s: James Golding. **Open:** all week L 12 to 2.15, D 6.30 to 9.30. **Meals:** alc (main courses £13 to £28). **Details:** 80 seats. 20 seats outside. Separate bar. Wheelchair access. Music. Car parking.

Symbols
🛏 Accommodation is available

£30 Three courses for less than £30

V Separate vegetarian menu

£5 OFF £5-off voucher scheme

🍷 Notable wine list

Droxford

The Bakers Arms
Beguiling village pub
High Street, Droxford, SO32 3PA
Tel no: (01489) 877533
www.thebakersarmsdroxford.com
Modern British | £28
Cooking score: 3

£30

It is almost nine years since the Corderys took over this heart-warming country inn, and readers are increasingly fulsome in their praise for a 'gem' that continues to 'delight in atmosphere, quality of food, good value and friendliness'. Adam Cordery knows what is required, and delivers in fine fashion – at well-judged prices – understanding what people want from a country-pub menu. The starting point is high-quality (often local) raw materials, perhaps Dorset snails with bacon and garlic butter or roast loin of Hampshire hare served with rösti potatoes and game sauce, but there could also be wild sea bass with lemon risotto. Desserts keep it old-fashioned with the likes of apple crumble and custard. It's the kind of place where just a pint at the bar is fine, too – beer is from the micro-brewery Bowman Ales, a mile away. Wines from £14.95.
Chef/s: Adam Cordery. **Open:** all week L 12 to 2 (3 Sun), Mon to Sat D 7 to 9. **Meals:** alc (main courses £10 to £19). Set L and D £13. Sun L £16. **Details:** 45 seats. 25 seats outside. Car parking.

Emsworth

Fat Olives
Imaginative championing of seasonal produce
30 South Street, Emsworth, PO10 7EH
Tel no: (01243) 377914
www.fatolives.co.uk
Modern British | £36
Cooking score: 2

There are some fat olives of the green variety waiting on the table at the Murphys' restaurant in a one-time fisherman's cottage on the lane down to the harbour. Tuck in as you study a menu filled with interesting combos and lots of local ingredients. It's a family affair where Lawrence is at the stove and Julia is out front, with a neutral décor that doesn't really bring anything to the table. Seafood gets a good showing, such as first-course skate in a fennel 'juice' with tapenade and little splashes of piquant smoked paprika oil, or a main of sea trout matched with lovage pesto. Not everything hits the heights (with some uneven cooking here and there), but there are lots of bright, creative ideas such as roast duck breast in the rich company of date purée and black treacle sauce. Desserts partner-up cherry Bakewell with crème brûlée. House Chilean is £15.25.

Chef/s: Lawrence Murphy. **Open:** Tue to Sat L 12 to 2, D 7 to 9. **Closed:** Sun, Mon, bank hols, 24 Dec to 1 Jan, 2 weeks Jun. **Meals:** alc (main courses £16 to £24). Set L £19 (2 courses) to £21. **Details:** 25 seats. 10 seats outside. Wheelchair access. Music. Children over 8 yrs only (except Sat L).

36 On The Quay
Destination restaurant-with-rooms
47 South Street, Emsworth, PO10 7EG
Tel no: (01243) 375592
www.36onthequay.co.uk
Modern European | £58
Cooking score: 5

Ramon and Karen Farthing's restaurant-with-rooms overlooking the harbour has bags of period charm with its bow windows and low ceilings. A former pub, it is now dedicated to fine dining. Sip a G&T in the small lounge area or head through to the creamy dining room, where pristine tables await and artworks bring splashes of colour to the soothing neutrality. The cooking is as rarefied as the setting, with amuse-bouches galore, pre-dessert (a zesty passion fruit posset with raspberry jelly, perhaps) and petits fours with coffee. First-class ingredients such as pink, gamey wood pigeon star in complex constructions that look pretty on the plate. The sea plays its part, too, providing the scintillating scallops served with little nori

rolls rich with crab. Main-course fallow deer arrives rare and tender, topped with a grassy knoll of lovage, and dessert might be a deconstructed cheesecake with apple foam and gel. House French is £21.50.

Chef/s: Ramon Farthing and Gary Pearce. **Open:** Tue to Sat L 12 to 1.45, D 7 to 9.30. **Closed:** Sun, Mon, 4 days Christmas, first 2.5 weeks Jan, last week May, last week Oct. **Meals:** Set L £24 (2 courses) to £29. Set D £48 (2 courses) to £58. **Details:** 50 seats. Separate bar. Wheelchair access.

▌Isle of Wight
The Crab Shed
Alfresco café with super-fresh seafood
Tamarisk, Love Lane, Steephill Cove, Isle of Wight, PO38 1AF
Tel no: (01983) 855819
www.steephillcove-isleofwight.co.uk
Seafood | £24
Cooking score: 1

If simplicity and provenance float your boat, head over to Steephill Cove for some freshly landed seafood at this splendid seaside café. The Crab Shed is right by the water's edge, where its own boat, *Endeavour*, lands a cargo of crab, lobster and mackerel. No frills, no fuss: everything takes place outdoors at rustic bench tables; it's 'worth visiting during good weather', as one reader points out. Expect salads filled with hand-picked crab or half a lobster, mackerel sandwiches and the trademark crab pasties. Wine starts at £14.50. Note, the place isn't called Steephill Cove for nothing (yes, it's steep).

Chef/s: Mandy Wheeler. **Open:** Wed to Mon L 12 to 3. **Closed:** Tue, Apr, Oct. **Meals:** alc (main courses £9 to £24). **Details:** Cash only. 34 seats outside.

▍▮ Average Price
The average price listed in main-entry reviews denotes the price of a three-course meal, without wine.

The Hambrough

Zeitgeist boutique cookery on the south coast
Hambrough Road, Ventnor, Isle of Wight,
PO38 1SQ
Tel no: (01983) 856333
www.thehambrough.com
Modern British | £55
Cooking score: 4

£5 OFF 🛏 V

Gazing out to sea on Wight's southern coast, the Hambrough is a boutique seaside hotel for the modern age. Its fresh contemporary dining room, furnished in silvery-grey and wood tones, makes a good foil for Darren Beevers' locally based interpretations of zeitgeist cookery. Dishes are acquisitive, complex mixtures whose occasionally aimless divergence is compensated by quality that rings true. First-off might be slow-cooked duck egg coated in powdered garlic leaf with blanched asparagus in soft cheese foam, a trio of snails and a giant pork scratching. Next could be excellent char-grilled sea bass with diced celeriac, confit chicken wing and spinach sauce. The limpid, milky clarity of lamb fillet is superb, as is its pressed shoulder and crisped rib, supported by broad beans and peas in minted garlic cream. A signature dessert is muscovado custard tart with torched lime segments and Earl Grey ice cream. Labour-intensive extras seal the deal. The French-led wine list opens at £26.
Chef/s: Darren Beevers. **Open:** Tue to Sat L 12 to 2, D 6 to 9.30. **Closed:** Sun, Mon, 2 weeks Jan, 1 week Nov. **Meals:** Set L £25 (2 courses) to £29. Set D £45 (3 courses) to £55. **Details:** 32 seats. 10 seats outside. Separate bar. Music.

Symbols

🛏 Accommodation is available

£30 Three courses for less than £30

V Separate vegetarian menu

£5 OFF £5-off voucher scheme

🍷 Notable wine list

Hillside Bistro

A bright seaside café making good use of local produce
30 Pier Street, Ventnor, Isle of Wight, PO38 1SX
Tel no: (01983) 853334
www.hillsideventnor.co.uk
Modern British | £25
Cooking score: 2

£5 OFF £30

A bright and pretty place, with an open kitchen to the rear, colourful, abstract paintings and a wood-tiled floor, Hillside is, according to one reporter, 'more of a seaside café than a bistro and a welcome addition to Ventnor'. A June lunch found cooking that 'made genuinely good use of local produce', from Ventnor crab cakes flavoured with ginger, chilli and garlic and teamed with nicely dressed local salad leaves, and three crisp-skinned fillets of sea bream atop cubes of beetroot mixed with a light mayo, to Godshill cherry clafoutis with milk ice cream. This is simple, modern British bistro stuff at fair prices, even in the evening when the likes of sea bream with Ventnor Bay crab risotto or roast lemon and thyme poisson with petits pois à la française pack a more gastronomic punch. There's a decent selection of wines, too (from £21, a figure the list barely goes above).
Chef/s: Gerald Fruitier. **Open:** all week 8 to 2, D 6 to 9. **Meals:** alc (main meals £11 to £14). **Details:** 24 seats.

NEW ENTRY

Isla's

Culinary modernism in a white room
The George Hotel, Quay Street, Yarmouth, Isle of Wight, PO41 0PE
Tel no: (01983) 760331
www.thegeorge.co.uk
British | £45
new chef/no score

🛏

Dianne Thompson, former CEO of lottery-runner Camelot, has given new purpose to this old stager, recruiting Robert Thompson (no relation) from the Hambrough, Ventnor (see entry). The once-stolid principal dining room has been bathed in purest white, with minimal flounces, though the harbour views remain generous and refreshing. Thorough-going gastro-modernism based on fine island produce is the imperative. Great depth is conjured from a terrine of smoked eel, ham hock, foie gras and apple with brioche and rémoulade ('a plate to linger over'), and from squab pigeon roasted pink, its confit legs on sprigs of Douglas fir, its jus infused with fragrant hay. Excellent breads and incidentals up the ante (and the prices), but there were early problems: crackled pork belly with lobster, peas and raw courgette carpaccio disintegrating into confused heterogeneity. Dessert might be bite-sized rum babas with rum and raisin ice cream and banana. Wines from £20. The Conservatory offers a simpler brasserie menu.

Chef/s: Robert Thompson. **Open:** Tue to Sat D only 6.30 to 9.30. Conservatory all week L 12 to 3, D 6.30 to 9.30. **Meals:** alc (£70, 3 courses). Conservatory alc (main courses £14 to £27). **Details:** 70 seats. 100 seats outside. Separate bar. Wheelchair access.

NEW ENTRY
The Pond Café
Village venue with a sunny disposition
Bonchurch Village Road, Bonchurch, Isle of Wight, PO38 1RG
Tel no: (01983) 855666
www.thehambrough.com
Italian | £22
Cooking score: 2
£30

In a 'gorgeous villagey setting' overlooking a lovely lily pond, the Pond Café is the sort of place that fits the bill for a family gathering, yet also for an impromptu lunch or dinner because there's nothing in the fridge (the bargain set menu is particularly welcome for the latter). Expect simple dishes with an Italian focus, say a 'first rate' ragù of local sausages on linguine, or spring pea and broad bean bruschetta with mozzarella. Main courses, too, deliver the kind of produce-led plates that

have widespread popularity these days, perhaps lamb's liver with parsley and smoked garlic risotto or Ventnor Bay pesce del Gorino. It's all 'served with smiles' in a dining room that is all white walls and clean-lined mahogany, from floor to furniture, encapsulating a look that is 'halfway between modern tea room and smart bistro'. Wines from £23.

Chef/s: Joanne Bennett. **Open:** Thur to Mon L 11 to 2, D 6 to 10. **Closed:** Tue, Wed. **Meals:** alc (main courses £5 to £17). Set L and D £18 (2 courses) to £22. Sun L £25. **Details:** 24 seats. 15 seats outside. Music.

LOCAL GEM
▲ Dan's Kitchen
Lower Green Road, St Helens, Isle of Wight, PO33 1TS
Tel no: (01983) 872303
www.danskitcheniow.com
Modern British | £28

Perched on a corner by the village green, Dan and Carla Maskell's neighbourhood joint is a cut above when it comes to culinary ambition. There's no shortage of bright ideas on the menu with the likes of smoked haddock and leek risotto preceding feather-blade steak with fondant potato and roasted root veg. It all happens in a cheery, no-frills room, and ends well with 'awesome' rice pudding with damson jam and grapes 'soaked in something fab'. Wines start at £17. Closed Sun and Mon.

¦¦● Please send us your feedback
To register your opinion about any restaurant listed in the Guide, or a new restaurant that you wish to bring to our attention, please visit the web address at the bottom of the page. Your feedback informs the content of the book and will be used to compile next year's reviews.

Longparish

The Plough Inn
A proper foodie pub
Longparish, SP11 6PB
Tel no: (01264) 720358
www.theploughinn.info
Modern British | £35
Cooking score: 5

V

James Durrant (ex-Maze) has made a good fist
of things since upping sticks from Mayfair and
taking over this 18th-century village boozer
in the bucolic Test Valley. With real ales on
draught, a sympathetic approach to kids,
classic grub in the bar and ample folksy beams
and fireplaces, the Plough feels like a proper
boozer. But order from the full menu and
you're in for a surprise: instead of belt-busting
fodder you'll find 'confident, refined and
skilful food' with plenty of panache and a
light, modern touch. Despite 'restaurant
prices' and occasionally 'shambolic' service, it's
well worth shelling out for eye-catching,
incisively flavoured plates of Lincolnshire
smoked eel with salt-baked beetroot,
horseradish snow and beetroot jelly or braised
ox cheek 'bourguignon' and artichoke purée
with glorious truffle mash. To finish, a
complex riff involving peanut-butter parfait
and cherry sorbet reminds you that Durrant
once worked for Jason Atherton. Wine
from £18.
Chef/s: James Durrant. Open: all week L 12 to 2.30
(4.30 Sun), Mon to Sat D 6 to 9.30. Closed: 25 Dec.
Meals: alc (main courses £14 to £30). Details: 48
seats. 20 seats outside. Wheelchair access. Music.
Car parking.

Lower Froyle

The Anchor Inn
Cracking country local for updated classics
Lower Froyle, GU34 4NA
Tel no: (01420) 23261
www.anchorinnatlowerfroyle.co.uk
Modern British | £30
Cooking score: 3

This lovingly restored 16th-century inn is
extremely good at winning converts with its
delightful location and agreeable blend of
rusticity, creature comforts and affluent vibes.
The easy-going style of the place is much
appreciated too, successfully bridging the
divide between country boozer and upper
crust inn-with-rooms. You can settle in for
drinks in the snug, low-beamed bar and salon
or eat at mismatched polished tables in the
candlelit, country-cosy dining room and
expect cosmopolitan food with a feel for
seasonality. British classics like steak and ale
pie have their say, but there's also cod fillet
with gnocchi, brown shrimps and cockles or
garlic and truffle chicken Kiev with braised
haricot beans, chorizo and parsley. An English
cheese plate is hard to resist, but then so is a
'perfect' pannacotta topped with poached
Yorkshire rhubarb and pine nut and almond
crumble. While output is generally consistent,
occasionally service has been found wanting.
House wines from £17.50.
Chef/s: Kevin Chandler. Open: all week L 12 to 2.30
(3 Sat, 4 Sun), D 6.30 to 9.30 (7 to 9 Sun). Closed:
25 Dec. Meals: alc (main courses £13 to £24). Sun L
£21 (2 courses) to £27. Details: 100 seats. 60 seats
outside. Separate bar. Music. Car parking.

▌Lymington

Egan's

Unpretentious neighbourhood eatery
24 Gosport Street, Lymington, SO41 9BE
Tel no: (01590) 676165
www.eganslymington.co.uk
Modern British | £31
Cooking score: 2

V

A well-liked bastion of the Lymington scene since 1999, John and Debbie Egan's unpretentious neighbourhood eatery occupies a late-Victorian building that once housed the local police station – you can still see the original blue lamp on display. Needless to say, everything is above board these days, and the kitchen stays firmly on the straight and narrow when it comes to matters gastronomic. The food is 'always reliably good', confirmed a regular who dined out on English asparagus with hollandaise, avocado and a truffle-dressed salad; pan-fried stone bass with caramelised brown shrimps; and a plate of venison loin accompanied by rabbit roulade and two kinds of cabbage. Menus evolve at a steady pace, but Egan's is also the kind of place where vegetables are brought to the table in separate dishes and the selection of desserts generally includes the likes of bread-and-butter pudding or chocolate torte. Easy-drinking wines (50 of them) start at £17.95.
Chef/s: John Egan. **Open:** Tue to Sat L 12 to 2, D 6.30 to 10. **Closed:** Sun, Mon, 25 Dec to 6 Jan.
Meals: alc (main courses £16 to £24). Set L £17 (2 courses) to £19. **Details:** 50 seats. 20 seats outside. Separate bar.

▌Lyndhurst

Hartnett Holder & Co.

Relaxed dining with an Italian accent
Lime Wood Hotel, Beaulieu Road, Lyndhurst,
SO43 7FZ
Tel no: (02380) 287167
www.limewoodhotel.co.uk
British-Italian | £55
Cooking score: 3

🛏 **V**

As you rattle over the cattle grid and head up the long drive, Lime Wood appears: a meticulously renovated Palladian country pile. As befits one of the new breed of country house hotels, luxurious trappings are *de rigueur*, but whispering reverence is supplanted by a happy hubbub and 'amazingly slick service' from smiling staff. And while it's 'not quite as casual as I had expected', the mood of understated elegance is seductive. Hartnett Holder & Co. relates to a group of comfortably appointed dining rooms where menus are under the supervision of Angela Hartnett – of London's Murano (see entry) – and executed by chef Luke Holder. The style is Hartnett's signature Italian, hammered home with pizzetta, agnolotti and vitello tonnato. Recent successes have included confit Dorset mackerel with a 'creamy, citrusy sauce', and 'very tender, very tasty braised rabbit' accompanied by mustard-glazed onions and 'a terrific jus'. A sweeping wine list opens at £18.95.
Chef/s: Angela Hartnett and Luke Holder. **Open:** all week 12 to 11. **Meals:** alc (main courses £16 to £45). Set L £20 (2 courses) to £25. Sun L £38. **Details:** 62 seats. 40 seats outside. Separate bar. Wheelchair access. Music. Car parking.

New Milton

Vetiver

Magpie food in an aristocratic retreat
Chewton Glen, Christchurch Road, New Milton,
BH25 6QS
Tel no: (01425) 275341
www.chewtonglen.com
Modern British | £50
Cooking score: 5

🍷 ➖ V

Given that it's ensconced within the
aristocratic surroundings of Chewton Glen's
old-money hospitality playground, Vetiver is
never likely to be an off-the-cuff destination
for passers-by – although there is much to
enjoy if you do fancy the trip. Spread over five
rooms, this set-up eschews formality in favour
of a luxe approach with a more easy-going
attitude. Bold contemporary furnishings set
the tone, and the kitchen plays magpie,
garnering ideas from far and wide. Don't be
surprised to see skate cheek tempura with soba
noodle salad alongside twice-baked
Emmental soufflé, or veal Holstein in
company with fish and chips or lamb tagine.
There are grills with old-school sauces, too,
plus daily roasts from the trolley and a battery
of desserts ranging from rice pudding to
Sicilian lemon tart with caipirinha-spiked
honey. The odd gripe suggests that 'badly
managed, sloppy service' can take the gloss off
proceedings, but the encyclopaedic wine list
(from £25) provides ample distraction with
its globetrotting array of gilt-edged vintages
and esteemed growers.
Chef/s: Luke Matthews. **Open:** all week L 12 to 2
(2.30 Sat and Sun), D 6 to 9.30 (10 Fri and Sat).
Meals: alc (main courses £21 to £35). Set L £25. Sun
L £40. Tasting menu £70 (6 courses). **Details:** 140
seats. 30 seats outside. Separate bar. Wheelchair
access. Music. Car parking. No children after 8.

Old Basing

★ TOP 50 PUB ★

NEW ENTRY
The Crown

Classy retro pub classics
The Street, Old Basing, RG24 7BW
Tel no: (01256) 321424
www.thecrownoldbasing.com
British | £28
Cooking score: 3

£5 OFF   £30 ⬇

Looking for all the world like an everyday sort
of boozer, the Crown has a couple of chefs
with experience at the fancy end of the
culinary spectrum who have helped put the
place on the map: 'The Crown is a real find.'
That's not to say they're cooking haute cuisine,
not a bit of it, for this place is all about classy
renditions of pub-style food made in-house.
Scotch egg with spicy ketchup and pickled
local mushrooms shows the way, as does Brie
and cranberry, so often a signpost to stay well
away, transformed into big, crisp wedges of
gooey Tunworth cheese from just up the road,
with an accompanying gem and celery salad
and beery chutney. The updated retro vibe
continues into main courses – the humble fish
goujon as moist pollack in an ultra-thin
crumb, and English beef braised in ale.
Funnily enough, the puds are a little more
highfalutin', rice pudding, for example, arrives
dotted with boozy Agen prunes and with a
crisp brûléed topping. The décor is decidedly
unreconstructed, the bar serves real ales and
wines kick off at £15.50.
Chef/s: Chris Barnes and Tom Wilson. **Open:** all
week L 12 to 2 (2.30 Fri to Sun), Mon to Sat D 6 to 9
(9.30 Fri and Sat). **Closed:** 1 Jan. **Meals:** alc (main
courses £13 to £18). **Details:** 55 seats. 40 seats
outside. Separate bar. Music. Car parking.

Petersfield

Annie Jones

Amicable local restaurant and tapas joint
Lavant Street, Petersfield, GU32 3EW
Tel no: (01730) 262728
www.anniejones.co.uk
Modern British | £35
Cooking score: 2

£5
OFF

An entirely appealing atmosphere of stylish domestic hospitality makes this all-purpose venue a treat, no matter whether you're in the market for tapas, coffee and patisserie, a drink in the bar overlooking the glorious gardens, or a full-on lunch or dinner in the restaurant. Banquettes scattered with brightly coloured cushions offset the whitewashed, brick-walled ambience. Steve Ranson's menus are all about vivid modern British combinations. Start with a tempura-battered courgette flower (remember them?) stuffed with goats' cheese, wild honey and almonds, and follow up with honey-roast duck with artichoke purée, girolles, blackberries and rhubarb, or roast cod in a mushroom and Parmesan crust with puréed cauliflower and sprouting broccoli. Desserts confidently push the right buttons with white chocolate mousse, oat shortcake and beetroot granita, or a serving of rice pudding yummied up with caramelised rum banana. Wines start at £15.50.
Chef/s: Steven Ranson. **Open:** all week L 10 to 3, Tue to Sat D 6 to 9.30 (10 Fri and Sat). **Closed:** Mon, 1 week Jan. **Meals:** Set L £15 (2 courses) to £18. Set D £28 (2 courses) to £35. **Details:** 30 seats. 80 seats outside. Separate bar. Music.

JSW

Contemporary cooking with a regional flavour
20 Dragon Street, Petersfield, GU31 4JJ
Tel no: (01730) 262030
www.jswrestaurant.com
Modern British | £40
Cooking score: 6

♦ ⇌ V

The one-time coaching inn has kept much of its period charisma, seen in oak beams and wonky lines, though the finish is all about comforting neutrality, with linen tablecloths and creamy décor. This reflects chef Jake Saul Watkins' belief that simplicity is king, and he also declares a passion for 'total simplicity' in his culinary output. Nevertheless, expect creative and well-crafted dishes such as scallops with cep 'pearls' and velouté, crisp Parmesan and textures of cauliflower. There are elements of French-inspired classicism throughout the menu, alongside first-class regional ingredients and flashes of brilliance. Dover sole is cooked with a light touch and arrives in the company of superb mussels in a 'chowder' with seawater 'pearls', sea purslane and samphire. Desserts run to a deconstructed cheesecake with admirably sharp rhubarb and ginger-beer jelly. Tasting menus lead the way (five or seven courses) with optional wine flights from the glitzy list; bottles start at £19.50.
Chef/s: Jake Saul Watkins. **Open:** Wed to Sun L 12 to 1.30, Wed to Sat D 7 to 9. **Closed:** Mon, Tue, 1 week Dec, 1 week Jan, 2 weeks Easter, 2 weeks Aug. **Meals:** alc L (2 courses £32; 3 courses £40), alc D (2 courses £40; 3 courses £50). Tasting menu £75 (7 courses). **Details:** 50 seats. 28 seats outside. Wheelchair access. Car parking. Children over 8 yrs only at D.

Portsmouth

LOCAL GEM
▲ Abarbistro
58 White Hart Road, Portsmouth, PO1 2JA
Tel no: (023) 9281 1585
www.abarbistro.co.uk
Modern British | £24

On a cobbled street corner, with street-side tables and a large conservatory-style eating area to the back, this former pub now provides a bright, breezy dining option within striking distance of Gunwharf Quays. The menu delivers bang-on flavours and doesn't aim to mess about with things too much. Korean-style crispy duck salad shows the global reach of the repertoire, while burgers or beer-battered fish and chips satisfy the homebodies. Wines get off the mark at £14.50. Open all week.

Preston Candover
Purefoy Arms
Spanish flavours in a Hampshire hostelry
Alresford Road, Preston Candover, RG25 2EJ
Tel no: (01256) 389777
www.thepurefoyarms.co.uk
Modern European | £27
Cooking score: 3

£30

The Purefoy Arms' red-brick exterior, black window frames, shabby-chic looks and 'naff' Muzak may suggest your average spruced-up country watering hole, but one glance at the spidery handwritten menu tells a different story. Spanish chef Andres Alemany and his partner Marie-Louise swapped London for this Hampshire backwater, and have imbued their boozer-turned-restaurant with a strong Iberian accent   although service needs sharpening. Tapas and nibbles such as Catalan tomato bread or Monte Ebro cheese with truffle honey give way to small plates and more substantial items ranging from a warm salad of baby gem hearts, black figs and sherry vinegar to an accomplished, 'generously proportioned' dish of line-caught pollack with

white beans, pata negra ham and romesco sauce. You can also get some generic European staples including braised shortrib of Angus beef with mash and green beans, while desserts jump from churros to tarte Tatin and pannacotta. Well-spread global wines start at £15.
Chef/s: Andres Alemany. Open: Tue to Sun L 12 to 3 (4 Sun), Tue to Sat D 6 to 10. Closed: Mon, 26 Dec, 1 Jan, Aug bank hol. Meals: alc (main courses £12 to £28). Set L £15 (2 courses) to £18. Details: 60 seats. 60 seats outside. Music. Car parking. No children after 7.

Romsey
The Three Tuns
Local with updated pub classics
58 Middlebridge Street, Romsey, SO51 8HL
Tel no: (01794) 512639
www.the3tunsromsey.co.uk
Modern British | £25
Cooking score: 2

£30

Mark Dodd, Damian Brown and Iain Longhorn from Winchester's Chesil Rectory (see entry) are the brains behind this 300-year-old listed pub set snugly amid the cottages on Middlebridge Street. It's a dream ticket for nostalgia-fuelled tourists with its dark beams, open fires and stone floors. The mood is leisurely, prices are fair and the food aims for generous, all-round satisfaction. Although the reference point is the classic pub repertoire, there's nothing quaint or archaic about the food. Fishcakes come with saffron aïoli and soft herb salad, a shepherd's pie is made with braised shoulder of lamb, and rump steak is served with dauphinois potatoes, kale and red wine shallot butter. Lemon curd fool with ginger crumb is one option for pudding, another is the crumble of the day, but there's also a good British cheeseboard. Drink local real ale or choose from the short, globetrotting wine list (bottles from £14.50).
Chef/s: Damian Brown and James Wills. Open: all week L 12 to 2.30 (3 Fri and Sat, 4 Sun), D 6 to 9 (9.30 Fri and Sat). Closed: 25 and 26 Dec. Meals: alc

(main courses £11 to £18). **Details:** 50 seats. 30 seats outside. Separate bar. Wheelchair access. Music. Car parking.

Southsea

Montparnasse

Smart, inventive and much-loved bistro
103 Palmerston Road, Southsea, PO5 3PS
Tel no: (023) 9281 6754
www.bistromontparnasse.co.uk
Modern European | £38
Cooking score: 4

It's a neighbourhood bistro inasmuch as it serves the people of Southsea very well indeed, but Montparnasse aims a little higher: 'laid-back fine dining' they say. The Victorian town house seats just 30 but manages to generate a happy hum. John Saunders opened up in 1999 and has ensured the kitchen's output has kept up with the times. Squid and mackerel ravioli in bonito broth with pak choi is a first course rich with the taste of the sea, while another opener combines slow-braised lamb with a mint gel and wild garlic profiterole. Main-course pan-fried fillet steak with Café de Paris butters shows the bistro tag is not entirely erroneous, and sea bass given a barbecue glaze is among the fish options. Familiar flavours come with a twist in a dessert of glazed toffee cake with an apple sorbet and candied apple. Wines prices start at £20.50.
Chef/s: Jake Tonkin. **Open:** Tue to Sat L 12 to 1.30, D 7 to 9.30. **Closed:** Sun, Mon. **Meals:** Set L and D £35 (2 courses) to £41. **Details:** 30 seats. Music.

Restaurant 27

Clever, high-definition cooking
Burgoyne Road, Southsea, PO5 2JF
Tel no: (023) 9287 6272
www.restaurant27.com
Modern French | £40
Cooking score: 5
V

The sparsely furnished dining room (formerly a chapel and once a gymnasium) is of barn-like proportions, but Kevin Bingham bowls almost everybody over with his innovative, provocative cooking. It's creative stuff, full of twists, turns and surprising technique, with a strong sense of freshness, flavour and balance. To find such cooking in Portsmouth is nothing short of a miracle. There are bold gestures aplenty, yet also delicacy, especially in the opening salvos – in canapés with drinks; in smoked salmon blinis with lemon, beetroot, caviar and sour cream; or an exquisite combination of whipped goats' cheese, pistachio shortbread and cumin honey. Reporters are unanimous in praising the roasted umami duck (with smoked leek, apple and feta), the way Bingham successfully mobilises slow, gentle cooking temperatures in his famous 30-hour belly of pork, and the fact that it's all good value. There's laudable service, too, and an interesting, broadly based wine list (from £19.50).
Chef/s: Kevin Bingham. **Open:** Sun L 12 to 2.30, Wed to Sat D 6.30 to 9.30. **Closed:** Mon, Tue, 25 and 26 Dec. **Meals:** Set D £44. Sun L £29. Tasting menu £39 to £50. **Details:** 34 seats. Separate bar. Music.

Sparsholt

The Avenue

Assured cooking in grand surroundings
Lainston House Hotel, Woodman Lane, Sparsholt, SO21 2LT
Tel no: (01962) 776088
www.lainstonhouse.com
Modern British | £55
Cooking score: 5
£5 OFF 🍷 🚃 V

The mile-long drive lined with lime trees creates a sense of expectation that the 17th-century Lainston House, not far from Winchester, does nothing to disappoint. Inside, the Avenue restaurant is easy on the eye, with dark mahogany panelled walls, red-leather chairs, white linen, old portraits and a brass chandelier. It provides a 'comfortable and unfussy', if slightly old-fashioned atmosphere in which to enjoy Olly Rouse's surprisingly light modern cooking. Food is both sophisticated and adventurous, showing layers of flavour, texture and colour wrought from

prime ingredients: some from the hotel's own kitchen garden. The prettily dressed plates live up to the stunning countryside outside – from mackerel with potato salad, parsley and cottage cheese to mains of rolled skate fillet teamed with perfect boulangère potatoes, pesto and iron-rich kale, and a dessert of 'wobbly pannacotta perfection', which comes pepped up by zesty blood orange, lychee and rhubarb. A cosmopolitan wine list opens at £23.50.
Chef/s: Olly Rouse. **Open:** all week L 12 to 2, D 6 to 10. **Meals:** Set L £23 (2 courses) to £33. Set D £45 (2 courses) to £55. Sun L £35. Tasting menu £60. **Details:** 70 seats. 100 seats outside. Separate bar. Wheelchair access. Car parking. Children at 6pm sitting only for D.

▌Stockbridge
The Greyhound on the Test
Rustic-chic pub with a local flavour
31 High Street, Stockbridge, SO20 6EY
Tel no: (01264) 810833
www.thegreyhoundonthetest.co.uk
Modern British | £35
Cooking score: 3

The river out back is a Mecca for fly-fishing folk and the Greyhound has rights to the holy land, but there's much more going on here than mere devotion to the art of angling. The pub has an opened-up contemporary attitude, with beams aplenty and a real fire or two, plus some smart bedrooms and a kitchen that shows confidence and direction. It's the kind of place where a pint at the bar is just fine, but with some good local nourishment on the menu, the food steals the show. Carpaccio of Hampshire beef with celeriac rémoulade is simplicity itself, satisfyingly so, while main courses like bream with salsa verde, or a daily special of beef shin pie, are just the ticket in this setting. A choc fondant with salted-caramel and peanut ice cream is a modern classic to bring things to a close. House wines start at £18.65.

Chef/s: Alan Haughie. **Open:** all week L 12 to 4, D 6.30 to 9. **Meals:** alc (main courses £13 to £24). Set L £14 (2 courses) to £19. Sun L £20 (2 courses) to £26. **Details:** 40 seats. 20 seats outside. Separate bar. Music. Car parking.

▌Stuckton
The Three Lions
Old-fashioned English auberge
Stuckton, SP6 2HF
Tel no: (01425) 652489
www.thethreelionsrestaurant.co.uk
Anglo-French | £40
Cooking score: 4
£5 OFF ▭

A New Forest institution – The Womersleys celebrate 20 years in 2015 – this ever-so English auberge attracts bags of local loyalty. While recent reports have been rather uneven, the balance is still tilted in the Three Lions' favour. Some quibbles relate to the prices and the décor (cluttered, loud carpets, pine furniture), but other customers are happy to report 'the food is always reliably superb and very classy'. On the day, Mike Womersley's cooking has a soundness to it – classically founded, slick and professional – and memorable results have included vermicelli with Dorset truffle and ceps in a creamy wine sauce; loin of venison with a 'lip sticking' jus; and 'wonderful fresh' wild turbot with tarragon and garlic. Desserts might encompass a perfectly executed individual tarte Tatin with verbena ice cream. And there's no questioning the quality and commitment of the wine list, with house selections starting at £15.75.
Chef/s: Mike Womersley. **Open:** Tue to Sun L 12 to 2, Tue to Sat D 7 to 9. **Closed:** Mon, last 2 weeks Feb. **Meals:** alc (main courses £19 to £27). Set L £24. Set D £30. **Details:** 60 seats. 12 seats outside. Separate bar. Wheelchair access. Music. Car parking.

EATING UNDERCOVER

One of our anonymous restaurant inspectors tips us off about their highlights this year.

Paul Ainsworth's 'My bread and butter'. The best version of bread-and-butter pudding in the world.

'Seafood Wreck' at the Springer Spaniel, Cornwall. Four pieces of fish, four intricate techniques; butter, mash, lemon, shrimp. Perfection.

Lamb at Antidote, London. The best lamb I have eaten anywhere this year. Belly, loin and faggot with potato gallette, lovage purée and onions.

Soy and mirin-marinated scallop sushi with truffle mayonnaise at the Dysart Arms, London. Best single bite of food I ate this year.

Strawberry cheesecake at the Freemasons at Wiswell. A slice of perfectly gooey, custard-like vanilla and Brillat-Savarin cheesecake glazed with strawberry jelly with all sorts of meringues and a popcorn ice cream. Dessert perfection.

▌West Meon
The Thomas Lord
Country-pub charm and local fare
High Street, West Meon, GU32 1LN
Tel no: (01730) 829244
www.thethomaslord.co.uk
British | £25
Cooking score: 2
£30

Thoroughly rooted in the village of West Meon, this modishly rustic pub (named after the founder of Lord's cricket ground) is an upbeat place that knows how to win friends. People love the way it strikes the right note between traditional and contemporary, and applaud the cooking from 'a burger through to a Sunday lunch'. Combined with the 'beautiful location and the friendly service', it's no wonder booking ahead is considered essential. The kitchen dishes up plates of beer-battered hake, steaks, and beef, ale, ox cheek and wild mushroom pie, but also turns its hand to flashier items such as Portland crab with brown crab custard, treacle bread and kohlrabi rémoulade, or pork loin with black pudding mousse and charred savoy cabbage. To conclude, try pumpkin rice pudding with Calvados caramel, pecan crumb and chai tea ice cream. Wines from £17.
Chef/s: Fran Joyce. **Open:** all week L 12 to 2.30 (3 Sat, 4 Sun), D 6 to 9.30 (10 Fri and Sat, 9 Sun). **Closed:** 25 Dec. **Meals:** alc (main meals £12 to £18). Set L and D £16 (2 courses) to £20. **Details:** 65 seats. 70 seats outside.

▌Winchester
The Black Rat
Culinary wit and inventiveness
88 Chesil Street, Winchester, SO23 0HX
Tel no: (01962) 844465
www.theblackrat.co.uk
Modern British | £40
new chef/no score

A converted white-faced pub, the Rat is furnished in farmhouse-kitchen fashion, with foursquare uncovered wood tables and exposed brick walls. For some years now the cooking has been at the leading edge of contemporary style, blowtorching pork back fat to accompany jamón-crusted cuttlefish, say, and garnishing with crushed artichokes, pistachios and crosnes, or utilising shoreline pickings to provide seaweed for poaching with lobster and tempura alexanders, as well as purslane for a partnership of chicken wings and lemon sole. However, we learned of the departure of Jamie Stapleton-Burns and the promotion of his sous chef Ollie Moore too late for us to arrange a visit, so reports of the new regime will be particularly welcome. On the wine front a decent international collection starts at £18.50.

Chef/s: Ollie Moore. **Open:** Sat and Sun L 12 to 2.30, all week D 7 to 9.30. **Closed:** 2 weeks Christmas and New Year, 1 week Easter, 1 week Oct. **Meals:** alc (main courses £19 to £28). **Details:** 40 seats. 20 seats outside. Separate bar. Music.

The Chesil Rectory

Half-timbered heritage and modern food
1 Chesil Street, Winchester, SO23 0HU
Tel no: (01962) 851555
www.chesilrectory.co.uk
Modern British | £32
Cooking score: 4

Dating from around 1450 and hailed as Winchester's oldest building, this venerable landmark drips heritage with its crooked half-timbered frontage, 'dangerously low' beams, dwarfish doorways and hunting-trophy taxidermy. But look closer and you'll also see vintage chandeliers, buttoned banquettes and assorted curios – plus a menu of bright, contemporary ideas with just enough spicy risk-taking to keep customers on their toes. White onion risotto is finished off with crisp shallot and burnt onion ash; rump of lamb gets a dose of sweet-and-sour garlic; and sea bream appears with crab tortellini, Stockbridge mushrooms and crisp cabbage. Readers also approve of the 'fantastic' set lunches – perhaps ewes' cheese, black pudding and ham croquette with rhubarb followed by roast breast of guinea fowl with peppered leeks

and potato purée. Desserts such as white chocolate cheesecake with blood orange also get the nod. Warm service is perfectly in tune with the mood. Carefully chosen wine from £19.95.

Chef/s: Damian Brown. **Open:** all week L 12 to 2.20 (3 Sun), D 6 to 9.30 (10 Fri and Sat, 9 Sun). **Closed:** 25 and 26 Dec, 1 Jan. **Meals:** alc (main courses £14 to £20). Set L and D £16 (2 courses) to £20. Sun L £22 (2 courses) to £27. **Details:** 65 seats. Separate bar. Music. Children at L only.

■ Woodlands

Hotel TerraVina

A destination for food lovers
174 Woodlands Road, Woodlands, SO40 7GL
Tel no: (023) 8029 3784
www.hotelterravina.co.uk
Modern European | £45
Cooking score: 4

🍷 ⊨ V

Master of Wine Gerard Basset's New Forest hotel not far from Southampton has grown organically (in every sense) since its purchase in 2007, into a place of stylish contemporary chic. The dining room, with its light woods and picture windows, resembles Basset's former Hotel du Vin restaurants, but with a lighter, fresher feel. In 2014, Gavin Barnes stepped up to become head chef, but the focus on eclectic modernist cooking of noticeable panache is maintained. That turns out to mean gazpacho with compressed watermelon and feta, followed by flamed black bream with pickled radish, miso and seaweed, on the tasting menu, but there are dishes that are more classically focused, as in a main course of cannon and breast of lamb with buttered greens, olive pommes Anna and shallots. The final flourish may be featherlight blackcurrant soufflé with white chocolate ice cream. Wines from a resourceful list start at £17.75.

Chef/s: Gavin Barnes. **Open:** all week L 12 to 2, D 7 to 9.45. **Meals:** alc (main courses £17 to £26). Set L £22 (2 courses) to £27. Tasting menu £65.
Details: 56 seats. 30 seats outside. Separate bar. Wheelchair access. Car parking.

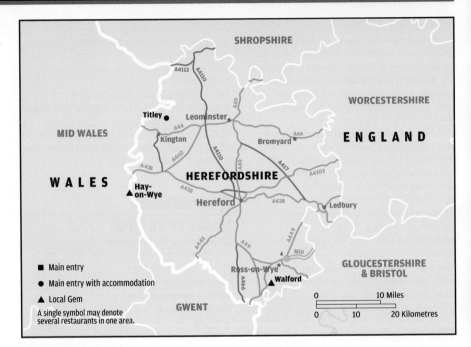

Hay-on-Wye

LOCAL GEM
▲ Richard Booth's Bookshop Café

44 Lion Street, Hay-on-Wye, HR3 5AA
Tel no: (01497) 820322
www.boothbooks.co.uk
Modern British | £18

'More of a snack place than a restaurant proper', readers are in complete agreement that this rustic, light-filled café is 'still worth a mention'. It is housed in the largest second-hand bookshop in Hay-on-Wye (entrance by the cookery section), winning many friends with its honest, good-value dishes: from favourites such as buttermilk pancakes, Welsh rarebit and the 'delicious' cakes, to the more substantial pheasant breast with lentil and bacon stew. Wines from £19. Closed Mon and D Sun to Thur.

Titley

★ TOP 50 PUB ★

The Stagg Inn

Herefordshire pub star
Titley, HR5 3RL
Tel no: (01544) 230221
www.thestagg.co.uk
Modern British | £33
Cooking score: 5
£5 OFF 🍷 ➡ V

Steve and Nicola Reynolds have been serving up damn fine, restaurant-style food within the bucolic confines of a handsome Herefordshire inn for 18 years. The Stagg still has the feel of a genuine watering hole, with excellent beer on tap, as well as three unshowy dining areas for those partaking of Steve's precise, uncluttered cooking. There is plenty of honest endeavour here and the regional larder gets a thorough workout – witness Madgett's Farm duck heart, duck livers and mushrooms on toast or Hereford beef fillet with salsa verde and chips.

Locally bagged game also features in season, and there's even Cornish fish on show (mackerel with smoked bone marrow and pickled cucumber, say). The cheese list celebrates the region's finest, while drinks include local ciders and perry from class acts such as Dunkertons. To top it all, the brilliant wine list punches well above its weight, with intelligent choices, a broad sweep of grape varieties and exceedingly enticing prices (from £17). **Chef/s:** Steve Reynolds. **Open:** Wed to Sun L 12 to 2 (2.30 Sun), D 6.30 to 9 (9.30 Sat, 8.30 Sun). **Closed:** Mon, Tue, 25 and 26 Dec, 1 Jan, 1 week Jan/Feb, first 2 weeks Nov. **Meals:** alc (main courses £17 to £28). Sun L £22. **Details:** 60 seats. 20 seats outside. Separate bar. Car parking.

■ Walford

LOCAL GEM
▲ The Mill Race
Walford, HR9 5QS
Tel no: (01989) 562891
www.millrace.info
Modern British | £40 £5 OFF

The owners of this village pub own a nearby farm, which supplies much of the meat, poultry and game on the menu. The kitchen makes the most of its Borders location (three miles from Ross-on-Wye), with producers from Herefordshire, Gloucestershire and Monmouthshire getting star billing. Dinner might kick off with pan-fried duck hash, duck liver pâté and fried duck egg on sourdough, followed by beef brisket and shin, horseradish mash and braised root vegetables. Wine from £15.50. Open all week.

GARETH FULFORD
Purslane, Cheltenham

What do you enjoy about being a chef?
I enjoy the pleasure of creating something from scratch, playing with ingredients and seeing what happens.

What inspired you to become a chef?
My grandparents owned several butcher shops and my nan was always in the kitchen when I was a kid.

What is your favourite time of year for food?
June, it's normally one of the calmer months for weather so it's great for landing fish. We can also source some great British fruits and Cotswold lambs.

What's your newest ingredient discovery?
Oxalis flowers. I love the sharp, citrus flavour and they look beautiful on the plate.

What food could you not live without?
Butter. It makes everything taste better.

Do you have a guilty foodie pleasure?
A whole block of marzipan in one evening.

Photo © Gerard Hughes

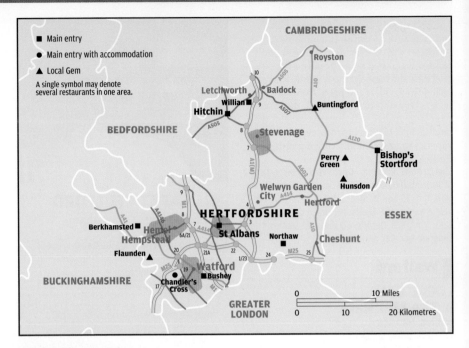

■ Berkhamsted

The Gatsby

Deco decadence and picture-pretty food
Rex Cinema, 97 High Street, Berkhamsted,
HP4 2DG
Tel no: (01442) 870403
www.thegatsby.net
Modern European | £35
Cooking score: 2

Occupying the original foyer and tea room
appended to Berkhamsted's gloriously
restored and multi-gonged Rex Cinema, the
Gatsby is a social hot spot of two halves. The
town's bright young things mingle, party and
sip cocktails in the rambunctious bar, while
those wanting something more sedate ascend
the stairs to the restaurant: a pillared white
room with ornate ceilings, a grand piano and
monochrome old photos. The food sometimes
feels too serious for the set-up (despite all that
Art Deco bling), but the kitchen makes a good
fist of things: fashioning intricate, picture-
pretty plates in the Anglo-European mould.

Starters of wild mushroom and leek risotto or
warm mackerel escabèche with pickled fennel,
cucumber and beetroot could precede saffron-
cured cod fillet with salt cod brandade and
white wine sauce, or beef bourguignon with
celeriac mash. After that, consider apple
crumble tart with cinnamon ice cream. Wines
from £15.95 (£4.15 a glass).
Chef/s: Matthew Salt. **Open:** Mon to Sat L 12 to
2.30, D 5.30 to 10.30. Sun 12 to 9. **Closed:** 25 and 26
Dec. **Meals:** alc (main courses £16 to £29). Set L and
D £15 (2 courses) to £21. Sun L £15. **Details:** 73
seats. 64 seats outside. Separate bar. Wheelchair
access. Music. Car parking. No children after 6.

Symbols

🛏 Accommodation is available

£30 Three courses for less than £30

V Separate vegetarian menu

£5 £5-off voucher scheme
OFF

🍷 Notable wine list

▌Bishops Stortford

LOCAL GEM
▲ Water Lane

31 Water Lane, Bishops Stortford, CM23 2JZ
Tel no: (01279) 211888
www.waterlane.co
Modern British | £20

A striking conversion of a former brewery, founded in 1780, is the setting for the fourth opening from the family behind the White Horse, Brancaster Staithe in Norfolk (see entry). Just a stroll from the town centre, Water Lane is geared to casual dining – sharing boards, small and large plates, steaks and seafood dishes or flatbreads with various toppings. Come evening and a few more imaginative dishes are tagged on, say roast stone bass with radicchio, Jersey Royals, fennel salad and lemon oil. House wine is £17.50. Open all week.

▌Buntingford

LOCAL GEM
▲ Pearce's Farmshop and Café

Hamels Mead, Buntingford, SG9 9ND
Tel no: (01920) 821246
www.pearcesfarmshop.com
British | £22 £5 OFF

A dedicated refuelling point beside the south carriageway of the A10, this simple and inexpensive café-cum-farm shop is a great draw, popular for the convivial way it is run as well as for its appealing food. The cooking takes in breakfast and brunch (both top shouts with reporters), together with sandwiches, salads, plates of beef and red wine pudding or salmon and crab fishcakes with aïoli and buttered samphire – plus traditional afternoon tea. Wines from £13.95. Open all week, daytime only.

▌Bushey

St James

Doing Bushey proud
30 High Street, Bushey, WD23 3HL
Tel no: (020) 8950 2480
www.stjamesrestaurant.co.uk
Modern European | £35
Cooking score: 1
V

Highly enjoyable, hugely popular and a boon for Bushey, St James may be opposite the church of the same name but effusive Alfonso La Cava ensures there's nothing reverential about eating in his long-serving bistro. A band of affable, prompt and 'coordinated' staff deliver plates of skilfully crafted, generous food to the assembled company. Grilled curried scallops with cauliflower couscous and raisin purée might be followed by calf's liver with parsley mash, braised red cabbage and bacon foam, while 'substantial' crème brûlée with blackberry compote makes a cracking finale. Set menus are appreciated, and 'very acceptable' house wines start at £15.95.
Chef/s: Matt Cook. **Open:** all week L 12 to 3, Mon to Sat D 6.30 to 10. **Closed:** 25 and 26 Dec, bank hols. **Meals:** alc (main courses £18 to £22). Set L £16 (2 courses) to £21. Set D £18 (2 courses) to £22.95. Sun L £21 (2 courses) to £26. **Details:** 100 seats. 30 seats outside. Separate bar. Wheelchair access. Music.

▌Chandler's Cross

The Grove, Colette's

Glamorous vibes and bold, creative food
Chandler's Cross, WD3 4TG
Tel no: (01923) 296010
www.thegrove.co.uk
Modern British | £75
Cooking score: 6
£5 OFF 🍽 V

Once *de rigueur* for a spiffing aristocratic weekend out of town, this expensively revitalised Georgian mansion is now a premier-league destination favoured by celebs and the Home Counties' nouveaux riches. The hotel's swanky flagship restaurant, Colette's, offers top-end cooking in an ever-so-trendy space complete with a suave bar, huge canvases and sizeable sculptures. Russell Bateman tops up his larder with pickings from the Grove's walled garden, and the result is a series of seriously priced tasting menus with names such as 'sonnet', 'symphony' and 'nature' (the veggie option). Even so, this is a kitchen with focus, creativity and the confidence to tackle bold ideas: organic salmon teriyaki with cucumber, avocado and peanut; rump of Cornish lamb with Wigmore cheese, artichokes and marjoram; hot chocolate mousse with crème fraîche, salt caramel and lime. There isn't a tiara in sight, but this is a 'hugely memorable experience', backed by an epic wine list (from £27).

Chef/s: Russell Bateman. **Open:** Tue to Sat D only 6.30 to 9.30. **Closed:** Sun, Mon, 25, 26 and 30 Dec, 1 Jan. **Meals:** Set D £75 (5 courses) to £85 (10 courses). **Details:** 42 seats. Separate bar. Wheelchair access. Music. Car parking. Children over 12 yrs only.

Flaunden

LOCAL GEM
▲ The Bricklayers Arms
Hogpits Bottom, Flaunden, HP3 0PH
Tel no: (01442) 833322
www.bricklayersarms.com
Modern British | £32 £5 OFF

Something about the Bricklayers Arms has chimed with readers this year. 'Little gem', thought one, 'rural delight', exclaimed another, and such praise has been echoed in many reports. Of particular attraction: the pub's relaxed feel, reasonable prices, commitment to fresh produce and the French chef's heritage (good terrines, salmon rillettes). There's also crab with home-smoked salmon and blinis, oxtail cooked in ale and honey, well-reported Sunday roasts, and a hearty English cheeseboard if apple and berry crumble doesn't tempt. Wines from £15.95. Open all week.

Hitchin

Hermitage Rd
Sparky food and feel-good vibes
20-21 Hermitage Road, Hitchin, SG5 1BT
Tel no: (01462) 433603
www.hermitagerd.co.uk
Modern British | £26
Cooking score: 2
£30

Ageing Hertfordshire rockers will remember the legendary Hermitage Ballroom – a muso's Mecca in the 1960s that once played host to Eric Clapton. It now functions as a cavernous feel-good restaurant and all-day bar done out in strikingly eccentric style (bicycles dangling from the ceiling, floral posies in milk bottles, arched windows and even the remnants of the original stage transformed into an exclusive nook). Some of the old razzmatazz has endured, thanks largely to current owners the Nye family who have already proved their worth at the White Horse, Brancaster Staithe and the Fox at Willian (see entries). The open kitchen knocks out sparky brasserie-style food ranging from 'amazingly presented' deli boards and barbecue pulled pork burgers with polenta chips, to Norfolk oysters and seafood specials – perhaps pan-fried sea trout with pesto-glazed potatoes, tomato and black bean salsa. To drink, craft beers and cocktails compete with a raft of wines from £17.

Chef/s: Kumour Uddin. **Open:** Mon to Fri L 12 to 2.30, D 6.30 to 10. Sat and Sun 12 to 10 (8 Sun). **Closed:** 25 Dec. **Meals:** alc (main courses £11 to £23). **Details:** 150 seats. Separate bar. Wheelchair access. Music.

SAVOURY COCKTAILS

Forget sugary syrups and tooth-achingly sweet drinks, this year the buzzword circulating the London cocktail scene is 'savoury'. But if your sugar-free drinks knowledge stretches only so far as the Bloody Mary, you'll be surprised how satisfying and moreish these cocktails can be.

Ease yourself into the savoury trend with the rye whiskey, amontillado sherry and bay leaf delight Rye Me To The Moon at Callooh Callay in Shoreditch.

If it's a meal-in-a-glass kinda drink you're after, hit up Bunga Bunga in Battersea for the Margherita, not Margarita – a Red Snapper of sorts featuring pizza-crust-infused savoury gin, Italian tomato sauce and a burrata foam.

But if you truly are a die-hard Bloody Mary fan looking for some sophistication, Islington's 69 Colebrooke Row does a sublime modern twist on a Prairie Oyster with a clarified tomato juice 'egg yolk', miso consommé, horseradish vodka, oloroso sherry, celery juice and Worcestershire sauce garnished with micro herbs and served on an oyster shell.

▌Hunsdon

LOCAL GEM
▲ Fox & Hounds
2 High Street, Hunsdon, SG12 8NH
Tel no: (01279) 843999
www.foxandhounds-hunsdon.co.uk
Modern British | £29

They've only gone and bought a Josper oven! Form an orderly queue for Dexter beef sirloin cooked on the bone. James and Bianca Rix have been at this roadside pub for ten years and made it an easy-going dining option in north Herts. The menu mixes British flavours with a bit of Med inspiration in dishes such as grey mullet with peperonata, blood orange and salsa verde, and Swaledale pork chops flavoured with anchovies and rosemary. Wines start at £16. No food Sun D or Mon.

▌Northaw

The Sun at Northaw
English rose of a pub
1 Judges Hill, Northaw, EN6 4NL
Tel no: (01707) 655507
www.thesunatnorthaw.co.uk
British | £29
Cooking score: 3

£5 OFF   £30

A charming 16th-century pub in a leafy, well-heeled village not far from Potter's Bar, the Sun is a proudly patriotic spot. Inside it's mildly cluttered, bunting adorns the walls, there's *Country Life* to hand and you might get a blast of Radio 3. As faithful to its home country, but far from stuffy, is the all-moods menu where fine British ingredients star in everything from sandwiches (Blythburgh ham and mustard), through to starters of wild mushrooms on toast with poached egg and hollandaise, seasonal salads (including Norfolk chicken, smoked bacon and poached egg), and mains such as East Coast hake fillet with Jersey Royals, sweet clams and crunchy samphire. For dessert, homemade ice cream comes in for high praise. The general consensus is that dishes are well presented, generous and feel like excellent value. In summary, it's a 'lovely local'. Doors open on to a fine garden, and there's wine from £17.50 a bottle.

Chef/s: Oliver Smith. **Open:** Tue to Sun L 12 to 3 (4 Sun), Tue to Sat D 6 to 10. **Closed:** Mon. **Meals:** alc (main courses £13 to £30). Set L £13 (2 courses) to £17. Sun L £28 (2 courses) to £35. **Details:** 80 seats. 40 seats outside. Separate bar. Music. Car parking.

Perry Green

LOCAL GEM
▲ The Hoops Inn
Perry Green, SG10 6EF
Tel no: (01279) 843568
www.hoops-inn.co.uk
British | £20

Visitors to the nearby Henry Moore Foundation flock to this white-painted Victorian village pub that was once the sculptor's local. The large terrace gets packed when the sun shines, but the open-plan interior provides plenty of room all year round to enjoy the seasonal menu. A light lunch might feature homemade soup or an antipasti platter, although seared haunch of local venison, carrot and horseradish purée and mushrooms is another option. Wines from £13.75. Closed Mon, Tue and D Sun.

St Albans

Lussmanns
Independently minded crusader
Waxhouse Gate, off High Street, St Albans, AL3 4EW
Tel no: (01727) 851941
www.lussmanns.com
Modern European | £25
Cooking score: 1

£5 OFF £30

A godsend for St Albans, Andrei Lussmann's welcoming modern brasserie is an agreeable bastion of good food. It draws locals and tourists (find it by the cathedral) for cooking that makes the most of super-fresh ingredients and cares about provenance. The food is straightforward: south coast sprats with lemon mayo or grilled haloumi with roasted vegetables, say, followed by bouillabaisse or steak-frites, crab linguine or duck with lyonnaise potatoes and pan-fried oranges. Pudding fans will love chocolate cheesecake with semifreddo berries and clotted cream ice cream. The zippy wine list starts at £15.80. There's another branch at 42 Fore St, Hertford, SG14 1BY; tel: (01992) 505329.

Chef/s: Max Slack. **Open:** all week 12 to 9.30 (10.30 Fri and Sat, 9 Sun). **Closed:** 25 and 26 Dec. **Meals:** alc (main courses £12 to £20). Set L and early D £12 (2 courses) to £14. **Details:** 105 seats. Wheelchair access. Music.

Thompson@Darcy's
Big modernist ideas in a posh bistro
2 Hatfield Road, St Albans, AL1 3RP
Tel no: (01727) 730777
www.thompsonatdarcys.co.uk
Modern British | £38
Cooking score: 5

V

Cobbled together from four pre-war cottages with a jutting timber upper storey, Darcy's was given a power boost when it was acquired in late 2013 by Phil Thompson, a chef with big ideas in the British modernist vein. Stripped-wood floors, grey-green walls and floral artworks establish a posh bistro feel that's pitched just right. Sunday suppers of lobster and steak are one way of building customer loyalty. Another is through resonantly successful contemporary offerings such as spring pea velouté with Cabernet vinegar jelly-cubes; seared yellowfin tuna with shaved bonito, daikon, puréed avocado and peanuts; and rolled guinea fowl breast in positively old-school mushroom cream sauce, with blanched garlic leaves and white asparagus. The balance and fine judgement in these dishes makes a bold statement of intent. Dessert might be a bowl of chocolate mousse topped with cherry sorbet with poached whole cherries and an almond wafer. An encouragingly varied wine list starts at £18.50 (£4.50 a glass).

Chef/s: Phil Thompson. **Open:** all week L 12 to 2.30 (4 Sun), D 6 to 10 (9.30 Sun). **Meals:** alc (main courses £17 to £25). Set L £17 (2 courses) to £21. Set D £19 (2 courses) to £23. **Details:** 90 seats. 20 seats outside. Separate bar. Wheelchair access. Music.

LOCAL GEM

▲ The Foragers

The Verulam Arms, 41 Lower Dagnall Street, St Albans, AL3 4QE
Tel no: (01727) 836004
www.the-foragers.com
Modern British | £32

A 'celebration of nature', the menu at this pub close to St Albans cathedral relies on the wild larder. Foraging walks, finishing with food here, are a feature. Without getting your boots muddy, try game meatballs with wild garlic crème fraîche and rosehip, raspberry and blackberry dressing, or hunters' stew with scrumpy. Pudding might be chocolate and elderberry posset with candied wild hazelnuts, and for afterwards bitters and liqueurs are homemade. Closed L Mon to Thur, no food Sun D. Wines from £16.95.

▮ Willian

The Fox

Dining-pub gem
Willian, SG6 2AE
Tel no: (01462) 480233
www.foxatwillian.co.uk
Modern British | £28
Cooking score: 2
£30

You can see why this place is popular. Dating from the 18th century and hard by the green, the Fox is a gentrified pub in two parts: a place where drinkers are welcome, and a smart dining room delivering a menu of contemporary brasserie-style dishes. Basic materials are well sourced (including a supply line from Norfolk for fish and shellfish) and well handled. The kitchen might come up with roasted quail with orange and carrot emulsion, braised chicory and crisp carrots,

ahead of venison (pan-fried loin and suet pudding) with creamed celeriac, roasted beetroot and redcurrant jus, or roasted supreme of coley teamed with Parma ham and potato terrine, buttered broad beans, crayfish and chive beurre blanc. For dessert there could be salted hazelnut parfait with caramelised pear, Earl Grey purée and hazelnut praline. Wines from £17. From the same stable as the White Horse and the Jolly Sailors, Brancaster Staithe, and Hermitage Rd, Hitchin (see entries).
Chef/s: Sherwin Jacobs. **Open:** all week L 12 to 2 (3 Sun), Mon to Sat D 6.45 to 9 (9.15 Fri and Sat). **Meals:** alc (main courses £13 to £21). **Details:** 120 seats. 80 seats outside. Separate bar. Wheelchair access. Music. Car parking.

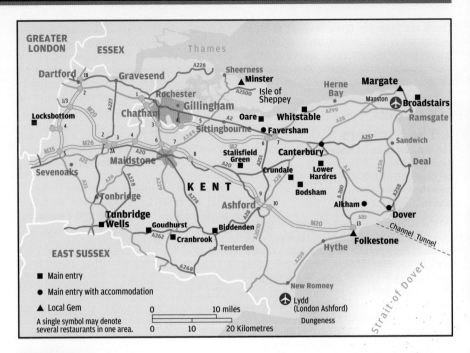

Alkham

The Marquis at Alkham

A new beginning
Alkham Valley Road, Alkham, CT15 7DF
Tel no: (01304) 873410
www.themarquisatalkham.co.uk
Modern British | £43
new chef/no score

Once a coaching inn, the Marquis at Alkham had a sharp makeover some years back – hence the stripped-back interior – emerging as a restaurant-with-rooms. For some it lacked character, displaying too much contemporary styling and not enough comfort, but there's no disputing that the place was a beacon for local food, its menus famous for warmly embracing rural Kent. However, just as we went to press, we learned that Charles Lakin had departed. His replacement, Michael Fowler, has emphasised his commitment to local produce and plans to make the Marquis more accessible by introducing an afternoon bar snack menu alongside the restaurant's tasting menu and à la carte. Reports, please, of the new regime. **Chef/s:** Michael Fowler. **Open:** Tue to Sun L 12 to 2.30 (3 Sun), all week D 6 to 9.30 (7 to 8.30 Sun). **Meals:** alc (main courses £18 to £25). Set L £10 (2 courses) to £13. Sun L £20 (2 courses) to £23. Tasting menu £55. **Details:** 55 seats. 30 seats outside. Wheelchair access. Music. Car parking. Children over 8 yrs only at D.

Biddenden

The West House

Innovative cooking in laid-back surrounds
28 High Street, Biddenden, TN27 8AH
Tel no: (01580) 291341
www.thewesthouserestaurant.co.uk
Modern European | £40
Cooking score: 5

It's easy to miss the Garretts' unassuming restaurant in a lovely Kentish weaver's cottage on Biddenden's high street. However, the half-timbered dining room – smart and uncluttered, furnished with wooden tables and high-backed leather chairs – is the setting for some serious culinary aspirations. A March lunch found a baffling variety of menus (set, tasting, main, garden) but a repertoire that celebrated seasonal produce. A 'truly beautiful plate' of beetroot (wood roast, pickled, cheesecake, sponge, ketchup) might precede 'soft, pink and beautifully tasty' venison haunch, served with a mini-mince pie, pickled red cabbage and a blob of silky-smooth cauliflower purée. Technically ingenious milk and honey, 'a vanilla-scented cloud of loveliness', makes quite a finale. However, reporters agree there's 'a disconnect between the vision and skill of the kitchen compared to a lack of the same careful eye on the front-of-house'. The wine list has generous range and good choice by the glass or carafe.

Chef/s: Graham Garrett. **Open:** Tue to Fri and Sun L 12 to 2 (2.30 Sun), Tue to Sat D 7 to 9 (9.30 Fri and Sat). **Closed:** Mon, 24 to 26 Dec, 1 Jan. **Meals:** Set L £25. Set D £40. Tasting menu £60. **Details:** 32 seats. Car parking.

Bodsham
The Timber Batts
Country pub, Anglo-French grub
School Lane, Bodsham, TN25 5JQ
Tel no: (01233) 750237
www.thetimberbatts.co.uk
Anglo-French | £35
Cooking score: 1

In a remote, rural and very beautiful location, this ancient pub-slash-restaurant may not be easy to find, but it's worth the effort. While still a proper watering hole with real ales, beams and a blazing fire, this is no ordinary Kent pub. Joël Gross has built up quite a following for his traditional French food. Firm favourites are crayfish in lobster bisque, fillet steak with Roquefort sauce, rack of lamb with gratin dauphinois, and apple tarte Tatin. Good-value set-lunch and weekday dinners soften the blow of the more expensive carte, and there's very good ham, egg and fries in the bar. Mainly French wines from £18.50.

Chef/s: Joël Gross. **Open:** Wed to Sun L 12 to 2.30 (3 Sun), Tue to Sat D 7 to 9 (9.30 Sat). **Closed:** Mon, 25 and 26 Dec. **Meals:** alc (main courses £13 to £25). Set L and weekday D £16 (2 courses) to £20. Sun L £21 (2 courses) to £26. **Details:** 50 seats. 50 seats outside. Separate bar. Music. Car parking.

Broadstairs
Albariño
Assured neighbourhood tapas joint
29 Albion Street, Broadstairs, CT10 1LX
Tel no: (01843) 600991
www.albarinorestaurant.co.uk
Tapas | £19
Cooking score: 3
£5 OFF £30

A welcome slice of Spain, within a stone's throw of Viking Bay, Albariño draws a loyal following for its confident, unfussy tapas. Presiding over the open kitchen and tiny, cramped dining room and bar, Steven Dray offers substantive Spanish fare with an unswerving dedication to sourcing the best local produce he can find. Tuck into a plate of the popular chickpea and fennel chips with aïoli or take your pick from top-drawer charcuterie and cheeses, but look to the daily changing specials, too – they proved to be a highlight at inspection, especially the local cod, potato and chorizo stew that came replete with nuggets of sweet, yielding fish. Tapas classics are also to be had, as well as more adventurous dishes such as ox cheek, cauliflower, liquorice and fried breadcrumbs. Creative puddings and homemade ice cream are worth saving room for, and wines from the Albariño region of Spain start at £15.

Chef/s: Steven Dray. **Open:** Sat L 12 to 3, Mon to Sat D 6 to 9.30 (10 Fri and Sat). **Closed:** Sun. **Meals:** alc (tapas £4 to £8). **Details:** 26 seats. 2 seats outside. Wheelchair access. Music.

NEW ENTRY
Wyatt & Jones
Confident harbourside British fare
23-27 Harbour Street, Broadstairs, CT10 1EU
Tel no: (01843) 865126
www.wyattandjones.co.uk
British | £27
Cooking score: 2
£5 OFF £30

You can't help but notice a cosmopolitan breeze as you cross the Farrow & Balled threshold into Wyatt & Jones' smart yet unflashy all-day diner. It may occupy a harbourside spot but it eschews the usual seaside clichés, opting for a more edgy, modern feel (note the ubiquitous dangling exposed-filament bulbs and open kitchen) and an unswerving commitment to British ingredients. Punters are welcomed from dawn to dusk, with vibrant daily changing menus adeptly traversing the day: from cooked breakfasts with homemade bread, through to fine lunchtime fare – ribeye steak and chips, perhaps, or a well-balanced dish of local sea bream in prawn butter with greens. Dinner is altogether more refined, with the chef's expertise fully on show. An appetite-teaser of anchovy toast might be followed by partridge with crab apple glaze and roasted Jerusalem artichokes. Pear and almond bake with rum and raisin ice cream makes for a great closing act. Wines from £15.

Chef/s: Jessica Leah. **Open:** all week L 12 to 3 (12.30 to 5 Sun), Mon to Sat D 6 to 10. **Closed:** Mon and Tue (autumn/winter), 25 and 26 Dec, 1 week Jan, 1 week Nov. **Meals:** alc (main courses £14 to £22). Set L £14 (2 courses) to £18. **Details:** 60 seats. Music.

▌Canterbury
The Goods Shed
Shedloads of good things
Station Road West, Canterbury, CT2 8AN
Tel no: (01227) 459153
www.thegoodsshed.co.uk
Modern British | £31
Cooking score: 2
£5 OFF

The Goods Shed is a joy for anyone interested in food. The curious setting is that of a cavernous Victorian railway shed, where natural light pours through large glass windows and most of the space is given over to a daily farmers' market. On the main floor, communal tables are scattered between stalls, and during the day you can eat very well, from bespoke sandwiches to the superb 'little plates' of impeccable market produce from the Wild Goose bar and counter. For a more substantial meal, head up the stairs to Raphael's Restaurant where the blackboard menu touts a regular line-up of house terrine or Rye Bay scallops thermidor among starters, then rack of lamb with leeks and nettle pesto, and wild bass with brown shrimps, lemon and parsley. British cheeses have that authentic artisan stamp, while desserts yo-yo between orange and almond cake and pear and walnut mess. Wines from £15.50.

Chef/s: Rafael Lopez. **Open:** Tue to Sun L 12 to 2.30 (3 Sat and Sun), Tue to Sat D 6 to 9.30. **Closed:** Mon, 25 to 27 Dec, 1 to 3 Jan. **Meals:** alc (main courses £14 to £22). **Details:** 72 seats. Car parking.

Michael Caines at ABode Canterbury

Fine-tuned cooking
High Street, Canterbury, CT1 2RX
Tel no: (01227) 766266
www.abodehotels.co.uk
Modern British | £45
Cooking score: 4

The building dates from 1469, but you wouldn't know it from the Tudorbethan frontage, and any medieval features within are decidedly muted. Michael Caines Restaurant takes up a fair amount of the ground floor of what is now a business- and function-orientated ABode Hotel, lacking a bit in atmosphere with its neutral palette but delivering cooking that's a cut above the norm for this chain-dominated tourist city. The menu invariably reads enticingly and ticks the right fashionable boxes with its modish ingredients and techniques, from a goats' cheese mousse with apple purée, candied hazelnuts and raisins to roasted chicken teamed with chicken wing, wild garlic, sweet chilli jam and a chicken jus that will have you mopping up the remnants. Momentum isn't lost at dessert stage and both a white chocolate and salted-caramel fondant, and passion fruit soufflé have been well reported. Well-priced set menus pull the crowds, too. Wines from £18.75.
Chef/s: Jauca Catalin. **Open:** all week L 12 to 2.30, Mon to Sat D 5.30 to 9.30 (10 Sat). **Meals:** alc (main courses £16 to £20). Set L £15 (2 courses) to £20. Set D £17 (2 courses) to £23. Sun L £20. Tasting menu £65 (7 courses). **Details:** 70 seats. Separate bar. Wheelchair access. Music. Car parking.

Cranbrook
Apicius

Big-statement cooking in a tiny space
23 Stone Street, Cranbrook, TN17 3HF
Tel no: (01580) 714666
www.restaurant-apicius.co.uk
Modern European | £45
Cooking score: 6

'A great little restaurant serving wonderful food' was one reporter's verdict on Faith Hawkins and Tim Johnson's converted 600-year-old cottage on the main road through Cranbrook. Named after Marcus Gavius Apicius, reputed author of the oldest collection of recipes to survive antiquity, it has a welcoming, hospitable atmosphere that makes everyone feel at home. Tim Johnson's menu, too, is appealing and modern – flavours are clear and well defined; portioning and presentation are spot-on; and there's an emphasis on seasonal ingredients. Indeed, the use of good raw materials is a strength, with Brixham crab boudin served with seared foie gras, pickled radish and apple purée a particular standout at a meal in May. Elsewhere, lambs' sweetbreads, deep-fried and served with celeriac purée, parsley salad and garlic crisps have pleased, as has a roast monkfish tail served with braised Puy lentils, pancetta, artichoke purée and red wine jus. Round things off with the impressive selection of cheeses, or a dark chocolate ganache with griottine cherries, salted candied walnuts, walnut coulis and tarragon ice cream, and 'exceptional' petits fours. Wines from £18.
Chef/s: Timothy Johnson. **Open:** Wed to Fri and Sun L 12 to 2, Wed to Sat D 7 to 9. **Closed:** Mon, Tue, 2 weeks Christmas, 2 weeks summer. **Meals:** Set L £27 (2 courses) to £32. Set D £34 (2 courses) to £40. **Details:** 30 seats. Wheelchair access. Children over 8 yrs only.

Crundale

NEW ENTRY
The Compasses Inn
Lost in the Garden of England
Sole Street, Crundale, CT4 7ES
Tel no: (01227) 700300
www.thecompassescrundale.co.uk
British | £27
Cooking score: 3
£30

This late-15th century pub is secreted away in glorious Kent countryside and oozes character. It comes with a full quota of hop-festooned beams and timbers, along with crackling winter fires and the option of a beer garden for fine days. The approach here is decidedly unpretentious, with hospitable service matched by some appealing, soothing food. Basic materials are well sourced (many locally) and well handled. There's no diffidence about serving an ox cheek bap with horseradish mayo and dripping chips, venison burger, or a well-reported honey-roast ham with champ potatoes, black pudding and poached duck egg at lunchtime. Other appearances might include duck liver parfait with pickled red cabbage, and loin of cod with spiced chickpeas and curried mussels. Puddings are pleasing, with particular praise going to ginger cake with poached pear brûlée. Shepherd Neame ales are served in the bar, along with wines from £14.
Chef/s: Rob Taylor. **Open:** Tue to Sun L 12 to 3 (4 Sun), Tue to Sat D 6 to 10. **Closed:** Mon. **Meals:** alc (main courses £11 to £15). **Details:** 16 seats. 60 seats outside. Separate bar. Wheelchair access. Music. Car parking.

Dover
The Allotment
Interesting, good-value food
9 High Street, Dover, CT16 1DP
Tel no: (01304) 214467
www.theallotmentdover.com
Modern British | £23
Cooking score: 3
£5 OFF   £30

'Always a warm welcoming atmosphere and impeccable service', was the verdict of one regular, while another praised a 'lovely evening with great food and drink'. So, hurrahs all round for this hard-working local asset opposite the Town Hall, which has been doing Dover proud since 2008. While much is made of local sourcing of ingredients, inspiration for dishes comes from wider-spread European roots, perhaps in the form of roasted Dungeness mackerel with potatoes and grain-mustard dressing or Trevélez ham and celeriac rémoulade. The open-plan kitchen can deliver real value in the shape of a Camargue-style beef or pot-roasted free-range chicken with vegetables and cider, and the complimentary salad to start 'is a lovely touch'. As for desserts, 'both the crumble and chocolate mousse are particularly good'. Smooth, attentive service is a bonus, as is the south-facing, flint-walled back garden – a natural suntrap in fine weather. Wines from £16.
Chef/s: David Flynn. **Open:** Tue to Sat 8.30am to 11pm. **Closed:** Sun, Mon, 24 Dec to 14 Jan. **Meals:** alc (main courses £9 to £16). **Details:** 26 seats. 24 seats outside. Wheelchair access. Music.

Faversham

Read's
Elevated dining at a Georgian manor house
Macknade Manor, Canterbury Road, Faversham,
ME13 8XE
Tel no: (01795) 535344
www.reads.com
Modern British | £60
Cooking score: 6

£5 OFF 🍷 🚍

Putting it in a nutshell, one visitor observed that this serene Georgian manor house on the outskirts of Faversham offers 'classy, elegant food with particularly fine service – good value lunch too'. This approach has kept David and Rona Pitchford's restaurant-with-rooms in the premier division for almost four decades. The food has always maintained a proudly British dimension – quality ingredients from a network of well-chosen suppliers – but these days the kitchen is not slow to take up other bright ideas and flavours: miso-cured salmon with pickled Asian pears, black radish and a Siamese dressing, say. But generally it's a classical style that turns up warm tartlet of duck livers, bourguignon-style, with pancetta and oil of fresh herbs or breast of corn-fed chicken with galette potato, button onions, bacon lardons and a lemon thyme sauce, followed by a superb rhubarb soufflé. The wine list oozes oenophile class, with an impressive range of half-bottles and a condensed list of Best Buys; house selections from £22.
Chef/s: David Pitchford. **Open:** Tue to Sat L 12 to 2, D 7 to 9. **Closed:** Sun, Mon, 25 to 27 Dec, first week Jan, first 2 weeks Sept. **Meals:** Set L £26. Set D £50 (2 courses) to £60. **Details:** 50 seats. 24 seats outside. Separate bar. Wheelchair access. Car parking.

🍴 **Visit us Online**
To find out more about
The Good Food Guide, please visit
www.thegoodfoodguide.co.uk

Folkestone

LOCAL GEM
▲ Rocksalt
4-5 Fishmarket Road, Folkestone, CT19 6AA
Tel no: (01303) 212070
www.rocksaltfolkestone.co.uk
Seafood | £28

Readers report 'this restaurant is well worth the effort', though it 'can be a bit hit or miss' – and with all the plate glass and wood, every little sound echoes. But when the sun shines on the boats bobbing in the harbour, and the kitchen is on form, it's hard to beat this 'modern and adventurous' place. Recent successes have been Romney Marsh beets, celery, Golden Cross (goats' cheese) and pennywort salad; fillet of cod with cockles and sea aster; and salted-caramel and white chocolate cheesecake. The set lunch is good value. Wines from £16.50. Closed Sun D.

Goudhurst

NEW ENTRY
The Vine
A welcoming beacon for drinkers and diners
High Street, Goudhurst, TN17 1AG
Tel no: (01580) 211753
www.thevinegoudhurst.com
Modern British | £32
Cooking score: 2

£5 OFF

The white-clapboarded Vine sits squarely in the centre of pretty Goudhurst, and with its potted vine tree out front ('looking uncannily like the White Tree of Minas Tirith'), the newly restored hostelry is a welcoming beacon for drinkers and diners. Inside, wooden floors and mismatched chairs may be ubiquitous these days, but much thought has gone into this lovely place – and the menu is no exception. A heritage beetroot salad with goats' curd, apple and toasted hazelnuts makes a fresh, pretty starter. To follow, you know you're in safe hands if you choose roast neck of lamb, confit belly, artichoke and fried potato, the latter a 'ruler-thin strip of crispy moreishness'. Elsewhere, braised ox cheek with rare onglet comes with delicate pickled onion rings in batter: another nice touch. The pudding menu has plenty of ideas to tempt, for instance cinnamon doughnuts with burnt coffee custard. Wine from £17.50.

Chef/s: Tobyn Excell. **Open:** Tue to Sun L 12 to 3 (4 Sun), Tue to Sat D 6 to 9.30. **Closed:** Mon. **Meals:** alc (main courses £15 to £22). Set L £17 (2 courses) to £20. **Details:** 60 seats. 20 seats outside. Separate bar. Music.

Locksbottom

Chapter One

Big-city cooking at local prices
Farnborough Common, Locksbottom, BR6 8NF
Tel no: (01689) 854848
www.chaptersrestaurants.com
Modern European | £39
Cooking score: 6

♦ V

It is hard to believe that such a gem resides in the heart of suburban Kent. All is relaxation, smiles and easy cooperation in the smart, spacious dining room. Here, Andrew McLeish's food takes an individual stance, his kitchen sending out quail Kiev with its roasted leg, a lick of herb mayonnaise, dandelion leaf and Gruyère, or teaming treacle-cured salmon with charred spring onions, coriander, ginger, lemongrass purée and sesame dressing, and matching Gloucester Old Spot pork belly with choucroute, silver-skin onions and devils on horseback. Surprises aplenty, then, but never novelty for its own sake. It's a measure of McLeish's finesse that while his cooking has unexpected twists it always retains a sense of proportion and balance. Hard-to-pass-up desserts include a rich milk chocolate and praline mousse with hazelnut cream and raspberry sorbet. Chapter One also scores with its reasonable prices, a policy extending to a stash of modern wines (prices from £17.50).

Chef/s: Andrew McLeish. **Open:** all week L 12 to 2.30 (2.45 Sun), D 6.30 to 10.30 (9 Sun). **Closed:** 2 to 4 Jan. **Meals:** alc (main courses £21 to £30). Set L

£20. Sun L £23. **Details:** 120 seats. 20 seats outside. Separate bar. Wheelchair access. Music. Car parking.

Lower Hardres

The Granville

A great local asset
Street End, Lower Hardres, CT4 7AL
Tel no: (01227) 700402
www.thegranvillecanterbury.com
Modern European | £28
Cooking score: 3
£5 OFF £30

This Kentish stalwart – now in its eleventh year – has much local support, a spacious, rustic interior and a reinvigorated kitchen since Dave Hart (formerly of the Fitzwalter Arms, Goodnestone) arrived. Sourcing good raw materials remains a priority, as befits a sibling of the acclaimed Sportsman (see entry). The blackboard menu centres on appetising combinations: wild sea bass fillet with crab bisque, say, or beef short rib in beer and onion. Kentish asparagus, simply served with butter and Parmesan, and a first-rate dish of wild garlic gnocchi and asparagus tips in a vivid green sauce, topped with a poached egg, speak of early summer, while a bowl of juicy mussels in a restrained broth of chilli, garlic and bay leaves, delicious homemade bread, and a delicate, silky buttermilk pudding (served with rhubarb) indicate a kitchen distinguishing itself with enthusiasm and honest effort. Shepherd Neame ales are on draught, and wines open at £15.50.

Chef/s: Dave Hart. **Open:** all week L 12 to 2.30 (3 Sun), Tue to Sat D 6.30 to 9. **Closed:** 25 and 26 Dec. **Meals:** alc (main courses £14 to £22). Set L £15 (2 courses) to £18. **Details:** 55 seats. 20 seats outside. Separate bar. Wheelchair access. Music. Car parking.

▌Margate

LOCAL GEM
▲ The Ambrette
44 King Street, Margate, CT9 1QE
Tel no: (01843) 231504
www.theambrette.co.uk
Indian | £27 £5 OFF

'Genuinely modern', Dev Biswal's
contemporary Indian cooking applies 'subtle
and aromatic' spicing to local goodies
including sea greens, game and orchard fruit.
These 'unique' combinations (also offered at
the Ambrette's posher branch in Rye, see entry
East Sussex) might take the form of a soft-
shell crab and sea purslane salad or slow-
cooked mallard leg with spiced courgette,
cauliflower purée and a lime leaf, lemongrass
and pepper sauce. Darjeeling chai jelly
wobbles alongside chocolate samosas for
dessert. House wine is £13.99. Open all week.

▲ GB Pizza Co
14a Marine Drive, Margate, CT9 1DH
Tel no: (01843) 297700
www.greatbritishpizzacompany.com
Italian | £15

'There is probably nowhere better if you're
heading to Margate.' Right on the seafront, a
plate-glass window taking in the sweep of
sand and huge skyscape, this small all-day
pizzeria mixes rough-round-the-edges
vintage with modern grit. It's all endearingly
unpretentious, with casual vibes, half a dozen
wood-fired, thin-crust pizzas and quality
British ingredients (even charcuterie is UK-
produced). 'Margate-rita' is the signature, but
there's also fennel salami, chorizo and chilli,
daily specials and 'amazing' brownies for
dessert. Drink Kentish ales, fruits juices or
organic house wine from £13. Open all week.

⫚ Average Price
The average price listed in main-entry
reviews denotes the price of a three-
course meal, without wine.

▌Minster

LOCAL GEM
▲ The Corner House
42 Station Road, Minster, CT12 4BZ
Tel no: (01843) 823000
www.thecornerhouseminster.co.uk
Modern British | £25

This simple bar-cum-restaurant-with-rooms
opposite the church is low-beamed and rustic
and offers short menus that seem to evolve
slowly. Chef/proprietor Matt Sworder knows
his customers and uses quality raw materials to
produce accomplished modern country
cooking; everything, from bread to ice cream,
is made in-house. Home in on a sharing board
that features sausage roll, potted shrimps and
rabbit and ham-hock terrine, move on to
venison and mushroom pudding, then
Kentish cheeses. Wines start at £14.
Accommodation. Closed Sun D and Mon.

▌Oare
The Three Mariners
The full country-pub package
2 Church Road, Oare, ME13 0QA
Tel no: (01795) 533633
www.thethreemarinersoare.co.uk
Modern British | £28
Cooking score: 2
🍷 £30

The Three Mariners commands a prime
position on the road that runs through this
village north of Faversham. It's a heart-
warming country pub with all the requisite
trappings – real ales (from Shepherd Neame),
roaring winter fire and summer terrace
looking towards Oare Creek. John
O'Riordan's vibrant, seasonal cooking is
assured and simple. He gets straight to the
point and seems to please with the likes of
local skate cheeks dressed with lemon, garlic
and parsley, local red mullet with salsa verde,
slow-braised ox cheeks and herb-crusted
rump of lamb. The cheap 'walkers' lunch'
(offered every day except Sunday) doesn't
muster the same enthusiasm, however. Several

reporters have complained its popularity puts pressure on the kitchen and that a little more attention to detail is required to maintain standards. But there are no complaints about the home-baked bread and the 'very welcoming' service. Wines from £14.50.
Chef/s: John O'Riordan. **Open:** all week L 12 to 2.30 (3 Sat and Sun), D 6.30 to 9 (9.30 Fri and Sat, 7 to 9 Sun). **Meals:** alc (main courses £13 to £22). Set L £13 and £18 (Mon to Sat). Set D £18 (Sun to Thur), £21 (Fri and Sat). Sun L £18 to £23. **Details:** 63 seats. 30 seats outside. Music. Car parking.

Sevenoaks

READERS RECOMMEND
Vine Restaurant
Modern British
11 Pound Lane, Sevenoaks, TN13 3TB
Tel no: (01732) 469510
www.vinerestaurant.co.uk
'Total experience was excellent – great choice of food, which was delicious, and good value. Service attentive but not overbearing.'

Stalisfield Green
The Plough
A convivial oasis
Stalisfield Green, ME13 0HY
Tel no: (01795) 890256
www.stalisfieldgreen.co.uk
British | £25
Cooking score: 2
£30

This medieval 'hall house' is found down narrow Kentish lanes and has everything you might expect from an ancient country hostelry: an ever-so-English village-green setting; all the beams and standing timbers you could wish for; real ales; real fires. There may have been a change of ownership since last year's Guide, but the air of no-nonsense simplicity has been retained and the Plough makes a convivial oasis. The cooking is appealing, too, and execution is generally on the money. Much of the menu runs along familiar lines, taking in excellent potted

shrimps or a thick slice of gin-cured Loch Duart salmon with horseradish cream and baby beets, then a main course of pink, tender Kentish lamb rump served with lightly spiced chickpeas and roast aubergine. There's homemade bread, too, and desserts such as chocolate mousse with sea-salt caramel and blood-orange sorbet.
Chef/s: Alex Windebank. **Open:** Tue to Sun L 12 to 2 (3 Sat and Sun), Tue to Sat D 6 to 9. **Closed:** Mon. **Meals:** alc (main courses £12 to £20). Set L and D £14 (2 courses) to £17. **Details:** 65 seats. 40 seats outside.

Tunbridge Wells
Thackeray's
Classy French food with a touch of 'Vanity Fair'
85 London Road, Tunbridge Wells, TN1 1EA
Tel no: (01892) 511921
www.thackerays-restaurant.co.uk
Modern European | £48
Cooking score: 5
V

'I booked a table for 8.30, which I consider relatively normal, but it's obviously radically late for this part of Kent as it was full to the brim and other diners were well on their way,' commented one visitor, who later stressed 'it made for a lovely buzz'. The wood floors and low ceilings of this 'beautiful space' – once home to the Victorian novelist – are brought together by twinkling lamps, candles and sumptuous wallpapers, and by Richard Phillips' intricate modern cooking. He fashions dishes that dovetail British ingredients with contemporary European technique, serving roasted saddle of Kentish rabbit with medjool dates and Gruyère bread sauce (with a crisp, gratinéed top), ahead of monkfish with calamari risotto, fennel (purée and pollen), avocado mousse, poached razor clams and fish velouté. Then he produces a 'perfect' Yorkshire rhubarb and tonka bean custard soufflé to finish. Brilliant-value lunches maintain the tempo, and the stylish, global wine list starts at £18.95.

Chef/s: Richard Phillips. **Open:** Tue to Sun L 12 to 2.30, Tue to Sat D 6.30 to 10.30. **Closed:** Mon. **Meals:** alc (main courses £25 to £29). Set L £17 (2 courses) to £19. **Details:** 68 seats. 30 seats outside. Separate bar. Music.

▌Whitstable

NEW ENTRY
East Coast Dining Room
Good food in up-coming Tankerton
101 Tankerton Road, Whitstable, CT5 2AJ
Tel no: (01227) 281180
www.eastcoastdiningroom.co.uk
Modern British | £33
Cooking score: 2

Claire Houlihan ran the Three Mariners at Oare (see entry) for several years, but in making the transition from pub to neighbourhood restaurant, she has really found her groove. There's an agreeably civilised feel to the two 'pleasant, light and bright' dining rooms with their hand-me-down chairs and white-clad tables. The kitchen looks to the locality for ingredients, yet mixes influences in true modern British style. Visitors tell of their sheer delight in a good-value set lunch that delivered a salad of curried smoked haddock with deep-fried quail's egg and fresh apple sticks, and roast pork tenderloin with creamy mash, savoy cabbage with pancetta and caramelised apple and ginger. Or a weekend brunch that opened with 'very good' goats' cheese custard with shaved fennel and black olive salad, and finished with an 'excellent' chocolate and espresso mousse with salted-caramel ice cream and cocoa nib crumbs. Wines from £16.
Chef/s: Ryan Smith. **Open:** Wed to Sun L 12 to 2.30 (3 Sat, 4 Sun), Wed to Sat D 6.30 to 9 (9.30 Fri and Sat). **Closed:** Mon, Tue, 25 Dec, 1 Jan, 2 weeks Jan. **Meals:** alc (main courses £15 to £21). Set L £13 (2 courses) to £16. **Details:** 38 seats. 16 seats outside. Wheelchair access. Music.

JoJo's
Top-notch tapas by the sea
2 Herne Bay Road, Whitstable, CT5 2LQ
Tel no: (01227) 274591
www.jojosrestaurant.co.uk
Tapas | £25
Cooking score: 4
£30

Housed in an imaginatively converted mini-supermarket overlooking the North Sea, Nikki Billington and Paul Watson's idiosyncratic tapas joint and coffee shop brightens up trendy Whitstable with its funky boho vibes and Mediterranean warmth. There's little in the way of décor (wood floors, farmhouse tables, white walls, an open kitchen), but an infectiously happy vibe prevails and the food says it all. The printed menu touts a regular line-up of wafer-thin cured meats and cheeses (served with homemade jellies), plus salads and meze plates ranging from stuffed red peppers, risotto balls and patatas bravas to mutton and feta koftas with spicy tomato sauce and tzatziki, or char-grilled sardines simply dressed with lemon and black pepper. Impeccable sourcing, seasonal diligence and honest-to-goodness craftsmanship put Jojo's in a league of its own – especially for its blackboard specials. To drink, there are some gluggable wines (from £15), although BYO is the default option (corkage £3). Note: no cards.
Chef/s: Nikki Billington and Jake Delaney. **Open:** Thur to Sun L 12.30 to 2, Wed to Sat D 6.30 to 9.30. **Closed:** Mon, Tue. **Meals:** alc (tapas £5 to £11). **Details:** Cash only. 60 seats. Wheelchair access. Music.

The Sportsman
Astonishing food in the most congenial pub
Faversham Road, Seasalter, Whitstable, CT5 4BP
Tel no: (01227) 273370
www.thesportsmanseasalter.co.uk
Modern British | £36
Cooking score: 6

Located on a quiet windswept road a few miles from Whitstable, this unremarkable roadside pub doesn't reveal the culinary quality within. Steve Harris's enterprise, hailed as a trailblazer when opening 15 years ago, has stood the test of time. The spare, scrubbed rustic interior has changed little, along with the paper napkins and laid-back feel. Harris remains obsessively influenced by the ingredients available on the doorstep, his cooking delightfully simple. Most plump for the carte – the dishes chalked on a blackboard to emphasise their daily-changing nature – but a tasting menu is available with 48 hours' notice. It's the sheer, dazzling flavours that stand out, whether the 'moreish' onion bhajia accompanying curried cauliflower soup, brill 'perfectly cooked and simply adorned', a superb saddle of lamb (cooked three ways) with creamed potato tart and greens, or a generous, rich tarte Tatin, for two. The short wine list opens at £16.95.
Chef/s: Steve Harris. **Open:** Tue to Sun L 12 to 2 (2.30 Sat, 3 Sun), Tue to Sat D 7 to 9. **Closed:** Mon, bank hols. **Meals:** alc (main courses £18 to £23). **Details:** 50 seats. Music. Car parking.

Wheelers Oyster Bar
British seaside through and through
8 High Street, Whitstable, CT5 1BQ
Tel no: (01227) 273311
www.wheelersoysterbar.com
Seafood | £36
Cooking score: 4

Oh, fortunate Whitstable residents to have such a restaurant on their doorsteps – remarkably down-to-earth and much praised by reporters for its lack of pretension and sensationally fresh fish. Behind the candyfloss-pink and blue frontage there's a tight squeeze at Wheelers, whether at tables in the 16-seater back parlour or perched on one of the four stools at the new seafood bar (repositioned to make better use of the space). However, the demand is such that 'it is well worth the effort and persistence to snag a table'. Mark Stubbs' brief menu is appealing: teriyaki scallops come with honey-glazed duck, oriental duck consommé and duck bonbon, as a possible prelude to fricassee of lemon sole, scallop and langoustine with fennel pollen, shellfish nage and saffron potatoes, or chorizo-crusted cod with squid-ink paint, smoked-prawn paella and 'piqiou' pepper purée. No licence means BYO (no corkage) and it's cash only.
Chef/s: Mark Stubbs. **Open:** Thur to Tue 1 to 7.30. **Closed:** Wed, 2.5 weeks in Jan. **Meals:** alc (main courses £19 to £24). **Details:** Cash only. 16 seats. 4 seats outside.

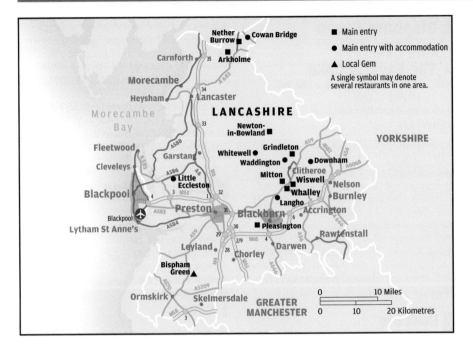

Nether Burrow · Cowan Bridge
Carnforth · 35 · Arkholme
Morecambe
Heysham · Lancaster
Morecambe Bay
LANCASHIRE
34
33
Fleetwood
Newton-in-Bowland
Garstang
Whitewell · Grindleton
Cleveleys
Waddington · Downham
Little Eccleston
Clitheroe
Mitton · Wiswell
Blackpool
32 · Nelson
Whalley · Burnley
Blackpool
Langho
Lytham St Anne's · Preston · Blackburn · Accrington
Pleasington
Rawtenstall
Leyland
Darwen
Bispham Green
Chorley
Ormskirk · Skelmersdale
GREATER MANCHESTER
YORKSHIRE

■ Main entry
● Main entry with accommodation
▲ Local Gem
A single symbol may denote several restaurants in one area.

0 ————— 10 Miles
0 ——— 10 —— 20 Kilometres

◼ Arkholme
The Redwell Inn

Modern robust flavours in a traditional setting
Kirkby Lonsdale Road, Arkholme, LA6 1BQ
Tel no: (015242) 21240
www.redwellinn.net
Modern British | £25
Cooking score: 2

£5 OFF · £30

'There is more to the place than first meets the eye,' confided a visitor to this old coaching inn in the Lune Valley. Within, it is all 'invitingly renovated' with a lovely double-sided woodburner and comfy sofas, a separate dining room and, behind the pub, its own smokehouse and shop. The kitchen is all about good hearty cooking with great local ingredients. In season, there might be butter-roasted pheasant breast served with squash, pine nuts and pancetta. Own-smoked provisions could include a simple 'creamy' smoked mackerel pâté or 'delicious' Morecambe Bay shrimp and smoked mussel risotto with crispy capers.

Mains deliver slow-cooked duck with creamed cabbage, quince and creamed potatoes, and a slow-cooked shin of beef. And for pudding? Mrs Talbot's award-winning sticky ginger and apple pudding might appear alongside pineapple parfait with pomegranate, yoghurt and chilli. As for wine, a French house duo start at £15.60.

Chef/s: Rob Talbot. **Open:** Wed to Sun L 12 to 2 (3 Sun), Wed to Sat D 6 to 9 (9.30 Sat). **Closed:** Mon, Tue. **Meals:** alc (main courses £13 to £24). Set L and D £20. Sun L £20. **Details:** 80 seats. 20 seats outside. Separate bar. Wheelchair access. Music. Car parking.

Symbols

🛏 Accommodation is available

£30 Three courses for less than £30

V Separate vegetarian menu

£5 OFF £5-off voucher scheme

🍷 Notable wine list

Bispham Green

LOCAL GEM
▲ The Eagle & Child
Malt Kiln Lane, Bispham Green, L40 3SG
Tel no: (01257) 462297
www.eagleandchildbispham.co.uk
British | £25

'Unpretentious' neatly sums up this cheery, whitewashed pub found down the unclassified lanes of west Lancashire. Inside, it's all low ceilings and old beams, with ancient wood partitions dividing the space. Service is swift and efficient, and food is freshly prepared, based on sound, often local, raw materials. Pub classics predominate (steak and ale pie, fish and chips), but specials run to cod, crayfish and pea fishcakes, and Goosnargh duck breast with confit leg, creamed potatoes and port. Wines from £15. Open all week.

Burrow

The Highwayman
Local flavours and local enterprise
Main Road, Burrow, LA6 2RJ
Tel no: (01524) 273338
www.highwaymaninn.co.uk
British | £27
Cooking score: 2
£30

Like the other pubs in Nigel Haworth's small chain of Ribble Valley Inns, the Highwayman serves consistently good food. The kitchen is firmly rooted in British cuisine and puts great emphasis on north-west suppliers, especially local producers: note Morecambe Bay potted shrimps (correctly served in just warmed butter), and 'damn good' Sandham's Tasty Lancashire cheese and onion pie (a generous portion served with a jacket potato), both popular menu fixtures according to reporters. Lancashire hotpot with pickled red cabbage is another star turn, alongside trusty grilled steaks, a 'hot dog' of pork and beef sausages in a brioche roll, and a rather nice smoked fish pie. This year reports suggest the Cumberland rum nicky with banana cream just about

trumps the famed sticky toffee pudding. 'Attentive and helpful' staff, winter fires and summer alfresco feature among the attractions, as do regional ales and a well-chosen, carefully annotated and kindly priced wine list (from £15.75).
Chef/s: Jason Burbeck. Open: Tue to Sat L 12 to 2, D 5.30 to 8.30 (9 Fri and Sat). Sun 12 to 8.30. Closed: Mon. Meals: alc (main courses £10 to £26). Sun L £20. Details: 110 seats. 45 seats outside. Separate bar. Wheelchair access. Music. Car parking.

Cowan Bridge

Hipping Hall
21st-century cooking/15th-century setting
Cowan Bridge, LA6 2JJ
Tel no: (01524) 271187
www.hippinghall.com
Modern British | £55
Cooking score: 5
🍷 🛏 V

Sitting on the borders of Lancashire, Cumbria and Yorkshire this 'very attractive, diminutive' country house hotel provides chef Brent Hulena with plenty of the fresh produce of which his menu boasts. The dining room is a traditionally furnished 15th-century hall, complete with minstrels' gallery and blazing winter fire. It makes quite a contrast to the impeccably 21st-century approach of Hulena's cooking. He sails confidently through the tricky waters of intricate modern cuisine, fashioning clever contemporary dishes from superlative raw materials: teaming home-smoked sea trout with kohlrabi and horseradish snow; matching roasted halibut with truffled pomme purée, hazelnuts and sea herbs; and lamb noisettes with confit shoulder, pickled onion and radicchio. From an amuse-bouche of blue cheese, quince and walnut, to desserts such as pear and ginger crumb with lime granita, and the slate of English cheeses, attention to detail is impressive. Clever wine suggestions are offered on a well-chosen list that opens at £21.

Chef/s: Brent Hulena. Open: Sat and Sun L 12 to 2, all week D 7 to 9. Meals: Set L £33. Set D £55. Sun L £33. Tasting menu £65. Details: 30 seats. Separate bar. Wheelchair access. Music. Car parking. Children over 12 yrs only at D.

Downham

The Assheton Arms

Traditional surroundings, modern food
Downham, BB7 4BJ
Tel no: (01200) 441227
www.asshetonarms.com
British | £28
Cooking score: 2

In a Ribble Valley village near Clitheroe, the Assheton is a grey-stone inn that has had a cool modern makeover, with light wood predominating. To a newbie, the whole experience was 'sublime', including the 'honest, down-to-earth cooking' of Antony Shirley. Flavours can arrive from afar, so expect salt-and-pepper squid with ginger dipping sauce, and Persian chicken done on the robata grill with pomegranate rice and almonds in yoghurt dressing. But rest assured that those in the market for dry-aged steak and onion rings, haddock and prawn fish pie under cheesy mash, or a snack treat of pork pie with brown sauce (both homemade) won't be sent away disappointed. The sweet-toothed can then opt for the syrup sponge and custard, or a lighter chocolate and cherry mousse with almond cookie crush. A commendable short wine list opens with house Spanish varietals – Verdejo and Bobal – for £15.10.
Chef/s: Antony Shirley. Open: all week L 12 to 3 (5 Sat and Sun), D 5 to 9 (10 Fri and Sat, 8.30 Sun). Meals: alc (main courses £11 to £24). Details: 100 seats. 60 seats outside. Separate bar. Wheelchair access. Music. Car parking.

Grindleton

★ TOP 50 PUB ★

The Duke of York Inn

Mellow pub with sharp seasonal food
Brow Top, Grindleton, BB7 4QR
Tel no: (01200) 441266
www.dukeofyorkgrindleton.com
Modern British | £31
Cooking score: 3

£5 OFF

Michael Heathcote's traditional hostelry in the Ribble Valley is the personification of an English pub, full of warmth, honest intent and gastronomic pleasures. The mood is mellow and Heathcote's respectful food is defined by clear flavours and a feel for what is right on the plate. He also sets great store by local ingredients: meat is from local valley farms, for example, and game from the Forest of Bowland. Lancashire cheese and caramelised onion soufflé could set the tone, before roasted and braised venison served with red cabbage, poached pear, fondant potato and a red wine chocolate sauce, then an excellent blood-orange curd meringue tart with blood-orange sorbet. As one fan notes: 'delicious food, great service, wonderful atmosphere – who could ask for more?' Local ales line up alongside a carefully annotated wine list offering seriously gluggable stuff from France, Italy, Spain and elsewhere; bottles from £16.50.
Chef/s: Michael Heathcote. Open: Tue to Sun L 12 to 2, D 6 to 9 (5 to 7.30 Sun). Closed: Mon, Tue after bank hols. Meals: alc (main courses £14 to £28). Set L and D £15 (2 courses) to £17. Sun L £20. Details: 70 seats. 20 seats outside. Separate bar. Wheelchair access. Car parking.

Langho

★ TOP 50 ★

Northcote

A smartly revitalised, timeless retreat
Northcote Road, Langho, BB6 8BE
Tel no: (01254) 240555
www.northcote.com
Modern British | £61
Cooking score: 6

🍷 🛏 V

With its meticulously tended grounds, carved-stone entrance and redbrick solidity, Northcote looks almost regal. This bushy-tailed bastion of reinvented British food is riding high following its vivacious makeover. Accrington-born Nigel Haworth is the main man, although his culinary ideas are brilliantly interpreted by head chef Lisa Allen. Just consider a superb trio of lamb involving slices of pink loin, a crisp roll of belly and a chunk of soft braised shoulder with peas in a soupy, 'milk-like' broth. Otherwise, it's all about the brave new world, as the kitchen fashions picture-perfect plates of scallop tempura with roast garlic and sorrel aïoli or char-grilled English veal rib with paprika butter and triple-cooked chips – plus extravagantly embellished desserts such as melting ginger pudding or a Valrhona chocolate cylinder with sheep's milk ice cream. Generous North Country hospitality abounds, and charmingly accommodating service makes everyone feel like royalty. To cap it all, the stupendous, passionately curated wine list is a labour of love, with 50 pages of mouth-watering oenophile opportunities; bottles from £25.
Chef/s: Lisa Allen. **Open:** all week L 12 to 2, D 7 to 9.30 (6.30 to 10 Sat, 7 to 9 Sun). **Closed:** 25 Dec, 10 days Jan. **Meals:** alc (main courses £29 to £40). Set L £28. Set D £60 (5 courses). Tasting menu £85 (7 courses). Sun L £36 (4 courses). **Details:** 60 seats. Separate bar. Wheelchair access. Music. Car parking.

Little Eccleston

The Cartford Inn

Handsome inn serving pub classics
Cartford Lane, Little Eccleston, PR3 0YP
Tel no: (01995) 670166
www.thecartfordinn.co.uk
Modern British | £28
Cooking score: 2

🛏 £30

Julie and Patrick Beaume imbue this 17th-century coaching inn with personality and quirkiness. It stands on the banks of the River Wyre amid the beauty of the Fylde Coast and is, in the words of several readers, 'quite simply one of my favourite places to eat'. Quality ingredients get standard modern treatment: a starter of Bury black pudding-flavoured gnocchi is teamed with scallops, lemon butter and crisp pancetta; Goosnargh duck breast arrives with pineapple and pepper skewers, vegetable stir-fry rice, light teriyaki and ginger. The kitchen generally makes a good fist at mainstream dishes too, such as oxtail and beef in real ale suet pudding or a fish pie made with cod, salmon and prawns – and steaks are highly recommended. Puddings, including brioche bread-and-butter pudding or chocolate fondant, push pleasure buttons rather than boundaries. The wine list opens with quaffable Chilean white and Italian red at £15.
Chef/s: Ian Manning. **Open:** Tue to Sat L 12 to 2, D 5.30 to 9 (10 Fri and Sat). Sun 12 to 8.30. **Closed:** Mon, 25 Dec. **Meals:** alc (main courses £12 to £21). **Details:** 80 seats. 30 seats outside. Separate bar. Wheelchair access. Music. Car parking.

▌Mitton

The Three Fishes
Flying the flag for regional food
Mitton Road, Mitton, BB7 9PQ
Tel no: (01254) 826888
www.thethreefishes.com
British | £23
Cooking score: 2
£30

The newly refurbished flagship of Nigel
Haworth's Ribble Valley Inns 'retains the
relaxed pub charm but with a contemporary
feel'. You can settle down in one of the many
nooks of this large, flagstoned pub and enjoy
'truly excellent' haddock and chips (cooked in
dripping) or Nigel's salt marsh lamb hotpot –
both still topping the bestseller list. But they
are strongly supported by many other regional
staples: Morecambe Bay potted shrimps, a
local Goosnargh duck platter or a twice-baked
Lancashire cheese soufflé with beetroot relish.
There is praise, too, for an 'excellent' gluten-
free menu. Along with local produce, seasonal
is a watchword, too – to be enjoyed in the
form of locally grown Formby asparagus, for
example. Desserts hark back to the days of
lemon curd tart, or perhaps Bramley apple
crumble. Capable, charming service, a 'flight'
of local cask ales and quaffable wines (from
£15.75) complete an admirable pub package.
Chef/s: Adam Edwards. **Open:** Mon to Fri L 12 to 2,
D 5.30 to 8.30 (9 Fri), Sat and Sun 12 to 9 (8.30
Sun). **Meals:** alc (main courses £10 to £21). Sun L
£16 (2 courses) to £20. **Details:** 120 seats. 55 seats
outside. Wheelchair access. Music. Car parking.

▌Newton-in-Bowland

NEW ENTRY
The Parkers Arms
Genial country pub, faultless cooking
Newton-in-Bowland, BB7 3DY
Tel no: (01200) 446236
www.parkersarms.co.uk
British | £26
Cooking score: 2
🛏 £30

Done up and given a new lease of life a few
years ago, this fine old pub in a pristine hamlet
in the Trough of Bowland continues to strike a
good balance between its restaurant and pub
personalities. In the bar there are flagstones,
log fires and real ales, contrasting with
polished boards and understated country
elegance in the dining room where proper pub
grub isn't overlooked. But alongside the oft-
reported Fleetwood haddock and chips, skirt
steak, and Goosnargh chicken and wild garlic
pie, there could be 'perfectly spiced and
seasoned pastrami' with treacle bread and
piccalilli; roast pheasant stuffed with herb
butter, wrapped in streaky bacon and served
on a bed of creamy mash, spring cabbage and a
scattering of diced roasted root veg; and
'delectable and flaky' Portuguese custard tart
or Wet Nelly (bread pudding). It all adds up to
'faultless cooking in genial surroundings'.
Wines from £15.75.
Chef/s: Stosie Madi. **Open:** Tue to Fri L 12 to 2.30, D
6 to 8.30. Sat and Sun 12 to 9 (8 Sun). **Closed:** Mon
(exc bank hols). **Meals:** alc (main courses £10 to
£17). **Details:** Separate bar.

█ Pleasington
The Clog & Billycock
Welcoming pub that champions local produce
Billinge End Road, Pleasington, BB2 6QB
Tel no: (01254) 201163
www.theclogandbillycock.com
British | £22
Cooking score: 2
£30

The Pleasington outpost of Nigel Haworth's
Ribble Valley Inns group is an old boozer
spruced up by this winning team who like
their establishments to remain rooted in the
community. The respect for the past extends
to decorative touches in the smart interior
relating to the weaving and cobbling heritage
round these parts. When it comes to the food,
there's evident passion for Lancashire produce.
The bright, contemporary output extends to
Morecambe Bay shrimps served warm with a
toasted English muffin, and a Scotch egg made
with venison and black pudding, but there's
also chicken kebab with spiced lentil sauce and
onion dabs. It's pub food with the rough edges
well and truly removed – beef shin, oxtail and
kidney pie, fish and chips with the spuds fried
in dripping, and Angus steaks cooked on the
char-grill. Finish with spotted dick and real
custard, and drink regional ales or global
wines from £15.50.
Chef/s: Matt Castelli. Open: Mon to Fri L 12 to 2, D
5.30 to 8.30 (9 Fri). Sat and Sun 12 to 9 (8.30 Sun).
Meals: alc (main courses £10 to £26). Set L £16 (2
courses) to £20. Sun L £16 (2 courses) to £20.
Details: 130 seats. 50 seats outside. Separate bar.
Wheelchair access. Music. Car parking.

¶¶● Please send us your
¶¶● feedback
To register your opinion about any
restaurant listed in the Guide, or a new
restaurant that you wish to bring to our
attention, please visit the web address at
the bottom of the page. Your feedback
informs the content of the book and will
be used to compile next year's reviews.

█ Waddington
The Waddington Arms
Lovely, welcoming village local
Waddington, BB7 3HP
Tel no: (01200) 423262
www.waddingtonarms.co.uk
Modern British | £23
Cooking score: 1
£5 OFF £30

This 'laid-back, proper country pub' has been
in the same hands since 1997 and is run with
great warmth. It's the genuine article:
centuries old with real ales, wood and stone
floors, polished tables, open fires and a menu
of sturdy agreeable pub food. Lancashire
hotpot, sausages with mash and onion gravy,
and steaks with all the trimmings are
satisfying, generously portioned staples, but
there's also seared scallops with crisp pork
belly and cauliflower purée, curry-spiced cod
loin with sag aloo and spicy tomato chutney,
and chocolate brownies with fudge sauce.
Wines from £15.25.
Chef/s: Thomas Steele. Open: Mon to Fri L 12 to
2.30, D 6 to 9.30. Sat and Sun 12 to 9.30 (9 Sun).
Closed: 25 Dec. Meals: alc (main courses £11 to
£19). Details: 82 seats. 120 seats outside. Car
parking.

█ Whalley
Food by Breda Murphy
Stonkingly good café and deli
Abbots Court, 41 Station Road, Whalley, BB7 9RH
Tel no: (01254) 823446
www.foodbybredamurphy.com
Modern British | £25
Cooking score: 2
V £30

A nondescript suburban house by a railway
bridge doesn't sound particularly enticing, but
the food in Breda Murphy's stonkingly good
café and deli is enough to stop you in your
tracks. Inside, it's bright, open and airy, with
music playing, a counter loaded with
comestibles and an all-day menu that cherry-
picks zingy, colourful ideas from the world

larder. Eclectic salads and open sandwiches on home-baked bread are the mainstays, while the seasonal roster promises everything from garden pea, courgette and Parmesan rösti with beetroot crème fraîche to herb-crusted rump of Bowland lamb with hummus, aubergine and feta salsa or the day's fish served with minted potato salad and fennel pesto. Breakfast and kids' meals, bookable afternoon teas, sharing platters and special fish and chip Fridays (from 4pm) are worth noting – likewise occasional themed suppers. Drinks cover everything from cappuccino and chamomile tea to Copper Dragon beer and keenly priced wines (from £14.95).
Chef/s: Gareth Bevan. **Open:** Tue to Sat 11 to 5.30, occasional evenings 7 to 9. **Closed:** Sun, Mon, 24 Dec to 3 Jan. **Meals:** alc (main courses £11 to £17). Set D £43 (5 courses). **Details:** 50 seats. 20 seats outside. Wheelchair access. Music. Car parking.

Whitewell
The Inn at Whitewell
A Lancashire hostelry for all seasons
Whitewell, BB7 3AT
Tel no: (01200) 448222
www.innatwhitewell.com
British | £35
Cooking score: 3

The 'keeper of the forest' once resided in this magnificent medieval pile, but these days the greatly extended Inn at Whitewell dishes out hospitality and also does duty as a vintner's and personal art gallery. Huge log fires, wooded vistas and gorgeous views of the River Hodder are highlights, but there's fine food to be had too. At lunchtime, visitors cram into the bars for upmarket pub grub and regional ales, while the more formal restaurant comes into its own for dinner. Lancastrian produce shows up well in capable dishes such as herb-crusted rump of Bowland lamb with crispy lamb breast, garlic mash and minted pea purée, or Goosnargh duck with baked beans, Anna potatoes and cauliflower cream. For afters, wholesome puds often look to the nursery for inspiration. Staff are 'fantastically

friendly and helpful', conversation is actively encouraged and the extensive wine list (from £13.95) treats the world as its cellar.
Chef/s: Jamie Cadman. **Open:** all week L 12 to 2, D 7.30 to 9.30. **Meals:** alc (main courses £16 to £27). **Details:** 60 seats. 40 seats outside. Separate bar. Car parking.

Wiswell
★ TOP 50 ★ PUB OF THE YEAR ★
Freemasons at Wiswell
High-impact food that's getting noticed
8 Vicarage Fold, Wiswell, BB7 9DF
Tel no: (01254) 822218
www.freemasonswiswell.co.uk
Modern British | £43
Cooking score: 7

Steven Smith's pub in a pretty Ribble Valley village is one of Lancashire's glories. It oozes character, the décor pitched agreeably somewhere between country interiors and rural inn, with equestrian pictures and stags' heads. There's a warmth to the greeting, and vigorous boundary-smashing in the kitchen. Dishes incorporate elements of the northern demotic, often in cheerily jumbled fashion, so expect Southport shrimps atop a warm pikelet with your just-cooked Wester Ross salmon, ponzu, elderflower and samphire. Other culinary traditions are jostled into service for heritage tomatoes with English mozzarella, aged balsamic, watermelon, summer fruits and black olives, or poached chicken breast studded with black garlic, leek and miso with summer greens, hen-of-the-woods and foie gras sauce. It all works because the precision and care shown in every dish, through to a perfect apricot soufflé, shines forth. A carefully constructed list covers the wine globe exhaustively from £15.50.
Chef/s: Steven Smith and Hywel Griffith. **Open:** Wed to Sat L 12 to 2.30, D 5.30 to 9 (6 to 9.30 Fri and Sat). Sun 12 to 7. **Closed:** Mon, Tue, 2 to 14 Jan. **Meals:** alc (main courses £22 to £35). Set L and D £20 (2 courses) to £22. Sun L £22 (2 courses) to £26. Tasting menu £60 (7 courses). **Details:** 70 seats. 24 seats outside. Separate bar. Wheelchair access.

LEICESTERSHIRE AND RUTLAND | England

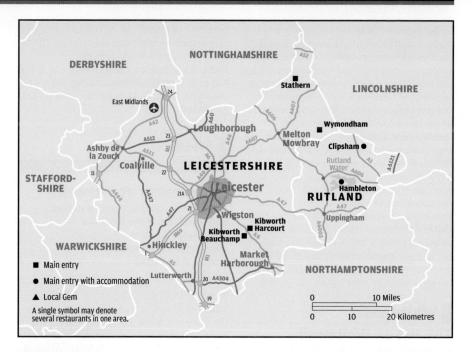

Clipsham
The Olive Branch
A well-honed country-pub operation
Main Street, Clipsham, LE15 7SH
Tel no: (01780) 410355
www.theolivebranchpub.com
British | £31
Cooking score: 3

🛏 V

A Rutland village inn that's only a couple of miles off the A1, the Olive Branch enjoys both accessibility and tranquillity. It was first knocked together as a pub in 1890, having originally been a trio of farm labourers' cottages. A notable part of the attraction is the drinking: refreshing lemonade, seasonal ales, decent wines and home-infused elderflower and cucumber gin are all on hand. Chef Sean Hope sees to it that there's something good to accompany these tipples, when it comes to imaginative productions like coffee-marinated pigeon breast with celeriac rémoulade, Loch Duart salmon with smoked bacon croquettes and fruity brown sauce, and pub favourites such as steak and kidney pie, served with swede and carrot crush, or impressive cod and chips with a minted pea dip. Finish with caramelised egg custard tart and blackcurrant sorbet. The wines are grouped by style, beginning with Spanish and Italian house selections at £18.50.

Chef/s: Sean Hope. **Open:** all week L 12 to 2 (2.15 Sat, 2.45 Sun), D 6.30 to 9.30 (7 Fri and Sat, 7 to 9 Sun). **Meals:** alc (main courses £14 to £25). Set L £17 (2 courses) to £20. Set D £25. Sun L £26. **Details:** 51 seats. 26 seats outside. Separate bar. Wheelchair access. Music. Car parking.

Symbols

🛏 Accommodation is available

£30 Three courses for less than £30

V Separate vegetarian menu

£5 OFF £5-off voucher scheme

🍷 Notable wine list

▌Hambleton

★ TOP 50 ★

Hambleton Hall

Country-house grandeur and fabulous food
Ketton Road, Hambleton, LE15 8TH
Tel no: (01572) 756991
www.hambleton.co.uk
Modern British | £65
Cooking score: 7

£5 OFF ⬥ ➴ V

'An awesome experience from start to finish', Hambleton Hall stands proud like some *petit château* transported to middle England. Glorious terraces and sculpted topiary, wondrous flowerbeds and landscaped gardens provide an aristocratic dreamscape, while the interior of this cherished Victorian edifice overlooking Rutland Water promises fine-looking features, polish and serenity – all backed by seamless, unobtrusive service. Much of the credit must go to hands-on owners Tim and Stefa Hart, who have transformed the venue into a spellbinding backdrop for out-of-town indulgence, although long-serving chef Aaron Patterson remains a key figure. Hambleton's menus are exceptionally pretty, their watercolour sketches a reminder that the seasons have a big impact on the kitchen's output. Images of feathers, russet leaves and sloes introduce winter's harvest – from a consommé of wild mushrooms with parsley root pannacotta to ruby-red loin of fallow deer with spiced lentils, caramelised endive and roasted celeriac. Arty presentation, perfect tuning and crystal-clear flavours also make their impact when it comes to the details: an ice-cold beetroot lollipop among the canapés; Stilton ice cream adding some pungent richness to a salad of walnut, celery and grapes; seared Scottish scallops pointed up with citrus fruit, fennel and almonds; and a 'fabulous' terrine of plums cleverly paired with prune sorbet. Hand-picked vintages from enterprising 'little guys' receive special treatment on Hambleton's prodigious list, from £21, although enticing 'wines of the moment' offer the best value.

Chef/s: Aaron Patterson. **Open:** all week L 12 to 1.30, D 6.45 to 9.30. **Meals:** Set L £26 (2 courses) to £32. Set D £65. Sun L £48. Tasting menu £75 (7 courses). **Details:** 60 seats. Separate bar. Wheelchair access. Car parking.

▌Kibworth Beauchamp

The Lighthouse

Bright and breezy seafood joint
9 Station Street, Kibworth Beauchamp, LE8 0LN
Tel no: (0116) 2796260
www.lighthousekibworth.co.uk
Seafood | £25
Cooking score: 3

£5 OFF £30

Judging by glowing reports of the new regime, Lino and Sarah Poli's decision to transform their 'fabulous' Firenze into a casual seafood restaurant was a wise move. It may be miles from the sea, but the owners have managed to establish some excellent supply lines – no doubt assisted by Leicester's renowned fish market. Seafood cookery is in Lino's blood, and he has imbued the dining room with bright and breezy interiors, nautical artwork and other suitable knick-knacks to match his vibrant menu. Go 'small or large' with plates of pan-fried scallops, haggis and cauliflower, cod fillet with porcini or gilthead bream with spinach and lobster sauce. Otherwise, nibble your way through tapas-style sharing plates: perhaps marinated anchovies, baby chilli peppers stuffed with tuna, game terrine or baked whole Camembert, washed down with a 'port and tonic' aperitif or something from the all-purpose wine list (from £16.95, £4.45 a glass). **Chef/s:** Lino Poli and Tom Wilde. **Open:** Tue to Sat D only 6 to 10. **Closed:** Sun, Mon, 25 and 26 Dec, 1 Jan, bank hols. **Meals:** alc (main courses £7 to £30). **Details:** 60 seats. Music.

⊌ STEVEN SMITH
Freemasons at Wiswell

What do you enjoy the most, and the least, about being a chef?
I enjoy the constant feeling of achievement that I get every day I'm in the kitchen. In terms of what I enjoy the least, it's never being able to switch off from food or from the restaurant.

What's your newest ingredient discovery?
Ponzu dressing - it's a mixture of a few ingredients but provides real umami and superb acidity.

What food could you not live without?
Bread - it makes the world go round.

Is there a dish that evokes strong memories for you?
Prawn cocktail - it's one of the very first dishes I ever made, and back then I really thought I'd reached the pinnacle of cooking.

And finally... tell us something about yourself that will surprise your diners.
I know every word to *Shang-a-Lang* by Bay City Rollers.

▊ Kibworth Harcourt
Boboli
All-day Italian bristling with artisan treats
88 Main Street, Kibworth Harcourt, LE8 0NQ
Tel no: (0116) 2793303
www.bobolirestaurant.co.uk
Italian | £25
Cooking score: 1
£5 OFF £30

With prices that keep locals returning, this unpretentious neighbourhood venue 'goes from strength to strength'. Expect straightforward, authentic Italian cuisine that pays attention to seasonality. The menu divides into antipasti, primi piatti, secondi, contorni and dolci, with a pizza list extending choice throughout the day. Start, perhaps, with bresaola with pecorino, rocket and lemon dressing, then a 'primi piatti', say the excellent lasagne. Main courses run to shin of veal with saffron risotto. Desserts are a high point: salame di cioccolato with nut and caramel semifreddo stands out. The all-Italian wine list opens at £15.50. Related to the Lighthouse in Kibworth Beauchamp (see entry).
Chef/s: Lino Poli and Sergio Gisbert. **Open:** all week 10 to 9.30. **Closed:** 25 and 26 Dec, 1 Jan. **Meals:** alc (main courses £7 to £17). Set L £14 (2 courses) to £19. Sun L £11 (1 course) to £19. **Details:** 90 seats. 28 seats outside. Separate bar. Music. Car parking.

▊ Stathern
Red Lion Inn
Village local, modern food
2 Red Lion Street, Stathern, LE14 4HS
Tel no: (01949) 860868
www.theredlioninn.co.uk
Modern British | £30
Cooking score: 2
£5 OFF

Described as a true village local by many reporters, Ben Jones and Sean Hope's 17th-century pub is nothing fancy. In the bar, the stone floor and open fire keep up traditional appearances, while in the beamed, wood-

floored dining room the short, daily changing menu is decidedly modern. The kitchen's repertoire is forever changing, reflecting the seasons as much as a prodigious talent for sourcing prime raw ingredients, many from local suppliers (check the map on the back of the menu). Thus a meal in winter might feature Cropwell Bishop Stilton pannacotta with cider caramel, apple and walnuts, and braised lamb shoulder with pearl barley, honey-roast parsnips and garlic. Desserts focus on tradition: sticky toffee pudding, hot chocolate fondant or a choice of homemade ice creams or sorbets, but there's also a cracking plate of British cheeses if you want to continue exploring the broad-minded and commendable wine list (from £16).
Chef/s: Jack Clayton. **Open:** Tue to Sun L 12 to 2 (3 Sun), Tue to Sat D 6.30 to 9 (7 to 9.30 Sat). **Closed:** Mon. **Meals:** alc (main courses £10 to £25). Set L £14 (2 courses) to £16. Set D £16. Sun L £16. **Details:** 60 seats. 40 seats outside. Separate bar. Music. Car parking.

▌Wymondham

The Berkeley Arms
Inviting country charmer
59 Main Street, Wymondham, LE14 2AG
Tel no: (01572) 787587
www.theberkeleyarms.co.uk
Modern British | £29
Cooking score: 3

V £30

It's five years since Louise and Neil Hitchen moved into this serenely located, 16th-century village pub. During their stewardship they have cared lovingly for the place – it shows in every detail – and everyone is put at ease by a mood that's as personable as can be. Indeed, the Hitchens have achieved the perfect balance: the pub dispenses real ale for locals yet also attracts long-distance diners with its no-frills modern dishes. As you might expect, Neil taps into the region's rich larder: witness twice-baked Lincolnshire Poacher cheese soufflé, perfectly rare wood pigeon with a Waldorf salad, and Launde Farm lamb shank with crushed root vegetables and rosemary

sauce. Desserts are equally assured, particularly an 'old favourite' of sticky toffee pudding with butterscotch sauce and vanilla ice cream. Readers continue to applaud the 'triumph' of Sunday lunch, the excellent British cheese plate and the decent wine list, which opens at £16.
Chef/s: Neil Hitchen. **Open:** Tue to Sun L 12 to 2 (3 Sun), Tue to Sat D 6 to 9 (9.30 Fri and Sat). **Closed:** Mon, first 2 weeks Jan, 1 week Aug, Tue after bank hols. **Meals:** alc (main courses £10 to £24). Set L £15 (2 courses) to £19. Set D £19 (2 courses) to £23. Sun L £20. **Details:** 48 seats. 24 seats outside. Separate bar. Wheelchair access. Car parking.

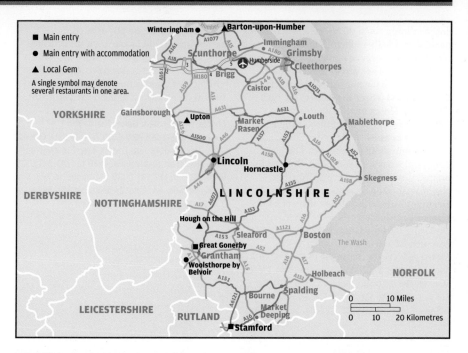

- ■ Main entry
- ● Main entry with accommodation
- ▲ Local Gem

A single symbol may denote several restaurants in one area.

■ Barton-upon-Humber

LOCAL GEM
▲ Elio's

11 Market Place, Barton-upon-Humber, DN18 5DA
Tel no: (01652) 635147
www.elios-restaurant.co.uk
Italian | £30

'These days, the traditional Italian meal is a rare beast,' observed one reader who enjoyed himself immensely at Elio Grossi's ever-reliable, long-serving trattoria-with-rooms. Famed for its conservatory/courtyard and daily board of fish specials, Elio's also pleases the punters with plates of egg florentine, porcini risotto, pizzas, steak Diane and tiramisu. Also check out the range of 'half-price, half-size' *assaggini* snacks. Service gets full marks for friendliness, and the all-Italian wine list offers sound regional drinking from £14.95. Open Mon to Sat D only.

■ Great Gonerby

Harry's Place

Homage to classic French cooking
17 High Street, Great Gonerby, NG31 8JS
Tel no: (01476) 561780
Modern French | £70
Cooking score: 4

Caroline Hallam's 'warm and wonderful' welcome awaits at the tiny restaurant she and her husband, the eponymous Harry, run from their Lincolnshire home. Come here to enjoy classic cooking at its traditional best. Harry couldn't give a fig for foams or smears or deconstructed rhubarb and custard puddings; his is a menu (just two choices per course) that offers the likes of seared king scallops, richly caramelised but textbook-soft inside, julienned orange and pepper and citrusy juices. Continue with loin of lamb, pink of course, or sautéed fillet of sea trout, both masterclasses in how first-rate ingredients, cooked to perfection, can sing for themselves (the fish comes with a simple white wine and shallot sauce and fine spears of just-steamed samphire, the lamb with a classic red wine and herb reduction). Finish with 'top-notch' apple soufflé or decadent prune and Armagnac ice cream, the sweetness cut with tangy passion fruit. Wine starts at £20.

Chef/s: Harry Hallam. **Open:** Tue to Sat L 12.30 to 2, D 7 to 9.30. **Closed:** Sun, Mon. **Meals:** alc (main courses £40). **Details:** 10 seats. Car parking. Children over 5 yrs only.

Great Limber

READERS RECOMMEND
The New Inn
Modern British
2 High Street, Great Limber, DN37 8JL
Tel no: (01469) 569998
www.thenewinngreatlimber.co.uk
'A significant, quality addition to eating houses in our area. There is an extremely pleasant atmosphere around the bar and in the restaurant.'

Horncastle

Magpies
Genuine warmth and quietly confident cooking
73 East Street, Horncastle, LN9 6AA
Tel no: (01507) 527004
www.magpiesrestaurant.co.uk
Modern British | £47
Cooking score: 5

⇌ V

'Never been disappointed,' commented one regular, as after 10 years at the helm Andrew and Caroline Gilbert continue to draw praise for their restaurant-with-rooms in a row of period cottages. It's the kind of place where you can sink into a cosy sofa in the lounge to peruse the menus, or sit out on the patio if you're lucky weather-wise. There's even afternoon tea if you're staying. Andrew Gilbert's cooking is not cutting-edge modern, but neither is it stuck in the past. Intelligent flavour combinations and a light touch are the hallmarks. A starter of roast pheasant breast with orange and beetroot salad comes with

little fritters filled with Langton goats' cheese, while main courses deliver John Dory with rösti Chinese greens and lime-fried scallops. Desserts are Caroline's department (as is front-of-house) with hot passion fruit soufflé on the cards. The wine list is terrific value, containing lots of good stuff from £16.35.

Chef/s: Andrew Gilbert. **Open:** Wed to Fri and Sun L 12 to 2, Wed to Sun D 7 to 9. **Closed:** Mon, Tue, 26 to 30 Dec, 2 weeks Jan. **Meals:** Set L £20 (2 courses) to £25. Set D £41 (2 courses) to £47. **Details:** 34 seats. 8 seats outside. Wheelchair access. Music.

Hough on the Hill

LOCAL GEM
▲ The Brownlow Arms
Grantham Road, Hough on the Hill, NG32 2AZ
Tel no: (01400) 250234
www.thebrownlowarms.com
British | £50

A diamond in the Lincolnshire countryside, this thoroughly likeable 17th-century inn is everything a decent, local restaurant should be. Dinner is the main event, with the kitchen producing a mixed bag of accessible dishes ranging from chicken liver parfait or pigeon breast with wild rocket, walnuts, purple sprouting broccoli and new potatoes, to wild garlic chicken Kiev, and slow-roasted pork cheeks with shallot and port, sweet potato gratin and roasted pear wrapped in pancetta. Wines from £16.50. Open Tue to Sat D and Sun L.

Kirby La Thorpe

READERS RECOMMEND
The Queens Head
British
Church Lane, Kirby La Thorpe, NG34 9NU
Tel no: (01529) 305743
www.thequeensheadinn.com
'Our regular restaurant, serving excellent, locally produced food. First class, friendly-but-professional, service.'

Legbourne

Michael Bullamore at the Queen's Head

Modern British
Station Road, Legbourne, LN11 8LL
Tel no: (01507) 604803
www.thequeensheadlegbourne.co.uk
'This place is value for money, absolutely delicious and very welcoming.'

Lincoln

The Old Bakery

Relaxed and idiosyncratic
26-28 Burton Road, Lincoln, LN1 3LB
Tel no: (01522) 576057
www.theold-bakery.co.uk
Modern British | £35
Cooking score: 2

£5 OFF

The flames went out in the original ovens back in 1956, but Ivano de Serio and his team still bake bread daily on the premises – and the old ovens are now a feature of the restaurant. The building's past life very much informs the present, with original features and a rustic finish creating something that feels suitably contemporary. There's accommodation, too, plus a conservatory-style dining room that cranks up the Mediterranean vibe. Ivano hails from Puglia and his menu shows flashes of the old country combined with modern British sensibilities. (Go for the five-course tasting menu if you really want to test his mettle.) Slow-roasted pork and black pudding terrine with a chorizo set cream shows ambition in the kitchen, with mains like rabbit loin stuffed with prunes served up with a beery stew and wild mushroom barley risotto. Finish with top-drawer British cheeses. Wines start at £17.95.
Chef/s: Ivano de Serio. **Open:** Tue to Sun L 12 to 1.30, Tue to Sat D 7 to 8.30. **Closed:** Mon, 2 weeks Jan, 2 weeks Aug. **Meals:** alc (main courses £16 to £26). Set L £13 (2 courses) to £17. Sun L £19. Tasting menu £39. **Details:** 60 seats. Wheelchair access. Music.

Stamford

Jim's Yard

Terrific neighbourhood eatery
3 Ironmonger Street, Stamford, PE9 1PL
Tel no: (01780) 756080
www.jimsyard.biz
Modern European | £27
Cooking score: 2

£5 OFF £30

There are plenty of reasons to linger in pretty Stamford – and Tim Luff's food is definitely one of them. Diners have been 'hugely impressed' by the 'finely judged' cooking coming out of this informal neighbourhood restaurant, tucked away in the town centre. Winking at Europe, the menu offers the likes of a porcini mushroom ravioli starter that you might follow with a fillet of sea bream served with sweet potato, chorizo and pak choi, or slow-cooked shoulder of lamb with mash, baby onions, garden peas and a rosemary gravy. Puddings come in for praise: try a chilled white chocolate and raspberry parfait, or a glazed lemon tart that for one happy diner was 'the best I've ever had anywhere – and I've had a lot'. A delightful courtyard garden, 'very attentive' service and a wine list that starts at a reasonable £15.45 for a French Colombard-Ugni Blanc complete the enticing picture.
Chef/s: Tim Luff. **Open:** Tue to Sat L 12 to 2.30, D 6 to 9.30. **Closed:** Sun, Mon, 2 weeks from 26 Dec, last week Jul, first week Aug. **Meals:** alc (main courses £13 to £22). Set L 15 (2 courses) to £18. Set D £20 (3 courses). **Details:** 65 seats. 18 seats outside. Separate bar. Wheelchair access. Music.

Upton

LOCAL GEM
▲ Upton Fish Shop
24 High Street, Upton, DN21 5NL
Tel no: (01427) 838607
www.uptonchippy.co.uk
Seafood | £10

Much more than a curiosity, Upton Fish Shop, in business since 1948, is billed as probably the UK's last fish and chip shop cooking with a coal-fired range and beef dripping. Reporters insist these are 'the best fish and chips in the country'. As the place only opens Friday evening and Saturday lunch, expect queues (a 30 to 40-minute wait is normal). You need to try them to understand the fuss – good fish, fresh from Grimsby (never frozen), real chips, hand-cut from locally grown Lincolnshire potatoes, are only part of the equation. Take-away only. Open Fri D and Sat L only.

Winteringham
Winteringham Fields
A shining star
1 Silver Street, Winteringham, DN15 9ND
Tel no: (01724) 733096
www.winteringhamfields.co.uk
Modern European | £59
Cooking score: 6
£5 OFF 🍽 V

Trompe l'oeil techno-artistry and home-reared pork aren't unfamiliar to British restaurant-goers, but it's rare to find both on the same menu. Just as Colin McGurran's Lincolnshire restaurant-with-rooms boasts both out-of-the-way charm and switched-on staff, his seven-course 'surprise' tasting menu features forward-thinking technique and the odd ruddy-cheeked touch. There's a 'low-key' atmosphere and 'deft' service in a fresh, comfortable dining room with tongue-in-cheek country references. Canapés are a mixed bag, but then the fun starts: spooning salmon tartare and pea purée with a touch of sesame and crunchy puffed rice out of a tiny glazed pot; tasting the garden in the gazpacho

'tomato' with feta dust; crunching prawn crackers and textures of cucumber with a perfect piece of stone bass. Winteringham pork loin and belly with garden veg is plain but convincingly done, and dessert might be an intense combination of pistachio ice cream and vivid apricot gel. Wine is from £26, with good advice on hand.
Chef/s: Colin McGurran. **Open:** Tue to Sat L 12 to 1.30 (2 Sat), D 7 to 10. **Closed:** Sun, Mon, 2 weeks Jan, 2 weeks Aug. **Meals:** Set L £40. Set D £59. Tasting menu £79. **Details:** 60 seats. Separate bar. Wheelchair access. Music. Car parking.

Woolsthorpe by Belvoir
Chequers Inn
Honest country pub with no-nonsense victuals
Main Street, Woolsthorpe by Belvoir, NG32 1LU
Tel no: (01476) 870701
www.chequersinn.net
Modern British | £28
Cooking score: 1
£5 OFF 🍽 £30

With Belvoir Castle and the village cricket pitch as neighbours, the 17th-century Chequers ticks all the 'quintessential inn' boxes, including roaring fires and an abundance of solid oak beams. There are real ales at the handpumps and a menu that delivers 'pub classics' such as local sausages with mash and onion gravy alongside more European-influenced stuff like pan-roasted breast of duck with a cassoulet of beetroot and morteau sausages. Goats' cheese and ratatouille lasagne is a veggie choice, with char-grilled ribeye and hand-cut chips at the other end of the spectrum. Finish with plum and rhubarb crumble. Wines start at £15.95.
Chef/s: Andrew Lincoln. **Open:** all week L 12 to 2.30 (4 Sun), D 6 to 9.30 (8.30 Sun). **Closed:** 25 and 26 Dec. **Meals:** alc (main courses £11 to £20). Set L £13 (2 courses) to £15. Set D £16 (2 courses) to £18. Sun L £14. **Details:** 90 seats. 100 seats outside. Separate bar. Wheelchair access. Music. Car parking.

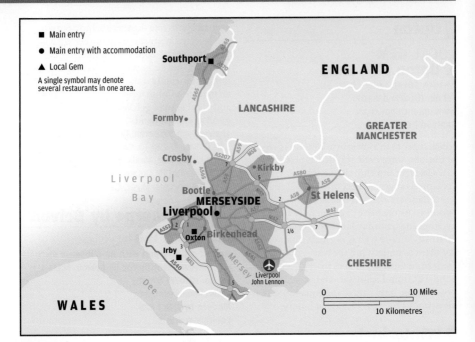

Irby

Da Piero
Tasty Italian home cooking
5 Mill Hill Road, Irby, CH61 4UB
Tel no: (0151) 6487373
www.dapiero.co.uk
Italian | £32
Cooking score: 4
£5 OFF V

There's a spotless feeling of freshness to the di Bellas' Sicilian restaurant on the Wirral, with its sparsely decorated white walls and laminate floor. You wouldn't expect too many locally sourced ingredients for such cuisine, and Piero Di Bella makes a virtue of bringing in vine tomatoes, anchovies, olives, extra-virgin olive oil and even salt from the volcanic island, with lemons from the Amalfi coast. And praise be, these raw materials are allowed to speak for themselves in the kinds of simple domestic treatments for which everyone loves Italian food. Start with beef carpaccio dressed in rocket and Parmesan, before continuing –

perhaps via lemon linguine – with herb-coated Admiral's tuna and braised fennel, or duck with sautéed red onions and mint. A vegan menu is a rare sight in Italian catering, ricotta cannolo a more comfortingly familiar one. Italian wines start at £19.20.
Chef/s: Piero Di Bella. **Open:** Tue to Sat D 6 to 11 (12 Sat). **Closed:** Sun, Mon, 25 and 26 Dec, 1 and 2 Jan, 2 weeks Aug. **Meals:** alc (main courses £14 to £22). **Details:** 32 seats.

Liverpool

Delifonseca
Vibrant international cooking at pleasing prices
Brunswick Quay, Liverpool, L3 4BN
Tel no: (0151) 2550808
www.delifonseca.co.uk
Modern European | £27
Cooking score: 2
£5 OFF V £30

In the five years since it opened, this café and adjoining food hall (deli, somehow, just doesn't sum it up) has gathered quite a following – but then Delifonseca did win our national Readers' Restaurant of the Year award in 2014. It's all rollickingly informal, the vibrant, internationally inspired menu aiming to please everybody. Prices are well pitched, from a well-reported po-boy filled with slow-roasted beef, gravy, lettuce, tomato and mayo, to a Cumbrian Herdwick mutton bhuna with spicy dhal and basmati rice. Successes have also included a cassoulet de printemps, featuring beer-brined pork, smoked pork, garlic sausage and beans in a clear broth; rabbit stew with creamy mash ('excellent hearty peasant food for a chilly day'); and a 'light and spicy' chocolate and ginger sponge. Breakfasts and Sunday roasts are outright winners and there's good choice for vegetarians. Wines open at £13.95; alternatively there are speciality and local beers.

Chef/s: Martin Cooper. **Open:** all week 8am to 9pm (9.30pm Fri and Sat, 9.30 to 5 Sun). **Closed:** 25 and 26 Dec, 1 Jan. **Meals:** alc (main courses £10 to £16). **Details:** 66 seats. 24 seats outside. Wheelchair access. Car parking.

Fonseca's
Hybrid deli/eatery with no airs and graces
12 Stanley Street, Liverpool, L1 6AF
Tel no: (0151) 2550808
www.delifonseca.co.uk
Modern European | £26
Cooking score: 2
£5 OFF £30

This hybrid deli/eatery operates variously as a lunchtime pit-stop, café, meeting place and evening restaurant. There are no airs and graces: the restaurant is wedged above the ground-floor deli, there's booth seating, a central communal table, and what's available that day is chalked up on blackboards. Like the no-frills décor there's nothing cluttered or fancy about the food, which aims to please with a mix of casual bistro favourites and more elaborately worked restaurant dishes. Sandwiches and salads are all-day staples. Also typical of the kitchen's output are 'perfectly cooked' rump of Herdwick lamb; bream with cockles, mussels and courgette in a light broth

'full of the flavours of the shellfish'; and a good lemon posset. Readers have been generally happy with the quality of food, but less forgiving of poor service, described this year as lacking the charm expected from a 'Liverpool institution'. Wines from £14.95.
Chef/s: Marc Paley. **Open:** Mon to Sat L 12 to 2.30 (5 Fri and Sat), Mon to Sat D 5 to 9 (10 Fri and Sat). **Closed:** Sun, 26 Dec to 30 Dec, bank hols. **Meals:** alc (main courses £10 to £16). Set L and D £20. **Details:** 50 seats. 60 seats outside. Separate bar. Music.

Hanover Street Social
Globetrotting all-day brasserie
Casartelli Building, 16-20 Hanover Street, Liverpool, L1 4AA
Tel no: (0151) 7098784
www.hanoverstreetsocial.co.uk
Modern European | £23
Cooking score: 1
£5 OFF £30

Given its location close to the L1 shopping centre and the city's trendy waterfront, it's no wonder that this all-day brasserie is a top shout for Liverpudlians. A high-decibel bar dispenses flashy cocktails for the party crowd, and lofty ceilings, bare brickwork, red leather banquettes and tiled floors tick all the boxes for modish urban design. The menu jump-starts proceedings with sausage sarnies, porridge and pancakes, before graduating to salads, small plates, grills, burgers and roasts – from pulled pork sliders with spare ribs and apple coleslaw, or wild mushroom tart with truffle mash, to cod fillet with sweet potato, mussels and chorizo. Wines from £14.95.
Chef/s: Simon Wood. **Open:** all week 12 to 10.30. **Closed:** 25 Dec. **Meals:** alc (main courses £10 to £17). Set L £11 (2 courses) to £14. Sun L £14 (2 courses) to £20. **Details:** 100 seats. Separate bar. Wheelchair access. Music.

The London Carriage Works

Stylish all-day dining
Hope Street Hotel, 40 Hope Street, Liverpool,
L1 9DA
Tel no: (0151) 7052222
www.thelondoncarriageworks.co.uk
Modern European | £40
Cooking score: 3

Last year we described the Carriage Works'
interior as 'understated'; a reporter begs to
differ, preferring 'dull . . . and very brown,
apart from some rather spectacular shards of
glass that separate bits of the dining area'. It
matters little: everyone is here for the food.
The all-day eating opportunities attract
shoppers, business folk and theatre-goers,
whether sharing a fish or meat platter or a
Caesar salad on a sofa in the bar or dining in
the restaurant. The kitchen aims to please,
celebrating local producers: Wirral pork belly
comes with pickled carrots; pan-roasted
Whitchurch chicken is served alongside black
pudding and wild garlic. Assiette of black-
faced Suffolk lamb – pink loin noisettes,
pulled shoulder and kidney with carrot purée,
caramelised onions, Puy lentils, leeks and
natural jus – was an inspection hit. To finish,
British cheeses feature alongside the likes of
silky vanilla pannacotta with strawberry and
balsamic sorbet and sweet basil purée. Wine
from £17.25.
Chef/s: David Critchley. **Open:** all week L 11 to 3, D 5
to 10 (9 Sun). **Meals:** alc (main courses £15 to £30).
Set L and D £18 (2 courses) to £23. Sun L £18.
Details: 52 seats. Separate bar. Wheelchair access.
Music.

★ READERS' RESTAURANT OF THE YEAR ★
NORTH WEST

Lunya

Vibrant Spanish eatery and deli
18-20 College Lane, Liverpool One, Liverpool,
L1 3DS
Tel no: (0151) 7069770
www.lunya.co.uk
Spanish | £18
Cooking score: 2
£5 OFF V £30

A Catalan deli and tapas joint in Liverpool
One – the city's gold-chip retail complex –
Lunya not only sells a prodigious assortment
of Spanish provisions, it also does a grand job
feeding shoppers and office workers. 'We wish
this place was in our home city,' commented
two Mancunians. Everyone loves the
authentic vibe, 'fantastic service' and 'genuinely
outstanding' food: especially the fried Catalan
breakfast (complete with chorizo). Otherwise,
exemplary cured meats, preserved fish and
regional cheeses share the billing with
memorable morcilla 'won tons', slow-roast ox
cheeks with cinnamon-infused sauce and
cauliflower purée, piquillo peppers stuffed
with tuna, and an immaculate 'mackerel
conception' comprising 'semen and eggs' (aka
soft and hard roe) on toast. Old faithfuls such
as albondigas, tortilla and croquetas also
feature, along with paella and traditional
desserts including chocolate and churros.
Regional 'gourmet banquets', terrific Spanish
wines (from £14.75) and a flamenco guitarist
on Saturday nights seal the deal.
Chef/s: Dave Upson. **Open:** Sun to Fri 10am to 9pm
(9.30pm Wed and Thur, 10pm Fri, 8.30pm Sun). Sat
9am to 10pm. **Meals:** alc (tapas £5 to £8). Set L £9
(2 courses) to £11. Tapas banquet £25. **Details:** 150
seats. 130 seats outside. Separate bar. Wheelchair
access. Music.

Salt House Tapas
Tapas with a buzz
1 Hanover Street, Liverpool, L1 3DW
Tel no: (0151) 7060092
www.salthousetapas.co.uk
Spanish | £20
Cooking score: 2
£30

It may be housed in a former bishop's residence, but this tapas bar opposite John Lewis is definitely part of 'new' Liverpool, drawing crowds with its 'buzzy atmosphere' and pleasing informality. Cutlery in paprika tins, sherries at the bar and mixologists who know how to shake a cocktail add to the cool urban vibe, while switched-on service, sound Spanish sourcing and a tuned-in kitchen ensure the food also scores highly. The menu takes some liberties with tapas, touting veal sliders and gin-cured salmon alongside sautéed baby chorizo with honey, patatas bravas and roast cod with mussel escabèche – but the results are bang on target. Breads, charcuterie and cheeses have that authentic artisan stamp, and desserts yo-yo between baked turrón cheesecake, churros and banoffi pots. If sherry isn't your tipple, jugs of sangria, bottles of Mahou beer or the aforementioned cocktails should do the business; otherwise, decent Spanish regional wines start at £14.95. **Chef/s:** Martin Renshaw. **Open:** all week 12 to 10.30 (11pm Fri and Sat). **Closed:** 25 Dec. **Meals:** alc (tapas £5 to £9). Set L £11. **Details:** 85 seats. 20 seats outside. Wheelchair access. Music.

The Side Door
Welcoming, good-value bistro
29a Hope Street, Liverpool, L1 9BQ
Tel no: (0151) 7077888
www.thesidedoor.co.uk
Modern European | £30
Cooking score: 2
£5
OFF

Comprising two floors of reclaimed furniture and stripped-wood flooring in a Georgian town house, the Side Door is a welcoming little bistro with bags of character and a kitchen that knows how to perform. There's nothing too ambitious here, but the food strikes a chord with readers – from bowls of sweetcorn and ginger soup or tempura scallops with sorrel aïoli to white chocolate mousse served with a macadamia nut cookie. In between, you might find balsamic calf's liver with leek and bacon mash; sea bass with Parmesan purée, fennel and cannellini beans; or 28-day-aged Lancashire steaks. At lunchtime you can pick up a burger or a plate of battered haddock and chips for a fiver, as well as club sandwiches and other fillers, while fixed-price theatre menus are a good-value ticket for culture vultures heading to the Everyman. A zesty wine list kicks off at £15. **Chef/s:** Michael Robinson and Matthew Manzanilla. **Open:** Mon to Sat L 12 to 2, D 5 to 9.30 (10 Thur to Sat). **Closed:** Sun, 25 and 26 Dec, bank hols. **Meals:** alc (main courses £13 to £20). Pre-theatre D £17 (2 courses) to £20. **Details:** 50 seats. 8 seats outside. Music.

Spire
Top Merseyside performer
1 Church Road, Liverpool, L15 9EA
Tel no: (0151) 7345040
www.spirerestaurant.co.uk
Modern European | £32
Cooking score: 4
£5
OFF

Since opening Spire on Church Road, brothers Adam and Matt Locke have established this 'warmly welcoming' contemporary eatery as a top Merseyside performer: a boon to the neighbourhood's regenerated social scene (Penny Lane just a stroll away). Inside, it's a smart mix of polished floors, abstract art and exposed brickwork, with a spiral staircase linking the two dining areas – perfect for food with a grown-up, cosmopolitan feel. To start, a warm salad of smoked haddock with poached quails' eggs received top marks from one reader, likewise a perfectly cooked main course of Cumbrian beef fillet with shallot purée and truffle confit. The kitchen's dedication to sourcing also shows in generous plates of hand-dived scallops with pork belly and celeriac purée, or Goosnargh chicken breast partnered by cauliflower and crispy black pudding. To finish, try apple cheesecake or 'excellent' hot chocolate fondant with marmalade ice cream. The wine list starts at £15.95.

Chef/s: Matt Locke. **Open:** Tue to Fri L 12 to 2, Mon to Sat D 6 to 9 (9.30 Fri and Sat). **Closed:** Sun, first week Jan. **Meals:** alc (main courses £14 to £22). Set L £12 (2 courses) to £15. Set D £15 (2 courses) to £18. **Details:** 70 seats. Music.

LOCAL GEM

▲ Etsu

25 The Strand (off Brunswick Street), Liverpool, L2 0XJ
Tel no: (0151) 2367530
www.etsu-restaurant.co.uk
Japanese | £27

Stylish simplicity is the watchword at this small, city-centre Japanese restaurant. Service is smiling, willing to guide diners around the menu, which offers a broad range: a revelation to people whose experience is limited to sushi bars. Expect 'spot-on' sushi and sashimi, well-seared gyoza dumplings, seared tuna with 'zingy sticky' ponzo (ginger, soy and vinegar sauce), chicken teriyaki, and grilled eel served on rice with crisp seaweed and Japanese pickles. Finish with goma ice cream (toasted black sesame seed). Drink saké or wine (£11.95). Closed Mon, Wed L, Sat and Sun.

Oxton

★ TOP 50 ★

Fraiche

Culinary wizardry on the Wirral
11 Rose Mount, Oxton, CH43 5SG
Tel no: (0151) 6522914
www.restaurantfraiche.com
Modern French | £65
Cooking score: 8
V

Out on a relative limb on the Wirral peninsula, Marc Wilkinson's Fraiche operates according to its own rules. The number of covers is limited, so a booking remains a covetable asset of north-western dining. An innovative approach to contemporary understatement is apparent in the interior design: from the glass artworks to the bespoke tableware that's for sale in the shop. Wilkinson's cooking style is powered by a heuristic drive for new methods and techniques, and a respect for natural, often unusual ingredients. A six-course fixed menu called 'Signature' is the mainstay, delivering much to beguile mind and palate: an apple cloud appetiser with apple gel and oyster leaf; pork popcorn with the provocative aftertaste of sumac; mussels and samphire on ginger and yuzu jelly; truffle-sprinkled cauliflower (Beaufort) cheese in mint and mustard dressing. Visually dramatic main courses brim with multi-faceted detail, as when brill is attended by orange-poached buckwheat and fennel macerated in blueberry vinegar, or duck coated in chocolate chips appears with kohlrabi purée, pickled and fresh cherries, smoked lettuce and maitake mushrooms. Familiar prototypes are redesigned even at dessert stage. Lemongrass pannacotta is lapped in sour cherry foam with flakes of dehydrated crêpe, or there may be a laboratory's worth of new textures of raspberry, with jasmine jelly and white chocolate ice. A shortish wine list opens at £18.

Chef/s: Marc Wilkinson. **Open:** Sun L 12 to 1, Wed to Sat D 7 to 8.30. **Closed:** Mon, Tue, 25 Dec, first week Jan. **Meals:** Set L £35. Tasting menu £65 (6 courses). **Details:** 14 seats. 6 seats outside. Children over 8 yrs only at D.

Southport

Bistrot Vérité

Homely eatery with Gallic classics
7 Liverpool Road, Birkdale, Southport, PR8 4AR
Tel no: (01704) 564199
www.bistrotverite.co.uk
French | £28
Cooking score: 3
£30

Marc Vérité's lively village bistro may feel as though it's straining to gallop off in the direction of the Boulevard St-Michel, but don't be deceived: it keeps its feet firmly in the Lancashire soil. Even if the name reads poisson et frites, you're not going to call the peas anything but mushy. That said, there is plenty of unalloyed Gallic charm to offerings such as moules provençale, boeuf lyonnaise, and canard aux pruneaux. You'll also find some successful detours into the modern repertoire: the likes of goats' cheese terrine with blood-orange, beetroot and candied walnuts, or roast hare with a bonbon of leg-meat, foie gras and cherries. It all happens in a bustling long room, with staff who keep their eye on the *ballon*, and will happily suzette your crêpes in Grand Marnier at the end. Look to the blackboard for the specials. The mostly French wines start at £16.75.

Chef/s: Marc Vérité. **Open:** Tue to Sat L 12 to 1.30, D from 5.30. **Closed:** Sun, Mon, 25 and 26 Dec, 1 Jan, 1 week Feb, 1 week Aug. **Meals:** alc (main courses £11 to £27). **Details:** 45 seats. 16 seats outside. Music.

The Warehouse
Bold British cooking by the seaside
30 West Street, Southport, PR8 1QN
Tel no: (01704) 544662
www.warehouserestaurant.co.uk
Modern British | £33
Cooking score: 2

Everybody seems to have a good word to say about this backstreet former clothing warehouse since Matt Worswick arrived from Glenapp Castle (see entry), though not everyone appreciates the 'rather dark décor'. The industrial ceiling is painted black, there are black tables and distressed mirrors; it makes for a smart if rather sombre atmosphere, 'not to mention reducing the ability to see the food'. A dinner in May produced a 'surprisingly winning combination' of wood pigeon, lovage, hummus and pickled apple, as well as a simple dish of fried duck egg, asparagus and little blobs of whipped buttermilk cream. Sea bream, with brown crab providing a rich backdrop, was teamed with squid-ink quinoa and marsh samphire and pronounced a 'great dish', while haunch of venison came with sturdy salt-baked beetroot,

pommes Anna and a slick of juniper jus. Chamomile pannacotta with apricot and burnt honey ice cream made a perfect finale. Wine from £19.

Chef/s: Matthew Worswick. **Open:** Tue to Sat L 12 to 2, D 6 to 10. **Closed:** Sun, Mon, 25 and 26 Dec. **Meals:** alc (main courses £14 to £22). Set L and D £15 (2 courses) to £19. **Details:** 80 seats. Separate bar. Wheelchair access. Music.

LOCAL GEM
▲ Bistro 21
21 Stanley Street, Southport, PR9 0BS
Tel no: (01704) 501414
www.bistro21.co.uk
Modern European | £32

Tucked just off the elegant Victorian boulevard of Lord Street, Bistro 21 is a well-run, appealing modern eatery with friendly staff and a menu of soundly rendered populist local food. Expect classic gravadlax with creamed goats' cheese and roasted beetroot; duck breast with char-grilled pineapple, cashews and coconut; and sticky toffee pudding with ginger ice cream. Simpler lunch dishes such as chicken in Thai-style coconut and chilli, or open steak and mushroom pie with chips, form the backbone of a top-value two-course deal (£8.95). House Spanish is £14.95. Open Wed-Sun L and Wed-Sat D.

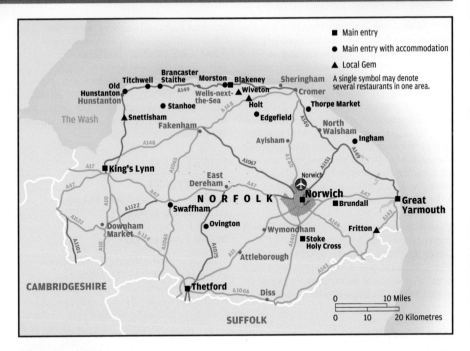

Main entry ■
Main entry with accommodation ●
Local Gem ▲
A single symbol may denote several restaurants in one area.

■ Blakeney
The Moorings

Endearing Norfolk bolt-hole
High Street, Blakeney, NR25 7NA
Tel no: (01263) 740054
www.blakeney-moorings.co.uk
Modern British | £30
Cooking score: 2

Richard and Angela Long make the most of
their location not far from Blakeney quay by
running the Moorings as a café by day and
restaurant in the evening. Fish specials, soups
and salads keep the lunch crowd happy, and as
darkness falls over the marshes it's on to
piscine-pleasers such as an 'excellent' spicy
Norfolk crab cake or fish soup with all the bits
and pieces. Attention to detail is especially
evident in the handling of veg and fish,
witness the 'superbly' cooked sea trout with
samphire and potted shrimp butter, and the
standout dauphinois potatoes. Local meat
receives classic treatment, too, as in roast fillet
of pork with sage and Parma ham and sauce
soubise. Angela's puddings and cakes are well
loved; try crème brûlée or plum and almond
tart. A neat wine list starts at £15.
Chef/s: Richard and Angela Long. Open: Tue to Sun
L 10.30 to 4.30, Tue to Sat D 6 to 9. Closed: Mon,
Mon to Thur (Nov to Mar), 3 weeks Jan. Meals: alc
(main courses £14 to £22). Sun L £18. Details: 55
seats. Music.

■ Brancaster Staithe
★ TOP 50 PUB ★
The White Horse

Simple cooking lets the flavours shine
Brancaster Staithe, PE31 8BY
Tel no: (01485) 210262
www.whitehorsebrancaster.co.uk
Modern British | £30
Cooking score: 3

Reporters enthuse about the hospitality at this
popular, well-established inn, where the
views across tidal salt marshes 150 metres away

are stunning. It has all-round appeal: a cracking bar where people pop in at any time for a bowl of local mussels or Norfolk beefburger, plus a pint of Brancaster Best; superb alfresco eating opportunities with front and rear terraces; and a conservatory dining room where Avrum Frankel delivers seriously good food. Monthly menus and daily specials favour local produce, especially seafood landed along the coast, with mussels, oysters and samphire harvested at the bottom of the garden. Asparagus (in season) comes from a nearby farm. There has been praise for hake served with locally made chorizo and mussel and bean stew, and slow-cooked Red Poll blade of beef, accompanied by smoked mash, local kale and textures of onion. To finish, try lemon tart with raspberry sorbet and buckthorn crisp. Wines from £17.

Chef/s: Avrum Frankel. **Open:** all week L 12 to 2 (2.30 Sun), D 6.30 to 9. **Meals:** alc (main courses £13 to £20). **Details:** 100 seats. 160 seats outside. Separate bar. Wheelchair access. Music. Car parking.

LOCAL GEM
▲ The Jolly Sailors
Brancaster Staithe, PE31 8BJ
Tel no: (01485) 210314
www.jollysailorsbrancaster.co.uk
British | £22

The roadside pub dates from the 18th century, shares owners with the upmarket White Horse down the road (see entry), but is run as a laid-back, family-focused local. The formula is simple: small rooms with wood fires, stone walls and a kitchen drawing on good local materials for honest pub grub, whether stone-baked pizzas, bowls of excellent Brancaster mussels, steak and ale pie, lamb curry or ploughman's, accompanied by Brancaster Brewery ales or house Georges Duboeuf (£16.50). No bookings. Open all week.

▌Brundall
The Lavender House
Delightfully unassuming foodie haven
39 The Street, Brundall, NR13 5AA
Tel no: (01603) 712215
www.thelavenderhouse.co.uk
Modern British | £45
Cooking score: 3

🍾 V

Richard Hughes' historic village restaurant has always punched above its weight. In the distant past, it was known as Old Beams, and offered haute cuisine in florid italics. These days, the formula makes a point of mixing old and new, so a country-pub ambience of exposed brick doesn't preclude a chef's table named in honour of an Austrian winemaker. The inspired menus are naturally overflowing with tastes of East Anglia, from Cley smoked salmon with brown shrimps and pickled fennel, to Blythburgh pork, the slow-cooked belly and loin served with smoked mash, a saffron pear and curly kale. Venison from a local estate shows up well too, enriched with chocolate, as well as hazelnut gnocchi, and desserts bring up the rear smartly with spiced Bramley apple cake and nougatine glacé. One of the Lavender House's glories is a wine list compiled by a true enthusiast: its tasting notes full of missionary zeal, the selections full of interest and character. Prices start at £22, or £5.50 a glass, for Chilean Sauvignon and Carmenère.

Chef/s: Richard Hughes. **Open:** Sun L 12 to 2, Thur to Sun D 6.30 to 10. **Closed:** Mon, Tue, Wed, 26 Dec to 9 Jan. **Meals:** Set D £45. Sun L £28. Tasting menu £55. **Details:** 48 seats. Separate bar. Car parking.

Edgefield

The Pigs

Gutsy food in a family-focused boozer
Norwich Road, Edgefield, NR24 2RL
Tel no: (01263) 587634
www.thepigs.org.uk
British | £30
Cooking score: 1
🛏

Strongly branded and much extended, this family-focused country pub has expanded over the years reflecting its huge popularity. You'll now find children's play areas, a covered terrace, accommodation and a spa – though victuals haven't been neglected, encompassing local real ale, a children's menu and a rangey repertoire of modern pub food. Good-value iffits ('Norfolk tapas') run from nibbles of deep-fried cockles or crispy pig's ear to a first-rate snack of baked eggs with smoky bacon, cream and spiced tomato chutney. A special of bream fillet with new potatoes and sea purslane might follow, with rhubarb and ginger crumble providing a sugary conclusion. Decent wine from £18.
Chef/s: Tim Abbott. **Open:** Mon to Sat L 11 to 2.30, D 6 to 9. Sun 12 to 9. **Meals:** alc (main courses £13 to £36). **Details:** 134 seats. 30 seats outside. Separate bar. Wheelchair access. Music. Car parking.

Fritton

LOCAL GEM
▲ The Fritton Arms

Church Lane, Fritton, NR31 9HA
Tel no: (01493) 484008
www.frittonarms.co.uk
Modern British | £22

A welcome addition to East Anglia, this former hotel on the Somerleyton Estate has been reincarnated with impeccable shabby-chic credentials. Executive chef Stuart Pegg brings classical skills to a clear, modern British menu that sources beef, game and much fresh produce from the estate itself. Pressed Swannington ham hock terrine with red onion marmalade could precede a Welsh Black burger with Norfolk Dapple cheese, bacon, slaw and chips. Indulge in a rhubarb crème brûlée before hiring a rowing boat on the exquisite Fritton Lake. There's plenty to drink by the glass, and 500ml carafes from £11. Open all week.

Great Yarmouth

Seafood Restaurant

Adorable seafood veteran
85 North Quay, Great Yarmouth, NR30 1JF
Tel no: (01493) 856009
www.theseafood.co.uk
Seafood | £35
Cooking score: 2

'One of the better reasons for visiting Great Yarmouth,' according to a reporter who travels over from France, Chris and Miriam Kikis' eatery has been doing the town proud since 1979. Many readers rate it as their 'all-time favourite' classic fish restaurant. High standards are a given, from the fastidiously sourced local catch to the personable service and passionate dedication of the owners. Good vibrations abound in this beautifully appointed Victorian building by Yarmouth's landmark railway bridge. Luxuriously sauced plates from the old school of seafood cookery arrive in the shape of 'sublime' lobster thermidor, turbot dressed with buttery, garlicky juices or monkfish spiced with curry. Alternatively, freshly grilled fish with ample vegetables might fit the bill, before one of Chris's desserts – perhaps 'excellent' crème brûlée, mixed berry Pavlova or orange and almond cake. To finish, don't miss the homemade chocolates with 'constantly refilled' coffee. Well-chosen, fish-friendly wines start at £16.50.
Chef/s: Christopher Kikis. **Open:** Mon to Fri L 12 to 1.45, Mon to Sat D 6.30 to 10.30. **Closed:** Sun, 24 Dec to 7 Jan, last 2 weeks May, bank hols. **Meals:** alc (main courses £12 to £35). **Details:** 42 seats. Separate bar. Wheelchair access. Music. Children over 7 yrs only.

Holt

LOCAL GEM
▲ Byfords
1 Shirehall Plain, Holt, NR25 6BG
Tel no: (01263) 711400
www.byfords.org.uk
Modern European | £24

It's a hive of activity – pop in for a coffee and cake, pick up something from the deli to eat on the hoof, fill your boots in the café or stay the night in one of the bedrooms. In a flint-faced building of considerable period charm, you can tuck into sandwiches (rare roast beef in a toasted flatbread, perhaps) or go for a sharing platter (local cheese), or something like kedgeree made with Cley smoked haddock and prawns. Wines from £18. Open all week.

Ingham

★ READERS' RESTAURANT OF THE YEAR ★
EAST ENGLAND

The Ingham Swan
Grown-up food in a medieval inn
Sea Palling Road, Ingham, NR12 9GA
Tel no: (01692) 581099
www.theinghamswan.co.uk
Modern European | £32
Cooking score: 3

£5 OFF 🍽

Seriously thatched, solidly antiquated and once linked to nearby Ingham Priory, this affable hostelry by the Broads feels like everyone's idea of a trusty village boozer. Ancient timbers, inglenook fireplaces and real ales from local heroes Woodforde's reinforce the theme – although the food tells a different story. Chef/proprietor Daniel Smith cooks free-ranging, restaurant-style dishes full of modern accents, so prepare yourself for crispy squid with roast pork belly, plum purée and pea shoot salad, or Dijon-crusted rack and noisette of lamb with fennel duxelle, broccoli and basil jus. Specialities such as longshore cod wrapped in pancetta with braised baby gem and Brancaster mussel broth show the kitchen has some regional leanings, although it's over to the sunny Med for affogato espresso shots, chocolate nemesis and Tuscan orange cake with poached pears. The accommodation comes highly recommended, likewise the cosmopolitan wine list (from £20), which offers thoughtful food-matching suggestions and plenty by the glass.
Chef/s: Daniel Smith. Open: all week L 12 to 2 (3 Sun), D 6 to 9 (8.30 Sun). Closed: 25 and 26 Dec. Meals: alc (main courses £15 to £25). Set L £15 (2 courses) to £19. Sun L £20 (2 courses) to £26. Details: 52 seats. 20 seats outside. Music. Car parking.

King's Lynn

Market Bistro
Welcoming, relaxed town-centre eatery
11 Saturday Market Place, King's Lynn, PE30 5DQ
Tel no: (01553) 771483
www.marketbistro.co.uk
Modern British | £27
Cooking score: 2

£5 OFF £30 🍷

A sunny spring lunchtime saw this 'gem of a place' fill quickly, and overwhelmingly with regular customers loyal to Richard Golding's reliable cooking and his wife Lucy's front-of-house warmth. Though a beetroot and goats' cheese starter at inspection veered towards bland, a plate of organic smoked salmon was a treat, the natural oiliness of the fish offset by tangy caperberries. Local ingredients shine: try Red Poll beef blade with skinny fries and vinegar slaw, or Cromer crab salad with potatoes, fennel and smoked paprika. A plump piece of pollack with crushed potatoes and wilted greens might be simplicity itself, but is all the more enjoyable for the absence of fuss. Puddings on the other hand do risk 'style over substance' for some, though a just-poached rhubarb with custard pannacotta, stem ginger and elderflower jelly deserves a thumbs-up for being as tasty as it is pretty. House wine from £16.95. Details overleaf.

Chef/s: Richard Golding. **Open:** Tue to Sun L 12 to 2 (3 Sun), D 6 to 8.30 (9 Fri and Sat). **Closed:** Mon, first 2 weeks Jan. **Meals:** alc (main courses £10 to £16). Set L £11. **Details:** 40 seats. Wheelchair access.

LOCAL GEM
▲ Marriott's Warehouse

South Quay, King's Lynn, PE30 5DT
Tel no: (01553) 818500
www.marriottswarehouse.co.uk
Modern British | £23 £5 OFF

Housed in a centuries-old warehouse, this quayside eatery marries fascinating maritime heritage with on-the-button food. Grilled sardines with garlic butter or pork and pistachio terrine start things off nicely, while mains rely on well-turned-out favourites such as sirloin (Ouse-grazed, we're told), lamb shanks or sea bass. Skate wing with roasted tomatoes and asparagus was flakily soft, any blandness in the fish offset by slivers of fiery chorizo and popplingly fresh pomegranate. A vanilla pannacotta perhaps lacked wobble, but its accompanying kiwi fruit jelly added plenty. Wines from £13.95. Open all week.

▮ Morston
Morston Hall

Classy, modern cooking near the coast
The Street, Morston, NR25 7AA
Tel no: (01263) 741041
www.morstonhall.com
Modern British | £66
Cooking score: 5

🛏 V

If consistency is one of the holy grails of the hospitality business (and it is), hats off to Galton and Tracy Blackiston for 22 years in the Guide. Morston Hall's position close to the north Norfolk coast puts them in reach of some top produce from land and sea, and the no-choice menu format means that prime ingredients in peak condition appear on the plate. The house, built of local flint, has conservatory dining areas overlooking the

garden. It's a place of low-key luxury. Arrival for dinner is 7.30 for 8, and what follows is some pinpoint, contemporary cooking. There's craft and attention to detail in dishes such as loin of Holkham venison rolled in liquorice with 96% cocoa chocolate and juniper jus, and North Sea plaice with local brown shrimps. British cheeses or frozen winter raspberries with white chocolate and celery granita is the only decision required. Wines start at £24.

Chef/s: Galton Blackiston and Richard Bainbridge. **Open:** Sun L 12.30 for 1 (1 sitting), Mon to Sat D 7.30 for 8 (1 sitting). **Closed:** 24 to 26 Dec, Jan. **Meals:** Set D £66. Sun L £36. **Details:** 50 seats. Wheelchair access. Car parking.

▮ Norwich
Roger Hickman's

Clean, clear seasonal flavours
79 Upper St Giles Street, Norwich, NR2 1AB
Tel no: (01603) 633522
www.rogerhickmansrestaurant.com
Modern British | £42
Cooking score: 5

£5 OFF

'Clever, inventive and exciting,' swooned one reader after experiencing Roger Hickman's cooking. His restaurant in picturesque Upper St Giles Street has neutral tones and moody artworks alongside tables that are generously spaced and dressed up for fine dining. The 'enthusiastic' service team ensure all is well. Hickman's menus – table d'hôte and tasting versions at both lunch and dinner – are rich with appealing combinations and creative flourishes, with everything looking as pretty as a picture on the plate. Mackerel is blow-torched to crispy perfection and comes with beetroot, puffed wild rice and nasturtiums. Main courses could bring pork belly with salt-baked turnip and salsify, or roast skate wing with charred leeks and a burnt butter crumb. There are amuse-bouches and pre-desserts before a stylish finale of poached pear with mascarpone mousse and thyme frangipane, topped with milk snow. The excellent wine list has concise tasting notes; prices from £22.

Chef/s: Roger Hickman. **Open:** Tue to Sat L 12 to 2.30, D 7 to 10. **Closed:** Sun, Mon, 25 to 27 Dec, 1 week Jan, 1 week Aug. **Meals:** alc (main courses £22). Set L £18 (2 courses) to £22. Set D £34 (2 courses) to £42. **Details:** 44 seats. Music.

LOCAL GEM

▲ Roots

6 Pottergate, Norwich, NR2 1DS
Tel no: (01603) 920788
www.rootsnorwich.co.uk
British | £25 £5 OFF

Pause as you explore Norwich's higgledy-piggledy Lanes at this 'difficult to praise too highly' bistro-cum-café-cum-farmers' shop. Jack of all trades? Reports suggest it's master of the robust breakfast and indulgent cream tea, and it certainly scores with a starter of freshly shucked oysters and main of line-caught sea bass served with a verdant abundance of perfectly steamed peas, beans and courgette ribbons. Honey and vanilla coconut pannacotta with local rhubarb finishes a meal well. Determinedly Norfolk sourcing extends to a wine list (from £18) that champions the local Winbirri vineyard. Closed Mon.

▲ Shiki

6 Tombland, Norwich, NR3 1HE
Tel no: (01603) 619262
www.shikirestaurant.co.uk
Japanese | £20

A rocking Japanese canteen opposite Norwich Cathedral, Shiki satisfies crowds of famished Asian students, tourists and locals with its forthright food and honest prices. At lunchtime, lacquered bento boxes, udon noodles and nutritious donburi rice bowls are the way to go. In the evening, tingling-fresh sushi and teppanyaki grills steal the show. The kitchen also hits the target with agedashi tofu, top-drawer tempura, crispy chicken kara-age and shogayaki (sliced pork in ginger sauce). Service is sharp, eager and streetwise. Drink beer, saké or tea. Closed Sun.

🍴 CRAFT BEERS

Craft beers are enjoying a renaissance among the nation's drinking cognoscenti, but can they be paired with haute cuisine? Michel Roux Jr thinks so: he recently collaborated with a London brewery to create Roux Brew, a grapefruit- and orange zest-infused beer that's the perfect partner to grilled fish and seafood dishes.

At Alyn Williams' Mayfair restaurant, you can opt for a beer flight to accompany the tasting menu. Sommelier Jess Kildetoft says the Sharp's Quadruple ale is a better match for a foie gras semi freddo than any wine.

At Quilon, a south Indian restaurant in Westminster, you'll find more than 20 world and vintage ales, including Chalky's Bark, a ginger-infused beer, commissioned by seafood chef Rick Stein, that works well with Asian flavours.

Will Beckett, co-founder of steakhouse chain Hawksmoor, says, 'When you think about it there's every reason to drink a classic London porter with a good British steak, or an IPA with some sticky Tamworth belly ribs'.

Old Hunstanton

The Neptune

Beautifully wrought, complex cooking near the coast

85 Old Hunstanton Road, Old Hunstanton, PE36 6HZ

Tel no: (01485) 532122

www.theneptune.co.uk

Modern British | £50

Cooking score: 4

£5 OFF

The ivy-clad former coaching inn on north Norfolk's coast road has been the setting for some rarefied cooking since Jacki and Kevin Mangeolles opened in 2007. Within, neutral tones, wooden flooring and raffia chairs decorate both the bar and little dining room. Jacki manages front-of-house with chatty informality, while – with an eye on fashion and a nod to seasonal and local ingredients – Kevin produces beautifully wrought, complex little dishes to please the area's gentlefolk (who seldom flinch at the prices). At inspection, textural contrasts brightened a starter of sweet, buttery-soft saké-poached salmon scattered with shredded white radish and crisp puffed rice; juicy, flavoursome Cumbrian rose veal starred among its supporting cast of dauphine potatoes, wild garlic, leeks and an aubergine and Parmesan purée; and mango mousse transcended its odd bedfellow of peanut-butter ice cream. Overall, flavours are restrained, with the admirable exception of a tangy pre-dessert of passion fruit jelly. Wines from £20.

Chef/s: Kevin Mangeolles. **Open:** Sun L 12 to 1.30, Tue to Sun D 7 to 9. **Closed:** Mon, 26 Dec, 2 weeks Nov, 3 weeks Jan. **Meals:** alc (main courses £25 to £30). Sun L £33. Tasting menu £70. **Details:** 22 seats. Separate bar. Music. Car parking.

¶¶¶ Average Price

The average price listed in main-entry reviews denotes the price of a three-course meal, without wine.

Ovington

The Café at Brovey Lair

Thrilling gastro-theatre

Carbrooke Road, Ovington, IP25 6SD

Tel no: (01953) 882706

www.broveylair.com

Pan-Asian seafood | £53

Cooking score: 6

In a world where restaurant design is a global business and menus have a familiar ring across the board, the Pembertons' place is about as far away from corporate uniformity as possible. For a start, Brovey Lair is their home (accommodation available) and the welcome is genuine. The restaurant/kitchen occupies an open-plan space, with Tina at the stove. Ask questions, walk about: that's the idea. Likes and dislikes are discussed when you book, to ensure the no-choice menu doesn't disappoint. Stunning seafood is at the heart of matters. You won't find anything 'domestic' about the cooking, as the world is Tina's oyster: ceviche of yellowfin tuna to begin, perhaps, followed by a soup of carrot and coriander fired up with ginger and turmeric. Next up, teppan-grilled monkfish, or sea bass tagine with almond and date couscous, followed by dessert of pear, polenta and Chardonnay cake. Wines from £19.50.

Chef/s: Tina Pemberton. **Open:** all week L 12.30 to 3 by special arrangement, D 7.45 (1 sitting). **Closed:** 25 and 26 Dec. **Meals:** Set L £45. Set D £53. **Details:** 24 seats. 20 seats outside. Wheelchair access. Car parking. Children over 13 yrs only.

Snettisham

LOCAL GEM

▲ The Rose & Crown

Old Church Road, Snettisham, PE31 7LX

Tel no: (01485) 541382

www.roseandcrownsnettisham.co.uk

Modern British | £27

Rose-covered, whitewashed, dog-friendly... what's not to love about this village pub-with-rooms? Friendly staff welcome guests hungry from bracing walks on the nearby north Norfolk beaches, tempting them maybe with a starter of local pigeon, wild mushrooms and wilted spinach, followed by tender new-season rack of lamb served with a Brie de Meaux gratin and greens. Portions are extremely generous, so the 'mini puds' option is welcome; try classic crème brûlée and shortbread biscuit. House wine from £15. Open all week.

▌Stanhoe

NEW ENTRY
The Duck Inn
Imaginative creations by the village duck pond
Burnham Road, Stanhoe, PE31 8QD
Tel no: (01485) 518330
www.duckinn.co.uk
British | £30
Cooking score: 3

'Very north Norfolk,' commented one seasoned observer, witnessing the grey-green colours of this modern pub-with-rooms and its scrubbed pine tables in both bar and dining area. A garden room attracts summertime customers who could wander across to the village duck pond. Prices might be pitched at second-home owners, but the quality of the 'fantastic imaginative' modern British cooking merits them. The concise menu entices (with baked cod, wild mushroom risotto and crisped braised ox cheeks a standout main course), but the specials hold yet more allure. Combinations can be brave – a fusion starter of precisely cooked hake in savoury dashi velouté with keta and dill – or more classic, as in an exploration of duck featuring sweet intense parfait, rillettes and juicy slices of breast. Puddings, too, catch the eye, especially a gratifying flourless chocolate tart teamed with chocolate mousse and peanut-butter sauce. Staff ('warm, friendly') and wine (from £14.50) provide admirable back-up.

Chef/s: Ben Handley. **Open:** all week L 12 to 2.30, D 6.30 to 9. Sun 12 to 8. **Closed:** 25 Dec. **Meals:** alc (main courses £13 to £20). **Details:** 60 seats. 86 seats outside. Separate bar. Wheelchair access. Music. Car parking.

▌Stoke Holy Cross

NEW ENTRY
Stoke Mill
Exciting new cooking in striking old mill
Mill Road, Stoke Holy Cross, NR14 8PA
Tel no: (01508) 493337
www.stokemill.co.uk
Modern British | £32
Cooking score: 4

Some 200 years ago, the air around this converted watermill would have pricked with mustard, for Jeremiah Colman first created his fiery, yellow condiment here. Now, Stoke Mill is where to enjoy the contemporary cooking of Andy Rudd. Fashionable Scotch egg gets a makeover, with crisp salt cod encasing a fragile quail's egg, served with chorizo and a punchy red pepper sauce. Follow with 'extremely tasty' delicate wild sea bass with Cromer crab cakes, white and green asparagus, samphire and roasted tomatoes on a luxuriously creamy lobster bisque, a dish of (too?) many parts, or loin of lamb (the perfect marriage of seared and pink) lifted with a smoky aubergine purée and early summer flavours of mint and peas. Chocolate dominates the puddings – apart from a textbook crème brûlée or praline parfait with exquisite honeycomb ice cream. The very reasonable wine list opens at £18, with ample choice at similar prices and by the glass.

Chef/s: Andy Rudd. **Open:** Thur, Fri and Sun L 12 to 2.30, Wed to Sat D 7 to 9.30. **Closed:** Mon, Tue. **Meals:** alc (main courses £13 to £19). **Details:** 80 seats. Separate bar. Music. Car parking.

Swaffham

Strattons
Quirky, tucked-away market town eatery
4 Ash Close, Swaffham, PE37 7NH
Tel no: (01760) 723845
www.strattonshotel.com
Modern British | £28
Cooking score: 2

Trust your SatNav, squeeze down the loke by the chippy and discover Swaffham's quirky Strattons. There's something of the louche boudoir about the half-basement dining room (fairy lights, velveteen upholstery, black walls, gilt mirrors), but the food is reassuringly conventional. Many ingredients are local, and newish chef Julia Hetherton lets ingredients speak for themselves. A sliver of grilled mackerel makes a gloriously simple starter even if the beetroot and pearled spelt accompaniment lacks gusto, and slow-cooked Scotts Field belly pork is deemed 'outstanding' by a finicky meat-eater. The menu will gladden vegetarians: follow a roasted tomato, olive, saffron tart with an 'exceptional' filo-pastry galette of wilted spinach, goats' cheese, crushed Maris Peers and sweet-savoury-spicy tomato and cardamom relish. To finish, a chocolate cookie/praline ice cream concoction is as overwhelming as a raspberry sorbet with chilled whisky custard is lip-smacking. Strattons' vegetarian and organic credentials stretch to the informative wine list (from £19.95). Service is exceptional.
Chef/s: Julia Hetherton. Open: Sun L 12 to 2.30, all week D 6.30 to 8.30 (9 Fri and Sat). Closed: 1 week Christmas. Meals: alc (main courses £14 to £19). Details: 40 seats. 12 seats outside. Separate bar. Music. Car parking.

Visit us Online
To find out more about
The Good Food Guide, please visit
www.thegoodfoodguide.co.uk

Thetford

NEW ENTRY
The Mulberry
Friendly, tucked-away neighbourhood treat
Thetford, IP24 2EA
Tel no: (01842) 824122
www.mulberrythetford.co.uk
Modern British | £31
Cooking score: 1

How lovely to put Thetford on the culinary map with this gem of a neighbourhood restaurant that has been quietly making its mark since opening some four years ago. Try the generously flavoured Mulberry salad of smoked duck breast, roasted beets, goats' cheese and endive to start, and perhaps follow with sirloin served unfussily with roast potatoes and red wine jus, or a piece of turbot, cooked just the right side of rare, with some local asparagus. To finish? A crème brûlée hits the spot sweetly, or try a zesty almond and orange cake with mascarpone cream. The wine list opens at £15.95.
Chef/s: Nathan Coleman. Open: Tue to Sat D only 6 to 9 (10 Sat). Closed: Sun, Mon. Meals: alc (main courses £11 to £22). Set D £20 (2 courses) to £25. Details: 45 seats. 8 seats outside. Separate bar. Music.

Thorpe Market

★ TOP 10 PUB ★

The Gunton Arms
Game-changer that fizzes with success
Cromer Road, Thorpe Market, NR11 8TZ
Tel no: (01263) 832010
www.theguntonarms.co.uk
British | £32
Cooking score: 5

In a glorious location on the edge of a 1,000-acre deer park, the Gunton Arms is a country pub reinvented for the 21st century — a mix of country house hotel, pub and restaurant. Its chill-out atmosphere and easy-going service work well with the quirky charm of the interior: all rich colours, leather, wood, the odd mod-Brit neon sign. There's fabulous theatre in watching chefs cook meat on the roaring fire in the Elk Room, and Norfolk's finest ales and venison sausage rolls are available in the bar. Stuart Tattersall's gutsy take on British cooking is distinguished by simplicity and full-on flavours. His exploration of our native larder continues to go down well with reporters – red deer loin with Jersey Royals and wild garlic, slip soles with brown shrimps and sea purslane, and roast suckling pig with rainbow chard and hotpot potatoes, for instance. The concise, spot-on wine list opens at £18.

Chef/s: Stuart Tattersall. **Open:** all week L 12 to 3, D 6 to 10 (9 Sun). **Closed:** 25 Dec. **Meals:** alc (main courses £12 to £23). **Details:** 60 seats. 150 seats outside. Separate bar. Wheelchair access. Music. Car parking.

▌Titchwell
Titchwell Manor
Ambitious, inventive cooking by the sea
Titchwell, PE31 8BB
Tel no: (01485) 210221
www.titchwellmanor.com
Modern European | £34
Cooking score: 3

£5
OFF

'Simply divine' is how one diner summed up a meal at this bright and welcoming restaurant a seagull's squawk from spectacular north Norfolk beaches. Self-taught Eric Snaith cooks up modern brasserie fare in his informal Eating Rooms, but keeps his showpieces for the Conservatory menu. Here – and on the eight-course Conversation menu – is where he creates the 'wonderful, innovative' dishes that are putting Titchwell Manor, and his name, firmly on the culinary map. Sweet, tender quail sits happily next to herby, fresh lovage and peppery roundels of radish, while dripping-poached pollack served with asparagus, watercress and delicate elderflower vinaigrette is a masterclass in balance and eye-appeal. Norfolk lamb with sweetbreads, lemon balm and courgette makes for a busy

plate, but the textures and flavours are memorable. Pick of the puds is a celebration of rhubarb with goats' cheese and pistachio. A Chilean Merlot kicks off the wine list at £17.50.

Chef/s: Eric Snaith. **Open:** all week 12 to 9.30. **Meals:** alc (main courses £8 to £27). Set D £55 (5 courses) to £65 (8 courses). Sun L £29. **Details:** 100 seats. 40 seats outside. Separate bar. Wheelchair access. Music. Car parking.

▌Wiveton

LOCAL GEM
▲ Wiveton Hall Café
Wiveton Hall, Wiveton, NR25 7TE
Tel no: (01263) 740525
www.wivetonhall.co.uk
Modern British | £25

'I ate lobster for lunch and rhubarb fool outside on a wonderful day,' mused a reader seduced by this wacky little café overlooking Wiveton Hall's PYO strawberry fields. 'Farm to table' is the message, which means a daily lunch menu featuring the likes of toasted Binham Blue cheese with red onion marmalade and walnut bruschetta, Weybourne crab salad or Wiveton pheasant with wild mushroom and chestnut soup. House wine £14.50. Open all week Mar to Dec (inc supper on Fri and Sat).

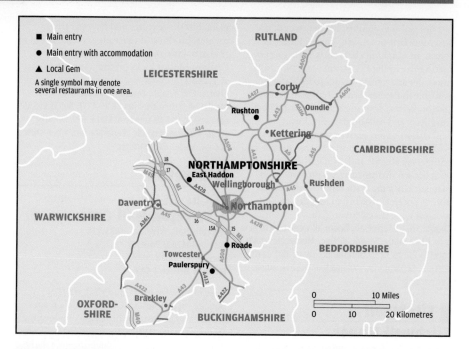

East Haddon
The Red Lion
A dining destination for the area
Main Street, East Haddon, NN6 8BU
Tel no: (01604) 770223
www.redlioneasthaddon.co.uk
Modern British | £27
Cooking score: 2

The former coaching inn dates from the 17th century and is a lovely, substantial building – golden sandstone topped with thatch, wooden floors and beams within – and is still very much a pub dispensing real ales and genuine hospitality. But it also successfully bridges the hard-to-achieve divide between village pub and stylish restaurant-with-rooms, helped, no doubt, by reasonable proximity to the M1. The kitchen is not trying to invent the culinary wheel, but the carefully sourced produce is precisely cooked, delivering pub classics such as Scotch egg with caper and parsley mayonnaise, fish and chips or confit pork belly – as well as smoked mackerel pâté, roasted salmon with a coconut and cauliflower curry, and poached and roasted chicken with a ham hock, leek and pearl barley risotto. Dessert could be Yorkshire rhubarb and custard trifle. The short, global wine list starts at £16.

Chef/s: Nick Bonner. **Open:** Mon to Fri L 12 to 2.30, D 6 to 9. Sat and Sun 12 to 9. **Closed:** 25 Dec. **Meals:** alc (main courses £11 to £26). **Details:** 80 seats. 50 seats outside. Separate bar. Wheelchair access. Music. Car parking.

Symbols

🛏 Accommodation is available

£30 Three courses for less than £30

V Separate vegetarian menu

£5 £5-off voucher scheme

🍷 Notable wine list

||| DUDE
||| FOOD

Once there was a time when fried chicken and burgers were the sole preserve of high street fast-food chains and a hot dog was something you bought from a cart at the fun fair. These days, you're as likely to find these junk-food classics, collectively known as 'dude food', in some of the hippest bricks-and-mortar eateries, if not more glitzy establishments. But don't expect rubbery chicken or thin, grey beef patties; the movement's acolytes take quality and authenticity to the nth degree.

The Meatliquor chain epitomises these dude food values with its menu of burgers, chilli dogs and 'house coated' chicken at its restaurants in London and Brighton. Likewise, Five Guys, a US chain that landed in Covent Garden in 2013 and now looks set to spread across the south-east. Even the Soho House Group has got in on the act with its Dirty Burger and Chicken Shop brands, whose branches have appeared in some of London's less chichi neighbourhoods. Meanwhile, in Knightsbridge, you'll find Yankee and Piggie burgers on the menu at Bar Boulud, though the foie gras and truffle-laden BB would never pass the authenticity test. Big fail, dude.

▌Paulerspury
The Vine House
Rural find with an offbeat approach
100 High Street, Paulerspury, NN12 7NA
Tel no: (01327) 811267
www.vinehousehotel.com
Modern British | £31
Cooking score: 4

£5 OFF 🛏

'A real find' in rural Northamptonshire, this 300-year-old farmhouse has been in the care of Marcus and Julie Springett since 1991. The restaurant-with-rooms has recently been refurbished, though in the kitchen Marcus's approach remains as offbeat (and as popular) as ever. Readers rate his knack with texture and flavour combinations which, as in a starter of home-smoked salmon with blue cheese and pineapple, follow a less-trodden path. Main courses include saddle of wild venison with a mushroom sausage roll and parsnip purée or skrei cod with lemon jam and Parmesan crackling, and local lamb is always a hit. A fondness for adding a savoury element to pudding shows in plum pie jelly with mustard mascarpone and pistachios, or chocolate terrine with hazelnuts, smoked bacon and sherry vinegar caramel. Service is capable and friendly, but if hell is other people, book the garden folly for two. Wine starts at £18.50.
Chef/s: Marcus Springett. **Open:** Tue to Sat L 12 to 2, Mon to Sat D 6.30 to 9. **Closed:** Sun. **Meals:** Set L and D £28 (2 courses) to £31. **Details:** 33 seats. Separate bar. Music. Car parking. Children over 8 yrs only.

Roade

Roade House
Respectable retreat with reassuring food
16 High Street, Roade, NN7 2NW
Tel no: (01604) 863372
www.roadehousehotel.co.uk
Modern British | £35
Cooking score: 2
£5 OFF

Chris and Sue Kewley celebrated 30 years at the Roade House in 2013 and continue to tread a steady path at their self-styled 'restaurant and hotel': a handy, custom-built retreat not far from Silverstone. Inside, the tidy beamed dining room feels calm, respectable and slightly old-fashioned, an impression reinforced by the reassuringly familiar menu. Chris dips into the European back catalogue for Hungarian goulash, navarin of lamb with Dijon mustard and pan-fried calf's liver with celeriac mash, 'various onions' and balsamic sauce, but he can also go global. Starters of lamb pastilla with harissa and yoghurt or fillet of saltfish with stir-fried greens, chilli, ginger and soy brighten the mood, while desserts stay closer to home for the likes of chocolate brownie with Guinness ice cream or apple and almond tart with Calvados syllabub. Fixed-price Sunday lunches often include some live jazz in the bar. Old World wines (from £16) dominate the mainstream list.
Chef/s: Chris Kewley. Open: Tue to Sun L 12.30 to 2 (2.30 Sun), Mon to Sat D 7 to 9.30. Closed: 26 Dec to 2 Jan, bank hols. Meals: alc (main courses £17 to £24). Set L £21 (2 courses) to £24. Sun L £21. Details: 45 seats. Separate bar. Wheelchair access. Music. Car parking.

Rushton

Rushton Hall, Tresham Restaurant
Satisfying food in venerable surroundings
Desborough Road, Rushton, NN14 1RR
Tel no: (01536) 713001
www.rushtonhall.com
Modern British | £55
Cooking score: 3
£5 OFF

Heritage means a lot at this stately Grade I-listed pile deep in the countryside. Now a leisure retreat, Rushton Hall was originally the medieval seat of the Tresham family. Carved stonework, gilded tapestries, cloistered hallways and a manicured grassy quad add gravitas to proceedings, while immaculately groomed staff lighten their politesse with chatty asides. Cocktails in lofty Great Hall is the drill, before repairing to the oak-panelled dining room for thoughtfully rendered, satisfying modern food with plenty of appeal but no shocks. Seasonal flavours ring true in a dish of seared hand-dived scallops with cauliflower, raisins and curry, as well as 'absolutely superb' loin of fallow deer with celeriac, juniper, red cabbage and chocolate. To finish, there are toothsome, technically astute assemblages such as cranberry cannelloni with clementine mousse and cranberry sorbet – but don't miss the display of English regional cheeses. A heavyweight, all-embracing wine list starts at £22.
Chef/s: Adrian Coulthard. Open: Sun L 12 to 2, all week D 7 to 9. Meals: Set D £55. Sun L £30. Details: 38 seats. Separate bar. Wheelchair access. Music. Car parking. No children under 10 yrs at D.

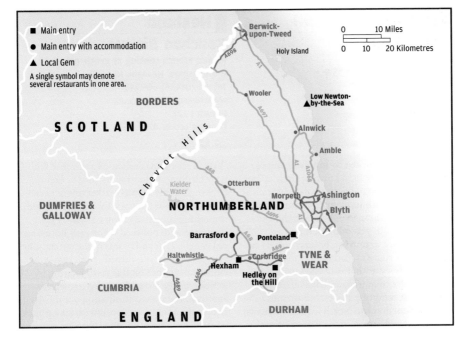

▮ Barrasford

The Barrasford Arms

Well-run, no-frills village inn
Barrasford, NE48 4AA
Tel no: (01434) 681237
www.barrasfordarms.co.uk
Modern British | £25
Cooking score: 2

Tony Binks acquired the rather majestic Victorian stone-built inn in 2006, and the place has become an obvious destination in a county still sparsely furnished with good eating. Hand-pulled ales help lubricate the evening convivium, when folk gather round the fire, and there's a choice of three dining areas. There are some stunning successes on the menu of modern country-pub food, as was discovered by one winter diner who began with Scotch egg made of black pudding, served on a slice of stuffed pheasant ballotine with apple purée: a bravura curtain-raiser. Other allurements have included mains of parsley-crusted sea bass with creamed leeks on roast pepper coulis, or grilled aged ribeye in hot peppercorn sauce. The dessert worth abandoning the diet for is a construction of sticky pistachio meringue with vanilla and orange mascarpone and poached rhubarb, and there are fine northern cheeses with chutney. Corney & Barrow house French is £14.95.
Chef/s: Tony Binks. **Open:** Tue to Sun L 12 to 2 (3 Sun), Tue to Sat D 6.30 to 9. **Closed:** Mon, 25 and 26 Dec, bank hols. **Meals:** alc (main courses £9 to £17). Set L £13 (2 courses) to £16. Sun L £15 (2 courses) to £17.50. **Details:** 65 seats. 20 seats outside. Separate bar. Music. Car parking.

▮▮▮ Visit us Online

To find out more about
The Good Food Guide, please visit
www.thegoodfoodguide.co.uk

Hedley on the Hill
The Feathers Inn

Industrious local inn
Hedley on the Hill, NE43 7SW
Tel no: (01661) 843607
www.thefeathers.net
British | £26
Cooking score: 3
£5 OFF £30

A cherished hub for the community, the Feathers houses the local knitting circle, a 'leek club' for gardeners and even a polling station at election time. With its exposed beams, open fires and old-fashioned pub games, this out-of-the-way, 200-year-old inn is also a favourite haunt of tourists, holidaymakers and sightseers en route to Hadrian's Wall or Hexham Abbey. Either way, the kitchen knows what is required, and delivers in fine fashion – at tempting prices. Industrious home production and North Country flavours speak loud and proud on the menu: from the renowned homemade black pudding with poached free-range egg and devilled gravy, or Craster kipper and whisky pâté, to slow-cooked Haydon Bridge beef in red wine with creamy mash, swede and horseradish; game pie with bilberries; or steamed gingerbread pudding. Cheeses from Northumberland and Durham also feature, alongside hand-pumped local ales. Wines from £15.

Chef/s: Rhian Cradock. **Open:** Tue to Sun L 12 to 2 (2.30 Sun), Tue to Sat D 6 to 8.30. **Closed:** Mon, first 2 weeks Jan. **Meals:** alc (main courses £11 to £15). Sun L £20. **Details:** 38 seats. 16 seats outside. Car parking.

Hexham
Bouchon Bistrot

Proper French cooking at gentle prices
4-6 Gilesgate, Hexham, NE46 3NJ
Tel no: (01434) 609943
www.bouchonbistrot.co.uk
French | £27
Cooking score: 4
£5 OFF £30

'Vive la Hexham!' exclaimed a traveller who stumbled upon a bastion of 'proper French cooking' in this hilltop market town. Loire-born proprietor Gregory Bureau has created something special: a vision of *la belle France* complete with polished mahogany floors, an old panelled bar and beams in the rafters. Chef Nicolas Duhil has returned after a two-year sabbatical and he's on fine form judging by recent reports. Many dishes have received approval, but it's worth singling out the deep, rich soupe à l'oignon topped with fat garlicky croûtes and 'volcanic' melted Gruyère – as well as a classic salade landaise loaded with cured duck breast, confit gizzards and chunks of cold, fried potatoes. Platters of charcuterie are much appreciated, rabbit with prunes and pommes dauphinois is an outright winner, and luscious îles flottantes provide an unmissable finale. 'Immensely efficient', chatty service helps things along nicely, while gentle pricing extends to the all-Gallic wine list (from £14.95).

Chef/s: Nicolas Duhil. **Open:** Mon to Sat L 12 to 2, D 6 to 9 (9.30 Fri and Sat). **Closed:** Sun, bank hols. **Meals:** alc (main courses £12 to £20). Set L £14 (2 courses) to £15. Set D £15. **Details:** 120 seats. Wheelchair access. Music.

LOCAL GEM
▲ The Rat Inn

Anick, Hexham, NE46 4LN
Tel no: (01434) 602814
www.theratinn.com
British | £24

Real ales, a real fire, stone flags and a village green add rustic cred to this centuries-old country boozer in the Tyne Valley. Don't expect culinary fireworks: instead, look forward to confident, unshowy pub classics from a kitchen that shows commitment to top-class regional materials – from Craster kippers via Richard Woodall's black pudding to local cheeses. Recent successes have included tender beer-braised beef, pink and tender lamb chops, and brown ale chocolate cake. Wines from £15.95. No food Sun D and Mon.

▌ Low Newton

LOCAL GEM
▲ The Ship Inn

Newton Square, Low Newton, NE66 3EL
Tel no: (01665) 576262
www.shipinnnewton.co.uk
British | £25

With an on-site micro-brewery and a quintessentially Northumbrian beachside location, the Ship is more than just a convenient stop for walkers on this glorious, unspoilt stretch of coast. 'Excellent food, freshly prepared' is the trademark, with lots of local smoked fish and Doddington cheese going into a simple lunch menu, and dishes such as Northumbrian venison with red wine sauce, spiced red cabbage and mash served at dinner. No cards, so go prepared. Wines from £15.95. No food D Sun to Tue.

▌ Ponteland

Café Lowrey

Setting the bar for neighbourhood eateries
33-35 The Broadway, Darras Hall, Ponteland, NE20 9PW
Tel no: (01661) 820357
www.cafelowrey.co.uk
Modern British | £29
Cooking score: 3
£30

Café Lowrey is a neighbourhood restaurant of generous spirit and stout heart. It's the sort of place that fits the bill for a celebratory meal, yet also for dinner on a Wednesday evening because there's nothing in the fridge (the bargain early-evening menu is particularly welcome for the latter). Expect bistro dishes with a French focus and pan-European leanings. There's a local flavour, too, as Ian Lowrey is an industrious chef who cures his own salmon and seeks out high-quality ingredients from the vicinity. Grilled black pudding with chorizo and potato salad makes a robust opener, or go for a Cheddar cheese and spinach soufflé. Main-course sea bass is ideally matched with an aubergine and tomato ragoût and a cumin cream. Otherwise, try the 10oz sirloin steak au poivre with confit tomato, flat-cap mushroom and hand-cut chips. Gooey chocolate fondant provides a comforting finish. Wines start at £16.50.
Chef/s: Ian Lowrey. **Open:** Fri to Sun L 12 to 2.30 (3 Sun), Tue to Sat D 5.30 to 10 (6 Sat). **Closed:** Mon. **Meals:** alc (main courses £15 to £25). **Details:** 70 seats. Wheelchair access. Car parking.

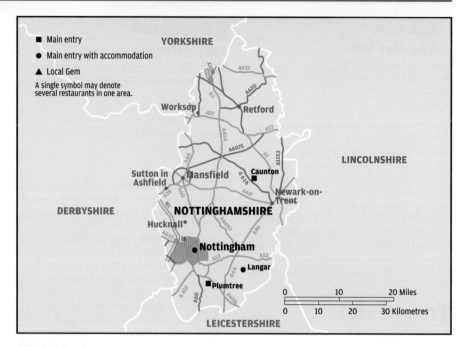

- ■ Main entry
- ● Main entry with accommodation
- ▲ Local Gem

A single symbol may denote
several restaurants in one area.

▌Caunton

Caunton Beck

All-day treats in a rural retreat
Main Street, Caunton, NG23 6AB
Tel no: (01636) 636793
www.wigandmitre.com
Modern European | £27
Cooking score: 2

£30

'Our favourite stopover when travelling on
the A1,' says one visitor to this meticulously
restored 16th-century cottage-cum-pub-
restaurant that serves food all day. Caunton
Beck is a welcoming free house occupying a
peaceful, out of the way rural setting, but one
that's 'worth the diversion' according to other
fans. The food is well prepared from high-
quality raw materials and the flexible menu
evolves throughout the day from breakfast
through to dinner. From the 'main' menu, a
starter of twice-baked chestnut mushroom
and Blacksticks Blue soufflé might be followed
by pan-seared Scottish salmon fillet, winter

greens, caviar and caper butter. Desserts,
including white fudge and rum-soaked raisin
crème brûlée, don't disappoint and service is
friendly and cheerful. As well as a range of
well-kept real ales dispensed from the bar, a
user-friendly and carefully selected wine list
offers plenty of good-value choices under
£20, starting at £14.95.
Chef/s: Andy Pickstop, Ben Hughes and Valerie
Hope. **Open:** all week 8.30am to 10.30pm (10pm
Sun). **Closed:** 25 Dec. **Meals:** alc (main courses £11
to £30). Set L and D £15 (2 courses) to £17.
Details: 36 seats. 100 seats outside. Separate bar.
Wheelchair access. Car parking.

Symbols

🛏 Accommodation is available

£30 Three courses for less than £30

V Separate vegetarian menu

£5 OFF £5-off voucher scheme

🍷 Notable wine list

Langar
Langar Hall
An aristocrat of East Midlands eating
Church Lane, Langar, NG13 9HG
Tel no: (01949) 860559
www.langarhall.com
Modern British | £40
Cooking score: 4

On a bright summer's day, Langar Hall appears the archetypal English country home: a dapper Victorian pile with a medieval church tower rising beyond, the clop of croquet mallets in the air and a heady scent of freshly trimmed lawns. But this is no prim, mind-your-manners place. Inside, eccentric trinkets decorate the surfaces, and flamboyant chandeliers dangle overhead: emblematic of the bonhomie that has sustained Langar through three decades of business. Start with an old favourite – twice-baked cheese soufflé – or else a simple construction like mackerel, beetroot, horseradish and dill. Mains flaunt their East Midlands roots: Langar lamb (cousins of whom can be heard baaing through the sash windows) with cumin gnocchi and homemade ricotta, or maybe Nottinghamshire beef with ox cheek, potato terrine and wild garlic. There are bright ideas among the puds (iced bergamot parfait with honey ice cream, for instance) and also in a scrupulously curated wine list (from £20).
Chef/s: Gary Booth and Ross Jeffery. **Open:** all week L 12 to 2, D 6 to 10. **Meals:** alc (main courses £14 to £26). Set D £25 (2 courses) to £30. **Details:** 60 seats. Separate bar. Car parking.

Readers Recommend
A 'readers recommend' review is a genuine quote from a report sent in by one of our readers. We intend to follow up these suggestions throughout the year to come.

Morton
READERS RECOMMEND
The Full Moon Inn
British
Main Street, Morton, NG25 0UT
Tel no: (01636) 830251
www.thefullmoonmorton.co.uk
'The facilities are good with ample parking, children's area and outdoor dining. The welcome and friendliness were nice. The food was well presented, served nicely and tasted delicious.'

Nottingham
Hart's
Putting on the style
Standard Hill, Park Row, Nottingham, NG1 6GN
Tel no: (0115) 9110666
www.hartsnottingham.co.uk
Modern British | £30
Cooking score: 5

A veritable veteran of Nottingham's restaurant scene, Tim Hart's stylish restaurant continues to be one of the city's most consistent places. This is a classy, modern and highly professional set-up that strikes a balance between the relaxed and smart-formal ends of the spectrum. Its neutral-toned décor is enlivened by colourful abstract paintings, its menu with some appealing ideas, such as Cornish crab salad with apple mayonnaise, blood orange and coriander, or guinea fowl galantine with redcurrant purée and duck liver parfait. First-class materials underpin the operation and results have included cod with potato gnocchi, cauliflower couscous and a lemon and hazelnut dressing, and roast pork collar served with a cider-cooked fondant potato, sauerkraut and marinated prunes. A 'wonderful' passion fruit soufflé with yoghurt sorbet has garnered praise, too. The wine list is reasonably priced throughout (from £17.50), well stocked with reliable producers from both hemispheres and completes an experience that reporters unanimously praise as destination stuff.

Chef/s: Dan Burridge. **Open:** all week L 12 to 2, D 6 to 10. **Meals:** alc (main courses £15 to £30). Set L £16 (2 courses) to £19. Set D £19 (2 courses) to £24. Sun L £23. **Details:** 65 seats. Separate bar. Wheelchair access. Car parking.

The Larder on Goosegate

Dependable city local with swagger to boot
16-22 Goosegate, Hockley, Nottingham, NG1 1FE
Tel no: (0115) 9500111
www.thelarderongoosegate.co.uk
Modern British | £28
Cooking score: 2

£5 OFF £30

With its striking cast-iron and plate-glass façade, the Larder on Goosegate has a touch of Victorian swagger about it – unsurprisingly as in a former life this was the first emporium of Nottingham pharmaceutical magnate Jesse Boot. He'd be chuffed to see his sign hanging in the first-floor dining room, a tasteful vision of bare wooden floors, whirring ceiling fans and twinkly chandeliers. These days, however, visitors to the airy mint-green space over an Oxfam shop are prescribed spirited modern British cooking. Start with ham hock with celeriac rémoulade or confit duck croquettes with plum sauce and pickled beech mushrooms. Mains are punchy in execution: lamb rump with caramelised onion, and onion and anchovy tart, say. Otherwise, pick from a formidable selection of steaks, including unlikely cameos from cuts such as picanha and hanger. House wines start at £15.50; alternatively choose from the extensive beer list, which flies the flag for Notts brews.

Chef/s: David Sneddon. **Open:** Thur to Sat L 12 to 2.30, Tue to Sat D 6 to 10. **Closed:** Sun, Mon. **Meals:** alc (main courses £13 to £20). Set L and D £14 (2 courses) to £16. **Details:** 65 seats. Music.

★ TOP 10 ★

Restaurant Sat Bains

An extraordinary personal endeavour
Lenton Lane, Nottingham, NG7 2SA
Tel no: (0115) 9866566
www.restaurantsatbains.com
Modern British | £89
Cooking score: 9

⇄ V

Everyone agrees it's an odd setting for one of Britain's top restaurants – on the industrial edge of Nottingham, bounded by an electricity pylon and the A52 flyover – and it's devilish hard to find without SatNav. Inside the redbrick Victorian farm building the pair of rather insular, detached dining rooms (one a conservatory) can sometimes make for a hushed start, but then the food has a colour and life all of its own. Sat Bains has perfected a culinary style full of understated personal flourishes and painstaking attention to detail: from the high degree of technical competence that suffuses everything, to the understanding that seasonal ingredients of unimpeachable quality come first. These ingredients are translated into dishes with real poise and superb balance. And the flavours Bains manages to evoke are strikingly vivid. His cooking has such exactitude that he creates flavours where others would lose them: in the umami hit of Parmesan layered with the sweetness of asparagus; in a stunning squid minestrone that is the pure essence of early summer; in the comforting amalgamation of baked potato, soft cheese and salty smoked roe; and in roe deer (loin, a small heap of tartare, a venison sausage) that gels impressively on the plate with a meaty slice of field mushroom, crisp lichen and an intense venison jus – and by the tiny iron pot of smoking pine needles on the side, giving off a heady scent. These are alpha dishes, no question, but each dish on the seven- or ten-course tasting menu shows the sheer vitality of the ingredients. A rich, sensuous chicken parfait, for example, underscores Bains' fondness for supple, silky textures contrasted with crunch, here supplied by crisp 'muesli' grains. It's a theme followed through in desserts that, at our inspection meal, included a smooth rice pudding with jam, icy saké granita and crisp, puffed rice; and a smooth, fruity pear finale given focus by toasted almonds and frozen pear snow. Masterful wine service is on hand to guide diners through a wine list that is sensitively tailored to the food. If your budget allows, go for the spot-on wine flight. Otherwise, there are good by-the-glass choices and bottles start at £25.

Chef/s: Sat Bains and John Freeman. **Open:** Tue to Sat L 12 to 1, D 7 to 9 (6 to 9.30 Fri and Sat). **Closed:** Sun, Mon, 2 weeks Dec to Jan, 1 week spring, 2 weeks Aug, 1 week autumn. **Meals:** Tasting menu £79 (7 courses) to £89 (10 courses). **Details:** 40 seats. Separate bar. Music. Car parking. Children over 12 yrs only.

LOCAL GEM

★ LOCAL GEM OF THE YEAR ★

▲ Delilah

12 Victoria Street, Nottingham, NG1 2EX
Tel no: (0115) 9484461
www.delilahfinefoods.co.uk
Modern European | £18

Delilah is an excellent, welcoming delicatessen, set in a tasteful bank-conversion beside Nottingham Council House. Among the tempting displays of pongy cheeses and fine wines you'll find tables where customers can graze (upstairs and down), and a bar with plenty of stools to scale for fast-paced grazing and drinking. The menu spans charcuterie and cheese platters, salads and bruschettas, as well as bistro classics like confit duck with melted Gruyère or pork cassoulet. It can get busy on weekend mornings when all of Nottingham piles in for hangover-busting breakfasts. 'Still the best (and only) of its kind in Nottingham, nay the East Midlands', Delilah is more than deserving of the Guide's inaugural Local Gem award for 2015. House wines start at £14. Open all week.

▌Plumtree

Perkins

Good-value family favourite
Station House, Station Road, Plumtree, NG12 5NA
Tel no: (0115) 9373695
www.perkinsrestaurant.co.uk
Modern European | £33
Cooking score: 2

The Victorian-era railway station, duly decommissioned, got a new lease of life in 1982 when it came into the hands of the Perkins family. It's run by the second generation these days (alongside chef-director Sarah Newman), and continues to deliver contemporary food made with due diligence. They have their own smokehouse, so the salmon eggs Benedict is a good bet – or else start with seared king scallops with carrot and cumin purée. Taste of pork (fillet, black pudding and cheek fritters) is a fashionable plate of porcine treats, while there's a decidedly Latin flavour to a dish of roast fillet of hake with avocado and lime purée. End in the feel-good zone with hot chocolate fondant with Kirsch-marinated cherries. It all takes place in a series of smart spaces replete with Victorian character, and there are outdoor tables on the one-time platform. The drinks list contains cocktails, and wines from £16.95.

Chef/s: Sarah Newham. **Open:** Sun L 12 to 3.30. Mon to Sat 12 to 10. **Meals:** alc (main courses £15 to £23). Set L £14 (2 courses) to £17. Set D £17 (2 courses) to £19. Sun L £16 (2 courses) to £19. **Details:** 73 seats. 22 seats outside. Separate bar. Wheelchair access. Music. Car parking.

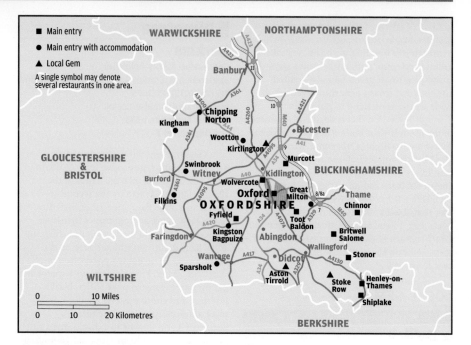

Map legend:
- ■ Main entry
- ● Main entry with accommodation
- ▲ Local Gem

A single symbol may denote several restaurants in one area.

■ Aston Tirrold

LOCAL GEM
▲ The Sweet Olive

Baker Street, Aston Tirrold, OX11 9DD
Tel no: (01235) 851272
www.sweet-olive.com
Modern European | £35

A restaurant in a pub run by two Frenchmen in a very English bit of England, the Sweet Olive is a curiosity, but a popular one. The Anglo–French menu is chalked up, and customers can pledge gastronomic allegiance with crispy duck salad and panache of fish in a Champagne saffron sauce, or local pork chop with apple and treacle sponge and custard. The wine list (from £18.95) knows which side it's on, with a special interest in Alsace. Closed all day Wed and Sun D.

■ Britwell Salome

The Red Lion

A well-groomed country pub
Britwell Salome, OX49 5LG
Tel no: (01491) 613140
www.theredlionbritwellsalome.co.uk
British | £30
Cooking score: 2

Looking every inch the well-groomed Oxfordshire country pub, with its pristine exterior and 'new 4WDs aplenty in the car park', the Red Lion, overseen by Andrew Hill and Eilidh Ferguson, is now a serious contender in the local food stakes. There's a stronger pub atmosphere than under its previous incarnation as the Goose, and the food delivers familiar British classics, including modish bar snacks such as black pudding Scotch egg, and Colston Bassett Stilton and fruitcake. The compact, seasonal menu is built around the very best from farms and producers in the area, perhaps home-smoked salmon with dill scone and cucumber,

or duck hearts on toast, while the prevailing mood is summed up by top rib steak with béarnaise sauce and chips, and turbot fillet with saffron potatoes, bouillabaisse sauce and rouille. Finish with a quince tart with St Clement's curd and crème fraîche. Wines from £16.50.
Chef/s: Andrew Hill. **Open:** Wed to Sun L 12 to 3 (5 Sun), Tue to Sat D 6 to 11 (5.30 Fri and Sat). **Closed:** Mon, first week Jan, week after Easter, week after Aug bank hol. **Meals:** alc (main courses £10 to £23). **Details:** 36 seats. 36 seats outside. Separate bar. Car parking.

Chinnor

★ TOP 50 PUB ★
The Sir Charles Napier
Eccentric Chiltern charmer
Sprigg's Alley, Chinnor, OX39 4BX
Tel no: (01494) 483011
www.sircharlesnapier.co.uk
Modern British | £44
Cooking score: 4

Julie Griffiths has been the life and soul of this deliciously oddball Chiltern charmer since the 1970s. Set high on Bledlow Ridge, with beech woods nearby and red kites soaring overhead, 'the Napier' offers an addictive blend of surreal sculptures, log fires and lazy pergolas. Menus follow the seasons as keenly as any forager: summer might bring Cornish mackerel on toast with tartare and gooseberry compote, superb lobsters or rack of lamb with minted broad beans; in winter, locally bagged game is the star, from partridge and woodcock to venison with bubble and squeak, braised red cabbage and parsley root. It's confident, full-blooded stuff, crowned by a stupendously whiffy Anglo-French cheese trolley. The sheer pressure of numbers occasionally wreaks havoc – although recent reports suggest the cooking is now sharper than ever and service has settled into a more dependable, kindly mode. The wine list oozes oenophile class,

with a particularly impressive range of half-bottles and 'stickies'; house selections from £19.50.
Chef/s: Chris Godfrey. **Open:** Tue to Sun L 12 to 2.30 (3.30 Sun), Tue to Sat D 6.30 to 9.30. **Closed:** Mon (exc bank hols), 25 to 28 Dec, first week Jan. **Meals:** alc (main courses £22 to £30). Set L and D Tue to Fri £18 (2 courses). **Details:** 70 seats. 60 seats outside. Separate bar. Music. Car parking. Children over 6 yrs only at D.

Chipping Norton
Wild Thyme
Sharply defined seasonal flavours
10 New Street, Chipping Norton, OX7 5LJ
Tel no: (01608) 645060
www.wildthymerestaurant.co.uk
Modern British | £35
Cooking score: 3

Nick and Sally Pullen's tidy little restaurant-with-rooms feels lived in, with its folksy coloured cushions, white-painted shabby-chic chairs and the odd chandelier adding a touch of class to the two brick-walled dining areas and covetable courtyard. Nick knows his region, chooses seasonal ingredients with care and can deliver some seriously good food with sharply defined flavours and flashes of Mediterranean sunshine. Star turns from recent visits have included his renowned twice-baked goats' cheese soufflé with baby beetroot and hazelnut gratin, crisply sautéed lamb's sweetbreads paired with minty crushed peas and Dijon mustard cream, and a 'sensational' plate of shaved Angus salt-beef fillet with tomato rosso purée, buffalo mozzarella, capers and rocket. Desserts also hit the target – from 'rhubarb, rhubarb, rhubarb' to a 'stunning' raspberry soufflé with milk chocolate ice cream. Locally sourced cheeses are worth a sniff and the commendable wine list starts at £15, with 11 offered by the glass.
Chef/s: Nicholas Pullen. **Open:** Tue to Sun L 12 to 2, Tue to Sat D 7 to 9. **Closed:** Mon. **Meals:** alc (main courses £14 to £22). Set L £18 (2 courses) to £23. Sun L £25 (2 courses) to £30. **Details:** 35 seats. 10 seats outside.

Filkins

★ TOP 50 PUB ★

The Five Alls

Confident, classy cooking in a Cotswolds inn
Filkins, GL7 3JQ
Tel no: (01367) 860875
www.thefiveallsfilkins.co.uk
Modern British | £30
Cooking score: 4

'Great hosts' Sebastian and Lana Snow, erstwhile escapees from the London restaurant scene, have hit the jackpot with the Five Alls, the Cotswolds country inn they took over in 2012. This artfully renovated spot, favoured by local celebs, is not your typical 'pint and a packet of crisps' boozer (though they'll gladly serve you a bag of Pipers and a pint of Brakspear), but nor is it a generic gastropub geared towards bulging wallets. The extensive menu covers everything from 'modern British to fusion' – from sashimi to steak and kidney – with a slight Italian accent, evidenced by antipasti platters, sea bream with salmoriglio, and Baileys ice cream 'affogato'. Proper pub grub isn't overlooked; Sunday roasts and fish and chips are favourites from the blackboard. Dogs are welcome; the locals are friendly; the fire's lit; and there's (usually) room to park. France and Italy are strengths on the global wine list, from £17.95.
Chef/s: Sebastian Snow and Piotr Skoczew. Open: all week L 12 to 2.30 (3 Fri to Sun), Mon to Sat D 6 to 10. Closed: 25 Dec. Meals: alc (main courses £14 to £23). Set L and D £16 (2 courses) to £21. Sun L £26. Details: 90 seats. 50 seats outside. Separate bar. Music. Car parking.

Fyfield

The White Hart

Historic hostelry in good hands
Main Road, Fyfield, OX13 5LW
Tel no: (01865) 390585
www.whitehart-fyfield.com
Modern British | £33
Cooking score: 3

'If we could eat here every day, we would,' enthused one regular of this historic 15th-century pub. The White Hart ticks every box, with beams, inglenooks and flag floors (even secret tunnels), and a kitchen garden, flower-filled patio and beer garden outside. There's good food to boot, with a menu that swings from pubby (though nonetheless appetising) predictability – chicken and duck liver parfait, fish and 'proper' chips, homemade ice cream – to dishes that elevate the pub to an 'unexpectedly good' place to eat. Try a starter of home-cured duck bresaola, blood oranges and duck leg rissole followed by monkfish wrapped in Parma ham, cockles, spinach and smoked potato croquettes. A gluten-free cherry and almond cake with plum ice cream and cherry essence would make a fitting finale, though the cheeseboard could well tempt too. Chilean Sauvignon Blanc or Merlot from the Maule Valley open the wine list at £17.50.
Chef/s: Mark Chandler. Open: Tue to Sun L 12 to 2.30 (3 Sun), Tue to Sat D 6.45 to 9.30. Closed: Mon (exc bank hols). Meals: alc (main courses £12 to £25). Set L £17 (2 courses) to £20. Sun L £23 (2 courses) to £26. Details: 60 seats. 40 seats outside. Separate bar. Music. Car parking.

Great Milton

★ TOP 50 ★

Le Manoir aux Quat'Saisons
Unashamed luxury and pure delight
Church Road, Great Milton, OX44 7PD
Tel no: (01844) 278881
www.manoir.com
Modern French | £115
Cooking score: 8

🍽 V

The Manoir has always had a finely developed
sense of its own appeal: 'Stepping-stone paths
[in the Japanese tea-garden] lead to a water-
basin where guests can clean their hands in
ritual ablution.' You won't get that in Hoxton.
Set amid kitchen gardens and lawns dotted
with sculptures, its soft-focus, all-round
loveliness, together with the abiding presence
of ever-genial Raymond Blanc, has kept the
venue popular for the fully 30 years it has now
clocked up. Monthly changing seasonal
menus are still the mainstay, where impeccable
ingredients find their apotheosis in
contemporary French compositions of
combined depth and subtlety. Beetroot terrine
and horseradish sorbet, spiced monkfish with
mussels in saffron-scented Gewürztraminer,
truffled venison loin with celeriac – all sprang
from the February Découverte seven-courser.
The style of dishes may be simpler these days,
as Gary Jones and Blanc have refined the
production, but dishes are still capable of
memorable impact: goats' cheese agnolotti
with artichoke and olives in tomato essence is a
winner, as is the fine Cornish sea bass with
langoustine and smoked butter mash in star
anise jus. Desserts include a daring take on
millionaire's shortbread, complete with
buttery ice cream. Reporters have been
known to query the slight air of detached
indifference with which they are approached,
or conversely a strangely hurried pace, as
though staff were hoping not to miss the last
bus back to Oxford. The gargantuan wine list
is one of the highly prized, and highly priced,
treasures of the Manoir, tickets beginning
somewhere in the region of £45.

Chef/s: Raymond Blanc and Gary Jones. **Open:** all
week L 11.45 to 2.15, D 6.45 to 9.15. **Meals:** alc
(main courses £48 to £54). Set L £79 (5 courses) to
£124 (7 courses). Set D £134 (5 courses) to £154 (7
courses). **Details:** 100 seats. Separate bar.
Wheelchair access. Car parking.

Henley-on-Thames

NEW ENTRY
Shaun Dickens at the Boathouse
Riverside dining now restored to terra firma
Station Road, Henley-on-Thames, RG9 1AZ
Tel no: (01491) 577937
www.shaundickens.co.uk
Modern British | £42
Cooking score: 2

£5 OFF V

Shaun Dickens' smart riverside restaurant is
most definitely in the boathouse. Although
arrivals in early 2014 found themselves
accommodated on a boat following the big
winter flood, dining is now restored to terra
firma. The views of the Thames are just as
lovely, whether from inside or from the
decked terrace. The menu of good-looking,
contemporary dishes might start with tuna
sashimi speckled with peanut crumbs and
pickled ginger, or pig terrine with gribiche
and braised snails. Main courses evince careful
attention to detail, as when monkfish turns up
with shredded braised fennel, hazelnuts and
segments of blood orange, or pork belly with
squid, spiked with pickled jalapeño, black basil
and caramelised onion. Desserts walk a fine
line between sophistication and outright
indulgence for peanut butter and jelly with
Graham cracker, raspberry sorbet and peanut
tuile, or deconstructed Bakewell tart with
almond ice cream and a gummy milk crisp.
Wines from £18.
Chef/s: Shaun Dickens. **Open:** Tue to Sun L 12 to 3
(3.30 Sun), Tue to Sat D 6.30 to 10. **Closed:** Mon, 24
to 26 Dec, 1 to 14 Jan. **Meals:** alc (main courses £19
to £24). Set L £22 (2 courses) to £25. **Details:** 45
seats. 30 seats outside. Separate bar. Wheelchair
access. Music.

EMILY WATKINS
The Kingham Plough

What do you enjoy about being a chef?
I love transforming raw ingredients into dishes, seeing and hearing the customers enjoying the food and the adrenaline of a busy service.

What's your newest ingredient discovery?
Chervil root, both in flavour and texture - a brilliant ingredient in both sweet and savoury dishes.

At the end of a long day, what do you like to cook?
Anything with my children - they love getting involved, too, especially making pizza.

Is there any dish that evokes strong memories for you?
The Sunday Roast - a hugely important meal that we always had growing up - probably the only meal of the week the whole family was there for. A tradition I keep with my family.

Do you have a guilty foodie pleasure?
Asian noodles - pure comfort food, the spicier the better.

Kingham

★ TOP 50 PUB ★

The Kingham Plough
A townie's rural dream
The Green, Kingham, OX7 6YD
Tel no: (01608) 658327
www.thekinghamplough.co.uk
Modern British | £32
Cooking score: 4

£5 OFF

This rambling golden-stoned hostelry feels both modern and venerable, the décor fresh, the original features lending a rustic burr – think pale walls, food-themed paintings, brick and sea grass floors, exposed beams, wood floors, and exposed brickwork. While the Kingham Plough still has the look and feel of a pub, food is at the heart of the operation, and the kitchen is crazy about sous-vide cooking – a slow and gentle technique that seals in flavour. It means the ingredients, particularly the meat, arrive warm, not hot, and retain a raw, fresh look. The technique shines in fish dishes such as a 'fresh and full-flavoured' lemon sole teamed with brown shrimps, potted shrimp butter and potted shrimp powder, as well as Jersey Royals and asparagus. While traditional recipes are a focus, there are touches of invention, too, as in a very simple and pretty starter of 'crab trifle' – dressed Cornish crab on wild garlic 'custard', with tomatoes and toasted tomato bread – or a dessert of hot chocolate-filled doughnuts with Crunchy Nut cornflake ice cream. Worth noting, too, are 'fantastic' bar snacks, particularly the cod cheeks and mini scotch eggs, and excellent bread. A decent list of international wines starts at £20.
Chef/s: Emily Watkins and Ben Dulley. **Open:** all week L 12 to 2 (3 Sat and Sun), Mon to Sat D 6 to 9. **Closed:** 25 Dec. **Meals:** alc (main courses £14 to £22). **Details:** 70 seats. 25 seats outside. Separate bar. Car parking.

NEW ENTRY
The Wild Rabbit
Classy pub food in stunning surroundings
Church Street, Kingham, OX7 6YA
Tel no: (01608) 658389
www.thewildrabbit.co.uk
British | £35
Cooking score: 3

This likeable Cotswolds offspring of Carole
Bamford's Daylesford Organic, dubbed 'the
poshest pub in Britain' by the *Daily Mail*,
draws the same tweedy toffs and Notting Hill
weekenders. It certainly walks the walk. The
interior is a dream − pale stone floors,
minimalist fireplaces and acres of wood and
exposed stonework − with the old building
segueing into a vast dining area, its gleaming
open kitchen juxtaposed, giving more than a
hint of a medieval dining hall. Posh and
peasant go hand in hand here: warm
sourdough may arrive on a trencher, but a
starter of mackerel ceviche with citrus
dressing, marinated fennel and a scattering of
pansies is pure class. The eclectic influences
continue with a main course of pollack with
crab and scallop cannelloni and langoustine
sauce, while steaks from the Josper grill come
with 'sensational' chips. To finish, sticky toffee
pudding is 'sheer perfection'. A short
international wine list opens at £24.
Chef/s: Adam Caisley. **Open:** Tue to Sun L 12 to 2.30
(3 Sun). Tue to Sat D 7 to 9. **Closed:** Mon. **Meals:** alc
(main courses £14 to £26). **Details:** 50 seats.
Separate bar. Car parking.

▌Kingston Bagpuize
NEW ENTRY
Fallowfields
Top-notch home-grown delights
Faringdon Road, Kingston Bagpuize, OX13 5BH
Tel no: (01865) 820416
www.fallowfields.com
Modern British | £55
Cooking score: 6

Country house hotels and Matt Weedon are a
perfect match. The former Glenapp Castle
chef (see entry, Scotland) is working the same
magic at this Oxfordshire beauty. The interior
is classically elegant yet feels fresh and light,
particularly in the restaurant with its
conservatory views of croquet lawns and
fields. Fallowfields produces much of its own
food and the menu shows gleeful engagement
with its farm and garden, from the 'kitchen
garden' amuse − a gardener's box containing,
in plant pots, pig's head croquettes, fat radishes
with lovage yoghurt, mini cornets of
artichoke and pear ice cream − to a ravioli of
Fallowfields egg and truffled potato with wild
mushrooms, char-grilled artichoke and
Parmesan. Classically inspired mains such as
pan-fried turbot with langoustine, fennel,
grilled artichoke and a langoustine and vanilla
sauce trumpet freshness and quality. For
dessert, blackcurrant soufflé and sorbet with
lemon meringue pie is powerfully fruity and
perfectly executed. A nicely annotated wine
list starts at £20.
Chef/s: Matt Weedon. **Open:** all week L 12 to 2.30, D
7 to 9.30 (9 Sun). **Meals:** alc (main courses £28 to
35). Set L £25 (2 courses) to £30. Sun L £30. Tasting
menu £65. **Details:** 30 seats. 20 seats outside.
Separate bar. Wheelchair access. Music. Car
parking.

▌Kirtlington

LOCAL GEM
▲ The Oxford Arms
Troy Lane, Kirtlington, OX5 3HA
Tel no: (01869) 350208
www.oxford-arms.co.uk
Modern British | £28 £5 OFF

A good showing of locals dining on a showery Tuesday lunchtime emphasises the popularity of this 19th-century village hostelry. It's an unpretentious, two-bar operation with real ale, stone walls, mismatched furniture and a brief menu of modern pub classics boosted by daily specials. The kitchen works well within its capabilities, judging from a test meal of light-as-mousse broccoli, leek and Binham Blue quiche; crisp-topped pork belly with Puy lentils and black pudding; and irresistible warm plum and almond tart with vanilla ice cream. Decent wines from £17.50. No food Sun D.

▌Murcott

★ TOP 50 PUB ★

The Nut Tree Inn
Pubby vitality and cooking with conviction
Main Street, Murcott, OX5 2RE
Tel no: (01865) 331253
www.nuttreeinn.co.uk
Modern European | £40
Cooking score: 5

£5 OFF V

A village pond, a whitewashed, thatched pub full of old beams and unforced charm – it's what most people hope to stumble across in the countryside. The Nut Tree Inn is just that: upbeat and modishly rustic in a 21st-century fashion, where a jaunty, smiling welcome greets newcomers, regulars and locals alike. Using local ingredients where possible, including own-grown vegetables and meat from his own pigs, Mike North injects vivid flavours and some bold combinations into his fiercely seasonally cooking. The quality is undeniably good, from excellent home-baked

breads via a 'superb' parfait of chicken livers with caramelised chutney to a 'perfectly cooked' rare fillet of aged Charolais beef. The bright, user-friendly repertoire also embraces plates of roast saddle and faggot of Oxford Down lamb, or cod with hispy cabbage, lardons and white wine sauce, while desserts promise the like of hot passion fruit soufflé. Well-considered wines start at £16.
Chef/s: Michael and Mary North. Open: Tue to Sun L 12 to 2.30 (3 Sun), Tue to Sat D 7 to 9. Closed: Mon, 27 Dec to 3 Jan. Meals: alc (main courses £17 to £30). Set L and D £18 (2 courses). Tasting menu £55 (7 courses). Details: 70 seats. 40 seats outside. Separate bar. Music. Car parking.

▌Oxford

Branca
Gregarious all-day Italian
111 Walton Street, Oxford, OX2 6AJ
Tel no: (01865) 556111
www.branca.co.uk
Italian | £23
Cooking score: 1

£5 OFF £30

'Everyone seems to have discovered cicchetti,' mused one reader as he tucked into the likes of tuna crostini. Those Venetian nibbles are very much at home at Branca, though: an Italian joint that positively hums with *bonomia*. There's an easy-going attitude all round, popular with students and anyone who fancies a stone-baked pizza or a table in the terrace garden. Main-course plates run to pink duck breast with crispy gnocchi and curly kale, and desserts don't stray very far from the classical comfort of rich chocolate torta. With its deli next door, Branca is an enterprising outfit. Wines start at £16.45.
Chef/s: E Blanders. Open: all week 10am to 11pm. Meals: alc (main courses £11 to £21). Set L and D £13. Sun L £13. Details: 110 seats. 75 seats outside. Separate bar. Wheelchair access. Music.

Cherwell Boathouse

Idyllic riverside favourite
50 Bardwell Road, Oxford, OX2 6ST
Tel no: (01865) 552746
www.cherwellboathouse.co.uk
Modern British | £32
Cooking score: 2

£5 OFF ♠ V

The tranquil location on the River Cherwell (handy for punting) has always been a major selling point for the Boathouse – backed up by the pristine look of the place and a killer wine list. Owned by Anthony Verdin since the 1960s, the venue has moved with the times as sedately as those punts bobbing outside. Nick Welford navigates the kitchen through its seasonal progress, and makes a confident fist of dishes such as crab and smoked salmon tian dressed in caviar; crisp-skinned cod in clam and potato chowder with blanched spring greens; and rump of lamb with aubergine caviar and baby courgettes in sauce vierge. Dessert might be plum fool with Champagne jelly, or Sussex pond pudding and custard. The now-legendary wine list is arranged by grape variety, and contains some of the world's greatest growers – Ostertag, Prüm, Ogier, Au Bon Climat, Vega Sicilia – at prices that often come as a pleasant surprise. Bottles begin at £14.75, standard glasses £4.50, for Languedoc house wines.
Chef/s: Nick Welford. **Open:** all week L 12 to 2 (2.30 Sat and Sun), D 6 to 9.30. **Closed:** 24 to 30 Dec. **Meals:** alc (main courses £17 to £24). Set L £14 (2 courses) to £18. Set D £22 (2 courses) to £27. Sun L £27. **Details:** 65 seats. 45 seats outside. Separate bar. Wheelchair access. Car parking.

Symbols

☞ Accommodation is available

£30 Three courses for less than £30

V Separate vegetarian menu

£5 OFF £5-off voucher scheme

♠ Notable wine list

Gee's

Oxford landmark with a flavour of the Med
61 Banbury Road, Oxford, OX2 6PE
Tel no: (01865) 553540
www.gees-restaurant.co.uk
Modern European | £28
Cooking score: 2

£30

Oxford is hardly short of venerable institutions, but it has another in Gee's, which has been feeding the city for over 30 years. The restaurant underwent a refurb in 2013 resulting in even more street cred, with a rustic-chic contemporary finish, but you don't go messing with a Grade II-listed glasshouse, and they haven't. These days a wood-fired oven and charcoal grill are the centrepieces of the kitchen and have helped bring a Mediterranean flavour to the menu. But you'll still find plenty of regional produce here. From the grill there might be prime rib chops with creamed spinach, while the wood oven works its magic on guinea fowl and wood pigeon. Pizzetta of speck and rocket pesto, Jersey crab on toast, Ibérico pork collar with pears and turnips – Gee's menu is packed with pan-European flavours, which also goes for desserts like croissant and chocolate pudding, or blood-orange tart. Wines from £18.
Chef/s: Richard Allen. **Open:** all week 12 to 10.30. **Closed:** 25 and 26 Dec. **Meals:** alc (main courses £10 to £18). Set L £13 (2 courses) to £17. **Details:** 80 seats. 35 seats outside. Separate bar. Wheelchair access. Music.

The Magdalen Arms

Med flavours, metropolitan assurance
243 Iffley Road, Oxford, OX4 1SJ
Tel no: (01865) 243159
www.magdalenarms.com
Modern European | £30
Cooking score: 2

Enter the Magdalen Arms' substantial Victorian premises and you might fancy yourself in a London food pub – such is its air of metropolitan assurance. But here, the cliché-free menu and keen pricing break the mould. Yes, there's mismatched furniture, bare boards (in front bar and rear restaurant), dark hues and an open-to-view kitchen – plus enticing real ales – but the menu changes twice daily and positively throbs with allure. Big earthy Mediterranean flavours shine forth in the likes of globe artichoke stuffed with goats' cheese and chewy olive 'crumbs', fennel-packed fish stew replete with flaky pollack and tender mussels, and a moist lemon polenta cake. Resolute meat eaters might precede pappardelle and venison ragù with brawn vinaigrette. With a few adjustments – less oven time for the artichoke; some lemony zest in the fish stew; shorter pauses between courses – this kitchen could trounce the local opposition. The wine list, too, is appealingly priced (from £15.40).

Chef/s: Tony Abarno. **Open:** Tue to Sun L 12 to 2.30 (3 Sun), all week D 6 to 10 (9.30 Sun). **Meals:** alc (main courses £11 to £28). **Details:** 100 seats. 80 seats outside. Separate bar. Wheelchair access. Music.

My Sichuan
Lip-numbing Szechuan adventure
The Old School, Gloucester Green, Oxford, OX1 2DA
Tel no: (01865) 236899
www.mysichuan.co.uk
Chinese | £20
Cooking score: 3
£30

No-holds-barred Szechuan cuisine is the sweat-inducing deal at this dramatic restaurant housed in a capacious Victorian schoolhouse near Oxford coach station. Lofty ceilings and a striking stained-glass dome add some gravitas to the space, while shiny mahogany furniture, Chinese-themed art and a curved bar are par for the course in the sprawling dining room. Pig's trotters, kidneys, tripe, ducks' tongues and other anatomical curiosities abound on the garishly illustrated menu, which parades its wares in all their lip-numbing, chilli-spiked glory: homemade spicy jelly tofu; sea snails with Szechuan

pepper; wok-grilled pig's intestines; fish slices 'lavishly' dressed with chilli oil . . . and more besides. At lunchtime, bowls of noodles and esoteric Szechuan dim sum are the main events (think 'drunken master' soup or crispy glutinous rice cakes with brown-sugar sauce). Our questionnaire was not returned, so check the restaurant's website for more details.
Chef/s: Jian Ju Zhou. **Open:** all week 12 to 11. **Closed:** 25 Dec. **Meals:** alc (main courses £7 to £19)

The Rickety Press
Reborn Jericho boozer
67 Cranham Street, Oxford, OX2 6DE
Tel no: (01865) 424581
www.thericketypress.com
Modern British | £26
Cooking score: 1
£5 OFF £30

Done up and dressed down, this old boozer was given a new name and a new lease of life some years ago, but continues to strike a good balance between its restaurant and pub personalities. A pint at the bar is still in order, though the conservatory restaurant is the big draw for a bit of refinement. Start with foie gras and chicken liver parfait, say, followed by wing of skate with spiced cucumber and shrimp butter, or a burger from the grill. Wines start at £18. Open all week.
Chef/s: Andrew Holland. **Open:** all week L 12 to 2.30 (3 Sun), D 6.30 to 9.30 (10 Fri and Sat). **Closed:** 25 and 26 Dec. **Meals:** alc (main courses £11 to £21). Set L and D £13 (2 courses) to £15. **Details:** 75 seats. Wheelchair access. Music.

LOCAL GEM
▲ Edamamé
15 Holywell Street, Oxford, OX1 3SA
Tel no: (01865) 246916
www.edamame.co.uk
Japanese | £16

A dinky eatery with a ring of authenticity and limited opening hours, Edamamé packs them in for tantalising Japanese food. The lunchtime deal is one-plate dishes such as pork shoyu ramen or chicken katsu, with first-rate sushi saved for Thursday evenings (super-fresh nigiri of freshwater shrimp, maybe). On Friday and Saturday evenings there are tapas-style sharing plates of squid in soy and ginger and deep-fried pork cutlet. There's take-away, too, and wines from £13. Open Wed to Sun L, Thur to Sat D.

▲ Sojo

6-9 Hythe Bridge Street, Oxford, OX1 2EW
Tel no: (01865) 202888
www.sojooxford.co.uk
Chinese | £25

Since launching in 2004, this unassuming little restaurant has carved out quite a niche for itself as a purveyor of authentic regional Chinese cuisine, rather than generic high-street fodder. Come here for Szechuan 'mouth-watery' chicken on the bone, Shanghai dong-po pork ('with a strip of fat'), oyster omelette, beef in 'godmother's chilli sauce' or foil-wrapped salt-baked mandarin prawns. There's also a popular dim sum menu (served until 5pm). Wines start at £18, but it's also worth investigating the saké list. Open all week.

▲ Turl Street Kitchen

16-17 Turl Street, Oxford, OX1 3DH
Tel no: (01865) 264171
www.turlstreetkitchen.co.uk
Modern British | £25 £5 OFF

Profits from this admirable neighbourhood eatery-with-rooms help to power the Oxford Hub charity situated in the same building, and Turl Street Kitchen also nails its colours to the mast when it comes to eco-friendly sourcing. 'Fresh, local, seasonal' trumpets the competitively priced menu, which changes every session as supplies come and go. A plate of beetroot, apple, radish and parsley dressed with Chiltern rapeseed oil might precede Spanish-style braised chicken with lentils, rocket and aïoli or lamb belly with black pudding and barley hotpot, while pud could be hazelnut Bakewell tart. Beers, ciders and wines (from £15.50) also follow the green code. Open all week.

▮ Shiplake

Orwells

Menus sparkling with culinary fireworks
Shiplake Row, Shiplake, RG9 4DP
Tel no: (01189) 403673
www.orwellsatshiplake.co.uk
Modern British | £40
Cooking score: 6

A beacon of quality since opening in 2010, Orwells has gained a reputation spreading far beyond its locale. The venue fits the rural location to a T, with a white-painted pub frontage and a simple dining room decorated in an effortlessly understated way. And in Ryan Simpson and Liam Trotman it has chef/proprietors delivering cooking that is current enough to stop passers-by in their tracks yet familiar enough to keep its loyal regulars (who name-check pub classics like mussels, and muntjac burger). An impressive range of calendar-correct materials and treatments make appearances, from cauliflower pannacotta with peanut and pickled mushrooms or a vibrant smoked eel and foie gras with tamarind, apple, barley and marinated mushrooms, to lamb rump with asparagus, chickpea, aubergine and tomato. Lunchtime tapas are a brilliant introduction – Wagyu beef salad, say, or crab fritters, and foie gras with liquorice, lentils and rhubarb – while a stash of modern wines (from £21) includes some classy organic and biodynamic choices and plenty by the glass.

Chef/s: Ryan Simpson and Liam Trotman. **Open:** Wed to Sun L 11.30 to 3 (3.30 Sun), Wed to Sat D 6.30 to 9 (9.30 Fri and Sat). **Closed:** Mon, Tue, first 2 weeks Jan, 1 week summer, first 2 weeks Sept. **Meals:** alc (main courses £13 to £26). Sun L £25 (2 courses) to £30. **Details:** 50 seats. 40 seats outside. Separate bar. Wheelchair access. Music. Car parking.

Sparsholt

★ TOP 50 PUB ★

The Star Inn
Gentrified boozer with smart cooking
Watery Lane, Sparsholt, OX12 9PL
Tel no: (01235) 751873
www.thestarsparsholt.co.uk
Modern British | £32
Cooking score: 4

'Beautifully styled', urbane interiors straight out of *Country Living* magazine have given this scrubbed-up village boozer a lift – although the real talking point is the food. Dave Watts has worked in some big-name kitchens (including Le Manoir aux Quat'Saisons, see entry) and his cooking has real zip, as well as an eye for detail. Standbys such as ham hock with piccalilli or T-bone steak with triple-cooked chips are well above the pub norm, but the menu also touts 'sublime', exquisitely presented dishes with a striking contemporary accent. Sample, perhaps, the crispy pig's head with salted cod, chorizo and red pepper dressing or Cornish day-boat brill accompanied by roasted salsify, millet, purple sprouting broccoli and buttermilk cream. For afters, don't miss the spectacular carrot cake with lime cream cheese: sophisticated comfort for Oxfordshire palates weaned on big-city food. Trendy snacks and real ales are available at the bar, and wine starts at £17.
Chef/s: Dave Watts. **Open:** Tue to Sun L 12 to 2 (2.30 Fri and Sat, 3.30 Sun), Tue to Sat D 6.30 to 9 (9.30 Fri and Sat). **Closed:** Mon, 2 weeks Jan. **Meals:** alc (main courses £9 to £27). Set L and D £17 (2 courses) to £20. **Details:** 45 seats. 20 seats outside. Separate bar. Wheelchair access. Music. Car parking.

Stoke Row

LOCAL GEM
▲ The Crooked Billet
Newlands Lane, Stoke Row, RG9 5PU
Tel no: (01491) 681048
www.thecrookedbillet.co.uk
Modern European | £32

'What a splendid place!' exclaimed one reader of this quirky gem, a lopsided, beamed and flagged rural inn and a screen star in its own right (*Patriot Games* and *Land Girls* being among its credits). 'A magical atmosphere and the most enthusiastic staff' are other reasons why crowds flock to order from a menu embracing everything from haggis on toast with fried egg and HP gravy, to roast pheasant, chestnuts, greens, smoked bacon and braised lentils. Wines from £22. Open all week.

Stonor
The Quince Tree
Country boozer turned foodie enclave
Stonor, RG9 6HE
Tel no: (01491) 639039
www.thequincetree.com
Modern British | £30
new chef/no score

The Quince Tree is quite a set-up these days: the original 17th-century coaching inn still does duty as a local boozer, with a jazzy dining room attached, while a modern glass extension houses a well-stocked farm shop and an all-day café dealing in breakfast, brunch, etc. With the departure of chef Peter Eaton, and no replacement as we went to press, changes may be in the pipeline. But in the past the pub has offered artisan deli boards and sandwiches at lunchtime, while dinner brings char-grilled Oxfordshire steaks, a few extra flounces, and rounds off proceedings with a 'card' of serious desserts. To drink, there are local ales on tap, plus a creditable assortment of wines from £16.

Open: all week L 12 to 2.45 (3 Sat and Sun), D 6.30 to 9. **Meals:** alc (main courses £12 to £26). Set D £14 (2 courses) to £18. Sun L £16. **Details:** 70 seats. 80 seats outside. Separate bar. Wheelchair access. Music. Car parking.

▌Swinbrook
The Swan Inn
Idyllic village pub
Swinbrook, OX18 4DY
Tel no: (01993) 823339
www.theswanswinbrook.co.uk
Modern British | £29
Cooking score: 2
🛏 £30

Ever so gently restored, this listed 16th-century inn alongside the River Windrush operates in a heritage setting of flagstones, settles, weathered timbers and log fires. It made the headlines in January 2014 when the Prime Minister lunched here with the President of France. Otherwise, there's little to disturb the gentrified rural peace in the bar or dining room, where honestly crafted food keeps customers well satisfied. The owner's uncle rears Aberdeen Angus cattle, fish comes up from the West Country, and the kitchen uses the local network for other seasonal supplies: from smoked meats to venison. Plates of home-cured bresaola, mixed antipasti or goats' cheese salad start things off invitingly, ahead of generous mains such as grilled bavette with skinny chips, saffron risotto with sun-blush tomatoes, or grilled whole plaice with green beans, shrimps, dill and lemon butter. Hook Norton ales bring smiles, and there are plenty of reasonably priced wines from £18.50.
Chef/s: Matthew Laughton. **Open:** all week L 12 to 2 (2.30 Sat, 3 Sun), D 7 to 9 (6.30 to 9.30 Fri and Sat, 8.30 Sun). **Meals:** alc (main courses £14 to £18). **Details:** 70 seats. 100 seats outside. Separate bar. Wheelchair access. Music. Car parking.

▌Toot Baldon
The Mole Inn
Pubby vibes and eclectic food
Toot Baldon, OX44 9NG
Tel no: (01865) 340001
www.themoleinn.com
Modern British | £30
Cooking score: 2
£5
OFF

'Clocking Pierre Koffmann at the next table should be a sign that you're about to eat well,' observed one eagle-eyed reporter who stumbled upon the Mole Inn. This reinvented 300-year-old village pub comes complete with inglenooks, winding corridors, scuffed stonework and a conservatory-style extension. Landlord/chef Gary Witchalls has an impressive CV, and his know-how shows in a menu that reflects thoughtful sourcing and an eye for value (all first courses come as starters or mains). It's an eclectic mix, pitched just right for the kitchen's ambitions – think shredded duck and beanshoot salad or smoked haddock and potato chowder with sweetcorn and curry oil, and then a generous fish mixed grill with potent lime and garlic mayo, or rosemary-crusted pork tenderloin and belly with mash, apple and onion soubise. Dry-aged Aberdeenshire steaks also figure, while desserts have yielded a properly gooey treacle tart with Carnation milk ice cream. International wines from £18.50.
Chef/s: Gary Witchalls. **Open:** all week L 12 to 2.30 (4 Sun), 7 to 9.30 (6.30 Fri and Sat, 6 to 9 Sun). **Closed:** 25 Dec. **Meals:** alc (main courses £13 to £19). Set L and D £20 (2 courses) to £25. Sun L £15. **Details:** 70 seats. 50 seats outside. Wheelchair access. Music. Car parking.

Wolvercote

NEW ENTRY
Jacob's Inn
Reinvented pub with rural-foodie appeal
130 Godstow Road, Wolvercote, OX2 8PG
Tel no: (01865) 514333
www.jacobs-inn.com
British | £24
Cooking score: 1
£30

A lot of work has gone in to reinventing the old Red Lion as a 'smart-meets-ramshackle' amalgam of oak floors, polished tables, scuffed bare brick, stone hearth and old advertising memorabilia. With pigs and chickens in the garden and a virtual farm shop, the owners are pushing the rural-foodie theme very hard. It's a modern refit that fills you with confidence, something the broad but compact menu does nothing to undermine. You can pick up steak and ale pie, Lancashire hotpot, a house burger or steak and chips, alongside veal schnitzel and scallop and monkfish skewers. House wine is £16.50.
Chef/s: Richard Burkert. **Open:** all week 9am to 10pm. **Closed:** 25 Dec. **Meals:** alc (main courses £9 to £22). **Details:** 140 seats. 60 seats outside. Separate bar. Wheelchair access. Music. Car parking.

Wootton

NEW ENTRY
The Killingworth Castle
Seductive cooking in a reborn inn
Glympton Road, Wootton, OX20 1EJ
Tel no: (01993) 811401
www.thekillingworthcastle.com
British | £28
Cooking score: 3
🛏 £30

Standing guard at the edge of a fetching little village, Wootton's 17th-century coaching inn was rescued from dereliction in 2012 by the couple behind Gloucestershire's Ebrington Arms (see entry). It features a welcoming stone-walled bar, a preponderance of scrubbed wooden benches and a succession of cosy, woody rooms where uncommonly fine food is served by clued-up staff. Order local real ale and peruse the seductive menu of Euro-accented British cooking. The kitchen needs a full skill set to produce the likes of 'excellent' cheesy smoked haddock soufflé with wilted spinach and crab bisque, followed by pink, juicy roast rump and confit shoulder of lamb, with bouncy (unadvertised) sweetbreads and anchovy boulangère potatoes – but head chef Phil Currie's team rarely slips. Finish with intense, expertly balanced chocolate and salted-caramel tart with hazelnut praline cream. Comfortably off locals create a warm buzz through the place, many of them sampling the extensive wine list (from £16.50).
Chef/s: Phil Currie and Andrew Lipp. **Open:** all week L 12 to 2.30 (3.30 Sun), D 6 to 9 (9.30 Fri and Sat, 8.30 Sun). **Meals:** alc (main courses £11 to £25). **Details:** 65 seats. 30 seats outside. Separate bar. Car parking.

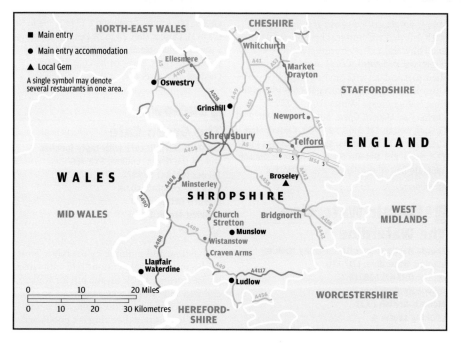

- ■ Main entry
- ● Main entry accommodation
- ▲ Local Gem

A single symbol may denote several restaurants in one area.

NORTH-EAST WALES

CHESHIRE

Whitchurch

Ellesmere

Market Drayton

Oswestry

STAFFORDSHIRE

Grinshill

Newport

Shrewsbury

Telford

ENGLAND

WALES

Broseley ▲

Minsterley

SHROPSHIRE

WEST MIDLANDS

MID WALES

Church Stretton

Bridgnorth

Munslow

Wistanstow

Craven Arms

Llanfair Waterdine

Ludlow

WORCESTERSHIRE

0   10   20 Miles
0 10 20 30 Kilometres

HEREFORD-SHIRE

■ Broseley

LOCAL GEM
▲ The King and Thai

The Forester Arms, Avenue Road, Broseley,
TF12 5DL
Tel no: (01952) 882004
www.thekingandthai.co.uk
Thai | £25

The old Forester Arms has been transformed.
It now houses Suree Coates' Thai restaurant
and comes with a classy interior that oozes
aspiration. Sourcing is as local as possible, with
local butcher's meat, game, free-range chicken
and eggs appearing on a short, easy to navigate
menu. Dishes are well prepared and fans
recommend the chicken green curry with
jasmine rice, 'weeping tiger', a 28–day aged
Shropshire beef fillet with a spicy chilli sauce,
and the excellent prawn fried rice. Wines from
£14.95. Closed Sun and Mon.

■ Grinshill

The Inn at Grinshill

Country inn with accomplished cooking
Grinshill, SY4 3BL
Tel no: (01939) 220410
www.theinnatgrinshill.co.uk
British | £30
Cooking score: 3

The old Georgian inn in a lush green valley has
been spruced up and kitted out for our times,
undergoing a makeover that hasn't sullied the
Grade II–listed charm of the place. It's still an
inn, albeit a food-focused one, with bedrooms
that have avoided the excesses of
boutiquification. When it comes to dining,
there are different spaces for different moods,
including linen-clad tables at the posher end
of the spectrum. The kitchen delivers a feel-
good output that presents itself very well
without showboating. A first-course dish of
mackerel with celeriac rémoulade comes
dressed in a mustard emulsion, while a main-

course whole grilled plaice arrives topped with café de Paris butter. There are steaks, fish and chips and a classy burger, too, served with triple-cooked chips. Local ingredients play their part and desserts can be as exotic as white chocolate and passion fruit gâteau with Kaffir lime leaf ice cream. Wines from £17.95.
Chef/s: Paul Maders. **Open:** Wed to Sun L 12 to 2.30 (3 Sun), Wed to Sat D 6.30 to 9.30. **Closed:** Mon, Tue, 2 Jan to 13 Jan. **Meals:** alc (main courses £12 to £22). Sun L £18. **Details:** 80 seats. 30 seats outside. Separate bar. Wheelchair access. Music. Car parking.

▌ Llanfair Waterdine
The Waterdine
Foodie destination with unflashy cooking
Llanfair Waterdine, LD7 1TU
Tel no: (01547) 528214
www.waterdine.com
Modern British | £33
Cooking score: 4
🛏

'We found this a lovely place to unwind,' remarked visitors to Ken and Isabel Adams' 16th-century long house found in a remote village on the Shropshire side of the Welsh border. With its rustic, old-fashioned look of rough stone walls, stone slabs and bare boards, the former drover's inn still feels like a village pub, but nowadays this agreeable country restaurant-with-rooms is known for its food. Much is made of fresh local ingredients, including own-grown herbs, vegetables and fruits, but inspiration for dishes comes from wider-spread roots, perhaps resulting in tomato, olive and feta tart or venison with vegetable pot-au-feu. When Sunday lunch includes slow-roasted pork belly in orange and Chinese spices on garlic and apple mash with glazed carrots, black pudding and mushroom spring roll – and dessert might be Wrekin Blue cheese with Eccles cake and pickled beetroot – it's clear that cooking is taken seriously. Wines from £18.50.

Chef/s: Ken Adams. **Open:** Sun L 12 to 3, Tue to Sat D 7 to 11. **Closed:** Mon, 24 to 26 Dec, 1 week spring, 1 week autumn. **Meals:** Set D £33. Sun L £23. **Details:** 20 seats. Separate bar. Car parking. Children over 8 yrs only at D.

▌ Ludlow
The Green Café
Lovely watermill café with tasty lunches
Mill on the Green, Ludlow, SY8 1EG
Tel no: (01584) 879872
www.thegreencafe.co.uk
Modern British | £19
Cooking score: 1
£30

A one-time mill building by the River Teme has become an 'unpretentious' café with tables by the water's edge. It fits the bill for walkers, children and canines who might not be so welcome elsewhere in the town, and is only open at lunchtimes (booking is a good idea). The service team 'clearly enjoy what they do' and the short menu is seasonal and cooked with care. Chicken liver pâté with fig chutney, squid and scallop risotto, and braised Barbary duck leg provide further reasons to visit. To drink, bottled beers and ciders are alternatives to the short wine list (starting at £17.50).
Chef/s: Clive Davis. **Open:** Tue to Sun L only 12 to 2.30. **Closed:** Mon, 24 Dec to 13 Feb. **Meals:** alc (main courses £7 to £12). **Details:** 30 seats. 25 seats outside. Wheelchair access.

Mr Underhill's
Bewitching waterside hideaway
Dinham Weir, Ludlow, SY8 1EH
Tel no: (01584) 874431
www.mr-underhills.co.uk
Modern British | £70
Cooking score: 6
🍾 🛏 V

Long before its ascent to gastronomic stardom, humble Ludlow was a twinkle in Mr Underhill's eye, the Bradleys' magically sited restaurant-with-rooms having been in operation since 1981. At the foot of the castle ramparts, within earshot of the rushing River Teme, yet minutes from the market square, it's in a lovely spot. What's more, the formula of a customised multi-course taster menu combining long-standing dishes and new, has been consistently successful over the years. Chris Bradley's carefully considered dishes take in the likes of white fish velouté with marmalade ice, crumbed hake with tomato and chorizo in sherry vinegar cream, and roast rack and braised shoulder of local lamb, spiced with ras-el-hanout and served with potato terrine and smoked aubergine. The ice cream cone variations (lemon meringue, apple crumble) are fun too. Tales of a frostier tone out front these days are worrying, but easily addressed. Wines are a labour of love, the selections chosen with discernment and described with unpretentious gusto. Prices open at £24 (glasses £6.50).

Chef/s: Chris Bradley. **Open:** Wed to Sun D only 7.30 to 8.15 (1 sitting). **Closed:** Mon, Tue, 25 to 31 Dec, 1 Jan, 2 weeks Jun, 1 week Oct. **Meals:** Set D £70 (9 courses). **Details:** 24 seats. 24 seats outside. Children over 6 yrs only.

Munslow
The Crown Country Inn
Quirky old inn with ambitions
Corvedale Road, Munslow, SY7 9ET
Tel no: (01584) 841205
www.crowncountryinn.co.uk
Modern British | £30
Cooking score: 1

A quirky mix of pub, restaurant and 'hideaway rooms' in an isolated village, this family-run inn was once a 'hundred house' presided over by the infamous Judge Jeffreys. There's much talk of ghosts in its atmospheric (some say 'gloomy') bar. Eat here or in the upstairs restaurant from a menu that tries hard to impress. Readers have praised Shropshire Blue cheese dumplings with walnut and apple salad, roast butternut squash risotto, and a hearty combo of pork belly, wild mushroom dauphinois and buttered leeks. To close, try

crème brûlée with hot fried churros. The beers are good, and wines (some creditable) start at £15.75.

Chef/s: Richard Arnold. **Open:** Tue to Sun L 12 to 2, Tue to Sat D 6.30 to 8.45. **Closed:** Mon, 25 to 28 Dec, 1 to 7 Jan. **Meals:** alc (main courses £15 to £20). Sun L £20. **Details:** 60 seats. 20 seats outside. Separate bar. Music. Car parking. No children under 12 yrs Fri and Sat D.

Oswestry
Sebastians
A petit slice of France
45 Willow Street, Oswestry, SY11 1AQ
Tel no: (01691) 655444
www.sebastians-hotel.co.uk
French | £45
Cooking score: 3
£5 OFF

There's a real sense of character about Mark and Michelle Fisher's restaurant-with-rooms in the borderland market town that considers itself the 'gateway to Wales'. A 17th-century coaching inn with half-panelled dining room, heavily beamed ceiling and winter fires, it nonetheless feels breezily modern in its decorative approach: helped by orange walls, blinded windows and entertaining pictures. A French-accented menu of modernish dishes opens with a three-way carpaccio (beef fillet, salmon and scallop), or goats' cheese pannacotta with apple and beetroot, before a sorbet heralds the arrival of mains such as sea bass and wilted spinach on black pasta in Pernod cream, or lamb duo (loin and shoulder) with glazed baby onions and puréed turnips in thyme jus. Finish with the all-out treat of baked chocolate moelleux in vanilla foam with malted chocolate ice cream, white chocolate sauce and crushed biscotti. House wines in all three colours from Chile's Santa Rita are £17.95.

Chef/s: Richard Jones. **Open:** Tue to Sat D only 6.30 to 9.30. **Closed:** Sun, Mon, 24 to 26 Dec, 1 Jan. **Meals:** Set D £23 (3 courses) to £45. **Details:** 35 seats. 20 seats outside. Music. Car parking. Children over 10 yrs only.

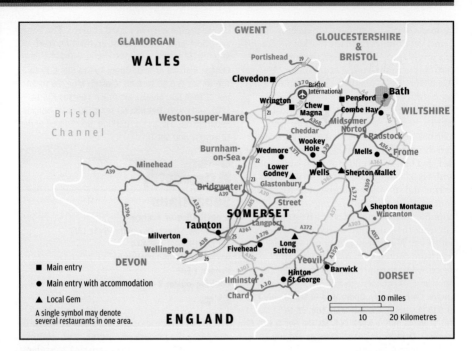

Main entry

Main entry with accommodation

Local Gem

A single symbol may denote several restaurants in one area.

Barwick
Little Barwick House
A little English idyll
Rexes Hollow Lane, Barwick, BA22 9TD
Tel no: (01935) 423902
www.littlebarwickhouse.co.uk
Modern British | £48
Cooking score: 5

Handsome and comfortable, with beautiful grounds, the Fords' old-fashioned country house is considered a 'gem of a place'. Drinks and canapés arrive at sofas in the homely sitting room and there are two dining rooms, one slightly formal, the other a pleasant conservatory. Emma Ford manages to create an enthusiastic but sincere, friendly and calm atmosphere. To match, there's a gently updated provincial style of cooking from Tim Ford. Familiar ideas typically form the menu's backbone: pan-fried foie gras, say, served on toasted orange brioche, while well-sourced materials include wild venison (with braised red cabbage, beetroot purée and rösti potatoes), and Cornish fish, perhaps turbot with basil-crushed new potatoes and a white wine sauce. Try chocolate tart with caramel sauce and prune and Armagnac ice cream for pudding, or vanilla and rhubarb pannacotta with rhubarb sorbet. Grouped in style, the wine list encompasses a broad sweep of flavours from across the globe, but prices are quite steep, with bottles from £19.95.
Chef/s: Tim Ford. **Open:** Wed to Sat L 12 to 2, Tue to Sat D 7 to 9. **Closed:** Sun, Mon. **Meals:** Set L £26 (2 courses) to £30. Set D £42 (2 courses) to £48. **Details:** 45 seats. 12 seats outside. Car parking. Children over 5 yrs only.

Average Price
The average price listed in main-entry reviews denotes the price of a three-course meal, without wine.

Bath

NEW ENTRY

Acorn Vegetarian Kitchen

Seriously exciting contemporary veggie food

2 North Parade Passage, Bath, BA1 1NX

Tel no: (01225) 446059

www.acornvegetariankitchen.co.uk

Vegetarian | £29

Cooking score: 3

£5 OFF **V** £30

For years, this listed Georgian building was home to Demuths, a meat-free restaurant with a loyal following. When the owner sold up in 2013, head chef Richard Buckley and a couple of like-minded pals jumped at the chance to pick up the baton, renaming it to signify a new chapter for this venerable veggie. The dining area is set across two floors, but the in-demand tables are those with views of the nearby abbey, visible over honey-coloured Bath stone rooftops. The menu of strictly seasonal and local produce generates inventive dishes that exhibit a firm understanding of textural contrast. A robust starter of spring herb-steamed beetroots with blackcurrant sorbet, red beet purée and dukkah might precede a curried cauliflower fritter with hickory-smoked potatoes, garlic dhal and greens with raisin and tamarind purée. To finish, the richness of a dark chocolate tart is countered by a sharp raspberry sorbet and crushed pistachios. Wine from £17.50.

Chef/s: Richard Buckley. **Open:** all week L 12 to 3 (3.30 Sat), D 5.30 to 9.30. **Closed:** 24 to 26 Dec. **Meals:** alc (main courses £10 to £16). Set L £14 (2 courses) to £17. Set D £24 (2 courses) to £29. Sun L £14. **Details:** 32 seats. Music.

Allium Brasserie

Big-city pizazz and attention-grabbing food

Abbey Hotel, North Parade, Bath, BA1 1LF

Tel no: (01225) 461603

www.abbeyhotelbath.co.uk

Modern British | £45

Cooking score: 4

Chris Staines was once a serious player on the London scene, and has brought some big-city pizazz to this spacious brasserie in Bath's revamped Abbey Hotel. Etruscan pots, edgy artwork and purple seating make a statement, while the menu is a modern-day gastro tour: eccentric, eclectic, attention-grabbing and full of surprises. Consider a 'revelatory' pressed terrine of coronation chicken with pickled carrots; perfectly spiced lamb rump with a braised lamb pastilla, spiced aubergine, mint yoghurt and compressed cucumber; or the barnstorming glazed quail with chilli caramel. This is cooking that 'lets rip', but holds a true line when it comes to balance. Desserts also go for broke: how about brown-sugar tart with date and tamarind purée, green apple sorbet and candied walnuts? Service delivers a 'rare blend of professionalism and hospitality', while the savvy wine list (from £20) keeps it interesting with plentiful half-bottles and by-the-glass selections. The adjoining terrace is a stunner.

Chef/s: Chris Staines. **Open:** all week L 12 to 3, D 5.30 to 9. **Meals:** alc (main courses £17 to £23). Set L and D £18 (2 courses) to £24. **Details:** 60 seats. 30 seats outside. Separate bar. Wheelchair access. Music.

Symbols

🛏 Accommodation is available

£30 Three courses for less than £30

V Separate vegetarian menu

£5 OFF £5-off voucher scheme

🍾 Notable wine list

The Bath Priory

Country-house elegance
Weston Road, Bath, BA1 2XT
Tel no: (01225) 331922
www.thebathpriory.co.uk
Modern European | £80
Cooking score: 4

🛏 V

Bath Priory is a pretty place with lovingly tended grounds. Paintings are displayed throughout the hotel, almost cluttered in the hallways and reception, and food-themed in the dining room. Here, tables are generously spaced, furnishings sumptuous and the brigade of staff well drilled yet friendly – in the context of traditional plush country-house dining. Come for lunch and the three courses (with excellent bread, canapés and a pre-dessert) are considered 'a bargain in this setting'. Elsewhere, Sam Moody showcases his fine-tuned modern cuisine by teaming scallops with cauliflower and hazelnut couscous, and delivering an 'enjoyable and luxurious' dish of Devon Red beef, which comes with bone marrow, wild garlic, asparagus, morels, Jersey Royals and red wine sauce. Although dishes may not always have the hoped-for impact, ingredients are of a high quality and technique sound. Some dozen wines by the glass open a pedigree list featuring peerless growers and top vintages; bottles from £31.50.
Chef/s: Sam Moody. Open: all week L 12 to 2.30, D 6.30 to 9.30. Closed: 2 weeks Jan. Meals: Set L Mon to Fri, £22 (2 courses) to £28, Sat £37. Set D £62 (2 courses) to £80. Sun L £37. Tasting menu £95 (7 courses). Details: 42 seats. Separate bar. Wheelchair access. Car parking. Children over 5 yrs only at L. Children over 12 yrs only at D.

🍴 **Average Price**
The average price listed in main-entry reviews denotes the price of a three-course meal, without wine.

Casanis

Charming bistro with Gallic classics
4 Saville Row, Bath, BA1 2QP
Tel no: (01225) 780055
www.casanis.co.uk
French | £30
Cooking score: 3

Occupying a handsome Georgian building in a lane adjacent to the city's Assembly Rooms, this charming bistro – named after a type of pastis – has a distinctly Gallic air. Antique chandeliers, splashes of duck-egg blue paintwork and sprigs of lavender on crisp white tablecloths provide a romantic Provençal feel. Former film-maker Jill Couvreur runs front-of-house, while husband Laurent cooks bistro classics. An early spring meal opened with a 'very fresh, assertively flavoured' crab and herb parfait with bouillabaisse vinaigrette, followed by an 'impressively tender' fillet of venison teamed with ceps and a 'perfect' pearl barley risotto, celeriac purée, braised endive and a glossy mulled wine and juniper sauce. A 'simple but delicious' warm apple tarte aux fines with vanilla ice cream made a 'well balanced' ending to a meal. The concise wine list kicks off at £18.50.
Chef/s: Laurent Couvreur. Open: Tue to Sat L 12 to 2, D 6 to 10. Closed: Sun, Mon, 25 and 26 Dec, 2 weeks Jan, 1 week Aug. Meals: alc (main courses £14 to £26). Set L £18 (2 courses) to £23. Set D £19 (2 courses) to £24. Details: 50 seats. 16 seats outside. Music.

The Circus Café & Restaurant

Refreshing two-pronged eatery
34 Brock Street, Bath, BA1 2LN
Tel no: (01225) 466020
www.thecircuscafeandrestaurant.co.uk
Modern British | £32
Cooking score: 3

£5 OFF

In a handsome Georgian building on the street linking The Circus and The Royal Crescent, this family-run café attracts locals and visitors in equal measure for elevenses and light lunches. The setting is relaxed – all heritage colours and original fireplaces. At night, however, it is transformed by means of candles and a menu that pays homage to Elizabeth David and other influential 20th-century cookery writers. Chef/patron Alison Golden understands the seasons and her concise, intelligent menus are backed up by service that is 'friendly and prompt without being overbearing'. Start with smoked haddock carpaccio, lime zest, green chilli, baby cress and saffron aïoli, perhaps, before moving on to pan-fried calf's liver with wilted spinach and sherry, anchovy and grain-mustard gravy. And for dessert? 'Perfect' crème brûlée with sultanas in sherry gets star notices. A wine list from small European growers starts at £17.30. **Chef/s:** Alison Golden. **Open:** Mon to Sat L 12 to 3, D 5.30 to 10.30. **Closed:** Sun, 23 Dec for 3 weeks. **Meals:** alc (main courses £17 to £19). **Details:** 50 seats. 8 seats outside. Music. Children over 10 yrs only.

NEW ENTRY

Clayton's Kitchen at The Porter

Food to suit all tastes, pockets and occasions
The Porter, 15A George Street, Bath, BA1 2EN
Tel no: (01225) 585100
www.theporter.co.uk
Modern British | £35
Cooking score: 3

In a former life, Rob Clayton won recognition at such notable local establishments as the Bath Priory (see entry). Now he's back behind the stoves, this time at a stylishly converted boozer. It's set across four floors, incorporating a speakeasy-style cocktail bar, lounge/bar and library and Clayton's Kitchen, which serves food from breakfast right through to dinner. Such multifarious dining options reflect the wide-reaching clientele, from business suits and local families to the ever-present tourist. It's a great addition to the Bath dining scene. An April meal opened with a 'superb' creamy asparagus soup topped with roasted hazelnuts and wild garlic oil, went on to precisely

cooked John Dory fillets with buttery, herb-flecked carrots, fennel and a light cream sauce, and finished with a praline crème brûlée accompanied by a crunchy salad of apple and walnut. Wines from £17.25.
Chef/s: Rob Clayton. **Open:** all week 12 to 10. **Closed:** 25 Dec. **Meals:** alc (main courses £12 to £24). Set L £15 (2 courses) to £19. **Details:** 60 seats. 20 seats outside. Separate bar. Music.

King William

No-nonsense cooking in a boho pub
36 Thomas Street, Bath, BA1 5NN
Tel no: (01225) 428096
www.kingwilliampub.com
British | £29
Cooking score: 1
£5 OFF   £30

This bustling little corner pub dates from 1827 and still has many original features. New head chef Scott Galloway and front-of-house manager Greg Bartholemew possess impressive pedigrees and seem to have adapted well to the King William's smart but pubby vibe. Broadly British in style, Galloway's cooking places strong emphasis on seasonal, local produce – maybe crispy pork shoulder with salsify and apple or whole pigeon with butternut squash, kale and shallots. Classic desserts include rice pudding and sticky toffee pudding. The substantial wine list includes a selection of 'natural' wines and kicks off at £13.50.
Chef/s: Scott Galloway. **Open:** all week L 12 to 2.30 (3 Sat and Sun), D 6 to 9. **Closed:** 25 and 26 Dec. **Meals:** alc (main courses £14 to £28). Set L £14 (2 courses) to £15. Set D £25 (2 courses) to £29. Sun L £20. **Details:** 50 seats. Separate bar. Music.

Visit us Online
To find out more about *The Good Food Guide*, please visit www.thegoodfoodguide.co.uk

The Marlborough Tavern

Swankily attired foodie pub
35 Marlborough Buildings, Bath, BA1 2LY
Tel no: (01225) 423731
www.marlborough-tavern.com
British | £32
Cooking score: 2

Built in the late 1700s, this Grade II-listed boozer has been feeding and watering the burghers of Bath for centuries – and continues to do a grand job. It is handily placed for the Royal Crescent and boasts one of the city's finest pub gardens. Inside, the décor is swanky: think textured wallpaper, vintage furniture and Farrow & Ball paintwork. Soups, burgers and sandwiches are the mainstays at lunchtime, but the kitchen ups its game for a more ambitious evening menu based on produce from West Country suppliers. Bypass the 'pub classics' in favour of, say, pickled and charred mackerel with smoked haddock fishcake, asparagus custard, cucumber and orange salad, or roasted fillet of pork with braised cheek, black pudding terrine, turnip, cabbage and apple. Breads are home-baked, cheeses are true to the region and desserts might offer anything from rhubarb crumble pie to Mocha crème brûlée with hazelnut cream. Wines from £16.50.
Chef/s: Sam Coltman. **Open:** all week L 12.30 to 2.30 (3 Sat, 4 Sun), D 6 to 9.30 (10 Fri and Sat, 9 Sun). **Meals:** alc (main courses £14 to £21). Set L £12 (2 courses) to £15. **Details:** 65 seats. 90 seats outside. Music. No children after 8pm.

Menu Gordon Jones

Innovative cooking with an element of surprise
2 Wellsway, Bath, BA2 3AQ
Tel no: (01225) 480871
www.menugordonjones.co.uk
Modern British | £45
Cooking score: 4

V

'A truly memorable dining experience' was the verdict of one visitor to Gordon Jones' self-styled restaurant, while another noted that a two-hour drive to lunch was 'the best investment of time we have made in a long while'. No longer simply worth a detour, this unprepossessing restaurant just outside Bath's city centre is now a gastronomic destination. The no-choice tasting menu offers an element of surprise and showcases Jones' highly individualistic dishes, while staff add a refreshingly unstuffy approach. From the diminutive open kitchen, Jones and his team 'take food to another level' with innovative flavour combinations such as a distinctive starter of wild mushroom mousse with smoked milk and onion madeleine. This might be followed by tandoori cod tongues with squid coleslaw, avocado yoghurt and smoked paprika taco or glazed rose veal cheek, truffled sticky rice, candied citrus and dried chervil roots. In addition, recent reports have praised the homemade bread and saffron butter, and a beautifully judged dessert of pannacotta, macaroon and red fruits. A compact wine list opens at £25.
Chef/s: Gordon Jones. **Open:** Tue to Sat L 12.30 to 2, D 7 to 9. **Closed:** Sun, Mon. **Meals:** Tasting menu £40 (5 courses) to £50 (6 courses). **Details:** 20 seats. Music. Children over 12 yrs only.

The Olive Tree

Comfort, quirks and eclectic cooking
The Queensberry Hotel, 4-7 Russel Street, Bath,
BA1 2QF
Tel no: (01225) 447928
www.olivetreebath.co.uk
Modern British | £45
Cooking score: 4
£5 OFF ♦ ➤ V

Tucked away in the basement of Bath's
Queensbury Hotel is the Olive Tree, the hotel's
serious, slick fine-dining restaurant. If its
formal tone and stiff staff seem somewhat at
odds with the quirky boutique hotel, the
room still offers 'a sense of romance' and, when
busy, a 'comfortable atmosphere'. The tasting
menu at inspection was a mixed bag, with
trendy twists occasionally hampering a dish's
success. Of the better creations, crisp quail,
asparagus and fried quail's egg atop mushroom
duxelle were 'sensible combinations that
worked', while herb-crumbed lamp rump
with morels, Little Gem and juicy braised
belly was 'dish of the evening'. Crab lasagne
also comes highly praised. On the downside,
beautiful caramelised scallops with
cauliflower were drowned out by
overpowering micro-herbs; and proportions
seemed 'out of kilter' in a halibut, snail and
rosemary gnocchi dish. The excellent wine list
(from £19.50) contains a huge variety
under £50.
Chef/s: Chris Cleghorn. **Open:** Fri to Sun L 12 to 2
(12.30 to 2.30 Sun), all week D 7 to 10. **Meals:** alc
(main courses £18 to £29). Set L £19 (2 courses) to
£25. Sun L £27. **Details:** 60 seats.

▮▮▮ Please send us your feedback

To register your opinion about any
restaurant listed in the Guide, or a new
restaurant that you wish to bring to our
attention, please visit the web address at
the bottom of the page. Your feedback
informs the content of the book and will
be used to compile next year's reviews.

The White Hart Inn

Old stager with assertive cooking
Widcombe Hill, Widcombe, Bath, BA2 6AA
Tel no: (01225) 338053
www.whitehartbath.co.uk
Modern British | £30
Cooking score: 2
£5 OFF ➤

'Simply well-cooked, well-sourced local
produce, served at a decent price,' ran the notes
of a regular, giving just one reason why this
cheery old-stager in the Widcombe area, not
far from the railway station, is a hit with locals
and visitors. The casual, 'basic, but not too
basic' pub (not only scuffed floorboards,
scrubbed tables, benches and junk-shop
chairs, but also candles and flowers) does a nice
line in freshly cooked, local eats. A monkfish
and chorizo skewer could open proceedings,
then chicken breast in Parma ham with
English asparagus and wild garlic pesto, or
harissa rump of lamb with herb couscous and
yoghurt and coriander dressing. Finish with
lemon polenta cake with rosemary ice cream
or honey and fig pannacotta. Sunday roasts
and a charming garden for when the weather
is kind have been applauded, as has the pride
with which this place is run. Wines start
at £16.50.
Chef/s: Rupert Pitt, Steve Wesley, Kirsty Fowle and
Luke Gibson. **Open:** all week L 12 to 2 (2.30 Sun),
Mon to Sat D 6 to 9 (10 Thur to Sat). **Closed:** 25 and
26 Dec, bank hols. **Meals:** alc (main courses £16 to
£19). Set L £13. **Details:** 50 seats. 40 seats outside.
Wheelchair access. Music.

LOCAL GEM

▲ Aió Sardinia

7 Edgar Buildings, Bath, BA1 2EE
Tel no: (01225) 443900
www.aiorestaurant.co.uk
Sardinian | £28

'Love at first sight' for one reader, Aió Sardinia
gives a taste of the Mediterranean island in a
Georgian town house, delivering it with
'irrepressible warmth'. There are a few knick-
knacks to recall the homeland, but the look is

modern with some tables on the pavement. Kick off with eel and swordfish carpaccio before a plate of pasta (linguine with Devon crab and bottarga, perhaps) followed by casserole of Somerset lamb with chard. Mostly Italian wines start at £16.25. Open all week L, Sat and Sun D.

▲ Yak Yeti Yak
12 Pierrepont Street, Bath, BA1 1LA
Tel no: (01225) 442299
www.yakyetiyak.co.uk
Nepalese | £21

Unpretentious and friendly – this Nepalese restaurant has found its groove and is a firm favourite in Bath. It occupies a series of cheerful basement rooms running across three 18th-century town houses. Service is smiling, Sunil Gurung's cooking homely and authentic. Start with delicately spiced potato and sesame salad, then a subtly spiced curry with rice and dhal: chicken stir-fried with fenugreek, perhaps, or slow-cooked lamb. There are enterprising vegetable dishes, too, and creamed saffron-spiced yoghurt to finish. Wines from £13.30. Open all week.

▋Chew Magna

★ TOP 50 PUB ★

The Pony & Trap
Versatile local food champion
Knowle Hill, Chew Magna, BS40 8TQ
Tel no: (01275) 332627
www.theponyandtrap.co.uk
Modern British | £30
Cooking score: 4

Just a 15-minute drive from Bristol, this 200-year-old cottage pub has become an increasingly popular venue for straight-forward but inventive cooking. The kitchen keeps a watchful eye on the seasons and takes local sourcing seriously, with a full list of suppliers written on the back of the daily changing menus. Josh Eggleton manages to keep locals happy with lunchtime pub classics such as ploughman's or a burger, while satisfying those looking for something a little

more ambitious. A starter of pigeon 'ham' with slow-cooked hen's egg and scalloped potatoes might be followed by fillet of sea bass with char-grilled ox tongue, mushroom and Worcestershire butter sauce; or toasted spelt and beetroot risotto, walnut, pickled beetroot and watercress. Desserts might offer rhubarb, white chocolate and hazelnut cheesecake with rhubarb sorbet, although a plate of quality cheeses with organic bread, biscuits and chutney is another way to round things off. Wines start at £14.75.
Chef/s: Josh Eggleton. Open: Tue to Sun L 12 to 2.30 (3.30 Sun), D 7 to 9.30. Closed: Mon. Meals: alc (main courses £13 to £20). Details: 60 seats. 30 seats outside. Separate bar. Music. Car parking.

▋Clevedon

Murrays of Clevedon
All-day Italian enterprise
87-93 Hill Road, Clevedon, BS21 7PN
Tel no: (01275) 341555
www.murraysofclevedon.co.uk
Italian | £22
Cooking score: 2
£30

The relaxed atmosphere of the Murray family's deli, bakery, wine shop and all-day café is greatly valued by regulars. There's comfort in the shelves laden with goodies, the reasonable prices and easy welcome. It's good for breakfast, but the kitchen proves its worth with a user-friendly lunch menu of deli-style sandwiches made with home-baked bread (try the hot pork with chutney); salads such as fennel with Sicilian orange, Taggiasca olives and radicchio; or Cornish crab with fennel and saffron tart. Alternatively, try a more substantial dish of potato gnocchi with a braised oxtail ragù and pecorino nero, or fillet of home-cured Cornish ling with chickpeas in a chilli, lemon and coriander mayonnaise. Occasional special evenings could hone in on a particular Italian region, perhaps featuring Florentine roast ribeye of beef with spiced Umbrian lentils, cremini mushrooms and sautéed spinach, followed by zuccotto (a traditional northern Italian dessert) with candied nuts. Italian wines from £12.

Chef/s: Reuben Murray. **Open:** Tue to Sat 8.30 to 5. **Closed:** Sun, Mon, 25 and 26 Dec. **Meals:** alc (main courses £9 to £18). **Details:** 45 seats. 6 seats outside. Wheelchair access. Music.

Combe Hay

★ TOP 50 PUB ★

The Wheatsheaf

Well-groomed inn with sophisticated food
Combe Hay, BA2 7EG
Tel no: (01225) 833504
www.wheatsheafcombehay.com
Modern British | £25
Cooking score: 4

£5 OFF £30

It's only four miles from genteel Bath, but hidden in a lush green valley – so 'give yourself plenty of time', advises one reader. This chic, well-groomed inn 'breathes new money', yet has bucolic charms too: from original stone floors and log fires in the bar to glorious three-tiered gardens, beehives and a productive vegetable patch. The kitchen deals in slick, big-city flavours, so expect Cornish mackerel snazzily dressed with beetroot, lime and a dab of wasabi mayonnaise, or a lasagne of wild mushrooms and Jerusalem artichokes drizzled with truffle oil, as well as muscular plates of Gloucester Old Spot pork with black pudding and swede, or steaks with 'fat chips' and an egg from the Wheatsheaf's chickens. Fish and veggie specials change daily; puds might bring lemon posset with rhubarb compote; and you can also 'chomp at the bar' during the lunchtime session. A well-considered, Euro-accented wine list starts at £16.50.

Chef/s: Eddy Rains. **Open:** Tue to Sun L 12 to 2, Tue to Sat D 6.30 to 9. **Closed:** Mon (exc bank hols), 25 and 26 Dec. **Meals:** alc (main courses £16 to £22). Set L and D £14 (2 courses) to £18. Sun L £20 (2 courses) to £25. **Details:** 55 seats. 75 seats outside. Music. Car parking.

Fivehead

NEW ENTRY

The Langford

Fresh, friendly country-house dining
Langford Fivehead, Lower Swell, Fivehead,
TA3 6PH
Tel no: (01460) 282020
www.langfordfivehead.co.uk
Modern British | £36
Cooking score: 5

£5 OFF

Hotels really don't come any more laid-back than at this rural 15th-century house. Sure, the sense of occasion is there – the generous sofas, the stone fireplaces, the luscious drapery – but the light fittings are funky, the artwork modern, the service relaxed and the home-from-home vibe could easily set you chatting with your fellow guests. Chef Olly Jackson made waves at New Yard in Cornwall (see entry) before landing here. He's already winning plaudits for his 'exemplary' cooking, that 'feels like a little secret everyone needs to know about'. Witness fat, seared scallops with cauliflower purée, crunchy florets and the glorious sweet, scented burst of jasmine-soaked raisins. A duo of pork (slow-roasted belly and pan-fried loin) arrives with 'exceptional' dauphinois, while Jackson's originality shines through in a playful riff on apple crumble: iced parfait, bramley compote, a sprinkling of crumble and a puffy cinnamon beignet. A gloriously Gallic wine list kicks off at £22.

Chef/s: Olly Jackson. **Open:** Tue to Sat D only 7 to 11. **Closed:** Mon, Sun, 25 and 26 Dec, Jan. **Meals:** Set D £36. **Details:** 16 seats. 10 seats outside. Car parking. Children over 12 yrs only.

Hinton St George

The Lord Poulett Arms

Appealing village pub with seasonal food
High Street, Hinton St George, TA17 8SE
Tel no: (01460) 73149
www.lordpoulettarms.com
Modern British | £27
Cooking score: 2

Not every old country pub has been lured into the modern era with chic minimalism. Some still look like old country pubs, like the Lord Poulett, which dates from the end of Charles II's reign. Standing in an unmolested hamstone Somerset village, it has a trio of fireplaces, original stone floors and walls in homely roughcast. Order at the bar from a menu that isn't shy of offering pub classics such as mussels cooked in local cider, chicken curry or chilli con carne, but lights out for more venturesome territory, too. Savoury cheesecake made with goats' cheese, served with red onion jam, makes an interesting departure, and mains follow on with venison and bacon meatloaf with Parmesan polenta in truffled jus, or herb-crusted hake with lyonnaise potatoes and Savoy cabbage. After that, it won't surprise you to find blood orange in the baked Alaska. Well-kept ales offer potent reassurance, and wines start at £16.
Chef/s: Philip Verden. **Open:** all week L 12 to 2.30 (3.30 Sun), D 7 to 9.15. **Closed:** 25 and 26 Dec, 1 Jan. **Meals:** alc (main courses £12 to £25). Sun L £18 (2 courses) to £22. **Details:** 65 seats. 50 seats outside. Separate bar. Wheelchair access. Car parking.

Long Sutton

LOCAL GEM
▲ The Devonshire Arms

Cross Lane, Long Sutton, TA10 9LP
Tel no: (01458) 241271
www.thedevonshirearms.com
Modern British | £28

Bang in the middle of a quintessential Somerset village (complete with a well-kept green), this prosperous-looking 400-year-old inn was once a hunting lodge for the Dukes of Devonshire (hence the name). These days, it feeds locals and travellers from a blackboard menu of upbeat country-pub dishes along the lines of warm crab and tomato tart, home-smoked chicken Caesar salad or fillet of gilthead bream with Jerusalem artichoke, fennel and Italian speck. Good West Country cheeses, too. Wines from £17.25. Accommodation. Open all week.

Lower Godney

LOCAL GEM
▲ The Sheppey Inn

Lower Godney, BA5 1RZ
Tel no: (01458) 831594
www.thesheppey.co.uk
Modern British | £27

'Somerset's best kept secret,' claims one reporter, but others have noted how busy this riverside pub gets – so it seems the secret is out. Live music and DJs, local ciders and craft ales draw crowds to this scruffy hostelry with a 'cool, quirky interior', but it's the generous, well-priced cooking that attracts locals. The kitchen makes admirable use of regional produce, say local lamb carpaccio, pork belly with black pudding mash, excellent steaks, fish from Cornwall, plus an all-Somerset cheeseboard. Closed Sun D and Mon.

Mells

Talbot Inn

Historic coaching inn oozing civilised charm
Selwood Street, Mells, BA11 3PN
Tel no: (01373) 812254
www.talbotinn.com
British | £28
Cooking score: 3

'Wonderful food, charming setting and delightful staff' – it seems the guys behind the Beckford Arms in Wiltshire (see entry) have done it again. With a full contingent of beams, timbers and roaring fires, this centuries-old, gentrified village inn-with-rooms certainly

puts on a convincing show. The aim is to combine first-rate, well-sourced materials with uncomplicated modern cooking to produce a menu with broad appeal. Pub classics have a please-all quality – for example, the well-reported burger with bacon, cheese and pickle – but the kitchen also turns out starters of potted ham hock with kohlrabi and apple salad, mains of roast roe deer with pearl barley, celeriac purée and roasted chicory, and Cambridge burnt cream to finish. There's 'a great vibe' in the Coach House Grill (Friday to Sunday only) where meat and fish are grilled on a magnificent open fire and served at long communal tables. Wines from £17.50.
Chef/s: Pravin Nayar. **Open:** all week L 12 to 2.30 (3 Sat and Sun), D 6 to 9.30 (10 Sat). **Closed:** 25 Dec. **Meals:** alc (main courses £10 to £19). **Details:** 45 seats. 20 seats outside. Separate bar. Wheelchair access. Music. Car parking.

Milverton
The Globe
Family-friendly attitude and a local flavour
Fore Street, Milverton, TA4 1JX
Tel no: (01823) 400534
www.theglobemilverton.co.uk
Modern British | £27
Cooking score: 2
£5 OFF

A four-square village pub with a Grade II-listed exterior, the Globe adds a Somerset flavour to its proceedings. You'll find a range of draught ales at the pumps and suppliers of regional produce duly name-checked on the menu. There's a family-friendly approach, too, with bespoke kids' dishes offered. A changing landscape of artworks (for sale) is displayed on the walls. The opened-up interior is warmed by a wood-burner in the cooler months, while tables on the terrace are a hit during warmer weather. The menu – supported by blackboard specials – deals in comforting stuff such as haddock and leek pie, burgers topped with local Cheddar, or slow-roasted glazed belly of pork with honey, shallots and garlic. Starters of twice-baked Cornish Blue soufflé with pear

salad, or tempura tiger prawns with sweet chilli sauce, show the range of the kitchen's output. Drink real ales, or wines from £14.50.
Chef/s: Mark Tarry and Kaan Atasoy. **Open:** Tue to Sun L 12 to 2, Mon to Sat D 7 to 9. **Meals:** alc (main courses £12 to £18). Sun L £16. **Details:** 50 seats. 20 seats outside. Separate bar. Wheelchair access. Music. Car parking.

Pensford
LOCAL GEM
▲ The Pig
Hunstrete House, Pensford, BS39 4NS
Tel no: (01761) 490490
www.thepighotel.com
British | £30

Part of a rapidly expanding litter of Pig hotels, this handsome Georgian house near Bath is surrounded by 20 acres of stunning woodland. The Victorian potting shed-style restaurant follows a 'field to fork' philosophy with a map of local suppliers on the back of the menu. Cured Mendip meats is one way to start, followed by 'Kentucky' fried wild rabbit and carrot purée. Apple pie with Somerset brandy and walnut ice cream is a show-stopping dessert. Wines from £16.50. Open all week.

Shepton Mallet
LOCAL GEM
▲ Blostin's
29-33 Waterloo Road, Shepton Mallet, BA4 5HH
Tel no: (01749) 343648
www.blostins.co.uk
Modern British | £30 £5 OFF

Nick and Lynne Reed have been serving classy bistro food for over a generation at Blostin's, hitting the 30-year mark in 2015. It's clearly a winning formula (the proof is in the pudding) and their charming cottage restaurant shows no sign of going off the boil. Nick's two- or three-course set menu is terrific value, featuring plenty of regional ingredients in dishes such as a classic French onion soup with cheese croûton and a main-course pheasant breast with celeriac mash. House wine is £16.50. Open Tue to Sat D only.

Shepton Montague

LOCAL GEM
▲ The Montague Inn
Shepton Montague, BA9 8JW
Tel no: (01749) 813213
www.themontagueinn.co.uk
Modern European | £28 £5 OFF

Head down winding lanes to reach a country pub and restaurant that fulfils both functions with good cheer: real ales and local produce winning the day. There are views over the Stourhead Estate, too. The kitchen team traverse the globe for inspiration if the mood takes them – beetroot and fennel risotto cake, Chinese-style BBQ pork pancakes – but are equally happy nearer to home with minced beef and onion suet pudding. Check out the range of local cheeses. Wines from £15. Closed Sun D.

Somerton

NEW ENTRY
The White Hart
Appealing cooking and pubby vitality
Market Place, Somerton, TA11 7LX
Tel no: (01458) 272273
www.whitehartsomerton.com
Modern British | £30
Cooking score: 2

Whether you are in for a swift pint in the 'busy, busy' bar, enjoying some beautiful cooked food, or staying in one of the boutique rooms, this smartly overhauled 18th-century market-town hostelry knows how to deliver satisfaction. That's not surprising given the White Hart is owned by the same team behind the Swan at Wedmore (see entry). Beams, plank floors and mismatched tables and chairs emphasise the pubby vitality, yet a serious approach to local sourcing and seasonality adds to the appeal of the cooking. A meal

'cooked to a delicious standard' might open with home-cured bacon and Cheddar croquettes with piccalilli, then continue along the lines of Cornish pollack fillet teamed with merguez-spiced sausage, River Fowey mussels and kale, and finish with lemon curd trifle, vanilla cream and Italian meringue. There has been praise, too, for the freshly baked bread, the hummus and the 'prompt' service. Wines from £15.35.
Chef/s: Tom Blake. Open: all week L 12 to 3, D 6 to 9.45. Meals: alc (main courses £12 to £22). Details: Separate bar.

Taunton

Augustus
Local heroes flying solo
3 The Courtyard, St James Street, Taunton, TA1 1JR
Tel no: (01823) 324354
www.augustustaunton.co.uk
Modern British | £25
Cooking score: 5
£5 OFF V £30

It may be named after food-loving Augustus Gloop in Roald Dahl's *Charlie and the Chocolate Factory*, but there's nothing whimsical about this dinky terraced restaurant in a tiny courtyard near the famous Castle Hotel. Chef Richard Guest and manager Cedric Chirossel made their reputations at the aforementioned pile before going solo, and their grown-up – but charming – approach continues to attract locals and visitors. The concise menu of finely tuned, bistro-style dishes fully lives up to expectations: from a plate of seared Brixham scallops embellished with parsley and garlic purée, or a homespun bacon, raclette cheese and onion bake with cornichon and potato salad, to slow-roast duck with confit fennel and glazed celeriac, or a 'celebration of British beef' in all its bovine glory. The spot-on delivery and assertive flavours are topped by textbook desserts such as tarte Tatin or chocolate soufflé with salted-caramel ice cream. Wines from £17.

Chef/s: Richard Guest. **Open:** Tue to Sat L 12 to 2.30, D 6 to 9.30. **Closed:** Mon, Sun, 25 and 26 Dec, 1 Jan, bank hols. **Meals:** alc (main courses £14 to £19). **Details:** 28 seats. 20 seats outside.

Castle Bow Restaurant
A special setting for outstanding dishes
Castle Green, Taunton, TA1 1NF
Tel no: (01823) 328328
www.the-castle-hotel.com/brazz
Modern British | £30
Cooking score: 5

The Castle is a Taunton institution, run by the Chapman family since 1950. Its restaurant is famed for launching the careers of Gary Rhodes and Phil Vickery, but since 2012, Irish chef Liam Finnegan has quietly made the place his own. A refurbishment some years ago has kept it current enough to attract first-timers, but the 1920s-style dining room is elegant enough to seduce well-heeled regulars. Finnegan's version of modern British is imaginative, well-executed and as joyous as it is seasonal. One reporter's ravioli of wild Quantock Hill rabbit with girolles, peas and chervil cream is a case in point, and the ever-popular Brixham crab and avocado salad always impresses. Sea bass with chard, mussels and parsnip purée 'with a hint of ginger', rare-breed Castlemilk Moorit lamb loin and braised shoulder, and a 'faultless' lemon tart also attract praise. Friendly food pricing is popular: a policy extending to the international list of wines (from £17.95).
Chef/s: Liam Finnegan. **Open:** Wed to Sat D only 7 to 9.30. **Closed:** Sun, Mon, Tue. **Meals:** alc (main courses £14 to £22). **Details:** 36 seats. Separate bar. Wheelchair access. Music. Car parking.

The Willow Tree
Modish cooking in a low-beamed setting
3 Tower Lane, Taunton, TA1 4AR
Tel no: (01823) 352835
www.thewillowtreerestaurant.com
Modern British | £33
Cooking score: 5

'A lovely, heart-warming, cheering, well-run place,' thought one visitor to this low-beamed, cottagey 17th-century town house behind the Castle. Another observed that it was 'deservedly popular with the locals, who are big fans of the signature dishes (the Cheddar soufflé and the bread and butter pudding)'. Darren Sherlock and Rita Rambellas have been here since 2002, which shows in their thoughtful approach to hospitality and in Darren's meticulous cooking based on carefully sourced, seasonal raw materials. Opening proceedings might be a classic pairing of smoked salmon and crab, served as a tian with horseradish, pickled cucumber and an avocado and crème fraîche cream. Mains run from fricassee of monkfish with caviar and saffron and a spaghetti of carrot, celeriac and courgette, to loin of venison teamed with Savoy cabbage creamed with bacon, carrots, onion and garlic. For a light finish, berries in Champagne jelly is recommended. Wines start at £18.95.
Chef/s: Darren Sherlock. **Open:** Tue, Wed, Fri and Sat D only 6.30 to 9. **Closed:** Mon, Thur, Sun, Jan, Aug. **Meals:** Set D £28. **Details:** 25 seats. 10 seats outside. Separate bar. Music.

▌Wedmore

The Swan
Simple, satisfying local food
Cheddar Road, Wedmore, BS28 4EQ
Tel no: (01934) 710337
www.theswanwedmore.com
Modern British | £25
Cooking score: 2
£5 OFF 🛏 £30 🔽

With a full quota of stone flags, bare boards, rugs, leather and wood (scrubbed and polished), this well-groomed Georgian coaching inn has urbane interiors straight out of *Country Living*. Yet the Swan is also a busy local watering hole, especially when the sun shines and the garden becomes an attraction. It's a true inn, bringing some classy food to the table, alongside smart accommodation. The kitchen certainly has its finger on the pulse, drawing from local farm supplies to create dishes that 'register way above the usual level for pub food' – witness the fried Quantock venison liver with grilled pear, bruschetta and apple balsamic, or the stuffed saddle of local lamb with dates, almonds, kale and potato hotpot. Don't worry if something simple will suffice: burgers, steaks and good old sticky toffee pudding are also present and correct. Wines from £15.95.

Chef/s: Tom Blake. **Open:** all week L 12 to 3, Mon to Sat D 6 to 10. **Meals:** alc (main courses £11 to £22). **Details:** 70 seats. 50 seats outside. Separate bar. Music. Car parking.

▌Wells

Goodfellows
Astute seafood cookery
5 Sadler Street, Wells, BA5 2RR
Tel no: (01749) 673866
www.goodfellowswells.co.uk
Modern British/Seafood | £42
Cooking score: 4

Adam Fellows is an industrious chap. His is the kind of place that covers every base: from coffee and croissant in the patisserie/café, via a light lunch, to a full-on seafood-focused feast, with just about everything made in-house. The ground floor has a central open kitchen to crank up the energy levels, while upstairs is more sedate, but the whole joint feels unpretentious and contemporary. There's some serious craft in the execution of dishes – 'beautiful textures and flavours' – try the tasting menu if you want to see the cut of Adam's jib. Raw tuna with soy and ginger jelly and wasabi crème fraîche is a starter that shows understanding of Asian flavours, and main-course roast hake with Moroccan spices and saffron-braised fennel is another fine piece of fish handled with skill. Meat eaters and

vegetarians don't miss out, and desserts such as blackcurrant pannacotta bring up the rear. Wine starts at £18.

Chef/s: Adam Fellows. **Open:** Tue to Sat L 12 to 2, Wed to Sat D 6.30 to 9.30. **Closed:** Sun, Mon, 25 and 26 Dec. **Meals:** alc (main courses £14 to £24). Set L £21 (2 courses) to £25. Set D £42. Tasting menu £65. **Details:** 40 seats. Music.

The Old Spot
Unfussy fine-tuned food
12 Sadler Street, Wells, BA5 2SE
Tel no: (01749) 689099
www.theoldspot.co.uk
Modern British | £28
Cooking score: 4
£30

If you manage to bag a table at the back of this congenial neighbourhood restaurant, you can view magnificent Wells Cathedral. If not, simply lap up the genuine hospitality radiating from the bow-fronted Georgian town house. Ian and Clare Bates have worked hard and established a loyal following since setting up the Old Spot in 2006, and the food still shows a sure touch – not to mention an affection for seasonal produce. Bare tables, bare floorboards and painted panelling set an unfussy tone, while the kitchen delivers classy, fine-tuned food without prissy posturing. Rillettes of pork with apricot chutney or smoked haddock fritters with tartare sauce could precede roast hake with brown shrimps and capers or roast breast and crépinette of pheasant with ceps and pearl barley. To finish, don't miss the tarte Tatin with Olive Farm cream. Prices are very accommodating, and the wine list offers inspired choices from £16.95.

Chef/s: Ian Bates. **Open:** Wed to Sun L 12.30 to 2.30, Tue to Sat D 6 to 10. **Closed:** Mon, 1 week Christmas. **Meals:** alc (main courses £13 to £22). Set L £16 (2 courses) to £19. Sun L £20 (2 courses) to £23. **Details:** 50 seats.

Wookey Hole
The Wookey Hole Inn
Wacky, fun-loving village pub
High Street, Wookey Hole, BA5 1BP
Tel no: (01749) 676677
www.wookeyholeinn.com
Modern British | £24
Cooking score: 1
🛏 £30

An endearing Somerset bolt-hole with good intentions and a big heart, Richard Davey's colourful and lively village hostelry deals in locally brewed ales and ciders and gutsy food. The menu delivers pub classics along the lines of various burgers, sausage and mash, fish and chips and ham and eggs, but it isn't all plain-speaking stuff. Witness sugar-cured salmon with pickled cucumber and horseradish cream, and roast rump of lamb with dauphinois potatoes and red onion tarte Tatin. To finish, there's stem ginger and treacle tart with cinnamon ice cream or a West Country cheese platter. Wines from £15.75.
Chef/s: Adam Kennington. **Open:** all week L 12 to 2.30 (3 Sun), Mon to Sat D 6.30 to 9 (7 to 9.30 Fri and Sat). **Closed:** 25 and 26 Dec. **Meals:** alc (main courses £13 to £25). Sun L £14. **Details:** 75 seats. 70 seats outside. Music. Car parking.

Wrington
The Ethicurean
Garden-grown ingredients cooked with flair
Barley Wood Walled Garden, Long Lane, Wrington, BS40 5SA
Tel no: (01934) 863713
www.theethicurean.com
British | £29
Cooking score: 2
£30

It may be *de rigueur* these days to claim that you supply your kitchen locally, but the Penningtons mean it. Their restaurant is in a Victorian walled garden, which you can stroll through if you will, perhaps buying fresh produce along the way. Local means seasonal of course, and what isn't in season is preserved by one of the multifarious ways in which households used to provision themselves through winter. Among the many surprises are starters of goat bacon with burnt chicory and pickled roots, or salt-baked celeriac in portobello mushroom and apple soup, before breast and confit leg of partridge with cavolo nero and bread sauce, or turmeric-fried ling and mussels with truffled toast and nigella seeds. The Ethicurean's own orchards furnish the main materials for sticky toffee apple cake, or pear tart with white chocolate and cardamom, served with clotted cream ice cream. A short wine list opens at £21.50.
Chef/s: Matthew and Iain Pennington. **Open:** Tues to Sun L 12 to 2.30, Fri and Sat D 7 to 9.30. **Closed:** Mon, 1 week mid Jan, bank hols. **Meals:** alc (main courses £15 to £19). **Details:** 60 seats. 32 seats outside. Wheelchair access. Music. Car parking.

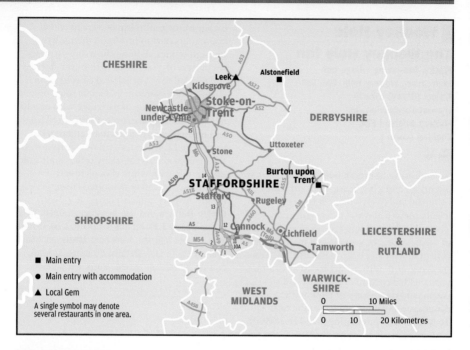

■ Alstonefield

The George

Village local with comfort food
Alstonefield, DE6 2FX
Tel no: (01335) 310205
www.thegeorgeatalstonefield.com
Modern British | £30
Cooking score: 2

It's little wonder that readers endorse Emily
Brighton's village hostelry as 'excellence from
beginning to end'. Step inside and you'll find a
'delightful' traditional pub with a beamed bar,
blazing fires, fresh flowers and a lovely
atmosphere. Food is treated in a simple,
forthright manner with a lunchtime menu
running from sandwiches to hearty pub meals
such as proper baked beans with poached egg
and crisp pancetta on toast, or Gloucester Old
Spot sausages with mash and onion gravy, and
beer-battered cod and chips. The kitchen ups
its game in the evening with a more ambitious
menu that could include brûlée of chicken
liver parfait or breast of wood pigeon (served
pink) with butternut squash, savoy cabbage,
walnuts and sorrel, then treacle-cured
Derbyshire beef fillet with saffron fondant and
bone marrow and horseradish butter. The
regional British cheeseboard has been praised,
but then so has the rhubarb crumble and
custard. Wines from £16.
Chef/s: Chris Rooney. **Open:** all week L 12 to 2.30, D
6.30 to 9 (8 Sun). **Closed:** 25 Dec. **Meals:** alc (main
courses £12 to £29). **Details:** 40 seats. 40 seats
outside. Separate bar. Car parking.

║● Please send us your feedback

To register your opinion about any
restaurant listed in the Guide, or a new
restaurant that you wish to bring to our
attention, please visit the web address at
the bottom of the page. Your feedback
informs the content of the book and will
be used to compile next year's reviews.

▌Burton upon Trent

99 Station Street

Outstanding value from an old-town asset
99 Station Street, Burton upon Trent, DE14 1BT
Tel no: (01283) 516859
www.99stationstreet.com
Modern British | £29
Cooking score: 1

£30

In a county not over-endowed with entries in this Guide, Daniel Pilkington's earnest approach to sourcing local ingredients is a breath of fresh air. The simple, contemporary décor and cheery service set the tone for Pilkington's gently modern bistro-style cooking, where chicken and leek terrine is wrapped in bacon and matched with a zesty tomato salsa, and main-course Packington pork is served three ways (roasted loin, confit belly and ham hock croquette). Finish with rice pudding with a brûlée-style topping and a little Kilner jar of raspberry jam. The set lunch is a bit of a bargain. Wines start at £12.75.
Chef/s: Daniel Pilkington. **Open:** Thur to Sun L 12 to 2, Wed to Sat D from 6.30. **Closed:** Mon, Tue, 26 to 30 Dec. **Meals:** alc (main courses £13 to £22). Set £13 (2 courses) to £14. Sun L £18. **Details:** 40 seats. Separate bar. Wheelchair access. Music.

▌Leek

LOCAL GEM
▲ Qarma

Cross Mill, Cross Street, Leek, ST13 6BL
Tel no: (01538) 387788
www.the-qarma.com
Indian | £20

A Bangladeshi and Indian restaurant and take-away that springs a few surprises, Qarma aims to impress with a menu that offers more than the tried-and-tested staples (though these are available, if you insist). Essa bora are like little fishy onion bhajias, and might precede Goan chicken or steak masala. The tandoor turns out chicken shashlik, plump king prawns and suchlike. Korma, vindaloo and other mainstays offer comfort to ardent traditionalists. Open all week D (lunch by reservation only).

▌Lichfield

READERS RECOMMEND
The Wine House
Modern British
27 Bird Street, Lichfield, WS13 6PW
Tel no: (01543) 419999
www.thewinehouselichfield.co.uk
'On Saturday night, it was ridiculously busy but the service was outstanding. Overall it was a fabulous evening, great food and a lovely setting.'

▌Walsall

READERS RECOMMEND
Five Rivers
Indian
11 Vicarage Place, Walsall, WS1 3NA
Tel no: (01922) 646164
www.thefiveriversgroup.co.uk
'The most important aspect, the food, is almost beyond reproach: sophisticated and complex, with a respect for the immense variations of cuisines that come under the "Indian" heading.'

🍴 Readers Recommend

A 'readers recommend' review is a genuine quote from a report sent in by one of our readers. We intend to follow up these suggestions throughout the year to come.

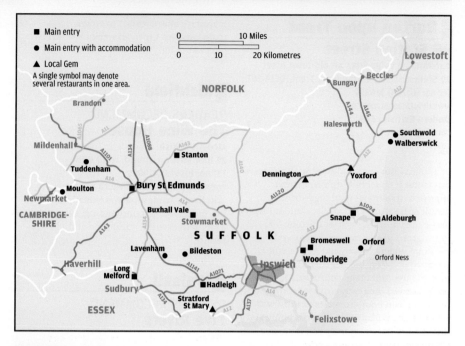

- ■ Main entry
- ● Main entry with accommodation
- ▲ Local Gem

A single symbol may denote several restaurants in one area.

▌Aldeburgh

Regatta

Bright and breezy seaside brasserie
171 High Street, Aldeburgh, IP15 5AN
Tel no: (01728) 452011
www.regattaaldeburgh.com
Modern British | £22
Cooking score: 1
£30

Even on a dismal off-season lunchtime, this embracing place transports you to the Med in a heartbeat. An assured kitchen brigade turns out familiar seaside bistro fare: classic moules marinière using plump rope-grown mussels; thick cod fillet (served with densely flavoured ratatouille) that's just the right side of rare; ditto seared scallops on celeriac purée. Warm brandon rost (hot-smoked salmon) with chilli chutney and crème fraîche, or whole smoked prawns with garlic mayonnaise, are top choices from the restaurant's excellent smokehouse, while a classic crème brûlée will finish a meal nicely. House wine from £15.50.

Chef/s: Robert Mabey. **Open:** all week L 12 to 2, D 6 to 10. **Closed:** 24 to 26 and 31 Dec, 1 Jan. **Meals:** alc (main courses £12 to £22). **Details:** 95 seats. Separate bar.

LOCAL GEM

▲ The Aldeburgh Market Café

170-172 High Street, Aldeburgh, IP15 5AQ
Tel no: (01728) 452520
www.thealdeburghmarket.co.uk
Modern British | £20 £5 OFF

Keeping the customer and the produce in close proximity, Sara Fox's place is a deli, fishmonger and fruit/veg shop where everything is fair game for the menu in the buzzy little café. Fish is the mainstay of the globetrotting repertoire, with classic fish soup with rouille and croûtons alongside pad Thai and a South Indian curry. There are cakes, too, plus local ice creams and hearty puddings such as seasonal fruit crumble. Drink wine (from £13.50) or Adnams beer. Open all week L.

Bildeston

The Bildeston Crown

Confident cooking at village favourite
High Street, Bildeston, IP7 7EB
Tel no: (01449) 740510
www.thebildestoncrown.co.uk
Modern British | £28
Cooking score: 4

There was barely a hiccup as Zack Deakins slid effortlessly back behind the Crown's stove – he was long-standing former chef Chris Lee's senior sous – to uphold this pub's fine foodie reputation. He's doing a grand job, skilfully turning out everything from sandwiches and bar lunches through to the show-stopping eight-course tasting menu where tantalisingly brief descriptions promise nuggets of brilliance using rabbit, halibut and beef. A midweek set menu offers a quicker option: start with a lobster bisque, the addition of lemongrass and a sesame prawn toast making a perfectly measured nod to Asia, and follow with globe artichoke and portobello mushroom on a perfectly crisp croûte with buttery, just-wilted spinach, or rump and tenderly braised shoulder of local Semer lamb. Apple crumble and custard is a prettily layered, vanilla-rich, sweet confection to finish. There is plenty of wine to drink by the glass, and bottles from £17.50.
Chef/s: Zack Deakins. **Open:** all week L 12 to 3, D 7 to 10 (9 Sun). **Meals:** alc (main courses £14 to £22). Set L £20. Set D £45 (3 courses) to £70. **Details:** 32 seats. Separate bar. Wheelchair access. Music. Car parking.

Bromeswell

The British Larder

Enterprising regional food forays
Orford Road, Bromeswell, IP12 2PU
Tel no: (01394) 460310
www.britishlardersuffolk.co.uk
British | £30
Cooking score: 4

'Quite excellent,' enthused one diner after eating at this unassuming roadside place where Ross Pike and Madalene Bonvini-Hamel have set out their very Suffolk stall. Vigorously championing the region's best producers, the menu takes you up the coast for smoked fish from Orford, swerves inland for superlative Blaxhall game (rabbit and smoked ham hock terrine makes a fine starter, while venison burger with red onion chutney, hand-cut chips and beer-battered onion rings is a triumphant take on a pub staple), and back into the Deben Valley for pork from the renowned Dingley Dell farm. Roasted boneless chicken leg (Sutton Hoo, naturally) is transformed into a perfect lunchtime dish, served with a syrupy-soft golden-yolked egg and just-picked asparagus. To finish? Capture early summer in an exquisite concoction of rhubarb gently roasted, creamed, iced, puréed and served with a scattering of meringue and a flutter of micro-coriander. A well-considered wine list starts at £17.25.
Chef/s: Ross Pike and Madalene Bonvini-Hamel.
Open: all week L 12 to 2.30 (2.15 Mon, 3 Sat and Sun), D 6 to 9 (9.30 Fri and Sat, 8 Sun). **Closed:** Jan, bank hols. **Meals:** alc (main courses £14 to £25). Set L £17 (2 courses) to £20. **Details:** 80 seats. 100 seats outside. Separate bar. Wheelchair access. Car parking.

Bury St Edmunds

Maison Bleue

The freshest fish, worth seeking out
30-31 Churchgate Street, Bury St Edmunds,
IP33 1RG
Tel no: (01284) 760623
www.maisonbleue.co.uk
Modern French | £43
Cooking score: 4

'An extraordinary outpost of France in
Suffolk,' thought one reporter of this popular
seafood restaurant a few minutes' walk from
St Edmundsbury Cathedral. Maison Bleue is
held in high affection, and its smart shopfront
topped by a blue awning looks instantly
appealing – although a modern tone prevails
inside. Affluent, bright and dressed-up, it's a
suitably discreet, very Gallic backdrop for
creative cooking that makes its mark through
painstaking detail and sound technique.
Poached Colchester Gigas oysters with cream
of parsley, Italian truffle and Jerusalem
artichoke espuma is an inimitable signature
dish, while halibut teamed with black olive,
carrot, lemon zest 'confit', cream of mooli and
wasabi, and a miso and mushroom dressing,
really works. Not in the mood for fish? There's
also Gressingham duck breast, venison or
Aberdeen Angus beef. Twelve-hour-cooked
Braeburn apple with salted-caramel ice cream
makes the perfect finale. Mainly French wines
start at £16.95.
Chef/s: Pascal Canevet. **Open:** Tue to Sat L 12 to 2,
D 7 to 9 (9.30 Sat). **Closed:** Sun, Mon, 3 weeks Jan,
2 weeks Aug. **Meals:** alc (main courses £18 to £30).
Set L £19 (2 courses) to £24. Set D £34. **Details:** 60
seats. Music.

Symbols

🛏 Accommodation is available

£30 Three courses for less than £30

V Separate vegetarian menu

£5 £5-off voucher scheme
OFF

🍾 Notable wine list

Pea Porridge

Something quite special
28-29 Cannon Street, Bury St Edmunds, IP33 1JR
Tel no: (01284) 700200
www.peaporridge.co.uk
Modern British | £30
Cooking score: 4
£5
OFF

'The best restaurant in Suffolk' is praise indeed
for this popular neighbourhood restaurant
opposite the Old Cannon brewery. There's
certainly much to like about Pea Porridge's
down-to-earth style: no posh table settings,
refreshingly unfussy décor and an absence of
pomp and ceremony. On the food front, it's all
about chef/proprietor Justin Sharp delving
into the British larder to produce creative
bistro cooking with French leanings.
Reporters have found plenty of top-drawer
stuff to applaud: from the 'freshly cooked
nibbles' via 'out of this world' squid-ink risotto
to slow-braised pig's cheeks teamed with soft
polenta, whole black pepper, crispy ears and
gremolata, or confit of duck with 'the best
mashed potato ever made'. There are plaudits,
too, for the 'fantastic bread', the 'sublime' tarte
Tatin, and the owners' knack of picking
'superb young staff'. The wine list is a sound
international jumble, with prices starting
at £15.95.
Chef/s: Justin Sharp. **Open:** Wed to Sat L 12 to 2,
Tue to Sat D 6.30 to 9.30. **Closed:** Sun, Mon, 2
weeks Christmas, 2 weeks Aug. **Meals:** alc (main
courses £13 to £20). Set L and D £13 (2 courses) to
£17. **Details:** 46 seats. 8 seats outside. Music.
Children at L only.

LOCAL GEM

▲ Benson Blakes

88-89 St John's Street, Bury St Edmunds,
IP33 1SQ
Tel no: (01284) 755188
www.bensonblakes.co.uk
Burgers | £18

'The kind of place I would normally walk
straight past, but my goodness the burgers!'
This high-street burger joint is a laudable

independent operation, strong on local sourcing (100% Suffolk beef, Suffolk black bacon, daily baked buns). While burgers dominate the long menu, there's also chicken and pulled pork (just as carefully sourced). It's family-friendly by day, but might be worth giving a miss come evening, when the youth of Bury pile in. Fantastic list of craft beers. Wines from £13.95. Open all week.

▌Buxhall Vale

Buxhall Coach House

Bold Italian flavours in the depths of Suffolk
Buxhall Vale, IP14 3DH
Tel no: (01449) 736032
www.honortownsend.com
Italian | £33
Cooking score: 1
£5
OFF

The parkland setting couldn't be more English, nor the food more Italian in this 'absolutely fabulous' family-run restaurant. Come here to absorb some authentic flavours of Italy, conjured up by Honor Townsend, back in her native Suffolk after years cooking in Umbria. Pan-seared scallops with truffle-scented cauliflower purée and spicy Italian sausage might precede a pesto-crusted rack of lamb with grilled marinated peppers. Portions are substantial, but leave room for Honor's memorable caramel and vanilla pannacotta with brandy-snaps. An all-Italian board includes Taleggio, fresh pecorino and pungent 'puzzone di Moena', served with ripe pear and homemade fig conserve. House wine starts at £22.
Chef/s: Honor Townsend. **Open:** Wed to Sun L 12 to 2.30, Wed to Sat D 7.30 to 9 (Wed bookings only). **Closed:** Mon, Tue. **Meals:** alc (main courses £16 to £29). **Details:** 28 seats. 28 seats outside. Wheelchair access. Music. Car parking.

▌Dennington

LOCAL GEM
▲ The Dennington Queen
The Square, Dennington, IP13 8AB
Tel no: (01728) 638421
www.thedenningtonqueen.co.uk
Modern British | £22

This 16th-century village pub has been brought up to date with more than just a lick of paint. Creature comforts may have been refined, but the charm is undisturbed and there remains a down-to-earth ambience lent by beams, standing timbers and open fires. The menu, too, is a mix of unfussy pub grub (fish and chips) and dishes with some neat tweaks: say, slow-roasted Cajun pork belly with pineapple and cucumber salsa or pheasant breast with grain-mustard and red wine jus. Wines from £14.50. Open all week.

▌Hadleigh

NEW ENTRY
The Hadleigh Ram
Refined but relaxed market-town eatery
5 Market Place, Hadleigh, IP7 5DL
Tel no: (01473) 822880
www.thehadleighram.co.uk
Modern European | £30
Cooking score: 2

Siblings Oliver and Lorna Macmillan have worked magic on this formerly very ordinary town-centre pub, fashioning a polished gem of an interior and turning out food that 'blew [the] socks off' one satisfied diner. There are 'stunning flavours' throughout – witness a smoked eel parfait starter, served with ham hock and quail's egg, or delightfully peppery haggis bonbons with gently pickled swede and confit turnip. You'll find echoes of sister restaurant, the Long Melford Swan, in an obvious commitment to local ingredients. A tasting of Dingley Dell pork (fillet, trotter, confit belly, plus all the trimmings), and the roasted breast and braised leg of Suffolk mallard are standout mains. Portions are generous, but it's wise to leave room for an

inventive take on rhubarb and custard or the 'wonderfully intense' mandarin sorbet served with an orange parfait. A bottle of Chilean Merlot opens the wine list at £15.50.
Chef/s: Oliver Macmillan and Nicholas Traher. **Open:** all week L 12 to 2.30 (4 Sun), Mon to Sat D 6 to 9. **Meals:** alc (main courses £13 to £22). Set L £16 (2 courses) to £18. Sun L £20 (2 courses) to £23. **Details:** 50 seats. 20 seats outside. Separate bar. Wheelchair access. Music.

Lavenham
The Great House
Impressive Gallic cooking
Market Place, Lavenham, CO10 9QZ
Tel no: (01787) 247431
www.greathouse.co.uk
Modern French | £43
Cooking score: 4

The market square of this medieval village is one of Suffolk's showpieces and the Great House occupies a prime corner site. Inside, exposed timbers point to the house's venerable age. Run by Régis and Martine Crépy as a restaurant with rooms for the past 30 years, it's a magnet for those in the know – being, in the words of one regular, 'a very stable ship'. The kitchen keeps abreast of the times and offers a wide-ranging daily changing menu: one that might bring both carrot, orange and coconut-milk soup, and scallops baked with garlic and parsley butter, to the table. Among main courses, fine materials are evident in a mint and marjoram-marinated local lamb saddle teamed with garden pea 'crémeux'. Then, if a plate of French cheeses doesn't tempt, try orange and mandarine Napoléon cheesecake with clementine jam and lime, ginger and chocolate sauce. The French-leaning wine list opens at £16.90.
Chef/s: Régis Crépy. **Open:** Wed to Sun L 12 to 2.30, Tue to Sat D 7 to 9 (9.30 Fri and Sat). **Closed:** Mon, Jan, 2 weeks summer. **Meals:** alc (main courses £20 to £29). Set L £19 (2 courses) to £24. Set D £34. Sun L £34. **Details:** 50 seats. 28 seats outside. Music. Car parking.

Long Melford
Scutchers
Quality ingredients and generous portions
Westgate Street, Long Melford, CO10 9DP
Tel no: (01787) 310200
www.scutchers.com
Modern British | £35
Cooking score: 2
£5 OFF

Parts of this converted village pub date back to the 15th century and the old exposed timbers lend plenty of character to the open-plan dining room. Nick and Di Barrett have run Scutchers as a country restaurant since 1991, though they now restrict opening times. Nick's cooking remains rooted in classic bistro style, but his menus continue to move with the times. Bold flavours dominate, with an emphasis on quality ingredients and generous portions. Dishes manage to achieve the tricky balance of being modern in style yet still appealing to more conservative palates. Thus, a typical menu might start with sautéed veal kidneys with mushrooms and a tarragon and Dijon mustard sauce, followed, perhaps, by fillet of halibut on lobster and chive risotto, with banana fritters, salted caramel and vanilla ice cream to finish. Wines from £17.
Chef/s: Nick Barrett. **Open:** Thur to Sat L 12 to 2, D 7 to 9.30. **Closed:** Sun to Wed. **Meals:** alc (main courses £18 to £27). **Details:** 50 seats. 25 seats outside. Separate bar. Wheelchair access. Car parking.

❙❙❘ Please send us your feedback
To register your opinion about any restaurant listed in the Guide, or a new restaurant that you wish to bring to our attention, please visit the web address at the bottom of the page. Your feedback informs the content of the book and will be used to compile next year's reviews.

Moulton

NEW ENTRY
The Packhorse Inn
Glamorous pub, thoroughbred cooking
Bridge Street, Moulton, CB8 8SP
Tel no: (01638) 751818
www.thepackhorseinn.com
Modern British | £35
Cooking score: 3

£5 OFF 🏠

Chris and Hayley Lee have upped sticks from
the Bildeston Crown (see entry) and now
produce skilful, if less flamboyant, cooking at
this once down-at-heel pub. Brought back to
glamorous life by financier and local resident,
Philip Turner, the Packhorse is as much a place
for pub staples (Red Poll burger with Suffolk
Gold cheese, say), as it is for Chris's more
refined food. The 'inspired' cooking might
tempt with seared foie gras, pain d'épices and
pineapple, or stone bass with carrot, artichoke
and braised red chicory. Cheffy, triple-cooked
chips come in a plant pot, steak and kidney pie
arrives as fillet steak with braised shin and
kidney pudding, and homemade fruit pastilles
(presented in a sweetie jar) make a fun 'mini
after'. House wine starts at £16.95.
Chef/s: Chris Lee. **Open:** all week L 12 to 2.30, D 7
to 10 (9 Sun). **Meals:** alc (main courses £14 to £22).
Details: 60 seats. 30 seats outside. Music. Car
parking.

Orford
The Trinity, Crown & Castle
Anglo-Italian flavours in a magical maritime
setting
Orford, IP12 2LJ
Tel no: (01394) 450205
www.crownandcastle.co.uk
Modern British | £35
Cooking score: 3

🏠 V

A little to the south of Aldeburgh, along the
windswept coast, you'll find this sturdy inn:
once part of Orford Castle, but now standing
proud of the keep. Orford is a hive of gastro-

activity (two smokehouses and a bakery), and
the Trinity does its bit too. Uncomplicated
brasserie-style cooking is the stock-in-trade,
with local materials to the fore. Fish is a strong
point, from skate in black butter with
cucumber and brown shrimps to sea bass with
caponata, but there are thoroughbred meats
too, as in Dingley Dell pork belly with proper
crackling and apple sauce. Reports have found
fluctuating standards of late, with certain
dishes failing to make the right impact, but
there's no lack of professionalism in the
service. The grown-up approach to desserts is
also something to cheer, producing razor-
sharp lemon jelly with lemon curd and
almond florentine. A graphically user-
friendly wine list begins at £17.95.
Chef/s: Charlene Gavazzi and Ruth Watson. **Open:**
all week L 12.15 to 2.15, D 6.30 to 9.15. **Meals:** alc
(main courses £15 to £25). **Details:** 50 seats. 50
seats outside.

Snape Maltings
The Plough & Sail
Making its mark by the Maltings
Snape Maltings, IP17 1SR
Tel no: (01728) 688413
www.theploughandsailsnape.com
Modern British | £20
Cooking score: 1

£5 OFF £30 ▼

Sitting cheek by jowl with the world-famous
Snape Maltings, this snug boozer is well
versed in providing for the Aldeburgh Festival
crowds, culture-hungry tourists and
binocular-toting walkers. Twins Alex and Oli
Burnside have made their mark since taking
over, and their efforts are being amply
rewarded. The food has a cosmopolitan accent,
although local supplies form the building
blocks for the likes of cod fillet on chickpea
and vegetable curry, sausage and mash or wild
duck breast and confit leg with roast beetroot
and orange jus. 'Light bites' are added at lunch,
Suffolk alemeister Adnams supplies the beers
and decent wines start at £11 a carafe. See
overleaf for details.

Chef/s: Oliver Burnside. **Open:** all week L 12 to 2.30 (3 Sun), D 6 to 9 (10 Sat). **Meals:** alc (main courses £11 to £19). **Details:** 100 seats. 40 seats outside. Separate bar. Wheelchair access. Music. Car parking.

▌Southwold

The Crown Hotel

Buzzy pub with good food
90 High Street, Southwold, IP18 6DP
Tel no: (01502) 722275
www.adnams.co.uk
Modern British | £30
Cooking score: 2

🍷 🛏 V

'It is wonderful to be able to book, particularly as the bar is so small' is a sentiment endorsed by many reporters this year. An engaging and popular all-rounder, the Crown Hotel has been the flagship of brewer and wine merchant Adnams for some three decades, and it puts on a visibly stylish and well-priced show for customers in search of food. There's a new chef in the kitchen, yet despite an early wobble during the changeover, the consensus is that things have settled down nicely. The kitchen doesn't try to reinvent the culinary wheel, though the carefully sourced, often local produce is precisely cooked: whether in pub classics such as confit duck leg or beef burger, or for something more adventurous, say lightly cured longshore cod with chorizo and bean stew. The Crown's jewel – its wine list – is defined by value and diversity, from oddball gems to classic beauties, plus good choice by the glass. Bottles start at £18.
Chef/s: Rory Whelan. **Open:** all week L 12 to 2 (2.30 Sat and Sun), D 6.30 to 9 (6 to 9.30 Sat). **Meals:** alc (main courses £13 to £20). Sun L £19 (2 courses) to £22. **Details:** 80 seats. 36 seats outside. Separate bar. Wheelchair access. Car parking.

Sutherland House

Oak-beamed heritage and low food miles
56 High Street, Southwold, IP18 6DN
Tel no: (01502) 724544
www.sutherlandhouse.co.uk
Modern British | £30
Cooking score: 2

£5 OFF 🛏

A doubly enviable position, in produce-rich Suffolk and in the oldest building in Southwold, gives this restaurant-with-rooms an effortless advantage. Chef Jed Tejada makes the most of it by highlighting local fish, seafood and meat, even going as far (or not) as totting up food miles for dishes that have their roots close by. Mussels from the Deben estuary go into moules marinière, while the black pudding served with scallops, foie gras and apricot purée is homemade. Sea bass with roasted artichoke, salsify and pancetta fritters, or halibut loin with tiger prawns and citrus butter, maintain the seafood focus, though for meat eaters there's belly and fillet of Blythburgh free-range pork with apple fondant. Desserts include a house speciality of bread-and-butter pudding with a crisp sugar top, and Suffolk ices made by Criterion in Bury St Edmunds. Wine from a short but accessibly priced list starts at £17.50.
Chef/s: Jed Tejada. **Open:** all week L 12 to 2, D 7 to 9. **Closed:** Mon (Oct to Mar), 2 weeks Jan. **Meals:** alc (main courses £17 to £25). **Details:** 40 seats. 30 seats outside. Wheelchair access. Music.

▌Stanton

The Leaping Hare

Charming vineyard eatery in 16th-century barn
Wyken Vineyards, Stanton, IP31 2DW
Tel no: (01359) 250287
www.wykenvineyards.co.uk
Modern British | £28
Cooking score: 3

£5 OFF £30 ▼

The well-heeled of Suffolk love coming here – and it's not surprising. The restaurant menu, served by 'smiling and attentive' staff, plunders

East Anglia for Cromer crab, Dingley Dell pork and Newmarket lamb, while game in season is from the Wyken Estate itself. A warm hint of spice makes a vivid pea purée a perfect foil for crisp lamb sweetbreads, while careful seasoning brings out the sweetness in pan-fried brill, served with a stuffed baked red pepper. Quicker searing might have prevented a bavette steak – flavoursome, but a tricky cut to get right – from being a tad tough, but all is forgiven with a taste of the rich, garlicky tarragon hollandaise and the crisp, just-made chips alongside. A lusciously creamy lemon posset, topped with sharpish blueberries, makes a fine end to a meal. Pay £20 for an uncomplicated fish-friendly Madeleine Angevine white from the Wyken Vineyards, or £18 for the house red.

Chef/s: Jon Ellis. **Open:** all week L 12 to 2.30, Fri and Sat D 7 to 9. **Closed:** 25 Dec to 5 Jan. **Meals:** alc (main courses £14 to £20). Set L £19 (2 courses) to £21. Set D £26 (Fri only). **Details:** 45 seats. 20 seats outside. Separate bar. Wheelchair access.

▮ Stratford St Mary

LOCAL GEM
▲ The Swan

Lower Street, Stratford St Mary, CO7 6JR
Tel no: (01206) 321244
www.stratfordswan.com
British | £26 £5 OFF

Mark Dorber, of the Anchor at Walberswick renown (see entry), has found a free house in which to indulge his passion for food and beer/wine pairing. Every dish on chef Steven Miles' refreshingly short menu is paired with something hoppy or vinous. A Trimbach Gewürztraminer makes a fragrant foil for pig's head croquette, while a robust ribeye steak matches well with Woodforde's Norfolk Nip. Dark ale – Mark suggests Trappist Rochefort 10 – works brilliantly with a bitter chocolate and salted-caramel tart. Wine from £15.50. Open Wed to Sun.

▮ Tuddenham

★ BEST SET LUNCH ★

Tuddenham Mill

Appealing cooking in seductive setting
High Street, Tuddenham, IP28 6SQ
Tel no: (01638) 713552
www.tuddenhammill.co.uk
Modern British | £40
Cooking score: 5

It would take a frosty heart not to be bewitched by Tuddenham Mill's swans-and-cygnets prettiness – and a jaded palate not to be thrilled by (relatively) new chef Lee Bye's cooking. Bye, who steps up after two years as sous chef, has steered the menu away from foraged ingredients to produce accessible, enjoyable food such as soft-as-you-like black bream with gently warming dhal and crisp lightly battered mussels, or tender bavette steak with triple-cooked chips. Dishes balance taste, texture and eye-appeal with easy confidence – witness a starter of crispy pig's head, smooth pale-green avocado, edgy red-rimmed radish and peppery watercress. 'You can taste every ingredient' commented one diner after eating Cullen skink with its crumbled oatcake, rich confit egg yolk and fresh cucumber gel. It's the same with puddings: Scottish cranachan elegantly combining nuttiness, bitter chocolatiness, satisfying crunch and uplifting raspberry pizazz. And the set lunch is one of the best-value deals in Suffolk, according to one who thought it 'amazing to eat this standard of food for these prices'. Enjoy it all with wine from a list that opens at £19.95.

Chef/s: Lee Bye. **Open:** all week L 12 to 2.15, D 6.30 to 9.15. **Meals:** alc (main courses £21 to £25). Set L and D £20 (2 courses) to £25. Sun L £25. **Details:** 54 seats. 40 seats outside.

Walberswick

The Anchor

Eco-friendly seaside getaway
The Street, Walberswick, IP18 6UA
Tel no: (01502) 722112
www.anchoratwalberswick.com
Modern British | £27
Cooking score: 3

🛏 £30

This welcoming place teems in summer, a Mecca for middle-class holidaymakers. Families pay homage to the skills of chefs Sophie Mellor and Andy Storer, whose ability to produce satisfying food using carefully sourced ingredients (many grown in an adjacent allotment) merits applause aplenty. Follow half a dozen West Mersea oysters with a Cromer crab and new potato salad (featuring lemony homemade mayonnaise), or go on a palate-pleasing tour of more global flavours: Peking glazed duck with mango salsa, or tempura mackerel with salsa verde and samphire, maybe. If, calamitously, the chocolate fondant with salted-caramel ice cream is finished, sticky toffee pudding is a sound alternative. Mark Dorber's inventive beer or wine pairings entice many; try a slug of Westmalle Dubbel ale with a lamb burger – or play it safe with a £15.95 vin de pays. **Chef/s:** Sophie Mellor and Andy Storer. **Open:** all week L 12 to 3, D 6 to 9. **Closed:** 25 Dec. **Meals:** alc (main courses £14 to £25). **Details:** 90 seats. 120 seats outside. Wheelchair access. Car parking.

Woodbridge

The Riverside

Meals and movies by the river
Quay Street, Woodbridge, IP12 1BH
Tel no: (01394) 382587
www.theriverside.co.uk
Modern British | £25
Cooking score: 1

£5 OFF £30

The Riverside inhabits a cinema and theatre venue not far from the station and offers film and dinner packages to lucky locals. Its menu of globally inspired, trending dishes is versatile enough to run from gravadlax cured in horseradish and vodka with potato raita, or chilli baby squid with watermelon and Thai basil, to sturdy, satisfying mains such as lamb rump with caponata, fried hake in beurre blanc with lyonnaise potatoes, and shallot Tatin with falafel and goats' cheese fritters. Finish with ginger cake frosted in cream cheese and orange. Lunchtime tapas are a strong draw. House Sicilian is £15. **Chef/s:** Luke Parsons. **Open:** all week L 12 to 2.15, Mon to Sat D 6 to 9.30 (10 Fri and Sat). **Closed:** 25 and 26 Dec. **Meals:** alc (main courses £10 to £22). Set D with film £30. **Details:** 65 seats. 30 seats outside. Wheelchair access. Music. Car parking.

Yoxford

LOCAL GEM
▲ Main's

High Street, Yoxford, IP17 3EU
Tel no: (01728) 668882
www.mainsrestaurant.co.uk
Modern British | £28

Saturday morning queues form for the bakery attached to Nancy Main's enterprising local restaurant, but this converted draper's shop is also known for its regular bread-making classes and wholesome evening meals. Local game and fish from the coast meet a larder full of fashionable ingredients – so expect anything from pan-fried squid with chorizo and chickpea salad to slow-braised shin of beef with soft polenta, or pigeon breasts with black pudding and turnip fondant. Wines from £14.50. Open Thur to Sat D only.

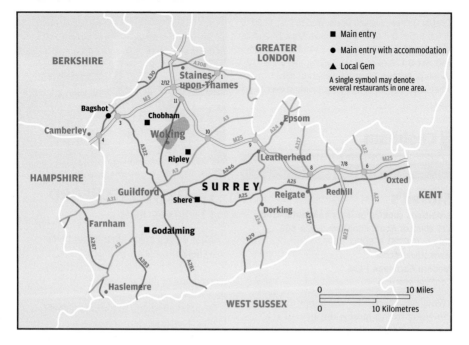

Bagshot

★ TOP 50 ★

Michael Wignall at the Latymer

Breathless displays of contemporary cuisine
Pennyhill Park Hotel, London Road, Bagshot,
GU19 5EU
Tel no: (01276) 486150
www.thelatymer.co.uk
Modern European | £78
Cooking score: 7

Built in the mid-19th century by a civil engineer, Pennyhill lies happily near the sporting lures of Wentworth, Ascot and Sunningdale. Over the years it has been extended in Bath stone, had an orangery added, the gardens formally terraced and the outer walls clad in foliage – the place might well have been in training to become a country house hotel. A choice of eating options culminates with the hot-ticket Latymer room, where Michael Wignall rules the roost (and there's also a chef's table seating up to eight). Wignall makes no bones about the fact that his food is complex, technically highly crafted, but for all that not intended to baffle or bemuse. What could be more heartening than a shellfish stew to begin, a marine cassoulet of razor clams, palourdes and cockles with cuttlefish gnocchi and a poached quail's egg? Or try poached rabbit loin with white polenta, rabbit 'chorizo' in oats, a little oyster mushroom, some truffled Brillat-Savarin, shaved Périgord and crisped milk skin. Main-course proteins are thoroughly explored, as in slow-roast suckling pig with Middle White fillet, caramelised onion and chicory, while desserts play harmonious variations on themes such as lemon (curd and cloud, soft meringue, crystallised rind and lemon thyme ice cream). The extensive wine list may well raise hackles, when tiny glasses start at £8.50, and bottles on the main list at £38. Details overleaf.

Chef/s: Michael Wignall. **Open:** Wed to Fri L 12.30 to 2, Tue to Sat D 7 to 9. **Closed:** Sun, Mon, 24 and 26 Dec, 1 to 15 Jan. **Meals:** Set L £34 (3 courses) to £60. Set D £78 (3 courses). Tasting menu £92 (10 courses). **Details:** 50 seats. Separate bar. Wheelchair access. Car parking. Children over 12 yrs only.

Chobham

★ READERS' RESTAURANT OF THE YEAR ★
SOUTH EAST

Stovell's

Ambitious cooking in leafy commuter-land
125 Windsor Road, Chobham, GU24 8QS
Tel no: (01276) 858000
www.stovells.com
Modern European | £38
Cooking score: 6

'Wow' was enough for one happy diner, emerging from a meal at this 'gem of a restaurant' that has been cheering up Surrey's culinary map since late 2012. There's endless praise for the friendly, knowledgeable staff. Chef Fernando Stovell's ears must be burning with the amount of glowing chatter about his culinary skills. His menu spices up a true marriage of style and substance with generous slugs of inventiveness. Start with a courgette carpaccio with buffalo burrata, 'light and fresh with a lovely kick in the dressing', and follow with beef Wellington from a grain-fed Cumbrian herd, served with truffle mash 'to die for', brassicas and oxtail jus. A 'sublime' rhubarb fool comes with yoghurt ice cream and honeycomb, while an exceptional French/English cheeseboard offers six cheeses and six paired garnishes: eat the nugget of nougat with nutty Comté, for example. The wine list matches the calibre of the food with global choices (from £17.50).
Chef/s: Fernando and Kristy Stovell. **Open:** Tue to Fri and Sun L 12 to 3.30 (4 Sun), Tue to Sat D 6 to 10. **Closed:** Mon, 26 Dec, 2 weeks Jan, Aug bank hol. **Meals:** Set L £16 (2 courses) to £20. Set D £30 (2 courses) to £38. Sun L £25. Tasting menu £60. **Details:** 74 seats. 20 seats outside. Separate bar. Car parking.

🍴 DAVID PITCHFORD
Read's, Kent

What do you enjoy most about being a chef?
I enjoy being self-employed and totally in control of my own destiny.

What inspired you to become a chef?
I had a very forward-thinking headmaster who was one of the first to get girls doing woodwork and boys doing domestic science. For the first time in my life I was the best in the class.

What's your newest ingredient discovery?
Tear-drop peas like they have in St Sebastian, Spain, served with finely chopped shallots in a little melted butter.

Is there any food that evokes strong memories for you?
Hot cross buns. When I was a young chef in the 60s, the Dorchester had its own in-house bakery that supplied most of the hotels and restaurants in London with bread and pastry products.

Do you have a guilty foodie pleasure?
A chicken vindaloo from my local takeaway. But I make my own chips to go with it.

▌Godalming

La Luna

Well-groomed Italian thoroughbred
10-14 Wharf Street, Godalming, GU7 1NN
Tel no: (01483) 414155
www.lalunarestaurant.co.uk
Italian | £30
Cooking score: 4

£5
OFF

La Luna has a contemporary sheen and wouldn't look out of place as some upmarket hotel dining room a few miles north in the metropolis. It's a long way from being a homely trattoria and does a cracking job at providing Surrey locals with Italian food that is a cut above. The fixed-price lunch menu is a veritable steal, while the carte isn't half bad in that department either, given the high-quality ingredients on show. Among antipasti, you can't go wrong with smoked tuna tartare with semi-dried cherry tomato and pickled artichoke heart, before a plate of pasta such as pappardelle with wild mushrooms and roasted butternut squash. Local South Downs lamb makes an appearance among secondi piatti, as roast cannon with a pistachio crust and slow-roasted belly, served with Umbrian lentils. Baked sea bream is among the fish options, and desserts are classy interpretations of classics. Drink regional Italian wines from £15.50.
Chef/s: Valentino Gentile. **Open:** Tue to Sat L 12 to 2, D 7 to 10 (6.30 Sat). **Closed:** Sun, Mon, 25 and 26 Dec, 1 week Jan, Easter, 1 week summer. **Meals:** alc (main courses £12 to £20). Set L £14 (2 courses) to £17. Tasting menu £85 (7 courses). **Details:** 58 seats. Music.

▌▮ Readers Recommend

A 'readers recommend' review is a genuine quote from a report sent in by one of our readers. We intend to follow up these suggestions throughout the year to come.

▌Redhill

READERS RECOMMEND
The Pendleton in St Johns

Modern British
26 Pendleton Road, St Johns, Redhill, RH1 6QF
Tel no: (01737) 760212
www.thependleton.co.uk
'Very friendly, excellent front-of-house and an innovative menu using local, seasonal ingredients. You need to book a few weeks in advance if you want a table on any day.'

▌Ripley

NEW ENTRY
The Anchor

Inviting dining pub with a touch of class
High Street, Ripley, GU23 6AE
Tel no: (01483) 211866
www.ripleyanchor.co.uk
British | £28
Cooking score: 3

£30
▼

An old hand reports that this rejuvenated pub on Ripley's high street is 'a great new find'. The lovingly revamped interior cleverly blends current fashion with original features (and includes understated imagery paying tribute to Ripley's heritage as a one-time cyclists' Mecca). Although related to Drake's across the road (see entry), the Anchor is no fine-dining extension. Mike Wall-Palmer (Drake's former head chef) has judged to a nicety what people want from a modern pub, offering simple yet innovative fare along the lines of cauliflower soup given an unusual spike by curried almond praline; the freshest wild sea bream teamed with watercress purée, parsnip and a splash of red wine sauce; or roast saddle of venison with sweet potato and pickled blackberries. To finish, 'not-to-be-missed' desserts include frozen ginger mousse with rhubarb and pistachios. Good local ales and a respectable wine list (from £18) complete a thoroughly satisfying picture. See overleaf for details.

Chef/s: Michael Wall-Palmer. Open: Tue to Fri and Sun L 12 to 2.30 (4 Sun), Tue to Fri D 6 to 9.30. Sat 12 to 9.30. Closed: Mon, 25 Dec. Meals: alc (main courses £14 to £19). Details: 40 seats. Separate bar. Wheelchair access. Music. Car parking.

Drake's Restaurant
Picture-perfect modern food
The Clock House, High Street, Ripley, GU23 6AQ
Tel no: (01483) 224777
www.drakesrestaurant.co.uk
Modern British | £60
Cooking score: 5
🍷 V

Steve and Serina Drake can feel proud of transforming Ripley's dining scene over the past few years. Their handsome Georgian restaurant may not suggest modern culinary pyrotechnics with its old timbers, pastel colours, white-clad tables and formal staff, but the kitchen produces course after course of intelligent, complex food. Two tasting menus (plus a veggie alternative) are built around a procession of small plates, delivering bright, contemporary ideas with just enough risk-taking to keep customers on their toes. A test meal produced real high points: lovely charred mackerel with 'fabulous' beetroot snow; 'sparklingly fresh' turbot with broccoli kombu, crisp mussels and sesame; and Scottish venison loin accompanied by a mini venison burger, celeriac, parsley and an 'awesome' orange purée. Bread and canapés were outstanding, as was a pre-dessert of grapefruit curd with peanut praline, passion fruit and condensed milk sorbet. The sommelier was 'on top form', too, advising on suitable wine matches from the patrician list; prices from £19.
Chef/s: Steve Drake. Open: Wed to Sat L 12 to 2, Tue to Sat D 7 to 9.30. Closed: Sun, Mon, 2 weeks Christmas, 2 weeks Aug. Meals: Tasting menu £60 (6 courses) to £80. Details: 40 seats. Separate bar. Music.

▌Shere

Kinghams
Cottagey restaurant, comforting cooking
Gomshall Lane, Shere, GU5 9HE
Tel no: (01483) 202168
www.kinghams-restaurant.co.uk
Modern British | £35
Cooking score: 1

Paul Baker has been the driving force behind this amenable 17th-century cottage restaurant since 1993. Found on the main road running around the edge of Shere, Kinghams delivers bags of original features across several small dining rooms (dark oak beams and timbers, ancient doorways, open fireplaces), and is popular with a generally affluent and self-confident crowd who appreciate the comforting (rather than assertive) cooking. Typical choices include smoked haddock and asparagus tart glazed with Welsh rarebit, char-grilled rump of lamb with swede and haggis mash, garlic potato purée and a rich jus, and a blackcurrant Bakewell tart to finish. Wines from £18.50.
Chef/s: Paul Baker. Open: Tue to Sun L 12 to 2, Tue to Sat D 7 to 9. Closed: Mon, 25 Dec to 4 Jan. Meals: alc (main courses £15 to £21). Set L and D £18 (2 courses) to £26. Sun L £25. Details: 48 seats. 20 seats outside. Music. Car parking.

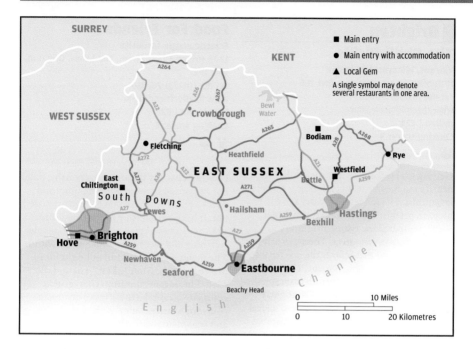

▌Bodiam

The Curlew

Contemporary cooking in the countryside
Junction Road, Bodiam, TN32 5UY
Tel no: (01580) 861394
www.thecurlewrestaurant.co.uk
Modern British | £39
Cooking score: 4

V

The one-time coaching inn with its pristine weatherboarded exterior delivers a thoroughly modern restaurant experience. Everything, from its smart décor to its pretty-as-a-picture culinary output, defies the splendid isolation of the location. You'll get glimpses into the kitchen from the sizeable L-shaped dining room (it's quite the Tardis, done out in a slick, country-chic manner), while the menus intrigue with their brevity. A first-course plate of Jersey Royals makes the potato the star attraction, but another starter of cured sea trout packs a little more punch. Modern cooking techniques are embraced with little piles of onion 'ash' accompanying organic chicken, and combinations such as goats' curd with meltingly soft lamb (and asparagus several ways) show a creative mind at work. Flavours hit the mark in a raspberry sorbet that comes with a textbook crème brûlée. The wine list has an interesting selection of organic and biodynamic bottles, with prices starting at £19.50.

Chef/s: Tony Parkin. **Open:** all week L 12 to 2.30, D 6 to 9.30 (9 Sun). **Closed:** 26 Dec, 1 Jan. **Meals:** alc (main courses £16 to £23). Set L and D £20 (2 courses) to £25. **Details:** 64 seats. 32 seats outside. Music. Car parking.

Symbols

🛏 Accommodation is available

£30 Three courses for less than £30

V Separate vegetarian menu

£5 OFF £5-off voucher scheme

🍷 Notable wine list

Brighton

The Chilli Pickle

Vibrant, idiosyncratic Indian
17 Jubilee Street, Brighton, BN1 1GE
Tel no: (01273) 900383
www.thechillipickle.com
Indian | £24
Cooking score: 3
£30

Getting a table for dinner at the Chilli Pickle usually requires forward planning – this place is rammed. The move a few years ago to modern premises attached to the myhotel hasn't hampered the rise of Brighton's favourite Indian restaurant. There's clearly an appetite for food that reflects the diversity and excitement of the Subcontinent. The modern curves of the room gain warmth from splashes of rich colours, and the buzz of contented customers confirms that this is indeed a local hot spot. Dishes range from recipes inspired by the streets of Mumbai (fragrant pav bhaji) to a luxe korma designed to impress the Nawabs of Lucknow. From the tandoor come platters of succulent meat (plus paneer or sea bream), and vibrant chutneys and pickles make for punchy accompaniments. Thalis are a lunchtime treat (staff will even deliver to your Brighton home), and there are interesting tea and beer options. Wines from £17.30.
Chef/s: Alun Sperring. **Open:** all week L 12 to 3, D 6 to 10.30 (10 Sun). **Closed:** 25 and 26 Dec. **Meals:** alc (main courses £11 to £18). Set L £14. Set D £24 (2 courses) to £28. **Details:** 115 seats. 8 seats outside. Wheelchair access. Music.

¶¶ Please send us your feedback

To register your opinion about any restaurant listed in the Guide, or a new restaurant that you wish to bring to our attention, please visit the web address at the bottom of the page. Your feedback informs the content of the book and will be used to compile next year's reviews.

Food For Friends

Eclectic veggie favourite
17-18 Prince Albert Street, The Lanes, Brighton, BN2 1PE
Tel no: (01273) 202310
www.foodforfriends.com
Vegetarian | £23
Cooking score: 1
V £30

Shaking off any feelings that vegetarian cooking can only be homely or worthy, Food For Friends has moved with the times and packs a punch as a 'restaurant', vegetarian or not. It has been a fixture in the Lanes since 1981, with curved glass windows for people-watching and plenty of natural wood within. The menu these days is full of bright ideas drawn from the Middle East, Asia and the Med. The output runs from char-grilled courgette escabèche to an 'inventive' main course of warm haloumi with avocado, mango and wasabi-roasted cashews. Wines start at £16.95.
Chef/s: Tomas Kowalski. **Open:** all week 12 to 10 (10.30 Fri and Sat). **Closed:** 25 and 26 Dec. **Meals:** alc (main courses £9 to £13). Set L and D £20. Sun L £11. Meze L £35. **Details:** 60 seats. 20 seats outside. Wheelchair access. Music.

The Gingerman

Jam-packed foodie hot spot
21a Norfolk Square, Brighton, BN1 2PD
Tel no: (01273) 326688
www.gingermanrestaurants.com
Modern European | £35
Cooking score: 3

The restaurant that spawned a mini empire, the Gingerman was set up by Ben McKellar back in 1998 and hit the ground running with its style of smart modern food. The other group members are pubs (see entries for the Ginger Pig and the Ginger Fox), but the original address is an oh-so-discreet restaurant. On a gently sloping side street heading down to the seafront, this remains an intimate dining spot, with relatively closely packed tables and stylish décor. The dinner menu constitutes very good value given the quality, while the set lunch is a bargain. There's much craft and creativity on show in dishes such as a starter of cod tongue and cheek with glazed fennel and a lemon and seaweed emulsion, or main course fillet of beef with black treacle. Masala chai tea soufflé with passion fruit kulfi maintains standards until the end. Wines start at £15.95.

Chef/s: Ben McKellar and Dan Kenny. **Open:** Tue to Sun L 12.30 to 2, D 7 to 10. **Closed:** Mon, 1 to 15 Jan. **Meals:** Set L £15 (2 courses) to £18. Set D £30 (2 courses) to £35. Sun L £23. **Details:** 32 seats. Wheelchair access. Music. Car parking.

NEW ENTRY
The Jolly Poacher
Easy-going pub with hearty food
100 Ditchling Road, Brighton, BN1 4SG
Tel no: (01273) 683967
www.thejollypoacher.com
Modern European | £29
Cooking score: 2
£5 OFF £30

With a menu that doesn't shy away from bold, earthy flavours, plus draught beers on tap, this old hostelry has bags of rustic appeal. It's more dining pub than boozer these days, but rough wooden tables and floorboards and modern artworks (for sale) combine to create an easy-going vibe that fits seamlessly into this part of town. The chef is happy using hearty ingredients like calf's brains and morcilla, but equally there's beer-battered cod and chips or char-grilled ribeye. Chilli-salt squid with aïoli packs a fiery punch, and another starter of leek and Roquefort tart shows sensitivity with powerful flavours. A main-course dish called 'The Jolly Choucroute' is full of rich, meaty things (including that wonderful morcilla), and desserts run to chocolate tart with honeycomb and crème fraîche. Wines start at £16.

Chef/s: Anthony Burns. **Open:** Tue to Sun L 12 to 2.30 (3 Sat, 3.30 Sun), Tue to Sat D 6 to 9.30 (10 Fri and Sat). **Closed:** Mon. **Meals:** alc (main courses £14 to £23). Set L £10. Set D £14 (2 courses) to £17. Sun L £20. **Details:** 55 seats. 17 seats outside. Music.

The Restaurant at Drakes
Fine dining at a classy boutique hotel
43-44 Marine Parade, Brighton, BN2 1PE
Tel no: (01273) 696934
www.therestaurantatdrakes.co.uk
Modern European | £44
Cooking score: 5
£5 OFF 🛏

The seaside hurly-burly seems a world away when seated in the basement restaurant of this cool boutique hotel. The Georgian town house, facing the sea and just a short stroll from the pier, is home to Brighton's most fine-dining of venues, where tables are dressed to impress and the décor mixes subtle Regency touches with today's fashionable neutrality. Chef Andrew MacKenzie adds freebie courses along the way to increase that special-occasion feeling, with his menu dealing in modern European constructions of some refinement. Chicken consommé with poached oysters and leek is a first course revealing classical intentions, followed by a main course of rabbit loin wrapped in pancetta and stuffed with pistachios and its own leg meat. There's a tasting menu, too, and desserts like Yorkshire rhubarb soufflé with custard ice cream show technical prowess. The ground-floor cocktail bar can top or tail (or both) a visit. Wines start at £25.

Chef/s: Andrew MacKenzie. **Open:** all week L 12.30 to 1.45, D 7 to 9.30. **Meals:** alc (main courses £20 to £25). Set L £20 (2 courses) to £25. Set D £30 (2 courses) to £40. Sun L £30. **Details:** 45 seats. Separate bar. Music.

Symbols
🛏 Accommodation is available

£30 Three courses for less than £30

V Separate vegetarian menu

£5 OFF £5-off voucher scheme

🍾 Notable wine list

NEW ENTRY
64 Degrees

Loud, packed and a lot of fun
53 Meeting House Lane, Brighton, BN1 1HB
Tel no: (01273) 767914
www.64degrees.co.uk
Modern British | £30
Cooking score: 4

£5
OFF

Fizzing with energy, Michael Bremner has given Brighton a restaurant with the sort of edge the city craves. This place is cool. A little glass box of a building with the kitchen at the back, it's loud, packed and great fun. A seat at the counter gives full view of all the cheffy action, and customers sit shoulder-to-shoulder with their fellow hipsters. Small plates is the deal, sharing the way to go, with dishes that pack a punch (chicken wings with a kim-chee marinade and foamy blue-cheese topping) and deliver bang-on flavours (soft and melting lamb with courgette-infused fregola and little pieces of feta adding a salty kick). Dishes arrive as and when, with not every plate reaching the same heights, but this is ambitious stuff made with the full armoury of current techniques. A dessert of 'textures of chocolate' comes in a tin cup. The short wine list starts at £20.
Chef/s: Michael Bremner. **Open:** all week L 12 to 3, D 6 to 9.45. **Closed:** 25 and 26 Dec. **Meals:** alc (main courses £5 to £12). **Details:** 27 seats. Music.

Terre à Terre

Quirky vegetarian favourite
71 East Street, Brighton, BN1 1HQ
Tel no: (01273) 729051
www.terreaterre.co.uk
Vegetarian | £28
Cooking score: 3

V £30

A trailblazer for vegetarian food since 1993, Terre à Terre has long been confounding cynics with its sheer invention. The restaurant was eco-friendly and ethically minded way before such things became *de rigueur*. There's no sense of worthiness, though, and no

preaching. The room heads back deep into the building, with space for 100-plus diners seated at wooden tables, surrounded by warming colours. The vibe is energetic, 'the staff are lovely'. The playful menu isn't always the easiest to interpret: 'brûlée vous', for example, is a savoury grana Padano version, with gingerbread crumbs, pickled Jerusalem artichokes and more; a main-course 'ding dong' proves to be a pie with mulled mushrooms and chestnut porcini foam. The kitchen has a love of global flavours, with the world its oyster – but no oysters, of course. 'The puddings are to die for', and there are cocktails, mocktails, organic beers and wines from £18.15.
Chef/s: György Gramán. **Open:** all week 12 to 10.30 (11 Sat, 10 Sun). **Closed:** 25 and 26 Dec. **Meals:** alc (main courses £14 to £15). Set L and D £36. **Details:** 100 seats. 15 seats outside. Wheelchair access. Music.

NEW ENTRY
Twenty Four St Georges

Ambitious cooking in the modern vein
24-25 St George's Road, Brighton, BN2 1ED
Tel no: (01273) 626060
www.24stgeorges.co.uk
Modern European | £32
Cooking score: 3

It's easy enough to find on the main drag through Kemptown, and helped by the fact the address is in the name. Brighton is relatively short on gaffs turning out sharp, modern food and Dean Heselden and Jamie Everton-Jones' place certainly delivers contemporary cooking with a bit of 21st-century swagger. A movable feast of local artworks (for sale) decorates the walls, and the menu also has a regional flavour, consisting of refined plates that mostly hit the target. A starter of pink and tender pigeon breast arrives pretty as a picture in a salad with leeks and asparagus, while main-course mackerel and clam 'Seasider' takes the beachy theme to the limit (and beyond). You'll find some very good cooking here, not least in a dessert of

lemon drizzle cake with a perky rhubarb ice cream. And the Menu du Jour option is amazingly good value. House French is £14.
Chef/s: Dean Heselden and Jamie Everton-Jones.
Open: Tue to Fri D only from 6. Sat from 12.30.
Closed: Mon, Sun. **Meals:** alc (main courses £12 to £24). Tue to Thur D and Sat L 'Menu du Jour' £19 (2 courses) to £22. **Details:** 50 seats.

▌East Chiltington
The Jolly Sportsman
Country-style pub-restaurant
Chapel Lane, East Chiltington, BN7 3BA
Tel no: (01273) 890400
www.thejollysportsman.com
Modern British | £29
Cooking score: 2
£30

This pastel green, part-weatherboarded and extended old cottage is found deep in the Sussex countryside in a truly tranquil spot. A blackboard listing the likes of lunchtime ploughman's and a serious dedication to local beers are two of its pubby attributes, but other than a few scrubbed tables (with candles) in the plank-floored bar, the 'cosy-dark and atmospheric' Jolly Sportsman has the look and feel of a country restaurant catering for a prosperous, gentrified crowd. Menus make good use of local, seasonal produce (including homegrown) and a reporter who visited for a mid-week lunch enjoyed mackerel and crab scotch egg with crab bisque, a 'beautifully cooked, crisp skinned' cod fillet topped with salsa verde and served with 'well-flavoured' shrimps, saffron vinaigrette, and 'delicious' Jersey Royals, and a Ditchling-fizz jelly chock full of raspberries with a well-made pannacotta. Service is 'very friendly and efficient.'
Chef/s: Bruce Wass. **Open:** Tue to Sun L 12.15 to 2.30 (3.30 Sun), Tue to Sat D 6 to 9.30 (10 Fri and Sat). **Closed:** Mon, 25 Dec. **Meals:** alc (main courses £14 to £20). Set L £15 (2 courses) to £17. Set D £20. Sun L £20. **Details:** 80 seats. 50 seats outside. Separate bar. Wheelchair access. Car parking.

▌Eastbourne
The Grand Hotel, Mirabelle
Gloriously traditional seafront hotel
King Edward's Parade, Eastbourne, BN21 4EQ
Tel no: (01323) 412345
www.grandeastbourne.com
Modern European | £45
Cooking score: 5
£5 OFF ▮ ▬

There's nothing like a grand old seafront hotel, and nothing else in Eastbourne looks remotely like the Grand, whose meringue-white tiers rise majestically above the western end of the esplanade. The Mirabelle, the hotel's full-dress dining room, has its own discreet side entrance. Within, aubergine and cream upholstery and immaculate table appointments set the tone, and Gerald Röser's modernisation of grand-hotel dining is as discreetly judged as that side entrance. You'll find plenty of assertive flavours, mind, and some unabashed richness, in dishes such as brandade fritters with warm potato salad, chorizo and grilled red pepper, or tapenade-crusted lamb rump with potato and rosemary tortilla. Set your taste-buds to stunned for the 'extra-bitter' Guayaquil chocolate fondant with pain d'épices parfait. The deeply classical wine list does homage to the French regions, before packing its bags for sunnier climes, scooping up Greek Assyrtiko, Israeli Syrah and Touriga Nacional from the Douro Valley along the way. Prices start at £26.50 and aim high, with standard glasses from £6.95.
Chef/s: Gerald Röser. **Open:** Tue to Sat L 12.30 to 2, D 7 to 10. **Closed:** Sun, Mon, first 2 weeks Jan.
Meals: Set L £21 (2 courses) to £25. Set D £42.
Details: 50 seats. Separate bar. Wheelchair access. Music.

Fletching

The Griffin Inn

Village inn with modern food and views
Fletching, TN22 3SS
Tel no: (01825) 722890
www.thegriffininn.co.uk
Modern British | £30
Cooking score: 3

£5 OFF 🍷 🛏

Maintaining its status as a local watering-hole and bringing some classy food to the table, alongside smart accommodation, the Griffin is a true inn. It has been in the hands of the Pullan family since 1979, and safe hands they have proved, keeping the historic feel of the place and showing attention to detail where it matters. Local beers, a serious wine list and some creative modern European cooking make a winning combination, with the terrace and garden providing great views when the weather allows. The kitchen sources a good amount of regional produce and takes time to cure its own gravadlax (served with citrussy fennel, capers and dill crème fraîche). Fillet of Sussex beef stars in a main course with shallot tarte Tatin, and desserts run to vanilla pannacotta with whisky and espresso ice cream. That excellent wine list kicks things off at £15.50, with twenty wines offered by the glass.
Chef/s: Matthew Sandells. Open: all week L 12 to 2.30 (3 Sat and Sun), Mon to Sat D 7 to 9.30, Sun pm bar menu only. Closed: 25 Dec. Meals: alc (main courses £14 to £25). Sun L £25 (2 courses) to £30. Details: 60 seats. 25 seats outside. Separate bar. Wheelchair access. Car parking.

🍴 Visit us
Online
To find out more about
The Good Food Guide, please visit
www.thegoodfoodguide.co.uk

Hove

The Foragers

Corner boozer with a local flavour
3 Stirling Place, Hove, BN3 3YU
Tel no: (01273) 733134
www.theforagerspub.co.uk
Modern British | £24
Cooking score: 3

£30

One half of the Foragers has classic pub appeal while the other goes for a rather more trendy dive-bar vibe. They both fall into the 'rough-and-ready' category, but in a nice way, and an easy-going attitude prevails throughout. The kitchen turns out some nifty plates of food that reflect a dedication to localism and sustainability. A blackboard menu in the bar deals in Welsh rarebit, burgers and the like, with the main menu offering some well-crafted stuff that makes this boozer in the Hove hinterland well worth knowing about. There's a terrace garden, too. Pan-seared scallops come in an inventive partnership with pea and ham purée and crispy caperberries, and a main-course daily special might be tender confit duck leg with herby mash and a silky red wine sauce. Wind up with home-made polenta cake with a perky apricot sorbet. Drink real ale or wine (from £16.50).
Chef/s: Patrick Calf and Danny Frape. Open: all week 12 to 10 (12 to 6 Sun). Meals: alc (main courses £12 to £20). Set L and D £12 (2 courses). Details: 90 seats. 90 seats outside. Separate bar. Music.

The Ginger Pig

All-rounder with punchy flavours
3 Hove Street, Hove, BN3 2TR
Tel no: (01273) 736123
www.gingermanrestaurants.com
Modern British | £30
Cooking score: 3

A big old boozer adjacent to the seafront, the Ginger Pig strikes a good balance between its pub and restaurant personalities. It's still a pub – unlike many other made-over establishments – with the front part of the premises pulling in the punters for a beverage or two, while the bulk of the place is given over to the business of eating. An easy-going brasserie vibe pervades, with wooden floors, banquette seating and dark wood tables setting the scene, along with a menu that aims to deliver punchy flavours and doesn't want for good ideas. Flame-grilled mackerel with satay sauce and Asian-spiced granola is a happy fusion to start, leading on to a trusty 35-day-aged ribeye with chips cooked in dripping, and winding up with an Earl Grey cheesecake. The Gingerman group (see entries) runs the gaff, with a bargain lunch and patio garden among the attractions. Wines start at £14.95.

Chef/s: David Moltersill and Ben McKellar. **Open:** all week L 12 to 2 (12.30 to 4 Sat and Sun), D 6 to 10. **Meals:** alc (main courses £13 to £19). **Details:** 80 seats. 30 seats outside. Separate bar. Wheelchair access. Music.

Graze
A romantic Regency-style showpiece
42 Western Road, Hove, BN3 1JD
Tel no: (01273) 823707
www.graze-restaurant.co.uk
Modern British | £35
Cooking score: 3
£5 OFF **V**

Kate Alleston's restaurant is named in honour of the small-plate concept of the tasting menu. That approach was relatively new when she opened in 1996, but the world has since caught up. There's a regular carte, too, so convention can be maintained. 'A cracking little find', as one reader put it, Graze takes the city's Regency past as inspiration for its décor, with lots of red velvet and gilt mirrors producing a boudoir vibe. The kitchen seeks out regional produce and turns the bounty into classy plates of contemporary food. Miso-cured mackerel, for example, is a bright idea, while another course from the tasting menu sees hand-dived scallops pimped up with a foie gras velouté and Jerusalem artichokes. Off the carte, duck is combined with octopus (plus kim-chee and

puffed rice) in a creative combo, and for dessert, textures of chocolate with rosemary is a little treasure trove. Wine starts at £19.
Chef/s: Adrian Hawkins. **Open:** Tue to Sun L 12 to 2 (12.30 to 3.30 Sun), D 6.30 to 9.30. **Closed:** Mon, 1 to 8 Jan. **Meals:** Set L £18. Set D £28 (2 courses) to £35. Sun L £15. Tasting menu £55 (7 courses). **Details:** 50 seats. 4 seats outside. Music.

The Little Fish Market
Classy seafood cookery in a former fish shop
10 Upper Market Street, Hove, BN3 1AS
Tel no: (01273) 722213
www.thelittlefishmarket.co.uk
Seafood | £40
Cooking score: 4
£5 OFF

Duncan Ray worked with Heston Blumenthal during the heady early years at the Fat Duck, but he's no fan of the science fandango. Here in a one-time fishmonger's by the old fish market, sparklingly fresh seafood is what to expect, cooked with precision and a light touch. Ray is all alone in the basement kitchen – it's OK, he likes it that way – with a solo server out front and no chip-and-pin machine in sight (cash only). The seafood is landed nearby (Newhaven or Brighton usually) and there's genuine refinement and skill in Ray's execution. Lobster ravioli is powered up with orange and basil, with pink grapefruit and pickled fennel doing the same for potted local crab. Cod is caught by hook and line and comes with crab mayonnaise and langoustine sauce, with desserts such as poached pear with gingerbread ice cream showing the same attention to detail. Wines start at £22.
Chef/s: Duncan Ray. **Open:** Wed to Sat L 12 to 2, Tue to Sat D 7 to 9.30. **Closed:** Sun, Mon, 1 week Mar, 1 week Aug, 1 week Sept, 1 week Dec. **Meals:** Set L £38 (2 courses). Set D £46 (3 courses). **Details:** Cash only. 22 seats. Music.

LOCAL GEM
▲ The Hove Kitchen
102-105 Western Road, Hove, BN3 1FA
Tel no: (01273) 725495
www.thehovekitchen.com
Modern European | £28

Occupying a row of shopfronts on Hove's main shopping, eating and drinking drag, the Hove Kitchen has pavement tables and windows that open up to bring the outside in (or the other way around). It's a chilled-out sort of place with a shabby-chic finish and can turn out a nifty cheeseburger with shoestring fries, knock up a cocktail or two, or up the ante for local scallops with cauliflower purée and crispy pancetta. Wines from £15.25. Open all week.

▌Rye
The Ambrette at Rye
Elegant Indian on top of its (local) game
White Vine House, 24 High Street, Rye, TN31 7JF
Tel no: (01797) 222043
www.theambrette.co.uk
Indian | £30
Cooking score: 1

£5
OFF

Dev Biswal is a chef who marinates chicken in coriander and wild garlic, cooks it sous-vide and serves it with a chicken roulade, lentil salad, raita and coriander chutney. And that's just a starter. The Ambrette is no ordinary Indian restaurant. The 450-year-old building has a stylish modern interior, so no curry-house clichés, just modern artworks and dark wood tables. The food is described as modern Indian fusion, which amounts to chicken pie (with local cauliflower and cashew nuts), and Kentish mutton and pearl barley biryani. There's a sister restaurant in Margate, Kent (see entry). Wines start at £14.95.
Chef/s: Dev Biswal and Deepak Suman. Open: all week L 11.30 to 2.30, D 6 to 9.30 (5.30 to 10 Fri to Sun). Meals: alc (main courses £12 to £19). Set L £15 (2 courses) to £20. Details: 46 seats. Music.

The George Grill
Bolt-hole with quality crowd-pleasers
The George Inn, 98 High Street, Rye, TN31 7JT
Tel no: (01797) 222114
www.thegeorgeinrye.com
Modern European | £32
Cooking score: 2

🛏

In the summer months you can eat in the Courtyard Garden, in winter in front of the log fire – this cleverly reworked 16th-century coaching inn has the seasons nicely covered. Likewise, the contrast between the hotel's Tudor heritage and the food served in the George Grill couldn't be more telling. While reports on the cooking have been mixed in the past, it looks like new chef Robert Wright is really finding his feet. His style is a self-assured take on the modern British theme and displays an admirable commitment to local produce. Alongside a streamlined collection of pub classics, there could be Rye Bay scallops teamed with boudin noir, samphire and celeriac, and Josper-baked Romney Marsh lamb with dauphinois potato, purple sprouting broccoli, anchovy dressing and red wine jus. Desserts take in vanilla bread-and-butter pudding with almond crème anglaise, and there are classy Sussex cheeses. Wines from £18.50.
Chef/s: Robert Wright. Open: all week L 12 to 3, D 6 to 9.30. Meals: alc (main courses £12 to £22). Details: 75 seats. 20 seats outside. Separate bar. Music.

Landgate Bistro
Landmark bistro that champions local food
5-6 Landgate, Rye, TN31 7LH
Tel no: (01797) 222829
www.landgatebistro.co.uk
Modern British | £29
Cooking score: 3

V £30

'My favourite place in Rye,' was the verdict of one visitor, who keeps returning to this small, unassuming neighbourhood restaurant overlooking the medieval Landgate, for the

high-quality service and excellent value. Martin Peacock clocks up ten years here in 2015, still doing what he does best: familiar combinations of quality ingredients, conscientiously sourced and cooked with care. A test meal found perfect fresh-from-the-oven bread; a precise, balanced starter of venison carpaccio with a dollop of horseradish cream and a sprinkling of Wensleydale cheese, thyme and peppery radish; then a main course of Romney Marsh lamb (pink chump chop, tender braised shoulder, fried sweetbreads, a little hotpot) that was a triumph of flavour and accuracy of cooking. Well-timed turbot served with a well-made chive hollandaise, green beans and sautéed new potatoes has been highly praised too, and the English cheese selection is superb. Wines from £17.80.
Chef/s: Martin Peacock. **Open:** Sat and Sun L 12 to 2.15, Wed to Sat D 7 to 9. Sun D 7 to 9 (bank hols only). **Closed:** Mon, Tue, 24 to 26 and 31 Dec, 1 Jan, bank hols. **Meals:** alc (main courses £13 to £20). Set L £16 (2 courses) to £19. Set D £18 (2 courses) to £21. **Details:** 32 seats. Separate bar. Music.

Webbe's at the Fish Café

Easy-going seafooder with strong local roots
17 Tower Street, Rye, TN31 7AT
Tel no: (01797) 222226
www.webbesrestaurants.co.uk
Seafood | £29
Cooking score: 2
£30

OK, so the name doesn't trip off the tongue, but it lays down a marker that this is part of Paul Webbe's local restaurant empire, which includes his original Wild Mushroom at Westfield (see entry). The name is a bit of a giveaway about the food too. Most of the fish and seafood dishes are in the modern British style, but the menu occasionally looks further afield, as in a bouillabaisse – 'an absolute belter of a dish' – and Indian-spiced mackerel fillet with cucumber, mint yoghurt and poppadom. A pair of reporters enjoyed 'simple, delicious' potted crab, 'lovely' steamed plaice fillets on a mix of summer vegetables, and Dover sole with a classic beurre blanc (note no

accompaniments, which means side dishes can bump up the bill), then a well-made raspberry crème brûlée. There's also char-grilled sirloin or slow-cooked ox cheek (for those who must), very good service, and wine starts at £16.50.
Chef/s: Matthew Drinkwater. **Open:** all week L 12 to 2.30, D 6 to 9.30. **Meals:** alc (main courses £12 to £17). Set L £15 (2 courses) to £20. **Details:** 60 seats. Music.

Westfield
The Wild Mushroom

Civilised country restaurant
Woodgate House, Westfield Lane, Westfield, TN35 4SB
Tel no: (01424) 751137
www.webbesrestaurants.co.uk
Modern British | £35
Cooking score: 2

Paul and Rebecca Webbe have been running their welcoming late-Victorian farmhouse for some 17 years, suggesting a rare level of reliability and consistency. People love the way it strikes the right note for a country restaurant – a little bit old-fashioned, with proper white tablecloths and pre-meal drinks in the conservatory or pretty garden when the weather obliges. They applaud pleasant service and the seasonal cooking, which takes full advantage of the superb raw materials on the doorstep. Local game gets standard modern treatment: a starter of cured venison and venison sausage is given a lift by wasabi cream and beetroot relish; pheasant breast arrives with chanterelle and cider sauce. The kitchen also delivers satisfaction with slow-braised ox cheek and beef with caramelised onions and claret jus, and desserts such as blood-orange bavarois with basil meringue or salted-caramel parfait. Wines from £16.95. See also Webbe's at the Fish Café in Rye.
Chef/s: Chris Weddle. **Open:** Wed to Sun L 12 to 2, Wed to Sat D 7 to 9.30. **Closed:** Mon, Tue. **Meals:** alc (main courses £13 to £20). Set L £17 (2 courses) to £20. Sun L £24. Tasting menu £34. **Details:** 40 seats. Separate bar. Wheelchair access. Music. Car parking.

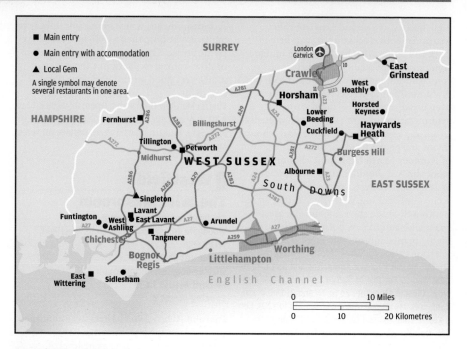

Map legend:
- ■ Main entry
- ● Main entry with accommodation
- ▲ Local Gem

A single symbol may denote several restaurants in one area.

SURREY
London Gatwick
Crawley
Horsham
West Hoathly
East Grinstead
Horsted Keynes
HAMPSHIRE
Fernhurst
Billingshurst
Lower Beeding
Cuckfield
Haywards Heath
Tillington
Petworth
Midhurst
WEST SUSSEX
Albourne
Burgess Hill
EAST SUSSEX
South Downs
Singleton
Lavant
Funtington
West Ashling
East Lavant
Arundel
Chichester
Tangmere
A259
Worthing
Bognor Regis
Littlehampton
East Wittering
Sidlesham
English Channel

0   10 Miles
0   10   20 Kilometres

▌ Albourne

The Ginger Fox

Country pub with urban roots
Muddleswood Road, Albourne, BN6 9EA
Tel no: (01273) 857888
www.gingermanrestaurants.com
Modern British | £30
Cooking score: 3

With its mop of neatly trimmed thatch and a garden serving up views over the South Downs, the Ginger Fox is a country pub that can provide you with a three-cheese ploughman's and a pint of local ale. But first and foremost it's a dining destination (that ploughman's is a classy version): part of Ben McKellar's group of 'Ginger' restaurants based in Brighton and Hove. The interior is pared down to fashionable rusticity and the menu strikes at the heart of the modern foodie – duck Scotch egg with confit gizzard preceding braised beef cheek with bone-marrow croquette, say. This is a kitchen that can turn out cod fillet with crispy chicken skin, salt-baked celeriac and mushroom consommé as a main course, and deliver a comforting dessert such as marmalade sponge pudding. Wines start at £14.95.
Chef/s: James Dearden. **Open:** all week L 12 to 2 (3 Sat, 4 Sun), D 6 to 10 (6.30 Sat, 9 Sun). **Closed:** 25 Dec. **Meals:** alc (main courses £14 to £20). Set L £15. **Details:** 80 seats. 100 seats outside. Separate bar. Wheelchair access. Music. Car parking.

▌ Arundel

The Town House

Resembling a classy Parisian brasserie
65 High Street, Arundel, BN18 9AJ
Tel no: (01903) 883847
www.thetownhouse.co.uk
Modern British | £30
Cooking score: 3
£5 OFF 🍴 V

Renaissance ceilings aren't exactly ten a penny in Sussex, but there's one here, and it's the genuine article too, shipped over from Florence. Its golden glow brings a touch of

16th-century glamour to the dining room of Lee and Katie Williams' restaurant-with-rooms opposite the castle. This is not a place preserved in aspic, though, as the engaging service team and Lee's well-crafted cooking provide an experience not a million miles from a classy Parisian brasserie. Fine dining is the name of the game, they say, with high-quality (and some local) ingredients turned into smart plates of classically inspired food. Foie gras with homemade brioche and onion chutney is an exemplary rendition, and there's pink and tender loin of local venison to follow, or sea bass with a chive butter sauce. Flavours hit the spot all the way to dessert of orange cheesecake with white chocolate ice cream. House French is £18.

Chef/s: Lee Williams. **Open:** Tue to Sat L 12 to 2.30, D 7 to 9.30. **Closed:** Sun, Mon, 25 and 26 Dec, 1 and 2 Jan, 2 weeks Easter, 2 weeks Oct. **Meals:** Set L £18 (2 courses) to £22. Set D £26 (2 courses) to £30. **Details:** 24 seats.

Cuckfield

Ockenden Manor

Confident cooking with panache
Ockenden Lane, Cuckfield, RH17 5LD
Tel no: (01444) 416111
www.hshotels.co.uk
Modern French | £56
Cooking score: 5

£5 OFF 🚗

Reached down a little lane in the centre of town, Ockenden is an Elizabethan manor house of great bucolic charm, comfortingly elegant rather than frighteningly grand. Despite the nine acres of grounds, and the oak panelling and log fires within, the cons are as mod as can be when it comes to spa treatments – and the extensive, but straightforwardly written menus of modern Anglo-French cooking in which Stephen Crane, incumbent here since 2000, specialises. Proceedings might kick off with Stilton dumplings, served with a salad of chicory, walnuts and pear, or with Carlingford oysters three ways: Rockefeller, beignets and as they come. Move on to cod forestière with crispy potato and

puréed onion, or a breast and pasty of local duck, served with kale, apple and celeriac. To close matters, it might be hazelnut dacquoise (layered sponge) with white chocolate ice cream. Five house wines come at £26.

Chef/s: Stephen Crane. **Open:** all week L 12 to 2, D 7 to 9 (6.30 Fri and Sat). **Meals:** Set L £20 (2 courses) to £26. Set D £56. Sun L £37. **Details:** 76 seats. Separate bar. Wheelchair access. Car parking.

East Grinstead

Gravetye Manor

Enchanting Elizabethan charmer
Vowels Lane, East Grinstead, RH19 4LJ
Tel no: (01342) 810567
www.gravetyemanor.co.uk
Modern British | £60
new chef/no score

🚗 V

It's a lovely old building, a many-gabled Elizabethan manor house set in meandering, beautiful grounds. Inside, dark oak panelling and ornate plaster mouldings predominate, with elegant proportions and period features providing plenty to catch the eye. George Blogg used to head the kitchen at Hotel TerraVina in Hampshire (see entry), where his formidable cooking built around foraged ingredients and local produce so impressed readers and inspectors that we made him our chef to watch for 2014. Now George has taken over the Gravetye kitchens too late for us to inspect properly. Early dishes, however, have included ravioli of white Brighton crab, scallop and lovage with a brown crab purée and garden herb flowers, and cannon of lamb with roasted garlic, rosemary crust, wilted greens and a croustillant of haggis and braised lamb. As for the wine list, there's an impeccable French starting point and peerless choice from around the globe; bottles from £30.

Chef/s: George Blogg. **Open:** all week L 12 to 2, D 6.30 to 9.30. **Meals:** alc (main courses £29 to £32). Set L £25 (2 courses) to £30. Set D £40. Sun L £35. **Details:** 40 seats. 20 seats outside. Separate bar. Wheelchair access. Music. Car parking. Children over 7 yrs only.

East Lavant
The Royal Oak Inn
Country inn focused on food
Pook Lane, East Lavant, PO18 0AX
Tel no: (01243) 527434
www.royaloakeastlavant.co.uk
Modern British | £29
Cooking score: 2
£5 OFF 🚗 £30

The Royal Oak's current owner admits that this gentrified country inn on the fringes of the Goodwood Estate is now primarily a restaurant-with-rooms rather than a local drinking den. It still has blazing fires in winter, real ales tapped from the cask and great views of the South Downs, but rustic-chic trappings and a conservatory dining room tell a rather different story. Menus change with the seasons, although old faithfuls such as burgers, 'long-aged' steaks or haddock and chips are year-round fixtures alongside the likes of shredded oriental duck salad, pea and pancetta risotto, slow-cooked local lamb or corn-fed chicken with tomato, chorizo and mixed-bean cassoulet. Desserts are comforting favourites such as fruit crumble or treacle tart with clotted cream. The wide-ranging 90-bin wine list is sourced from Berkmann Cellars in London; bottles start at £16.95.
Chef/s: Daniel Ward. **Open:** all week L 12 to 2.30 (3 Sun), D 6 to 9 (9.30 Sat, 6.30 Sun). **Meals:** alc (main courses £14 to £28). **Details:** 50 seats. 30 seats outside. Music. Car parking.

East Wittering
Samphire
Laid-back by the beach
57 Shore Road, East Wittering, PO20 8DY
Tel no: (01243) 672754
www.samphireeastwittering.co.uk
Modern British | £25
Cooking score: 2
£5 OFF £30

Only 50 metres from the beach, chef/ proprietor David Skinner's tiny village restaurant prides itself on serving fish and seafood supplied by the fishermen at the end of the road. With its rustic, driftwood-style tables and cushioned benches, the comfortable dining room and tiny terrace provide an appropriately laid-back, no-frills backdrop for 'varied and innovative' dishes that show a strong seasonal awareness. Everything from bread to ice cream is made in the open-plan kitchen, which might deliver a winter meal of baked scallop and Selsey crab soufflé with pickled samphire salad, followed by pan-fried cod with crispy pig's cheek, crab rösti, buttered greens and parsley sauce. Chocolate fondant, teamed with a rhubarb ice cream and rhubarb coulis, could end matters. Service is friendly and efficient, and staff 'really care about food'. Wine from £15.
Chef/s: David Skinner. **Open:** Mon to Sat L 12 to 2, D 6 to 10. **Closed:** Sun, 25 and 26 Dec, 2 weeks Jan. **Meals:** alc (main courses £11 to £18). Set L £13 (2 courses) to £16. **Details:** 28 seats. 10 seats outside. Music.

Fernhurst
★ TOP 50 PUB ★
The Duke of Cumberland Arms
Archetypal country pub with high aspirations
Henley, Fernhurst, GU27 3HQ
Tel no: (01428) 652280
www.dukeofcumberland.com
Modern British | £35
Cooking score: 4

This charming, 16th-century country pub in the South Downs National Park appears rustic and unassuming – an impression reinforced by beams, log fires, bare tables and cask-drawn ales. But press through to the modern dining extension and you'll discover some accomplished cooking. Simon Goodman's kitchen concentrates on excellent raw materials and details are not overlooked: praise is heaped on the bread, the house honey-roasted ham and the all-British cheeseboard. Pub staples such as the local sausages, mash and rich onion gravy on the lunch menu are done very well, but expect, too, precise up-to-date cooking that comes with bright ideas and assured style: perhaps sea bass teamed with a fricassee of samphire, spinach, green beans, monk's beard, new potatoes and caviar velouté. To finish, there could be a well-reported Baileys liqueur bread-and-butter pudding with crème anglaise, or warm chocolate fondant with chocolate soil and ice cream. Wines from £15.50.

Chef/s: Simon Goodman. **Open:** all week L 12 to 2, Tue to Sat D 7 to 9. **Closed:** 25 and 26 Dec. **Meals:** alc (main courses £14 to £30). **Details:** 66 seats. 140 seats outside. Separate bar. Wheelchair access. Music. Car parking.

Funtington
Hallidays

Local produce in an ancient setting
Watery Lane, Funtington, PO18 9LF
Tel no: (01243) 575331
www.hallidays.info
Modern British | £37
Cooking score: 2
£5 OFF

Andy Stephenson is the kind of guy who likes to get his hands dirty, whether that's rooting around for foraged ingredients or stoking his wood-fired oven. His restaurant in a row of 13th-century former cottages within the South Downs National Park seems straight out of central casting for a period drama, with a mop of thatch and shimmering flint. However, the 'tired' interior lacked the same charm for one reader. There's evident passion for local produce in dishes such as Selsey crab cakes with watercress and tomato salsa, and a main-course duo of Racton Park Farm lamb with a sauce soubise and glazed shallots. The locally sourced menu changes weekly and everything from bread to ice cream is made in-house, with the latter turning up as a praline version, served alongside a butterscotch-roasted pineapple perked up with spiced rum. The set lunch menu is cracking value, and wines begin at £19.50.

Chef/s: Andrew Stephenson. **Open:** Wed to Fri and Sun L 12 to 2, Wed to Sat D 7 to 9.30. **Closed:** Mon, Tue, 1 week Mar, 2 weeks Aug. **Meals:** alc (main

courses £18 to £22). Set L £16 (2 courses) to £23. Set D £21 (2 courses) to £28. Sun L £24. **Details:** 24 seats. Separate bar. Wheelchair access. Music. Car parking.

Haywards Heath
Jeremy's Restaurant

Special-occasion dining at everyday prices
Borde Hill Garden, Balcombe Road, Haywards Heath, RH16 1XP
Tel no: (01444) 441102
www.jeremysrestaurant.co.uk
Modern British | £38
Cooking score: 4
£5 OFF

The location is a pretty enough picture at any time of year, but not to be missed in high summer, when the surrounding Borde Hill gardens are in full shimmering bloom, and the Victorian walled garden teems with fruit and vegetable life. In what was the estate's stable block, Jeremy and Vera Ashpool's welcoming restaurant has been well bedded in since 1998. The seasonally inspired menus draw on modern British thinking to show off their plenteous fresh produce to its best advantage. Chicory and Jerusalem artichoke are the garnishes for a salad and parfait of Gressingham duck, which might set the ball rolling towards brill in mussel and dill velouté with fennel, black beans and sea veg, or tenderloin and slow-roast belly of Plumpton pork with beetroot, cavolo nero and gnocchi in Calvados sauce. If you liked the beetroot, have a little more with dark chocolate mousse and orange mascarpone. Wines open at £18.

Chef/s: Jimmy Grey. **Open:** Tue to Sun L 12.30 to 2.30, Tue to Sat D 7 to 10. **Closed:** Mon, first 2 weeks Jan. **Meals:** alc (main courses £19 to £23). Set L and D £17 (2 courses) to £20. Sun L £26 (2 courses) to £32. **Details:** 55 seats. 55 seats outside. Separate bar. Wheelchair access. Music. Car parking.

▌Horsham

Restaurant Tristan
Outstanding cooking at moderate prices
3 Stans Way, Horsham, RH12 1HU
Tel no: (01403) 255688
www.restauranttristan.co.uk
Modern British | £45
Cooking score: 6

Tristan Mason served time at the stove with
Marco Pierre White, picking up a thorough
understanding of classical culinary matters.
But since striking out on his own in 2008, he
has embraced the innovative techniques that
define our time. The results are 'great', 'lovely'
and 'fabulous'. It all takes place on the first floor
of a 16th-century building (above the buzzy
all-day café-bar), where chunky oak rafters
combine with chic wallpaper to give a
contemporary sheen. This is a thoroughly
modern kind of gaff, with a menu that makes a
virtue of brevity – 'hake, parsley, turnip'.
Expect precision timing, quality produce,
balanced flavours and everything to look
stunning on the plate. A first-course duck egg
is cooked at 64°C to oozing perfection (with
white asparagus and morels), while main-
course 'lamb, kid, goat' is a truly creative
combo. The classy desserts run to blood-
orange soufflé with fennel granita. Wine
from £24.
Chef/s: Tristan Mason. **Open:** Tue to Sat L 12 to 2.30,
D 6.30 to 9.30. **Closed:** Sun, Mon, first 2 weeks Jan,
27 Jul to 9 Aug. **Meals:** Set L £18 (2 courses) to £25.
Set D £38 (2 courses) to £45. **Details:** 42 seats.
Separate bar. Music. No children.

▌Horsted Keynes

NEW ENTRY
The Crown Inn
Food very much at the top of the agenda
The Green, Horsted Keynes, RH17 7AW
Tel no: (01825) 791609
www.thecrown-horstedkeynes.co.uk
Modern British | £25
Cooking score: 2
£5 OFF 🍽 £30

Recently spruced up, the Crown boasts an
opened-up interior rich with fabulous
fireplaces and copious beams – the old girl has
plenty of character. There's room enough in
the 16th-century inn for both drinkers and
diners, though food is very much top of the
agenda. The menu combines classy renditions
of pub classics with a bit of brasserie-style
razzle-dazzle. A starter of braised ham hock
terrine is as pretty as a slice of French
patisserie, with a cauliflower mousse and
meaty jelly perched on top. Mains might
deliver a rump steak burger topped with
smoked Goodwood cheese, or fillet of bream
with cockles and prawns. There are daily
specials, too (if the staff remember to mention
them), and desserts such as an underwhelming
vanilla pannacotta. A terrace backs on to the
village cricket green, and accommodation
consists of four bedrooms. House Spanish
is £18.50.
Chef/s: Mark Raffan. **Open:** all week L 12 to 2 (2.30
Fri and Sat, 4 Sun), Mon to Sat D 6 to 9 (9.30 Fri
and Sat). **Meals:** alc (main courses £13 to £23).
Details: 80 seats. 70 seats outside. Wheelchair
access. Music. Car parking.

Lavant

The Earl of March
Finely honed seasonal dishes
Lavant Road, Lavant, PO18 0BQ
Tel no: (01243) 533993
www.theearlofmarch.com
Modern British | £32
Cooking score: 4

£5 OFF **V**

The village location near Chichester has the verdant South Downs as a backdrop, the original 'green and pleasant land' that William Blake apostrophised from the east bay window here in 1803. A Georgian coaching inn that once sustained travellers on the Midhurst road, the Earl is nowadays the image of a modern country pub. The bar has Sussex ales on tap, and serves pub snacks, but the focus of the dining operation is Luke Gale's seasonally evolving contemporary menus. Humorous appropriations being the current mood, you might start with 'fish and chips' (tempura sea bass with pea gel and a sweet-potato chip), while the serious business emerges in seared venison loin with celeriac dauphinois in beetroot and port jus. Pear poached in star anise and vanilla is accompanied by popcorn ice cream and berry purée. Slow, inattentive service can be a letdown, especially when it means waiting for something from the decent wine list (bottles from £18).
Chef/s: Luke Gale. Open: all week L 12 to 2.30 (3 Sun), D 5.30 to 9.30 (9 Sun). Meals: alc (main courses £15 to £25). Set L and D £18 (2 courses) to £20. Sun L £15.50. Details: 60 seats. 60 seats outside. Separate bar. Music.

Lower Beeding

The Crabtree
A genuine hostelry with sound culinary talent
Brighton Road, Lower Beeding, RH13 6PT
Tel no: (01403) 892666
www.crabtreesussex.co.uk
Modern British | £32
Cooking score: 2

England is hardly deficient in old coaching inns, but few come as idyllically situated as the Crabtree, an originally Tudor hostelry in the countryside outside Horsham. 'It has the most amazingly beautiful garden, with cosy sheepskin throws on picnic benches and quirky hammocks to relax in after lunch,' confides a local regular. You might think it's the hammocks that swing it, but that would be to overlook a menu of modern British food that's teeming with good ideas. Hay-smoked mackerel in chorizo oil with shaved fennel, pickled cucumber and aïoli might be the overture to mains such as roast wood pigeon with celeriac purée and potato gratin, or Loch Duart salmon with a bunch of seafood for company (razor clams, mussels, baby squid), as well as char-grilled leeks in chervil-lemon butter. Finish with blood-orange and poppy-seed tart, served with marmalade ice cream. A commendably broad-based wine selection opens at £17.
Chef/s: Mark Wadsworth. Open: Mon to Sat L 12 to 2.30, D 7 to 10. Sun 12 to 7. Closed: 25 Dec. Meals: alc (main courses £15 to £50). Set L £15 (2 courses) to £18. Set D £22 (2 courses) to £30. Sun L £14. Details: 75 seats. 150 seats outside. Separate bar. Wheelchair access. Music. Car parking.

LOWER BEEDING

★ TOP 50 ★
The Pass
Fireworks and fun in the kitchen
South Lodge Hotel, Brighton Road, Lower
Beeding, RH13 6PS
Tel no: (01403) 891711
www.southlodgehotel.co.uk
Modern British | £65
Cooking score: 7

🍴 V

One of the biggest changes in British
restaurant culture over recent years is our
seemingly insatiable desire to get up close and
personal to the action. If once we didn't care
what went on behind the swing doors, now
we want a piece of it. The Pass was specifically
designed to meet that need: a restaurant in the
kitchen, just 26 seats, right by the pass. Blood,
sweat and tears (actually, nothing of the sort –
more like cool, calm and creative), as Matt
Gillan and his team knock up some mightily
impressive things. It all takes place in the sort
of swanky country hotel that meets your every
need before you realise the need itself. The Pass
feels startling modern in this rather dignified
setting. Screens show the cheffy business in
glorious close-up, so everyone gets a gander.
Tasting menus are the way: small plates of
phenomenally dynamic food. Dish
descriptions are brief – extremely so on 'The
Surprise Experience' menu ('Trout', followed
by 'Langoustine' . . . you get the idea) – and
high-quality ingredients impress throughout.
Some combinations such as pork, apple and
celeriac may sound traditional, but what
arrives is inventive, clever and full of flavour.
Clam, kiwi and radish is a heart-stoppingly
creative trio, with the thrills continuing into
desserts such as parsnip, pistachio and passion
fruit. The wine list has a global spread, prices
starting at £28.
Chef/s: Matt Gillan. **Open:** Wed to Sun L 12 to 1.30,
D 7 to 8.30. **Closed:** Mon, Tue, first 2 weeks Jan.
Meals: Set L £25 (3 courses) to £55. Set D £65 (6
courses) to £85. Sun L £35 (5 courses) to £55.
Details: 26 seats. Separate bar. Wheelchair access.
Car parking. Children over 12 years only.

▌Petworth

NEW ENTRY
The Leconfield
Smart cooking and surroundings
New Street, Petworth, GU28 0AS
Tel no: (01798) 345111
www.theleconfield.co.uk
Modern British | £30
Cooking score: 3

In a town filled with antique shops, boutiques
and tea shops, the Leconfield restaurant and
bar fits in perfectly. Its 17th-century features
are enhanced by wide limed-oak boards,
leather, pastel shades and modern art. The
kitchen displays a passion for seasonality and
local produce (south-coast fish, locally reared
meats), and skilfully blends simplicity with
colour, texture and flavour. The cooking is
underpinned by classic influences, with a nod
to the Med (and beyond). A summer lunch
produced a lovely light dish of heritage
tomatoes, buffalo mozzarella, Parma ham and
basil, as well as some green asparagus teamed
with poached egg, smoky bacon crumb and an
elegant petit salad. 'Lovely, crisp-skinned' grey
mullet fillet was next, with the smoothest,
buttery mash complemented by the citrus-
liquorice hit of a fennel and grapefruit salad
with wild-garlic croûton. A 'wibbly-wobbly'
vanilla pannacotta finished with mixed berry
compote and almond tuile made the perfect
conclusion. Admirable wines from £19.
Chef/s: David Craig-Lewis. **Open:** Tue to Sun L 12 to
2.30 (3 Sun), Tue to Sat D 6 to 9.30. **Closed:** Mon, 25
and 26 Dec. **Meals:** alc (main courses £11 to £24).
Details: 70 seats. Wheelchair access. Music.

🍴 Please send us your feedback
To register your opinion about any
restaurant listed in the Guide, or a new
restaurant that you wish to bring to our
attention, please visit the web address at
the bottom of the page. Your feedback
informs the content of the book and will
be used to compile next year's reviews.

▌Sidlesham

The Crab & Lobster

Contemporary seafood by a nature reserve
Mill Lane, Sidlesham, PO20 7NB
Tel no: (01243) 641233
www.crab-lobster.co.uk
Modern European | £55
Cooking score: 3

Pagham Harbour is a tidal inlet and nature reserve rich with birdy action, and the 300-year-old Crab & Lobster occupies a plum spot on the water's edge (check out the outside tables). It's a smart place with a contemporary sheen amid the low ceilings and open fireplaces, and bedrooms come with telescopes to enable closer inspection of the abundant wildlife. The restaurant takes a modern tack, with lots of regional ingredients to boost the sense of place, and a decidedly pan-European spin to proceedings. Potted rabbit is pointed up by an accompanying shallot marmalade, and Selsey crab cakes get a kick from mango, sesame and chilli jam. Fish is a good bet – loin of hake in beer batter or a bouillabaisse-style fish stew – while Southdown lamb might crop up as roasted rump, confit shoulder and shepherd's pie with black cabbage and Madeira jus. Finish with plum tarte Tatin. Wines from £16.50.
Chef/s: Clyde Hollett. Open: Mon to Fri L 12 to 2.30, D 6 to 9.30 (10 Fri). Sat and Sun 12 to 10 (9 Sun). Meals: alc (main courses £17 to £31). Set L £22 (2 courses) to £26. Details: 48 seats. 48 seats outside. Wheelchair access. Music. Car parking.

▌Singleton

LOCAL GEM
▲ The Partridge Inn

Grove Road, Singleton, PO18 0EY
Tel no: (01243) 811251
www.thepartridgeinn.co.uk
British | £25 £5 OFF

The traditional Tudor village inn is located on the Goodwood Estate in a pretty Sussex village near Chichester. Run by a former executive chef of the London Ritz, it has an old-school panelled country ambience that provides the backdrop for modern pub dishes such as tiger prawns in garlic and herb butter, heartily sustaining steak, mushroom and ale pie with chips, or black bream with crushed potatoes and wilted spinach in sauce vierge. End with a double chocolate brownie and cream. Wine from £16. Open all week.

▌Tangmere

Cassons

Small restaurant run with evident passion
Arundel Road, Tangmere, PO18 0DU
Tel no: (01243) 773294
www.cassonsrestaurant.co.uk
Modern British | £39
Cooking score: 3
£5 OFF

A pair of converted 18th-century farm cottages, two miles east of Chichester on the busy A27 dual carriageway, create an unusual rustic restaurant. Run with evident passion and hands-on dedication by chef Vivian Casson, and with husband 'Cass' making a genial front-of-house, this is a homely, cosy sort of place, devoid of any affectation. An 'unbelievable value' set lunch and a fixed-price à la carte come packed with seasonal ideas. Among starters, mini Yorkshire puddings filled with foie gras mousse, shallot marmalade, rémoulade, Sauternes jelly and pear competes for attention with more trendy Selsey crab with asparagus, lime mayonnaise, cucumber, potato glass and lemon gel. There's sirloin steak and twice-cooked chips to follow, or loin of rabbit with leg croustade, grain mustard, lemon thyme sauce and fondant potato. Finish with lemon curd ice cream wrapped in rhubarb sorbet, with rhubarb crumble and milk chocolate aero. Wines start at £21.
Chef/s: Vivian Casson. Open: Wed to Sun L 12 to 2, Tue to Sat D 7 to 9.30. Closed: Mon, 25 to 30 Dec. Meals: Set L £17 (2 courses) to £20. Set D £31 (2 courses) to £39. Sun L £23 (2 courses) to £28. Details: 36 seats. 16 seats outside. Separate bar. Wheelchair access. Music. Car parking.

▌Tillington

NEW ENTRY
The Horse Guards Inn
Best kind of independently owned village inn
Upperton Road, Tillington, GU28 9AF
Tel no: (01798) 342332
www.thehorseguardsinn.co.uk
Modern British | £28
Cooking score: 2

A stone-built 17th-century hostelry next to Petworth House, the Horse Guards is the best kind of independently owned village inn. Inside, a mass of homespun detail charms – muntjac skulls, cheese-graters as candlesticks, vintage china and glassware. Chickens scurry about the pretty garden, where a summerhouse is full of antique miscellanea with a box for stuffing cash into if anything catches your eye. Local buying buttresses Mark Robinson's menus, as do veg and herbs from the pub's own allotment. Sussex Charmer cheese is in the fondue, and a version of 'chorizo' made from local goat meat serves as a topping for rosemary and onion flatbread. Brill grilled on the bone arrives with very garlicky alexanders in mayo, while silky ham and a soft-yolked, new-laid egg come with triple-cooked chips. Finish with something light and fresh, such as blood-orange and mint salad with medjool dates, yoghurt and local honey. A serviceable wine list opens at £16.
Chef/s: Mark Robinson. **Open:** all week L 12 to 2.30 (3 Sat, 3.30 Sun), D 6.30 to 9 (9.30 Fri and Sat). **Closed:** 25 Dec. **Meals:** alc (main meals £10 to £21). **Details:** 50 seats. 50 seats outside. Music.

▌West Ashling

★ TOP 50 PUB ★
The Richmond Arms
Globetrotting, free-spirited food
Mill Road, West Ashling, PO18 8EA
Tel no: (01243) 572046
www.therichmondarms.co.uk
Modern British | £32
Cooking score: 4

Local lad William Jack and his wife Emma have scored a resounding hit since taking over this tidy-looking pub-with-rooms at the foot of the South Downs National Park. A pint-sized bar accommodates local drinkers, while pastel shades and solid wood furniture provide the setting for free-spirited food loaded with globetrotting flavours. Small plates start things off – from Kentucky-fried quail with sweetcorn emulsion and tiny peas, to Selsey crab spring rolls with miso mayonnaise – while mains keep it proudly local and seasonal. How about T-bone of Sussex fallow deer with Manchego croquette, mushrooms and Gentleman's Relish, or sticky, slow-cooked brisket with autumn slaw and dripping chips? The Jacks recently converted their skittle alley into a self-contained bar, which is fed by pizzas and other wood-fired goodies from a vintage Citroën H Van parked outside. Drinks also cast the net widely, from Sussex-brewed ales and 'hedgerow'eaux de vie to international wines (from £15.95).
Chef/s: William Jack. **Open:** Wed to Sun L 12 to 2 (3 Sun), Wed to Sat D 6 to 9. **Closed:** Mon, Tue, 23 Dec to 15 Jan, 23 to 31 Jul. **Meals:** alc (main courses £15 to £22). **Details:** 41 seats. 60 seats outside. Separate bar. Music. Car parking.

▌West Hoathly

The Cat Inn

A cracking village pub
Queen's Square, West Hoathly, RH19 4PP
Tel no: (01342) 810369
www.catinn.co.uk
Modern British | £35
Cooking score: 2

This ancient inn at the heart of a village in the Ashdown Forest is an appealing, tile-hung, former medieval hall house. Inside, there's a refreshingly traditional bar – massive inglenook, plank floor, beams and panelling, simple wooden tables and chairs. Food is served on old dark-wood dining tables in the modernised Victorian rear extension or in the smart new conservatory where glass doors open on to a terrace, giving alfresco opportunities in fine weather. Regular visitors value the reassuring consistency of the food, be they in for lunchtime sandwiches, classics like beer-battered cod or fish pie, or a spring risotto verde of asparagus, samphire, wild garlic, broad beans and peas. Local ingredients and produce from other corners of the UK form the backbone of the menu: Romney Marsh lamb and Rye Bay fish could appear on the specials board, for example. Wines from £16, including a selection from Sussex.
Chef/s: Max Leonard. **Open:** all week L 12 to 2 (2.30 Fri to Sun), Mon to Sat D 6 to 9 (Fri and Sat 9.30). **Closed:** 25 Dec. **Meals:** alc (main courses £10 to £22). **Details:** 102 seats. 40 seats outside. Separate bar. Car parking.

▌Worthing

Crescent Road Restaurant

Modern British
14 Crescent Road, Worthing, BN11 1RL
Tel no: (01903) 204194
www.crescentroad.co.uk
'Octopus with guacamole, belly pork with rhubarb, textures of strawberries – just one of the amazing meals at this lovely restaurant.'

⅏ WILLIAM JACK
The Richmond Arms

What do you enjoy about being a chef?
The freedom of creativity, and the privilege of catering for special occasions in people's lives.

What inspired you to become a chef?
My grandparents in Australia were a very traditional farming family and I was always intrigued by the game they would have hanging in the larder and its plucking and preparation.

What food trends are you spotting at the moment?
There will always be new trends, but thankfully pride in local produce and producers continues to grow.

What is your favourite time of year for food?
Autumn, we pick wild mushrooms that go into the wood-fired oven and we have the first woodcock and snipe sent down from the family in Anglesey.

What food could you not live without?
Salt, olive oil and lemon... You can make anything taste great with these three ingredients.

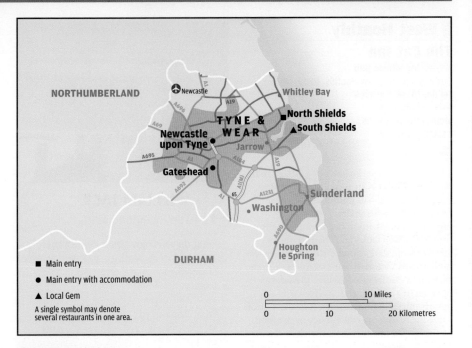

NORTHUMBERLAND

Newcastle

Whitley Bay

A19

TYNE &
WEAR

North Shields
South Shields

Newcastle
upon Tyne

Jarrow

Gateshead

Sunderland

Washington

DURHAM

Houghton
le Spring

■ Main entry

● Main entry with accommodation

▲ Local Gem

A single symbol may denote
several restaurants in one area.

0   10 Miles
0   10   20 Kilometres

▌Gateshead

Eslington Villa

Dependable cooking in a Victorian villa
8 Station Road, Low Fell, Gateshead, NE9 6DR
Tel no: (0191) 4876017
www.eslingtonvilla.co.uk
Modern British | £28
Cooking score: 2

Built in 1880 as an out-of-town bolt-hole for a
northern industrialist, Eslington Villa still
enjoys views over the leafy Team Valley –
although the faraway horizon is now blighted
by Geordie urban sprawl. Reports suggest this
place is a diamond for big birthdays and
anniversaries, although the kitchen is fully
geared up whatever the occasion. Friendly staff
go about their duties efficiently, and the food
also makes a glowing impression. Dishes such
as ham knuckle and foie gras terrine with
pease pudding and Melba toast, or venison
haunch with Macsween haggis, neeps and
tatties show a liking for regional ideas, but the
epigrammatic menu also plunders Europe for
blue cheese pannacotta with red wine jelly,
slow-cooked duck leg with Savoy cabbage and
cherries, or chocolate délice with milk purée,
banana bread and cinder toffee. The
atmosphere and location can't be faulted, and
the wine list does its job: bottles from £17.50.
Chef/s: Jamie Walsh. **Open:** Mon to Sat L 12 to 2.30,
D 5.30 to 10 (6.30 Sat). Sun 12 to 10. **Closed:** 25 and
26 Dec, 1 Jan. **Meals:** Set L £14 (2 courses) to £17.
Set D £23 (2 courses) to £28. Sun L £20. **Details:** 80
seats. 20 seats outside. Separate bar. Wheelchair
access. Music. Car parking.

Symbols

🛏 Accommodation is available

£30 Three courses for less than £30

V Separate vegetarian menu

£5 OFF £5-off voucher scheme

🍾 Notable wine list

READERS RECOMMEND
Six
Modern British
Baltic Centre for Contemporary Arts, South Shore Road, Gateshead Quays, Gateshead, NE8 3BA
Tel no: (0191) 4404948
www.sixbaltic.com
'Went as part of a family of five for Sunday lunch. Good impression – fantastic venue and good food.'

■ Newcastle upon Tyne
Blackfriars Restaurant
Modern food where medieval monks dined
Friars Street, Newcastle upon Tyne, NE1 4XN
Tel no: (0191) 2615945
www.blackfriarsrestaurant.co.uk
British | £28
Cooking score: 3
£5 OFF £30

Once a friary for Dominican monks, the building dates from the 13th century and is the real deal when it comes to historic medieval ambience – this is no theme park reconstruction. The main restaurant over two levels is in the former refectory, and the old banqueting hall is bookable for parties and functions (tread in the footsteps of Edward III). The kitchen deals in spirited flavours wrought from regional ingredients, but there's creativity too. Cauliflower, for example, is slow-roasted for a soup that comes with a Montgomery Cheddar fritter and truffle oil, and main-course smoked haddock is matched with a herb-crusted chicken lollipop and mustard sauce. Northumbrian ribeye steak is jazzed up with crispy marrow and peppercorn sauce, and, for dessert, there's ginger parkin with salted-caramel custard and banana ice cream. The set lunch and early evening menu is a steal (or a gift, as a monk might say). Wines from £17.50.
Chef/s: Dan Duggan. **Open:** all week L 12 to 2.30 (4 Sun), Mon to Sat D 5.30 to 10. **Closed:** 25 and 26 Dec, 1 Jan, bank hols. **Meals:** alc (main courses £12

to £25). Set L and D £15 (2 courses) to £18. Sun L £12. **Details:** 72 seats. 30 seats outside. Separate bar. Music.

★ TOP 50 PUB ★
★ BEST NEW ENTRY: PUB ★
NEW ENTRY
The Broad Chare
Big-boned British pub food
25 Broad Chare, Newcastle upon Tyne, NE1 3DQ
Tel no: (0191) 2112144
www.thebroadchare.co.uk
Modern British | £25
Cooking score: 4
£30

'Proper pub, proper beer, proper food' is the mantra at this cracking venture – a tie-in between local hero Terry Laybourne's '21' group and the Live Theatre events enterprise. Located opposite Laybourne's Café 21 (see entry), it occupies a beautifully restored three-storey building with plants spilling from the balcony, a ground-floor dedicated to real ales and an upstairs dining room tricked out in 'Dickensian chophouse chic'. Bare floorboards and roughly sanded tables suit a mass-appeal, nose-to-tail menu bursting with appetising stuff. Crunchy crackling, crispy pig's ears and cauliflower fritters are spot-on for nibbling, while the rest is a creative mix of dishes with 'bang-on' flavours and generous helpings of big-boned Britishness: haggis with fried duck egg and HP sauce; tangy soused mackerel with potato salad; ox heart cooked long with a light, buttery sauce, peas and braised lettuce; even good old strawberry sundae. This is great cooking, exactly what you want in an historic, town-centre pub. Staff are efficient and super-friendly, the beer list is a must-try and quirky wines start at £16.60
Chef/s: Christopher Eagle. **Open:** all week L 12 to 2.30 (5.30 Sun), Mon to Sat D 5.30 to 10. **Meals:** alc (main courses £11 to £19). **Details:** 50 seats. Separate bar. Music.

Café 21

Stylish quayside favourite
Trinity Gardens, Quayside, Newcastle upon Tyne,
NE1 2HH
Tel no: (0191) 2220755
www.cafetwentyone.co.uk
Modern British | £41
Cooking score: 4

V

The flagship of Terry Laybourne's fleet of
restaurants, now firmly settled in Trinity
Gardens, offers a menu of beautifully balanced
and well-presented dishes in the smart grey
and citrus-themed dining room. A concise
but carefully constructed menu at lunch or
early evening may start with potted rabbit
with rosemary and pickled vegetables,
followed by cod, celeriac purée, buttered
cabbage and hazelnut pesto. Price, choice and
complexity rattle up a little in the evening
with the likes of monkfish 'osso buco' with
saffron risotto, gremolata and veal jus, or
partridge pie, wild mushrooms and Madeira.
Vegetarians are well considered on the regular
menu and are offered a dedicated menu, too. A
sharp, well-informed young team operate
front-of-house. Wines start with a carafe at
£12.90 and rise to what they call 'big guns' at
£60 or more, but with plenty of mid-priced
bottles on an intelligent list.
Chef/s: Chris Dobson. **Open:** all week L 12 to 2.30 (3
Sun), D 5.30 to 10.30 (9.30 Sun). **Closed:** 25 and 26
Dec, 1 Jan, Easter Mon. **Meals:** alc (main courses
£16 to £30). Set L £17 (2 courses) to £20. Set D £18
(2 courses) to £21. Sun L £22. **Details:** 129 seats.
Separate bar. Wheelchair access. Music.

NEW ENTRY

House of Tides

Finely tuned concept dining on the quayside
28-30 The Close, Newcastle upon Tyne, NE1 3RF
Tel no: (0191) 2303720
www.houseoftides.co.uk
Modern British | £55
Cooking score: 4

A Grade I-listed 16th-century merchant's
town house on the historic quayside near the
Tyne Bridge is the latest home for Kenny
Atkinson, a much-lauded chef who has traded
in his country-house background for a
rougher-and-readier urban posting. Eating
mainly occurs in the bipartite first-floor room
where brownish-orange banquettes and
lightweight tables provide the setting.
Atkinson's style is finely tuned concept dining
based on deconstructions and reimaginings,
but founded on familiar enough ideas:
mackerel with gooseberries, lemon and
mustard; quail with apple, celeriac, hazelnuts
and foie gras; spring chicken with macaroni,
baby onions, peas and summer truffle. Not
everything is successful. An overheated
reworking of fish pie with lobster and bony
kipper under Parmesan mash let the side down
at inspection, but a dessert of chocolate délice
with pistachio paste and cherry sorbet was
back on song. The blustering, florid service
approach might set Newcastle teeth on edge.
Wines start at £19.
Chef/s: Kenny Atkinson. **Open:** Tue to Sat D only
5.30 to 9.30. **Closed:** Sun, Mon. **Meals:** Set D £55 (4
courses, Tue to Fri only). Tasting menu £65 (7
courses, Tue to Sat). **Details:** 50 seats. Separate
bar.

Jesmond Dene House
Pretty plates of smart, metropolitan food
Jesmond Dene Road, Newcastle upon Tyne,
NE2 2EY
Tel no: (0191) 2123000
www.jesmonddenehouse.co.uk
Modern European | £50
Cooking score: 5

A self-appointed country house in the city,
this rather grandiose Arts and Crafts mansion
overlooks the sylvan expanses of Jesmond
Dene Park: a landscaped riverside retreat
within easy reach of Newcastle. Inside, it has
been lavishly recast as a boutique hotel with
gorgeous public areas, elegant restaurant and a
summery garden room with sun terrace.
Despite the occasional misfire, the kitchen
delivers pretty plates of smart, metropolitan
food, embellishing top-drawer regional
ingredients with herbs, flowers and conceits:
from Northumberland venison carpaccio with
pickled plums, beetroot and horseradish or
hand-dived scallops with pork belly, Puy
lentils, Pedro Ximénez sherry and nasturtiums
to Galloway beef fillet with leeks, crisp bone
marrow and shallots or honey and lemon
parfait with parsnip ice cream. An all-
inclusive, no-bookings daytime menu touts
everything from Welsh rarebit and pulled
pork sliders to doughnuts and macarons.
Commendable wines by the glass or carafe
open the enterprising wine list; bottles
from £29.
Chef/s: Michael Penaluna. **Open:** all week L 12 to 2
(12.30 Sat, 12.30 to 3.15 Sun), D 7 to 9.30 (6.30 to
10 Fri and Sat). **Meals:** alc (main courses £16 to
£35). Sun L £28. **Details:** 70 seats. 28 seats outside.
Separate bar. Wheelchair access. Music. Car
parking.

Visit us Online
To find out more about
The Good Food Guide, please visit
www.thegoodfoodguide.co.uk

LOCAL GEM
▲ Caffè Vivo
29 Broad Chare, Newcastle upon Tyne, NE1 3DQ
Tel no: (0191) 2321331
www.caffevivo.co.uk
Italian | £28

Terry Laybourne offers up a slice of *la dolce vita*
at his buzzy enoteca in a former warehouse
near the Tyne. It's a casual sort of place with an
urban vibe (exposed brick, cast-iron pillars),
where sandwiches, coffee and an ace-value
fixed menu rule the roost during the day.
Things crank up in the evening for cicchetti,
pasta, sharing planks and whole sea bass
cooked on the grill. Booze sticks to the Italian
theme, with wines from £16. Closed Sun and
Mon.

North Shields
Irvins Brasserie
Cheery all-day brasserie with serious food
Union Road, The Fish Quay, North Shields,
NE30 1HJ
Tel no: (0191) 2963238
www.irvinsbrasserie.co.uk
Modern British | £25
Cooking score: 3
£30

Occupying the whole ground floor of an
imposing listed trawlerman's building at the
edge of North Shields Fish Quay, Irvins is a
slick, expansive brasserie that has garnered a
bulging inbox of praise from readers. There's a
'buzzy but relaxed atmosphere', helped by
sweeping stone arches, floor-to-ceiling
windows, a white-tiled open kitchen and an
attractively priced set lunch menu. From this
you might pick pristine grilled hake served
atop couscous dotted with still-crunchy dice
and strips of carrot, broccoli, spring cabbage
and broad beans and given a lift by basil
gremolata, or slow-roast pork belly.
Elsewhere, there's corned beef and salad
cream; dry-aged beef rib with cheek, broad
beans and salsify; presa steak (acorn-fed
Iberian pork), potato gratin and cabbage; and

even Craster kipper salad with poached egg: evidence of the accomplished produce-led school-of-St-John fare offered. Better still, most of the dishes come in small or large portions at very reasonable prices. Incidentals shine, too, with own-baked bread including a 'superbly gooey, light and crisp on top' cheese, tomato and basil focaccia. The short wine list (from £16.95) packs in decent variety and provides 15 options by the glass.

Chef/s: Graeme Cuthell. **Open:** Wed to Sun 10 to 10 (midnight Fri, 9am to midnight Sat, 9 to 7.30 Sun). **Closed:** Mon and Tue. **Meals:** alc (main courses £9 to £21). Set L and D £12 (2 courses) to £16. **Details:** 60 seats. Separate bar. Wheelchair access. Music.

LOCAL GEM
▲ The Staith House

57 Low Lights, North Shields Fish Quay, North Shields, NE30 1JA
Tel no: (0191) 2708441
www.thestaithhouse.co.uk
Modern British | £27 £5 OFF

The Staith House is a pub that spent 150 years as the Dolphin, but now it's back to its original name and in the hands of John Calton, a former finalist of *MasterChef: The Professionals*. There's much reclaimed wood and a seafaring vibe within (it's on the Fish Quay after all), with the kitchen serving substantial portions of fish and chips alongside more adventurous stuff (Shields crab with fennel and blood orange, hake with wild garlic and walnut pesto). Wines from £15.50. Closed Sun D.

▌ South Shields

LOCAL GEM
▲ Colmans

182-186 Ocean Road, South Shields, NE33 2JQ
Tel no: (0191) 4561202
www.colmansfishandchips.com
Seafood | £15

With a jovial atmosphere and 'no lack of professionalism from the staff', Colmans (established 1926), continues to be a 'local favourite and a bit of a community hub'. It remains true to its original chip shop character, still noted for 'beautiful fresh fish and chips', but, with a smartened-up dining room, now presents itself as a more 'upmarket restaurant'. Expect generous portions, very fresh fish (either battered or grilled) alongside Thai prawn cakes, crab salad and seafood platters. Wines from £12.95. Open all week.

‖● Please send us your feedback

To register your opinion about any restaurant listed in the Guide, or a new restaurant that you wish to bring to our attention, please visit the web address at the bottom of the page. Your feedback informs the content of the book and will be used to compile next year's reviews.

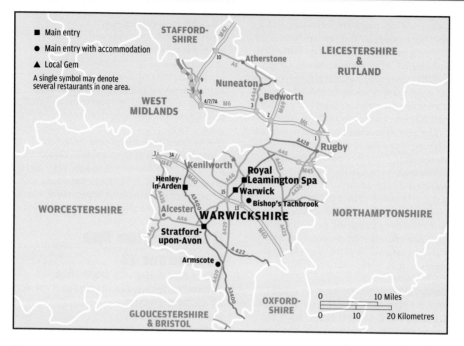

- ■ Main entry
- ● Main entry with accommodation
- ▲ Local Gem

A single symbol may denote several restaurants in one area.

■ Armscote

NEW ENTRY

The Fuzzy Duck

Smart foodie inn with good intentions
Ilmington Road, Armscote, CV37 8DD
Tel no: (01608) 682635
www.fuzzyduckarmscote.com
Modern British | £35
Cooking score: 1

Recently rebooted with a natural eye for style and lashings of Farrow & Ball, this immaculate 18th-century coaching inn is brimful of good intentions – though the venue is now far removed from its humbler watering-hole beginnings. Localism is the buzzword. The kitchen majors in modern pub classics – duck Scotch egg, duck liver parfait, steak, risotto of wild garlic and goats' cheese, an 'excellent' raspberry trifle – alongside provenance-marked snacks including 'Aubrey Allen' black pudding fritters and baked Cotswold cheese. More reports please. House wine £16.

Chef/s: Joe Adams. **Open:** all week L 12 to 2.30 (3 Sun), Mon to Sat D 6.30 to 9. **Meals:** alc (main courses £13 to 27). Sun L £16. **Details:** 60 seats. Separate bar. Wheelchair access. Music. Car parking.

■ Bishop's Tachbrook

The Dining Room at Mallory Court

Pedigree package for country-house fans
Harbury Lane, Bishop's Tachbrook, CV33 9QB
Tel no: (01926) 330214
www.mallory.co.uk
Modern British | £65
Cooking score: 5

£5 OFF 🛏 V

Just outside Leamington, Mallory Court is an ivy-smothered country house in the Lutyens style, sitting in ten acres of landscaped lushness. Water plashes in fountains, and the summer gardens are fragrant with roses. Arriving in February 2014, Paul Foster (ex-Tuddenham Mill, Suffolk) brings a finely honed instinct for clean, natural modernism to the ornate dining room. Shredded poached skate with spiky-sweet grapefruit gel and pickled fennel is a study in sharp edges, offset by the gentler succeeding course of salmon with apple and cucumber in intensely fragrant lovage soup. A piece of positively gamey sirloin with braised oxtail topped in crisp onions and slivered turnip makes a more inspired beef dish than the fillet norm, or there may be venison haunch bolognaise in peppery port reduction. The grand finale is white chocolate mousse with passion fruit granita and light caramel. A global wine list with plenty of half-bottles starts at £22.50, or £6.75 a glass.

Chef/s: Paul Foster. **Open:** Sun to Fri L 12 to 1.30, all week D 6.30 to 9. **Meals:** Set L £28 (2 courses) to £33. Set D £48 (3 courses) to £70. Sun L £40. **Details:** 56 seats. 20 seats outside. Wheelchair access. Music. Car parking.

Henley-in-Arden

The Bluebell

Upbeat and modishly rustic hostelry
93 High Street, Henley-in-Arden, B95 5AT
Tel no: (01564) 793049
www.bluebellhenley.co.uk
Modern British | £30
Cooking score: 3

Leigh and Duncan Taylor's half-timbered coaching inn on Henley's Tudor high street is well worth seeking out. Now an upbeat and modishly rustic hostelry with striking original features and a superb atmosphere, it's a welcoming place much loved by locals and visitors who appreciate the 'good, helpful' service and the 'sense of very good value'. The modern menu showcases carefully sourced ingredients – Cornish mussels, Loch Duart salmon, Jimmy Butler's pork – keeps an eye on the seasons and reveals realistic ambition. Warwickshire lamb faggot with pearl barley and pickled red cabbage, followed by stone

bass with roast parsnip purée, curly kale, beurre noisette, hazelnuts and cockles typifies the predominantly British style, although a sharing board of Spanish tapas brings a Mediterranean feel. There's a good selection of British cheeses if puddings such as passion fruit cheesecake with passion fruit curd and lime ice cream don't appeal. Wines from £15.75.

Chef/s: James Devonshire. **Open:** Tue to Sun L 12 to 2.30 (3.30 Sun), Tue to Sat D 6 to 9.30. **Closed:** Mon. **Meals:** alc (main courses £13 to £25). Set L and D £15 (2 courses) to £18. Sun L £25. **Details:** 52 seats. 40 seats outside. Wheelchair access. Music. Car parking. No children after 8.

Leamington Spa

Restaurant 23

Serious food fizzing with bright ideas
34 Hamilton Terrace, Leamington Spa, CV32 4LY
Tel no: (01926) 422422
www.restaurant23.co.uk
Modern European | £38
Cooking score: 4

Restaurant 23's location within a lavishly restored Grade II-listed Victorian building suggests serious intent. The dining room puts on a grand show with its centrepiece wine displays, ornate architrave and dramatic circular lampshades hanging from a floridly decorated ceiling. Peter Knibb's cooking aims high and his kitchen delivers progressive, serious food fizzing with bright ideas. Attention is paid to sourcing, and it shows in smart, contemporary dishes such as seared diver-caught scallops with cavolo nero, ginger purée and tempura squid, or a fashionable seasonal pairing of roast duck with pancetta terrine, salt-baked vegetables, Brussels sprouts and chestnuts. Dry-aged beef fillet with triple-cooked chips is a fixture, while clever desserts reveal the kitchen's lighter side: witness lemon tartlet with toasted meringue, blackcurrant ripple ice cream and candied lemon zest. Prices are set fair (particularly for the 'express' lunch), and the substantial Eurocentric wine list offers classy drinking from £20. For cocktails or digestifs, head upstairs to Morgan's Bar.

Chef/s: Peter Knibb. **Open:** Tue to Sun L 12.15 to 2 (3 Sun), Tue to Sat D 6.15 to 9.45. **Closed:** Mon, 25 and 26 Dec, 1 to 3 Jan. **Meals:** alc (main courses £18 to £27). Set L £16 (2 courses) to £19. Sun L £26. **Details:** 65 seats. 20 seats outside. Separate bar. Wheelchair access. Music. No children under 8.

▌Stratford-upon-Avon
No 9 Church St
Capable food and keen prices
9 Church Street, Stratford-upon-Avon, CV34 6HB
Tel no: (01789) 415522
www.no9churchst.com
Modern British | £30
Cooking score: 1

Occupying the upper levels of a quaint listed building in Stratford's old town, this venue has become a spiffing refuge for shoppers, tourists and budget-conscious Bard disciples. Great-value lunch and pre-theatre deals aim for no-frills satisfaction (fish pie, homemade venison sausages, apple crumble), but that's only half the story. Come nightfall, the kitchen dives headlong into the flashier world of smoked beetroot salad with whipped goats' cheese, slow-cooked collar of free-range pork with Savoy cabbage, or spiced fillet of ling with braised jasmine rice, mussels, coconut and coriander. For afters, try the 'Irish coffee' dessert with hot doughnuts. Gluggable wines start at £15.50.

Chef/s: Wayne Thomson. **Open:** Mon to Sat L 12 to 2, D 5 to 9 (9.30 Thur to Sat). **Closed:** Sun, 25 and 26 Dec, bank hols. **Meals:** alc (main courses £13 to £22). Set L £13 (2 courses) to £18. Tasting menu £38 (5 courses) to £50 (9 courses). **Details:** 40 seats. Separate bar. Music.

¡¡¡ BESPOKE SPIRITS

Ant gin and tonic anyone? Skip across the ocean to Denmark's Noma and that's one of the delightful offerings you'll find on the famed restaurant's cocktail menu. It features a bespoke gin - made exclusively for the Nordic restaurant - that's infused with ants for an alternative citrus hit (apparently the flavour is concentrated in their bottoms!).

But if Noma's creepy-crawly concoction is a stretch too far - for your wallet and your stomach - there are a number of unique spirits available to try right here in the UK, but only at the bars that created them.

Pop into Roast in London for an Aviation made with Roast's own gin and a maraschino liqueur, then swing by Trailer Happiness for an El Presidente made with a Plantation Rum blended especially for the bar.

Outside London visit Canary Bar in Bath for a unique Bath G&T garnished with a kaffir lime leaf, or Alimentum in Cambridge for a Truffle and Lady Grey Gin Martini.

▌Warwick

High Pavement

Cooking with metropolitan sophistication
3 High Street, Warwick, CV34 4AP
Tel no: (01926) 494725
www.highpavementwarwick.com
Modern British | £28
Cooking score: 2

£5 OFF £30

This handsome town house has been flamboyantly converted from high-street pizzeria to style-conscious bar and restaurant. The building itself has good bones, now enhanced by bold fabrics, bare brick, eye-catching artworks and industrial lights. Modern, if mainstream, European bistro fare features in both bar and restaurant. The former's menu encompasses 'bar bowls' (tapas, basically) such as ham hock croquettes and breaded squid, alongside roast meat sandwiches, burgers and Caesar salads. In the restaurant, diners are presented with attractive, interesting plates including scallops, cauliflower and belly pork, and balsamic-glazed duck breast with shallot Tatin. Dessert is fun: take your pick of four from a choice of ten mini puds. Two years in, High Pavement is already 'very popular', with quite a scene developing around the bar – drinkers ordering anything from a 'well-kept' ale to an 'impressive' cocktail. Wines come from an easy-drinking and sensibly priced list (from £14.95).

Chef/s: Martin Connolly. **Open:** Mon to Sun L 12 to 3 (5 Sun), Mon to Sat D 6 to 9.30. **Closed:** 25 Dec. **Meals:** alc (main meals £11 to £20). **Details:** 75 seats. 20 seats outside. Separate bar. Music.

Tailors

Dynamic duo's ritzy contemporary food
22 Market Place, Warwick, CV34 4SL
Tel no: (01926) 410590
www.tailorsrestaurant.co.uk
Modern British | £38
Cooking score: 3

V

Long-term mates Dan Cavell and Mark Fry's restaurant in Warwick's market square may well look like a trad joint from the outside, but it's nothing of the sort. For a start, Tailors sports a smart-rustic finish within, including big and bold artworks on the walls – and then there's the dazzlingly contemporary food. Via a tasting menu, an 'unbelievable value' set lunch, midweek early-evening menu and carte, the lads deliver ambitious and complex plates that reveal a sense of fun. 'Duck and orange' is a rich parfait served with crispy brioche and the flavours of orange and bay, while 'corned beef hash 99' arrives looking like a classic children's treat, but delivers a savoury hit. There are bold flavour combinations throughout. Main-course 'Highland game venison' matches roasted haunch with blue cheese, 'black fruits' and chocolate; and, for dessert, the 'Waggon Wheel' is unsurprisingly a creative interpretation. Wines start at £18.95.

Chef/s: Dan Cavell and Mark Fry. **Open:** Tue to Sat L 12 to 1.45, D 6.30 to 9. **Closed:** Sun, Mon, 25 Dec to 1 Jan. **Meals:** Set L £15 (2 courses) to £19. Set D £30 (2 courses) to £38. **Details:** 28 seats. Music.

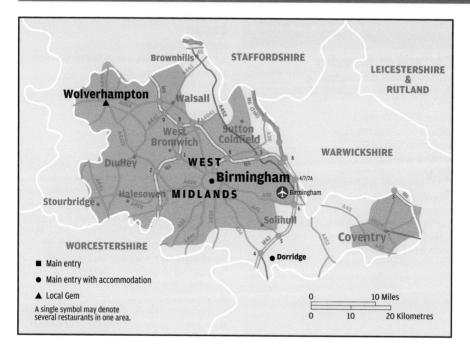

- ■ Main entry
- ● Main entry with accommodation
- ▲ Local Gem

A single symbol may denote
several restaurants in one area.

■ Birmingham

Adam's

Utterly brilliant eatery for a short time only
21a Bennetts Hill, Birmingham, B2 5QP
Tel no: (0121) 6433745
www.adamsrestaurant.co.uk
Modern British | £50
Cooking score: 6

£5
OFF

It may be a pop-up looking for a permanent
home, but much effort has been put into
giving Adam's a classy, modern feel, with faux
marble, mirrors and trompe l'oeil. Colours are
muted, but Adam Stokes' impressive cooking
has vibrancy all of its own. Lunch is a three-
course bargain, but dinner brings a choice of
two tasting menus of five or nine courses with
succinct, intense add-ons – perhaps vivid
beetroot and goats' cheese macaroons or a
memorable 'roast chicken dinner on a stick'.
After the overtures, the subtle hits of sweet-
and-sour work their magic in an escabeche of
sea bream with sea vegetables and orange

buckwheat, but equally deft is the textural
contrasts in a dish of Jerusalem artichoke,
chorizo and egg yolk; the fantastic flavours of
crisp-skinned pheasant breast and
accompanying celeriac purée, tarragon and
button mushrooms; and the whiskey, cream,
chocolate and honey confection that 'drew
sighs of sheer wonderment from around the
table after the first mouthful'. Wine from £23.
Chef/s: Adam Stokes. **Open:** Tue to Sat L 12 to 2, D 7
to 9. **Closed:** Sun, Mon, 3 weeks Dec to Jan, 2 weeks
summer. **Meals:** Set L £28 (2 courses) to £32. Set D
£45. Tasting menu £50 (5 courses) to £80 (9
courses). **Details:** 24 seats. No children.

Symbols

🍴 Accommodation is available

£30 Three courses for less than £30

V Separate vegetarian menu

£5
OFF £5-off voucher scheme

🍾 Notable wine list

Carters of Moseley
Food to capture the imagination
2c Wake Green Road, Moseley, Birmingham,
B13 9EZ
Tel no: (0121) 4498885
www.cartersofmoseley.co.uk
Modern British | £45
Cooking score: 3
£5 OFF **V**

'You can see how it is so popular with the locals,' noted a first-time visitor to Brad Carter and Holly Jackson's restaurant, located in a suburban parade of shops just a few minutes' walk from the centre of Moseley. Inside it is small, smart-casual, with 'exceptionally friendly staff who seem really eager to please'. Ever-changing menus maintain interest, and the kitchen can deliver some seriously good food. Readers praise the black pudding Scotch eggs, smoked wood pigeon and soft hen's egg with wild garlic barley risotto, and the British Isles cheeseboard. The accomplished partnerships continue with 'a lovely combination' of devilled crab with samphire and new potatoes; a very fresh-tasting dish of Cornish lamb, peas and lamb bacon with some wonderful mint sauce ('the best I've had'); and a refreshing dessert of sheep's-curd mousse, sea buckthorn and small meringue balls. The set lunch menu is good value. Wines from £19.95.
Chef/s: Brad Carter. **Open:** Wed to Sun L 12 to 2 (3 Sun), D 6.30 to 9.30 (7 Sun). **Closed:** Mon, Tue, 1 to 8 Jan, 11 to 27 Aug. **Meals:** Set L £18 (2 courses) to £20. Set D £45 (5 courses) to £85 (with wine). Sun L £25. Sun D £30 (5 courses). **Details:** 34 seats. Wheelchair access. Music. Car parking. Children over 8 yrs only.

Lasan
Stylish Indian eatery
3-4 Dakota Buildings, James Street, St Paul's Square, Birmingham, B3 1SD
Tel no: (0121) 2123664
www.lasan.co.uk
Indian | £35
Cooking score: 3
£5 OFF **V**

'If we can blow people away with exotic flavour combinations,' declares Aktar Islam, 'I'm a very happy man.' Lasan certainly blew away Gordon Ramsay, when its fine-tuned pan-Indian cooking won it Local Restaurant of the Year in 2013 on Channel 4's *The F Word*. The restaurant is located in the jewellery quarter. Its deep windows and plush, chic interiors set the tone for cooking that showcases tiptop ingredients, and is alive with the pungency and bite of freshly ground and roasted spices. Chilli-battered soft-shell crab with a pea and potato cake and sour mango chutney, or coriander-marinated red mullet with lemony beetroot purée, are starters to make the taste-buds pay attention. The must-have main course is elaichi beef: braised blade and marinated sirloin of Hereford with tandoori sweetbread and a bone-marrow pakora in cashew sauce. Sides include Punjabi pumpkin, and okra in coconut and yoghurt, and there's gulab jamun to finish. Wines from £17.99.
Chef/s: Aktar Islam. **Open:** Sun to Fri L 12 to 2.30 (1 Sun), all week D 6 to 11 (9 Sun). **Closed:** 25 Dec. **Meals:** alc (main courses £13 to £22). **Details:** 64 seats. Separate bar. Wheelchair access. Music. Children over 8 yrs only.

Loves

Intimate vibes and intricate food
Browning Street, Canal Square, Birmingham,
B16 8FL
Tel no: (0121) 4545151
www.loves-restaurant.co.uk
Modern British | £48
Cooking score: 5

£5 OFF | V

In the four years since Steve and Claire Love
moved to Birmingham's rejuvenated canal
basin they have propelled their converted
woollen-mill restaurant firmly on to the
national radar, thanks to a sense of space, an
affable demeanour and sharply defined
cooking. Clean, clear flavours are Steve Love's
culinary trademarks, whether he is fashioning
'delicious' pig's cheek and foie gras with crisp
smoked eel and a small radish and celery salad
or a broad-shouldered plate of impressively
rich venison, haunch and braised shoulder,
served with beetroot, celeriac, apple and
parsnip ('some of the best that I've had this
year'). He can also conjure up delicacy and
spirit-level balance when required, as in a
'light and delicious' dessert of pineapple and
rum sponge with little meringues and palm-
sugar ice cream. The wine list also comes up
trumps, a cherry-picked selection that oozes
class, from some of the world's most exciting
and reputable producers to some astonishing
acquisitions from artisan winemakers around
the globe. Prices from £25.
Chef/s: Steve Love. **Open:** Fri and Sat L 12 to 1.45,
Wed to Sat D 7 to 9 (6 to 9.30 Fri and Sat). **Closed:**
Sun, Mon, Tue, 1 week Jan, 1 week Easter, 2 weeks
Aug. **Meals:** Set menu £40 (2 courses) to £48.
Tasting menu £55 to £75. **Details:** 44 seats.
Separate bar. Wheelchair access. Music. Children
over 8 yrs only at D.

Visit us Online
To find out more about
The Good Food Guide, please visit
www.thegoodfoodguide.co.uk

Opus

Bullish Brummie brasserie
54 Cornwall Street, Birmingham, B3 2DE
Tel no: (0121) 2002323
www.opusrestaurant.co.uk
Modern British | £31
Cooking score: 2

£5 OFF

A fixture of Birmingham's commercial
district for the past decade, this large-scale
brasserie is thoroughly urban with its floor-
to-ceiling windows, skylights and spacious
dining area. Cheerful service keeps the
atmosphere buzzy and it all makes for an
engaging venue in which to enjoy the modern
British approach of the kitchen. Typical of the
output is a starter of tian of Brixham crab,
vierge dressing and salad, which could be
followed by cannon of Cornish lamb, slow-
cooked belly, potato fondant, cauliflower
purée, creamed cabbage and bacon; or fillet of
turbot, ricotta and basil gnocchi, spinach and
chorizo and tomato cream. For dessert, there
may be chocolate cheesecake and kumquat
marmalade or you could choose from the
board of British cheeses. From a French-heavy
list with plenty of interesting bottles under
£25, wines start at £17.95.
Chef/s: David Colcombe. **Open:** Mon to Fri and Sun
L 12 to 2.30 (3 Sun), Mon to Sat D 6 to 9.30. **Closed:**
25 Dec to 1 Jan, bank hols. **Meals:** alc (main courses
£10 to £28). Set L and D £14 (2 courses) to £16. Sun
L £25. **Details:** 80 seats. Separate bar. Wheelchair
access. Music.

Purnell's

No-holds barred approach to cooking
55 Cornwall Street, Birmingham, B3 2DH
Tel no: (0121) 2129799
www.purnellsrestaurant.com
Modern British | £65
Cooking score: 5

Glynn Purnell's financial-district restaurant
has been a beacon of Brummie gastronomy
since 2007. The dining room is modern,
understated, patrolled by surprisingly formal
staff given the maverick personality of the

chef/patron, who revels in a no-holds barred approach to cooking. Fixed tasters are the format, with menus evolving slowly but retaining the all-important seasonal note. 'Emotions of cheese and pineapple' (on sticks, 1970s-style) is an indelible memory, so too the monkfish masala, which is brilliantly partnered by red lentils, pickled carrot, coconut and coriander. And the riot of flavours that accompanies carpaccio of beef with red wine octopus, home-cured beef, salt beef, sour cream and sweet-and-sour onions 'really did work'. That these dishes succeed indicates novelty isn't pursued for its own sake, but we must report this year that we found the Purnell's experience 'nice enough', yet less than breathtaking for a restaurant operating at such a high level: 'less of a Grand Tour, more of a package tour'. On the wine front, France is in the ascendancy with good New World and European support; bottles from £22.95.

Chef/s: Glynn Purnell. **Open:** Tue to Fri L 12 to 1.30, Tue to Sat D 7 to 9. **Closed:** Sun, Mon, 2 weeks at Christmas, Easter and summer. **Meals:** Set L £32 (3 courses) to £42. Tasting menu £65 (6 courses) to £85. **Details:** 45 seats. Wheelchair access. Music. Children over 10 yrs only.

Purnell's Bistro

Glynn Purnell's own brand of bistro
11 Newhall Street, Birmingham, B3 3NY
Tel no: (0121) 2001588
www.purnellsbistro-gingers.com
Modern French | £30
Cooking score: 2

V

The Bistro is a horse of a different colour to Glynn Purnell's principal restaurant (see entry), a place where 'hearty portions, simple bold flavours and welcoming surroundings' are the prime assets, in the words of a reader. The last include the 1930s-themed Ginger's (as in Rogers) cocktail bar, the babbling buzz of which spills convivially into the dining room. Menus are similarly vivacious, mobilising familiar techniques in all sorts of tempting ways. Starters of grilled black pudding with a

Scotch egg, onion soup and sour apple, or goats' cheese ravioli in tomato salsa, are straightforward and direct. Mains might be braised shoulder of lamb with lentils and roasted roots, or poached cod with butter beans, chorizo and spinach. Dishes aren't unduly fancy, and are all the better for it. Desserts follow suit with properly caramelised crème brûlée offset with the warming note of spiced poached pear. House Languedoc in three colours is £17.50.

Chef/s: Micheal Dipple. **Open:** Sun to Fri L 12 to 2 (4 Sun), Mon to Fri D 6.30 to 9.30. Sat 12 to 9.30. **Meals:** alc (main courses £15 to £19). **Details:** 90 seats. Separate bar.

Saffron

Creative Indian cookery, with glitz
909 Wolverhampton Road, Oldbury, Birmingham, B69 4RR
Tel no: (0121) 5521752
www.saffron-online.co.uk
Indian | £20
Cooking score: 2

£5 OFF   **V**   £30

Saffron has set out its stall firmly on the 'modern' side of the Indian restaurant spectrum, with an approach combining a décor that aspires to sophistication with a menu that offers plenty of interesting combinations not seen elsewhere around these parts. Presentation is pretty nifty, too, with tawa scallops – pan-fried Scottish ones, served with cauliflower and red pepper relish – looking good on the plate. The tandoori mixed grill covers all the bases, or go for assam ka gosht (a spicy curry with, unusually, beef as the central ingredient), or tawe ki bathak (braised Barbary duck in a smoky sauce). There are classics, too, such as well-made versions of chicken korma and lamb passanda. Vegetarian dishes, breads and the like show equal attention to detail. Desserts go the fusion way: carrot halwa with raspberry fool. The wine list kicks off at £10.50 for house French.

Chef/s: Avijit Mondal. **Open:** all week L 12 to 2.30, D 5.30 to 11. **Meals:** alc (main courses £8 to £24). **Details:** 90 seats. Wheelchair access. Music. Car parking.

Simpsons
Formidably accomplished suburban restaurant
20 Highfield Road, Edgbaston, Birmingham,
B15 3DU
Tel no: (0121) 4543434
www.simpsonsrestaurant.co.uk
Modern British | £60
Cooking score: 6
🛏 V

'Impeccable' service (one reader reports never having seen so many staff in a restaurant), a tranquil suburban setting and accomplished cooking continue to make Simpsons the grown-up option in Birmingham. Mature gardens and a glazed terrace surrounding the converted Georgian town house, along with 'delightful touches all round', are appreciated by correspondents who also rate the spanking-fresh fish and deconstructed desserts. To start, duck egg gets the cold-weather treatment with mushrooms, parsley root, duck confit, cep and chestnut velouté, and there's a nod to the wider city in a main course of lamb with a samosa, yellow-lentil dhal, burnt aubergine, yoghurt and curry oil. Passion fruit soufflé with coconut sorbet lets the kitchen flex some of the impressive classical muscle that underpins every dish. A streamlined French-leaning wine list (no half-bottles, and not much to play with at the lower end) starts at £27, with glasses from £11.
Chef/s: Luke Tipping and Matt Cheal. **Open:** all week L 12 to 2 (2.30 Sun), Mon to Sat D 7 to 9.30. **Closed:** 24 to 26 Dec, 31 Dec to 2 Jan, bank hols. **Meals:** alc (main courses £21 to £27). Set L £40. Tasting menu £90. **Details:** 70 seats. Wheelchair access. Car parking.

Turners Restaurant
Assured and contemporary
69 High Street, Harborne, Birmingham, B17 9NS
Tel no: (0121) 4264440
www.turnersrestaurantbirmingham.co.uk
Modern British | £50
Cooking score: 5

One of the exclusive group of restaurants that keep Birmingham on the fine-dining map, Turners may lack an apostrophe but otherwise excels in attention to detail. Richard Turner has cooked here, on Harborne's main street, for seven years and his dining room, dark and bold, has an assured air. A menu of Turners classics (the entry level is two courses for £40; lunch is cheaper) includes squab with turnip, peanut and mustard seed – you can picture the bird pecking at its own garnishes – and a smoky take on hogget with chickpeas, smoked aubergine, goats' curd and charred leeks. A tasting menu offers a slight shift, with more technical flourishes and wholly contemporary dishes like delicately plated scallop with garlic, chicken skin and Parmesan custard or veal tongue with smoked marrow, onions and tarragon. As the end nears, chocolate with banana, miso and lime demonstrates a theatrical flair. Wine is from £29.
Chef/s: Richard Turner. **Open:** Fri and Sat L 12 to 2, Tue to Sat D 7 to 9.30. **Closed:** Sun, Mon, 25 and 26 Dec, 1 to 7 Jan. **Meals:** Set L £25 (2 courses) to £33. Set D £40 (2 courses) to £50. Tasting menu £85. **Details:** 26 seats. Wheelchair access. Music. Car parking. No children.

▍Dorridge
The Forest
On the right track
25 Station Approach, Dorridge, B93 8JA
Tel no: (01564) 772120
www.forest-hotel.com
Modern European | £32
Cooking score: 3
£5 OFF 🛏

The Forest has travelled a long way since its days as a prim and proper Victorian station hotel, and is now something of a hot-ticket destination for weary commuters and locals in search of invigorating modern food. Chef Dean Grubb's kitchen runs on supplies of top produce – including beef from gold-standard butcher Aubrey Allen – for a menu that delivers everything from eggs Benedict to char-grilled piri-piri chicken. Along the way, you might also encounter beetroot tarte Tatin with goats' curd, kumquat and pickled walnut dressing; game pie with elderberry jus; or rump of lamb with sweetbreads, confit shoulder, aubergine and Moroccan spices. The polished tables and standard lamps also chime well with 'classics' such as salmon and prawn fishcakes, burgers and wild mushroom linguine, while puds chug their way through dark chocolate délice, lemon meringue pie, rhubarb soufflé and tiramisu. The food is bolstered by a list of commendable wines from £15.95.

Chef/s: Dean Grubb. **Open:** all week L 12 to 2.30 (4 Sun), Mon to Sat D 6.30 to 9.30. **Closed:** 25 Dec. **Meals:** alc (main courses £12 to £23). Set L and D £14 (2 courses) to £16. Sun L £17 (2 courses) to £20. **Details:** 60 seats. 60 seats outside. Separate bar. Music. Car parking.

▮ Hampton-in-Arden

READERS RECOMMEND
Peel's Restaurant

Modern British
Hampton Manor, Shadowbrook Lane, Hampton-in-Arden, B92 0DQ
Tel no: (01675) 446080
www.hamptonmanor.eu

'An old-fashioned but elegant room. Six superb amuse-bouches, very small, freshly baked bread loaves and freshly churned butter created a wonderful start to the meal.'

▮ Wolverhampton

LOCAL GEM
▲ Bilash

2 Cheapside, Wolverhampton, WV1 1TU
Tel no: (01902) 427762
www.thebilash.co.uk
Indian | £30

First opening its doors in the year 'Come on Eileen' held the Number One spot (1982), Bilash has a track record second to none in the city. Bangladeshi and Indian cuisine is the name of the game, with a menu that avoids lazy cliché and delivers interesting recipes such as neza kebab (chicken leg flavoured with cardamom), Goan tiger prawn masala and laziz pasliyan (spicy lamb with cashew nuts). There are pre-theatre and bargain lunch menus, and wines from £18.90. Closed Sun.

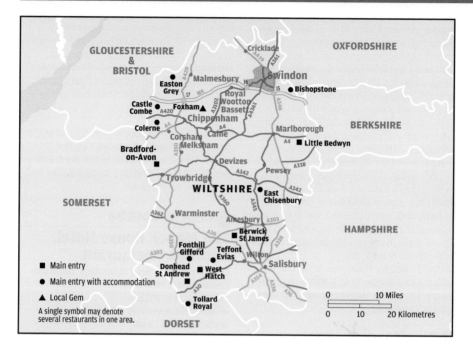

Berwick St James

The Boot Inn

Appealing pub with home cooking
High Street, Berwick St James, SP3 4TN
Tel no: **(01722) 790243**
www.bootatberwick.co.uk
British | £24
Cooking score: 1

£5 OFF £30

The Dickinsons extend a warm welcome at their Georgian coaching inn, located in a Till Valley village near Salisbury. Low ceilings and tiled floors set the colourful scene within, and the culinary compass points firmly to home cooking, with hearty propositions such as platters of home-smoked and cured meats, fish and cheese with relishes and toast as starter or main, as well as whole grilled plaice with potted shrimps and sprouting broccoli, or local sirloin steak with snails in garlic butter. Finish with marmalade-glazed bread-and-

butter pudding and orange custard. The little wine list does its job, with house Chileans at £16.90.

Chef/s: Giles Dickinson. **Open:** Tue to Sun L 12 to 2.15 (2.30 Sun), Tue to Sat D 6.30 to 9.15 (9.30 Sat). **Closed:** Mon, 25 Dec, 1 to 13 Feb. **Meals:** alc (main courses £10 to £18). **Details:** 34 seats. 24 seats outside. Music. Car parking.

Bishopstone

Helen Browning at the Royal Oak

Cheery organic pub-cum-B&B
Cues Lane, Bishopstone, SN6 8PP
Tel no: **(01793) 790481**
www.helenbrowningorganics.co.uk
British | £29
Cooking score: 3

£5 OFF   £30

A partnership made in heaven – or at least on the Wilts-Oxon borders – this reconfigured country pub and B&B is a thriving adjunct of organic pioneer Helen Browning's Eastbrook Farm. Full use is made of the farm's organically reared meats, and of locally grown fruit and vegetables (often the result of bartering deals). It's a fruitful tie-in that regularly yields satisfying dishes, from spiced pumpkin soup to asparagus with morels, hazelnuts and a morel sauce. Game fans might fancy risotto of pheasant and red wine with gremolata; fish lovers might prefer roast pollack with mussel chowder – in the words of one regular, this is 'plain pub cooking raised to remarkable heights by quality ingredients'. Sweet hits such as apple tart or impressive buffalo-milk ice creams, and details such as the regional cheeseboard, help make a meal a 'joy'. To cap it all, the organic wine list is a cracker with bottles from £18.

Chef/s: Ed McCrea. **Open:** Mon to Sat L 12 to 3 (4 Sat), D 6 to 9.30. Sun 12 to 7. **Meals:** alc (main courses £11 to £26). **Details:** 50 seats. 50 seats outside. Car parking.

∎ Bradford-on-Avon

NEW ENTRY

The Three Gables

Resurrected charmer with a French accent
St Margaret's Street, Bradford-on-Avon, BA15 1DA
Tel no: (01225) 781666
www.thethreegables.com
Modern European | £35
Cooking score: 3

£5 OFF 🍷

This lovingly resurrected listed building is a charmer. In the centre of town, just across from the River Avon, the 'delightfully tucked away' dining room occupies the first floor and feels 'wonderfully archaic' with its beams, bare stone walls, leaded windows and double-white clothed tables. The food is eclectic, with France taking the lead. Popular set lunches offer the likes of grilled Cornish mackerel with curried sweet potato and onion bhajia, then truffled veal sausage with champ and onion gravy, and Bakewell tart with vanilla ice cream. The à la carte is considerably more ambitious – but not excessively so. Diver-caught scallops come with smoked haddock

velouté and croûtons; roast monkfish is teamed with an onion bhajia, coriander and mussel butter and a sweet potato purée; coffee meringue arrives with mandarin curd and walnut praline. Fans of pricey French and Italian wines will find serious meat on the bulky, well-researched wine list, which starts at £21.

Chef/s: Marc Salmon. **Open:** Tue to Sat L 12 to 2, D 6 to 9.30 (10 Fri and Sat). **Closed:** Sun, Mon. **Meals:** Set L £12 (2 courses) to £16. Set D £30. **Details:** 55 seats. 25 seats outside. Separate bar. Wheelchair access. Music.

∎ Castle Combe

The Manor House Hotel, Bybrook Restaurant

Complex modern food in heritage surrounds
Castle Combe, SN14 7HR
Tel no: (01249) 782206
www.manorhouse.co.uk
Modern British | £60
Cooking score: 5

£5 OFF 🛏 V

A country seat of the powerful since medieval times, this imposing Cotswold manor house looks a picture. A river runs through its trimly landscaped grounds, and Italianate gardens add to the pleasing prospect. The Bybrook Restaurant announces its heritage with carved stonework, varnished panelling, stained-glass windows and glittering chandeliers, but there's nothing antiquated about the food. The kitchen fashions complex, multi-layered dishes from top-end ingredients, as in a torchon of duck liver with orange and gingerbread or pan-fried Gigha halibut with chorizo risotto and braised baby gem. Pork from the hotel's Gloucester Old Spot pigs might appear with pickled white cabbage, carrot purée and five-spice, while slow-cooked rump of Wiltshire lamb could be teamed with cauliflower couscous, golden raisins and chocolate. Prettily plated desserts such as lemon cheesecake with anise ice cream and candied fennel exhibit bright, frisky flavours. The heavyweight wine list deals in serious vintages at serious prices (from £25). **Chef/s:** Richard Davies. **Open:** Wed to Sun L 12.30 to 2, all week D 7 to 9 (6.30 to 9.30 Fri and Sat). **Meals:** Set L £25 (2 courses) to £30. Set D £52 (2 courses) to £60. Sun L £35. Tasting menu £74 (7 courses). **Details:** 70 seats. Separate bar. Car parking. No children at D.

▌Colerne
Lucknam Park
Palatial grandeur and intricate food
Colerne, SN14 8AZ
Tel no: (01225) 742777
www.lucknampark.co.uk
Modern British | £75
Cooking score: 5

⇌ V

'An absolute picture of palatial smart,' drooled one visitor after surveying this Palladian mansion set in 500 acres of grounds with oak-flanked driveways, woodland copses and striped lawns. The big-time hospitality package boasts everything from an equestrian centre to a spa with a decent brasserie. The main action occurs in the full-dress Park Restaurant: a riot of crystal chandeliers and gold drapes occupying the former ballroom. Chef Hywel Jones is capable of producing fabulous food full of intricate detailing: witness golden-roasted turbot fillet on braised iceberg lettuce with charred baby artichoke, hand-rolled macaroni and truffle butter sauce. But there's also a feeling he's 'on a treadmill', sending out impressive, but predictable, renditions of country-house classics: poached rose veal with glazed sweetbreads and marinated salsify; red mullet with langoustines, broad beans and girolles; banana soufflé with salted caramel ice cream. The sommelier knows his way around the heavyweight wine list, which includes a few sub-£30 bottles.

Chef/s: Hywel Jones. **Open:** Sun L 12 to 2, Tue to Sat D 6 to 10. **Closed:** Mon. **Meals:** Set D £75. Sun L £39. Tasting menu £90 (7 courses). **Details:** 80 seats. Wheelchair access. Music. Car parking. Children over 5 yrs only.

▌Donhead St Andrew
The Forester
Well-tended country boozer
Lower Street, Donhead St Andrew, SP7 9EE
Tel no: (01747) 828038
www.theforesterdonheadstandrew.co.uk
Modern British | £29
Cooking score: 2

V £30

Hidden down a network of tiny lanes on the Wiltshire/Dorset border, this 16th-century village pub looks every inch the well-tended country boozer: from its neatly trimmed thatched roof to its blackened beams, plank floors, stone walls and mighty inglenook. The kitchen feeds trencherman appetites with 30-day aged Dexter steaks, burgers and roast pork belly with bubble and squeak, although seafood from the West Country boats gets star billing on the menu, perhaps including pan-fried fillets of John Dory with pea risotto, prime turbot with spinach and hollandaise, or herb-crumbed cod with black olive mash, sprouting broccoli and sauce vierge. Cheeky touches such as cockle popcorn nibbles or plates of rabbit haggis with swede purée and whisky-laced onion marmalade raise a smile, although it's back to basics for the likes of sticky toffee pudding or warm raspberry Bakewell tart with honeycomb ice cream. Drink local ales, cider or keenly priced wines (from £17).
Chef/s: Andrew Kilburn. **Open:** all week L 12 to 2, Mon to Sat D 6.30 to 9. **Closed:** Mon (Jan to Mar). **Meals:** alc (main courses £14 to £25). Set L and D £17 (2 courses) to £20. **Details:** 60 seats. 40 seats outside. Separate bar. Car parking.

East Chisenbury

★ TOP 10 PUB ★

The Red Lion

Much more than your average free house
East Chisenbury, SN9 6AQ
Tel no: (01980) 671124
www.redlionfreehouse.com
Modern British | £35
Cooking score: 6

£5 OFF 🛏

This lovely thatched village pub (and guesthouse) in an Area of Outstanding Natural Beauty, our 2014 'Pub of the Year' winner, continues to draw effusive praise from readers. Chef Guy Manning will either be pleased or put out to discover his 'enthusiastic', 'passionate' front-of-house staff have almost as many fans as he does. *Almost*. It is Manning's smart, resolutely seasonal cooking that really lures diners across county lines. Beginning with 'beautifully done' snacks such as pig's head Scotch egg, the cooking is 'exceptional'. And from the daily menu, dishes like beef shin and tendon pappardelle, and guinea fowl with farfalle, broad beans, ramsons and meat juices demonstrate serious skills and a respect for raw ingredients. To finish, choose crème brûlée or 'beautifully balanced' Seville orange mille-feuille. The easily navigated wine list (from £18.50) is an excellent pub list: not encyclopaedic but with plenty sub-£35 and some real finds among the 'specials'.
Chef/s: Guy Manning. **Open:** all week L 12 to 2.30, D 6.30 to 9 (8 Sun). **Meals:** alc (main courses £15 to £30). Set L £16 (2 courses) to £20. **Details:** 50 seats. 20 seats outside. Music. Car parking.

Symbols

🛏 Accommodation is available

£30 Three courses for less than £30

V Separate vegetarian menu

£5 OFF £5-off voucher scheme

🍾 Notable wine list

Easton Grey

★ TOP 50 ★

Whatley Manor, The Dining Room

Truly astounding food
Easton Grey, SN16 0RB
Tel no: (01666) 822888
www.whatleymanor.com
Modern French | £85
Cooking score: 8

£5 OFF 🍾 🛏

More than a decade after joining this 'exemplary' country house hotel, Martin Burge still has a trick or two up his sleeve. His precise, clever cooking sits comfortably against the smart backdrop of oak panelling and mullioned windows – although the modern artwork and slick young staff are perhaps a hint that the food will be no slave to tradition. Begin in the improbably large lounge with its clustered armchairs and flickering candles, where foie gras mousse comes with teriyaki jelly, or a poached quail's egg might sport a topping of smoked eel and kipper foam. Burge has a knack for squeezing an extra flavour or two out of each dish, nudging it beyond the obvious into the sublime. Brillat-Savarin and truffle ravioli, perfectly silky and satisfying on its own, is elevated with a tang of apple and an intense cauliflower ice cream. A crisp-skinned fillet of sea bass with caramelised langoustine tail and a velveteen langoustine reduction is made unforgettable by the umami-laden truffle and shellfish macaroni on the side. Lemon and olive oil raviolis with tangy blood-orange sorbet, olive oil ice cream and pine nut foam typifies Burge's ability to come up with combinations that surprise yet, on tasting, make perfect sense. The sommelier draws the best out of a truly international wine list, priced from £30 to nearly £1,000 and offering 15 options by the glass.
Chef/s: Martin Burge. **Open:** Wed to Sun D only 7 to 10. **Closed:** Mon, Tue. **Meals:** Set D £85. Tasting menu £110. **Details:** 40 seats. Separate bar. Wheelchair access. Music. Children over 12 yrs only.

Fonthill Gifford

★ TOP 50 PUB ★

Beckford Arms

Upper-crust rural inn
Fonthill Gifford, SP3 6PX
Tel no: (01747) 870385
www.beckfordarms.com
British | £28
Cooking score: 3

There's nothing like a beautiful rural location to induce a feeling of relaxed contentment, and this creeper-clad 18th-century coaching inn on the edge of the Fonthill Estate maximises that happy state. With an acre of mature garden, a full contingent of beams, wooden flooring and open fires, plus bags of atmosphere throughout, it's easy to see why the Beckford is popular. Traditional pub trappings (rustic bar, real ales) are successfully blended with swish boutique bedrooms and appealingly soothing food. The kitchen champions seasonal, often local produce, including locally bagged game. Beckford-smoked trout rillettes is served with beetroot and herb crème fraîche; Creedy Carver duck breast arrives with salsify, kale and sautéed potatoes; or there could be roast leg of locally shot deer teamed with dauphinois potatoes and garden-grown purple sprouting broccoli. Everything – from hams and pies, bread and ice cream, to chutneys and jams – is homemade. Wines from £17.50.
Chef/s: Carl Thompson. **Open:** all week L 12 to 2.30 (3 Sat and Sun), D 6 to 10 (9 Sun). **Closed:** 25 Dec. **Meals:** alc (main courses £10 to £22). **Details:** 65 seats. 26 seats outside. Separate bar. Wheelchair access. Music. Car parking.

Visit us Online
To find out more about
The Good Food Guide, please visit
www.thegoodfoodguide.co.uk

Foxham

LOCAL GEM
▲ **The Foxham Inn**
Foxham, SN15 4NQ
Tel no: (01249) 740665
www.thefoxhaminn.co.uk
Modern British | £28

The Coopers' prettily located country-pub-with-rooms is run with great warmth. Within, it includes a traditional pub bar with a cosy wood-burner, a modern dining room with open-to-view kitchen and a menu of no-nonsense modern British cooking. Native ingredients appear in the shape of Dorset snails (with a ragoût of pearl barley, chorizo and local smoked bacon), and Tiddenham duck (with maple-glazed salsify, cherry sauce and dauphinois potatoes). Sunday lunch remains a high point. Drink real ales or good-value wines from £14.50. Closed Mon.

Little Bedwyn

The Harrow at Little Bedwyn

Real food and extraordinary wines
High Street, Little Bedwyn, SN8 3JP
Tel no: (01672) 870871
www.theharrowatlittlebedwyn.com
Modern British | £55
Cooking score: 6

Since opening in 1998, Roger and Sue Jones have made the Harrow a model of the modern country restaurant. The splendid tranquillity of the location, near Marlborough, is a tonic, but the pursuit of blue-riband local produce and a true expert's approach to wine elevate the place out of the bucolic norm. The integrity of ingredients is respected in dishes like deep-fried Pembroke lobster seasoned with Asian spices, or tuna tartare with wasabi curd and caviar. Main courses follow with fillet and belly of Kelmscott pork deepened by the earthier notes of faggot and black pudding, or sea bass and shrimps with grilled courgettes and white asparagus in lemon oil. A tasting of thoroughbred chocolate items seems the

obligatory self-indulgence at dessert. Wines pop up all over the menu, making it hard not to opt for a flight. If you prefer to exercise the right to choose, be prepared for a list of gargantuan breadth and rare discernment, from £25. Themed evenings with global wine VIPs are an abiding feature.
Chef/s: Roger Jones. **Open:** Wed to Sat L 12 to 2, D 7 to 9. **Closed:** Sun, Mon, Tue, 24 Dec to 3 Jan. **Meals:** alc (main courses £30). Set L £40. Set D £50. Tasting menu £75. **Details:** 32 seats. 30 seats outside. Music.

Rowde

The George & Dragon
Proper local with top-notch seafood
Church Lane, Rowde, SN10 2PN
Tel no: (01380) 723053
www.thegeorgeanddragonrowde.co.uk
Modern British | £35
Cooking score: 3

⇆ V

Stark, faded white and imposing alongside the main road through a Wiltshire village, this amenable 16th-century inn is not necessarily somewhere you'd expect to specialise in fish. While it shores up boozy credentials with real ales, blazing fires and panelled walls, the kitchen promises the daily catch from St Mawes chalked up on boards above the bar, perhaps 'so fresh' megrim sole brushed with butter and grilled whole on the bone. John Dory with asparagus and hollandaise, whiting done as fish and chips, and butterflied mackerel with garlic butter could also be on offer. To start there's 'fishy hors d'oeuvres', a spot-on, simple preparation of good-quality smoked salmon, plenty of crayfish, a little pile of very fresh white crabmeat, some pickled octopus and mussels. Alternatively, go for venison terrine followed by slow-roast pork belly with Chinese cabbage and red wine jus and finish with banana sponge with jersey cream. Wines from £14.50.
Chef/s: Christopher Day. **Open:** all week L 12 to 3 (4 Sat, 5 Sun), Mon to Sat D 6.30 to 11. **Meals:** alc (main courses £11 to £22). Set L and D £17 to £20.

Sun L £20. **Details:** 50 seats. 30 seats outside. Separate bar. Wheelchair access. Music. Car parking.

Teffont Evias

Howard's House Hotel
Country comforts and quietly confident food
Teffont Evias, SP3 5RJ
Tel no: (01722) 716392
www.howardshousehotel.co.uk
Modern European | £45
Cooking score: 3

⇆ V

A late Jacobean dower house by a burbling brook in a rather fetching Wiltshire village sounds like a good place to recharge the batteries, and the family-owned Howard's House rises to the occasion. Furnished and run with creature comforts in mind, and featuring views over the well-maintained gardens, it makes a seductive showcase for some fine West Country produce. The culinary style is more informed by classicism than modernity, so proceedings may open with a starter serving of beef bourguignon, or lemon-battered king prawns with guacamole. At main, game features strongly in season, when the choice extends to guinea-fowl in thyme jus, partridge with game chips and bread sauce, and sika venison loin with dauphinois in Cassis jus – or there could be saffron-scented fish stew. Finish on a lighter note with a cranberry soufflé served with raspberry yoghurt. Wines are arranged by style and start at £17 (£4.25 a glass).
Chef/s: Nick Wentworth. **Open:** all week L 12 to 2, D 7 to 9. **Closed:** 24 to 27 Dec. **Meals:** alc (£36 2 courses, £45 3 courses) Set L £20. Set D £25 to £30. Tasting menu £65. Sun L £30. **Details:** 40 seats. 24 seats outside. Music. Car parking.

Average Price
The average price listed in main-entry reviews denotes the price of a three-course meal, without wine.

▌Tollard Royal

The King John Inn
Popular village inn with unusual flair
Tollard Royal, SP5 5PS
Tel no: (01725) 516207
www.kingjohninn.co.uk
Modern British | £35
Cooking score: 3

This Victorian brick-and-flint inn set in a beautiful Wiltshire village certainly makes an impression. There's a good rustic feel inside, with tiled floors, scrubbed wooden tables, open fires, big windows and a very civilised atmosphere. True food values and a passion for sourcing the finest seasonal produce are at the heart of Simon Trepess' cooking, and the accomplished chef has a raft of appealing ideas up his sleeve. Devilled fallow deer kidneys on fried bread or Portland crab on toast, for example, and mains of warm Sika venison salad with greens, beets, bacon and carrots, or lobster and sole ravioli with thermidor sauce, are the kind of dishes to expect – food with its roots in the region. Apple doughnuts with toffee sauce and mulled cider continues to be the most reported dessert, but there's also a featherlight elderflower soufflé. House wines start at £16.95.
Chef/s: Simon Trepess. **Open:** all week L 12 to 2.30 (3 Sat and Sun), D 7 to 9.30 (10 Fri and Sat, 9 Sun). **Closed:** 25 Dec. **Meals:** alc (main courses £15 to £29). **Details:** 60 seats. 60 seats outside. Separate bar. Wheelchair access. Car parking. Children over 8 yrs only at D.

▌West Hatch

Pythouse Kitchen Garden Shop and Café
Quaint kitchen garden eatery
West Hatch, SP3 6PA
Tel no: (01747) 870444
www.pythouse-farm.co.uk
British | £25
Cooking score: 2

Formerly the potting shed in the magical Victorian walled garden on the Pythouse Estate, this delightful little café also doubles up as a shop selling pickles and preserves, in addition to fruit, vegetables and flowers grown outside the door. It is by no means your typical garden centre café, as evidenced by flagstone floors, exposed bricks, wood-burner and a dresser laden with enticing homemade cakes. The chefs have a close relationship with the gardeners, which means the daily changing menu works in tandem with the seasons and keeps in step with garden produce as it appears: perhaps a warm heritage-carrot salad with Rosary goats' cheese and date purée, followed by grilled Pythouse Estate lamb chump chop with roasted mixed beetroots, cavolo nero and salsa verde. Finish with toasted fruit brioche with dark chocolate and blood-orange mousse, roasted fig and salted-caramel ice cream. Wines from £16.95 (£3.75 a glass).
Chef/s: Toby Rogers. **Open:** Wed to Mon L 12 to 3, D Thur to Sat 6 to 10. **Closed:** Tue, 25 and 26 Dec. **Meals:** alc (main courses £7 to £12). **Details:** 60 seats. 40 seats outside. Wheelchair access. Car parking.

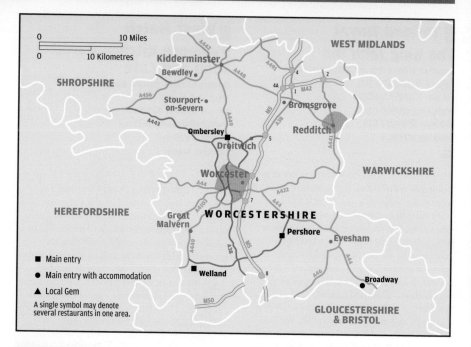

Broadway

Russell's

Inviting boutique brasserie
20 High Street, Broadway, WR12 7DT
Tel no: (01386) 853555
www.russellsofbroadway.co.uk
Modern British | £35
Cooking score: 4

£5 OFF

Named after renowned furniture designer, Sir
Gordon Russell, whose workshop and
showroom once occupied the premises, this
boutique brasserie-with-rooms is now a
pleasing prospect for locals and out-of-
towners. Plush upholstery, a massive open
fireplace and pieces of original furniture create
a relaxed, comforting vibe in the two
interconnecting dining rooms, while there's a
charming decked courtyard for alfresco
dining. Chef Neil Clarke is in tune with
current trends, embellishing his menus with
fashionable extras such as smoked pineapple,
pickled mushrooms and spiced popcorn,
although his smart dishes always hang
together convincingly. Home-cured pulled
beef comes with potatoes, peas, crispy quail's
egg and herb emulsion; halibut arrives atop
bone-marrow risotto. Vegetarians might be
tempted by crisp polenta with Kalamata
olives, roasted beetroot and purple sprouting
broccoli. Dry-aged steaks also have their fans,
while desserts might bring cherry Bakewell
tart with clotted cream or elderflower
pannacotta accompanied by apricot biscotti.
House wines from £21.50.
Chef/s: Neil Clarke. **Open:** all week L 12 to 2.30,
Mon to Sat D 6 to 9.30 (6.30 Sat). **Closed:** bank
hols. **Meals:** alc (main courses £17 to £28). Set L
and D £17 (2 courses) to £24. Sun L £25. **Details:** 60
seats. 20 seats outside. Separate bar. Wheelchair
access. Car parking.

▌Ombersley
The Venture In

Gently modernised food
Main Road, Ombersley, WR9 0EW
Tel no: (01905) 620552
www.theventurein.co.uk
Modern European | £39
Cooking score: 3

Dating from 1430, this crooked, half-timbered medieval dwelling comes suitably endowed with heavy sandstone walls, wonky floors, an inglenook and (naturally) a resident ghost. However, there's nothing spooky about the gently modernised Anglo-European food here. Chef/proprietor Toby Fletcher has been calming nerves and feeding the crowds since 1995, matching classic themes with a few bright ideas from his culinary box of tricks. Dishes such as crispy fried herring roes with rocket salad and fennel chutney, or pan-fried duck breast with sage polenta and pickled carrot purée, are unlikely to give anyone goose bumps – although they are rendered with confidence and a sure touch. Fish specials along the lines of monkfish wrapped in Parma ham with sautéed squid and lemon oil dressing depend on the market, while the choice of puds might run from warm pear and frangipane tart to iced praline parfait with apple and blackberry crumble. The wide-ranging wine list starts at £18.
Chef/s: Toby Fletcher. **Open:** Tue to Sun L 12 to 2, Tue to Sat D 7 to 9.30. **Closed:** Mon, 1 week Mar, 1 week Jun, 2 weeks Aug, 1 week Dec. **Meals:** Set L £25 (2 courses) to £29. Set D £39. Sun L £29.
Details: 32 seats. Separate bar. Music. Car parking. Children over 10 yrs only.

▌Pershore
Belle House

Value as well as contentment
5 Bridge Street, Pershore, WR10 1AJ
Tel no: (01386) 555055
www.belle-house.co.uk
Modern British | £32
Cooking score: 3

Arched front windows and a bell high on the brick wall mark out this tastefully converted Georgian building on Pershore's main drag. Inside all is classy and pleasing, with lofty ceilings, gilt-framed mirrors, the occasional blown-up foodie print on ochre-toned walls and a menu that promises value and contentment. Britain, France and the Med all have their say as the kitchen delivers plates of roast scallops with crab bisque and tomatoes followed by roast loin of pork with braised cheek, pressed apple and sage jus. Seafood and saffron stew with pungent aïoli, or macaroni with artichokes, wild mushrooms and Parmesan crisps sing of the south, and lemon meringue pie with passion fruit granita does duty for dessert. The well-judged wine list has been cleverly tailored to match the food, with bottles from £18.95. Steve Waites also runs the traiteur next door, selling deli provisions and take-away meals for those who fancy eating 'chez moi'.
Chef/s: Steve Waites. **Open:** Tue to Sat L 12 to 2, D 7 to 9.30. **Closed:** Sun, Mon, 25 to 30 Dec, first 2 weeks Jan. **Meals:** Set L £16 (2 courses) to £24. Set D £25 (2 courses) to £32. **Details:** 80 seats. Separate bar. Wheelchair access. Music.

▌Welland

The Inn at Welland
Country pub that's a great food destination
Drake Street, Welland, WR13 6LN
Tel no: (01684) 592317
www.theinnatwelland.co.uk
Modern British | £25
Cooking score: 3
£5 £30
OFF

David and Gillian Pinchbeck's style-conscious
country inn in bucolic Welland 'has really
come on this year', suggest local reports. The
Pinchbecks took over in 2011 giving the
stone-floored pub and terraced garden a nifty
makeover and reinvigorating the kitchen with
an everything-from-scratch philosophy. Now
'the place is full of life', 'a fantastic asset badly
needed in this area' – not only for Sunday
roast but during weekday lunchtime, when
the generously filled sandwiches (rare roast
beef and fresh horseradish mayo, for instance)
and 'British pub classics' (home-cured ham,
egg and chips and the like) keep the regulars
smiling. The carte takes a modern British tack,
teaming Cornish scallops with squid-ink
spaghetti, local venison with root vegetable
strudel and griottine cherry jus, and salted-
caramel pannacotta with gingerbread for
afters. Local cheese 'slates' also come
recommended. Enjoy with cask-conditioned
ales or 'a good selection of wines by the glass'.
Bottles from £14.95.
Chef/s: Chris Exley. Open: Tue to Sun L 12 to 2.30,
Tue to Sat D 6 to 9.30. Closed: Mon. Meals: alc
(main courses £12 to £22). Set L £21. Set D £25.
Details: 50 seats. 30 seats outside. Wheelchair
access. Music. Car parking.

▏▎ Readers Recommend
A 'readers recommend' review is a
genuine quote from a report sent in by
one of our readers. We intend to follow
up these suggestions throughout the
year to come.

▌Worcester

READERS RECOMMEND
Old Rectifying House
Modern British
North Parade, Worcester, WR1 3NN
Tel no: (01905) 619622
www.theoldrec.co.uk
'We liked the menu of this city-centre bar and
restaurant. Good because the menu is short so
the kitchen can concentrate on doing things
well; good because there's no stinting on big,
bold flavours.'

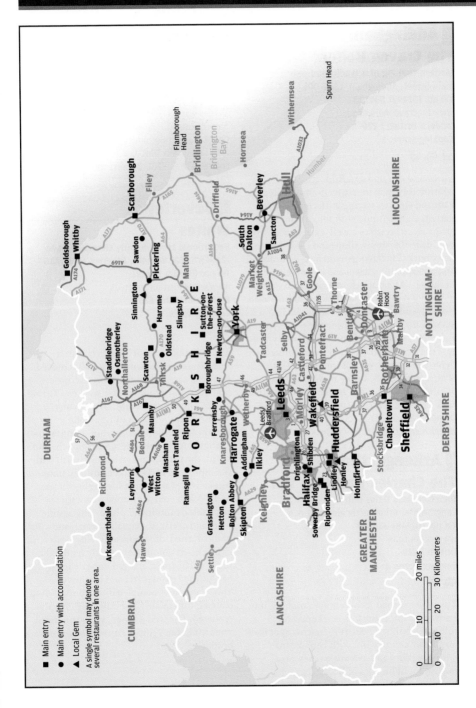

Addingham

The Craven Heifer

Modern cooking in a traditional pub
Main Street, Addingham, LS29 0PL
Tel no: (01943) 830106
www.thecravenheifer.com
Modern British | £29
Cooking score: 1
£5 OFF 🛏 £30

Visitors to this updated Addingham pub can comfortably tuck in to a well-constructed ham and chicken terrine with chicken liver parfait, and continue with loin of lamb and crispy sweetbreads or a well-executed 'surf and turf' dish of seared scallops and cider-braised belly pork. Pub favourites such as gammon and pineapple or scampi and chips are available in the bar. Alternatively, choose from smaller £3 and £4 plates of, say, black pudding with rhubarb and savoury granola, smoked salmon and potato salad or mini cottage pie. Over-fussy presentation and 'lots of flummery' can mar the experience (witness the deconstructed 'lemon meringue pie'). Wines from £14.
Chef/s: Mark Owens. **Open:** all week L 12 to 2 (6 Sun), Mon to Sat D 6 to 9. **Meals:** alc (mains £16 to £23). Set L and D £12 (2 courses) to £15. Sun L £18. **Details:** 80 seats. 32 seats outside. Separate bar. Wheelchair access. Music. Car parking.

Arkengarthdale

The Charles Bathurst Inn

Unpretentious Dales pub
Langthwaite, Arkengarthdale, DL11 6EN
Tel no: (01748) 884567
www.cbinn.co.uk
British | £28
Cooking score: 1
🛏 £30

The whitewashed 18th-century coaching inn, known locally as the CB, is set amid the rolling Yorkshire Dales. It's a bracing spot for a hospitable country inn with bare-board floors, log fires and a menu written on a mirror. Light lunches of Scotch egg and piccalilli, or crab and avocado tian, give way to more ambitious evening fare such as scallops with celeriac purée and chorizo, shank and neck of local lamb with carrot and swede mash and dauphinois, and tempting finishers like white chocolate and Amaretto crème brûlée. Local cheeses come with homemade chutney. Wines start at £15.95 for a Languedoc Sauvignon.
Chef/s: Gareth Bottomley. **Open:** all week L 12 to 2.30 (6 Sat and Sun), D 6 to 9. **Meals:** alc (main courses £12 to £20). **Details:** 100 seats. Separate bar. Car parking.

Beverley

Whites

Exceptional food on daily changing menu
12a North Bar Without, Beverley, HU17 7AB
Tel no: (01482) 866121
www.whitesrestaurant.co.uk
Modern British | £25
Cooking score: 4
🛏 £30

The evening menu at Whites' compact, sparsely decorated dining room has moved from à la carte to a 'surprise' four-course midweek and a nine-course weekend tasting menu. The midweek deal, in particular, represents tremendous value as John Robinson's cooking goes from strength to strength. After first-rate amuse-bouche and bread, the Parmesan and barley risotto with shrimps, wild garlic and beautifully smoky smoked eel was the first highlight of a test meal. A fish course of stone bass with sea vegetables, cauliflower purée, langoustine foam and caviar was equally strong, and a plate of unadorned, 36-hour, sous-vide lamb with char-grilled onions was sweetly tender. The finale of chocolate and red wine délice with hay-infused pannacotta and crumbs of 'chocolate snow' completed four outstanding courses: top-quality ingredients, perfectly rendered. The well-chosen, well-annotated wine list (from £18.95) contains some unusual bottles.

Chef/s: John Robinson. **Open:** Sat L 12 to 1.30, Tue to Sat D 6.30 to 11. **Closed:** Sun, Mon, 2 weeks Christmas, 1 week Aug. **Meals:** Set L £20. Set D £24 (4 courses) to £50. **Details:** 25 seats. Wheelchair access. Music.

▌Bolton Abbey

The Burlington at the Devonshire Arms
New chef steering a polished flagship
Bolton Abbey, BD23 6AJ
Tel no: (01756) 710441
www.burlingtonrestaurant.co.uk
Modern French | £65
Cooking score: 5

🍷 🛏

Adam Smith arrived here in 2013 fresh from the Ritz to run one of Yorkshire's hautest kitchens at the Duke and Duchess of Devonshire's polished flagship hotel. Expect fine wines, exacting service, intricate little dishes and impeccable sourcing. A test meal began with a taster of chilled potato soup with shrimp, black olive and potato crisp, followed by the knockout freshness of a sliced marinated scallop, interleaved with peppery radish, pickled cucumber, tiny pork croquettes and drops of whipped avocado. Next, three cuts of lamb arrived with white asparagus, wild garlic leaf, broad beans, smoked aubergine and lamb jus. A 'stunning' pre-dessert of rhubarb foam and gin sorbet garners praise, though for one reporter, puddings – deconstructed cheesecake, and chocolate ganache – didn't reach such heights. That said, Smith looks set to maintain the Burlington's reputation as one of Yorkshire's premium tables. The legendary wine list starts at £17, with dozens by the glass.
Chef/s: Adam Smith. **Open:** Tue to Sun D only 7 to 9.30. **Closed:** Mon, 25 Dec. **Meals:** Set D £65. **Details:** 70 seats. Separate bar. Wheelchair access. Car parking.

The Devonshire Brasserie
Ducal eatery with a metropolitan edge
Bolton Abbey, BD23 6AJ
Tel no: (01756) 710710
www.devonshirebrasserie.co.uk
Modern British | £30
Cooking score: 2

🛏

Transformed by the Duchess of Devonshire into a chic, country bolt-hole, the Devonshire Arms' second restaurant (see entry, The Burlington) has settled into a rhythm over the years. A vibrantly decorated bar and a slightly more formal dining room create a smart yet relaxed look. The place is enduringly popular, making a great setting at the gateway to the Dales. The food is all about brasserie favourites with much input from Yorkshire's larder, the emphasis on simple classics with a please-all appeal. Nidderdale-reared chicken liver parfait with spiced apple and shallots and toasted sultana brioche starts things off with a zing, while mains might offer roasted lamb rump with buttered and thyme fondant potato, smoked aubergine purée and truffled cabbage, or good old beer-battered fish, chunky chips and garden peas, and then a tangy iced lemon parfait with Earl Grey sorbet and ginger-poached pear to finish. Wine from £15 a bottle.
Chef/s: Charlie Murray. **Open:** all week L 12 to 2.30 (4 Sun), D 6 to 9.30 (9 Sun). **Meals:** alc (main courses £14 to £19). **Details:** 70 seats. 40 seats outside. Separate bar. Wheelchair access. Music. Car parking.

▌Boroughbridge

The Dining Room
Welcoming family-run restaurant
20 St James Square, Boroughbridge, YO51 9AR
Tel no: (01423) 326426
www.thediningroomonline.co.uk
Modern British | £30
Cooking score: 2

A listed Queen Anne house in the centre of a small market town, the Astleys' Dining Room might convey a touch of domesticity in its name, but it's a rather refined spot. The venue is smartly turned out in crisp whites with swagged curtains, and there's a suntrap terrace for aperitifs and/or summer dining. The menu looks simple, though the brasserie-style dishes arrive in polished presentations. Starter could be venison terrine with redcurrant jelly, or a bowl of lightly spiced smoked haddock chowder, prior to mains such as sea bass and samphire in lemon and thyme, duck confit with cider-apple compote, or something from the char-grill, which busily turns out anything from steaks to whole Dover soles. Finish with affogato, or a slice of glazed lemon tart. A concise wine selection appears on the back of the menu, with house Australian at £19 (£5.25 a standard glass).

Chef/s: Chris Astley. **Open:** Sun L 12 to 3, Tue to Sat D 6 to 9.15. **Closed:** Mon, 26 Dec to 1 Jan, bank hols. **Meals:** alc (main courses £10 to £30). Early D £16 (2 courses) to £20. **Details:** 32 seats. 22 seats outside. Separate bar. Music.

Chapeltown
Greenhead House
Dinner-party vibes in a cottagey setting
84 Burncross Road, Chapeltown, S35 1SF
Tel no: (0114) 2469004
www.greenheadhouse.com
Modern European | £49
Cooking score: 2

Greenhead House feels entirely un-urban, with its walled garden and 17th-century bearing. It is easy to forget you're in a Sheffield suburb. Since the early 1980s, the restaurant has been run by Neil and Anne Allen who ensure a traditional, dinner-party style prevails, from the taking of drinks in the cosy lounge to the countrified charms of the dining room. There's a reassuring formality to the place. Mr Allen works the stoves, Mrs Allen manages front-of-house and everything runs smoothly. The cooking takes a classical Anglo-French approach in a four-course format (plus canapés, coffee and petits fours). Begin with smoked salmon cannelloni topped with a béchamel sauce and browned under the grill, before a soup – smoked aubergine with

parsley oil, perhaps – or a fruity sorbet. Main-course venison casserole is flavoured with juniper, cinnamon and cloves, and, for dessert, spiced hazelnut meringues are layered with chocolatey mascarpone cream. Wines start at £23.

Chef/s: Neil Allen. **Open:** Fri L 12 to 1, Wed to Sat D 7 to 8.30. **Closed:** Sun to Tue, 1 week Christmas and New Year, 2 weeks May to Jun, 2 weeks Sept. **Meals:** Set L and D £49 (four courses). **Details:** 30 seats. Wheelchair access. Car parking. Children over 8 yrs only.

Drighlington
Prashad
Cooking from Gujarat and South India
137 Whitehall Road, Drighlington, BD11 1AT
Tel no: (01132) 852037
www.prashad.co.uk
Indian Vegetarian | £26
Cooking score: 3
V £30

Prashad's appeal is rooted both in the Patel family's warm, time-served approach to hospitality and the deft, well-rounded spicing of chef Minal's menu. Now fully settled into the three floors of a converted Leeds pub, the restaurant continues to offer dishes from the family's Gujarati homeland alongside food from South India – all vegetarian, of course. Although the menu 'hasn't expanded very much', the dominant theme is still 'fab', with a delicacy and range extending to rarely seen items such as hara bara kebabs: a belting mash-up of spiced cauliflower and pea with a dark, crisp exterior. Masala dosa with the traditional potato and onion stuffing, coconut and yoghurt chutney and spicy lentil soup is the complete textural experience, while chickpea chole has a streak of sharpness against the fragrance of cumin. Stuffed Gujwari naan, nutty and sweet, is a Gujarati take on the Peshwari version. House wine is £13.95.

Chef/s: Minal Patel. **Open:** Fri to Sun L 12 to 5, Tue to Sun D 5 to 11.30 (10.30 Tue, 12 Fri and Sat, 9 Sun). **Closed:** Mon, 25 Dec. **Meals:** alc (main courses £7 to £10). **Details:** 70 seats. Wheelchair access. Music. Car parking.

Ferrensby

★ TOP 50 PUB ★

The General Tarleton
High-profile foodie beacon
Boroughbridge Road, Ferrensby, HG5 0PZ
Tel no: (01423) 340284
www.generaltarleton.co.uk
Modern British | £35
Cooking score: 4

Not far from Harrogate, the Tarleton is a
carefully restored Georgian coaching inn in a
captivating rural setting. It's a maze of
interlinked rooms inside, with walls a mix of
smooth coffee-cream and exposed brick,
internal windows and a fireplace with logs
stacked up against the Yorkshire chill. Virtually
everything in John Topham's kitchen is as
Yorkshire as the moorland winds. The
appropriate instinct of the cooking even
runs to including provençale fish soup under
'Food with Yorkshire Roots'. Apart from one
or two such traditional touches, bold culinary
modernism runs through the menus. There's
crab and scallop lasagne in chive beurre blanc
to start, and mains such as rabbit (loin, cutlets,
a pie and a pancetta-packaged leg) in game jus,
or halibut with mussels and red pepper in
saffron broth. Pub classics will reassure the
cautious, as will finishers like tarte Tatin with
apple pannacotta and vanilla ice cream. Wines
start at £18.85.
Chef/s: John Topham and Marc Williams. **Open:** all
week L 12 to 2, D 5.30 to 9 (9.15 Sat, 8.30 Sun).
Meals: alc (main courses £14 to £23). Set L and D
£15 (2 courses) to £19. Sun L £25. **Details:** 120 seats.
60 seats outside. Car parking.

Goldsborough

The Fox & Hounds
No fuss, just high-quality food
Goldsborough, YO21 3RX
Tel no: (01947) 893372
www.foxandhoundsgoldsborough.co.uk
Modern European | £38
Cooking score: 5

Holding the line between Sandsend and
Runswick Bay on the North Yorkshire coast,
Sue and Jason Davies' country restaurant is
worth hunting down. The place has survived a
decade serving what the menu calls 'supper'
four evenings a week. Locally sourced organic
produce is the mainstay of the concise menus,
which offer a trio of choices at each stage.
Italianate simplicity informs the openers,
which might see bruschetta piled with chicken
livers, anchovies and capers, or smoked
haddock served carpaccio fashion, dressed
with wild rocket, tomato and lemon. At main,
fish is a hot ticket, perhaps perfectly timed
Dover sole on the bone with fennel potatoes
and sprouting broccoli, while meat eaters
dither between milk-braised suckling pig on
smashed cannellini beans, lemon and sage, and
the dry-aged rare-breed beef fillet with grilled
radicchio, proper chips and a splotch of
horseradish cream. Finish with almond and
lemon polenta cake. A compact wine list
opens at £18.
Chef/s: Jason Davies. **Open:** Wed to Sat D only 6.30
to 8.30. **Closed:** Sun, Mon, Tue, Christmas, bank
hols. **Meals:** alc (main courses £18 to £30).
Details: 26 seats. Car parking.

▌Grassington

Grassington House Hotel
Impressive field-to-fork food
5 The Square, Grassington, BD23 5AQ
Tel no: (01756) 752406
www.grassingtonhousehotel.co.uk
Modern British | £33
Cooking score: 3

£5 OFF 🛏

There's a true sense of dedication about John and Sue Rudden's carefully refurbished Georgian town house in the heart of a lovely Dales village. In their hands the house has flourished as an unstuffy hotel, offering just the sort of hospitality that both travellers and locals appreciate. It's a very personal operation, with attentive service and good, modern British food in the elegantly appointed dining room – 5 The Square. And good it is, too. The cooking is based on sound technique and an abundance of regional materials, delivering seared potted hog roast wrapped in cured ham and served with toffee apple jus, ahead of best end and loin of Pateley lamb teamed with artichokes, aubergines and rosemary Anna potatoes. Straightforward desserts – like baked plum and warm spiced treacle cake with vanilla ice cream – continue the theme. Wines offer a decent spread of contemporary styles from £15.75.
Chef/s: John Rudden. **Open:** all week L 12 to 2.30 (4 Sat and Sun), D 6 to 9.30 (8.30 Sun). **Closed:** 25 Dec. **Meals:** alc (main courses £13 to £24). Set L and D £15 (2 courses) to £17. Sun L £15 to £18. **Details:** 48 seats. 36 seats outside. Separate bar. Wheelchair access. Music. Car parking.

▌Halifax

NEW ENTRY
Ricci's Place
Tapas in a converted mill
4 Crossley House, Crossley Street, Halifax, HX1 1UG
Tel no: (01422) 410203
www.riccis-place.co.uk
Mediterranean | £25
Cooking score: 2

£5 OFF £30 ▼

Arrive at this handsomely renovated 19th-century former carpet mill on a good day and you'd be forgiven for imagining yourself somewhere much further south than Halifax. The vast square is fringed with cafés, food shops and Michael Ricci's cheerful eatery located in part of the mill. Unsurprisingly, the style is post-industrial, with vaulted brick ceilings, bare walls, tall windows letting in lots of light, the obligatory pipework – and a bar lined with high stools. It feels cosmopolitan and is highly popular. The place-mat menu promises hugely appealing tapas and cicchetti – the spiced cauliflower fritters with saffron and vanilla aïoli, and porcini gnocchi with wood pigeon are both beautifully presented and full of flavour – but there are also pig's head croquettes with apple purée, stuffed sea bass with Israeli couscous, and giambotta (Italian vegetable) stew. Service is excellent, and wines start at a gentle £11.50 a bottle.
Chef/s: Michael Ricci. **Open:** Mon to Sat 9 to 9. **Closed:** Sun, 25 and 26 Dec, 1 Jan. **Meals:** alc (main courses £10 to £16). **Details:** 70 seats. Music. Car parking.

Harome

The Pheasant Hotel

Country inn with a modern British menu
Mill Street, Harome, YO62 5JG
Tel no: (01439) 771241
www.thepheasanthotel.com
Modern British | £40
Cooking score: 4

🍷 🛏 V

With its muted Yorkshire tartans and hunting-lodge air, this is a thoroughly cosseting location. Dinner is served in the conservatory or the refined and modishly redecorated dining room. Lunch can also be taken by the fireside or on a terrace overlooking the village duck pond. It's all 'really delightful'. Menus, created by chef and co-owner Peter Neville (with Jacquie Pern), change seasonally and are beautifully balanced. From the market menu comes hot-smoked salmon simply served with soft-boiled egg, hollandaise and thinly sliced treacle bread, or Scarborough woof with morels and new-season asparagus. More elaborate dishes appear on the tasting menu and à la carte. Children and vegetarians are welcomed with their own menus, service is 'immaculate', and there are 16 comfortable bedrooms. An excellent wine list has good explanations and wines by the glass or carafe. Bottles start at £17.50.

Chef/s: Peter Neville. **Open:** all week L 12 to 2, D 6.30 to 9.30 (9 Sun). **Meals:** alc (main courses £19 to £24). Set L £24 (2 courses) to £29. Set D £36. Sun L £29 (2 courses) to £34. **Details:** 70 seats. 40 seats outside. Separate bar. Music. Car parking.

★ TOP 50 PUB ★

The Star Inn

Thatched inn with top-class food
High Street, Harome, YO62 5JE
Tel no: (01439) 770397
www.thestaratharome.co.uk
Modern British | £45
Cooking score: 5

🛏

'Faultless dinner on a midweek evening. Busy even at 7pm and service was fine. Couldn't fault it.' So ran the notes of one reporter, who found this venerable thatched inn (with nine bedrooms) on robust good form – despite concerns that chef/proprietor Andrew Pern has been distracted by his new opening in York (Star Inn the City, see entry). Steamed Argyll 'spoots' (razor clams) with local salami; slow-roast hogget with sheep's curd, pickled celeriac and blackened leeks; and potted wild rabbit with Whitby lobster and a mustard and cep cream proved that, despite 18 years here, Pern has lost little of his inventiveness with local, seasonal produce. New dishes continue to appear on the specials board. The Market menu is sound value, and the wine list (from £18.95) is reliable. Alternatively, try the excellent 'Two Chefs' honey beer created by Pern and James Mackenzie from the Pipe and Glass (see entry).

Chef/s: Andrew Pern. **Open:** Tue to Sun L 12 to 2 (6 Sun), Mon to Sat D 6.30 to 9.30. **Meals:** alc (main courses £18 to £27). Set L and D £20 (2 courses) to £25. Sun L £19. **Details:** 100 seats. 40 seats outside. Separate bar. Music. Car parking.

▌Harrogate

Orchid Restaurant

Well-crafted oriental cooking
Studley Hotel, 28 Swan Road, Harrogate, HG1 2SE
Tel no: (01423) 560425
www.orchidrestaurant.co.uk
Pan-Asian | £30
Cooking score: 2

£5 OFF 🚗

Harrogate is well served by this elegant, modern restaurant in the Studley Hotel. The Orchid is westernised in mood and atmosphere, with service that is charming and very accommodating. Much of the appeal derives from Kenneth Poon's satisfying pan-Asian cooking. Fine ingredients and assured technique are strengths, though with flavours aimed at Western palates, the kitchen is not pushing at any boundaries; instead it explores familiar territory, giving people what they know and like. The lengthy menu covers all staples, making a success of dishes as diverse as Malaysian chicken satay or Szechuan aromatic lamb pancakes, a Thai red duck curry, Cantonese black pepper sizzling beef, and chicken with black bean sauce from Hong Kong. The various set menus are a cut above the norm, and chilled mango pudding makes a refreshing dessert. Fairly priced New World wines stand out on the shortish list, with bottles from £18.40.
Chef/s: Kenneth Poon. **Open:** Mon to Fri and Sun L 12 to 2, all week D 6 to 10. **Closed:** 25 and 26 Dec. **Meals:** alc (main courses £10 to £25). Set L £11 (2 courses) to £14. Sun L £17. **Details:** 70 seats. 24 seats outside. Separate bar. Music. Car parking.

Sasso

Distinctive regional Italian cooking
8-10 Princes Square, Harrogate, HG1 1LX
Tel no: (01423) 508838
www.sassorestaurant.co.uk
Italian | £25
Cooking score: 3

£5 OFF   £30 ▼

Buried in a smart, uncluttered basement beneath one of Harrogate's Georgian terraces, Stefano Lancellotti's contemporary trattoria/enoteca never puffs itself up. Instead, the kitchen proves its worth with some highly distinctive Italian regional cooking – particularly in the pasta department. Specials such as lobster and courgette ravioli with tarragon and lobster bisque are always worth a go, in addition to favourites such as tagliolini with sweet chorizo, prawns, roasted peppers and saffron. Sasso's seasonal salad with smoked chicken, artichoke hearts and bagna cauda dressing provides a sprightly opener, while secondi might range from slow-cooked lamb shank in Tuscan tomato and porcini sauce, or a duo of marinated duck breast and pork belly, to veal burgers topped with ripe Gorgonzola and crispy pancetta. To finish, don't miss the homemade ice creams or signature tiramisu doused in aniseed and sambuca sauce. Italy and France claim pole position on the wine list, with prices from £13.95 (£3.75 a glass).
Chef/s: Stefano Lancellotti. **Open:** Mon to Sat L 12 to 2 (2.30 Sat), D 5.45 to 10 (10.30 Fri and Sat). **Closed:** Sun, 25 and 26 Dec, 1 Jan. **Meals:** alc (main courses £13 to £22). Set L and early D £9 (2 courses). **Details:** 90 seats. 20 seats outside. Music.

Van Zeller

A chef firing on all cylinders
8 Montpellier Street, Harrogate, HG1 2TQ
Tel no: (01423) 508762
www.vanzellerrestaurants.co.uk
Modern British | £50
Cooking score: 6

£5 OFF **V**

'Van Zeller really is a breath of fresh air.
Although Harrogate boasts many restaurants,
these are geared very much to tourists, not at
locals who want to eat and appreciate great
food.' So writes one of Tom Van Zeller's
growing army of fans. The surrounds may lack
zest – the dining room is small and tables
quite close together – but it hardly matters, as
the cooking is triumphant, explosively
exciting. Take dark pink salmon, sharing its
zone with bacon jam, little domes of bright
white-green avocado mayonnaise forming a
coded pattern around the immaculately placed
watercress shoots of varying graded shades: 'it
was almost a shame to eat it, but when we did,
the cleverly provided flavours twirled around
like a kaleidoscope'. Elsewhere, a beautifully
judged dish of rabbit with marmalade and
carrot soil could light the path for a following
course of duck served several ways and given a
lift by mango, spring onion, pak choi and
five-spice. And Mr Van Zeller proves his
pedigree by following the calendar
unerringly: game season, for example, has
delivered a fabulous red-legged partridge with
malt, liquorice, chanterelles and hay.
Technically ingenious chocolate with coffee
and salted caramel might close the deal. A
short list of thoroughbred wines starts
at £19.50.
Chef/s: Tom Van Zeller. **Open:** Tue to Sat L 12 to
2.30, D 6 to 10. **Closed:** Sun, Mon, first 10 days Jan.
Meals: Set L £35. Set D £50. Tasting menu £85 (10
courses). **Details:** 34 seats. Music.

▌Hetton

The Angel Inn

Honest-to-goodness country-pub food
Hetton, BD23 6LT
Tel no: (01756) 730263
www.angelhetton.co.uk
Modern British | £30
Cooking score: 2

The Watkins family's agreeable Dales pub-
with-rooms has been a consistent entry in the
Guide for many years. At one end is an
'elegant, olde-worlde, low-ceilinged village
pub' (aka bar-brasserie), at the other 'a rather
formal dining room'. Most prefer the bar-
brasserie for its 'atmosphere and roaring range
fire'. Here, real ales rubber-stamp the pub
credentials and the kitchen delivers classy
renditions of pub staples – black pudding
Scotch egg, fish pie, steak au poivre; it is for
the bar-brasserie that the score relates. Here,
too, is brasserie-style razzle-dazzle in a crisp
confit Goosnargh duck leg with cassoulet,
while honey-roast ham sandwiches draw the
lunchtime ramblers, and there's praise for the
banana pannacotta (served with banana bread
and caramel ice cream). The wine list has its
heart in France and opens with some 20 or so
wines by the glass, giving 'immense
encouragement to diversify one's food
choices'. Prices from £17.25.
Chef/s: Bruce Elsworth. **Open:** all week L 12 to 2, D
6 to 9 (9.30 Sat, 8.30 Sun). **Closed:** 4 days Jan.
Meals: alc (main courses £12 to £27). Set L and D
£15 (2 courses) to £19. Sun L £25. **Details:** 120 seats.
30 seats outside. Separate bar. Wheelchair access.
Car parking.

Holmfirth

NEW ENTRY
The Spiced Pear
Single-minded class on a Yorkshire hillside
Sheffield Road, Holmfirth, HD9 7TP
Tel no: (01484) 683775
www.thespicedpearhepworth.co.uk
British | £36
Cooking score: 2

V

On a West Yorkshire hillside near Huddersfield, this multi-faceted operation aims to change the way modern eateries work. Comprising a cocktail bar, vintage tea room and spacious restaurant with arboreally themed wallpaper, it has in Timothy Bilton a single-minded chef/patron who aims to make the place self-sustaining from its own smallholding within the next few years. There's a welcome hankering after big earthy flavours in the cooking, seen to exemplary effect in a bowl of thick wild garlic velouté with malty bread and a spoonful of pesto. The natural, seasonal focus also shines forth in a starter of William pear and onion tart with a salad of blue cheese, walnuts and wild flowers. Main courses step up a gear for the likes of sea bass with clams in a marine-fragranced velouté with samphire and powdered seaweed, while meats offer butter-fried brisket with a flat-iron steak, horseradish mash and tomato gravy. The *de rigueur* chocolate plate to finish has marquise, brûlée and a tart, along with popping candy, praline ice cream and macadamias. Glass-cloched artisan cheeses offer notable value. Afternoon teas with Moët & Chandon sound the last word in decadent delight. Good drinking otherwise includes interesting beers and a short wine list from £17.
Chef/s: Timothy Bilton. Open: Wed to Sun L 12 to 2 (5 Sun), D 6 to 9.30 (5.30 to 7 Sun). Closed: Mon, Tue. Meals: alc (main courses £18 to £22). Set L and

D £18 (2 courses) to £21. Sun L £29. Details: 88 seats. 20 seats outside. Separate bar. Music. Car parking.

Honley

LOCAL GEM
▲ Mustard & Punch
6 Westgate, Honley, HD9 6AA
Tel no: (01484) 662066
www.mustardandpunch.co.uk
British | £35

This bustling, bistro-style restaurant of some 14 years standing is the brainchild of Richard Dunn and Wayne Roddis. An absolute godsend for this small village, it offers a promising menu, taking in black pudding Scotch egg with roast onion purée and béarnaise sauce, outstanding seasonal game (from perfect pigeon breasts to pheasant with crushed new potatoes, streaky bacon and a rich game sauce), and local lamb rump, crisp belly and pressed potato terrine. The chocolate assiette has found favour, too. Wines from £17.50. Open Tue to Sat D.

Huddersfield
Bradley's
Boisterous basement brasserie
84 Fitzwilliam Street, Huddersfield, HD1 5BB
Tel no: (01484) 516773
www.bradleysrestaurant.co.uk
Modern British | £29
Cooking score: 2

V £30

'We come back time and time again,' enthused one fan of this Huddersfield veteran – open for just over 20 years. Whether it's Michael Bublé tribute acts or Friday steak nights, Andrew Bradley ensures that regular themed events liven up proceedings at this animated town-centre brasserie. Good-value, eclectic menus keep the locals happy in the cheery split-level dining room set in the basement of a converted mill. Wide-ranging influences are apparent in starters that range from French black pudding with Parma ham, red onion marmalade and wholegrain mustard to ham hock and pea risotto with mint. To follow, roast rump of lamb with dauphinois potatoes, sautéed spinach and red wine jus lines up alongside grilled fillets of sea bream with sautéed king prawns and smoked salmon cream. Meals might end with apple and raisin crumble and custard. Wines from £15.95.

Chef/s: Ben Flintoff and Hayden Satterley. **Open:** Tue to Fri L 12 to 2, Tue to Sat D 6 to 10. **Closed:** Sun, Mon, 27 Dec for 1 week, bank hols. **Meals:** alc (main courses £11 to £24). Set L £9 (2 courses) to £11. Set D £16 (2 courses) to £22 (3 courses with wine). Early D £15, Thur to Tue. **Details:** 120 seats. Separate bar. Wheelchair access. Music.

▮ Ilkley

The Box Tree

One of Yorkshire's finest
35-37 Church Street, Ilkley, LS29 9DR
Tel no: (01943) 608484
www.theboxtree.co.uk
Anglo-French | £60
Cooking score: 6

🍷 V

An idiosyncratic icon of the Yorkshire restaurant scene since the 1960s, the Box Tree still looks as if it's suspended in a time warp of paisley upholstery and striped wallpaper, but the food tells a very different story. Main man Simon Gueller upped the ante in 2013 by recruiting Lawrence Yates from multi-gonged Midsummer House (see entry) to run the kitchen – and it shows. Recent reports of 'immaculate service and beautifully judged dishes' prove the venue is riding high on confidence. Refinement and technical prowess are a given as the team delivers everything from an exquisitely presented tranche of wild turbot with orange, fennel and coriander to fillet of grass-fed local beef ('what flavour!') with a rustic daube, wild mushrooms and red wine sauce. After that, prepare yourself for the grand finale: a conversation-stopping raspberry soufflé, perhaps. Ever-attentive staff also know their way around the distinguished wine list – a classy compendium of French grandees, Aussie big boys and other oenophile treasures, priced from £22.

Chef/s: Simon Gueller and Lawrence Yates. **Open:** Fri to Sun L 12 to 1.30 (2 Sun), Tue to Sat D 7 to 9.30 (6.30 Sat). **Closed:** Mon, 26 to 30 Dec, 1 to 5 Jan. **Meals:** Set L £30. Set D £60. Sun L £35. Gourmand menu £70 (6 courses). **Details:** 60 seats. Separate bar. Music. No children under 10 yrs at D.

Ilkley Moor Vaults

Home-grown flavours and catchy ideas
Stockeld Road, Ilkley, LS29 9HD
Tel no: (01943) 607012
www.ilkleymoorvaults.co.uk
Modern British | £22
Cooking score: 2

£5 OFF £30

Handily placed at the start of the Dales Way, Joe McDermott's revitalised boozer not only provides a cracking pit-stop for thirsty walkers, but also hits the bull's-eye when it comes to food and atmosphere. Inside, original flagstone floors, open fires and weathered beams set the scene, old-fashioned standard lamps add a touch of sitting-room nostalgia and blackboards advertise the day's specials. This is a productive set-up, with its own kitchen garden and smokehouse – so expect honest home-grown flavours and some catchy international ideas from the 'slow food' school of cookery. Beef and ale pie rubs shoulders with Spanish chicken stew; smoked haddock with mustard sauce pleases the fish brigade; and there are also excellent cuts of prime Yorkshire beef. If available, the pub's homemade sausages are worth ordering, too. Desserts keep it simple with the likes of lemon posset or sticky toffee pudding. Two dozen workaday wines start at £14.90.

Chef/s: Sabi Janak. **Open:** Tue to Sat L 12 to 2.30 (3 Sat), D 5.30 to 9. Sun 12 to 7. **Closed:** Mon. **Meals:** alc (main courses £10 to £21). Set D £12 (2 courses) to £15. **Details:** 65 seats. 30 seats outside. Car parking.

Leeds

Brasserie Forty 4
Long-standing brasserie on the waterfront
44 The Calls, Leeds, LS2 7EW
Tel no: (0113) 2343232
www.brasserie44.com
Modern European | £30
Cooking score: 2

This converted corn mill on the banks of the
Aire is a Leeds stalwart. It was in the vanguard
of the new-wave contemporary bistros of the
mid-1990s and has continued to fly the flag
ever since. Exposed brick, industrial ironwork
and arched windows overlooking the river
make for an attractive setting, and there's a
balcony for sunny days. The à la carte features
salt cod croquettes or oxtail and truffle risotto
followed, perhaps, by venison haunch with
Madeira sauce or a pleasing puff pastry tart of
tomatoes, mushrooms and rocket. The three-
course set menu at lunch and early evening
offers good value as it includes a bottle of wine
between two and a choice from the likes of
chicken liver parfait with Armagnac prunes,
pork fillet and cannellini beans in a cream and
mustard sauce, and a classic crème brûlée.
Wines start at £17.15, with a dozen by the
glass.
Chef/s: David Robson. Open: Mon to Sat L 12 to 2 (1
to 3 Sat), D 6 to 9.30 (5 to 10 Sat). Closed: Sun, 25
and 26 Dec, bank hols (exc Good Friday). Meals: alc
(main courses £13 to £24). Set L and D £24 (3
courses, inc half-bottle of wine). Details: 120 seats.
18 seats outside. Separate bar. Children over 2 yrs
only.

Crafthouse
Slick, stylish cosmopolitan eatery
Level 5, Trinity Leeds, 70 Boar Lane, Leeds,
LS1 6HW
Tel no: (0113) 8970444
www.crafthouse-restaurant.com
Modern British | £37
Cooking score: 3

The first provincial outing for D&D London
(Almeida, Coq d'Argent, Launceston Place etc,
see entries), slick, stylish Crafthouse struts its

cosmopolitan stuff on the fifth floor of Trinity
Leeds (the city's flashy new shopping
complex). Cool polished interiors, swathes of
glass and metal, wraparound views, 'charming
staff' and an open kitchen set the scene for
grown-up Anglo-European food majoring in
meat and seafood from the Josper grill. If
you're not sold on well-hung steaks (from
Ginger Pig), burgers, sticky ribs or king
prawns, the extensive repertoire also
encompasses ham hock and dandelion salad
with Colman's mustard dressing; pea and
broad bean risotto; and baked sea bass fillet 'in
paper' with bouillabaisse, grilled courgettes
and saffron potatoes. Likewise, desserts range
from sherry trifle to pistachio soufflé with
chocolate sorbet. On the sixth floor is little
sibling Angelica: a more informal, cheaper
eatery dealing in sharing plates, salads, pasta
and grills. Knowledgeably chosen wines start
at £17.
Chef/s: Lee Bennett. Open: Tue to Sat L 12 to 3, Mon
to Sat D 5 to 11. Sun 12 to 10. Closed: 25 Dec.
Meals: alc (mains £15 to £40). Set L £19 (2 courses)
to £23. Details: 120 seats. 20 seats outside.
Wheelchair access. Music.

The Reliance
Well-chosen beers and reliably good food
76-78 North Street, Leeds, LS2 7PN
Tel no: (0113) 2956060
www.the-reliance.co.uk
Modern British | £23
Cooking score: 3
£30

Drinkers fairly drown in choice at this former
cloth mill turned bar and dining room on the
fringes of the city centre. Well-chosen beers
(hailing from Ilkley to San Francisco) and
wines don't so much take the edge off the no-
reservation policy as induce comfortable stasis
in the bar, where snacks include excellent
home-cured charcuterie. Those who make it
through to the restaurant will find
contemporary, solid-but-smart pub food,
cooked and served with eyes wide open. Try
heritage beetroot with grilled mackerel and
horseradish, or luxurious bone-marrow

risotto with oxtail and grilled shallot; to follow, a venison and kidney suet pudding is a 'standout', while breezier options include roast cod with cider, salsify and seaweed. Puddings such as chocolate orange ganache with orange jelly and hazelnut conclude a congenial experience. The fact that prices are keen helps make this 'a great place to spend an evening'. Wine is from £14.75.

Chef/s: Verdine Etoria. **Open:** all week L 12 to 5 (11 to 4 Sun), D 5.30 to 10 (6 to 9.30 Sun). **Closed:** 25 and 26 Dec, bank hols. **Meals:** alc (main courses £10 to £14). Pre-theatre D £15 (2 courses) to £19. **Details:** 128 seats. 6 seats outside. Separate bar. Music. Car parking.

Salvo's

Fantastic pizzas and budget prices
115 Otley Road, Headingley, Leeds, LS6 3PX
Tel no: (0113) 2755017
www.salvos.co.uk
Italian | £28
Cooking score: 2
£30

It's not all about the pizza, but they are very, very good – strongly recommended is the 'Buongiorno' with pancetta and free-range egg or 'Posillipo' with a mix of seafood and roast peppers. Going strong for almost 40 years, Salvo's has pictures of the old days on the walls and remains fun and full of life. The menu has much to catch the eye other than those pizzas, with antipasti such as octopus, potato and samphire salad, and homemade liver pâté with spiced orange marmalade, plus a secondi of pot-roast shoulder of lamb with artichokes and capers. Local supply networks are well trusted by now and other stuff is shipped over from Milan market. Pasta is a winner, too (rigatoni with cremini mushrooms and a creamy truffle sauce), and there's a kids' menu – 'it's a great family place'. Salumeria (the linked, very good café-deli) is nearby. Italian wines start at £16.95.

Chef/s: Gip Dammone and Giuseppe Schivripa. **Open:** Mon to Sat L 12 to 2, D 6 to 10.30 (5.30 to 11 Fri and Sat). Sun 12 to 9. **Closed:** 25 and 26 Dec, 1 Jan. **Meals:** alc (main courses £9 to £20). Set L £12.

Set D £15 (2 courses) to £18. Sun L £15 (2 courses) to £18. **Details:** 88 seats. 20 seats outside. Separate bar. Wheelchair access. Music.

LOCAL GEM
▲ Hansa's

72-74 North Street, Leeds, LS2 7PN
Tel no: (0113) 2444408
www.hansasrestaurant.com
Indian Vegetarian | £15 £5 OFF

Reporters agree that Hansa Dabhi's long-running Gujarati restaurant is the most consistent address for vegetarian food in Leeds. The dining room is charmingly dated, with family photos emphasising its homely qualities. Stuffed paratha, chilli paneer, pani puri with lashings of tamarind sauce, and masala dosa represent one aspect of the menu; curries of fresh vegetable (aubergine and potato, say) or pulses (chickpea koftas and potatoes) are the other. It's all great value. There's a popular Sunday L buffet, otherwise it's D only. Wine from £15.25.

▌Leyburn
The Sandpiper Inn

Highly polished Dales inn
Market Place, Leyburn, DL8 5AT
Tel no: (01969) 622206
www.sandpiperinn.co.uk
Modern British | £32
Cooking score: 3

A right and proper old stone pub in the middle of Leyburn, the Sandpiper has sturdy beams, nooks, crannies and the kind of rustic finish that almost seems contemporary. But this place is no designer recreation: it's the real deal. Draught ales are dispensed from the bar and the log fire glows, while the restaurant turns out some modern British plates that impress with their ambition and execution. 'Textures of parsnip' accompany a first-course caramelised pork belly with seared queen scallops in a trendy and well-judged combo, and a main course of slow-cooked

Wensleydale beef with black pudding might follow. There are local ingredients aplenty, from Swinton Park venison to Washfold Farm pheasant, and pubby dishes such as haddock in real ale batter are served in the bar. Good-looking desserts run to a Knickerbocker glory. Wines start at £15.95.

Chef/s: Jonathan Harrison. **Open:** Tue to Sun L 12 to 2.30, D 6.30 to 9 (9.30 Sat). **Closed:** Mon, Tue (winter). **Meals:** alc (main courses £15 to £22). Sun L £20 (2 courses) to £29. **Details:** 56 seats. 20 seats outside. Separate bar. Music.

▌Lindley
Eric's
In tune with its customers
75 Lidget Street, Lindley, HD3 3JP
Tel no: (01484) 646416
www.ericsrestaurant.co.uk
Modern British | £35
Cooking score: 3

A 'great atmosphere', 'friendly, attentive staff' and 'good value for money' are big selling points at this smart, contemporary restaurant found in a suburban parade of shops. Eric Paxman has a passion for local, seasonal ingredients and delivers the kind of must-eat, big-hearted dishes that win many friends. Light lunches and early-bird dinners please the locals, but the kitchen ups its game with a carte that mixes standards with more contemporary ideas. The quality of ingredients always beams forth. Successful dishes this year have been a warm salad of streaky bacon with merguez sausage, blue cheese and mustard dressing ('superb flavour combinations'); a 'standout' pot-roast chicken served with braised red peppers, saffron gnocchi, baby leeks and roast garlic mayonnaise; 'perfectly cooked' fillet steak with triple-cooked chips; and a chocolate and beetroot mousse with pistachio meringue that was 'possibly the most sublime morsel to ever pass my lips'. Wines start at £16.50.

Chef/s: Eric Paxman, Paul Cookson, James Thompson and Thomas Badger. **Open:** Tue to Fri and Sun L 12 to 2 (4 Sun), Tue to Sat D 6 to 10 (5.30 Sat). **Closed:** Mon. **Meals:** alc (main courses £16 to £28). Set L £16 (2 courses) to £18. Set D £19 (2 courses) to £23. Sun L £19 (2 courses) to £23. **Details:** 80 seats. Wheelchair access. Music.

▌Masham
Samuel's at Swinton Park
Artful cooking and Gothic grandeur
Swinton Park, Masham, HG4 4JH
Tel no: (01765) 680900
www.swintonpark.com
Modern British | £52
Cooking score: 5
£5 OFF ═ V

The ancestral home of the Earls of Swinton since the 1880s, this grandiose country pile flaunts its aristocratic credentials with a full complement of battlements, turrets, gatehouses and parkland: think blue-blooded heritage wearing sporting togs. Chef Simon Crannage reaps rich rewards with produce from the estate and the walled garden, loading his menus with artful, sense-of-occasion dishes that chime with the surroundings. Seasonal game is a sound choice: perhaps garlic-braised pigeon with black pudding, milk-poached celeriac, crisp potato and watercress; or pheasant with charred leeks, truffle butter sauce and kale. There's Swinton trout too, as well as fish from further afield (fillet of halibut with barley, root vegetables, oxtail and garlic purée) – not forgetting Yorkshire beef, lamb and Middle White pork. For afters, marvel at the artistic desserts: roasted pineapple with almond cake, anise ice cream, pineapple gel and almonds, for example. Around 20 inviting house selections (from £18) open the heavy-duty wine list.

Chef/s: Simon Crannage. **Open:** Tue to Sun L 12.30 to 2, all week D 7 to 9.30. **Meals:** Set L £22 (2 courses) to £26. Set D £52. Sun L £28. Tasting menu £60 (7 courses) to £70 (10 courses). **Details:** 60 seats. Separate bar. Wheelchair access. Car parking. Children over 8 yrs only at D.

Vennell's

Bringing metropolitan chic to Masham
7 Silver Street, Masham, HG4 4DX
Tel no: (01765) 689000
www.vennellsrestaurant.co.uk
Modern British | £28
Cooking score: 5

£5 OFF £30

The purple frontage stands out strikingly on a Grade II-listed stone building in the North Yorkshire brewing and market town, not far from Ripon. Inside is as elegant as can be, with aubergine walls, little round mirrors and jazzily patterned upholstery. There's a mood of relaxing civility. Jon Vennell's impulse to please extends to devising bespoke menus for special occasions. Theme nights linked to the cycles of the gastronomic year are a feature. The evolution of modern British cooking, to include retrospective glances at classical modes, produces here a starter of whole Dover slip sole dressed in lemon, parsley, capers and butter, as well as devilled kidneys on toast. After those might come venison haunch with Savoy cabbage and wild mushrooms in apricot jus, or sea bass with aubergine confit and dried tomatoes. Finish with meltingly luscious chocolate fondant and caramel ice cream. Fairly priced wines are classified by grape, starting at £19.50.

Chef/s: Jon Vennell. **Open:** Sun L 12 to 4, Wed to Sat D 7.15 to 12. **Closed:** Mon, Tue, 26 to 30 Dec, 2 weeks Jan, 1 week Aug. **Meals:** Set D £25 (2 courses) to £28. Sun L £23. **Details:** 30 seats. Separate bar. Music. Children over 4 yrs only.

■ Maunby

NEW ENTRY

The Buck Inn

Extraordinary cooking in an ordinary pub
Maunby, YO7 4HD
Tel no: (01845) 587777
www.thebuckinnmaunby.co.uk
British | £30
Cooking score: 2

£5 OFF

Handy for the A1, the Buck is smack in the centre of pretty Maunby village. It's one of those 'never judge a book by its cover' kind of places – not the prettiest pub with its red-brick 1980s roadhouse vibe – but the cavernous interior (all open fires, beams and squashy leather sofas, plus two dining rooms) has a comfy vibe. Sammy Clark and Matthew Roath know a thing or two about hospitality and good food. From Sammy comes a welcome that is genuinely warm, and Matthew's cooking impresses. Readers have nothing but praise for his homemade soda bread and house hummus, and the devotion to local and seasonal produce shows in beautifully presented plates. Locally shot confit rabbit with smoked artichoke risotto has 'stunning depth of flavour', and there could be hake fillet with pommes Anna, Whitby crabmeat tortellini and watercress velouté. The wine list opens at £16.

Chef/s: Matthew Roath. **Open:** Tue to Sun L 12 to 2.30 (5 Sun), Tue to Sat D 5 to 9.30 (6 Sat). **Closed:** Mon, 26 Dec, 1 Jan. **Meals:** alc (main courses £12 to £21). Set L and early weekday D £13 (2 courses) to £16. Sun L £10 (1 course) to £17. **Details:** 48 seats. 5 seats outside. Separate bar. Music. Car parking.

Newton-on-Ouse

The Dawnay Arms

Brit cooking with verve and gusto
Moor Lane, Newton-on-Ouse, YO30 2BR
Tel no: (01347) 848345
www.thedawnayatnewton.co.uk
Modern British | £26
Cooking score: 3

V £30

City chef turned country-pub landlord Martel Smith and his wife seem happy and contented in this elegant Georgian hostelry. And why not, given the desirable village location and pretty gardens running down to the banks of the River Ouse? Inside, funky cushions and pastel colours sit comfortably with the original flagstone floors, church pews and chunky wooden tables in the bar and dining room. The kitchen deploys ingredients with verve and gusto for a menu of sturdy Brit-accented dishes in nifty new guises: steamed steak, kidney and stout pudding is embellished with onion purée and carrot fondant; chunks of Whitby cod are teamed with braised oxtail, herb gnocchi and red wine sauce; wild mushroom risotto is finished with thyme velouté. Dry-aged steaks and plates of fish and chips also rate highly in the popularity charts, while desserts are wholesome old faithfuls such as sticky toffee pudding or treacle tart with custard. Wines from £16.95.
Chef/s: Martel Smith. **Open:** Tue to Sun L 12 to 2.30 (6 Sun), Tue to Sat D 6 to 9.30. **Closed:** Mon, 1 Jan. **Meals:** alc (main courses £13 to £25). Set L £13 (2 courses) to £16. Set D £14 (2 courses) to £18. Sun L £15 (2 courses) to £19. **Details:** 60 seats. 30 seats outside. Separate bar. Wheelchair access. Music. Car parking.

Oldstead

★ TOP 50 PUB ★

The Black Swan

From family inn to garlanded restaurant
Oldstead, YO61 4BL
Tel no: (01347) 868387
www.blackswanoldstead.co.uk
Modern British | £46
Cooking score: 4

V

A family-owned stone-built inn in a village not far from York, the Swan is a graceful old bird. Kitted out with Persian rugs and brass candleholders, it makes an easy impression on the eye. Tommy Banks is the latest scion of the family to step up to the stoves, bringing renewed energy and creativity to the cooking. Dishes built on local ingredients find unlikely partners, so butternut squash, shiitakes and pumpkin seeds are added to a smoked scallop; and carrots, kohlrabi and five-spice are teamed with a starter serving of rabbit. Mains might be either richly accompanied white fish such as halibut or brill done with Cheddar and truffles, or perhaps saddle and sausage of venison with celeriac, hazelnuts and pear. To finish, variants on classic baking produce the likes of Black Forest gâteau or carrot cake with walnuts and mascarpone. A stylistically arranged list of dependable wines opens at £19.
Chef/s: Tommy Banks. **Open:** Thur to Sun L 12 to 2 (3 Sun), all week D 6 to 9. **Closed:** 1 to 2 weeks Jan. **Meals:** alc (main courses £24 to £29). Set L and D £28. Tasting menu L £48, D £75. **Details:** 40 seats. 20 seats outside. Separate bar. Wheelchair access. Music. Car parking.

▌Osmotherley
Golden Lion
Warm-hearted watering hole
6 West End, Osmotherley, DL6 3AA
Tel no: (01609) 883526
www.goldenlionosmotherley.co.uk
Anglo-European | £30
Cooking score: 2

🛏 V

Walkers and tourists rub shoulders with locals in this 18th-century sandstone inn overlooking Osmotherley village square. The Golden Lion is a warm-hearted watering hole that knows a few things about country hospitality. Real ales, varnished woodwork and roaring fires shore up its pubby credentials, but most people come for the good-value food: nothing too fancy or outré, just big, honest flavours and carefully handled ingredients from a menu that rarely changes as the years roll by. Head here for bowls of mussels, suet-crusted steak and kidney pud, salmon fishcakes with chive beurre blanc or even a burger and chips; otherwise, take the European path by ordering a salad of goats' cheese, chorizo and peppers ahead of whole poussin roasted with rosemary and garlic. For afters, keep it traditional with two scoops of homemade ice cream or ginger sponge with stewed plums and custard. The 30-bin wine list offers sound drinking from £16.95.
Chef/s: Christopher Wright. **Open:** Wed to Sun L 12 to 2.30 (3 Sun), all week D 6 to 9 (8.30 Sun). **Closed:** 25 Dec. **Meals:** alc (main courses £10 to £20). **Details:** 68 seats. 16 seats outside. Wheelchair access. Music.

▌Pickering
The White Swan Inn
Big-hearted Yorkshire hospitality
Market Place, Pickering, YO18 7AA
Tel no: (01751) 472288
www.white-swan.co.uk
Modern British | £36
Cooking score: 3

🛏

There's a palpable sense of history here, but that isn't too surprising given the White Swan has been offering hospitality to weary travellers since the 16th century. Run by the Buchanan family since the early 1980s, the hotel today has a broadly contemporary finish to contrast with all the antiquity – smart and a little posh. The kitchen makes much of the local provenance of its ingredients and puts them to very good use in a menu that skilfully strikes a balance between rusticity and refinement. A jar of Ginger Pig pork with piccalilli and sticky apple and crackling salad is typical of the output. Alternatively, go for a fabulous piece of ox tongue that melts in the mouth (served with wild garlic pesto). Main-course bacon chop is just the job, too, with roasted skate as a fish option. The wine list includes a section devoted to Saint-Emilion. House wine is £17.25.
Chef/s: Darren Clemmit. **Open:** all week L 12 to 2, D 6.45 to 9. **Meals:** alc (main courses £13 to £28). **Details:** 65 seats. 25 seats outside. Separate bar. Car parking.

Ramsgill

★ TOP 50 ★

The Yorke Arms
A chef with stellar talents
Ramsgill, HG3 5RL
Tel no: (01423) 755243
www.yorke-arms.co.uk
Modern British | £65
Cooking score: 6

£5 OFF 🍷 🛏

The Nidderdale Valley is the green, pleasant home of the Yorke Arms, a Georgian coaching inn that adds to the verdant scene with its creeper-covered walls and neatly trimmed hedges. Run by Gerald and Frances Atkins since 1997, it's a restaurant-with-rooms that packs a culinary punch. Mrs Atkins is a stellar chef who takes prime Yorkshire produce – there's a fruitful kitchen garden, too – and delivers modern food rooted in classical technique and regional provenance. The 'Classics' menu might include lamb as slow-cooked shoulder, loin and sweetbread, while the carte produces a Med-inspired tuna dish with squid and chorizo, followed by saddle of venison with oxtail and the delicately judged additions of blackcurrant and liquorice. Traditional, elegant dining rooms and sharp presentation make for an upmarket experience. Lychee soufflé with jasmine tea sorbet and almond pastry provides a creative finish. 'The best in Yorkshire' for one reader. Wines kick off at £25.
Chef/s: Frances Atkins. **Open:** all week L 12 to 2, D 7 to 9 (Sun D residents only). **Meals:** alc (main courses £35 to £39). Set L £40. Sun L £50. Tasting menu £85. **Details:** 40 seats. 20 seats outside. Music. Car parking.

🍴 **Visit us Online**
To find out more about
The Good Food Guide, please visit
www.thegoodfoodguide.co.uk

Ripon

Lockwoods
Café-restaurant that aims to please
83 North Street, Ripon, HG4 1DP
Tel no: (01765) 607555
www.lockwoodsrestaurant.co.uk
Modern British | £30
Cooking score: 1

Matthew Lockwood's joint is a thriving café-bar during the day, with sandwiches, fish pie and suchlike, morphing seamlessly into a restaurant in the evening. Whatever the time of day, there's dedication to local ingredients and a focus on British and Med flavours. The period building has a modern finish – zinc-topped bar, bold colours – and everything from the Yorkshire game terrine (packed with pheasant, rabbit and pigeon) to main-course sea bream with celeriac purée and gnocchi is cooked with verve. There are cocktails, too, and desserts such as spiced rhubarb and vanilla crumble. Wines open at £15.95.
Chef/s: John Malia. **Open:** Tue to Sat L 12 to 2.30 (10 to 3 Sun), D 5 to 9.30 (10 Fri and Sat). **Closed:** Mon, 25 and 26 Dec, 1 Jan. **Meals:** alc (main courses £11 to £20). Set D £13.50 (2 courses) to £16.50. **Details:** 65 seats. Wheelchair access. Music.

Ripponden

El Gato Negro
No clichés, just sharp, honest tapas
1 Oldham Road, Ripponden, HX6 4DN
Tel no: (01422) 823070
www.elgatonegrotapas.com
Spanish | £25
Cooking score: 4

£5 OFF £30 ▼

Ripponden may be a long way from the backstreets of Barcelona, but Yorkshireman Simon Shaw has done his best to create a little corner of Spain in this former Pennine village boozer. With its 'tick the boxes' place-mat menus and casual tapas-bar vibe, El Gato Negro has become a firm favourite locally and regionally – it's handy for the M62. The list kicks off with impeccably sourced bar snacks, charcuterie and cheeses. One reporter hailed the pan catalana as 'the best I've had' and was equally impressed by a 'nicely garlicky' roast rump of lamb with rosemary and alubia blanca beans. More technical dishes such as sous-vide whole rack of baby pork ribs in Pedro Ximénez glaze, and whole roasted black bream with fennel, lemon, garlic and thyme show the owner's fine-dining background. Wine from £15.95, and there's an extensive range of sherries.

Chef/s: Simon Shaw. **Open:** Sat L 12 to 2, Tue to Sat D 6 to 9.30 (10 Fri and Sat). **Closed:** Mon, Sun, 3 weeks Jan, 10 days Aug. **Meals:** alc (tapas £5 to £15). **Details:** 52 seats. Wheelchair access. Music.

▌Sancton

★ TOP 50 PUB ★

The Star @ Sancton

Appealingly local menus and sound cooking
King Street, Sancton, YO43 4QP
Tel no: (01430) 827269
www.thestaratsancton.co.uk
British | £34
Cooking score: 4

V

It goes from strength to strength, this traditional roadside pub set in the gentle Yorkshire Wolds. Refreshingly unfussy décor, polished tables, a wood-burner and an absence of pomp or ceremony are plus points. Ben Cox's cooking is equally straightforward, his menus revealing a passion for seasonal foods and local producers. The robust repertoire stretches from Peck's of Beverley smoked haddock risotto with poached egg, mustard and chervil, and Black Sheep beer-battered haddock and chips from the blackboard in the bar, to Yorkshire pudding filled with braised oxtail, and East Coast monkfish with paprika, Kirkby Malham chorizo and crispy York ham on the evening à la carte. Puddings embrace crème brûlée with banana and peanut-butter cookie, and sticky toffee pudding with rich vanilla toffee sauce, espresso foam and local

clotted cream. Staff are friendly and interested, the atmosphere warm and welcoming, and the fairly priced, global wine list opens at £14.95.

Chef/s: Ben Cox. **Open:** Tue to Sun L 12 to 2 (3 Sun), D 6 to 9.30 (8 Sun). **Closed:** Mon, first week Jan, bank hols. **Meals:** alc (main courses £16 to £23). Set L £17 (2 courses) to £19. **Details:** 80 seats. 36 seats outside. Separate bar. Wheelchair access. Music. Car parking.

▌Sawdon

The Anvil Inn

Satisfying food in a former smithy
Main Street, Sawdon, YO13 9DY
Tel no: (01723) 859896
www.theanvilinnsawdon.co.uk
Modern European | £29
Cooking score: 2

🛏 £30

Forged from the remains of a 200-year-old smithy, the Anvil Inn prospers as a smart boozer and country restaurant-with-rooms a short hike from Scarborough. The old blacksmith's workshop is now the bar, complete with oak pews and assorted tools of the trade. You can drop in here for a proper pub lunch of steak pie or a pulled pork sandwich washed down with local ale from the likes of World Top and Daleside. In the evening, the kitchen rolls up its sleeves for a restaurant menu with a tad more culinary sophistication – think pigeon carpaccio with venison sausage roll and duck liver parfait, sautéed medallions of Scarborough woof in tartare butter with purple potatoes and spider crab rémoulade, or slow-braised beef brisket with horseradish mash and red onion gravy. For afters, try something plain (treacle and nut tart) or something fancy (liquorice bavarois with pear and flapjack). Wines cost from £16.50.

Chef/s: Mark Wilson. **Open:** Wed to Sun L 12 to 2 (2.30 Sun), D 6.30 to 9 (6 to 8 Sun). **Closed:** Mon, Tue, 25 and 26 Dec, 1 Jan, 2 weeks summer, 1 week Nov. **Meals:** alc (main courses £12 to £25). **Details:** 34 seats. 12 seats outside. Separate bar. Music. Car parking.

Scarborough

Eat Me Café

Cool, kitsch café on the Yorkshire coast
1 Hanover Road, Scarborough, YO11 1LS
Tel no: (01723) 373256
www.eatmecafe.com
Modern British | £22
Cooking score: 2

£5 OFF £30

It's a café all right – cash only, unlicensed and you might have to share a table with a new best friend – located behind the town's famous Stephen Joseph Theatre. And the people, they do come. Eat Me is open for breakfasts ranging from the classic English variety (including a vegetarian alternative) to the more EU-friendly eggs with chorizo and potato, while the lunchtime menu incorporates burgers, sarnies and 'tin plate' dishes of chicken satay or chilli. Most things are made in-house and local ingredients play their part – 'there always seems to be something new to try'. Thursday to Saturday evenings is 'Eat Me Social' time (until 7pm), when the café stays open later for a host of burgers (sloppy, bacon or haloumi and mushroom), and bowls of ramen noodles. There's a specials board, too, perhaps featuring oven-roasted cod with dauphinois potatoes, and desserts such as pear and almond tart with homemade custard.
Chef/s: Martyn Hyde and Emily Webster. **Open:** Mon to Sat L 10 to 5 (9am Sat), Thur to Sat D 5.30 to 7. **Closed:** Sun, 3 weeks Christmas. **Meals:** alc (main courses £10 to £18). **Details:** Cash only. 34 seats. Music.

Lanterna

A proper Piedmontese ristorante
33 Queen Street, Scarborough, YO11 1HQ
Tel no: (01723) 363616
www.lanterna-ristorante.co.uk
Italian | £35
Cooking score: 3

£5 OFF

'We have been coming back for years!' trumpets one admirer of this cheery, centrally located Scarborough stalwart. Chef/patron Giorgio Alessio took over Lanterna in 1997, but the restaurant has been around for much longer, celebrating its recent 40th anniversary with a tasteful revamp. The kitchen concentrates on robust regional dishes that reflect Giorgio's Piedmontese upbringing. Top-quality Yorkshire ingredients are used (including locally caught fish), as well as produce imported from Italy – the prized white truffle from Piedmont taking star billing in its short season. The result is unpretentious dishes including homemade pasta, which might appear in a signature starter of spaghetti with velvet crab. Medallions of rare fillet steak pan-fried with butter and garlic is a typical main course, followed by a classic zabaglione, made to order at your table. The all-Italian wine list opens at £14.95.
Chef/s: Giorgio Alessio. **Open:** Mon to Sat D only 7 to 9.30. **Closed:** Sun, 25 and 26 Dec, 1 Jan, last 2 weeks Oct. **Meals:** alc (main courses £14 to £45). **Details:** 35 seats. Music.

Scawton
The Hare Inn
Foodie pub with big ambitions
Scawton, YO7 2HG
Tel no: (01845) 597769
www.thehare-inn.com
Modern British | £40
Cooking score: 2

V

At first glance, this 17th-century village hostelry could be mistaken for an archetypal Yorkshire watering hole with its dark-red walls, brass trinkets, cosy corners and scrubbed tables. Look closer, though, and you'll discover a serious foodie destination with big ambitions. One reader reckoned the cooking was 'absolutely top class', following a meal that included highly imaginative touches such as an amuse-bouche of beef consommé with horseradish 'that looked like Guinness'. The terse, voguish menu is guaranteed to raise a few local eyebrows: how about hare with walnut, spinach, truffle, king oyster and Yorkshire Blue cheese; or halibut partnered by octopus, broccoli, chorizo, rooster potato and shiitake mushrooms? The kitchen also proves its worth for pudding – witness a gin-and-tonic sorbet tinged with basil, or a deconstructed lemon meringue with fennel, white chocolate and rose-water. House wine is £20 (£4.95 a glass).
Chef/s: Paul Jackson. Open: Wed to Sat L 12 to 2.30, Tue to Sat D 6 to 9. Closed: Sun, Mon, Tue D (winter) 2 weeks Jan. Meals: alc (main courses £20 to £26). Set L and D £21 (2 courses) to £26. Sun L £16. Details: 36 seats. 10 seats outside. Separate bar. Wheelchair access. Music. Car parking.

Symbols
🛏 Accommodation is available
£30 Three courses for less than £30
V Separate vegetarian menu
£5 OFF £5-off voucher scheme
🍾 Notable wine list

Sheffield
Rafters
New-found confidence and ambition
220 Oakbrook Road, Nether Green, Sheffield, S11 7ED
Tel no: (0114) 2304819
www.raftersrestaurant.co.uk
Modern British | £39
Cooking score: 3
£5 OFF 🍾

'An unexpected gem in a pleasant and leafy Sheffield suburb,' thought one reporter of this old neighbourhood favourite, which was given a new lease of life when Alistair Myers and Thomas Lawson took over in November 2013. There is a new-found confidence and ambition, and Rafters now feels like a place that's really aspiring to be a go-to dining venue in Sheffield. Skill and creativity pour out of the kitchen. A pair of canapés starts the ball rolling, and imaginative bread such as black pudding rolls 'leaves you wanting more'. Presentation of dishes is accomplished too: notably in the 72-hour pork belly with sweet potato and peanuts. Local lamb, braised shoulder and roasted rump, might follow, with the accompanying gratin, carrots and greens 'just right'. To conclude, a well-made baked egg custard with rhubarb was 'a nice surprise'. The interesting and fairly priced wine list starts at £16.50.
Chef/s: Thomas Lawson. Open: Sun L 12 to 2, Wed to Sun D 6.30 to 8.30 (9 Fri and Sat, 8 Sun). Closed: Mon, Tue. Meals: Set D £39 (3 courses). Sun L £28 (2 courses) to £34. Details: 36 seats. Music. Children at Sun L only.

LOCAL GEM
▲ The Broadfield Ale House
452 Abbeydale Road, Sheffield, S7 1RF
Tel no: (0114) 2550200
www.thebroadfield.com
British | £20

It used to have a bad reputation, but this traditional pub just outside the city centre has been cleaned up (think scrubbed oak floors and glorious stained-glass windows) and is now the hub of local social life. Drinkers can enjoy an impressive array of Yorkshire beers, while the kitchen turns out homemade pork sausage sandwiches, fabulous pies (the beef, ale and mushroom is a 'belter'), as well as fish and chips, whole maple-glazed ham hock, and a smashing baked egg custard for afters. Service is kind. Wines from £14. Open all week.

▲ Lokanta
478-480 Glossop Road, Sheffield, S10 2QA
Tel no: (0114) 2666444
www.lokanta.co.uk
Turkish | £24 £5 OFF

'Like I'm back on holiday in rural Turkey,' commented one globetrotting reader after tucking into the likes of octopus and dill salad, and grilled lamb fillet with smoked aubergine purée. The owners used to run a place on the Turkish coast (she's a Sheffield lass, he's from Ankara), opening in Broomhill in 2009. It's a smart, modern place, with a long menu offering meze galore, kebabs and grills. Everything from hummus to bread is made in-house. Wines from £16. Open all week D and Sun L.

▊ Shibden
Shibden Mill Inn
Captivating inn with solid cooking
Shibden Mill Fold, Shibden, HX3 7UL
Tel no: (01422) 365840
www.shibdenmillinn.com
Modern British | £30
Cooking score: 3

🍴 V

Squirrelled away in a lush Yorkshire fold, this 17th-century spinning mill promises bags of heritage appeal, a bubbling stream, homely surrounds and a kitchen with its finger on the pulse. You can still come here for 'comforts and favourites' (goats' cheese muffins, battered haddock sandwiches, bangers with champ), but it pays to try the more adventurous, modish stuff – perhaps red mullet with Morecambe Bay clams and saffron broth,

dried chilli and coriander shoots; or a plate of Shibden Valley rare-breed pork with quail's egg, baby vegetables, char-grilled pineapple and beetroot purée. While there's still a lot happening on the plate, one regular reckons the kitchen has 'cut back on unnecessary complication' and applied a more earthy streak of late – to good effect. Artisan Yorkshire cheeses, a 'little people's menu', breakfast and afternoon tea earn bonus points for enterprise, and the wine list promises generous global pickings from £17.35 (£4.30 a glass).
Chef/s: Darren Parkinson. **Open:** Mon to Sat L 12 to 2 (2.30 Fri and Sat), D 5.30 to 9 (9.30 Fri and Sat). Sun 12 to 7.30. **Meals:** alc (main courses £13 to £19). Set L £12 (2 courses) to £15. Sun L £13. **Details:** 86 seats. 60 seats outside. Separate bar. Music. Car parking.

▊ Sinnington
LOCAL GEM
▲ Fox & Hounds
Main Street, Sinnington, YO62 6SQ
Tel no: (01751) 431577
www.thefoxandhoundsinn.co.uk
Modern British | £28 £5 OFF

With its hop garlands, real ales and double-sided log-burner, this sturdy 18th-century inn sends out all the right signals as a welcoming country boozer – although most people are here for the bistro-style food served in the dining room. Lunch is no-frills pub grub, but the evening menu moves up a notch for the likes of twice-baked cheese soufflé with beetroot and pine nut salad, pheasant breast with apple and salame risotto, then chocolate truffle torte with mango sorbet. Wines from £15.95. Accommodation. Open all week.

▎▎▌ Average Price
The average price listed in main-entry reviews denotes the price of a three-course meal, without wine.

Skipton

Le Caveau

Retro bistro in a secret cellar
86 High Street, Skipton, BD23 1JJ
Tel no: (01756) 794274
www.lecaveau.co.uk
Anglo-French | £30
Cooking score: 1

This likeable subterranean bistro occupies a 16th-century cellar, complete with barrel-vaulted ceiling, mighty beams and rugged stone walls. Richard Barker and co have resided here since 1997, leavening their retro menu with voguish flourishes. Breadcrumbed goats' cheese gets a watermelon salsa, hot-smoked cod is served on lightly spiced pea risotto with a poached egg, and salmon is wrapped in filo pastry with Thai vegetables, plus lime and sushi-ginger crème fraîche on the side. Roast duck with orange sauce or char-grilled Dales sirloin steak keep traditionalists happy, while desserts see Eton mess pitched alongside raspberry pannacotta with white chocolate sorbet. House wine is £14.95. **Chef/s:** Richard Barker. **Open:** Tue to Fri L 12 to 2, Tue to Sat D 7 to 9.30 (5 to 9.45 Sat). **Closed:** Sun, Mon, 25 Dec, first week Jan, first week Jun, first 2 weeks Sept. **Meals:** alc (main courses £14 to £23). Set L £11 (2 courses) to £15. Set D £17 (2 courses) to £20. **Details:** 26 seats. Separate bar. Music.

Slingsby

NEW ENTRY
The Grapes Inn

Pub classics in vintage surroundings
Railway Street, Slingsby, YO62 4AL
Tel no: (01653) 628076
www.thegrapesinn-slingsby.co.uk
British | £20
Cooking score: 1

£30

Leigh and Catharine Spooner dealt antiques in a previous life, so there's no surprise that antique and vintage furniture – looking 'as if it's been in place for centuries' – is spread throughout three comfortable rooms in this good-looking Georgian village pub. Oak settles and Windsor chairs on flagged floors are inviting, wood stoves belt out cheer, and there are candles and flowers everywhere. This is home cooking: nothing fancy mind, the tiny back kitchen delivering simple pub classics of the burger, fish and chips and steak pie with herb suet crust variety. Wines from £13.95. **Chef/s:** Samantha Buckley. **Open:** Tue to Sun L 12 to 2 (3 Sun), Tue to Sat D 6 to 8.30. **Closed:** Mon. **Meals:** alc (main courses £10 to £16). **Details:** 50 seats. Separate bar. Car parking.

South Dalton

★ TOP 10 PUB ★

The Pipe and Glass Inn

Dazzle at a refined country pub
West End, South Dalton, HU17 7PN
Tel no: (01430) 810246
www.pipeandglass.co.uk
Modern British | £30
Cooking score: 5

V

On the site of the gatehouse to Lord Hotham's estate, the 17th-century inn was where his Lordship's guests were once lodged. It makes a commodious, refined country pub nowadays, accoutred with buttoned leather sofas and pine flooring. James Mackenzie's modern British cooking is all about showmanship and dazzle, with a chef's table and private room for the bespoke tasting menus. The food is pleasingly direct, though: witness a starting pot of creamy pork rillettes and shallots with dried apple salad, or cider-marinated sea trout tartare with samphire and dots of dill cream. Main courses are expertly judged, whether for guinea-fowl breast with a crisp parcel of leg meat (served with devils on horseback and buttered kale in sherry cream), or halibut with queenies and asparagus – everything tasting of what it is. 'The second-best sticky toffee pudding I have ever had' is the kind of seasoned eater's accolade you can't buy. Wines from £15.95. Details overleaf.

Chef/s: James Mackenzie. **Open:** Tue to Sun L 12 to 2 (4 Sun), Tue to Sat D 6 to 9.30. **Closed:** Mon (exc bank hols), 25 Dec, 2 weeks Jan. **Meals:** alc (main courses £11 to £27). **Details:** 100 seats. 60 seats outside. Separate bar. Wheelchair access. Music. Car parking.

■ Sowerby Bridge

Gimbals

Upbeat neighbourhood bistro
76 Wharf Street, Sowerby Bridge, HX6 2AF
Tel no: (01422) 839329
www.gimbals.co.uk
Modern European | £28
Cooking score: 4
£5 OFF £30

Gimbals' seductive retro décor shows an eye for interior design (courtesy of co-owner Janet Baker), with a huge Union Jack that served aboard one of Her Majesty's battleships at the entrance, and a rustic-chic finish that gives the place a sense of occasion. The kitchen delivers bucolic, creative and rather dynamic constructions such as pan-seared 'scarlet' salmon with a hot carpaccio of purple beetroot, goats' cheese bonbons and rocket purée. You might find woof, too: Scarborough woof that is, salt-and-pepper style with squid, tartare salsa verde and samphire. There's a fearless global reach to the output here, with home-grown and home-smoked ingredients adding a Yorkshire earthiness and a feeling of place. For dessert, a plate of passion fruit goodies confirms this to be an ambitious venue reaching the heights. Cocktails and sharing boards are served in the lounge area, and wines start at £16.90.
Chef/s: Mark Ferrier. **Open:** Tue to Sat D only 6.30 to 10. **Closed:** Sun, Mon, 24 to 26 Dec, bank hols. **Meals:** alc (main courses £13 to £22). Set D £17 (2 courses) to £20. **Details:** 50 seats. Separate bar. Wheelchair access. Music. Car parking.

■ Staddlebridge

Cleveland Tontine

Glam refurb of much loved hotel/bistro
Staddlebridge, DL6 3JB
Tel no: (01609) 882671
www.theclevelandtontine.co.uk
French | £35
Cooking score: 3
🛏

After 35 years running this eccentric and much-loved roadhouse, the McCoy brothers have moved on, leaving the new owners to spend the year revamping the bedrooms and public rooms – all to good effect. Apart from a lick of paint, they have left the lovely basement dining room intact so that it still glows invitingly with glass, polished silver and candlelight. The menu, too, remains French-bistro in style, with vintage dishes like prawn cocktail, rabbit terrine, sole meunière and steak and chips. Everything is well executed by chef James Cooper, who has taken local traditions to new lengths with his 'Posh Parmo', a riff on the north-east chip shop special of breadcrumbed chicken breast. Here he stuffs it with garlic and truffle, wraps it in prosciutto and serves it on a bed of Little Gem. Starting point on an individual and largely Old World wine list is £21.50.
Chef/s: James Cooper. **Open:** all week L 12 to 2.30, D 6.30 to 9. **Meals:** alc (main courses £17 to £35). Set L £18 (2 courses) to £20. Set D £18 (Sun, Mon, 2 courses) to £22. Sun L £24 (2 courses) to £27. **Details:** 88 seats. 20 seats outside. Separate bar. Music. Car parking.

Sutton on the Forest

NEW ENTRY
The Park
Inventive cooking in rural setting
Sutton Park, Sutton on the Forest, YO61 1DP
Tel no: (01347) 810852
www.theparkrestaurant.co.uk
British | £48
Cooking score: 3

After praise and prizes at the Black Swan at
Oldstead (see entry), chef Adam Jackson has
jumped ship to launch his own restaurant at
Sutton Park – sadly not in the Georgian
stately home itself but, rather anti-
climactically, in a building in the grounds that
serves as a visitors' tea room by day. With 16
covers and a no-choice, eight-course tasting
menu (three courses available midweek), it's a
high-wire act that starts with good bread and
substantial pork rillettes and proceeds through
seven small, precise and highly accomplished
courses. Two standout plates were the puréed
broccoli, with stems of purple sprouting,
finished with goats' cheese and almonds, and
tender beef fillet with asparagus and black
truffle. A pre-dessert was less impressive, with
strawberry and lemon given an overpowering
basil granita. Service is by a young enthusiastic
team. Choose from a list of decent wines
(from £23 a bottle) or a £35 flight that
follows the menu.
Chef/s: Adam Jackson. **Open:** Tue to Sat D only 7 to
9. **Closed:** Sun, Mon, 3 to 24 Jan. **Meals:** Set D (8
courses) £48. **Details:** 16 seats. Separate bar.
Wheelchair access. Music. Car parking. Children
over 14 yrs only.

Symbols
🛏 Accommodation is available

£30 Three courses for less than £30

V Separate vegetarian menu

£5 £5-off voucher scheme

🍷 Notable wine list

Wakefield

LOCAL GEM
▲ Iris
12 Bull Ring, Wakefield, WF1 1HA
Tel no: (01924) 367683
www.iris-restaurant.com
British | £23 £5 OFF

Once the administrative capital of West
Yorkshire, Wakefield has seen better days, and
the Bull Ring is littered with empty shops and
generic pubs. Chic Iris, with its bare floors,
contemporary lighting, abstract photographs
on walls and well-spaced tables is an oasis. This
is chef Liam Duffy's first solo venture and he
has created a Yorkshire-centric menu, along
the lines of Grimsby-landed hake with
crushed potatoes and paprika, 'just perfect'
steak from local butcher Allums, and
Pontefract liquorice cake. Service is friendly
and accommodating. Wines from £14.95.
Open all week D only.

West Tanfield
The Bruce Arms
Striking pub with splendidly rustic food
Main Street, West Tanfield, HG4 5JJ
Tel no: (01677) 470325
www.thebrucearms.com
Modern British | £29
Cooking score: 3
🛏 £30

Since taking over in 2009, Hugh Carruthers
has really put this 18th-century village pub-
with-rooms on the map. He captures the style
and the atmosphere of an English inn
perfectly: all beams and log fires, polished,
mismatched tables and chairs, sporting prints
and bric-à-brac alongside some striking
modern art. Britain, France and the
Mediterranean basin all have their say as the
kitchen delivers pork rillettes or ribollita
(Tuscan vegetable and bean stew) followed by
plates of herb-crusted loin of lamb with
pommes Anna and provençale vegetables, or
calf's liver with butternut, bacon, sage and red
wine jus. The south is also represented by

Moroccan-style steamed mussels or roast cod with ham hock, chickpeas, tomatoes, smoked paprika and black pudding, while vanilla pannacotta with poached rhubarb makes a fine finale. The set-lunch deal is very good value, but lamentably slow service remains a regular gripe. Wines from £14.95.

Chef/s: Hugh Carruthers. **Open:** Tue to Sun L 12 to 3, D 5 to 11. **Closed:** Mon, 10 days Feb, 10 days Nov. **Meals:** alc (main courses £13 to £27). Set L £10 (2 courses). Set D £23 (inc wine). Sun L £19. **Details:** 45 seats. 30 seats outside. Separate bar. Music. Car parking.

■ West Witton
The Wensleydale Heifer
Seafood and chic vibes in the country
Main Street, West Witton, DL8 4LS
Tel no: (01969) 622322
www.wensleydaleheifer.co.uk
Seafood | £35
Cooking score: 3
£5 OFF 🛏 V

You're more likely to whiff farmer's muck than briny ozone hereabouts, yet this gentrified 17th-century Dales inn (now a boutique hotel) still manages to fill its kitchen with fresh seafood – and visitors love the results. 'Consistently fabulous, quirky, fun and gorgeous,' declares one regular who has probably eaten her way through most of the menu: from assorted lunchtime tapas to the famous beer-battered fish and chips with 'posh' peas and hand-cut chips cooked in goose fat. In between, there are bowls of Mediterranean fish soup, gargantuan seafood platters and daily specials such as pan-fried lemon sole fillets with buttered spinach, brown shrimps, scallop and herb cream. Fancy a change? Try panko-crusted goats' cheese fritters with red onion jam followed by slow-braised beef ribs with horseradish mash, perhaps rounded off with iced pear parfait and Kirsch cherries. Read about the wines in the Heifer's rib-tickling house mag; bottles from £21.50.

Chef/s: David Moss and Craig Keenan. **Open:** all week L 12 to 2.30, D 6 to 9.30. **Meals:** alc (main courses £17 to £31). Set L and D £20 (2 courses) to £23. Sun L £22. **Details:** 90 seats. 50 seats outside. Separate bar. Wheelchair access. Music. Car parking.

■ Whitby
The Woodlands CaféBar
Endearing eatery by the sea
East Row, Sandsend, Whitby, YO21 3SU
Tel no: (01947) 893438
thewoodlands-sandsend.com
Modern British | £27
Cooking score: 1
£30

It's a refuelling point for holidaymakers staying at the nearby Woodlands B&B, but this endearing whitewashed cottage just a pebble's throw from the sea is also a proper eatery. Bold seasonal flavours are the order of the day, from small plates of roast beetroot, Yellison goats' curd and honeycomb to fish stew with fennel, orange and aïoli or onglet steak with girolles, artichokes and crisp polenta. Coffee, cake and sandwiches fill the daytime gaps. Behind the 'chocolate box' exterior is a chic, trendy space filled with cool music, and a lovely decked garden beckons on fine days. Around 20 zippy wines start at £16.

Chef/s: Alexander Perkins. **Open:** Tue to Sun L 10 to 5 (4 Fri to Sun), Fri and Sat D 6 to 9. **Closed:** Mon, 25 Dec. **Meals:** alc (main courses £11 to £16). **Details:** 30 seats. 30 seats outside. Separate bar. Wheelchair access. Music. Car parking.

LOCAL GEM
▲ Magpie Café
14 Pier Road, Whitby, YO21 3PU
Tel no: (01947) 602058
www.magpiecafe.co.uk
Seafood | £25 £5 OFF

A Georgian merchant's house overlooking Whitby harbour is a fitting location for this much-loved seafood restaurant. Magpie inspires fierce loyalty among its regulars, who say it offers 'the best fish and chips in the world'. But other seafood shouldn't be overlooked: Whitby kipper and potato soup (à la Cullen skink), crab and prawn salads, and a main-course hotpot of haddock, salmon, squid and various shellfish in garlicky, buttery wine liquor. Beef in ale provides the meat eaters' alternative. Finish with spotted dick. Wines from £14.95. Open all week.

▲ The Moon and Sixpence

Marine Parade, Whitby, YO21 3PR
Tel no: (01947) 604416
www.moon-and-sixpence.co.uk
British | £21

It's hard to imagine a better location. On a clear day (even night), the view across the harbour to Whitby old town and the Abbey is stunning. Try and bag a window seat in this handsome Georgian building and order a Prosecco cocktail. Then tuck into carefully prepared rustic food, with seafood to the fore. Bouillabaisse arrives loaded with squid, prawns and cod; sea bass (two fat, pearly fillets) come with mash, creamed leeks and bacon. Pork chop with bubble and squeak is a meaty alternative, and there's crème brûlée to finish. Wines from £17.

■ York

Le Langhe

Artisan foodie enterprise
The Old Coach House, Peasholme Green, York, YO1 7PW
Tel no: (01904) 622584
www.lelanghe.co.uk
Italian | £32
Cooking score: 5

£5 OFF 🍷

Ottavio Bocca is committed to showing off good food and top ingredients and over the years his well-stocked deli-cum-café/restaurant has built up a loyal following. Fans are drawn back time and again by simple, modern food that has its roots in Piedmont and stays true to the seasons. There are no pizzas, no heavy sauces – this is elegant

cooking where simplicity, along with impeccable sourcing, can be seen in the selection of Italian charcuterie and cheeses, in a simple salad of mozzarella, tomatoes and basil, in a standout game ragù with superbly fashioned pasta, and in wonderful classics such as calf's liver with pancetta and onions. Cakes and tarts feature for dessert, as does rice pudding with poached rhubarb. The tasting menus offered at lunch and dinner (Friday and Saturday evenings only) are 'truly excellent', and the all-Italian wine list teems with quality and value; bottles from £15.
Chef/s: Ottavio Bocca. **Open:** Mon to Sat L 12 to 3, Fri and Sat D 6.45 to 10. **Closed:** Sun, 25 to 27 Dec, 1 to 14 Jan, Easter, bank hols. **Meals:** alc (main courses £14 to £20). Set L £20 (2 courses) to £24. Set D £25 (2 courses) to £27. Tasting menu L £24, D £39. **Details:** 50 seats. 20 seats outside. Wheelchair access. Music.

Melton's

Top-class cooking at fair prices
7 Scarcroft Road, York, YO23 1ND
Tel no: (01904) 634341
www.meltonsrestaurant.co.uk
Modern British | £34
Cooking score: 5

£5 OFF 🍷

After 25 years, the enduring appeal of Michael and Lucy Hjort's reliable and relaxed neighbourhood restaurant shows no sign of diminishing. 'Always interesting, always a delight!' confided one regular who has been visiting Melton's since it opened in 1990. In a Victorian terrace close to the racecourse, this unassuming venue may have close-packed tables and timeworn furnishings, but its intimate quirkiness adds to the charm. Top-drawer Yorkshire ingredients take centre stage on a menu that's modern and British. Dinner might start with home-smoked ox tongue, pickled vegetables and horseradish snow, followed by a main-course belly pork, warm ham hock terrine, pork and cep ballotine with soured cabbage and boulangère potatoes. There's always a 'worth the wait' soufflé offered, perhaps prune and brandy, although it vies for attention with the slate of artisan North Country cheeses. A global wine list contains plenty of sub-£20 bottles, with house recommendations at £17.

Chef/s: Calvin Goddard and Michael Hjort. **Open:** Tue to Sat L 12 to 2, D 5.30 to 10. **Closed:** Sun, Mon, 2 weeks Dec. **Meals:** alc (main courses £16 to £23). Set L £23 (2 courses) to £26. Tasting menu £38. **Details:** 40 seats. Music.

Melton's Too

Flexible drop-in bistro with freewheeling food
25 Walmgate, York, YO1 9TX
Tel no: (01904) 629222
www.meltonstoo.co.uk
Modern European | £24
Cooking score: 2
£30

The easy-going sister gaff to the high-flying Melton's (see entry), Michael and Lucy Hjort's all-day café-bar-bistro takes up several floors of a former workshop dating from the 1790s. The *au naturel* décor heralds what is to come: simply presented dishes with full-on flavours at 'good Yorkshire prices' (as one reader put it). Brunch, lunch and dinner deliver food of reliable provenance and pan-European scope, such as Yorkshire burger with Wensleydale cheese, fried potato and herb gnocchi, or pork and bean cassoulet. There are tapas options, too (garlic and paprika squid with tartare sauce, or piquillo peppers stuffed with haddock brandade), and you can even pop in for a scone with Yorkshire jam and clotted cream. Homemade sticky toffee pudding comes with Yorvale vanilla ice cream (from just outside the city), with Yorkshire cheeses as an alternative. Local real ales are served at the bar, plus various bottled beers, and wines from £14.95.

Chef/s: Michael Hjort. **Open:** all week 10.30 to 10.30. **Closed:** 25 and 26 Dec, 1 Jan. **Meals:** alc (main courses £13 to £18). Set L and D £14. Sun L £14. **Details:** 120 seats. Wheelchair access. Music.

NEW ENTRY
The Star Inn the City

A taste of Yorkshire in a winning location
Lendal Engine House, Museum Street, York, YO1 7DR
Tel no: (01904) 619208
www.starinnthecity.co.uk
British | £44
Cooking score: 3

This restored brick engine house in Museum Gardens opened with much fanfare in late 2013. With a glitzy glass and timber add-on giving views down the river, it's a winning location. The Garden Room has floor-to-ceiling windows, tasselled lampshades and chairs of Yorkshire tweed. Yes, the 'baht 'at' flat-cap bread baskets and the bibulous cartoons might make you squirm, but Andrew Pern's food soon distracts. His posh prawn cocktail puts hot-smoked salmon, pea purée, Bloody Mary sorbet and Marie Rose sauce in a martini glass. Ale-braised ox cheek is impressively paired with blue Wensleydale. Readers have been 'generally impressed with the quality of food' but have been less forgiving of poor service ranging from 'a considerable wait' to booking errors. Whether it's understaffing, poor training or the pressure of all-day opening, the Star needs to polish this aspect to shine as brightly as its revered rural parent (see entry, Star at Harome).

Chef/s: Andrew Pern and Matthew Hunter. **Open:** all week 12 to 10 (8.30 Sun). **Meals:** alc (main courses £15 to £20). **Details:** 130 seats. 60 seats outside. Separate bar. Wheelchair access. Music.

SCOTLAND

Borders, Dumfries & Galloway,
Lothians (inc. Edinburgh),
Strathclyde (inc. Glasgow), Central, Fife,
Tayside, Grampian, Highlands & Islands

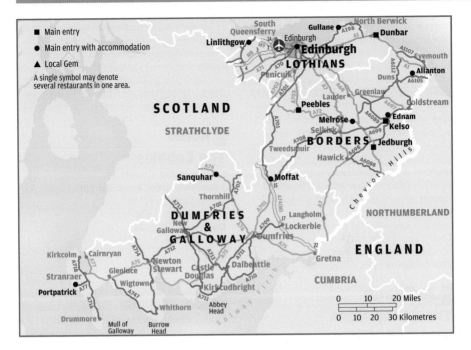

Allanton

The Allanton Inn

Hearty food with bags of local sourcing
Allanton, TD11 3JZ
Tel no: (01890) 818260
www.allantoninn.co.uk
Modern British | £25
Cooking score: 2

A charming village inn with six bedrooms, the Allanton has a pleasantly updated interior, a garden with views across Border country, and a bar that equally welcomes families, touring weekenders and check-shirted farmers on a night out. A local's local then, but with a restaurant that mostly punches above its weight. At a test meal, smoked ham and Italian sausage Scotch egg with a creamy celeriac rémoulade was exemplary, and a caramelised chicory tart with walnut and pear salad alongside tiny herb-crusted Roxburgh Roondie cheese fritters also impressed. There were inconsistencies, however, like the belly pork that came minus both crackling and apple compote. Nevertheless, the inn's virtues more than compensate, and portions are generous to a fault – too large to do justice to all three courses. Wines start at £14.
Chef/s: Craig Rushton. **Open:** all week L 12 to 2, D 6 to 9. **Closed:** 25 and 26 Dec. **Meals:** alc (main courses £10 to £23). **Details:** 50 seats. 40 seats outside. Wheelchair access. Music.

Ednam

Edenwater House

Personally run borderland retreat
Ednam, TD5 7QL
Tel no: (01573) 224070
www.edenwaterhouse.co.uk
Modern British | £40
Cooking score: 4

Locals and tourists seem to have genuine affection for this foursquare converted manse hidden in the Upper Tweed Valley. Jeff and Jacqui Kelly have stayed true to their original

purpose, giving precedence to residents but also feeding visitors in their petite dining room. He plays host, while she takes care of business in the kitchen. Dinner is a thoughtful, unhurried four-course affair with plenty of bright ideas and evidence of a sure hand at the stove. Meals begin with a demi-tasse of soup, before a serving of fish such as sea bass and rösti stack with confit cherry tomatoes, lemon and dill salsa. Scottish meat and game provide the centrepiece, from roast duck breast to rack of lamb with a warm summer salad, celeriac gratin and pickled carrots. Dessert might be iced nougat and mango terrine with passion fruit coulis. An authoritative wine list starts at £20.
Chef/s: Jacqui Kelly. **Open:** Thur to Sat D only 6 to 10. **Closed:** Sun to Wed, Nov to Feb. **Meals:** Set D £40. **Details:** 16 seats. Car parking.

Jedburgh
The Caddy Mann
Quirky local restaurant
Mounthooly, Jedburgh, TD8 6TJ
Tel no: (01835) 850787
www.caddymann.com
Modern British | £24
Cooking score: 2

V £30

Formed from three old crofters' cottages (and handy for the A68), this quirky Jedburgh favourite may be quaintly old-fashioned but chef/proprietor Ross Horrocks' food more than makes up for the wonky interiors and eclectic curios. Horrocks honed his skills at Gleneagles and has a passion for cooking seasonal game; his roast grouse has won particular praise from reporters. Borders produce dominates the menu and a starter of seared hand-dived scallops, Stornoway black pudding, cauliflower purée and foie gras jus is a firm favourite. This might be followed by venison 'cooked three ways' – rare roasted rack, shepherd's pie and ravioli of confit shin – with wine-braised sticky red cabbage and rowanberry jus. Lemon crêpe soufflé flambéed

in suzette sauce with Grand Marnier ice cream and pink grapefruit confit is one of the well-executed desserts. House wine is £13.50.
Chef/s: Ross Horrocks. **Open:** all week L 12 to 2, Fri and Sat D 7 to 12. **Closed:** 1 to 3 Jan. **Meals:** alc (main courses £11 to £20). **Details:** 50 seats. 20 seats outside. Wheelchair access. Car parking.

Kelso
The Cobbles
Local beer and victuals
7 Bowmont Street, Kelso, TD5 7JH
Tel no: (01573) 223548
www.thecobbleskelso.co.uk
Modern British | £25
Cooking score: 1

£30

In the heart of Kelso, this relaxed, buzzy pub has an attractive slate-floored bar and a larger dining area where a broad and gutsy range of food is served. Cream walls and wood panelling create a light, modern atmosphere and service is charming. Starters range from falafel to traditional Cullen skink, while lunchtime mains take in burgers, bagels and fish and chips. Evening options are more ambitious – maybe pan-roast pheasant breast with a haggis bonbon, heritage potatoes and red wine and port jus – and there's double chocolate fondant for dessert. Wine starts at £14.95, or try the selection of Tempest ales.
Chef/s: Ross Birrell. **Open:** all week L 12 to 2.30, D 5.45 to 9 (9.15 Fri and Sat, 8.30 Sun). **Closed:** 25 and 26 Dec. **Meals:** alc (main courses £13 to £20). Sun L £21. **Details:** Cash only. 70 seats. 16 seats outside. Separate bar. Wheelchair access. Music.

❚❙❙ Visit us Online
To find out more about
The Good Food Guide, please visit
www.thegoodfoodguide.co.uk

Melrose
Burt's Hotel
Culinary satisfaction in a grand old inn
Market Square, Melrose, TD6 9PL
Tel no: (01896) 822285
www.burtshotel.co.uk
Modern British | £36
Cooking score: 2

Owned and run by members of the
Henderson family since 1971, this
quintessential Borders inn is very much the
hub of Melrose life. Weekday shoppers,
business lunchers and families with kids avail
themselves of brasserie-style pub grub in the
bar (think BBQ chicken, beef bourguignon or
beer-battered haddock), while the restaurant
offers evening meals with bigger ambitions.
The dining room is a picture of elegant, if old-
fashioned gentility, and the menu aims for
safe-and-sound satisfaction. Grills (including
Borders lamb) hold centre stage, but the daily
line-up might also feature the likes of crispy
pork belly with caramelised apples and
hazelnut salad, roast salmon with lyonnaise
potatoes, tomato and chive butter sauce or
saddle of Highland venison with red cabbage
and juniper jus. For dessert, perhaps try sticky
toffee pudding or white chocolate and Baileys
mousse with dark chocolate ice cream and nut
brittle. The well-spread global wine list starts
with house selections from £17.25.
Chef/s: Trevor Williams. **Open:** Sat and Sun L 12 to
2, all week D 7 to 9 (9.30 Fri and Sat). **Closed:** 26
Dec, 5 to 11 Jan. **Meals:** alc (main courses £15 to
£28). **Details:** 65 seats. 24 seats outside. Separate
bar. Music. Car parking. Children over 10 yrs only.

Readers Recommend
A 'readers recommend' review is a
genuine quote from a report sent in by
one of our readers. We intend to follow
up these suggestions throughout the
year to come.

Peebles
Osso
Café by day, bistro by night
Innerleithen Road, Peebles, EH45 8BA
Tel no: (01721) 724477
www.ossorestaurant.com
Modern British | £28
Cooking score: 3

£30

Bustling Osso has stayed true to its
neighbourhood roots and continues to serve
daytime nourishment to a motley crew of
office workers, shoppers and mums with
toddlers. That said, the menu is far from
predictable café fodder: how about snacking
on a hot sandwich of crispy monkfish cheek
with 'damn good' chilli jam, rocket and
Monterey Jack cheese, followed by warm
tapioca with poached Yorkshire rhubarb?
Come evening, the kitchen turns up the heat
and the whole place morphs into an upbeat
bistro with serious aspirations. There's plenty
of creativity and smart thinking on show –
witness crispy spiced rabbit 'in a box' with
thrice-cooked chips; udon noodles with
spiced broth and tofu; or free-range chicken
with spelt risotto, charred leeks and truffle. To
start, consider crispy pork with Jerusalem
artichoke purée and gooseberries; to finish,
try dark chocolate and salted-caramel tart
with brown-sugar ice cream. Wines from £15.
Chef/s: Ally McGrath. **Open:** all week L 10 to 4.30,
Tue to Sat D 6 to 9. **Closed:** 25 Dec, 1 Jan. **Meals:** alc
(main courses £12 to £25). **Details:** 38 seats. 6 seats
outside. Wheelchair access. Music.

Swinton
READERS RECOMMEND
Wheatsheaf at Swinton
Modern European
Swinton, TD11 3JJ
Tel no: (01890) 860257
www.wheatsheaf-swinton.co.uk
'We have been using this restaurant for six
years and have been unable to find better food
and hospitality in the eastern borders.'

▌Moffat
The Limetree Restaurant
Assertive cooking of local ingredients
Hartfell House, Hartfell Crescent, Moffat,
DG10 9AL
Tel no: (01683) 220153
www.hartfellhouse.co.uk
Modern British | £28
Cooking score: 4

£5 OFF 🍴 £30

Even if you are not staying at this handsome
greystone Victorian guesthouse on the edge of
Moffat, its intimate, no-frills dining room is
well worth a detour. Chef Matt Seddon cooks
solo in the kitchen (he even does his own
washing up) and although much of the tiptop
raw materials are from the immediate area, his
food has a more international scope. A starter
of brandade of smoked haddock and tapenade
crostini offers more than a hint of Provence,
while one reporter praised the 'beautifully
cooked and well presented' roast chump of
Cumbrian lamb, grilled Parmesan polenta,
ratatouille vegetables, puttanesca sauce and
basil. End with praline honey parfait,
brandied prunes and peanut-butter cookie or a
board of quality artisanal Scottish cheeses. The
whole experience is enhanced by 'gracious and
efficient service' according to another visitor.
The reliable and 'fairly priced' wine list starts
at £16.
Chef/s: Matt Seddon. **Open:** Sun L 12 to 2, Tue to Sat
D 6.30 to 8.30. **Closed:** Mon, 21 Dec to 15 Jan, 2
weeks Oct. **Meals:** Set L £20 (2 courses) to £23. Set
D £23 (2 courses) to £28. **Details:** 24 seats.
Wheelchair access. Music. Car parking.

▌Portpatrick
Knockinaam Lodge
Thrilling, windswept views and refined food
Portpatrick, DG9 9AD
Tel no: (01776) 810471
www.knockinaamlodge.com
Modern British | £65
Cooking score: 5

£5 OFF 🍴 V

With a beach all to itself and views across to
Ireland – as well as 30 acres of gardens and
gorse to call its own – Knockinaam Lodge is a
destination that lingers in the memory. Built
by a Victorian with a good eye for a location,
today's luxury hotel is on a human scale, with
oak panels and period details to maintain a
traditional feel. In the kitchen, chef Tony
Pierce procures bang-on regional ingredients
and turns them into refined, gently modern
Scottish dishes. The no-choice menu (until the
dessert or cheese dilemma), might kick off
with Luce Bay sea bass with a citrus emulsion,
preceding a soupy interlude (cauliflower,
parsley and truffle). The intelligent
combinations continue with main courses
such as roast Goosnargh duck breast with
sweet-and-sour red cabbage and coriander
and ginger reduction, followed by a hot apple
crumble soufflé dessert. Wines start at £24.
Chef/s: Tony Pierce. **Open:** all week L 12 to 2, D 7 to
9. **Meals:** Set L £40 (4 courses). Set D £65 (5
courses). Sun L £30. **Details:** 20 seats. Separate
bar. Wheelchair access. Music. Car parking. Children
over 12 yrs only at D.

Sanquhar
Blackaddie House Hotel
Foodie oasis in the borderlands
Blackaddie Road, Sanquhar, DG4 6JJ
Tel no: (01659) 50270
www.blackaddiehotel.co.uk
Modern British | £52
Cooking score: 4

'What a little gem', is the heartfelt declaration
of one reader, summing up the fondness with
which regulars view Ian McAndrew's country
house hotel. The 16th-century stone manse is
set in grounds where 'the view from the
conservatory looking out over the River Nith
as the sun goes down' makes a charming
backdrop for this personable operation. The
drill is daily changing, fixed-price menus,
which allows McAndrew's finely honed
cooking skills and dedication to seasonal
produce to be used to their best effect. A
typical evening's dinner might begin with
slow-braised pressed and pan-fried beef
terrine with red cabbage and lightly pickled
carrots, followed by beetroot sorbet, then
fillet of wild halibut with parsley risotto and a
salad of confit chicken, concluding with early
rhubarb (sorbet, purée, poached) with lemon
cheesecake. The excellent wine list starts at
£19.95, though there's a brief 'private cellar
selection' for those with deeper pockets.
Chef/s: Ian McAndrew. **Open:** all week L 12 to 2, D
6.30 to 9. **Meals:** Set L £25 (2 courses) to £30. Set D
£25 (2 courses) to £52 (4 courses). **Details:** 20
seats. Separate bar. Wheelchair access. Music. Car
parking.

ROY BRETT
Ondine, Edinburgh

What inspired you to become a chef?
I met Alan Hill (now at Gleneagles) at
the Caledonian Hotel and he showed me
around his impressive kitchens. He's a
legend, I have never looked back.

**What is your favourite time of year
for food?**
Spring time. As you know, Scotland is
pretty dark and wet in the winter. Spring
evokes our great Scottish larder, bringing
to mind too many products to mention.

What's your newest ingredient discovery?
Mara seaweed. I helped the girls at Mara
develop outstanding, natural, sea shore
flavours.

What food could you not live without?
Oysters, these wonderful animals are the
heart of Ondine. No oysters mean
no Ondine.

**Is there a dish that evokes strong
memories for you?**
For me, caramelised rice pudding made
by my late grandmother. So honest and
delicious.

Dunbar

The Creel

Spanking-fresh food and keen prices
25 Lamer Street, Dunbar, EH42 1HJ
Tel no: (01368) 863279
www.creelrestaurant.co.uk
Modern British | £27
Cooking score: 3

£5 OFF £30

Almost every surface in this small street-corner restaurant is wood – the floor, the panelled walls and the boarded ceiling. Throw in a few nautical knick-knacks and small, glinting lights and everything looks shipshape. The Formica-topped tables may give a slightly institutional look, but the overall feel is warm and inviting, setting the scene for good, honest cooking – nothing fancy, but plenty of it. Consider a platter of crab claws and over a dozen fat prawns, served with an excellent mayonnaise; or a bowl brimful with pan-fried gnocchi, fresh tomato sauce, mushrooms and melting blue cheese. The little extras are lovely too, from peppered bread to a free glass of 'Creel Royale': dry cider with Cassis. Classic desserts are well handled: maybe a smooth crème brûlée with a crisp, caramelised top. A choice of nearly 30 international wines starts at £16.50.
Chef/s: Logan Thorburn. **Open:** Wed to Sun L 12 to 2.30, Wed to Sat D 6.30 to 9.30. **Closed:** Mon, Tue. **Meals:** Set L £17 (2 courses) to £20. Set D £25 (2 courses) to £28. Sun L £20 (2 courses) to £25. **Details:** 36 seats. Wheelchair access. Music.

Edinburgh

Angels with Bagpipes

Uptown meets Old Town
343 High Street, Royal Mile, Edinburgh, EH1 1PW
Tel no: (0131) 2201111
www.angelswithbagpipes.co.uk
Modern European | £30
Cooking score: 3

There really is an angel holding a set of bagpipes in St Giles' church, just across the Royal Mile from this 16th-century town house. Candlesticks in the form of winged angels light the scene here, and there's a beguiling fin-de-siècle feeling to the decorative scheme. Fraser Smith's cooking draws on pedigree Scottish produce for a rendition of the modern European mode, bringing on goats' cheese yoghurt with beetroot, hazelnuts and verjus jelly, as well as a voguish partnering of Orkney scallop and pig's cheek with pickled walnut, parsnip and vanilla. Venison from the Cairngorms turns up with turnips and purple kale in redcurrant jus with a little suet pudding for a fortifying main course, or there may be Loch Duart salmon with its roe, alongside parsley root risotto. Finish with passion fruit cheesecake and lime sorbet, or chocolate mousse, salted caramel and peanut-butter ice cream. Wines start at £19 for a Spanish Verdejo.
Chef/s: Fraser Smith. **Open:** all week 12 to 9.30. **Closed:** 23 to 25 Dec. **Meals:** alc (main courses £13 to £22). Set L £15 (2 courses) to £19. **Details:** 77 seats. 16 seats outside. Separate bar. Wheelchair access. Music.

NEW ENTRY

Bistro Moderne

Modern cooking in a buzzy bistro
15 North West Circus Place, Edinburgh, EH3 6SX
Tel no: (0131) 2254431
bistromoderne.co.uk
Modern French | £30
Cooking score: 2

The high ceilings and parquet flooring of Mark Greenaway's second Edinburgh restaurant (see entry, Restaurant Mark Greenaway) maintain the look and feel of the bank it once was. However, a granite-topped bar, open kitchen and the Greenaway trademark of innovative and unlikely pairings add the *moderne* to this agreeable Stocksbridge bistro. Battered soft-shell Scottish crab with a tartare sauce infused with fresh crabmeat was highly praised at inspection, and the Aberdeen Angus carpaccio, accompanied by Parmesan ice cream, was excellent. Mains were strong too, with accurately roasted cod on pea purée and polenta chips, and a generous dish of tender caramelised duck breast served with watermelon, salsify and a duck neck sausage roll. Despite some absent-minded service and an absent dessert (the tonka bean crème brûlée had failed to set) there's plenty to like about Greenaway's confident new venture. Wines begin at £18 and the cocktail menu is worth investigating.

Chef/s: Scott Catchpole and Mark Greenaway. **Open:** Mon to Sat L 12 to 2.30, D 5.30 to 10. Sun 12 to 9. **Closed:** 25 and 26 Dec, 1 and 2 Jan. **Meals:** alc (main courses £12 to £19). Set L £13 (2 courses) to £15. Sun L £25. **Details:** 60 seats. 16 seats outside. Wheelchair access. Music.

Café St Honoré
Scottish produce in a Parisian setting
34 North West Thistle Street Lane, Edinburgh, EH2 1EA
Tel no: (0131) 2262211
www.cafesthonore.com
French | £35
Cooking score: 3

£5 OFF

All the prerequisites of a classic French bistro can be ticked off at Café St Honoré in Edinburgh's New Town. Bentwood chairs? Check. Black-and-white tiles? Check. Distressed mirrors? Check. All that's missing is a predictable menu of réchauffé standards. Chef Neil Forbes leaves that to the chains; his kitchen doesn't put all that effort into butchering in-house and sourcing fine local and organic ingredients to play it safe. 'There's a real sense of "what's in the market today",' observes one enamoured reader. That might mean an impressive vegetarian choice of purple sprouting broccoli and Lanark Blue with wild garlic and potato croquette; a considered starter of Aberdeen Angus beef, air-dried in-house, with heritage potato salad; or an inventive sweet cicely-infused set custard with candied peel and cat's tongue biscuit. Service is 'cordial' and 'sincere'. The wine selection lists French classics (from £17.90) alongside surprises from Lebanon, England and even Scotland.

Chef/s: Neil Forbes. **Open:** all week L 12 to 2, D 5.15 to 10 (6 Sat and Sun). **Closed:** 25 to 27 Dec, 1 and 2 Jan. **Meals:** alc (main courses £16 to £23). Set L £16 (2 courses) to £20. Set D £18 (2 courses) to £24. Sun L £16. **Details:** 48 seats. Music.

Castle Terrace
Superlative modern cooking
33-35 Castle Terrace, Edinburgh, EH1 2EL
Tel no: (0131) 2291222
www.castleterracerestaurant.com
Modern British | £57
Cooking score: 6

V

Dominic Jack's town house restaurant near the Castle is part of Tom Kitchin's stable (see entry, Kitchin) and, for all its faint air of a homely pub dining room, is equally ambitious. Staff are welcoming and knowledgeable, and the place is relaxing, though you might find yourself shoehorned into an awkward alcove. It hardly matters, as the cooking is explosively exciting. Jack takes fine Scottish regional produce and alchemises it into dishes of compelling power and impact. Scallops lifted by a beautifully judged curry dressing might light the way for a following course of spelt risotto with crisped ox tongue and confit veal heart. Hake comes zested up with celeriac, lemon and lime, while the game season brought on fabulous partridge breast stuffed with foie gras, served bravely with the brain. Technically ingenious chocolate and orange pavé with orange sorbet might close the deal. A long list of thoroughbred wines starts at £22.50.

Chef/s: Dominic Jack. **Open:** Tue to Sat L 12 to 2, D 6.30 to 10. **Closed:** Sun, Mon, Christmas. **Meals:** alc (main courses £25 to £42). Set L £28.50. Tasting menu £75 (6 courses). **Details:** 65 seats. Separate bar. Wheelchair access. Music. Children over 5 yrs only.

Centotre

Lively all-day Italian eatery
103 George Street, Edinburgh, EH2 3ES
Tel no: (0131) 2251550
www.centotre.com
Italian | £25
Cooking score: 1
£30

There's certainly no denying the glamour of the pink cocktails amid the Corinthian pillars of this old George Street bank, but others love Centotre for its assiduous Italian sourcing and unpretentious cooking. Without doubt, this is a good fun place, though 'service could cheer up'. Start with arancini stuffed with four DOP cheeses and porcini, continue with a main-course special of salmon linguine or the self-described house classic contadino of orecchiette with piccante sausage, cremini mushrooms and cream. Breads, pizza, gelati and sorbets more than measure up, and the wine list offers an exemplary tour of Italian varieties (from £17).
Chef/s: Ferrigno Prisco. **Open:** all week 7.30am to midnight. **Closed:** 25 and 26 Dec. **Meals:** alc (main courses £12 to £25). Set L £14 (2 courses) to £19. Sun L £25. **Details:** 100 seats. 30 seats outside. Separate bar. Music.

David Bann

Globetrotting contemporary veggie
56-58 St Mary's Street, Edinburgh, EH1 1SX
Tel no: (0131) 5565888
www.davidbann.co.uk
Vegetarian | £24
Cooking score: 2
V £30

David Bann's forward-thinking vegetarian restaurant puts a very different spin on eating without meat. The dining room eschews rough-hewn rusticity in favour of sexy lighting, cool aubergine colour schemes and minimalist trappings, while the menu is stuffed with exuberant global flavours and bright ideas. Dishes are often described down to the last detail, without resorting to overkill. How about a red lentil pancake filled with butter beans, kidney beans and red chilli sauce, served with grilled sweet potato, courgette, crème fraîche, salsa and chocolate sauce? Starters roam freely, from Thai broccoli and smoked tofu fritters to olive polenta with basil pesto and homemade goats' curd, although fancy desserts such as lemon and raspberry posset or hot apple, cinnamon and Calvados tart follow a more orthodox European path. The eclectic wine list (from £15.50) is also true to the cause, touting organic, vegetarian and vegan tipples from around the globe.
Chef/s: David Bann. **Open:** all week 12 to 10 (10.30pm Fri, 11 to 10.30 Sat, 11am Sun). **Closed:** 25 and 26 Dec, 1 Jan. **Meals:** alc (main courses £12 to £13). **Details:** 80 seats.

The Dogs

Hearty casual dining
110 Hanover Street, Edinburgh, EH2 1DR
Tel no: (0131) 2201208
www.thedogsonline.co.uk
Modern British | £22
Cooking score: 1
£30

Since it opened in 2008, this city-centre eatery has been popular with students, tourists and locals, attracted by the kind prices, relaxed atmosphere and welcoming service (though perhaps not by the 'uncomfortable, crowded seating'). Hearty, slow-cooked dishes are always the best: the likes of rich, melting braised oxtail with celeriac mash and spinach fitting the bill nicely. Warm salad of grilled squid comes with well-flavoured paprika potatoes and broad bean vinaigrette, while at dessert stage 'simple creations' like lemon posset with farmhouse ice cream are 'preferred to the more elaborate affairs'. Wines from £14.95.
Chef/s: Aitor Lozano Rodrigo. **Open:** all week L 12 to 4, D 5 to 10. **Closed:** 25 Dec, 1 Jan. **Meals:** alc (main courses £11 to £15). **Details:** 58 seats.

Fishers in Leith

Quirky seafood bistro
1 The Shore, Leith, Edinburgh, EH6 6QW
Tel no: (0131) 5545666
www.fishersrestaurantgroup.co.uk
Seafood | £30
Cooking score: 1

V

An old-stager on the Leith scene, this branch of Fishers sits cosily at the foot of a 17th-century windmill overlooking the old docks. Inside, a mermaid figurehead, scallop motifs, nautical prints and maritime-blue chairs leave punters in no doubt that seafood is the kitchen's forte. Fish soup, shellfish platters and East Neuk smoked salmon are bolstered by more elaborate dishes along the lines of Scrabster hake fillet with charred ratatouille, aïoli and polenta chips or Peterhead sea trout with Wye asparagus, pea, broad bean and radish panzanella. Meat eaters aren't overlooked and there are a few regulation puds, too. Wines from £14.95.
Chef/s: Andrew Bird. **Open:** all week 12 to 10.30 (12.30 Sun). **Closed:** 25 and 26 Dec, 1 Jan. **Meals:** alc (main courses £12 to £24). Set L £13 (2 courses) to £16. **Details:** 40 seats. 12 seats outside. Separate bar. Music. No children after 8.

Galvin Brasserie de Luxe

Big on flavour and quality
The Caledonian, Princes Street, Edinburgh, EH1 2AB
Tel no: (0131) 2228988
www.galvinbrasseriedeluxe.com
French | £34
Cooking score: 3

£5 OFF 🛏

The Galvin brothers have pulled off a characteristically successful riff on their Baker Street original. More spacious than its London counterpart, the interconnecting dining rooms here hark back to when the Caledonian Hotel was a grand railway hotel (for the now-defunct Princess Street station) and suffer a little from the perfunctory old railway design. For some it's a 'soulless space', but for others the muted French bistro look (small tables, bentwood chairs) allows 'the food and the polished staff to shine'. The kitchen belts out some cracking French regional classics like escargots de Bourgogne, white onion velouté, and crab lasagne with beurre nantaise. It's a tried-and-trusted repertoire at main-course stage, too, with robust versions of daube of ox cheek, and confit duck leg with boudin noir and couscous. Desserts play it straight with raspberry soufflé and apple tarte Tatin. On the wine front, France is the main contender with bottles from £19.
Chef/s: Craig Sandle. **Open:** all week L 12 to 2.30 (12.30 to 3 Sat and Sun), D 6 to 10 (9.30 Sun). **Meals:** alc (main courses £13 to £28). Set L and D £17 (2 courses) to £20. **Details:** 130 seats. Separate bar. Wheelchair access. Music. Car parking.

The Gardener's Cottage

Rural vibe in the heart of the city
1 Royal Terrace Gardens, London Road, Edinburgh, EH7 5DX
Tel no: (0131) 5581221
www.thegardenerscottage.co
British | £30
Cooking score: 2

'Just an amazing place,' purred one reader after six earthy courses for 30 quid. The former gardener's residence has surely never been so busy. Now a cottage restaurant, it is furnished in rustic neutrality complete with an open-to-view kitchen and long, communal wooden tables. Many ingredients are grown in the garden, and the others won't have come too far – this joint has a real sense of place. So it's elbow to elbow with your new best friend before tucking in to celeriac soup enriched with hazelnuts; a quiche rich with onion, bacon and cheese; or roe deer with hay-smoked potato dumplings. The evening menu (the 30 quid job) includes a cheese course, perhaps featuring the Camembert-like Tunworth from Hampshire, served with carrot jam and Bath Olivers, and winds up with a dessert such as the intriguing-sounding potato and chocolate slice. Wines start at £17.90.

Chef/s: Dale Mailley and Edward Murray. **Open:** Thur to Mon L 12 to 2.30, D 5 to 10. **Closed:** Tue, Wed, 25 Dec to 8 Jan. **Meals:** Tasting menu £30 (6 courses). **Details:** 30 seats. 10 seats outside. Music.

La Garrigue
A taste of the Midi off the Royal Mile
31 Jeffrey Street, Edinburgh, EH1 1DH
Tel no: (0131) 5573032
www.lagarrigue.co.uk
French | £30
Cooking score: 3

Jean-Michel Gauffre's popular city-centre restaurant with views towards Calton Hill looks rather grander than a bistro, with high-backed chairs, violet walls and attractive village scenes of Gauffre's native Languedoc. Nevertheless, the cooking certainly has its heart in the bistro idiom. A seasonal *menu du patron* prefaces the bilingual prix fixe and, although there are forays beyond the Midi, the kitchen faithfully returns to the favoured dishes of the deep south. Setoise crab and squid tart in cumin and anise tomato sauce might set the ball rolling, perhaps with proper cassoulet to follow, replete with confit duck, pork and Toulouse sausage and served with walnut salad. It all ends with pear poached in red wine, served with apple and goats' cheese mousse and sweet red wine sorbet. Languedoc heads the wine list with Daumas Gassac and Domaine de Clovallon in the vanguard. Prices start at £16 for a Syrah rosé.
Chef/s: Jean-Michel Gauffre. **Open:** all week L 12 to 2.30, D 6 to 9.30. **Meals:** Set L £13 (2 courses) to £16. Set D £25 (2 courses) to £30. Sun L £13. **Details:** 45 seats. Wheelchair access. Car parking.

Symbols
🛏 Accommodation is available
£30 Three courses for less than £30
V Separate vegetarian menu
£5 £5-off voucher scheme
🍷 Notable wine list

The Kitchin
Star player on the waterfront
78 Commercial Quay, Leith, Edinburgh, EH6 6LX
Tel no: (0131) 5551755
www.thekitchin.com
Modern European | £65
Cooking score: 7
🍷 V

There seems to be some debate among readers as to whether Edinburgh chef Tom Kitchin's strength lies in seafood or whether his game cookery has the edge. And then there are others who'd be quite content with just his crudités for their desert island dish. Yes, 'perfectionist', personable chef Tom Kitchin has an enthusiastic fanbase, one that has steadily grown since he and wife Michaela opened the Kitchin on Leith waterfront in 2006. If his fans have a gripe, it's that several months' notice is now required to snag a weekend table in the comfortable, contemporary dining room. Kitchin has forged a style that might be called Scottish haute cuisine. French techniques are everywhere – in the artichoke barigoule with cod cheeks and the hare à la royale – but his 'impeccably sourced' ingredients are Scotland's finest. Visit during the game season for Borders woodcock, classically presented, the entrails spread atop a croûton, or tender roe deer loin with chestnuts, blackberry and apple. For seafood, there's the 'marvellous signature dish' of shellfish rock pool with sea vegetables, and a 'true highlight', lobster with snail butter. A fittingly seasonal dessert might be blueberry cheesecake on a 'real shortbread crust' with cobnuts. Set lunch and vegetarian menus are no afterthought, and the modern global wine list (from £28 a bottle) is as good a guide as you'll find to what to drink now.
Chef/s: Tom Kitchin. **Open:** Tue to Sat L 12.15 to 2.30, D 6.30 to 10 (10.30 Fri and Sat). **Closed:** Sun, Mon. **Meals:** alc (main courses £28 to £45). Set L £29. Tasting menu £75. **Details:** 55 seats. 32 seats outside. Separate bar. Wheelchair access. Music. Children over 5 yrs only.

Number One

Subtly inventive cooking that really surprises
The Balmoral, 1 Princes Street, Edinburgh,
EH2 2EQ
Tel no: (0131) 5576727
www.restaurantnumberone.com
Modern European | £68
Cooking score: 6

£5 OFF 🍷 ⇄ V

Dinner at Number One, the flagship restaurant of Edinburgh's landmark Balmoral Hotel, will undoubtedly give your credit card a hammering. Nevertheless, Jeff Bland's assured contemporary take on Scottish ingredients in one of the city's most glamorous dining rooms, is the lasting memory. It's not easy to beautify a windowless basement, but Olga Polizzi has pulled it off with red lacquered walls, original artwork, golden banquettes and acres of space. The surroundings are complemented by service that manages to be relaxed and unstuffy yet utterly professional. A spring menu featured a fragrant dish of Scottish crab and heirloom tomatoes garnished with violet blossoms and crab foam, and a near-definitive Blairgowrie beef fillet with barley and green bean risotto, red wine sauce, black truffle and foie gras. Desserts range from the intricate gariguette strawberries with a lemon posset-filled cylinder of meringue to a simpler pistachio sponge with crowdie mousse, rhubarb gel and vanilla ice cream. The approachable sommelier oversees choice on the predominantly French wine list, with bottles from £30.

Chef/s: Brian Grigor and Jeff Bland. **Open:** all week D only 6.30 to 10 (6 Fri to Sun). **Closed:** 2 weeks Jan. **Meals:** alc (main courses £36). Set D £68. Tasting menu £75. **Details:** 55 seats. Separate bar. Wheelchair access. Music.

🍴 **Average Price**

The average price listed in main-entry reviews denotes the price of a three-course meal, without wine.

Ondine

Sustainable seafood favourite
2 George IV Bridge, Edinburgh, EH1 1AD
Tel no: (0131) 2261888
www.ondinerestaurant.co.uk
Seafood | £30
Cooking score: 4

Perched above the Royal Mile, with panoramic windows providing views of George IV Bridge, this clean-lined, contemporary dining room comes with a funky side order of jaunty art and baroque fabrics. Most attention, however, focuses on the glistening crustacea bar. Sustainable seafood is a passion here, and the kitchen sets out its sophisticated stall with mighty roast shellfish platters as well as 'grand fruits of sea' for those wanting to impress their companions. Otherwise, the menu casts its net widely, pulling in bowls of fragrant steamed mussels masala, roast monkfish with a punchy tomato, chorizo and chickpea stew, or Eyemouth lobster and chips. Fillet of Orkney beef and steak tartare offer satisfaction for carnivores, while desserts might bring treacle tart or ginger crème brûlée. Cleansing aperitifs top the smart, brasserie-style wine list, which kicks off at £19.50. Be warned: the noise and general hubbub can be deafening at weekends.
Chef/s: Roy Brett. **Open:** Mon to Sat L 12 to 3, D 5.30 to 10. **Closed:** Sun, 24 to 26 Dec, 1 to 9 Jan. **Meals:** alc (main courses £14 to £39). Set L £22 (2 courses) to £25. **Details:** 70 seats. Separate bar. Wheelchair access. Music.

Plumed Horse

Harnessing powerful, sculpted flavours
50-54 Henderson Street, Edinburgh, EH6 6DE
Tel no: (0131) 5545556
www.plumedhorse.co.uk
Modern European | £55
Cooking score: 5

Tony Borthwick's place not far from the Leith waterfront has plenty of competition within Edinburgh's nerve-centre restaurant district, but stands out for its genuine character. Occupying the ground floor of a traditional

apartment building, in two snug, haphazardly shaped rooms, Plumed Horse benefits from the proprietor's personal touch, with arresting modern artworks and cooking of evident distinction. Borthwick chooses prime Scottish materials, as may be seen in an ingenious starter of duck confit and foie gras, served with a poached egg and hollandaise en cocotte, and purple sprouting broccoli for dipping. Mains might bring bacon-wrapped monkfish and smoked eel with white bean cassoulet, or royally treated roe deer loin with clapshot, beetroot and kale. Desserts could woo you in the obvious way with a chocolate brownie, or more enterprisingly with pineapple tart, jasmine and lemongrass pannacotta, coconut and rum sorbet and puréed coriander. A refined French-led wine list starts at £22.
Chef/s: Tony Borthwick and William Grubb. **Open:** Tue to Sat L 12.30 to 1.30, D 7 to 9 (6.30 Fri and Sat). **Closed:** Sun, Mon, Christmas, 2 weeks Jul. **Meals:** Set L £24. Set D £55. Tasting menu £69. **Details:** 36 seats. Wheelchair access. Music. No children after 8.

The Pompadour by Galvin

Big-ticket luxury and fabulous French flavours
The Caledonian, Princes Street, Edinburgh, EH1 2AB
Tel no: (0131) 2228975
www.thepompadourbygalvin.com
French | £58
Cooking score: 5
£5 OFF 🍴 V

The Pompadour at the legendary Caledonian opened in 1925 and immediately started seducing generations hungry for glamour and fanciful distraction. Now the grand old lady of Auld Reekie gastronomy is back in the limelight, with London-based dynamic duo Chris and Jeff Galvin at the helm. Big-ticket luxury is a given here, and the amply proportioned first-floor dining room exudes primped-up, *belle époque* affluence – from the wedding-cake corniching and pink chandelier to the hand-painted Chinese panels. The food is fabulously French, but with typical dedication to British sourcing and

freewheeling ideas: think roast John Dory with pig's trotter, veal sweetbread, parsnip purée and apple fondant, or loin of Borders venison with cocoa nib and Brazil nut crumb, pommes Anna, quince and orange jus, followed by Valrhona and mandarin bombe with white chocolate and ginger ice cream. The cheeseboard is 'brilliant', service faultless and the masterly wine list (from £26) breathes pure-bred Galvin pedigree.
Chef/s: Craig Sandle. **Open:** Tue to Sat D only 6.30 to 10 (6 Fri and Sat). **Closed:** Mon, Sun, 2 weeks Jan. **Meals:** Set D £58 (3 courses) to £68 (7 courses). **Details:** 60 seats. Separate bar. Wheelchair access. Music. Car parking.

Purslane

Basement eatery with big ideas
33a St Stephen Street, Stockbridge, Edinburgh, EH3 5AH
Tel no: (0131) 2263500
www.purslanerestaurant.co.uk
Modern British | £28
Cooking score: 2
£5 OFF £30 🍴

A perfect fit for Edinburgh's trendy Stockbridge district, bijou Purslane plies its trade in a cosy but smart basement furnished in pleasantly informal, metropolitan style. Chef/proprietor Paul Gunning is a protégé of high-flying Jeff Bland (see entry Number One at the Balmoral Hotel), and it shows in a menu that aims high. Expect simple ideas dressed up to the nines: as in sea bream with squid, confit pepper and fennel compote, or braised beef faggots with seared foie gras, parsley mash and red wine jus. Classics such as braised venison with Cumberland sauce or roast pork loin with celeriac dauphinois and curly kale also appear, while desserts mix familiarity with a touch of brio – from prune and Armagnac rice pudding with candied rosemary to lemon posset with a gin-and-tonic granita. Prices are pegged back, the tasting menu offers splendid value, and the wine list promises sound drinking from £15.95.

Chef/s: Paul Gunning. **Open:** Tue to Sun L 12 to 2, D 6 to 11 (11.30 Fri and Sat). **Closed:** Mon, 25 and 26 Dec, 1 and 2 Jan. **Meals:** Set L £15 (2 courses) to £18. Set D £24 (2 courses) to £28. Tasting menu £50. **Details:** 24 seats. Music. Children over 6 yrs only.

Restaurant Mark Greenaway
Harmonious food in elegant surrounds
69 North Castle Street, Edinburgh, EH2 3LJ
Tel no: (0131) 2261155
www.markgreenaway.com
Modern British | £40
Cooking score: 4

Mark Greenaway and front-of-house partner Nicola Jack are clearly on song in their elegant new home – a converted bank in Edinburgh's Old Town, complete with warm muted colours, the chef's signature emblazoned above the fireplace and a specially designed wine vault. Greenaway has a reputation for classy contemporary cooking and clear-sighted, harmonious ideas, but his dishes are also 'accessible to everyone'. Top calls from the 'market menu' have included a cheeky riff involving pan-fried duck egg with duck croquette, brioche, duck ham and baby celery leaves; salmon fillet with soft-shell crab tempura; and an 'astounding' plate of deeply flavoured 11-hour pork belly with pommes purée, Savoy cabbage and toffee apple jus. After that, don't miss the peanut caramel cheesecake with toffee sauce and roasted peanuts (shades of a Snickers bar, perhaps). 'Unbelievably superb service' has turned reporters' heads, too. The cosmopolitan wine list has laudably gentle mark-ups (bottles from £22).
Chef/s: Mark Greenaway. **Open:** Tue to Sat L 12 to 2.30, D 5.30 to 10. **Closed:** Sun, Mon, 24 to 26 Dec, 1 and 2 Jan. **Meals:** alc (main courses £20 to £29). Set L £17 (2 courses) to £20. Tasting menu £66 (8 courses). **Details:** 60 seats. Music.

Restaurant Martin Wishart
Inspired cooking from a Caledonian star
54 The Shore, Leith, Edinburgh, EH6 6RA
Tel no: (0131) 5533557
www.martin-wishart.co.uk
Modern French | £70
Cooking score: 7
♦ V

'There's something warm and comforting about high-end restaurants like Martin Wishart,' commented an admirer of this Caledonian star overlooking Leith's re-energised waterfront. The suave, low-key dining room may not suggest culinary pyrotechnics with its neutral colours, gentle music and formal French staff, but the kitchen delivers course after course of superlative, intelligent and complex food. As well as three tasting menus (including fish and veggie options), there's a refreshingly concise carte for those who simply want 'three great plates without bells and whistles'. Recommendations are many and varied – from precisely seared scallops on Puy lentils (cooked in a rich, savoury sauce enhanced by pig's trotter), to roast leg of Pyrenean lamb, 'bang-on for pinkness', carved at table and served with 'perfect discs of cooked spud', asparagus, artichokes and morels. Fish fans have been enraptured by the 'truly fabulous' ceviche of halibut with mango and passion fruit, while vegetarians admire the urbane, wafer-thin take on rustic flammekuchen tart with sliced Vivaldi potato, caramelised onion, Comté cheese and pumpkin purée. As for dessert, some enthuse about the tonka bean brûlée topped with rhubarb compote to cut through the richness; others crave chocolate in myriad forms. Thoughtful extras add to the pleasure, while the comprehensive, cosmopolitan wine list turns up rare tipples and vintage classics from around the globe; prices start at £27 and half-bottles are numerous. Details overleaf.

Chef/s: Martin Wishart. **Open:** Tue to Sat L 12 to 1.30, D 7 to 9 (6.30 to 9.30 Fri and Sat). **Closed:** Sun, Mon, 24 to 26 Dec, 2 weeks Jan. **Meals:** Set L £29. Set D £70. Tasting menu £75 (6 courses). **Details:** 50 seats. Wheelchair access. Music.

Rhubarb at Prestonfield
Unrestrained opulence and luxurious food
Prestonfield House, Priestfield Road, Edinburgh, EH16 5UT
Tel no: (0131) 2251333
www.prestonfield.com
Modern British | £55
Cooking score: 4

Lavishly extravagant décor complements the grandiose baroque style of this palatial edifice: built in 1687 for Edinburgh's Lord Provost, but now an opulent country-house retreat in the city. The hotel is a vision of unrestrained opulence, complete with oil paintings, antique furniture and boudoir-esque trappings, while Rhubarb itself comprises two oval-shaped Regency dining rooms overlooking the grounds. Dusky red, green and aubergine colour schemes, gold-trimmed drapes and impeccable table settings provide the backdrop for luxurious, highly worked modern cooking – from galantine of duck and foie gras with prunes, salted lemon, pistachio and gingerbread to caramelised white chocolate with sea buckthorn, hazelnut crumble and clotted cream parfait. In between, aged steaks, game birds and venison loom large, but there's also room for fish: perhaps sea bream with butternut squash, lime and sage butter sauce. Cheeses celebrate the Auld Alliance, while the mighty wine list (from £23) reads like a gazetteer of global oenology.
Chef/s: John McMahon. **Open:** all week L 12 to 2 (1 to 3 Sun), D 6.30 to 10 (6 to 11 Fri and Sat). **Meals:** Set L £19 (2 courses) to £35. Set D £35. Sun L £19. **Details:** 80 seats. 20 seats outside. Separate bar. Wheelchair access. Music. Car parking.

NEW ENTRY
The Scran and Scallie
Tom Kitchen's lively dining pub
1 Comely Bank Road, Edinburgh, EH4 1DT
Tel no: (0131) 3326281
www.scranandscallie.com
Modern British | £30
Cooking score: 3

Tom Kitchin's eagerly awaited offshoot – a 'public house with dining' – gets its definition the wrong way round. As Stockbridge's middle classes fight for a table, and for attention from overrun staff (the policy of mixing reservations with first-come, first-served doesn't help), there's not much room for a quiet pint. Nor does a £32 langoustine main-course special sound too pubby, although superior bangers and mash and crumble desserts more broadly typify the menus. The £16 steak pie (with side dishes extra) better justified its tag: big enough for Desperate Dan and satisfyingly accomplished from crust to core. The main dining room is an easy-going mix of exposed brick and mellow tartan. Draught beer is sensibly limited to a few proven Scottish indies, and the cost of wine accelerates fast from £18 for a humble Karrikiri from Navarra. Probably best to go off-peak until the fuss settles.
Chef/s: David Umpherston. **Open:** Mon to Fri L 12 to 3, D 6 to 10. Sat and Sun 12 to 10. **Closed:** 25 Dec. **Meals:** alc (main courses £10 to £19). Set L £15. **Details:** 110 seats. Separate bar. Wheelchair access. Music.

NEW ENTRY
Timberyard
Nordic-inspired food in a rustic setting
10 Lady Lawson Street, Edinburgh, EH3 9DS
Tel no: (0131) 2211222
www.timberyard.co
Modern European | £39
Cooking score: 4

'This is a restaurant for the future, respecting the environment, customers and the food it serves,' enthused one visitor to this rambling, Nordic-inspired family restaurant. The 1895 former wood store remains artfully shabby:

rustic beams, industrial lighting and whitewashed brick, warmed by a stove, sofa and tartan throws. An outdoor dining courtyard has fire-pits and vegetable beds. Dishes come in three sizes, starting with a 'bite' of, say, 'exquisite' raw scallop, cucumber, watercress, scurvy grass and crème fraîche. 'Small' could feature roast pigeon, mushroom, charred leek and chickweed, and a 'large' involves the likes of 'exemplary' mackerel, beetroot, apple, shrimps and samphire. Throughout, execution matches originality, including some esoteric foraged ingredients like the knockout dessert of buttermilk, crowdie, carrots, oats and vibrant-orange sea buckthorn. An admirable wine list (from £17) and brilliant cocktails (both alcoholic and none), plus 'staff and customers sharing a communal, happy experience', make a meal an 'uplifting' occasion.
Chef/s: Ben Radford. **Open:** Tue to Sat L 12 to 2, D 5.30 to 9.30. **Closed:** Sun, Mon, 25 Dec to 1 Jan, 1 week Apr, 1 week Oct. **Meals:** alc (main course £16 to £21). Set L and D £19 (2 courses) to £27. **Details:** 80 seats. 30 seats outside. Wheelchair access. Music.

21212

Artful, offbeat food in sumptuous surrounds
3 Royal Terrace, Edinburgh, EH7 5AB
Tel no: (0131) 5231030
www.21212restaurant.co.uk
Modern French | £49
Cooking score: 6

The supremely elegant town house on the Royal Terrace extends over four floors of spacious, stylish rooms, looking towards the Firth of Forth from the higher storeys. Reporters rarely fail to mention the sophisticated feel, which extends to an industrious kitchen on view behind a spotted glass partition. Paul Kitching's restlessly innovative account of contemporary cuisine brings on dishes composed of multifarious ingredients, often rooted in the demotic. Cauliflower cheese in risotto guise with black pudding, sultanas and walnuts makes perfect

sense, as does a reworking of beef olives, the superb fillet appearing with actual olives, macadamias and a pasta salad. A fish double-act teams halibut and smoked haddock with barley pudding, pear and pimento in sauce soubise, and desserts aim to please with the likes of almond shortbread brûlée, or an alliterative trifle of cream cheese, chocolate, cottage cheese, custard and cake with pecans and pineapple. Wines from a compendious list start at £26.
Chef/s: Paul Kitching. **Open:** Tue to Sat L 12 to 1.45, D 6.45 to 9.30. **Closed:** Sun, Mon. **Meals:** Set L £22 (2 courses) to £53 (5 courses). Set D £49 (3 courses) to £69 (5 courses). **Details:** 38 seats. Children over 5 yrs only.

Valvona & Crolla Caffè Bar

Pioneering Neapolitan blockbuster
19 Elm Row, Edinburgh, EH7 4AA
Tel no: (0131) 5566066
www.valvonacrolla.co.uk
Italian | £23
Cooking score: 3
£5 OFF | £30

Members of the Contini dynasty have been doing Edinburgh proud since setting out their stall as market traders in 1934. They are now the undisputed godfathers of the city's Italian foodie scene, and this original outlet is still 'numero uno' with its jam-packed caffè-bar attracting throngs of shoppers, tourists and arty types. Casual, all-day eating is the deal, and everything hinges on top-drawer Italian ingredients – plus ample Scottish produce. Drop by for a signature 'panatella' sandwich with excellent coffee, or try some spot-on pasta: perhaps tagliolini with crab and chilli. There are bespoke pizzas too, and hefty plates of seasonal rusticity in the shape of frittata or grlled polenta with endive and sausages. To finish, V&C's bombolone doughnuts and luscious cakes are a must, as are the locally made gelati. The Continis are also wine merchants, with the finest Italian cellar in town – so cruise round the shop or pick from the pared-down caffè list: prices from £15.95 (£4.40 a glass). Note: extended opening hours in August.

Chef/s: Mary Contini and Pina Trano. **Open:** Mon to Sat 8.30 to 5.30 (8 to 6 Fri and Sat). Sun 10.30 to 4. **Closed:** 25 and 26 Dec, 1 and 2 Jan. **Meals:** alc (main courses £10 to £14). **Details:** 55 seats. Music.

The Witchery by the Castle
Tricks and treats
Castlehill, Royal Mile, Edinburgh, EH1 2NF
Tel no: (0131) 2255613
www.thewitchery.com
Modern British | £45
Cooking score: 2

🍷 🍽

There's more than a splash of Hogwarts hocus-pocus about Edinburgh's most magical restaurant – an atmospheric hideout stowed away in a 16th-century building just off the Royal Mile. Eat in the Gothic oak-panelled Witchery itself, surrounded by tapestries, drapes and bagpipe-playing cherubs, or descend a stone staircase to the enchanting Secret Garden: an enclosed courtyard replete with a pulpit, extraordinary painted ceilings and an urn-filled terrace. Either way, the food covers all bases: simple and complex, traditional and modern, homespun and exotic, with Scottish produce as the common thread. Among the culinary tricks and treats are Oban oysters Rockefeller, grilled Orkney lobster with sherry hollandaise, and Borders beef Rossini, but also expect weighty seafood platters, a version of haggis blended with chicken mousse, and desserts such as rhubarb Savarin with crème fraîche. The wine list is a mighty 1,000-bin tome as thick as a book of spells, embracing the world's most esteemed producers, grape varieties and styles; 17 house selections start at £21.50 (£5.25 a glass).

Chef/s: Douglas Roberts. **Open:** all week 12 to 11.30. **Meals:** alc (main courses £15 to £42). Set L £16 (2 courses). Set D £35. **Details:** 95 seats. 20 seats outside. Music. Children over 8 yrs only after 8.

LOCAL GEM

▲ Tanjore
6-8 Clerk Street, Edinburgh, EH8 9HX
Tel no: (0131) 4786518
www.tanjore.co.uk
Indian | £15

Fresh ingredients, well-balanced spicing, unusual Tamil dishes and good value are key to the enduring success of this unpretentious, welcoming south Indian eatery. Tanjore happily accommodates vegetarians, vegans and meat eaters. Spinach paneer dumplings, idli (rice and lentil cakes) steaming with freshness, and madurai kothu parotta (a bread biryani) continue to draw enthusiastic reports. Other highlights include massive rolled-up dosas (one comes stuffed with curried chicken pieces), and the splendidly generous thalis. Drink lassi or BYO (unlicensed) and enjoy the laid-back atmosphere. Open all week.

▌Gullane

Chez Roux
Golfing Mecca with French food
Greywalls Hotel, Muirfield, Gullane, EH31 2EG
Tel no: (01620) 842144
www.greywalls.co.uk
French | £35
Cooking score: 4

🍽 V

Designed by Sir Edwin Lutyens in 1901 and owned by the Weaver family since 1946, honey-coloured Greywalls sits proud amid sunken gardens imagined by Gertrude Jekyll – although most of its kudos now comes from nearby Muirfield golf course. Four smart dining areas have views of the fairways. Culinary branding comes courtesy of French master Albert Roux, whose fingerprints are all over the menu. Red chairs, starched napkins and twinkling glassware provide a suitably polished setting for food that will have fans of Gavroche-style *cuisine ancienne* licking their lips. Pike quenelles with mushroom duxelles, brown shrimps and sauce Nantua could precede roast saddle of French farmed rabbit with sautéed kidneys and carrot mousse, or turbot T-bone with creamed parsnips, confit garlic and chicken jus. No meal would be complete without a soufflé: perhaps the iconic twice-baked suissesse version to start. Wines from £22.

Chef/s: Derek Johnstone. **Open:** all week L 12 to 2.30, D 7 to 10. **Meals:** alc (main courses £15 to £24). Set L £27. Set D £30. **Details:** 80 seats. 20 seats outside. Separate bar. Car parking.

La Potinière

A cavalcade of immensely pleasurable food
34 Main Street, Gullane, EH31 2AA
Tel no: (01620) 843214
www.la-potiniere.co.uk
Modern British | £38
Cooking score: 6

Lauded as 'one of Scotland's best', redoubtable La Potinière is enjoying something of an Indian summer under the shrewd stewardship of Mary Runciman and Keith Marley. It might initially be mistaken for a private house: an impression reinforced by pretty interiors, gracious service and the immensely comforting pleasure of eating here. The owners' reputation hinges on accumulated culinary wisdom and diligent sourcing (suppliers are name-checked), plus great consistency. In the evening that might mean a cavalcade of finely honed dishes ranging from warm beetroot pannacotta with beetroot salad and horseradish crème fraîche, to poached and seared loin of roe deer with parsnip mash, hazelnut and cranberry relish and spiced cherry sauce. Lunch finds the kitchen on top form, judging by reports of steamed lemon sole with braised fennel and asparagus followed by 'warm-centred' chocolate moelleux with caramelised banana and coffee sauce. The knowledgeable wine list is split into price brackets, starting at £17.

Chef/s: Mary Runciman and Keith Marley. **Open:** Wed to Sun L 12.30 to 1.30, Wed to Sat D 7 to 8.30. **Closed:** Mon, Tue, 24 Dec to 26 Dec, Jan, 1 week Oct, bank hols. **Meals:** Set L £20 (2 courses) to £26. Set D £38 to £43 (4 courses). **Details:** 24 seats. Wheelchair access. Car parking.

▌Linlithgow

Champany Inn

Pioneering steakhouse
Champany Corner, Linlithgow, EH49 7LU
Tel no: (01506) 834532
www.champany.com
British | £75
Cooking score: 3
🛏

Bullish patriotic steakhouses and their ritzy transatlantic cousins are currently all the rage, so it's easy to forget that Clive and Anne Davidson have been showing everyone the way for more than three decades. Fashioned from a collection of 16th-century farm buildings, the tourist-friendly Champany has become synonymous with some of the best beef in the land – courtesy of prime Aberdeenshire beasts reared on home turf. The carcasses are aged for three weeks in an ionised chill room and grilled on specially designed stoves. Simply peruse the chilled counter with its slabs of sirloin, porterhouse, T-bones and whole ribs, pick your sauce and brace yourself for a hefty bill. The kitchen also offers home-cured fish from the 'smokepot', Brechin black pudding with rösti, herb-crusted Dornoch lamb and butter-poached lobster – plus Loch Gruinart oysters and old-school puddings such as cheesecake with quince compote. The epic 50-page wine list opens at £21.90.

Chef/s: Clive Davidson and David Gibson. **Open:** Mon to Fri L 12 to 2, Mon to Sat D 6.30 to 10. **Closed:** Sun, 25 and 26 Dec, 1 and 2 Jan. **Meals:** alc (main courses £31 to £45). Set L £26 (2 courses). Set D £43. **Details:** 50 seats. 20 seats outside. Separate bar. Wheelchair access. Car parking. Children over 8 yrs only.

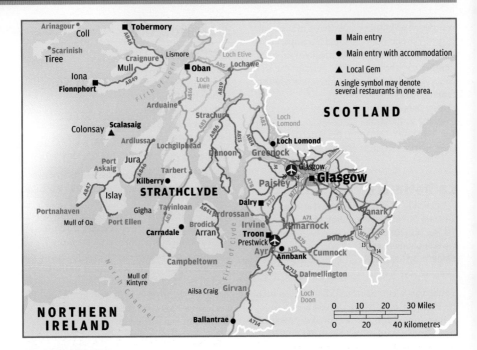

Annbank

Enterkine House

Splendour, charm and sophisticated cooking
Enterkine Estate, Annbank, KA6 5AL
Tel no: (01292) 520580
www.enterkine.com
Modern European | £38
Cooking score: 4

£5 OFF

Originally built for a P&O shipping magnate, this sparkling 1930s residence stands proud at the heart of a 300-acre estate with enchanting views over the River Ayr and ample opportunities for bracing Scottish-style R&R. It may exude baronial country-house splendour, but Enterkine House also has personal charms in abundance and a forward-thinking attitude to food. Pine floors and bare tables set a relaxed tone in the restaurant, although Paul Moffat's Euro-accented cooking aims for sophistication and impact. Scottish ingredients get full exposure in complex, thoughtful dishes ranging from

Jerusalem artichoke velouté with Marrbury smoked salmon, caramelised roots and sherry caramel, to iced honey parfait with granola crumble, toffee sauce and golden raisins. In between, mature Orkney Gold beef cheek might appear with parsnip purée, wild leeks and shallots, while loin of moorland hare could be accompanied by aromatic red cabbage, salsify and potato fondant. The illustrated international wine list opens at £21.95.
Chef/s: Paul Moffat. **Open:** all week L 12 to 2, D 6.30 to 9.30. **Meals:** alc (main courses £15 to £25). Set L £17 (2 courses) to £19. Set D £25 (2 courses) to £38. Sun L £19. **Details:** 40 seats. 20 seats outside. Music. Car parking.

Visit us Online

To find out more about
The Good Food Guide, please visit
www.thegoodfoodguide.co.uk

Ballantrae
Glenapp Castle
Formidable cooking at a top-notch hotel
Ballantrae, KA26 0NZ
Tel no: (01465) 831212
www.glenappcastle.com
Modern British | £65
Cooking score: 6

£5 OFF ⊨ V

For a slice of the aristocratic life, Glenapp Castle is just the ticket: a long, winding drive, towering turrets, oil paintings, chandeliers and antiques, and smart, attentive staff. Sumptuous, classic, elegant, as country house hotels go, this really is in a class of its own. Tyron Ellul has taken over from Matt Worswick, and his classic but inventive cooking is built on the best the area can offer: an exceptional cauliflower velouté with Mull Cheddar and a rarebit beignet; tender pig's cheek and Arran mustard cromesquis, sweetened with apple and vanilla purée; wild mushroom risotto, umami-rich and luxuriant; and superb, tender roasted breast of Gressingham duck with confit leg pithiviers, sweet red onion and wild asparagus (achieving textural contrast as well as deep, rounded flavours). To finish, maybe gloriously rich chocolate Palet d'Or, lightened by sweet milk crumble and salted-caramel ice cream. The wine list offers interesting finds from £29.
Chef/s: Tyron Ellul. **Open:** all week L 12 to 2, D 7 to 9. **Closed:** 23 to 28 Dec, 3 Jan, late Mar. **Meals:** Set L £40, Set D £65, Sun L £30. **Details:** 34 seats. Wheelchair access. Car parking.

Bothwell

READERS RECOMMEND
Grapevine Restaurant
Modern British
27 Main Street, Bothwell, G71 8RD
Tel no: (01698) 852014
www.grapevinebothwell.com
'Amazing. New owners have brought a modern flavour of Scotland to the menu, showing their commitment to good quality.'

Cameron House, Loch Lomond
Martin Wishart at Loch Lomond
Poised cooking in a baronial pile
Cameron House, Loch Lomond, G83 8QZ
Tel no: (01389) 722504
www.martinwishartlochlomond.co.uk
Modern French | £70
Cooking score: 6

⊨ V

Nowadays, everybody who's anybody in the culinary world has one foot in the metropolis and the other in the country, and so it is with Martin Wishart, whose self-named Leith restaurant (see entry) has long been one of Edinburgh's ornaments. At Cameron House, with its simultaneously soothing and exhilarating views over Loch Lomond, the bucolic component is achieved in style: minimally so in Ian Smith's interior design (the monochrome palette relieved by some leafy-green upholstery), and thrillingly in Graeme Cheevers' execution of Wishart's dynamic contemporary Scottish cooking. Start with bracing roe deer tartare with pear, chestnuts and smoked crème fraîche, followed by skate in seaweed butter with razor clams, shrimps and ginger, or an in-vogue combination of pig's cheek and langoustines with choucroute. You'll positively radiate health after a dessert of yuzu and pink grapefruit curd with goji berries and coriander-mint ice cream. The impressive Francocentric wine list opens at £27.
Chef/s: Graeme Cheevers. **Open:** Sat and Sun L 12 to 2 (2.30 Sun), Wed to Sun D 6.30 to 10 (7 Sun). **Closed:** Mon, Tue, first 2 weeks Jan. **Meals:** Set L £24 (2 courses) to £29. Set D £55 (2 courses) to £70. Sun L £29. Tasting menu £75. **Details:** 40 seats. Wheelchair access. Music. Car parking.

Carradale

Dunvalanree

Enchanting clifftop home from home
Port Righ, Carradale, PA28 6SE
Tel no: (01583) 431226
www.dunvalanree.com
Modern British | £28
Cooking score: 2

🛏 V £30

Perched on the edge of the Mull of Kintyre, with sweeping views across to Arran and the Argyll coast, the Milsteads' beautifully remote hotel is a place to escape to. Dunvalanree has a homely and welcoming air, and was a founder member of the Seafood Trail group, celebrating the bounteous fish and shellfish of western Scotland. Ravishing views and smartly laid tables with tartan runners make a fine setting for Alyson Milstead's freshly cooked three-course menus. Those seafood specialities might take in Etive mussels in coconut and coriander broth, followed by prosciutto-wrapped sea bass filled with lime and tarragon butter. A meatier proposition could start with spicy pork meatballs in tomato and smoked garlic, perhaps followed by breast and confit leg of duck with roasted orange in red wine sauce. Thoroughbred Scottish cheeses and oatcakes are good enough to tempt you away from desserts such as tangy lemon posset. Wines from £16.50.
Chef/s: Alyson Milstead. Open: all week D only 7 (1 sitting). Closed: Christmas. Meals: Set D £24 (2 courses) to £28. Details: 24 seats. Car parking.

Dalry

Braidwoods

Precision-tuned cooking and incisive flavours
Drumastle Mill Cottage, Dalry, KA24 4LN
Tel no: (01294) 833544
www.braidwoods.co.uk
Modern British | £45
Cooking score: 6

Half an hour's drive south-west of Glasgow brings you to a single-track road, where, in an ancient whitewashed miller's cottage, Keith and Nicola Braidwood have run their discreet country restaurant for over 20 years. The classy, slightly old-fashioned feel strikes a chord with reporters, who love the comfortable surroundings, professional service and the splendid isolation. The Braidwoods believe a restaurant should reflect its location, use local and regional produce and respond to the seasons. This gives the food its identity, which here includes a 'gloriously tender' fillet of roe deer and best end of Ayrshire lamb with a confit of the neck. Flavours impress from the beginning – a warm timbale of Arbroath smokies perhaps, then a tart of Parmesan with red pepper coulis – and reach their zenith in a 'wonderful' chilled and caramelised rice pudding with warm prunes in Armagnac. The wine list (from £23.95) offers value across the board.
Chef/s: Keith Braidwood. Open: Wed to Sat L 12 to 1.45, Tue to Sat D 7 to 9. Closed: Sun, Mon, 4 weeks from 24 Dec, first 2 weeks Sept. Meals: Set L £25 (2 courses) to £28. Set D £45. Sun L £35. Details: 24 seats. Car parking. Children over 12 yrs only at D.

Glasgow

Brian Maule at Chardon d'Or

Pleasing French food and exemplary wines
176 West Regent Street, Glasgow, G2 4RL
Tel no: (0141) 2483801
www.brianmaule.com
French | £40
Cooking score: 4

🍷 V

Brian Maule's city-centre restaurant, near Blythswood Square, has been a beacon of Glasgow gastronomy since 2001. A light, breezy backdrop of russet-coloured panelling, good pictures and exuberant floral adornments makes for relaxed, appreciative dining. Maule's French-influenced modern Scottish cooking is full of highlights. Starter could be as bistro-simple as smoked salmon with a baby leek salad and herbed cream cheese, or as thought-provoking as the trio of duck (cured fillet, confit terrine and foie gras with a scattering of pistachios). Whatever the level of intricacy, the tendency to make

strange bedfellows of ingredients is resisted, so main-course lamb comes with Jerusalem artichokes and wild mushroom persillade, while grilled bream appears in recognisably provençale guise, with braised fennel, courgette and tomato. Desserts are unabashedly classical: crème brûlée, tarte Tatin, creamed rice pudding with prunes and brandy. Cheeses come from either Scotland or France. Clear thinking is also brought to the wine list, which is ordered by style and finds room for plenty of inspiring flavours from authoritative names. Prices from £19.
Chef/s: Brian Maule. **Open:** Mon to Sat L 12 to 2.30 , D 6 to 10. **Closed:** Sun, 25 and 26 Dec, 1 and 2 Jan, bank hols. **Meals:** alc (main courses £26 to £28). Set L and D £19 (2 courses) to £22. **Details:** 140 seats.

Cail Bruich

Swanky brasserie aiming high
725 Great Western Road, Glasgow, G12 8QX
Tel no: (0141) 3346265
www.cailbruich.co.uk
Modern British | £38
Cooking score: 3
£5 OFF

Swanky Cail Bruich's arty photographs, smart red banquettes, worn floorboards and dim lighting chime perfectly with the upmarket boho vibe of Glasgow's West End. The food is suitably on-trend too. Chef/proprietor Chris Charalambous makes much about sourcing and provenance, embellishing his menus with hand-dived Tarbert scallops, Glenapp Estate partridge, Highland venison and other seasonal pleasures. The result is a roster of ambitious, Anglo-European combos with complex nuances – although some readers have reported occasional 'nondescript' flavours. Expect plenty of tricksy bells and whistles in dishes such as Loch Duart salmon with crab cannelloni, cucumber, burnt apple and rye crumb, or roast pheasant breast with spelt grain, smoked celeriac, chestnut and truffle sauce – plus some sparky ideas in the dessert department (chocolate and caramel tart

with blackberry sorbet and malt crumble, say). Service is 'second to none', even when the place is packed to the rafters. Wines from £18.
Chef/s: Chris Charalambous. **Open:** Tue to Sun L 12 to 2.15 (12.30 to 3.30 Sun), D 5.30 to 9.30 (5.30 to 7.30 Sun). **Closed:** Mon, 25 and 26 Dec, 1 and 2 Jan. **Meals:** alc (main courses £18 to 24). Set L £15 (2 courses) to £18. Set D £17 (2 courses) to £20. Sun L £17 (2 courses) to £20. **Details:** 48 seats. Music.

Central Market

Cool, all-purpose eatery
51 Bell Street, Glasgow, G1 1PA
Tel no: (0141) 5520902
www.centralmarketglasgow.com
Modern British | £30
Cooking score: 2
£5 OFF

Coffee shop, deli, oyster bar, slick metropolitan bistro – Central Market aims to be all things to all people, and manages to keep everyone happy. The interior might be described as 'urban cool', with slate floors, grey steel pillars, functional furniture and an open kitchen, while the menu sends out all the right signals for on-trend global flavours and ideas. There are eggs, waffles and pastries for breakfast, and the all-day line-up is big on deli-style sandwiches (pastrami with Gruyère and coleslaw, say). Otherwise, the choice runs from appetisers such as crispy beef brisket with sriracha chilli mayo, mushroom kim-chee and gem lettuce, to braised neck of lamb with apricots, Israeli couscous and rocket pesto. Burgers, Ibérica pluma steaks and spatchcock chicken receive the char-grill treatment, while fancy-pants desserts might include chocolate salame with toasted hazelnuts and mascarpone. Enterprising wines from £14.95.
Chef/s: Neil Palmer and Andrew Lambert. **Open:** all week 11am to 10pm (8pm Sun). **Closed:** 25 Dec, 1 Jan. **Meals:** alc (main courses £11 to £15). Set D £16 (2 courses). **Details:** 50 seats. 10 seats outside. Wheelchair access. Music.

NEW ENTRY
Crabshakk

Fish, fish and more fish
1114 Argyle Street, Glasgow, G3 8TD
Tel no: (0141) 3346127
www.crabshakk.com
Seafood | £44
Cooking score: 3

With a small interior that's been cleverly designed to maximise space over ground- and first-floor dining areas, and a menu that is 'fish, fish and more fish' – anything from Champagne and oysters to plain fish and chips – this West End seafooder exudes confidence. Tables are squeezed in everywhere and 'there is a very intimate feel', but this all adds to the charm. For one reporter, 'zingy, fresh' razor and surf clams topped with finely diced chorizo in a butter sauce was his star dish, though there was strong competition from two plump fillets of perfectly cooked John Dory served atop a delicate celeriac purée with Puy lentils, braised bacon and some wilted spinach leaves. 'Full of flavour' moules marinière might kick things off, while a 'perfectly wobbly' vanilla pannacotta, served with a wedge of spice-roasted pear, made a 'fitting end to a well-executed meal'. Wines from £19.50.
Chef/s: David Scott. **Open:** Tue to Sat 11 to midnight, Sun 12 to 12. **Closed:** Mon. **Meals:** alc (main courses £10 to £44). **Details:** 53 seats. Separate bar. Wheelchair access. Music.

Gamba

Glasgow seafood stalwart
225a West George Street, Glasgow, G2 2ND
Tel no: (0141) 5720899
www.gamba.co.uk
Seafood | £44
Cooking score: 3
£5
OFF

Derek Marshall has been peddling his wares to fish-loving Glaswegians since 1998, and his flatteringly lit, soft-toned basement now ranks as something of a local institution. Given that 'gamba' is Spanish for 'prawn',

there's no concealing the menu's allegiances – so expect lots of eclectic influences, exotic flavours and hints of luxury, with prices to match. Marshall's take on fish soup is a legendary broth loaded with crabmeat, ginger and prawn dumplings (naturally), but his kitchen also shows its class with plates of Loch Duart salmon tartare, sea bass Caesar salad or red mullet with honey mustard sauce and chanterelles. Away from the sea, you might find Scotch beef fillet with peppered wild mushrooms, or sweet potato, lentil and coriander cakes with creamed spinach and pine kernels. Desserts could promise chocolate tart with honeycomb ice cream or cinnamon-poached pears with crème fraîche. Corney & Barrow house wines from £21.
Chef/s: Derek Marshall. **Open:** Mon to Sat L 12 to 2.15, all week D 5 to 10 (9 Sun). **Closed:** 25 and 26 Dec, 1 to 8 Jan. **Meals:** alc (main courses £11 to £32). Set L £18 (2 courses) to £21. Set D £18 (2 courses) to £25. **Details:** 65 seats. Separate bar.

Stravaigin

Global food from prime Scottish ingredients
28 Gibson Street, Glasgow, G12 8NX
Tel no: (0141) 3342665
www.stravaigin.com
Modern European | £26
Cooking score: 2
£30
▼

Covering two floors on Gibson Street, Stravaigin strives to 'think global, eat local', which amounts to cracking seasonal Scottish ingredients and a 'world is your oyster' policy when it comes to culinary inspiration. There's a buzzy café-bar and a restaurant with décor that defies easy classification – modern art, quirky bits and pieces. Everything, from the brunch menu to cool cocktails, impresses with its attention to detail. If haggis seems a little obvious, it's nevertheless a good 'un (with mashed neeps and champit tatties, and an optional whisky sauce), while pan-fried baby squid with Kalamata olives recalls Mediterranean climes. Sea bream is pan-seared and served with lemon-roast fennel and dilled labneh, and there's an oriental flavour to braised pork belly with sticky rice cakes and an apple and ginger relish. Finish with a whizzo dessert such as hibiscus soup with white peach sorbet and white chocolate mousse. Wines from £17.25.

Chef/s: Kenny Mackay. **Open:** all week 9am to 11pm (11am Sat and Sun). **Closed:** 25 Dec, 1 Jan. **Meals:** alc (main courses £9 to £19). Set L £14 (2 courses) to £16. **Details:** 130 seats. 25 seats outside. Separate bar. Wheelchair access. Music.

Ubiquitous Chip

Glasgow icon
12 Ashton Lane, Glasgow, G12 8SJ
Tel no: (0141) 3345007
www.ubiquitouschip.co.uk
Modern British | £36
Cooking score: 4

♦ V

You have to hand it to the team at this gastronomic veteran. Four decades down the line the sprawling, buzzy, versatile space is still charming visitors, who find it 'very enjoyable', and 'all in all one of my favourite places'. Head to the Courtyard Restaurant for a broadly contemporary menu that delivers 'delicious' creamed langoustine bisque with brown shrimp dauphine and shellfish oil; 'a very good' guinea fowl breast with a ballotine of the leg, mustard barley, poached celery and tarragon gravy; or a well-reported monkfish and slow-braised ox cheek. A flexible, well-priced brasserie menu is served all day in the various bars, mezzanine and roof terrace: perhaps a charcuterie sharing platter, venison haggis with neeps 'n' tatties, steamed mussels or confit duck leg. The substantial wine list is a veritable encyclopedia of mature clarets and Burgundies, alongside wines plucked from all corners of the world (prices from £18.85).

Chef/s: Andrew Mitchell. **Open:** all week 11 to 11. **Closed:** 25 Dec, 1 Jan. **Meals:** alc (main courses £16 to £35). Set L and early D £16 (2 courses) to £20. Sun L £20. **Details:** 100 seats. Separate bar. Wheelchair access. Music.

LOCAL GEM
▲ Number 16

16 Byres Road, Glasgow, G11 5JY
Tel no: (0141) 3392544
www.number16.co.uk
Modern British | £28 £5 OFF

The neighbourhood is very well served by the presence of this feisty little two-floor bistro, with urban décor and a menu packed with creative little numbers. The kitchen's output runs to interesting combinations such as a starter of pan-fried mackerel with beetroot gazpacho and horseradish granita. Inspiration is drawn from far and wide: Gressingham duck with aromatic sauerkraut, braised pork belly with a Shaoxing broth and, for dessert, moist sweet potato and almond cake. Wines from £15.95. Open all week.

▌ Isle of Colonsay

LOCAL GEM
▲ The Colonsay

Scalasaig, Isle of Colonsay, PA61 7YT
Tel no: (01951) 200316
www.colonsayestate.co.uk
Modern British | £30

Set in splendid isolation between Jura and Mull, the island of Colonsay has rugged charm and offers terrific hospitality at its only hotel. The whitewashed inn first opened in 1750 and continues to serve the community in its lively bar and restaurant. There's a real Scottish flavour to the straightforward culinary output, which uses produce from the kitchen garden and runs from ham hock terrine with celeriac rémoulade through to scallops with black pudding, and rhubarb fool for dessert. Wines start at £13.50. Closed Nov to Feb.

Isle of Mull

Café Fish
Fantastic no-frills seafood
The Pier, Main Street, Tobermory, Isle of Mull, PA75 6NU
Tel no: (01688) 301253
www.thecafefish.com
Seafood | £30
Cooking score: 3

Occupying the upper floor of the old CalMac ferry ticket office, and overlooking Tobermory harbour, Jane McDonald and Liz McCougan's small, no-nonsense restaurant celebrates 10 years in 2015. Its raison d'être is to provide the freshest of fresh fish and crustaceans, delivered daily and cooked with simplicity and skill. There's usually a meat dish or two as a concession to those dragged along by fish-eating friends (roast chicken or locally reared ribeye steak), but the menu focuses firmly on the likes of oysters, creel-caught squat lobster, mussels, and gloriously unadorned main courses such as whole lobster served with hot garlic butter, or a roast shellfish platter. Those seeking greater complexity might prefer peat-smoked haddock, rolled and stuffed with squat lobster and baked in cream. Everyone finishes with something like a Tobermory whisky-laced chocolate pot. Wines start at £16.
Chef/s: Liz McGougan. **Open:** all week L 11 to 3, D 5.30 to 10. **Meals:** alc (main courses £12 to £30). **Details:** 34 seats. 50 seats outside.

NEW ENTRY
Ninth Wave
A unique and fabulous place
Bruach Mhor, Fionnphort, Isle of Mull, PA66 6BL
Tel no: (01681) 700757
www.ninthwaverestaurant.co.uk
Modern British | £44
Cooking score: 4

'You can literally feel the skill and love that converts ingredients into dishes.' So concluded a contented visitor to this stunningly located, lovingly renovated 200-year-old crofter's bothy at the end of a 37-mile single-track road. Menus are dictated by the availability of ingredients, which can be a lottery when you use only seasonal, local or wild produce. Here, however, John and Carla Lamont have the advantage of their own seven-acre croft and kitchen garden, excellent local meat and game, John's daily haul of creel-caught seafood and the fact that Carla is a busy and accomplished cook. Reporters have praised everything from the homemade bread, garden pea and sea lettuce soup with smoked haddock and seaweed croûtons, the soufflé-style crab cheesecake, and lobster 'that is beyond compare', to meadowsweet and honey ice cream, the beetroot chocolates served with coffee and the warmth of the service. Wines from £15.95.
Chef/s: Carla Lamont. **Open:** Tue to Sun D only 7 to 11. **Closed:** Mon, Nov to Easter. **Meals:** Set D £44 to £52 (4 courses). **Details:** 18 seats. Wheelchair access. Car parking. Children over 12 yrs only.

Kilberry

The Kilberry Inn
Dream destination with superlative seafood
Kilberry Road, Kilberry, PA29 6YD
Tel no: (01880) 770223
www.kilberryinn.com
Modern British | £30
Cooking score: 3
£5 OFF

Located on the Argyll coast, the Kilberry Inn is a stone cottage with a distinctive red-tin roof. It's a haven of tranquillity, reached via a 15-mile single-track road; views out over the islands of Islay, Jura and Gigha are spectacular. The atmosphere is warm and homely, with open fires, soft lighting and attentive hosts: David Wilson looks after front-of-house, while Clare Johnson employs her skills in the kitchen. Sourcing local seafood is part of the plan and the no-nonsense menu concentrates on stalwarts of the repertoire, from fish soup or mussels in white wine to Loch Fyne queenie scallops toasted with a Mull Cheddar and herb crust. There might be belly of pork slow-braised in Marsala with orange and cardamom, and served with sweet winter slaw

for those not in the mood for fish, and blackberry frangipane tart to finish. The fairly priced wine list starts at £18.
Chef/s: Clare Johnson. **Open:** Wed to Sun L 12 to 2, Tue to Sun D 6.30 to 10. **Closed:** Mon, 1 Jan to mid Mar. **Meals:** alc (main courses £13 to 22). **Details:** 30 seats. 10 seats outside. Wheelchair access. Music. Car parking.

▌Oban

Waterfront Fishouse Restaurant
Minimal frills, super-fresh seafood
1 Railway Pier, Oban, PA34 4LW
Tel no: (01631) 563110
www.waterfrontoban.co.uk
Seafood | £22
Cooking score: 1
£30

With fishing boats right outside the window, there's really no need to ask where the Fishouse gets its supplies. The restaurant occupies the first floor of a former fisherman's mission. There's no interior-design frills, but that's just fine when the food is all about provenance and simplicity. The view across the Sound of Mull is 'just the icing on the cake'. Whole local langoustines are a treat when available, or go for smoked haddock chowder. There are oysters, too, plus mains such as grilled Dover sole and grilled sea bass. Wines from £15.99.
Chef/s: Alex Needham. **Open:** Sun to Fri L 12 to 2.15, D 5.30 to 9.30. Sat 12 to 9.30. **Closed:** 25 Dec. **Meals:** alc (main courses £12 to £22). Set L and D £12 (2 courses) to £15. **Details:** 80 seats. Separate bar. Music. Car parking.

LOCAL GEM

▲ Ee-Usk
North Pier, Oban, PA34 5QD
Tel no: (01631) 565666
www.eeusk.com
Seafood | £32

Set at the end of Oban's pier, this purpose-built restaurant makes the most of sea views and, naturally, gives seafood top billing. The

daily haul generally yields Loch Creran oysters, salmon from the local smokehouse and locally caught prawns (aka langoustines), served hot or cold. Also expect seafood platters, scallops with mornay sauce and dishes like oven-baked halibut with creamed leeks. Ribeye steak with pepper sauce satisfies meat-eaters, and to finish there's sticky toffee pudding. Wines from £16.50. Open all week.

▌Troon

MacCallums Oyster Bar
No fancy posturing, just prime seafood
The Harbour, Troon, KA10 6DH
Tel no: (01292) 319339
Seafood | £27
Cooking score: 1
£30

Down by Troon harbour, where the fishing boats tie up, this appealingly informal seafood restaurant is housed in an old pumping station. The freshest of fresh fish and crustaceans are delivered here daily and cooked with simplicity and skill. Beef and ale pie usually accounts for the meat dish, but the menu focuses firmly on the likes of oysters, whole grilled langoustine or steamed mussels, and mains such as char-grilled lemon- and garlic-marinated monkfish with aromatic rice or 'perfect as one would expect' fish and chips – also available from the Wee Hurrie, the owners' popular chip shop next door. Wine from £15.95.
Chef/s: Michael Tracey. **Open:** Tue to Sun L 12 to 2.30, Tue to Sat D 6.30 to 9.30. **Closed:** Mon, 3 weeks from 25 Dec. **Meals:** alc (main courses £13 to £20). Set L £11 (2 courses). **Details:** 43 seats. Music. Car parking.

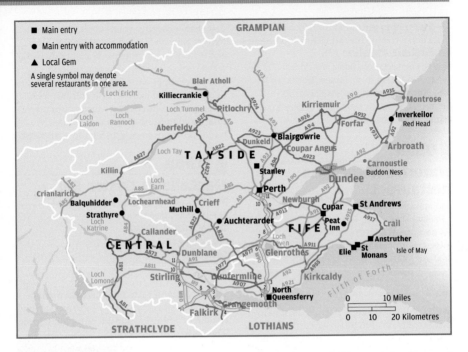

Balquhidder

Monachyle Mhor

Family enterprise with a foodie heart
Balquhidder, FK19 8PQ
Tel no: (01877) 384622
www.mhor.net
Modern British | £55
Cooking score: 5

🍷 ⌷ V

The Lewis family's Mhor portfolio now includes a fish restaurant and bakery in Callander as well as a roadside motel, but this pink-washed farmhouse hotel in the Trossachs is the heartbeat of their foodie enterprise. Tom Lewis and co rear their own livestock, maintain a smallholding, shoot game and undertake all kinds of home production to support their culinary endeavours. The result is food that sings with clean, natural flavours and sharp contrasts: crispy pork belly from their own pigs is simply embellished with a quail's egg and pea shoots; Monachyle venison carpaccio comes with Puy lentils and white truffle dressing; and Blairgowrie beef is served with garden potatoes, pearl onions and kohlrabi tops. Fish from the Scottish ports also has its say, and the seasons shine through in desserts such as pear and spiced pumpkin soufflé with roast quince and ginger custard. Pithy quotes add spice to the highly personal wine list, which mixes blue-chip vintages with unusual varietals and assorted 'oddballs'. Bottles from £22.
Chef/s: Tom Lewis and Marysia Paszkowska. **Open:** all week L 12 to 2, D 7 to 9. **Closed:** 5 to 24 Jan. **Meals:** alc (main courses £18 to £26). Set L £24 (2 courses) to £30. Set D £40 (2 courses) to £55. Sun L £34. **Details:** 34 seats. 10 seats outside. Separate bar. Wheelchair access. Music. Car parking.

🍴 Average Price

The average price listed in main-entry reviews denotes the price of a three-course meal, without wine.

Strathyre

Creagan House

Delightful farmhouse with standout food
Strathyre, FK18 8ND
Tel no: (01877) 384638
www.creaganhouse.co.uk
Modern European | £35
Cooking score: 4

£5 OFF 🚗

The best way to appreciate the pleasures of Gordon and Cherry Gunn's lovingly maintained 17th-century farmhouse is to stay a while – to enjoy the 'wonderful breakfasts' and local sights (including Loch Lomond and the Rob Roy trail). Cherry oversees the lavishly appointed, high-baronial dining room with charm and professionalism, while Gordon keeps things fresh in the kitchen, absorbing influences from afar for a short daily menu. Spanish-style slow-braised pork cheek in Pedro Ximénez sherry might open proceedings, ahead of Perthshire lamb cutlets with a Kiev-style burger, kidney and mustard sauce or 'gorgeous' turbot fillet en papillote on Moroccan couscous, served with vegetables from Creagan's garden. Scottish cheeses are given serious attention, while traditional desserts such as chocolate and hazelnut délice generally come with a twist – although fresh strawberries with homemade ice cream is hard to trump. The substantial wine list (from £18.65) includes plenty by the glass or carafe. **Chef/s:** Gordon Gunn. **Open:** Fri to Tue D only 7.15 for 8 (1 sitting). **Closed:** Wed, Thur, 1 Jan to 26 Mar, 28 Oct to 31 Dec. **Meals:** Set D £35. **Details:** 14 seats. Separate bar. Wheelchair access. Car parking. Children over 10 yrs only.

🍴 SAY WHAT?

Waiters confirm that many customers are reluctant to order something they can't pronounce – and also that there's a limit to how much the staff really care. But if you flail between having a go at the native pronunciation or just ordering the soup instead, it helps to have things spelt out.

Chorizo (chore-reeth-oh): if you want to upset a purist, saying chorizo wrong is a good start. And given how much it's used, 'Spanish pork sausage spiked with garlic and smoked paprika' is not a practical alternative.

Escabeche (esk-a-besh): pickling and sousing are all the rage, and some chefs are turning to the Spanish way of applying vinegar-based marinades to cooked fish.

Kara-age (ka-ra-ah-ge): done right, this Japanese fried chicken is crisp, tender and addictive.

Prosciutto (pro-shoot-oh): Crudo is cured and raw, cotto is cooked, and it's all delicious. If you still find it a mouthful, wait until you spot some speck.

▌Anstruther

NEW ENTRY
The Cellar
Fresh flavours and technical precision
Anstruther, KY10 3AA
Tel no: (01333) 310378
www.thecellaranstruther.co.uk
Modern British | £42
Cooking score: 6

Billy Boyter's arrival here in early 2014 marked a new beginning for the Cellar, a renowned seafood restaurant run by the late Peter Jukes for over 30 years. An instantly loveable, low-beamed space brightened by candles and wood-burning stoves, it has fallen into good hands. Boyter's experience at two top Edinburgh restaurants (Restaurant Martin Wishart and Number One, see entries) has forged a distinctive cooking style that takes wonderful local ingredients and makes their flavours sing. Scottish crab with rapeseed mayonnaise, Thai basil and heirloom tomatoes is a case in point, but nowhere does Boyter's technical precision shine brighter than in a main of brill with truffle and pea macaroni, fat mussels and wild garlic. Extras, notably a crunchy-runny black pudding Scotch egg, are faultless, while vanilla pannacotta with coconut and Malibu tapioca and mango sorbet makes a fresh, interesting finale. A modest wine list opens at £16, with excellent local craft beers an alternative.
Chef/s: Billy Boyter. **Open:** Thur to Sun L 12.30 to 1.45, Wed to Sun D 6.30 to 9. **Closed:** Mon, Tue.
Meals: Set L £24 (3 courses). Set D £42 (3 courses).
Details: 25 seats. Separate bar. Wheelchair access. Music.

Symbols

🛏 Accommodation is available

£30 Three courses for less than £30

V Separate vegetarian menu

£5 £5-off voucher scheme

🍷 Notable wine list

LOCAL GEM
▲ Anstruther Fish Bar
42-44 Shore Street, Anstruther, KY10 3AQ
Tel no: (01333) 310518
www.anstrutherfishbar.co.uk
Seafood | £12 £5

So close to Anstruther's charming harbour that you can watch the boats coming and going while you eat, this family-run fish bar is a local institution. There's a traditional chippy feel to the place: from its brass rails and Formica tables, right down to the friendly, if inconsistent, waitress service in the restaurant area. Golden-crumbed Scottish lemon sole or crisp battered local haddock can be followed by one of 50 homemade ice creams. Wines from £9. Open all week.

▌Cupar
Ostlers Close
Characterful cooking from a local hero
25 Bonnygate, Cupar, KY15 4BU
Tel no: (01334) 655574
www.ostlersclose.co.uk
Modern British | £43
Cooking score: 5

Cupar in the Howe of Fife has proved a hospitable billet for Jimmy and Amanda Graham since 1981. The Close is an amalgam of Stuart-era private houses that once served time as the scullery of a temperance hotel. (Don't worry, there's a wine list now.) Jimmy grows much of his own produce, extending the seasons' bounty of vegetables, saladings and soft fruits, and he occasionally forages for wild mushrooms. These might appear in a starter of seared Mull scallops with saffron risotto and winter chanterelles. To follow, a bouquet of roasted root veg and red cabbage could adorn a plate of roast roe deer, its game-stock reduction scented with juniper. Fish might be turbot fillet with asparagus and bouillabaisse, and the dessert a modernising take on tarte Tatin, the caramelised top echoed in salted-caramel ice cream and a sauce of PX caramel. A broadly based wine list opens with house Chileans at £18.50.

Chef/s: Jimmy Graham. **Open:** Tue to Sat D only 7 to 9.30. **Closed:** Sun, Mon, 25 and 26 Dec, 1 and 2 Jan. **Meals:** alc (main courses £22 to £26). **Details:** 28 seats.

Elie
Sangster's
Appealing Fife fixture
51 High Street, Elie, KY9 1BZ
Tel no: (01333) 331001
www.sangsters.co.uk
Modern British | £40
Cooking score: 4

An intimate, appealing fixture of Fife since 2003, Bruce and Jacqueline Sangster's personable town house remains a good friend to its many regulars. The homely interior hints at cosmopolitan chic and Bruce's cooking generally rises to the occasion. His ever-popular twice-baked cheese soufflé made with Tobermory Cheddar, and his 'full-flavoured' Ibérico pig's cheek with Ayrshire pork fillet, crushed winter roots, glazed apple and red wine sauce have both been received with pleasure. There's precision and satisfaction in the fish department too – witness halibut fillet on 'nutty' cabbage with dauphinoise potatoes, or herb-crusted hake surrounded by a vivid Mediterranean mélange of braised butter beans, peppers, courgettes, chorizo and basil pesto. To finish, fragrant strawberry parfait is recommended, although you might also find lemon and sour cream mousse with saffron-poached pear and lemon-curd ice cream. Service is charming, and the knowledgeably chosen, global wine list is stuffed with commendable bottles from £21.50.

Chef/s: Bruce Sangster. **Open:** Sun L 12.30 to 1.30, Tue to Sat D 7 to 8.30. **Closed:** Mon. **Meals:** Set D £33 (2 courses) to £40. Sun L £28. **Details:** 28 seats. Children over 12 yrs only.

North Queensferry
The Wee Restaurant
A diamond under the Forth Rail Bridge
17 Main Street, North Queensferry, KY11 1JG
Tel no: (01383) 616263
www.theweerestaurant.co.uk
Modern European | £34
Cooking score: 3
£5 OFF

Craig and Vikki Wood's 100-year-old building 'almost' underneath the Forth Rail Bridge is an unassuming little gem, a simply stylish space with polished wood tables and food that shows some real star quality. There's a rustic integrity to Craig Wood's output with much input from seasonal Scottish ingredients. Intense, precise flavours come through strongly, perhaps in a disarmingly simple black pudding and duck egg salad with celeriac rémoulade and micro greens, or a splendid smoked wood pigeon 'cassoulet' with Toulouse sausage, Puy lentils and herb gnocchi. Seafood is a strength: mussels with bacon, basil, pine nuts and Parmesan cream continues to delight reporters, or there could be sea bass with Thai broth, udon noodles, baby shrimps and oriental vegetables. Desserts are equally assured, particularly the bread-and-butter pudding with sultanas and vanilla ice cream. Service ensures that a happy mood prevails, and prices are 'very reasonable'. Wine from £16.75.

Chef/s: Craig Wood. **Open:** Tue to Sun L 12 to 2, D 6.30 to 9. **Closed:** Mon. **Meals:** Set L £17 (2 courses) to £20. Set D £27 (2 courses) to £34. **Details:** 36 seats. Music.

Peat Inn

★ TOP 50 ★

The Peat Inn
Blue-chip gourmet destination
Peat Inn, KY15 5LH
Tel no: (01334) 840206
www.thepeatinn.co.uk
Modern European | £55
Cooking score: 7

🍶 ⊏ V

'An exquisite all-round performance', proclaimed one reader after visiting this blue-chip 18th-century inn: a premier-league gourmet destination run with confidence and panache by Geoffrey and Katherine Smeddle. Muted colours, fresh flowers, tweed fabrics and other homely touches soften the mood in the three intimate, interlinked dining rooms, where guests are treated to a procession of precisely honed gastronomic delights. Geoffrey's cooking yields a 'plethora of tastes and textures', underpinned by his acute knowledge of the seasons and their bounty: witness braised veal cheek and crisp sweetbreads with roast cauliflower, young turnip and hazelnut dressing or loin of Cairngorm roe deer with Hispi cabbage, quince and a venison haggis. To begin, a warm salad of quail with roast pepper purée, couscous and black olive dressing had one reporter reaching for the superlatives: likewise a stunningly constructed dish of slow-braised veal shank with creamed onions, roast courgettes, confit tomatoes and pancetta dressing. After that, a trolley of Scottish farmhouse cheeses awaits, although the exotic prospect of mango meringue tart with passion fruit sorbet and candied chilli or coconut mousse with pineapple sorbet and lemongrass syrup is hard to resist. Capable, expertly trained staff show 'highly impressive' knowledge when recommending wines from the astutely assembled list – a global compendium led by French aristocrats from Bordeaux and Burgundy. Prices start at £19, with a laudable choice of half-bottles too.

Chef/s: Geoffrey Smeddle. Open: Tue to Sat L 12.30 to 1.30, D 7 to 9. Closed: Sun, Mon, 24 to 26 Dec, 1 to 9 Jan. Meals: alc (main courses £15 to £26). Set L £19. Set D £45. Tasting menu £65 (6 courses). Details: 40 seats. Wheelchair access. Car parking.

St Andrews
The Seafood Restaurant
Sustainable seafood in a spectacular setting
The Scores, Bruce Embankment, St Andrews, KY16 9AB
Tel no: (01334) 479475
www.theseafoodrestaurant.com
Seafood | £35
Cooking score: 3

At first glance, this dramatic glass cube overlooking St Andrews' seafront may remind you of a certain high-jeopardy TV game show, but inside it tells a less risky story. Views across rock pools and golf courses add a thrill to proceedings, though the restaurant itself is a curious mix of formal posturing and garrulous activity. To one side are rows of heavily clothed tables; to the other, a buzzy, counter-height open kitchen at full tilt. Such refreshing modernity chimes perfectly with a menu that majors in sustainable seafood, although the kitchen can also turn its hand to other stuff. Expect West Coast oysters, home-cured salmon and capably executed, mainstream ideas such as seared scallops with cauliflower purée or fillet of hake with braised fennel and orange. Otherwise, consider a Scottish steak or, perhaps, asparagus, pea and mint risotto. The wine list has depth without being overstuffed, and prices (from £14) are commendable.

Chef/s: Colin Fleming. Open: all week L 12 to 2.30 (12.30 to 3 Sun), Mon to Sat D 6 to 10. Closed: 25 and 26 Dec, 1 Jan. Meals: alc (main courses £13 to £28). Details: 50 seats. 20 seats outside. Wheelchair access. Car parking.

St Monans

Craig Millar @ 16 West End

Dazzling seafood, spectacular views
16 West End, St Monans, KY10 2BX
Tel no: (01333) 730327
www.16westend.com
Modern British | £42
Cooking score: 5

£5
OFF

Things get a bit hairy when there's a storm in the offing, but it all adds to the excitement, for Craig Millar's restaurant sits right by the harbour with views over the mouth of the Firth of Forth to the distant Isle of May. The former fisherman's cottage has kept its rugged charms while bringing in enough creature comforts to satisfy 21st-century sybarites. The eponymous Mr Millar is an exponent of refined and dazzlingly contemporary cooking that delivers pretty plates of full-flavoured food. There's a tasting menu (with optional wine flight) and a short, punchy carte that sees pea mousse with pickled shallots and focaccia precede stone bass with spiced Israeli couscous and satay sauce. Seafood is a particular passion, but there are fine meat dishes too (suprême of guinea fowl with Puy lentils), and winning desserts such as mulled bramble parfait. The excellent, French-focused wine list starts at £22.

Chef/s: Craig Millar. **Open:** Wed to Sun L 12.30 to 2, D 6.30 to 9. **Closed:** Mon, Tue, 25 and 26 Dec, 1 and 2 Jan. **Meals:** Set L £22 (2 courses) to £26. Tasting menu £60. **Details:** 44 seats. 32 seats outside. Separate bar. Wheelchair access. Car parking. Children over 12 yrs only at D.

THE FLEXITARIAN OPTION

The consensus that too much meat does no-one any favours has coincided with a creative phase among veg-loving chefs. Getting your flexitarian fix is now as easy as pearl barley pie.

The menu at Bruno Loubet's Grain Store gives vegetables equal billing alongside meat and fish, which is often used as a garnish. Herb and aubergine salad with pea and broad bean ragout, piquillo pepper purée, lamb confit and pine needle salt is a dish in point.

Shove up and prepare to eat falafel at Honey & Co, the little Middle Eastern café that offers plenty of zingy meat-free fritters, salads and hot assemblies like cauliflower shawarma with tahini, caramelized onion and crispy pitta.

At Gauthier Soho, Alexis Gauthier's vegetable tasting menus are inventive, and those who are flexing for health will note there are calorie counts, too.

Ollie Dabbous might be big on ribs at his second restaurant, Barnyard, but the vegetable is king at the original, where avocado, basil and almonds in a chilled osmanthus broth is one of the draws.

Auchterarder

★ TOP 50 ★

Andrew Fairlie at Gleneagles
Awe-inspiring, luxurious French cuisine
Auchterarder, PH3 1NF
Tel no: (01764) 694267
www.andrewfairlie.co.uk
Modern French | £95
Cooking score: 8

V

Gleneagles is a spectacular high-gloss hotel, set deep in acres of sprawling golf course (one of the world's most famous) interspersed with beautiful parkland. At its heart is Andrew Fairlie's 'otherworld built for pleasure'. Here are fantasy chandeliers, black walls (on which glowing, gold-framed paintings seem to hover against the darkness) and perfect staff appearing and disappearing as if by magic. But it's the cooking that draws gasps of delight – ethereal yet grounded, inventive yet access-ible, subtle yet strong. Perfect canapés set the stage: a light-as-air gougère with a warm Gruyère filling; radishes filled with butter and smoked salt; and a potato cracker topped with salmon and scallop tartare. The smoked lobster is a classic Fairlie starter, but there are other delights: the pea and crowdie ziti gratin with Parmesan and truffle thrilled with its 'tightly packed flavours and unctuous juices'. The simplest-sounding descriptions conceal surprises: 'sea trout fillet, sea vegetables, roast langoustines' includes a ravioli made from celeriac and kohlrabi. Flavours and textures are arrayed with pinpoint accuracy as in a riff on banana – fluffy cake, silky ice cream – with salty peanut-butter mousse and peanut sugar tuiles. The wine list favours the better-known regions, and includes a good selection of Champagnes plus plenty by the glass. Bottles start at £35.
Chef/s: Andrew Fairlie and Stephen McLaughlin. **Open:** Mon to Sat D only 6.30 to 10. **Closed:** Sun, 3 weeks Jan. **Meals:** alc (main course £46). Set D £95 (6 courses) to £125 (8 courses). **Details:** 52 seats. Wheelchair access. Music. Car parking. Children over 12 yrs only.

Blairgowrie

Kinloch House Hotel
Grand Scottish hospitality
Dunkeld Road, Blairgowrie, PH10 6SG
Tel no: (01250) 884237
www.kinlochhouse.com
Modern British | £53
Cooking score: 5

A grand and hefty property with a creeper-covered façade, Kinloch House has 25 acres of prime Perthshire countryside all to itself. Tradition rules the roost within, with a preponderance of burnished panels, antique furniture, tartan fabrics and portraits of serious folk from times gone by. 'Discreet and polite' service sets the tone. The kitchen – headed by Steve MacCallum – impresses with its refined and regionally focused output, where game is a seasonal treat and the kitchen garden makes a contribution. Arbroath lobster stars in a first course with roast fennel, chicory and a citrus dressing, and there's roast fillet and slow-cooked feather-blade of beef to follow (with a potato fondant and truffled leeks). For afters, iced rhubarb parfait with ginger snaps competes with the comforts of sticky toffee pudding and cheeses from Scotland, England and Ireland. 'The set lunch menu is a bargain.' Wine (from £27.50) leans towards France.
Chef/s: Steve MacCallum. **Open:** all week L 12 to 2, D 7 to 9. **Closed:** 14 to 29 Dec. **Meals:** Set L £20 (2 courses) to £26. Set D £43 (2 courses) to £53. Sun L £30. **Details:** 30 seats. Separate bar. Wheelchair access. Car parking. Children over 5 yrs only at D.

Please send us your feedback
To register your opinion about any restaurant listed in the Guide, or a new restaurant that you wish to bring to our attention, please visit the web address at the bottom of the page. Your feedback informs the content of the book and will be used to compile next year's reviews.

Little's Restaurant

Known for its fresh and varied fish
4 Wellmeadow, Blairgowrie, PH10 6ND
Tel no: (01250) 875358
www.littlesrestaurant.co.uk
Modern British | £35
Cooking score: 2

£5
OFF

'Nice place, prices firm side of good, excellent choice of (predominantly) fish dishes, nice staff . . . all in all an asset for Blairgowrie,' was the endorsement of one regular visitor to this simple restaurant – all white walls and plain sensible furnishings. Chef/proprietor Willie Little 'really knows fish' and while one reporter finds it hard to get past either the 'very fresh' sea trout or halibut if they are on the menu, there were no regrets on trying 'a gamey hare with black pudding and Puy lentils'. Others have praised the baked goats' cheese tart with red onion, roast monkfish with squid and leek risotto and, from a selection of unusual pizzas 'straight from the oven', a chorizo, black pudding, scallop and apple pizza that 'really worked'. To finish, there's banana and carrot cake with banana ice cream. Wines start at £15.95.
Chef/s: William Little. **Open:** Fri and Sat L 12 to 2.30, Tue to Sat D 4 to 9.30 (6 to 9.30 Fri and Sat). **Closed:** Sun, Mon, 25 and 26 Dec, 1 and 2 Jan. **Meals:** alc (main courses £10 to £20). **Details:** 40 seats. Wheelchair access. Music.

▌Inverkeilor

Gordon's

Cooking with vitality and dazzle
Main Street, Inverkeilor, DD11 5RN
Tel no: (01241) 830364
www.gordonsrestaurant.co.uk
Modern British | £55
Cooking score: 5

🛏

Maria and Gordon Watson have run this 18th-century dwelling house as a relaxed restaurant-with-rooms for nigh on three decades, creating an enterprise of great self-

assurance and charm. They enthusiastically celebrate the best of Scotland, from Stornaway black pudding to Loch Duart salmon and the many fine regional cheeses. It all happens in a smart, rustic-chic room where the mood is intimate and personable. Everyone has a good word to say about the service. Son Garry now does the majority of the cooking and vigorously follows modern lines. Quail is boned and teamed with black pudding and Puy lentils, for example, while loin of Highland roe deer comes with mushroom ravioli, nutty cabbage, celeriac purée, Chantenay carrots and Rioja sauce. In addition, there could be 'delicious' Tobermory Cheddar soufflé, roast pepper and vine tomato velouté, and Valrhona chocolate parfait, poached red-blushed pear and chocolate sorbet to finish. Wines from £18.95.
Chef/s: Gordon and Garry Watson. **Open:** Wed to Fri and Sun L 12 to 1.45, Tue to Sun D 7 to 9. **Closed:** Mon, last 3 weeks Jan. **Meals:** Set L £29. Set D £55 (4 courses). **Details:** 24 seats. Music. Car parking. Children over 9 yrs only at D.

▌Killiecrankie

Killiecrankie House

Personally run Victorian retreat
Killiecrankie, PH16 5LG
Tel no: (01796) 473220
www.killiecrankiehotel.co.uk
Modern British | £42
Cooking score: 3

🛏 V

Out in the Perthshire wilds, the appealing white house was built for a minister of the kirk in the early Victorian era, and has been a hotel since the eve of the Second World War. It's in a beautiful spot, not far from the River Garry, with lush, well-tended gardens that can be enjoyed from the dining room. Here, Mark Easton cooks a vigorous, modern Scottish menu that draws inspiration from classical Italian technique. Risottos and pasta dishes buttress the vegetarian and vegan menus; otherwise, choose from the likes of king scallops and black pudding with apple bonbons and pea shoots, followed perhaps by

venison fillet with dauphinois, a wild mushroom and leek tartlet and pink peppercorn cream, or crisp-skinned sea bream with pea and shallot tortellini in sweet chilli sauce. To finish, there may be pear frangipane tart with heather honey ice cream. Wines on a stylistically grouped list start at £20.
Chef/s: Mark Easton. **Open:** all week L 12.30 to 2, D 6.30 to 8.30. **Closed:** 3 Jan to mid Mar. **Meals:** alc (main courses £12 to £18). Set D £42. **Details:** 35 seats. Separate bar. Wheelchair access. Car parking.

▊ Muthill
Barley Bree
Scottish inn with French connections
6 Willoughby Street, Muthill, PH5 2AB
Tel no: (01764) 681451
www.barleybree.com
Anglo-French | £39
Cooking score: 3
£5 OFF ➤ V

The Bouteloups' Perthshire restaurant-with-rooms was built at the beginning of the 19th century by a local joiner, yet looks considerably older. However, its gnarled beams and brick pillars have been thrown into relief by stylish decorative modernisation to stop it appearing at all grim. Fabrice Bouteloup cooks in contemporary French vein, with a similar kind of eclectic resourcefulness used in modern British food. Start with iced goats' curd, beetroot and broad bean salad perfumed with marjoram, or lemon sole with kombu seaweed and rouille, before the organic and locally gleaned main-course meats and fish steam into view. Monkfish tail comes with curried cauliflower and chickpeas, while venison saddle is accompanied by pumpkin purée and kale. Stay off the beaten track at dessert with cardamom pannacotta, honeyed pineapple and coconut ice cream, or exclaim '*Vive la tradition!*' over a wodge of tarte Tatin and vanilla ice cream. A French-led wine list opens at £19.

Chef/s: Fabrice Bouteloup. **Open:** Wed to Sun L 12 to 2 (6 Sun), Wed to Sat D 6.45 to 9. **Closed:** Mon, Tue, 31 Mar to 10 Apr, 7 to 22 Jul, 20 to 23 Oct. **Meals:** alc (main courses £22 to £28). **Details:** 32 seats. 12 seats outside. Music. Car parking.

▊ Perth
Deans @ Let's Eat
City-centre restaurant, modern flavours
77-79 Kinnoull Street, Perth, PH1 5EZ
Tel no: (01738) 643377
www.letseatperth.co.uk
Modern British | £32
Cooking score: 3
£5 OFF

The Deans family celebrates ten years at Deans @ Let's Eat in 2015. From the start they gained plaudits for the family feel, the reasonable prices and the accomplished modern cooking. The short carte is peppered with ideas that attempt to please all palates – a policy that seems to work, as crowds of regulars keep the mood buoyant. Willie Deans, an old hand at the restaurant game, moves with the times, although his style is one of gradual change rather than revolution. Dishes are based on impressive ingredients, from Arbroath smokies via Orkney beef to Ochil venison (served with spring cabbage, toffee apple caramel, turnip and potato mash and pearl barley). Readers relish the food: from beautifully cooked twice-baked Cheddar and cauliflower soufflé with spicy Macsween's haggis, turnip mash, whisky and cream to the warm chocolate fudge cake with red berry ice cream and chocolate sauce. Wines from £18.
Chef/s: William Deans. **Open:** Tue to Sat L 12 to 2, D 6 to 10. **Closed:** Sun, Mon, last 2 weeks Jan. **Meals:** alc (main courses £14 to £24). Set L £13 (2 courses) to £17. Set D £16 (2 courses) to £21. **Details:** 70 seats. Separate bar. Wheelchair access. Music.

Stanley

The Apron Stage

Small is beautiful
5 King Street, Stanley, PH1 4ND
Tel no: (01738) 828888
www.apronstagerestaurant.co.uk
French | £28
Cooking score: 3

£30

Shona Drysdale and Jane Nicoll hit on a winning formula in 2006, with their *hommage* to the French neighbourhood restaurant. They cater for just 18 covers from a tiny kitchen, and do virtually everything themselves, with a little culinary guidance from Tony Heath. There's an indelible streak of Francophilia in menus that come up with spinach and leek soup with herbes de Provence, or warm goats' cheese, pear and walnut salad, to start. Main courses follow suit, bringing guinea fowl breast with black pudding and boulangère potatoes in Calvados jus, or Fraserburgh cod fillet with pea purée, slow-roast cherry tomatoes and red pepper dressing. It's robust, lively bistro cooking with bags of appeal, founded on quality Scottish ingredients such as Angus beef fillet, served with braised oxtail and caramelised shallots. To finish, there could be dark chocolate tart with coffee sauce or perhaps a seasonal trio of rhubarb desserts. House South African is £15.
Chef/s: Shona Drysdale. **Open:** Thur to Sat D only 6.30 to 9.30. **Closed:** Sun to Wed, Jan, 1 week Oct. **Meals:** alc (main courses £15 to £20). **Details:** 18 seats. Wheelchair access. Music. No children.

MARCELLO TULLY
Kinloch Lodge

What do you enjoy about being a chef?
The buzz and atmosphere in my kitchen. Working with the best quality local and natural ingredients.

What food trends are you spotting at the moment?
There's a lean towards healthier and fresher, cleaner flavours.

Do you have a guilty foodie pleasure?
Eating too much cheese at the end of an evening - with lashings of rhubarb jam and a good vintage port.

What's your newest ingredient discovery?
Fennel pollen, it has notes of liquorice, curry and honey. It's very versatile and a little goes a long way.

Is there a dish that evokes strong memories for you?
I serve a fine-dining version of Coxinha - a Brazilian street food I have loved from my childhood. I make it using Orkney smoked Cheddar - it is delicious!

What would you be if you weren't a chef?
A racing driver for Mercedes!

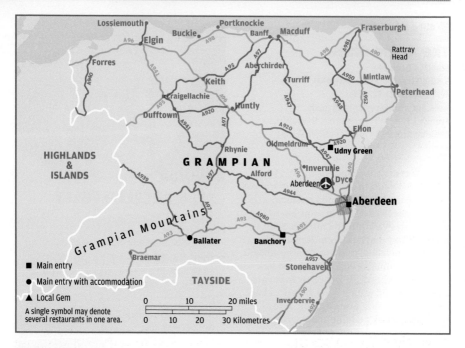

Aberdeen

Silver Darling
Redoubtable seafood veteran
Pocra Quay, North Pier, Aberdeen, AB11 5DQ
Tel no: (01224) 576229
www.thesilverdarling.co.uk
Seafood | £48
Cooking score: 3

Perched atop Aberdeen's old customs house, with floor-to-ceiling windows providing views over the harbour and bay, Didier Dejean's redoubtable seafood veteran is perfect for its location. 'Silver darling' was the old Scots nickname for a herring, although these beauties rarely grace the menu nowadays; instead, expect a plentiful daily haul ranging from squid and oysters to rock turbot and sea bream. Didier's food takes inspiration from his Gallic homeland and there's usually a lot happening on the plate: witness herb-crusted roast cod with cockles, kedgeree 'risotto', wilted spinach and veal jus. Seasonal game specials such as roast partridge with cep

spätzle, watercress velouté and soft-boiled quail's egg should satisfy meat eaters. To conclude, classic tarte Tatin and crème brûlée share the billing with exotica such as mango and passion fruit cheesecake with chocolate sorbet. Wines from £19.50.
Chef/s: Didier Dejean. **Open:** Mon to Fri L 12 to 1.45, Mon to Sat D 6.30 to 9.30. **Closed:** Sun. **Meals:** alc (main courses £16 to £26). Set L £20 (2 courses) to £24. **Details:** 50 seats. Music. No children after 8.

Ballater

Darroch Learg
Bastion of Scottish hospitality
56 Braemar Road, Ballater, AB35 5UX
Tel no: (013397) 55443
www.darrochlearg.co.uk
Modern British | £45
Cooking score: 5

The name means 'the oak wood on the sunny hillside', with the former very much in evidence, but the latter entirely in the lap of

the gods. The house was built in Victorian times in a prime spot with glorious views. It has been in the Franks family for half a century, and Nigel and Fiona Franks run the place with seasoned charm and professionalism. This is the sort of country-house hotel where it feels like you're staying with (posh) friends. The restaurant, with distant views during daylight hours, is the setting for modern Scottish food of style and invention. There's a local flavour and classical refinement to wood pigeon, foie gras and shallot pie (served with fig jam), and main-course roast monkfish with pomme purée and chorizo. A tasting menu is offered, too, plus desserts like classic lemon tart. The wine list has vintage charts and a global reach; prices from £22.
Chef/s: John Jeremiah. **Open:** Sun L 12.30 to 2, all week D 7 to 9. **Closed:** 1 week Christmas, last 3 weeks Jan. **Meals:** Set D £45. Sun L £28. **Details:** 48 seats. Wheelchair access. Car parking.

Banchory

Cow Shed Restaurant
Robustly seasonal, sharply contemporary
Raemoir Road, Banchory, AB31 5QB
Tel no: (01330) 820813
www.cowshedrestaurant.co.uk
Modern British | £30
Cooking score: 2
£5 OFF

This long, lofty building may have cowshed proportions, but any rustic aesthetics are left at the door. Beneath the high ceiling are chrome chairs set around modern wood tables, a vast glass-walled wine cellar and a sparkling kitchen on full view through an automatic glass door. In this metropolitan-cum-farmyard setting, yawning windows look out over lush, undulating fields, and the menu offers hearty, juicy steaks served with 'superbly crunchy' French fries. There's much more besides: from a faultless, paprika-spiked prawn cocktail to a tender chicken breast with a punchy peppercorn sauce, a rustic chunk of pancetta and sides of new potatoes and precisely cooked seasonal vegetables. This is gutsy, deceptively simple cooking with

rounded flavours and carefully chosen ingredients. Proportions are generous – especially at dessert, when a smooth, crisp-topped crème brûlée could easily feed two. Wines start at just £14 a bottle.
Chef/s: Neil Hudson. **Open:** Sat and Sun L 12 to 3, Wed to Sat D 6 to 9.30. **Closed:** Mon, Tue. **Meals:** alc (main courses £15 to £20). Set L £12 to £16. Set D £16 to £20. **Details:** 70 seats. 40 seats outside. Wheelchair access. Music. Car parking.

Udny Green

Eat on the Green
Convivial village restaurant
Udny Green, AB41 7RS
Tel no: (01651) 842337
www.eatonthegreen.co.uk
Modern European | £40
Cooking score: 2

Nicknamed 'the kilted chef' following his TV appearances, Craig Wilson is the driving force behind this likeable village restaurant housed in Udny Green's old stone post office. Inside all is warm and convivial in a thoroughly Scottish way, with candles illuminating the lounge and handsome tartan carpets throughout the dining room – although a chef's table signifies serious culinary intent. The menu contains plenty of sound ideas, with native ingredients given a proper showing in dishes such as char-grilled Aberdeen Angus beef fillet with slow-braised blade, carrot and cardamom purée, duck-fat chips and port jus. But the kitchen doesn't like to be tethered, so expect flashes of faraway inspiration such as lime, coconut and chilli-marinated salmon with ginger, apple and pak choi salad; or courgette, red onion and feta strudel with roasted sweet potato. To finish, try the dark chocolate and salted-caramel parfait with orange segments and blueberries.
Chef/s: Craig Wilson. **Open:** Wed to Fri and Sun L 12 to 2, Wed to Sun D 6.30 to 8.30 (9 Fri, 5.30 to 9.30 Sat). **Closed:** Mon, Tue, 1 to 7 Jan. **Meals:** alc (main courses £23 to £28). Set L £24 (2 courses) to £27. Sun L £27 (2 courses) to £32. **Details:** 80 seats. Separate bar. Wheelchair access. Music. Car parking.

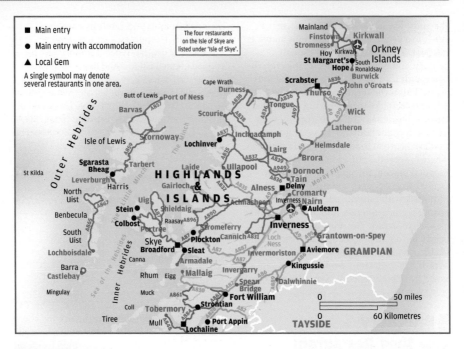

- ■ Main entry
- ● Main entry with accommodation
- ▲ Local Gem

A single symbol may denote several restaurants in one area.

The four restaurants on the Isle of Skye are listed under 'Isle of Skye'.

Auldearn

Boath House

Distinguished retreat with chic cooking
Auldearn, IV12 5TE
Tel no: (01667) 454896
www.boath-house.com
Modern European | £30
Cooking score: 5

Surrounded by 20 acres of manicured grounds, complete with an ornamental lake and a walled garden, Boath House is among the most distinguished and beautiful country piles in Scotland. Dutiful custodians Don and Wendy Matheson have contributed much to its success as a desirable Highland retreat, while long-serving chef Charlie Lockley continues to keep things fresh and modern in the kitchen. Lunch is relatively simple, but the place shows its mettle for dinner with a six-course menu of tersely worded contemporary dishes: from 'pheasant, foie gras, quince' to 'rhubarb, almond, bergamot'. Flavours are

true, technique is sharply honed and dishes look sparkling. Lockley also pays homage to Scotland's larder: serving roe deer with Jerusalem artichoke and liquorice, pairing langoustines with burnt celeriac, and allowing native cheeses to have their say (Clava Brie with figs and oatmeal biscuits, for example). The global wine list reads well, with sound vintages and fair prices (from £25).
Chef/s: Charlie Lockley. **Open:** all week L 12 to 2, D 7 to 10. **Meals:** Set L £24 (2 courses) to £30. Set D £45 to £70 (6 courses). **Details:** 26 seats. Separate bar. Car parking.

Symbols

- ⊨ Accommodation is available
- £30 Three courses for less than £30
- V Separate vegetarian menu
- £5 OFF £5-off voucher scheme
- ♠ Notable wine list

Aviemore
Mountain Café

A jewel in the midst of Aviemore
111 Grampian Road, Aviemore, PH22 1RH
Tel no: (01479) 812473
www.mountaincafe-aviemore.co.uk
British | £24
Cooking score: 1

£5 OFF V £30

Something about the Mountain Café hits exactly the right spot with readers. It's as busy and buzzy at breakfast as for lunch, and while it may not have the space to cope, folk are happy to queue. 'They know what they're doing, and they do it magnificently,' confided one fan. New Zealander Kirsten Gilmour is noted for her 'towering' all-day breakfast (including local sausages, black pudding and hash browns), very good banana bread, 'wonderful' cakes and lunches of salmon and haddock chowder, Kiwi sweetcorn fritter stack or grilled Moroccan-style chicken salad, all 'beautifully served'. Wines from £14.
Chef/s: Kirsten Gilmour. **Open:** all week 8.30 to 5.30. **Closed:** 25 and 26 Dec, 1 Jan. **Meals:** alc (main courses from £6 to £13). **Details:** 52 seats. 12 seats outside. Music. Car parking.

Delny

★ READERS' RESTAURANT OF THE YEAR ★
SCOTLAND

The Birch Tree

Country restaurant with confident food
Delny Riding Centre, Delny, IV18 ONP
Tel no: (01349) 853549
www.the-birch-tree.com
Modern British | £28
Cooking score: 2

£5 OFF V £30

The Birch Tree proves that decent local restaurants can pop up in the most unlikely places. Chef/proprietor Barry Hartshorne created this 'new build' from a stable block appended to his parents' riding centre just off the A9 near Invergordon. Views of green pastures and paddocks come with the territory, but all the talk is about the increasingly confident food at this clean-lined, contemporary venue. A glance at the menu will tell you the kitchen is dedicated to proper sourcing: Ardgay venison loin might appear with boudin noir, celeriac gratin and burnt onion mayo, while roast cod could be paired with squid-ink and razor-clam risotto, jamón crumbs and a poached egg. Strathdon Blue cheese soufflé is a bestseller, and Morangie Brie stars in a veggie pithiviers with spinach and watercress emulsion. If sweetness is required, try the crème caramel with Muscat jelly and pear sorbet. House wine is £15.95.
Chef/s: Barry Hartshorne. **Open:** Tue to Sat L 12 to 2, D 6 to 10. **Closed:** Sun, Mon. **Meals:** alc (main courses £13 to £21). Set L £13 (2 courses) to £16. Set D £22 (2 courses) to £27. **Details:** 32 seats. Wheelchair access. Music. Car parking.

Fort William
Crannog

Fun fish restaurant on the pier
Town Pier, Fort William, PH33 6DB
Tel no: (01397) 705589
www.crannog.net
Seafood | £32
Cooking score: 1

The white building perched at the end of the town pier and topped by a bright-red roof is perfectly positioned to make the most of the view across Loch Linnhe. Plenty of the water's luminous glow finds its way into the simple, timbered dining room, where a log burner belts out warmth in winter and the service is homely and personal. Super-fresh fish and shellfish are the star turns: mussels steamed with white wine and garlic and finished with cream, 'very tasty' Cullen skink, platters of shellfish, and lightly spiced Mallaig monkfish with pilaf rice and a tomato and chilli salsa. Wines from £17.75.
Chef/s: Stewart MacLachlan. **Open:** all week L 12 to 2.30, D 6 to 9. **Closed:** 25 and 26 Dec, 1 Jan. **Meals:** alc (main courses £15 to £20). Set L £15 (2 courses) to £19. **Details:** 60 seats. Separate bar. Wheelchair access. Music. Car parking.

Inverlochy Castle

Baronial pile with high-end contemporary food
Torlundy, Fort William, PH33 6SN
Tel no: (01397) 702177
www.inverlochycastlehotel.com
Modern British | £67
Cooking score: 6

🛏 V

If the budget stretches to being collected from the airport by the resident Rolls-Royce Phantom, you may as well go for it. There has been no hiding of lights under bushels at Inverlochy, from the moment of its Victorian inception as a magnificent Scots baronial mansion near the old ruined castle just outside Fort William. The interiors are fine enough to have been furnished by one of the kings of Norway, but are more accommodating softness than Gothic terror. Philip Carnegie's cooking is a nice balance of old-school country-house grandeur and intelligently worked modernism, producing scallops in Champagne velouté, and Angus fillet with oxtail in sauce bordelaise, but also veal sweetbread raviolo with watercress purée and broad beans, and Gigha halibut with Parmesan gnocchi in truffled cauliflower sauce. The results achieve high impact, right through to desserts such as passion-fruit cheesecake with lime ice cream. A fine global wine list starts at £35.
Chef/s: Philip Carnegie. **Open:** all week L 12.30 to 1.30, D 6 to 10. **Meals:** Set L £28 (2 courses) to £38. Set D £67. **Details:** 40 seats. Wheelchair access. Music. Car parking. Children over 6 yrs only.

▌Inverness

Rocpool

Eye-catching riverside restaurant
1 Ness Walk, Inverness, IV3 5NE
Tel no: (01463) 717274
www.rocpoolrestaurant.com
Modern European | £37
Cooking score: 2

£5 OFF

Rocpool brings a touch of contemporary brasserie style and spirit to Inverness. A highlight are the views of the castle and the River Ness, which flows from the legendary loch out to the Beauly Firth. The décor doesn't let the side down when it comes to delivering a cool, metropolitan setting for the kitchen's modern – and regionally focused – output. A first course of spiced crab and sweetcorn soup demonstrates the readiness to cross international borders, but there are Scottish ingredients at the heart of it all. Much is made of sustainability and seasonality in menus that run to Cromarty crab in a risotto, crispy haggis Scotch egg with black pudding, and loin of Speyside venison. Setting the pace among desserts is honeycomb ice cream with caramel popcorn and hot chocolate sauce. Early-evening and lunchtime set menus catch the eye for their great value. Wines start at £16.50.
Chef/s: Steven Devlin. **Open:** Mon to Sat L 12 to 2.30, D 5.45 to 10. **Closed:** Sun, 25 and 26 Dec, 1 to 5 Jan. **Meals:** alc (main courses £13 to £25). Set L £15 (2 courses). Set D £17 (2 courses). **Details:** 55 seats.

Isle of Harris
Scarista House
Gorgeous getaway showcasing island bounty
Scarista, Isle of Harris, HS3 3HX
Tel no: (01859) 550238
www.scaristahouse.com
Modern British | £44
Cooking score: 2

🛏 V

The serene white Georgian manse was once home to a minister of the kirk, and its soul-sustaining location overlooking three miles of sandy Harris beaches and the Atlantic swell must have been popular with members of his congregation. Its reputation for hospitality is maintained today by the Martins' classy hotel and self-catering cottage business. Tim Martin busies himself in the kitchen making bread, pasta and ice creams, as well as growing herbs and saladings: a resourceful approach for somewhere so remote. French-inflected modern Scottish cooking in fixed three-course dinner menus is the day's order. One evening, this might entail langoustine bisque with crab mayonnaise, Angus fillet in Burgundy with celeriac mash, and lemon tart in strawberry and pink peppercorn coulis. Another night might bring pigeon breast salad in bread sauce, turbot and asparagus in sauce vierge, and Drambuie praline parfait with raspberries. The wine list contains some classy French merchandise. House Chilean is £19.
Chef/s: Tim Martin. **Open:** all week D only 8 (1 sitting). **Closed:** mid Dec to end Feb. **Meals:** Set D £44. **Details:** 20 seats. Car parking. Children over 8 yrs only.

Isle of Skye
Creelers of Skye
Delightful French-style seafood
Broadford, Isle of Skye, IV49 9AQ
Tel no: (01471) 822281
www.skye-seafood-restaurant.co.uk
French | £28
Cooking score: 2

£5 OFF £30

David Wilson and Ann Doyle run their smashing little seafood eatery from 'little more than a shack' (their own words), so don't come to Creelers anticipating fancy napkins, starched tablecloths or sharp-suited waiters. Instead, enjoy the simple pleasures of prime Scottish fish cooked with a pronounced French accent and served with lots of smiles. If you feel like splashing out, try the magnificent Marseilles bouillabaisse: a feast for two served authentically in two stages with aïoli, rouille and garlic toast on the side. Otherwise, the menu varies with the catch, so expect anything from steamed razor clams and queen scallops to Cajun-spiced haddock, sea bass provençale or halibut poached in Chardonnay on tagliatelle with langoustine and saffron velouté. If you must have meat, look for the daube of lamb or 28-day-aged Angus steaks before concluding with crème brûlée or chocolate mousse; alternatively, there's the Auld Alliance cheeseboard. Wines from £15.50.
Chef/s: David Wilson. **Open:** Mon to Sat 12 to 10. **Closed:** Sun, Nov to Feb. **Meals:** alc (main courses £14 to £19). Set L £10 (2 courses) to £18. **Details:** 26 seats. Wheelchair access. Music. Car parking.

Kinloch Lodge

Remote retreat with finely crafted food
Sleat, Isle of Skye, IV43 8QY
Tel no: (01471) 833214
www.kinloch-lodge.co.uk
Modern British | £70
Cooking score: 5

♦ ⇆ V

As the ancestral seat of the Macdonald clan for generations, this enviably remote 17th-century hunting lodge overlooking Loch na Dal has plenty of baronial tartan pomp, but it's also a genuinely hospitable family affair. Lady Claire Macdonald – with recipe books and TV appearances by the score – was once dubbed 'the cook for all seasons', although she has now handed over most of the cheffing duties to Brazilian-born Marcello Tully. The result is finely crafted food with a classical slant and a fondness for seasonal Highland produce: think warm West Coast crab and langoustine mousse; nut- and herb-crusted Black Isle lamb; or Speyside beef fillet with a mini kidney pie, slow-roast tongue, raisin purée and port sauce. Fixed-price dinner menus bring a multitude of courses, culminating in desserts such as apple crumble parfait with a dinky cinnamon doughnut. The magisterial wine list is a highly knowledgeable thoroughbred stuffed with gold-standard producers and peerless vintages; house selections from £26.
Chef/s: Marcello Tully. **Open:** all week L 12 to 2, D 6 to 9.30. **Meals:** Set L £33 (2 courses) to £38. Set D £70 (5 courses) to £80 (7 courses). Sun L £33. **Details:** 45 seats. Separate bar. Wheelchair access. Music. Car parking.

‖• Visit us
‖‖ Online
To find out more about
The Good Food Guide, please visit
www.thegoodfoodguide.co.uk

Loch Bay

Honest-to-goodness seafood bistro
1-2 Macleod Terrace, Stein, Isle of Skye, IV55 8GA
Tel no: (01470) 592235
www.lochbay-seafood-restaurant.co.uk
Seafood | £33
Cooking score: 2

⇆

A converted 18th-century fisherman's cottage in a conservation village overlooking the Outer Isles is the rather romantic pitch for David and Alison Wilkinson's honest-to-goodness seafood bistro. Comprising just one room with a few wooden tables, some artwork on the walls and local pottery dotted here and there, the set-up couldn't be more unassuming – and the look matches perfectly with the roster of simply rendered Scottish fish. Menus vary with the market, but dinner might promise grilled oysters, steamed mussels or fish soup, ahead of grilled Isle of Gigha halibut, a duo of sea bass and plaice with vermouth sauce, or fillet of salmon with lime, ginger and spring onions. There are also extravagant shellfish platters for sharing, while desserts might include crème brûlée with Skye rhubarb or sticky ginger pudding doused with ginger wine and brandy sauce. The modest wine list includes some decent fish-friendly numbers from £17.50.
Chef/s: David Wilkinson. **Open:** Wed to Sat D only 6.30 to 8.30. **Closed:** Sun, Mon, Tue, mid Oct to Easter. **Meals:** Set D £33. **Details:** 23 seats. Music. Car parking. Children over 8 yrs only.

The Three Chimneys

Original food and matchless hospitality
Colbost, Isle of Skye, IV55 8ZT
Tel no: (01470) 511258
www.threechimneys.co.uk
Modern British | £60
Cooking score: 6

♦ ⇆

Visitors to the Three Chimneys might feel like James Boswell and Dr Johnson as they take a mini tour of the Western Isles, trekking over the sea to Skye. Eddie and Shirley Spear's remote retreat was once a crofter's cottage, but since 1985 it has played host to crowds of like-minded gastronauts who come to sample the original food and matchless hospitality. Low ceilings and seagrass flooring create a peaty vibe that belies the kitchen's highly sophisticated endeavours. There's much to savour on the fish front: try the top-class Scottish 'fruits de mer' with Glendale organic mesclun or Mallaig red mullet and Sconser scallop with asparagus, kale, pink grapefruit and seaweed dressing. Black Isle beef and Blackface lamb also feature (the latter with pearl barley, neeps and nettles), and it would be rude to miss the legendary hot marmalade pudding with Drambuie custard. The wine list is a prestigious, globe-spanning labour of love with France in the ascendancy, but the New World also waxing strongly. Bottles start at £25 and there's a top-drawer selection by the glass.

Chef/s: Michael Smith. **Open:** all week L 12.15 to 1.45 (mid Mar to end Oct only), D 6.15 to 9.45. **Closed:** 1 to 23 Jan. **Meals:** Set L £29 (2 courses) to £37. Set D £60 (5 courses). Tasting menu £90 (8 courses). **Details:** 48 seats. Separate bar. Wheelchair access. Car parking. Children over 5 yrs only at L, over 8 yrs at D.

Kingussie
The Cross
Assured cooking in a peaceful setting
Ardbroilach Road, Kingussie, PH21 1LB
Tel no: (01540) 661166
www.thecross.co.uk
Modern British | £55
Cooking score: 4

A glorious setting by the River Gynack in the Cairngorms is only the half of it. The Kitchingmans' 2012 acquisition of the long-running Cross, a converted late-Victorian tweed mill, effected a seamless transition, and the consensus is that Ross Sutherland's kitchen is on song. His modern Scottish approach teams up prime Highland ingredients with a resourceful range of techniques. Proceedings might open with Ullapool scallops served

with chorizo, king prawn, sweet potato and black garlic, prior to local venison with a gamey stuffing and butternut squash in port jus, or stone bass accompanied by crab cannelloni with broccoli and almonds in shrimp butter sauce. It all concludes with the fragrant likes of rose-water and lychee pannacotta garnished with passion fruit and coconut. Artisan Scottish cheeses are worth leaving room for. A dazzling wine list arranged by style hauls in New Zealand Gewürztraminer, excellent Brunello and Austrian botrytised nectar among the French classics, at fair prices, from £22 a bottle. A few more by the glass would help.

Chef/s: Ross Sutherland. **Open:** All week L 12 to 2, D 7 to 8.30. **Closed:** Christmas, 2 Jan to mid Feb. **Meals:** Set L £23 (2 courses) to £25. Set D £55. Tasting menu £58. **Details:** 26 seats. 10 seats outside. Wheelchair access. Car parking.

Lochaline
The Whitehouse
The Highland larder on a plate
Lochaline, PA80 5XT
Tel no: (01967) 421777
www.thewhitehouserestaurant.co.uk
Modern British | £40
Cooking score: 3

Perched up the hill from the Mull ferry, this pretty, plain whitewashed restaurant matches stunning harbour views with old stonework, rustic furnishings and a menu that celebrates the Scottish seasonal larder. Seafood from the local boats is a star turn, perhaps pan-roast Lochaline scallops with cauliflower purée and sweet cicely, pollack poached in seawater with 'rock pool' broth or a mammoth crab salad with gazpacho dressing – thoughtful, uncluttered dishes topped up with pickings from the owners' greenhouse and veg patch. There's plenty of meat and game, too, from short ribs of Lochaber beef with Kelpie ale and wild mushrooms to pan-seared Ardtornish stag's liver and kidneys with capers and a shot of Tomatin whisky jus. Cheeses are fervently Scottish, and the accompanying chutneys are all homemade, while puds are boozy affairs –

from flaming crème brûlée to Shetland gin fizz with raspberries and a Highland berry sorbet. Wines start at £17.

Chef/s: Mike Burgoyne. **Open:** Tue to Sat L 12 to 2.30, D 6 to 10. **Closed:** Sun, Mon, Nov to Easter. **Meals:** alc (main courses £14 to £25). Set L £17 (2 courses) to £21. **Details:** 24 seats. 8 seats outside. Wheelchair access.

Lochinver
Albannach

Solace, sustenance and fine hospitality
Baddidarroch, Lochinver, IV27 4LP
Tel no: (01571) 844407
www.thealbannach.co.uk
Modern British | £68
Cooking score: 6

🛏 V

When Colin Craig and Lesley Crosfield describe their cooking as 'informed by moorland, croft and sea', that is no mere lip service, for this is an establishment firmly rooted in its environment. The house has stood for a couple of hundred years, the views of peaks and sea unchanged, while the interior maintains the traditions of the past with its respectful formality. Home-grown ingredients come from their croft, and what isn't from down the road won't have travelled far if they can help it. The five-course menu includes a cheese course – Criffel, perhaps, or Blue Monday – and might kick off with a mousseline of wild halibut with a lobster bisque sauce. The moors provide the roe deer, whose saddle is served with braised garden roots and a potato galette. The refined modern Scottish style continues with desserts like caramelised pear tart with pear gelato and salted caramel. Wines from £21.

Chef/s: Colin Craig and Lesley Crosfield. **Open:** Tue to Sun D only 8 (1 sitting). **Closed:** Mon, Mon to Wed (Nov and Dec exc Christmas), Jan to mid Mar. **Meals:** Set D £68 (5 courses). **Details:** 20 seats. Car parking. Children over 12 yrs only.

Orkney Islands
The Creel

Orcadian oasis dedicated to island produce
Front Road, St Margaret's Hope, Orkney Islands, KW17 2SL
Tel no: (01856) 831311
www.thecreel.co.uk
British | £40
Cooking score: 6

🛏

The Creel is testament to the single-minded persistence of Alan and Joyce Craigie and is warmly appreciated by its faithful followers. What awaits, according to one reporter, is 'lovely food'. Their simple, white-walled restaurant sits on the harbour, offers priceless sea views and is imbued with the confidence that comes from longevity – the Craigies have been here since 1985. Alan Craigie starts with the pick of the island's produce, showcased on a short menu with a pair of choices at each course. Everyone praises the home-baked sourdough, the freshness of the fish and shellfish, and the rich, tasty flavour of the seaweed-fed North Ronaldsay mutton. Or there could be smoked haddock soup to start, then slow-cooked Aberdeen Angus brisket and cheeks, served with carrots, peas and mushroom relish. Conclude with a tart, say rhubarb and custard or the famous lemon with marmalade ice cream. House wine selections start at £18.

Chef/s: Alan Craigie. **Open:** Tue to Sat D only 6 to 8. **Closed:** Sun, Mon, mid Oct to Easter. **Meals:** Set D £36 (2 courses) to £40. **Details:** 16 seats. Wheelchair access. Car parking.

READERS RECOMMEND
The Foveran

Modern British
Kirkwall, St Ola, Orkney Islands, KW15 1SF
Tel no: (01856) 872389
www.foveranhotel.co.uk
'Owned and run by chef Paul Doule. Much local produce including seafood, but also local mutton and fillet steak, all cooked in a straightforward way.'

Plockton

Plockton Inn
Proving that simple can be best
Innes Street, Plockton, IV52 8TW
Tel no: (01599) 544222
www.plocktoninn.co.uk
Seafood | £24
Cooking score: 2

£5 OFF   £30

It makes sense anywhere, but here particularly, to use local produce and cook it simply. And the Plockton Inn's location, some 100 metres from the harbour, is a reminder, if one were needed, that fresh supplies are never far away. After 18 years, Mary Gollan continues to deliver food that draws plaudits from reporters: from locally caught langoustine served with hot garlic butter, to her own-smoked seafood platter; from a classic skate wing with black butter, to superb king scallops with bacon, garlic and cream. There's also very good haddock and chips with homemade tartare sauce, but diners not in the mood for fish are catered for with lamb, steak and chicken. For dessert, choose from the likes of sticky toffee pudding, cranachan ice cream or chocolate cheesecake. This is the kind of place visitors love to stumble across in any fishing village: family-run, unassuming and welcoming. Wines from £14.95.
Chef/s: Mary Gollan. **Open:** all week L 12 to 2.15, D 6 to 9. **Closed:** 25 and 26 Dec. **Meals:** alc (main courses £16 to £34). **Details:** 60 seats. 20 seats outside. Wheelchair access. Music. Car parking.

Port Appin

Airds Hotel
Former ferry inn full of delights
Port Appin, PA38 4DF
Tel no: (01631) 730236
www.airds-hotel.com
Modern British | £55
Cooking score: 6

V

The location is sensational, complete with loch views, lighthouse and dotted islands – the Airds' petite garden is a gem amid the wilds of western Scotland. From the outside, the hotel resembles a wayside inn: low, whitewashed and unassuming. Inside, though, it's a smart retreat: all plush carpets and big sofas, bookshelves and coffee tables, the décor light and fresh, the staff sporting tartan. Canapés of haggis bonbon, Parmesan and chorizo doughnut, and hummus with dukkah spices, showcase Jordan Annabi's 'ambitious, reliable' cooking. The style fits its Scottish location yet also draws ingredients from farther afield. West Coast crab, for instance, comes with crunchy Welsh asparagus, Parmesan custard and a deep, musky truffle dressing, while stone bass fillet is matched with haricot bean and horseradish purée, pancetta, Puy lentils, baby onions and Parmentier potatoes. Strawberry soufflé with white chocolate mousse, fresh berries and yoghurt sorbet makes a flawless finale. The substantial wine list starts at £27.
Chef/s: Jordan Annabi. **Open:** all week L 12 to 1.45, D 7.15 to 9.15. **Closed:** 2 days each week Dec and Jan. **Meals:** Set L £18. Set D £55. Sun L £18. **Details:** 36 seats. 20 seats outside. Separate bar. Car parking. Children over 9 yrs only at D.

Scrabster
The Captain's Galley
Terrific harbourside eatery
The Harbour, Scrabster, KW14 7UJ
Tel no: (01847) 894999
www.captainsgalley.co.uk
Seafood | £49
Cooking score: 3

Chef/proprietor Jim Cowie heads down to the nearby fish market on the pier every day to pick out the seafood he'll be serving. Alternatively, he buys directly from the boats, looking for the best seasonal stuff from sustainable sources. Most of the other ingredients are sourced from within a 50-mile radius of Scrabster. With your environmental concerns assuaged, look forward to impressive plates of seafood prepared with skill. The fixed-price carte and tasting menus run to successful combos such as crab cakes with crispy calamari, and cod with slow-braised oxtail (Chinese style). There might be grilled lobster with garlic butter and home-cut chips, too, plus a stellar take-away option. Meaty choices are available (wild duck with choucroute, for instance), plus creative desserts such as 'expressions' of hazelnut. It all takes place in a charming Georgian building by the harbour: a one-time ice house and salmon store with a barrel-vaulted ceiling. Wines from £16.75.
Chef/s: Jim Cowie. Open: Tue to Sat 12.30 to 9 (9.30 Fri). Closed: Sun, Mon, 25, 26 and 31 Dec, 1 and 2 Jan. Meals: alc (main courses £18 to £25). Set L £25. Set D £49. Tasting menu £61 (7 courses). Details: 25 seats. 25 seats outside. Wheelchair access. Music. Car parking.

Strontian
Kilcamb Lodge
Welcoming retreat of the best Highland kind
Strontian, PH36 4HY
Tel no: (01967) 402257
www.kilcamblodge.co.uk
Modern British | £50
Cooking score: 4

If you like elegant surroundings and loch views, Kilcamb Lodge's pretty little restaurant – all cerise walls, floral swags and classic furnishings – is where to be. For something more relaxed, try the brasserie with its cream wood panelling and well-stocked bar. Either way, there's a versatile menu that favours seafood but does much more besides. A 'silky, vivid' pea velouté with fresh crab sums up the kitchen's general approach, which is fresh, interesting and classically inspired. As you'd hope, seafood is deftly handled: a pearly piece of sea bass is cooked 'to perfection' and served with a fat langoustine, tomato and olive tart, fresh broad beans and lentils; monkfish comes with aubergine purée, onion rings, asparagus and green olive sauce. A dessert of lemon posset, jelly, meringue and white chocolate mousse is the perfect palate cleanser. Drinks include excellent Scottish bottled beers, plus a decent wine list, divided by type and opening at £21.50.
Chef/s: Gary Phillips. Open: all week L 12 to 2, D 6 to 9. Closed: Jan. Meals: alc (main courses £16 to 24). Set L £19. Set D £52. Sun L £19. Details: 36 seats. 12 seats outside. Separate bar. Music. Car parking. Children over 10 yrs only in restaurant.

WALES

Glamorgan, Gwent, Mid-Wales, North-East Wales, North-West Wales, West Wales

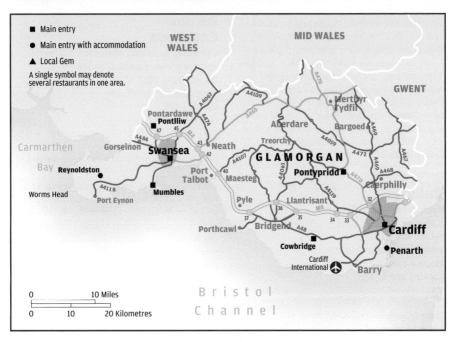

Barry

The Gallery
Modern British
2 Broad Street, Barry, CF62 7AA
Tel no: (01446) 735300
www.the-gallery-restaurant.co.uk

'Excellent trout goujons starter, beautifully cooked sea bass main and rhubarb four-ways for pud – crumble, frangipane, trifle and sorbet. All of this served by a friendly and knowledgeable front-of-house team.'

‖● Please send us your feedback

To register your opinion about any restaurant listed in the Guide, or a new restaurant that you wish to bring to our attention, please visit the web address at the bottom of the page. Your feedback informs the content of the book and will be used to compile next year's reviews.

Cardiff
Arbennig
Classy, colourful cooking in a modern setting
6-10 Romilly Crescent, Cardiff, CF11 9NR
Tel no: (029) 2034 1264
www.arbennig.co.uk
Modern British | £25
Cooking score: 4
£30

Its name means 'special' in Welsh and Arbennig doesn't disappoint. Formerly Oscar's, it has shifted up a gear under the new ownership, offering classy but unpretentious cooking in an airy, modern setting. Expect charming, efficient service and views of leafy suburbia (though the city centre is not far away). A 'great value' lunch could kick off with a broad bean and pea bruschetta with ricotta, young herbs and a lemon dressing – a 'perfect mix of crunch, creaminess and fresh flavours'. Sourcing is taken seriously here, so a main of grilled brill is pearly fresh, and comes with tender cuttlefish beurre noisette, toasted almonds, sparky little capers and broccoli. If you possibly can, squeeze in dessert – the individual lemon meringue pie, its pastry crisp, its topping a fluffy pavilion, is 'faultless'. The international wine list offers a good selection by the glass. Bottles start at £15.95. **Chef/s:** John Cook. **Open:** Wed to Sun 12 to 11 (6 Sun). **Closed:** Mon, Tue, 25 and 26 Dec, 2 weeks Aug, bank hols. **Meals:** alc (main courses £10 to £22). Set L £10 (2 courses). **Details:** 60 seats. 12 seats outside.

Bully's
Powerful French allegiances
5 Romilly Crescent, Cardiff, CF11 9NP
Tel no: (029) 2022 1905
www.bullysrestaurant.co.uk
Modern French | £40
Cooking score: 2
£5
OFF

'Pan-fried foie gras on anything' says the menu – a reminder that this long-running neighbourhood restaurant has powerful French allegiances. The interior may look shabby-chic with its grey banquettes, gilded mirrors and jumble of pictures covering all wall space, but there's nothing slapdash about the kitchen's approach to things gastronomic. Goats' cheese, walnut and pomegranate mille-feuille is dressed with toasted walnut vinaigrette; Welsh venison comes with coffee jus; and fillet of sea bass is paired with braised butter beans and poached egg. Even haggis gets a Gallic makeover with salad mâche and a smear of Dijon mustard sauce. To finish, readers reckon the tarte Tatin is 'simply divine' – or you might prefer griottine cherry clafoutis with Kirsch reduction and mandarin ice cream. Service gets top marks and the international wine list has ample fairly priced French classics; house selections start at £11.50 a carafe (£3.90 a glass). **Chef/s:** Gareth Farr. **Open:** Mon to Sun L 12 to 2 (3.30 Sun), Mon to Sat D 6.30 to 9. **Closed:** 23 to 26 Dec, first week Jan. **Meals:** alc (main courses £14 to £26). Set L £14 (2 courses) to £18. Set D £15 (2 courses) to £20. Sun L £16 (2 courses) to £20. **Details:** 40 seats. Music.

NEW ENTRY
Casanova
Charming, authentic city-centre Italian
13 Quay Street, Cardiff, CF10 1EA
Tel no: (029) 2034 4044
www.casanovacardiff.com
Italian | £28
Cooking score: 1
£30

As Italian as mozzarella – from its waiters to its wine list – this homely little treasure is a far cry from central Cardiff's chain restaurants. A free glass of Prosecco on arrival puts you in the mood, as do fat olives and crusty bread. A generous set-price menu offers traditional regional dishes, but specials such as seared tuna steak with an umami-laden soft bean salad deserve serious consideration. Simplicity and balance are the watchwords: think pasta with sweet roast pumpkin, punchy garlic and chilli and salty pancetta, or a boozy tiramisu, served with a smile. Wine (from £20) mostly sticks below £30. **Chef/s:** Antonio Cersosimo. **Open:** Mon to Sat L 12 to 2.30, D 5.30 to 10. **Closed:** Sun, 24 to 26 Dec, 31 Dec, 1 Jan. **Meals:** alc (main courses £18). Set L £12 (2 courses) to £16. Set D £22 (2 courses) to £28. **Details:** 13 seats.

Chapel 1877
Classic flavours in a unique setting
Churchill Way, Cardiff, CF10 2WF
Tel no: (029) 2022 2020
www.chapel1877.com
Modern British | £30
Cooking score: 2
£5
OFF

Chapel 1877 is an establishment of two very distinct parts: the ground floor is a lively bar; upstairs is luxurious, quieter, offering the choice of secluded booths or tables with a view of the throng below. There may have been grumbles about bouncers and slow service in the past year, but readers report that the food remains sound. An 'attractively presented' courgette flower tempura with chilli sauce has been endorsed, while a 'generous portion' of cod fillet with chorizo, squid and samphire, 'all seemingly fresh and with a bit of zip and zing' also satisfied. Alternatively, steaks (28-day aged) are always an option, paired with an 'excellent' béarnaise sauce. Desserts deliver a twist on classics such as raspberry crème brûlée or warm dark chocolate and beetroot fondant with tonka bean ice cream and a pink peppercorn and sea salt tuile. A decent international selection of wines commences at £15.

Chef/s: Kieran Harry. **Open:** Sun to Thur L 12 to 2.30 (5.30 Sun), Mon to Thur D 5.30 to 10. Fri and Sat 12 to 10. **Meals:** alc (main courses £6 to £30). Set L £13 (2 courses) to £16. Sun L £13. **Details:** 106 seats. Separate bar. Music.

ffresh
Flag-waving minimalist eatery
The Wales Millennium Centre, Bute Place, Cardiff, CF10 5AL
Tel no: (029) 2063 6465
www.ffresh.org.uk
Modern British | £24
Cooking score: 3

V £30

The Wales Millennium Centre is the place for a spot of opera but it's also good for a bite to eat, thanks to this pleasant modern restaurant with snappy minimalist styling. Expect it to be rammed before performances – no surprise, given the good-value pre-show 'express dinner'. Confit duck and prune terrine with apricot syrup and micro salad has been well reported, as has breast of chicken with bubble and squeak cake and mustard jus: 'outstanding, generous helping with top-quality chicken'. The main thrust of the menu is British, with a few European inflections, as in spiced pumpkin tortellini with pesto cream and shaved fennel. Old-fashioned desserts include warm ginger cake, treacle tart and lemon posset. If you'd prefer a light bite, plump for the bar where pizzas, charcuterie boards and burgers are offered. Wines start at £16.95 a bottle.

Chef/s: Jenni Trottman and Dave Richardson. **Open:** Tue to Sun L 12 to 3 (4 Sun), Tue to Sat D 5 to 9. **Closed:** Mon, 25 Dec. **Meals:** alc (main courses £12 to £18). Set L £17 (2 courses) to £20. Set D £20 (2 courses) to £24. Sun L £17. **Details:** 120 seats. 40 seats outside. Separate bar. Wheelchair access. Music.

Fish at 85
Marine life fresh from the fishmonger's counter
85 Pontcanna Street, Cardiff, CF11 9HS
Tel no: (029) 2002 0212
www.fishat85.co.uk
Seafood | £30
Cooking score: 3

£5 OFF

The fish counter, piled high with the day's catch, sets out the stall for this cutesy neighbourhood restaurant in the Cardiff suburb of Pontcanna. Whitewashed wood, slate floors and simple white furniture add to the fishmonger vibe, as does the helpful chap in wellies and overalls who will talk you through your options. Pick your fish, select a cooking method, sauce and side and you're away. Or opt for specials such as a big, crisp-skinned sea bass fillet with sautéed potatoes, samphire, leek and a beurre blanc sauce. Freshness, generosity and precision are the watchwords here. While most flavours are European, there are occasional jaunts to Asia as in crisp battered squid with nam prik sauce. As a finale, rich, gluten- and flour-free chocolate nemesis takes the curtain call with a flourish. There's a snappy selection of international wines starting at £15.95, so a little tipple shouldn't break the bank.

Chef/s: Dan Howell. **Open:** Tue to Sat L 12 to 2.30, D 6 to 9. **Closed:** Mon, Sun, 2 weeks Christmas, bank hols. **Meals:** alc (main courses £20 to £40). Set L £13 (2 courses) to £16. **Details:** 30 seats. 8 seats outside. Music.

Mint & Mustard

Pan-Indian cooking given a contemporary spin
134 Whitchurch Road, Cardiff, CF14 3LZ
Tel no: (029) 2062 0333
www.mintandmustard.com
Indian | £20
Cooking score: 2

V £30

The sleek, contemporary look of Mint & Mustard's Cardiff venue (there are other branches in Penarth and Taunton) suits its modern approach to pan-Indian cooking. A spacious room in mustard (of course) and aubergine is decorated with pictures of Indian river scenes, and cloth-less tables are lined up against comfortable banquettes. Prime the palate with starter nibbles such as Bombay chaat with yoghurt and relishes, or scallops variously grilled and splashed with orange coulis or simmered in coconut milk and lemon. Next come assiduously spiced, richly satisfying main dishes like Pondicherry lamb curry, flaky-crusted biryanis, and swordfish in mango and ginger. Principal ingredients gain resonant depth of flavour through marinating and roasting – as with the salmon steak that's soaked in honey, dill and spices and then finished in the tandoor. Finish with the famous sweet samosas filled with chocolate ganache and flaked almonds. House wines are £15.95.
Chef/s: Santhosh Nair. **Open:** all week L 12 to 2, D 5 to 11. **Closed:** 25 and 26 Dec, 1 Jan. **Meals:** alc (main courses £8 to £15). Set L £13 (2 courses) to £35. Set D £35. **Details:** 90 seats. Music.

The Potted Pig

Generous cooking and a lively atmosphere
27 High Street, Cardiff, CF10 1PU
Tel no: (029) 2022 4817
www.thepottedpig.com
Modern British | £35
Cooking score: 2

Housed in a cavernous former bank vault close to the Millennium Stadium, this atmospheric eatery has certainly won over the locals by dispensing easy-to-like European brasserie dishes in generous portions. Starters are of the rich variety: try potted pig with toast and pickles, smoked haddock kedgeree with a poached egg, or whole pigeon with lentils, bacon and green sauce. Mains might range from a simple sea bass with courgettes, peas and cockle butter via rabbit served three ways with chunky chips, to a whole suckling pig, which can be pre-ordered by groups of eight or more. The set lunch is considered good value, and desserts might be a simple lemon posset or poached pear with Amaretto ice cream and toasted almonds. The restaurant can get very noisy with all that bare brick and those large dining groups, but there's always the gin menu to take the edge off. Wine opens at a reasonable £16.
Chef/s: Gwyn Myring and Tom Furlong. **Open:** Tue to Sun L 12 to 2, Tue to Sat D 7 to 9 (6.30 to 9.30 Fri and Sat). **Closed:** Mon, 23 Dec to 3 Jan. **Meals:** alc (main courses £12 to £27). Set L £12 (2 courses). Sun L £15. **Details:** 80 seats. Wheelchair access. Music.

Purple Poppadom

Indian invention and surprises
Upper Floor, 185a Cowbridge Road East, Cardiff, CF11 9AJ
Tel no: (029) 2022 0026
www.purplepoppadom.com
Indian | £35
Cooking score: 3

£5 OFF

'Oxtail odyssey duo'; 'scallops chou-fleur'; 'fresh from the creamery' – not phrases often found in a Cardiff curry house. But the Purple Poppadom is no ordinary tandoori joint: chef/proprietor Anand George made his name at Mint & Mustard (see entry), and he's raising the bar again at this vibrant first-floor eatery in the city's Canton district. The dish descriptions may be OTT, but they signal serious ambition as the kitchen plays tricks with Indian flavours, packs many contrasting ideas on the plate and presents dishes in modern European style. How about crispy soft-shell crab alongside a crab cake and a warm salad of crabmeat with sweetcorn, or chicken tikka 'half and half', or a trio of

venison involving a burger, grilled haunch and a pastry-topped, oven-baked curry? To finish, freshen up with green tea and rose-petal crème brûlée. India and Wales are both represented on the eclectic wine list; prices from £15.95.
Chef/s: Anand George. **Open:** Sat L 12 to 2.30, Tue to Sat D 5.30 to 11. Sun 1 to 9. **Closed:** 25 and 26 Dec, 1 Jan. **Meals:** alc (main courses £8 to £18). **Details:** 74 seats. Music.

▌Cowbridge

★ READERS' RESTAURANT OF THE YEAR ★
WALES

Bar 44
Enjoyable, cheery tapas joint
44c High Street, Cowbridge, CF71 7AG
Tel no: (01446) 776488
www.bar44.co.uk
Tapas | £20
Cooking score: 2
£5 OFF V £30

Cowbridge's Bar 44 doesn't just serve authentic *tapas y copas* (tapas and drinks), it has a genuine understanding of Spain's eating and drinking culture. The details matter here. From the generous pour of the 'San Sebastian' style G&T to the hand-carving of the jamón de Teruel and the triple-cooking of the patatas bravas, the owners have exacting standards. Interiors – modern but modest with tiles and blackboards – aren't as trendy as at the newer Penarth branch, but they're versatile. As are the menus, which encompass Spanish 'Sunday lunch', a £10 'menu del dia' and daily specials. Tapas rarely top £5. Among the best are medium-rare Ibérico pork shoulder with cauliflower purée and pine nuts, arroz negro with cuttlefish and allioli, Spanish artisan cheeses and, for afters, PX chocolate mousse with olive oil, sea salt and toast. Sherry, cava, cider and beer join the all-Spanish contingent on the drinks side. Wine from £14.95.
Chef/s: Tommy Heaney. **Open:** all week 9.30 to 9 (5 Mon, 10 Fri and Sat). **Closed:** 25 Dec. **Meals:** Tapas (£3 to £8). Mon to Fri set L £10 (3 dishes, 10 to 4). Sun L £11 to £12. **Details:** 55 seats. Music.

Oscars of Cowbridge
Bright, breezy and imaginative cooking
65 High Street, Cowbridge, CF71 7AF
Tel no: (01446) 771984
www.oscarsofcowbridge.com
Modern European | £24
Cooking score: 1
£30

The aim is to provide something for everyone at this charming High Street eatery. Oscars' industrious kitchen can do you a bowl of mussels or a plate of Welsh lamb rump with five-spiced lentils and chickpeas, but reporters have also emerged full of praise for generous lunchtime sandwiches, evening burgers, and sustainably and locally sourced fresh fish. You can expect early-bird meal deals, morning coffee and warm chocolate brownies, too – it's an all-day formula that has served Cowbridge well for 13 years. The reasonably priced, globetrotting wine list opens at £15.95.
Chef/s: Gareth Chivell. **Open:** Mon to Sat 10am to 11pm. **Closed:** Sun. **Meals:** alc (main courses £9 to £20). **Details:** 50 seats. 24 seats outside. Wheelchair access. Music. Car parking.

▌Mumbles
Munch of Mumbles
Skilled cooking at a bargain price
650 Mumbles Road, Mumbles, SA3 4EA
Tel no: (01792) 362244
www.munchofmumbles.com
British | £27
Cooking score: 2
£5 OFF £30

This 'great local restaurant' is one of many vying for attention along the seafront in Mumbles, the upmarket fishing village at Swansea's western edge. There's an emphasis here on value for money; £27 will buy a three-course dinner and you can bring your own wine, although the restaurant does have its own modest selection (from £12.95). While there's nothing slick about the interior, the 'faultless hospitality' more than makes up for it and there's a happy, unbuttoned vibe to the

place. Chef/owner Ben Griffiths and his wife Jacquie have built a solid local following, with praise being heaped on everything from the 'very knowledgeable' staff to the local produce on the menu. Typical choices are smoked haddock arancini with curry spices; sea bream with carrot and ginger purée, beansprouts and Thai coconut emulsion; and chocolate terrine with peanut crumble and salted-caramel ice cream.
Chef/s: Ben Griffiths. **Open:** Wed to Sun L 12 to 2.15, Wed to Sat D 6.30 to 9.15. **Closed:** Mon, Tue, 25 and 26 Dec, 1 week Feb, 2 weeks Oct, bank hols. **Meals:** Set L £15 (2 courses) to £19. Set D £24 (2 courses) to £27. Sun L £16 (2 courses) to £20. **Details:** 40 seats. Music.

▮ Penarth

The Fig Tree
Panoramic views and confident seasonal food
The Esplanade, Penarth, CF64 3AU
Tel no: (029) 2070 2512
www.thefigtreepenarth.co.uk
Modern British | £28
Cooking score: 3
£30

A converted Victorian beach shelter overlooking the Bristol Channel isn't exactly the obvious choice for a serious neighbourhood restaurant, but the Fig Tree succeeds splendidly in all departments. The views are tremendous, although Mike Caplan-Hill's confident food never plays second fiddle to the setting – particularly as the kitchen has bumper supplies of locally sourced produce. Queen scallops are baked in white wine, dill and laverbread sauce; Gower mussels are given the provençale treatment; and slow-cooked shoulder of Carmarthenshire lamb is served with boulangère potatoes, curly kale and rosemary jus. Prime Welsh beef also grabs attention, while peckish vegetarians might order beetroot and goats' cheese tarte Tatin followed by wild garlic, spring onion, broad bean and cashew risotto. For afters, the sweet-toothed of every persuasion can look forward to the likes of lemon posset, fruit crumble or

bara brith bread-and-butter pudding with crème anglaise. Around 50 wines offer reasonably priced drinking from £14.
Chef/s: Mike Caplan-Hill. **Open:** Tue to Sun L 12 to 3 (4 Sat and Sun), Tue to Sat D 6 to 9. **Closed:** Mon, 25 and 26 Dec. **Meals:** alc (main courses £11 to £20). Set L £11 (2 courses) to £14. Sun L £20. **Details:** 54 seats. 28 seats outside. Wheelchair access. Music.

★ TOP 50 ★

NEW ENTRY

Restaurant James Sommerin
Sommerin is back and on top form
The Esplanade, Penarth, CF64 3AU
Tel no: (029) 2070 6559
www.jamessommerinrestaurant.co.uk
Modern British | £55
Cooking score: 7

For anyone who loved his cooking at the Crown at Whitebrook, James Sommerin's new restaurant was a long time coming – but well worth the wait. The seafront in well-to-do Penarth is a sensible choice of location, and the restaurant's slick, minimalist styling (pale walls, hidden lighting, white linen) makes it clear you can expect something special. The service is perfectly pitched between friendly and formal. Staff are knowledgeable, confident and happy to chat about the food. In matters culinary, Sommerin and his team have hit the ground running. Operating from a kitchen that's visible through a wide window, they turn out food that excites and satisfies in equal measure. If anything, the cooking is more interesting than it was at the Crown: expect a virtuoso show of flavours and techniques, with clever, subtle use of spices and wonderful interplays of texture. Top choices from the set-price tasting menu include sea bass with broccoli, melt-in-the-mouth aubergine and spiced butter, topped with salty, crunchy broccoli florets; succulent lamb with peas, broad beans, sweet roasted garlic, sweetbread, lentils and a perfumed cumin sauce; and an 'utterly divine' dessert of macerated strawberries in rose-water with an Italian meringue shard, cream-cheese mousse, rose-water jelly and strawberry syrup. The

decent selection of international wines covers most prices and includes some lesser-known finds, starting at £24.

Chef/s: James Sommerin. **Open:** Tue to Sun L 12 to 2.30, D 7 to 9 (6.30 Fri to Sun). **Closed:** Mon. **Meals:** Set L and D £55 (5 courses) to £85 (10 courses). **Details:** 70 seats.

▌ Pontlliw

Rasoi

Lively Indian creations
Bryntirion Road, Pontlliw, SA4 9DY
Tel no: (01792) 882409
www.rasoiwales.co.uk
Indian | £23
Cooking score: 2
£30

If you fancy arriving in style, it's worth noting that Rasoi is one of the few Indian restaurants in the land with its own helipad. In fact, this personally run eatery a few miles from Swansea is full of surprises. The rambling dining room embraces the look currently favoured by many provincial curry houses – idiosyncratic carved wooden furniture and patterned panels – while the open kitchen produces some unusual, lively creations. Sound ingredients and pinpoint spicing ensure that staples such as onion bhajias, rogan josh, chicken dhansak and seafood biryani are a cut above the norm, but it pays to investigate the less familiar stuff: seared scallops 'royale' with mango and chilli salsa, beetroot sauce and mint chutney; crispy duck breast with garlic potato and confit duck spring roll; and honey and ginger prawns with green rice. Wines start at £13.95, but don't miss the New Delhi ice tea and other glamorous cocktail thrills.

Chef/s: Kunwar Singh. **Open:** Mon to Thur L 12 to 2.30, D 5.30 to 10.30. Fri to Sun 12 to 11 (10.30 Sun). **Closed:** 25 Dec. **Meals:** alc (mains £8 to £15). Set L £9 (2 courses) to £11. **Details:** 190 seats. 90 seats outside. Separate bar. Wheelchair access. Music. Car parking.

⑂ EATS, SHOOTS AND LEAVES

Finding mystery greenery strewn over your starter? Then it's bang on trend. Here's what to expect from the most modish of leaves, and where to find them in restaurant captivity.

Did you know monk's beards were edible? At Polpetto, Florence Knight pairs creamy burrata with red chilli and vivid green agretti, aka saltwort or monk's beard. It's got a mineral flavour and gentle crunch.

Lovage is the wild man's celery and can grow as tall as a strapping forager. At the Ethicurean, it's used as 'crackling' in a ham-hock broth, and served with lamb sweetbreads with onion kefir milk. You'll also spot sweet cicely, nasturtiums and bronze dill here.

Simon Rogan leads the field of cheffy grower-gatherers. The most obscure greenery on his menu at Fera at Claridges is probably the melilot, or sweet clover, served with rhubarb, linseed and sweet cicely. The flavour? Similar to woodruff – obviously.

Pontypridd
Bunch of Grapes
Hostelry that does the neighbourhood proud
Ynysangharad Road, Pontypridd, CF37 4DA
Tel no: (01443) 402934
www.bunchofgrapes.org.uk
Modern British | £30
Cooking score: 3

Now here's a pub whose gastronomic adventures have not trampled on its role as a cosy local. You enter through a soothingly shady bar complete with wood-burner and acres of exposed wood. It would be easy to settle here, but the main event is in the adjoining rooms, where a stylishly rough-hewn restaurant, half of it in a conservatory, offers countless blackboard menus of imaginative, earthy cooking. Try the wonderful bread, baked on site (and for sale), and then perhaps a tumble of cockles, leek and crisp bacon piled high on toast, the flavours fresh and vivid. Next, maybe a stonking smoked salmon and cod lasagne, still bubbling hot, with a cooling salad of new potatoes, samphire and spring onions. For dessert, a great slab of sticky toffee pudding with a slick of glossy sauce is a good way to go. The nicely annotated international wine list starts at £15.90.
Chef/s: Sebastien Vanoni. **Open:** all week L 12 to 2.30 (3 Sat, 3.30 Sun), Mon to Sat D 6.30 to 9.30. **Meals:** alc (main courses £15 to £24). **Details:** 60 seats. 24 seats outside. Separate bar. Music.

Reynoldston
Fairyhill
Smart hotel with clear-flavoured cooking
Reynoldston, SA3 1BS
Tel no: (01792) 390139
www.fairyhill.net
Modern British | £45
Cooking score: 4
🍷 🛏

Andrew Hetherington and Paul Davies have done the Gower Peninsula proud during their two-decade residency at this smart country

house hotel. Fairyhill stakes its claim as one of the region's prime hotel destinations and its many fans are drawn back time and again for top-drawer food. The kitchen taps into the locality's rich larder and delivers a style of modernised country-house cooking perfectly in keeping with the surroundings. Carrot purée, buttermilk, peanuts and bisque might be added to scallops, but classic gestures assuage more conservative tastes – Brecon venison with creamed potatoes and red cabbage, or loin and rissole of Welsh lamb with aubergine, roasted garlic, cabbage and thyme jus, say. For dessert, dark chocolate truffle with mandarin jelly and blood-orange sorbet has been singled out. The wine list is a majestic selection representing the great and the good from France, backed up by stellar pickings from around the globe. Prices start at £19.50.
Chef/s: David Whitecross. **Open:** all week L 12 to 2 (3 Sun), D 7 to 9. **Closed:** 26 Dec, 3 weeks Jan. **Meals:** Set L £20 (2 courses) to £25. Set D £35 (2 courses) to £45. Sun L £28. **Details:** 60 seats. 20 seats outside. Separate bar. Wheelchair access. Music. Car parking. Children over 8 yrs only at D.

Swansea
Didier & Stephanie
Tasteful French cuisine
56 St Helen's Road, Swansea, SA1 4BE
Tel no: (01792) 655603
French | £30
Cooking score: 4

This classy little French restaurant has a sleek new look. Gone are the acres of stripped wood, replaced by carpets, cool grey walls and modern lighting. It all hangs together beautifully, as does Didier's modern French cooking, which remains as precise and satisfying as ever. Certain favourites are constant – notably the melt-in-the-mouth croustillant of French black pudding with mustard dressing – but much of the menu shifts with the seasons. Regional French classics (maybe raclette melted on potatoes and bacon) are produced using beautiful Welsh ingredients such as lamb, braised and served with rosemary and tomatoes, or sea bass fillet with Noilly Prat sauce. A perennial dessert is pear, perhaps poached in spices and honey and served with ice cream. Pistachio crème brûlée is another classic, but the selection of French cheese also deserves careful consideration. The substantial wine list runs to 10 pages and kicks off at a reasonable £15.90.

Chef/s: Didier Suvé. **Open:** Tue to Sat L 12 to 3, D from 7. **Closed:** Sun, Mon, Christmas to New Year, 2 weeks summer. **Meals:** alc (main courses £17 to £19). Set L £16 (2 courses) to £19. **Details:** 25 seats. Music.

Hanson at the Chelsea

Unfussy but sophisticated bistro
17 St Mary Street, Swansea, SA1 3LH
Tel no: (01792) 464068
www.hansonatthechelsea.co.uk
Modern European | £30
Cooking score: 3

£5
OFF

Squirrelled away in a little street just off Swansea's party central, Andrew and Michelle Hanson's cosy yellow-walled bistro is a welcome retreat. Inside, the dining room's understated mix of clean-lined New England simplicity and Art Deco style allows Andrew's unfussy but sophisticated food to take centre stage. Seafood is a strong suit, from regular items such as roast scallops with smoky grilled pancetta and a deep-fried strudel of cockles and laverbread to daily specials posted on the big blackboard (sea bass with spicy vegetables and saffron rice, perhaps). Otherwise, the kitchen produces finely judged versions of confit duck on Savoy cabbage with duck-fat chips; char-grilled beef fillet; or eight-hour, honey-glazed pork belly with apple compote, black pudding, apple velouté and crackling. To finish, the trio of mini desserts is tempting, and the Welsh cheeseboard is also well worth a punt. A fairly priced, carefully sourced global wine list starts at £13.95.

Chef/s: Andrew Hanson. **Open:** Mon to Sat L 12 to 2, D 7 to 9.30. **Closed:** Sun. **Meals:** alc (main courses £13 to £22). Set L £13 (2 courses) to £17. Set D £20. **Details:** 42 seats. Music.

Pant-y-Gwydr Restaurant

French cooking that hits the spot
Oxford Street, Swansea, SA1 3JG
Tel no: (01792) 455498
www.pantygwydr.co.uk
French | £35
Cooking score: 3

The Victorian pub on a Swansea corner has been a *travail d'amour* for Jacques and Michèle Abdou. They acquired the place in 2007 and set about converting it into a sympathetically run homage to traditional French gastronomy, respectfully retaining its Welsh name in the process. Inside, they have made creative use of the solid stone walls and pine floors, lightening the space with a mural of Swansea Bay. Jacques' food harks back to earlier eras of French bistro cooking, starting with frogs' legs in garlic and parsley, or coquilles St Jacques in beurre blanc, followed by monkfish casseroled with squid and mussels, or Barbary duck leg confit with sautéed potatoes. The menu helpfully describes the origins of certain dishes, and even more helpfully concludes with gâteau Opéra, and delicately constructed tarte fine aux pommes with apricot sorbet. Languedoc house wines in all three shades cost £16.80, heading a short French list.

Chef/s: Jacques Abdou. **Open:** Wed to Sat L 12 to 2, D 6 to 10. **Closed:** Sun, Mon, Tue, 2 weeks early Sept. **Meals:** alc (main courses £8 to £28). **Details:** 53 seats. Wheelchair access.

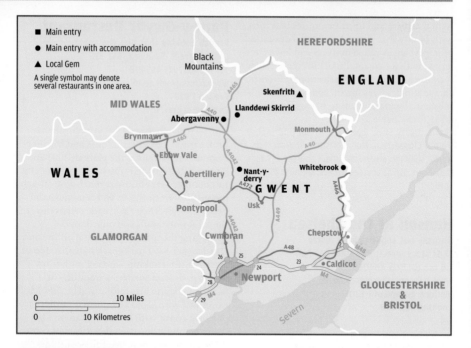

■ Main entry
● Main entry with accommodation
▲ Local Gem

A single symbol may denote
several restaurants in one area.

Abergavenny

★ TOP 50 PUB ★

The Hardwick
An all-round Welsh winner
Old Raglan Road, Abergavenny, NP7 9AA
Tel no: (01873) 854220
www.thehardwick.co.uk
Modern British | £40
Cooking score: 5

TV appearances by chef/patron Stephen Terry
may help keep this former pub on the radar,
but there's no doubt that the food is the
Hardwick's best publicist. Terry's style remains
as distinctive as ever: generous, full flavoured
and fresh, with a clear focus on sourcing.
Flavours straddle the globe, from spiced
pastilla of local lamb with spiced lentils,
aubergine, cucumber, yoghurt and harissa, to
a veal burger with Swiss cheese, cowboy
pickles and skinny fries. Starters show the
same scope, running from pork meatloaf to

crab linguine with brown–butter
breadcrumbs. Each dessert reads like a list of
home comforts: baked stem ginger cheesecake
and shortbread crumble with poached
rhubarb; and rice pudding and caramelised
salted apple with baked shortbread crumble.
Like the service and the décor, the food is very
slick and polished, yet succeeds in seeming
rustic and relaxed. A substantial international
wine list, divided by style, starts at £19.
Chef/s: Stephen Terry. **Open:** all week L 12 to 3, D
6.30 to 9 (6 Sun). **Closed:** 25 and 26 Dec. **Meals:** alc
(main courses £17 to £27). Set L £19 (2 courses) to
£24. Sun L £21 (2 courses) to £26. **Details:** 100
seats. 25 seats outside. Separate bar. Wheelchair
access. Music. Car parking.

Average Price
The average price listed in main-entry
reviews denotes the price of a three-
course meal, without wine.

Restaurant 1861
Homely roadside restaurant
Cross Ash, Abergavenny, NP7 8PB
Tel no: (0845) 3881861
www.18-61.co.uk
Modern European | £38
Cooking score: 3
£5 OFF **V**

Built in 1861, this attractive black-and-white roadside building is full of original features, but chef-owner Simon King and his wife Kate have added modern touches to the interior, creating a setting that feels relaxed but has a sense of occasion. The green hills that unroll on all sides hide a number of good restaurants – perhaps the richest concentration in Wales – but 1861 has made its mark with a combination of Simon's classically inspired cooking and Kate's front-of-house charm. Pan-fried ethically produced foie gras with braised lentils is a good way to start, while a main course of fricassee of pheasant with grain-mustard cream is typical of the rich and comforting style. To finish, maybe choose acorn pannacotta with pumpkin ice cream or pear tarte Tatin with quince sorbet. The international wine list includes a number of Welsh wines, with prices from £17.50.
Chef/s: Simon King. **Open:** Tue to Sun L 12 to 2, Tue to Sat D 7 to 9. **Closed:** Mon, 26 Dec to 10 Jan. **Meals:** alc (main courses £19 to £24). Set L £19 (2 courses) to £25. Set D £35. Sun L £22. **Details:** 35 seats. Separate bar. Music. Car parking.

Llanddewi Skirrid
The Walnut Tree
Re-energised Welsh icon
Llanddewi Skirrid, NP7 8AW
Tel no: (01873) 852797
www.thewalnuttreeinn.com
Modern British | £45
Cooking score: 6

The Walnut Tree has lost none of its pilgrimage status over the years, and the prospect of bookable cottages nearby is an added incentive for city folk to head for the foothills of the Black Mountains. Shaun Hill and his team have worked wonders since 2007, re-energising this unaffected rural eatery and putting it back in the big time. All the trademarks are here: genuine warmth, brilliant value, an honest respect for seasonal ingredients, straight-talking flavours and full-frontal impact without unnecessary flourishes. Hill's remit is broad: he serves squid with salt-cod croquettes, parsley and garlic sauce; pairs wild duck with morels; and matches Dover sole with Jansson's temptation (a potato-based Scandi favourite). There are salads, charcuterie boards and savoury tarts, too, plus generous sides and irresistible puddings ranging from chocolate and amaretti trifle to apple parfait with salted-caramel sauce. Set lunches are a bargain, and the barnstorming wine list touts 'essentials' and 'shining stars' at enticing prices. Carafes from £10.
Chef/s: Shaun Hill and Roger Brook. **Open:** Tue to Sat L 12 to 2, D 6.30 to 9.30. **Closed:** Sun, Mon, 1 week Christmas. **Meals:** alc (main courses £15 to £26). Set L £22 (2 courses) to £28. **Details:** 50 seats. 10 seats outside. Separate bar. Wheelchair access. Car parking.

Nant-y-derry
★ TOP 50 PUB ★

The Foxhunter
Sheer indulgence and thoughtful food
Nant-y-derry, NP7 9DN
Tel no: (01873) 881101
www.thefoxhunter.com
Modern British | £35
Cooking score: 4

'This is a venue where I am willing to step out of my comfort zone and try new things,' a regular visitor tells us, which must be music to a chef's ears. Matt and Lisa Tebbutt's stone-built village restaurant was originally the stationmaster's house, when somewhere as tiny as Nant-y-derry had the luxury of its own railway stop. It makes a charming setting for

Matt's highly crafted modern British cooking, some of which is provisioned by items foraged on tutored trips into the wilds. Hearty soups of celeriac or spiced pumpkin are a traditional way to start, or there may be a starter serving of lasagne made with Dexter beef and pecorino. Follow on with haunch of Brecon venison on braised Puy lentils and salsa verde, or turbot in shellfish broth, and then prepare for a seductive finisher like rice pudding with Armagnac prunes. Wines start at £19.95, or £4.95 a glass.
Chef/s: Matt Tebbutt. **Open:** Tue to Sun L 12 to 2, Tue to Sat D 6 to 9. **Closed:** Mon, 25 and 26 Dec, bank hols. **Meals:** alc (main courses £18 to £25). Set L £23 (2 courses) to £28. Sun L £24 (2 courses) to £30. **Details:** 40 seats. 12 seats outside. Separate bar. Wheelchair access. Music. Car parking.

Skenfrith

LOCAL GEM
▲ The Bell at Skenfrith
Skenfrith, NP7 8UH
Tel no: (01600) 750235
www.skenfrith.co.uk
Modern British | £27 £5 OFF

The management may be new but the Bell's rustic-chic styling, warm welcome and focus on dining remain constant. Settle in easy chairs by the fire for a pre-dinner drink, then move to the dining area with its pretty garden views. Typical dishes are Lyme Bay crab mayo on toast; pan-fried John Dory, braised salsify and asparagus with crayfish zabaglione; and apple sauce-filled doughnuts with a toffee dipping sauce and a shot glass of malted cider. Wines from £16. Closed Tue Jan to mid Feb.

Whitebrook

NEW ENTRY
The Crown at Whitebrook
Foraged food and fresh flavours
Whitebrook, NP25 4TX
Tel no: (01600) 86025
www.crownatwhitebrook.co.uk
British | £54
Cooking score: 5
£5 OFF 🍽 V

New chef/proprietor Chris Harrod is carving a niche for himself at this rural restaurant-with-rooms – it looks set to regain the special status achieved under James Sommerin. Harrod has kept the fine-dining flag flying, but the place feels more relaxed. The carpets have been replaced with wood floors, the staff are chatty and you get to unfold your own napkin. While the Crown's branding remains the same, Harrod's style is emphatically his own: expect classic techniques, interesting flavours and plenty of foraging. Laver seaweed, turnip and burnt apple give depth and zing to a fillet of flame-grilled mackerel, while turbot on smoked roe purée with smashed Jersey Royals and challengingly woody ground elder is the only time the foraged element falls short of wonderful. An admirable lightness of touch shines through in a lemon mousse with fizzy apple honeycomb, jellied Tintern mead and elderflower. The wine list kicks off at £23.
Chef/s: Chris Harrod. **Open:** Tue to Sun L 12 to 2, D 7 to 9. **Closed:** Mon, 2 to 15 Jan. **Meals:** Set L £19 (2 courses) to £24. Set D £48 (2 courses) to £54. Sun L £34. Tasting Menu £65. **Details:** 30 seats. 16 seats outside. Separate bar. Music. Car parking.

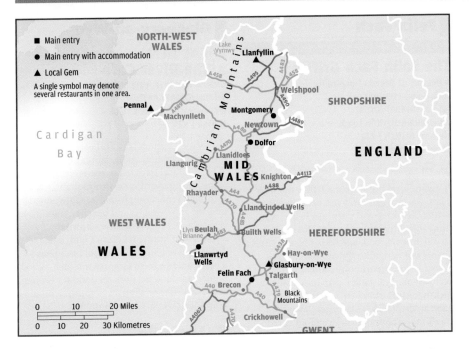

■ Dolfor

The Old Vicarage Dolfor
Folksy, food-loving Welsh hideaway
Dolfor, SY16 4BN
Tel no: (01686) 629051
www.theoldvicaragedolfor.co.uk
Modern British | £30
Cooking score: 2

£5 🛏
OFF

Tim and Helen Withers opted for the good life back in 2005 after making a name for themselves as food-loving pub landlords in Wiltshire. Almost 10 years later, they are still happy in their converted Victorian vicarage: tending to their increasingly productive kitchen garden and polytunnels, rearing chickens and supporting organically minded endeavours around their adopted home. They have even found time to create a wildlife pond for the amusement of guests. You need to book 24 hours in advance if you want to sample Tim's cooking, but it's worth the effort for a modest, daily menu of thoughtfully crafted dishes based on home-grown and name-checked regional produce – perhaps avocado and celeriac timbale with sweet chilli and tomato dressing followed by Cornish hake with roast tomato sauce, purple sprouting broccoli and cauliflower. After that, some Welsh farmhouse cheeses or sticky toffee pudding should suffice. Wines from £15.
Chef/s: Tim Withers. **Open:** Sun L 1, all week D 7.30 (1 sitting). **Closed:** 20 Dec to 5 Jan. **Meals:** Set D £25 (2 courses) to £30. Sun L £30. **Details:** 12 seats. 8 seats outside. Car parking.

Symbols

🛏 Accommodation is available

£30 Three courses for less than £30

V Separate vegetarian menu

£5 £5-off voucher scheme
OFF

🍾 Notable wine list

Felin Fach

★ TOP 50 PUB ★

The Felin Fach Griffin
A beacon of Brecon hospitality
Felin Fach, LD3 0UB
Tel no: (01874) 620111
www.felinfachgriffin.co.uk
Modern British | £32
Cooking score: 4

£5 OFF 🛏

A hub of local life since the 1780s, and now a heart-warming country inn dedicated to 'eating, drinking and sleeping', Felin Fach shines brightly in the Brecons. It's located on an old drovers' road, and boasts blazing fires, beams and agricultural memorabilia, but there's serious gastronomic intent too: a certified organic garden provides seasonal pickings for the kitchen, and the food has its roots in the Welsh countryside. That said, there's nothing rough-hewn about cured salmon and duck with potato salad and quail's egg mayonnaise or haunch of Bwlch venison with cabbage, black pudding, chanterelles and hazelnut sauce. Some ingredients have farther to travel (dressed Portland crab, for example), but puds such as treacle tart with clotted cream bring it back home. Service is kind and accommodating, especially concerning special diets, while drinks range from Welsh real ales and ciders to sherries and a compendium of idiosyncratic wines from £18.50.
Chef/s: Ross Bruce. Open: all week L 12 to 2.30, D 6 to 9 (9.30 Fri and Sat). Closed: 25 Dec, 4 days early Jan. Meals: alc (main courses £17 to £20). Set L £18 (2 courses) to £21. Set D £23 (2 courses) to £29. Sun L £25. Details: 58 seats. 20 seats outside. Separate bar. Wheelchair access. Music. Car parking.

Glasbury-on-Wye

LOCAL GEM
▲ The River Café
Glasbury-on-Wye, HR3 5NP
Tel no: (01497) 847007
www.wyevalleycanoes.co.uk
Italian | £25 £5 OFF

Wye Valley Canoes is at the heart of this bustling operation on the banks of the River Wye, but local spies tell us the River Café across the boatyard is no afterthought. Informal, with a rough-and-ready wooden interior of bare tables and benches, plus riverside decking, it becomes a proper restaurant at lunch and dinner with daily dishes chalked on an old school blackboard. There could be fresh Cornish mussels, a good homemade lasagne, pork tenderloin cassoulet, and treacle tart or affogato to finish. House wines are £14.95. Closed Sun D.

Llanfyllin

LOCAL GEM
▲ Seeds
5 Penybryn Cottages, High Street, Llanfyllin, SY22 5AP
Tel no: (01691) 648604
Modern British | £30

Mark and Felicity Seager have been driving this amenable village restaurant since 1991 and continue to win friends for their warm hospitality and good-value bistro cooking. The short-choice, set-price menus (supplemented by blackboard specials) fit the bill perfectly, typical choices being ricotta and pumpkin pasta parcels followed by sea bass on wilted spinach and sun-dried tomato sauce or fillet steak with brandy and cream. A rather good crème brûlée will round things off. The international wine list (from £14) won't break the bank, either. Closed Sun to Tue and Wed L.

🍴 STÉPHANE BORIE
The Checkers, Powys

What inspired you to become a chef?
My grandfather Marcel was a keen hunter and he had a potager in Mussidan, France, that was my first memory of food. But the one that inspired me the most was my aunt Jacqueline - an excellent home cook who makes the best prune jam in Agen.

What is your favourite time of year for food?
For me summer food is the best - the light, fresh, and beautifully ripe fruit is second to none.

What's your newest ingredient discovery?
Methyl cellulose; it enables us to make the most delicious beetroot meringues.

At the end of a long day, what do you like to cook?
I love Chinese food - and a Pot Noodle is never too far away at the end of a busy day!

Are there any ingredients that evoke strong memories for you?
Being from Agen, les pruneaux (prunes) will always be associated with me.

▌Llanwrtyd Wells

Carlton Riverside
Smart yet homely riverside retreat
Irfon Crescent, Llanwrtyd Wells, LD5 4SP
Tel no: (01591) 610248
www.carltonriverside.com
Modern British | £31
Cooking score: 5

£5 OFF

A restaurant-with-rooms by the River Irfon (the second oldest property in town, they say, which is itself the smallest town in Wales), Carlton Riverside is easy to spot thanks to its sky-blue paintwork picked out on the granite façade. Alan and Mary Ann Gilchrist are experienced hands and deliver a compelling package of comfortable rooms, a lively bar serving pizzas all day and a civilised restaurant that impresses with its vibrant modern British output. There's plenty of Welsh produce to be had, such as the Carmarthen ham that comes as a first course in the company of a pea mousse, or a main-course roast rump of lamb with an accompanying Madeira jus. Dishes can be as simple as lemon linguine with cream and Parmesan, while desserts run to chilled caramelised rice pudding with whinberry compote. The wine list, compiled by Alan, has a global spread with prices starting at £16.95. **Chef/s:** Mary Ann Gilchrist. **Open:** Mon to Sat D only 7 to 8.30. **Closed:** Sun, 21 to 30 Dec. **Meals:** alc (main courses £13 to £27). **Details:** 16 seats. Music.

Lasswade Country House
Seasonal food without gimmickry
Station Road, Llanwrtyd Wells, LD5 4RW
Tel no: (01591) 610515
www.lasswadehotel.co.uk
Modern British | £34
Cooking score: 2

£5 OFF

Once a spa and regularly paraded as 'the smallest town in Britain', Llanwrtyd Wells is also home to Roger and Emma Stevens' gently nurtured restaurant-with-rooms: a tall Edwardian residence near the railway station.

Comforting interiors and log fires set the scene for evening meals in Lasswade's candlelit, Regency-style dining room, where the short daily menu showcases seasonal food without gimmickry. Roger flies the flag for organic produce, is on first-name terms with his suppliers and uses produce from the family's cottage garden in Cilycwm. He has also teamed up with the Cambrian Mountains Initiative, so his hill lamb is among the region's best – no wonder it's given 'celebratory' billing in dishes such as herb-crusted best end with confit shoulder, baby shepherd's pie and Madeira reduction. To begin, you might try roasted Tally goats' cheese and asparagus with Carmarthen air-dried ham; to finish, perhaps ginger-poached pears with dark chocolate and honey ganache. Wines from £15.75.
Chef/s: Roger Stevens. **Open:** all week D only 7.30 to 9. **Closed:** 25 and 26 Dec. **Meals:** Set D £28 (2 courses) to £34. **Details:** 20 seats. Wheelchair access. Car parking.

Montgomery

The Checkers
Faultless French food
Broad Street, Montgomery, SY15 6PN
Tel no: (01686) 669822
www.thecheckersmontgomery.co.uk
French | £50
Cooking score: 6

A genuine feeling of affection radiates from readers' reports we receive about 'this quaint restaurant-with-rooms' occupying a former 18th-century coaching inn. To be sure, the Checkers is a smart place with its country-style lounge and gracefully appointed dining areas, but what it is primarily all about is excellent French cuisine. Stéphane Borie and Sarah Francis deal in precision-tuned cooking, with sound materials and technical ability providing the impetus. From homemade boudin noir with pommes mousseline and Madeira sauce, to an avidly reported roasted saddle of rabbit with confit shoulder, tarragon butter beans and smoked belly lardons, white wine and thyme jus, this is food that pleases, excites and soothes in equal measure. Desserts are equally captivating, whether a billowingly light dark chocolate soufflé (with Baileys ice cream) or mélange of ginger and rhubarb desserts. Wines on a reasonably priced, globetrotting list (with France to the fore) start at £17.
Chef/s: Stéphane Borie. **Open:** Thur to Sat L 12 to 1.45, Tue to Sat D 6 to 9. **Closed:** Sun, Mon, 25 and 26 Dec, 2 weeks Jan. **Meals:** alc (main courses £20 to £28). **Details:** 48 seats. Children over 8 yrs only at D.

Pennal

LOCAL GEM
▲ Glan Yr Afon
Pennal, SY20 9DW
Tel no: (01654) 791285
www.riversidehotel-pennal.co.uk
Modern British | £25

Glan Yr Afon ('the Riverside') is a solid-looking 16th-century country pub and hotel in the centre of the village by the River Sychan (a tributary of the Dyfi). It has nailed its colours to the foodie mast, but a pint of real ale in the bar is still on the cards: positively encouraged in fact. Expect duck confit with tarragon couscous, or pie of the day, and a local flavour here and there. Wines start at £14.50. Open all week.

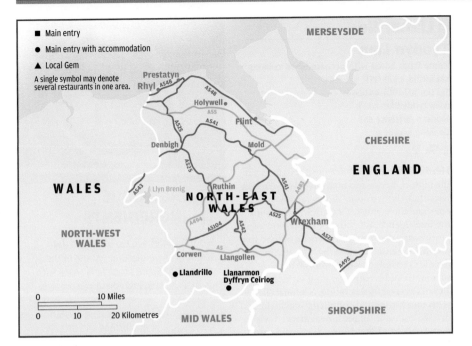

Llanarmon Dyffryn Ceiriog

The West Arms Hotel
Characterful inn with fine local food
Llanarmon Dyffryn Ceiriog, LL20 7LD
Tel no: (01691) 600665
www.thewestarms.co.uk
Modern British | £25
Cooking score: 3
£5 OFF 🛏 £30

A 'homely, traditional' pub in a quiet Welsh village, this former drovers' inn dates from the 16th century. Stunning countryside unfolds outside, and the interior retains a host of original features, including chunky beams and real fires. The bar menu is full of hearty comfort food (steak and mushroom pie, gammon and chips), while the restaurant menu favours Welsh ingredients and classic recipes – maybe a soufflé made from Perl Las cheese with warm pear chutney, and then seared fillet of Welsh Black beef with confit of wild mushrooms, oxtail fondant and port wine jus. The kitchen becomes more inventive at dessert, when ricotta doughnuts with warm chocolate sauce and clotted cream ice cream, or iced praline parfait with espresso foam, might be offered. The wine list is wide-ranging and provides plenty of choice, much of it under £25, with bottles from £16.95.
Chef/s: Grant Williams. **Open:** Bar meals: all week 12 to 9. Restaurant: D only 6 to 9. Sun 12 to 9. **Meals:** alc (main courses £12 to £23). Set D £30 (2 courses) to £35. Sun L £11. **Details:** 50 seats. 20 seats outside. Separate bar. Wheelchair access. Music. Car parking.

Symbols
🛏 Accommodation is available

£30 Three courses for less than £30

V Separate vegetarian menu

£5 OFF £5-off voucher scheme

🍷 Notable wine list

▌Llandrillo

Tyddyn Llan

Home from home with accomplished cooking
Llandrillo, LL21 OST
Tel no: (01490) 440264
www.tyddynllan.co.uk
Modern British | £55
Cooking score: 6

🍷 🍴 **V**

Head and shoulders above most restaurants in the region, Bryan and Susan Webb's Georgian restaurant-with-rooms shows exactly how to combine the virtues of a country hotel with the intelligence and culinary know-how of a serious-minded eatery. 'It's a menu of food that just makes sense,' says one fan. The attention to detail is 'second to none', from smart surrounds and accommodating service to Bryan's ever-skilful cooking. Seasonal clarity is his touchstone and simplicity is evident in dressed crab and langoustine enhanced with a fennel salad and pea shoots. Successful main courses have included roast turbot with leek risotto and red wine sauce ('did exactly what it said on the tin'), and a plate of local pork: fillet, long-braised cheek, breaded trotter, roasted belly, crisp crackling, black pudding and apple purée. To finish, rhubarb and Champagne jelly trifle is 'sweet, fruity and boozy in every mouthful'. The wine list is a delight, shining brightest in France, with kind mark-ups; bottles from £23.50.
Chef/s: Bryan Webb. **Open:** Fri to Sun L 12.30 to 2 (2.30 Sun), all week D 7 to 9 (9.30 Fri and Sat). **Closed:** last 2 weeks Jan. **Meals:** alc (main courses £10 to £29). Set L £22 (2 courses) to £29. Set D £45 (2 courses) to £55. Sun L £29. **Details:** 40 seats. 12 seats outside. Separate bar. Wheelchair access. Car parking.

🍴 INGENIOUS INGREDIENTS

From the wild and wonderful to the scientifically molecular – some of the *Good Food Guide's* top chefs share with us their newest ingredient discoveries.

Scurvy grass is a favourite of Tristan Mason. Found at clifftops and on salt marshes, scurvy grass is peppery with a taste akin to watercress or horseradish.

Paul Ainsworth recommends ice wine vinegar. Grapes are harvested and pressed whilst frozen, and fermented slowly, resulting in a sweet, dark vinegar which can be used similarly to balsamic.

Gareth Fulford loves oxalis flowers, which 'have a sharp, citrus flavour and look beautiful on the plate'. The flower is not the only edible part, oxalis root is also rather tasty and quite popular as a vegetable in New Zealand.

Shaun Rankin and Mark Jordan are big fans of ormers. Ormers, (taken from the French 'oreille de mer' – ear of the sea) are best eaten either slow cooked or flash fried. These meaty sea snails are a delicacy of the Channel Islands since they are not able to live any further north.

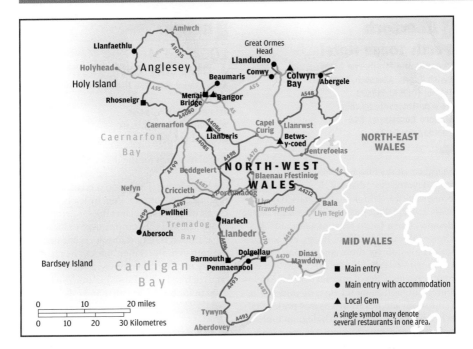

Abergele

★ TOP 50 PUB ★

The Kinmel Arms
Revitalised inn with fulfilling Welsh food
St George, Abergele, LL22 9BP
Tel no: (01745) 832207
www.thekinmelarms.co.uk
Modern British | £30
Cooking score: 4

Tucked neatly into the north Wales hinterland
between mountains and sea, the hamlet of St
George is home to a 17th-century sandstone
inn, its mullioned windows and carriage-
lamps contrasting with a more contemporary
look inside. Co-proprietor Tim Watson's
artworks add to the elegant, clean-lined
interiors. In the kitchen, Heddwen Wheeler
makes best use of north Walian and Cheshire
produce for appealing modern bistro dishes.
Start with seared breast of wood pigeon in a
mélange of wild mushrooms, pickled baby

turnips and puréed carrots, or maybe Menai
mussels in creamy Thai-spiced sauce. Next
comes sea bream marinated in lemon and
thyme with scallops and Jerusalem artichokes
in watercress velouté, or braised shank and
shoulder ragoût of fine Welsh lamb, with
sautéed Savoy cabbage, cubes of mint jelly and
rosemary pastilles. A citrus assiette to finish
contains lemon posset, Key lime pie, orange
and white-chocolate parfait, and pink
grapefruit sherbet. The thoughtfully written
wine list opens at £17.50.
Chef/s: Heddwen Wheeler. **Open:** Tue to Sat L 12 to
2, D 6 to 9.30. **Closed:** Sun, Mon, 25 Dec, 1 Jan, bank
hols. **Meals:** alc (main courses £15 to £23).
Details: 88 seats. 24 seats outside. Separate bar.
Music. Children before 9pm only.

Average Price
The average price listed in main-entry
reviews denotes the price of a three-
course meal, without wine.

Abersoch
Porth Tocyn Hotel
Redoubtable family-run hotel
Bwlch Tocyn, Abersoch, LL53 7BU
Tel no: (01758) 713303
www.porthtocynhotel.co.uk
Modern European | £46
Cooking score: 3

🛏

Members of the Fletcher–Brewer family have
been devoted custodians of this country-
house retreat overlooking Cardigan Bay since
1948 – with Guide recognition for nigh on six
decades. Porth Tocyn remains a dependable
choice for seaside family holidays, but also cuts
it as a bolt-hole for those appreciating capable
cooking in relaxed, 'dinner party' surrounds.
Staff serve up plates of uncontroversial Anglo-
European food along the lines of wild
mushroom and pea risotto, seared pork fillet
with red onion mash and wholegrain mustard
reduction or roast guinea fowl breast with
black pudding hotpot, artichokes and spring
onion jus. There's decent local fish, too
(poached lemon sole with spring vegetables,
pak choi, saffron potatoes and lemon butter,
perhaps), while dessert might bring warm
treacle tart with Amaretto ice cream or
lavender crème brûlée with lime shortbread.
Light lunches, Sunday buffets, kids' high teas
and an imposing list of knowledgeably chosen
wines (from £17.50) complete the picture.
Chef/s: Louise Fletcher-Brewer and Martin
Williams. **Open:** all week L 12 to 2.30, D 7 to 9.
Closed: early Nov to week before Easter. **Meals:** Set
D £39 (2 courses) to £46. Sun L £26. **Details:** 50
seats. 20 seats outside. Separate bar. Car parking.

Symbols
🛏 Accommodation is available
£30 Three courses for less than £30
V Separate vegetarian menu
£5 £5-off voucher scheme
🍷 Notable wine list

Bangor
LOCAL GEM
▲ Blue Sky Café
Ambassador Hall, 236 High Street, Bangor,
LL57 1PA
Tel no: (01248) 355444
www.blueskybangor.co.uk
British | £14 £5

Regulars vouch for the 'delicious food' at this
well-regarded café tucked up a little alley off
the High Street. The mood is relaxed – think
roaring wood-burner, slouchy leather sofas,
bare wooden floor, plain tables – prices are
reasonable and the commitment to local and
organic food is important. Everyone praises
the corn-fed, free-range 'chicken in a basket',
the organic Welsh beefburgers, the lovely BLT
sandwich and well-dressed salads. You can also
drop in for breakfast, coffee and cakes. Wine
from £11.75. Closed Sun and all evenings.

Barmouth
Bistro Bermo
Pint-sized local bistro
6 Church Street, Barmouth, LL42 1EW
Tel no: (01341) 281284
www.bistrobarmouth.co.uk
Modern British | £32
Cooking score: 2

Emma and Paul Ryder's pint-sized restaurant
runs along merrily, a hard-working local asset
on Barmouth's main street. The couple take
care of just about everything themselves,
putting in the hours and delivering capable
cooking with a real sense of pride. Provenance
and seasonality are to the fore on the
approachable menus and the food is
accomplished without being pretentious – a
mix of traditional British with modern
European touches, so most people find
something they like. Booking is essential, as
'everyone knows about it in the area'. Start,
perhaps, with tempura prawns with a sweet
chilli sauce; follow with pork belly teamed
with scallops and a pork reduction or a boned
and braised shoulder of lamb that comes with

apple and mint gravy; finish with dark chocolate and raspberry crème brûlée, although the all-Snowdonia cheeseboard is an impressive finishing touch. Wines from £15.50.
Chef/s: Paul Ryder. **Open:** Tue to Sun D 5 to 10. **Closed:** Mon. **Meals:** alc (main courses £14 to £23). **Details:** 18 seats. 2 seats outside. Music.

Beaumaris

Ye Olde Bull's Head Inn, Loft Restaurant
Bull with a pull
Castle Street, Beaumaris, LL58 8AP
Tel no: (01248) 810329
www.bullsheadinn.co.uk
Modern British | £45
Cooking score: 5

This pedigree inn dates from the 15th century and is a rather grand edifice, converted and encompassing a 'cheerful and pleasant' brasserie in the former stables, and the smart, contemporary Loft Restaurant, shoehorned into the hayloft. The latter, a long dining room, feels very Sunday best, but without the stiff-collared formality, and service runs along unobtrusively. Chef Hefin Roberts has a sharp eye for local detail, his field-to-fork commitment to local produce seen in roast loin and rump of Anglesey lamb, which arrives with wild mushroom and tongue risotto, charred vegetables and rosemary oil. 'Bang on' starters could include smoked pork belly with a chorizo beignet and an onion and parsley risotto, preceded by an amuse-bouche of parsnip soup – 'so good it should serve as a masterclass in parsnip soup making'. Finally, there's always a plate of fine Welsh cheeses, along with cleanly presented desserts such as lemon mousse with Cointreau savarin, blood-orange curd and root-ginger arlette, or a 'perfectly balanced' chocolate and hazelnut gateau. The French-led wine list starts at £19.50.

Chef/s: Hefin Roberts. **Open:** Tue to Sat D only 7 to 9.30 (6.30 Fri and Sat). **Closed:** Sun, Mon, 25 and 26 Dec, 1 Jan. **Meals:** Set D £45 (3 courses). **Details:** 45 seats. Separate bar. Car parking. Children over 8 yrs only.

Betws-y-Coed

LOCAL GEM
▲ Bistro Betws-y-Coed
Holyhead Road, Betws-y-Coed, LL24 0AY
Tel no: (01690) 710328
www.bistrobetws-y-coed.co.uk
British | £23 £5 OFF

Chef Gerwyn Williams has recently taken over this bistro in the touristy village of Betws-y-Coed where he conjures up fairly extensive menus of simple dishes based on locally sourced raw materials. Start perhaps with Penmachno wild pigeon (served with bubble and squeak, crispy bacon and homemade chilli-spiced plum jam), follow with a trio of local lamb (roast rack, braised lamb shank, fritter) and finish off with a traditional lemon flummery with raspberry cream. Wines from £13.95. Open all week summer. Accommodation.

Colwyn Bay

LOCAL GEM
▲ Hayloft
Bodnant Welsh Food, Furnace Farm, Tal-y-Cafn, Colwyn Bay, LL28 5RP
Tel no: (01492) 651100
www.bodnant-welshfood.co.uk
Modern British | £25

Bodnant Welsh Food Centre is sited in a handsomely renovated 18th-century farm in the glorious Conwy Valley. Its well-endowed estate and farm shop (based around local producers) provides for both a café and the spacious Hayloft restaurant. Here, menus display commendable seasonal focus and starters such as Anglesey mussels cooked in leeks and Taffy cider, and served with Bodnant leek and Aberwen (cheese) bread, show quality from the off. There's also Welsh Black ribeye, slow-roasted lamb Henry and desserts such as bara brith crème brûlée. Wines from £12.75. Closed Mon and Tue.

Conwy

Dawsons at the Castle Hotel
Designer décor and local produce
High Street, Conwy, LL32 8DB
Tel no: (01492) 582800
www.castlewales.co.uk
Modern British | £30
Cooking score: 2

£5 OFF

The Castle sports a distinctive red-brick and granite façade courtesy of the Victorians, but the origins of the building go back much further. It has been a source of hospitality in the town for a long while and continues today with a touch of 21st-century boutique glamour. The dining option, Dawsons (named after a Victorian illustrator whose work adorns the restaurant), has been visited by the interior designers and dressed up to the nines, while the menu takes a broad approach to satisfy the modern customer. Among starters, a classy prawn cocktail competes for attention with the more trendy scallops with butternut squash purée and confit chorizo. There's char-grilled steak to follow, or pot-roasted pheasant with smoked pancetta-enriched cabbage. A decent showing of local ingredients helps give a sense of place. Finish with sticky toffee pudding or a slate of Welsh cheeses. Wines start at £16.50.
Chef/s: Andrew Nelson. Open: all week 12 to 9.30. Closed: 25 and 31 Dec. Meals: alc (main courses £15 to £23). Details: 86 seats. 34 seats outside. Separate bar. Music. Car parking.

Dolgellau

Bwyty Mawddach
Mediterranean flavours on a family farm
Llanelltyd, Dolgellau, LL40 2TA
Tel no: (01341) 421752
www.mawddach.com
Modern British | £32
Cooking score: 2

Ifan Dunn's decision to return to the family farm and open a restaurant has created a venue that feels entirely rooted in its landscape. The 17th-century barn received a stylish makeover, maintaining the rustic feel of the spaces (over two floors) while adding a bit of contemporary swagger. The views from here are quite something – the Cader Idris mountain and Mawddach estuary – and, given those farming connections, there's a genuinely local flavour to the menu. That said, Dunn cooks with a modern European/Med focus, producing the likes of deep-fried risotto with smoked haddock and black pudding, or free-range chicken with polenta and anchovies. Trusted local supply lines deliver Welsh Black beef (served as ribeye with triple-cooked chips and béarnaise), while the farm itself is the source of the lamb served in a pie with arborio rice and salsa verde. Wine from £15.
Chef/s: Ifan Dunn. Open: Wed to Sun L 12 to 2.30, Wed to Sat D 6 to 9. Closed: Mon, Tue. Meals: alc (main courses £14 to £21). Sun L £22. Details: 75 seats. 50 seats outside. Separate bar. Wheelchair access. Music. Car parking.

Dylanwad Da
Covering all the gastronomic bases
2 Ffôs-y-Felin, Dolgellau, LL40 1BS
Tel no: (01341) 422870
www.dylanwad.co.uk
Modern British | £28
Cooking score: 1

£5 OFF £30

Dylanwad Da covers all the gastronomic bases, serving the community as café, bar, restaurant and wine shop. Dylan Rowlands

has been on hand here for more than 25 years and his establishment has become part of Dolgellau's DNA. It's not a complicated formula – fresh food, simple combinations and a local flavour. Rarebit comes with apple chutney as a starter, followed by a sirloin steak (from Bala) with trad trimmings, or spiced fillet of salmon. The mostly European wine list is full of good stuff, with prices starting at £15.50.
Chef/s: Dylan Rowlands. **Open:** Tue to Sat L 10 to 3, D 7 to 10. **Closed:** Sun, Mon, Feb. **Meals:** alc (main courses £15 to £21). Set D £26. **Details:** 26 seats. Separate bar. Music.

Harlech
Castle Cottage
Accomplished restaurant-with-rooms
Y Llech, Harlech, LL46 2YL
Tel no: (01766) 780479
www.castlecottageharlech.co.uk
Modern British | £40
Cooking score: 2

🛏

Readers continue to sing the praises of the Roberts' long-established restaurant-with-rooms overlooking Harlech Castle. It's a polished set-up, the smartly modernised dining room all soft furnishings and soft lighting under a low-beamed ceiling – an indicator of the age of the building. The place runs trippingly along under the watchful eye of Jaqueline Roberts and is open for dinner only. In the kitchen, husband Glyn's cooking will not amaze for its adventure but will satisfy for its technique. His style is simple, seasonally aware and uses mainly Welsh produce. The fixed-price menu brings lovely own-baked bread and canapés, then risotto of smoked haddock with a poached egg and light curry sauce ahead of loin of local lamb or excellent Welsh Black steak. Desserts have been a particular highlight, and the date sponge with warm butterscotch sauce garners as much praise as the high-quality Welsh cheeses. Wines from £16.

Chef/s: Glyn Roberts. **Open:** all week D only 7 to 9 (8 Sun). **Closed:** 24 to 26 Dec, 3 weeks Nov. **Meals:** Set D £35 (2 courses) to £40. Tasting menu £50 (5 courses). **Details:** 35 seats. Separate bar. Music. Car parking.

Llanberis
LOCAL GEM
▲ The Peak
86 High Street, Llanberis, LL55 4SU
Tel no: (01286) 872777
www.peakrestaurant.co.uk
Modern British | £15 £5 OFF

If the Snowdonia peaks bring you to this part of the world, it's worth knowing you can eat well in between all the exertion at Angela Dwyer's restaurant. This homely place, with no airs or graces, has an open kitchen showing the experienced chef/patron at work. Welsh produce shines in dishes that cross international borders: crab cakes with herby mayonnaise, bouillabaisse packed with local seafood or roasted lamb shank with roasted winter vegetables. Wine from £14.95. Open Tue to Sat D.

Llandudno
NEW ENTRY
Jaya
Lovingly cooked North Indian food
36 Church Walks, Llandudno, LL30 2HN
Tel no: (01492) 818198
www.jayarestaurant.co.uk
Indian | £26
Cooking score: 2
£30

'The food here is much better than what one finds in a routine Indian restaurant in the UK,' thought one reader, of this 'unique' eatery located in a 19th-century town house in the middle of a residential area. The ground floor is divided into a modern cocktail bar and dining room, which has glass-topped tables and high-backed cream chairs. Indian taped music plays in the background. Dishes are 'authentic and freshly cooked', for Sunita

Katoch recreates her family's lovingly guarded recipes, mainly north Indian food with some Kenyan influences, and meat and fish are well sourced. Start with a Kenyan-inspired pili pili boga (fried aubergine, cauliflower, peppers and mushrooms in a tamarind sauce), followed perhaps by a North Indian karahi lamb, some mattar paneer (peas and homemade Indian cheese in a spicy gravy) and tandoori naan. Wine from £13.95.

Chef/s: Sunita Katoch. **Open:** Wed to Sat D only 6 to 9. **Closed:** Sun, Mon, Tue. **Meals:** alc (main courses £10 to £13). **Details:** 20 seats. Separate bar. Music. Car parking.

St Tudno Hotel, Terrace Restaurant
Traditional hotel with well-judged dishes
Promenade, Llandudno, LL30 2LP
Tel no: (01492) 874411
www.st-tudno.co.uk
Modern British | £36
Cooking score: 2
🍷 ⇆ V

St Tudno is the best of the bunch of hotels on Llandudno's seafront promenade, occupying pride of place facing the pier and gardens. It might strike some as being in a time warp (one reporter thought the 'whole feel of the place was tired and dated'), but options are limited for an authentic Victorian hotel in this kind of location. The Lake Como mural in the ground-floor Terrace Restaurant extends over two walls and is there to compensate for the lack of a view, but the room is pretty enough with its chandeliers and draped tables – and Andrew Foster's cooking still delivers. His mature, modern British style produced well-judged dishes at inspection: pan-seared Anglesey scallops with streaky bacon, oven-roast loin of Welsh lamb, then lemon and raspberry posset (deemed a lighter pudding than apple crumble parfait). Bottles on the well-researched wine list start at £18.50.

Chef/s: Andrew Foster. **Open:** all week L 12 to 1.45, D 5.30 to 9. **Closed:** 1st week Jan. **Meals:** alc (main courses £18 to £28). Set L and D £15 (2 courses) to

£20. Sun L £18. **Details:** 45 seats. 12 seats outside. Separate bar. Wheelchair access. Music. Car parking. Children over 11 yrs only after 7.

▌Llanfaethlu

The Black Lion Inn
Simple food in a lovely 18th-century pub
Llanfaethlu, LL65 4NL
Tel no: (01407) 730718
www.blacklionanglesey.com
Modern British | £26
Cooking score: 1
£5 OFF ⇆ £30

Business has been brisk since Leigh and Mari Faulkner renovated this derelict 18th-century country inn. It can be thought of as a gentrified pub in two parts – a pleasant, traditional, slate-floored bar and a modern dining extension – though reporters recommend the fire-warmed bar as the place to eat. Basic materials are well sourced (many locally) and well handled, the kitchen coming up with Menai Strait mussels served Thai-style, roast garden beetroot with locally made goats' cheese, and braised lamb Henry with a tomato and basil sauce. Bara brith bread-and-butter pudding gets an honourable mention too. Wines from £14.95.

Chef/s: Robert Alexander. **Open:** Tue to Sun L 12 to 2 (5 Sat, 3 Sun), Tue to Sat D 6 to 8 (9 Fri, 5 to 9 Sat). **Closed:** Mon and Mon, Tue (Nov to Mar), 6 to 15 Jan. **Meals:** alc (main courses £11 to £19). Sun L £15. **Details:** 80 seats. 35 seats outside. Wheelchair access. Music. Car parking.

▌Menai Bridge

Sosban and the Old Butcher's

Surprises all the way
Trinity House, 1 High Street, Menai Bridge, LL59 5EE
Tel no: (01248) 208131
www.sosbanandtheoldbutchers.com
Modern British | £44
Cooking score: 4

V

A Grade II-listed Anglesey butcher's shop, complete with an original tiled frieze; a young couple at the helm; limited opening times; an impromptu seasonal menu – no wonder fans insist 'there's nothing quite like Sosban'. Bethan Stevens runs front-of-house with real personality and charm, while husband Stephen mans the stoves, delivering a six-course no-choice tasting menu full of creativity and surprises. Summer visitors tell wondrous tales of caramelised onion and goats' cheese tart, lamb with crunchy (and smooth) peanut paste, strawberry and cream lollipops, and rice pudding with warm grapes. But drop by in autumn and you might be offered crispy pork belly with kipper and smoked apple; mushroom risotto with apricot and rosemary; monkfish with ox tongue, celeriac and celery – ahead of blackberry crumble and a confection of chocolate and milk. There are Neal's Yard Dairy cheeses, too, plus a modest collection of quaffable wines from £15.45.
Chef/s: Stephen Stevens. **Open:** Thur to Sat D only 7 to 11. **Closed:** Sun to Wed, 22 Dec to mid Feb. **Meals:** Tasting menu £44 (6 courses). **Details:** 16 seats. Wheelchair access.

▌Penmaenpool

Penmaenuchaf Hall

Old-fashioned elegance and modern menus
Penmaenpool, LL40 1YB
Tel no: (01341) 422129
www.penhall.co.uk
Modern British | £45
Cooking score: 2

£5 OFF 🍷 🛏

Pen Hall is enviably situated in the Snowdonia National Park, with wonderful views of the Mawddach estuary and the mountains beyond. The gabled Victorian mansion is all about old-fashioned elegance – comfortable lounges, properly attired staff, white linen and silver plate in the conservatory dining room – and it operates to its own rhythm. Concise, daily changing menus are what to expect, the culinary style of simple, modern food underpinned by well-sourced ingredients. Baked beetroot and Per Las tartlet with dill crème fraîche, say, ahead of a complimentary butternut squash velouté, then roasted rump of Rhug Estate organic lamb with ratatouille, fondant potato and redcurrant jus are typical choices, with orange, chocolate and tuile biscuit mille-feuille to finish. As you would hope, there is an impressive wine list – a line-up from passionate winemakers around the world, offering good drinking at all price levels from £20.95.
Chef/s: Justin Pilkington. **Open:** all week L 12 to 2, D 7 to 9.30 (9 Sun). **Closed:** 15 to 22 Dec, 3 to 17 Jan. **Meals:** alc (main courses £27). Set L £17 (2 courses) to £19. Set D £36 (2 courses) to £45. Sun L £19. **Details:** 36 seats. 20 seats outside. Separate bar. Wheelchair access. Music. Car parking. Children over 6 yrs only.

▌ Pwllheli

Plas Bodegroes

Landmark hotel with impressive food
Efailnewydd, Pwllheli, LL53 5TH
Tel no: (01758) 612363
www.bodegroes.co.uk
Modern British | £45
Cooking score: 5

🍷 ▭

Chris and Gunna Chown are into their third decade as custodians of this Grade I-listed Georgian manor house, which stands in Arcadian tranquillity on the Llyn Peninsula. Woodland paths and beech avenues may distract the eye, likewise the hotel's fabulous art collection, but Plas Bodegroes also has a serious foodie reputation. Chris applies years of experience to a larder loaded with Welsh ingredients, delivering intelligent, sharply executed and flavoursome dishes with orthodox leanings. Seared scallops with braised leeks, laver cakes and crispy Carmarthen ham is as patriotic as a rousing rendition of 'Cwm Rhondda' by a male-voice choir, while roast breast and confit mallard with Jerusalem artichoke gratin and wild mushroom sauce keeps its eye on the calendar. There's also a touch of class about desserts such as apricot and ginger parfait or chocolate fondant with Amaretto ice cream. Treasures from French regional vineyards loom large on the prestigious wine list, with 20 house recommendations from £19.50 (£5 a glass).
Chef/s: Chris Chown. **Open:** Sun L 12.30 to 2, Tue to Sat D 7 to 9. **Closed:** Mon, 1 Dec to early Mar. **Meals:** Set D £45. Sun L £23. **Details:** 56 seats. Separate bar. Wheelchair access. Car parking. No children under 8 yrs at D.

▌ Rhosneigr

The Oyster Catcher

Please-all food with principles
Rhosneigr, LL64 5JP
Tel no: (01407) 812829
www.oystercatcheranglesey.co.uk
Modern British | £25
Cooking score: 1

£5 OFF   £30

In a modern Huf Haus-designed building with environmental credentials, the Oyster Catcher has an amazing location amid shifting sand dunes. The place works along the lines of Jamie Oliver's Fifteen – it's a chef's academy and social enterprise, as well as a restaurant. The kitchen can turn out a jellied ham hock terrine with piccalilli among first courses, followed by a burger or roasted and braised chicken in a white wine sauce. There are pasta options, too, and a kids' menu, plus lunchtime charcuterie and fish boards. To finish, check out the team's baking skills with spiced orange cake. Wines from £16.50.
Chef/s: Clare Lara. **Open:** Mon to Fri L 12 to 2.30, D 6 to 9. Sat and Sun 12 to 9. **Closed:** 25, 26 Dec. **Meals:** alc (main courses £10 to £16). Sun L £25. **Details:** 129 seats. 100 seats outside. Separate bar. Wheelchair access. Music. Car parking.

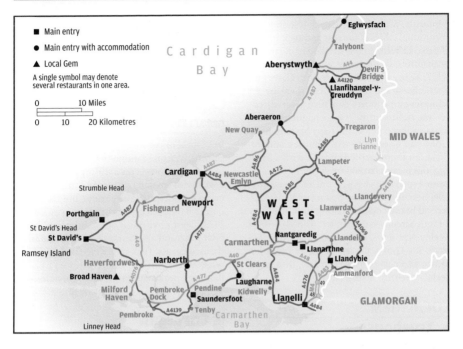

- ■ Main entry
- ● Main entry with accommodation
- ▲ Local Gem

A single symbol may denote several restaurants in one area.

0   10 Miles
0   10   20 Kilometres

C a r d i g a n
B a y

Eglwysfach
Talybont
Aberystwyth▲
Devil's Bridge
Llanfihangel-y-Creuddyn ▲ A4120
Aberaeron
New Quay
Tregaron
MID WALES
Llyn Brianne
Lampeter
Cardigan Newcastle Emlyn
Llandovery
Strumble Head
Newport
Fishguard
Llanwrda
Llandeilo
W E S T W A L E S
Porthgain
St David's Head
St David's
Carmarthen
Nantgaredig
Llanarthne
Llandybie
Ramsey Island
Haverfordwest
Narberth
St Clears
Ammanford
Broad Haven▲
Milford Haven
Pembroke Dock
Pendine
Laugharne
Kidwelly
Llanelli
GLAMORGAN
Saundersfoot
Pembroke
Tenby
Linney Head
Carmarthen Bay

Aberaeron

Harbourmaster

Sleek harbourside hotel
Pen Cei, Aberaeron, SA46 OBT
Tel no: (01545) 570755
www.harbour-master.com
Modern British | £30
Cooking score: 1

Painted in a striking cobalt blue, this listed former harbourmaster's house stands out on Aberaeron's colourful Georgian quayside. The wooden-floored, fire-warmed bar serves a selection of Welsh ales, while the blue-panelled restaurant is proud of its use of native ingredients, particularly seafood – say sea bass, garlic and chilli seafood linguine or fillet of cod with chorizo cassoulet. But there's also leek and potato soup with Welsh rarebit croûton; pork cheeks with crushed celeriac, apples, carrots, leeks and braising juices; a

super selection of local cheeses; and a highly popular chocolate fondant pudding with salted-caramel ice cream. Wines from £15.
Chef/s: Ludo Dieumegard. **Open:** all week L 12 to 2.30, D 6.30 to 9. **Closed:** 25 Dec. **Meals:** alc (main courses £11 to £25). Set D £25 (2 courses) to £30. Sun L £17 (2 courses) to £23. **Details:** 95 seats. 15 seats outside. Separate bar. Wheelchair access. Music. Car parking.

Aberystwyth

Ultracomida

Well-endowed deli and tapas joint
31 Pier Street, Aberystwyth, SY23 2LN
Tel no: (01970) 630686
www.ultracomida.co.uk
Spanish | £18
Cooking score: 2

V £30

An enterprising outfit, with a brace of addresses and an online presence, Ultracomida is a deli, wine merchant, café and tapas joint that revels in the flavours of the Iberian peninsula. Walk through the deli to the communal tables at the rear and tuck into chorizo in Welsh cider, smoked ham croquetas with allioli, Teruel rabbit with garlic and white beans, or a salad made with Caws Ffetys goats' cheese and beetroot. And there are fabulous cured meats, too, such as air-dried cecina. At lunchtime try the baguette-like barra gallega filled with crispy Serrano ham or Gorwydd Caerphilly with chutney, and for breakfast there's grilled chorizo with a fried egg and patatas fritas. Drink sherry and wines from España, or choose from an interesting selection of beers from Spain and Wales. A second branch operates along the same lines at 7 High Street, Narberth; tel: (01834) 861491. **Chef/s:** Aled Jones. **Open:** Mon to Sat 10 to 9 (5 Mon). Sun 12 to 4. **Closed:** 25 and 26 Dec, 1 Jan. **Meals:** alc (main courses £3 to £10). **Details:** 32 seats. Wheelchair access. Music.

LOCAL GEM
▲ Treehouse
14 Baker Street, Aberystwyth, SY23 2BJ
Tel no: (01970) 615791
www.treehousewales.co.uk
British | £16 £5 OFF

Above a popular organic food shop and offering more veg than meat, the Treehouse is a wholesome daytime option with a sense of place. Long-standing employee Matthew Williams has recently moved up to head chef and cooks local dishes such as spinach and potato omelette with a laver bread sauce alongside exotica including Jamaican curried mutton with coco bread and salads. Vegetarian breakfasts, café-style lunches and kids' plates keep things flexible. Wines from £11. Open all day Mon to Sat.

¦¦ Visit us Online
To find out more about *The Good Food Guide*, please visit www.thegoodfoodguide.co.uk

▌Broad Haven

LOCAL GEM
▲ The Druidstone
Broad Haven, SA62 3NE
Tel no: (01437) 781221
www.druidstone.co.uk
Global | £28

In a world of corporate blandness, the Dru is a shining beacon of individuality and character. Its location alone – on a clifftop above a sandy beach with amazing views (and sunsets) – could encourage the easy route, but the Bell family have been going their own way since 1972. There's live music, art exhibitions, basic bedrooms and a restaurant hosting regular themed events. Tuck into wok-fried squid with sweet chilli and garlic, followed by flambéed pork with prunes and Calvados. Wines start at £14. Open all week.

▌Cardigan

NEW ENTRY
The 25 Mile
Cool pub serving local delights
1 Pendre, Cardigan, SA43 1JL
Tel no: (01239) 623625
www.the25mile.com
British | £28
Cooking score: 3
£5 OFF £30

If ever proof were needed that the 'fresh and local' mantra can equal fabulous food as well as ethical brownie points, this is it. Maps chalked on the wall plot the short (25 miles or less) journeys most ingredients make from supplier to kitchen. 'Stunning' sourdough is baked on site, and the fittings – all stripped wood and fairy lights – transmit exactly the kind of slouchy cool you'd expect from the people who founded the Howies ethical clothing label. Portions are staggeringly large, but if you get past starters such as a doorstep slab of venison terrine with onion marmalade, there's more wholesome goodness to follow: maybe pan-fried gnocchi with local shiitake mushrooms and Perl Las cheese, and then apple charlotte with 'wonderful crisp pastry' and silky, unctuous clotted cream ice cream. There are local ales from the barrel, but also a respectable selection of international wines, starting at £15 a bottle.

Chef/s: Rhydian Jones. **Open:** all week L 12 to 3 (4 Sun), Mon to Sat D 6 to 9. **Closed:** 25 and 26 Dec, 1 Jan. **Meals:** alc (main courses £12 to £21). Sun L £18 (2 courses) to £21. **Details:** 58 seats. Wheelchair access. Music.

Eglwysfach

★ TOP 50 ★

★ CHEF TO WATCH ★

Ynyshir Hall
Cooking that's moving into top gear
Eglwysfach, SY20 8TA
Tel no: (01654) 781209
www.ynyshirhall.co.uk
Modern British | £73
Cooking score: 7

Once a country retreat for Queen Victoria, Ynyshir Hall is an island of manicured beauty in the wilderness of Wales' mid-western flank. From spring to summer the gardens are ablaze with colour – as are the walls of the hotel all year round, the vivid colour schemes mirroring the hues of co-owner Rob Reen's sheep-themed paintings. The smart, turquoise-walled dining room is now the domain of chef Gareth Ward. Hailing from Restaurant Sat Bains (see entry), he has arrived aglow with fresh ideas, delivering an eight-course, no-choice menu and shorter alternative lunch option. Ward knows when to play it simple (as with airy, crusty sourdough with irresistible Wagyu beef fat), but can also dazzle with a scintillating play of flavours and textures: maybe 'not French onion soup' (puréed 'miso onions' with tofu and croûtons, and a dashi stock on the side) or a piece of Wagyu beef with a sashimi prawn, pickled red cabbage and sea purslane. Foraged foods are a favourite; fall-apart hogget comes with purslane and sea aster, gravy-rich mince, wild garlic purée and sparky little capers. A

deconstructed tiramisu, with icy granita and a masala and egg yolk spray added at the table, is a charming finale. The huge international wine list covers France in detail, with prices from £24 (to £2,000).

Chef/s: Gareth Ward. **Open:** all week L 12.30 to 3.30, D 7 to 9. **Meals:** Set L £30 (5 courses) to £73. Set D £73 (7 courses) to £90. **Details:** 25 seats. Separate bar. Wheelchair access. Music. Car parking.

Laugharne

The Cors
Tucked-away restaurant-with-rooms
Newbridge Road, Laugharne, SA33 4SH
Tel no: (01994) 427219
www.thecors.co.uk
Modern British | £35
Cooking score: 3

Nick Priestland's 'quirky' Victorian house is considered a great special-occasions restaurant locally, according to one reporter. At the end of a long drive, in a huge Harry Potterish glade-like garden, the building has a wonderfully bohemian interior: rambling, candlelit, with abstract paintings on the blood-red walls, tiled floors, mermaid statue lamps and Art Deco touches. The eccentric but romantic setting is perfectly complemented by the robust, unpretentious cooking, which puts local, seasonal produce in the spotlight – and the kitchen clearly prepares the food with passion. Dinner could start with hot, seared locally smoked salmon of 'excellent quality' (served with wild rocket and tartare sauce), go on to beautifully cooked roasted fillet of Welsh beef with green peppercorns and a red wine jus, and finish with a zingy lemon tart or a wedge of chocolate torte. The concise but interesting wine list offers value, starting at £16.50.

Chef/s: Nick Priestland. **Open:** Thur to Sat D only 7 (1 sitting). **Closed:** Sun to Wed, first 2 weeks Nov. **Meals:** alc (main courses £16 to £26). **Details:** 24 seats. 10 seats outside. Children over 12 yrs only.

Llanarthne
Wright's Food Emporium
Gutsy favourites at a cheerful deli/café
Golden Grove Arms, Llanarthne, SA32 8JU
Tel no: (01558) 668929
www.wrightsfood.co.uk
Modern British | £15
Cooking score: 3
£30

Recently relocated to the Golden Grove Arms, Wright's has really found its form. The pale, airy pub rooms provide breathing space for the food store, deli counter and wine shop, plus the hungry regulars clustered around rustic tables. There's a hipsterish edge to the place – guests are encouraged to set their own soundtrack in the record room, for instance. Although it stays open some way into the evening, Wright's is essentially a deli café serving gutsy, rustic and utterly indulgent comfort food, often with a US accent. The Cubano – caramelised pork belly crammed in a roll with melting Cheddar – is a winning choice, but specials such as a mountainous poached sewin tartine also deserve attention. There are stonking burgers, meat and cheese platters crammed with interesting finds, and for those who have room, a table groaning with excellent homemade cakes. Accompany the feast with wine from the barrel (£12 a bottle).
Chef/s: Maryann Wright, Tom Mason and Phoebe Powell. **Open:** Sun to Tue 11 to 7 (5 Sun). Wed to Sat 9 to 7 (10pm Fri and Sat). **Closed:** 25 and 26 Dec, 1 Jan. **Meals:** alc (main courses £7 to £9). **Details:** 60 seats. 20 seats outside. Wheelchair access. Music. Car parking.

Llandybie
Valans
Good-looking neighbourhood eatery
29 High Street, Llandybie, SA18 3HX
Tel no: (01269) 851288
www.valans.co.uk
Modern European | £25
Cooking score: 2
£30

Dave and Remy Vale have pitched their personally run neighbourhood eatery at the heart of village life in Llandybie. Valans cuts quite a dash with its sleek layout, shiny red-and-black chairs, crisp napery and bare polished tables. Welsh beef, Gower lamb and locally landed fish all make their presence felt on the concise, regularly changing menu. The repertoire might wend its way from pan-fried scallops with cauliflower purée, Carmarthen air-dried ham and chilli dressing, via duck ravioli with red pepper sauce, to bowls of bouillabaisse or honey-glazed duck breast on vegetable, mixed bean and sausage cassoulet. Generous quantities of home-baked bread and Welsh butter are always on hand, and meals conclude with platters of regional Welsh cheeses and desserts such as sticky toffee pudding, chocolate crème brûlée or vanilla pannacotta with mango and passion fruit sauce. Look out for special events including French-style Sunday lunches. House wines are £14.60.
Chef/s: Dave Vale. **Open:** Tue to Sat L 12 to 3, D 7 to 11. **Closed:** Sun, Mon, 26 Dec to 6 Jan, 26 to 31 May. **Meals:** alc (main courses £15 to £22). Set L and midweek D £12 (2 courses) to £16. Sat D £19 (2 courses) to £23. **Details:** 35 seats. Wheelchair access. Music.

Llanelli

Sosban

Slick dockside contender
North Dock, Llanelli, SA15 2LF
Tel no: (01554) 270020
www.sosbanrestaurant.com
French | £30
Cooking score: 3

You could almost imagine yourself to be in New York – well, you know what we mean: the old pump house has been stripped back to its bricks and bones, sleek modern furniture added and arty lighting strung from the ceiling. The building may be part of Wales' industrial history, but the menu has a distinctly European bent, albeit with the benefit of some wonderful Welsh ingredients. Monmouthshire ham is served with celeriac rémoulade, for instance, or Perl Las cheese might be paired with poached pear in a salad starter. Mains plough a similar furrow, but the European theme is not rigid, so you may find tagine of Gower lamb with couscous and aubergine caviar alongside beef bourguignon or cheese soufflé. And dessert? Maybe classic tarte Tatin with vanilla ice cream or fresh madeleines. The substantial international wine list (from £15) offers numerous choices for under £30 and plenty by the glass.
Chef/s: Sian Rees and Ian Wood. **Open:** all week L 12 to 2.45, Mon to Sat D 6 to 9.45 (5.30 Fri and Sat). **Closed:** 25 Dec, 1 Jan. **Meals:** alc (main courses £15 to £22). Set L and D £16 (2 courses) to £19. **Details:** 90 seats. 80 seats outside. Separate bar. Wheelchair access. Music. Car parking.

Llanfihangel-y-Creuddyn

LOCAL GEM
▲ Y Ffarmers

Llanfihangel-y-Creuddyn, SY23 4LA
Tel no: (01974) 261275
www.yffarmers.co.uk
Modern British | £24 £5 OFF

The bilingual Y Ffarmers is a proper pub, a white-painted local that has been revamped by Rhodri Edwards and Esther Prytherch to become, once again, the 'hub' of the community. It's right on the village square, opposite the 13th-century church. Within, there's a wood-burning stove, real ales and a menu of gently updated Welsh dishes with a local flavour. Expect the likes of devilled whitebait, pheasant casserole, homemade pies and sirloin steaks. Wines start at £14. No food Sun D and Mon.

Nantgaredig

Y Polyn

Broad-shouldered regional cooking
Capel Dewi, Nantgaredig, SA32 7LH
Tel no: (01267) 290000
www.ypolynrestaurant.co.uk
Modern British | £33
Cooking score: 3

The one-time tollhouse is no architectural gem from the outside, despite the exposed timber frames, but that matters not, for Y Polyn has got its priorities right. Within, all is rustic neutrality and the menu packs a punch with its robust flavours and trencherman attitude – as they say: 'Fat equals flavour. Live with it.' Local ingredients get a good outing, inspiration comes from classic combinations and the broader European continent, and just about everything is made in-house. A starter of wild rabbit ragù with tagliatelle sits comfortably on the menu alongside a zesty salad with shaved celeriac, golden beetroots and blood oranges (enriched with truffle oil). Venison pithiviers, duck shepherd's pie, Carmarthenshire ribeye with cured ox tongue . . . these are good things, cooked by a sure hand. There are cracking Sunday lunches, and proper beer too. To finish, desserts like custard tart with blackberry ice cream vie with Welsh cheeses. House French is £15.
Chef/s: Susan Manson and Alix Alliston. **Open:** Tue to Sun L 12 to 2 (2.30 Sat and Sun), Tue to Sat D 7 to 9 (9.30 Fri and Sat). **Closed:** Mon. **Meals:** alc (main courses £13 to £18). Set L £12 (2 courses) to £15. Set D £26 (2 courses) to £33. Sun L £18 (2 courses) to £24. **Details:** 45 seats. 15 seats outside. Separate bar. Wheelchair access. Music. Car parking.

Narberth

The Grove

Gastronomic getaway and chill-out retreat
Molleston, Narberth, SA67 8BX
Tel no: (01834) 860915
www.thegrove-narberth.co.uk
Modern British | £49
Cooking score: 5

🍷 🍽 V

Brought back to life by a go-getting couple with big ideas, this highly desirable boutique hotel has established itself as a gastronomic getaway and chill-out retreat par excellence. The Grove is enticingly stowed away in a nook of the Pembrokeshire boondocks, with the Preseli Mountains looming on the horizon – although most people set their SatNavs to Narberth in search of Duncan Barham's highly complex contemporary cooking. Seasonal Welsh produce, foraged pickings and trug-loads of fresh stuff from the garden come together on a menu that yields surprises at every turn. Tea-cured pheasant boudin is offset by pickled red cabbage and a pear tart; monkfish gains some eastern promise from lentil dhal, spinach, mango and cucumber; and parsley root, carrot, chocolate and spiced oats contribute to a dish of Rhug Estate venison. After that, explore the sweet possibilities of vanilla pannacotta with cherry jelly, cola sorbet and warm doughnuts. Serious, helpfully annotated wines from across the globe add extra clout to proceedings; prices start at £21.
Chef/s: Duncan Barham. **Open:** all week L 12 to 2.30, D 6 to 9.30. **Meals:** Set L £20 (2 courses) to £25. Set D £39 (2 courses) to £49. Sun L £25. Tasting menu £70 (7 courses). **Details:** 60 seats. 30 seats outside. Separate bar. Wheelchair access. Car parking.

🍴 DUNCAN BARHAM
The Grove, Narberth

What inspired you to become a chef?
A combination of things: both my parents are great home cooks and food was always central to our family life as I grew up. My Saturday job all the way through school was in a butcher's shop where I was taught the trade, how to respect all cuts of meat, and the animals they came from. Couple that with my desire to be creative and a piggish appetite, I was destined to be a chef!

What food trends are you spotting at the moment?
There seems to be a real move towards simplifying food on the plate. Getting more out of fewer ingredients without losing any of the technical content.

At the end of a long day, what do you like to cook?
Toasted bagel, plenty of butter, scrambled eggs and brown sauce.

Is there any dish or ingredient that evokes strong memories for you?
A foie gras dish that I had in a beautiful little village restaurant in Brittany. It brings back memories of being happy... and a little drunk.

Newport

Cnapan
Home from home with excellent ingredients
East Street, Newport, SA42 0SY
Tel no: (01239) 820575
www.cnapan.co.uk
Modern British | £32
Cooking score: 2

£5 OFF ⊨ V

Michael and Judith Cooper have run their restaurant-with-rooms for 30 years. The listed Georgian house, centrally located in Newport, is a welcoming place, much loved by locals and visitors and valued for its old-fashioned feel, its superb atmosphere and its good food. Judith's menu showcases local produce and reveals realistic ambition; her clear focus is greatly appreciated. Spicy chowder with mussels, hot-smoked salmon and crevette, or chicken, port and pistachio terrine, followed by roast breast of guinea fowl with a red onion, thyme and leek ragoût, crispy smoked bacon and an elderflower jus typifies the finely tuned cooking. In addition, reporters praise the decadent dark chocolate and Amaretto dessert, the all-Welsh cheeseboard and the confidence (born of longevity) that infuses the whole operation. Wines from £15.
Chef/s: Judith Cooper. **Open:** Wed to Mon D only 6.30 to 9. **Closed:** Tue, Christmas to mid Mar. **Meals:** Set D £26 (2 courses) to £32. **Details:** 36 seats. Separate bar. Wheelchair access. Music. Car parking.

Llys Meddyg
Clever flavour-balancing in a Georgian inn
East Street, Newport, SA42 0SY
Tel no: (01239) 820008
www.llysmeddyg.com
British | £33
Cooking score: 3

£5 OFF ⊨

Lou and Ed Sykes are Pembrokeshire natives who wandered out into the world, but were drawn back to this beautiful corner of Wales. Their stone-built Georgian coaching inn incorporates a flagstoned cellar bar in a room dating from the 16th century. Soft woods with old-fashioned black radiators and industrial-chic lamps make a distinctive statement in the dining room, where Patrick Szenasi rustles up appealing country cooking based on thoroughbred regional ingredients. Open with a lusciously rich brûlée of brown crab, topped with white meat and garnished with daikon and pickled cucumber, before a two-way taster dish of venison and mallard, with fondant potato, chestnut purée and apple, or wild mushroom gnocchi with spinach dressed in truffle oil. A clever way with flavour-balancing produces a finisher of caramelised pear with blue cheese ice cream and a honey tuile. Four house wines at £17.50 (£4.90 a glass) head a short list.
Chef/s: Patrick Szenasi. **Open:** all week D only 6 to 9. **Closed:** Mon and Tue (Nov to Apr). **Meals:** alc (main courses £14 to £25). **Details:** 40 seats. Separate bar. Music. Car parking.

Porthgain

The Shed
Homespun seafood cookery by the harbour
Porthgain, SA62 5BN
Tel no: (01348) 831518
www.theshedporthgain.co.uk
Seafood | £27
Cooking score: 1

£5 OFF £30 ⏷

'Nice place, good simple food, friendly staff, wonderful situation alongside the quay. What more could you want?' So ran the notes of one fan of this charmingly rustic, rough-round-the-edges seafood restaurant. Readers have enthused about the fresh battered fish and chips, but the kitchen is capable of much more – for example, samosas made with own-caught crab; fish stew stuffed with sustainable local marine life and served in a rich fennel and tomato sauce; delicate lemon sole meunière. There are non-fish dishes (sausages, steak) too, and the chance to walk off the calories along the coastal path. Wines from £15.50. Details overleaf.

Chef/s: Matthew Devonald. **Open:** all week L 12 to 3, D 5.30 to 9. **Meals:** alc (main courses £11 to £28). **Details:** 46 seats. 30 seats outside. Wheelchair access. Music. Car parking.

St David's
Cwtch

Hearty, wholesome local food
22 High Street, St David's, SA62 6SD
Tel no: (01437) 720491
www.cwtchrestaurant.co.uk
Modern British | £30
Cooking score: 3

£5
OFF

Readers continue to sing the praises of Cwtch, the well-established restaurant on St David's main street, relieved that since being taken over by Jackie and John Hatton-Bell in May 2013, nothing has changed. Andy Holcroft continues to head the kitchen and his unfussy menus produce some very good things to eat indeed. The style is simple, seasonally aware and looks to the locality for ingredients, but also mixes influences in true modern British style. Mulligatawny soup with root vegetables, red lentils and yoghurt dressing rubs shoulders with scallops served with chorizo, pea purée and chervil, while perfectly timed lemon sole (teamed with Penclawdd cockles, laverbread, smoked bacon, oatcake and mornay sauce) lines up alongside slow-braised shoulder of Welsh lamb with fondant potato, salsa verde and red wine gravy. To finish, the oft-reported iced raspberry soufflé hits the right note. Wines from £18.
Chef/s: Andy Holcroft. **Open:** Sun L 12 to 2.30, all week D only 6 to 9.30. **Closed:** 25 and 26 Dec. **Meals:** Set D £26 (2 courses) to £30. Set early D £22 (2 courses) to £26. Sun L £20 (2 courses) to £24. **Details:** 50 seats. Wheelchair access. Music.

Saundersfoot

NEW ENTRY
Coast

Assured cooking in a breathtaking location
Coppet Hall Beach, Saundersfoot, SA69 9AJ
Tel no: (01834) 810800
http://coastsaundersfoot.co.uk
Modern British | £35
Cooking score: 4

Occupying an unbeatable location overlooking Saundersfoot Bay, this contemporary restaurant opened in April 2014 and has fast become a hit with the locals. A curving glass-fronted wooden building with suntrap terrace allows light to pour into the spacious dining room, which is all sandy wood floors, white tongue-and-groove panels and beach-like blue and beige furnishings. Will Holland made a name for himself at La Bécasse in Ludlow, but while he retains a commitment to classic modern dishes, his style is much more relaxed here. Prime local ingredients, including seafood from the bay outside, now take the spotlight. A test meal opened with 'remarkably fresh' griddled squid teamed with pink grapefruit and shaved fennel, went on to roast John Dory with confit fennel, capers and 'spice of the angels', and finished with an inventive and perfectly executed dark chocolate fondant with a delicate Turkish delight ice cream. Wine from £17.
Chef/s: Will Holland. **Open:** all week L 12 to 2.30, D 6 to 9.15. **Meals:** alc (main courses £13 to £25). Tasting menu £60. **Details:** 64 seats. Separate bar. Music.

CHANNEL ISLANDS

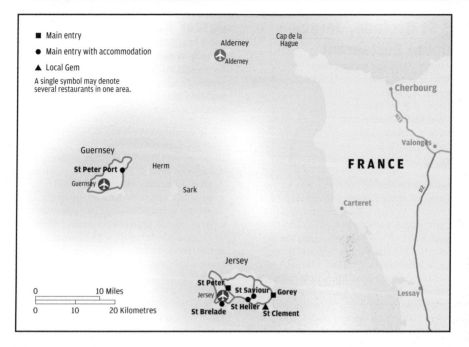

- ■ Main entry
- ● Main entry with accommodation
- ▲ Local Gem

A single symbol may denote
several restaurants in one area.

Alderney
✈ Alderney
Cap de la Hague

Cherbourg

Valognes

FRANCE

Guernsey
St Peter Port ●
Guernsey ✈
Herm
Sark
Carteret

Jersey
St Peter
Jersey ✈
St Saviour
St Helier ▲
St Brelade
■ Gorey
St Clement
Lessay

0   10 Miles
0   10   20 Kilometres

■ Gorey, Jersey

Sumas
No question, it's a beautiful spot
Gorey Hill, St Martin, Gorey, Jersey, JE3 6ET
Tel no: (01534) 853291
www.sumasrestaurant.com
Modern European | £36
Cooking score: 2

V

'With its terrace overlooking the busy harbour
and bobbing yachts, Sumas seemed to be by
far the busiest restaurant/hotel in this seaside
village full of restaurants', noted one spring
visitor to Patrice Bouffaut's splendidly located
eatery. The place operates as an all-day café,
but tables are smartly laid for lunch and
dinner, the menu delivering straightforward
fare with a Mediterranean tilt and a forte in
locally caught fish. Evening menus are slightly
more ambitious, perhaps local fish soup, hand-
dived scallops or twice-baked cheese soufflé,
followed by line-caught sea bass with crab or
roast loin of lamb wrapped in Serrano ham.

Lunch could start with roast tomato and
pepper soup, continue with loin of pork with
sautéed potatoes, red cabbage and apple sauce,
and end with a homemade vanilla ice cream.
There's a good choice of wine from a balanced
list: not too pricey, but offering the chance to
splash out (from £17).
Chef/s: Patrice Bouffaut. **Open:** all week L 12 to
2.30 (3.30 Sun), Mon to Sat D 6 to 9.30. **Closed:** 21
Dec to mid Jan. **Meals:** alc (main courses £15 to
£26). Set L £15 (2 courses) to £19. Set D £19 (2
courses) to £23. Sun L £19 (2 courses) to £23.
Details: 35 seats. 16 seats outside. Music.

¶¶● Please send us your feedback

To register your opinion about any
restaurant listed in the Guide, or a new
restaurant that you wish to bring to our
attention, please visit the web address at
the bottom of the page. Your feedback
informs the content of the book and will
be used to compile next year's reviews.

St Brelade, Jersey

Ocean Restaurant
Holiday views and serious food
Atlantic Hotel, Le Mont de la Pulente, St Brelade, Jersey, JE3 8HE
Tel no: (01534) 744101
www.theatlantichotel.com
Modern British | £65
Cooking score: 5

🛏 V

From an unrivalled position overlooking St Ouen's Bay, the Atlantic Hotel commands amazing sea views. Within, it is tastefully understated, with 'the feel of an old-school posh hotel'. A 'lovely, very elegant' dining room with well-spaced tables and proper, accomplished service makes a fitting backdrop to Mark Jordan's cooking, which combines native produce with a resourceful range of techniques. Everything, from the excellent bread and 'serious' canapés to the final petits fours, shows Jordan's flair for blending flavours. There's much to savour from the sea: perhaps brill with braised oxtail, salsify and wild mushrooms and Parmesan shavings. But proceedings might open with a trio of duck (parfait, terrine, foie gras with a fig gel and brioche), prior to an assiette of Jersey beef with lobster ravioli and beef consommé ('a real delight') then a chocolate, coffee and dulcey (blond chocolate) mousse, with crystalised hazelnuts and milk sorbet. The pedigree wine list starts at £24.
Chef/s: Mark Jordan. **Open:** all week L 12.30 to 2.30, D 6.30 to 10. **Closed:** 5 Jan to 5 Feb. **Meals:** Set L £20 (2 courses) to £25. Set D £55. Sun L £30. Tasting menu £80. **Details:** 60 seats. Separate bar. Music. Car parking.

🍴 **Visit us Online**
To find out more about
The Good Food Guide, please visit
www.thegoodfoodguide.co.uk

Oyster Box
Perky beachside haven
Route de la Baie, St Brelade, Jersey, JE3 8EF
Tel no: (01534) 850888
www.oysterbox.co.uk
Seafood | £31
Cooking score: 3

Perched right on the beach at St Brelade, with dioramic views of the sands and the bay from all tables, the Oyster Box caters to the widespread appetite for waterside locations. Against the beatific blue backdrop, it's no surprise to find seafood features strongly, shown off to best advantage in the house cocktail of crab, prawns and smoked salmon, or plancha-grilled squid with chorizo, rocket and Parmesan in lemony dressing. If the sea's bounty isn't your thing, turn to grilled baby artichokes with piquillo peppers and little mozzarella balls. An extensive spread of main-course options takes in sea bass with braised Little Gem and smoked pancetta in oxtail jus, as well as reliable steaks, braised lamb shank and seasonal game such as grouse with truffled pea purée. Spins on dessert classics include peach Melba and vanilla cheesecake with blackberries. Jersey wines appear on a global list that opens at £16.50.
Chef/s: Patrick Tweedie. **Open:** Tue to Sun L 12 to 2.30 (3 Sun), Mon to Sat D (Apr to Oct only) 6 to 9 (9.30 Fri and Sat). **Closed:** 25 and 26 Dec, 1 Jan. **Meals:** alc (main courses £12 to £28). **Details:** 90 seats. 60 seats outside. Separate bar. Wheelchair access. Music.

St Clement, Jersey

LOCAL GEM
▲ Green Island Restaurant
Green Island, St Clement, Jersey, JE2 6LS
Tel no: (01534) 857787
www.greenisland.je
Seafood | £37 £5 OFF

'Such a lovely location on a fine day', thought one visitor to this pleasant café-cum-restaurant perched atop the slipway to Green Island, with splendid views out to sea and plenty of alfresco space. There may be an ice cream kiosk in the forecourt, but inside the dining room is smartly kitted out and seafood the star of the menu: home-cured salmon, say, then a Singapore-style monkfish and tiger prawn curry, with lemon posset to finish. Wines from £15.95. Closed D Sun and Mon.

▌St Helier, Jersey

Bohemia
Fine-tuned contemporary cooking
The Club Hotel & Spa, Green Street, St Helier, Jersey, JE2 4UH
Tel no: (01534) 876500
www.bohemiajersey.com
Modern European | £59
Cooking score: 6
£5 OFF 🍽 V

Bohemia is St Helier's prime spot for special occasions. Rich upholstery and classy tableware lend lustre to the dining room, its seriousness somewhat diluted by noise from the adjoining bar, but service is attentive. The food, possibly the 'best dining experience all year' for one reporter, showcases Steve Smith's creative modern cooking. An inspection meal found great technical skill, good combinations and interesting ingredients. There's a welcome lightness of touch, given all the extras (canapés, two amuse-bouches, a pre-dessert, petits fours, 'lovely' bread), so 'one was never overwhelmed'. Scallop teamed with celeriac, apple, smoked eel and truffle, and beautifully presented langoustine with parsnip, smoked butter and sea herbs, have been hits from the 'prestige' menu. From the 'classic' menu comes 'a memorable meal' of quail with girolles, sweetcorn and purslane, followed by veal textures, with white asparagus, black garlic, girolles and Madeira, then gariguette strawberries with fromage blanc and Lanique rose vodka. Wines on a pedigree list start at £18.
Chef/s: Steve Smith. **Open:** Mon to Sat L 12 to 2.30, D 6.30 to 10. **Closed:** Sun, 24 to 30 Dec. **Meals:** alc (main courses £30 to £35). Set L £20 (2 courses) to £25. Set D £50 (2 courses) to £59. Sun L £30. Tasting

menus £75 (8 courses) to £85. **Details:** 60 seats. Separate bar. Wheelchair access. Music. Car parking.

Ormer
High-spec dining with brasserie-style buzz
Don Street, St Helier, Jersey, JE2 4TQ
Tel no: (01534) 725100
www.ormerjersey.com
Modern French | £45
Cooking score: 6
V

Big-hitting Shaun Rankin shot to fame while cooking in the glitzy, clubby surrounds of Bohemia (see entry), but this is his own gaff – a high-spec venture in the centre of St Helier, with a sophisticated look courtesy of designer Martin Brudnizki. Silk wallpaper and distressed oak panelling point up the expansive blue and yellow-toned dining room, while the kitchen delivers Rankin's trademark interpretations of contemporary French cuisine. The restaurant is named after one of the Channel Islands' most covetable seafood delicacies, although more familiar Jersey produce provides inspiration for the innovative and 'exciting' food: Dover sole with 'fishy pie flavours', charred leeks, sea vegetables and parsley oil; lobster salad, fennel ceviche and crab linguine; beef cheek with oyster beignet, curly kale, radish and parsley velouté. To finish, go off-piste with a sweet/savoury confection of Roquefort, raspberries, beetroot salad, malt bread and chickweed. The deeply serious, 300-bin wine list starts at £20 (£5 a glass).
Chef/s: Shaun Rankin. **Open:** Mon to Sat L 12 to 2.30, D 6.30 to 10. **Closed:** Sun, 25 and 26 Dec, 1 Jan. **Meals:** alc (main meals £24 to £30). Set L £19 (2 courses) to £24. Set D £30. **Details:** 50 seats. 20 seats outside. Separate bar. Wheelchair access. Music.

Tassili

Headline restaurant at a luxury spa hotel
Grand Jersey, The Esplanade, St Helier, Jersey,
JE2 3QA
Tel no: (01534) 722301
www.grandjersey.com
Modern European | £49
Cooking score: 4

🛏 V

It may look a little like a post-war resort hotel,
but the Grand Jersey was built in 1890, as its
majestic lobby more readily indicates. There's
no denying the impressive location: overlooking St Aubin's Bay opposite the island
landmark of Elizabeth Castle. The hotel's
flagship dining room is Tassili, an understated
space furnished in soothing white and pastel
peach. Chef Richard Allen's family ran a
Dorset bakery, and his culinary instinct is
deeply driven, eventually leading to the
thoroughgoing vanguard cooking produced
here. Unimpeachable island produce is the
foundation of dishes such as turbot with
chancre crab, black quinoa, saffron textures
and pennywort; or belly and braised cheek of
Classic Herd pork with poached langoustine,
chorizo and pork popcorn. Topping and
tailing those could be foie gras parfait with
smoked duck, 100% chocolate and pine nut
butter and irresistible pistachio and olive oil
cake with orange gel and chocolate sorbet.
Well-chosen wines open at £18.50.
Chef/s: Richard Allen. **Open:** Fri and Sat L 12 to
1.45, Tue to Sat D 7 to 10. **Closed:** Sun, Mon, first 2
weeks Jan. **Meals:** Set L £19 (2 courses) to £25. Set
D £49. Tasting menu £67. **Details:** 28 seats.
Separate bar. Wheelchair access. Music. Car
parking.

Symbols

🛏 Accommodation is available

💷30 Three courses for less than £30

V Separate vegetarian menu

£5 £5-off voucher scheme

🍷 Notable wine list

LOCAL GEM
▲ The Green Olive

1 Anley Street, St Helier, Jersey, JE2 3QE
Tel no: (01534) 728198
www.greenoliverestaurant.co.uk
Mediterranean | £25 £5off

Paul and Anna Le Brocq's charming first-floor
restaurant overlooking St Helier's town centre
specialises in vegetarian and seafood dishes.
Chef Paul is constantly developing his modern
repertoire, which leans towards Asia via the
Mediterranean, although Jersey produce is at
the fore. Pan-fried sea bass with pine nut crust,
celeriac purée, grapefruit and orange segments
and crab fritters could be followed by basil
crème brûlée with a strawberry and cream
'shooter'. House wine is £16.95. Closed Sat L,
Sun and Mon.

∎ St Peter Port, Guernsey
La Frégate

Stunning seascapes and complex cooking
Beauregard Lane, Les Cotils, St Peter Port,
Guernsey, GY1 1UT
Tel no: (01481) 724624
www.lafregatehotel.com
Modern British | £38
Cooking score: 4

🛏

'It's well worth the trek up narrow streets to
this lovely hotel overlooking the harbour,'
thought one reporter, who relished the
striking view from the dining room. The food
continues to draw attention, too. Long-
standing chef Neil Maginnis favours clear
flavours, well-honed technique, intricate
detailing – and local sourcing. Scallops are
regularly mentioned in dispatches, perhaps
teamed with sun-dried tomato salsa, crisp
pancetta and sauce vierge, but if you're not in
the mood for fish there's a combo of foie gras
and chicken liver parfait and pan-fried foie
gras (with smoked duck salad and kumquat
sauce). Readers have raved about sea bass
served with fresh mussels, sun-dried
tomatoes, creamed baby spinach and pesto,

and the 'surf and turf': a choice of king prawns or seared scallops with fillet, sirloin or ribeye steak, plus a choice of sauces. Assiette gourmande (a trio of three desserts) is a popular way to finish. Wines from £20.
Chef/s: Neil Maginnis. **Open:** all week L 12 to 1.30, D 7 to 9.30. **Meals:** alc (main courses £19 to £24). Set L £18 (2 courses) to £24. Set D £34. Sun L £24. **Details:** 70 seats. 20 seats outside. Music. Car parking.

LOCAL GEM
▲ Da Nello
46 Lower Pollet, St Peter Port, Guernsey, GY1 1WF
Tel no: (01481) 721552
www.danello.gg
Italian | £25 £5 OFF

'This pleasant Italian restaurant comes with the gusto one would expect, a warm welcome and good service,' noted one spring visitor. Housed in a 500-year-old building near the centre of St Peter Port, Da Nello is surprisingly spacious, with two main dining areas and a lovely courtyard. Long-standing chef/proprietor Tim Vidamour is noted for straightforward, authentic cooking: Italian fish soup, say, then entrecôte with red wine, brandy cream and green pepper sauce, or fegato milanese (breadcrumbed calf's liver). House wines are £16.95. Open all week.

▲ Fermain Beach Café
Fermain Lane, St Peter Port, Guernsey, GY1 1ZZ
Tel no: (01481) 238636
Italian | £30

'This is definitely what I call a hidden gem,' exclaimed one reporter of this all-day beach café in a 'magical setting'. Though there's an indoor dining area, most come to eat by the sea (supported by blankets and outdoor heating in less favourable weather). Many will have walked along the coastal path – otherwise take a taxi from the Fermain Hotel. The good, simple fare includes sandwiches, salads, pasta such as seafood linguine, risottos, and

perhaps salmon and crab with sweet chilli and asparagus. Wines from £14.95. Open all week, no D.

■ St Peter, Jersey
Mark Jordan at the Beach
Down-to-earth venue, crowd-pleasing brasserie dishes
La Plage, La Route de la Haule, St Peter, Jersey, JE3 7YD
Tel no: (01534) 780180
www.markjordanatthebeach.com
Modern British | £35
Cooking score: 4

Mark Jordan is better known as the head chef of the Ocean Restaurant at the Atlantic Hotel (see entry), but his more affordable, casual dining place is proving a favourite haunt for both tourists and locals. The 'lurid red' painted venue in a lovely beachside setting ('especially if you can bag a window seat looking out to the beach and boats'), offers first-class alfresco opportunities as well as a down-to-earth dining room with beach-themed artwork, oak floors and high-backed wicker chairs. The menu showcases Jersey produce and the kitchen knows what is required, and delivers in fine fashion – at tempting prices. That said, there's nothing humble or penny-pinching about the results, with a spring lunch producing Jersey crab cake, then honey-glazed duck leg served with pak choi and butternut squash purée, and pineapple croquant to finish. The relaxed but reassuringly professional tone carries through to staff. Wines from £16.
Chef/s: Mark Jordan and Benjamin Crick. **Open:** all week L 12 to 2.30, D 6 to 9.30. **Closed:** Jan. **Meals:** alc (main courses £15 to £22). Set L £20 (2 courses) to £25. Set D £28. Sun L £30. **Details:** 50 seats. 30 seats outside. Separate bar. Music. Car parking.

MARK JORDAN
Ocean Restaurant &
Mark Jordan at the Beach

What do you enjoy about being a chef?
For me it's the creation of something really special that gives people enjoyment. I am so lucky with the location of both Ocean and Mark Jordan at the Beach. You couldn't get more spectacular coastal views and inspiring local produce.

What's your newest ingredient discovery?
Sustainable ormers from the Jersey Ormer Hatchery. They have been commercially farming ormers for the last four years, taking ormers through the full life cycle from spawning to plate. It's an incredible achievement and totally unique. In fact, ormers cannot survive any further north than the Channel Islands.

Are there any ingredients that evoke strong memories for you?
King prawns. Whenever I cook them it takes me back to the days working for Keith Floyd and grilling them outside by the River Dart with garlic butter and lemon.

Do you have a guilty foodie pleasure?
Baked beans and prawn cocktail crisps!

▌St Saviour, Jersey

Longueville Manor
A new broom at an old favourite
St Saviour, Jersey, JE2 7WF
Tel no: (01534) 725501
www.longuevillemanor.com
Modern British | £60
Cooking score: 4

🛏 V

This beautiful, small-scale medieval manor house has passed from one generation to the next. Malcolm Lewis is now at the helm and has great plans for the place. Thankfully, Longueville remains the best venue in Jersey for a grand and cocooning experience. Chef Andrew Baird has been here for years, and continues to makes deft use of local produce (including ingredients from the hotel's kitchen garden). Two dining rooms – the dark-panelled Oak Room, and the lighter Garden Room – are the setting for his luxurious style of cooking, which matches sense of place and occasion. Complexity is a given, as in hand-dived North Coast scallops served with slow-cooked belly pork, black pudding and apple, or roast saddle of rabbit wrapped in Parma ham with rabbit 'bonbon' and butternut squash. A beautifully wrought Valrhona chocolate sphere with Baileys ice cream and hazelnut mousse makes a fitting finale. Wines start at £25 a bottle.
Chef/s: Andrew Baird. **Open:** all week L 12 to 2, D 6 to 10. **Meals:** Set L £25 (2 courses) to £30. Set D £53 (2 courses) to £60. Sun L £40. Tasting menu £80. **Details:** 90 seats. 35 seats outside. Separate bar. Music. Car parking.

NORTHERN IRELAND

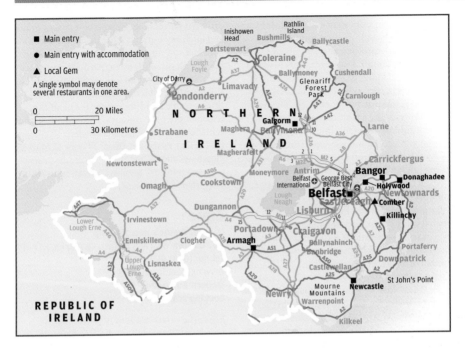

Armagh, Co Armagh
Uluru Bistro
Aussie tucker in Armagh
16 Market Street, Armagh, Co Armagh, BT61 7BX
Tel no: (028) 3751 8051
www.ulurubistro.com
Australian | £25
Cooking score: 2

V £30

Standing in the shadows of St Patrick's Cathedral, this Aussie-run bistro brings some swagger to the centre of Armagh. Whether you fancy a Bondi burger or a plate of char-grilled kangaroo with kumera chips, Uluru is where to come. The kitchen also mixes and matches ingredients at will, pulling in 'amazing' ideas from the Pacific Rim, the Med and beyond. Start with crispy chilli chicken, nappa slaw and chilli plum jam, or sticky Malaysian-style pork belly with citrus salad, before going walkabout in search of char-grilled venison haunch with whipped potatoes, port and raisin jus. There's plenty of

well-hung Irish beef too, while desserts might usher in 'decadent' chocolate tart with cherry coulis and berry sorbet. Cheers for the terrific prices and 'awesome, friendly service'. House wine is £15.
Chef/s: Dean Coppard. **Open:** Tue to Sat L 12 to 3, Tue to Sun D 5 to 9 (10 Fri and Sat). **Closed:** Mon, 25 and 26 Dec, 31 Dec, 1 Jan. **Meals:** alc (main courses £15 to £24). Set D £17. **Details:** 32 seats. 12 seats outside. Separate bar. Wheelchair access. Music.

Bangor, Co Down
The Boat House
Cooking with big ambitions
1a Seacliff Road, Bangor, Co Down, BT20 5HA
Tel no: (028) 9146 9253
www.theboathouseni.co.uk
Modern British | £30
Cooking score: 6

Dutch-born brothers Jasper and Joery Castel pitched up at the old Boat House overlooking Bangor marina in 2008. They have since transformed this former harbourmaster's office

into a hot-ticket restaurant sought-after by sailors, tourists and itinerant foodies. Joery made his name cooking at celeb retreat Castle Leslie in Glaslough, but now tailors his food to a different audience – matching brilliant technical wizardry with careful sourcing, while keeping prices pegged back. This is cooking with big ambitions, an open mind and confidence: evidenced in whipped goats' cheese and vanilla mousse with truffle honey, toasted hazelnuts and beetroot in various forms; or brill fillet with 'salty vegetables', borage crème, saffron potato, blood orange, caper powder and parsley oil. Joery also likes creating spiky South-East Asian flavours, as in seared duck breast with steamed duck bun, Malaysian potato sticks and kumquat gel. The food is matched by a list of equally complex, imaginatively chosen wines from £17.50.
Chef/s: Joery Castel. **Open:** Tue to Sat L 12.30 to 2.30, D 5.30 to 9.30, Sun 1 to 8. **Closed:** Mon, Tue (winter). **Meals:** Set L £20 (2 courses) to £25. Set D £30. **Details:** 36 seats. 8 seats outside. Separate bar. Music. Car parking.

Belfast, Co Antrim
The Bar & Grill at James Street South
Please-all steakhouse with a Josper grill
21 James Street South, Belfast, Co Antrim, BT2 7GA
Tel no: (028) 9560 0700
www.belfastbargrill.co.uk
Modern British | £28
Cooking score: 3
£30

The more informal counterpoint to Niall McKenna's James Street South (see entry), housed in the same former Victorian linen mill, the Bar & Grill is loosely based on a New York steakhouse. The stripped-back ground-floor dining room ticks all the right on-trend boxes with its exposed brickwork, sea-blue panelling and comfortable leather banquette seating. The charcoal-fuelled Josper oven and grill is the workhorse of the kitchen, with locally sourced steaks served with seven

different sauces including bone-marrow gravy and anchovy butter. Other dishes offer both comfort and nostalgia in the shape of potted duck with piccalilli or pappardelle with duck ragù, which might be followed by mixed grilled fish with lemon and tartare sauce. Sticky toffee pudding sundae is one of the reassuringly retro desserts. The concise, global wine list starts at £15 for a bottle.
Chef/s: Carl Johannsen. **Open:** all week 12 to 10.30. **Closed:** 25 and 26 Dec, 1 Jan. **Meals:** alc (main courses £11 to £23). **Details:** 50 seats. Separate bar. Wheelchair access. Music.

Eipic
Michael Deane's new flagship
28-40 Howard Street, Belfast, Co Antrim, BT1 6PF
Tel no: (028) 9033 1134
www.michaeldeane.co.uk
Modern European | £40
Cooking score: 4

From the smart modern brasserie that is Deanes at Queens to the Italian-accented Deane & Decano, via the more casual Deanes Deli Vin Cafe and Deanes Deli Bistro, chef-restaurateur Michael Deane, a long-term contributor to Belfast's quality-restaurant scene, has successfully spread his name across the city. His former self-named Howard Street flagship has undergone a costly revamp, extended into adjacent premises and emerged as three new concepts. Meat Locker and Love Fish are buzzy steak and seafood casual-dining rooms, while Eipic, with its sponsored Champagne bar and crisp linen, is a much more luxurious, ambitious concern. Here, the kitchen, overseen by Danni Barry, sends out sharply defined modern food. Pretty haute plates star the likes of Strangford Lough langoustines, Fermanagh chicken and beef from Peter Hannon. Apart from an all-French cheeseboard, everything champions local produce. House wine is £19.50.
Chef/s: Danni Barry. **Open:** Fri L 12 to 3, Wed to Sat D 5.30 to 10. **Closed:** Sun, Mon, Tue. **Meals:** Set L £20 (2 courses) to £25. Set D £40. Tasting menu £70. **Details:** 30 seats. Separate bar.

NEW ENTRY
Hadskis
Bright wine bar from Belfast's top chef
33 Donegall Street, Belfast, Co Antrim, BT1 2NB
Tel no: (028) 9032 5444
www.hadskis.co.uk
Modern European | £30
Cooking score: 3

The latest venture from Niall McKenna of James Street South and The Bar & Grill (see entries) is located off a cobbled alley in the Cathedral Quarter. Named after the family who once ran an iron foundry on the premises (manufacturing pot and pans until the late 18th century), Hadskis is a bright, modern all-day wine bar dominated by a stool-lined kitchen counter that makes the most of the long, narrow space. The kitchen offers an eclectic menu where obvious crowd-pleasers such as smoked salmon and wheaten bread, confit duck, bacon, egg and chips, steaks and a whole thyme- and lemon-roasted chicken sit alongside more off-kilter charmers such as rabbit, chicken and pork-belly kebabs, and oxtail with roast scallops and mushy peas. Charcuterie and daily seafood specials are always to the fore, and the tarte Tatin has been highly praised. The globetrotting wine list is good value, with bottles from £15.
Chef/s: David Scott. **Open:** all week 12 to 10.30 (11 to 10.30 Sun). **Meals:** alc (main courses £11 to £22). **Details:** 40 seats. 10 seats outside. Separate bar. Wheelchair access. Music.

Il Pirata
Casual 'small plates' Italian
279-281 Upper Newtownards Road,
Ballyhackamore, Belfast, Co Antrim, BT4 3JF
Tel no: (028) 9067 3421
www.ilpiratabelfast.com
Italian | £20
Cooking score: 3
£30

There's a 'real air of fun' about Il Pirata, a young Italian eatery in trendy east Belfast. Diners in the white-tiled, distressed-wood space are encouraged to share a selection of small dishes,

helping themselves to plates and cutlery from the middle of the table as they get stuck in. There's snacky stuff to start, perhaps pork and fennel sliders or smoked eel Caesar crostini, with powerful flavours dominating the 'pizzetta', pasta and 'piatto' sections, too. Penne with Sicilian lamb ragù, guanciale and Taleggio pizzetta, and chicken scaloppine with Marsala sauce are pretty representative dishes. The international wine list (from £17.50) covers all styles for a sub-£30 budget, but a sharper regional Italian focus might be more inspiring. Sister establishment Coppi can be found in the Cathedral Quarter.
Chef/s: Jonny Phillips. **Open:** all week 12 to 10 (11 Fri and Sat). **Closed:** 25 and 26 Dec. **Meals:** alc (main courses £9 to £15). **Details:** 80 seats. Separate bar. Wheelchair access. Music. Car parking.

★ **READERS' RESTAURANT OF THE YEAR** ★
NORTHERN IRELAND

James Street South
Serious cooking at accessible prices
21 James Street South, Belfast, Co Antrim,
BT2 7GA
Tel no: (028) 9043 4310
www.jamesstreetsouth.co.uk
Modern European | £32
Cooking score: 6

James Street South's Niall McKenna is no longer simply one of Belfast's finest chefs, he has also become one of the city's most influential restaurateurs with the opening of the Bar & Grill (adjacent to James Street South) in 2011 and newcomer Hadskis in 2013 (see separate entries). Ten-year-old James Street South continues to woo Belfast epicureans with all the confidence of the cherished first-born. Its monochrome dining room, hung with paintings, makes a stylish backdrop to McKenna's French-inspired technique, 'fabulous flavours' and fine Irish produce. Highly praised, fairly priced dishes include Portavogie crab wrapped in charred gem leaves with cucumber and shallot, served with a brown crab brioche 'sandwich'; monkfish with lemon prawns, chorizo and

fennel croquettes; and pear délice, whipped Amaretto and William pear sorbet. Readers speak highly of 'first-rate service' and flexibility from the kitchen, but could do without the 'canned music'. Approachably priced wines from £16.50.
Chef/s: David Gillmore. **Open:** Mon to Sat L 12 to 2.45, D 5.45 to 10.45. **Closed:** Sun, 25 and 26 Dec, 1 Jan. **Meals:** alc (main courses £15 to £33). Set L and early D £19. **Details:** 72 seats. Separate bar. Wheelchair access. Music.

Molly's Yard
Unpretentious bijou bistro
1 College Green Mews, Botanic Avenue, Belfast, Co Antrim, BT7 1LW
Tel no: (028) 9032 2600
www.mollysyard.co.uk
Modern British | £35
Cooking score: 2

V

Lisburn's Hilden Brewing Co produces wonderfully named craft beers – Headless Dog, Twisted Hop, Titanic Quarter – which can be sampled here in the brewery's own joint, occupying a prime position in Belfast's University Quarter. This former Victorian stable has been transformed into a buzzy little restaurant with a modern Irish approach to its food. The bistro attitude is confirmed by daytime offerings such as the classy burger, while the ante is upped a little in the evening. Potted smoked ham hock comes as a starter with pickled local (and organic) veg and stout wheaten bread. Main courses might include venison with sage and potato gnocchi, or fish of the day ('depending on the tides'). There's a rustic integrity to the kitchen's output, and a sense of fun in desserts such as rum and raisin sundae with whiskey ice cream. Prices won't break the bank of mum and dad, either. Wines from £15.
Chef/s: Ciarán Steele. **Open:** Mon to Sat 12 to 9 (9.30 Fri and Sat). **Closed:** Sun, 24 to 26 Dec, 1 Jan, 12 Jul. **Meals:** alc (main courses £18 to £25). Set D £15 (2 courses) to £18. **Details:** 50 seats. 20 seats outside. Wheelchair access. Music.

Mourne Seafood Bar
Local seafood hero
34-36 Bank Street, Belfast, Co Antrim, BT1 1HL
Tel no: (028) 9024 8544
www.mourneseafood.com
Seafood | £25
Cooking score: 3

V **£30**

Fish and shellfish landed at Annalong and Kilkeel find their way here for the lucky folk of Belfast. The Mourne group also has its own oyster beds in Carlingford Lough (as well as restaurants in Dundrum and Dublin – and a new partnership with chef Chris Bell at the Eagle Bar & Grill at Galgorm Castle Golf Club, see entry). There's an easy-going attitude at this city venue, and lots of cracking seafood to be had, either in the ground-floor bar or (slightly) swankier upstairs restaurant. Oysters come as you fancy, with starters running to piri-piri prawns or seafood chowder. Hearty mains include beer-battered fish and chips, or a whole sea bass with crab and avocado salsa. There are also wet fish sales, should you want to take something home, and a cookery school to show you what to do with it when you get there. Wines from £25.
Chef/s: Andy Rea. **Open:** Fri and Sat L 12 to 4, D 5 to 10.30. Mon to Thur 12 to 9.30. Sun 1 to 6. **Meals:** alc (main courses £8 to £20). **Details:** 80 seats. Separate bar. Wheelchair access.

OX
Creative, ingredients-led seasonal food
1 Oxford Street, Belfast, Co Antrim, BT1 3LA
Tel no: (028) 9031 4121
www.oxbelfast.com
Modern European | £32
Cooking score: 6

£5 OFF **V**

Launched by 'two guys making an effort', trendsetting OX sits pretty in downtown Belfast, with views over the River Lagan and the Beacon of Hope sculpture, from plate-glass windows. Inside, it's comfortably pared back in Scandi style with sparse furnishings, hard lines and an open kitchen dedicated to 'creative seasonality'. One look at the Irish cheeses (served with fermented celeriac) will tell you they care about ingredients here. Chef/co-proprietor Stephen Toman made his name at James Street South (see entry), and his menu speaks the current lingua franca: 'celeriac, seared scallop, sea urchin, sorrel'; 'sprouting broccoli, cod, egg, crispy chicken skin'. . . you get the picture. This is assertive, accomplished, 'desirable' stuff; just consider a beautifully crafted plate of pigeon, foie gras, salsify and chicory, with warm fig purée served separately. Desserts also keep it serious, as in a mini buttermilk pudding with caramelised beetroot and pistachio biscotti. The enterprising wine list favours 'artisan' over 'classic', with agreeable prices from £17; also check out the gin menu.

Chef/s: Stephen Toman. **Open:** Tue to Sat L 12 to 3 (1 Sat), D 6 to 9.45. **Closed:** Sun, Mon, 24 to 30 Dec, 21 to 27 Apr, 14 to 27 Jul. **Meals:** alc (main courses £15 to £22). Set L £13 (2 courses) to £16. Pre-theatre D £16 (2 courses) to £20. **Details:** 40 seats. Separate bar. Wheelchair access. Music.

The Potted Hen

Lively contemporary bistro
11 Edward Street, Belfast, Co Antrim, BT1 2LR
Tel no: (028) 9023 4554
www.thepottedhen.co.uk
Modern European | £28
Cooking score: 3

V £30

St Anne's Square is among Belfast's most sought-after locations, and the faint air of a film set hangs over the meringue-white colonnades encasing the Potted Hen. The setting is ideal for outdoor summer dining, and there are alfresco tables for soaking up the Irish sun. Inside, by contrast, is all muted modern industrial, with iron columns and exposed duct-work: an apposite backdrop for the kitchen's contemporary brasserie food. Potted items seem the obvious way in, whether shrimps, salmon or pork rillettes. Alternatively, take a bowl of chunky seafood chowder. Crowd-pleasing mains such as slow-cooked pork belly with buttered Savoy,

puréed shallots, mashed celeriac and toffee apple compete with spiced haddock fritters, skinny chips, curried slaw and saffron mayo. It culminates in the calorific frenzy of chocolate and peanut-butter tart with vanilla ice cream. House Chilean is £16.95.

Chef/s: Dermot Regan. **Open:** Mon to Sat L 12 to 3 (2.45 Sat), D 5 to 9.30 (10 Fri and Sat). Sun 12 to 9. **Closed:** 24 to 26 Dec, 1 and 2 Jan, 12 and 13 Jul. **Meals:** alc (main courses £12 to £24). Set D £16 (2 courses) to £18. Sun L £19 (2 courses) to £22. **Details:** 160 seats. 44 seats outside. Wheelchair access. Music.

LOCAL GEM
▲ The Ginger Bistro

7-8 Hope Street, Belfast, Co Antrim, BT12 5EE
Tel no: (028) 9024 4421
www.gingerbistro.com
Modern European | £30

Simon McCance's bistro has an easy-going attitude and a menu that reveals a carefree attitude about international borders. It's all about the craic and producing winning flavour combinations. Oriental duck fritters arrive as a starter in the company of roasted plums and spiced pickled carrot, followed by main courses such as grilled smoked haddock with a crab and pea risotto, or local sirloin steak with chips. Finish with an individual sticky toffee pudding. Wines start at £16.50. Closed Mon L and Sun.

Comber, Co Down

LOCAL GEM
▲ The Old Schoolhouse Inn

100 Ballydrain Road, Comber, Co Down, BT23 6EA
Tel no: (028) 9754 1182
www.theoldschoolhouseinn.com
Modern British | £30 £5 OFF

Housed in what was Ballydrain Primary School, Will Brown's restaurant-with-rooms recently underwent a massive transformation, with a new bar/lounge now added to the mix alongside the original floors, windows and radiators. The kitchen sticks to its task, delivering inventive modern dishes along the lines of a trio of quail with raisin, turnip and radish; roast Ballydugan Estate pheasant with mushroom purée and pan juices; or hake with cured cucumber, carrot, celeriac, shrimps and langoustine froth. Wines from £17. Closed Mon.

Donaghadee, Co Down
The Governor Rocks
Generous portions of fantastic fish and seafood
27 The Parade, Donaghadee, Co Down, BT21 0HE
Tel no: (028) 9188 4817
www.thegovernorrocks.com
Seafood | £25
Cooking score: 3
£5 OFF £30

Sitting on the seafront in an attractive little coastal town on the north-eastern Ards Peninsula, just a few miles from Bangor, Jason More's venue enjoys sweeping views of the Copeland Islands and the western coast of Scotland. It's an appetising location for some appetisingly fresh fish and seafood dishes that draw inspiration from far and wide. Crab claws and langoustines in garlic butter is a reassuringly classic starter, but there might also be tom yum soup with cod and salmon in a welter of lemongrass, galangal and chilli. Main course could be a duo of monkfish and sea bass in crisped Parma ham with pea and Parmesan risotto or, if you're the meaty type, braised Dexter beef with duck-fat roasties and Yorkshire pudding. A treat is in store at dessert stage, with chocolate marquise in chocolate sauce, garnished with fresh berries and vanilla ice cream. House Chilean is £12.95.
Chef/s: Conal Boyle. **Open:** Mon to Sat L 12 to 3, D 5.30 to 8.30 (9.30 Wed and Thur, 10 Fri and Sat). Sun 12 to 8. **Closed:** 25 Dec. **Meals:** alc (main courses £10 to £23). **Details:** 115 seats. Wheelchair access. Music.

Galgorm, Co Antrim
NEW ENTRY
The Eagle at Galgorm
Teeing off with country-sized portions
Galgorm Castle, Galgorm, Co Antrim, BT42 1HL
Tel no: (028) 2563 0173
www.theeagleatgalgorm.com
Modern British | £25
Cooking score: 2
£30

The first floor of this modern but rather unspectacular-looking club house for Galgorm Castle golf course incorporates a surprisingly handsome dining room. Since early in 2014, chef Chris Bell (in partnership with Mourne Seafood, see entry) has been sending out country-sized portions of good local produce from the kitchen here. The bar menu – Ulster Fry, fish pie, battered scampi and haddock – keeps the golfers happy all year round, but in the main restaurant, seafood and seasonal game are the speciality and the daily changing specials blackboard reflects the seasons. Expect bold flavours in the likes of Irish stew, roasted scallops with herb gnocchi and a basil and white wine cream, or a wild mushroom risotto. Sweets such as red berry meringue, or plum crumble with gingerbread-man ice cream, are no less generously proportioned.
Chef/s: Chris Bell. **Open:** all week 8.30am to 9pm. **Meals:** alc (main courses £9 to £23). **Details:** 80 seats. Music.

Holywood, Co Down
The Bay Tree
Idiosyncratic indie cafe
118 High Street, Holywood, Co Down, BT18 9HW
Tel no: (028) 9042 1419
www.baytreeholywood.co.uk
Modern British | £25
Cooking score: 1
£30

Open for breakfast, lunch and afternoon treats throughout the week, the Bay Tree is an idiosyncratic indie café of the best sort: part neighbourhood drop-in, part unofficial art gallery and local hub. It is famously home to some of the best cinnamon scones in the land, and pleases early birds with bowls of porridge, bacon and banana toasties and fry-ups. Lunch brings open sandwiches, salads, baked potatoes and sweet delights ranging from coffee cake to meringues with cream and fruit compote. For Friday supper there's home-smoked chicken Caesar salad or spicy braised Irish pork shoulder with green rice and pink pickled onions. Wine from £15.

Chef/s: Glen Potts. **Open:** all week 8 to 5 (9.30pm Fri, 9am Sat, 10 to 3 Sun). **Closed:** 25 and 26 Dec, 1 Jan, 12 and 13 Jul. **Meals:** alc (main courses £10 to £19). **Details:** 60 seats. 12 seats outside. Music. Car parking.

Killinchy, Co Down
Balloo House
Classy old coaching inn
1 Comber Road, Killinchy, Co Down, BT23 6PA
Tel no: (028) 9754 1210
www.balloohouse.com
Modern British | £23
Cooking score: 3

V £30

A converted coaching inn of two halves, Balloo House occupies an atmospheric 400-year-old former farmhouse within wind-whistling distance of Strangford Lough. Sturdy stone walls, ancient flagstones, a warming range and beers on tap set the tone in the ground-floor bar, which doubles as a jolly bistro. Head here for robust, gutsy dishes ranging from local mussels cooked in Armagh cider to slow-cooked Dexter beef cheeks with garlic mash and stout gravy or Thai-spiced chicken breast with basil and coconut curry. Alternatively, ascend the stairs for something more refined. Upstairs at Balloo (evenings only) deals in more elaborate ideas with lots of cheffy primping – as in roast veal sweetbread with pea velouté, field mushrooms and summer truffle or butter-poached Strangford lobster with black rice, Parmesan and sautéed squid. To finish, have some fun with a combo

of lemon and Szechuan-pepper financier, aerated chocolate, candied popcorn and popcorn ice cream. House wines from £15.95.

Chef/s: Danny Millar. **Open:** all week 12 to 9 (9.30 Fri and Sat). **Closed:** 25 Dec. **Meals:** alc (main courses £10 to £22). Set L £14 (2 courses) to £18. Set D £15 (2 courses) to £19. Sun L £23. **Details:** 70 seats. Separate bar. Wheelchair access. Music. Car parking.

Newcastle, Co Down
Vanilla
Colourful surrounds, colourful food
67 Main Street, Newcastle, Co Down, BT33 0AE
Tel no: (028) 4372 2268
www.vanillarestaurant.co.uk
Modern British | £31
Cooking score: 3

A 'culinary oasis' not far from Newcastle promenade ('where the Mountains of Mourne sweep down to the sea'), Darren Ireland's bistro is nattily garbed in rich gold, copper, purple and green tones, with smart fittings and 'linear seating'. It provides a colourful backdrop for an equally colourful menu that roams far in search of inspiration – from satay chicken and noodle spring rolls with Asian 'slaw and curry dressing, or crispy squid and stir-fried beef salad with smoked aubergine dressing, to slow-cooked pork belly with Clonakilty black pudding, or a rack of aged sirloin with garlic and Irish cheese dauphinois, buttered cabbage and tobacco onions. Lunch brings sandwiches, wraps and easy pickings such as steak sandwiches or Creole chicken burgers, while puddings keep it global with the likes of mango pannacotta or passion fruit and coconut crème brûlée. Also check out the espresso martinis for a dessert cocktail kick. Wines from £15.95.

Chef/s: Darren Ireland. **Open:** all week L 12 to 3.30, D 5 to 9 (6 to 9.30 Fri and Sat). **Closed:** 25 Dec. **Meals:** alc (main courses £16 to £22). Set L and D £16 (2 courses) to £20. **Details:** 40 seats. 8 seats outside. Wheelchair access. Music. Car parking.

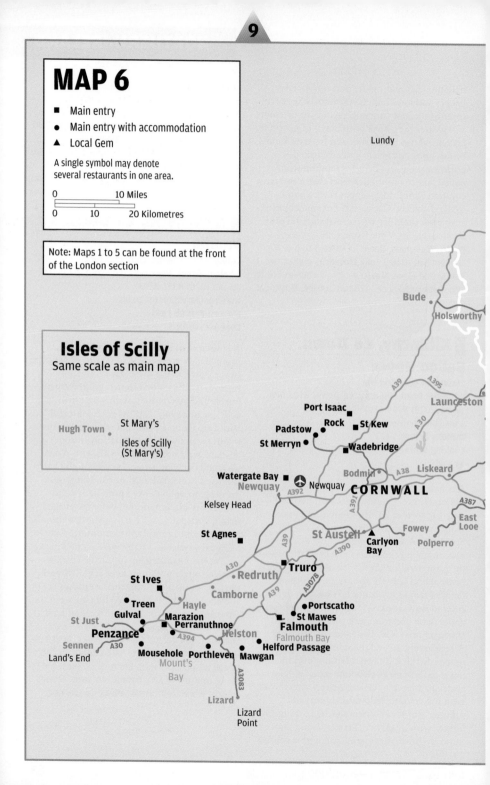

MAP 6

- ■ Main entry
- ● Main entry with accommodation
- ▲ Local Gem

A single symbol may denote
several restaurants in one area.

0		10 Miles
0	10	20 Kilometres

Note: Maps 1 to 5 can be found at the front
of the London section

Isles of Scilly
Same scale as main map

Hugh Town

St Mary's

Isles of Scilly
(St Mary's)

Lundy

Bude

Holsworthy

A39   A395

A39   Launceston

A30

Port Isaac
Rock   St Kew
Padstow
St Merryn   Wadebridge

Bodmin   A38   Liskeard

Watergate Bay
Newquay   A392   Newquay   CORNWALL

Kelsey Head   A392   A387

East
Looe

St Agnes   St Austell   Fowey
A390   Carlyon   Polperro
Bay

A30   Redruth   Truro

Camborne   A39   A3078

St Ives   Portscatho
Treen   Hayle   St Mawes
Gulval   Marazion   Helston   Falmouth
St Just   Perranuthnoe   Falmouth Bay
Penzance   A394   Helford Passage
Sennen   A30
Land's End   Mousehole   Porthleven   Mawgan
Mount's
Bay

A3083

Lizard
Lizard
Point

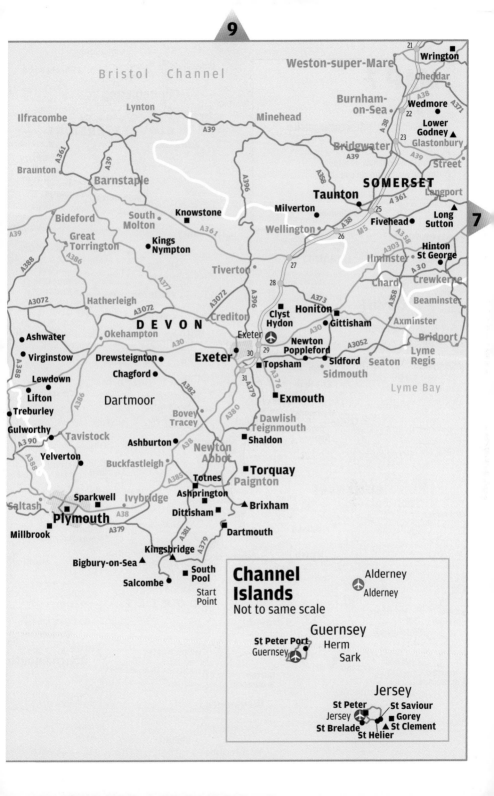

7

Bristol Channel

Weston-super-Mare

Wrington ■

Cheddar

Burnham-
on-Sea

Wedmore

A38

A371

Minehead

Lower
Godney ▲

22

Ilfracombe

Lynton

A39

Glastonbury

23

Bridgwater

Street

A39

A39

Braunton

A361

A39

Barnstaple

SOMERSET

A361

Langport

A396

Taunton

A368

Milverton

Long
Sutton ▲

Bideford

South
Molton

Knowstone ■

A361

Wellington

Fivehead ●

25

Great
Torrington

A39

A388

A386

Kings
Nympton ●

26

M5

A358

A303

Hinton
St George

Ilminster

Tiverton

27

Crewkerne

A30

A3072

Hatherleigh

A3072

A377

28

Chard

A358

Beaminster

Ashwater ●

D E V O N

A3072

Crediton

A396

Clyst
Hydon ■

Honiton ■

Axminster

Bridport

Okehampton

Gittisham ●

A30

Exeter ●

A30

Newton
Poppleford ●

A3052

Lyme
Regis

Virginstow ●

Drewsteignton ●

A382

Topsham ■

Sidford ●

Seaton

Lewdown ●

Chagford ●

29

30

31

Sidmouth

Lyme Bay

Lifton ●

A386

Dartmoor

A379

Exmouth ■

Treburley ●

Bovey
Tracey

A376

Gulworthy ●

A390

Tavistock

A380

Dawlish
Teignmouth

Yelverton ●

Buckfastleigh

Ashburton ●

A38

Shaldon ■

Newton
Abbot

Saltash

Sparkwell ■

Ivybridge

A385

Totnes ■

Torquay ■

Paignton

Plymouth

A38

Ashprington ■

Millbrook ■

A388

A379

A381

Dittisham ■

▲ Brixham

Dartmouth ■

Kingsbridge ▲

A379

Bigbury-on-Sea ▲

South
Pool ■

Salcombe ●

Start
Point

**Channel
Islands**
Not to same scale

Alderney

Alderney

Guernsey

St Peter Port

Herm

Guernsey

Sark

Jersey

St Peter

St Saviour

Jersey

■ Gorey

St Brelade

▲ St Clement

St Helier

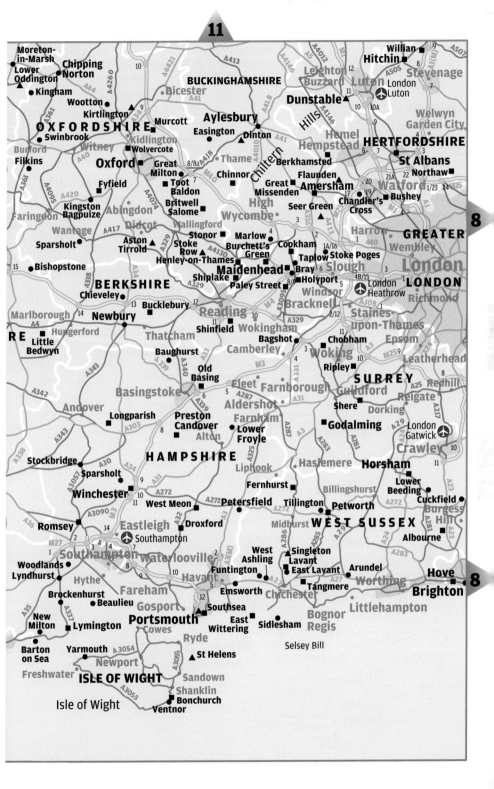

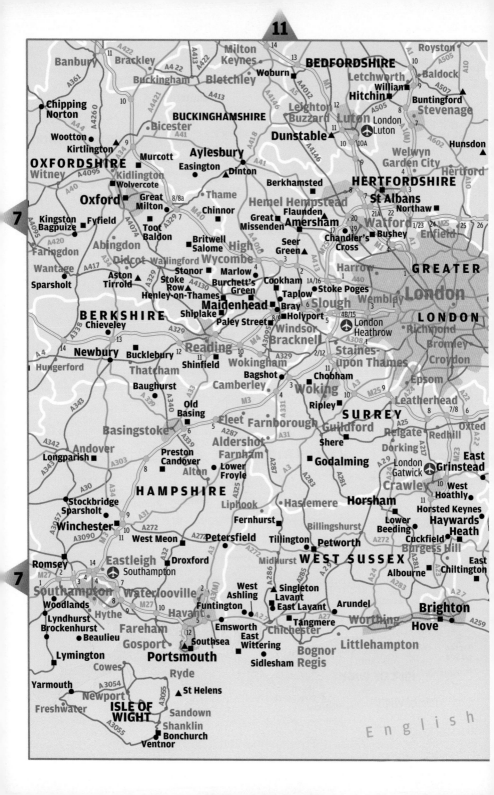

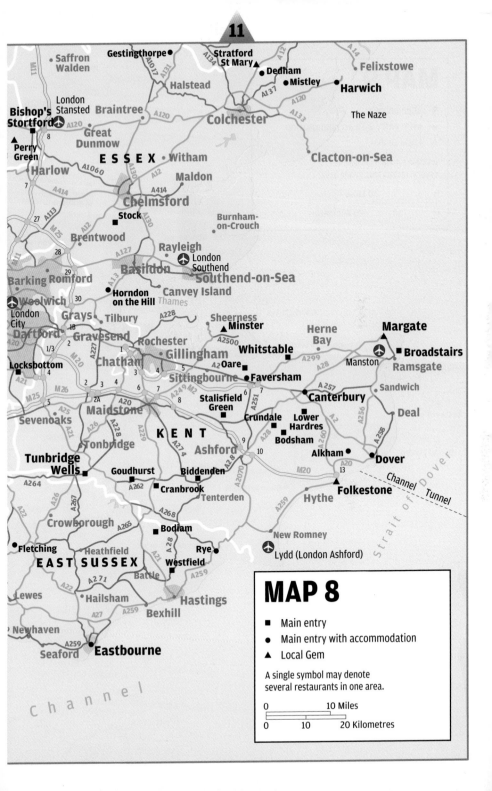

Saffron Walden

Gestingthorpe

Stratford St Mary

Dedham

Mistley

Felixstowe

Halstead

Harwich

London Stansted

Braintree

A120

Colchester

The Naze

Bishop's Stortford

A120

Great Dunmow

Clacton-on-Sea

Perry Green

8

E S S E X · Witham

A1060

Harlow

7

A414

Maldon

A414

27

A113

Chelmsford

Stock

Burnham-on-Crouch

M25

Brentwood

A127

Rayleigh

London Southend

28

Basildon

29

Southend-on-Sea

Barking Romford

30

Horndon on the Hill

Canvey Island

Thames

Woolwich

London City

Grays

Tilbury

A228

Sheerness

Minster

Herne Bay

Margate

Broadstairs

18

Dartford

1/3

2

Gravesend

A227

Rochester

A2500

Whitstable

A299

Manston

Ramsgate

Locksbottom

A21

M25

A25

M20

A227

1

Chatham

Gillingham

A2

Oare

A28

Sandwich

2

3

4

2A

A20

3

4

Sittingbourne

A249 M2

Faversham

A257

Canterbury

Deal

Sevenoaks

A26

A228

A229

Maidstone

5

6

7

8

Stalisfield Green

A251

6

7

A2

A256

Tonbridge

A274

K E N T

Ashford

Crundale

Lower Hardres

A260

Bodsham

9

10

Alkham

Dover

Tunbridge Wells

A264

Goudhurst

A262

Biddenden

Cranbrook

A2070

A28

M20

13

A20

Channel Tunnel

A26

A267

A22

Crowborough

A265

A268

Bodiam

Tenterden

A259

Hythe

Folkestone

Fletching

Heathfield

A28

Rye

New Romney

Strait of Dover

E A S T S U S S E X

A271

Westfield

Lydd (London Ashford)

Lewes

A22

Hailsham

A27

A259

Battle

Bexhill

A259

Hastings

Newhaven

A259

Seaford

Eastbourne

C h a n n e l

MAP 8

■ Main entry

● Main entry with accommodation

▲ Local Gem

A single symbol may denote
several restaurants in one area.

0   10 Miles

0   10   20 Kilometres

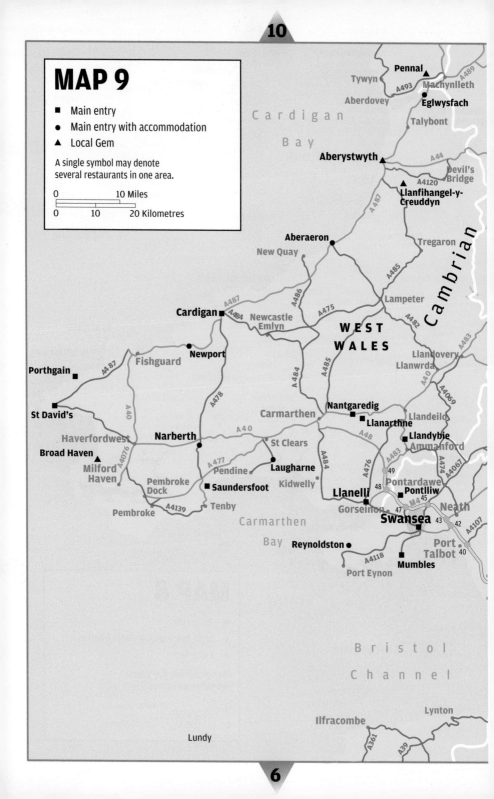

MAP 9

- ■ Main entry
- ● Main entry with accommodation
- ▲ Local Gem

A single symbol may denote
several restaurants in one area.

0   10 Miles
0   10   20 Kilometres

Cardigan

Bay

Pennal
Tywyn   Machynlleth
Aberdovey   Eglwysfach
Talybont

Aberystwyth
Devil's
Bridge
Llanfihangel-y-
Creuddyn

Aberaeron
New Quay

Tregaron

Lampeter

WEST
WALES

Cardigan
Newcastle
Emlyn

Porthgain
Fishguard   Newport

St David's

Llandovery
Llanwrda

Nantgaredig
Carmarthen   Llanarthne
Llandeilo
Llandybie
Ammanford

Haverfordwest
Narberth
St Clears
Broad Haven
Milford
Haven
Pembroke
Dock
Laugharne
Pendine
Kidwelly
Saundersfoot

Pembroke
Tenby

49
Llanelli   48   Pontardawe
Gorseinon   47   Pontlliw
Carmarthen   Swansea   43 42 Neath
Bay   Reynoldston   Port
Mumbles   Talbot 40
Port Eynon

Bristol

Channel

Lynton

Ilfracombe

Lundy

CAMBRIAN

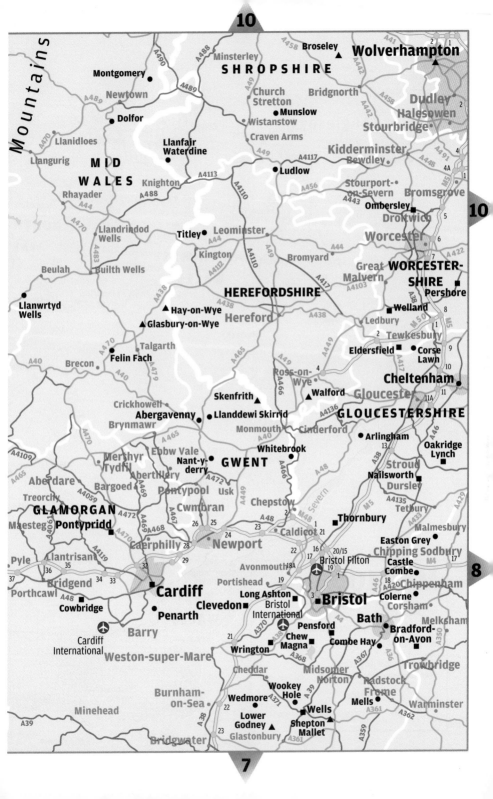

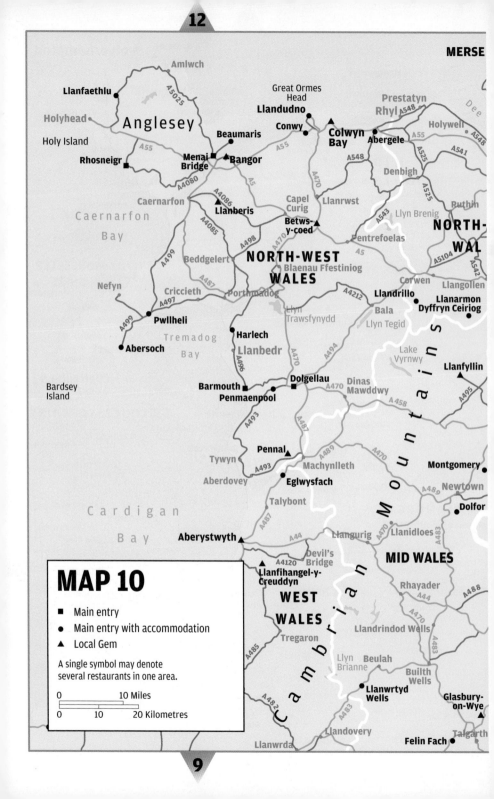

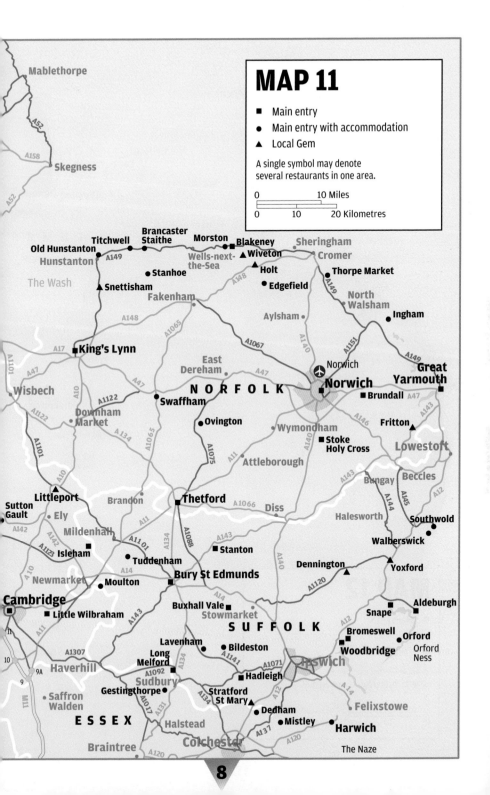

MAP 11

- ■ Main entry
- ● Main entry with accommodation
- ▲ Local Gem

A single symbol may denote
several restaurants in one area.

0   10 Miles

0   10   20 Kilometres

Mablethorpe

A52

A158

Skegness

A52

The Wash

Brancaster
Staithe   Morston   Blakeney   Sheringham
Titchwell   Cromer
Old Hunstanton   Wells-next-   Wiveton
Hunstanton   A149   the-Sea   Holt
                    Stanhoe   Edgefield   Thorpe Market
Snettisham   North
Fakenham   Aylsham   Walsham
                                                                 Ingham
A148   A1067
A1065
King's Lynn   East   A1067   A149
A17   Dereham   Norwich   Great
A47   A47   Yarmouth
Wisbech   NORFOLK   Norwich
A10   Swaffham   Brundall   A47
A1122
Downham   Ovington   Wymondham   Fritton
Market   A134   A146
A1101   A1065   A1075   Stoke   Lowestoft
A10   Holy Cross
                                Attleborough   Beccles
Littleport   A143   Bungay
Sutton   Southwold
Gault   Ely   Brandon   Thetford   A1066   Diss
A142   Halesworth
Mildenhall   A11   A134   A143   Walberswick
Isleham   A1101   A1088   Dennington Yoxford
Newmarket   Tuddenham   Stanton
Moulton   A14   Bury St Edmunds   A1120
Cambridge   A14
Little Wilbraham   A143   Buxhall Vale   Snape   Aldeburgh
                               Stowmarket   Orford
11   SUFFOLK Bromeswell Orford
A11   Lavenham   Bildeston   Woodbridge   Ness
10   Long   A1071
9A   A1307   Melford   A1141   Ipswich
9   Haverhill A1092   Hadleigh
M11   Sudbury   Stratford   A12
          Saffron Gestingthorpe St Mary   Felixstowe
          Walden   Dedham
ESSEX   Halstead   Mistley   Harwich
Braintree   A120   Colchester   The Naze
A137

8

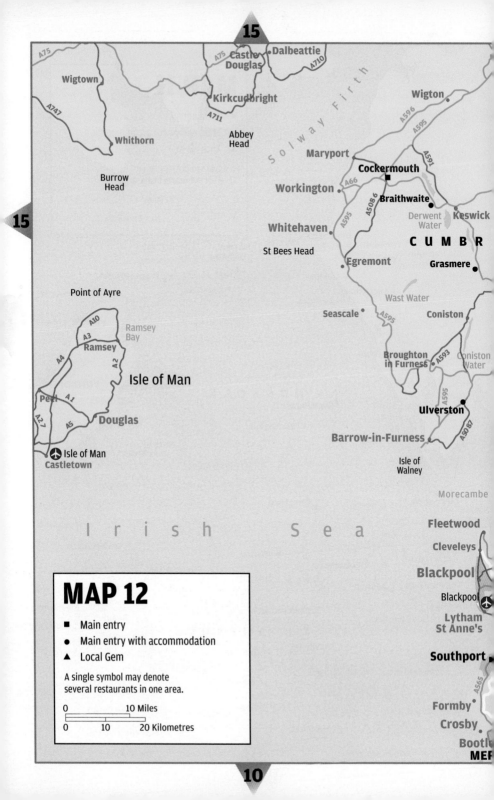

A75

Wigtown

A75 · Castle Douglas · Dalbeattie

A75 · Kirkcudbright

A711 · A710

A747

Whithorn

Abbey Head

Solway Firth

Wigton

A596 · A595

Burrow Head

Maryport

Cockermouth ■

A66 · A5086 · A595 · A591

Workington ·

Braithwaite ·

Derwent Water · Keswick ·

Whitehaven ·

C U M B R

St Bees Head

Egremont ·

Grasmere ·

Point of Ayre

Wast Water

A10

A3 · Ramsey Bay

Ramsey

A2

A4

Isle of Man

Seascale ·

A595

Coniston ·

Broughton in Furness ·

A593 · Coniston Water

A595

Peel · A1

A27 · A5

Douglas ·

A5087

Ulverston ·

✈ Isle of Man

Castletown

Barrow-in-Furness ·

Isle of Walney

Morecambe

I r i s h   S e a

Fleetwood ·

Cleveleys ·

Blackpool

MAP 12

Blackpool ✈

■ Main entry

● Main entry with accommodation

▲ Local Gem

Lytham St Anne's

A single symbol may denote
several restaurants in one area.

Southport ■

0 _____ 10 Miles

A565

0 ____ 10 ____ 20 Kilometres

Formby ·

Crosby ·

Bootle

MEF

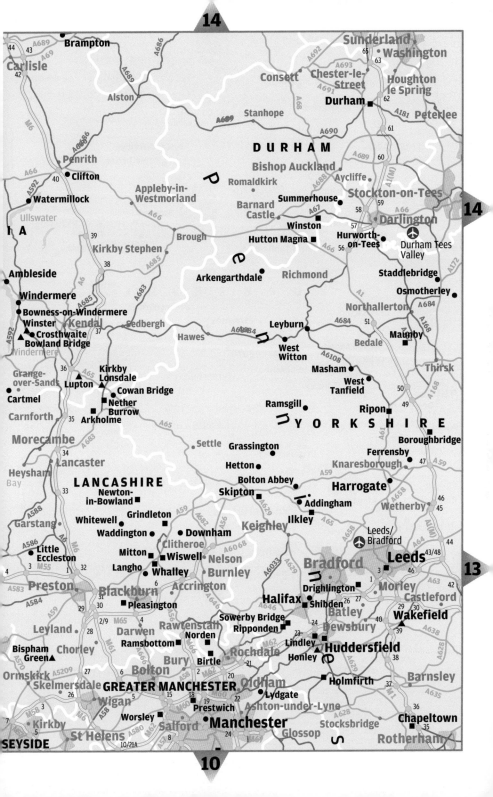

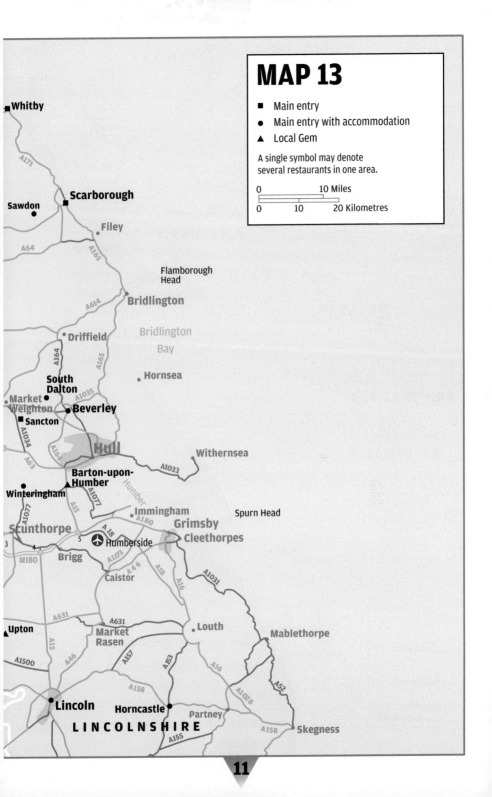

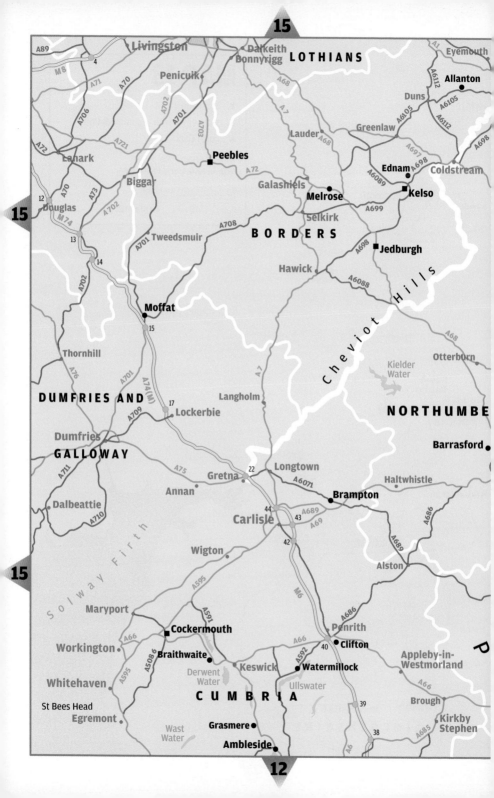

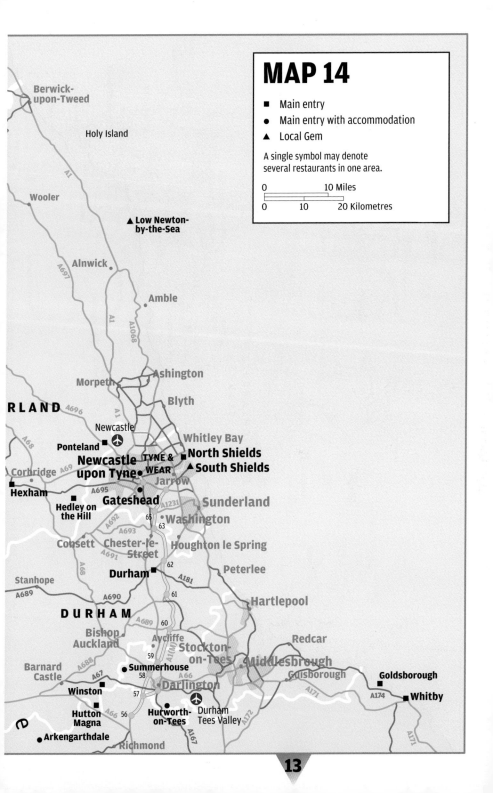

MAP 14

- ■ Main entry
- ● Main entry with accommodation
- ▲ Local Gem

A single symbol may denote
several restaurants in one area.

```
0              10 Miles
0      10      20 Kilometres
```

Berwick-upon-Tweed

Holy Island

Wooler

▲ Low Newton-by-the-Sea

Alnwick

Amble

Morpeth

Ashington

RLAND   A696

Blyth

Newcastle

Ponteland ■

Whitley Bay

Corbridge A69

Newcastle upon Tyne

TYNE & WEAR

■ North Shields
▲ South Shields

Hexham ■

Jarrow

A695

Hedley on the Hill

Gateshead

A1231

Sunderland

A692

65

A693

•Washington
63

Consett

Chester-le-Street

A691

Houghton le Spring

Stanhope

A689

A68

62

Durham ■

A181

Peterlee

A690

61

D U R H A M   A689

60

Hartlepool

Bishop Auckland

Aycliffe

59

Stockton-on-Tees

Redcar

Barnard Castle

A688

Summerhouse
58

A66

Middlesbrough

Guisborough

Goldsborough

A67

Winston

57

Darlington

A171

A174

■ Whitby

Hutton Magna

A66   56

Hurworth-on-Tees

Durham Tees Valley

A172

• Arkengarthdale

Richmond

A167

A171

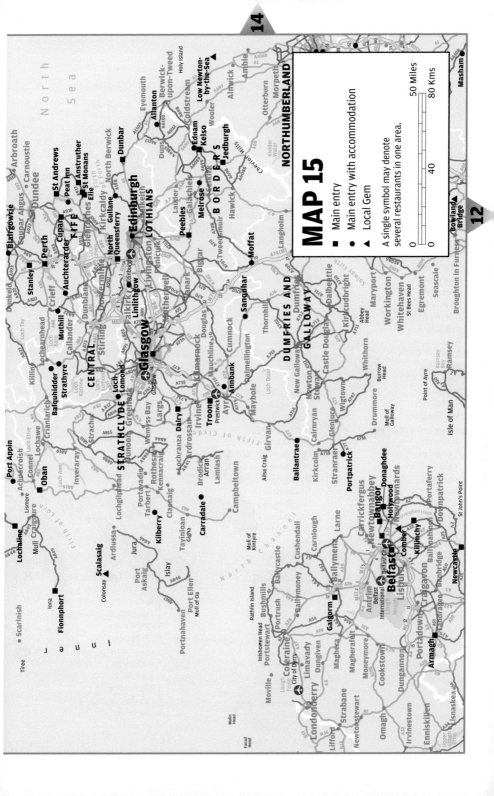

Note: The INDEX BY TOWN does not include London entries.

The Good Food Guide 2015

TOWN | Index

The Good Food Guide 2015

The Good Food Guide 2015

Thank you

This book couldn't have happened without a cast of thousands. Our thanks are due to the following contributors, among many others.

Roger Aardestiy
Ben Aardewerk
Ben Abbott
Nick Abercrombie
Laura Abert
Anthony Abrahams
Carol Absott
Martin G Ackroyd
Jonathan Acton
Davis QC
David Adair
Alasdair Adam
Barbara Adams
Christine Adams
Dan Adams
Fenella Adams
Jan Adams
Karen Adams
Myan Adams
Matt Adamson-Drage
Kirstie Addis
Liz Addison
Robert Addlestone
Jennifer Adrian
Carrie Afrin
Kevan Alderman
Melanie Alderson
Brett Alderton
Richard Aldous
Lee Alesbury
Sally Alexander
Simon Alexander
Mo Ali
Jane Alison
Haval Al-Khalifa
Andrea Allan
Isabel Allan
Roger Allcock
Dale Allen
Ian Allen
Ian Allison
Julie Allman
Debra Allonby
Lucia Allum
Rosert Ambrose
Glyn Amphlett
Amina Amrani
Sanjiv Anchal
Gillian Anderson
Leslie Anderson
Sarah Anderson
Helen Anderson
Jose Andres
Jonathan Andrews
Nicki Andrews
William Andrews
Ellen Andronov
Pauline Anne
Frederick Anslow
Sebastian Anstey
Douglas Anthony
Julie Anthony
Alex Antrobus
Jane Appleby

Linda Arch
Sally Archer
Stuart Archibald
Dryvers Ariane
Danielle Arkwright
Steve Armitage
Claire Armstrong
Graham Armstrong
Hilary Armstrong
Teresa Armstrong
Jacqueline Arnold
Amy Arora
Haz Arshad
Charlotte Ashe
David Ashford
Kenneth Ashken
Kirsty Ashman
Carey Ashworth
Anthony Askew
Neil Askham
Emily Asquith-Fox
Rachel Astbury
Siobhan Astbury
Margaret Atherton
Sally Atherton
Kim Atkins
Paul Atkins
Michelle Atkinson
Frank Attwood
Helen Auchland
Arsha Aulakh
Angela Austin
Glynis Austin
Pat Auty
Siri Avends
Deryn Averill
Steven Axford
Madeleine Aylett
Lyn Ayrton
Sam Aziz
Michele Backer
Keri Backhouse
Diane Backler
Beverley Bacon
Sean Badrick
Nicholas Baer
Jona Bagham
Christopher Baigent
Gary Bailey
Jason Bailey
Pat Bailey
Richard Bailey
Carmel Baillum
Adrian Bain
James Baird
Briana Baker
Caryle Baker
Margaret Baker
Simon Baker
Ravi Bala
Judith Balfour
David Ball
Yasmin Ball
Amanda Ballard-Stuart

Anne Balls
Richard Barnes
Heather Bamford
Hans Raj Bance
Sam Band
Nicki Bane
Barbara Banks
Catherine Bannan
Nattalie Barbara
Helen Barber
Janice Barbour
James Barclay
Rachel Barclay
Wesley Bardoe
Jack Bardrick
Marie Barker
Melanie Barker-Dobson
Nadia Barkot
Vivien Barlow
John Barnard
Amy Barnes
Derek Barnes
Paul Barnes
Robert Barnes
Roseanna Barnes
Paul Barnett
Ajay Barolia
Mat Barow
Brian Barr
Jane Barrett
Sarah Barrett
David Barron
Jane Barry
Buz Barstow
Gus Bartholomew
Helen Bartlett
Brian Barton
Philip Barwood
Martin Bashall
Nicola Bashall
April Baskind
Katie Batchelor
Ros Bate
Phil Bateman
Simon Bates
Anne Bate-Williams
Andy Batley
Joanne Batten
Chris P Batter
John Batters
Cynthia Battersby
Nicholas Battige
Tim Battle
Alison Battrick
Paul Baumgartner
Peter Baxter
Valerie Baxter
Rosie Baylies
Laura Bea
Jessica Beaghen
Tracy Beal
Emma Beale
Scott Bean
Elaine Beardall

Richard Beardon
Sally Beasmont
Butch Beaton Brown
Judith Beatty
Maria Beaumont
Jane Beck
Stuart Beckess
Clare Beckman
Dr & Mrs G J Bedford
Tanya Bedford
Andy Beesley
Bryan Bell
Chris Bell
Daniel Bell
Stephanie Bell
Janet Bellamy
Loretta Bellman
Charlotte Bemon
John Bence
Irene Bendler
Valerie Benguerel
Jacolyn Benn
Alison Bennett
Charlotte Bennett
Ian Bennett
Katryn Bennett
Rachel Bennett
Rebecca Bennett
Robin Bennett
Camille Bensley
Clive Benson
Sally Benson
Stephen Benson
Fred Bent
Philip Bentley
Carole Benyon
Kitty Benzecry
Sharon Berford
Barrie Bernstein
Bec Berrett
Emma Berry
Jan Berry
Peter Bessey
Muriel Best
Martin Bett
Anne Bettridge
Andrew Betts
Jean Betts
Elaine Beveridge
Maria Bez
P Bhati
Aditi Bhattacharya
Alessandro Bianchi
Jonathan Bibbings
James Bickers
Doug Bickley
James Biddlecombe
Timothy Bigelow
David Bigmore
Pete Biller
Dougal Binech
Aileen Binner
Sheila Binns
Evonne Birch-Jackson

Sue Bird
Jenny Birnie
Sue Bishop
Kate Bishop
Christopher Black
Margaret Black
Brenda Blackburn
June Blackburn
Catherine Blackman
Sarah Blackwell
Michael Blagden
Mark Blake
Nigel Blake
Nicki Blayber
Angela Blaze
Jackie Blease
Samantha Blenkinsopp
Heather Bliss
Sarah Blomiley
Aileen Bloomer
Elena Bloomfield
Robert Bluner
Elena Blunsum
Jamie Blyth
Sarah Blythe
Andy Boase
Michael Boatwright
Marco Bode
John Boden
Cathy Bodikian
Mark Boffin
Rosa Bolger
Francesca Bonatti
Frankie Bond
Geoff Bond
Malcolm Bonder
Napier Bonnet
Edward Bonnett
Neil Bontoft
Bev Boon
Derek Boorman
Jane Boorman-Dhillon
Ben Booth
Jason Booth
Kat Booth
Ken Booth
Nick Booth
Robert Booth
Claire Boother
Julie Boreham
Jill Boswell
Samuel Botham
Ella Bothing
Nicola Bothwell
Ian Bottle
Karen Bottomley
Faye Boucher
John Boulter
Sylvia Bound
Aisling Bourne
Diane Boustead
Anne Bowden
Tanya Bowell
Caroline Bowen

Teral Bowen
Linzi Bower
Jane Bowers
Jackie Bowes
Laurence Bowes
Lyn Bowker
Aly Boyle
Nick Boyle
Chris Boyne
Danielle Boyne
Gill Bracey
Anthony Bradbury
John Bradbury
Janet Bradford
Chris Bradley
Mark Bradley
Bradley Braithwaite
Karen Braithwaite
Ann Bramfitt
Ewan Bramley
Chris Bramwell
Sophie Brandreth
Beth Bray
Heather Bray
Martin Brayshaw
Tony Brazendale
Ian Breckon
David Bremner
Stuart Brenna
Alex Brennon
Alan Brentnall
Blair Breton
Wendy Brett
Joanne Brewer
Paul J M Brewer
Jessica Brick
Michael Bridge
Sandra Bridge
Jane Bridge
Lavinia Bridges
Beth Berry Jones
David John Brigg
Andrew Brookes
Candyce Brooks
Caul Brooks
Karen Brooks
Christine Broom
Amy Broomfield
David Brougham
Mairin Broughton
April Browell
Alan Brown
Amanda Brown
Andy Brown
John Brown
Julian Brown
Kirkham Brown
Mary Brown
Nicola Brown
Shoina Brown
Tim Brown
Alex Browne
Daniel Browne
Jordan Brownlee

Jane Brunton
Polly Bryan
John Bryant
Doug Bryson
Jayne Buchanan
Sally Buck
Chris Buckley
Grainne Buckley
Kirsten Buckley
James Budd
James Budern
Moira Budge
Frances Bull
Ruth Bull
Sam Bulloch
Matt Bulmers
Sarah Bundy
Paul Burbridge
Samuel Burdge
Daphne Burgess
Dale Burke
Paul Burmester
Emma Burnaby-Atkins
John Burnham
Fran Burns
Grace Burns
Kathleen Burns
Oliver Burns
Gordon Burnside
Karl Burnside
Stanley Burnton
Richard Burridge
Mairi Burrow
Eric Burrows
Nicola Burrows
Jill Burry
Julia Burt
Christine Burton
Trudi Burton
Margaret Bury
Julie Bush
Sharyn Butcher
Jason Butler
Sharon Butler
Eugene Butlerworth
Steve Butterfield
Bev Butterworth
Andy Button
Gareth Byrne
Richard Byrne
Jacqueline Byrom
Adam Byron
Roy Caddy
Kathy Cadwallader
Catriona Cahill
Christine Cairns
John Calder
Alysia Calderwood
Mike Caldwell
Christine Campbell
Laura Campbell
Margret Campbell
Sheree Campbell
Jacqui Campbell Martin
James Camwell
James Cannon
Nigel Cant
Jane Cantellow
Ros Caplan
Kate Capper
Emily Card
Natasha Card
Heather Carne
Laura Carney
Frank Carnie
Leslie Caroline
Joanne Carpanini
Rachael Carr
Anna Carriero
Bradley Carroll
Steve Carroll
Mik Carson
Jane Carter
Julie Carter
Lewis Carter
Ronnie Carter
Sarah Carter
Deborah Cartwright
Mike Carwithen
Michael Casey
Tony Casey
Dawn Casson
Elian Castaing
Rebecca Castle
Tony Castro
Peter Causnett
Andy Cave
Mark Caven
Mary-Jane Cembrowicz

Emma Chadderton
Hollie Chadderton
Paul Chambers
Steven Chambers
Kerry-Jane Chandler
Tom Chandler
Jane Chandley
Lionel Chaplin
Laura Chapman
Philip Chapman
Robin Chapman
Zoë Chappell
Gill Charlton
John Charnock
Naomi Chatterley
Harshida Chavd
Peter Checkley
Edna Cheer
Eddie Cheng
Chantelle Chester
Lucy Chester
Sue Chesterman
Franck Chevallier
Casey Child
Elizabeth Childs
Paul Chilton
Jack Chilvers
Sarah Chisnall
Dawn Chivers
Nik Chotai
Chris Chowney
Deborah Christie
Maureen Christie
Ben Citarelli
Margaret Clamp
Margaret Clancy
Mike Clapp
Elaine Clark
Lionel Clark
Natasha Clark
Anne Clarke
David Clarke
John Clarke
Matt Clarke
Yuette Clarke
Caroline Clayton
Suzanne Clayton
Jem Clear
Susan Clegg
Hannah Clemit
Patricia Cleverley
Gordon Clifford
Gail Clinch
John Clough
Wendy Clubley
Sam Coates
Ray Coats
David Cockburn
Dee Cocking
Richard Coe
Clare Cohen
Claire Colclough
Ian Cole
Nath Cole
Zoe Cole
Jennifer Coleman
John Coleman
Julie Coleman
Roger Coleman
Tom Coleman
Jennifer Coles
Jane Coller
Terence Collie
Cameron Collier
Anne Collins
Emma Collins
Hannah Collins
Martha Collins
Suzanne Collins
Lorrone Collor
Sam Complin
Alex Conboy
Amy Connell
Patricia Connell
Heather Connor
Chris Conroy
Anne Conway
David Cook
Gary Cook
Jim Cook
Martin Cook
Alysit Cooke
John Cooke
Theresa Cooke
Derek Cooknell
Iain Cookson
Adrian Cooling
Barry Cooper
David Cooper

Helen Cooper
Jane Cooper
Olivia Cooper
Sandra Cooper
Sarah Cooper
Susan Cooper
Rob Copeland
Charlotte Copson
Jennifer Corbett
Matthew Corder
Clare Cork
John Cormack
Barry Corner
Tina Corney
Nicola Cosgrave
Gerard Costello
Laura Costello
Zoe & Elliot Costello
Lee Cotle
Neil Cottow
Sophie Coulombeau
Eddy Coulson
Kay Coupe
Dominie Court
Ashley Courtney
Emma Coutts
Nick Cowan
David Cox
Harry Cox
Jon Cox
Laura Cox
Nichola Cox
Sheena Cox
Steven Cox
Tom Cox
Simon Coxon
Derek Crabb
Sarah Crabb
John Craig
Amanda Craigs
Sarah Cranness
Michael Craven
Neil Crawford
Norman Crawford
Stephen Creed
Ian Crewe
Rachael Crewe
David Crimble
Olivia Critchley
Beverley Croft
Peta Croft
Stephen Cromie
Richard Crone
Linda Crosby
Richard Crosby
John Crosfield
Andy Cross
Emily Cross
Rose Cross
Eleanor Crossland
Marilyn Crowder
Dawn Crowe
Jane Crowson
Rosanna Cruci
Gemma Crump
Katie Crump
Lee Cubley
Andrew Cumming
Michael Cundey
Lionel Cunnington
William Cupit
Lynn Curnow
Catherine Curry
S H Curry
Belinda Curtis
Nick Curtis
Sam Curtis
Mike Cushman
James Cutforth
Lucy Cuthbert
Thomas Cutts
Liane Dabbous
Harry Dadak
Adam Dakin
Anthony Dale
Leone Dale
Teri Dale
Rebecca Dallman
Amber Dalton
Morag Dalton
Jason Daly
Jeffrey Daly
Michael Daly
Jessie Damman
Victoria D'Angelo
Catherine Daniel
Vicci Daniels
Elizabeth Darby
Catherine D'Arcy

Clair Darke
Alice Darrington
Daniel Darwood
Tom Daukes
Jay Dave
Carol Davey
Clement Davey
Giles Davey
Matt Davey
Stephen Davidson
Freida Davie
Alun Davies
Beverley Davies
Dave Davies
Debbie Davies
Ian Davies
Jill Davies
Kirsty Davies
Natalie Davies
Rebecca Davies
Sally Davies
Kirsty Davies-Chinnock
Anna Davis
Barbara Davis
Cl Davis
Iona Davis
Luan Davis
Mary Davis
Paul Davis
Sarah Davis
Hilary Davison
Karen Davison
Kathy Davison
Lance Davison
Esme Dawber
Andrew Dawson
Ursula Dawson
Geoffrey Day
Glenys Day
Laura Day
Mark Day
Pauline Day
Tom Day
Gloria Dayman
Rudolf De Lange
Simon De Pinna
Mark De Wesselow
Kristy Dean
Rob Dean
Karen Dearman
Georgina Dee
Nicholas Dee
Alastair Deller
Iain Denby
Kathy Denman
John Denmark
John & Sue Denmark
Roy Dennis
Deborah Denny
Sam Derbyshire
Brian Devany
Victoria Devenish
Dawn Devine
Ian Dewey
Amar Dhami
Ailsa Di Emidio
Evelyn Dick
William Dick
Simon Dickens
Lucy Dickinson
Joanne Dicterson
Rhiannon Dillon
Louise Dilworth
Allison Dingle
Claire Dinsdale
Cardelia Ditton
Colin Divall
Tina Divito-Lones
Lisa Dixon
Sue Dixon
G M Dobbie
Martin Doble
Angela Dobson
Lisa Docherty
Claire Dockett
Martin Dodd
Debbie Dodge
Andy Dodson
Steve Doherty
Julie Dolling
Sophie Donnelly
James Doody
Mindy Doon
Dawn Doran
John Doran
Kathleen Dore
Lynn Dorling
Dereen Doward
Phil Dowling

James Downie
Helen Dowson
Dean Doyle
Elizabeth Doyle
Ben Drahe
Karrie & Adam Drake
Phil Drake
Sally Drake
Tony Draper
Dudley Drayson
Stephen Drew
Ruth Dryga
Guillaume Ducasse
Jay Duckett
Kenneth Duckett
Caroline Duckworth
Mike Dudley
Sheila Dudley
Lynda Duffield
Peter Duffy
Neil Dugard
Susan Dugher
Lindsay Dunlop
Alan Dunn
Pamella Dunn
Sally Dunstone
Teresa Dupay
Tom Durkin
Donna Duslea
Rebecca Duxbury
Emma Dwan O'Reilly
Ann Dyer
Catherine Dyer
Anna Dyson
Antony Dyson
Lorraine Dyson
Caroline Eaden
Mel Ealey
Russell Earnshaw
Wendy Eastlake
Lindsay Easton
Paul Easton
Chris Easy
Hannah Eaton
Ruth Ebdon
Rachel Eburne
Amanda Edwards
Jacquelin Edwards
Jane Edwards
Rachel Edwards
Mark Egan
Helen Eger
Debbie Egerton-Morris
Anthony Elbra
Sarah Eley
Gary Elflett
Cynthia Elkington
James Elliman
Katie Elliot
David Elliott
Alea Ellis
Chris Ellis
Mark Ellis
Richard Ellis
Steve Ellison
Francesca Ellitt
Jamie Ells
Martin Elsender
Daniel Embleton
John Emms
Lisa Emsley
Anne Endres
Sue Erins
Bibi Evans
Catherine Evans
Jo Evans
Peter Evans
Richard Evans
Maureen Everson
Sharon Ewens
Phil Extance
Sonya Exton
Tracy Facey
Kathy Fackler-Chapman
Guy Fairbank
Donna Fairley
Angus Falconer
Catrina Falconer
Charlotte Falconer
Angus Falconer
Kirrilly Falivene
Gary Fall
Jacqueline Faller
Ramune Farnan
Nadir Farrell
Margaret R Farrelly
Karen Farrow
Sally Farrow
Tariq Faruque

Jay Faulkner
Linda Favill
Paddy Fay
Jefrey Fazal
Clairi Fearon
Chris Feeley
Fiona Feeney
Sue Fells
Rachel Fennant
A B X Fenwick
Debbie Fenwick
Mike Fenwick
Donilla Ferfier
Irene Ferla
Giuseppe Ferraro
Charmian Ferrett
David Fettes
J Fiddian
Gordon Field
Maureen Field
Richard Fielding
Michael Fields
Neville Filar
Samantha Finch
Valerie Finch
Marc Findlay
Roxane Fish
Emma Fisher
Andrew Fishwick
Christopher Fishwick
Ian Fitzgerald
Bill Fitzpatrick
Terence Flanagan
Mark Flannagan
David Flannery
Emma Flather
Roz Flawty
Adelaide Flaxman
Jes Fleming
Philip Fleming
Dave Fletcher
Janis Fletcher
Charlotte Fleur
Adam Flint
Jamie Flodman
Anne-Marie Flood
Amanda Fluck
Helene Flynn
Pam Foden
Barry Fogg
Stephanie Fokinther
Vikki Fold
Nicola Folley
Michael Foot
Peter Footitt
Kitty Forbes
Gail Ford
Lindsey Ford
Andy Fordham
Leigh Forman
Ian Foster
Rachel Foster
Anne Fouche
Mike Fountain
Michael Fourman
Chris Fowkes
Heline Fowkes
Kim Fowler
Kirsteen Fox
Simon Fox
Tessa Fox
Rich Foxcroft
Rachel Frame
Howard Frances
Cath Francis
Peter & Pauline Frank
Mark Frankel
Dale Franks
Francine Franks
Kristy Franks
Roz Frankun
Colin Fraser
Joan Fraser
John Fraser
Jonathan Freeland
Carole Frelder
Steph French
Rachel Fripp
Cara Froggatt
James Frost
Frank Froud
Carol Fry
Norman Fry
Emrys Fuge
John Fullerton
Maggie Fullerton
Kate Fulwell
Rachael Fundrey
Deborah Funnell

Bernadette Gaffney
Jane Gaffney
Miriam Gage
Phil Gage
Nick Gale
Jessica Gallienne
Georgina Gamble
Lynda Gardner
Barry Garfield
Edith Gargaud
Carys Garner
Emma Garner
Jan Garner
Patricia Garner
Isobel Garvie
Rosie Gatensbury
Peter Gates
Rebecca Gautch
Vernon Gayle
Laura Gaynor
Rory Gazzard
Keily Geary
Gabriele Gell
Tony Gelsthorpe
Shaw Geo
Seamus Geoghegan
Hilary George
Wendy George
Mari Geraint
Brendan Gerrard
Christine Gerrard
Mary Gerrard
Steve Gerrard
Stuart Gerrett
Helen Gibb
Grahame Gibbins
Tina Gibbins
Elspeth Gibbon
Daphne Gibbs
Angela Gibson
Ann Gibson
Clara Gibson
Keith Gibson
Tracy Gifford
Preetha Gigo
Emma Gilbert
Nick Gilbody
Judy Giles
Alan Gill
Brett Gill
James Gill
Steve Gill
Emily Gill
Holly Gillan
Liz Gilley
Liz Gillgrass
Zoe Gillon
Era Gjurgjeala
Jehona Gjurgjeala
Andrea Glass
John Glass
Martin Glassborow
Mike Glasspole
John Glazebrook
David Gleave
Catherine Gledhill
Bryan Anthony Glister
Alessandra Giordano
Kelly Glover
Roger Glover
Sam Goates
Ben Goddard
Jim Godsell
David Gold
Bruce Goldman
Anne Goldshy
Lauren Goldsworthy
Lisa Goldsworthy
Eduardo Gomes
Marta Gonzalez
David Gonzalez-Bello
Jessica Goodfellow
Kate Goodfellow
Gareth Goodhead
Tim Goodson
Claire Goodwin
Laura Goodwin
Margaret Goodwin
Lionel Gorick
Carole Gorman
Rob Gornall
Brody Gospel
Chris Goss
Chris Gottard
Paul Gough
Emma Gould
Dan Graham
Laurie Graham
Margaret Graham

Muriel Graham
Nigel Graham
Jackie Grahm
Gwendoline Gralton
Dario Grandich
J Grant
Marc Grant
Rachel Grant
Susan Grant
Lucrezia Grasso
Emily Gravenor
Fiona Gravette
Catherine Gray
Elizabeth Gray
Jeanette Gray
Nicola Gray
Philip Gray
Fay Grayer
Alison Green
Carole Green
Chris Green
Helen Green
Jacqueline Green
Jonathan Green
Peter & Margaret
 Green
Susan Green
Chloe Greene
Eric Greenhill
Lizzie Greenstreet
Anne Greenwood
Jan Greenwood
Miriam Greenwood
Sharow Greenwson
Helen Greer
John Gregory
Matt Gregory
Rachel Gregory
Anne Gregson
Adam Grieve
Jane Griffeths
Christine Griffin
Sophie Griffin
Barbara Griffiths
Hannah Griffiths
Jane Griffiths
Martin Griffiths
Michael Griffiths
Sabina Griffiths
Susan Griffiths
Samantha Grffiths
Lorna Grimes
Elaine Grinwell
Sue Groves-Phillips
Gregory Grzesiczek
Vicki Gubert
Damian Guilfoyle
Kyle Gumersall
Emma Gundry
Alan Gurnett
David Thomas Guthrie
Natalie Hackett
Brian Haddok
Katherine Haddrell
Katie Hadfield
Terry Hagedorn
Marianne Haggstrom
Adrian Haigh
Ron Haigh
Tim Hailstone
Kaye Haite
Steve Hales
Geoff Halfhide
Elizabeth Halksworth
Alexander Hall
Angela Hall
Barbara Hall
Danny Hall
Em Hall
Jeremy Hall
Julie Hall
Lena Hall
Lynn Hall
Simona Hall
Tina Hall
Mel Hallett
Susan Hallworth
Linda Hamadache
Sarah Hamber
Claire Hambly
Christopher Hamer
John Hamer
Maha Hamer
Anne Hamilton
Dorothy Hamilton
Katie Hamilton
Neil Hamilton
Sophia Hamilton
Steven Hamilton

Pieter Hamman
Catherine Hammond
Kendra Hammond
Sophie Hammond
Zenobia Hammond
Lynne Hampshire
Bob Hampson
Lesley Hampson
Mary Hampton
Carl Hancock
David Hancock
Joanna Hancock
Michelle Hancox
Megan Hand
Bruno Handley
Lynn Handley
Noel Handley
Sarah Handley
Karen Hands
Sarah Hanison
Michael Paulie
 Hanmod
Ian Hannah
Kevin Hannan
Sarah Hanrahan
Dr Catherine Hanratty
Jennifer Hansell
Sissel Hansen
Paul Haper
Angie Harbury
Bechy Harding
Maura Harding
Rhonda Hards
Carole Hardwick
Rhianne Haresign
Dorothy Hargreaves
Linda Hargreaves
Eleanor Harland
Jane Harmston
Daniel Harper
Penny Harri Taylor
Charlie Harris
Ian Harris
Jane Harris
Lewis Harris
Alan Harrison
Brian Harrison
Emma Harrison
Hazel Harrison
Karen Harrison
Rebecca Harrison
Rob Harrison
Stuart Harrison
Anne Harrop
Alison Hart
Anelay Hart
David Hart
Jonathan Hart
Sharon Hart
Vanessa Hart
Bev Hartley
John Hartley
Robyn Hartley
Susie Hartley
Tina Hartridge
Barry Hartshorne
Brigid Harty
Ben Harvey
Camilla Harvey
Kathryn Harvey
Caroline Harvie
Liz Harvie
Jo Haslam
Chris Hasluck
Matt Hatin
Stuart Hatzel
Paul Haut
Neil Havercroft
Abbie Haward
G Hawes
Richard Hawes
Kevin Hawking
Judith Hawkins
Stuart Hawkins
Graham Hawkswell
Faith Hawksworth
Emma Haworth
Ann Hawson
Jon Hayden
Alice Hayes
Elaine Hayes
Natalie Hayes
Shirley Hayes
Will Hays
Andy Hayler
Tony Haynes
Lee Hayward
Richard Hazeldine
Stuart Hazeldine

Laura Head
Wendy Headley
Elaine Healey
Phil Healing
Julia Heap
Joanna Heard
Sylvia Heathcote
Julie Heaton
Will Heeley
Karl Hegarty
Rado Heidler
Robert Hellen
Katie Hellon
David Hempel
Donia Henderson
Elouise Henderson
Jen Hendry
Andy Henk
Mary Hennedy
Alistair Henry
Jacqueline Henry
Judith Henshaw
Susan Heppenstall
James Hepworth
Jeremy Herbert
Kelly Herbert
Marwell Herding
Avril Hermann
Alison Hernandez
Ruth Herringer
Katrina Hervey
Ruth Hesketh
David Heslop
Michael Hession
Helena Hetherington
Chloe Hewitt
Glen Hewlett
Nick Hewson
Nick Hex
Geoff Hickman
Sharon Higginbotham
Anna Higgins
Pippa Higgs
Jane Higham
Kevin Highton
Rebecca Hildred
Allen Hill
Christine Hill
Dennis Hill
Rachel Hill
Shirley Hill
Oliver Hinchcliff
Danielle Hincliffe
Amy Hind
Lucy Hindle
Mark Hines
Suzie Hingley-Wilson
Gwen Hinton
Edwina Hirst
David Hiscox
Caroline Hitch
David Hitchcock
Cheryl Hitchcock-
 Smith
Peter Hoare
Phil Hobbis
Michael Hobbs
Tom Hobson
John Hoccingdale
David Hocken
Diane Hodge
Margaret Hodge
Stephanie Hodgetts
Donald Hodgson
Philip Hodgson
Bob Hoggatt
James Holden
June Holden
Lorraine Holder
Kate Holgate
P Holgate
Lizzy Holiday
Lorraine Holland
Richard Holland
Carole Holliday
Andrew Hollingsworth
Jeff Hollingworth
Anthea Holloway
Tom Holloway
Carly Holman
David Holmes
Joy Holmes
Louise Holmes
S Holmes
Vanessa Holmes
Ruth Holmstock
Lea Holt
Susan Holt
Tracy Holt

Will Holt
Seina Holtz
Nicky Homer
Veronica Hood
Mike Hookway
Kate Hooper
Terry Hooper
Alex Hopkins
Sally Hopkinson
Emma Hopson
Janet Hopwood
Chris Horan
Wayne Hornigold
Chris Horton
Steve Hoselitz
Esther Hothersall
S Houlder
Carl Housbey
Valerie House
Janet Houston
Erica Howard
Paul Howard-Beald
David Howarth
Andrew Howat
Megan Howe
Paul Howe
Victoria Howe
Loran Howells
Kelly Howett
Susan Howlet
Ken Howman
John Hoyle
Laura Hubbard
Michael Hudley
Andreas Hudson
Ashley Hudson
Carl Hudson
Claire Hudson
Donald Hudson
Liam Hudson
Barbara Hughes
Barry Hughes
Chris Hughes
Dollna Hughes
Emma Hughes
Jane Hughes
Jill Hughes
Neil Hughes
Paula Hughes
Rob Hughes
Roger Hughes
Susanna Hughes
Thomas Hughes
Amy Hugill
Sarah Hull
Ailsa Hulme
Julie Humphereys
Anne Humphreys
Helen Humphreys
Vida Humphreys
David Hunt
Martin Hunt
Nigel Hunt
Ross Hunt
Abigail Hunter
Crystal Hunter
Nina Hunter
Pauline Hunter
Victoria Hunter
Sharon Hurren
Victoria Hurst
Gerard Hussey
Edna Hutchinson
Paul Hutchinson
Peter Hutchinson
Fiona Hutchison
Lisa Hutchison
Nikki Hutchison
Emma Hutter
Stephen Hyett
Susan I'Anson
Sophie Ibbotson
Valerie Iddom
Alako Ikeda
Jo Ingham
Emma Inglis
Fred Inglis
Trevor Ingram
Tim Ionlson
Gabriella Ireland
John Irlam
Stewart Irvine
Gwyn Irving
Nicol Irwin
Reiko Itoh
Josephine Ives
Peter Ivey
Matthew Jack
Carl Jackson

David Jackson
Garth Jackson
Grace Jackson
Julia Jackson
Louise Jackson
Martin Jackson
Rachel Jackson
Hilda & Bill Jackson
Helen Jackson-Garside
Jennifer Jacobs
Lee Jacobs
Simon Jacobson
Mathiew Jacques
Saurabh Jain
Rita Jakes
Ann Jakic
Jan James
Michelle James
Paula James
Ralph James
Rebecca James
Susan James
Mika Jameson
Robert Jamieson
Tom Jamieson
David Janata
Eileen Jaques
Jack Jarvis
Jon Jasson
Caroline Jaycock
Stuart Jebb
Andrew Jefferson
Nicholas Jeffery
Tony Jeffires
David Jenkins
Milly Jenkins
Steven Jenkins
Tracey Jenkins
John Jennings
Camilla Jessel
Kenneth Jeyaretnam
Pam Jibson
Maria Joergensen
Lucy Johns
Russell Johns
Carol Johnson
Chris Johnson
Dominik Johnson
Graeme Johnson
Jane Johnson
Jennifer Johnson
Peter Johnson
Keith Johnston
T Johnston
William Johnston
Tracey Johnstone
Kirsty Joly
Alison Jones
Alvin Jones
Anne Jones
Bethany Jones
Carol Jones
Clare Jones
Frederic T Jones
Gareth Jones
Helen Jones
Hugh Jones
Ian Jones
John Jones
Jonathan Jones
Laura Jones
Meryl Jones
Neil Jones
Oxana Jones
Philip Jones
Rachel Jones
Sharon Jones
Tracy Jones
June Jordan
Mary Joseph
Liz Joy
Becky Joyce
Michelle Juett
Mackay Julia
Mikko Juusola
Abi Kadri
Christian Kafanke
Jess Kaler
Becka Kane
Paul Kane
Sejal Kankali
Michael Kann
Norman Kaphan
Vicky Karkow
Yashmir Kashan
Andy Kassube
Amerjit Kaur
Sarah Kay
Chris Kaye

Simon Kayman
Judy Keap
Gillian Keating
Leslie Keeble
Lucy Keeble
Toni Keech
Alexandra Keeler
Grace Keeler
Duncan Keelins
Kay Keith-Wilby
Chris Keller-Jackson
Audrea Kelly
Karen Kelly
Mel Kelly
Patrick Kelly
Sarah Kemble
William Kemp
Geraldine Kennedy
Marie Kennedy
Chris Kenny
Alainée Kent
Michael Kent
Sharon Kent
Janet Kenworthy
Christopher Kerr
David Kerr
Tom Kerr
Emily Kerrigan
Fiona Kersh
Andrew Kershaw
Peter Kershaw
Robert Kerslake
Dayana Kevin
Peter Keynton
Dee Khatri
Valerie Kidd
John Kiely
Anthony Kiernan
John Kilby
Tessa Kilgour
Kathy Kilpatrick
Ed Kilsby
Jill Kinder
David King
Doug King
Hayley King
Jane King
Jennifer Mary King
Karen King
Mary King
Samantha Kinghorn
Andrew Kingston
Martin Kingston
Fiona Kinnear
Emma Kinsley
Anne Kirk
Giseca Kirk
Nigel Kirk
Louise Kirkham
Daniel Kirman
James Kisback
Rajesh Kishan
Hannah Kitson
Paul Knifton
Adam Knight
Clare Knight
Vanessa Knight
Sally Knill
Martin Knoester
Belinda Knott
Chris Knott
Jessica Knowes
John Knowles
Jonathan Knowles
Natalie Knowles
Shena Knowles
Tracy Knowles
Aimee Kong
Joanna Kostka
Babis Koukakis
Jonathan Kourad
Katarina Kovacova
Raluca Kovacs
Elena Krasnova
Alyssa Kreutier
Zia Kruger
Sally Kynaston
Marin Kynch
Heather Lacey
Samantha Lacobacci
Beverly Lagna
Gemma Laing
Georgina Lamb
Lorna Lamb
Mary Lamb
Steven Lamb
Lesley Lambert
Dawn Marie Lamonica

Tony Lancaster
Nicola Lang
Ulla Lang
Susan Langfield
Jasmine Langley-Smith
Yvonne Lankry
Heather Lankston
Bill Lanyon
Abby Large
Chloe Large
Graham Large
Terry & Sally Larkham
Darren Lashford
Rachael Laurie
Ann Law
Rachel Law
Adam Lawrence
Michael Lawrence
Caroline Lawrie
Brian Lawson
Matthew Lawson
Richard Lawton
James Le Couteur
Helen Le Gal
Malcolm Lea
Elizabeth Leadbeater
Alan Leading
Claire Learner
Wayne Leatherland
Jean Lecot
Janice Lee
Simon Lee
Yvonne Lee
Howard Leech
Kay Leech
Georgina Leeming
Bill Lees
Martin Lees
Mark Leese
Matt Leigh
Ray Leighton
Malcolm Lendon
Amanda Leon
John Leonard
Sophie Leung
Maralyn Lever
Janet Leversidge
James Lewellyn
Stephen Lewin
Jacek Lewinson
Jonathan Lewis
Leanne Lewis
Mark Lewis
Nicola Lewis
Stewart Lewis
Val Lewis
Wendy Lewis
Cedric Lherbier
Liz Liddall
Colin Liddy
Stafford Lightman
Julia Lilley
Rupert Limon
Vander Lindey
Roy Lindop
David Lindridge
Jean Lindsay
Sarah Lindsay
Shane Linford
Dr John R Ling
Maureen Ling
Joan Lipp
Suzanne Rose List
A Lister
Charlotte Litteck
Dave Little
Geoffrey Little
Julie Little
Amy Littlehead
Richard Littlejohns
Deborah Liu Liu
Neil Livesey
Jessica Lloyd
Theo Lloyd
Malcolm Loades
John Locan
Rebecca Locke
Arcadia Lockhart
Susie Lockie-Bloore
Nigel Lockley
Alistair Lockwood
Malcolm Lockwood
Adrian Lockyer
Annabel Lofthouse
Marie-Louise Logan
Mike Logan
Robin Logie
Maricel Lomibao
Richard Long

Penny Longhurst
Ian Longley
Ian Lonsley
Darren Lord
Helen Lord
Louise Lord
Sarah Lotherington
Liam Loudlaw
Ashleigh Louw
Tim Love
Judy Lowe
Stephen Lowe
Nicola Loweth
Jake Lowndes
Marion Lowrence
Steve Lowry
Claire Lucas
Daren Luckings
Catherine Ludman
Alan Ludwains
Sheila Lumb
Jo Lune
Sandy Luthe-Hughes
Joanna Luxton
Rachael Luxton
Rob Lynch
Alison Lynn
Glenda Lyons
Julian Lyons
Suzanne Lyons
David Mabey
Morag MacAskill
Lesley MacBean
Kenneth MacCrimmon
Heather MacDonald
Isabel MacDonald
Nick Mace
Andrew Macer
John Macey
Isobel MacFarlane
Helen Macfield
James Machin
Lina Machnicki
Chris Machon
Kristen Macintosh
Christopher Mack
Jonathan Mack
Alison Mackay
Julia Mackay
Sheila Mackay
Berry Mackenzie
Adrian Mackie
Janet Mackley
Ross Maclaverty
Katie Maclean
Beverley Maclennan
Lady Helen Maclennan
Of Rosart
John Macleod
Roy Macleod
Anna MacMillan
Valerie Macniven
James Macpherson
Brian Macreadie
Michael Macveigh
Paul Madden
Tamara Madej
Anthony Madeley
Terence Madge
Paul Madley
Nancy Magiver
Mruyunjaya Maharana
Erica Mahony
Rod Main
Pamle Maire
Matej Majercik
Susan Major
Peter Makin
Simba Makwembere
James Malcolm Green
Shahid Malik
Ethel Mallett
John Mallett
Zoe Mallinson
G Malone
Ian Malyk
Susan Manasian
Susan Manktelow
Alex Mann
Anne Mann
Jocasta Mann
Andrew Manners
Paul Mansell
Julie Mansfield
Estella March
Mike Mardesich
Caroline Marding
Adrian Markley
Cheryl Markosky

Ray Marks
Charles Markus
Louise Markus
Debbie Marland
Richard Marley
Jess Marlow
Annita Marquardt
Elena Marris
Rob Marsden
Linda Marsh
Philip Marsh
Stanley Marsh
Tony & Leela Marsh
Claire Marshall
Gerry Marshall
Robert Marshall
Sarah Marshall
Simon Marshall
Kelsey Marsland
Ruth Marsland
St John Marston
Judy Martel
Lois Marter
Andrew Martin
Basil Martin
Ben Martin
Debbie Martin
Graham Martin
Helen Martin
Lily Martin
Linda Martin
Martina Martin
Nigel Martin
Peter Martin
Samantha Martin
Valerie Martin
David Martinez
Andrew Martlew
C Massey
Andrea Mason
Lynn Mason
Rob Mastrodomenilo
William Mather
Murdo Mathewson
Rakesh Mathur
Ann Matthews
Jill Matthews
Nicola Matthews
Tom Matthews
Gisela Matthias
Julie Maxwell
Gillian May
Ian May
Michael May
Susan May
Karen Mayger
Bea Maynard
Louvain Mayne
Michael McAlister
Linzi McAlister
Glynis McAndrew
Greg McAteer
Sam McBratney
Aideen McBride
Karina McCaig
Robyn McCarroll
Karenza McCarthy
Rosemary McCartney
Paul McCauley
Julia McColl
Chris McCormack
Karen McCormack
Fiona McCowan
Walter McCrindle
Anne McCullagh
Janet McCunn
Gary McDermott
Yvonne McDermott
Irene McDonald
Nicky McDonald
Simon McDonnell
Cara McDonough
Sheron McDougall
Paul McElvenney
Kelly McFarland
Devon McFarlane
Shona McFarlane
Alan McFerran
Michelle McGahan
Alison McGarthy
Andrew McGavin
Katie McGill
Sarah McGowan
John McGrath
Pat McGrath
Laura McGreevy
Shauna McGuinness
Craig McHale
Charlotte McIlroy

Trish McIntosh
Alice McIntyre
Tonia McKechnie-
Sharma
Maura McKendry
Emma McKenna
Lesley McKeown
John McKie
Lynne McKissock
Pip McKnight
Mark McLarty
Ken McLean
Ailsa McLellan
Joan McLoughlin
Peter McLoughlin
Helen McLure
Gerard McMenemy
Luke McMenemy
Amanda McMillan
Mark McNally
Nick McNally
Andrew McNeil
Rosie McNeil
Anthony McNicholas
Jill McPhail
Andrew McPherson
John McSherry
Kathryn McWer
David Mead
Philip Meade
Chris Meads
Lynn Mears
Annie Medcalf
Jane Medhurst
Kay Meeler
Jennifer Mehta
Kunal Mehta
Graham Meiklejohn
Hugh Mellor
Tammy Mellor
Daniel Mellward
Christine Menzies
Joanne Merchant
Lynn Meredith
Jim Meronik
Am Merrick
Samantha Merridale
Jerome Merrow
Michele Mervin
Ian Mewse
Mashuk Miah
Aimee Michel
Jane Middleton
Keith Middleton
Margaret Mieras
Ryan Miler
Sabbir Milad
Alana Miles
Chris Miles
Michelle Miles
Rachel Miles
Rob Miles
Sara Miles Bishop
Mark Milhofer
John Mill
Hugh Millar
Rhian Millar
Emily Millen
Alice Miller
Gary Miller
Marianne Miller
Mary Miller
Rhona Miller
Rose Miller
Mary Millichip
Mike Millington
Andrew Mills
Gemma Mills
Lucy Mills
Victoria Mills
Tom Millward
Lynda Milner
Wendy Milnes
Richard Mindel
Antoine Miribel
Liz Missen
Jinesh Mistry
Nicola Mitcham
Andrew Mitchell
Charlotte Mitchell
Grant Mitchell
Jonathan Mitchell
Karen Mitchell
Pete Mitchell
Sue Mitchell
Jana Moffett
James Mohammed
Bob Mole
Maria Mollaghan

Louis Molloy
Patricia Molloy
Tom Monaghan
Graham Monro
Zac Monro
Russell Montague
Nicola Monteiro
Alan Montgomery
Stephen Montgomery
John Moody
Ellen Moon
Alison Moore
Alun Moore
Andy Moore
Carl Moore
Jenny Moore
Kate Moore
Sean Moore
Sharon Moore
Tommy Moore
Wendy Moore
Tim Moorey
Angela Moran
Angie Moran
Tony Moran
Phil Morcumb
Catherine Morgan
Diana Morgan
John Morgan
Lisa Morgan
Peter Morgan
Stephen Morgan
Victoria Morgan-
Cummins
Jerry Morley
David Morpand
Ashley Morris
Esther Morris
Grant Morris
Janet Morris
Jennifer Morris
Row Morris
Debbie Morrison
Donald Morrison
Maggie Morrison
Susie Morrison
Pat Mortimer
Val Mortmer
David Morton
Steve Morton
Anne Moss
Tim Moss
Lauren Mothershaw
Leona Motrshall
Peter Moulam
Giles Mountford
Adrienne Moyce
Martin Muers
Audrey Muir
Stewart Muir
Helen Mulholland
Tracey Mulholland
Lisa Mullaney
Bertie Muller
Toni Mullins
Terry Mulvenna
Rachel Mundy
Derek Munn
Susana Munoz
Catherine Munro
Jenny Munro-Hunt
Alicia Munson
Andi Murch
Anne Murdoch
Caroline Murphy
Gareth Murphy
Rose Murphy
Ben Murray
Dee Murray
Les Murray
Robin Murray
Sharon Musgrove
Calire Mykel
Sue Myles
Anzhelika Nabozhina
Kaustubh Naik
Katy Nally
Dominic Nancekievill
Jennifer Nash
Jody Nason
Fernando Nasso
Anna Nayler
Rob Naylor
Wendy Naylor
Martin Neal
Karen Neale
Carol Needham
Heikola Neer
Jeff Neill

Penny Nelson
Maff Nesham
Jackie Neve
Maria Gloria Neves
Diane Neville
Philippa Neville
Sally Nevitt
Peter & Pauline Newbury
Alex Newby
John Newby
Adrian Newell
Catherine Newman
Jo Newman
Colin Newstead
Angela Newton
Jo Newton
Keith Newton
Jeffrey Ng
Craig Nichol
Lesley Nicholls
Chris Nicholson
Eugene Nicholson
Wendy Nicholson
Laura Nickoll
Joy Nicoll
Alan Nightingale
Andy Niven
Dudley Nixon
Fiona Nixon
Franck Nlanak
Eileen Noble
Jane Noddings
Roger Nolan
Joyce Norfolk
Samantha Norman
Joan Norris
Sue North
Sarah Northover
Jane Norton
Caroline Nunns
Sally Oakes
Alan O'Brien
Julie O'Brien
Louise O'Connor
Graham Oddey
Kevin Odean
Michael Odey
Marty O'Doherty
Elaine O'Donnell
Heather O'Donnell
Sean O'Donnell
Ian Ody
Jerome O'Garro
Liz Ogilvie
Klaudia O'Gorman
Michael Ohagan
Yvonne O'Hara
Daniel O'Keefe
Funmi Okunola
Denise O'Leary
Kayleigh O'Leary
Diojo Olival
Diana Oliveria
Paul Olson
Michael Oneill
Lynne & Jen O'Neill
Ted Oram
David Orchard
Beatriz Orejana
David Orgles
Dave Ormesher
James Orpin
Jonny Orr
Nicky Ortiz
Alan Osborne
Sascha Ostbero
Robbie O'Sullivan
Claire Ottley
Samuel Outtridge
Ed Ovenden
David Over
Peter Overall
Olga Owen
Greg Pack
Pau Padam
David Page
Johanne Page
Linda Page
Clementine Paine
Abigail Palmer
Desmond Palmer
Jasmine Palmer
Mitchell Palmer
Neil Palmer
Victorie Pandes
Chinmay Pandit
Harvinder Panesar
Lucy Pannell Woodward

Lee Pardoe
Jess Parish
Susan Park
David Parker
Katrina Parker
Loraaine Parker
Sophie Parker
Hannah Parkes
Robert Parkins
Andy Parkinson
Stuart Parkinson
Jane Parmiter
Jamila-Alice Parr
Clive Parry
Hayley Parry
Julie Parry
Marc & Stacey Parry
Andrew Parsons
Gabrielle Parsons
John Parsons
Sharon Parton
Chris Pascall
Becky Paskin
Kate Pass
David Passmore
Dev Patel
Mehul Patel
Shimeem Patel
Urmish Patel
Roger Pateman
Gorden Paterson
Nigel Patrick
Sam Patrick
Darren Patt
Andre Pattenden
Linda Patterson
Shonadh Patterson
Mali Pattinson
Lou Paul
Emma Pauley
Lauren Paull
Christina Paumgarten
Rajan Paw
Debbie Payne
Linda Payne
Mandy Payne
Vickie Peace
Alexandra Pearce
Howard Pearce
Lisa Pearson
Heather Peattie
Jennifer Peed
Juliet Peel
Martin Pendered
Stephen Penfold
Jonathan Pengelly
Mary Penn
Harry Pennington
Jane Pennington
John Penny
Kate Pepper
Phillipa Peppermint
Peter Perchard
Nicola Perkin
Cheryl Perkins
Helen Perkins
Malcolm Perks
Sally Perrett
Keith Perry
Linda Perry
Nicky Perry
Phil Perry
Terence Perry
Kaylee Petch
Catherine Peterkin
John Peters
Kim Peters
William Peters
Charles Peters
Katrine Peterson
Kiel Peterson
Alex Petheram
Elaine Peto
Irina Petrova
Kate Phelan
Susan Phelps
Dominic Philbin
Suman Philip
Charlotte Phillips
Jim Phillips
Julia Phillips
Samantha Phillips
Simon Phillips
Thomas Phillips
Valentine Mark Phillips
Gwynneth Picken
David Pickup
Jeanette Pickup
Julia Pickup

Will Piersenne
John Pigott
Martin Pilarski
Mark Pilgrim
Keith Pinching
Jennie Pinho
Jonathan Pink
Nancy Pinnock
Clare Pipe
Elizabeth Pirie
Rosamunde Pitcher
Sara Pitts
Tim Place
Mike Plant
Roger Plastow
Anna Plater
Sharon Pledge
Susan Plowman
Martin Pocock
Ann Pointing
Nik Pole
Lynn Polkey
Adrian Pollitt
Wayne Pollock
Stuart Pomeroy
Dallas Ponds
Alice Poole
Sean Poole
Mark Porgeous
Eric Porter
Margret Porter
Jeremy Posnansky
Lynne Potter
Rosie Potts
Jessica Poulter
David Pound
Andrew Powell
Brooke Powell
Darren Powell
Lynn Powell
Ellie Powler
Michael Precord
Michael Prescott
Jo Prest
Katy Prewett
Aimee Price
Danielle Price
G W Price
Greg Price
Heather Price
Helen Price
Katherine Price
Morgan Price
Philip Price
Robert Pride
Emma Prince
Ben Prior
David & Janet Pritchard
Lucy Pritchard
Ceri Pritchett
Paula Prunty
Abigail Prymaka
Russell Pullan
Liz Pullar
Victoria Pullar
Gemma Pulling
Mary-Alice Pulsford
Christopher Purcell
Penny Purdam
David Purser
Ann Purvis
Noreen Purvis
Frank Putman
Roy Puttoch
Douglas Pye
Mike Pye
Sonya Pye
Barbara Pytches
Marek Pytel
Emma Queenan
Susan Quigley
Beryl Quilter
Thelma Quince
Fiona Quincey
Karen Quinn
Keith Quinn
Gabbriel Ractery
Chris Radford
Shirley Radforth
Elizabeth Rafferty
Pat Rallinson
Marianne Ramsay
Olivia Rana
Joshua Randell
T A Rankin
Alice Ranson
Libby Raphel
Rob Ratcliff

Eleanor Ratcliffe
Elinda Ratcliffe
K Raven
John Rawlings
A Rayer
Steve Raymond
Jenny Raynes
Paul Reaney
Lesley Reardon
Merci Rebati
Sarah Reddall
Nick Redfern
Steve Redgrave
Philip Redhaw
Caroline Redman
Lucy Redshaw
Andrew Reed
Derek Reed
Max Reed
Marian Reene
Sam Rees
Paul Reeve
Mathew Reeves
Roger Reeves
Gill Regan
Ailsa Reid
Alison Reid
Carolyn Reid
Cathy Reid
Rebecca Reidy
Steve Rencontre
Gordon Rennie
Nicola Renshaw
Luise Renwick
Lizzie Reuben
Ann Reynolds
Tom Reynolds
Gloria Rhodes
Karen Rhodes
Michael Rhodes
James Rice
Phil Rice
Angela Richards
Carol Richards
Charles Richards
Kathleen Richards
Lee Richards
Sophia Richards
Hannah Richardson
John Richardson
Stephanie Richardson
Norman Riches
Trish Riching
Andy Ricketts
Caroline Ricketts
Mark Riddles
Aaron Riding-Brown
Elisabeth Ries
Nichola Rigden
David Riggs
Florence Riley
Martin Riley
Sarah Riley
Wendy Riley
John Rivers
Elaine Rivett
Wendy Roach
Nic Roberti
Hilary Roberts
Jane Roberts
Jenny Roberts
Liam Roberts
Sarah Roberts
Tim Roberts
Tom Roberts
Vicki Roberts
Deborah Robertson
John Robertson
Kelly Robertson
Barbara Robinson
Malcolm Robinson
Rachael Robinson
Shelagh Robinson
Stuart Robinson
Tim Robinson
Victoria Robinson
Lee Robinson-Walton
Lucia Rodan
Barrie Roderick
Anne Rodger
Tracey Rodgers
Kirsten Roebuck
Amy Rogers
C Rogers
Clive Rogers
David Rogers
Michael Rogers
Mark Rolery
Oliver Rosaire

Hannah Rose
Randall Rose
Sue Rose
Michael Rosenthal
Alison Rosie
Ian Ross
Murray Ross
Alison Ross
John Rossell
Duncan Rothery
Sarah Rothery
Helen Rough
Becky Round
Christina Routledge
Evelyn Rowand
Carole Rowe
Delroy Rowe
John Rowe
Laura Rowe
John Rowlands
Sian Rowlands
Joan Rowley
Rachel Rowley
Denise Roxburgh
Jocelyn Ruddell
Sarah Rudley
Wendy Rule
Georgette Rundle
Beverley Russell
Dave & Kath Russell
Howard Russell
Jane Russell
Sheila Russell
Roy Rust
Ildiko Rusvai
Derek & Vicky Rutherford
Jenny Rutland
Ruby Rutter
Nick Ryalls
Anna Ryan
Jill Ryan
Zoe Ryan
James Rymell
Gwen Rymill
Isabel Sadler
Karen Sadler
Lee Sainsbury
Lizzie Sale
Mike Sales
Pauline Salisbury
Sarah Salman
Ellie Salter-Jones
Eric Saltmagh
Keith Salway
Melissa Sampson
David Sandars
Jeremy Sanders
Ian Sanderson
Vanessa Sanderson
Liam Sandie
Nick Sands
Jamie Sangeter
Clare Sangster
Emma Sansom
Carol Sansum
Beatrice Santell
Jane Saunders
Robert Savage
Stephen Savory
Laura Sayed
Huw Sayer
Jessica Saynor
Wendy Scarborough
Joachim Schafheitle
Britta Schieffer
Adam Schiff
Heidi Schmit
Angela Schofield
Damon Schofield
Debbie Schofield
Mary Schofield
Rynda Schofield
Breda Scholes
Vanessa Schotes
Jenna Scoble
Dr M J S Scorer
Denise Scott
Fiona Scott
Helen Scott
John Scott
Julian Scott
Kelly Scott
N Scott
Pat Scott
Robert Scott
Laura Scotter
Geoffrey Scoynes
Michelle Scrimshaw

Shauna Scroggie
Lynn Seaton
Hazel Seddon
Trevor Seed
David Sefton
Kirat Sekhon
Val Self
Robert Selle
David Sellick
Sally Semple
Dr A K Sethi
Nisha Sethi
Superna Sethi
Michelle Settle
Neil Sewell
Carol Seymour
Dipan Shah
Scott Shand
Phil Shannon
Vikrant Sharma
Janet Sharp
Oliver Sharp
Karen Sharpe
Laura Sharpe
Alaine Shaw
Kevin Shaw
Rachel Shaw
Robert Shaw
Sue Shaw
Derek Sheard
William Shearer
Jo Sheeran
Monica Shelley
Andrew Shephard
Amy Shepherd
Marc Shepherd
Paula Shepherd
Wendy Sheppard
Laura Shervin
Tomas Sherwood
Jamie Shields
Martin Shirley
Gilbert Short
Sara Shorten
Sue Shove
Jo Shrimpion
Michael Shun
Janet Shuttleworth
Moira Siddons
Sarpreet Sidhu
John Sieczkowski
Victoria Silcock
Anne Silps
Lee Simmonds
Sally Simmonds
Christina Simmons
Lee Simon
Shona Simon
Mare Simonitsch
Ann Simonsen
Christopher Simpson
Evelyn Simpson
Joe Simpson
Neil Simpson
Penelope Simpson
Phil Simpson
Sarah Simpson
J Simpson
Mary Sinclair
Richard Sinclair
Adam Singer
Dal Singh
Graham Singleton
Gregory Sion
Cheryl Sitkowski
Robert Skeel
Marc Skeldon
Clare Skelly
Pam Skett
Campbell Skinner
Patrick Skinner
Claire Slater
Wendie Slater
Niki Slemeck
Jennifer Slivenslay
Paul Sloan
Alan Slomson
Kay Sly
Edward Smalley
Lucy Smart
Krystal Smedley
Andy Smerdon
Aaron Smith
Alex Smith
Angela Smith
Anjelah Smith
Brenda Smith
Carol Smith
Derek Smith

Fred Smith
Gemma Smith
Geoff Smith
Helen Smith
James Smith
Janis Smith
Jim Smith
John Smith
Kiv Smith
Lisa Smith
Louise Smith
Margaret Smith
Michaela Smith
Michela Smith
Nick Smith
Oliver Smith
Ollie Smith
Richard Smith
Roselynn Smith
Vivien Smith
Sarah Smithies
Corolyn Snaith
Michael Snelgrove
Laura Snelling
Sue Snook
Diane Snow
Liane Solmson
Derek Somerville
Pash Sonigra
Maninder Soor
Jered Sorkin
Lucinda Southall
John Southern
Anna Sowray
Samia Soyer
Christopher Spalding
Royston Sparkes
Christine Sparrowhawk
Marlian Speak
Alan Spedding
Tracy Spencer
Ray Speneer
Alan Spillar
Rebecca Spittle
Elaine Spooner
Angela Spray
Elaine Srig
Maurice Stagg
Anthony Stanbury
Richard Standen
Anne Stanley
Eric Stansfield
Jonathan Staples
Katie Starkey
Mathew Starr
Kathy Stayle
Andrew Stead
Emma Stead
Paul Steadman
John Stedman
Maureen Steel
Rachael Steenson
Jane Steggles
Gillian Stemp
Robert Stemp
Barbara Stenhouse
Heidi Stenhouse
Claire Stentiford
Nicola Stentiford
Carole Stephens
Mary Stephens
Graham Stephenson
Tim Steven
Carol Stevens
Lisa Stevens
Lloyd Stevens
Sarah Stevens
Nicola Stevenson
Emily Stever
Elizabeth Stewart
Gary Stewart
Nick Stewart
Allen Stidwill
Adam Stiff
Alexandra Stiver
Alan Stockford
Roy Stockwell
Caroline Stoddart
Jan Stokoe
Rob Stone
Liz Stones
Quentin Stoper
Heather Storer
Graham Storey
Paul Storman
Jayne Stoten
Wendy Stoten
Jo Stovell
John Strange

Raymond Stratfull
Anne Streatfield
Kevin Street
Andrew Stride
Heather Stride
Gillian Strudwick
Caroline Stryjak
Adrienne Stuart
Carol Stuart
Luke Stuart-Smith
Patricia Studley
Greg Stump
Bob Sturges
Lynne Stutter
Alan Styles
Elizabeth Suarez
Jeremy Sudlow
Tim Sudworth
Jasmine Suleyman
Linda Sullivan
Ben Sulston
Nick Summerscales
Leena Surelia-Manners
Gemma Surtees
Sheryl Surue
Michael Sutcliffe
William Sutheraland
Daniel Sutherland
Pam Sutton
Suzanne Swan
Eleanor Swann
Charlotte Swarbnick
Mark Swarwick
Michael Sweasey
Robyn Sweeney
Amanda Sweet
Emma Sweet
Helen Swift
Johnathan Swift
Julia Swift
Kerenza Swift
Shelagh Swindells
Audrey Sykes
Karen Sykes
Penny Sykes
Sabrina Sykes
Stuart Sykes
Paul Symington
Chris Symonds
Alan Tait
Douglas Talintyre
John Tamplin
Nora Tandberg
Emmaniel Tangoy
Abi Tanguy
Siôn Tansley
Adrian Tantrum
Mike Tarbard
Sandra Tarigo
Jean Tarry
Richard Tasker
Dan Tate
Rodney Tatman
Lewis Tattersall
Adam Taylor
Angie Taylor
Cheryl Taylor
Dennis Taylor
George Taylor
Helen Taylor
Jean Taylor
Jeffrey Taylor
Jessica Taylor
John Taylor
Josh Taylor
Katie Taylor
Laura Taylor
Linda Taylor
Mark Taylor
Michael Taylor
Rosemary Taylor
Steven Taylor
Trish Taylor
Vince Taylor
Diane Teale
Susan Teare
Georgina Teary
Angela Tebboth
Barbara Tee
Sophie Teear
Suen Teisen
Susan Tello
Elizabeth Terry
Danilo Tersigni
Alison Theaker
Dianne Thew
Chrissy Thirlaway
Alex Thomas
Chrisitna Thomas

Christine Thomas
Clare Thomas
David Thomas
Fiona Thomas
Jade Thomas
Katie Thomas
Louise Thomas
Lucy Thomas
Mary Thomas
Sally Thomas
Jenni Thomas-Davey
Gary Thomassen
Christine Thomasson
Sam Thome
Carol Thompson
Emma Thompson
Fiona Thompson
Jane Thompson
Katharine Thompson
Kathryn Thompson
Marc Thompson
Nick Thompson
Pauline Thompson
Roger Thompson
Rosalind Thompson
Tina Thompson
Deborah Thomson
Jess Thomson
Paula Thomson
Anna Thorne
Mark Thornhill
Zoe Thornhill
Camilla Thornton
Charles Rodney Thornton
David Thornton
F P & E M Thornton
Matthew Thorpe
Bob Thurlow
Mark Tibbenham
Jennifer Tickle
Jonathan Tides Well
Michael Tilney
Maggie Timlin
Floyd Timms
Graham Timms
Anthony Timoney
Robert Tims
Katie Tindle
Aimee Tinker
James Tinker
Kris Tisdale
Jay Titterington
Nick Tocker
Elizabeth Todd
Mike Todd
Juliette Toft
Ciara Toland
Robin Tomkins
Michael Tomlinson
Sarah Tomsent
Catherine Took
Paul Toomer
Robert Topping
Julie Torpy
Ben Toth
Matthew Towler
Rachel Towler
Sue Townsend
Maryjane Traber
Peter & Ruth Tracey
Becky Tracy
Lucie Trapp
Anna Travis
Steve Trayler
Mark Tredgat
Charlie Tresham
Marion Trimm
Karel Trott
Sue Trott
Christopher Trotter
David Truscott
Ian Tucker
Ginny Tudor
John Tullett
Karen Tulloch
Sarah Tumbull
Sarah Turiver
Bernard Turner
David Turner
Emma Turner
Jean Turner
Kate Turner
Marie & David Turner
Nick Turner
Richard Turner
Sarah Turner
Wendy Turner
Jill Turton

Katie Turton
Paul Turton
Tony Tween
Pauline Twentyman
Andrew Tye
Mic Tyler
Beth Tynegate
John Underwood
Su Underwood
Suzy Unwin
John Urry
Ian Usher
Mark Uytenhaak
Heather Vale
Mark Vallance
Chris Valle
Gerard Van Dam
Matthew Van Matre
Bernice Van Rooben
Fiona Vandermeer
Arcangelo Varamo
Phoebe Vardigans
Jonathan Varey
Karen Varley
Paul Varman
Jane Vaughan
Tom Vaughan
Germana Veneziano
Heather Venezio
Maureen Vento
Marie-Claude Verdier
Hugh Vere Nicoll
Brian Verry
Moira Viggers
Dennis Vincent
Simon Vittelch
Steven Voller
Michael Wace
Alan Waddington
Ella Wade
Jo Wade
Johan Wadsten
Linsey Wadsworth
Patricia Wainman
Narina Waite
Sue Walbcoff
David Walden
Chris Waliger
Angela Walker
Caroline Walker
David Walker
Joanne Walker
Maxine Walker
Mel Walker
Susie Walker
Marynka Wall
Matthew Wall
Nicholas Wall
Noelle Wall
Ray Wall
Richard Wall
Beverley Waller
Rebecca Waller
Lizzie Walmsley
Robert Walpole
Ann Walsh
Jo Walsh
Stephen Walsh
Jean Walters
Steve Walters
Robert Walton
Tony Walton
Laura Wanny
Chris Ward
Cyril Ward
Esther Ward
Karen Ward
Karl Ward
Lizzie Ward
Martin Ward
Sheena Ward
Timothy Ward
Tracy Ward
Diane Wardman
Chris Ware
Janet Waring
John Warner
Carol Warren
Russell Warren
Jane Warrington-Smith
Josephine Warrior
Davina Warwick
Joe Warwick
Di Wasae
Beryl Waterhouse
Norman Waterman
Ian Waters
Rob & Carol Watkin
David Watkins

Nicola Watkins
Rowena Watkins
Sharon Watkins
Jane Watson
Malcolm Watson
Peter Watson
Trevor Watson
Fiona Watson-Smyth
Alexandra Watson-
   Usher
Andrew Watt
Dol Watt
James Watt
Abbi Watts
Kate Watts
Val Waugh
Benjamin Ways
Sarah Weaver
Carolyn Webb
Elizabeth Webb
Kate Webb
Katie Webber
Susan Webber
Oliver Webster
Rachel Webster
Ben Weeks
David Weeks
Dr Paul Weeks
Linda Wei
Philip Welch
Jason Wells
Jeanette Wells
Keith Wells
Louise Wells
Rob Wells
Claire Welsh
Yvonne Welsh
Bryan Wendon
Patricia Wenworth
Daniel West
David West
Dean West
Christine Westerland
Joanna Westlake
Stuart Westley
Charles Weston
Sidriey Weston
Jennifer Westwood
Rachel Whaiotes
Simon Whalley
Robert Whaton
Carol Wheeler
Oliver Wheeler
Caroline & Bryan
   Whelan
Kathleen White
R White
Simon White
Susan White
Joanne Whitehead
Mark Whitehead
Christopher
   Whitehouse
David Whitehouse
Helen Whitehouse
George Whitelaw
John Scott Whiteley
Jeanette Whitelocks
Bernard Whiteside
Richard Whitley
Duncan Whitney-
   Groom
Lizzie Whitson Cloud
Sarah Whitten
David Whittle
Tom Whittle
Andy Wiens
Andrew Wigfall
Anna Wiggins
Lucy Wiggins
Jenny Wigginton
Catherine Wigington
Liz Wigley
Caroline Wilbraham
Alex Wilby
Laura Wilchan
Emma Wilcox
Deborah Wilde
Eileen Wilde
Sue Wilkins
Carol Wilkinson
David Wilkinson
Elizabeth Wilkinson
Emma Wilkinson
Gemma Wilkinson
Jennifer Wilkinson
Karen Wilkinson
Lauren Wilkinson
Margaret Wilkinson

Miles Wilkinson
Steve Wilkinson
Lauren Wilkison
John Will
Dianne Willcocks
Daniel Willett
Martyn Willey
Gemma Williams
Graham Williams
Jenny Williams
Lynsey Williams
Mary Williams
Oliver Williams
Peter Williams
Richard Williams
Sylvia Williams
Tony Williams
Anne Williamson
Justin Williamson
Adam Willis
Anzelika Willmore
Alam Wills
Mark Wills
Glynn Willson
Lorelei Wilmot-Smith
Aliza Wilson
Emily Wilson
Gavin Wilson
Helen Wilson
Jane Wilson
John Wilson
Kerry Wilson
Suzanne Wilson
Tim Wilton
Richard Winborn
Ellen Wing
Linda Winn
Deborah Winson
Glen Winter
Trevor Woodward
Dominic Wishlade
John Wolfe
Jiri Wolker
Tana Wollen
Dean Womack
A Wong
Sherlin Wong
Adam Wood
Amanda Wood
Christopher Wood
Ean Wood
John Wood
Maggie Wood
Martin Wood
Rebecca Woodhead
Richard Woodings
Joanna Woods
David Woodward
Peter Woodward
Stephanie Woodward
Trevor Woodyard
Deborah Woodyatt
Sophie Woolcock
Candida Woolcott
Rachel Woollacott
Ingrid Woolley
Steven Woolrich
Mandy Wragg
Helen Wray
Julie Wright
Katie Wright
Leanne Wright
Peter Wright
Tania Wright
Nigel Wrighton
Pam Wyatt
Robert Wyatt
Michael Wyldbore-
   Wood
Amanda Xiong
Charlie Yates
Christina Yates
Helen Yates
Mark Yates
Arabella Yelland
Tristan Yelland
Belinda Yeo
Christine Yeo
Andrew Yeoman
Richard York
Debra Yorke
Heather Youd
Allison Young
Grace Young
J Young
Dave Youngs
Katy Yoxall
Mehreen Yusuf
Vicky Zimmerman

Waitrose
GOOD FOOD
GUIDE
2015
£5 VOUCHER

Waitrose
GOOD FOOD
GUIDE
2015
£5 VOUCHER

Waitrose
GOOD FOOD
GUIDE
2015
£5 VOUCHER

Waitrose
GOOD FOOD
GUIDE
2015
£5 VOUCHER

Waitrose
GOOD FOOD
GUIDE
2015
£5 VOUCHER

Waitrose
GOOD FOOD
GUIDE
2015
£5 VOUCHER

Waitrose
GOOD FOOD
GUIDE
2015
£5 VOUCHER

Waitrose
GOOD FOOD
GUIDE
2015
£5 VOUCHER

Waitrose
GOOD FOOD
GUIDE
2015
£5 VOUCHER

Waitrose
GOOD FOOD
GUIDE
2015
£5 VOUCHER

Waitrose
GOOD FOOD GUIDE
2015

TERMS & CONDITIONS

This voucher can only be used in participating restaurants, highlighted by the £5 OFF symbol. It is redeemable against a pre-booked meal for a minimum of two people, provided the customer highlights the intention to use the voucher at the time of booking. Only one voucher may be used per table booked. This voucher may not be used in conjunction with any other scheme.
Offer valid from 01/09/2014 to 01/09/2015.
For additional terms and conditions, see below.

TERMS & CONDITIONS

This voucher can only be used in participating restaurants, highlighted by the £5 OFF symbol. It is redeemable against a pre-booked meal for a minimum of two people, provided the customer highlights the intention to use the voucher at the time of booking. Only one voucher may be used per table booked. This voucher may not be used in conjunction with any other scheme.
Offer valid from 01/09/2014 to 01/09/2015.
For additional terms and conditions, see below.

TERMS & CONDITIONS

This voucher can only be used in participating restaurants, highlighted by the £5 OFF symbol. It is redeemable against a pre-booked meal for a minimum of two people, provided the customer highlights the intention to use the voucher at the time of booking. Only one voucher may be used per table booked. This voucher may not be used in conjunction with any other scheme.
Offer valid from 01/09/2014 to 01/09/2015.
For additional terms and conditions, see below.

TERMS & CONDITIONS

This voucher can only be used in participating restaurants, highlighted by the £5 OFF symbol. It is redeemable against a pre-booked meal for a minimum of two people, provided the customer highlights the intention to use the voucher at the time of booking. Only one voucher may be used per table booked. This voucher may not be used in conjunction with any other scheme.
Offer valid from 01/09/2014 to 01/09/2015.
For additional terms and conditions, see below.

TERMS & CONDITIONS

This voucher can only be used in participating restaurants, highlighted by the £5 OFF symbol. It is redeemable against a pre-booked meal for a minimum of two people, provided the customer highlights the intention to use the voucher at the time of booking. Only one voucher may be used per table booked. This voucher may not be used in conjunction with any other scheme.
Offer valid from 01/09/2014 to 01/09/2015.
For additional terms and conditions, see below.

TERMS & CONDITIONS

This voucher can only be used in participating restaurants, highlighted by the £5 OFF symbol. It is redeemable against a pre-booked meal for a minimum of two people, provided the customer highlights the intention to use the voucher at the time of booking. Only one voucher may be used per table booked. This voucher may not be used in conjunction with any other scheme.
Offer valid from 01/09/2014 to 01/09/2015.
For additional terms and conditions, see below.

TERMS & CONDITIONS

This voucher can only be used in participating restaurants, highlighted by the £5 OFF symbol. It is redeemable against a pre-booked meal for a minimum of two people, provided the customer highlights the intention to use the voucher at the time of booking. Only one voucher may be used per table booked. This voucher may not be used in conjunction with any other scheme.
Offer valid from 01/09/2014 to 01/09/2015.
For additional terms and conditions, see below.

TERMS & CONDITIONS

This voucher can only be used in participating restaurants, highlighted by the £5 OFF symbol. It is redeemable against a pre-booked meal for a minimum of two people, provided the customer highlights the intention to use the voucher at the time of booking. Only one voucher may be used per table booked. This voucher may not be used in conjunction with any other scheme.
Offer valid from 01/09/2014 to 01/09/2015.
For additional terms and conditions, see below.

TERMS & CONDITIONS

This voucher can only be used in participating restaurants, highlighted by the £5 OFF symbol. It is redeemable against a pre-booked meal for a minimum of two people, provided the customer highlights the intention to use the voucher at the time of booking. Only one voucher may be used per table booked. This voucher may not be used in conjunction with any other scheme.
Offer valid from 01/09/2014 to 01/09/2015.
For additional terms and conditions, see below.

TERMS & CONDITIONS

This voucher can only be used in participating restaurants, highlighted by the £5 OFF symbol. It is redeemable against a pre-booked meal for a minimum of two people, provided the customer highlights the intention to use the voucher at the time of booking. Only one voucher may be used per table booked. This voucher may not be used in conjunction with any other scheme.
Offer valid from 01/09/2014 to 01/09/2015.
For additional terms and conditions, see below.

Vouchers are valid from 01/09/2014 to 01/09/2015. Only one £5 voucher can be used per table booked (for a minimum of 2 people). No photocopies or any other kind of reproduction of vouchers will be accepted. Some participating establishments may exclude certain times, days or menus from the scheme so long as they a) advise customers of the restrictions at the time of booking and b) accept the vouchers at a minimum of 70% of sessions when the restaurant is open. Please note that the number of participating restaurants may vary from time to time.